Financial Accounting Standards Board (FASB), Statements of Financial Accounting Standards (1973–1979)

Refer to Index for page citations

Financial Accounting Standards Board (FASB), Interpretations (1974–1979)

June,	1974	No. 1	Accounting Changes Related to the Cost of Inventory (APB Opinion No. 20)
June,	1974	No. 2	Imputing Interest on Debt Arrangements Made Under the Federal Bankruptcy Act (APB Opinion No. 21)
Dec.,	1974	No. 3	Accounting for the Cost of Pension Plans Subject to the Employee Retirement Income Security Act of 1974 (APB Opinion No. 8)
Feb.,	1975	No. 4	Applicability of FASB Statement No. 2 to Purchase Business Combinations
Feb.,	1975	No. 5	Applicability of FASB Statement No. 2 to Development Stage Enterprises
Feb.,	1975	No. 6	Applicability of FASB Statement No. 2 to Computer Software
Oct.,	1975	No. 7	Applying FASB Statement No. 7 in Statements of Established Enterprises
Jan.,	1976	No. 8	Classification of a Short-Term Obligation Repaid Prior to Being Replaced by a Long-Term Security (FASB Std. No. 6)
Feb.,	1976	No. 9	Applying APB Opinions No. 16 and 17 when a Savings and Loan or Similar Institution is Acquired in a Purchase Business Combination (APB Op. No. 16 & 17)
Sept.,	1976	No. 10	Application of FASB Statement No. 12 to Personal Financial Statements (FASB Std. No. 12)
Sept.,	1976	No. 11	Changes in Market Value after the Balance Sheet Date (FASB Std. No. 12)
Sept.,	1976	No. 12	Accounting for Previously Established Allowance Accounts (FASB Std. No. 12)
Sept.,	1976	No. 13	Consolidation of a Parent and Its Subsidiaries Having Different Balance Sheet Dates (FASB Std. No. 12)
Sept.,	1976	No. 14	Reasonable Estimation of the Amount of a Loss (FASB Std. No. 5)
Sept.,	1976	No. 15	Translation of Unamortized Policy Acquisition Costs by a Stock Life Insurance Company (FASB Std. No. 8)
Feb.,	1977	No. 16	Clarification of Definitions and Accounting for Marketable Equity Securities That Become Nonmarketable (FASB Std. No. 12)
Feb.,	1977	No. 17	Applying the Lower of Cost or Market Rule in Translated Financial Statements (FASB Std. No. 8)
March,	1977	No. 18	Accounting for Income Taxes in Interim Periods (APB Op. No. 28)
Oct.,	1977	No. 19	Lessee Guarantee of the Residual Value of Leased Property (FASB Std. No. 13)
Nov.,	1977	No. 20	Reporting Accounting Changes under AICPA Statements of Position (APB Op. No. 20)
April,	1978	No. 21	Accounting for Leases in a Business Combination (FASB Std. No. 13)
April,	1978	No. 22	Applicability of Indefinite Reversal Criteria to Timing Differences (APB Op. No. 11 and 23)
Aug.,	1978	No. 23	Leases of Certain Property Owned by a Governmental Unit or Authority (FASB Std. No. 13)
Sept.,	1978	No. 24	Leases Involving Only Part of a Building (FASB Std. No. 13)
Sept.,	1978	No. 25	Accounting for an Unused Investment Tax Credit (APB Op. No. 2, 4, 11, and 16)
Sept.,	1978	No. 26	Accounting for Purchase of a Leased Asset by the Lessee during the Term of the Lease (FASB Std. No. 13)
Nov.,	1978	No. 27	Accounting for a Loss on a Sublease (FASB Std. No. 13 and APB Op. No. 30)
Dec.,	1978	No. 28	Accounting for Stock Appreciation Rights and Other Variable Stock Option or Award Plans (APB Op. No. 15 and 25)
Feb.,	1979	No. 29	Reporting Tax Benefits Realized on Disposition of Investments in Certain Subsidiaries and Other Investees (APB Op. No. 23 and 24)
Sept.,	1979	No. 30	Accounting for Involuntary Conversions of Nonmonetary Assets to Monetary Assets (APB Op. No. 29)

INTERMEDIATE ACCOUNTING

INTERMEDIATE ACCOUNTING
Third Edition

Donald E. Kieso, Ph.D., C.P.A.

Northern Illinois University
DeKalb, Illinois

Jerry J. Weygandt, Ph.D., C.P.A.

University of Wisconsin
Madison, Wisconsin

JOHN WILEY & SONS

New York   Chichester   Brisbane   Toronto

Dedicated to

C. A. Moyer and Arthur R. Wyatt

For their many contributions to
accounting education and the accounting
profession and for their influence
in our lives.

and to

Donna,	Enid,
Douglas,	Matthew,
and Debra	Erin,
	and Lia

Library of Congress Cataloging in Publication Data:

Kieso, Donald E.
    Intermediate accounting.

    Includes bibliographical references and index.
    1. Accounting.   I. Weygandt, Jerry J., joint author.
II. Title.
HF5635.K5 1980   657'.044   79-26817
ISBN 0-471-04819-4

Printed in the United States of America

10 9 8 7 6 5 4 3 2

Preface

The third edition of *Intermediate Accounting* discusses in depth the traditional (intermediate) financial accounting topics as well as the recent developments in accounting valuation and reporting practices promulgated by the leading professional accounting organizations and applied by practitioners in public accounting and industry. Explanations and discussions of financial accounting theory are supported and illustrated by examples taken directly from practice and authoritative pronouncements.

Continuing to keep pace with the complexities of the modern business enterprise, we have added many new topics, clarified some of the existing coverage, added numerous illustrations, and updated all material where necessary. To make the book even more comprehensive than the earlier editions, we have made greater use of judiciously selected appendices. The fifteen appendices are concerned primarily with complex subjects, lesser used methods, or specialized topics. Our intent in using the appendices is to provide the instructor with greater flexibility in choosing topics to cover or omit.

The text is organized into six major parts.

1. Financial Accounting Functions and Basic Theory
   (Chapters 1 to 6)
2. Current Assets and Current Liabilities
   (Chapters 7 to 10)
3. Plant Assets and Long-Term Liabilities
   (Chapters 11 to 14)
4. Stockholders' Equity, Dilutive Securities, and Investments
   (Chapters 15 to 18)
5. Issues Related to Income Determination
   (Chapters 19 to 23)
6. Preparation and Analysis of Financial Statements
   (Chapters 24 to 27)

NEW FEATURES

Some of the additions, significant revisions, and new features of this edition are as follows. In Chapter 1 we have added an updated discussion on the accounting profession's responses to recent governmental interest in accounting and auditing, including the reports of the Moss Committee, the Metcalf Committee, and the Cohen Commission. In Chapter 2 we have integrated coverage of recent FASB Statements and Exposure Drafts of Financial Accounting Concepts on (a) objectives and (b) elements of financial statements and (c) qualitative criteria for evaluating accounting policies. Chapter 3 has been reorganized slightly. The preparation of a work sheet has been integrated into the chapter and specialized journals are discussed in an appendix; our coverage of "conversion of cash basis to accrual basis" has been expanded. The "statement of changes in financial position" has been added to Chapter 5, where the presentation focuses on the content and interpretation of this statement (Chapter 24 is still devoted to the preparation of this statement). Minor additions to Chapter 6 concern the form of "computing unknown interest rates, number and amount of annuities," "interpolation," and a complete annuity due table has been included.

Chapter 8 has been updated by coverage of "capitalization of interest cost," expanded by adding topics on "special sale agreements," and clarified by simplifying our presentation of "dollar-value LIFO" and adding a graphic comparative analysis of the effect of major inventory methods. We have added a new appendix on "special LIFO reporting problems" to Chapter 9 that covers "initial adoption of LIFO," "LIFO reserves," "interim reporting problems," and "index determination for dollar-value LIFO." LIFO retail, formerly an appendix, has been integrated into Chapter 9.

"Capitalization of interest cost" has been integrated into our coverage of acquisition of plant and equipment in Chapter 11. To Chapter 12 we have added discussions on "discovery value" and "reserve recognition accounting (RRA)" for natural resources. The "methods of measuring goodwill" in Chapter 13 are better organized and presented in this edition. Two appendices have been added to Chapter 14: "Illustration of Serial Bond Amortization and Redemption Before Maturity" and "Accounting for Troubled Debt Restructurings."

Chapters 15 and 16 on stockholders' equity have been slightly expanded with coverage on "redeemable preferred stock," the "nature of stockholders' equity" and many new illustrations on disclosure. "Employee compensation and stock option plans" in Chapter 17 has been revised, updated, and expanded to include a section on "stock appreciation rights (SARs)."

Chapter 19 on revenue recognition has been reorganized around "product sales transactions" and "service sales transactions" to include new coverage of "accounting for service sales transactions." In order to integrate the tax effect into our coverage of "accounting changes and error analysis," we have moved our coverage on income tax allocation ahead of our chapter on accounting changes. Our presentations on "gross and net change tax computation methods" have been greatly clarified. Our coverage of "pension costs" has been revised slightly with some discussions being shortened ("two views of pension cost"), some being simplified ("normal, past, and prior service cost"), and some being expanded ("accounting for actuarial gains and losses" and "effects of the Pension Reform Act of 1974"). Accounting for leases, Chapter 22, has been completely rewritten in order to update and integrate the many FASB statements and interpretations issued since Statement No. 13; also added to our lease chapter is coverage of "guaranteed and unguaranteed residual values," "bargain purchase options," and "initial direct costs."

Chapter 24 on "statement of changes in financial position" has been completely revised along with the appendix so that the "work sheet approach" and the "T-account approach" are comparable. Because of the issuance of FASB Statement No. 33, we present in Chapter 25 all new, up-to-date coverage of financial accounting and changing prices" including comprehensive illustrations of "constant dollar" and "current value accounting." To Chapter 26 we have added a new appendix on "fundamental analysis versus capital market analysis." Chapter 27 on "Full Disclosure" has been expanded to include new coverage of "related party transactions," "illegal acts," "management's responsibilities for financial statements," and "criteria for making accounting and reporting choices."

QUESTIONS, CASES, EXERCISES, AND PROBLEMS

At the end of each chapter we have provided a comprehensive set of review and homework material consisting of questions, cases, exercises, and problems. For this edition all exercises and problems have been revised, and the end-of-chapter material has been supplemented with many new cases and problems, nearly all of which have been class tested.

The questions are designed for review, self-testing, and classroom discussion purposes as well as homework assignments. The cases generally require essay as opposed to quantitative solutions; they are intended to confront the student with situations calling for conceptual analysis and the exercise of judgment in identifying problems and evaluating alternatives. Typically, an exercise covers a specific topic and requires less time and effort to solve than cases and problems. The problems are designed to develop a professional level of achievement and are more challenging to solve than the exercises.

Probably no more than one-fourth of the total case, exercise, and problem material must be used to cover the subject matter adequately; consequently, problem assignments may be varied from year to year.

SUPPLEMENTARY MATERIALS

Accompanying this textbook is an improved and expanded package of supplements consisting of instructional aids for either students or instructors: (1) a *Student Study Guide* (written by Raymond J. Clay, Jr., of Texas Tech University), (2) a booklet of "Examination Questions and Achievement Tests," (3) a comprehensive "Solutions Manual" for the end-of-chapter material, (4) ruled "Working Papers" for all problems, (5) a "Practice Set" (with solutions) designed to accompany Chapter 3, (6) overhead projector transparencies for selected problems, (7) a "Checklist of Key Figures," and (8) a new separate "Instructor's Manual" containing lecture outlines, an annotated bibliography, and other enrichment materials.

ACKNOWLEDGEMENTS

We thank the many users of our second edition who contributed to this revision through their comments and constructive criticism. Special thanks are extended to the primary reviewers of our third edition manuscript: Thomas Barton, Florida State University; Floyd A. Beams, Virginia Polytechnic Institute and State University; Willard H. Galliart, Loyola University of Chicago; Mary Noble, Southwest Missouri State University; LeRoy F. Imdieke and Ralph E. Smith, Arizona State University; and Mary Ellen Phillips, Oregon State University.

Other colleagues in academe who have read portions of this work and made valuable suggestions include: Ernest I. Hanson, David Koeppen, and Raghavan D. Nair, University of Wisconsin—Madison; John Borke, Martin A. Bubley, Patrick R. Delaney, Cathy Geddeis, James M. Lahey, Shirley Mecklenburg, Curtis L. Norton, Nicholas Polydoros, and John Simon, Northern Illinois University; Laurel Brown, Arizona State University; John E. Delaney, University of Texas—Austin; Jerry Hamsmith, Aurora College; and M. Zafar Iqbal, California Polytechnic State University.

From the field of professional accountancy we owe thanks to the following practitioners: Arthur R. Wyatt and John E. Stewart, Arthur Andersen & Co.; Margaret Pfau and Richard Thompson, Coopers & Lybrand; Kenneth I. Solomon, Laventhol & Horwath; and James A. Miller, Price Waterhouse & Co.

We especially appreciate the exemplary support and commitment given us by Carol Cardella, Jackie Remmers, Donna Reichenbacher, and Enid Stottrup as typists and proofreaders; and by the production and editorial staffs, including Richard Palmer, Romayne Ponleithner, Judy Nolan, John Beresford, Don Ford, and Howard Smith.

We appreciate the cooperation of the American Institute of Certified Public Accountants and the Financial Accounting Standards Board in permitting us to quote from their pronouncements. We also acknowledge permission from the American Institute of Certified Public Accountants and the Institute of Management Accounting to adapt and use material from the Uniform CPA Examinations and the CMA Examinations, respectively.

If this book helps teachers instill in their students an appreciation for the challenges and limitations of accounting, if it encourages students to evaluate critically and understand financial accounting theory and practice, and if it prepares students for advanced study, professional examinations, and the successful pursuit of their careers in accounting or business, then we will have attained our objective.

Suggestions and comments from users of this book will be appreciated.

Donald E. Kieso

Jerry J. Weygandt

DeKalb, Illinois
Madison, Wisconsin
January, 1980

About the Authors

Donald E. Kieso, Ph.D., CPA, received his doctorate in accounting from the University of Illinois. He is currently Professor of Accountancy at Northern Illinois University. He has public accounting experience with Price Waterhouse & Co. (San Francisco and Chicago) and Arthur Andersen & Co. (Chicago) and research experience with the Research Division of the American Institute of Certified Public Accountants (New York). He has done postdoctorate work as a Visiting Scholar at the University of California at Berkeley and is a recipient of NIU's Teaching Excellence Award. Professor Kieso is the author of other accounting and business books and is a member of the American Accounting Association, the American Institute of Certified Public Accountants, the Financial Executives Institute, and the Illinois CPA Society. Most recently he has served as a member of the Board of Directors of the Illinois CPA Society, the Board of Governors of the American Accounting Association's Administrators of Accounting Programs Group, the Board of Directors of Aurora College, the State of Illinois Comptroller's Commission, and as Secretary-Treasurer of the Federation of Schools of Accountancy.

Jerry J. Weygandt, Ph.D., CPA, is Professor of Accounting at the University of Wisconsin—Madison. He holds a Ph.D. in accounting from the University of Illinois. Articles by Professor Weygandt have appeared in the *Accounting Review, Journal of Accounting Research*, the *Journal of Accountancy*, and other professional journals. These articles have examined such financial reporting issues as accounting for price-level adjustments, pensions, convertible securities, stock option contracts, and interim reports. He is a member of the American Accounting Association, the American Institute of Certified Public Accountants, and the Wisconsin Society of Certified Public Accountants. He has served on numerous committees of the American Accounting Association and as a member of the editorial board of the *Accounting Review*. In addition, he is actively involved with the American Institute of Certified Public Accountants and recently was appointed to the Accounting Standards Executive Committee (AcSEC) of that organization. He has served as a consultant to a number of businesses and state agencies on financial reporting issues.

Contents

PART 3
PLANT ASSETS AND LONG-TERM LIABILITIES

Financial Accounting Functions and Basic Theory

1

The Environment of Accounting and the Development of Accounting Standards

Is accounting a service activity, a descriptive/analytical discipline, or an information system? It is all three. **As a service activity,** accounting provides interested parties with quantitative financial information that helps them to make decisions about the deployment and use of resources in business and nonbusiness entities and in the economy. **As a descriptive/analytical discipline,** it identifies the great mass of events and transactions that characterize economic activity and, through measurement, classification, and summarization, reduces those data to relatively small, highly significant, and interrelated items that, when properly assembled and reported, describe the financial condition and results of operation of a specific economic entity. **As an information system,** it collects and communicates economic information about a business enterprise or other entity to a wide variety of persons whose decisions and actions are related to the activity.

Although each of these descriptions of accounting appears unlike the others, no contradiction exists between them. Each definition contains the three essential characteristics of accounting: (1) **measurement and communication of financial information about** (2) **economic entities to** (3) **interested persons.** These characteristics have been peculiar to accounting for hundreds of years. Yet, in the last fifty years economic entities have increased so greatly in size and complexity, and the interested persons have increased so greatly in number and diversity, that the responsibility placed on the accounting profession is greater today than ever before.

Financial Accounting

For purposes of study and practice the discipline of accounting is commonly divided into the following areas or subsets: financial accounting, managerial (cost) accounting, tax accounting, and nonprofit or fund accounting. This textbook concentrates on financial accounting. Financial accounting has been characterized as "the branch of accounting that focuses on the general-purpose reports on financial position and results of operations known as financial statements."[1] These statements provide "a continual history quantified in money terms of economic resources and obligations of a business enterprise and of economic activities that change these resources and obligations."[2] **Financial accounting** is the process that culminates in the preparation of financial reports relative to the enterprise as a whole for use by parties both internal and external to the enterprise. In contrast, **managerial accounting** pertains most directly to the accumulation and communication of information relative to subsystems of the entity for use by internal parties (management).[3]

Financial Statements and Financial Reporting

The principal means of communicating financial information to those outside an enterprise are through financial statements. The **financial statements** most frequently provided are (1) the balance sheet, (2) the income statement, (3) the statement of changes in financial position, and (4) the statement of changes in owners' or stockholders' equity. Appropriate footnote disclosures are an integral part of each of these four basic financial statements.

But some financial information is better provided, or can be provided only, by means of **financial reporting** other than formal financial statements either because it is required by authoritative pronouncement, regulatory rule, or custom, or because enterprise management wishes to disclose it voluntarily. Financial reporting other than financial statements (and related footnotes) may take various forms and relate to various matters. Common examples are contained in corporate annual reports (e.g., the president's letter or supplementary schedules), prospectuses, annual reports filed with government agencies, news releases, management's forecasts or plans or expectations, and descriptions of an enterprise's social or environmental impact.[4]

The primary but not exclusive focus of this textbook is on the development of financial information that is reported in the basic financial statements and the related disclosures.

---

[1]"Basic Concepts and Accounting Principles Underlying Financial Statements of Business Enterprises," *Statement of the Accounting Principles Board No. 4* (New York: AICPA, 1970), par. 9.

[2]*Ibid.*, par. 41.

[3]*Report of the Committee on Courses in Financial Accounting* (Evanston, Ill.: American Accounting Association, 1971), pp. 3–9.

[4]"Objectives of Financial Reporting by Business Enterprises," *Statement of Financial Accounting Concepts No. 1* (Stamford, Conn.: FASB, November, 1978), pars. 5–8.

Objectives of Financial Reporting

In a recent attempt to establish a foundation upon which financial accounting and reporting standards will be based the accounting profession has identified a set of **objectives of financial reporting by business enterprises.** The objectives state that financial reporting should provide information:

(a) that is useful to present and potential investors and creditors and other users in making rational investment, credit, and similar decisions. The information should be comprehensible to those who have a reasonable understanding of business and economic activities and are willing to study the information with reasonable diligence.

(b) to help present and potential investors and creditors and other users in assessing the amounts, timing, and uncertainty of prospective cash receipts from dividends or interest and the proceeds from the sale, redemption, or maturity of securities or loans. Since investors' and creditors' cash flows are related to enterprise cash flows, financial reporting should provide information to help investors, creditors, and others assess the amounts, timing, and uncertainty of prospective net cash inflows to the related enterprise.

(c) about the economic resources of an enterprise, the claims to those resources (obligations of the enterprise to transfer resources to other entities and owners' equity), and the effects of transactions, events, and circumstances that change its resources and claims to those resources.[5]

In summary, the objectives of financial reporting are to provide (1) information that is useful in investment and credit decisions, (2) information that is useful in assessing cash flow prospects, and (3) information about enterprise resources, claims to those resources, and changes in them. The above emphasis on "assessing cash flow prospects" should not be interpreted as meaning that the cash basis is being advocated. It is generally believed that accrual accounting provides a better indication of an enterprise's ability to generate cash in the present and the future than a simple cash receipts and cash disbursements statement.

ENVIRONMENT OF FINANCIAL ACCOUNTING

Accounting, like other social science disciplines and human activities, is largely a product of its environment. The environment of accounting consists of social-economic-political-legal conditions, restraints, and influences, which have varied from time to time. As a result, accounting objectives and practices are not the same today as they were in the past, **because accounting theory has evolved to meet changing demands and influences.**

Modern financial accounting is the product of many influences and conditions, three of which deserve special consideration. **First, accounting recognizes that people live in a world of scarce means and resources.** Because resources exist in limited supply, people try to conserve them, to use them effectively, and to identify and encourage those who can make efficient use of these resources. This stress on efficiency and effectiveness in economic activities leads to the use of income measurement as an indicator of success. Accounting measures and communicates the costs of efforts and resources that have been used or consumed in the production of

---

[5]*Ibid.*, p. viii.

goods, services, or desired conditions. Similarly, accounting is involved with the distribution and disposition of the values or other benefits represented by the goods, services, and conditions.

Second, accounting recognizes and accepts society's current legal and ethical concepts of property and other rights as standards in determining equity among the varying interests in the enterprise or entity. Accounting looks to its environment for its standards in regard to what property rights society protects, what society recognizes as value, and what society acknowledges as equity and fairness.

Third, accounting recognizes that in highly developed, complex economic systems, some (owners and investors) entrust the custodianship of and control over property to others (managers). One of the results of the corporate form of organization has been the tendency in large enterprises to divorce ownership and management. Thus, the function of measuring and reporting information to absentee investors, called the **stewardship function,** has been added to that of recording and presenting financial data for owner-manager use. This development greatly increased the need for accounting standards. The absentee investor, unlike the owner-operator, has no opportunity to combine reported information with first-hand knowledge of the conditions and activities of the enterprise.[6] Accounting has become responsible for providing standards that insure the fairness, objectivity, and comparability of this reported information. The public accountant (auditor) plays a major role in meeting this responsibility by attesting to the fairness of financial statements and their conformity to generally accepted accounting principles.

The foregoing three qualitative conditions are impressed on financial accounting by the environment within which it operates and which it is intended to reflect.[7] The following environmental aspects, although not as basic as the three qualitative conditions just discussed, also shape financial accounting to a significant extent:

1.   The many uses and users that accounting serves.
2.   The overall organization of economic activity.
3.   The nature of economic activity in individual business enterprises.
4.   The means of measuring economic activity.[8]

The basic features, elements, and principles of accounting reflect these aspects of the environment.

Many Uses and Users

Some users of financial accounting information have (or contemplate having) a direct interest[9] in economic entities. Other users[10] have an interest in such entities because their function is to assist or protect persons who have or contemplate

---

[6]W. A. Paton and A. C. Littleton, *An Introduction to Corporate Accounting Standards,* American Accounting Association, 1940, pp. 1–2.

[7]A Study Group at the University of Illinois, *A Statement of Basic Accounting Postulates and Principles* (Urbana, Ill.: Center for International Education and Research in Accounting, 1964), pp. 4–6.

[8]*APB Statement No. 4,* par. 42.

[9]*Direct interest users*—owners; creditors; suppliers; potential owners, creditors, and suppliers; management; taxing authorities; employees; and consumers.

[10]*Indirect interest users*—financial analysts; stock exchanges; lawyers, regulatory and registration authorities; financial press and reporting agencies; trade associations; and labor unions.

having a direct interest in them. In order to provide the most useful and equitable information, the accountant must know the nature of user needs, the decision process employed by users, and the information that best serves their needs.

Organization of Economic Activity

All societies engage in the fundamental economic activities of production, income distribution, exchange, consumption, saving, and investment. In a highly developed economy like that of the United States these activities become specialized, complex, and intertwined. Because the activities are continuous, relationships and accomplishments associated with intervals of time (such as a year or portions of a year) can be measured only on the basis of assumptions or conventional accounting allocations. Because the activities are so interdependent and intertwined, the computation of the precise effects of a particular event, transaction, or process is impossible except on an arbitrary basis. This problem is intensified in a dynamic economy because the outcome of economic activity is uncertain at the time decisions are made or even when action has been taken. Fortunately, the continuity of enterprise existence and the framework of law, custom, and traditional patterns of action help to stabilize many aspects of the economic environment. The degree of uncertainty is reduced (and the accounting function greatly assisted) when the society ensures the protection of property rights, the fulfillment of contracts, and the payment of debts.

Economic Activity in Individual Enterprises

Business enterprises are the units that conduct economic activity; they consist of economic resources (assets), economic obligations (liabilities), and residual interests (owners' equity); these elements are increased or decreased by the economic activities of the enterprise. The resources, obligations, and residual interests (balance sheet items) of an enterprise are the basis for the results of operations—revenue, expenses, and net income (income statement items)—and other changes in financial position with which financial accounting is concerned.

Measuring Economic Activity

Accounting facilitates the comparison and evaluation of diverse economic activities by the **measurement** (or valuation) of an enterprise's resources and obligations and the events that increase or decrease them. As already indicated, the complexity, continuity, and joint nature of economic activity create problems in measuring the effects of these activities and associating them with specific enterprises, processes, and products and with relatively short time periods. Measuring the resources and obligations of an enterprise and measuring the changes in them are two aspects of the same problem; hence, there is an inseparable connection between the accountant's statement of financial position (balance sheet), the statement indicating the results of activities (income statement), and the statement of changes in financial position (often called the funds statement). Money offers a simple solution to the selection of a common standard for purposes of measurement. **Money permits the measurement of qualitative and quantitative attributes of economic events, resources, and obligations.** Thus, the unit of measurement in accounting is expressed in terms of money or exchange price. Of course, some important activities of enterprises are not measurable in terms of money (e.g., appointing a new president, adopting a tradename or trademark).[11]

Accounting is not critical or important because it is a product of its environment, but rather because it shapes its environment and plays a significant role in the conduct of economic, social, political, legal, and organizational decisions and actions. **Accounting is a system that feeds back information to organizations and individuals, which they can use to reshape their environment.** It provides information for the reevaluation of social, political, and economic objectives as well as the relative costs and benefits of the alternative means of achieving these objectives.[12] Because accounting is influenced by, and simultaneously influences, its environment, there is a tremendous interest in the formulation of accounting standards and in the practice of accounting. Let us examine the manner in which accounting standards have been and are being developed. (The terms **principles** and **standards** are used interchangeably in practice and throughout this textbook.)

THE DEVELOPMENT OF ACCOUNTING STANDARDS

The Need To Develop Standards

The users of financial accounting statements have coinciding and conflicting needs for statements of various types. To meet these needs, and to satisfy the fiduciary reporting responsibility of management, accountants prepare a single set of **general-purpose financial statements.** These statements are expected to present fairly, clearly, and completely the economic facts of the existence and operations of the enterprise. **In preparing financial statements, accountants (like those involved in any communication process) are confronted with the potential dangers of bias, misinterpretation, inexactness, and ambiguity.** In order to minimize these dangers and to render financial statements that can be reasonably compared between enterprises and between accounting periods, the accounting profession has attempted to develop a body of theory that is generally accepted and universally practiced. Without this body of theory, each accountant or enterprise would have to develop its own theory structure and set of practices. If this happened, readers of financial statements would have to familiarize themselves with every company's peculiar accounting and reporting practices. As a result, comparability would be nearly impossible.

---

[11]Qualitative attributes, as well as quantitative ones, are measurable (valued) in money terms. For instance, in October 1979, one ounce of gold measured $400 in money terms while one ounce of silver measured $18. (Obviously, two ounces of gold, or double the quantity, was valued at $800, double the amount of money.) And as another example, one of Van Gogh's paintings (*La fin de la journeé*—1890) was sold recently at auction for $800,000, while the author's brother had difficulty selling one of his paintings for $50 at an art fair. Money measures both quality and quantity.

[12]Report of the Study Group on Introductory Accounting, *A New Introductory Accounting* (New York: Price Waterhouse Foundation, 1971), pp. 16–17.

The accounting profession, therefore, has attempted to establish a body of theory and practice that acts as a general guide. Its efforts have resulted in the adoption of a common set of accounting concepts, standards, and procedures called **generally accepted accounting principles (GAAP).** Although the principles have provoked both debate and criticism, most accountants and members of the financial community recognize them as the theories, methods, and practices that, over time, have proved to be most useful.

Historical Perspective

A historical perspective of the interaction between accounting and its environment would foster a greater appreciation of accounting's heritage and conventions. Because of space limitations, however, we shall confine our discussion to the development of the current generally accepted accounting principles in the United States, which are primarily a product of the years since 1930.

Before 1900 the economy of the United States required a relatively unsophisticated type of accounting function, and an accounting profession per se was virtually nonexistent. Before the beginning of this century, single ownership was the predominant form of business organization in our economy. Accounting reports emphasized solvency and liquidity and were limited to internal use and scrutiny by banks and other lending institutions. From 1900 to 1929 the growth of large corporations, with their absentee ownership and the increasing investment and speculation in corporate stocks, resulted in the demand for greater disclosure and a change in the concern with solvency to a concern with income-producing ability. The constitutional amendment in 1913 authorizing the federal government to impose an income tax on businesses and individuals intensified the emphasis on income measurement. As a result of the stock market crash of 1929, the Great Depression, and widespread dissatisfaction with accounting reports, the federal government, the stock exchanges, and the accounting profession all made efforts to improve accounting. Since that time, the environmental influences on the development of accounting principles have been primarily institutional (or organizational).

Although the needs of interested parties have been the focus in the development of accounting principles, certain professional organizations, governmental agencies, and legislative acts have exerted a significant influence also.

The AICPA

The efforts of the **American Institute of Certified Public Accountants (AICPA),** the national professional organization of practicing Certified Public Accountants (CPAs), have been vital to the development of "generally accepted accounting principles" in the United States. In 1905 the Institute began monthly publication of **The Journal of Accountancy,** which has been the most popular forum for the practicing CPA since then. In 1917 an Institute committee, at the request of the Federal Trade Commission, prepared a pamphlet on "Uniform Accounting," which suggested procedures for standardizing the preparation of financial statements. In 1930 the Institute appointed a special committee to cooperate with the New York Stock Exchange on matters of common interest to accountants, investors, and the exchanges. An outgrowth of this special committee was the Committee on Accounting Procedure which, during the years 1939 to 1959, issued 51 **Accounting Research Bulletins** (see list on inside of front cover) dealing with a variety of timely account-ing problems. These bulletins, however, were not directives to the members of the Institute. Their authority rested only on their general acceptance by the profession. Although these bulletins narrowed the range of alternative practices to some ex-tent, this problem-by-problem approach of the Committee on Accounting Proce-dure failed to provide the well-defined and well-structured body of accounting principles that was so badly needed and desired.

GAAP

In 1959 the AICPA created the **Accounting Principles Board (APB)** and a new Accounting Research Division as part of a program to advance the written expres-sion of accounting principles, to determine appropriate practices, and to narrow the areas of difference and inconsistency in practice.[13] The objectives of this reor-ganization were fourfold: (1) to establish basic postulates,[14] (2) to formulate a set of broad principles, (3) to set up rules to guide the application of principles in specific situations, and (4) to base the entire program on research. Accordingly, a perma-nent accounting research staff was employed to carry on the research and to pub-lish research studies.

Accounting Research Studies

Research projects were conducted by independently employed consultants or by members of the research staff under the guidance of the Director of Accounting Research and a project advisory committee. Research usually was undertaken on a subject to be considered and acted on by the APB. (The APB was designated as the AICPA's sole authority for public pronouncements on accounting principles.) Upon completion of a research project, the results of the study and the conclusions and recommendations were published and circulated for comment and discussion. The published **Accounting Research Studies** were not official pronouncements of the AICPA; they were the responsibility of their authors and were published under the authority of the Director of Accounting Research. Fifteen research studies were published between 1960 and 1975 (see list on inside of back cover).

APB Opinions

The APB had more authority and responsibility than did its predecessor, the Com-mittee on Accounting Procedures. The Board's 18 to 21 members were selected primarily from public accounting but also included representatives from industry and the academic community. The Board's official pronouncements, called **APB Opinions,** were intended to be based mainly on research studies and to be sup-ported by reasoning. The adoption of an opinion required a two-thirds majority consent of the Board; minority dissents were published as part of the opinion.

---

[13]*Organization and Operation of the Accounting Research Program and Related Activities* (New York: AICPA, 1959), p. 9.

[14]Postulates are basic assumptions of self-evident propositions that are generally accepted as valid. Few in number and broad in nature, they provide the basis from which principles or standards may be deduced.

Between its inception in 1959 and its dissolution in 1973, the APB issued 31 opinions (see complete list inside front cover).

APB Opinions were enforced primarily through the prestige of the AICPA, and its APB, which was recognized as the body that regulated the accounting profession and determined and enforced accounting principles. Probably the most critical and the most important enforcement pressure resulted from the Securities and Exchange Commission's willingness to recognize the AICPA and to support APB Opinions.

In 1964 the Council (the governing body) of the AICPA circumscribed the long-used but officially undefined term **"generally accepted accounting principles."** In a document published as a Special Bulletin in 1964 and later as an appendix to **APB Opinion No. 6,** the Council adopted the following resolution:

1. "Generally accepted accounting principles" are those principles which have substantial authoritative support.
2. Opinions of the Accounting Principles Board constitute "substantial authoritative support."
3. "Substantial authoritative support" can exist for accounting principles that differ from Opinions of the Accounting Principles Board.
4. No distinction should be made between the Bulletins issued by the former Committee on Accounting Procedure on matters of accounting principles and Opinions of the Accounting Principles Board.

More important, the Council and the APB declared that all material departures by companies from APB Opinions and effective Research Bulletins must be disclosed and explained in the companies' published financial statements. Although the AICPA recognizes other sources as constituting substantial authoritative support, the decision and burden of proof in these cases rest with the reporting member.[15] Because of this burden of proof and the related risk of liability from lawsuits, the pronouncements issued to that date and since have been followed. Thus, the policy of strong **persuasion** gave way to a more effective one of professional (not legislative) **compulsion.**

Financial Accounting Standards Board

The APB was beleaguered throughout its 13-year existence. It came under fire early, charged with lack of productivity and failing to act promptly to correct alleged accounting abuses. Later the APB tackled numerous thorny accounting issues, only to meet a buzz saw of industry opposition and occasional government interference. In 1971 the accounting profession's leaders, anxious to avoid governmental rule-making, responded by appointing a Study Group on Establishment of Accounting Principles (commonly known as the Wheat Committee) "to examine the organization and operation of the Accounting Principles Board and determine what changes are necessary to attain better results faster." The Study Group's rec-

[15]Failure to follow generally accepted accounting principles may invoke the application of Rule 203 of the Rules of Conduct of the Code of Professional Ethics of the AICPA. Rule 203 prohibits a member of the AICPA from expressing an opinion that financial statements conform with generally accepted accounting principles if those statements contain a material departure from an accounting principle promulgated by the FASB, unless the member can demonstrate that because of unusual circumstances the financial statements otherwise would have been misleading.

ommendations were submitted to the AICPA Council in the spring of 1972, adopted totally, and implemented by early 1973.

The result of the Wheat Committee's recommendation was the demise of the APB and the creation of the **Financial Accounting Standards Board (FASB).** There was widespread support for the creation of the unprecedented private, independent board. The expectations of success and support for the new FASB were based upon several significant differences between it and its predecessor APB:

1. **Smaller membership.** The FASB is composed of seven members, replacing the relatively large 18-member APB.
2. **Full-time, remunerated membership.** FASB members are well-paid, full-time members appointed for renewable five-year terms, whereas the APB members were unpaid and part-time.
3. **Greater autonomy.** The APB was a senior committee of the AICPA, whereas the FASB is not an organ of any single professional organization. It is appointed by and answerable only to the Financial Accounting Foundation.[16]
4. **Increased independence.** APB members had retained their private positions with firms, companies, or institutions; FASB members must sever all such ties.
5. **Broader representation.** All APB members were required to be CPAs and members of the AICPA; only four of the seven members of the FASB must be CPAs (this requirement is now eliminated).

In recognition of the misconceptions caused by the term "principles," the FASB utilizes the term **financial accounting standards** in its pronouncements. Financial support for the new Board, averaging in excess of $4 million annually, is borne by the private sector (public accounting and industry) through contributions to the Financial Accounting Foundation.

Two of the basic premises of the FASB are that in establishing financial accounting standards: (1) it should be responsive to the needs and viewpoints of the entire economic community, not just the public accounting profession, and (2) it should operate in full view of the public through a "due process" system that gives interested persons ample opportunity to make their views known. To insure the achievement of these goals, the following steps are taken in the evolution of a typical FASB Statement:

1. A topic or project is identified and placed on the Board's agenda.
2. A task force of experts from various sectors is assembled to define problems, issues, and alternatives related to the topic.
3. Research and analysis are conducted by the FASB technical staff.
4. A **discussion memorandum** is drafted and released.
5. A public hearing is often held, usually 60 days after release of the memorandum.
6. The Board analyzes and evaluates the public response.
7. The Board deliberates on the issues and prepares an **exposure draft** (prepublication copy) for release.
8. After a 30-day (minimum) exposure period for public comment, the Board evaluates all of the responses received.

---

[16]The Financial Accounting Foundation members are appointed by representatives of the American Accounting Association, the American Institute of CPAs, the Financial Executives Institute, the National Association of Accountants, the Financial Analysts Federation, and the Securities Industry Association.

9. A committee studies the exposure draft in relation to the public responses, reevaluates its position, and revises the draft if necessary.
10. The full Board gives the revised draft final consideration and votes on issuance of a **Standards Statement.**

The passage of a new accounting standard in the form of an FASB Statement requires the support of four of the seven Board members. FASB Statements are considered GAAP and thereby binding in practice. All ARBs and APB Opinions that were in effect when the FASB became effective continue to be effective until amended or superseded by FASB pronouncements.

The FASB took one full year to become operational after its establishment on June 30, 1972, officially replacing the Accounting Principles Board on July 1, 1973. Since that time the FASB has issued 16 discussion memoranda, 34 statements, and 30 interpretations (see a complete list inside front cover).

Since it has become operational, the FASB has undeniably been hard at work and quite productive. However, that the Board's effectiveness and productivity are any more free of criticism than were those of the APB is debatable. Like the APB, the FASB in its first six years adopted the "problem-by-problem approach" in establishing standards and has been under constant pressure to perform more expeditiously and be more responsive and productive. Both critics and supporters agree that **the FASB will have the best chance of survival if it deals with problems promptly, sets proper priorities, takes whatever action it thinks is right and in the public interest, and handles pressures responsibly without overreacting to them.**

Statements of Financial Accounting Concepts

As part of a long-range effort to move away from the "problem-by-problem approach," the FASB in November 1978 issued the first in a series of **Statements of Financial Accounting Concepts.** The purpose of the series is to set forth fundamental objectives and concepts that the Board will use in developing future standards of financial accounting and reporting.[17] Individual concept statements will be issued serially; they are intended to form a cohesive set of interrelated concepts, a body of theory or a conceptual framework, that will serve as tools for solving existing and emerging problems in a consistent, sound manner. Unlike a Statement of Financial Accounting **Standards,** a Statement of Financial Accounting **Concepts** does not establish generally accepted accounting principles.

Interpretations of APB Opinions and FASB Standards

During the years the APB was in existence, the AICPA staff was authorized to issue **interpretations** of accounting questions that were of general interest to the profession. The interpretations were intended to provide guidance without the lengthy formal procedures required for an APB Opinion and to clarify points that were misunderstood by practitioners or about which practitioners disagreed. These interpretations were not pronouncements of the Board, did not have the same signifi-

---

[17]"Objectives of Financial Reporting by Business Enterprises," *Statement of Financial Accounting Concepts No. 1* (Stamford, Conn.: FASB, November, 1978), p. i.

cance as opinions, and did not establish standards enforceable under the AICPA's Code of Professional Ethics. But, where no clear answer was available from an opinion, interpretations were considered authoritative. The APB's administrative director, in whom the responsibility for their preparation rested, issued 101 interpretations during the Board's existence.

FASB interpretations, on the other hand, are pronouncements of the Board, requiring the votes of at least four of the seven members, and they have the same authority as statements. Interpretations appear to represent modifications or extensions of existing statements.

The Effect of Pressure Groups on Accounting Standards

The earlier discussion of the environment of accounting disclosed some of the factors that shape and influence the nature and development of accounting standards and practice. Possibly the most influential environmental force flows from various pressure groups (Figure 1–1). Pressure groups consist of the parties who are most interested in or affected by accounting standards, rules, and procedures. Pressure groups play a significant role because the setting of accounting standards is a social decision; that is, it is as much a product of political action as of careful logic or empirical findings.[18]

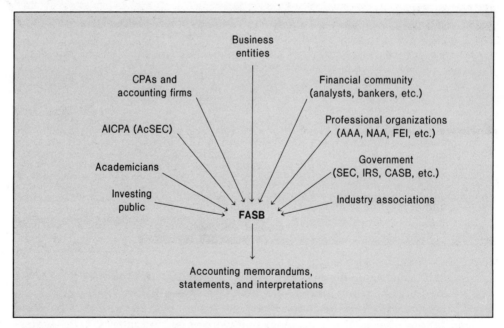

FIG. 1–1. Pressure groups that influence the formulation of accounting standards.

Pressure groups want particular economic events accounted for or reported in a particular way, and they fight hard to get what they want. They know that the most effective way to influence the standards that dictate accounting practice is to par-

[18]Charles T. Horngren, "The Marketing of Accounting Standards," *Journal of Accountancy* (October, 1973), p. 61.

ticipate in the formulation of these standards or to bring influence or persuasion on the formulator of them. Therefore, the FASB has become the target of many pressures and efforts to influence changes in the existing standards and the development of new ones.[19] Because of the accelerated rate of change in our economy, the increased complexity and interrelatedness of our economic activity, and the ever-increasing dependence on accounting, these pressures have been multiplying. Some influential groups demand that the accounting profession act more quickly and decisively to solve its problems and remedy its deficiencies; other groups resist such action, preferring to implement change more slowly, if at all.

The sources of pressure are innumerable, but the most intense and continuous pressure comes from governmental agencies, financial analysts, bankers, industry associations, clients of CPAs, individual companies, academicians, other accounting organizations, and public opinion. Several of these pressure groups significantly influence accounting standards.

The Securities and Exchange Commission

The Great Depression of the 1930s, which resulted in the widespread collapse of businesses and the securities market, was the impetus for government intervention and regulation of business. This intervention and regulation involved a good deal of concern with financial statements and accounting principles. A direct result was the creation of the **Securities and Exchange Commission (SEC)** as an independent regulatory agency of the United States government to administer the Securities Act of 1933, the Securities Exchange Act of 1934, and several other acts. Companies that issue securities to the public or are listed on stock exchanges are required to file annual audited financial statements with the SEC. The SEC, in turn, was given broad powers to prescribe, in whatever detail it desires, the accounting practices and principles to be employed by companies that fall within its jurisdiction. The SEC filing requirements and accounting opinions are published in (1) its **Accounting Series Releases,** of which more than 250 have been issued since 1937, (2) **Regulation S-X,** which contains instructions and forms for filing financial statements, and (3) decisions on cases coming before the SEC. Yet, the SEC until recently acted with remarkable restraint in the area of developing accounting principles. For the most part, it relied on the AICPA to regulate the accounting profession and develop and enforce accounting principles.

In late 1975 the SEC initiated a series of **Staff Accounting Bulletins (SABs).** By the end of 1978, 25 SABs had been issued. The Bulletins, through a question-and-answer format, provide examples of answers or interpretations given by the SEC staff in specific situations. Release No. 1 bears the warning:

> "The statements in the Bulletin are not rules or interpretations of the Commission nor are they published as bearing the Commission's official approval; they represent interpretations and practices followed by the Division and the Chief Accountant in administering the disclosure requirements of the federal securities laws."

Nevertheless, these releases carry significant authority.

---

[19]Former FASB chairman Marshall S. Armstrong acknowledged that several of the Board's projects, including "Accounting for Contingencies," "Accounting for Changes in General Purchasing Power," and "Accounting for Certain Marketable Equity Securities," were targets of political pressure.

Changing Role of the AICPA

For several decades the AICPA provided the leadership in the development of accounting principles and rules; it regulated the accounting profession and developed and enforced accounting practice more than did any other professional organization. The Accounting Principles Board was a standing committee of the AICPA. When the APB was dissolved and replaced with the FASB, the AICPA established the Accounting Standards Division to act as its official voice on accounting and reporting issues. The **Accounting Standards Executive Committee (AcSEC)** was established within the Division and was designated as the senior technical committee authorized to speak for the AICPA in the area of financial accounting and reporting.

During the first five years of its operation, AcSEC (1) responded to pronouncements of both the FASB and the SEC and (2) devoted attention to emerging problems not addressed by the FASB or the SEC through the issuance of **Statements of Position (SOP).** Unlike FASB pronouncements, the SOPs do not represent enforceable standards required of AICPA members; they are issued with the objective of influencing the development of accounting and reporting standards and of providing guidance where none exists. By the end of 1978, AcSEC had issued 33 SOPs and had about as many more in draft form or under study (see list inside back cover).

Because of this proliferation, the FASB in late 1978 publicly expressed concerns that the AICPA was evolving into a competing standard-setting body. The FASB proposed first to consolidate that work into a single standard-setting body—its own—by rewriting the SOPs into FASB style and format. After exposure to public comment they would be issued as final Statements of Financial Accounting Standards. Second, the FASB proposed to establish a new series of "FASB Technical Bulletins" that would offer timely guidance on preferred accounting and reporting practice.[20]

The AICPA agreed in general with the FASB proposal, urging that the FASB adopt existing SOPs as authoritative as it did with Accounting Research Bulletins and APB Opinions. In 1979 "the FASB agreed to exercise responsibility for the specialized accounting and reporting principles and practices in AICPA Statements of Position and Guides on accounting and auditing matters by extracting those specialized principles and practices from those documents and issuing them as FASB Statements, after appropriate due process."[21] In the meantime, until due process is accomplished, the Board issued **Statement No. 32** which designated a large number of SOPs and Guides on accounting and auditing as containing preferable accounting principles for purposes of justifying a change in accounting principles.

The FASB, recognizing that it must leverage the resources of the AICPA and others, has taken steps to increase its productivity. For example, a new series entitled **Invitations to Comment** was initiated by the FASB in 1978 with the issuance of

[20]Financial Accounting Standards Board, "Request for Written Comments on an FASB Proposal for Dealing with Industry Accounting Matters and Accounting Questions of Limited Application" (Stamford, Conn.: FASB, Nov. 7, 1978), 6 pages.

[21]"Specialized Accounting and Reporting Principles and Practices in AICPA Statements of Position and Guides on Accounting and Auditing Matters," *Statement of Financial Accounting Standards No. 32* (Stamford, Conn.: FASB, 1979).

"Accounting for Certain Service Transactions," which was written by an AICPA task force. Unlike a Discussion Memorandum, the Invitation to Comment is not a product of an FASB task force nor does it include alternative accounting methods for the issues under consideration. And, unlike an Exposure Draft, the conclusions set forth in an Invitation to Comment have not been deliberated by the Board.[22] The "Invitation to Comment" has no authoritative status—if, after exposure, the comment appears to have been formulated appropriately, an FASB standard would then be issued.

In addition, the AICPA has started publishing **Accounting Research Monographs** which are intended to provide background material and to elicit discussion on significant accounting problems. These research monographs are similar in purpose to the Accounting Research Studies mentioned earlier. At the present time, three monographs have been issued dealing with (1) accounting for depreciable assets, (2) intercorporate investments, and (3) financial reporting and the evaluation of solvency. These monographs are not authoritative in nature but rather provide a basis for discussion on important reporting problems in accounting.

The AICPA is still the leader in developing auditing standards through its **Auditing Standards Executive Committee (AudSEC)**, in regulating accounting practice, in developing and enforcing professional ethics, and in providing continuing professional education programs. The AICPA also develops and grades the CPA examination, which is administered in all fifty states.

The American Accounting Association

The **American Accounting Association (AAA)**, an organization of college professors and practicing accountants, seeks, as part of its stated objective, to influence the development of accounting theory by encouraging and sponsoring accounting research. Functioning through a series of committees, the Association has published numerous monographs and committee reports and a series of statements on accounting principles, standards, and theory. In 1936 the Association published "A Tentative Statement of Accounting Principles Underlying Corporate Financial Statements" as its first attempt to set forth a consistent, coordinated statement of accounting principles. This statement was first revised in 1941 and 1948, and then more extensively in 1957. A new approach to theory formulation was taken in the Association's 1966 extension in this series of statements entitled **A Statement of Basic Accounting Theory.** The authors determined four attributes that information must possess to be useful in accounting. These four attributes—relevance, verifiability, freedom from bias, and quantifiability—were presented, along with five guidelines to communication. The most recent publication in this AAA series is the 1978 **Statement on Accounting Theory and Theory Acceptance** which emphasizes the difficulty of developing a theory structure for accounting.

The AAA in its role as critic appraises accounting practice and recommends improvements through its quarterly publication, **The Accounting Review,** and the work of its committees. Its concern is more for "what should be, as opposed to what

---

[22]"Accounting for Certain Service Transactions," *FASB Invitation to Comment* (Stamford, Conn.: FASB, 1978), 22 pages. In addition, for purposes of leveraging the resources of others, respected academicians have been consulted to develop materials on the conceptual framework study on such topics as qualitative characteristics of accounting information and revenue recognition criterion.

was, or what is." Unconcerned about immediate adoption of its proposals, the AAA takes a long-range point of view and attempts to lead practice rather than follow it.

During the past decade the AAA has given greater emphasis and encouragement to independent research in all areas of accounting through an ambitious program of financing research and sponsoring publication of the results. The first of the AAA **Studies in Accounting Research,** published in 1969, initiated a continuing series of contributions to accounting theory. The AAA also appoints from its membership ad hoc committees that draft responses to specific FASB discussion memorandums and exposure drafts.

Cost Accounting Standards Board

The **Cost Accounting Standards Board (CASB)** is a relatively new organization established in 1970 as an agency of the U.S. Congress. The CASB is authorized to promote uniformity and consistency in the cost accounting practices applied to negotiated defense contracts in excess of $100,000 by establishing **Cost Accounting Standards.** Any company that engages in government contracting, either as a prime contractor or as a subcontractor, must become familiar with the CASB and its pronouncements. Although our interest in this textbook is focused on financial accounting rather than cost accounting, the CASB's interest in any cost that may be charged to a government contract necessarily overlaps topics relevant to financial accounting and reporting.

As a condition of contracting, the CASB requires government contractors and subcontractors to file an extensive **Disclosure Statement** setting forth their cost accounting practices. Such practices must be in compliance with the Board's Standards, which are established to:

1. Measure the amount of costs which may be allocated to cover contracts,
2. Determine the accounting period to which costs are allocable, and
3. Determine the manner in which allocable costs can be allocated to covered contracts.

The Board consists of five appointed members who hold 4-year terms. The Board is supported by a full-time staff of professionals with backgrounds in industry, public accounting, government, and education. Since its organization in 1971 the CASB has issued 17 Standards (see complete list inside back cover). These Standards are monitored and enforced by the individual government contracting agencies, such as the Defense Contract Audit Agency. Unlike Financial Accounting Standards, which are dependent upon "general acceptance," Cost Accounting Standards, like SEC Accounting Series Releases, derive their authority from legislation.

Other Influential Organizations

Several other organizations also have been influential in the development of accounting theory. The **National Association of Accountants**—NAA—(formerly the National Association of Cost Accountants) has been interested in research primarily in cost accounting and in managerial accounting since its origin in 1919. **Management Accounting** is the monthly publication of the NAA. In 1968 the NAA broadened its research program to "encompass the entire range of socioeconomic information needed by those who manage a business and by those who provide its capital."[23] Undoubtedly this step will make the NAA more influential in the development of accounting standards in the future.

The **Financial Executives Institute**—FEI—(formerly the Controllers Institute of America) and its subsidiary, the Financial Executives Research Foundation, have published several interesting accounting and reporting studies. The FEI's monthly publication is **The Financial Executive.** The FEI has influenced the development of accounting standards through its Panel on Accounting Principles. This panel reviews the Discussion Memorandums and the prepublication drafts of proposed pronouncements of the FASB and submits its views and recommendations. More recently the FEI established committees to parallel task forces of the FASB that are responsible for developing various standards.

The state societies of CPAs also provide sounding boards and forums for the airing of support and criticism of FASB exposure drafts on accounting standards. Comments and proposals are formally obtained by each state CPA society and submitted to the FASB, thus providing the Board with a grassroots reaction to its proposed opinions.

The **Internal Revenue Service (IRS),** which derives its authority from the Internal Revenue Code and its amendments and legal interpretations, constitutes one of the strongest influences on accounting practice. In an effort to lessen the impact of taxes, and to avoid keeping two sets of books, business managers frequently adopt "acceptable" accounting procedures that minimize taxable income. Because the objectives of the tax law differ from the objectives of financial accounting, however, "good tax accounting" is not necessarily "good financial accounting." As noted throughout this textbook, tax laws and "tax effects" are a pervasive influence in business decision-making and on the selection of accounting methods. Differences between tax accounting and financial accounting are generally permissible; therefore, in the preparation of financial statements tax considerations must give ground to the requirements of sound accounting.

Governmental Interest in the Accounting Profession: Public Sector Versus Private Sector

All professions have come under increasing scrutiny by the government in the last ten years. Whether it be the legal profession because of Watergate, the medical profession because of high costs and medicare or medicaid frauds, or engineers because of their failure to consider environmental or societal consequences in their technical projects, all have come under the attention of the government as it has assumed an increasingly active role in protecting the public interest. The accounting profession has not been ignored. Owing to some well-publicized instances of corporate fraud, domestic and foreign bribery, and sudden bankruptcies, critics of the accounting profession started to question our dedication and performance. Add to this the general societal desire for more accountability from all institutions, and it is not surprising that Congress began to inquire into the structure and practices of the accounting profession, the accounting and auditing standard-setting process, and the role of the accounting profession in the business world.

[23]"Report and Recommendations of the Long-Range Objectives Committee of the NAA," *Management Accounting*, 1968, Section 3.

In 1976, for example, a House of Representatives committee chaired by Representative John E. Moss **(Moss Committee)** issued a report critical of the FASB for not moving quickly enough to eliminate some of the alternative reporting practices in accounting. It recommended that the SEC take a more active role in establishing accounting principles and that a framework for uniform accounting principles be developed. In 1977 a Senate committee chaired by Senator Lee Metcalf **(Metcalf Committee)** also examined the accounting profession and arrived at a number of conclusions that were not only critical but also inaccurate. The accounting profession was warned that, unless substantial changes were made in its self-regulation process, Congress would legislate (1) the setting of accounting and auditing standards for publicly held companies and (2) the regulation of CPA firms that audit financial statements of publicly held companies.

The private sector response has been direct and immediate. Even before these Congressional committees began investigating the profession's problems, the AICPA had established an independent **Commission on Auditor's Responsibilities** (referred to as the Cohen Commission) to review the function and responsibilities of the public accountants and to clarify the role of the auditor. Recommendations of the Cohen Commission that are currently in various stages of implementation include:

1. Modify the current standard auditor's report to make it a more effective means of communicating with users.
2. Develop a model code of conduct for use by client companies in adopting policy statements as to employee conduct.
3. Develop criteria for judging the adequacy of internal control systems.
4. Complete, as soon as possible, a publication of guidelines for audit committees.
5. Study significant frauds and audit failures and publish analysis for the guidance of practitioners on methods of detecting frauds and the need for new or revised auditing standards.

As part of its self-reform, the AICPA has established a new Accounting Firms Division (in addition to the existing division for individual AICPA members) with two sections: one for firms auditing SEC clients (called the **SEC Practice Section**) and the other for firms auditing privately owned, non-SEC, clients (called the **Private Companies Section**).[24] To qualify for membership in the **SEC Practice Section,** a CPA firm must:

1. Submit to an independent review of the quality controls over its audit practice at least once every three years (peer review).
2. Rotate the partner in charge of the audit for each SEC client at least every five years.
3. Provide mandatory continuing education for all levels of its professional staff.
4. Carry certain minimum amounts of liability insurance.
5. Comply with certain measures designed to safeguard independence and audit quality.

To help assure the public that the SEC Practice Section is meeting its responsibilities, the AICPA established as part of this structure an independent **Public Oversight Board.** The Board, composed of distinguished nonaccountants, has its own staff and is free to conduct its own inquiries and to report publicly as it wishes. The

---

[24]CPA firms that audit SEC registered firms must join the SEC Practice Section and thereby must comply with more comprehensive practice requirements (such as compulsory peer practice review) than are required by the Private Companies Section.

Private Companies Section also has its own quality control standards and peer review requirements.

During this same period of time the Financial Accounting Foundation (the body responsible for organizing, funding, and exercising general oversight of the FASB):

1. Opened FASB meetings to the public.
2. Changed the voting requirement for adoption of FASB pronouncements from five affirmative votes among the seven members to a simple majority.
3. Eliminated the requirement that at least four of the FASB members be CPAs principally experienced in public accounting.
4. Replaced the Board of the AICPA as the sole elector of the Foundation's Trustees with a panel of six representatives from six sponsoring organizations.
5. Approved a plan to obtain broader based financing for the FASB's operations.

Never before has the accounting profession acted so quickly and so constructively on so many fronts. Apparently these actions have satisfied some of our most severe critics and averted sweeping Congressional action to reform and control the accounting profession. The latest reports from the Congressional committees now downplay the possibility of any new legislation and support the notion that the accounting profession and the SEC be given the opportunity to fulfill their "pledges of timely action . . . to achieve reform."

In 1979, the SEC issued a report on its oversight of the accounting profession and the accounting standard-setting process, noting that the initiative for standard setting belongs in the private sector. The SEC indicated that the private sector's performance has been satisfactory and responsive to the recommendations for self-reform and self-regulation.

A delicate balance now exists between the private sector and the public sector. The private sector because of its substantive resources, expertise, and desire should be better able to develop and maintain high standards; yet, some people in government and the financial community demand that the accounting profession assume more responsibility and be more responsive to the needs of the public. At present, the accounting profession is reacting responsibly and effectively to remedy identified shortcomings, and the government appears willing to permit it to develop its own standards and regulate itself with minimal intervention.

Questions

1. In what ways is accounting a service activity? A descriptive/analytical discipline? An information system?
2. What is it in today's environment that places a greater responsibility upon accounting now than ever before?
3. Into what areas can the discipline of accounting be divided?
4. Differentiate broadly between financial accounting and managerial accounting.
5. Differentiate between "financial statements" and "financial reporting."
6. Accounting is an unchanging discipline independent of its environment and other influences. Comment.
7. Name several environmental conditions that shape financial accounting to a significant extent.
8. It is an acknowledged fact that we live in a world of scarce means and resources. In what ways is this fact recognized by accounting?
9. How are the current legal and ethical standards related to the basic nature of accounting?

10. In what way does accounting shape its environment and play a role in the conduct of economic, social, political, and legal actions?

11. Of what value is a common body of theory in financial accounting and reporting?

12. What is the likely limitation of "general-purpose financial statements"?

13. What are some of the developments or events that occurred between 1900 and 1930 that helped bring about changes in accounting theory or practice?

14. What was the Committee on Accounting Procedure and what were its accomplishments and failings?

15. For what purposes did the AICPA in 1959 create the Accounting Principles Board and a new Accounting Research Division?

16. Distinguish between Accounting Research Bulletins, Accounting Research Studies, Opinions of the Accounting Principles Board, and Statements of the Financial Accounting Standards Board.

17. How were APB opinions enforced?

18. If you had to explain or define "generally accepted accounting principles or standards" to a nonaccountant, what essential characteristics would you include in your explanation?

19. In what ways was it felt that the statements issued by the Financial Accounting Standards Board would carry greater weight than the opinions issued by the Accounting Principles Board?

20. How are FASB "discussion memorandums" and FASB "exposure drafts" related to FASB "statements"?

21. Distinguish between FASB "statements of financial accounting **standards**" and FASB "statements of financial accounting **concepts.**"

22. What are "interpretations" of APB opinions and "interpretations" of FASB statements and how much authority do they have?

23. What are the sources of pressure that change and influence the development of accounting principles and standards?

24. In what way is the Securities and Exchange Commission concerned about and supportive of accounting principles and standards?

25. Differentiate between the Financial Accounting Standards Board and the Cost Accounting Standards Board.

26. What is AcSEC and what is its relationship to the FASB? Include in your answer a discussion of AcSEC's apparent conflict with the FASB.

27. Explain how the Internal Revenue Code affects financial accounting standards and practices.

28. If you were given complete authority in the matter, how would you propose that accounting principles or standards should be developed and enforced?

Cases

C1-1   At the completion of the Wetzel Industries, Inc. audit, the president, Thomas Wetzel, Sr., asks about the meaning of the phrase "in conformity with generally accepted accounting principles" that appears in your audit report on the management's financial statements. He observes that the meaning of the phrase must include more than what he thinks of as "principles."

Instructions

(a) Explain the meaning of the term "accounting principles" as used in the audit report. (Do **not** discuss in this part the significance of "generally accepted.")

(b) President Wetzel wants to know how you determine whether or not an accounting principle is generally accepted. Discuss the sources of evidence for determining whether an accounting principle has substantial authoritative support. Do **not** merely list the titles of publications.

(c) President Wetzel believes that diversity in accounting practice always will exist among independent entities despite continual improvements in comparability. Discuss the arguments that **support** his belief.

(AICPA adapted)

C1-2 Some accountants have said that politicization in the development and acceptance of generally accepted accounting principles (i.e., standard-setting) is taking place. Some use the term "politicization" in a narrow sense to mean the influence by governmental agencies, particularly the Securities and Exchange Commission, on the development of generally accepted accounting principles. Others use it more broadly to mean the compromising that takes place in bodies responsible for developing generally accepted accounting principles because of the influence and pressure of interested groups (SEC, American Accounting Association, businesses through their various organizations, National Association of Accountants, financial analysts, bankers, lawyers, etc.).

Instructions

(a) The Committee on Accounting Procedures of the AICPA was established in the mid to late 1930s and functioned until 1959, at which time the Accounting Principles Board came into existence. In 1973, the Financial Accounting Standards Board was formed and the APB went out of existence. Do the reasons these groups were formed, their methods of operation while in existence, and the reasons for the demise of the first two indicate an increasing politicization (as the term is used in the broad sense) of accounting standard-setting? Explain your answer by indicating how the CAP, the APB and the FASB operated or operate. Cite specific developments that tend to support your answer.

(b) What arguments can be raised to support the "politicization" of accounting standard-setting?

(c) What arguments can be raised against the "politicization" of accounting standard-setting?

(CMA adapted)

C1-3 A press release announcing the appointment of the trustees of the new Financial Accounting Foundation stated that the Financial Accounting Standards Board (to be appointed by the trustees) ". . . will become the established authority for setting accounting principles under which corporations report to the shareholders and others" (AICPA news release, July 20, 1972).

Instructions

(a) No mention is made of the SEC in the press release. What role does the SEC play in setting accounting principles?

(b) How have accounting principles been set in the past ten years? In your answer identify the body performing this function, the sponsoring organization, the method by which the body arrives at its decisions.

(c) What methods have management and management accountants used to influence the development of accounting principles in the past ten years?

(CMA adapted)

Basic Theory Underlying
Financial Accounting

Accounting may appear to be primarily procedural in nature. The visible portion of accounting—record keeping and preparation of financial statements—too often suggests the application of a low-level skill in an occupation devoted to mundane objectives and devoid of challenge and imagination. In accounting a large body of theory does exist, however. Philosophical objectives, normative theories, interrelated concepts, precise definitions, and rationalized rules comprise this body of theory, which may be unknown to many people in the business community.[1] Thus, **accountants philosophize, theorize, judge, create, and deliberate as a significant part of their professional practice.** The subjective aspects that are so critical to current accounting practice, such as searching for truth and fact, judging what is fair presentation, and considering the behavior induced by presentations, are overshadowed by the appearance of exactitude, precision, and objectivity that accompanies the use of numbers to express the financial results of the enterprise.

Although the practice of accounting is considered an art, the development of accounting theory is more scientific. Even so, the principles of accounting are unlike the principles of the natural sciences and mathematics, because they cannot be

---

[1]Perhaps the most significant documents in this area are: Maurice Moonitz, *Accounting Research Study No. 1: The Basic Postulates of Accounting* (New York: AICPA, 1961); Robert T. Sprouse and Maurice Moonitz, *Accounting Research Study No. 3: A Tentative Set of Broad Accounting Principles for Business Enterprises* (New York: AICPA, 1962); *APB Statement No. 4: Basic Concepts and Accounting Principles Underlying Financial Statements of Business Enterprises* (New York: AICPA, 1970); "Objectives of Financial Reporting by Business Enterprises" *Statement of Financial Accounting Concepts No. 1* (Stamford, Conn.: FASB, 1978); and "Conceptual Framework for Financial Accounting and Reporting: Elements of Financial Statements and Their Measurement," *FASB Discussion Memorandum,* (Stamford, Conn.: FASB, 1976). These studies, as well as related documents, are summarized in the appendix to this chapter and provide useful reference material to those wishing to explore this area in greater depth.

derived from or proved by the laws of nature, and they are not viewed as fundamental truths or axioms. Accounting principles have not been discovered; they have been created, developed, or decreed. Accounting principles are supported and justified by intuition, authority, and acceptability. Because it is difficult to substantiate accounting principles objectively or by experimentation, arguments concerning them can degenerate into quasi-religious dogmatism. As a result, the sanction for and credibility of accounting principles rest upon their general recognition and acceptance, which depend upon such criteria as usefulness, fairness, and feasibility.

Development of a Framework

Many are critical of the accounting profession standard-setting process because no overall framework has been developed to guide the formation of consistent financial reporting standards. Recognizing the necessity for this framework, the FASB in December 1976 issued a massive three-part discussion memorandum entitled **Conceptual Framework for Financial Accounting and Reporting: Elements of Financial Statements and Their Measurement,** which detailed the major issues considered necessary to establish a basic framework for resolving financial reporting controversies. The purpose of this project was to lead to FASB pronouncements on the following matters:

1. **Establishment of the objectives of financial statements.** It is necessary to determine (a) for what purposes financial statements are intended to be used; (b) to whom should they be directed; (c) what information should be included; and (d) the limitations of financial statements.
2. **Determination of the essential qualitative characteristics of financial statement information.** What qualities (such as relevance, objectivity, and comparability) make accounting information useful to financial statement readers and what are the appropriate trade-offs that are necessary when conflicts between these characteristics (such as relevance and objectivity) occur?
3. **Definition of the basic elements of accounting.** What is an asset, liability, revenue, or expense? Are some of these elements more important than others in determining net income? For example, should net income be defined in terms of changes in an enterprise's net assets (excluding capital transactions) over a period of time, or should assets and liabilities be determined only after revenues, expenses, and net income are defined?
4. **Determination of the basis of measurement.** Even after the basic elements are developed, how should assets be measured? For example, should we use historical cost, replacement cost, current selling price, expected cash flows, present value of expected cash flows, or some other valuation system?
5. **Change in the measuring unit.** Should the basic measuring unit of accounting be adjusted for changes in purchasing power of the dollar, should these changes be ignored, or should information on a supplementary basis be presented?

The accounting profession has struggled with these questions for many years without much success. However, there is cause for optimism now because the FASB has already issued one pronouncement, **Statement of Financial Accounting Concepts No. 1,** "Objectives of Financial Reporting by Business Enterprises," which identifies a set of objectives for financial reporting. As indicated in Chapter 1, these objectives suggest that financial reporting should provide information useful in investment and credit decisions being made by individuals who have a reasonable understanding of business, rather than naive or unsophisticated investors. In addition, financial reporting should help users assess the amount, timing, and uncertainty of future cash flows and should provide information about economic resources, the claims to them, and the changes in them. Recently the FASB issued **Statement No. 33,** "Financial Reporting and Changing Prices," which requires increased disclosure of price-level information in the financial statements.[2] Such action by the FASB indicates that answers to other issues discussed above are under serious consideration.

Theoretical Framework

As indicated, no well-defined framework exists at present to guide the standard setting process. There are, however, certain fundamentals that accountants generally recognize and apply in practice. We have classified these fundamentals of financial accounting into **five major categories: objectives, elements, assumptions, principles, and modifying conventions.** Others might term them postulates, procedures, rules, and so on. Whatever terminology is used, the content of the basic theory does not change significantly.

Accountants who have attempted to develop a general theory establish somewhat similar categories to classify the theoretical concepts of their discipline. We have selected a classification framework that makes useful differentiations within the theory structure, but we have not provided a complete system in this chapter. This framework is presented as an aid to understanding the basic theory of financial accounting; it serves as a reference for examining the situations and problems that are covered in intermediate accounting. Because the objectives of financial reporting are presented in Chapter 1, page 5, we will start with the basic elements of financial accounting theory.

BASIC ELEMENTS

An important aspect in developing any theoretical structure is the establishment of a body of elements or definitions. FASB Chairman Donald Kirk noted that the establishment of definitions for such items as assets, liabilities, and earnings may be the most important phase of the FASB Conceptual Framework Study.[3] At present, accounting uses many terms that have peculiar and specific meanings, terms that constitute the language of business or the jargon of accounting. One such term is **asset.** Is it something we own? If the answer is yes, can we assume that any asset leased would never be shown on the balance sheet? Is it something we have the right to use, or is it anything of value used by the enterprise to generate earnings? If the answer is yes, then why should the management of the enterprise not be considered an asset? It seems necessary, therefore, to develop a basic defini-

---

[2]"Financial Reporting and Changing Prices" *Statements on Financial Accounting Standards No. 33* (Stamford, Conn.: FASB, 1979).

[3]Speech by FASB Chairman Donald J. Kirk before the Financial Executives Institute International Conference, summarized in *FASB Viewpoints* (Stamford, Conn.: FASB, 1978), p. 3.

tional framework for the **elements of accounting.** The following definitions for the elements have been developed in an FASB exposure draft:

Assets—Financial representations of economic resources—cash and future economic benefits—the beneficial interest in which is legally or equitably secured to a particular enterprise as a result of a past transaction or event.

Liabilities—Financial representations of obligations of a particular enterprise to transfer economic resources to other entities in the future as a result of a past transaction or event affecting the enterprise.

Owners' Equity—Residual interest in the enterprise's assets remaining after deducting liabilities. It is the interest of owners who bear the ultimate risks and uncertainties of enterprise earning and financing activities and the effect of other events and circumstances that may affect the enterprise and who obtain the reward from enterprise successes.

Revenues—Gross increases in assets or gross decreases in liabilities (or a combination of both) from delivering or producing goods, rendering services, or other earning activities of an enterprise during a period.

Expenses—Gross decreases in assets or gross increases in liabilities (or a combination of both) from delivering or producing goods, rendering services, and other earning activities and from imposition of taxes by governmental units.

Gains and Losses—Gains are increases in net assets other than from revenues or investments by owners. Losses are decreases in net assets other than from expenses or withdrawals by owners.

Earnings—Revenues minus expenses plus gains minus losses (all pertaining to the same period).[4]

The definition of these basic elements depends to a great extent on an individual's belief in how net income should be measured. One approach, referred to as the **asset and liability view,** contends that net income is a measure of the changes in net economic resources (net assets) from one period to another (with limited exceptions); thus, net income is defined in terms of changes in assets and liabilities. Definitions of revenues, expenses, gains or losses, although useful for providing additional information, are not considered necessary for determining net income or loss.

Another approach, referred to as the **revenue and expense view,** argues that net income should be a measure of the effectiveness of an enterprise in producing and distributing goods or rendering services during a period and should not limit itself to changes in the net economic resources (net assets) of a business enterprise. Thus, definitions of revenues, expenses, gains, and losses are essential to the revenue and expense view. Net income (loss) is defined as the difference between revenues (inflow of resources) and expenses (outflow of resources). In the revenue and expense approach, the matching of cost and revenues is of primary importance and, therefore, the recording of deferred charges and credits is permitted to ensure proper matching. Conversely, the asset and liability view would not record deferred charges or credits because such items are not considered to be assets or liabilities.

[4]These definitions are taken from "Objectives of Financial Reporting and Elements of Financial Statements of Business Enterprises," FASB Exposure Draft (Stamford, Conn.: FASB, 1977). Subsequently the objectives were restated in final form in *Statement of Financial Accounting Concepts No. 1*, but because there was disagreement about the elements, the Board delayed issuing a Statement of Financial Accounting Concepts on them. The Board plans to reexpose the elements study; undoubtedly some definitions will change, particularly regarding liabilities. However, the above definitions provide a reasonable perspective of the general nature of these items.

BASIC ASSUMPTIONS OF ACCOUNTING

What are the basic assumptions of accounting? In most cases, they are so obvious that we might ask why they have to be stated at all. But, because these assumptions are critical to the development of proper and consistent accounting, they merit special attention. If we do not understand the basic assumptions made by accountants, we cannot understand why the data are presented in a given manner.

Four basic assumptions that seem to underlie the financial accounting structure are (1) **an economic entity assumption,** (2) **a going concern assumption,** (3) **a monetary unit assumption,** and (4) **a periodicity assumption.**

Economic Entity Assumption

A major assumption in accounting is that economic activity can be identified with a particular unit of accountability. In other words, the activity of a business enterprise can be kept separate and distinct from its owners and any other business unit.[5] If there were no meaningful way to separate all of the economic events that occur, no basis for accounting would exist. Accounting as a system for providing information for and about a given company simply would not exist. Imagine the results, for example, if the activities of General Motors could not be distinguished from those of Ford, Chrysler, or American Motors.

The entity concept does not apply solely to the segregation of activities among given business enterprises. Generally we think of entities as business enterprises; but an individual, a department or division, or an entire industry could be considered a separate entity if we chose to define the unit in such a manner. Thus **the entity concept is not necessarily a legal-entity concept;** a parent and its subsidiaries are separate **legal** entities, but merging their activities for accounting and reporting purposes is not a violation of the **economic entity** assumption.

Going Concern Assumption

Most accounting methods are based on **the assumption that the business enterprise will have a long life.** Experience indicates that, in spite of numerous business failures, companies have a fairly high continuance rate, and it has proved useful to adopt a going concern or continuity assumption for accounting purposes. Although accountants do not believe that business firms will last indefinitely, they do expect them to last long enough to fulfill their objectives and commitments.

The implications of adopting this assumption are critical. Acceptance of this assumption provides credibility to the historical cost principle, which would be of limited usefulness if eventual liquidation were assumed. Under a liquidation approach, for example, asset values are better stated at net realizable value (sales price less costs of disposal) than at acquisition cost. **Only if we assume some per-**

---

[5]Surprisingly, such a distinction is not always made in practice. A recent *Wall Street Journal* article, for example, noted that audit committees of six publicly held companies want their chief executive to reimburse the companies an additional $1 million in personal expenses for such items as company yachts, speedboats, refurbishing, and rent money on personal apartments. "Posners Asked to Repay Firms 1.1 Million More," *Wall Street Journal*, November 27, 1978, p. 6.

manence to the enterprise are depreciation and amortization policies justifiable and appropriate. If a liquidation approach were adopted, the current-noncurrent classification of assets and liabilities would lose much of its significance. Labeling anything a fixed or long-term asset would be difficult to justify. The listing of the liabilities on the basis of priority in liquidation, for example, is more reasonable.

The going concern assumption is generally applicable in most business situations. Only where liquidation appears imminent is the assumption inapplicable, and in these cases a total revaluation of the assets and liabilities can provide information that closely approximates net realizable value of the entity. Most of the accounting problems related to an enterprise in liquidation are presented in advanced accounting.

Monetary Unit Assumption

Accounting is based on the assumption that money is the common denominator by which economic activity is conducted, and that the monetary unit provides an appropriate basis for accounting measurement and analysis. This assumption implies that the monetary unit is the most effective means of expressing to interested parties changes in capital and exchanges of goods and services. Support for this assumption lies in the fact that the monetary unit is relevant, simple, universally available, understandable, and useful. Application of this assumption is dependent on the even more basic assumption that quantitative data are useful in communicating economic information and in making rational economic decisions.

In the United States, accountants have chosen generally to ignore the phenomena of price-level change (inflation and deflation) by adopting the monetary unit assumption that assumes that the unit of measure—the dollar—remains reasonably stable. This second assumption about the monetary unit allows the accountant to add 1952 dollars to 1980 dollars without any adjustment. Arguments submitted in support of the stability assumption are that the effects of price-level changes are not significant and that presentation of price-level data is not easily understood.

Whether the stable monetary assumption will continue in accounting is difficult to predict. This assumption has come under increasing criticism in the United States because of the increased inflation rate, which has doubled prices in the last ten years. Recent studies indicate that significant variances in reporting can develop from omission of price-level data. Several countries adopting the monetary unit as the basis of accounting measurement do not assume its stability and, therefore, make adjustments for price-level changes as standard procedure. The assumption that the monetary unit remains stable will be followed throughout this textbook to emphasize the basis of the historical cost system. The FASB recently issued FASB Statement No. 33, "Financial Reporting and Changing Prices," which requires supplemental price-level disclosures by certain large enterprises. Chapter 25 discusses the accounting problems and benefits of adjusting for price-level changes.

Periodicity Assumption

The most accurate way to measure the results of enterprise activity would be to measure them at the time of the enterprise's eventual liquidation. Business, government, investors, and various other user groups, however, cannot wait indefinitely for such information. If accountants did not provide financial information periodically, someone else would.

The periodicity or time period assumption simply implies that **the economic activities of an enterprise can be divided into artificial time periods.** These time periods vary, but the most common are monthly, quarterly, and yearly. Because accountants have to divide continuous operations into arbitrary time periods, they must determine the relevance of each business transaction or event to one specific accounting period. The shorter the time period, the more difficult it becomes to determine the proper net income for the period. Because of problems of allocation, a month's results are usually less reliable than a quarter's results, and a quarter's results are likely to be less reliable than a year's results. This phenomenon provides an interesting example of the trade-off between reliability and timeliness in preparing financial data. Investors desire and demand that information be quickly processed and disseminated; yet the quicker the information is released, the more subject it is to error.

BASIC PRINCIPLES OF ACCOUNTING

In view of the basic assumptions of accounting, what are the principles or guidelines that the accountant follows in recording transaction data? These principles can be classified as (1) **the historical cost principle,** (2) **the revenue realization principle,** (3) **the matching principle,** (4) **the consistency principle,** (5) **the full disclosure principle,** and (6) **the objectivity principle.** The principles relate basically to how assets, liabilities, revenues, and expenses are to be identified, measured, and reported.

The Historical Cost Principle

The determination of the amounts to be recorded and reported for various assets and liabilities creates one of the most difficult problems in accounting. A wide range of values may exist for a single item: replacement cost, current selling price, present value of future cash flows, and original cost less depreciation. Which should the accountant use? Which will best serve the several interests in the enterprise to the mutual benefit of all?

Accountants, business managers, taxing authorities, and others have found that cost is generally the value most useful as a basis for accounting records. The first principle, then, is that assets and liabilities are accounted for on a basis of cost. **Cost has this important advantage over other valuations: it is definite and determinable.** To illustrate the importance of this advantage, let us consider the problems that would arise if we adopted some other basis for keeping records. If we were to select current selling price, for instance, we might have a difficult time in attempting to establish a sales value for a given item without selling it. Every member of the accounting department might have his or her own opinion of the proper valuation of the asset, and management might desire still another figure. And how often would we find it necessary to establish sales value? All companies close their accounts at least annually, and some compute their net income every month. These companies would find it necessary to place a sales value on every asset each time they wished to determine income—a laborious task and one that would result in a figure of net income materially affected by opinion on sales value of the many assets involved. Similar objections have been leveled against use value, cost to replace, or any other basis of valuation except cost.

Cost is definite and objective, not a matter for conjecture or opinion. Once established, it is fixed as long as the asset remains the property of the company. These two characteristics are of real importance to those who use accounting data. To rely on the information supplied, both internal and external parties must know that the information is accurate and based on fact. **By using cost as their basis for record keeping, accountants can provide objective and verifiable data in their reports.**

Although there is general agreement that assets and liabilities should be accounted for on the basis of cost, there is also considerable criticism of this practice. Some accountants and others point out that accounting records kept on the basis of historical costs have severe disadvantages. Criticism is especially strong during a period when general price levels are changing substantially. At such times **cost is said to go "out of date" almost as soon as it is determined.** In a period of rising or falling prices, the cost figures of the preceding year are viewed as not comparable with current cost figures. Financial statements that present the cost of fixed assets acquired 20 or 30 years ago may even be misleading, because readers of such statements tend to think in terms of current price levels, not in terms of the price levels at the time the fixed assets were purchased. A further complication follows from the fact that depreciation figures are based on recorded costs. As depreciation expense enters into income calculations, even the net income figure is suspect because of price-level changes.

The question of "what is cost" is not always easy to answer; a variety of problems arises. If fixed assets are to be carried in the accounts at cost, are cash discounts to be deducted in determining cost? Does cost include freight and insurance? Does it include cost of installation as well as the price of a machine itself? And what of the cost of reinstallation if the machine is later moved? When land is purchased for a building site and is already occupied by old structures, is the cost of razing these structures part of the cost of the land? These and similar questions must be considered and answered in arriving at cost figures for assets purchased.

Furthermore, purchase is not the only method of acquiring assets. How do we determine the cost of items received as a gift? It is not unusual for a developing community to offer plant sites free as an inducement to companies to establish themselves in that locality. At what price should such assets be carried? Again, certain assets may be acquired by the issuance of the capital stock of the acquiring company or perhaps through the issuance of bonds or notes payable. If no money price is stated in the transaction, how is cost to be established? These questions are answered in later chapters; they are raised here only to point out some of the difficulties regularly encountered in accounting for costs.

The basic financial statements include liabilities and assets. We ordinarily think of cost as relating only to assets, and so it may seem strange that liabilities too are accounted for on a basis of cost. **If we convert the term "cost" to "exchange price," we will find that it applies to liabilities as well.** Liabilities, such as bonds, notes, and accounts payable, are issued by a business enterprise in exchange for assets, or perhaps services, upon which an agreed price has usually been placed. This price, established by the exchange transaction, is the "cost" of the liability and provides the figure at which it should be recorded in the accounts and reported in financial statements.

The Revenue Realization Principle

The revenue realization principle provides the answer to the question of when revenue should be recognized. Revenue is realized when (1) **the earning process is virtually complete** and (2) **an exchange transaction has occurred.**

Generally, an objective test, confirmation by a sale to independent interests, is adopted as the test to indicate realization of revenue. Any basis for revenue realization short of actual sale opens the door to wide variations in practice. Conservative business individuals might wait until sale of their securities; more optimistic individuals could watch market quotations and take up gains as market prices increased; yet others might recognize increases that are merely rumored; and unscrupulous persons could "write up" their investments as they please to suit their own purposes. To give accounting reports uniform meaning, a rule of income realization comparable to the cost rule for asset valuation is essential. **Realization through sale provides a uniform and reasonable test.**

There are, however, exceptions to the rule and, at times, the basic rule is difficult to apply.

Percentage-of-Completion Approach   Realization of revenue is allowed in certain long-term construction contracts before the contract is completed. The advantage of this method is that income is recognized periodically on the basis of the percent that the job is complete instead of only when the entire job is finished. Although technically an exchange transaction has not occurred (transfer of ownership), the earning process is substantially completed as construction progresses. Naturally, if it is not possible to obtain dependable estimates of cost and progress, then the accountant should wait and record the revenue at the completion date.

End of Production   At times, revenue might be considered realized before sale, but after the production cycle has ended. This is the case where the price is certain as well as the amount. An example would be the mining of certain minerals for which, once the mineral is mined, a ready market at a standard price exists. The same holds true for some artificial price supports set by the government in establishing agricultural prices.

Receipt of Cash   Receipt of cash is another basis for revenue recognition. The cash basis approach should be used only when it is impossible to establish the revenue figure at the time of sale because of the uncertainty of collection. This approach is commonly referred to as the installment sales method where payment is required in periodic installments over a long period of time. Its most common use is in the retail field where all types of farm and home equipment and furnishings are sold on an installment basis. The installment method is frequently justified on the basis that the risk of not collecting an account receivable may be so great that the sale is not sufficient evidence that realization has taken place. In some instances, this reasoning may be valid but not in a majority of such transactions. If a sale has been completed, it should be recognized; and if bad debts are expected, they should be recorded as separate estimates of uncollectibles.

Revenue, then, is recorded in the period in which an exchange takes place and the earning process is virtually complete. Normally, this is the date of sale, but circumstances may dictate application of the percentage-of-completion approach, the end-of-production approach, or the receipt-of-cash approach.

Conceptually, the proper accounting treatment for revenue realization should be apparent and should fit nicely into one of the conditions mentioned above, but often it does not. For example, consider two recent developments on the business scene—**franchises** and **motion picture sales to television.**

During the 1960s, franchising appeared to be the "updated version of the American dream." Franchising operations were established for a wide variety of businesses from restaurants to pet-care centers. One need not have traveled too widely to appreciate the significant increases in fast-food chains such as McDonald's, Shakey's, Kentucky Fried Chicken, Wendy's, and so on. One of the problems that faced accountants of the franchisor (seller of the franchise) was when to recognize revenue from the sale of a franchise. In nearly all cases, as soon as the franchisor found an individual franchisee (buyer of the franchise) and received a down payment (no matter how small), the entire franchise price was treated as realized income. Consequently, to avoid any income slump that could impair their growth reputation, many franchisors signed up franchisees at an accelerating rate each year to perpetuate growth in earnings. This was necessary because the initial franchise fees were treated immediately as revenue—even though in many situations those fees were payable over a period of years, were refundable or uncollectible in the case of franchises that never got started, or were earned only as certain services were performed by the franchisor. In effect the franchisors were counting their fried chickens before they were hatched.

Because of the abuses that developed in the area of franchise accounting, accountants had to change the basis for revenue recognition from the date the franchise contract is signed to a basis that more clearly represents earnings and the earning process. It appears that accountants eventually will allow revenue recognition only when the franchisor has made substantial performance of services to meet the obligations under the franchise agreement. The franchisor also will be required to deduct from its revenue an allowance for losses on uncollectible notes, especially if it is a new company.

How should motion picture companies such as Metro-Goldwyn-Mayer Inc., Warner Bros., and United Artists account for the sale of rights to show motion picture films on television networks such as ABC, CBS, or NBC? Should the revenue from the sale of the rights be reported when the contract is signed, when the motion picture film is delivered to the network, when the cash payment is received by the motion picture company, or when the film is shown on television? The problem of revenue recognition is complicated because the TV networks are often restricted to the number of times the film may be shown and over what period of time.

For example, Metro-Goldwyn-Mayer Inc. (MGM) recently sold to CBS the rights to show "Gone With The Wind" for $35 million. For this $35 million, CBS is permitted to show this classic movie twenty times over a twenty-year period. MGM contends that revenue reporting should coincide with the right to telecast on first and subsequent showings as included in the license agreement. They argue that the right to show "Gone With The Wind" twenty times over a twenty-year period is a significant contract restriction and, therefore, revenue recognition should coincide with the showings. The accounting profession on the other hand argues that when (1) the sales price and cost of each film is known, (2) collectibility is assured, and (3) the film is available and accepted by the network, revenue recognition should occur. The restriction that "Gone With The Wind" be shown only once a year for twenty years is not considered significant enough or appropriate justification for deferring revenue recognition. It is interesting to note that MGM, Inc., in the first quarter of 1979, reported essentially the entire $35 million in revenue in one period as the following headline in the *Wall Street Journal* reports, "MGM's Net Tripled in the First Quarter That Ended Nov. 30."

The Matching Principle

A year is the accepted fiscal period for almost every type of business. Occasionally 52 weeks instead of 365 days is considered to be a year, but in general the fiscal period is 12 consecutive months. The 12-month period may or may not coincide with the calendar year. Many concerns use a "natural business year" that ends at a time of low business activity, when their normal business cycle has been completed.

The popularity of the calendar year as a fiscal period is partly due to the collection of federal income taxes on a calendar-year basis. If proper application is made, however, the Internal Revenue Service will permit a company to file its tax return on the basis of a business year instead of a calendar year.

Whether the fiscal year is a calendar year or a natural business year, its importance to accountants follows from its acceptance as the term or period for which net income should be computed. At annual intervals, the results of operations are computed as accurately as possible. The net income figure (together with details of the income and expense considered in arriving at net income) is used by the board of directors to determine whether dividends should be declared, by governments to levy taxes, and by investors and creditors to appraise the efforts of management. Net income is perhaps the most important single factor in establishing a value for the business and for shares of its stock. In the single figure of net income is condensed the result of the operations of the company for the year; the importance of an accurate computation of net income cannot be overemphasized.

In making an accurate computation of net income for a year, accountants face a problem in trying to include all revenue and expenses, items that belong within the year, and to exclude all revenue and expenses that do not belong within the given year. The term accrual basis of accounting describes the accounting procedures that are used to allocate revenue and expense properly among the years that an enterprise is in operation.

Under a **cash basis of accounting** the total outflow of cash during the period is considered the expense incurred. The **accrual basis of accounting modifies this approach by adopting the revenue realization principle that revenue is recorded when earned, and uses the matching principle to indicate that expenses may be**

incurred and matched against revenue even though no cash outflow has occurred.[6]

Most companies use the accrual basis of accounting; very small enterprises and practicing professionals usually use a strict or modified cash basis approach. Under a strict cash basis, all expenditures are expensed when paid; under a **modified cash basis** certain expenditures may be capitalized and amortized in the future. For example, under a strict cash basis, the purchase of a plant asset such as equipment for cash is expensed immediately; under a modified cash basis, the purchase of equipment is recorded as an asset and not considered an expense even though the item is fully paid for. Several service enterprises such as firms of physicians, lawyers, or accountants employ the modified cash basis, because their transactions are relatively simple and straightforward and no significant differences normally exist between the modified cash method and the accrual basis of accounting for their type of enterprise. Note that the modified cash basis is the method followed by the average taxpayer in determining taxable income for the Internal Revenue Service.

Accountants generally use the accrual basis of accounting, recognizing that many arbitrary decisions will have to be made, but hoping that a better indicator of the financial position and results of operations can be achieved than would be possible if a strict or modified cash basis were employed.

The problem of allocating revenue and expenses to the proper fiscal period is difficult and ever present in accounting. When the accrual system is used, certain tests or standards aid the accountant in determining the proper method of handling any given item. The previously discussed revenue realization principle covered the bases used for revenue realization.

In allocating expenses to accounting periods we use a somewhat different type of test. The basic principle is to match expenses with the revenues; "let the expense follow the revenue." Thus, the expense should be recognized not when wages are paid or necessarily when the work is performed, but when that work actually makes its contribution to revenue. In some cases, determining the period in which an expense contributes to the generation of revenue is difficult, but many expenses can be associated with particular revenues. **The matching principle thus dictates that efforts (expenses) be matched with accomplishments (revenues) if feasible.**

For those costs for which it is difficult to adopt some type of rational association between the expense and revenue, some other approach must be developed. Often, the accountant must develop a "rational and systematic" allocation policy that will approximate the matching principle. This type of expense recognition pattern always involves assumptions about the benefits that are being received as well as the cost associated with those benefits. The cost of a long-lived asset, for example, must be allocated over all of the accounting periods during which the asset is used because the asset contributes to the generation of revenue throughout its useful life.

Some costs are charged to the current period as expenses (or losses) simply because no future benefit is anticipated or no apparent connection with revenue is

---

[6]*Statement of Financial Accounting Concepts No. 1* indicated that information about enterprise earnings based on accrual accounting generally provides a better indication of an enterprise's present and continuing ability to generate favorable cash flows than information limited to the financial effects of cash receipts and payments.

available. Examples of these types of costs are officers' salaries and advertising and promotion expenses.

Summarizing, we might say that costs are analyzed to determine whether a relationship exists with revenue. Where this association holds, the costs are expensed and matched against the revenue in the period when the revenue is recognized. If no connection appears between costs and revenues, an allocation of cost on some systematic and rational basis might be appropriate. Where, however, this method does not seem desirable, the cost may be expensed immediately. Notice that costs are generally classified into two groups: **product costs and period costs.** Product costs such as material, labor, and overhead attach to the product and are carried into future periods if the revenue from the product is realized in subsequent periods. Period costs such as officers' salaries and selling expenses are charged off immediately to income because no direct relationship between cost and revenue can be determined.

The problem of expense recognition is as complex as that of revenue recognition. For example, at one time a large oil company spent a considerable amount of money in an introductory advertising campaign in Hawaii. The company obviously hoped that this advertising campaign would attract new customers and develop brand loyalty. Over how many years, if any, should this outlay be expensed? For another example, Delta Air Lines depreciates its planes over 10 years, while United Air Lines, at the other end of the spectrum, writes off its B727 jets over periods as long as 16 years.

The point again seems clear: we have a fairly definitive principle that conceptually appears useful; yet certain items do not fit into any neat classification framework.

The Consistency Principle

Accounting reports for any given year are useful in themselves, of course, but they are much more useful if they can be compared with similar reports for prior years and with reports for other companies. The consistency principle of accounting requires that accounting entities give accountable events the same accounting treatment from period to period. To achieve comparability, alternative accounting practices must be minimized and then consistently applied period by period. Reports prepared on a basis of cost in one year, for example, and on a price-level adjusted basis in another year cannot be compared without modifying one or the other. In the following chapters, a number of alternative practices with respect to inventory pricing, depreciation policies, and expensing versus capitalizing are available to companies in keeping their accounts. Switching from one alternative to another, year after year, results in accounting data that are not at all comparable. Thus accountants place considerable emphasis on consistency from one year to another.

The consistency principle means that a company applies the same methods from period to period, but it does not mean that companies cannot switch from one method of accounting to another. Companies can change, but the changes are restricted to situations in which it can be demonstrated that the newly adopted principle is preferable to the old. And then, the nature and effect of the accounting change as well as the justification for it must be disclosed in the financial statements for the period in which the change is made.

The standard opinion rendered by independent certified public accountants also refers to consistency. The relevant portion of this opinion is: "In our opinion, the accompanying financial statements present fairly the financial position and results of operations for the period under review in accordance with generally accepted accounting principles applied on a **basis consistent with that of the preceding year.**" Beyond the requirements of good theory, little can be done to insist that one company keep its accounts on a basis that is consistent with that of another. Thus, in comparing the reports of different companies, the similarity or dissimilarity of their respective accounting practices must be determined.

The Full Disclosure Principle

Because numerous alternative accounting treatments are available, and because their selection is frequently subjective or capricious, there is always the possibility that another accountant might have chosen a different treatment. It is also true that many readers of financial reports do not appreciate the existence of the number of alternatives from which the accountant selected a given practice. Unless explicitly informed, a reader might assume that an entirely different practice had been followed. To offset this possibility, accountants have adopted a principle of full disclosure that generally calls for revealing in financial statements any facts of sufficient importance to influence the judgment of an informed reader. Thus, the full disclosure principle requires the presentation of sufficient information to permit the knowledgeable reader to reach an informed decision instead of indulging in a guessing game. The common methods of disclosure are (1) **presenting an account with a balance,** (2) **parenthetical disclosure,** and (3) **footnote disclosure.**

Excessive disclosure is also a possibility. Reasonable condensation and summarization of the details of a company's operations and financial position are essential to readability and comprehension. Thus, in determining what is adequate disclosure, the accountant makes decisions on the basis of whether omission would cause a misleading inference by the reader of the statement.

Adequate disclosure includes not only more information but also more descriptive captions, brief parenthetical notations and explanations, logical arrangement and format, and concise yet complete footnotes. For example, it is generally considered desirable to disclose the composition of a manufacturing firm's inventory classified as raw materials, work in process, and finished goods, and to include a statement of the method of pricing as well as the basis of valuation. Details of bond issues, full descriptions of capital stock, and detailed classification of current assets are the standard practice instead of the exception in reports.

The accountant's problem is compounded by the complexity and dynamic nature of the business environment. During the past decade the increased occurrence of business combinations has produced innumerable conglomerate-type business organizations and financing arrangements that demand new and peculiar accounting and reporting practices and principles. Leases, investment credits, pension funds, franchising, options, and mergers have had to be studied and proper reporting practices have had to be developed. In each of these situations, the accountant is faced with the problem of making sure that enough information is presented so that the mythical **reasonably prudent investor** will not be misled.

A classic illustration of the problems of determining adequate disclosure guidelines is the recent turmoil related to bribes and political gifts to foreign countries. How much disclosure, if any, is necessary in the financial statements for these types of expenditures? On the one hand, it is contended that payoffs are unavoidable in business abroad, and sometimes in the United States, and should be looked upon as a cost of doing business. In addition, many of the transactions are generally small in comparison with the corporation's revenues and are not considered material in relation to the financial statements of the corporation. Conversely, others argue that these types of payoffs raise questions about the quality of management and the quality of earnings. It is contended that stockholders have the right to know if the continuation of a company's operations in a foreign country depends on making payoffs and what effect stopping the payoffs might have on the financial statements. The emergence of such a problem demonstrates the complexity and subjectivity of devising disclosure rules that meet the needs of society.[7]

The Objectivity (Verifiability) Principle

Accountants recognize that the usefulness of accounting information is dependent on providing data that are objectively determined and verifiable. Verifiability is concerned with the availability and adequacy of evidence attesting the validity of the data being considered. If the information is objective and verifiable, **essentially similar measures and conclusions would be reached if two or more qualified persons examined the same data.** To rely on the information supplied, users must know that the information is based on fact and is unbiased.

No information is ever completely objective. When financial statements are prepared for short time periods, estimates must be made of such items as depreciation charges, amortization, and deferrals and accruals of cost and revenue items. These allocations must be based on the use of the accountant's judgment, observation, and experience. The process of measuring and presenting financial information, therefore, loses some objective reality. But, **as long as the estimate, forecast, or measurement process is based on data and methodology that can be corroborated by outside parties, the information is considered verifiable and objective.**

The principle of objectivity is a necessity for individuals who have neither the time nor the expertise to evaluate the factual content of the information. In particu-

---

[7]The Foreign Corrupt Practices Act of 1977, which resulted from these developments, has been called by many the most significant piece of legislation affecting business enterprise in the last twenty years. This legislation requires business enterprises to keep books and records accurately to reflect accounting transactions and to maintain a system of internal accounting controls sufficient to provide reasonable assurance that transactions are handled properly. It establishes criminal penalties for making payments to foreign officials, political parties, or candidates in order to obtain or retain business. Such legislation provides guidance to accountants who, prior to this legislation, often were forced to make their own moral judgments on these questions. Additional guidance is now given to auditors in "The Independent Auditor's Responsibility for the Detection of Errors or Irregularities," *Statement on Auditing Standards No. 16,* (AICPA, January, 1977) and "Illegal Acts by Clients," *Statement on Auditing Standards No. 17* (AICPA, 1977).

lar, objectivity is extremely important to the independent audit process. Auditors would have a difficult time justifying their opinion in regard to financial information unless the information were verifiable.

CONSIDERATIONS MODIFYING BASIC THEORY

This brief discussion of basic accounting theory cannot be regarded as a series of infallible rules to be followed in every situation. There are certain exceptions in the practical application of these theories. A young and growing profession, accounting is still developing its theory and rationale. Leaders in the profession, who are continually questioning the purpose and objectives of accounting, disagree on some basic principles. Accounting theory is also affected by certain practical considerations that merit our attention. These are referred to as **modifying conventions.**

Materiality

Accounting is not intended to be an abstract, theoretical study; it is a practical, useful technique to aid in the communication and control of business activities. Therefore, precise attention to theory may be quite unreasonable in specific instances. One point of basic theory maintains that all costs of producing a given revenue should be applied against that revenue to determine a net result for the operations producing the revenue, but it is not always feasible to do so. A large concern will have numerous operations from which it derives revenue and to which it allocates costs. For example, let us assume that the sale of certain waste materials as scrap produces a small, regular income. Strict adherence to theory would require that the cost of the scrap material sold and the expenses of collecting and selling it be carefully determined and deducted from the amount received. Unless the amount of scrap sales or the expenses connected are material, this determination would not be reasonable, necessary, or particularly helpful. The added complication and expense involved in attempting to determine the expense of such a minor and unimportant activity are not justified by the benefit to be derived.

The point involved here is one of **materiality, of relative size and importance.** If the amount involved is significant when compared with the other revenues and expenses, assets and liabilities, or net income of the entity, theory should be followed; if the amount is so small that it is quite unimportant when compared with other items, requirements of theory may be considered of less importance. This policy is sometimes called the **doctrine of materiality.** It is difficult to give firm guides in judging when any given item is not material because materiality varies both with relative amount and relative importance; thus, much depends not only on the size of the item but also on the size of the company under consideration. To some extent it also varies with the nature of the item itself. Consider the following illustration.

	Company A	Company B
Sales	$10,000,000	$100,000
Costs and expenses	9,000,000	90,000
Net income from operations	$ 1,000,000	$ 10,000
Unusual gain	$ 20,000	$ 5,000

During the period in question, the income and expenses and, therefore, the net income of Company A and Company B have been proportional. Each has had an unusual gain. In looking at the abbreviated income figures for Company A, it does not appear significant whether the amount of the unusual gain is set out separately or merged with the regular operating income. It amounts to only 2% of the net income and, if merged, would not seriously distort the net income figure. Company B has had an unusual gain of only $5,000, but it is relatively much more significant than the larger gain realized by A. For Company B, an item of $5,000 amounts to 50% of its net income. Obviously, the inclusion of such an item in ordinary operating income would affect the amount of that income materially. Thus we see the importance of the **relative size** of an item in determining its materiality.

Materiality is a difficult concept to grasp, as these practical examples indicate: (1) General Dynamics disclosed that at one time its Resources Group had improved its earnings by $5.8 million at the same time that its Stromberg Datagraphix subsidiary had taken write-offs of $6.7 million. Although both numbers were far larger than the $2.5 million that General Dynamics as a whole earned for the year, neither was disclosed as an unusual or nonrecurring item in the annual report; apparently the net effect on net income was not considered material. (2) In the first quarter, GAC's earnings rose from 76 cents to 77 cents a share. Nowhere did the annual report disclose that a favorable tax carry-forward of 4 cents a share prevented GAC's earnings from sliding to 73 cents a share. The company took the position that this carry-forward should not be shown as an extraordinary item because it was not material (6%). As one executive noted, "You know that accountants have a rule of thumb that says that anything under 10% is not material." The examples should illustrate one point: in practice, the answer to what is material is not clear-cut, and difficult decisions must be made each period. Only by the exercise of good judgment and professional expertise can the accountant arrive at answers that are reasonable and appropriate.

The nature of the item may also be important. If a gain occurred from a transaction that would happen only once in the life of the enterprise, it would be relatively less significant than if it occurred from a new type of transaction or activity into which the management had ventured on an experimental basis. If it were the latter, perhaps it would be of such importance that management would want it segregated for study and review so that the profitability of the new venture could be determined.

Materiality is a factor in a great many accounting decisions, only some of which are concerned with reporting items in the financial statements. For example, the amount of classification required in a subsidiary expense ledger, the degree of accuracy to be required in prorating expenses among the departments of a business, or the extent to which adjustments should be made for accrued and deferred items should finally be determined on a basis of reasonableness and practicability, which is the materiality convention sensibly applied.

Industry Practices

Another practical consideration, which sometimes requires departure from basic theory, is the **peculiar nature of some industries and business concerns.** Meat packing, for example, is considerably different from manufacturing. In a manufacturing plant, various raw materials and purchased parts are put together to create a finished product. Because the cost of each individual component part is known, the various items in inventory, whether completely or partially finished, can be accounted for on a basis of cost as required by basic theory. In a packing house a different situation prevails. The "raw material" consists of cattle, hogs, or sheep, each unit of which is purchased as a whole and then divided into parts that are the products. Instead of one product out of many parts, many products are made from one "unit" of raw material. To allocate the cost of the animal "on the hoof" into the cost of ribs, chucks, and shoulders, for instance, is a practical impossibility. It is much easier and more useful to determine the market price of the various products and value them in the inventory at selling price less the various costs, such as shipping and handling, necessary to get them to market. Hence, because of a peculiarity of the industry, **inventories are sometimes carried at sales price less distribution costs in the meat-packing industry,** which is a departure from basic theory. Such variations from basic theory are not many; yet they do exist, and so, whenever we find what appears to be a violation of basic accounting theory, it is well to determine whether it is explained by some peculiar feature of the type of business involved before being critical of the procedures followed.

We must be constantly alert to the necessity of departing from basic theory because of the immateriality of the amounts involved or because of the peculiarities of the given business. An attitude of reasonableness toward practical problems is essential, but we also must be wary of being so reasonable that the standards of good theory are neglected completely.

Conservatism

Few conventions in accounting are as misunderstood as the convention of conservatism. The practicing accountant must make many decisions, some of them very difficult. For example, in a particular case the accountant may be in doubt about whether a given purchase should be charged to an expense account or to an asset account. In reaching a decision he or she uses accounting theory as modified by materiality, industry practices, consistency, and the influence that this item will have on the financial statements. If this approach does not give the accountant a clear decision, he or she then tends to rely on the convention of conservatism which says, in effect: **when in doubt choose the solution that will be least likely to overstate assets and income.** Note that there is nothing in the conservatism convention urging the accountant to understate assets or income. Unfortunately it has been interpreted by some accountants to mean just that. All that conservatism does, properly applied, is to give the accountant a guide in difficult situations, and then the guide is a very reasonable one: refrain from overstatement of net income and net assets. Examples of conservatism in accounting are the use of the lower of cost or market approach in valuing inventories and the rule that accrued net losses should be recognized on firm purchase commitments for goods for inventory. If the issue is in doubt, it is better to understate than overstate. Of course, if there is no doubt, there is no need to apply this convention.

Summary of the Structure

The figure on page 43 illustrates the essentials of the theoretical framework developed thus far. We cannot overemphasize the usefulness of this theory framework in understanding many of the problem areas that are examined in subsequent chapters.

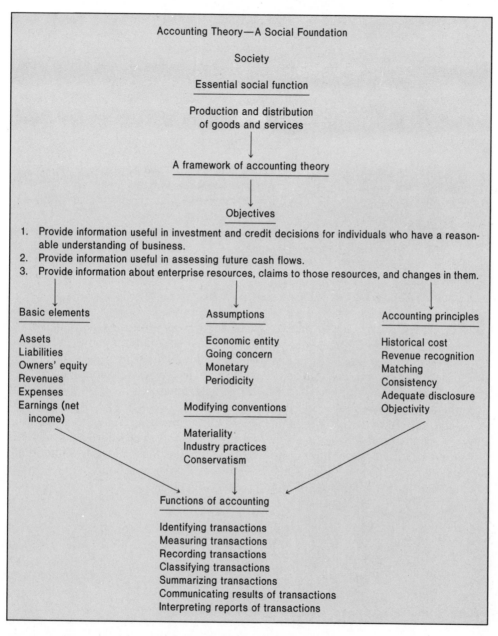

Accounting Theory—A Social Foundation

Society

Essential social function

Production and distribution
of goods and services

A framework of accounting theory

Objectives

1. Provide information useful in investment and credit decisions for individuals who have a reasonable understanding of business.
2. Provide information useful in assessing future cash flows.
3. Provide information about enterprise resources, claims to those resources, and changes in them.

Basic elements

Assets
Liabilities
Owners' equity
Revenues
Expenses
Earnings (net
 income)

Assumptions

Economic entity
Going concern
Monetary
Periodicity

Modifying conventions

Materiality
Industry practices
Conservatism

Accounting principles

Historical cost
Revenue recognition
Matching
Consistency
Adequate disclosure
Objectivity

Functions of accounting

Identifying transactions
Measuring transactions
Recording transactions
Classifying transactions
Summarizing transactions
Communicating results of transactions
Interpreting reports of transactions

Source: Adapted from materials of Professor Thomas
Hubbard, University of Nebraska, Lincoln, Nebraska.

APPENDIX

Approaches to Accounting Theory Formulation

As indicated in Chapter 2, accountants have attempted to develop a general theory to resolve the many financial accounting issues facing the accounting profession. At present, no generally accepted well-defined structure exists, although there are certain basic elements, principles, and assumptions that accountants recognize and apply in practice.

The purpose of this appendix is to show that the proper approach to accounting theory formulation is very much a matter of debate and that different individuals have quite different perceptions about what approaches the profession should take to resolve financial accounting issues. The different views of accounting theory can be classified in the following manner:[1]

1. True income approach.
2. Decision model approach.
3. Individual user approach—behavioral.
4. Aggregate user approach—efficient markets.
5. Information economics approach.

True Income Approach

Some accountants argue that if we search long enough, we will ultimately find the one proper method to account for various business transactions. This approach has been referred to as the **true income approach** because it implies that there is a single accounting method that will correctly identify the economic substance of a business transaction.

Many of the writings in the early and mid-1900's, for example, seemed to adopt

---

[1]The general approach to this section was heavily influenced by the AAA Committee on Concepts and Standards for External Financial Reports, *Statement on Accounting Theory and Theory Acceptance* (Sarasota: American Accounting Association, 1977).

this position.[2] No consideration was given to the fact that information requirements might be different for different users of financial statements. These writers generally agreed that current values were superior to historical cost, although they differed as to how current values should be implemented. In short, the true income approach adopts the position that there is one correct reporting method and that research should be directed to finding this method.

Decision Model Approach

In the **decision model** or **decision usefulness approach** to accounting theory formulation, an appropriate decision model based on the hypothesized needs of financial statement users is developed. For example, one theorist might argue that the greatest concern of users is that a company maintain its physical capacity. Using physical capacity as the economic attribute of interest to financial statement users, the theorist might then argue that replacement cost is the appropriate method for the valuation of business transactions. Conversely, another theorist might argue that command over consumer goods is the most important economic attribute of interest to financial statement users, and would suggest that selling prices or exit values are the appropriate bases for the valuation of business transactions. In other words, the decision model theorist establishes a set of normative assumptions about the goals, decisions, and information needs of users, and, given these assumptions, derives the accounting methods best suited for meeting these needs.

The decision model approach has been used to justify accounting methods based on (1) replacement cost, (2) selling price, and (3) present value of future cash flows.[3] The proponents of each accounting method argue forcefully that their method is correct, given their underlying assumptions as to what users of financial statements desire. Unlike the proponents of the true income approach, the decision model theorists acknowledge that different information may be needed for different users of the financial statements or for different kinds of decisions.

Individual User Approach—Behavioral

Some accountants have suggested that accounting theory should be developed not by postulating a set of normative assumptions about how accounting information is used (decision model approach) but rather by examining actual user decision behavior. This approach has sometimes been referred to as the **individual user** or **behavioral approach** to accounting theory formulation.

To illustrate this approach, consider the current controversy over whether some form of price-level adjusted information should be reported in the financial statements. The behavioral/accounting theorist might solicit opinions from various financial statement users, primarily financial analysts and bankers, about the useful-

[2]See, for example, John B. Canning, *The Economics of Accountancy* (New York: Ronald Press, 1929); Henry W. Sweeney, *Stabilized Accounting* (New York: Harper, 1936); Kenneth MacNeal, *Truth in Accounting*, (New York: Ronald Press, 1939).

[3]See, for example, Lawrence Revsine, *Replacement Cost Accounting* (Englewood Cliffs, N.J.: Prentice-Hall, 1973); Robert R. Sterling, *Theory of the Measurement of Enterprise Income* (Lawrence: University Press of Kansas, 1970); George J. Staubus, *A Theory of Accounting to Investors* (Berkeley: University of California Press, 1961).

ness of price-level adjusted information. If the majority of users indicated that price-level adjusted information would be useful, it would then be argued that this information should be provided. Another technique used by behavioral theorists is to ask a group of financial statement users to make a series of investment or loan decisions based on some accounting information set, e.g., conventional financial statements. Another group of users are then asked to make the same decisions on the basis of a different information set, e.g., price-level adjusted financial statements. The decisions are then compared and the behavioral theorist attempts to infer which information set (conventional or price-level adjusted) is most useful.

Aggregate User Approach—Efficient Markets

The **aggregate user** or **efficient market approach**[4] holds that all publicly available information about a company is quickly incorporated into its stock price because of the sophistication of the many financial analysts and individual investors who comprise the stock market. This approach does not say that the price of the stock is necessarily "correct" but rather that it reflects all publicly available information.

To illustrate the implications of the efficient market approach, suppose that we were concerned about whether price-level adjustments should be used to report financial information. Advocates of the efficient market approach would argue that, if reporting price-level adjusted information is a costless venture, both conventional and price-level adjusted information should be disclosed. Because the market is efficient, the marketplace will decide on what information to use. In other words, why be concerned about a specific reporting approach? Disclose the alternatives and the marketplace (aggregate users) will decide what information is useful.

Implicitly this approach suggests that if the information is publicly disclosed the market as a whole cannot be fooled, although particular individual investors may be. For example, assume that two companies are exactly alike in all respects except that one company uses straight-line depreciation and the other accelerated depreciation. In such a case, one company will have higher reported profits than the other, but efficient market theorists would argue that the stock price would be the same as long as the alternative reporting methods are disclosed or can be computed from available financial information. The market is not fooled by this difference in accounting methods.

Information Economics Approach

The **information economics approach** to accounting theory maintains that all accounting reporting decisions should be evaluated within a cost-benefit framework. Essentially this approach looks upon accounting information as a commodity, just as bread and butter are commodities, and asks what the costs of producing this commodity are and what the benefits are.[5] For example, comments are often made

[4]See, for example, William H. Beaver, "What Should Be the FASB Objectives" *The Journal of Accountancy* (August, 1973), for a simplified explanation of this approach.

[5]See, for example, Joel Demski, "Choice Among Financial Reporting Alternatives," *Accounting Review* (April, 1974).

that a given reporting alternative is too costly in view of the benefits obtained, but few attempts have been made to measure the costs and benefits. Conversely, to say simply that a reporting method reflects the economic substance of a transaction and, therefore, should be used is equally inappropriate. What must be considered are all the possible ramifications (costs and benefits) of reporting this approach.[6]

To illustrate, recently the FASB mandated that ordinarily all research and development costs should be expensed as incurred. Assuming that this treatment reflects the economic substance of the situation, does it necessarily follow that we should adopt the FASB's mandate? One might argue that to report research and development expenditures in such a manner might incur social costs that far outweigh the benefits. For example, forcing companies to expense research and development costs as incurred might result in curtailment of their research and development projects, which might produce long-run social consequences that are undesirable.

In the FASB's study on foreign currency translation **(Statement No. 8)** two studies were commissioned. The first tried to determine whether stock price behavior is significantly affected by the manner in which foreign exchange gains and losses are reported. This stock market study concluded that the method of reporting translation gains and losses had no significant effect on the stock price of the company involved. A second study attempted to determine whether companies would forego profitable investments overseas or employ foreign exchange practices that might be considered uneconomical because of the way foreign translation gains and losses were reported. The conclusion was that **FASB Statement No. 8** was causing business enterprises to make bad economic decisions.

Concluding Remarks

We have attempted to provide a brief overview of the alternative approaches to theory formulation currently being discussed in the accounting literature. Although the descriptions are necessarily brief, it is hoped that they provide sufficient insight into the essence of each approach. Exposure to these ideas and thoughts develops a broader and better framework for judging the advancement of the accounting profession.

---

[6]Recently the FASB has become involved in attempting to assess the economic consequences of accounting standards issued. To illustrate, studies were commissioned on *FASB Statement No. 5*, "Accounting for Contingencies"; *FASB Statement No. 8*," Accounting for the Translation of Foreign Currency Transactions and Foreign Financial Statements"; and *FASB Statement No. 19*, "Financial Reporting by Oil and Gas Producing Companies."

APPENDIX

Review of Professional Literature on Theoretical Structures

As indicated in Chapter 2, accountants currently do not have a well defined theoretical structure to guide the standard setting process. Many believe that such a structure is badly needed if accounting standards are to be consistent and useful in producing reliable financial statements. Recognizing this deficiency and solving it, however, are two different matters. To illustrate the attempts that accountants have made to develop such a framework, we present a brief review of the most often quoted and currently discussed theoretical structures. Our discussion of these structures is adapted from the following pronouncements:

1. **Accounting Research Studies No. 1 (1961) and No. 3 (1962).**
2. **Accounting Principles Board Statement No. 4 (1970).**
3. **Conceptual Framework for Financial Accounting and Reporting: Elements of Financial Statements and Their Measurement (1976).**

ACCOUNTING RESEARCH STUDIES NO. 1 AND NO. 3

Research Studies No. 1 and No. 3 were commissioned by the AICPA in 1959–1960 in an effort to develop the basic structure of financial accounting theory. At the time these statements were being developed, there was hope that these research studies would provide the cornerstore on which the AICPA's Accounting Principles Board could base its standard setting.

Basic Postulates of ARS No. 1

ARS No. 1 attempts to set forth the basic assumptions or postulates that constitute the foundation of accounting. The postulates are classified into three categories— Group A, B, and C—sometimes referred to as environmental, supplementary, and imperative postulates. These postulates, which are somewhat similar to the basic assumptions presented in Chapter 2 of this book, are as follows:

1. **Group A (Environmental).** These postulates are relevant to accounting, although in form they refer to the political and economic environment. To illustrate, such postulates as quantification, exchange, entities, time period, and unit of measure are discussed.
2. **Group B (Supplementary).** The first set of postulates deals only indirectly with accounting. This set and the next deal directly with accounting. The basic postulates of this group are financial statements, market prices, entities, and tentativeness.
3. **Group C (Imperatives).** These postulates are separated from the first two (Groups A and B) because they refer to areas of what ought to be. The other postulates were almost simple statements of fact. Because these postulates stress what ought to be, they are called "imperatives." These basic postulates are continuity, objectivity, consistency, stable unit, and disclosure.

Principles of ARS No. 3

ARS No. 3 is essentially an extension of **ARS No. 1.** It attempts to answer the question: In view of the basic postulates established in **ARS No. 1,** what are the broad principles of accounting? Thus **ARS No. 3** builds on the initial analysis in **ARS No. 1** and develops the principles on the basis that the postulates or assumptions of accounting have been properly stated. For this reason the basic postulates established in **ARS No. 1** are an essential part of **ARS No. 3.** Examples of principles developed in **ARS No. 3** are as follows:

1. Profit is attributable to the whole process of business activity. Any rule or procedure, therefore, that assigns profit to a portion of the whole process should be continuously reexamined to determine the extent to which it introduces bias into the report of the amount of profit assigned to specific periods of time.
2. Changes in resources should be classified among the amounts attributable to certain causes. They include:
   (a) Changes in the dollar (price-level changes) that lead to restatements of capital but not to revenues or expenses.
   (b) Changes in replacement costs (above or below the effect of price-level changes) that lead to elements of gain or loss.
   (c) Sale or other transfer, or recognition of net realizable value, all of which lead to revenue or gain.
   (d) Other causes, such as accretion or the discovery of previously unknown natural resources.
3. All assets of the enterprise, whether obtained by investments of owners or of creditors, or by other means, should be recorded in the accounts and reported in the financial statements. The existence of an asset is independent of the means by which it was acquired.

ARS No. 1 and No. 3 did not attempt to describe existing practice; they were an attempt to determine what ought to be. Evidence of this normative rather than descriptive approach to practice is the **ARS No. 3** recommendation that in most situations replacement cost as basis of measurement should be substituted for historical cost. These two studies ran into opposition from practicing accountants and the business community. Such terms as "too theoretical," "impractical of implementation," and even "conceptually deficient" were used to describe them. Conversely, others believed that these studies were "forward thinking," "conceptually accurate," and "provide a basis for standard setting in the future." The APB chose to ignore the recommendations of these studies and worked without an official conceptual framework throughout its years of deliberations.

APB Statement No. 4

Statement No. 4's basic framework is similar to the elements, assumptions, principles, and modifying conventions developed in Chapter 2, with some minor differences. This Statement was developed primarily from observation of existing accounting practice, and no attempt was made to develop a framework for financial accounting.

Statement No. 4, develops a descriptive framework of accounting consisting of basic features, basic elements, and generally accepted accounting principles. **Basic features,** for example, attempt to describe the fundamentals of an accounting system. **Basic elements** are the definitions of terms used in accounting, such as assets, liabilities, and owners' equity. **Generally accepted accounting principles** constitute at a given point in time a consensus of how financial transactions should be recorded. A diagram of the contents of **Statement No. 4** is presented on page 51.

The principles are comprised of three groups as follows:

1. **Pervasive principles.** These are broad concepts which provide the basis upon which general and detailed rules are established. The pervasive principles are divided into (a) pervasive measurement principles, and (b) modifying conventions.
2. **Broad operating principles.** These are derived from the basic pervasive principles and govern application of detailed principles. For example, general discussions of how revenue and costs should be measured are presented in this area.
3. **Detailed principles.** These are the numerous rules and procedures that develop from the broad operating principles. Examples are the use of LIFO instead of FIFO in certain circumstances, or vice versa.

Statement No. 4 is widely employed by practitioners as a basis for resolving accounting controversies. For example, this Statement discusses how costs should be matched with revenues. If a specific relationship exists with revenues, costs are expensed in the period that the revenue is recognized. If it is difficult to associate expense and revenue, a rational and systematic method of allocating costs can be used. And costs are charged to expense immediately if no future benefit is anticipated or if no apparent connection with revenue is available. Such guidelines are extremely valuable to practitioners and, therefore, **Statement No. 4** is generally considered a useful resource document.

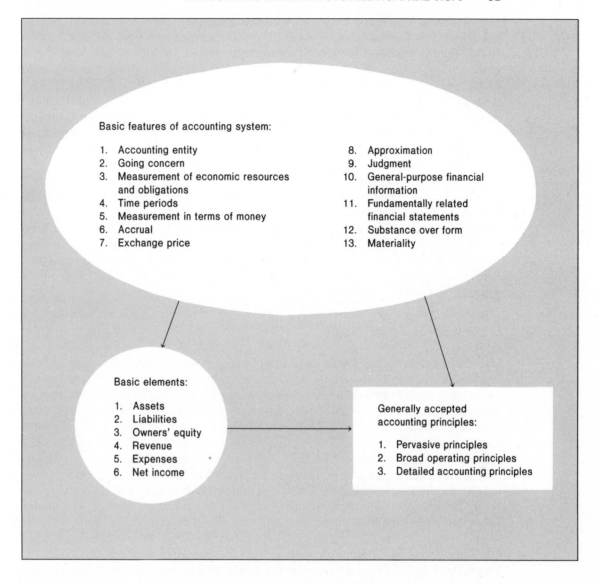

Objectives of Financial Statements (SFAC No. 1)

Statement No. 4 included a section on objectives including seven qualitative objectives: relevance, understandability, verifiability, neutrality, timeliness, comparability, and completeness. These objectives were stated in such relatively abstract terms, however, that little if any guidance for financial reporting could be inferred. Further, **Statement No. 4** stated objectives in terms of what was considered acceptable and did little to indicate what was needed in financial reports.

A Study Group on Objectives of Financial Statements (the Trueblood Committee) was therefore appointed by the AICPA to develop a set of objectives for financial reporting. This Study Group identified a set of objectives for financial reporting which initiated much discussion in accounting and the business community. Subsequently, the FASB issued (1) a discussion memorandum on the "Objectives of Financial Statements" in 1974, (2) tentative conclusions on "Objectives of Financial Statements of Business Enterprises" in 1976, (3) an exposure draft on "Objectives of Financial Reporting and Elements of Financial Statements of Business Enterprises" in 1977, and finally (4) **Statement of Financial Accounting Concepts No. 1 (SFAC No. 1)** in 1978, which detailed the "Objectives of Financial Reporting by Business Enterprises." A condensation of these objectives is presented in Chapter 1, page 5.

The efforts required to develop just a set of objectives for financial reporting illustrates that the task of establishing a complete theoretical structure for accounting will be both slow and arduous. The accounting professsion has taken years and spent countless dollars to arrive at the objectives embodied in **SFAC No. 1.** Still, many contend that **SFAC No. 1's** objectives are so broad that they provide little guidance of practical value. Others, of course, believe that the document provides the beginnings of a framework that can be employed as a basis for establishing accounting standards in the future.

Conceptual Framework Study

The FASB's Conceptual Framework Study encompasses much more than the development of a set of objectives for financial statements. As indicated earlier, the issues remaining to be resolved include: the essential qualitative characteristics of financial information, definitions for the basic elements of accounting, the proper basis of measurement, and the treatment, if any, for changes in the monetary unit. As this textbook is being written, the FASB is issuing various documents and conducting research to find the answers to these questions. A brief perspective of where the FASB appears to be headed is provided below.

First, as indicated earlier, the FASB has issued **SFAC No. 1,** which identifies the broad objectives of financial reporting and **FASB Statement No. 33,** "Financial Reporting and Changing Prices." Second, the FASB will probably issue another SFAC on "Qualitative Characteristics: Criteria for Selecting and Evaluating Financial Accounting and Reporting Policies" by the time this textbook is published. Third, the FASB will soon reexpose for comment an exposure draft on the elements of financial statements which should provide definitions of such items as assets, liabilities, and so on.

In addition, the Board is currently examining many other issues: (1) reporting earnings, (2) funds flows and liquidity, and (3) information in financial statements and in financial reporting other than financial statements. The issues are as follows:[1]

> **Reporting Earnings**—Determination of the appropriate display of information about earnings, focusing on the kinds of revenues, gains, expenses, and losses that should be displayed in the context of objectives of financial reporting. Views about whether an earnings statement should focus primarily on current operating performance or on the

---

[1]"Plan for FASB Technical Projects and Other Technical Activities," *FASB Status Report*, No. 80 (Stamford, Conn.: FASB, January 31, 1979), pp. 1–3.

earnings effects of all events and circumstances will be reexamined. The relationship between earnings information and funds flow information will be considered, as will the display of per share information, extraordinary items, infrequent and unusual items, prior period adjustments, and similar items.[2]

Funds Flows and Liquidity—Consideration of the information about an enterprise's flow of funds and its liquidity position that would be helpful to financial statement users. The project reconsiders matters covered in APB Opinion No. 19, "Reporting Changes in Financial Position." Statements on elements and qualitative characteristics preferably should precede a Statement on funds flows and liquidity. Also, this project is closely related to that on reporting earnings, and further progress on the latter is expected to be helpful.

Information in Financial Statements and in Financial Reporting Other Than Financial Statements—Development of guidelines for (1) identifying financial information that should be disclosed outside the financial statements and (2) distinguishing between information that all enterprises should be required to disclose and information that only certain designated types of enterprises should be required to disclose. Special attention is being given to the financial statements and financial reporting of small or closely held enterprises.

Conclusions

It has been suggested frequently that present-day generally accepted accounting principles should be made more consistent internally and should provide more useful information. Because accounting is a social discipline, the best way to report a given item or event is often difficult to determine because different users have different perspectives and different sets of objectives. That is why it is considered important to establish some framework on which to base the standard-setting process. Some believe that the search for a framework is hopeless and that an issue-by-issue approach is the only practical method of resolving accounting controversies. Only one thing appears certain at this point—accounting principles and procedures will grow and change as internal attempts at improvement continue and external pressures for change persist.

Note: All **asterisked** questions, cases, exercises, or problems relate to material contained in the appendix to each chapter.

Questions

1. What are the primary objectives of financial reporting as indicated in *Statement of Financial Accounting Concepts No. 1?*
2. The fundamentals of financial accounting theory may be classified into five major categories. What are the five categories and what purpose does each serve?
3. If the going-concern assumption is not made in accounting, what difference does it make in the amounts shown in the financial statements for the following items?
   (a) Unamortized bond premium.
   (b) Land.
   (c) Depreciation expense on equipment.
   (d) Long-term investments in common stocks of other companies.
   (e) Prepaid insurance.
   (f) Merchandise inventory.

[2]The Board has issued a discussion memorandum on reporting earnings: "Reporting Earnings," FASB Discussion Memorandum (Stamford, Conn.: FASB, 1979).

4. What is the "asset and liability view"? How is it distinguished from the "revenue and expense view"?

5. Develop an argument supporting the adjustment of cost figures in financial statements for general price-level changes, or at least, the preparation of supplementary statements adjusted for changes in the general price level.

6. The life of a business is divided into specific time periods, usually a year, to measure results of operations for each such time period and to portray financial conditions at the end of each period.
   (a) This practice is based on the accounting assumption that the life of the business consists of a series of time periods and that it is possible to measure accurately the results of operations for each period. Comment on the validity and necessity of this assumption.
   (b) What has been the effect of this practice on accounting? What is its relation to the accrual system? What influence has it had on accounting entries and methodology?

7. The chairman of the board of directors of the company for which you are chief accountant has told you that he is entirely out of sympathy with accounting figures based on cost. He believes that replacement values are of far more significance to the board of directors than "out-of-date costs." Present some arguments to convince him that accounting data should still be based on cost.

8. Which items in the income statement represent "old dollars" and therefore are most subject to misunderstanding during a period of inflation or deflation? Which items represent "current dollars"?

9. Pizer Company paid $73,000 for a machine in 1976. The Accumulated Depreciation account has a balance of $27,000 at the present time. The company could sell the machine today for $94,000. The company president believes that the company has a "right to this gain." What does the president mean by this statement? Do you agree?

10. Why has the date of sale been chosen as the point at which to recognize the revenue resulting from the entire producing and selling process?

11. What is the justification for the following deviations from recognizing revenue at the time of sale?
    (a) Installment sales method of recognizing revenue.
    (b) Recognition of revenue during production for certain agricultural products.
    (c) The percentage-of-completion basis in long-term construction contracts.

12. Discuss the revenue realization principle and its significance to the process of periodic income determination. Discuss the effect of the realization principle on the valuation of assets for balance sheet purposes.

13. Explain how you would decide whether to record each of the following expenditures as an asset or an expense.
    (a) Ireland, Inc. paves the driveway leading to the office building at a cost of $7,300.
    (b) Legal fees paid in connection with the purchase of land are $325.
    (c) A meat market purchases a meat-grinding machine at a cost of $160.
    (d) On June 30, Cook and Foster, medical doctors, pay six months' office rent to cover the month of June and the next five months.
    (e) The Martin Hardware Company pays $2,700 in wages to laborers on a building to be used in the business.
    (f) Felly Florists pays wages of $1,400 for November to an employee who serves as driver of their delivery truck.

14. Three expense recognition points (associating cause and effect, systematic and rational allocation, and immediate recognition) were discussed in the text under the matching principle. Indicate the basic nature of each of these types of expenses and give two examples of each.

15. What is the objective of requiring an independent certified public accountant to make a statement about consistency?

16. Discuss whether the changes described in each of the cases below require recognition in the CPA's opinion as to consistency (assume that the amounts are material).

    (a) After three years of computing depreciation under the declining balance method for income tax purposes and under the straight-line method for reporting purposes, the company adopted the declining balance method for reporting purposes.

    (b) The company disposed of one of the two subsidiaries that had been included in its consolidated statements for prior years.

    (c) The estimated remaining useful life of plant property was reduced because of obsolescence.

    (d) The company is using an inventory valuation method that is different from all those used by other companies in their industry.

17. In February 1980, Dain, Inc. doubled the amount of its outstanding stock by selling on the market an additional 10,000 shares to finance an expansion of the business. You propose that this information be shown by a footnote on the balance sheet as of December 31, 1979. The president objects, claiming that this sale took place after December 31, 1979 and, therefore, should not be shown. Explain your position.

18. How are materiality (and immateriality) related to the proper presentation of financial statements? What factors and measures should the CPA consider in assessing the materiality of a misstatement in the presentation of a financial statement?

19. The president of Hilton Enterprises has heard that conservatism is a doctrine that is followed in accounting and, therefore, proposes that several policies be followed that are conservative in nature. State your opinion with respect to each of the policies listed below.

    (a) A personal liability lawsuit is pending against the company. The president believes there is an even chance that the company will lose the suit and have to pay damages of $70,000 to $120,000. The president recommends that a loss be recorded and a liability created in the amount of $120,000.

    (b) The inventory should be valued at "cost or market whichever is lower" because the losses from price declines should be recognized in the accounts in the period in which the price decline takes place.

    (c) The company gives a two-year warranty to its customers on all products sold. The estimated warranty costs incurred from this year's sales should be entered as an expense this year instead of an expense in the period in the future when the warranty is made good.

    (d) When sales are made on account, there is always uncertainty about whether the accounts are collectible. Therefore, the president recommends recording the sale when the cash is received from the customers.

*20. What is the difference between the true income and the decision model approach to resolving accounting controversies?

*21. Indicate the basic similarities between **Statement No. 4: Basic Concepts and Accounting Principles Underlying Financial Enterprises** and **Accounting Research Studies No. 1 and No. 3.** What are the major differences?

*22. What differences exist among pervasive principles, broad operating principles, and detailed principles as indicated by **Statement No. 4: Basic Concepts and Accounting Principles Underlying Financial Statements of Business Enterprises?** What are the major classifications of postulates used in **Accounting Research Study No. 1, The Basic Postulates of Accounting?** Why are they grouped in this manner?

Cases

C2-1 Two students are discussing various aspects of the FASB's recent pronouncement, *Statement of Financial Accounting Concepts No. 1,* "Objectives of Financial Reporting by Business Enterprises." One student indicates that this new pronouncement provides little, if any, guidance to the practicing professional in resolving accounting controversies. This student believes that the statement provides such broad guidelines that it would be impossible to apply the objectives to present-day reporting problems. The other student concedes this point, but indicates that objectives are still needed to provide a starting point for the FASB in helping to improve financial reporting.

Instructions

(a) Indicate the basic objectives established in *Statement of Financial Accounting Concepts No. 1.*

(b) What do you think is the meaning of the second student's statement that the FASB needs a starting point to resolve accounting controversies?

C2-2   Even though insurance is available, some businesses adopt a policy of self-insurance. Self-insurance is based on the belief that the losses will be less over an extended period of time than the premiums that would have to be paid to insure against such losses. Some individuals then argue that to avoid the irregular effects on net income resulting from nonrecurring uninsured losses, an expense should be accrued annually for a portion of the unanticipated losses. When the company charges insurance expense each year with this hypothetical amount, a credit is made to a liability account entitled Accumulated Provision for Self-Insured Risks or Allowance for Uninsured Losses. When the casualty losses occur, they are charged against the liability account.

Instructions

Assume that you are a proponent of the asset and liability view rather than the revenue and expense view. Would you be in favor of the approach described above in accounting for self-insurance? Explain.

C2-3   In this chapter, numerous attempts have been made to develop a theory framework to help in resolving accounting controversies. Much study has therefore taken place in developing basic assumptions and principles of accounting that might be universally applied. Such a task is not easy because the users of the financial statements may have different needs for financial information.

Instructions

(a) Discuss (1) the purpose of developing basic assumptions and principles of accounting, and (2) the benefits to be derived from their development.

(b) Frequently advanced as a basic assumption is a general proposition dealing with "objectivity." Under what conditions, in general, is information arising from a financial transaction considered to be objective in nature?

(c) Accountants acknowledge that financial statements reporting the results of operations for relatively short periods of time, say one year, are tentative whenever allocations between past, present, and future periods are required. On the other hand the "objectivity" assumption leads to the logical deduction that changes in assets and liabilities, and the related effects (if any) on revenues, expenses, retained earnings, and the like, should not be given formal recognition in the accounts earlier than the point of time at which they can be measured in objective terms. Can this apparent conflict be resolved? Discuss.

C2-4   The president of the Martin Manufacturing Company received an income statement from his controller. The statement covered the calendar year 1980. "Sally," he said to the controller, "this statement indicates that a net income of two million dollars was earned last year. You know the value of the company is not that much more than it was this time last year."

"You're probably right," replied the controller. "You see, there are factors in accounting that sometimes keep reported operating results from reflecting the change in the value of the company."

Instructions

Prepare a detailed explanation of the accounting factors to which the controller referred. Include justification, to the extent possible, for the generally accepted accounting methods.

C2-5 Presented below is a statement that appeared about Weyerhaeuser Company in a financial magazine.

> The land and timber holdings are now carried on the company's books at a mere $422 million. The value of the timber alone is variously estimated at from $3 billion to $7 billion and is rising all the time. "The understatement of the company is pretty severe," conceded Charles W. Bingham, a senior vice-president. Adds Robert L. Schuyler, another senior vice-president: "We have a whole stream of profit nobody sees and there is no way to show it on our books."

Instructions

(a) What does Schuyler mean when he says that "we have a whole stream of profit nobody sees and there is no way to show it on our books?"

(b) If the understatement of the company's assets is severe, why does accounting not report this information?

C2-6 On June 8, 1980, Larson Corporation signed a contract with Flad Associates under which Flad agreed (1) to construct an office building on land owned by Larson, (2) to accept responsibility for procuring financing for the project and finding tenants, and (3) to manage the property for 35 years. The annual net income from the project, after debt service, was to be divided equally between Larson Corporation and Flad Associates. Flad was to accept its share of future net income as full payment for its services in construction, obtaining finances and tenants, and management of the project.

By May 31, 1981, the project was nearly completed and tenants had signed leases to occupy 90% of the available space at annual rentals aggregating $3,000,000. It is estimated that, after operating expenses and debt service, the annual net income will amount to $1,100,000. The management of Flad Associates believed that the economic benefit derived from the contract with Larson should be reflected on its financial statements for the fiscal year ended May 31, 1981 and directed that revenue be accrued in an amount equal to the commercial value of the services Flad had rendered during the year, that this amount be carried in contracts receivable, and that all related expenditures be charged against the revenue.

Instructions

(a) Explain the main difference between the economic concept of business income as reflected by Flad's management and the measurement of income under generally accepted accounting principles.

(b) Discuss the factors to be considered in determining when revenue has been realized for the purpose of accounting measurement of periodic income.

(c) Is the belief of Flad's management in accord with generally accepted accounting principles for the measurement of revenue and expense for the year ended May 31, 1981? Support your opinion by discussing the application to this case of the factors to be considered for asset measurement and revenue and expense recognition.

(AICPA adapted)

C2-7 After the presentation of your report on the examination of the financial statements to the board of directors of the Strother Publishing Company, one of the new directors expresses surprise that the income statement assumes that an equal proportion of the revenue is earned with the publication of every issue of the company's magazine. He feels that the "crucial event" in the process of earning revenue in the magazine business is the cash sale of the subscription. He says that he does not understand why most of the revenue cannot be "realized" in the period of the sale.

Instructions

(a) List the various accepted methods for recognizing revenue in the accounts and explain when the methods are appropriate.

(b) Discuss the propriety of timing the realization of revenue in the Strother Publishing Company's account with:

1. The cash sale of the magazine subscription.
2. The publication of the magazine every month.
3. Both events, by realizing a portion of the revenue with cash sale of the magazine subscription and a portion of the revenue with the publication of the magazine every month.

(AICPA adapted)

C2-8 A common objective of accountants is to prepare income statements that are as accurate as possible. A basic requirement in preparing accurate income statements is to match costs against revenues properly. Proper matching of costs against revenues requires that costs resulting from typical business operations be recognized in the period in which they expired.

Instructions

(a) List three criteria that can be used to determine whether such typical costs should appear as charges in the income statement for the current period.

(b) As generally presented in financial statements, the following items or procedures have been criticized as improperly matching costs with revenues. Briefly discuss each item from the viewpoint of matching costs with revenues and suggest corrective or alternative means of presenting the financial information.

1. Cash discounts on purchases.
2. Valuation of inventories at the lower of cost or market.
3. Receiving and handling costs.

C2-9 An accountant must be familiar with the concepts involved in determining earnings of a business entity. The amount of earnings reported for a business entity is dependent on the proper recognition, in general, of revenue and expense for a given time period. In some situations, costs are recognized as expenses at the time of product sale; in other situations, guidelines have been developed for recognizing costs as expenses or losses by other criteria.

Required:

(a) Explain the rationale for recognizing costs as expenses at the time of product sale.

(b) What is the rationale underlying the appropriateness of treating costs as expenses of a period instead of assigning the costs to an asset? Explain.

(c) In what general circumstances would it be appropriate to treat a cost as an asset instead of as an expense? Explain.

(d) Some expenses are assigned to specific accounting periods on the basis of systematic and rational allocation of asset cost. Explain the underlying rationale for recognizing expenses on the basis of systematic and rational allocation of asset cost.

(e) Identify the conditions in which it would be appropriate to treat a cost as a loss.

(AICPA adapted)

C2-10 Pick Homes sells and erects shell houses, that is, frame structures that are completely finished on the outside but are unfinished on the inside except for flooring, partition studding, and ceiling joists. Shell houses are sold chiefly to customers who are handy with tools and who have time to do the interior wiring, plumbing, wall completion and finishing, and other work necessary to make the shell houses livable dwellings.

Pick buys shell houses from a manufacturer in unassembled packages consisting of all lumber, roofing, doors, windows, and similar materials necessary to complete a shell house. Upon commencing operations in a new area, Pick buys or leases land as a site for its local warehouse, field office, and display houses. Sample display houses are erected at a total cost of from $3,600 to $7,700 including the cost of the unassembled packages. The chief element of cost of the display houses is the unassembled packages, inasmuch as erection is a short low-cost operation. Old sample models are torn down or altered into new models every three to seven years. Sample display houses have little salvage value because dismantling and moving costs amount to nearly as much as the cost of an unassembled package.

Instructions

(a) A choice must be made between (1) expensing the costs of sample display houses in the periods in which the expenditure is made and (2) spreading the costs over more than one period. Discuss the advantages of each method.

(b) Would it be preferable to amortize the cost of display houses on the basis of (1) the passage of time or (2) the number of shell houses sold? Explain.

(AICPA adapted)

C2-11   You are engaged in the audit of Compet, Inc., which opened its first branch office in 1981. During the audit Sharon Walters, president, raises the question of the accounting treatment of the operating loss of the branch office for its first year, which is material in amount.

The president proposes to capitalize the operating loss as a "starting-up" expense to be amortized over a five-year period. She states that branch offices of other firms engaged in the same field generally suffer a first-year operating loss that is invariably capitalized, and you are aware of this practice. She argues, therefore, that the loss should be capitalized so that the accounting will be "conservative"; further, she argues that the accounting must be "consistent" with established industry practice.

Instructions

Discuss the president's use of the words "conservative" and "consistent" from the standpoint of accounting terminology. Discuss the accounting treatment you would recommend.

(AICPA adapted)

C2-12   The general ledger of MBS, Inc., a corporation engaged in the development and production of television programs for commercial sponsorship, contains the following accounts before amortization at the end of the current year:

Account	Balance (Debit)
Monk & Cindy	$48,000
Supertown	39,000
The Badman	21,500
Spacetrack	9,000
Studio Rearrangement	4,000

An examination of contracts and records revealed the following information:

1. The first two accounts listed above represent the total cost of completed programs that were televised during the accounting period just ended. Under the terms of an existing contract Monk & Cindy will be rerun during the next accounting period, at a fee equal to 50% of the fee for the first televising of the program. The contract for the first run produced $400,000 of revenue. The contract with the sponsor of Supertown provides that he may, at his option, rerun the program during the next season at a fee of 75% of the fee on the first televising of the program.

2. The balance in The Badman account is the cost of a new program that has just been completed and is being considered by several companies for commercial sponsorship.

3. The balance in the Spacetrack account represents the cost of a partially completed program for a projected series that has been abandoned.

4. The balance of the Studio Rearrangement account consists of payments made to a firm of engineers that prepared a report relative to the more efficient utilization of existing studio space and equipment.

Instructions

(a) State the general principle (or principles) of accounting that are applicable to the first four accounts.

(b) How would you report each of the first four accounts in the financial statements of MBS, Inc.? Explain.

(c) In what way, if at all, does the Studio Rearrangement account differ from the first four? Explain.

(AICPA adapted)

*C2-13 Two students in intermediate accounting are arguing about the merits of various theory approaches to resolving financial reporting controversies. The first student indicates that we should develop some type of normative criterion, such as prediction of cash flows, and then decide which accounting procedure or which reporting approach best meets this criterion. The second student believes that an analysis of the costs and the benefits of a proposed accounting alternative should be determined, and then, after assessing the costs and benefits, it can be determined whether or not this alternative should be selected.

Instructions

(a) What general type of theory approach involves the establishment of some normative criterion, such as prediction of cash flows, to resolve accounting controversies? Discuss.

(b) What general approach is employed when the costs and benefits of a proposed accounting standard are examined? Discuss.

Problems

P2-1 Each of the following statements represents a decision made by the controller of Sampson Enterprises on which your advice is asked.

1. A flood during the year destroyed or damaged a considerable amount of uninsured inventory. No entry was made for this loss because the controller reasons that the ending inventory will, of course, be reduced by the amount of the destroyed or damaged merchandise, and therefore its cost will be included in cost of goods sold and the net income figure will be correct. *disagree - not part of operations*

2. The company provides housing for certain employees and adjusts their salaries accordingly. The controller contends that the cost to the company of maintaining this housing should be charged to "Wages and Salaries." *disagree - need keep maintenance on in separate so know how much costs start comb*

3. Material included in the inventory that cost $70,000 has become obsolete. The controller contends that no loss can be realized until the goods are sold, and so the material is included in the inventory at $70,000. *Recognize loss use net realizable value*

4. Inasmuch as profits for the year appear to be extremely small, no depreciation of fixed assets is to be recorded as an expense this year. *violates consistency principle*

5. The company occupies the building in which it operates under a long-term lease requiring annual rental payments. It sublets certain office space not required for its own purposes. The controller credits rents received against rents paid to get net rent expense. *full disclosure other income operating expense include net expe Footno rent rent*

6. The entire cost of a new delivery truck is to be charged to an expense account. *need be italiz capitaliz*

7. The company has paid a large sum for an advertising campaign to promote a new product that will not be placed on the market until the following year. The controller has charged this amount to a prepaid expense account. *Since not on market until next year, match expense + revenue use prepaid - ad*

8. A customer leaving the building slipped on an icy spot on the stairway and wrenched his back. He immediately entered suit against the company for permanent physical injuries and claims damages in the amount of $96,000. The suit has not yet come to trial. The controller has made an entry charging a special loss account and crediting a liability account. *contingent liability — if measurable + probable — record*

if probable + not measurable disclose but no amount

9. A building purchased by the company five years ago at $64,000, including the land on which it stands, can now be sold for $103,000. The controller instructs that the new value of $103,000 be entered in the accounts.

10. The company operates a cafeteria for the convenience of its employees. Sales made by the cafeteria are credited to the regular sales account for product sales; food purchased and salaries paid for the cafeteria operations are recorded in the regular purchase and payroll accounts.

Instructions

You are to state (a) whether you agree with his decision and (b) the reasons supporting your position. Consider each decision independently of all others.

P2-2 Presented below are a number of facts related to Rotterman Co. Assume that no mention of these facts was made in the financial statements and the related footnotes.

(a) The company is a defendant in a patent-infringement suit involving a material amount; you have received assurance from the company's counsel that the possibility of loss is remote.

(b) During the year, an assistant controller for the company embezzled $5,000. Rotterman's net income for the year was $1,400,000. The assistant controller and the money have not been found.

(c) Because of the recent gasoline shortage, it is possible that Rotterman may suffer a costly shutdown in the near future similar to those suffered by other companies both within and outside the industry.

(d) Rotterman has reported its ending inventory at $1,300,000 in the financial statements. No other information related to inventories is presented in the financial statements and related footnotes.

(e) The company changed its method of depreciating equipment from the double-declining balance to the straight-line method. No mention of this change was made in the financial statements.

(f) The company decided that, for the sake of conciseness, only net income should be reported on the income statement. Details as to revenues, cost of goods sold, and expenses were omitted.

(g) Equipment purchases of $70,000 were partly financed during the year through the issuance of a $60,000 notes payable. The company offset the equipment against the notes payable and reported plant assets at $10,000.

Instructions

Assume that you are the auditor of Rotterman Co., and that you have been asked to explain the appropriate accounting and related disclosure necessary for each of these items.

P2-3 Presented below is information related to Sanchez, Inc.

(a) Materials were purchased on January 1, 1980 for $42,000 and this amount was entered in the Materials account. On December 31, 1980, the materials would have cost $49,000, so the following entry is made.

historical cost, revenue recognition

Inventory	7,000	
Gain on Inventories		7,000

(b) An order for $10,000 has been received from a customer for products on hand. This order was shipped on January 3, 1981. The company made the following entry in 1980. *change hands 81 record 81*

Accounts Receivable	10,000	
Sales		10,000

(c) During the year, the company purchased equipment through the issuance of common stock. The stock had a par value of $100,000 and a fair market value of $300,000. The fair market value of the equipment was not easily determinable. The company recorded this transaction as follows: *should be 300,000*

Equipment	100,000	
Common Stock		100,000

(d) Depreciation expense on the building for the year was $17,000. Because the building was increasing in value during the year, the controller decided to charge the depreciation expense to retained earnings instead of to net income. The following entry is recorded.   *unacceptable*

Retained Earnings	17,000	
Accumulated Depreciation—Buildings		17,000

(e) During the year, the company sold certain equipment for $100,000, recognizing a gain of $6,000. Because the controller believed that new equipment would be needed in the near future, the controller decided to defer the gain and amortize it over the life of any new equipment purchased.   *gain should be recognized*

Instructions

Comment on the appropriateness of the accounting procedures followed by Sanchez, Inc.

P2-4   Each of the items below involves the question of materiality to Carlson, Inc.

1.   The amount of $600 is paid during 1980 for an assessment of additional income taxes for the year 1978. The amount originally paid in 1978 was $18,000, and the amount of this year's income taxes will be $26,000.

2.   Land that had originally been purchased for expansion is sold in 1981 at a gain of $7,000. Net income for the year is $53,000, including the gain of $7,000. The company has experienced similar types of gains in the past.

3.   It is expected that purchase returns and allowances made in 1980 in the amount of $4,400 will represent returns and allowances on purchases made in 1981. This is a typical amount of returns and allowances made at the beginning of each year on sales made in the preceding year.

4.   The company purchases hundreds of items of equipment each year that cost less than $90 each. Most of them are used for several years, but some of them last for less than a year. The total cost of these purchases is about the same each year.

Instructions

State your recommendation as to how each item should be treated in the accounts and in the statements, giving proper consideration to materiality and practicability aspects.

P2-5   A number of accounting procedures and practices are described below:

1.   Ken Janson, manager of University Bookstore, Inc., bought a radio for his own use. He paid for the set by writing a check on the Bookstore checking account and charged the "Office Equipment" account. *economic entity assumption*

2.   Goldman, Inc. recently completed a new 120-story office building which houses their home offices and many other tenants. All the office equipment for the building which had a per item or per unit cost of $900 or less was expensed as immaterial even though the office equipment has an average life of 10 years. The total cost of such office equipment was approximately $25 million. (Do not use the matching principle.)   *materiality*

3. A large lawsuit has been filed against Losso Corp. by Rand Co. Losso has recorded a loss and related estimated liability equal to the maximum possible amount it feels it might lose. They are confident, however, that either they will not lose the suit or they will owe a much smaller amount. (Do not use the "objectivity" principle.)   *matching*

4. The AICPA, in a recent audit guide for brokers and other dealers in securities, stated that "the trading and investment accounts . . . should be valued at market or fair value for financial reporting purposes. . . ." The brokerage firm of Heneman and Cummings, Inc. continues to value its trading and investment accounts at cost or market, whichever is lower.   *Industry Practice*

5. Savco Discount Centers buys its merchandise by the truck and train-carload. Savco does not defer any transportation costs in computing the cost of its ending inventory. Such costs, although varying from period to period, are always material in amount.   *matching*

6. Rollet, Inc., a fast-food company, sells franchises for $60,000, accepting a $500 down payment and a 50-year note for the remainder. Rollet promises within 3 years to assist in site selection, building, and management training. Rollet records the $50,000 franchise fee as revenue in the period in which the contract is signed.   *revenue realization*

7. Heber Chemical Company "faces possible expropriation [i.e., take-over] of foreign facilities and possible losses on sums owed by various customers on the verge of bankruptcy." The company president has decided that these possibilities should not be noted on the financial statements because Heber still hopes that these events will not take place.   *full disclosure*

8. The treasurer of Montalavi Co. wishes to prepare financial statements only during downturns in their wine production, which occur periodically when the rhubarb crop fails. He states that it is at such times that the statements could be most easily prepared. In no event would more than 30 months pass without statements being prepared.   *periodicity*

9. "Eastman Kodak Co. said it plans to adopt complete LIFO inventory accounting . . . that is expected to reduce 1974 net income about $41 million . . . Kodak said that the 'appropriate portion' of the change will be reflected in the financial statements. . . . Kodak has been using FIFO inventory accounting." (**Wall Street Journal** 9/18/74.)   *consistent*

10. The LPS Power & Light Company has purchased a large amount of property, plant, and equipment over a number of years. They have decided that because the general price level has changed materially over the years, they will issue only price-level adjusted financial statements.   *historical cost*

11–12. Wright Manufacturing Co. decided to manufacture its own widgets because it would be cheaper to do so than to buy them from an outside supplier. In an attempt to make their statements more comparable with those of their competitors, Wright charged its inventory account for what they felt the widgets would have cost if they had been purchased from an outside supplier. (List **two** terms for this situation.)

Instructions   *Objectivity, Historical Cost*

For each of the foregoing, list the assumption, principle, or modifying convention that has been violated. In each case, except where noted, list only one term.

P2-6 Presented below are a number of accounting procedures and practices that have developed over time.

1. All payments out of petty cash are charged to Miscellaneous Expense. (Do not use conservatism.)

2. The use of consolidated statements is justified.   *Parent Co includes subsidiary in statements*

3. Reporting must be done at defined time intervals.

4. An allowance for doubtful accounts is established.

5. Changes cannot be made from FIFO to LIFO back to FIFO.

6. Anticipate no profits and recognize all possible losses.

7. Goodwill is recorded only at time of purchase. (Do not use objectivity principle.)   *historical cost ^ conservatism*

8. Brokerage firms use market value for purposes of valuation of all marketable securities.
9. Each enterprise is kept as a unit distinct from its owner or owners.
10. It is essential if financial statements of successive periods are to be comparable.
11. All significant postbalance sheet events are reported.
12. Revenue is recorded at point of sale.
13. Price-level changes are not recognized in the accounting records. (Do not use objectivity principle.)
14. Lower of cost or market is used to value inventories.
15. Financial information is presented so that reasonably prudent investors will not be misled.
16. Intangibles are capitalized and amortized over periods benefited.
17. Repair tools are expensed when purchased.
18. Financial forecasts are not recorded because of their subjective nature.
19. All important aspects of bond indentures are presented in financial statements.
20. Rationale for accrual accounting is stated.

Instructions

Select the assumption, principle, or modifying convention that most appropriately justifies these procedures and practices.

P2-7 Presented below are a number of business transactions that occurred during the current year for Tuttle, Inc.

1. Because of a "fire sale," equipment obviously worth $140,000 was acquired at a cost of $110,000. The following entry was made:

Equipment	140,000	
Cash		110,000
Income		30,000

2. Merchandise inventory which cost $380,000 is reported on the balance sheet at $460,000, the expected selling price less estimated selling costs. The following entry was made to record this increase in value:

Merchandise Inventory	80,000	
Income		80,000

3. Tuttle, Inc. has been concerned about whether intangible assets could generate cash in case of liquidation. As a consequence, goodwill arising from a purchase transaction during the current year and recorded at $600,000 was written off as follows:

Retained Earnings	600,000	
Goodwill		600,000

4. Because the general level of prices increased during the current year, Tuttle, Inc. determined that there was a $8,000 understatement of depreciation expense on its equipment and decided to record it in its accounts. The following entry was made:

Depreciation Expense	8,000	
Accumulated Depreciation		8,000

5. The company is being sued for $90,000 by a customer who claims damages for personal injury apparently caused by a defective product. Company attorneys feel extremely confident that the company will have no liability for damages resulting from the situation. Nevertheless, the company decides to make the following entry:

Loss from Lawsuit	90,000	
Liability for Lawsuit		90,000

6. The president of Tuttle, Inc. used his expense account to purchase a new boat solely for personal use. The following entry was made:

Miscellaneous Expense	8,000	
Cash		8,000

Instructions

In each of the situations above, discuss the appropriateness of the journal entries in accordance with generally accepted accounting principles.

P2-8 You are engaged to review the accounting records of Dennis Corporation prior to the closing of the revenue and expense accounts as of December 31, the end of the current fiscal year. The following information comes to your attention.

1. For a number of years the company had used the average cost method for inventory valuation purposes. During the current year, the president noted that all the other companies in their industry had switched to the LIFO method. The company decided not to switch to LIFO because net income would decrease $280,000. *could go either way*

2. During the current year, Dennis Corporation changed its policy in regard to expensing purchases of small tools. In the past, these purchases had always been expensed because they amounted to less than .01% of net income, but the president has decided that capitalization and subsequent depreciation should now be followed. It is expected that purchases of small tools will not fluctuate greatly from year to year. *materiality*

3. Dennis Corporation constructed a warehouse at a cost of $350,000. The company had been depreciating the asset on a straight-line basis over ten years. In the current year, the controller doubled depreciation expense because the replacement cost of the warehouse had increased significantly. *should base depreciation on historical cost*

4. The company decided in October of the current fiscal year to start a massive advertising campaign to enhance the marketability of their product. In November, the company paid $400,000 for advertising time on a major television network to advertise their product during the next twelve months. The controller expensed the $400,000 in the current year on the basis that "once the money is spent, it can never be recovered from the television network." *matching*

5. In preparing the balance sheet, detailed information as to the amount of cash on deposit in each of several banks was omitted. Only the total amount of cash under a caption "Cash in banks" was presented. *Don't need state particular banks*

6. On June 6 of the current year, Dennis Corporation purchased an undeveloped tract of land at a cost of $285,000. The company spent $60,000 in subdividing the land and getting it ready for sale. An appraisal of the property at the end of the year indicated that the land was now worth $400,000. Although none of the lots were sold, the company recognized revenue of $115,000, less related expenses of $60,000, for a net income on the project of $55,000. *Revenue realization*

Instructions

State whether or not you agree with the decisions made by Dennis Corporation: Support your answers with reference whenever possible to the generally accepted principles and assumptions applicable in the circumstances.

A Review of the Accounting Process

Accounting systems vary widely from one business to another, depending on the nature of the business and the transactions in which it engages, the size of the firm and the volume of data to be handled, and the informational demands that management and others place on the system.

The broadest definition of an accounting system includes all of the activities required to provide management with the quantified information needed for planning, controlling, and reporting the financial condition and operations of the enterprise. Managers and investors, confronted with questions such as those listed below, depend on the accounting system for the answers.

What is the composition of our asset structure?
What is the amount of invested and earned capital?
Did we make a profit last period?
What did it cost us to produce one unit of product?
Were our sales higher this period than last?
Are any of our product lines or divisions operating at a loss?
Can we safely increase our dividends to stockholders?
Is our rate of return on net assets increasing?

Many similar questions can be answered when there is an efficient accounting system to provide the data. A well-devised accounting system is a necessity for every business enterprise. A company that does not keep an accurate record of its business transactions is likely to lose revenue and operate inefficiently. Although most companies have satisfactory accounting systems, many companies are inefficient partly because of poor accounting procedures. Consider, for example, the Long Island Railroad,[1] the nation's busiest commuter line, which lost money at one time because its cash position was unknown; large amounts of money owed the

[1]"Long Island Railroad Is Said to Be Losing Revenue Due to 'Weak' Accounting System," *The Wall Street Journal*, February 19, 1971, p. 4.

railroad had not been billed; some payables were erroneously recorded twice; and redemptions of bonds were not recorded. Although this situation is rare in large enterprises, it illustrates our point: accounts and detailed records must be kept by every business enterprise.

Procedures Employed in Accounting

Financial accounting rests on a framework of rules for identifying, recording, classifying, and interpreting transaction data relating to enterprises. These rules are derived from the concepts discussed in Chapter 2. It is important that the accountant understand the basic terminology employed in collecting accounting data. Here are the terms most commonly used.

Transactions. Changes in assets, liabilities, and equities that are recorded. A transaction is financial in nature, is expressed in terms of money, and generally results in the transfer of values between parties. The two types of transactions are **external transactions** in which other entities participate and **internal transactions** in which only the enterprise participates.

Account. A systematic arrangement that shows the effect of transactions on a specific asset or equity. A separate account is kept for each asset, liability, revenue, expense, and for capital (owners' equity).

Real and nominal accounts. Real accounts are asset, liability, and equity accounts and they appear on the balance sheet. Nominal (also called temporary) accounts are revenue and expense accounts and they appear on the income statement. Nominal accounts are periodically closed; real accounts are not.

Ledger. The book (or computer print outs) containing the accounts is called a ledger. It usually has a separate page for each account. A **general ledger** is a collection of all the asset, liability, owners' equity, revenue, and expense accounts. A **subsidiary ledger** contains a group of accounts that constitute the details related to a specific general ledger account.

Journal. The book of original entry where the essential facts and figures in connection with all transactions are initially recorded. From the book of original entry the various amounts are transferred to the ledger.

Posting. The mechanical process of transferring the essential facts and figures from the book of original entry to the accounts in the ledger.

Trial balance. A list of all open accounts in the ledger and their balances. A trial balance may be prepared at any time. A trial balance taken immediately after all adjustments have been posted is called an **adjusted trial balance.** A trial balance taken immediately after closing entries have been posted is designated an **after-closing** or **post-closing trial balance.**

Adjusting entries. Entries made at the end of an accounting period to bring all accounts up to date on an accrual accounting basis so that correct financial statements can be prepared.

Financial statements. Statements that reflect the collection, tabulation, and final summarization of the accounting data. Basically four statements are involved: (1) the **balance sheet,** which shows the financial condition of the enterprise at the end of the year, (2) the **income statement,** which measures the results of operations during the year, (3) the **statement of changes in financial position,** which measures the resources provided during the period and uses to which they are put, and (4) the **statement of retained earnings,** which reconciles the balance of the retained earnings account from the beginning to the end of the year.

Closing entries. The formal process by which all nominal accounts are reduced to zero and the net income or net loss is determined and transferred to the Capital account is known as "closing the ledger," "closing the books," or merely "closing."

Utilizing these definitions, accountants have established procedures for the periodic reporting of recorded transaction data in the form of financial statements. The basic procedures normally used to insure that the transaction data are recorded correctly and transmitted to the user are often called the steps in the accounting cycle. The accounting cycle presented in Figure 3–1 (which is completed at least once each year) illustrates the necessary procedures followed from one accounting period to another.

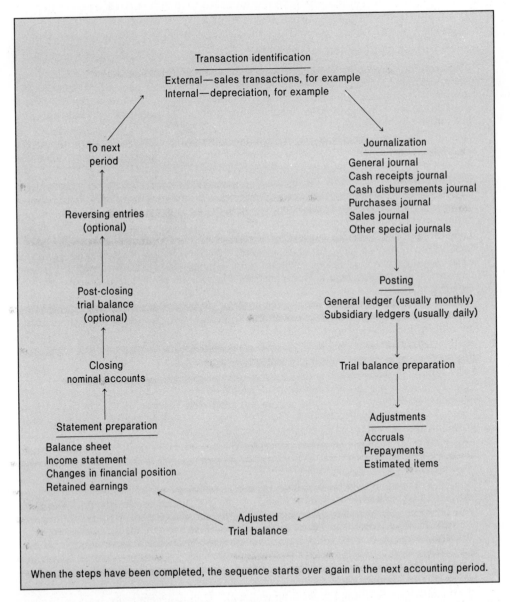

FIG. 3–1. The accounting cycle.

Transaction Identification—What to Record

The first step in the accounting cycle is transaction analysis. The problem is to determine what to record, that is, to **identify recordable events.** No simple rules exist for stating whether an event should be recorded. For example, most accountants agree that changes in personnel, changes in managerial policies, and the value of human resources are important; but none of these items are recorded in the accounts. On the other hand, when the company makes a cash sale, we have no reservations about recording this transaction.

What makes the difference? Generally, two criteria are applied in determining whether an event or item should be recorded: Can the event or item **be measured objectively** in financial terms? And does this event or item **affect the financial position** of the company? If the answer is no to either question, the event should not be recorded. Events that can be measured and that directly affect the financial statements are generally called business transactions and are reducible to dollars and cents. To illustrate, consider the problem of human resources. Should human resources be recognized on financial statements? R. G. Barry & Co., for example, at one time reported as supplemental data total assets of $14,055,926, including $986,094 for "net investments in human resources." Other companies such as American Telephone and Telegraph and Mobil Oil Company have also experimented with human resource accounting. Should accountants value employees for balance sheet purposes and also for income statement purposes? Certainly skilled employees are an important asset, but the problems of determining their value and measuring it objectively have not yet been solved. Consequently, human resources are not recorded; perhaps when measurement techniques become more sophisticated and accepted, such information will be presented, if only in supplemental form.

There are two types of transactions: (1) **external transactions** in which other entities participate, such as sales, purchases, or receipts and disbursements of cash; and (2) **internal transactions** in which only the enterprise participates, such as the process of production in which raw material, labor, and overhead are combined to make a new product. Most external events are easy to recognize, because they encompass any transfer of goods, services, money, or exchange of one obligation for another. An external transaction also occurs when the enterprise receives cash from an owner to increase the investment in the enterprise, or when the enterprise transfers resources to owners and their interests decrease, such as in a declaration of dividends or a transfer from an ownership interest to a creditorship position.

Internal transactions are more difficult to isolate and record. The most obvious examples of internal transactions are the recording of the depreciation, depletion, and amortization. Another illustration is any recombination of existing assets such as in a production process, where each of the activities results in a product that has a price greater than the costs associated with making it.

In short, accountants record as many events as possible that affect the financial position of the enterprise, but events or items are often omitted because the problems of measuring them are complex. The accounting profession, through the efforts of individuals and numerous organizations, as indicated in Chapter 1, is continually working to refine its measurement techniques.

Double-Entry Accounting

There are established rules for recording transactions as they occur. These rules, often referred to as double-entry accounting, are the ones you probably learned in your basic principles course. Debit and credit in accounting simply mean left and right or, depending on the account, positive and negative. The left side of any account is the debit side; the right side, the credit side. In arithmetic, plus and minus signs indicate addition and subtraction; in accounting, addition or subtraction is indicated by the side of the account on which the amount is shown. All asset and expense accounts are increased on the left or debit side and decreased on the right or credit side. Conversely, all liability, revenue, and capital accounts are increased on the right or credit side and decreased on the left or debit side. The basic guidelines for an accounting system are presented below.

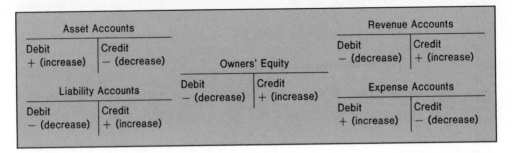

Assume a transaction in which service is rendered for cash. Two accounts are affected; both an asset account (Cash) and a revenue account (Sales) are increased. Cash is debited and Sales is credited. Therein are revealed the essentials of a **double-entry system**—for every debit there must be a credit and vice versa.

This leads us, then, to the basic equality in accounting,

$$\text{assets} = \text{liabilities} + \text{owners' equity}$$

or simply

$$\text{assets} = \text{equities}$$

Every time a transaction occurs, the elements of the equation change, but the basic equality remains. To illustrate, here are seven different transactions.

1. Deposit by the owner of $30,000 for use in the business:
    assets = liabilities + owners' equity
    +30,000   +30,000

2. Disburses $600 cash for secretarial wages:
    assets = liabilities + owners' equity
    −600   −600 (expense)

3. Purchases office equipment priced at $5,200 giving a 10% promissory note in exchange:
    assets = liabilities + owners' equity
    +5,200   +5,200

4. Pays off a short-term liability of $7,000:
    assets = liabilities + owners' equity
    −7,000   −7,000

5. Declares a cash dividend of $5,000:

$$\text{assets} = \text{liabilities} + \text{owners' equity}$$
$$+5,000 \qquad -5,000$$

6. Converts a long-term liability of $9,000 into common stock:

$$\text{assets} = \text{liabilities} + \text{owners' equity}$$
$$-9,000 \qquad +9,000$$

7. Pays cash of $8,000 for a delivery van:

$$\text{assets} = \text{liabilities} + \text{owners' equity}$$
$$-8,000$$
$$+8,000$$

Revenue and expense accounts are elements of owners' equity—revenues being the increases or credits to owners' equity and expenses being the decreases or debits. The difference between revenues and expenses for a period of time is the net increase (income) or net decrease (loss) in owners' equity.

The Journal—Book of Original Entry

Accounts are the means by which differing effects on the basic business elements (assets, liabilities, and equities) are categorized and collected. The **general ledger** is a collection of all the asset, liability, owners' equity, revenue, and expense accounts. A **"T" account** (as illustrated on page 73) is a convenient method of illustrating the effect of transactions on particular asset, liability, equity, revenue, and expense items.

In practice, transactions are not recorded directly in the ledger because a transaction affects two or more different accounts, each of which is on a different page in the ledger. To circumvent this problem and to have a complete record of each transaction in one place, a **journal** is employed. The simplest form of a journal is a chronological listing of transactions expressed in terms of debits and credits to particular accounts. This type of journal is called a **general journal** and is illustrated on page 72 for the following transactions.

Nov. 1 Buys a new delivery truck on account from Chevy Motor Co., $8,700.
    3 Receives an invoice from the *Evening Journal* for advertising, $80.
    4 Returns merchandise to Crane Supply for credit, $175.
  16 Receives a $45 debit memo from Stafford & Co., indicating that freight on a purchase from Stafford & Co. was prepaid, terms, f.o.b. shipping point.

Transactions entered in the general journal record much the same data as are recorded in the "T" accounts. Each general journal entry consists of four parts: (1) the accounts and amounts to be debited (Dr.), (2) the accounts and amounts to be credited (Cr.), (3) a date, and (4) an explanation. The debit account titles and amounts are entered first, followed by the credit account titles and amounts, which are slightly indented to differentiate them from debits. The explanation is begun on the line below the name of the last account to be credited and may take one or more lines. The "Acct. No." column is completed at the time the accounts are posted.

GENERAL JOURNAL		Page 12		
Date 1981		Acct. No.	Amount	
			Dr.	Cr.
Nov. 1	Delivery Equipment	8	8,700	
	Accounts Payable	34		8,700
	(Purchased delivery truck on account from Chevy Motor Co.)			
3	Advertising Expense	65	80	
	Accounts Payable	34		80
	(Received invoice for advertising from *Evening Journal*)			
4	Accounts Payable	34	175	
	Returned Purchases	53		175
	(Returned merchandise for credit to Crane Supply)			
16	Transportation-In	55	45	
	Accounts Payable	34		45
	(Received debit memo for freight on merchandise purchased f.o.b. shipping point from Stafford & Co.)			

Specialized Journals

Most businesses use special journals in addition to the general journal. Special journals permit greater division of labor, reduce the time necessary to accomplish the various bookkeeping tasks, and summarize transactions possessing a common characteristic. The coverage of specialized journals, which could be inserted at this point, is located in Appendix D at the end of this chapter.

Posting to the Ledger

The items entered in a general journal must be transferred to the general ledger. This procedure, **posting,** is considered part of the summarizing and classifying activity of the accounting process. Because the debit and credit analysis of the transaction takes place as the entry is recorded in the general journal, posting consists of transferring to the proper ledger accounts the amounts entered in the general journal.

For example, the November 1 entry in the general journal expressed a debit to Delivery Equipment of $8,700 and a credit to Accounts Payable of $8,700. This entry indicates that the amount in the debit column is posted from the journal to the debit side of the ledger account, and that the amount in the credit column is posted from the journal to the credit side of the ledger account.

The numbers in the "Acct. No." column refer to the accounts in the ledger to which the respective items are posted. For example, the "8" to the right of the words "Delivery Equipment" means that Delivery Equipment is account No. 8 in the ledger, to which the $8,700 was posted. Similarly, the "34" placed in the column to the right of "Accounts Payable" indicates that this $8,700 item was posted to account No. 34 in the ledger. The posting of the general journal is completed when all of the posting reference numbers have been recorded opposite the account titles in the journal. Thus the number in the posting reference column serves two purposes: (1) to indicate the ledger account number of the account involved, and (2) to indicate that the posting has been completed for the particular item. Each business enterprise selects its own numbering system for its ledger accounts. One practice is to begin numbering with asset accounts and to follow with liabilities, owners' equities, revenue, and expense accounts, in that order.

The various ledger accounts affected by the journal entries in the preceding illustration appear as below after the posting process is completed. The source of the data transferred to the ledger account is indicated by the reference GJ12 (General Journal, page 12).

Delivery Equipment						No. 8
Nov. 1	GJ 12	8,700				
			Accounts Payable			No. 34
Nov. 4	GJ 12	175	Nov. 1	GJ 12		8,700
			3	GJ 12		80
			16	GJ 12		45
			Returned Purchases			No. 53
			Nov. 4	GJ 12		175
			Transportation-In			No. 55
Nov. 16	GJ 12	45				
			Advertising Expense			No. 65
Nov. 3	GJ 12	80				

Trial Balance

As soon as the entries have been recorded in the journal and posted to the ledger for a given period, it is customary and desirable to prepare a trial balance. A trial balance is a list of all open accounts in the general ledger and their balances. The trial balance accomplishes two principal purposes:

1. It proves that debits and credits of an equal amount are in the ledger.
2. It supplies a listing of open accounts and their balances that are the basis for any adjustments and are used in preparing the financial statements and in supplying financial data about the concern.

The trial balance for Ruddy Bros. Wholesale is illustrated on page 74.

Need for Adjusting Entries

The employment of an accrual system means that numerous adjustments are necessary before financial statements are prepared because certain accounts are not accurately stated. For example, if we handle transactions on a cash basis, only cash transactions during the year are recorded. Consequently, if a company's employees are paid every two weeks and the end of an accounting period occurs in the middle of these two weeks, neither liability nor expense is shown for the last week. In order to bring the **accounts** up to date for the preparation of financial statements, both the wage expense and the wage liability accounts need to be increased. This change is accomplished by means of an adjusting entry.

Ruddy Bros. Wholesale
TRIAL BALANCE
December 31, 1981

Cash	$ 13,000	
Accounts Receivable	14,650	
Notes Receivable	8,000	
Inventory, January 1, 1981	89,500	
Office Equipment	16,000	
Furniture and Fixtures	12,300	
Accounts Payable		$ 14,100
Notes Payable		24,000
Ruddy Bros. Capital		91,240
Sales		896,000
Returned Sales	3,760	
Sales Allowances	960	
Purchases	713,450	
Returned Purchases		4,140
Transportation-In	6,570	
Sales Salaries Expense	65,700	
Traveling Expenses	4,900	
Advertising Expense	21,200	
General Office Salaries	39,800	
Rent Expense	18,000	
Insurance Expense	2,780	
Utilities Expense	4,310	
Telephone Expense	1,260	
Auditing and Legal Expense	2,780	
Miscellaneous Administrative Expense	2,200	
Purchases Discount		13,500
Sales Discount	1,860	
	$1,042,980	$1,042,980

A necessary step in the accounting process, then, is the adjustment of all accounts to an accrual basis. **Adjusting entries** are therefore necessary to achieve a proper matching of revenues and expenses in the determination of net income for the current period and to achieve an accurate statement of the assets and equities existing at the end of the period. Each adjusting entry affects both a real (asset or equity) account and a nominal (revenue or expense) account.

Normally the adjustments are classified in the following manner:

Prepaid (deferred) items:
   Prepaid expenses
   Unearned revenues
Accrued items:
   Accrued liabilities (expenses)
   Accrued assets (revenues)
Estimated items

Prepaid Expenses   A prepaid expense is an item paid and recorded in advance of its use or consumption in the business, part of which properly represents expense of the current period and part of which represents an asset on hand at the end of the period. If a three-year insurance premium is paid in advance at the beginning of the current year, one-third of the amount paid represents expense of the current year and two-thirds is an asset at the end of the year, an amount properly to be deferred to and expensed in future years.

   Illustration. If insurance for three years is purchased for $1,200 on January 2, 1981, and the books are closed annually on December 31, the asset account appears as follows on December 31, 1981, before the adjusting entry is made:

Unexpired Insurance		
1981 Jan. 2	Cash	1,200

   Because one-third of the three-year period has now passed, one-third of the amount paid is shown as an expense for 1981, and the asset account is reduced by the same amount. The adjusting entry required on December 31, 1981, is:

Dec. 31

Insurance Expense	400	
Unexpired Insurance		400
(To charge one-third of insurance premium to expense)		

   The ledger now shows an expense for insurance of $400 and an asset, Unexpired Insurance, of $800.

Unexpired Insurance					
1981 Jan. 2	Cash	1,200	1981 Dec. 31	To Insurance Expense	400
Insurance Expense					
1981 Dec. 31	Insurance Expired	400			

Unearned Revenue   Unearned revenue is revenue received and recorded as a liability or as a revenue before the revenue has been earned by providing goods or services to customers. As dictated by the "matching principle" in accounting, revenue is reported in the period in which it is earned; therefore, when it is received in advance of its being earned, the amount applicable to future periods is deferred to future periods. The amount unearned is considered a liability because it represents an obligation to perform a service in the future.

Some common unearned revenue items are rent received in advance, interest received in advance on notes receivable, subscriptions and advertising received in advance by publishers, and deposits from customers in advance of delivery of merchandise.

Illustration. Assume that a business rented part of a building for a three-year period from January 3, 1981, for $6,000 to a tenant who paid the full three years' rent in advance. The business made the following entry.

	Jan. 2	
Cash	6,000	
Unearned Rent Income		6,000
(To record rent received for three years in advance)		

At the end of 1981 one-third of this amount is earned and, therefore, an adjusting entry is made.

	Dec. 31	
Unearned Rent Income	2,000	
Rent Income		2,000
(To take up as income one-third of $6,000)		

The entry also records $2,000 in the Rent Income account, which represents the amount of income earned during the year. These two accounts now show the following balances after adjustment.

Unearned Rent Income					
1981 Dec. 31	Adjusting	2,000	1981 Jan. 2	Cash	6,000
Rent Income					
			1981 Dec. 31	Adjusting	2,000

For prepaid items, it makes no difference if an original transaction entry is recorded in a real account (asset or liability) or in a nominal account (revenue or expense). After adjusting entries, the balances of the respective accounts are the same, regardless of the original entry.

Accrued Liabilities or Expenses Accrued liabilities or accrued expenses are items of expense that have been incurred during the period, but have not yet been recorded or paid. As such, they represent liabilities at the end of the period. The related debits for such items are included in the income statement as expenses.

Some common accrued liabilities are interest payable, wages and salaries payable, and property taxes payable.

Illustration. When employees are paid on a monthly basis on the last day of the month, there are no accrued wages and salaries at the end of the month or year because all employees will have been paid all amounts due them for the month or the year. When they are paid on a weekly or biweekly basis, however, it is usually necessary to make an adjusting entry for wages and salaries earned but not paid at the end of the fiscal period.

Assume that a business pays its sales staff every Friday for a five-day week, that the total weekly payroll is $2,000, and that December 31 falls on Thursday. On December 31, the end of the fiscal period, the employees have worked four-fifths of a week for which they have not been paid and for which no entry has been made. The adjusting entry on December 31 is:

Dec. 31

Sales Salaries Expense	1,600	
Salaries Payable		1,600
(To record accrued salaries as of Dec. 31: 4/5 x $2,000)		

As a result of this entry, the income statement for the year includes the salaries earned by the sales staff during the last four days in December and the balance sheet shows as a liability salaries payable of $1,600.

Sales Salaries Expense			
1981			
Paid in 1981	103,000		
Dec. 31 Adjusting entry	1,600		
Total 1981	104,600		
Salaries Payable			
	1981		
	Dec. 31 Adjusting entry	1,600	

Accrued Assets or Revenues   Items of income that have been earned during the period but that have not yet been collected are called accrued assets, accrued revenues, or revenues receivable. Adjusting entries must be made for these items to record the revenue that has been earned but not yet received and to record as an asset the amount receivable.

Some examples of accrued assets are rent receivable and interest income receivable.

Illustration. Assume that office space is rented to a tenant at $1,000 per month, that the tenant has paid the rent for the first 11 months of the year, and that the tenant has paid no rent for December. The adjusting entry on December 31 is:

Dec. 31

Rent Income Receivable	1,000	
Rent Income		1,000
(To record December rent)		

As a result of this entry, an asset of $1,000, Rent Income Receivable, appears on the balance sheet disclosing the amount due from the tenant as of December 31. The income statement discloses rent income of $12,000, the $11,000 received for the first 11 months and the $1,000 for December entered by means of the adjusting entry. After adjustment the accounts appear as follows.

Rent Income		
	1981	
	Received in 1981	11,000
	Dec. 31 Adjusting entry	1,000
	Total 1981	12,000
Rent Income Receivable		
1981		
Dec. 31 Adjusting entry 1,000		

Estimated Items

Uncollectible accounts and depreciation of fixed assets are ordinarily called estimated items because the amounts are not exactly determinable. In other words, an **estimated item** is a function of unknown future events and developments, which means that current period charges can be evaluated on a subjective basis only. It is known, for example, that some accounts receivable arising from credit sales will prove to be uncollectible. To prevent an understatement of expenses and losses of the period, it is necessary to estimate and record the bad debts that are expected to result.

Also, when a long-lived fixed asset is purchased, it is assumed that ultimately it will be scrapped or sold at a price much below the purchase price. This difference between an asset's cost and its scrap value represents an expense to the business that should be apportioned over the asset's useful life. We must estimate the probable life of the fixed asset and its scrap value to determine the expense that is charged in each period.

Adjusting Entries for Bad Debts   Proper matching of revenues and expenses dictates recording bad debts as an expense of the period in which the sale is made instead of the period in which the accounts or notes are written off. This method requires an adjusting entry.

At the end of each period an estimate is made of the amount of current-period sales on account that will later prove to be uncollectible. The estimate is based on the amount of bad debts experienced in one or more past years, general economic conditions, the age of the receivables, and other factors that indicate the element of uncollectibility in the receivables outstanding at the end of the period. Usually it is expressed as a certain percent of the sales on account for the period, or it is computed by adjusting the account for Allowance for Doubtful Accounts to a certain percent of the trade accounts receivable and trade notes receivable at the end of the period.

Assume, for example, that experience reveals that bad debts usually approximate one-half of one percent of the net sales on account and that net sales on account for the year are $300,000. The adjusting entry for bad debts is:

Dec. 31

Bad Debts Expense	1,500	
Allowance for Doubtful Accounts		1,500
(To record estimated bad debts for the year: $300,000 × .005)		

Adjusting Entries for Depreciation   Entries for depreciation are similar to those made for reducing the prepaid expenses in which the original amount was debited to an asset account. The principal difference is that for depreciation the credit is made to a separate account, Accumulated Depreciation, instead of to the asset account.

In estimating depreciation, the original cost of the property, its length of useful life, and its estimated salvage or trade-in value is used. Assume that a truck costing $9,000 has an estimated life of five years and an estimated trade-in value of $1,000 at the end of that period. Because the truck is expected to be worth $8,000 less at the time of its disposal than it was at the time of its purchase, the amount of $8,000 represents an expense that is apportioned over the five years of operations. It is neither logical nor good accounting practice to consider the $8,000 as an expense entirely of the period in which it was acquired or the period in which it was sold, inasmuch as the business receives the benefit of the use of the truck during the entire five-year period.

If the widely used straight-line method of depreciation is used, each year shows as an expense one-fifth of $8,000, or $1,600. Each full year the truck is used the following adjusting entry is made.

Dec. 31

Depreciation Expense—Delivery Equipment	1,600	
Accumulated Depreciation—Delivery Equipment		1,600
(To record depreciation on truck for the year)		

Similarly, depreciation on a building costing $200,000 with an estimated life of fifty years and no scrap value is recorded by the following entry at the end of each year:

Dec. 31

Depreciation Expense—Building	4,000	
Accumulated Depreciation—Building		4,000
(To record depreciation of building for the year)		

Summary of Adjustments Section   As a review, we have summarized the basic adjustments and defined them individually:

Prepaid expense. An expense paid in cash and recorded in advance of its use or consumption.

Unearned revenue. A revenue received and recorded before it is earned.

Accrued liabilities (expenses). Expense incurred but not yet paid.

Accrued assets (revenues). Revenue earned but not yet received.

Estimated items. An expense recorded on the basis of subjective estimates because the expense is a function of unknown future events or developments.

As soon as these adjusting entries have been recorded and posted, another trial balance is prepared before closing. The second or **adjusted trial balance** is used to prepare the financial statements. The basic set of financial statements is discussed in the next two chapters.

Year-End Procedure for Inventory

When the inventory records are maintained on a **perpetual inventory system,** purchases and issues are recorded directly in the inventory account as the purchases and issues occur. Therefore, the balance in the inventory account should represent the ending inventory amount and no adjusting entries are needed. No Purchases account is used because the purchases are debited directly to the inventory account. However, a Cost of Goods Sold account is used to accumulate the issuances from inventory.

When the inventory records are maintained on a **periodic inventory system,** a Purchases account is used and the inventory account is unchanged during the period. The inventory account represents the beginning inventory amount throughout the period. At the end of the accounting period the inventory account must be adjusted by closing out the **beginning inventory** amount and recording the **ending inventory** amount. The ending inventory is determined by physically counting the items on hand and valuing them at cost or at the lower of cost or market. Under the periodic inventory system, cost of goods sold is, therefore, determined by adding the beginning inventory together with net purchases and deducting the ending inventory.

Computation of cost of goods sold under periodic inventory accounting has the characteristics of both an adjusting entry and a closing entry; thus, there is more than one way to prepare the entries that update inventory, record cost of goods sold, and close the other related nominal accounts. To illustrate, Collegiate Apparel Shop has a beginning inventory of $30,000; Purchases $200,000; Transportation-In $6,000; Returned Purchases $1,200; Purchase Allowances $800; Purchase Discounts $2,000; and the ending inventory is $26,000. One method of transferring the various merchandise accounts into the Cost of Goods Sold account is as follows.

Inventory (ending)	26,000	
Purchase Discounts	2,000	
Purchase Allowances	800	
Returned Purchases	1,200	
Cost of Goods Sold	206,000	
Inventory (beginning)		30,000
Purchases		200,000
Transportation-In		6,000

   (To transfer beginning inventory and net purchases to
   Cost of Goods Sold and to record the ending inventory)

After the foregoing entry, only the Cost of Goods Sold account remains to be closed.

The following diagram illustrates in T-account form the process of adjusting the inventory balance, and determining cost of goods sold, and closing the related nominal accounts.

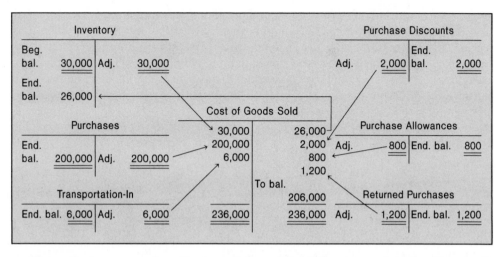

Alternatively, a second method consisting of the following series of entries could be prepared to adjust inventory and to determine cost of goods sold under a periodic inventory system:

Cost of Goods Sold	30,000	
Inventory (beginning)		30,000
(To transfer beginning inventory to Cost of Goods Sold)		
Inventory (ending)	26,000	
Cost of Goods Sold		26,000
(To record the ending inventory balance)		
Purchase Discounts	2,000	
Purchase Allowances	800	
Returned Purchases	1,200	
Cost of Goods Sold	202,000	
Purchases		200,000
Transportation-In		6,000
(To transfer net purchases to Cost of Goods Sold)		

The first two entries adjusting the Inventory account are generally viewed as adjusting entries, while the third entry transferring net purchases to Cost of Goods Sold is viewed as a closing entry.

The balance of Cost of Goods Sold will be the same whether the method of its determination is considered a part of the adjusting process or a part of the closing process. Unless you are specifically directed to treat the transfer of inventory to Cost of Goods Sold as an adjusting entry, you will be expected to prepare an entry similar to the first alternative above and include it as part of the closing process when working the problems at the end of this chapter.

The Closing Process

The procedure generally followed to reduce the balance of nominal (temporary) accounts to zero in order to prepare the accounts for the next period's transactions is known as the **closing process.** In the closing process all of the revenue and expense account balances (income statement items) are transferred to a Revenue and Expense Summary account, which is used only at the end of each accounting period. Revenues and expenses are matched in the Revenue and Expense Summary account and the net result of this matching, which represents the net income or net loss for the period, is then transferred to an owners' equity account (retained earnings for a corporation, and capital accounts normally for proprietorships and partnerships).

For example, assume that revenue accounts of Collegiate Apparel Shop have the following balances, after adjustments, at the end of the year:

Revenue from Sales	$280,000
Rental Revenue	27,000
Interest Income	5,000

These **revenue accounts** would be closed and the balances transferred through the following closing journal entry:

Revenue from Sales	280,000	
Rental Revenue	27,000	
Interest Income	5,000	
Revenue and Expense Summary		312,000
(To close revenue accounts to Revenue and Expense Summary)		

Assume that the expense accounts, including Cost of Goods Sold, have the following balances, after adjustments, at the end of the year:

Cost of Goods Sold	$206,000
Selling Expenses	25,000
General and Adm. Expenses	40,600
Interest Expense	4,400
Income Tax Expense	13,000

These **expense accounts** would be closed and the balances transferred through the following closing journal entry:

Revenue and Expense Summary	289,000	
Cost of Goods Sold		206,000
Selling Expenses		25,000
General and Adm. Expenses		40,600
Interest Expense		4,400
Income Tax Expense		13,000
(To close expense accounts to Revenue and Expense Summary)		

The Revenue and Expense Summary account now has a credit balance of $23,000 which is net income. The **net income is transferred to owners' equity** by closing the Revenue and Expense Summary account to Retained Earnings as follows:

Revenue and Expense Summary	23,000	
Retained Earnings		23,000
(To close Revenue and Expense Summary to owners' equity)		

After the closing process is completed, each income statement (i.e., nominal) account is balanced out to zero and is ready for use in the next accounting period.

The following diagram illustrates in T-account form the closing process.

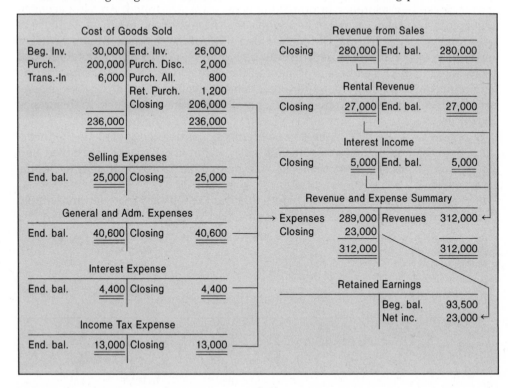

Trial Balance After Closing

We already mentioned that a trial balance is taken after the regular transactions of the period have been entered and that a second trial balance (the adjusted trial balance) is taken after the adjusting entries have been posted. A third trial balance may be taken after posting the closing entries; often called the **postclosing trial balance,** it shows that equal debits and credits have been posted to the Revenue and Expense Summary. The postclosing trial balance consists only of asset, liability, and owners' equity accounts.

Reversing Entries

After the financial statements have been prepared and the books closed, it is customary and desirable to reverse some of the adjusting entries before entering the regular transactions of the next period. Such entries are called reversing entries.

Adjusting entries are made for prepaid, accrued, and estimated items, whereas reversing entries are usually made only for accrued items and for some prepaid items. The prepaid items that are reversed are those in which the amounts arising from the original transactions were initially entered in expense or income accounts, as opposed to asset or liability accounts.

Reversing Entries for Prepaid Expenses   Earlier in this chapter the adjusting entry for unexpired insurance (a prepaid expense) was illustrated. An asset account, Unexpired Insurance, was debited when the three-year premium of $1,200 was paid in advance. At the end of the year, one-third of that amount, $400, was transferred from the asset account to Insurance Expense, and Insurance Expense was then closed to the Revenue and Expense Summary account in the closing process. This adjusting entry does not require reversing; at the end of the next year the asset account is reduced by another $400 and that amount is debited to Insurance Expense.

Suppose, however, that the insurance premium was debited initially to the Insurance Expense account. In the adjusting entry Insurance Expense is credited and Unexpired Insurance is debited for the unexpired portion of the insurance coverage.

After the books are closed and before any transactions are recorded in the next period, a reversing entry is recorded.

Jan. 1

Insurance Expense	800	
Unexpired Insurance		800
(To reverse the adjusting entry of Dec. 31)		

After we post this entry, the two accounts appear as below.

Insurance Expense					
First year			First year		
Jan. 2	Cash paid	1,200	Dec. 31	Adjusting entry	800
			Dec. 31	To R & E	
				Summary	400
		1,200			1,200
Second year					
Jan. 1	Reversing entry	800			
Unexpired Insurance					
First year			Second year		
Dec. 31	Adjusting entry	800	Jan. 1	Reversing entry	800

Here a reversing entry was made to return to the expense account the cost of unexpired insurance at the beginning of the second year of the policy. The business continues to debit Insurance Expense for purchases of other insurance during the second year; to be consistent, the unexpired insurance at the beginning of the year is shown in the same account as the insurance purchased; both can be used during the second year.

Reversing entries are also made for prepaid revenue transactions if the initial entry is made to the revenue account.

Avoidance of Reversing Entries   With respect to prepaid items, why are all such items not entered originally into real accounts (assets and liabilities), thus making reversing entries unnecessary? This practice is sometimes followed. It is particularly advantageous for items that need to be apportioned over several periods.

Other items, however, that do not follow this regular pattern and that may or may not involve two or more periods, are ordinarily entered initially in income or expense accounts. The income and expense accounts may not require adjusting and are systematically closed to Revenue and Expense Summary.

Accrued Items Are Reversed   Because each accrued item involves either a later receipt of cash for income or a later disbursement of cash for expense, a reversing entry is made to offset part of the credit to income or part of the debit to expense. In that way, the net balance that develops in the income or expense account in the later period represents the income earned or expense incurred for that period. To illustrate, we continue with the Sales Salaries account after the adjustment that was shown previously (page 77). The Sales Salaries Expense account, being an expense account, is closed to Revenue and Expense Summary on December 31. On January 1 this reversing entry is made.

Jan. 1

Salaries Payable	1,600	
Sales Salaries Expense		1,600
(To reverse the adjusting entry of Dec. 31)		

This entry closes the Salaries Payable account and puts a credit balance of $1,600 in the Sales Salaries Expense account. On January 1, after we post the reversing entry the accounts appear as follows.

Sales Salaries Expense						
1981			1981			
Paid in 1981		103,000	Dec. 31	To Rev. and Exp.		
Dec. 31	Adjusting entry	1,600		Summary	104,600	
		104,600			104,600	
			1982			
			Jan. 1	Reversing entry	1,600	

Salaries Payable						
			1981			
			Dec. 31	Adjusting entry	1,600	
1982						
Jan. 1	Reversing entry	1,600				

On Friday, January 1, the weekly payroll of $2,000 is paid, and the usual debit to Sales Salaries Expense and credit to Cash are recorded. The Sales Salaries Expense account now contains a debit of $2,000 and a credit of $1,600. The balance of $400 represents the expense incurred during the first day of January. This is illustrated below.

Sales Salaries Expense					
1982			1982		
Jan. 1	Cash paid	2,000	Jan. 1	Reversing entry	1,600

This item was reversed so that the entry for payment of salaries on the first Friday in 1982 is the same as that for any other payroll. If the entry had not been reversed, it would have been necessary to debit Salaries Payable for part of the amount, $1,600, and Sales Salaries Expense for $400. Analysis of this sort can be time-consuming and impractical.

In general, all adjusting entries for prepaid items for which the original amount was entered in an income or expense account and for *all* accrued items should be reversed. It follows, of course, that all other adjusting entries are not reversed; in other words, adjusting entries for prepaid items for which the original amount was entered in a real account and for estimated items are not reversed.

Some accountants avoid reversing entries entirely, but generally it is desirable to use them under the conditions described to ensure consistent treatment of the accounts and to establish standardized procedures for transactions that occur regularly.

The Accounting Cycle

A summary of the steps in a complete accounting cycle shows a logical sequence of the accounting procedures used during a fiscal period.

1. Enter the transactions of the period in appropriate journals.
2. Post from the journals to the ledger.
3. Take a trial balance (first trial balance).
4. Prepare adjusting journal entries and post to the ledger.
5. Take a trial balance after adjusting (second trial balance).
6. Prepare the financial statements from the second trial balance.
7. Prepare closing journal entries and post to the ledger.
8. Take a trial balance after closing (third trial balance).
9. Prepare reversing entries and post to the ledger.

This list of procedures constitutes a complete accounting cycle that is normally performed in every fiscal period.

USING A WORK SHEET TO PREPARE FINANCIAL STATEMENTS

To facilitate the end-of-period accounting and reporting process, accountants frequently use a work sheet. A **work sheet** is a columnar sheet of paper that may be used to help in adjusting the account balances and preparing the financial statements. The **ten-column work sheet** illustrated in this chapter provides columns for the first trial balance, adjustments, adjusted trial balance, income statement, and balance sheet. The work sheet does not in any way replace the financial statements; instead it is the accountant's informal device for accumulating and sorting the information that is needed for the financial statements. The satisfactory completion of the work sheet provides considerable assurance that all of the details related to the end-of-period accounting and statement preparation have been properly brought together.

Adjustments Entered on the Work Sheet

The information that serves as the basis for the adjusting entries made in the work sheet illustration on page 90 follows:

(a) Furniture and equipment is depreciated at the rate of 10% per year based on original cost.

(b) Estimated bad debts, one-quarter of 1% of sales.

(c) Insurance expired during the year, $360.

(d) Interest accrued on notes receivable as of December 31, $800.

(e) The Interest Expense account contains $500 interest paid in advance, which is applicable to next year.

(f) Property taxes accrued December 31, $2,000.

The adjusting entries shown on the work sheet are:

(a)

Depreciation Expense—Furniture and Equipment	6,700	
Accumulated Depreciation of Furniture and Equipment		6,700

(b)

Bad Debts Expense	1,000	
Allowance for Doubtful Accounts		1,000

(c)

Insurance Expense	360	
Unexpired Insurance		360

(d)

Interest Receivable	800	
Interest Income		800

(e)

Prepaid Interest Expense	500	
Interest Expense		500

(f)

Property Tax Expense	2,000	
Property Tax Payable		2,000

These adjusting entries are transferred to the Adjustments columns of the work sheet, and each may be designated by letter. The accounts that are set up as a result of the adjusting entries and that are not already in the trial balance are listed below the totals of the trial balance, as illustrated on page 90. The Adjustments columns are then totaled and balanced.

The illustration does not include in the Adjustments columns the adjustments for cost of goods sold. Although these adjustments are sometimes included in these columns on a ten-column work sheet, this illustration assumes that these entries will be made during the closing process.

Adjusted Trial Balance Columns

The amounts shown in the Trial Balance columns are combined with the amounts in the Adjustments columns and are extended to the Adjusted Trial Balance columns. For example, the amount of $2,000, shown opposite the Allowance for Doubtful Accounts in the Trial Balance Cr. column, is added to the $1,000 in the Adjustments Cr. column, and the total of $3,000 is extended to the Adjusted Trial Balance Cr. column. Similarly, the $900 debit opposite Unexpired Insurance is reduced by the $360 credit in the Adjustments column, and the $540 is shown in the Adjusted Trial Balance Dr. column. The Adjusted Trial Balance columns are then totaled and determined to be in balance.

Income Statement and Balance Sheet Columns

All the debit items in the Adjusted Trial Balance are extended into one of the two debit columns to the right, depending on the financial statement in which the items will appear. Similarly, all the credit items in the Adjusted Trial Balance are extended into one of the two credit columns to the right. It should be observed that the January 1 inventory, which was the inventory at the beginning of the year, is extended to the Income Statement Dr. column, because this item will appear as an addition in the cost of goods sold section of the income statement.

Ending Inventory

The December 31 inventory, which is the inventory at the end of the year, is not in either of the trial balances but is listed as a separate item below the accounts already shown. In the illustration the amount of the ending inventory is assumed to be $40,000, and this amount is shown on the work sheet as both debit and credit. It is listed in the Balance Sheet Dr. column because it is an asset at the end of the year, and in the Income Statement Cr. column because it will be used as a deduction in the cost of goods sold section of the income statement.

Income Taxes and Net Income

The next step is to total the Income Statement columns; the figure necessary to balance the debit and credit columns is the income or loss for the period before income taxes. In this illustration the income before income taxes of $15,640 is shown in the Income Statement Dr. column because the revenues exceeded the expenses by that amount.

The income tax expense and related tax liability are then computed (in this case an effective rate of 22% was applied). Because the Adjustments columns have been balanced, this adjustment is entered in the Income Statement Dr. column as Income Tax Expense $3,440 and in the Balance Sheet Cr. column as Income Tax Payable $3,440. Next the Income Statement columns are balanced with the income taxes included. The $12,200 difference between the debit and credit columns in this illustration represents net income. The net income of $12,200 is entered in the Income Statement Dr. column to achieve equality and in the Balance Sheet Cr. column as the increase in retained earnings. The following adjusting journal entry is recorded and posted to the general ledger as well as the work sheet.

	(g)	
Income Tax Expense	3,440	
Income Tax Payable		3,440

Eight-Column and Twelve-Column Work Sheets

An eight-column instead of a ten-column work sheet may be used to accumulate the same information. The only difference between the two is that the eight-column work sheet omits the Adjusted Trial Balance columns. The amounts shown in the Trial Balance columns (the first two columns) are combined with the amounts in the Adjustments columns and are extended directly into the Income Statement and Balance Sheet columns.

A twelve-column work sheet may be prepared to accommodate increases and decreases in retained earnings by merely adding Retained Earnings Dr. and Cr. columns. Dividends and net income would appear as adjustments to the beginning retained earnings.

Preparation of Financial Statements from Work Sheet

The work sheet provides the information needed for preparation of the financial statements without reference to the ledger or other records. In addition, the data have been sorted into appropriate columns, which facilitates the preparation of the statements.

The financial statements prepared from the ten-column work sheet illustrated are:

Statement of Income for the Year Ended December 31, 1981.

Balance Sheet as of December 31, 1981.

Statement of Retained Earnings for the Year Ended December 31, 1981.

The Spencer Company
TEN-COLUMN WORK SHEET

December 31, 1981

Accounts	Trial Balance Dr.	Trial Balance Cr.	Adjustments Dr.	Adjustments Cr.	Adjusted Trial Balance Dr.	Adjusted Trial Balance Cr.	Income Statement Dr.	Income Statement Cr.	Balance Sheet Dr.	Balance Sheet Cr.
Cash	1,200				1,200				1,200	
Notes receivable	16,000				16,000				16,000	
Accounts receivable	41,000				41,000				41,000	
Allowance for doubtful accounts		2,000		(b) 1,000		3,000				3,000
Inventory, Jan. 1, 1981	36,000				36,000		36,000			
Unexpired insurance	900			(c) 360	540				540	
Furniture and equipment	67,000				67,000				67,000	
Accumulated depreciation of furniture and equipment		12,000		(a) 6,700		18,700				18,700
Notes payable		20,000				20,000				20,000
Accounts payable		13,500				13,500				13,500
Bonds payable		30,000				30,000				30,000
Common stock		50,000				50,000				50,000
Retained earnings		14,200				14,200				14,200
Sales		400,000				400,000		400,000		
Purchases	320,000				320,000		320,000			
Sales salaries expense	20,000				20,000		20,000			
Advertising expense	2,200				2,200		2,200			
Traveling expense	8,000				8,000		8,000			
Salaries, office and general	19,000				19,000		19,000			
Telephone and telegraph expense	600				600		600			
Rent expense	4,800				4,800		4,800			
Property tax expense	3,300		(f) 2,000		5,300		5,300			
Interest expense	1,700			(e) 500	1,200		1,200			
Totals	541,700	541,700								
Depreciation expense— furniture and equipment			(a) 6,700		6,700		6,700			
Bad debts expense			(b) 1,000		1,000		1,000			
Insurance expense			(c) 360		360		360			
Interest receivable			(d) 800		800				800	
Interest income				(d) 800		800		800		
Prepaid interest expense			(e) 500		500				500	
Property tax payable				(f) 2,000		2,000				2,000
Totals			11,360	11,360	552,200	552,200				
Inventory, Dec. 31, 1981								40,000	40,000	
Totals							425,160	440,800		
Income before income taxes							15,640			
Totals							440,800	440,800		
Income before income taxes								15,640		
Income tax expense			(g) 3,440				3,440			
Income tax payable				(g) 3,440						3,440
Net income							12,200			12,200
							15,640	15,640	167,040	167,040

Statement of Income

The income statement presented here is that of a trading or merchandising concern; if a manufacturing concern were illustrated, three inventory accounts would
be involved: raw materials, work in process, and finished goods. When these accounts are used, a supplementary statement entitled cost of goods manufactured
must be prepared.

The Spencer Company
INCOME STATEMENT
For the Year Ended December 31, 1981

Net sales			$400,000
Cost of goods sold			
Inventory, Jan. 1, 1981		$ 36,000	
Purchases		320,000	
Cost of goods available for sale		356,000	
Deduct inventory, Dec. 31, 1981		40,000	
Cost of goods sold			316,000
Gross profit on sales			84,000
Selling expenses			
Sales salaries expense		20,000	
Advertising expense		2,200	
Traveling expense		8,000	
Total selling expenses		30,200	
Administrative expenses			
Salaries, office and general	$19,000		
Telephone and telegraph expense	600		
Rent expense	4,800		
Property tax expense	5,300		
Depreciation expense—furniture and equipment	6,700		
Bad debts expense	1,000		
Insurance expense	360		
Total administrative expenses		37,760	
Total selling and administrative expenses			67,960
Income from operations			16,040
Other income			
Interest income			800
			16,840
Other expense			
Interest expense			1,200
Income before income taxes			15,640
Income taxes			3,440
Net income			$ 12,200

Balance Sheet

The balance sheet prepared from the ten-column work sheet contains more new
items resulting from year-end adjusting entries. Interest receivable, unexpired insurance, and prepaid interest expense are included as current assets, because these

assets will be converted into cash or consumed in the ordinary routine of the business within a relatively short period of time. The amount of Allowance for Doubtful Accounts is deducted from the total of accounts, notes, and interest receivable because it is estimated that only $54,800 of the total of $57,800 will be collected in cash.

In the property, plant, and equipment section the accumulated depreciation is deducted from the cost of the furniture and equipment; the difference represents the book or carrying value of the furniture and equipment.

Property tax payable is shown as a current liability because it is an obligation that is payable within a year. Other short-term accrued liabilities would also be shown as current liabilities.

The bonds payable, due in 1985, are long-term or fixed liabilities and are shown in a separate section. (Interest on the bonds was paid on December 31.)

The Spencer Company
BALANCE SHEET

As of December 31, 1981

Assets

Current assets			
Cash			$ 1,200
Notes receivable	$16,000		
Accounts receivable	41,000		
Interest receivable	800	$57,800	
Less allowance for doubtful accounts		3,000	54,800
Merchandise inventory on hand			40,000
Unexpired insurance			540
Prepaid interest expense			500
Total current assets			97,040
Property, plant, and equipment			
Furniture and equipment		67,000	
Less accumulated depreciation		18,700	
Total property, plant, and equipment			48,300
Total assets			$145,340

Liabilities and Stockholders' Equity

Current liabilities			
Notes payable			$ 20,000
Accounts payable			13,500
Property tax payable			2,000
Income taxes payable			3,440
Total current liabilities			38,940
Long-term liabilities			
Bonds payable, 8%, due June 30, 1985			30,000
Total liabilities			68,940
Stockholders' equity			
Common stock $1.00 par value issued and outstanding, 50,000 shares		$50,000	
Retained earnings		26,400	
Total stockholders' equity			76,400
Total liabilities and stockholders' equity			$145,340

The Spencer Company is a corporation, and the capital section of the balance sheet, called the stockholders' equity section in the illustration, is somewhat different from the capital section for a proprietorship. The total capital or stockholders' equity consists of the common stock, which is the original investment by stockholders, and the earnings retained in the business.

Statement of Retained Earnings

The net income earned by a corporation may be retained in the business or it may be distributed to stockholders by payment of dividends. In the illustration the net income earned during the year was added to the balance of retained earnings on January 1, thereby increasing the balance of retained earnings to $26,400 on December 31. No dividends were declared or paid during the year.

The Spencer Company
STATEMENT OF RETAINED EARNINGS

For the Year Ended December 31, 1981

Retained earnings, Jan. 1, 1981	$14,200
Add net income for 1981	12,200
Retained earnings, Dec. 31, 1981	$26,400

Closing and Reversing Entries

The entries for the closing process are as follows:

General Journal

Inventory (December 31)	40,000	
Cost of Goods Sold	316,000	
Inventory (January 1)		36,000
Purchases		320,000
(To record ending inventory balance and to determine cost of goods sold)		
Interest Income	800	
Sales	400,000	
Cost of Goods Sold		316,000
Sales Salaries Expense		20,000
Advertising Expense		2,200
Traveling Expense		8,000
Salaries, Office and General		19,000
Telephone and Telegraph Expense		600
Rent Expense		4,800
Property Tax Expense		5,300
Depreciation of Furniture and Equipment		6,700
Bad Debts Expense		1,000
Insurance Expense		360
Interest Expense		1,200
Income Tax Expense		3,440
Revenue and Expense Summary		12,200
(To close revenues and expenses to Revenue and Expense Summary)		
Revenue and Expense Summary	12,200	
Retained Earnings		12,200
(To close Revenue and Expense Summary to Retained Earnings)		

After the financial statements have been prepared, the enterprise may use reversing entries to facilitate the accounting next period. The following reversing entries would be made if a reversing system were used.

(1)

Interest Income	800	
Interest Receivable		800

(2)

Interest Expense	500	
Prepaid Interest Expense		500

(3)

Property Tax Payable	2,000	
Property Tax Expense		2,000

Reversing entries would not appear on the ten-column work sheet because they are recorded in the next year (1982). The main object of the work sheet is to obtain the correct balances at the end of the year for financial statement presentation for the current year (1981).

Monthly Statements, Yearly Closing

The use of a work sheet at the end of each month or quarter permits the preparation of *interim financial statements* even though the books are closed only at the end of each year. For example, assume that a business closes its books on December 31 but that monthly financial statements are desired. At the end of January a work sheet similar to the one illustrated in this chapter can be prepared to supply the information needed for statements for January. At the end of February a work sheet can be used again. Because the accounts were not closed at the end of January, the income statement taken from the work sheet on February 28 will present the net income for two months. An income statement for the month of February can be obtained by subtracting the items in the January income statement from the corresponding items in the income statement for the two months of January and February.

A statement of retained earnings for February only also may be obtained by subtracting the January items. The balance sheet prepared from the February work sheet, however, shows the assets and equities as of February 28, the specific date for which a balance sheet is desired.

The March work sheet would show the revenues and expenses for three months, and the subtraction of the revenues and expenses for the first two months could be made to supply the balance needed for an income statement for the month of March only.

APPENDIX

Conversion of Cash Basis to Accrual Basis

As part of the discussion of the matching principle in Chapter 2, we briefly contrasted the accrual basis of accounting with the cash basis of accounting. Most large companies use the **accrual basis of accounting,** recording revenue when it is realized (earned) and recognizing expenses in the period incurred, without regard to the time of receipt or payment of cash. Many small enterprises, however, use a strict or modified cash basis approach. Under the **strict cash basis,** revenue is recorded only when the cash is received and expenses are recorded only when the cash is paid. The determination of income on the cash basis rests upon the collection of revenue and the payment of expenses, and the matching principle is ignored. Consequently, cash basis financial statements are not in conformity with generally accepted accounting principles.

The **modified cash basis,** a mixture of cash basis and accrual basis, is the method followed by service enterprises and by the average individual taxpayer in determining taxable income for income tax purposes. Expenditures having an economic life of more than one year are capitalized as assets and depreciated or amortized over future years. Prepaid expenses and accrued expenses are not treated in a consistent manner. Prepayments of expenses are deferred and deducted only in the year to which they apply, while expenses paid after the year of incurrence (accrued expenses) are deducted only in the year paid. Revenue is reported in the year of receipt. For tax purposes, however, any business in which inventory is a significant factor must use the accrual basis of accounting in reporting revenue from sales and cost of goods sold.

Not infrequently an accountant is required to convert a cash basis set of financial statements to the accrual basis for presentation and interpretation to a banker or for audit by an independent CPA. The simplified diagram below illustrates how cash basis financial data are converted to the accrual basis through various types of adjusting items.

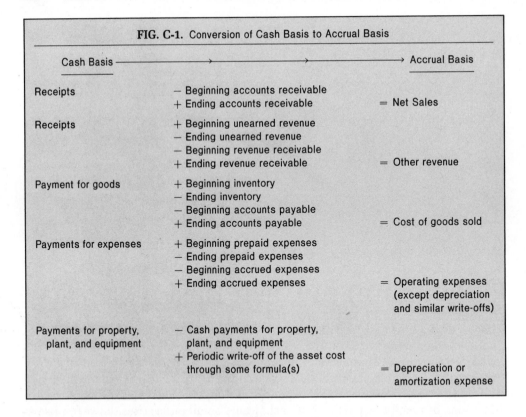

FIG. C-1. Conversion of Cash Basis to Accrual Basis

In Figure C-1 cash receipts are converted to **net sales** by subtracting beginning accounts receivable and adding ending accounts receivable. By expanding the formula to include all of the accounts related to sales, cash receipts can be converted to **gross sales,** as shown below.

Cash receipts from customers		xxx
Plus: Cash discounts	xx	
Sales returns and allowances	xx	
Accounts written off	xx	
Ending accounts receivable	xx	xx
		xxx
Less: Beginning accounts receivable		xx
Gross sales		xxx

Cash receipts from customers can be converted to net sales also merely by adding or subtracting the change in the balance of accounts receivable from the beginning to the end of the year, as shown below.

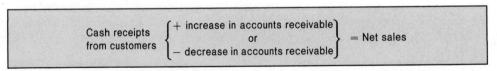

ILLUSTRATION   **97**

Similarly cash payments for goods can be converted to cost of goods sold by adding or deducting the change from the beginning to the end of the year in the accounts payable balance and in the inventory balance as follows.

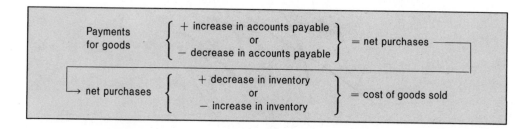

Figure C-1 presents the conversion of cash payments for *all* expenses to the accrual basis operating expenses in the aggregate and, therefore, involves both prepaid and accrued expenses in the conversion. Generally, each expense item is affected by a related accrual or a related prepayment, but not both. For example, the conversion of wages expense and the conversion of insurance expense are illustrated separately below.

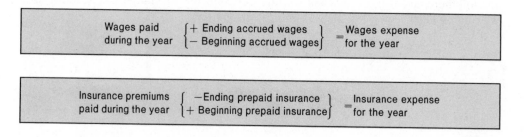

Illustration. Conversion of cash basis income statement data to the accrual basis will be illustrated for Olivia Newton, D.D.S., a dentist who keeps her accounting records on a cash basis. During 1980, Dr. Newton collected $80,000 from her patients and paid $30,000 for operating expenses, resulting in a cash basis net income of $50,000. At January 1 and December 31, 1980, she has fees receivable, unearned fees, accrued expenses, and prepaid expenses as follows:

	January 1, 1980	December 31, 1980
Fees receivable	$12,000	$5,000
Unearned fees	–0–	1,000
Accrued expenses	3,800	6,800
Prepaid expenses	2,000	3,000

Restatement of Olivia Newton's income statement data is presented in work sheet form below:

Olivia Newton, D.D.S.
Conversion of Income Statement from Cash Basis to Accrual Basis
For the Year 1980

	Cash Basis	Adjustments Add	Adjustments Deduct	Accrual Basis
Revenue from fees:	$80,000			
— Fees receivable, Jan. 1			$12,000	
+ Fees receivable, Dec. 31		$5,000		
— Unearned fees, Dec. 31			1,000	
Restated				$72,000
Operating expenses:	30,000			
— Accrued expenses, Jan. 1			3,800	
+ Accrued expenses, Dec. 31		6,800		
+ Prepaid expenses, Jan. 1		2,000		
— Prepaid expenses, Dec. 31			3,000	
Restated				32,000
Net income—cash basis	$50,000			
Net income—accrual basis				$40,000

The computation of income on the cash basis can result in a material misstatement when there is a lag in time between the exchange transactions and the related cash receipt or disbursement transactions.

APPENDIX

Specialized Journals and Methods of Processing Accounting Data

SPECIAL JOURNALS

Most businesses use special journals in addition to the general journal. Special journals permit greater division of labor, reduce the time necessary to accomplish the various bookkeeping tasks, and summarize transactions possessing a common characteristic. Therefore, the special journals used by any given business depend largely on the specific transactions common to that business. Most trading concerns have many transactions grouped into these categories:

> Receipts of cash
> Sales on account
> Purchases on account
> Payments of cash

A business that engages in many of each of these transactions is likely to use the following five journals.

1. **Cash receipts journal.** Receives entries for all cash received by the business.
2. **Sales journal.** Receives entries for all sales of merchandise on account.
3. **Purchases journal.** Receives entries for all purchases of merchandise on account.
4. **Cash payments journal** (check register). Receives entries for all cash paid.
5. **General journal.** Receives entries for all transactions that cannot be recorded in any of the special journals.

The general journal, special journals, and posting to the general and subsidiary ledgers are eliminated or altered in an automated or computerized system. The following discussion concerns a manual system normally used by small businesses.

Cash Receipts Journal

Every transaction entered in the cash receipts journal represents a debit to cash and a credit to each of the accounts in the "account credited" column. In other words, the cash receipts journal is the book of original entry in which **all** receipts of cash are recorded before being posted to the ledger. Special columns are used in the cash receipts journal to save time in posting. Although all transactions entered in this journal are based on receipts of cash, not all cash receipts are necessarily from customers. Thus a one-column journal is not sufficient to accommodate all cash receipts transactions; columns must be provided for cash and the common sources of cash as illustrated below.

				CASH RECEIPTS JOURNAL					Page 8
Date 1981	L.F.	Account Title	Explanation	Cash Dr.	Sales Discount Dr.	Accounts Receivable Cr.	Sales Cr.	Sundry Cr.
April 7	208	M. L. King	In full	182.28	3.72	186.00		
8	✔	Sales	Per cash register	25.00			25.00	
9	16	Notes Payable	60-day, 12%, First Nat'l	300.00				300.00
16	206	J. Lahey	On account	200.00		200.00		
18	204	A. Pushkin	In full	735.00	15.00	750.00		
19	✔	Sales	Per cash register	185.00			185.00	
				1,627.28	18.72	1,136.00	210.00	300.00
				(1)	(74)	(3)	(20)	✔

The columns in the cash receipts journal indicate that the business receives cash from customers (credits to Accounts Receivable), sells goods for cash (credit Sales), and has miscellaneous sources of cash (credits entered in the Sundry column). Additional specific credit columns are used if business needs demand them. For example, if cash were borrowed from the bank frequently, a separate Notes Payable, Credit column could be used.

Posting from Cash Receipts Journal

The posting procedures from a cash receipts journal are relatively simple. The totals of the columns for Cash, Sales Discount, Accounts Receivable, and Sales are posted to those general ledger accounts at the end of the month. Amounts entered in the Sundry Credit column must be posted to the general ledger as individual amounts to the accounts named in the Account Title column, because the ledger does not contain a Sundry account and because the purpose of this column in the journal is to provide a place to identify miscellaneous sources of cash receipts. The use of a Sundry column avoids having to have a column for every different credit account entered in the journal.

In addition to these general ledger postings, all amounts in the Accounts Receivable Credit column are posted to the credit side of the subsidiary ledger account named in the Account Title column. A **subsidiary ledger** is a group of accounts with a common characteristic (e.g., all are accounts receivable) assembled together principally to facilitate the accounting process by freeing the general ledger from details concerning individual balances. Business concerns of medium and large size frequently have accounts with thousands of customers and hundreds of creditors. A continuous record of the transactions affecting each customer and each creditor is necessary, and individual accounts with each customer and each creditor are better kept in ledgers separate from the ledger containing other asset, liability, and nominal accounts. Thus the average trading concern has one or more subsidiary ledgers containing nothing but accounts with customers, one or more subsidiary ledgers containing nothing but accounts with creditors, and one general ledger containing the other accounts of the business. The enterprise still maintains a **controlling account** in the general ledger that summarizes the same arithmetical results that the customers' or creditors' ledgers contain in detail. A general ledger is self-balancing (debit balances equal credit balances); subsidiary ledgers are not self-balancing.

The **advantages of subsidiary ledgers** are that they:

1. Permit the transactions affecting a single customer or single creditor to be shown in a single account.
2. Free the general ledger of details relating to accounts receivable and accounts payable.
3. Assist in locating errors in individual accounts by reducing the number of accounts combined in one ledger and by using controlling accounts.
4. Permit the division of labor by separating groups of accounts.

A business may establish and use controlling accounts and subsidiary ledgers for other than accounts receivable and accounts payable, such as for inventory, property, plant and equipment, investments, general expenses, and selling expenses.

In the illustrated Cash Receipts Journal the page numbers in the "Acct. No." column opposite the names of individual customers refer to page numbers in the customer's subsidiary ledger. Care must be taken to post the amount appearing in the Accounts Receivable Credit column. These postings are generally made on a daily basis, if possible, so that information on the status of any customer's account is up to date. Because each amount in the Accounts Receivable Cr. column is posted as a part of the column total to the Accounts Receivable (control account) in the general ledger and also to the individual customer account in the subsidiary ledger, each amount may be said to be **double posted.**

Check marks are used in the ledger folio column opposite the two items titled "Sales." These check marks indicate that these items should not be posted individually to the Sales account because they are posted in total as a credit to the Sales account. Thus, individual postings would merely duplicate the amounts posted to Sales. Also, a check mark below the Sundry Credit total indicates that the item is not to be posted. Here the individual amounts that make up this total have been posted to the specific general ledger accounts identified in the entry.

The totals of the columns of the Cash Receipts Journal are then posted to the account involved. Cash is posted to account 1 in the general ledger; Sales Discount to account 74; Accounts Receivable to account 3; Sales to account 20; and the

Sundry total is not posted, because it was posted on a transaction-by-transaction basis. The total debited to various general ledger accounts equals the total credited.

The Sales Journal

Entries in the sales journal are based on sales invoices or charge sales issued. Remember that the sales journal is used only for sales of merchandise on account. Sales of merchandise for cash are entered in the cash receipts journal.

The sales journal may take a variety of forms, depending on the specific needs of a business. In its simplest form it has an amount column on the right side of the page, with space for the date, posting reference, account title, and explanation to the left. If a business concern wishes to accumulate the sales according to the major types of merchandise sold, several amount columns are used, each denoting sales of one type of merchandise.

The following illustration shows the headings employed in a simple sales journal for a business concern that maintains only one Sales account.

		SALES JOURNAL			Page 6
Date 1981	Acct. No.	Account Debited	Explanation	Sales Invoice No.	Amount
April 1	208	M. L. King	2/10,n/30	62	186
2	202	Randy Ryan	Net	63	910
4	206	J. Lahey	2/10,n/30	64	816
6	204	A. Pushkin	2/10,n/30	65	750
	3/20				2,662

Notice that the sales journal follows basically the same procedure for posting as the cash receipts journal. The "T" accounts on page 103 illustrate how these postings are recorded in the general and subsidiary ledger.

Purchases Journal and Voucher Register

The purpose of a purchases journal is to record entries for all purchases of merchandise on account. Each invoice received for purchases of merchandise is the basis for an entry in the purchases journal. Transactions for purchases on account are entered in a separate journal in a manner similar to that described for the sales journal. The columns in a purchases journal are similar to those in a sales journal. If the business concern requires an analysis of purchases by product or department, the purchases journal is expanded to contain a separate money column for each product or department. The headings for a purchases journal are shown below.

GENERAL LEDGER

Cash   No. 1

1981					
March 31	Balance	600.00			
April 30	CR8	1,627.28			

Accounts Receivable   No. 3

1981					
March 31	Balance	672.00	April 30	CR8	1,136.00
April 30	S6	2,662.00			

Notes Payable   No. 16

			1981		
			April 9	CR8	300.00

Sales   No. 20

			1981		
			March 31	Balance	7,826.00
			April 30	S6	2,662.00
			April 30	CR8	210.00

Sales Discount   No. 74

1981					
April 30	CR8	18.72			

Accounts Receivable
SUBSIDIARY LEDGER

Randy Ryan   202

1981					
March 31	Balance	520			
April 2	S6	910			

A. Pushkin   204

1981					
March 31	Balance	30	April 18	CR8	750
April 6	S6	750			

J. Lahey   206

1981					
March 31	Balance	122	April 16	CR8	200
April 4	S6	816			

M. L. King   208

1981					
April 1	S6	186	April 7	CR8	186

PURCHASES JOURNAL				
Date 1981	Acct. No.	Name of Creditor	Explanation	Amount
Nov. 1	105	Hendricks Produce	Oct. 30, n/30	765.00

Each entry in this journal is recorded on one line to show each purchase invoice received. The total of the items entered in the purchases journal represents the total purchases on account for the month or other accounting period. At the end of each accounting period, the purchases journal is totaled and posted to the purchases and accounts payable accounts in the general ledger. At frequent intervals during the accounting period, the accounts payable are posted to the individual accounts in the subsidiary ledger.

A **voucher register** is a book of original entry that often replaces the purchases journal. Entries in the voucher register are not limited to purchases of merchandise on account but include purchases of services, supplies, and fixed assets. In other words, credit purchases of all descriptions are properly entered in the voucher register. In addition, when the voucher system operates in its most complete form, a voucher is prepared for every payment, so that cash purchases also are entered in the voucher register. To voucher such a payment it is necessary only to make out a voucher form giving the facts about the amount to be paid. The types of columns generally employed in a voucher register are illustrated below.

VOUCHER REGISTER									
			Payment Made		Vouchers Payable	Purchases	Advertising	Sundry Items Dr.	
Date 1981	Voucher No.	Creditor	Check No.	Date	Cr.	Dr.	Dr.	Account Title	Amount
Jan. 2	200	W. C. Crane	205	Jan. 5	343.00	343.00			
Jan. 3	201	R. M. Higgins	206	Jan. 6	150.00		150.00		
Jan. 4	202	R. Haugen	208	Jan. 9	200.00		200.00		
Jan. 5	203	C. Kroncke	209	Jan. 10	285.00	285.00			

Each voucher is numbered consecutively for control purposes and the entries are made in numerical order. Also, two columns are provided for Payment Made—one for the number of the check used to pay the voucher, and one for the date of payment. Because all entries made in the voucher register are for vouchers to be paid, the single credit money column needed is for Vouchers Payable. Also, because the vouchers are prepared for several different items, we find several money debit columns, as shown in the illustration.

The use of the voucher system assumes that with few exceptions all current obligations are set up as liabilities in the form of vouchers payable, and that cash payments reduce liabilities thus set up. In other words, expressed in general journal form, the voucher system requires the following entries for every payment:

In the Voucher Register		
Expense (or asset)	xxx	
Vouchers Payable		xxx
In the Cash Payments Journal (Check Register)		
Vouchers Payable	xxx	
Cash		xxx

In this procedure the only items that appear in the cash payments journal express a debit to Vouchers Payable, a credit to Cash, and a credit to Purchase Discounts.

Cash Payments Journal

Every transaction entered in the cash payments journal represents a credit to Cash and a debit to each of the accounts named in the Account Debited column. Any transaction that does not stand this test of debits and credits cannot be entered in the cash payments journal. Here is the basic format of a cash payments journal (without a voucher system):

CASH PAYMENTS JOURNAL							
Date 1981	Acct. No.	Account Title	Explanation	Cash Cr.	Purchase Discounts Cr.	Accts. Payable Dr.	Sundry Dr.
April 1	302	Bennett Co.	In full	514.50	10.50	525.00	
April 3	65	Advertising	Star Times	173.00			173.00

The cash payments journal operates in principle much like the cash receipts journal. The totals of the Cash Credit, Purchase Discounts Credit, and Accounts Payable Debit columns are posted at the end of the month. The items in the Sundry Debit column are posted as individual items from time to time during the month. The amounts entered in the Accounts Payable Debit column are posted daily, if possible, as debits to the individual accounts in the accounts payable subsidiary ledger.

Whenever a voucher system is employed, the enterprise replaces accounts payable with vouchers payable and adds another column to its cash payments journal (often called a check register in a voucher system) entitled Voucher Number to indicate which voucher is being paid. The column headings are illustrated below.

CASH PAYMENTS JOURNAL
(or check register)
Entries for Vouchers Paid

Date 1981	Acct. No.	Check No.	Payee	Voucher No.	Cash Cr.	Purchase Discounts Cr.	Vouchers Payable Dr.	Sundry Dr.
Jan. 5		205	W. C. Crane	200	336.14	6.86	343.00	
Jan. 6		206	R. M. Higgins	201	150.00		150.00	
Jan. 8		207	Pappas Supply	195	190.00		190.00	
Jan. 9		208	R. Haugen	202	196.00	4.00	200.00	
Jan. 10		209	C. Kroncke	203	280.00	5.00	285.00	

Flexibility in Selection of Journals

In addition to the journals described in this chapter, other specialized journals are required by various businesses. For example, if a business found that it had a large volume of returned sales or returned purchases, it could use a returned sales journal or a returned purchases journal. A notes receivable journal could be used by a business that regularly receives notes.

Each business decides on the appropriate journals to use after a study of the transactions in which it regularly engages. Most businesses have a general journal and the cash journals, whereas many trading companies also find a sales and a purchases journal necessary. A cash-and-carry grocery, on the other hand, has no need for a sales journal, because no sales are made on account. Thus, there is no established rule for a business to follow in choosing its books of original entry. It selects the books that result in the greatest convenience and saving of time in processing the many transactions in which it engages. The design of the journals and ledgers is part of the work involved in the design of an accounting system.

Journals Not Always "Books"

Journals are usually called books of original entry, but some "books" of original entry are in reality not books at all; they are merely **files of business papers** preserved in an orderly manner in a filing or binding device.

For example, some concerns use carbon copies of sales invoices as a sales journal. These invoices give the essential facts about the sale, and a copy (usually a carbon) of each sales invoice for the period provides the data necessary to debit Accounts Receivable and credit Sales for the period. Thus the principle of the sales journal is applied in handling the sales transactions even though a journal is not used.

In a similar manner loose-leaf purchase invoice records, returned sales records, and purchase allowance records, for example, may take this form. Regardless of the arrangement used for the initial recording of transactions, all transactions are ultimately posted to the ledger accounts in accordance with the principles developed in this chapter for the several journals. These principles are fundamental; they do not change when a different means of recording and processing the data are used, whether it be loose-leaf records, adding machine tapes, bookkeeping machines, punched cards, or other mechanical or electrical devices.

METHODS OF PROCESSING

The principles of recording, classifying, and summarizing large quantities of accounting data described in this chapter are those applicable to a situation where sophisticated types of accounting machinery are not needed. In many business enterprises, the mass of data is so great that it is simply too time-consuming to post the entries manually, add the columns, update the files, and summarize the information. For this reason, accountants have now resorted to more sophisticated devices to process the data quickly and efficiently. Our purpose now is to provide only a brief outline of the general types of equipment used for data processing, such as accounting machines, punched-card or tape systems, and EDP systems. No attempt is made to determine what machinery is best for a given situation because this question is complex and better left for an accounting systems course. Regardless of the devices used to process the data, the basic principles developed in this chapter apply.

Accounting or Bookkeeping Machines   Accounting or bookkeeping machines are essentially posting machines operated by a clerk. They make it possible to post a transaction simultaneously to several different records. For example, a purchase invoice is recorded in the purchases journal that is posted to the subsidiary accounts payable ledger at the same time. Summary totals are then posted manually either daily or monthly to the purchases account and the accounts payable control account in the general ledger. The major benefits of an accounting or bookkeeping machine are that (1) the posting process is expedited, (2) the records are neater and easier to read, and (3) the equality of debits and credits is maintained.

Punched-Card Equipment   A punched-card or tape system involves information that is punched onto various cards or tapes by means of holes arranged in a definite pattern. The punches identify the name of the customer, the item sold, the date, the amount, and other relevant data. For example, when a purchase order is received, the name of the customer, the type of item involved, and the dollar amount of the order are punched into a card. These cards are then processed through different types of machinery to arrive at the necessary grouping and summarized totals needed to determine the total purchases for the day, the various types and percentages of items sold in a given day, the percent of goods sold on a cash basis versus a credit basis, the geographical area where the goods were sold, and other pertinent information. Different types of machinery that reproduce, verify, collate, and tabulate the punched cards facilitate the analysis. The advantages of a punched-card or tape system are (1) flexibility, since many different procedures can be employed on this one card to develop different types of information, and (2) speed and accuracy, since this information can be easily summarized with little chance of error.

Computers   A computer is a machine that can perform with amazing speed many internal operations from a specific set of instructions. The computer has revolutionized data-processing not only because of its speed and accuracy in processing data, but also because it can be programmed to process the data in almost any manner desired by management. "Programmed" means that a data processor can write instructions to the computer to handle the data in a certain way. Essentially these instructions are all of a *yes* and *no* variety. For instance, if a certain sales level is achieved, a report might be issued warning of possible stockout on inventory items. One of the more interesting developments in the computer area has been the development of **on-line computer systems.** In this system, the transaction is immediately recorded in the computer as it occurs without the use of any basic source document. The advantages of a computer are that it can take different courses of action depending on the results of data collected previously and can process data more quickly and efficiently than other types of business equipment.

Nearly every medium- or large-sized business owns or rents a computer, but until recently a computer was too expensive for a small business to own or rent. Small businesses generally avoided investing large sums of money yet gained the use of computers through **EDP service centers** or through **time-sharing arrangements.** However, with the recent emergence of **mini-computers** and **microprocessors,** even small businesses can own a computer and obtain the operating and record-keeping efficiencies provided by computers.

Note: All **asterisked** questions, cases, exercises, or problems relate to material contained in the appendix to each chapter.

Questions

1. Why are revenue and expense accounts called temporary or nominal proprietorship accounts?
2. Do the following events represent business transactions? Explain your answer in each case.
   (a) Merchandise is ordered for delivery next month.
   (b) A truck is purchased on account.
   (c) A customer returns merchandise and is given credit on account.
   (d) A prospective employee is interviewed.
   (e) The owner of the business withdraws cash from the business for personal use.
3. Give an example of a transaction that results in
   (a) A decrease in one asset and an increase in another asset.
   (b) A decrease in an asset and a decrease in a liability.
   (c) A decrease in one liability and an increase in another liability.
4. Name the accounts debited and credited for each of the following transactions:
   (a) Purchase of office supplies on account.
   (b) Purchase of 10 gallons of gasoline for the delivery truck.
   (c) Billing a customer for work done.
   (d) Receipt of cash from customer on account.

5. Is it necessary that a trial balance be taken periodically? What purpose does it serve?

6. Indicate whether each of the items below is a real or nominal account and whether it appears in the balance sheet or the income statement.
   (a) Furniture.
   (b) Income from Services.
   (c) Office Salaries.
   (d) Supplies on Hand.
   (e) Prepaid Insurance Expense.
   (f) Wages Payable.
   (g) Merchandise Inventory.
   (h) Accumulated Depreciation.

7. Employees are paid every Saturday. If a balance sheet is prepared on Wednesday, December 31, what does the amount of wages earned during the first three days of the week (12/29, 12/30, 12/31) represent? Explain.

8. Why is the Purchases account debited both when merchandise is purchased for cash and when it is purchased on account? Why is the inventory amount as determined at the end of the fiscal period under a periodic inventory system deducted from the cost of goods available for sale?

9. What is the purpose of the Cost of Goods Sold account?

10. Under a periodic system is the amount shown for Inventory the same in a trial balance taken before closing as it is in a trial balance taken after closing? Why?

11. If the cost of a new typewriter ($300) purchased for office use were recorded as a debit to Purchases, what would be the effect of the error on the balance sheet and income statement in the period in which the error was made?

12. What differences are there between the trial balance before closing and the trial balance after closing with respect to the following?
    (a) Revenue accounts.
    (b) Retained earnings account.
    (c) Cash.
    (d) Expense accounts.
    (e) Accounts payable.

13. What are "adjusting entries" and why are they necessary?

14. What are "closing entries" and why are they necessary?

15. What are "reversing entries" and why are they necessary?

*16. List two types of transactions that would receive different accounting treatment using (a) strict cash basis accounting and (b) a modified cash basis.

*17. Why are beginning accrued wages subtracted from, and ending accrued wages added to, wages paid during the year when wages expense for the year is computed?

*18. Why would a company use several journals instead of only a general journal? How would the company determine which special journals it should use?

*19. When the special journals illustrated in this chapter are used, how many postings are made to the Cash account? Why?

*20. For each of the following transactions name the book of original entry and the accounts to be debited and credited, assuming that the five journals discussed in this chapter are used:
    (a) Sale of merchandise for cash.
    (b) Purchase of office equipment on account.
    (c) Payment of cash to a creditor, no discount.
    (d) Receipt of cash from customer on account.
    (e) Loan from bank on a promissory note; interest payable at maturity date.
    (f) Purchase of merchandise on account (periodic inventory system).
    (g) Return of damaged merchandise from a supplier.

*21. What is a controlling account? What is its relationship to a subsidiary ledger?

*22. How does the use of controlling accounts and subsidiary ledgers affect (a) the taking of a trial balance, (b) the appearance of the trial balance, and (c) the equality of debits and credits in the trial balance?

*23. Differentiate between a purchase order, a purchase invoice, a voucher, and a check. What journal entry, if any, generally results from each of these documents (assume a periodic inventory system)?

Exercises

E3-1   The trial balance of the Wirlwind Company does not balance.

Wirlwind Co.		
TRIAL BALANCE		
April 30		
Cash	$ 5,762	
Accounts Receivable	6,400	
Supplies on Hand	1,600	
Furniture and Equipment	5,200	
Accounts Payable		$ 4,400
Wirlwind Co., Capital		10,000
Income from Fees		4,700
Office Expenses	1,880	
	$20,842	$19,100

An examination of the ledger shows these errors.

1. Cash received from a customer on account was recorded (both debit and credit) as $1,300 instead of $1,120.
2. The purchase on account of a typewriter costing $680 was recorded as a debit to Office Expenses and a credit to Accounts Payable.
3. Services were performed on account for a client, $1,780, for which Accounts Receivable was debited $1,780 and Income from Fees was credited $178.
4. A payment of $60 for telephone charges was entered as a debit to Office Expenses and a debit to Cash.
5. The Income from Fees account was totaled at $4,700 instead of $4,720.

Instructions

From this information prepare a corrected trial balance.

E3-2   Information concerning the first month of operations of Linda Lahey Boutique is presented below:

Transportation-in	$ 450
Total purchases on account	18,000
Purchase returns on account	720
Transportation-out	540
Total recorded as cash purchases	8,280
Purchase allowances on account	630
Inventory at the end of the month	3,600
Sales discounts	585
Refunds for defective items purchased for cash	378
Error made by bookkeeper debiting Supplies Expense, when in reality the item was a cash purchase of merchandise	288

Instructions

(a) Prepare a cost of goods sold "T" account.

(b) Prepare the cost of goods sold section of the income statement.

(c) Indicate in which section of the income statement items not used in the cost of goods sold section of this exercise should appear.

E3-3   When the accounts of Bubba's Spudnut Shoppe are examined, the adjusting data listed below are uncovered on December 31, the end of an annual fiscal period.

1. The unexpired insurance account shows a debit of $900, representing the cost of a 3-year fire insurance policy dated September 1 of the current year.
2. On November 1, Rental Income was credited for $1,200, representing income from a subrental for a 3-month period beginning on that date. Dr *Rental Income*   Cr *Unearned Revenue*
3. Purchase of advertising materials for $800 during the year was recorded in the advertising expense account. On December 31, advertising materials of $120 are on hand.
4. Interest of $90 has accrued on notes payable.

Instructions

Prepare in general journal form: (a) the adjusting entry for each item; (b) the reversing entry for each item where appropriate.

*E3-4   Cricket Company maintains its books on the accrual basis. The company reported insurance expense of $17,450 in its 1980 income statement. Prepaid insurance at December 31, 1980 amounted to $3,220; cash paid for insurance during the year 1980 totaled $19,800. There was no accrued insurance expense either at the beginning or at the end of 1980.

Instructions

What was the amount, if any, of prepaid insurance at January 1, 1980? Show computations.

*E3-5   Needles Corporation, which uses the accrual basis of accounting, reported interest expense of $90,280 in its 1980 income statement. Accrued interest at December 31, 1980 amounted to $14,710; cash paid for interest during 1980 totaled $84,400. There was no prepaid interest either at the beginning or at the end of 1980.

Instructions

What was the amount, if any, of accrued interest at January 1, 1980? Show computations.

*E3-6   Cat Nip Corp. maintains its financial records on the cash basis of accounting. Interested in securing a long-term loan from its regular bank, Cat Nip Corp. requests you as its independent CPA to convert its cash basis income statement data to the accrual basis. You are provided with the following summarized data covering 1978, 1979, and 1980.

	1978	1979	1980
Cash receipts from sales:			
On 1978 sales	$240,000	$ 45,000	$15,000
On 1979 sales	-0-	270,000	90,000
Cash payments for expenses:			
On 1978 expenses	150,000	21,000	9,000
On 1979 expenses	18,000[1]	150,000	42,000
On 1980 expenses		15,000[2]	

[1]Prepayments of 1979 expense.
[2]Prepayments of 1980 expense.

Instructions

(a) Using the data above, prepare abbreviated income statements for the years 1978 and 1979 on the cash basis.
(b) Using the data above, prepare abbreviated income statements for the years 1978 and 1979 on the accrual basis.

*E3-7   Presented below are the following transactions of the Spanish Company.

Sept. 1   Purchases office equipment for cash, $706.

   3   Sells merchandise on account to S. Adams, $1,063, f.o.b. shipping point.

   3   Pays freight on sale to S. Adams, $56.

   4   Receives a refund of $52 on office equipment because of a difference in the speci-
        fications of equipment ordered and received.

   7   Purchases merchandise on account from R. Barnes, $1,500, 2/10, n/30, f.o.b. desti-
        nation (record at gross amount).

   9   R. Barnes has paid freight on shipment, $44. *no entry*

  13   Receives a check in full of account from S. Adams.

  18   Because of increased business, Spanish Company purchases additional office
        equipment at a price of $600, giving in exchange shares of its own no-par stock
        having a total market price of $310, with the balance payable in 30 days.

  21   Cash sales of $6,250 are made.

  25   An invoice for heat, light, and water of $50 is received.

  27   Pays R. Barnes in full of account.

  29   Office salaries of $438 and the utilities bill received on September 25 are paid.

Instructions

Prepare journal entries for each transaction and indicate in which journal they normally are
recorded. (Spanish Company uses a periodic inventory system.)

*E3-8   The general ledger of the Watts Company contains the following Accounts Payable
control account. Also shown is the related subsidiary ledger.

Accounts Payable

Feb. 28	General journal	13,500	Feb.	1	Balance	37,538
28		33,450		5	General journal	180
				11	General journal	53
				28	Cash receipts	300
				28	General journal	990
				28	Purchases	21,750

Creditor's Ledger

French	Greek	Elliott
Balance 4,783	Balance 8,417	Balance ?

Instructions

For the data above:

   (a) Indicate the missing posting reference in the control account and the missing ending
       balance in the subsidiary ledger.

   (b) Indicate the amounts in the control account that were double posted.

   (c) What is meant by "double posting"? (Explain in full.)

*E3-9   Here are selected records and documents for the voucher system of the John
            Penkowski Company.

VOUCHER REGISTER

Date Feb. 1977	Vou. No.	Creditor	Payment Made		Vouchers Payable Cr.	Purchases Dr.	Sundry Items Dr.	
			Check No.	Date			Account Title	Amount
2/5	300	Russell Supply	113	2/7	900		Supplies	900
2/9	301	Dick & Jane	114	2/26	2,340	2,340		
2/15	302	Betts & Bore	115	2/26	5,220	5,220		
2/17	303	Capps Co.	117	2/28	3,150		Furniture	3,150
2/20	304	Daily Courier			450		Advertising	450
2/24	305	K. Comfort			63		Miscellaneous expenses	63
2/25	306	Dick & Jane			1,980	1,980		
2/28	307	Otey Realty	116	2/28	2,430		Rent	2,430

UNPAID VOUCHERS

Voucher No. 304	Voucher No. 305
Date: 2/20 To: Daily Courier	Date: 2/24 To: K. Comfort
Amount $450	Amount $63
Acct. Dr. Advertising	Acct. Dr. Miscellaneous Expenses
Voucher No. 301	Voucher No. 299
Date: 2/9 To: Dick & Jane	Date: 2/3 To: Jeri Delaney
Amount $2,340	Amount $423
Acct. Dr. Purchases	Acct. Dr. Repair Expenses

GENERAL LEDGER
Vouchers Payable

1974			1974		
Feb. 28	CP	13,680	Feb. 28	VR	16,533

Instructions

(a) Determine the balance in the control account.

(b) Prove the vouchers payable account by reconciling the voucher file with the detail in the register.

(c) Determine the causes of any lack of agreement between the control account and subsidiary records. (Label all amounts.)

(d) What is the correct vouchers payable balance?

Problems

P3-1 The accounts listed appeared in the December 31 trial balance of the Egyptian Theater.

Equipment	180,000	
Accumulated Depreciation of Equipment		54,000
Notes Payable		72,000
Income from Admissions		378,000
Income from Concessions		18,000
Advertising Expense	13,680	
Salaries Expense	57,600	
Interest Expense	1,080	

Instructions

(a) From the account balances listed above and the information given below prepare the adjusting entries necessary on December 31.

1. The equipment has an estimated life of 20 years and a trade-in value of $36,000 at the end of that time. (Use straight-line method.)
2. The note payable is a 90-day note given to the bank October 22 and bearing interest at 6%.   *Dr Interest Expense   Cr Interest Payable*
3. In December 1,000 coupon admission books were sold at $18 each; they could be used for admission any time after January 1.
4. The concession stand is operated by a concessionaire who pays 10% of gross receipts for the privilege of selling popcorn, candy, and soft drinks in the lobby. Sales for December were $21,600, and the 10% due for December has not yet been received or entered.   *Dr Income Receivable   Cr Income*
5. Advertising expense paid in advance, $900.
6. Salaries accrued but unpaid, $3,100.

(b) What amounts should be shown for each of the following on the income statement for the year:

1. Interest expense. *1,920*
2. Income from admissions. *360,000*
3. Income from concessions. *20,160*
4. Advertising expense. *12,780*
5. Salaries expense. *60,700*

P3-2   Presented below are the trial balance and the other information related to I. M. Amazing, a consulting engineer.

I. M. Amazing, Consulting Engineer
TRIAL BALANCE
December 31, 1980

Cash	$ 37,800	
Accounts Receivable	13,100	
Allowance for Doubtful Accounts		$ 486
Engineering Supplies Inventory	1,980	
Unexpired Insurance	666	
Furniture and Equipment	24,660	
Accumulated Depreciation of Furniture and Equipment		3,960
Notes Payable		5,400
I. M. Amazing, Capital		18,914
Revenue from Consulting Fees		90,000
Rent Expense	9,360	
Office Salaries	29,880	
Heat, Light, and Water	1,080	
Miscellaneous Office Expense	234	
	$118,760	$118,760

1. Fees received in advance from clients, $2,700.
2. Services performed for clients that were not recorded by December 31, $3,600.
3. The Allowance for Doubtful Accounts account should be adjusted to 7% of the accounts receivable balance (adjusted).
4. Insurance expired during the year, $234.
5. Furniture and equipment is being depreciated at 10% per year.
6. I. M. Amazing gave the bank a 90-day, 6% note for $5,400 on December 1, 1980.
7. Rent of the building is $720 per month. The rent for 1980 has been paid, as has that for January 1981.
8. Office salaries earned but unpaid December 31, 1980, $540.

Instructions

(a) From the trial balance and other information given prepare adjusting entries as of December 31, 1980.

(b) Prepare a single-step income statement for 1980, a balance sheet, and a statement of capital. I. M. Amazing withdrew $18,000 cash for personal use during the year.

P3-3 Following is the December 31 trial balance of Brighter TV Store.

	Brighter TV Store TRIAL BALANCE December 31	
Cash	$ 6,000	
Accounts Receivable	56,000	
Allowance for Doubtful Accounts		$ 3,400
Inventory, January 1	70,000	
Furniture and Equipment	60,000	
Accumulated Depreciation of Furniture and Equipment		24,000
Prepaid Insurance	3,600	
Notes Payable		20,000
I. M. Brighter, Capital		56,000
Sales		600,000
Purchases	400,000	
Sales Salaries	40,000	
Advertising	1,800	
Administrative Salaries	60,000	
Office Expenses	6,000	
	$703,400	$703,400

Instructions

(a) Construct "T" accounts and enter the balances shown.

(b) Prepare adjusting journal entries for the following and post to the "T" accounts. (The books are closed yearly on December 31.)
  1. Adjust the Allowance for Doubtful Accounts to 10% of the accounts receivable.
  2. Furniture and equipment is depreciated at 10% per year.
  3. Insurance expired during the year, $1,600.
  4. Interest accrued on notes payable, $800.
  5. Sales salaries earned but not paid, $1,200.
  6. Advertising paid in advance, $600.
  7. Office supplies on hand, $1,000, charged to Office Expenses when purchased.

(c) Prepare closing entries and post to the accounts. The inventory on December 31 was $80,000.

P3-4   Listed below are the transactions of E. Z. Out, D.D.S., for the month of September:

Sept. 1   E. Z. Out begins practice as a dentist and invests $10,800 cash.

   2   Purchases furniture and dental equipment on account from Meyer Co. for $17,280.

   4   Pays rent for office space, $540 for the month.

   4   Employs a receptionist.

   5   Purchases dental supplies for cash, $756.

   8   Receives cash of $306 from patients.

  10   Pays miscellaneous office expenses, $126.

  14   Bills patients $1,620 for services performed.

  18   Pays Meyer Co. on account, $3,600.

  19   Withdraws $1,800 cash from the business for personal use.

  20   Receives $720 from patients on account.

  25   Bills patients $1,530 for services performed.

  30   Pays the following expenses in cash: office salaries, $900; miscellaneous office expenses, $72.

  30   Dental supplies used during September, $144.

Instructions

(a) Enter the transactions shown above in appropriate ledger accounts. Allow 10 lines for the Cash account and five lines for each of the other accounts needed. Record depreciation using an 8-year life on the furniture and equipment, the straight-line method, and no salvage value.

(b) Take a trial balance.

(c) Prepare an income statement, a balance sheet, and a statement of capital.

(d) Close the ledger.

(e) Take a postclosing trial balance.

P3-5   The balance sheet of Dawna Company as of December 31, 1980, is presented below.

Dawna Company
BALANCE SHEET AS OF DECEMBER 31, 1980

Assets		Liabilities and Capital	
Cash	$ 3,900	Accounts payable	$ 2,325
Accounts receivable	4,395	Notes payable	3,000
Inventory	2,250	Total liabilities	$ 5,325
Office equipment	3,600		
Accum. depr.	(975)		
Furniture and fixtures	6,300		
Accum. depr.	(1,500)	Dawna, capital	12,645
Total assets	$17,970	Total liabilities and capital	$17,970

The following transactions occurred during the month of January, 1981.

Jan. 2   Receives payment of $750 on accounts receivable.

   3   Purchases merchandise on account from R. Walsh for $1,875, 2/30, n/60 f.o.b. shipping point (record at gross amount).

   4   Receives an invoice from **Tops,** a trade magazine, for advertising, $24.

   4   Sells merchandise on account to Marvin Roy for $825, 2/10, n/30 f.o.b. shipping point.

   4   Makes a cash sale to Phil Remmers for $1,523.

   6   Sends a letter to R. Walsh regarding a slight defect in one item of merchandise received.

9 Purchases merchandise on account from Heather's Novelty Company, $563.

11 Pays freight on merchandise received from R. Walsh, $53.

11 Receives a credit memo from R. Walsh granting an allowance of $18 on defective merchandise (see transaction of January 6).

15 Receives $450 on account from Marvin Roy.

19 Sells merchandise on account to R. Urban, $713, 2/10, n/30.

21 Pays display clerk's salary of $488.

25 Sells merchandise for cash, $1,312.

27 Purchases office equipment on account, $750 (begin depreciating in February).

29 Pays R. Walsh in full of account.

30 Receives a note from R. Urban in full of account.

31 A count of the inventory on hand reveals $2,490 of salable merchandise.

Instructions

(a) Open ledger accounts at January 1, 1981.

(b) Enter the transactions into ledger accounts.

(c) Take a trial balance and adjust for depreciation; use 10-year life, straight-line method, and no salvage for all long-term assets.

(d) Close the ledger for preparation of the monthly financial statements.

(e) Prepare a balance sheet and income statement.

(f) Take a postclosing trial balance.

P3-6 On January 1, 1981, after reversing entries were made, the third trial balance of Scott Grometer Co. contained the following account balances, all of which relate to prepaid or unearned items.

Interest Expense	$ 60	
Prepaid Insurance ($480 was paid Oct. 1,		
1980 for one year's premium)	360	
Subscription Income		$2,200
Newsprint on Hand (balance was $7,600 before adjusting)	4,400	
Stationery and Postage Expense	1,220	
Unearned Advertising Revenue (balance was		
$36,000 before adjusting)		6,000

Instructions

(a) Give the December 31, 1980, adjusting entry that involved each of the accounts shown.

(b) Which of the adjusting entries shown in (a) were probably reversed on January 1, 1981?

P3-7 Presented below is information related to Noel Batten, realtor, at the close of the fiscal year ending December 31.

1. He had paid the local newspaper $108 for an advertisement to be run in January of the next year, charging it to Advertising Expense.

2. On October 31 he had his three-month note for $3,000 discounted at the bank at 6% and received cash for the proceeds (Interest Expense was debited).

3. Salaries and wages due and unpaid December 31: sales, $950; office clerks, $750.

4. Interest accrued to date on Nick Company's note, which he holds, $150.

5. Estimated loss on bad debts, $1,120 for the period.

6. Stamps and stationery on hand, $180, charged to Stationery and Postage Expense account when purchased.

7. He has not yet paid the December rent on the building his business occupies, $800.

8. Insurance paid November 1 for one year, $648, charged to Unexpired Insurance when paid.
9. Property taxes accrued, $1,400.
10. On December 1 he gave Carol & Company his 60-day, 6% note for $5,000 on account.
11. On October 31 he received $2,040 from Eric Grinter in payment of six months' rent for office space occupied by him in the building and credited Unearned Rent Income.
12. On September 1 he paid six months' rent in advance on a warehouse, $9,000, and debited Prepaid Rent Expense.
13. The bill from the City Light & Power Company for December has been received but not yet entered or paid, $470.
14. Estimated depreciation on furniture and equipment, $1,150.

Instructions

(a) Prepare adjusting entries as of December 31.

(b) List the numbers of the entries that would be reversed.

P3-8   The following list of accounts and their balances represent the unadjusted trial balance of Omeomy Company at December 31, 1981.

	Dr.	Cr.
Cash	$ 83,124	
Accounts Receivable	106,200	
Allowance for Doubtful Accounts		$ 3,060
Merchandise Inventory	59,400	
Prepaid Insurance	2,232	
Investment in India Inc. Bonds	22,000	
Land	27,000	
Building	121,500	
Accumulated Depreciation—Building		13,500
Equipment	32,400	
Accumulated Depreciation—Equipment		5,400
Goodwill	30,600	
Accounts Payable		117,000
Bonds Payable (20-year; 6%)		180,000
Discount on Bonds Payable	14,400	
Common Stock		162,000
Retained Earnings		36,211
Sales		180,000
Rental Income		4,860
Advertising Expense	27,000	
Supplies Expense	10,800	
Purchases	97,200	
Purchase Discounts		1,800
Office Salary Expense	18,900	
Sales Salary Expense	42,300	
Interest Expense	8,775	
	$703,831	$703,831

Additional information:

1. Actual advertising costs amounted to $1,800 per month. The company has already paid for advertisements in **People Magazine** for the first quarter of 1982.
2. The building was purchased and occupied January 1, 1979 with an estimated life of 18 years. (The company uses straight-line depreciation.)
3. Prepaid insurance contains the premium costs of two policies: Policy A, cost of $756, 1-year term taken out on Sept. 1, 1980; Policy B, cost of $1,728, 3-year term taken out on April 1, 1981.

4. A portion of their building has been converted into a snack bar that has been rented to the Yummy Tummy Food Corp. since July 1, 1980 at a rate of $3,240 per year payable each July 1.

5. One of the company's customers declared bankruptcy December 30, 1981, and it has been definitely established that the $2,700 due from them will never be collected. This fact has not been recorded. Omeomy estimates that 4% of the Accounts Receivable balance on December 31, 1981 will become uncollectible.

6. Nine hundred dollars, which was advanced to a salesperson on December 31, 1981, was charged to Sales Salary Expense. Sales salaries are paid on the 1st and 16th of each month for the following half month.

7. When the company purchased a competing firm on July 1, 1979, it acquired goodwill in the amount of $36,000, which is being amortized.

8. On October 1, 1977, Omeomy issued 180, $1,000 bonds at 90% of par value. Interest payments are made semiannually on March 31 and September 30. (Use straight-line method for amortization of the bond discount.)

9. On August 1, 1981, Omeomy purchased 22, $1,000, 10% bonds maturing on August 31, 1986, at par value. Interest payment dates are July 31 and January 31.

10. The physical inventory on hand at December 31, 1981 was $82,800 per a physical inventory. Record the adjusting entry for inventory by using a "Cost of Goods Sold" account.

Instructions

(a) Prepare adjusting and correcting entries in general journal form using the information above.

(b) Indicate which of the adjusting entries will probably be reversed.

P3-9 The following list of accounts and their balances represent the unadjusted trial balance of Rita Co. at December 31, 1981:

	Dr.	Cr.
Cash	$ 5,000	
Accounts Receivable	46,000	
Allowance for Doubtful Accounts		$ 720
Inventory	55,000	
Prepaid Insurance	2,760	
Prepaid Rent	14,400	
Investment in Zorp. Corp. Bonds	10,000	
Property, Plant, and Equipment	104,000	
Accumulated Depreciation		15,600
Accounts Payable		10,930
Bonds Payable		50,000
Premium on Bonds Payable		950
Capital Stock		100,000
Retained Earnings		51,600
Sales		216,000
Rent Income		7,200
Purchases	170,000	
Purchase Discounts		3,400
Transportation-out	10,000	
Transportation-in	4,400	
Salaries and Wages	32,000	
Interest Expense	1,950	
Miscellaneous Expense	890	
	$456,400	$456,400

Additional data:

1. On November 1, 1981, Rita received $7,200 rent from its lessee for an 18-month lease beginning on that date, crediting Rent Income.

2. Rita estimates that 4% of the Accounts Receivable balances on December 31, 1981, will become uncollectible. On December 28, 1981, the bookkeeper incorrectly credited Sales for a receipt on account in the amount of $1,000. This error had not yet been corrected on December 31. _Closing process_

3. Per a physical inventory, inventory on hand at December 31, 1981, was $54,000. Record the adjusting entry for inventory by using a cost of goods sold account.

4. Prepaid insurance contains the premium costs of two policies: Policy A, cost of $840, 1-year term, taken out on September 1, 1981; Policy B, cost of $1,920, 3-year term, taken out on April 1, 1981.

5. The regular rate of depreciation is 10% per year. Acquisitions and retirements during a year are depreciated at half this rate. There were no retirements during the year. On December 31, 1980, the balance of Property, Plant, and Equipment was $96,000. _104,000 96,000 8000 ne_

6. On April 1, 1981, Rita issued 50, $1,000, 8% bonds, maturing on April 1, 1991, at 102% of par value. Interest payment dates are April 1 and October 1.

7. On August 1, 1981, Rita purchased 10, $1,000, 10% Zorp. Corp. bonds, maturing on August 31, 1983, at par value. Interest payment dates are July 31 and January 31.

8. On May 30, 1981, Rita rented a warehouse for $600 per month, paying $14,400 in advance, debiting Prepaid Rent.

Instructions

(a) Prepare adjusting and correcting entries in general journal form using the information above.

(b) Indicate the adjusting entries that would be reversed.

P3-10 Following is the trial balance of the Recluse Country Club as of December 31. The books are closed annually on December 31.

Recluse Country Club
TRIAL BALANCE
December 31

Cash	$ 16,000	
Dues Receivable	13,200	
Allowance for Doubtful Accounts		$ 1,200
Land	400,000	
Buildings	120,000	
Accumulated Depreciation of Buildings		40,000
Equipment	160,000	
Accumulated Depreciation of Equipment		70,000
Unexpired Insurance	6,000	
Capital		562,800
Dues Income		180,000
Income from Greens Fees		6,000
Rent Income		13,200
Utilities Expense	54,000	
Salaries Expense	80,000	
Maintenance	24,000	
	$873,200	$873,200

Instructions

(a) Enter the balances in ledger accounts. Allow five lines for each account.

(b) From the trial balance and the information given, prepare adjusting entries and post to the ledger accounts.

1. The buildings have an estimated life of 40 years with no salvage value (straight-line method).
2. The equipment is depreciated at 10% per year.
3. Insurance expired during the year, $2,000.
4. The rent income represents the amount received for 11 months for dining facilities. The December rent has not yet been received.
5. It is estimated that 20% of the dues receivable will be uncollectible.
6. Salaries earned but not paid by December 31, $2,400.
7. Dues paid in advance by members, $3,000.

(c) Prepare an adjusted trial balance.

(d) Prepare closing entries and post.

(e) Prepare reversing entries and post.

(f) Prepare a trial balance.

P3-11 Presented below is the trial balance for Lisa Poe, proprietor.

Lisa Poe
TRIAL BALANCE
December 31, 1981

Cash	$ 11,100	
Accounts Receivable	64,800	
Allowance for Doubtful Accounts		$ 1,900
Inventory, January 1	76,000	
Land	27,000	
Building	90,000	
Accumulated Depreciation of Building		14,400
Furniture and Fixtures	17,300	
Accumulated Depreciation of Furniture and Fixtures		5,700
Unexpired Insurance	7,700	
Accounts Payable		32,400
Notes Payable		27,000
Mortgage Payable		36,000
Lisa Poe, Capital		79,380
Sales		720,000
Sales Returns and Allowances	3,600	
Purchases	558,000	
Purchase Returns and Allowances		5,900
Transportation-in	14,800	
Sales Salaries	21,600	
Advertising	4,700	
Salaries, Office and General	16,200	
Heat, Light, and Water	4,300	
Telephone and Telegraph	1,600	
Miscellaneous Office Expenses	2,000	
Purchase Discounts		8,600
Sales Discount	9,500	
Interest Expense	1,080	
	$931,280	$931,280

Instructions

  (a) Copy the trial balance above in the first two columns of a ten-column work sheet.

  (b) Prepare adjusting entries in journal form from the following information. (The fiscal year ends December 31.)
    1. Estimated bad debts, one-quarter of 1% of sales less returns and allowances.
    2. Depreciation on building, 2% per year; on furniture and fixtures, 10% per year.
    3. Insurance expired during the year, $2,500.
    4. Interest at 6% is payable on the mortgage on January 1 of each year.
    5. Sales salaries accrued, December 31, $1,400.
    6. Advertising expenses paid in advance, $700.
    7. Office supplies on hand December 31, $1,000. (Charged to Miscellaneous Office Expenses when purchased.)
    8. Interest accrued on notes payable December 31, $1,300.

  (c) Transfer the adjusting entries to the work sheet and complete it. Merchandise inventory on hand December 31, $50,000.

  (d) Prepare an income statement, a balance sheet, and a statement of capital.

  (e) Prepare closing journal entries.

  (f) Indicate the adjusting entries that would be reversed.

P3-12 The Saddle Up Co. closes its books only once a year on December 31 but prepares monthly financial statements by estimating month-end inventories and by using work sheets.

    The company's trial balance on January 31, 1980, is presented below. Selling Expenses and Administrative Expenses are controlling accounts.

Saddle Up Company
TRIAL BALANCE
January 31, 1980

Cash	$ 1,150	
Accounts Receivable	10,000	
Notes Receivable	2,600	
Allowance for Doubtful Accounts		$ 1,250
Inventory, Jan. 1, 1980	15,000	
Furniture and Fixtures	25,000	
Accumulated Depreciation of Furniture and Fixtures		5,000
Unexpired Insurance	600	
Supplies on Hand	1,050	
Accounts Payable		6,000
Notes Payable		5,000
Common Stock		20,000
Retained Earnings		10,125
Sales		101,600
Sales Returns and Allowances	1,600	
Purchases	70,000	
Transportation-in	2,000	
Selling Expenses	11,000	
Administrative Expenses	9,000	
Interest Income		75
Interest Expense	50	
	$149,050	$149,050

Instructions

   (a) Copy the trial balance in the first two columns of an eight-column work sheet.

   (b) Prepare adjusting entries in journal form (administrative expenses includes bad debts, depreciation, insurance, supplies, and office salaries).

      1. Estimated bad debts, one-quarter of 1% of net sales.

      2. Depreciation of furniture and fixtures, 12% per year.

      3. Insurance expired in January, $60.

      4. Supplies used in January, $250.

      5. Office salaries accrued, $400.

      6. Interest accrued on notes payable, $110.

      7. Interest unearned on notes receivable, $65.

   (c) Transfer the adjusting entries to the work sheet.

   (d) Estimate the January 31 inventory and enter it on the work sheet. The average gross profit earned by the company is 35% of net sales.

   (e) Complete the work sheet.

   (f) Prepare a balance sheet, an income statement, and a statement of retained earnings. Dividends of $2,000 were paid on the common stock during the month.

*P3-13 On January 2, 1980, Wetzel-Pretty, Inc. was organized with two stockholders, Thomas Wetzel and Mary Ann Pretty. Thomas Wetzel purchased 500 shares of $100 par value common stock for $50,000 cash; Mary Ann Pretty received 500 shares of common stock in exchange for the assets and liabilities of a men's clothing shop that she had operated as a sole proprietorship. The trial balance immediately after incorporation appears on the work sheet.

     No formal books have been kept during 1980. The following information has been gathered from the checkbooks, deposit slips, and other sources:

1. Most balance sheet account balances at December 31, 1980 have been determined and recorded on the work sheet.

2. Cash receipts for the year are summarized as follows:

Advances from customers	$ 700
Cash sales and collections on accounts receivable (after sales discounts of	
$1,520 and sales returns and allowances of $1,940)	126,540
Sale of equipment costing $5,000 on which $1,000 of depreciation had	
accumulated	4,500
	$131,740

3. During 1980, the depreciation expense on the building was $400; the depreciation expense on the equipment was $1,750.

4. Cash disbursements for the year are summarized as follows:

Insurance premiums	$ 825
Purchase of equipment	18,000
Addition to building	4,600
Cash purchases and payments on accounts payable (after purchase discounts	
of $1,150 and purchase returns and allowances of $1,800)	82,050
Salaries paid to employees	38,620
Utilities	1,850
Total cash disbursements	$145,945

5. Bad debts are estimated to be 1.2% of total sales for the year. The ending accounts receivable balance of $18,700 has been reduced by $650 for specific accounts that were written off as uncollectible.

Instructions

Complete the work sheet for the preparation of accrual basis financial statements. Formal financial statements and journal entries are not required.

(AICPA adapted)

Wetzel-Pretty, Inc.
WORK SHEET FOR PREPARATION OF ACCRUAL BASIS
FINANCIAL STATEMENTS
For the Year 1980

	Balance Sheet January 2, 1980		Adjustments		Income Statement 1980		Balance Sheet December 31, 1980	
	Debit	Credit	Debit	Credit	Debit	Credit	Debit	Credit
Cash	$ 50,000							
Accounts receivable	12,400						18,700	
Merchandise inventory	23,000						24,500	
Unexpired insurance	350						200	
Land	15,000						15,000	
Buildings	20,000							
Accumulated depreciation— buildings		$ 7,000						
Equipment	8,000							
Accumulated depreciation— equipment		2,400						
Accounts payable		17,850						9,229
Advances from customers		900						550
Salaries payable		600						1,595
Capital stock		100,000						100,000
	$128,750	$128,750						

(Prepare your own work sheet, because you will need additional accounts)

*P3-14   Presented below is information related to the Colonial Company.

Journals

Sales journal	Page 17
Purchases journal	Page 8
Cash receipts journal	Page 43
Cash payments journal	Page 44
General journal	Page 12

Ledger Accounts

Title	Balance July 1	Acct. No.
Cash	$6,000	2
Accounts Receivable	8,000	5
Delivery Equipment	7,000	8
Sales Equipment	1,000	21
Accounts Payable	5,000	35
Advertising Expense	0	65
Purchases	0	52
Purchase Returns	0	53
Sales	0	69
Transportation-in	0	70

The following transactions occurred during the month of July.

July 1   Sells merchandise for cash, $9,000.

    3   Buys a new delivery truck on account from L. Canary Motors, $9,000.

3   Receives an invoice from the **Daily Advertiser** for a full-page advertisement, $150, which appeared in the paper on July 2.

5   Receives a purchase requisition for display equipment from the sales manager; the equipment sells for $1,130.

6   Returns merchandise for credit of $130 on a cash purchase.

7   Sells merchandise on account to Peggy Graham, $10,000.

8   Purchases merchandise on account from Kelly Smith, $9,000, f.o.b. shipping point.

10   Receives cash of $130 for merchandise returned July 6.

11   Receives a debit memo for $70 from Kelly Smith, indicating that the merchandise purchased July 8 was shipped with freight prepaid.

13   Purchases display equipment for $1,130; the invoice is paid immediately. (See July 5 information.)

17   Sells merchandise on account to Lisa Jacobson, $1,000.

20   Pays Kelly Smith in full of account.

24   Purchases merchandise on account from Sherrie Strain, $3,400.

28   Pays the **Daily Advertiser.**

31   Receives full payment from Peggy Graham.

Instructions

Complete the following:

(a) Open ledger accounts and enter the July 1 balances.

(b) Record the July transactions in appropriate journals.

(c) Post from the journals to the ledger with posting references in good form (omit subsidiary ledger postings).

*P3-15   The E. T. Elsner Company maintains a voucher register with debit columns for Purchases, Office Salaries, Sales Salaries, Advertising Expense, Office Supplies Expense, and Sundry, and a credit column for Vouchers Payable. The check register contains a debit column for Vouchers Payable and credit columns for Cash and Purchase Discounts.

May 3   Purchases merchandise from the Finnel Company for $10,800, terms 1/10, n/30 (purchases are recorded at gross amount).

6   Purchases merchandise from F. Kort for $6,300, 2/10, n/30.

9   Pays office payroll of $2,160 and sales payroll of $4,500.

11   Purchases office equipment for $3,600 from Duncan Equipment Company, terms 1/15, n/45.

12   Returns damaged merchandise of $800 to the Finnel Company and pays the balance due.

15   Receives an invoice from the Power and Light Company for utilities of $41.

17   Pays Duncan Equipment Company the full amount due.

20   Purchases office supplies of $1,000 from Office Equipment Company, making immediate payment by check.

21   Receives an invoice for advertising from WGSN Radio Station, $270.

23   Pays F. Kort in full of account.

27   Pays the telephone bill of $47 received from the telephone company.

28   Pays the invoices for utilities and advertising.

31   Supplies on hand are valued at $558.

Instructions

Record the transactions in the books of original entry of the E. T. Elsner Company beginning with voucher number 1 and check number 101.

Statement of Income and
Retained Earnings

The statement of income, or statement of earnings as it is frequently called,[1] is the report that measures the success of enterprise operations for a given period of time. The business and investment community uses this report to measure investment value, credit worthiness, and income success, for instance. Whether this confidence is well-founded is a matter of conjecture, because the derived income is at best a rough estimate, and great caution should be exercised not to give it more significance than it deserves.

As indicated in Chapter 2, the measurement of income in accounting is a reflection of the many assumptions and principles (standards) established over the years by accountants, such as the periodicity assumption, the revenue realization principle, and the matching principle. If for any reason the assumptions and principles are ill-founded, weaknesses will appear in the income statement.

Measurement of Income

Economists have often criticized accountants for their definition of income, because accountants do not include many items that contribute to the general growth and well-being of an enterprise. For example, the noted economist, J. R. Hicks, has defined income as the maximum value a person can consume during a period and still be as well off at the end as at the beginning.[2] This definition provides the essential elements of measuring an individual's income. Any effort to measure how

---

[1] *Accounting Trends and Techniques—1978* (New York: AICPA), p. 237, indicates that for the 600 companies surveyed in 1977 the term *income* is employed in the title of 357 income statements. The term *earnings* is second in acceptance with 179, while the term *operations* is used by 60 companies.

[2] J. R. Hicks, *Value and Capital* (Oxford: Clarendon Press, 1946), p. 172.

well-off an individual is at any point in time, however, will prove fruitless unless certain restrictive assumptions are developed and applied.

For example, what was your net income for last year? Let us suppose that you worked during the summer and earned $2,100. Because you paid taxes and incurred tuition and living expenses for school, your income statement may show a loss for the year, if measured in terms of straight dollar value. But have you sustained a loss? How do you value the education obtained during this one year? One interpretation of Hicks's definition states that you would measure not only monetary income but also psychic income. Psychic income is defined as a measure of increase in net wealth arising from qualitative features, in this case the value of your educational experience.

Accountants undoubtedly recognize that the measurement of such experiences may be useful, but the problem of measurement has not been solved. Items that cannot be quantified with any degree of objectivity have been discarded as impractical to measure.

Capital Maintenance Approach vs. Transaction Approach

Hicks's definition of income assumes that net income is measured by subtracting beginning net assets (assets minus liabilities) from ending net assets and adjusting for any additional investments during the period. When income is calculated in this manner, accountants state that a capital maintenance approach to income measurement is employed. The **capital maintenance approach** (sometimes referred to as the change-in-equity approach) takes the net assets or capital values based on some valuation (e.g., historical cost, discounted cash flows, current cost, or fair market value) and measures income by the difference in capital values at two points in time.[3] Here is an illustration, assuming the use of historical costs.

Suppose that a corporation had beginning net assets of $10,000 and end of the year net assets of $18,000, and that during this same period additional owners' investments of $5,000 were made. Calculation of the net income for the period, employing the capital maintenance approach, is shown below.

Net assets, December 31, 1980	$18,000
Net assets, January 1, 1980	10,000
	8,000
Less:	
Owners' investments during the year	5,000
Net income for 1980	$ 3,000

With the capital maintenance approach we compute the net income for the period, but there is one important drawback. Detailed information concerning the composition of the income is not evident; all of the revenue and expense amounts are not presented to the financial statement reader.

[3]The Internal Revenue Service uses the capital maintenance approach to identify unreported income and refers to its approach as a "net worth check." See Joseph Karasyk, "The Net Worth Method in Tax Evasion Cases," *The CPA Journal*, Vol. XLIX, No. 4, April 1979, pp. 35–40.

An alternative procedure measures the basic income related transactions that occur during a period and summarizes them in an income statement. This method is normally called the **transaction approach.** This approach focuses on the activities that have occurred during a given period; instead of presenting only a net change, the components that comprise the change are disclosed. Income may be classified by customer, product line, or function. In addition, classification into groupings such as ordinary and extraordinary is developed to aid user groups. The transaction approach to income measurement is the method that you learned in your basic accounting course.

Single-Step Income Statements

The transaction approach to income measurement is superior to the capital maintenance approach because it provides more information. One problem with the transaction approach involves the determination of the proper format for this information. Many accountants prefer a statement format entitled the **single-step** income statement.

In this statement, two groups exist: revenues on the one hand, and cost and expenses on the other. The expenses are deducted from the revenues to arrive at the net income or loss; the expression "single-step" is derived from the single subtraction necessary to arrive at net income. Frequently, however, income taxes are shown as a separate last item.

For example, here is the income statement of Kaiser, Inc.

Kaiser, Inc. INCOME STATEMENT For the Year Ended December 31, 1980	
Net sales	$343,000
Other revenue	6,000
Total revenue	349,000
Expenses	
Cost of goods sold	258,000
Selling and administrative expenses	49,000
Interest on long-term debt	3,961
Other expenses	1,104
Total expenses	312,065
Income before taxes	36,935
Income taxes	16,000
Net income	$ 20,935
Earnings per share	$1.36

The use of the single-step form of income statement is predominant in business reporting today; in recent years, however, the multiple-step form has regained some of its former popularity.[4]

___

[4]*Accounting Trends and Techniques—1978, op. cit.,* p. 237. Of the 600 companies surveyed in 1977, 371 employed the single-step form and 229 employed the multiple-step income statement format.

The primary advantage of the single-step format lies in the simplicity of presentation and the absence of any implication of the priority of one type of revenue or expense item over another. Potential classification problems are thus eliminated.

Multiple-Step Income Statements

Some accountants contend that additional important relationships exist in income and expense data and that when the income statement shows these relationships it becomes more informative and more useful. Further classification and association of data within the statement make the report even more informative. Among the features are:

1. A separation of results achieved through regular operations and those obtained through the subordinate or nonoperating activities of the company. This separation is helpful because it provides a sound basis for evaluating the results of nonoperating activities as well as the regular activities. For example, enterprises often present an income from operations figure and then a section entitled other income or expense that includes interest income and expense, and sales of miscellaneous items and dividends received.

2. A classification of expenses by functions, such as merchandising or manufacturing (cost of goods sold), selling, and administration. This presentation of the total expense of each activity permits immediate comparison with costs of previous years and with the cost of other departments during the same year.

Accountants who show these additional relationships in the operating data favor what is called a **multiple-step** income statement, rather than the single-step statement. In a multiple-step statement the basic division is between operating and nonoperating activities, with both revenues and expenses separated into these two groups. And, whenever practicable, costs and expenses are classified and grouped within each major division. This statement is recommended because it recognizes a separation of operating transactions from nonoperating transactions and matches costs and expenses with related revenues to provide more information to the financial statement reader. To illustrate, the Caine Company's multiple-step statement of income is presented on page 130.

For a manufacturing company, the section concerned with the cost of goods manufactured and sold is usually too extensive to include in the income statement. Normally, a separate schedule is required for the presentation of this data, if it is presented at all.

Sections of the Income Statement

The development of sections and subsections within the income statement is described below.

1. Operating section. A report of the revenues and expenses of the company's principal operations. (This section may or may not be presented on a departmental basis.)
   a. Sales or revenue section. A subsection within the operating section to present the pertinent facts about sales, discounts, allowances, returns, and other related information, and to arrive at the net amount of sales revenue.
   b. Cost of goods sold section. A subsection within the operating section that shows the cost of goods that were sold to produce the sales, and that shows in adequate detail the components of this cost figure.

Caine Company
INCOME STATEMENT
For the Year Ended December 31, 1980

Sales			
Sales			$3,053,081
Less: Sales discount		$ 44,241	
Sales returns and allowances		36,427	80,668
Net sales			2,972,413
Cost of Goods Sold			
Merchandise inventory, Jan. 1, 1980		461,219	
Purchases	$1,989,693		
Less purchase discounts	19,270		
Net purchases	1,970,423		
Freight and transportation-in	40,612	2,011,035	
Total merchandise available for sale		2,472,254	
Less merchandise inventory, Dec. 31, 1980		489,713	
Cost of goods sold			1,982,541
Gross profit on sales			989,872
Operating Expenses			
Selling expenses			
Sales salaries and commissions	202,644		
Sales office salaries	59,200		
Travel and entertainment	48,940		
Advertising expense	38,315		
Freight and transportation-out	41,209		
Shipping supplies and expense	24,712		
Postage and stationery	16,788		
Depreciation of sales equipment	9,005		
Telephone and telegraph	12,215	453,028	
Administrative expenses			
Officers' salaries	186,000		
Office salaries	61,200		
Legal and professional services	23,721		
Utilities expense	23,275		
Insurance expense	7,029		
Depreciation of building	8,059		
Depreciation of office equipment	6,000		
Stationery, supplies, and postage	2,875		
Miscellaneous office expenses	2,612	320,771	773,799
Income from operations			216,073
Other income			
Dividend income		8,500	
Rental income		2,910	11,410
			227,483
Other Expense			
Interest on bonds and notes			26,060
Income before taxes			201,423
Income taxes			102,000
Net income for the year			$ 99,423
Earnings per share			$3.06

    c. Selling expenses. A subsection within the operating section that states expenses resulting from the company's efforts to make sales.

    d. Administrative or general expenses. A subsection within the operating section reporting expenses of general administration of the company's operations.

    e. Special gains or losses that are material in amount and unusual or infrequent—but not both—are generally shown in this section.

2. Nonoperating section. A report of the revenues and expenses resulting from secondary or auxiliary activities of the company. Generally these break down into two main subsections:

    a. Other income. A list of the incomes earned, generally net of related expenses, from nonoperating transactions.

    b. Other expenses. A list of the expenses, or losses incurred, generally net of any related incomes, from nonoperating transactions.

3. Income taxes. A short section to report as a separate item the amount of federal and state taxes levied on income.

4. Discontinued operations. Material gains or losses resulting from the disposition of a segment of the business.

5. Extraordinary items. Unusual and infrequent gains and losses of material amounts.

6. Cumulative effect of a change in accounting principle.

7. Earnings per share.[5]

Although the content of the operating section is always the same, the organization of the material need not be as described. The breakdown above uses a **natural expense classification** and is commonly used for manufacturing concerns and for merchandising companies in the wholesale trade. Another classification of operating expenses recommended for retail stores uses a **functional expense classification** of administrative, occupancy, publicity, buying, and selling expenses. Thus any reasonable classification that serves to inform those who use the statement is satisfactory. The present tendency in statements prepared for management is to present considerable detailed expense data grouped along lines of responsibility. This permits evaluation of the effectiveness of the work of individuals and departments according to work done and amount expended.

Whether a single-step or a multiple-step income statement is used, unusual transactions such as discontinued operations, extraordinary items, and cumulative effect of changes in accounting principles should be reported separately following income from continuing operations.

Refer to the income statement of Tenneco, Inc., Appendix E, p. 194, for an illustration of an income statement from practice.

Condensed Income Statements

In some cases it is impossible to present in a single report of convenient size all of the detailed expenses that are desirable in the statement of income. This problem is solved by including only the totals of expense groups in the statement of income and preparing supplementary schedules of expenses to support the totals in the statement. When this is done, the income statement proper may be reduced to only a few lines on a single sheet. For this reason, readers who study all the reported data on operations must give their attention to the supporting schedules of ex-

---

[5]*APB Opinion No. 15* requires that earnings per share or net loss per share be included on the face of the income statement.

penses as well. The income statement below for Caine Company is a condensed version of the more detailed statement presented earlier and is more representative of the type found in practice. If used, it should be accompanied by supporting schedules to present as much detail as desirable.

Caine Company
INCOME STATEMENT
For the Year Ended December 31, 1980

Net sales		$2,972,413
Cost of goods sold		1,982,541
Gross profit		989,872
Selling expense	$453,028	
Administrative expense	320,771	773,799
Income from operations		216,073
Other income		11,410
		227,483
Other expense		26,060
Income before taxes		201,423
Income taxes		102,000
Net income for the year		$ 99,423
Earnings per share		$3.06

There is always a problem concerning the amount of detail to include in the financial statements. On the one hand, we want to present a simple, summarized statement so that a reader can readily discover the facts of importance. On the other hand, there is the necessity for full disclosure of the results of all activities and a desire to provide more than just a skeleton report. Supplementary schedules that provide the detailed information that cannot fit conveniently into the principal statement satisfy both requirements. They make it possible to present brief summarized statements and to report as much additional detail as desired separately from but in conjunction with the basic statement.[6]

Current Operating versus All-Inclusive

Another question concerning the income statement is, what should be included in income? For years a controversy has existed in accounting circles about whether certain gains and losses and corrections of income and expenses of prior years should be closed directly to Retained Earnings and therefore not be reported in the income statement. Or, should they first be presented in the income statement and then carried to Retained Earnings along with the net income or loss for the period? When all the items are first presented in the income statement, the Retained Earnings account normally includes for any given year only the net income (or loss) for

[6]For ideas on how to measure information gains and losses on the introduction or deletion of certain financial material, see Baruch Lev, "The Aggregation Problem in Financial Statements: An Informational Approach," *Journal of Accounting Research* (Autumn, 1968), pp. 247–61, and Baruch Lev, "The Informational Approach to Aggregation in Financial Statements: Extensions," *Journal of Accounting Research* (Spring, 1970).

the year and any dividends declared. Thus the advocates of this latter procedure were said to favor an **all-inclusive** income statement.

On the other hand, those who advocated closing such gains and losses directly to Retained Earnings were said to favor a **current operating performance** income statement. Under this procedure unusual gains and losses of material amounts that are recognized during the period do not appear in any income statement but are charged or credited directly to the Retained Earnings account.

To illustrate, Harrison Corporation has a retained earnings balance on January 1, 1981 of $80,000. For 1981, the corporation has earned revenue of $100,000 and incurred expenses of $30,000, exclusive of an extraordinary gain on the condemnation of properties of $10,000, net of tax. All-inclusive and current operating statements are illustrated below.

	All-Inclusive	Current Operating
Revenues	$100,000	$100,000
Expenses	30,000	30,000
Income before extraordinary item	70,000	70,000
Extraordinary item:		
Gain on condemnation of properties (net of tax)	10,000	
Net income	$ 80,000	$ 70,000
Beginning retained earnings	$ 80,000	$ 80,000
Add:		
Net income	80,000	70,000
Extraordinary gain on condemnation of properties (net of tax)		10,000
Ending retained earnings	$160,000	$160,000

Here is the essence of the controversy. During the life of any enterprise some relatively large unusual and nonrecurring gains and losses are experienced. In general, these extraordinary items are not directly identified with the ordinary operations of the enterprise for the current year, yet they must be considered in determining the overall profitability of the enterprise's activities during its life span. Do such extraordinary items contribute to the net income or loss of the enterprise for the period in which they appear?

Advocates of the current operating performance concept exclude all such items from the income calculation and from the income statement. They say that the net income figure should show the regular, recurring earnings of the business based on its normal operations. Extraordinary gains and losses are neither representative nor reflective of an enterprise's future earning power. Therefore, they should not be included in computing net income but should be carried directly to Retained Earnings as special items. In addition, they note that many readers are not trained to differentiate between ordinary and extraordinary items and, therefore, would be confused.

Advocates of the all-inclusive income statement insist that such items be included along with net income as a part of the long-range income-producing ability of the enterprise. They state that any gain or loss experienced by the concern, whether directly or indirectly related to operations, contributes to its long-run profitability and should be included in its computation. They point out that nonrecurring and extraordinary gains and losses can be separated from the results of ordinary operations to arrive at a figure of income from operations, but that in determining the net income for the year, all transactions should be included. They believe that when judgment is allowed to determine extraordinary items, differences develop in treatment of questionable items and, as a result, a danger of manipulating income data arises. For example, at one time American Standard wrote off $17.9 million in losses from discontinued operations directly to Retained Earnings. This enabled the company to report earnings per share of $1.01; if the write-off had been charged against income, American Standard would have reported a loss of 78 cents per share. If permitted, it could be to the advantage of the corporation to run losses through retained earnings, but gains through income. Supporters of the all-inclusive concept argue that this flexibility should not be allowed because it leads to poor financial reporting practices. In other words, Gresham's law applies; poor accounting practices drive out good ones.

For many years practicing accountants apparently favored the current operating performance income statement. For example, in 1953 the Committee on Accounting Procedure stated that the preferred method of treating extraordinary items is to "carry all such charges and credits directly to the surplus [retained earnings] account with complete disclosure as to their nature and amount."[7]

Recently, however, the most convincing arguments must have been given by those who favor the all-inclusive concept. **APB Opinion No. 9,** issued in 1967, **adopted the all-inclusive concept and requires application of this approach in practice with a few exceptions.** Subsequently, a number of pronouncements were issued that directly or indirectly involved the classification of unusual items. For purposes of discussion, we will classify these items into six general categories:

1. Extraordinary items related to the current period.
2. Certain gains and losses that do not constitute extraordinary items even though they are material in amount.
3. Prior-period adjustments.
4. Normal, recurring corrections and adjustments.
5. Changes in accounting principle.
6. Discontinued operations.

Extraordinary Items Related to the Current Period   These are defined as **material** items "of a character significantly different from the typical or customary business activities of the entity" and "which would not be expected to recur frequently and which would not be considered as recurring factors in any evaluation of the ordinary operating processes of the business."

In **Opinion No. 30** the following criteria for extraordinary items were developed:

Extraordinary items are events and transactions that are distinguished by their unusual nature **and** by the infrequency of their occurrence. Thus, **both** of the following criteria should be met to classify an event or transaction as an extraordinary item:

(a) **Unusual nature**—the underlying event or transaction should possess a high degree of abnormality and be of a type clearly unrelated to, or only incidentally related to, the ordinary and typical activities of the entity, taking into account the environment in which the entity operates.

---

[7]*Accounting Research Bulletin No. 43,* "Restatement and Revision of Accounting Research Bulletins" (New York: AICPA, 1953), Ch. 8, par. 11.

(b) **Infrequency of occurrence**—the underlying event or transaction should be of a type that would not reasonably be expected to recur in the foreseeable future, taking into account the environment in which the entity operates.[8]

For further clarification, the Board specified that the following gains and losses do not constitute extraordinary items:

(a) Write-down or write-off of receivables, inventories, equipment leased to others, deferred research and development costs, or other intangible assets.
(b) Gains or losses from exchange or translation of foreign currencies, including those relating to major devaluations and revaluations.
(c) Gains or losses on disposal of a segment of a business.
(d) Other gains or losses from sale or abandonment of property, plant, or equipment used in the business.
(e) Effects of a strike, including those against competitors and major suppliers.
(f) Adjustment of accruals on long-term contracts.[9]

The items listed above do not constitute extraordinary items in an ongoing business "because they are usual in nature and may be expected to recur as a consequence of customary and continuing business activities." Only in rare situations will an event or transaction occur that clearly meets the criteria specified in **Opinion 30** and thus gives rise to an extraordinary gain or loss.[10] In these circumstances, gains or losses such as (a) and (d) above should be classified as extraordinary if they are a **direct result of a major casualty** (such as an earthquake), **an expropriation, or a prohibition under a newly enacted law or regulation** that clearly meets the criteria of unusual and infrequent.

In determining whether an item is an extraordinary item, **the environment in which the entity operates is of primary importance.** The environment of an entity includes such factors as the characteristics of the industry or industries in which it operates, the geographical location of its operations, and the nature and extent of governmental regulations. Thus, extraordinary item treatment is accorded the loss arising from hail damages to a tobacco grower's crops because severe damage from hailstorms in the locality is rare. On the other hand, frost damage to a citrus grower's crop in Florida does not qualify as extraordinary because frost damage is normally experienced every three or four years. In this environment, the criterion of infrequency is not met. Similarly, when a company sells the only security investment it has ever owned, the gain or loss meets the criteria of an extraordinary item. Another company, however, that has a portfolio of securities which it has acquired for investment purposes, would not have an extraordinary item upon the sale of such securities. Because the company owns several securities for investment purposes, sale of such securities is considered part of its ordinary and typical activities in the environment in which it operates.

It should be noted that there are **exceptions** to the general rules provided above. As indicated earlier, the **disposal of a segment of a business** [item (c) above], which is not an extraordinary item, requires special accounting treatment unlike any of

---

[8]"Reporting the Results of Operations," *Opinions of the Accounting Principles Board No. 30* (New York: AICPA, 1973), par. 20.

[9]*Ibid.*, par. 23.

[10]Some accountants have concluded that the extraordinary item classification is so restrictive that only such items as a single chemist who knew the secret formula for an enterprise's mixing solution but was eaten by a tiger on a big game hunt or a plant facility that was smashed by a meteor would qualify for extraordinary item treatment.

the other items resulting in a gain or loss. In addition, **material gains and losses from early extinguishment of debt** ordinarily should be reported as an extraordinary item even though these gains or losses do not meet the criteria mentioned above for extraordinary items.[11] The rationale for this position will be discussed in Chapter 14. In addition, the **tax benefits of loss carryforwards** recognized in periods subsequent to the loss must be reported as an extraordinary item in those periods (discussed in Chapter 20).[12]

Unfortunately, it is often difficult to determine what is extraordinary because accountants have never clearly defined materiality. As indicated in Chapter 2, firm guidelines to follow in judging when an item is or is not material have not been established. For example, companies have shown as extraordinary gains or losses items that accounted for less than 1% of income before extraordinary items. Our point is that as long as the definition of materiality is not sharply outlined, it will be difficult in some cases to differentiate an ordinary from an extraordinary item.[13] In determining whether an extraordinary event or transaction is material in relation to income before extraordinary items, to the trend of earnings, or by other appropriate criteria, items should be considered individually and not in the aggregate.[14]

In addition, considerable judgment must be exercised in determining whether an item should be reported as extraordinary. For example, some paper companies have had their forest lands condemned by the government for state or national parks or forests. Is such an event extraordinary or is it part of normal operations? Such determination is not easy; much depends on the frequency of previous condemnations, the expectation of future condemnations, materiality, etc.

Extraordinary items are to be shown net of taxes in a separate section in the income statement, just before net income. After listing the usual revenues, costs and expenses, and income taxes, the remainder of the statement shows:

```
Income before extraordinary items
Extraordinary items (less applicable income taxes of $_____)
Net income
```

For example, Keystone Consolidated Industries, Inc. presented its extraordinary loss in this manner in a recent annual report:

---

[11]"Reporting Gains and Losses from Extinguishment of Debt," *Statement of Financial Accounting Standard No. 4* (Stamford, Conn.: FASB, 1975), par. 8.

[12]"Accounting for Income Taxes," *Opinions of the Accounting Principles Board No. 11* (New York: AICPA, 1967), par. 45.

[13]For an interesting discussion of some of the weaknesses of earlier pronouncements, see Leopold A. Bernstein, "Reporting the Results of Operations—A Reassessment of APB *Opinion No. 9,*" *The Journal of Accountancy* (July 1970), pp. 57–61. Another problem deals with what is referred to as the "big-bath" approach. Many companies, if they see that a large loss is inevitable, write off as much as possible on the theory that investors do not make that great a distinction between a small loss and a larger one. Future statements are also relieved of these charges and provide a company with a quick earnings injection.

[14]"Reporting the Results of Operations," *op. cit.,* par. 24.

Keystone Consolidated Industries, Inc.	
Income before extraordinary item	$11,638,000
Extraordinary item—flood loss (Note E)	1,216,000
Net income	$10,422,000

Note E. *Extraordinary Item.* The Keystone Steel and Wire Division's Steel Works experienced a flash flood on June 22. The extraordinary item represents the estimated cost, net of related income taxes of $1,279,000, to restore the steel works to full operation.

Material Gains and Losses Not Constituting Extraordinary Items   Because of **Opinion No. 30**'s narrow criteria for extraordinary items, financial statement users now must examine carefully the financial statements for items that are **unusual or infrequent but not both.** As indicated earlier, the Opinion provides examples of items such as write-downs of inventories and gains and losses from fluctuation of foreign exchange that should be reflected in the determination of income before extraordinary items. Thus, these items are shown with the normal, recurring revenues, costs, and expenses. If they are not material in amount, they are combined with other items in the statement. If they are material, they must be disclosed separately, but are shown above "income (loss) before extraordinary items."

For example, Cosco, Inc. presented an unusual charge in the following manner:

Net sales		$56,961,631
Cost and expenses		
Cost of sales	43,254,687	
Marketing, general and administrative	13,876,172	
Unusual charges (Note 4)	685,931	
Interest	1,686,669	
		59,503,459
Loss from operations before income taxes		(2,541,828)

Note 4. *Unusual charges.* Cost of businesses acquired in excess of values assigned to assets was written down by $685,931 representing amounts applicable to businesses, which, in management's opinion, no longer have significant intangible value.

In dealing with events that are either unusual or nonrecurring but not both, the Board attempted to prevent a practice that many accountants believed was misleading. Companies often reported these transactions on a net-of-tax basis and prominently displayed the earnings per share effect of these items. Although not captioned extraordinary items, they were presented in the same manner as extraordinary items. Some had referred to these as "first cousins" to extraordinary items. As a consequence, the Board specifically **prohibited a net-of-tax treatment for such items** to insure that users of financial statements can easily differentiate extraordinary items from material items that are unusual or infrequent, but not both.

Prior Period Adjustments   The accounting treatment for prior period adjustments is relatively straightforward. **FASB Statement No. 16** requires that items of profit and loss related to the following shall be accounted for and reported as prior period adjustments and excluded from the determination of net income for the current period:

(a) Correction of an error in the financial statements of a prior period and
(b) Adjustments that result from realization of income tax benefits of pre-acquisition operating loss carry forwards of purchased subsidiaries.

In addition, certain accounting changes required or permitted by an FASB Statement, an FASB Interpretation, or an APB Opinion are required to be accounted for retroactively and reported similar to prior period adjustments.[15]

Prior period adjustments should be charged or credited to the opening balance of retained earnings net of tax and, thus, excluded from the determination of net income for the current period. To illustrate, in 1981, Nevin Enterprises determined that it had overstated its depreciation expense in 1980 by $75,000 owing to an error in computation. The error affected both the income statement and the tax return for 1980. Adjustment for this error is presented in the financial statements for 1981 as follows (all other figures are assumed):

Retained earnings, January 1, 1981, as previously reported	$130,000
Correction of an error in depreciation in prior period (net of $35,000 tax)	40,000
Adjusted balance of retained earnings at January 1, 1981	170,000
Net income	27,000
Retained earnings, December 31, 1981	$197,000

As a practical illustration, a recent annual report of Lafayette Radio Electronics Corporation presented a revised balance sheet, a revised income statement, and a revised statement of changes in financial position with the accompanying footnote explaining the nature of the prior period adjustment that necessitated the revised statements.

Note 6—*Revision of 1977 Financial Statements:* Subsequent to the issuance of its financial statements the Company discovered a computational error in the amount of $1,046,000 in the calculation of its July 2, 1977 inventory used to determine cost of sales for the year then ended. Accordingly, the 1977 statements have been restated. The effect of the correction of the error resulted in an increase in the 1977 net loss from $3,101,000 to $3,621,000 or from $1.42 to $1.65 per share.

The accounting treatment for prior period adjustments provides an interesting illustration of the evolutionary nature of accounting principle formulation. In 1966, **Opinion No. 9** identified certain criteria that had to be met before an item could be classified as a prior period adjustment.[16] These criteria permitted, for example, settlements of law suits in litigation to be reported as prior period adjustments but did not permit such treatment of corrections of errors. After considerable concern had been expressed about how corrections of errors should be handled, **Opinion**

---

[15]"Prior Period Adjustments," *Statement of Financial Accounting Standards Board No. 16* (Stamford, Conn.: FASB, 1977), pars. 11 and 12.

[16]"Reporting the Results of Operations," *Opinions of the Accounting Principles Board No. 9* (New York: AICPA, 1966).

No. 20, "Accounting Changes," was issued in 1971; it required that corrections of errors related to a previous period be reported as prior period adjustments.[17]

Subsequently, the SEC began to challenge prior period classification for litigation settlements, arguing that the outcome of litigation could not have been determined in a prior period and, therefore, these items should be run through the current year's income statement. The real concern was that adverse effects on net income could be partially hidden by direct charges to retained earnings. The FASB then reconsidered this issue, but only four of the seven members voted in late 1976 to eliminate litigative suits as prior period adjustments. According to the then existing by-laws of the FASB, five votes were required to establish a new standard; therefore, no change in the accounting for prior period adjustments was made. In early 1977, the trustees of the Financial Accounting Foundation in reviewing their operating procedures, decided that a simple majority vote of the FASB was sufficient to establish a new standard and that this change in the by-laws should be retroactive. Thus, what did not become an accounting standard in late 1976 did become an accounting standard in early 1977 **because of a change in the voting rules.** As a result, the number of prior period adjustments will be reduced, because generally only corrections of errors related to a prior period are accorded this treatment. The foregoing narrative illustrates the tenuous nature of accounting standard-setting.

Normal, Recurring Corrections and Adjustments   Adjustments that grow out of the use of estimates in accounting are not classified as prior period adjustments and, therefore, are used in the determination of income for the current period and future periods and not charged or credited directly to Retained Earnings. Items resulting from changes in the estimated lives of fixed assets, adjustment of the costs, realizability of inventories believed to be obsolete in preceding years, and similar items are accounted for in the period of the change if they affect only that period, or in the period of change and future periods if the change affects both. Note that **changes in estimate should not be treated as extraordinary items.**

Changes in Accounting Principle   As just indicated, changes in accounting occur frequently in practice, because at the statement date important events or conditions may be in dispute or uncertain. One type of accounting change, therefore, comprises the normal recurring corrections and adjustments that are made by every business enterprise. Another accounting change is a change in accounting principle that results when an accounting principle is adopted that is different from the one previously used. Changes in accounting principle are, for example, a change in the method of inventory pricing from FIFO to average cost or a change in depreciation from the double-declining to the straight-line method.[18]

These types of changes are recognized generally by including in the income statement of the current year net of tax the cumulative effect, based on a retroactive computation, of changing to a new accounting principle. **The effect on net**

---

[17]"Accounting Changes," *Opinions of the Accounting Principles Board No. 20* (New York: AICPA, 1971).

[18]*Ibid.*, par. 18. Chapter 23 examines in greater detail the problems related to accounting changes; our purpose now is to provide general guidance for the major types of transactions affecting the income statement.

income of adopting the new accounting principle should be disclosed as a separate item following extraordinary items in the income statement.

To illustrate, Arco decided at the beginning of 1981 to change from the sum-of-the-years'-digits method of computing depreciation on their plant assets to the straight-line method. The assets originally cost $100,000 and have a service life of four years. Here are the data assumed for this illustration and the manner of reporting the change.

Year	Sum-of-the-Years'-Digits Depreciation	Straight-Line Depreciation	Excess of Sum-of-the-Years'-Digits over Straight-Line Method
1979	$40,000	$25,000	$15,000
1980	30,000	25,000	5,000
Total			$20,000

The information is shown on the 1981 financial statements as follows (tax rate, 48%):

Income before extraordinary item and cumulative effect of a change in accounting principle	$120,000
Extraordinary item—casualty loss (net of $19,200 tax)	(20,800)
Cumulative effect on prior years of retroactive application of new depreciation method (net of $9,600 tax)	10,400
Net income	$109,600

Discontinued Operations   One of the most common types of unusual items has been the disposal of a business or a product line. Because of the increasing importance of this type of event, **Opinion No. 30** developed a set of classification and disclosure requirements to provide the information necessary to assess the impact of discontinued operations on the business enterprise.[19] Discontinued operations refer to those of a separate line of business or class of customers.

A separate income statement category for the gain or loss from **disposal of a segment of a business** must be provided. In addition, the **results of operations of a segment that has been or will be disposed of** is reported in conjunction with the gain or loss on disposal and separated from the results of continuing operations. The effects of discontinued operations are shown net of tax as a separate category in the income statement after continuing operations but before extraordinary items.

To illustrate, ATS, Inc., a highly diversified company, decides to discontinue its electronics division. During the current year, the electronics division lost $300,000 (net of tax) and was sold at the end of the year at a loss of $500,000 (net of tax). The information is shown on the 1981 income statement as follows:

[19]The reporting requirements for discontinued operations are complex; only the major provisions are provided in this discussion.

Income from continuing operations (after related taxes)		$20,000,000
Discontinued operations		
Loss from operation of discontinued electronics division (net of tax)	$300,000	
Loss from disposal of electronics division (net of tax)	500,000	800,000
Net income		$19,200,000

The assets, results of operations, and activities of a segment of a business must be clearly distinguishable, physically, operationally, and for financial reporting purposes, from the other assets, results of operations and activities of the entity to qualify for discontinued operations treatment. Disposal of assets incidental to the evolution of the entity's business is not considered to be disposal of a segment of the business. **Disposals of assets that do *not* qualify as disposals of a segment** of a business include the following:

1. Disposal of *part* of a line of business.
2. Shifting of production or marketing activities for a particular line of business from one location to another.
3. Phasing out of a product line or class of service.
4. Other changes occasioned by a technological improvement.

Examples that would qualify as a disposal of a segment of a business are: (a) sale by a meat-packing company of a 53% interest in a professional football team, or (b) sale by a communications company of all of its radio stations but none of its television stations or publishing houses.

Conversely, examples that would not qualify are (1) discontinuance by a children's wear manufacturer of its operations in Italy but not elsewhere, or (2) sale by a diversified company of one furniture-manufacturing subsidiary but not all furniture-manufacturing subsidiaries. Note that judgment must be exercised in defining a disposal of a segment of a business because the criteria in some cases are difficult to apply.

Summary

The public accounting profession now tends to accept a modified all-inclusive income concept instead of the current operating performance concept. The only items ordinarily charged or credited directly to Retained Earnings are **prior period adjustments** that are essentially error corrections, and certain accounting changes that require restatement of prior period financial statements. All other unusual gains or losses or nonrecurring items are closed to Revenue and Expense Summary and are included in the income statement. Of these, the **unusual, material, nonrecurring items** that are significantly different from the typical or customary business activities are shown in a separate section for "extraordinary items" in the income statement just before net income. Other items of a material amount that are of an **unusual or nonrecurring** nature and are **not considered extraordinary** are separately disclosed. In addition, the cumulative adjustment that occurs when a change in accounting principles develops is disclosed as a separate item before net income. Finally **discontinued operations of a segment** of a business are classified as a separate item in the income statement after continuing operations but before extraordinary items.

The following chart summarizes the basic concepts previously examined. Although the chart is simplified, it provides a useful framework for determining the proper treatment of special items affecting the income statement.

SUMMARY OF APB OPINIONS AND FASB STANDARDS[a]

Type of Situation	Criteria	Examples	Placement on Financial Statements
Extraordinary items	Material; unusual; nonrecurring (infrequent).	Gains or losses resulting from casualties, an expropriation, or a prohibition under a new law.[b]	Separate section in the income statement entitled extraordinary items. (Shown net of tax)
Material gains or losses, not considered extraordinary	Material; character typical of the customary business activities; unusual or infrequent but not both.	Write-downs of receivables, inventories; adjustments of accrued contract prices; gains or losses from fluctuations of foreign exchange; gains or losses from sales of assets used in business.	Separate section in income statement above income before extraordinary items. (Not shown net of tax)
Prior period adjustments and accounting changes that require restatement	Material corrections of errors applicable to prior periods or accounting changes required or permitted by an FASB Statement or an APB Opinion to be handled retroactively.	Corrections of errors; retroactive restatements per *APB Opinion No. 20* or other authoritative pronouncements.	Adjust the beginning balance of retained earnings. (Shown net of tax)
Changes in estimates	Normal, recurring corrections and adjustments.	Changes in the realizability of receivables and inventories; changes in estimated lives of equipment, intangible assets; changes in estimated liability for warranty costs, income taxes, and salary payments.	Change in income statement only in the account affected. (Not shown net of tax)
Changes in principle[c]	Change from one generally accepted principle to another.	Changing the basis of inventory pricing from FIFO to average cost; change in the method of depreciation from accelerated to straight-line.	Cumulative effect of the adjustment is reflected in the income statement between the captions extraordinary items and net income. (Shown net of tax)
Discontinued operations	Disposal of a segment of a business constituting a separate line of business or class of customer.	Sale by diversified company of major division which represents only activities in electronics industry. Food distributor that sells wholesale to supermarket chains and through fast-food restaurants decides to discontinue the division that sells to one of two classes of customers.	Shown in separate section of the income statement after continuing operations but before extraordinary items. (Shown net of tax)

[a]This summary provides only the general rules to be followed in accounting for the various situations described above. Exceptions do exist in some of these situations.

[b]Material gains and losses from extinguishment of debt and tax benefits of loss carryforwards are considered extraordinary, even though criteria for extraordinary items may not be met.

[c]The general rule per *APB Opinion No. 20* is to use the cumulative effect approach. However, all the recent FASB pronouncements require or permit the retroactive method whenever a new standard is adopted for the first time.

INTRAPERIOD TAX ALLOCATION

Allocation Within a Period

Whenever an extraordinary item, prior period adjustment, change in accounting principle, or discontinued operation occurs, most accountants believe that the resulting income tax effect should be directly associated with that event or item. In other words, the tax expense for the year should be related, where possible, to specific items on the income statement to provide a more informative disclosure to statement users. This procedure is called **intraperiod tax allocation.** Its main purpose is to relate the income tax expense to the following items which affect the amount of the tax provisions: (1) income from continuing operations, (2) discontinued operations, (3) extraordinary items, (4) changes in accounting principle, (5) net income, and (6) prior period adjustments. The general concept is "let the tax follow the income."

The income tax expense attributable to "income from continuing operations" is simply computed by ascertaining the income tax expense related to revenue and to expense transactions entering into the determination of this income. In this computation, no effect is given to the tax consequences of the items excluded from the determination of "income from continuing operations." The income tax expense attributable to other items is determined by the tax consequences of transactions involving these items. Because all these items are ordinarily material in amount, the applicable tax effect is also material and is disclosed separately and in close association with the related items.

Extraordinary Losses   For example, assume that a company has income before extraordinary items of $250,000 and an extraordinary loss from a major casualty of $100,000. Because the casualty is not expected to recur frequently, has a material effect, and is not considered a recurring factor in any evaluation of the ordinary operating processes of the business, it is reported as an extraordinary item. The loss is deductible for tax purposes, however. Therefore, if the income tax rate is assumed to be 48%, the income tax payable for the year will be calculated as follows:

Income before loss deduction	$250,000
Less loss from casualty	100,000
Taxable income	$150,000
Income tax payable at 48%	$ 72,000

The income tax expense applicable to the $250,000 income before extraordinary items is $120,000, and the tax reduction applicable to the loss of $100,000 from the major casualty is $48,000. If the tax reduction of $48,000 is **not** associated with the extraordinary loss, the income statement would appear incorrectly as follows:

Income before tax and extraordinary item	$250,000
Income tax	72,000
Income before extraordinary item	178,000
Loss from casualty	(100,000)
Net income	$ 78,000

The report above does not disclose an appropriate relationship between the income tax expense and "income before extraordinary item" and the "loss." Without the tax benefit of the loss, the $250,000 of operating income would have been taxed at the 48% rate for an income tax of $120,000. The income before extraordinary item then would have appeared as $130,000 instead of $178,000. Thus we have the paradoxical situation of a loss of $100,000 making the income before extraordinary item appear larger by $48,000 instead of smaller.

To avoid such a misleading presentation, we report the tax effect in the income statement along with the loss in the following way.

Income before tax and extraordinary item		$250,000
Income tax		120,000
Income before extraordinary item		130,000
Loss from casualty	$100,000	
Less applicable income tax reduction	48,000	(52,000)
Net income		$ 78,000

Or, it may be reported "net of tax" with footnote disclosure as illustrated below.

Income before tax and extraordinary item	$250,000
Income tax	120,000
Income before extraordinary item	130,000
Extraordinary item, less applicable income tax (note 1)	(52,000)
Net income	$ 78,000

Note 1. During the year the Company suffered a major casualty at a net loss of $52,000 after applicable income tax reduction of $48,000.

An example of a comprehensive footnote accompanying an "Extraordinary Charge . . . $262,000" reported by The Penn Traffic Company in its 1978 annual report is presented below.

Note 11—Extraordinary Charge: On July 20, 1977 a flash flood in the Johnstown, Pennsylvania area damaged the Company's milk processing and ice cream manufacturing plant and its largest department store. The resultant extraordinary charge is computed as follows:

Physical damage and other losses (net)		$2,039,000
Business interruption		525,000
Flood loss		2,564,000
Less: Insurance proceeds	$2,000,000	
Income tax benefits	302,000	2,302,000
Extraordinary charge		$ 262,000

Following the flood, the Company suspended all retail operations in the downtown area. The Company currently owns the building formerly used for the department store (239,700 square feet) and a supporting warehouse building (41,300 square feet). Disposition or alternative use of the two buildings is presently being investigated. The Company's milk and ice cream manufacturing plant was back in operation by September 1977.

Extraordinary Gains If a company realizes an extraordinary gain, the tax expense is allocated between the gain and the income before gain. If we assume a $100,000 extraordinary gain, the income statement disclosure is as follows.

Income before tax and extraordinary item		$250,000
Income tax (48%)		120,000
Income before extraordinary item		130,000
Extraordinary gain	$100,000	
Less applicable income tax	48,000	52,000
Net income		$182,000

Prior Period Adjustments The possibility of misleading reports resulting from carrying prior period adjustments directly to retained earnings also results unless the related tax effect is reported with the adjustment. Again, "let the tax follow the income" expresses the basic idea. A prior period adjustment having a current tax effect is disclosed in this statement of retained earnings as follows.

Retained earnings at beginning of year:		
As previously reported		$2,000,000
Correction of an error	$200,000	
Less applicable income tax reduction	96,000	(104,000)
Adjusted balance of retained earnings at beginning of year		1,896,000
Net income		160,000
Retained earnings at end of year		$2,056,000

Under this arrangement the net income for the year shows the income tax expense related to the revenue and expense transactions that determine such income.

Earnings Per Share

The results of a company's operations are customarily summed up in one important figure: net income. As if this condensation were not enough of a simplification of a complex operation, the financial world has widely accepted an even more distilled and compact figure as its most significant business indicator, "earnings per share."

"Net income per share" or "earnings per share" is a ratio commonly used in prospectuses, proxy material, and annual reports to stockholders, and in the compilation of business earnings data for the press and other statistical services. Because of the inherent dangers of focusing attention on earnings per share by itself, the profession concluded that **earnings per share must be disclosed on the face of the income statement.** In addition to net income per share, per share amounts should be shown for "income from continuing operations," "income before extraordinary items and cumulative effect of accounting changes," and "cumulative effect of changes in accounting principles." Reporting per share amounts for gain or loss on discontinued operations and gain or loss on extraordinary items is optional.

To illustrate comprehensively both the income statement order of presentation and the earnings per share data assume that Juarez Industries, Inc. had the following condensed income statement shown on page 147 and that 100,000,000 shares of stock have been outstanding for the entire year.

The earnings per share data also may be disclosed parenthetically by a corporation, as illustrated below (this form is especially applicable when only one per share amount is involved):

Net Income (per share $4.02)	$804,000

As indicated earlier, amounts for discontinued operations and extraordinary items need not be stated on a per-share basis. These per-share amounts can be determined simply by subtraction if not reported as separate per-share amounts. For example, General Mills reported $1.77 earnings per share before an extraordinary item and net income of $1.83. This means it had an extraordinary gain of $.06 per share net of income tax. It should be emphasized that the Juarez illustration is highly condensed, and that items such as the "Unusual Charge," "Discontinued Operation," "Extraordinary Item," and the "Change in Accounting Principle" would have to be described fully and appropriately in the statement or related footnotes. Additional earnings per share computations are also required for certain types of accounting changes which will be discussed in Chapter 23.

Many corporations have simple capital structures that include only common stock. For these companies, a presentation such as "earnings per common share" is appropriate on the income statement. In an increasing number of instances, however, companies' earnings per share are subject to dilution (reduction) in the future because existing contingencies permit the further issuance of common shares.[20] Examples of such instances are (1) outstanding preferred stock or debt that is convertible into common shares, (2) outstanding stock options or warrants, and (3)

[20]"Earnings Per Share," *Opinions of the Accounting Principles Board No. 15* (New York: AICPA, 1969), pars. 14 and 15.

Juarez Industries, Inc.
INCOME STATEMENT
For the Year Ended December 31, 1981
(000 Omitted)

Sales		$1,480,000
Cost of goods sold		600,000
Gross profit		880,000
Selling and administrative expenses		320,000
Income from operations		560,000
Other income and expense		
Interest income	$10,000	
Loss on disposal of part of Steel Division	(5,000)	
Unusual charge—loss on sales of investments	(45,000)	(40,000)
Income from continuing operations before income taxes		520,000
Income taxes		208,000
Income from continuing operations		312,000
Discontinued operations		
Income from operations of Hartley Division, less		
applicable income taxes of $36,000	54,000	
Loss on disposal of Hartley Division, less		
applicable income taxes of $60,000	(90,000)	(36,000)
Income before extraordinary item and cumulative		
effect of accounting change		276,000
Extraordinary item—loss from earthquake, less		
applicable income taxes of $30,000		(45,000)
Cumulative effect in prior years of retroactive application of new		
depreciation method, less applicable income taxes of $40,000		(60,000)
Net income		$ 171,000
Per Share of Common Stock		
Income from continuing operations		$3.12
Income from operations of discontinued division, net of tax		.54
Loss on disposal of discontinued operation, net of tax		(.90)
Income before extraordinary item and cumulative effect		2.76
Extraordinary loss, net of tax		(.45)
Cumulative effect of change in accounting principle, net of tax		(.60)
Net income		$1.71

agreements for the issuance of common shares for little or no consideration in the satisfaction of certain conditions (e.g., the attainment of specified levels of earnings following a business combination). The computational problems involved in accounting for these dilutive securities in earnings per share computations are discussed in Chapter 17.

In summary, the simplicity and availability of figures for per-share earnings lead inevitably to their widespread use. Because of the undue importance that the public, even the well-informed public, attaches to earnings per share, accountants have an obligation to make the earnings per share figure as meaningful as possible.

STATEMENT OF RETAINED EARNINGS

Reconciling Beginning and Ending Balances

A statement of retained earnings is generally included, together with an income statement and a balance sheet, in the financial statements of an enterprise. Actually, instead of being a statement that reports related data, it is a reconciliation of the balance of the retained earnings account from the beginning to the end of the year.

Every effort should be made to prepare as useful and informative a statement of retained earnings as possible. If the retained earnings account is to receive direct charges and credits for certain prior period adjustments, the income statement will not reveal all the necessary information about income. The statement of retained earnings must be studied in conjunction with the income statement; otherwise, important components of the results of operations may be overlooked. Therefore, the statement of retained earnings makes full use of descriptive terminology so that readers can relate the appropriate items to the income statement.

Some of the significant relationships and data recorded in the account for retained earnings that should be clearly disclosed in the statement are:

1. **Prior period adjustments.** Any adjustment that relates to prior periods indicates that one or more income statements for prior years was incorrect, and that the amounts shown as prior period adjustments do not appear in any prior income statement. Such items should be described clearly. Prior period adjustments normally require the restatement of prior period financial statements that are presented for comparative purposes.

2. **The relationship of dividend distributions to net income for the period.** An association of these two items indicates whether management is distributing all earnings, is "plowing" part of the earnings back into the business, or is distributing not only current income but also the accumulated earnings of prior years.

3. **Transfers to and from retained earnings.** Transfers to and from retained earnings may be made in accordance with contract requirements, a continuing policy, or the apparent necessity of the moment. In any case, the amounts of retained earnings appropriated for stated reasons and the amounts returned should be clearly arranged for evaluation by the user of the statement.

An example of a statement of retained earnings is as follows:

Fairfield Corporation		
STATEMENT OF RETAINED EARNINGS		
For the Year Ended December 31, 1981		
		(000's omitted)
Retained earnings January 1, 1981		$ 21,159
Add net income for the year		99,423
		120,582
Deduct dividends declared on:		
Preferred stock, at $5 per share	$15,000	
Common stock, at $7 per share	28,000	43,000
Retained earnings December 31, 1981		$ 77,582

Combined Statement of Income and Retained Earnings

Some accountants believe that the statements of income and retained earnings are so closely related that they present both statements in one combined report. The principal advantage of a combined statement is that all items affecting income, including operating items and prior period adjustments, appear in one statement. On the other hand, the figure of net income for the year is "buried" in the body of the statement, a feature that some find objectionable. There once was a definite trend toward this method of presentation, but at present this method is not gaining in favor. When a combined statement is prepared, the income statement is presented as if it were to be issued as an independent report but, instead of closing that statement with the amount of net income, the reconciliation of retained earnings is stated as below.

The Magnavox Company COMBINED STATEMENT OF INCOME AND RETAINED EARNINGS (lower portion only)	
Net income for the year	$ 42,290,385
Retained earnings at beginning of the year	106,734,310
	149,024,695
Cash dividends paid	15,764,250
Retained earnings at end of year	$133,260,445

If the company has other capital accounts such as Additional Paid-In Capital, a good practice is to present a statement of these accounts reconciling the beginning and ending balances. **APB Opinion No. 12,** for example, indicates that when both a balance sheet and income statement are presented, disclosure of changes in the separate accounts comprising stockholders' equity (such as Additional Paid-In Capital) is required to make the financial statement sufficiently informative. Disclosure of such changes takes the form of separate statements or is made either in the basic financial statements or in the footnotes.

Examples of income statements, retained earnings sections, and additional paid-in capital sections are presented in Appendix E (page 196) of Chapter 5 and in Chapter 16.

Questions

1. Why should caution be exercised in the use of the income figure derived in an income statement? What are the objectives of generally accepted accounting principles in their application in the income statement?
2. What is the difference between the capital maintenance approach to income measurement and the transaction approach? Is the final income figure the same under both approaches?
3. What are the advantages and disadvantages of the "single-step" income statement?
4. What usually are the main sections of a multiple-step income statement?

5. What are the advantages and disadvantages of a combined statement of income and retained earnings? What is the basis for distinguishing between operating and nonoperating items?

6. Distinguish between the "all-inclusive" income statement and the "current operating performance" income statement. According to present generally accepted accounting principles, which is recommended? Explain.

7. What is the significance of the materiality of an item in deciding the proper placement of a nonrecurring item in the statement of retained earnings or in the income statement? Explain.

8. How should prior-period adjustments be reported in the financial statements? Give an example of a prior period adjustment.

9. Discuss the appropriate treatment in the financial statements of each of the following:
   (a) Rent received from subletting a portion of the office space.
   (b) A patent infringement suit, brought two years ago against the company by another company, was settled this year by a cash payment of $108,000.
   (c) A reduction in the Allowance for Doubtful Accounts balance, because the account appears to be considerably in excess of the probable loss from uncollectible receivables.
   (d) An amount of $48,000 realized in excess of the cash surrender value of an insurance policy on the life of one of the founders of the company who died during the year.
   (e) A profit-sharing bonus to employees computed as a percentage of net income.
   (f) Additional depreciation on factory machinery because of an error in computing depreciation for the previous year.

10. Give the section of a multiple-step income statement in which each of the following is shown.
   (a) Loss on sale of machinery.
   (b) Interest expense.
   (c) Depreciation expense.
   (d) Material write-offs of notes receivable.
   (e) Bad debt expense.
   (f) Loss on disposal of a segment of the business.
   (g) Loss on inventory writedown.
   (h) Loss from strike.

11. Indicate where the following items would ordinarily appear on the financial statements of Fry Limited for the year 1980:
   (a) Fry Limited changes its depreciation from straight-line to double-declining on machinery in 1980. The cumulative effect of the change is $300,000 (net of tax).
   (b) In 1977, a supply warehouse with an expected useful life of seven years was erroneously expensed.
   (c) An income tax refund related to the 1977 tax year was received.
   (d) In 1980 the company wrote off one million dollars of inventory that was considered obsolete.
   (e) In 1980 an earthquake destroyed a warehouse that had a book value of $200,000. Earthquakes are rare in this locality.
   (f) The service life of certain equipment was changed from seven to five years. If a five-year life had been used previously, additional depreciation of $35,000 would have been charged.

12. What is meant by "tax allocation within a period"? What is the justification for such practice?

13. When does tax allocation within a period become necessary? How should this allocation be handled?

14. During 1980, the Jones Company earned income of $400,000 before federal income taxes and realized a gain of $300,000 on a government-forced condemnation sale of a division plant facility. The income is subject to federal income taxation at the rate of 48%; the gain on the sale of the plant is taxed at 25%. Proper accounting suggests that

the unusual gain be reported as an extraordinary item. Illustrate an appropriate presentation of these items in the income statement.

15. Recently Scott Paper Company decided to close two small pulp mills in Oconto Falls, Wisconsin and Anacortes, Washington. Would these closings be reported in a separate section entitled Discontinued Operations after Income from Continuing Operations? Discuss.

16. On January 30, 1979, a suit was filed against Olin Corporation under the Equal Rights amendment. On August 6, 1979, Olin Corporation agreed to settle the action and pay $180,000 in damages to certain current and former employees. How should this settlement be reported in the 1979 financial statements? Discuss.

17. What major types of items are reported in the retained earnings statement?

18. The controller for Harlight, Inc. is discussing the possibility of presenting a combined statement of income and retained earnings for the current year. Indicate a possible advantage and disadvantage of this presentation format.

19. Generally accepted accounting principles usually require the use of accrual accounting to "fairly present" income. If the cash receipts and disbursements method of accounting will "clearly reflect" taxable income, why does this method not usually also "fairly present" income?

20. State some of the more serious problems encountered in seeking to achieve the ideal measurement of periodic net income. Explain what accountants do as a practical alternative.

Cases

C4-1 Information concerning the operations of a corporation is presented in an income statement or in a combined "statement of income and retained earnings." Income statements are prepared on a "current operating performance" basis ("earning power concept") or an "all-inclusive" basis ("historical concept"). Proponents of the two types of income statements do not agree upon the proper treatment of material nonrecurring charges and credits.

Instructions

(a) Define "current operating performance" and "all-inclusive" as used above.

(b) Explain the differences in content and organization of a "current operating performance" income statement and an "all-inclusive" income statement. Include a discussion of the proper treatment of material nonrecurring charges and credits.

(c) Give the principal arguments for the use of each of the three statements, "all-inclusive" income statement, "current operating performance" income statement, and a combined "statement of income and retained earnings."

(AICPA adapted)

C4-2 The Ace Company was incorporated and began business on January 1, 1980. It has been successful and now requires a bank loan for additional working capital to finance expansion. The bank has requested an audited income statement for the year 1980. The bookkeeper for Ace Company provides you with the following income statement which Ace plans to submit to the bank:

INCOME STATEMENT

Sales		$932,100
Dividends		12,300
Gain on recovery of insurance proceeds from flood loss (extraordinary)		28,400
		972,800
Less:		
Selling expenses	$101,100	
Cost of goods sold	532,200	
Advertising expense	13,700	
Loss on obsolescence of inventories	34,000	
Loss on discontinued operations	48,600	
Administrative expense	73,400	803,000
Income before income taxes		169,800
Income taxes		84,300
Net income		$ 85,500

Instructions

Indicate the deficiencies in the income statement presented above. Assume that the company desires a single-step income statement.

C4-3 Holmes, Inc. is a real estate firm which derives approximately 30% of its income from the Executive Management Division, which manages apartment complexes. As auditor for Holmes, Inc., you have recently overheard the following discussion between the controller and financial vice-president.

VICE-PRESIDENT: If we sold the Executive Management Division, it seems ridiculous to segregate the results of the sale in the income statement. Separate categories tend to be absurd and confusing to the stockholders. I believe that we should simply report gain on the sale as other income or expense.

CONTROLLER: Professional pronouncements would require that we disclose this information separately in the income statement. If a sale of this type is considered unusual and infrequent, it must be reported as an extraordinary item.

VICE-PRESIDENT: What about the walkout we had last month when our employees were upset about their commission income? Would this situation not also be an extraordinary item?

CONTROLLER: I am not sure whether this item would be reported as extraordinary or not.

VICE-PRESIDENT: Oh well, it doesn't make any difference because the net effect of all these items is immaterial, so no disclosure is necessary.

Instructions

(a) Based on the foregoing discussion, answer the following questions: Who is correct about handling the sale? What would be the income statement presentation for the sale of the Executive Management Division?

(b) How should the walkout by the employees be reported?

(c) What do you think about the controller's observation on materiality?

(d) What facts can you give the group about the earnings per share implications of these topics?

C4-4 The vice-president of finance for Sloan, Inc. has recently been asked to discuss with the company's division controllers the proper accounting for extraordinary items. The vice-president prepared the factual situations presented below as a basis for discussion.

1. A large diversified company sells a block of shares from its portfolio of securities acquired for investment purposes.   *not extraordinary*
2. A company sells a block of common stock of a publicly traded company. The block of shares, which represents less than 10% of the publicly held company, is the only security investment the company has ever owned.   *extraordinary*
3. A company that operates a chain of warehouses sells the excess land surrounding one of its warehouses. When the company buys property to establish a new warehouse, it usually buys more land than it expects to use for the warehouse with the expectation that the land will appreciate in value. Twice during the past five years the company sold excess land.   *not extraordinary*
4. A textile manufacturer with only one plant moves to another location and sustains relocation costs of $400,000. *not extraordinary*
5. A company experiences a material loss in the repurchase of a large bond issue that has been outstanding for three years. The company regularly repurchases bonds of this nature.   *not extraordinary exception because of bond.*
6. A railroad experiences an unusual flood loss to part of its track system. Flood losses normally occur every three or four years.   *not extraordinary*
7. A machine tool company sells the only land it owns. The land was acquired ten years ago for future expansion, but shortly thereafter the company abandoned all plans for expansion but decided to hold the land for appreciation.   *extraordinary*
8. An earthquake destroys one of the oil refineries owned by a large multinational oil company. Earthquakes are rare in this geographical location.   *extraordinary*
9. A publicly held company has incurred a substantial loss in the unsuccessful registration of a bond issue.   *not extraordinary*
10. A large portion of a cigarette manufacturer's tobacco crops are destroyed by a hailstorm. Severe damage from hailstorms is rare in this locality.   *extraordinary*

Instructions

Determine whether the foregoing items should be classified as extraordinary items. Present a rationale for your position.

C4-5 The following financial statement was prepared by employees of the Cason Corporation.

Cason Corporation
STATEMENT OF INCOME AND RETAINED EARNINGS
Year Ended December 31, 1981

Revenues	
Gross sales, including sales taxes	$877,900
Less returns, allowances, and cash discounts	19,800
Net sales	858,100
Dividends, interest, and purchase discounts	30,250
Recoveries of accounts written off in prior years	13,850
Total revenues	902,200
Costs and expenses	
Cost of goods sold, including sales taxes	415,900
Salaries and related payroll expenses	60,500
Rent	19,100
Freight-in and freight-out	3,400
Bad debt expense	24,000
Addition to reserve for possible inventory losses	3,800
Total costs and expenses	526,700
Income before extraordinary items	375,500

Extraordinary items	
Loss on discontinued styles (note 1)	27,000
Loss on sale of marketable securities (note 2)	49,050
Loss on sale of warehouse (note 3)	86,350
Retroactive settlement of federal income taxes for 1980 and 1979 (note 4)	34,600
Total extraordinary items	197,000
Net income	178,500
Retained earnings at beginning of year	310,700
Total	489,200
Less: Federal income taxes	120,000
Cash dividends on common stock	21,900
Total	141,900
Retained earnings at end of year	$347,300
Net income per share of common stock	$1.81

Notes to the Statement of Income and Retained Earnings:

1. New styles and rapidly changing consumer preferences resulted in a $27,000 loss on the disposal of discontinued styles and related accessories.
2. The corporation sold an investment in marketable securities at a loss of $49,050. The corporation normally sells securities of this nature.
3. The corporation sold one of its warehouses at an $86,350 loss.
4. The corporation was charged $34,600 retroactively for additional income taxes resulting from a settlement in 1981. Of this amount, $17,000 was applicable to 1980, and the balance was applicable to 1979. Litigation of this nature is recurring for this company.

Instructions

Identify and discuss the weaknesses in classification and disclosure in the single-step Statement of Income and Retained Earnings above. You should explain why these treatments are weaknesses and what the proper presentation of the items is in accordance with recent professional pronouncements.

C4-6 As audit partner for Check and Doublecheck, you are in charge of reviewing the classification of unusual items that have occurred during the current year. The following items have come to your attention:

1. A construction company, at great expense, prepares a major proposal for a government loan. The loan is not approved. *operating expense, or other expense*
2. A water pump manufacturer has had large losses resulting from a strike by its employees early in the year. *operating expense*
3. Depreciation for a prior period was incorrectly understated by $47,000. The error was discovered in the current year. *retained earnings adjust retained Earnings beginning balance*
4. A large cattle rancher suffered a major loss because the state required that all cattle in the state be killed to halt the spread of a rare disease. Such a situation has not occurred in the state for twenty years. *extraordinary expense*
5. A food distributor that sells wholesale to supermarket chains and to fast-food restaurants (two major classes of customers) decides to discontinue the division that sells to one of the two classes of customers. *Disposal, operations discontinued operations*

6. An automobile dealer sells for $86,000 an extremely rare 1926 Type 37 Bugatti which it purchased for $15,000 ten years ago. The Bugatti is the only such display item the dealer owns. *Extraordinary*

7. A drilling company during the current year extended the estimated useful life of certain drilling equipment from 9 to 14 years. As a result, depreciation for the current year was materially lowered. *Operating Expense*

8. A food-processing company incorrectly overstated its ending inventory two years ago by a material amount. Inventory for all other periods is correctly computed. *offsetting error counterbalancing*

9. A retail outlet changed its computation for bad debt expense from 1% to ½ of 1% of sales because of changes in their customer clientele. *Operating Expense*

10. A mining concern sells a foreign subsidiary engaged in gold mining, although it (the seller) continues to engage in gold mining in other countries. *Operating Income other income*

11. A steel company changes from accelerated depreciation to straight-line depreciation in accounting for its plant assets. *Cumulative effect of changes in accounting principle*

Instructions

From the foregoing information, indicate in what section of the income statement or retained earnings statement these items should be classified. Provide a brief rationale for your position.

C4-7 R. D. Nair, controller for W & M, Inc., has recently prepared an income statement for 1981. Mr. Nair admits that he has not examined any recent professional pronouncements, but believes that the following presentation presents fairly the financial progress of this company during the current period.

W & M, Inc.
INCOME STATEMENT
For the Year Ended December 31, 1981

Sales			$347,852
Less: sales returns and allowances			6,320
Net sales			341,532
Cost of goods sold:			
Inventory, January 1, 1981		$ 50,235	
Purchases	$182,143		
Less: purchase discounts	3,142	179,001	
Cost of goods available for sale		229,236	
Inventory, December 31, 1981		37,124	
Cost of goods sold			192,112
Gross profit			149,420
Selling expenses		41,850	
Administrative expenses		32,142	73,992
Income before taxes			75,428
Other income			
Dividends received			31,000
			106,428
Income taxes			41,342
Net income			$ 65,086

W & M, Inc.
STATEMENT OF RETAINED EARNINGS
For the Year Ended December 31, 1981

Retained earnings, January 1, 1981			$176,000
Add			
Net income for 1981	$65,086		
Gain from casualty (net of tax)	10,000		
Gain on sale of plant assets	21,400	$ 96,486	
Deduct			
Loss on expropriation (net of tax)	8,000		
Cash dividends on common stock	30,000		
Correction of mathematical error in depreciating plant assets in 1979 (net of tax)	7,186	(45,186)	51,300
Retained earnings, December 31, 1981			$227,300

Instructions

(a) Determine whether these statements are prepared under the "current operating" or "all-inclusive" concept of income. Cite specific details.

(b) Which method do you favor and why?

(c) Which method must be used, and how should the information be presented? Common shares outstanding for the year are 100,000 shares.

For questionable items, use the classification that ordinarily would be appropriate.

Exercises

E4-1   Presented below is certain information pertaining to the Outer Space Attire Company:

Cash balance, January 1, 1981	$ 8,000
Accounts receivable, January 1, 1981	20,000
Collections from customers in 1981	180,000
Capital account balance, January 1, 1981	40,000
Total assets, January 1, 1981	60,000
Cash investment added, July 1, 1981	4,000
Total assets, December 31, 1981	68,000
Cash balance, December 31, 1981	10,000
Accounts receivable, December 31, 1981	27,000
Merchandise taken for personal use during 1981	10,000
Total liabilities, December 31, 1981	26,000

Instructions

Compute the net income for 1981.

E4-2   Presented below are changes in the account balances of Antler Manufacturing Co. during the current year, except for retained earnings.

	Increase (Decrease)		Increase (Decrease)
Cash	$ 80,000	Accounts payable	$ (26,000)
Accounts receivable (net)	14,000	Bonds payable	80,000
Inventory	126,000	Common stock	120,000
Investments	(42,000)	Additional paid-in capital	11,000

Instructions

Compute the net income for the current year, assuming that there were no entries in the retained earnings account except for a dividend payment of $26,000.

E4-3   Presented below are certain account balances of Dwyer, Inc.

Sales returns	$ 7,200	Ending inventory	$ 50,700
Sales discounts	18,100	Rental income	8,400
Selling expenses	98,800	Interest expense	10,300
Sales	372,400	Purchase allowances	8,200
Income taxes	33,000	Beginning retained earnings	105,300
Beginning inventory	42,400	Ending retained earnings	124,100
Purchases	184,200	Freight-in	10,100
Purchase discounts	17,300	Dividends earned	74,000
Administrative expenses	82,000		

Instructions

From the foregoing, compute the following: (a) Net revenue; (b) Cost of goods sold; (c) Net income; (d) Dividends declared during the current year.

E4-4   The financial records of Harbor, Inc. were destroyed by fire at the end of the current year. Fortunately the controller had kept certain statistical data related to the income statement as presented below.

1. The income tax rate is 45%.
2. Cost of goods sold amounts to $460,000.
3. Administrative expenses are 20% of cost of goods sold but only 8% of gross sales.
4. Four-fifths of the operating expenses relate to sales activities.
5. The beginning merchandise inventory was $88,000 and decreased 25% during the current year.
6. Sales discounts amount to $17,800.
7. 20,000 shares of common stock were outstanding for the entire year.
8. Interest expense was $28,000.

Instructions

From the foregoing information prepare an income statement for the current year in single-step form.

E4-5   Two accountants for the firm of Foot and Crossfoot are arguing about the merits of presenting an income statement on the basis of a multiple-step versus a single-step format. The discussion involves the following information related to Davis Company.

Administrative expense	
Officers' salaries	$ 6,000
Depreciation of office furniture and equipment	4,250
Purchase returns	6,150
Purchases	51,250
Rental revenue	16,650
Selling expense	
Transportation-out	4,450
Sales commissions	7,320
Depreciation of sales equipment	5,850
Merchandise inventory, beginning inventory	12,550
Merchandise inventory, ending inventory	14,150
Sales	77,450
Transportation-in	2,280
Income taxes	13,360
Interest expense on bonds payable	1,860

Instructions

(a) Prepare an income statement for the year 1981 using the multiple-step form. Common shares outstanding for 1981 are 50,000 shares.

(b) Prepare an income statement for the year 1981 using the single-step form.

(c) Which one do you prefer? Discuss.

E4-6 The bookkeeper of Kin-So Enterprises has compiled the following information from the company's records as a basis for an income statement for the year ended 12/31/81.

Merchandise inventory, 1/1/81	$ 85,000
Merchandise inventory, 12/31/81	71,000
Purchase returns and allowances	9,000
Net sales	952,000
Sales taxes payable	40,000
Depreciation on plant assets	
(75% selling, 25% administrative)	52,000
Dividends declared	22,000
Rental revenues	17,000
Interest on notes payable	10,000
Market appreciation on temporary investments	18,000
Merchandise purchases	389,000
Transportation-in—merchandise	45,000
Wages and salaries—sales	104,000
Materials and supplies—sales	29,500
Common stock outstanding (no. of shares)	10,000*
Income taxes	53,300
Wages and salaries—administrative	142,000
Other administrative expense	45,000

* Remained unchanged all year.

Instructions

(a) Prepare a multiple-step income statement.

(b) Prepare a single-step income statement.

(c) Which format do you prefer? Discuss.

E4-7 Presented below is information related to Sampler Square, Inc. for the year 1981. There were 10,000 shares of common stock outstanding during 1981. Assume that the loss due to damage from fire is an extraordinary item.

Purchases	$26,000
Interest income	6,000
Selling expense	20,000
Sales	80,000
Transportation-in	4,000
Administrative expenses	11,000
Income tax expense	12,000
Inventory, January 1, 1978	4,000
Inventory, December 31, 1978	6,000
Cash dividend paid ($5,000 declared)	4,000
Loss due to uninsured fire loss (net of tax)	10,000
Accrued rent payable	2,000
Appropriation for contingencies	12,000

Instructions

(a) Prepare a multiple-step income statement.

(b) Prepare a single-step income statement.

(c) Which format do you prefer? Discuss.

E4-8 Presented below is income statement information related to Fallon Corporation for the year 1981.

Earthquake damage (pretax extraordinary item, tax rate 25%)	$ 50,000
Purchases	575,000
Sales	850,000
Transportation-in	10,000
Purchase discounts	7,000
Inventory (beginning)	135,000
Sales returns and allowances	17,000
Selling expenses:	
Sales salaries	55,000
Depreciation expense—store equipment	12,000
Store supplies expense	9,000
Administrative expenses:	
Officers' salaries	45,000
Depreciation expense—building	11,900
Office supplies expense	7,000
Income tax applicable to uninsured earthquake	12,500
Inventory (ending)	140,000

In addition, the corporation has other income from dividends received of $30,000 and other expense of interest on notes payable of $9,000. There are 10,000 shares of common stock outstanding for the year. The tax rate on income is 40%.

Instructions

(a) Prepare a multiple-step income statement for 1981.

(b) Prepare a single-step income statement for 1981.

(c) Discuss the relative merits of the two income statements.

E4-9 Presented below is information related to O'Reilly, Inc. for the year 1981.

Net sales	$1,500,000
Cost of goods sold	900,000
Selling expenses	110,000
Administrative expenses	60,000
Dividend revenue	15,000
Interest revenue	6,000
Write-off of inventory due to obsolescence	60,000
Depreciation expenses omitted by accident in 1980	15,000
Casualty loss (extraordinary item)	20,000
Dividends declared	30,000
Retained earnings at December 31, 1980	2,500,000
Federal tax rate of 40% on all items	

Instructions

(a) Prepare a multiple-step income statement for 1981. Assume that 100,000 shares of common stock are outstanding.

(b) Prepare a separate statement of retained earnings at December 31, 1981.

E4-10 The following balances were taken from the books of the Modern Health Studios Corporation on December 31, 1981:

Interest income	$ 70,000
Sales	1,200,000
Sales returns and allowances	200,000
Sales discount	30,000
Inventory 1/1/81	225,000
Inventory 12/31/81	320,000
Purchases	700,000
Purchases returns and allowances	125,000
Purchase discounts	55,000
Selling expenses	150,000
Administrative and general expenses	100,000
Interest expense	30,000
Loss from flood damage (extraordinary item)	120,000

Income tax rates are:
(1) 50% on ordinary income.
(2) 25% on extraordinary gains and losses.

Instructions

Prepare a multiple-step income statement. Assume that 100,000 shares of common stock were outstanding during the year.

E4-11 During 1981 Becker Enterprises had pretax earnings of $500,000 exclusive of a realized and tax deductible loss of $200,000 from the condemnation of properties (extraordinary item). In addition, the company discovered that depreciation expense was overstated by $100,000 in 1976. Retained earnings at January 1, 1981, amounted to $1,000,000; dividends of $150,000 were paid on common stock during 1981. One hundred thousand shares of common stock were outstanding during 1981.

Assume that the income tax rate on income is 45% for both 1976 and 1981.

Instructions

Prepare a combined statement of income and retained earnings.

E4-12 The stockholders' equity section of Danna Corporation appears below as of December 31, 1981:

5% cumulative preferred stock, $50 par value, authorized 100,000 shares, outstanding 90,000 shares		$ 4,500,000
Common stock, $1.00 par, authorized and issued 10 million shares		10,000,000
Additional paid-in capital		20,000,000
Retained earnings Dec. 31, 1980	$200,000,000	
Net income	20,000,000	2,200,000
		$254,500,000

Net income for 1981 reflects a tax rate of 50%. Included in the net income figure is a loss of $10,000,000 (before tax) as a result of a major casualty loss (extraordinary item).

Instructions

Compute earnings per share data as it should appear on the financial statements of the Danna Corporation.

E4-13 The following information was taken from the records of Logan, Inc. for the year 1981. Income tax applicable to income from continuing operations, $250,000; income tax applicable to loss on discontinued operations, $30,000; income tax applicable to extraordinary gain, $40,000; income tax applicable to extraordinary loss, $20,000.

Retained earnings January 1, 1981	$ 500,000
Cost of goods sold	800,000
Selling expenses	200,000
Sales	1,600,000
Extraordinary gain	90,000
Loss on discontinued operations	100,000
Administrative expenses	110,000
Rent income	35,000
Extraordinary loss	50,000
Cash dividends declared	40,000

Shares outstanding during 1981 were 10,000 shares.

Instructions

(a) Prepare a single-step income statement for 1981. Include per share data.

(b) Prepare a combined single-step income and retained earnings statement.

(c) Which one do you prefer? Discuss.

Problems

P4-1 Selected accounts and related amounts appearing in the income statement and balance sheet columns of Roth Corporation for December 31 are listed in alphabetical order below.

Administrative expenses (total)	$105,000	Purchase discounts	$ 13,000
Capital stock	300,000	Rent income	15,000
Dividends declared and paid	40,000	Retained earnings (1/1)	230,000
Freight-in	10,500	Salaries payable	11,000
Gain on sale of land	10,000	Sales	960,000
Merchandise inventory (1/1)	87,500	Sales discounts	7,500
Merchandise inventory (12/31)	92,500	Sales returns	13,500
Purchases	587,500	Selling expenses (total)	186,000

The gain on sale of land is not an extraordinary item. All income is taxed at a uniform rate of 45% except for the gain on sale of land, which is taxed at a 30% rate.

Instructions

Prepare a combined statement of income and retained earnings using the single-step form. Assume that the only change in the unappropriated retained earnings balance during the current year was for dividends. Ten thousand shares of common stock were outstanding during the entire year.

P4-2 The president of Sue Kinney Corporation provides you with the following account balances as of 12/31/81.

	Dr.	Cr.
Sales		$2,500,000
Sales office salaries	$ 180,000	
Officers' salaries	195,000	
Building depreciation (50% of building is directly related to sales)	90,000	
Freight-out	50,000	
Cost of goods sold	1,050,000	
Dividends paid	75,000	
Dividends received		45,000
Interest expense—7% bonds	60,000	
Retained earnings—1/1/81		250,000
Expropriation of foreign holdings (extraordinary item)	500,000	
Damages payable from litigation		75,000
Federal income taxes paid	172,500	

The president informs you that the damages payable from litigation arose in 1981 out of a lawsuit initiated in 1977, and the bookkeeper debited retained earnings for $75,000. Assume that the company is continually involved in litigation of this nature. The bookkeeper had also credited cash for $172,500 in payment of the federal income taxes for 1981. The president requests your help in constructing an income statement. She advises you that the corporation had 100,000 shares of common stock outstanding, and was taxed at a straight rate of 50% on all income-related items.

Instructions

(a) Prepare a combined statement of income and retained earnings in multiple-step form.

(b) Prepare a combined statement of income and retained earnings in single-step form.

P4-3 The following account balances were included in the trial balance of the Stender Equipment Corporation at June 30, 1981.

Sales	$1,485,625
Sales returns	18,352
Purchases	895,450
Freight-in	20,500
Purchase returns	5,150
Purchase discounts	18,670
Sales salaries	31,750
Sales commissions	88,700
Travel expense—salespersons	23,650
Freight-out	19,500
Entertainment expense	15,150
Telephone and telegraph—sales	8,700
Depreciation of sales equipment	4,980
Building expense—prorated to sales	6,200
Miscellaneous selling expenses	2,980
Office supplies	3,450
Telephone and telegraph—administration	2,820
Depreciation of office furniture and equipment	5,340
Real estate and other local taxes	6,525
Bad debt expense—administrative	4,315
Building expense—prorated to administration	8,210
Miscellaneous office expenses	3,570
Sales discounts	22,450
Dividends received	25,000
Bond interest expense	14,000
Income taxes	93,400
Depreciation understatement due to error—1978 (net of tax)	6,680
Dividends on preferred stock	9,000
Dividends on common stock	32,000
Merchandise inventory—July 1, 1980	225,000

The merchandise inventory at June 30, 1981 amounted to $255,000. The Unappropriated Retained Earnings account had a balance of $195,000 at June 30, 1981, before closing; the only entry in that account during the year was a debit of $35,000 to establish an Appropriation for Bonded Indebtedness. There are 100,000 shares of common stock outstanding.

Instructions

(a) Using the multiple-step form, prepare a combined statement of income and unappropriated retained earnings for the year ended June 30, 1981.

(b) Using the single-step form, prepare a combined statement of income and unappropriated retained earnings for the year ended June 30, 1981.

P4-4   Below is the Retained Earnings account for the year 1981 for Haley, Inc.

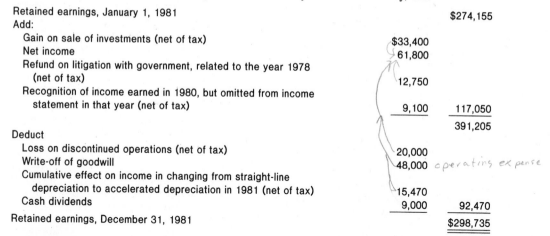

Retained earnings, January 1, 1981		$274,155
Add:		
Gain on sale of investments (net of tax)	$33,400	
Net income	61,800	
Refund on litigation with government, related to the year 1978		
(net of tax)	12,750	
Recognition of income earned in 1980, but omitted from income		
statement in that year (net of tax)	9,100	117,050
		391,205
Deduct		
Loss on discontinued operations (net of tax)	20,000	
Write-off of goodwill	48,000	*operating expense*
Cumulative effect on income in changing from straight-line		
depreciation to accelerated depreciation in 1981 (net of tax)	15,470	
Cash dividends	9,000	92,470
Retained earnings, December 31, 1981		$298,735

Instructions

(a) Prepare a statement of Retained Earnings. Haley, Inc. normally sells investments of the type mentioned above.

(b) State where the items that do not appear in the Retained Earnings statement should be shown.

P4-5   Presented below is information related to the Hope Company for 1981.

Retained earnings balance January 1, 1981	$ 980,000
Sales for the year	25,000,000
Cost of goods sold	17,000,000
Interest income	50,000
Selling and administrative expenses	5,000,000
Write-off of goodwill (not tax deductible)	500,000
Federal income taxes for the year	1,100,000
Assessment for additional 1977 income taxes (normally recurring)	250,000
Gain on the sale of investments	90,000
Loss from operation of discontinued foreign subsidiary (net of tax)	350,000
Loss from disposal of foreign subsidiary (net of tax)	450,000
Dividends declared on common stock RE	250,000
Dividends declared on preferred stock RE	75,000

Instructions

Prepare a combined statement of income and retained earnings using the single-step form. Hope Company ordinarily sells investments of the type mentioned above. The loss from disposal of a foreign subsidiary should be considered a loss from discontinued operations. There were 500,000 shares of common stock outstanding during 1981.

P4-6   Mandell Company has 100,000 shares of common stock outstanding. In 1981, the company reports income from continuing operations before taxes of $1,570,000. Additional transactions not considered in the $1,570,000 are as follows:

1. In 1981, Mandell Company sold equipment for $86,000. The machine had originally cost $68,000 and had accumulated depreciation of $26,000. The gain or loss (considered ordinary) is taxed at the rate of 40%.

2. The company discontinued operations of one of its subsidiaries during the current year at a loss of $180,000 before taxes. Assume that this transaction meets the criteria for discontinued operations. The loss on operations of the discontinued subsidiary was $80,000 before taxes; the loss from disposal of the subsidiary was $100,000 before taxes.

3. The sum of $84,000, applicable to a breached 1977 contract, was received as a result of a lawsuit. Prior to the award, legal counsel was uncertain about the outcome of the suit and had not established a receivable.

4. In 1981 the company reviewed its accounts receivable and wrote off as an expense of that year $18,400 of accounts receivable that had been carried for years and appeared unlikely to be collected.

5. An internal audit discovered that amortization of intangible assets was understated by $32,000 (net of tax) in a prior period. The amount was charged against retained earnings.

6. The company sold its only investment in common stock during the year at a gain of $120,000. The gain is taxed at a rate of 25%. Assume that the transaction meets the requirements of an extraordinary item.

Instructions

Prepare an income statement for the year 1981 starting with income from continuing operations before taxes. Compute earnings per share as it should be shown on the face of the income statement. (Assume a tax rate of 40% on all items, unless indicated otherwise.)

P4-7 The Gabriel Corporation reported income from continuing operations before taxes during 1981 of $720,000. Additional transactions occurring in 1981 but not considered in the $720,000 are as follows:

1. Securities sold as a part of its portfolio resulted in a loss of $80,000 (pretax).

2. When its president died, the corporation realized $90,000 in an insurance policy. The cash surrender value of this policy had been carried on the books as an investment in the amount of $51,000 (the gain is nontaxable).

3. The corporation disposed of its recreational division at a loss of $80,000 before taxes. Assume that this transaction meets the criteria for discontinued operations.

4. The corporation decided to change its method of inventory pricing from average cost to the FIFO method. The effect of this change on prior years is to increase 1979 income by $60,000 and decrease 1980 income by $20,000 before taxes. The FIFO method has been used for 1981. The tax rate on these items is 40%.

5. The corporation experienced an uninsured flood loss (extraordinary) in the amount of $50,000 during the year. The tax rate on this item is 45%.

6. At the beginning of 1979, the corporation purchased a machine for $72,000 (salvage value of $6,000) that had a useful life of six years. The bookkeeper uses straight-line depreciation, but failed to deduct the salvage value in computing the depreciation base.

Instructions

Prepare an income statement for the year 1981 starting with income from continuing operations before taxes. Compute earnings per share as it should be shown on the face of the income statement. Common shares outstanding for the year are 10,000 shares. (Assume a tax rate of 45% on all items, unless indicated otherwise.)

P4-8 The Merill Corporation commenced business on January 1, 1977. Recently the corporation has had several unusual accounting problems related to the presentation of their income statement for financial reporting purposes.

You have been the CPA for Merill Corporation for several years and have been asked to examine the following data.

Merill Corporation
STATEMENT OF INCOME
For the Year Ended December 31, 1981

Sales	$9,500,000
Cost of goods sold	6,000,000
Gross profit	3,500,000

Selling and administrative expense	1,250,000
Income before income taxes	2,250,000
Income tax (40%)	900,000
Net income	$1,350,000

In addition, this information was provided:

1. Retained earnings as of January 1, 1981 was $3,600,000. Cash dividends of $500,000 were paid in 1981.

2. In January, 1981, Merill Corporation changed its method of accounting for plant assets from the straight-line method to the accelerated method (double-declining balance). The controller has prepared a schedule indicating what depreciation expense would have been in previous periods if the double-declining method had been used. (The effective tax rate for 1978, 1979, and 1980 was 30%.)

	Depreciation Expense under Straight-Line	Depreciation Expense under Double-Declining	Difference
1978	$ 90,000	$140,000	$50,000
1979	90,000	121,000	31,000
1980	90,000	105,000	15,000
	$270,000	$366,000	$96,000

3. In 1981, Merill discovered that two errors were made in previous years. First, when it took a physical inventory at the end of 1978, one of the count sheets was apparently lost. The ending inventory for 1978 was therefore understated by $80,000. The inventory was correctly taken in 1979, 1980, and 1981. Also, the corporation found that in 1980 it had failed to record $16,000 as an expense for sales commissions. The effective tax rate for 1978, 1979, and 1980 was 30%. The sales commissions for 1980 are included in 1981 expenses.

4. The controller mentioned that the corporation has had difficulty in collecting on several of their receivables. For this reason, the bad debt write-off was increased to 1½% of sales from 1%. The controller estimates that if this rate had been used in past periods, an additional $25,000 worth of expense would have been charged. The bad debt expense for the current period was calculated and is part of selling and administrative expense.

5. Common shares outstanding at the end of 1981 totaled 1,000,000. No additional shares were purchased or sold during 1981.

6. Merill noted also that

   (a) Inventory in the amount of $48,000 was obsolete.

   (b) The major casualty loss suffered by the corporation was partially uninsured and cost $60,000, net of tax (extraordinary item).

Instructions

Prepare the income statement for Merill Corporation in accordance with professional pronouncements. Do not prepare footnotes.

P4-9 A condensed statement of income and retained earnings of the Macon Company for the year ended December 31, 1981 is presented below.

Presented below are three unrelated situations involving accounting changes and classification of certain items as ordinary or extraordinary. Each situation is based upon the condensed statements of income and retained earnings of the Macon Company shown above and requires revisions of these statements.

The Macon Company
CONDENSED STATEMENTS OF INCOME
AND RETAINED EARNINGS
For The Year Ended 1981

Sales	$5,000,000
Cost of goods sold	2,800,000
Gross margin	2,200,000
Selling, general, and administrative expenses	1,500,000
Income before extraordinary item	700,000
Extraordinary item	(500,000)
Net income	200,000
Retained earnings, January 1	800,000
Retained earnings, December 31	$1,000,000

Situation A

At the end of 1981, Macon's management decided that the estimated loss rate on uncollectible accounts receivable was too low. The loss rate used for the years 1980 and 1981 was 1% of total sales, and owing to an increase in the write-off of uncollectible accounts, the rate has been raised to 3% of total sales. The amount recorded in bad debt expense under the heading of selling, general, and administrative expenses for 1981 was $50,000 and for 1980 was $30,000.

The extraordinary item in the condensed statement of income and retained earnings for 1981 relates to a loss incurred in the abandonment of outmoded equipment formerly used in the business.

Situation B

On January 1, 1979, Macon acquired machinery at a cost of $200,000. The Company adopted the double-declining balance method of depreciation for this machinery, and had been recording depreciation over an estimated life of ten years, with no residual value. At the beginning of 1981, a decision was made to adopt the straight-line method of depreciation for this machinery. Owing to an oversight, however, the double-declining balance method was used for 1981. For financial reporting purposes, depreciation is included in selling, general, and administrative expenses.

The extraordinary item in the condensed statement of income and retained earnings relates to shutdown expenses incurred by the Company during a major strike by its operating employees during 1981.

Situation C

During the latter part of 1981, the company discontinued its retail and apparel fabric divisions. The results of such operations and the loss on sale of these two discontinued divisions amounted to a total loss of $500,000. This amount was considered part of selling, general, and administrative expenses. The transaction meets the criteria for discontinued operations.

The extraordinary item in the condensed statement of income and retained earnings for 1981 relates to a loss sustained as a result of damage to the company's merchandise caused by a tornado that struck its main warehouse in Beaumont City. This natural disaster was considered an unusual and infrequent occurrence for that section of the country.

Instructions

For each of the three unrelated situations, prepare a revised condensed statement of income and retained earnings of the Macon Company. Ignore income tax considerations and earnings per share computations.

(AICPA adapted)

5

Balance Sheet and Statement of Changes in Financial Position

Investors have often directed their attention primarily toward examination of the income statement and earnings per share to the virtual exclusion of the balance sheet and statement of changes in financial position. However, the recent high inflation rates, coupled with the related credit "crunches of the 1970's," have taught investors an important lesson—many surprises in earnings per share could have been discovered if more attention had been given to these forgotten financial statements. Liquidity and financial flexibility are necessary conditions for any profitable enterprise, and only through careful analysis of balance sheets and statements of changes in financial position can this information be obtained.

Usefulness of the Balance Sheet[1]

Although the income statement is generally conceded to be the most important financial statement for judging the economic well-being of an enterprise, the balance sheet also provides useful information if examined carefully. Evaluation of liquidity, which is a measure of the cushion available to meet debt as due, is extremely important. Therefore, both short-term and long-term credit grantors will be interested in such short-term measures as cash or near cash to current liabilities to assess the enterprise's cushion to meet obligations in case of financial difficulties. In addition, long-term creditors and present or prospective stockholders can

---

[1]*Accounting Trends and Techniques—1978* indicated that 89% of the companies surveyed used the term "balance sheet." The term "statement of financial position" is used infrequently, although it is conceptually appealing.

employ the balance sheet to evaluate the **financial flexibility** of the enterprise. For example, some companies become so loaded with debt that their sources of monies to finance expansion or to pay off maturing debt are limited or nonexistent. Such situations lead to the subsequent sale of stock which often substantially dilutes the earnings per share figure. In evaluating liquidity and financial flexibility, the balance sheet then provides a basis for **predicting or forecasting future events.** For example, a recent examination of General Motors' balance sheet indicated that it had approximately $1.6 billion in excess cash. This may suggest the possibility of either an increase in dividends or the initiation of new investment projects.

Management must also be concerned about the composition of the assets and liabilities for the reasons mentioned above. The balance sheet provides useful measures for controlling enterprise solvency, analyzing the cost of new financing, and determining the flexibility available for altering the basic capital structure.

Limitations of the Balance Sheet

The AICPA has stated that a balance sheet "presents an indication in conformity with generally accepted accounting principles of the financial status of the enterprise at a particular point of time."[2] Herein lie many of the criticisms concerning the balance sheet.

As indicated in Chapter 2, the balance sheet **does not reflect current value** because accountants have adopted an historical cost basis in valuing and reporting the assets and liabilities. When a balance sheet, for example, is prepared in accordance with generally accepted accounting principles, most assets are stated at cost; exceptions are receivables, marketable securities, and some long-term investments. Many accountants believe that all the assets should be restated in terms of current values; there are, however, widely different opinions about the exact type of valuation basis to be employed. Some contend that historical statements should be adjusted for constant dollars (general price-level changes) when inflation is significant; others believe that a current cost concept (specific price-level changes) is more useful; and yet others believe that a fair market value concept should be adopted. Regardless of the method favored, all are significantly different from the historical cost approach. Each approach has the advantage over the historical cost basis of presenting a more accurate assessment of the current value of the enterprise, although the question of whether objective values can be obtained is still unresolved. These issues are discussed further in Chapter 25.

Another basic limitation of historical cost statements is that **estimates must be utilized.** Even if significant changes in the price level do not occur, the determination of the collectibility of receivables, the salability of inventory, and the useful life of long-term tangible and intangible assets are difficult to determine. Although the depreciation of long-term assets is a generally accepted practice, the recognition of accretion and enhancement in value is generally ignored by accountants for similar fixed assets.

In addition, the balance sheet necessarily **omits many items that are of financial value to the business** but cannot be recorded objectively. As indicated earlier, the

[2]Accounting Principles Board, *Basic Concepts and Accounting Principles Underlying Financial Statements of Business Enterprises,* Statement No. 4 (New York: AICPA, 1970), par. 3.

value of a company's human resources is certainly significant, but it is omitted because such assets are difficult to quantify as a result of the uncertainty surrounding their ultimate value.

CLASSIFICATION IN THE BALANCE SHEET

In the balance sheet accounts are classified so that similar items are grouped together to arrive at significant subtotals; furthermore, the material is arranged so that important relationships are shown and attention is focused on the most important items.

The three general classes of items included in the balance sheet are assets, liabilities, and owners' equity. Here is how we defined them in Chapter 2.

1. **Assets.** Financial representations of economic resources—cash and future economic benefits—the beneficial interest in which is legally or equitably secured to a particular enterprise as a result of a past transaction or event affecting the enterprise.
2. **Liabilities.** Financial representations of obligations of a particular enterprise to transfer economic resources to other entities in the future as a result of a past transaction or event affecting the enterprise.
3. **Owners' Equity.** Residual interest in the enterprise's assets remaining after deducting liabilities. It is the interest of owners who bear the ultimate risks and uncertainties of enterprise earning and financing activities and the effect of other events and circumstances that may affect the enterprise and who obtain the rewards from enterprise successes.

These items are then divided into several subclassifications that provide the reader with additional information. The table below indicates the general format of balance sheet presentation.

BALANCE SHEET	
ASSETS	LIABILITIES AND OWNERS' EQUITY
Current assets	Current liabilities
Noncurrent assets	Noncurrent liabilities
Investments	Owners' equity
Property, plant, and equipment	Capital stock
Intangible assets	Additional paid-in capital
Other assets	Retained earnings

The balance sheet may be classified in some other manner, but these are the major subdivisions of this statement, and there is very little departure from them in practice. If a proprietorship or partnership is involved, the classifications within the owners' equity section are presented slightly differently.

Current Assets

Current assets are cash and other assets that are expected to be converted into cash, sold, or consumed either in one year or in the operating cycle, whichever is longer. For this purpose, the operating cycle of any given enterprise is considered to be the average time between the acquisition of materials and supplies and the realization of cash through sales of the product for which the materials and supplies were acquired. Thus the time it takes to process the material, to sell the product, and to collect from customers is included in the operating cycle. The cycle operates from cash through inventory and receivables back to cash. This definition ignores the arbitrary one-year period except when there are several operating cycles within one year; then the one-year period is used. If the operating cycle is more than one year, the longer period is used.

Current assets are presented in the balance sheet in the order of their liquidity. The five major items found in the current section are cash, marketable securities, receivables, inventories, and prepayments. **Cash** is included at its stated value; **marketable securities** are valued at cost or the lower of cost or market; **accounts receivable** are stated at the estimated amount collectible; **inventories** generally are included at cost or the lower of cost or market; and **prepaid items** are valued at cost.

These items are not considered current assets if they are not realized in one year or in the operating cycle, whichever is longer. For example, cash restricted for purposes other than payment of current obligations or for use in current operations is excluded from the current asset section. **Generally, the rule is that if an asset is to be turned into cash or is to be used to pay a current liability within a year or the operating cycle, whichever is longer, it is classified as current.** This requirement is subject to exceptions. Marketable securities, for example, pose a problem. Depending on the intent of management, an investment in common stock is classified as either a current asset or a noncurrent asset. The problem is especially difficult when a company has small holdings of common stocks or bonds of another company. Should these assets be classified as current? At this point, the differentiation can be made only on the basis of intent: What does the company plan to do with these securities?

Note also that although a current asset is well defined, certain theoretical problems develop. One problem is justifying the inclusion of prepaid expense in the current asset section. The normal justification is that if these items had not been paid in advance, they would require the use of current assets during the operating cycle. If we follow this logic to its ultimate conclusion, however, any asset purchased previously saves the use of current assets during the operating cycle and is considered current. Prepaid expenses are not material in amount, however, and their placement on the balance sheet has been of little concern.

Another problem occurs in the current asset definition when fixed assets are consumed during the operating cycle. A literal interpretation of the accounting profession's position on this matter would indicate that an amount equal to the current depreciation and amortization charges on the noncurrent assets should be placed in the current asset section at the beginning of the year, because they will be consumed in the next operating cycle. This conceptual problem is generally ignored, which illustrates that the formal distinction made between current and noncurrent assets is, nonetheless, "flexible."[3]

[3]For an interesting discussion of the shortcomings of the current and noncurrent classification framework, see Loyd Heath, "Financial Reporting and the Evaluation of Solvency," *Accounting Research Monograph No. 3* (New York: AICPA, 1978), pp. 43–69. The principal recommendation is that the current and noncurrent classification be abolished, and that assets and liabilities simply be listed without classification in their present order. This approach is justified on the basis that any classification scheme is arbitrary and that users of the financial statements can assemble the data in the manner they believe most appropriate.

Cash Any restrictions on the general availability of cash or any commitments on its probable disposition must be disclosed.

Current assets		
Cash		
Restricted in accordance with terms of the purchase contract	$48,500.00	
Unrestricted—available for current use	14,928.92	$63,428.92

In the example above, it was assumed that the necessary amount of cash ($48,500) was restricted to meet an obligation due currently and, therefore, the restricted cash was included under current assets. If cash is restricted for purposes other than current obligations, it is excluded from the current assets, as shown below:

Current assets		
Cash	$78,327.45	
Less cash restricted for additions to plant	45,000.00	$33,327.45
Other assets		
Cash restricted for additions to plant in accordance with action of the board of directors		$45,000.00

Short-Term Investments The basis of valuation and any differences between cost and current market value should be included in the balance sheet presentation of short-term investments. The generally accepted method for accounting for short-term investments, often referred to as marketable securities, is cost or market, whichever is lower.[4]

Current assets	
Marketable securities—at cost which approximates market	$26,342.00

Receivables Any anticipated loss due to uncollectibles, the amount and nature of any nontrade receivables, and any amounts pledged or discounted should be clearly stated.

---

[4]Special rules that apply for both short-term and long-term marketable securities are discussed in Chapters 7 and 18. "Accounting for Certain Marketable Securities," *Statement of Financial Accounting Standards No. 12* (Stamford, Conn.: FASB, 1975).

Current assets		
Notes and accounts receivable		
Customers—		
Notes	$ 35,000.00	
Accounts (of which $40,000 are pledged as		
security for a note payable)	146,528.75	
Subsidiary company	18,247.12	
Officers and employees	17,912.11	
	217,687.98	
Less allowance for doubtful accounts	11,200.00	$206,487.98

Inventories For a proper presentation of inventories, the basis of valuation, the method of pricing, and, for a manufacturing concern, the stage of completion of the inventories are disclosed.

Current assets		
Inventories—at the lower of cost (determined		
by the first-in, first-out method) or market		
Finished goods	$ 47,258.91	
Work in process	12,246.88	
Raw materials	188,764.21	$248,270.00

Some accountants contend that, in a company that assembles a final product from both purchased and manufactured parts and also sells some of these parts, a distinction among work in process, finished goods, and raw materials is arbitrary and misleading. They prefer a classification that indicates the source or nature of the inventory amount as shown below.

Current assets		
Inventories—at the lower of cost (determined		
by the first-in, first-out method) or market		
Materials	$103,856.18	
Direct labor	74,212.11	
Manufacturing overhead	70,201.71	$248,270.00

Current Liabilities

Current liabilities are the obligations that are reasonably expected to be liquidated either through the use of current assets or the creation of other current liabilities. This concept includes:

1. Payables resulting from the acquisition of goods and services: accounts payable, wages payable, taxes payable, and so on.
2. Collections received in advance for the delivery of goods or performance of services; for example, prepaid rent income or prepaid subscriptions income.

3. Other liabilities whose liquidation will take place within the operating cycle. This includes long-term liabilities such as bonds to be paid in the current period, or short-term obligations arising from purchase of equipment.

At times, even though a liability will be paid next year, it is not included in the current liability section. This occurs either when the debt is expected to be refinanced through another long-term issue,[5] or when the retirement of the debt occurs out of noncurrent assets. This approach is used because liquidation does not result from the use of current assets or the creation of other current liabilities. Current liabilities frequently are reported on the balance sheet in the order they will be paid.

Here is an example of a current liability section.

Current liabilities		
Notes payable to bank (secured by pledge of raw materials inventory)		$ 45,000.00
Accounts payable		
Trade	$185,917.18	
Customers' deposits and advances	32,412.81	
Employees' payroll deductions	18,912.88	237,242.87
Bank overdraft		7,245.12
Current maturities of installment note payable, secured by lien against land and buildings		50,000.00
Dividend payable		18,000.00
Income taxes		23,000.00
Miscellaneous accrued liabilities		17,245.86 $397,733.85

Current liabilities include such items as trade payables, nontrade notes and accounts payable, advances received from customers, and current maturities of long-term debt. Income taxes and other accrued items are classified separately, if material. Any secured liability, e.g., stock held as collateral on notes payable, is fully described so that the assets providing the security can be determined.

Long-Term Investments

Long-term investments, often referred to simply as investments, normally consist of one of three types:

1. Investments in securities such as bonds, common stock, or long-term notes.
2. Investments in tangible fixed assets not currently used in operations, such as land held for speculation.
3. Investments set aside in special funds such as a sinking fund, pension fund, or plant expansion fund. The cash surrender value of life insurance is included here.

Long-term investments are to be held for many years, and are not acquired with the intention of disposing of them in the near future. Long-term investments are

---

[5]A detailed discussion of accounting for debt expected to be refinanced is found in Chapter 10 and in "Classification of Short-term Obligations Expected to Be Refinanced," *Statement of Financial Accounting Standards No. 6* (Stamford, Conn.: FASB, 1975).

usually presented on the balance sheet just below Current Assets in a separate section called Investments. Many securities that are properly shown among the long-term investments are readily marketable but should not be included as current assets if they were not acquired or are not held with the intention of converting them to cash in a year or in the operating cycle, whichever is longer.

Investments			
Investments in subsidiary companies—at equity			
Leelco, Inc.			
1,000 shares (45%) of			
capital stock	$86,425		
Cash advance	10,000	$96,425	
Career Co., Inc.			
2,000 shares (40%) of capital stock		42,000	$138,425
Miscellaneous other investments—			
at cost,[6] which is approximately			
$13,500 below current market value		84,600	$223,025

Property, Plant and Equipment and Intangible Assets

Property, plant and equipment are properties of a durable nature used in the regular operations of the business. These assets consist of physical property such as land, buildings, machinery, furniture, tools, and wasting resources (timberland, minerals). With the exception of land, most assets are either depreciable (e.g., buildings) or consumable (e.g., timberlands).

Property, plant and equipment			
Land		$ 80,000	
Buildings	$420,000		
Less accumulated depreciation	176,000	244,000	
Buildings in process of construction—			
at cost to date (subject to the first			
mortgage lien of $200,000)		230,000	$554,000
Intangible assets			
Franchise—			
at cost less amortization of $4,712		8,244	
Licenses, trademarks, and patents—			
at cost less amortization of $12,444		16,556	
Goodwill—at cost less amortization of $10,000		70,000	94,800

Intangible assets lack physical substance. They include, for example, patents, copyrights, franchises, goodwill, trademarks, trade names, and secret processes.

---

[6]Noncurrent investments in marketable equity securities are required to be reported at the lower of cost or market unless the equity method of accounting is used. See discussion of *FASB Statement No. 12* in Chapter 18.

Generally, all of these intangibles are written off (amortized) against income. Intangibles can represent significant economic resources, yet financial analysts often ignore them, and accountants write them down or off arbitrarily because valuation is difficult. Intangibles are not generally capitalized and amortized unless acquired in arm's-length transactions.

The basis of valuing the property, plant and equipment and intangible assets, any liens against the properties, and accumulated depreciation should be shown. It is seldom advisable to show a detailed classification of the property, plant and equipment in the balance sheet; a supplementary schedule or analysis generally provides a better means of presenting such information.

Other Assets

The items included in the section "Other Assets" vary widely in practice. Some of the items commonly included are deferred charges (long-term prepaid expenses), noncurrent receivables, intangible assets, assets in special funds, and advances to subsidiaries. Such a section unfortunately is too general a classification. Instead, this classification should be restricted to unusual items sufficiently different from assets included in the categories above. Some deferred costs such as organization costs incurred during the early life of the business are commonly classified here. Even these costs, however, are more properly placed in the intangible asset section.

Long-Term Liabilities

Long-term liabilities are obligations that are not reasonably expected to be liquidated within the normal operating cycle of the business but, instead, are payable at some date beyond that time. Bonds payable, notes payable, deferred income taxes, lease obligations, and pension obligations are the most common long-term liabilities. Generally, a great deal of supplementary disclosure is needed for this section because most long-term debt is subject to various covenants and restrictions for the protection of the lenders. Long-term liabilities that mature within the current operating cycle are classified as current liabilities if their liquidation requires the use of assets included in the current asset group.

Generally, **long-term liabilities are of three types:**

1. Obligations arising from specific financing situations where additional assets are acquired, such as the issuance of bonds, long-term lease obligations, and long-term notes payable.
2. Obligations arising from the ordinary operations of the enterprise such as pension obligations and deferred income taxes.
3. Obligations that are dependent upon the occurrence or nonoccurrence of one or more future events to confirm the amount payable, or the payee, or the date payable, such as service or product warranties.

For issued bonds payable it is desirable to report any premium or discount separately as an addition to or subtraction from the bonds payable. The terms of all long-term liability agreements including maturity date or dates, rates of interest, nature of obligation, and any security pledged to support the debt should be described as illustrated below.

Long-term liabilities			
First mortgage 9% notes payable in semiannual installments of $25,000	$500,000		
Less current maturities	50,000	$450,000	
Bond payable 9½% (due in 1986)		850,000	$1,300,000

Notes in the amount of $50,000, which mature currently and have been deducted above, are shown as current liabilities.

Owners' Equity

The complexity of capital stock agreements and the various restrictions on residual equity imposed by state corporation laws, liability agreements, and voluntary actions of boards of directors make the owners' equity (stockholders' equity) section one of the most difficult sections to prepare and understand. The section is usually divided into three parts:

1. **Capital stock.** The par or stated value of the shares issued.
2. **Additional paid-in capital.** Primarily the excess of the amounts paid in over the par or stated value.
3. **Retained earnings.** The undistributed earnings of the corporation.

The major requirements for reporting the capital stock account are that the par value amounts authorized, issued, and outstanding be disclosed. In addition, any capital stock reacquired (treasury stock) is shown as a reduction of stockholders' equity. The additional paid-in capital is usually presented in one amount, although breakdowns are informative if the sources of additional capital obtained are varied and material. The retained earnings section may be divided between the unappropriated (the amount that is available for dividend distribution) and any amounts that are restricted (such as for future plant expansion).

The ownership or stockholders' equity accounts in a corporation are considerably different from those in a partnership or proprietorship. Partners' permanent capital accounts and the balance in their temporary accounts (Drawing accounts) are shown separately. Proprietorships ordinarily use a single capital account that handles all of the owners' equity transactions.

Presented below are illustrations of various owners' equity sections.

Capital investment		
Capital stock, par value $5		
Authorized and issued, 100,000 shares	$500,000.00	
Additional paid-in capital	40,000.00	
Earnings reinvested in the business (of which $16,500 is not available for dividends on capital stock under terms of the bank loan payable)	27,200.00	$567,200.00

Investment of stockholders, represented by			
Cumulative 6% preferred stock, par value $25			
Authorized and issued 10,000 shares		$250,000.00	
Common stock, par value $1.00			
Authorized 500,000 shares;			
issued and outstanding,			
450,000 shares		450,000.00	
Premium on common stock		33,000.00	
Earnings retained in the business:			
Appropriated for future inventory losses	$20,000.00		
Unappropriated	15,000.00	35,000.00	$768,000.00

Stockholders' equity			
Paid in on capital stock:			
6% cumulative preferred—			
Authorized, 2,500 shares of $50			
par value; issued 2,000 shares	$100,000.00		
(Aggregate involuntary liquidation			
value, $105,000)[7]			
Less 200 shares reacquired			
and held in treasury	10,000.00		
	90,000.00		
Common—			
Authorized, 60,000 shares without			
par value; issued and			
outstanding, 50,000 shares at a			
stated value of $2.50 a share	125,000.00		
Excess of issue price over stated			
value of common stock	45,000.00	$260,000.00	
Retained earnings:			
Restricted by purchase of			
treasury stock	10,000.00		
Appropriated in accordance with			
terms of 8% sinking fund bonds	87,000.00		
Appropriated for plant expansion	50,000.00		
Unrestricted	107,314.12	254,314.12	$514,314.12

Additional Information Reported

The balance sheet is not complete simply because a listing of the assets, liabilities, and owners' equity accounts has been presented. Great importance is given to supplemental information that is completely new or is an elaboration or qualification of items in the balance sheet. There are normally four types of information that are supplemental to account titles and amounts presented in the balance sheet.

[7]"Omnibus Opinion—1966," *Opinions of the Accounting Principles Board, No. 10* (New York: AICPA, 1966), par. 10, recommends that the liquidation value of preferred stock be disclosed in the equity section of the balance sheet in the aggregate.

1. **Contingencies.** Events that have an uncertain outcome that may have a material effect on financial position.
2. **Valuations and accounting policies.** Explanations of the valuation methods used or the basic assumptions made concerning, for example, inventory valuations, depreciation methods, investments in subsidiaries.
3. **Contractual situations.** Explanations of certain restrictions or covenants attached either to specific assets or, more likely, to liabilities.
4. **Post-balance sheet disclosures.** Disclosures of certain events that have occurred after the balance sheet date but before the financial statements have been issued.

Chapter 27 on full disclosure discusses these subjects and additional topics on disclosure.

Gain Contingencies   The term **gain contingencies** designates claims or rights whose existence is uncertain but which may become valid property rights eventually.

The typical gain contingencies are:

1. Possible receipts of monies from gifts, donations, bonuses, and so on.
2. Possible refunds from the government in tax disputes.
3. Pending court cases where the probable outcome is favorable.

Accountants have adopted a conservative policy in this area. Gain contingencies are not recorded and are disclosed only when the probabilities are high that a gain contingency will become reality.

Loss Contingencies   **FASB Statement No. 5** requires that an estimated loss from loss contingencies be accrued by a charge to income and the recording of a liability if both of the following conditions are met:

1. Information available prior to issuance of the financial statements indicates that it is **probable** that a liability had been incurred at the date of the financial statements.
2. The amount of loss can be **reasonably estimated.**[8]

As indicated earlier, the establishment of a liability for service or product warranties would ordinarily meet the two conditions mentioned above and thus qualify as a liability.

In most loss contingency cases, however, one or both of the conditions will not be present. For example, assume that a company is involved in a lawsuit with one of its competitors. The company's lawyer indicates that a reasonable possibility exists that they could lose. In such a case, there is only a **reasonable possibility** of loss rather than a **probable** one and, therefore, a liability should not be recorded. Disclosure of the nature of the contingency and, where possible, the amount involved, however, should be made. If a reasonable estimate of the amount of the contingency is not possible, disclosure is made in general terms, describing the loss contingency and explaining that no estimated amount is determinable. Because these types of contingencies are only possibilities, they should not enter into the determination of net income.

Diversity in practice exists in accounting for contingencies because varied interpretations are made of the words "probable" and "reasonably possible." As a result,

---

[8]"Accounting for Contingencies," *Statement of Financial Accounting Standards No. 5* (Stamford, Conn.: FASB, 1975), par. 8.

the contingencies reported and disclosed vary somewhat. This area of practice requires that the accountant use professional judgment because the determination of what constitutes full and proper accounting and disclosure is accompanied with a high element of subjectivity.

Some of the more common sources of **loss contingencies that ordinarily will not be accrued as liabilities are:**

1. Guarantees of indebtedness of others.
2. Obligations of commercial banks under "standby letters of credit" (commitments to finance projects under certain circumstances).
3. Guarantees to repurchase receivables (or any related property) that have been sold or assigned.
4. Disputes over additional income taxes for prior years.
5. Pending lawsuits whose outcome is uncertain.

It should be noted that the reporting rules for loss contingencies are complex and are presented here only in general terms. In Chapter 10 the subject is discussed at great length. **General risk contingencies** that are inherent in business operations, such as the possibility of war, strike, losses from catastrophes not ordinarily insured against, or a business recession, are not reflected in financial statements either by incorporation in the accounts or by other disclosure.

Valuations and Accounting Policies   As subsequent chapters of this textbook indicate, accountants utilize many different methods and bases in valuing assets and allocating costs. For instance, inventories can be computed under several flow assumptions (e.g., LIFO and FIFO), plant and equipment can be depreciated under several accepted methods of cost allocation (e.g., double-declining balance and straight line), and investments can be carried at different valuations (e.g., cost, equity, and market). Many users of financial statements know of these possibilities and examine the statements closely to determine the methods used.

Generally, specific requirements have been established to make certain that these valuation methods are disclosed either in the statement itself or in the footnotes to the statements. **APB Opinion No. 22** recommends that specific identification and description of all significant accounting principles and methods that involve selection from among alternatives and/or those that are peculiar to a given industry be disclosed in the annual report.[9] The APB believes that the disclosure is particularly useful if given in a separate **Summary of Significant Accounting Policies** preceding the footnotes to the financial statement or as the initial footnote. See the specimen financial statements in Appendix E following this chapter for an example of such a summary (pages 198–199) and further discussion of this topic in Chapter 27.

Contracts and Negotiations   In addition to the contingencies and different methods of valuation disclosed as supplementary data to the financial statements, any contracts and negotiations of significance are disclosed in the footnotes to the statements. **It is mandatory, for example, that the essential provisions of lease contracts,**

---

[9]"Disclosure of Accounting Policies," *Opinions of the Accounting Principles Board No. 22* (New York: AICPA, 1972).

pension obligations, and stock option plans be clearly stated in the footnotes to the financial statements. The analyst who examines a set of financial statements wants to know not only the amount of the liabilities, but also how the different contractual provisions of these debt obligations affect the company at present and in the future.

As just indicated, the profession has spelled out exacting disclosure requirements for certain obligations. In addition, many other items may have an important and significant effect on the enterprise, and this information should be disclosed. It is here that the accountant must exercise considerable judgment about whether omission of such information is misleading to the financial statement user. The axiom "When in doubt, disclose" is appropriate here; it seems better to disclose a little too much information than not enough.

Post-Balance Sheet Events   Footnotes to the financial statements should include adequate explanations of any significant financial events taking place after the formal date of the balance sheet, but before it is finally issued.

A period of several weeks, and sometimes months, may elapse after the end of the year before the financial statements are issued. Problems involved in taking and pricing the inventory, reconciling subsidiary ledgers with controlling accounts, preparing necessary adjusting entries, assuring that all transactions for the period have been entered, obtaining an audit of the financial statements by independent certified public accountants, and printing the annual report all take time. During the period between the balance sheet date and its distribution to stockholders and creditors, important transactions or other events may have occurred that materially affect the company's financial position or operating situation.

Those who read a balance sheet (if it is fairly recent) may think of the balance sheet condition as remaining constant, and project it into the future. Numerous events or transactions may make this projection inappropriate, however. If the company has sold one of its plants, acquired a subsidiary, suffered extraordinary losses, settled significant litigation, or experienced any other important event in the post-balance sheet period, such an event should be brought to the attention of financial statement readers. Without an explanation of such an occurrence in a footnote, the reader (not knowing of its existence) might easily be misled and might make conclusions that could be avoided if all the facts were disclosed.

Two types of events or transactions occurring after the balance sheet date (commonly referred to as **subsequent events**) may have a material effect on the financial statements or may need to be considered to interpret these statements accurately.

The first type of event or transaction consists of events that (1) provide additional evidence about conditions that existed at the balance sheet date, (2) affect the estimates that are used in preparing financial statements, and (3) result in adjustments of the financial statements. The accountant is obliged to use all of the information that is available prior to the issuance of the financial statements in evaluating estimates previously made. To ignore these subsequent events is to pass up an opportunity to improve the accuracy of the financial statements. This first type encompasses information that would have been recorded in the accounts had it been available at the balance sheet date: for example, subsequent events that affect the realization of assets such as receivables and inventories or the settlement of estimated liabilities. Such events typically represent the culmination of conditions that existed for some time.

The second type consists of the events that provide evidence about conditions that (1) did not exist at the balance sheet date but arise subsequent to that date and (2) do not require adjustment of the financial statements. Some of these events may have to be disclosed to keep the financial statements from being misleading. These disclosures take the form of footnotes, supplemental schedules or, possibly, even pro forma (as if) financial data that make it appear as if the event had occurred on the date of the balance sheet. Below are examples of such events that require disclosure (but do not result in adjustment):

   a. Sale of bonds or capital stock.
   b. Purchase of a business.
   c. Settlement of litigation when the event giving rise to the claim took place subsequent to the balance sheet date.
   d. Loss of plant or inventories as a result of fire or flood.
   e. Losses on receivables resulting from conditions (such as a customer's major casualty) arising subsequent to the balance sheet date.
   f. Gains or losses on certain marketable securities.[10]

Identifying events that require adjustment of or disclosure in the financial statements under the criteria stated above calls for the exercise of judgment and knowledge of the facts and circumstances. For example, if a loss on an uncollectible trade account receivable results from a customer's deteriorating financial condition, leading to bankruptcy subsequent to the balance sheet date, the financial statements are adjusted before their issuance because the event (bankruptcy) indicates conditions existing at the balance sheet date. A similar loss resulting from a customer's major casualty, such as a fire or flood, after the balance sheet date is not indicative of conditions existing at that date, however, and adjustment of the financial statements is not necessary: disclosure is appropriate depending on the materiality of the loss. The same criterion applies to settlements of litigation. If the events that gave rise to the litigation, such as personal injury or patent infringement, took place prior to the balance sheet date, adjustment of the financial statements is necessary. If the event giving rise to the claim took place subsequent to the balance sheet date, no adjustment is necessary but disclosure is. Subsequent events such as changes in the quoted market prices of securities ordinarily do not result in adjustment of the financial statements because such changes typically reflect a concurrent evaluation of new conditions.

In addition to the events noted above, **many subsequent events or developments are not likely to require either adjustment of or disclosure in the financial statements.** These are nonaccounting events or conditions that managements normally communicate by other means. These events include legislation, product changes, management changes, strikes, unionization, marketing agreements, and loss of important customers.

---

[10]"Subsequent Events," *Statement on Auditing Standards No. 1* (New York: AICPA, 1973), pp. 123–124, and "Accounting for Certain Marketable Securities," *op. cit.,* par. 17.

Techniques of Disclosure

The effect of various contingencies on financial condition, the methods of valuing assets, and the companies' contracts and agreements should be disclosed as completely and as intelligently as possible in the balance sheet. These methods of disclosing pertinent information are available:

> Parenthetical explanations
> Footnotes
> Supporting schedules
> Cross reference and contra items
> Showing items "short"

Appendix E contains specimen financial statements that illustrate these methods.

Parenthetical Explanations   Additional information or description is often given by means of parenthetical explanations following the item. For example, investments in common stock are shown on the balance sheet under Investments as below.

> Investments in Common Stock (market value, $330,586)—at cost $280,783

This device permits disclosure of additional pertinent information that adds clarity and completeness to the balance sheet. It has an advantage over a footnote because it brings the additional information into the body of the statement where it is less likely to be overlooked. Of course, inasmuch as lengthy parenthetical explanations might distract the reader from or even appear to contradict the balance sheet information, they must be used with care.

Footnotes   If additional explanations or descriptions cannot be shown conveniently as parenthetical explanations, footnotes are used. For example, inventories are shown in this balance sheet as follows:

> Inventories—See Note 2 $8,380,576

On the same page as the balance sheet or on the following page "Note 2" appears:

> "Note 2. Inventories were priced at cost of $8,380,576. The market price, or cost to replace the inventory as of the balance sheet date, was $8,780,635. The Company has consistently followed a policy of determining cost on the basis of specific lots on hand, and this policy was followed in arriving at the cost of $8,380,576, shown on the balance sheet."

Footnotes are commonly used to present other information such as the existence and amount of any preferred stock dividends in arrears, the terms of or obligations imposed by purchase commitments, special financial arrangements, depreciation policies, any changes in the application of accounting principles, and the existence of contingencies. The following footnotes indicate a common method of presenting such information.

> "Note 3. The Company has entered into a loan agreement with certain banks, which agreement makes available to the Company until January 31, 1985, sums not to exceed $5,000,000 outstanding at any one time. Borrowings may be made to mature, at the Company's option, before January 31, 1986, or in five equal annual installments commencing on that date. The Company pays interest at 9% on all amounts borrowed under this agreement and pays a commitment fee of ¾ of 1% annually on all the unused amount available. As of December 31, 1981, $1,800,000 has been borrowed under this agreement.

> "Note 4. During the year ended December 31, 1981 the Company changed from the first-in, first-out method of pricing inventories to the last-in, first-out method. This reduced the December 31, 1981, inventory valuation from approximately $18,275,800 under the first-in, first-out method to $16,935,250 under the last-in, first-out method, thereby reducing net income for the year by approximately $1,340,550.

> "Note 5. Provisions for depreciation of plant facilities and equipment charged to cost of goods sold amounted to $386,520 in 1981 and $327,840 in 1980."

In the preparation of footnotes, we must be sure that they present all essential facts as completely and succinctly as possible. Careless wording may result in misleading instead of aiding readers. Footnotes should add to the total information made available in the financial statements, not raise unanswered questions or contradict other portions of the statements.

Cross Reference and Contra Items   A direct relationship between an asset and a liability is called to the attention of the balance sheet reader by use of cross-referencing. For example, on December 31, 1981, among the current assets this might be shown:

Cash on deposit with sinking fund trustee for redemption of bonds payable—see current liabilities	$800,000

Included among the current liabilities is the amount of bonds payable to be redeemed currently:

Bonds payable to be redeemed in 1982—see current assets	$2,300,000

This cross reference points out that $2,300,000 of bonds payable are to be redeemed currently, for which only $800,000 in cash has been set aside; therefore the additional amount of cash needed must come from the general cash, from sales of investments, or from some other source. The same information can be shown parenthetically, if this device is preferred.

Another procedure that is often used is to establish contra or adjunct accounts. A **contra account** is an account that reduces either an asset or liability on a balance sheet. As examples, Accumulated Depreciation is considered a contra account; Discount on Bonds Payable also is a contra account. Contra accounts provide the accountant with some flexibility in presenting the financial information. With the use of the Accumulated Depreciation account, for example, a reader of the statement can see the original cost of the asset as well as the depreciation to date.

An **adjunct account,** on the other hand, increases either an asset or a liability. An example is Premium on Bonds Payable which when added to the Bonds Payable account provides a picture of the total liability of the enterprise.

Showing Items "Short"   Items shown short on the balance sheet are listed and described, but no amounts are extended to the column used in arriving at totals or subtotals. In other words, items that are shown short are not included in the totals of the balance sheet. An example of such an item is a claim for a federal income tax refund that has not been allowed as yet by the Internal Revenue Service. Since this claim may be disputed, it is not listed as an asset in the ordinary sense. Instead, it is listed among the assets as a separate item with the amount shown short, as follows:

Claim for refund of federal income taxes of 1978	$23,000

Similarly, certain loss contingencies may be shown short among the liabilities in the balance sheet:

Loss contingencies	
Accommodation endorsements on notes	$10,000
Damage suits filed against the company	15,000
	$25,000

In both of these examples the amounts shown are not included in the totals of the balance sheet. The showing of items short is generally not looked on favorably because it is usually inadvisable to state definite amounts with respect to such items, and also it is generally possible to give more complete explanations through the use of footnotes.

Supporting Schedules   Often a separate schedule is needed to present more detailed information about certain assets or liabilities. Here is a single item in the balance sheet for long-term tangible assets that might be appropriate:

Property, plant and equipment	
Land, building, equipment, and other fixed assets (see Schedule 3)	643,300

A separate schedule then might be presented as follows:

Schedule 3
LAND, BUILDINGS, EQUIPMENT, AND OTHER FIXED ASSETS

	Total	Land	Buildings	Equip.	Other Fixed Assets
Balance January 1, 1981	$740,000	$46,000	$358,000	$260,000	$76,000
Additions in 1981	161,200		120,000	38,000	3,200
	901,200	46,000	478,000	298,000	79,200
Assets retired or sold in 1981	31,700			27,000	4,700
Balance December 31, 1981	869,500	46,000	478,000	271,000	74,500
Depreciation taken to January 1, 1981	196,000		102,000	78,000	16,000
Depreciation taken in 1981	56,000		28,000	24,000	4,000
	252,000		130,000	102,000	20,000
Depreciation on assets retired in 1981	25,800			22,000	3,800
Depreciation accumulated December 31, 1981	226,200		130,000	80,000	16,200
Book value of assets	$643,300	$46,000	$348,000	$191,000	$58,300

Balance Sheet Form

One common arrangement followed in the presentation of the balance sheet is called the **account form.** It lists the assets by sections on the left side and the liabilities and stockholders' equity by sections on the right side. To avoid the use of facing pages, another arrangement lists the liabilities and stockholders' equity directly below the assets and on the same page, in what is often called the **report form.**[11] This arrangement is illustrated on page 186. Other presentations have infrequently been used in practice. For example, current liabilities are sometimes deducted from current assets to arrive at the amount of working capital, or all liabilities are deducted from all assets. Refer to the financial statements of Tenneco, Inc., Appendix E, page 195 for a practical illustration of a balance sheet presentation in report form.

Questions on Terminology

The account titles in the general ledger do not necessarily represent the best terminology for balance sheet purposes. Account titles are often brief and include technical terms that are understood only by those keeping the records and by other accountants who are familiar with such technical expressions. Balance sheets are examined by many persons who are not acquainted with the technical vocabulary of accounting and, therefore, should contain descriptions that will be generally

[11]*Accounting Trends and Techniques—1978* indicates that 98% of the companies surveyed use the "report or account form," sometimes collectively referred to as the "customary form."

Ecological Management, Inc.
BALANCE SHEET

December 31, 1981

Assets

Current assets

Cash		$ 42,485
Marketable securities—cost which		
approximates market value		28,250
Accounts receivable	$165,824	
Less allowance for doubtful accounts	1,850	163,974
Notes receivable		23,000
Inventories—at average cost		489,713
Supplies on hand		9,780
Prepaid expenses		16,252
Total current assets		$ 773,454

Long-term investments

Securities at cost (market value $94,000)		87,500

Property, plant and equipment

Land—at cost		125,000
Buildings—at cost	975,800	
Less accumulated depreciation	341,200	634,600
Property, plant and equipment		759,600

Intangible assets

Goodwill		100,000
Total assets		$1,720,554

Liabilities and Stockholders' Equity

Current liabilities

Notes payable to banks		$ 50,000
Accounts payable		197,532
Accrued interest on notes payable		500
Accrued federal income taxes		62,520
Accrued salaries, wages, and other expenses		9,500
Deposits received from customers		420
Total current liabilities		$ 320,472

Long-term debt

Twenty-year 8% debentures, due January 1, 1986		500,000
Total liabilities		820,472

Stockholders' equity

Paid in on capital stock		
Preferred, 7%, cumulative		
Authorized and outstanding,		
30,000 shares of $10 par value	$300,000	
Common		
Authorized, 500,000 shares of $1.00 par value;		
issued and outstanding, 400,000 shares	400,000	
Additional paid-in capital	37,500	737,500
Earnings retained in the business		
Appropriated	85,000	
Unappropriated	77,582	162,582
Total stockholders' equity		900,082
Total liabilities and stockholders' equity		$1,720,554

understood and not be subject to misinterpretation. Accountants are becoming aware of the need for better terminology in financial statements. This awareness is evident in the helpful descriptions used in recent published financial statements and in the attention given this subject by professional groups, periodicals, and textbooks.

For example, the AICPA recommended that the word "reserve" be used only to describe an appropriation of retained earnings. This term had been used in several ways: to describe amounts deducted from assets (contra accounts such as accumulated depreciation, and allowance for doubtful accounts), as a part of the title of contingent liabilities, and to describe certain charges in the income statement. Because of the different meanings attached to this term, its significance in the balance sheet was questionable, and misinterpretation often resulted from its use. The use of "reserve" only to describe appropriated earnings has resulted in a better understanding of its significance when it appears in a balance sheet. Perhaps the use of the word should be discontinued entirely, because to the nonaccountant a reserve is something quite different from what is signified by a reserve on a balance sheet. The term "appropriated" appears more logical and its use should be encouraged.

For years the AICPA has recommended that the use of the word "surplus" be discontinued in balance sheet presentations of owners' equity. This term has a connotation outside accounting that is quite different from its meaning in the accounts or in the balance sheet. The use of the terms capital surplus, paid-in surplus, and earned surplus is confusing to the nonaccountant and leads to misinterpretation. Although condemned by the AICPA, these terms appear all too frequently in current financial statements and in current literature. We have discussed them only to enable you to understand these terms when you encounter them in practice.

The AICPA recommendations relating to changes in terminology have been directed primarily to the balance sheet presentation of stockholders' equity so that the words or phrases used for these unique accounts describe more accurately the nature of the amounts shown.

STATEMENT OF CHANGES IN FINANCIAL POSITION

If you were asked to determine the additions to or dispositions of property, plant and equipment for the past year at B. F. Goodrich Company or the amount of money borrowed or capital stock issued by General Electric Company during the year, you would best proceed by analyzing their **statements of changes in financial position.** The statement of changes in financial position provides the answers to these questions because it (1) summarizes information concerning the **financing** and **investing** activities of the company and (2) completes the **disclosure of changes** in financial position during the period.[12]

Although the income statement, balance sheet, and statement of retained earnings contain information on financing and investing activities, they present this information only in a partial, fragmented manner. Only the statement of changes in financial position indicates where the resources (funds) came from during the pe-

---

[12]"Reporting Changes in Financial Position," *Opinions of the Accounting Principles Board No. 19* (New York: AICPA, 1971), par. 4. Procedures for preparing this statement are discussed in more detail in Chapter 24. The major purpose of this discussion is to focus on the content and use of the statement.

riod and how they were used. Since 1971 **(APB Opinion No. 19)**, the statement of changes in financial position has been a mandatory accompaniment to the balance sheet and statement of income and retained earnings, which means that it can be considered as **a basic financial statement.**

The statement of changes in financial position summarizes the changes between the beginning and ending balance sheets in addition to the changes summarized by the income statement. The financing and investing activities are usually summarized on the basis of either **changes in cash** or **changes in working capital** (current assets minus current liabilities). Regardless of the basis used in preparation of the statement, **all** financing and investing activities must be incorporated in the statement even though neither cash nor working capital was directly affected: this is referred to as the **all-financial resources concept.** Examples of transactions that must be reflected although they do not affect cash or working capital are: acquisition of property in exchange for other property, issuance of stock for property, and conversion of long-term debt to common stock.

When the all-financial resources concept is employed concurrently with the working capital approach, the major resources provided and applied transactions are classified as follows:

Resources provided by	Resources applied to
Income from operations	Loss from operations
Sale of noncurrent assets	Purchase of noncurrent assets
Increase in long-term debt	Retirement of long-term debt
Issuance of additional capital stock	Retirement of capital stock
	Dividends on capital stock

The statement of changes in financial position for Indiana-Lambert, Inc. on page 189 illustrates the typical form and content.

Note that the statement of changes in financial position begins with resources provided from operations. In the operations section, income is the usual starting point (unless there is an extraordinary item, in which case income before extraordinary item is the starting point) to which nonworking capital items are added or deducted. For example, depreciation is added back to income before extraordinary item in arriving at working capital from operations exclusive of extraordinary item because depreciation expense is a nonworking capital charge. After the operations section is completed, extraordinary items and all other financing and investing transactions should be disclosed individually when material. The arrangement of these items is kept somewhat flexible so that any significant changes that might develop in a particular year can be highlighted. The statement generally ends with an increase or decrease in working capital for the year. A schedule detailing the changes in the individual items comprising working capital is also reported in the statement or in a separate tabulation accompanying the statement.

Appendix E, page 197, provides another illustration of a statement of changes in financial position. Chapter 24 presents a comprehensive discussion of this subject and illustrates the techniques of preparing the statement of changes in financial position on both the cash and the working capital basis.

Indiana-Lambert, Inc.
STATEMENT OF CHANGES IN FINANCIAL POSITION
For the Year 1981

Resources provided by:
Operations:
Income before extraordinary item $55,458
Add or (deduct) items not affecting working capital:

Income before extraordinary item		$55,458
Add or (deduct) items not affecting working capital:		
Depreciation expense	$11,250	
Bond discount amortization	486	
Equity in earnings of 25%-owned company	(5,880)	5,856
Working capital provided by operations, exclusive of extraordinary item		61,314
Extraordinary item—Condemnation of land, including extraordinary gain of $8,500 (net of $3,000 tax)		21,300
Sale of bonds		63,560
Issuance of common stock to retire preferred stock (Note 5)		30,000
Total resources provided		$176,174
Resources applied to:		
Purchase of equipment		81,500
Cash dividends		8,000
Payment on long-term note		21,674
Preferred stock retired by issuance of common stock (Note 5)		30,000
Total resources applied		141,174
Increase in working capital		$ 35,000

SCHEDULE OF WORKING CAPITAL CHANGES
For the Year 1981

	Working Capital Change	
Current Assets	Increase	Decrease
Increase in cash	$35,426	
Decrease in marketable securities		$ 9,200
Increase in accounts receivable	25,000	
Increase in inventory	17,500	
Current Liabilities		
Decrease in accounts payable	3,890	
Increase in dividends payable		8,000
Increase in income taxes payable		29,616
Totals	81,816	46,816
Increase in working capital		35,000
	$81,816	$ 81,816

Notes to the financial statements.
Note 5. All of the 8% preferred stock was retired through the issuance of two shares of common stock ($1.00 par) for each share of preferred. Retirement required the issuance of 18,000 shares of common stock. No cash was paid or received incidental to this retirement.

APPENDIX

E

Specimen Financial Statements

To the student—

The following 17 pages contain the financial statements and accompanying notes of a complex industrial conglomerate—Tenneco, Inc. Because of the diversity and worldwide scope of its operation in many industries, Tenneco's accounting and reporting practices are affected by most accounting topics covered in this text and by nearly every facet of generally accepted accounting principles, as well as many specialized industry accounting requirements. Of all U.S. companies, Tenneco, Inc. is the 19th largest in sales dollars (8.8 billion), 23rd largest in terms of net income ($466 million), 15th largest in dollars of assets ($10 billion), and 22nd largest with 104,000 employees in 1978.

We do not expect that you will comprehend Tenneco, Inc.'s financial statements and the accompanying notes in their entirety at your first reading. But we expect that by the time you complete the coverage of the material in this text your level of understanding and interpretive ability will have grown enormously.

At this point we recommend that you take 20 to 30 minutes to scan the statements and notes to familiarize yourself with the contents and accounting elements. Throughout the following twenty-two chapters when you are asked to refer to specific parts of Tenneco's financials, do so! Then, when you have completed reading this book, we challenge you to reread Tenneco's financials to see how much greater and more sophisticated is your understanding of them.

Tenneco Inc 34th Annual Report Summary

Financial Highlights—(Millions Except Per Share Amounts)

Consolidated Results	1978	1977	Per Cent Change
Net sales and operating revenues	$ 8,762	$7,408	+18%
Net income	466	427	+ 9
Preferred and preference stock dividends	31	20	+55
Net income to common stock	435	407	+ 7
Earnings per share of common stock—			
Average shares outstanding	4.53	4.38	+ 3
Fully diluted	4.30	4.11	+ 5
Average number of shares outstanding	96	93	+ 3
Capital expenditures	1,008	714	+41
Total assets	10,134	8,278	+22
Return on average common stockholders' equity	14.5%	15.2%	

Results by Major Business	Total Revenues 1978		Total Revenues 1977		Income* 1978		Income* 1977	
Integrated oil	$2,015	23%	$1,708	23%	$ 481	43%	$ 399	38%
Natural gas pipelines	2,013	23	1,815	24	293	26	278	27
Construction and farm equipment	1,985	22	1,519	20	128	11	111	11
Automotive	747	9	658	9	78	7	72	7
Chemicals	827	9	499	7	66	6	52	5
Agriculture, land management	258	3	214	3	25	2	20	2
Packaging	533	6	486	6	25	2	45	4
Shipbuilding	733	8	786	11	14	1	50	5
Investments	36	—	20	—	18	2	8	1
Intergroup sales	(270)	(3)	(225)	(3)	—	—	—	—
	$8,877	100%	$7,480	100%	$1,128	100%	$1,035	100%

*Before interest, federal income taxes and minority interests.

Financial Review

Tenneco Inc

Tenneco's consolidated operating revenues, net income and earnings per share reached new highs in 1978.

Consolidated operating revenues rose to $8.8 billion, an 18% increase over 1977 revenues of $7.4 billion. Revenues have attained record levels in each year of the Company's history.

Net income increased 9% to $466 million from $427 million in 1977. Net income available to the common stock, after provision for preferred and preference stock dividends, was $435 million. This was 7% greater than the $407 million reported the previous year.

Fully diluted earnings per common share were $4.30, compared with $4.11 in 1977, a gain of 5%. Fully diluted earnings reflect the effect of the anticipated issuance of additional common shares for convertible or exchangeable securities, stock options and warrants.

The return on average net assets employed for 1978 was 15.1%, a decrease from 16.1% in 1977. The return on average common stockholders' equity declined from 15.2% in 1977 to 14.5% in 1978. These returns declined principally due to an aggressive capital expenditure program and recent acquisitions which will not reach their full potential until future periods.

Financial Position

The consolidated assets of the Company increased 22% during 1978 to $10.1 billion, up from $8.3 billion at year-end 1977. Working capital rose to $731 million from $567 million at December 31, 1977, and funds provided from operations increased 13% — to $1.0 billion in 1978 from $890 million in 1977.

Commercial paper issued and outstanding by Tenneco Inc. at year-end totaled $169 million. The proceeds of a long-term financing in early 1979 were used to repay commercial paper outstanding at year-end. Accordingly, the balance has been reclassified from short-term to long-term debt in the year-end balance sheet.

Bank credit lines arranged by the Company during 1978 for short-term borrowing requirements include

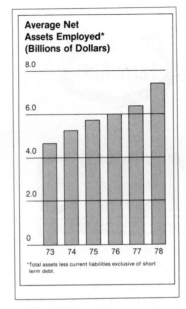

Average Net Assets Employed* (Billions of Dollars)

*Total assets less current liabilities exclusive of short term debt.

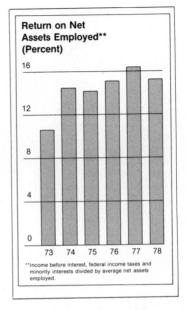

Return on Net Assets Employed** (Percent)

**Income before interest, federal income taxes and minority interests divided by average net assets employed.

twelve revolving credit lines with domestic banks totaling $110 million and seven Eurodollar term lines totaling $80 million.

On August 1, the Company entered into a revolving credit and term loan arrangement with a number of major domestic banks, which committed a $600 million line of credit. The funds will be available to the Company on a revolving credit or term loan basis through August 1, 1982, at which time any unused part of the commitment will be available as term loans. None of these loans were outstanding at year-end.

The sound financial position of the Company and its subsidiaries is evidenced by the $554 million of short-term credit available and the $121 million in cash and temporary investments on hand at year-end.

Oil and Gas Accounting Rule

In August, 1978, the Securities and Exchange Commission announced plans to develop a method of accounting that would recognize valuations of proved oil and gas reserves in the financial statements of oil and gas producers. During the interim period while this accounting method is being developed, companies may follow either the suc-

cessful efforts method as prescribed by the Financial Accounting Standards Board or the full-cost method as prescribed by the Securities and Exchange Commission. The Company intends to continue following the full-cost method of accounting for financial reporting purposes.

A full discussion of the matter is found in the Notes to Financial Statements.

Change in Inventory Method

Effective January 1, 1979, the Company changed its method of accounting for a substantial portion of its inventories from the first-in, first-out (FIFO) method to the last-in, first-out (LIFO) method. Under the LIFO method of inventory valuation, the cost of inventories sold reflects the latest cost of goods acquired or produced. With a strong probability that inflation will continue in the future, it is expected that the use of LIFO will result in lower reported earnings but significantly improved cash flow resulting from a decrease in federal income tax payable.

Capital Expenditures

A total of $1.0 billion was spent in 1978 for expansion and improvement of facilities and for the explora-

Tenneco Inc

tion and development of natural resources. This was an increase of 41% from the $714 million spent in 1977.

Of the total, $558 million, or approximately 55%, was spent for the exploration for and development of oil and gas reserves and for refining and marketing facilities. Pipeline system expenditures for facilities and gas supply additions were $137 million, or approximately 14% of the total. These capital commitments, which together represent approximately 69% of our total capital outlay, illustrate the Company's continuing effort to satisfy the energy demands of our customers.

The chemicals, packaging and agriculture/land management businesses accounted for $180 million or 18% of the total, and the remaining $133 million or 13% was shared by the construction and farm equipment, automotive, and shipbuilding businesses. These funds were used to build and modernize plants and facilities for new products, to expand production capacity and to increase the efficiency of existing operations.

Depreciation, depletion and amortization amounted to $449 million in 1978, up 13% from $396 million in 1977. Net plant, property and equipment increased 20% to $5.7

billion, from $4.8 billion in 1977.

Financing

Three major debt financings were consummated in 1978. In January, 1978, $200 million of 8⅝% promissory notes due 1998 were privately placed with institutional investors. Another financing occurred in April, when Tenneco sold to the public $200 million principal amount of 8⅞% debentures due 2003. The proceeds from these two financings were added to the general funds of the Company and made available for general corporate purposes, including capital expenditures and working capital requirements. The third major debt financing occurred in September, when a subsidiary acquired all of the stock of Albright & Wilson, Ltd., which Tenneco did not previously own. The acquisition was financed by a British sterling borrowing equivalent to approximately $232 million.

In March, 1978, Tenneco Inc. acquired full ownership of Philadelphia Life Insurance Company with the issuance of 1,951,555 shares of a new issue of $7.40 Cumulative Preference Stock having a total market value of approximately $170 million. Holders of Philadelphia Life capital stock received .25 of a share of the $7.40 preference stock for each share of Philadelphia Life stock. Tenneco had previously owned approximately 24% of Philadelphia Life Insurance Company.

Tenneco Inc. also arranged a private placement with institutional investors for $225 million of 9⅝% promissory notes due 1999. Of this amount, $153 million was received in January, 1979, and the balance was received in March.

Capitalization

Capitalization totaled $6.6 billion at the end of 1978, including common stockholders' equity of $3.1 billion, minority stockholders' equity of $27 million, preferred and preference stock of $385 million, and long-term debt of $3.1 billion. As a result of financings in 1978, long-term debt as a proportion of total capitalization increased from 43.5% at year-end 1977 to 46.3%.

The number of common shares

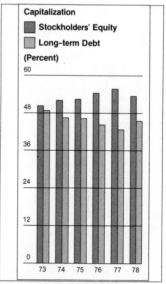

Capitalization
■ Stockholders' Equity
■ Long-term Debt
(Percent)

outstanding increased by 2.4 million shares to 98.6 million shares at year-end, with 1.1 million shares issued in exchange for Tenneco Inc. and Tenneco Corporation convertible securities and 1.3 million shares sold to benefit and investment plans of Tenneco employees and common shareholders.

The book value of the common stock was $32.30 per share at December 31, 1978, up 8% from $30.00 at year-end 1977. The book value has increased each year since the Company began operations and has nearly doubled in the last 10 years.

Dividends

Effective in the fourth quarter of 1978, the common stock dividend was increased 10% to an annual rate of $2.20 per share from the previous rate of $2.00, which had been in effect since the third quarter in 1977. This brought the total 1978 dividend payment to common shareholders to $2.05 per share, which included 50 cents per share in each of the first three quarters and the new rate of 55 cents per share in the last quarter.

The 1978 dividend rate increase marked the seventh consecutive year in which an increase was made and the rate has gone from $1.32 in 1971 to $2.20 in 1978, a rise of more than 66%.

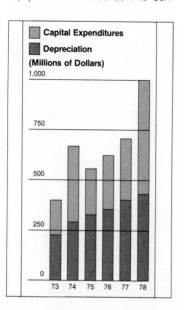

■ Capital Expenditures
■ Depreciation
(Millions of Dollars)

Financial Statements

Tenneco Inc. and Consolidated Subsidiaries
Statement of Income
Year Ended December 31, 1978 and 1977
(Millions Except Per Share Amounts)

STATEMENT OF INCOME

	1978	1977
Revenues:		
Net sales and operating revenues—		
Integrated oil	$2,010	$1,704
Natural gas pipelines	1,991	1,804
Construction and farm equipment	1,968	1,506
Automotive	740	657
Chemicals	808	480
Agriculture, land management	252	210
Packaging	530	482
Shipbuilding	733	785
Investments	—	5
Intergroup sales	(270)	(225)
	$8,762	$7,408
Other income, net	115	72
	$8,877	$7,480
Operating Expenses:		
Cost of sales and operating expenses	$6,489	$5,420
Selling, general and administrative expenses	828	654
Depreciation, depletion and amortization	432	371
	$7,749	$6,445
Income Before Interest, Federal Income Taxes and Minority Interests	$1,128	$1,035
Interest, Federal Income Taxes and Minority Interests:		
Interest expense	$ 345	$ 269
Interest capitalized	(24)	(18)
Federal income taxes	339	354
Minority interests	2	3
	$ 662	$ 608
Net Income	$ 466	$ 427
Preferred and Preference Stock Dividends	31	20
Net Income to Common Stock	$ 435	$ 407
Earnings Per Share of Common Stock:		
Average shares outstanding	$ 4.53	$ 4.38
Fully diluted	$ 4.30	$ 4.11

See notes to consolidated financial statements.

Tenneco Inc. and Consolidated Subsidiaries
Balance Sheet
December 31, 1978 and 1977
(Millions)

BALANCE SHEET

	1978	1977
ASSETS		
Current Assets:		
Cash	$ 90	$ 68
Temporary cash investments	31	14
Notes receivable	138	93
Accounts receivable	1,140	883
Shipbuilding contracts in progress, less billings	178	220
Inventories—		
Raw materials, work in process and finished products	1,520	1,203
Materials and supplies	131	85
Prepayments and other	160	112
	$ 3,388	$2,678
Investments and Other Assets:		
Investments in affiliated companies	$ 444	$ 323
Long-term receivables and other investments	243	159
Advances to secure future natural gas pipeline supply	177	201
Excess of cost over net assets of businesses acquired	83	63
Unamortized debt and preferred stock expense	25	25
Other	48	46
	$ 1,020	$ 817
Plant, Property and Equipment	$ 9,101	$7,790
Less—Reserves for depreciation, depletion and amortization	3,375	3,007
	$ 5,726	$4,783
	$10,134	$8,278
LIABILITIES AND STOCKHOLDERS' EQUITY		
Current Liabilities:		
Current maturities on long-term debt	$ 234	$ 163
Commercial paper	—	52
Notes payable	503	359
Accounts payable	1,101	771
Taxes accrued	291	386
Interest accrued	70	48
Natural gas pipeline revenue refund reservation	159	145
Other	299	187
	$ 2,657	$2,111
Long-term Debt	$ 3,067	$2,391
Deferred Income from Production Payments	$ 31	$ 63
Deferred Federal Income Taxes	$ 625	$ 445
Deferred Credits and Other Liabilities	$ 192	$ 164
Minority Interests	$ 27	$ 24
Stockholders' Equity:		
Preferred stock	$ 190	$ 201
Second preferred stock	10	11
Preference stock	185	17
Common stock	493	481
Premium on capital stock and other capital surplus	807	760
Retained earnings	1,880	1,642
	$ 3,565	$3,112
Less—Parent company stock held by a subsidiary, at cost	30	32
	$ 3,535	$3,080
	$10,134	$8,278

See notes to consolidated financial statements.

Tenneco Inc. and Consolidated Subsidiaries
Statement of Changes in Stockholders' Equity
Year Ended December 31, 1978 and 1977
(Millions Except Share Amounts)

STATEMENT OF SHAREHOLDERS' EQUITY

	1978		1977	
	Shares	Amount	Shares	Amount
Preferred Stock:				
Balance January 1	2,005,510	$ 201	2,091,604	$ 209
Acquired for sinking fund	(110,834)	(11)	(86,094)	(8)
Balance December 31	1,894,676	$ 190	2,005,510	$ 201
Second Preferred Stock:				
Balance January 1	115,025	$ 11	221,447	$ 22
Converted to common stock	(9,336)	(1)	(104,890)	(11)
Retired	(1,676)	—	(1,532)	—
Balance December 31	104,013	$ 10	115,025	$ 11
Preference Stock:				
Balance January 1	691,183	$ 17	946,996	$ 24
Converted to common stock	(161,428)	(4)	(255,813)	(7)
Issued to acquire Philadelphia Life Insurance Company	1,951,555	170	—	—
Other	3,734	2	—	—
Balance December 31	2,485,044	$ 185	691,183	$ 17
Common Stock:				
Balance January 1	96,186,591	$ 481	92,240,583	$ 461
Conversion of Tenneco Inc. securities	629,344	3	1,299,734	7
Exchange of Tenneco Corporation securities	480,638	2	1,077,030	5
Issued to employee benefit plans	939,999	5	1,096,806	6
Issued to the Dividend Reinvestment Plan	348,766	2	162,588	1
Issued to acquire Midwestern Gas Transmission Company	—	—	274,586	1
Other	27,103	—	35,264	—
Balance December 31	98,612,441	$ 493	96,186,591	$ 481
Premium on Capital Stock and Other Capital Surplus:				
Balance January 1		$ 760		$ 682
Premium on common stock issued:				
Upon conversion of Tenneco Inc. securities		2		10
Upon exchange of Tenneco Corporation securities		11		25
To employee benefit plans		24		30
To the Dividend Reinvestment Plan		9		4
To acquire Midwestern Gas Transmission Company		—		8
Other		1		1
Balance December 31		$ 807		$ 760
Retained Earnings:				
Balance January 1		$1,642		$1,412
Net income		466		427
Dividends—				
Preferred stock		(14)		(14)
Second preferred stock		—		(1)
Preference stock		(15)		(5)
Common stock		(197)		(177)
Other		(2)		—
Balance December 31		$1,880		$1,642
Less—Parent Company Stock Held by a Subsidiary, at Cost:				
Balance January 1	1,178,940	$ 32	1,178,940	$ 32
Issued in acquisition	(95,049)	(2)	—	—
Balance December 31	1,083,891	$ 30	1,178,940	$ 32
Total Stockholders' Equity		$3,535		$3,080

See notes to consolidated financial statements.

Tenneco Inc. and Consolidated Subsidiaries
Statement of Changes in Financial Position
Year Ended December 31, 1978 and 1977
(Millions)

STATEMENT OF CHANGES IN FINANCIAL POSITION

	1978	1977
Source of Working Capital:		
Net income	$ 466	$ 427
Items which did not affect working capital:		
Depreciation, depletion and amortization	449	396
Deferred federal income taxes	132	93
Undistributed earnings of affiliated companies	(43)	(30)
Other	4	4
Working capital provided from operations	$1,008	$ 890
Common stock issued	59	97
Preference stock issued	170	—
Long-term debt incurred	718	353
Short-term debt refinanced in 1979	225	—
Disposal of properties	20	15
Other (net)	26	28
	$2,226	$1,383
Use of Working Capital:		
Natural gas pipeline cash refund	$ 276	$ 144
Less—Amount reflected in other working capital accounts	204	102
Refund charged to depreciation reserve	$ 72	$ 42
Capital expenditures for plant, property and equipment	1,008	714
Net assets purchased in acquisitions	469	129
Working capital of acquired companies	(181)	(26)
Reduction of long-term debt	356	290
Retirement of production payments	32	68
Dividends	226	197
Preferred and preference stock reacquired or exchanged for common stock	19	31
Investments and other assets	61	(20)
	$2,062	$1,425
Increase (Decrease) in Working Capital	$ 164	$ (42)
Changes in Components of Working Capital:		
Cash and temporary cash investments	$ 39	$ (46)
Notes and accounts receivable	302	126
Inventories	363	258
Current maturities on long-term debt	(71)	(60)
Commercial paper	52	5
Notes and accounts payable	(474)	(228)
Taxes accrued	95	(76)
Other current assets and liabilities	(142)	(21)
	$ 164	$ (42)

See notes to consolidated financial statements.

Tenneco Inc. and Consolidated Subsidiaries
Notes to Financial Statements

NOTES TO FINANCIAL STATEMENTS

SUMMARY OF ACCOUNTING POLICIES:
Consolidation

The consolidated financial statements include all majority-owned subsidiaries other than finance, insurance and inactive subsidiaries. Reference is made to the caption "Unconsolidated Subsidiaries" for summarized financial information of J I Case Credit Corporation and Philadelphia Life Insurance Company, unconsolidated wholly-owned subsidiaries.

Unconsolidated majority-owned subsidiaries and companies in which at least a 20% voting interest is owned are carried at cost plus equity in undistributed earnings since date of acquisition. Such equity in undistributed earnings amounted to $139 million and $127 million at December 31, 1978 and 1977, respectively.

Currency Translation and Foreign Operations

Foreign currency transactions and foreign currency financial statements are translated into U.S. dollars using applicable current and historical rates. The resulting gains or losses are included in the determination of income for the period in which the exchange rate changes. Translation losses were approximately $16 million and $6 million for 1978 and 1977, respectively.

At December 31, 1978, the combined net assets of subsidiaries and branches engaged in foreign operations approximated $712 million. Net sales from such operations were approximately $1.7 billion and $1.0 billion for 1978 and 1977, respectively. Corresponding net income was $34 million and $36 million, respectively.

Acquisitions

In June 1977, a subsidiary of Tenneco Inc. completed its acquisition of a 40% interest in Poclain, S.A., a French construction machinery firm, through the purchase of newly issued shares of Poclain capital stock, at a purchase price of approximately $40 million. In addition to acquisition of the Poclain stock, the subsidiary subsequently acquired certain subsidiaries of Poclain, at a purchase price of approximately $18 million.

In December 1977, Tenneco Inc. purchased the remaining 50% interest in Petro-Tex Chemical Corporation for approximately $35 million. Tenneco owned 50% of Petro-Tex since its formation.

In March 1978, Philadelphia Life Insurance Company became a wholly-owned subsidiary of Tenneco Inc. through the exchange of 1,951,555 shares of Tenneco Inc. $7.40 preference stock for all of the remaining shares of Philadelphia Life not already owned by Tenneco Inc. At year-end 1977, Tenneco Inc. owned 24% of the Philadelphia Life shares outstanding.

In August 1978, Tenneco Inc. increased its voting interest in Albright & Wilson, Ltd. (A & W) common stock from 49.8% to 50.5% through the conversion of loan stock. In September 1978, Tenneco Inc. acquired all of the remaining stock of A & W for approximately $232 million financed by a British sterling long-term borrowing. Net sales of A & W for the five months ended December 31, 1978 included in the Statement of Income were approximately $284 million.

None of the above acquisitions had a significant effect on net income in the year of acquisition.

Federal Income Taxes

The companies follow deferred tax accounting for timing differences in the recognition of revenues and expenses for tax and financial reporting purposes, except for certain timing differences resulting from Federal Energy Regulatory Commission (FERC) rate regulatory practices and unremitted earnings of foreign subsidiaries.

Prior to 1974, the companies did not provide deferred federal income taxes with respect to intangible drilling costs and other oil and gas exploration and development costs which enter into the determination of taxable and financial income in different periods. At December 31, 1978, the cumulative amount of unamortized costs which have previously been deducted for tax purposes for which deferred tax has not been provided is approximately $500 million ($240 million of deferred tax at the 1978 statutory rate of 48%). Reference is made to the subcaption "Full-Cost Accounting and Depreciation, Depletion and Amortization", concerning rules which will require that deferred taxes which have not been previously provided be included in the retroactive restatement to adopt the SEC's specified form of the full-cost method.

No provision has been made for U.S. income taxes on unremitted earnings of foreign subsidiaries (approximately $205 million at December 31, 1978) since it is the present intention of management to reinvest a major portion of such unremitted earnings in foreign operations.

The companies follow the flow-through method of accounting whereby the benefit of the investment tax credit is currently recognized in the income statement. At December 31, 1978, the companies had no unused investment tax credits.

Full-Cost Accounting and Depreciation, Depletion and Amortization

In accordance with the full-cost method of accounting, Tenneco Inc. and its subsidiaries capitalize all productive and nonproductive costs incurred in connection with the acquisition, exploration and development of oil and gas reserves and amortize such costs associated with each cost center, exclusive of certain undeveloped offshore leases, over the life of the companies' estimate of proved oil and gas reserves using the unit-of-production method. When a lease is abandoned, all costs incurred in connection with its acquisition, exploration and development are charged to the reserve for depreciation, depletion and amortization. The United States properties, Canadian properties and each foreign concession are accounted for as separate cost centers.

Effective for the fiscal year ending December 31, 1979, the Securities and Exchange Commission (SEC) announced its decisions relating to financial accounting and reporting practices for oil and gas producing activities and adopted rules that provide the following: (1) oil and gas producers must adopt retroactively either a form of the successful efforts method of accounting as specified by the Financial Accounting Standards Board or a form of the full-cost method of accounting as specified by the SEC; (2)

producers must adopt retroactively comprehensive inter-period allocation of income taxes using the deferred method; (3) producers must disclose in financial statements extensive information on proved reserves including quantities and valuations and historical costs and revenues. Further, the SEC initiated an effort seeking the development of a method of accounting that would recognize valuations of proved reserves in balance sheets and income statements.

Certain elements of the SEC's specified form of the full-cost method differ from that presently followed by Tenneco Inc. Tenneco Inc. is currently conducting a study to determine the impact of applying the SEC's full-cost method. While the results of the study are incomplete and subject to change, preliminary information indicates that application of the SEC's full-cost method, including comprehensive inter-period allocation of income taxes, will result in a noncash reduction of Tenneco Inc. stockholders' equity at December 31, 1978, of approximately 11 percent and in a reduction of reported net income of approximately 2 percent in both 1978 and 1977. Any reduction in stockholders' equity would reduce by an equal amount costs and taxes which would otherwise be charged to future periods. Tenneco Inc. believes that such reduction will have no effect on its dividend policy or its ability to comply with covenants in its debt and other agreements and will not significantly affect Tenneco Inc.'s future operations and programs.

Depreciation of the other properties is provided on a straightline basis in amounts which, in the opinion of management, are adequate to allocate the cost of properties over their estimated useful lives.

Long-Term Shipbuilding Contracts

Newport News Shipbuilding and Dry Dock Company (Newport), a subsidiary, reports profits on its long-term shipbuilding contracts on the percentage-of-completion method of accounting, determined on the basis of costs incurred to date to estimated final costs. Newport reports losses on such contracts when first estimated. The performance of such contracts may extend over several years; therefore, periodic reviews of estimated final revenues and costs are necessary during the term of the contracts. Final contract settlements and periodic reviews may result in revisions to estimated final contract profits or losses which have the effect of including cumulative adjustments of income in the period in which the revisions are made.

In October 1978, Newport reached agreement with the U.S. Navy to end long-standing disputes over the costs of additional work and delays incurred during the construction of 12 nuclear-powered vessels. This agreement settled claims and resolved change orders and other outstanding items on the five shipbuilding contracts involved. All of the vessels covered by the contracts have been delivered to the Navy. Newport received $105 million in payments of which $45 million represented provisional payments on account of these claims and $60 million as partial payment on the settlement. Under the agreement the Navy is required to pay an additional $90 million to Newport. The settlement is subject to (1) notice by the Navy to Newport no later than March 31, 1979, that the Navy's obligation to pay such

amount has been fully funded and (2) payment of such amount within 60 days after notice is given.

The after-tax effect of the claim settlement was a reduction in previously reported income of approximately $9 million and is reflected in the accompanying financial statements for the year ended December 31, 1978.

In October 1978, a federal grand jury in Virginia commenced an investigation to determine whether Newport submitted fraudulent claims under contracts involved in this settlement. Newport has supplied certain documents to the grand jury and certain of its employees and former employees have testified.

Tenneco Inc. believes that final resolution of the above matters will have no material adverse effect on the financial position or results of operations of Tenneco Inc. and its consolidated subsidiaries.

Inventories

Inventories are stated at the lower of cost ("first-in, first-out" or "average" methods) or market (determined on the basis of estimated realizable values).

Interest Capitalized

Interest capitalized on regulated gas transmission construction projects amounted to approximately $2 million in both 1978 and 1977. Such interest represents the cost of funds used for construction. Under established regulatory practices, the companies are permitted to earn a fair return on such costs and to recover them in rates charged their customers.

Interest capitalized on nonregulated projects amounted to approximately $22 million and $16 million for 1978 and 1977, respectively. Such interest represents the cost of borrowed funds utilized in acquiring and carrying offshore oil and gas leases until development is substantially completed, in acquiring and carrying real estate held for resale and in the construction of major capital additions. Net income was increased approximately $16 million and $11 million in 1978 and 1977, respectively, due to capitalizing interest on nonregulated projects as compared to charging interest to expense as incurred.

PROVISION FOR FEDERAL INCOME TAXES:

Following is an analysis of the components of federal income tax expense:

	1978	1977
	(Millions)	
Current before investment tax credit—		
U.S.	$157	$299
Foreign	29	35
	$186	$334
Investment tax credit	$ (41)	$ (35)
Deferred—		
U.S.	$192	$ 53
Foreign	2	2
	$194	$ 55
	$339	$354

Following is a reconciliation of the current U.S. federal income tax rate of 48% to the effective tax rate reflected in the statement of income:

	1978	1977
Current U.S. federal income tax rate	48%	48%
Increases (reductions) in tax rate resulting from:		
Investment tax credit	(5)	(4)
Equity in earnings of unconsolidated subsidiaries included in income on an after-tax basis	(3)	(2)
Other	2	3
Effective federal income tax rate	42%	45%

Deferred tax expense results from timing differences in the recognition of revenues and expenses for tax and financial reporting purposes. The differences and the tax effect of each were as follows:

	1978	1977
	(Millions)	
Difference in timing of recognition of income on long-term shipbuilding contracts	$ (4)	$(40)
Difference in timing of recognition of income and expense relative to operations regulated by the FERC	58	(11)
Excess of tax over financial deductions for oil and gas exploration, development and production costs	106	58
Excess of tax depreciation at accelerated rates over tax depreciation at straightline rates applicable to operations regulated by the FERC	9	10
Excess of tax depreciation over book depreciation applicable to operations not regulated by the FERC	26	27
Transactions reported on the installment basis for tax purposes	17	10
Other	(18)	1
	$194	$ 55

FEDERAL ENERGY REGULATORY COMMISSION RATE MATTERS:

At December 31, 1978, Tenneco Inc. had an application for a rate increase pending before the FERC. Such rates were placed in effect, subject to refund, on November 1, 1977.

The proposed increase is based, among other things, upon (1) an increase in the rate of return to 11.67%, (2) increased operating expenses and (3) a reflection of the effects of curtailment. While Tenneco Inc. believes the requested rates are justified, reported revenues and net income have been reduced by a reserve for rate refund which takes into consideration probable adverse regulatory decisions.

In July 1976, the FERC issued an opinion with respect to an earlier rate case. Such opinion disallowed the cost of service effect of certain advance payments made to producers. Tenneco Inc. filed an appeal with the United States Circuit Court of Appeals for the District of Columbia and also requested that the Court stay the FERC requirement of immediate refunds relating to the disputed advance payments issue. The Court denied the request for stay and in 1977, Tenneco Inc. refunded to its customers approximately $144 million including interest of $31 million. Of the amount

of such refunds, $82 million is attributable to a reduction in the applied-for rates of depreciation.

Approximately $32 million of the above refund (including interest) related to the advance payments issue. It is the opinion of Tenneco Inc. that the Court's denial of the requested stay of these refunds will have no effect on the Court's ultimate resolution of this matter on the basis of its merits. If Tenneco Inc. prevails on this issue, the FERC has represented to the Court that the $32 million will be recoverable from Tenneco Inc.'s customers.

In May 1978, the FERC issued an order approving a settlement of three prior rate increase applications as well as the rates of depreciation in the November 1, 1977 application. Tenneco Inc. made refunds of approximately $266 million, including interest of $27 million. Of the amount of such refunds, $133 million is attributable to a reduction in the applied-for rates of depreciation. This settlement resolves all issues relating to these three prior rate increases except the treatment of research and development expenditures and advance payments to producers. The determination of these issues has been reserved pending the outcome of a hearing before the FERC and pending the aforementioned litigation.

Revenues, depreciation, interest expense, other income and taxes have been restated in the accompanying statement of income for 1977 to reflect the provisions of the FERC's opinions. Neither the restatement nor the refunds had any effect on previously reported net income.

At December 31, 1978, Tenneco Inc. had collected approximately $210 million applicable to contested rate matters. Should Tenneco Inc. be unsuccessful in all of the contested issues, refunds of approximately $230 million including interest would be required. After taking into consideration amounts reserved of $157 million at December 31, 1978, earnings would be reduced by approximately $35 million. Tenneco Inc. believes that the ultimate resolution of these rate increase applications (taking into account revenues and net income reserved) will have no significant effect on its consolidated financial position or reported net income. Tenneco Inc. presently intends to reflect any impact on net income in the period in which these matters are ultimately resolved.

On January 29, 1979, Tenneco Inc. filed for an increase in rates expected to become effective August 1, 1979. The rates in this case were designed to produce annual revenues of approximately $14 million above those which would be produced by pre-filing rates. This rate filing included, among other things, a rate of return of 12.13%.

LONG-TERM DEBT, INTERIM FINANCING AND SHORT-TERM DEBT:
Long-Term Debt

A summary of long-term debt outstanding at December 31, 1978, is set forth in the following tabulation:

(Millions)

Tenneco Inc.—

First mortgage pipeline bonds due 1979 through 1991, average interest rate 7.14%	$ 248
Debentures due 1979 through 2003, average interest rate 7.89%	852

Notes due 1980 through 1998, average interest rate 10.18%	888
Tenneco International Holdings Ltd.— 10.51% British sterling notes due 1985	240
Tenneco Corporation— Debentures due 1990 through 1993, average interest rate 6.45%	141
Tenneco International N.V.— Notes and debentures due 1979 through 1987, average interest rate 7.72%	147
Tenneco International Inc.— 8¾% Eurodollar loan due 1981	43
Other subsidiaries due 1979 through 2008, average interest rate 7.75%	518
Short-term debt (refinanced from proceeds of long-term debt issued in 1979)	225
Unamortized discount and premium (net)	(1)
	$3,301
Less—Current maturities	234
	$3,067

At December 31, 1978, approximately $3.2 billion of gross plant, property and equipment was pledged as collateral to secure $448 million principal amount of long-term debt.

Tenneco Inc. has issued $225 million principal amount of 9⅝% long-term notes due 1999 of which $153 million was issued in January 1979 and $72 million was issued in March 1979. Tenneco Inc. repaid commercial paper from the initial proceeds of such financing and intends to use the remainder of such financing to repay additional commercial paper or short-term debt. Accordingly, commercial paper and short-term debt in the amount of $225 million have been classified as long-term debt in the accompanying balance sheet at December 31, 1978.

Interim Financing

Tenneco Inc. has arranged a loan agreement which provides for bank loans up to an aggregate principal amount of $600 million. These funds will be available to Tenneco Inc. and Tenneco Corporation on a revolving credit basis and to Tenneco Inc. on a term loan basis through August 1, 1982. On August 2, 1982, all or any part of these funds not then outstanding as term loans will be available to Tenneco Inc. as term loans which would mature on July 31, 1988. The agreement provides for a commitment fee on the unused portion of the total commitment in an amount equal to ½ of 1% per annum plus a fee on the total commitment less the outstanding term loans in an amount equal to 6½% of the prime rate from August 1, 1978, to August 1, 1982. From August 1, 1978, until all of the term loans are paid in full, a fee will be charged on the unpaid balance of the term loans at a rate per annum equal to 6½% of the prime rate. Interest is payable quarterly and is based on the prime rate from August 1, 1978, through July 31, 1982. Interest is based on an ascending rate from prime to 107% times prime from August 1, 1982, through July 31, 1988. At December 31, 1978, no loans were outstanding under this agreement.

Short-Term Debt

The companies have lines of credit with various banks and also sell commercial paper to provide short-term financing. The credit agreements provide for borrowings at various rates and commitment fees on the unused amount of the commitments are required on certain lines. Information for 1978 regarding the lines of credit and commercial paper issued follows:

	Lines of Credit	Commercial Paper
	(Millions)	
Outstanding borrowings at end of year	$392*	$169*
Average interest rate on outstanding borrowings at end of year	10.1%	10.2%
Approximate maximum month-end outstanding borrowings during year	$475	$169
Approximate average month-end outstanding borrowings during year	$301	$ 60
Weighted average interest rate on approximate average borrowings during year	8.6%	8.7%
Approximate unused portion of lines of credit at end of year—		
Tenneco Inc. (available for direct borrowings or support of commercial paper)	$288	
Subsidiary companies	266	
	$554	

*All of the commercial paper and $56 million of short-term debt has been classified as long-term debt in the accompanying balance sheet at December 31, 1978. Reference is made to the subcaption "Long-Term Debt" in this note for additional information.

Included in the lines of credit existing at December 31, 1978, are approximately $610 million which expire in 1979 and may be extended annually at the election of the participating banks and approximately $336 million which expire subsequent to December 31, 1979. Additionally, at December 31, 1978, the companies had other short-term borrowings of $167 million.

At December 31, 1978, approximately $52 million of compensating balances, all subject to legal withdrawal, were maintained in connection with lines of credit.

Tenneco International Inc., a subsidiary, has guaranteed short-term debt of Tenneco International Finance, Ltd., an unconsolidated finance subsidiary, in the principal amount of $138 million.

RESTRICTIONS ON PAYMENT OF DIVIDENDS:

At December 31, 1978, under its most restrictive dividend provisions, Tenneco Inc. had approximately $880 million of retained earnings available for the payment of dividends on common stock. At such date, if all subsidiaries had paid dividends to Tenneco Inc. equal to their unrestricted retained earnings, Tenneco Inc. would have had approximately $1.1 billion of retained earnings available for the payment of dividends on common stock. Reference is made to the caption "Full-Cost Accounting and Depreciation, Depletion and Amortization".

PENSION PLANS:

The companies have several retirement plans which cover substantially all of their employees. Costs of all plans are actuarially determined, and it is the companies' policy to fund all pension costs accrued.

The unfunded prior service cost of the plans is estimated to be approximately $190 million at December 31, 1978, and is generally being amortized over periods ranging from 30 to 40 years. The excess of actuarially computed vested benefits over funded amounts and accruals is approximately $50 million at December 31, 1978. Total pension expense was approximately $79 million and $64 million for 1978 and 1977, respectively.

PREFERRED AND PREFERENCE STOCK:
Preferred Stock
At December 31, 1978 and 1977, there were authorized 3,620,750 and 3,703,250 shares, respectively, of cumulative preferred stock, par value $100 per share, of which 2,013,750 and 2,096,250 shares were outstanding at the respective dates. At December 31, 1978 and 1977, 119,074 and 90,740 shares, respectively, were held for sinking fund requirements.

At December 31, 1978, there were thirteen issues of cumulative preferred stock outstanding with annual dividend rates ranging from 4.60% to 8.52% (average dividend rate of 7.10%). The aggregate redemption value was $198 million which declines at various future dates. The preference in involuntary liquidation is the par value of each issue. Tenneco Inc. is required to retire a portion of the outstanding preferred stock each year; sinking fund requirements for 1979 amount to $9 million.

Second Preferred Stock
At December 31, 1978 and 1977, there were authorized 2,000,000 shares of cumulative second preferred stock, par value $100 per share, of which 104,013 and 115,025 shares were outstanding at the respective dates.

At December 31, 1978, there were five series of cumulative second preferred stock outstanding with annual dividend rates ranging from 4.50% to 5.36% (average dividend rate of 5.16%). Each share of the 5.36% series is convertible into 2.95 Tenneco Inc. common shares on or before December 31, 1982. Conversion rights have expired on all other series. The aggregate redemption value was $11 million which declines at various future dates.

Preference Stock
At December 31, 1978 and 1977, there were authorized 10,000,000 shares of preference stock, without par value.

At December 31, 1978, there were two series of preference stock outstanding, designated as $5.50 Cumulative Convertible Preference Stock, of which 529,755 and 691,183 shares were outstanding at December 31, 1978 and 1977, respectively, and $7.40 Cumulative Preference Stock of which 1,955,289 shares were outstanding at December 31, 1978. The $5.50 preference stock has a stated value of $25 per share and a liquidating value of $100 per share (liquidating value of $53 million and $69 million at December 31, 1978 and 1977, respectively). Each $5.50 preference share is convertible into 3.73 Tenneco Inc. common shares. At December 31, 1978, the aggregate redemption value of the $5.50 preference stock was $58 million which declines at various future dates. The $7.40 preference stock has a

mandatory redemption value of $100 per share (mandatory redemption value of $196 million at December 31, 1978). Tenneco Inc. has the option of redeeming the $7.40 preference stock from March 1, 1988, until March 1, 1993, for $101 per share and from March 1, 1993, until March 1, 1998, for $100 per share. Within each twelve-month period commencing with the twelve-month period ending on March 1, 1989, Tenneco Inc. must redeem at $100 per share, plus accrued and unpaid dividends, 10% of the number of shares of preference stock originally issued. At December 31, 1978, options for the purchase of 2,468 shares of $7.40 preference stock were outstanding.

COMMON STOCK, EARNINGS PER SHARE AND STOCK OPTION PLAN:
Common Stock
At December 31, 1978 and 1977, there were authorized 150,000,000 shares of common stock, par value $5 per share, of which 98,612,441 and 96,186,591 shares were outstanding at the respective dates. A subsidiary held 1,083,891 and 1,178,940 shares at December 31, 1978 and 1977, respectively.

At December 31, 1978, the shares of Tenneco Inc. common stock reserved for issuance were as follows:

Conversion of 5.36% second preferred stock	182,820
Conversion of $5.50 preference stock	1,975,986
Exercise of common stock warrants (at $30.07 per share through April 1, 1979)*	2,670,499
Exchange of Tenneco Corporation second preferred stock, stated value $27.75 (1.03 shares of common stock issuable for each share of second preferred stock to May 1, 1983)	289,820
Exchange of Tenneco Corporation debentures (at $28.49 per share through September 30, 1992)	936,295
Conversion of Tenneco Inc. 10% loan stock through December 24, 1995	514,866
Other	1,838,107
	8,408,393

_____

*Cash proceeds from exercise of these warrants are required to be applied to the retirement of Tenneco Inc. 6% Debentures due 1979.

The number of shares issuable, as set forth above, is subject to adjustment under certain conditions to protect against dilution.

Reference is made to the caption "Commitments and Contingencies—Tenneco Offshore" concerning Tenneco Inc.'s contingent obligations and possible future issuances of its common stock.

Cash dividends on common stock have been paid at a quarterly rate of 47¢ per share through June 30, 1977, and 50¢ per share through September 30, 1978. In December 1978, a fourth quarter dividend of 55¢ per share was paid.

Earnings Per Share
Earnings per share of common stock are based on the average number of shares of common stock outstanding during each period. Such average shares outstanding were 95,999,290 and 92,956,464 shares for 1978 and 1977, respectively. Earnings per share computations assuming full dilution additionally include the average common shares is-

suable for convertible or exchangeable securities, stock options and warrants during each period and the elimination of the related dividend and interest requirements, less applicable federal income taxes. Such average shares assuming full dilution were 103,245,561 and 101,885,226 shares for 1978 and 1977, respectively. Net income to common stock assuming full dilution was approximately $444 million and $418 million for the corresponding periods.

Stock Option Plan

Tenneco Inc. initially reserved an aggregate of 500,000 shares of common stock under a Qualified Stock Option Plan which provided for the granting of options at 100% of the fair market value at date of grant. All options have been granted under such plan. Options for the purchase of 15,000 shares have been cancelled and are not reissuable. At December 31, 1978, options for the purchase of 448,750 shares had been exercised.

Option changes during 1978 were as follows:

Shares issuable at beginning of year	64,750
Options exercised	(26,000)
Options cancelled	(2,500)
Shares issuable at end of year	36,250

COMMITMENTS AND CONTINGENCIES:
Capital Commitments

Tenneco Inc. estimates that expenditures aggregating approximately $740 million will be required after December 31, 1978, to complete facilities and projects authorized at such date and substantial commitments have been made in connection therewith.

In connection with Tenneco Inc.'s advance payments to producers to secure future natural gas pipeline supply, it may be required to make up to approximately $175 million of additional advances after December 31, 1978, based on gas reserves discovered.

Lease Commitments

At December 31, 1978, the companies had long-term leases covering certain of their facilities and equipment. The minimum rental commitments under noncancellable operating leases with lease terms in excess of one year are approximately $44 million, $36 million, $31 million, $26 million and $22 million for 1979, 1980, 1981, 1982 and 1983, respectively, and $92 million for subsequent years. Commitments under capital leases were not significant to the accompanying financial statements. Total rental expense for 1978 and 1977 was approximately $86 million and $67 million, respectively.

Litigation

Tenneco Inc. and certain of its subsidiaries are defendants to related lawsuits filed in 1975 by Air Products and Chemicals, Inc. (Air Products) in a state and a federal court in Louisiana, involving disputed contractual obligations of Tenneco Oil Company to supply, under certain circumstances, natural gas to Creole Gas Pipeline Company for delivery to Air Products at a price which is currently 20¢ per MCF. Air Products claims that it is entitled to deliveries of

22,500 MCF per day from October 1973 through June 1990. In April 1975, due to legal, regulatory and other restraints, Tenneco Oil Company substantially reduced its deliveries under this contract. The claims asserted are based on alleged breaches of contract and related violations of antitrust laws. The actions seek specific performance and damages totaling $881 million, of which $8 million is alleged as losses to date of filing the actions, $286 million is alleged as future losses for breach of contract through June 30, 1990, and $588 million is alleged to be added as trebling under the antitrust allegations.

In the opinion of counsel for Tenneco Inc. based upon discovery and factual investigation completed to date, (i) the antitrust allegations and claims for future losses are highly speculative and the chances of successfully defending against these claims are very favorable; and (ii) with regard to other allegations, Tenneco Inc. has substantial defenses.

In June 1978, the FERC commenced a private investigation to determine among other things, whether the delivery and transportation of natural gas by Tenneco Inc. to Creole Gas Pipeline Company for delivery to Air Products was in violation of the Natural Gas Act. The FERC has issued subpoenas requiring production of various documents and Tenneco Inc. has substantially responded to such subpoenas.

Tenneco Inc. is confident of its ability to comply with any final orders of the courts and further believes that the final resolution of these matters will not have a material adverse effect on Tenneco Inc. and its consolidated subsidiaries' financial position or results of operations.

Packaging Corporation of America (Packaging), a subsidiary of Tenneco Inc., in July 1976 pleaded *nolo contendere* to an indictment by the Federal Government before the U.S. District Court for the Northern District of Illinois. The indictment charged that Packaging and other corporate defendants conspired to fix prices of folding cartons in violation of the Sherman Act. The Court accepted such plea, entered a judgment of guilty and assessed a fine of $50 thousand against Packaging. Packaging, together with other corporations, is also a defendant in numerous private antitrust suits filed in various U.S. District Courts based on similar allegations, which seek treble damages in unspecified amounts. In most of such suits, the plaintiffs purport to represent a class of purchasers of folding cartons which allegedly was damaged as a result of the alleged antitrust violations. These private actions have been transferred to the U.S. District Court for the Northern District of Illinois for consolidated pretrial discovery. Packaging and the plaintiffs representing the class of purchasers of folding cartons have agreed to a settlement relating to these actions. Such settlement, which must be approved by the court, requires Packaging to pay approximately $11 million in damages and interest and has been reflected in the 1978 financial statements.

Packaging is also one of many corporate defendants in numerous private antitrust suits, commenced at various times since March 1977 in various U.S. District Courts, all of which have been transferred to the U.S. District Court for the

Southern District of Texas for consolidated pretrial discovery. These suits allege in effect that the defendants conspired to fix prices of corrugated containers and corrugated sheets in violation of the Sherman Act. In most of such suits, the plaintiffs purport to represent a class consisting of persons who purchased corrugated containers or corrugated sheets from the defendants and seek injunctive relief and treble damages in unspecified amounts. These suits are in the preliminary stage.

Since November 1976, Packaging has received and responded to subpoenas from the U.S. Department of Justice, Antitrust Division, to produce documents in connection with a federal grand jury investigation of practices relating to the production and sale of paper and paperboard.

Tenneco Inc. believes that the resolution of these actions against Packaging will have no material effect on the financial position or results of operations of Tenneco Inc. and its consolidated subsidiaries.

In August 1978, Amoco Gas Company (Amoco) filed an amended petition in a lawsuit originally instituted in September 1976 in the District Court of Harris County, Texas, against Tenneco Inc. and certain of its affiliates or subsidiaries, including Channel Industries Gas Company (Channel). The suit relates to a 1966 fixed-price gas purchase contract between Amoco and Channel which, together with Channel's contracts with its other principal customers, was amended in 1973 to reflect a settlement of certain disputes among Channel and its customers. In 1978, Channel's sales to Amoco constituted approximately 16% of Channel's total gas sales. In its amended petition, Amoco alleges (i) breach of the 1966 contract, as amended, and tortious interference with the Channel/Amoco contractual relationship for which it seeks actual damages "in excess of" $42 million and punitive damages of $85 million and (ii) fraud in the inducement of the 1973 Channel contract amendments, for which it seeks rescission of the 1973 amendment and restitution of the amount paid by Amoco to Channel in excess of the fixed prices provided for in the 1966 contract in an amount exceeding $102 million through April 1978 and punitive damages in the amount of $200 million. Additionally, Amoco seeks to compel the defendants to restore certain low-cost gas reserves to Channel which it alleges were illegally transferred or released or, alternatively, actual damages in an unspecified amount. Finally, Amoco seeks to recover in excess of $307 million as treble damages for alleged violations of Texas deceptive trade practice statutes.

Certain of Channel's other customers, whose contracts were also amended to reflect the 1973 settlement referred to above, have informed Tenneco Inc. that, in order to protect their rights, they may be obliged to commence legal proceedings based on claims similar to those asserted by Amoco. Tenneco Inc. has given assurance that no settlement of Amoco's litigation will be concluded without the prior approval of all of Channel's customers whose contracts were similarly amended in 1973.

The above-described claims concerning Channel involve complex issues of law and fact. This litigation is in a pretrial stage and discovery has commenced but is far from completion. In the opinion of counsel for Tenneco Inc., the defendants have substantial defenses. Tenneco Inc. and other defendants intend to defend vigorously against these claims. In view of the present stage of this litigation, and the number and complexity of the issues involved, such counsel is unable to express an opinion as to its ultimate outcome, or, if unfavorable, the amount of damages which might ultimately be assessed. Tenneco Inc., however, believes that the resolution of these claims will have no material effect on Tenneco Inc. and its consolidated subsidiaries' financial position or results of operations.

In preparing for the defense of the above litigation, it came to the attention of counsel for Tenneco Inc. that certain volumes of natural gas purchased by Channel have been produced from acreage or reservoirs which were, or may have been, at one time dedicated to interstate commerce under contracts between various producers and Tenneco Inc.'s interstate pipeline division. It appears that such gas was released from any such dedication to interstate commerce under a variety of procedures, some of which involve transactions which may have failed to meet all regulatory requirements therefor under the Natural Gas Act. The transactions in question were initiated several years ago, one dating back as far as 1958; Tenneco Inc. and its consolidated subsidiaries' records concerning them may be incomplete, and the surrounding circumstances and legal implications thereof are presently unclear. Tenneco Inc. and its consolidated subsidiaries have conducted an investigation of these transactions and on the basis of their review presently estimate that Channel's purchases of gas in such transactions have amounted to an aggregate of approximately 390 billion cubic feet over a period commencing in 1965.

In February 1977, Tenneco Inc. petitioned the Federal Power Commission (FPC) for a determination as to whether additional regulatory authority was required as to certain of these transactions under the circumstances and, if so, for the issuance of any such authority required. The FPC instituted an investigation into the matters set forth in Tenneco Inc.'s petition, and ordered that various producers involved, as well as Channel and Tenneco Oil Company, be made parties to the proceeding; in addition other parties intervened. Hearings on these matters were commenced before the FERC. In January 1979, the FERC suspended the administrative proceeding and commenced a private investigation to determine, among other things, whether there have been transfers of gas between Tenneco Inc. and Channel without the authorization of the FERC and whether a significant imbalance of gas may have developed between Channel and Tenneco Inc. Counsel for Tenneco Inc. and its consolidated subsidiaries are unable to express an opinion as to the ultimate outcome of this investigation, or the nature or extent of any charges or claims which might be asserted against Tenneco Inc. and its consolidated subsidiaries in connection therewith or as a result thereof. However, based upon information available to date, Tenneco Inc. believes that the resolution of this matter will have no material effect on Tenneco Inc. and its consolidated subsidiaries' financial position or results of operations.

Prior to the acquisition during 1977 of Monroe Auto Equipment Company (Monroe), the Federal Trade Commission (FTC) commenced an administrative proceeding to determine if such acquisition violated the federal antitrust laws; thereafter the FTC petitioned the U.S. District Court for the District of Columbia for a preliminary injunction against such acquisition, which was denied. A subsequent motion by the FTC to the U.S. Court of Appeals to enjoin temporarily such acquisition was also denied. The administrative proceeding is still pending and hearings have commenced. In the event the FTC finds the acquisition violated the antitrust laws, it could order a number of remedies, including divestiture of Monroe. Tenneco Inc. is unable to predict the outcome of such administrative proceeding, but intends to appeal if a materially adverse decision is issued by the FTC.

Tenneco Inc. and its subsidiaries are parties to numerous other lawsuits arising from their operations. Tenneco Inc. believes that the outcome of these suits will have no material effect on Tenneco Inc. and its consolidated subsidiaries' financial position or results of operations.

Questionable Payments

Tenneco Inc. has conducted an investigation into so-called "questionable" payments made in the operations of Tenneco Inc. and its subsidiaries. The results of this investigation were included in various reports filed in 1976 by Tenneco Inc. with the SEC, and additional information has been supplied on behalf of Tenneco Inc. and certain of its subsidiaries to the Division of Enforcement of the Securities and Exchange Commission, which is investigating the matters so reported by Tenneco Inc. In addition, the Internal Revenue Service commenced an investigation in 1976 to determine whether Tenneco Inc. and certain of its subsidiaries, and possibly their officers and employees, have violated the civil fraud provisions of the Internal Revenue Code. As of the date hereof, these governmental investigations are continuing. Tenneco Inc. believes that the final resolution of these investigations will not have a material adverse effect on Tenneco Inc.'s financial position or results of operations.

In November 1978, after trial in the U.S. District Court for the Eastern District of Louisiana, Tenneco Oil Company was convicted of utilizing facilities of interstate commerce to commit the offense of public bribery under Louisiana law in connection with payments made to a Louisiana sheriff who was also a licensed attorney. Sentencing is scheduled for March 1979; the maximum fine which could be imposed as a result of the conviction is $300,000.

Federal Energy Administration

The operations of several subsidiaries of Tenneco Inc., including Tenneco Oil Company, are subject to regulations adopted by the Federal Energy Administration (FEA). Tenneco Inc. believes that the subsidiaries have complied, in all material respects, with the terms and conditions of such regulations. However, the complexity of the regulations, lack of guiding precedent and attendant uncertainty concerning application of the regulations may expose the companies to interpretations by regulatory authority which differ from those of management. In this connection, the FEA has is-

sued Notices of Probable Violation which have not yet been resolved and remedial orders adverse to Tenneco. Additionally, Tenneco Oil Company initiated court proceedings with respect to FEA orders relating to pricing of gasoline and crude oil sales. Tenneco Inc. believes, however, that it has no exposure in such matters which could materially affect its financial position or results of operations.

Tenneco Offshore

Tenneco Offshore Company, Inc. (Offshore), a corporation organized by Tenneco Inc. to invest in oil and gas exploration in the Gulf of Mexico, sold to the public shares of its common stock and $95 million principal amount of convertible debentures due 1980. Tenneco Inc. and its subsidiaries own none of such common stock or convertible debentures. Tenneco Oil Company, a subsidiary of Tenneco Inc. and the General Partner of Tenneco Exploration, Ltd., a limited partnership in which Offshore is the Limited Partner, has a contingent obligation to cause such partnership to distribute cash or, at the option of Tenneco Inc., shares of Tenneco Inc. common stock equivalent to the principal amount of Offshore debentures (which have not been previously retired by Offshore or converted into Offshore's common stock) when the principal amount of such debentures becomes due in 1980.

Tenneco Offshore Company, Inc. organized a wholly-owned subsidiary corporation, Tenneco Offshore II Company, for the purpose of expanding its investment in oil and gas exploration in the Gulf of Mexico. Tenneco Offshore II Company sold $100 million principal amount of long-term notes due 1984 and contributed the $100 million to a limited partnership, Tenneco Exploration II, Ltd., in which it is the Limited Partner and Tenneco Oil Company is the General Partner. Tenneco Oil Company has a contingent obligation to cause such partnership to distribute cash or, at the option of Tenneco Inc., shares of Tenneco Inc. common stock to retire the principal amount of any notes which may remain outstanding at maturity.

Tenneco Exploration, Ltd. and Tenneco Exploration II, Ltd. have not completed development of their offshore oil and gas properties, and additional drilling is required in order to make a definitive estimate of reserves ultimately recoverable. Based on results of drilling to date and Tenneco Oil's present estimate of recoverable reserves and assuming crude oil, condensate and natural gas prices remain at the same levels as stipulated under presently existing regulations, Tenneco Inc. is of the opinion that any required cash advances to Tenneco Exploration, Ltd. in order to retire any debentures which are outstanding at maturity will be recovered through cash distributions from the partnership; however, Tenneco Inc. believes that a portion of cash advances to Tenneco Exploration II, Ltd. to retire outstanding notes of Tenneco Offshore II Company may not be recovered through cash distributions from the partnership. Accordingly, Tenneco Oil has recognized a liability of $50 million and increased its investment in offshore oil and gas properties for the projected future cash advances.

ASSET REPLACEMENT COST (Unaudited):

The companies have been subject to increasing operating costs as a result of the impact of inflation. However, the companies (in the aggregate) have historically been able to compensate for such cost increases by increasing sales prices in amounts sufficient to maintain an approximately constant gross profit percentage on sales.

Replacing items of plant and equipment with assets having equivalent productive capacity has usually required a substantially greater capital investment than was required to purchase the assets which are being replaced. The additional capital investment principally reflects the cumulative impact of inflation on the long-lived nature of these assets.

Tenneco Inc.'s annual report on Form 10-K (a copy of which is available upon request to the Tenneco Inc. Corporate Secretary) contains specific information by major businesses with respect to replacement cost of inventories and productive capacity (generally plant, machinery and equipment) at December 31, 1978 and 1977, and the approximate effect which replacement cost would have had on the computation of cost of sales and depreciation expense for the years then ended.

PLANT, PROPERTY AND EQUIPMENT:

Details of plant, property and equipment and related reserves for depreciation, depletion and amortization by major business at December 31, 1978, were as follows:

	Gross	Less Reserves	Net
		(Millions)	
Integrated oil	$3,405	$ 960	$2,445
Natural gas pipelines	2,761	1,452	1,309
Construction and farm equipment	573	221	352
Automotive	333	127	206
Chemicals	771	233	538
Agriculture, land management	215	50	165
Packaging	546	201	345
Shipbuilding	497	131	366
	$9,101	$3,375	$5,726

UNCONSOLIDATED SUBSIDIARIES:

Summarized financial information of J I Case Credit Corporation, an unconsolidated wholly-owned finance subsidiary and Philadelphia Life Insurance Company, an unconsolidated wholly-owned insurance subsidiary, at December 31, 1978 and 1977, and for the years then ended is as follows:

J I Case Credit Corporation

	1978	1977
	(Millions)	
Assets	$746	$690
Liabilities	643	599
Equity in net assets	103	91
Net income	12	10

Philadelphia Life Insurance Company

Assets	$779	$714
Liabilities	619	578
Equity in net assets	160	136
Net income	25	20

QUARTERLY FINANCIAL DATA:

Unaudited quarterly financial data for 1978 and 1977 is presented on page 43.

SEGMENT AND GEOGRAPHIC AREA INFORMATION:

Segment and geographic area information at December 31, 1978 and 1977, and for the years then ended is presented on pages 46 and 47.

(The above notes are an integral part of the foregoing financial statements.)

ARTHUR ANDERSEN & CO.
HOUSTON, TEXAS
February 20, 1979

To the Stockholders and
Board of Directors,
Tenneco Inc.:

We have examined the balance sheet of Tenneco Inc. (a Delaware corporation) and consolidated subsidiaries as of December 31, 1978 and 1977, and the related statements of income, stockholders' equity and changes in financial position for the years then ended. Our examinations were made in accordance with generally accepted auditing standards and accordingly included such tests of the accounting records and such other auditing procedures as we considered necessary in the circumstances.

In our opinion, the accompanying financial statements present fairly the financial position of Tenneco Inc. and consolidated subsidiaries as of December 31, 1978 and 1977, and the results of their operations and the changes in their financial position for the years then ended, in conformity with generally accepted accounting principles applied on a consistent basis during the years.

Arthur Andersen & Co.

Quarterly Data

QUARTERLY FINANCIAL DATA—(Millions Except Per Share Amounts)

Quarter	Net sales and operating revenues	Income before interest, federal income taxes and minority interests	Net income	Earnings per share of common stock	
				Average shares outstanding	Fully diluted
1978					
1st	$2,037	$ 265	$110	$1.10	$1.04
2nd	2,155	288	118	1.14	1.09
3rd	2,113	249	103	.98	.93
4th	2,457	326	135	1.31	1.24
	$8,762	$1,128	$466	$4.53	$4.30
1977					
1st	$1,826	$ 252	$105	$1.10	1.02
2nd	1,904	260	106	1.10	1.03
3rd	1,759	238	97	.98	.92
4th	1,919	285	119	1.20	1.14
	$7,408	$1,035	$427	$4.38	$4.11

QUARTERLY PER SHARE MARKET PRICES AND DIVIDENDS*

Quarter	Common Stock			$5.50 Preference Stock			$7.40 Preference Stock**		
	Market Prices			Market Prices			Market Prices		
	High	Low	Dividends	High	Low	Dividends	High	Low	Dividends
1978									
1st	$30⅞	$28	$.50	$112	$104	$1.375	$88⅛	$86¼	$ .6167
2nd	33¾	29½	.50	123	113	1.375	88⅛	86½	1.85
3rd	33¼	30	.50	123	110½	1.375	89½	81⅜	1.85
4th	34½	29	.55	128½	109	1.375	89	83¼	1.85
1977									
1st	$37¼	$31¾	$.47	$138	$121	$1.375			
2nd	35½	31½	.47	130	117	1.375			
3rd	35½	29¾	.50	131	112	1.375			
4th	33¼	28½	.50	119	108½	1.375			

Source of Market Prices: National Quotation Bureau Incorporated

Principal Market: New York Stock Exchange

*Five series of second preferred stock are outstanding (aggregating 104,013 and 115,025 shares at December 31, 1978 and 1977, respectively) with annual dividend rates ranging from $4.50 to $5.36. Very limited market information is available on these issues.

**Issued March 1, 1978.

Questions

1. Of what use is a balance sheet to creditors? Management? Investors?

2. What are the major limitations of the balance sheet as a source of information?

3. If cash is restricted for purposes other than to pay current obligations, should it be classified as a current asset?

4. State the generally accepted accounting principle (standard) applicable to the balance sheet valuation of each of the following assets.
   (a) Inventories.
   (b) Prepaid expenses.
   (c) Trade accounts receivable.
   (d) Machinery and equipment.
   (e) Marketable securities.

5. In what section of the balance sheet should the following items appear, and what balance sheet terminology would you use?
   (a) Checking account at bank.
   (b) Land (held as an investment).
   (c) Reserve for sinking fund.
   (d) Unamortized premium on bonds payable.
   (e) Investment in copyrights.
   (f) Employees' pension fund (consisting of cash and securities).
   (g) Premium on capital stock.
   (h) Long-term investments (pledged against bank loans payable).
   (i) Treasury stock (entered at cost, which is below par).

6. Where should the following items be shown on the balance sheet, if shown at all?
   (a) Allowance for doubtful accounts receivable. *current assets*
   (b) Merchandise held on consignment. *would not appear*
   (c) Advances received on sales contract. *current liability*
   (d) Cash surrender value of life insurance. *noncurrent* *but should be disclosed (footnote)*
   (e) Accommodation endorsement on note. *not recorded*
   (f) Merchandise out on consignment. *current asset*
   (g) Pension fund on deposit with a trustee (under a trust revocable at depositor's option). *noncurrent asset*
   (h) Intangible assets. *grouped with other intangibles*
   (i) Accumulated depreciation of plant and equipment. *in noncurrent asset*
   (j) Materials in transit—f.o.b. shipping point. *current asset*

7. What is the relationship between a current asset and a current liability?

8. The creditors of a company agree to accept promissory notes for the amount of its indebtedness with a proviso that three-fourths of the annual profits must be applied to their liquidation. How should these notes be shown on the balance sheet of the issuing company? Give a reason for your answer.

9. What are some of the techniques of disclosure for the balance sheet?

10. What does showing items "short" mean? Give an example.

11. What are the major types of subsequent events? Indicate how each of the following "subsequent events" would be reported.
    (a) Collection of a note written off in a prior period.
    (b) Issuance of a large preferred stock offering.
    (c) Acquisition of a company in a different industry.
    (d) Destruction of a major plant in an earthquake.
    (e) Death of company president.
    (f) Settlement of a four-week strike at additional wage costs.
    (g) Settlement of a federal income tax case at considerably more tax than anticipated at year-end.
    (h) Change in the product mix from consumer goods to industrial goods.

12. What is a gain contingency? A loss contingency? Give two examples of each.

13. What is the difference between the report form and the account form for the purpose of balance sheet presentation?

14. What is a "Summary of Significant Accounting Policies"?

15. What types of contractual obligations must be disclosed in great detail in the footnotes to the balance sheet? Why do you think these detailed provisions should be disclosed?

16. What is the purpose of the statement of changes in financial position? How does it differ from a balance sheet or income statement?

17. The net income for the year for Largo Enterprises is $900,000, but the statement of changes in financial position indicates that the resources provided by operations is $960,000. What might account for the difference?

18. Each of the following items must be considered in preparing a statement of changes in financial position. State where each item is to be reported in the statement, if at all.
    (a) During the year, 1,000 shares of common stock with a stated value of $25 a share were issued at $40 per share.
    (b) The company had a net income for the year of $90,000. Depreciation expense amounted to $14,000 and bond premium amortization to $6,000.
    (c) Uncollectible accounts receivable in the amount of $12,000 were written off against the Allowance for Doubtful Accounts.

19. The president of your company has recently read an article that disturbs him greatly. The author of this article stated that "although the balance sheet and income statement balance to the penny, they are full of estimates and subject to material error." Indicate items found in these statements that are based on estimates and explain why you must resort to "guessing" these amounts.

Cases

C5-1 At December 31, 1980, Buckley, Inc. has assets of $9,000,000, liabilities of $6,000,000, common stock of $2,000,000 (representing 2,000,000 shares of $1.00 par common stock), and retained earnings of $1,000,000. Net sales for the year 1980 were $18,000,000 and net income was $800,000. As auditors of this company, you are making a review of subsequent events of this company on February 13, 1981 and find the following.

1. On February 3, 1981, one of Buckley's customers declared bankruptcy. At December 31, 1980, this company owed Buckley $200,000, of which $20,000 was paid in January, 1981.

2. On January 18, 1981, one of the three major plants of the client burned.

3. On January 23, 1981, a strike was called at one of Buckley's largest plants which halted 30% of its production. As of today (February 13) the strike has not been settled.

4. A major electronics enterprise has introduced a line of products that would compete directly with Buckley's primary line, now being produced in a specially designed new plant. Because of manufacturing innovations, the competitor has been able to achieve quality similar to that of Buckley's products, but at a price 50% lower. Buckley officials say they will meet the lower prices, which are high enough to cover variable manufacturing and selling costs but which permit recovery of only a portion of fixed costs.

5. Merchandise handled by the company had been traded in the open markets in which it procures its supplies at $1.40 on December 31, 1980. This price had prevailed for two weeks, after release of an official market report that predicted vastly enlarged supplies; however, no purchases were made at $1.40. The price throughout the preceding year had been about $2.00, which was the level experienced over several years. On January 18, 1981, the price returned to $2.00, after public disclosure of an error in the official calculations of the prior December, correction of which destroyed the expectations of excessive supplies. Inventory at December 31, 1980 was on a cost or market basis.

6. On February 1, 1981, the board of directors adopted a resolution accepting the offer of an investment banker to guarantee the marketing of $1,000,000 of preferred stock.

Instructions

State in each case what notice, if any, you would make in your report affecting the year 1980.

C5-2 The following items were brought to your attention during the course of the year-end audit:

1. Because of a general increase in the number of labor disputes and strikes, both within and outside the industry, it is very likely that the client will suffer a costly strike in the near future.

2. Trade accounts receivable include a large number of customers' notes, many of which had been renewed several times and may have to be renewed continually for some time in the future. The interest is settled on each maturity date and the makers are in good credit standing.

3. At the beginning of the year the client entered into a ten-year nonrenewable lease agreement. Provisions in the lease require the client to make substantial reconditioning and restoration expenditures at the termination of the lease.

4. Inventory includes retired equipment, some at regularly depreciated book value, and some at scrap or sale value.

5. The client expects to recover a substantial amount in connection with a pending refund claim for a prior year's taxes. Although the claim is being contested, counsel for the company has confirmed this expectation.

6. Your client is a defendant in a patent infringement suit involving a material amount; you have received from the client's counsel a statement that the loss can be reasonably estimated and that a reasonable possibility of a loss exists.

7. Cash includes a substantial sum specifically set aside for immediate reconstruction of plant and renewal of machinery.

Instructions

For each of the situations above describe the accounting treatment you recommend for the current year. Justify your recommended treatment for each situation.

C5-3 In an examination of the Davis Corporation as of December 31, 1981, you have learned that the following situations exist. No entries have been made in the accounting records.

1. On December 15, 1981, the Davis Corporation declared a common stock dividend of 1,000 shares per 100,000 of its common stock outstanding, payable February 1, 1982, to the common stockholders of record December 31, 1981.

2. Davis Corporation, which is on a calendar-year basis, changed its inventory method as of January 1, 1981. The inventory for December 31, 1980, was costed by the FIFO method, and the inventory for December 31, 1981, was costed by the average method.

3. Davis Corporation has guaranteed the payment of interest on the 20-year first mortgage bonds of the Poper Company, an affiliate. Outstanding bonds of the Poper Company amount to $150,000 with interest payable at 8% per annum, due June 1 and December 1 of each year. The bonds were issued by the Poper Company on December 1, 1977, and all interest payments have been met by the company with the exception of the payment due December 1, 1981. The Davis Corporation states that it will pay the defaulted interest to the bondholders on January 15, 1982.

4. During the year 1981, the Davis Corporation was named as a defendant in a suit for damages by the Long Company for breach of contract. The case was decided in favor of Long Company, and it was awarded $60,000 damages. At the time of the audit, the case was under appeal to a higher court.

5. The corporation erected its present factory building in 1966. Depreciation was calculated by the straight-line method, using an estimated life of 35 years. Early in 1981, the board of directors conducted a careful survey and estimated that the factory building had a remaining useful life of 25 years as of January 1, 1981.

6. An additional assessment of 1981 income taxes was levied and paid in 1981.

7. When calculating the accrual for officers' salaries at December 31, 1981, it was discovered that the accrual for officers' salaries for December 31, 1980, had been overstated.

Instructions

Describe fully how each of the items above should be reflected in the financial statements of Davis Corporation for the year 1981.

C5-4 The assets of Loghorn, Inc. are presented below:

Loghorn, Inc.
BALANCE SHEET
December 31, 1981

Assets

Current Assets

Cash		$ 80,000
Unclaimed dividend checks		7,500
Marketable securities (cost $20,000) at market		24,500
Accounts receivable (less bad debt reserve)		75,000
Inventories—at lower of cost (determined by the next-in, first-out method) or market		250,000
Total current assets		437,000

Tangible Assets

Land (less accumulated depreciation)		70,000
Buildings and equipment	$800,000	
Less accumulated depreciation	300,000	500,000
Net tangible assets		570,000

Long-Term Investments

Stocks and bonds		100,000
Treasury stock		40,000
Total long-term investments		140,000

Other Assets

Discount on bonds payable		14,200
Claim against U.S. government (pending in 3rd Dist.)		975,000
Total other assets		989,200
Total Assets		$3,136,200

Instructions

Indicate the deficiencies, if any, in the foregoing assets of Loghorn, Inc.

C5-5   Presented below is the balance sheet of Widener Corporation:

Widener Corporation
BALANCE SHEET
December 31, 1981

Assets

Current assets:		
Cash	$ 9,000	
Marketable securities	9,000	
Accounts receivable	25,000	
Merchandise inventory	20,000	
Supplies inventory	4,000	
Stock investment in Subsidiary Company	20,000	$ 87,000
Investments:		
Treasury stock		26,000
Property, plant, and equipment:		
Buildings and land	71,000	
Less: Reserve for depreciation	20,000	51,000
Deferred charges:		
Unamortized discount on bonds payable		1,000
Other assets:		
Cash surrender value of life insurance		18,000
		$183,000

Liabilities and Capital

Current liabilities:		
Accounts payable	$15,000	
Reserve for income taxes	14,000	
Customers' accounts with credit balances	1	$ 29,001
Long-term liabilities:		
Bonds payable		46,000
Total liabilities		75,001
Capital stock:		
Capital stock, par $5	75,000	
Earned surplus	24,999	
Cash dividends declared	8,000	107,999
		$183,000

Instructions

Indicate your criticism of the balance sheet presented above. State briefly the proper treatment of the item criticized.

C5-6 The financial statement below was prepared by employees of your client, Godfrey Manufacturing Company. The statement is unaccompanied by footnotes.

Godfrey Manufacturing Company
BALANCE SHEET
As of November 30, 1981

Current assets			
Cash		$ 179,200	
Accounts receivable (less allowance of $15,000 for doubtful accounts)		240,700	
Inventories		2,554,000	$2,973,900
Less current liabilities			
Accounts payable		206,400	
Accrued payroll		8,260	
Accrued interest on mortgage note		12,000	
Estimated taxes payable		66,000	292,660
Net working capital			2,681,240
Property, plant, and equipment (at cost)			

	Cost	Depreciation	Value	
Land and buildings	$ 983,300	$310,000	673,300	
Machinery and equipment	1,135,700	568,699	567,001	
	$2,119,000	$878,699		1,240,301

Deferred charges			
Prepaid taxes and other expenses		11,700	
Unamortized discount on mortgage note		10,800	22,500
Total net working capital and noncurrent assets			3,944,041
Less deferred liabilities			
Mortgage note payable		300,000	
Unearned revenue		1,898,000	2,198,000
Total net assets			$1,746,041
Stockholders' equity			
6% Preferred stock at par value			$ 400,000
Common stock at par value			697,000
Paid-in surplus			210,000
Retained earnings			483,641
Treasury stock at cost (370 shares)			(44,600)
Total stockholders' equity			$1,746,041

Instructions

Indicate the deficiencies, if any, in the balance sheet above.

C5-7 The following balance sheet, which was submitted to you for review, has been prepared for inclusion in the published annual report of the Drives Corporation for the year ended December 31, 1981.

Drives Corporation
BALANCE SHEET
As of December 31, 1981

ASSETS

Current assets		
Cash		$ 1,800,000
Accounts receivable	$3,900,000	
Less reserve for bad debts	50,000	3,850,000
Inventories—at the lower of cost (determined by the first-in, first-out method) or market		3,600,000
Total current assets		9,250,000
Plant assets		
Land (at cost)	200,000	
Building, machinery and equipment, and furniture (at cost)	4,200,000	
Less reserve for depreciation	(1,490,000)	2,910,000
Deferred charges and other assets		
Cash surrender value of life insurance	20,000	
Unamortized discount on first mortgage note	42,000	
Prepaid expenses	40,000	102,000
		$12,262,000

LIABILITIES

Current liabilities		
Notes payable to bank—unsecured		$ 750,000
Current maturities of first mortgage note		600,000
Accounts payable—trade		1,900,000
Reserve for income taxes for the year ended December 31, 1981		700,000
Accrued expenses		550,000
		4,500,000
Long-term debt		
8% first mortgage note payable in quarterly installments of $150,000	$4,200,000	
Less current maturities	600,000	3,600,000
Reserves		
Reserve for contingencies	500,000	
Reserve for additional federal income tax	100,000	950,000
Reserve for damages	50,000	
Reserve for possible future inventory losses	300,000	
Capital		
Capital stock—authorized, issued, and outstanding 100,000 shares of $10 par value	1,000,000	
Capital surplus	300,000	
Earned surplus	1,912,000	3,212,000
		$12,257,000

Additional Data

1. Reserve for contingencies was set up by charges against earned surplus over a period of several years by the board of directors to provide for a possible future recession.

2. Reserve for federal income taxes was set up in prior years and relates to additional taxes that the Internal Revenue Service contends the company owes. The company believes that the department will settle for the amount of $100,000 set up on the balance sheet.

3. Reserve for damages was setup by a charge against current fiscal year's net income to cover damages possibly payable by the company as a defendant in a lawsuit in progress at the balance sheet date. Suit was subsequently compromised for $50,000 prior to the issuance of the statement.

4. Reserve for possible future inventory losses was set up in prior years by action of the board of directors by charges against earned surplus. No charges occurred in the account during the current year.

5. Capital surplus consists of the difference between the par value of $10 per share of stock and the price at which the stock was actually issued.

Instructions

State what changes in classification or terminology you advocate in the presentation of this balance sheet to make it conform with generally accepted accounting principles and with present-day terminology. State your reasons for your suggested changes.

C5-8 The following year-end financial statements were prepared by the Warren Corporation's bookkeeper. The Warren Corporation operates a chain of retail stores.

Warren Corporation
BALANCE SHEET
June 30, 1981

ASSETS

Current assets		
Cash		$ 100,000
Notes receivable		100,000
Accounts receivable, less reserve for		
doubtful accounts		75,000
Inventories		395,500
Investment securities (at cost)		100,000
Total current assets		770,500
Property, plant, and equipment		
Land (at cost) (note 1)	$180,000	
Buildings, at cost less accumulated depreciation		
of $350,000	500,000	
Equipment, at cost less accumulated depreciation		
of $180,000	400,000	1,080,000
Intangibles		450,000
Other assets		
Prepaid expenses		6,405
Total assets		$2,306,905

LIABILITIES AND OWNERS' EQUITY

Current liabilities			
Accounts payable			$ 25,500
Estimated income taxes payable			160,000
Contingent liability on discounted notes receivable			75,000
Total current liabilities			260,500
Long-term liabilities			
9% serial bonds, $50,000 due annually on December 31			
Maturity value		$865,000	
Less unamortized discount		35,000	830,000
Total liabilities			1,090,500
Owners' equity			
Common stock, stated value $10			
(authorized and issued, 75,000 shares)		750,000	
Retained earnings			
Appropriated (note 2)	$110,000		
Free	356,405	466,405	1,216,405
Total liabilities and owners' equity			$2,306,905

Warren Corporation
INCOME STATEMENT
As at June 30, 1981

Sales			$2,500,000
Interest income			6,000
Total revenue			2,506,000
Cost of goods sold			1,780,000
Gross margin			726,000
Operating expenses			
Selling expenses			
Salaries	$ 95,000		
Advertising	85,000		
Sales returns and allowances	50,000	$230,000	
General and administrative expenses			
Salaries	84,000		
Property taxes	38,000		
Depreciation and amortization	86,000		
Rent (note 3)	75,000		
Interest on serial bonds	48,000	331,000	561,000
Income before income taxes			165,000
Income taxes			80,000
Net income			$ 85,000

Notes to financial statements:

Note 1.   Includes a future store site acquired during the year at a cost of $80,000.

Note 2.   Retained earnings in the amount of $110,000 have been set aside to finance expansion.

Note 3.   During the year the corporation acquired certain equipment under a long-term lease.

Instructions

Identify and discuss the defects in the financial statements above with respect to terminology, disclosure, and classification. Your discussion should explain why you consider them to be defects. Do not prepare revised statements.

(AICPA adapted)

C5-9   Below are the account titles of a number of debit and credit accounts as they might appear on the balance sheet of the Pappas Corporation as of October 31, 1981.

Debits	Credits
Cash in bank *current asset*	Accrued payroll *current liability*
Land	Provision for renegotiation of U.S. government *cl*
Inventory of operating parts and supplies *current asset*	contracts
Inventory of raw materials *asset current*	Notes payable *depends*
Patents	Accrued interest on bonds *cl*
Cash and U.S. government bonds set aside for	Accumulated depreciation
property additions	Accounts payable *cl*
Investment in subsidiary	Capital in excess of par
Accounts receivable	Accrued interest on notes payable *cl*
U.S. government contracts	8% first mortgage bonds to be redeemed in 1981
Regular *current asset*	out of current assets
Installments—due in 1981 *current asset*	Capital stock—preferred
Installments—due in 1982-1983 *current asset*	9½% first mortgage bonds due in 1988
Goodwill	Preferred stock dividend, payable Nov. 1, 1981 *cl*
Inventory of finished goods *current asset*	Allowance for doubtful accounts receivable *reduction ca*
Inventory of work in process " "	Provision for federal income taxes *cl*
Deficit	Customers advances (on contracts to be com-
Interest accrued on U.S. government securities *current asset*	pleted in 1982) *cl*
Notes receivable *depends*	Appropriation for possible decline in value of raw
Petty cash fund *current asset*	materials inventory
U.S. government securities *probably current*	Premium on bonds redeemable in 1981 *cl*
Treasury stock	Officers' 1981 bonus accrued *cl*
Unamortized bond discount	

Instructions

Select the current asset and current liability items from among these debits and credits. If there appear to be certain borderline cases that you are unable to classify without further information, mention them and explain your difficulty, or give your reasons for making questionable classifications, if any.

(AICPA adapted)

Exercises

E5-1   Presented below are the captions of a balance sheet:

A. Current assets	F. Current liabilities
B. Investments	G. Noncurrent liabilities
C. Property, plant, and equipment	H. Capital stock
D. Intangible assets	I. Additional paid-in capital
E. Other assets	J. Retained earnings

Instructions

Indicate by letter where each of the following items would be classified:

1. Goodwill
2. Preferred stock
3. Wages payable
4. Trade accounts payable
5. Buildings
6. Marketable securities
7. Current portion of long-term debt
8. Premium on bonds payable
9. Allowance for doubtful accounts
10. Appropriation for contingencies
11. Cash surrender value of life insurance
12. Notes payable (due next year)
13. Taxes payable
14. Land
15. Bond sinking fund
16. Merchandise inventory
17. Office supplies
18. Prepaid insurance
19. Bonds payable
20. Common stock

E5-2   Presented below are a number of balance sheet accounts:

1. Investment in Common Stock	8. Marketable Securities (short-term)
2. Treasury Stock	9. Income Taxes Payable
3. Common Stock Distributable	10. Accrued Interest on Notes Payable
4. Accumulated Depreciation	11. Unearned Subscription Income
5. Warehouse in Process of Construction	12. Work in Process
6. Petty Cash	13. Accrued Vacation Pay
7. Deficit	14. Cash Dividends Payable

Instructions

For each of the accounts above, indicate the proper balance sheet classification. In the case of borderline items, indicate the additional information that would be required to determine the proper classification.

E5-3   Assume that Rothschild, Inc. has the following accounts at the end of the current year.

1. Common Stock	15. Accumulated Depreciation— Buildings
2. Discount on Bonds Payable	
3. Treasury Stock	16. Notes Receivable Discounted
4. Common Stock Subscribed	17. Cash Restricted for Plant Expansion
5. Raw Materials	18. Land Held for Future Plant Site
6. Preferred Stock Investments— Long-term	19. Allowance for Doubtful Accounts— Accounts Receivable
7. Unearned Rent Income	20. Retained Earnings—Unappropriated
8. Appropriation for Plant Expansion	21. Discount on Common Stock
9. Work in Process	22. Unearned Subscription Income
10. Copyrights	23. Receivables—Officers (due in one year)
11. Buildings	
12. Notes Receivable (short-term)	24. Finished Goods
13. Cash	25. Accounts Receivable
14. Accrued Salaries Payable	26. Bonds Payable (due in four years)
	27. Stocks Subscriptions Receivable

Instructions

Prepare a balance sheet in good form (no monetary amounts are necessary).

E5-4   Assume that Harlow Enterprises uses the following headings on its balance sheet:

A. Current assets	F. Current liabilities
B. Investments	G. Long-term liabilities
C. Property, plant, and equipment	H. Capital stock
D. Intangible assets	I. Paid-in capital in excess of par
E. Other assets	J. Retained earnings

Instructions

Indicate by letter how each of the following usually should be classified. If an item should appear in a note to the financial statements, use the letter "N" to indicate this fact. If an item need not be reported at all on the balance sheet, use the letter "X".

1. Advances to suppliers.
2. Unearned rental income.
3. Treasury stock.
4. Unexpired insurance.
5. Stock owned in affiliated companies.
6. Unearned subscriptions revenue.
7. Premium on preferred stock.
8. Copyrights.
9. Bond sinking fund.
10. Sale of large issue of common stock 15 days after balance sheet date.
11. Accrued interest on notes receivable.
12. Twenty-year issue of bonds payable which will mature within the next year. (No sinking fund exists and refunding is not planned.)
13. Machinery retired from use and held for sale.
14. Fully depreciated machine still in use.
15. Organization costs.
16. Salaries which company budget shows will be paid to employees within the next year.
17. Company is a defendant in a lawsuit for $1 million (possibility of loss is remote).
18. Discount on bonds payable. (Assume related to bonds payable in No. 12.)
19. Accrued interest on bonds payable.
20. Accumulated depreciation.

E5-5 Focus Company has decided to expand their operations. The bookkeeper recently completed the balance sheet presented below in order to obtain additional funds for expansion.

Focus Company
BALANCE SHEET
For the Year Ended 1981

Current assets	
Cash (net of bank overdraft of $40,000)	$180,000
Accounts receivable (net)	325,000
Inventories at lower of average cost or market	420,000
Marketable securities—at market (cost $110,000)	125,000
Property, plant, and equipment	
Building (net)	460,000
Office equipment (net)	185,000
Land held for future use	150,000
Intangible assets	
Goodwill	75,000
Cash surrender value of life insurance	64,000
Prepaid expenses	2,200
Current liabilities	
Accounts payable	95,000
Notes payable (due next year)	100,000
Pension obligation	71,000
Rent payable	85,000
Premium on bonds payable	68,000
Long-term liabilities	
Bonds payable	500,000
Reserve for plant expansion	75,000
Stockholders' equity	
Common stock, $1.00 par, authorized 400,000 shares, issued 280,000	280,000
Additional paid-in capital	70,000
Retained earnings	?

Instructions

Prepare a revised balance sheet given the available information. Assume that the accumulated depreciation balance for the buildings is $95,000 and for the office equipment, $55,000. The allowance for doubtful accounts has a balance of $25,000. The pension obligation is considered a long-term liability.

E5-6 The bookkeeper for the Warwick Company has prepared the following balance sheet as of July 31, 1981:

Warwick Company
BALANCE SHEET
as of July 31, 1981

Cash	$ 54,000	Notes and accounts payable	$ 41,000
Accounts receivable (net)	38,000	Long-term liabilities	64,000
Inventories	50,000	Stockholders' equity	130,000
Equipment (net)	73,000		
Patents	20,000		
	$235,000		$235,000

The following additional information is provided:

1. Cash includes $800 in a petty cash fund and $10,000 in a bond sinking fund.
2. The net accounts receivable balance is comprised of the following three items: (a) accounts receivable—debit balances $45,000; (b) accounts receivable—credit balances $5,000; (c) allowance for doubtful accounts $2,000.
3. Merchandise inventory costing $2,400 was shipped out on consignment on July 31, 1981. The ending inventory balance does not include the consigned goods. Receivables in the amount of $3,200 were recognized on these consigned goods.
4. Equipment had a cost of $95,000 and an accumulated depreciation balance of $22,000.
5. Taxes payable of $4,000 were accrued on July 31. The Warwick Company, however, had set up a cash fund to meet this obligation. This cash fund was not included in the cash balance, but was offset against the taxes payable amount.

Instructions

Prepare a corrected balance sheet as of July 31, 1981 from the available information.

E5-7 The current asset and liability sections of the balance sheet of Olson, Inc. appear as follows:

Olson, Inc.
PARTIAL BALANCE SHEET
December 31, 1981

Cash		$ 30,000	Accounts payable	$48,000
Accounts receivable	$80,000		Notes payable	70,000
Less allowance for doubtful acounts	6,000	74,000		
Inventories		170,000		
Prepaid expenses		10,000		
		$284,000		$118,000

The following errors in the corporation's accounting have been discovered:

1. Sales for the first four days in January 1982 in the amount of $26,000 were entered in the sales book as of December 31, 1981. Of these, $23,000 were sales on account and the remainder were cash sales.

2. Cash, not including cash sales, collected in January 1982 and entered as of December 31, 1981, totaled $30,384. Of this amount, $20,384 was received on account after cash discounts of 2% had been deducted; the remainder represented the proceeds of a bank loan.

3. January 1982 cash disbursements entered as of December 1981 included payments of accounts payable in the amount of $37,000, on which a cash discount of 2% was taken.

4. The inventory included $24,000 of merchandise that had been received at December 31 but for which no purchase invoices had been received or entered. Of this amount, $10,000 had been received on consignment; the remainder was purchased f.o.b. destination, terms 2/10, n/30.

Instructions

(a) Restate the current asset and liability sections of the balance sheet in accordance with good accounting practice. (Assume that both accounts receivable and accounts payable are recorded gross.)

(b) State the net effect of your adjustments on the Olson, Inc.'s retained earnings balance.

E5-8   Condensed financial data of the Baker Company for the years ended December 31, 1980 and December 31, 1981, are presented below:

Baker Company
Comparative Balance Sheet Data
as of December 31, 1980 and 1981

	1980	1981
Cash	$ 18,400	$134,800
Receivables, net	49,000	83,200
Inventories	61,900	92,500
Investments	100,000	90,000
Plant assets	220,000	240,000
	$449,300	$640,500
Accounts payable	$ 67,300	$100,000
Mortgage payable	73,500	50,000
Accumulated depreciation	50,000	30,000
Common stock	125,000	175,000
Retained earnings	133,500	285,500
	$449,300	$640,500

Baker Company
INCOME STATEMENT
For the Year Ended December 31, 1981

Sales	$300,000	
Interest and other revenue	10,000	$310,000
Less:		
Cost of goods sold	$100,000	
Selling and administrative expenses	10,000	
Depreciation	22,000	
Income taxes	5,000	
Interest charges	3,000	
Loss on sale of plant assets	8,000	148,000
Net income		$162,000
Dividends		10,000
Income retained in business		$152,000

Additional information:
New plant assets costing $80,000 were purchased during the year. Investments were sold at book value.

Instructions

From the foregoing information, prepare a statement of changes in financial position (working capital approach).

Problems

P5-1   Presented below is a list of accounts in alphabetical order.

Accounts payable	Gain on sale of equipment
Accounts receivable	Interest receivable
Accrued wages	Inventory—beginning inventory
Accumulated depreciation—buildings	Inventory—ending inventory
Accumulated depreciation—equipment	Land for future plant site
Advances to employees	Patent
Advertising	Pension fund
Allowance for doubtful accounts	Pension obligations
Appropriation for possible inventory price declines	Petty cash
	Preferred stock
Appropriation for plant expansion	Premium on bonds payable
Bond sinking fund	Premium on preferred stock
Bonds payable	Prepaid expenses
Buildings	Purchases
Cash in bank	Purchase returns and allowances
Cash on hand	Retained earnings—unappropriated
Cash surrender value of life insurance	Sales
Commission expense	Sales discounts
Common stock	Sales salaries
Dividends payable	Temporary investments
Equipment	Transportation-in
FICA taxes payable	Treasury stock
Franchise	Unearned subscription income

Instructions

Prepare a balance sheet in good form (no monetary amounts are to be shown).

P5-2 Presented below are a number of balance sheet items for Anderson, Inc. for the current year, 1981.

Notes receivable *ca*	$ 627,905	Accumulated depreciation— *nca*	
Notes payable to banks *cl*	241,652	equipment	$272,084
Accounts payable *cl*	701,244	Inventories *ca*	225,468
Equipment *nca*	1,766,874	Rent payable—short-term *cl*	33,600
Marketable securities *ca*		Taxes payable *cl*	70,541
(short-term)	96,000	Long-term rental obligations *ncl*	460,296
Accumulated depreciation— *nca*		Common stock, $.10 par value *se*	156,162
building	80,800	Preferred stock, $10 par value *se*	160,000
Building *nca*	1,802,823	Prepaid expenses *ca*	109,662
Retained earnings *se*	?	Goodwill *intangible*	124,263
Refundable federal and state		Payroll taxes payable *cl*	168,000
income taxes *ca*	92,632	Bonds payable *ncl*	240,000
Unsecured notes payable due		Discount on bonds payable *ncl*	12,000
after one year *ncl*	1,633,154	Cash *ca*	240,000
		Land *nca*	280,000

Instructions

Prepare a balance sheet in good form. Common stock authorized was 35,000,000 shares and preferred stock authorized was 30,000 shares. Assume that notes receivable and notes payable are short-term, unless stated otherwise.

P5-3 Presented below is the balance sheet of Krainer Corporation as of December 31, 1981:

Krainer Corporation
BALANCE SHEET
December 31, 1981

ASSETS

Building (note 1)	$1,425,000
Land	823,500
Treasury stock (50,000 shares, no par)	91,500
Cash on hand	187,500
Assets allocated to trustee for plant expansion	
Cash in bank	60,000
U.S. Treasury notes, at cost	165,000
Accounts receivable	130,500
Inventories	151,500
Goodwill (note 2)	108,000
	$3,142,500

EQUITIES

Common stock, authorized and issued, 1,000,000 shares, no par	$1,650,000
Notes payable (note 3)	480,000
Federal income taxes payable	46,500
Reserve for repairs of machinery (note 4)	39,000
Reserve for contingencies	67,500
Reserve for depreciation of building	315,000
Appreciation capital (note 1)	288,000
Retained earnings	256,500
	$3,142,500

Note 1. Buildings are stated at cost, except for one building that was recorded at appraised value. The excess of appraisal value over cost was $288,000.

Note 2. Goodwill in the amount of $108,000 was recognized because the company believed that their book value was not an accurate representation of the fair market value of the company.

Note 3. Notes payable are long-term except for the current installment due of $15,000.

Note 4. A reserve for repairs was set up by a charge to income. Upon consultation with the company's auditors, it was determined that this contingency did not meet the criteria of a loss contingency. The company still wishes to show this amount in stockholders' equity.

Instructions

Prepare a corrected balance sheet in good form.

P5-4 Presented below is the balance sheet of Buttars Corporation for the current year, 1981.

Buttars Corporation
BALANCE SHEET
December 31, 1981

Current assets	$ 420,000	Current liabilities	$ 380,000
Investments	640,000	Long-term liabilities	1,040,000
Property, plant, and equipment	1,720,000	Stockholders' equity	1,640,000
Intangible assets	280,000		
	$3,060,000		$3,060,000

The following information is presented:

1. The current asset section includes: cash $100,000, accounts receivable $170,000 less $10,000 for allowance for doubtful accounts, inventories $180,000, and prepaid income 20,000. The cash balance is comprised of $116,000, less a bank overdraft of $16,000. Inventories are stated on the lower of FIFO cost or market.

2. The investments section includes the cash surrender value of a life insurance contract $40,000, investments in common stock, short-term $80,000 and long-term $140,000, bond sinking fund $200,000, and organization costs $180,000.

3. Property, plant, and equipment includes buildings $1,040,000 less accumulated depreciation $360,000, equipment $420,000 less accumulated depreciation $180,000, land $500,000, and land held for future use $300,000.

4. Intangible assets include a franchise $140,000, goodwill $100,000, and discount on bonds payable $40,000.

5. Current liabilities include accounts payable $90,000, notes payable—short-term $120,000 and long-term $80,000, taxes payable $40,000, and appropriation for short-term contingencies $50,000.

6. Long-term liabilities are comprised solely of 10% bonds payable due 1992.

7. Stockholders' equity has preferred stock, no par value, authorized 300,000 shares, issued 150,000 shares for $450,000, and common stock, $1.00 par value, authorized 400,000 shares, issued 100,000 shares at an average price of $10. In addition, the corporation has retained earnings of $190,000.

Instructions

Prepare a balance sheet in good form.

P5-5 Below is the trial balance of Wollman Bros. and other related information for the year 1981.

Wollman Bros.
TRIAL BALANCE
December 31, 1981

Cash	$ 18,000	
Accounts Receivable	144,000	
Allowance for Doubtful Accounts		$ 5,940
Prepaid Expenses	1,620	
Inventory	270,000	
Long-term Investments	324,000	
Land	72,000	
Construction Work in Progress	108,000	
Patents	18,000	
Equipment	360,000	
Accumulated Depreciation of Equipment		108,000
Unamortized Discount on Bonds Payable	7,200	
Accounts Payable		162,000
Accrued Expenses		3,600
Notes Payable		72,000
Bonds Payable		360,000
Capital Stock		540,000
Premium on Capital Stock		23,400
Retained Earnings		37,080
Reserve for Contingencies		10,800
	$1,322,820	$1,322,820

Additional information is given as follows:

1. The inventory has a replacement market value of $320,400. The LIFO method of inventory value method is used.
2. The market value of the long-term investments that consist of stocks and bonds is $330,000.
3. The amount of the Construction Work in Progress account represents the costs expended to date on a building in the process of construction. (The company rents factory space at the present time.) The land on which the building is being constructed cost $72,000, as shown in the trial balance.
4. The patents were purchased by the company at a cost of $28,800 and are being amortized on a straight-line basis.
5. Of the unamortized discount on bonds payable, $600 will be amortized in 1982.
6. The notes payable represent bank loans that are secured by long-term investments carried at $144,000. These bank loans are due in 1982.
7. The bonds payable bear interest at 11% and are due January 1, 1992.
8. Six hundred thousand shares of common stock of a par value of $1.00 were authorized, of which 540,000 shares were issued and are outstanding.
9. The Reserve for Contingencies was created by action of the board of directors.

Instructions

Prepare a balance sheet as of December 31, 1981 so that all important information is fully disclosed.

P5-6 The Haveman Corporation is primarily a sales organization. The corporation has approximately 1,000 stockholders, and its stock, which is traded "over the counter," sold throughout 1981 at about $7 a share with little fluctuation.

Below is the corporation's balance sheet at December 31, 1980.

Haveman Corporation
BALANCE SHEET
December 31, 1980

Assets

Current assets		
Cash		$ 4,386,040
Accounts receivable	$3,150,000	
Less allowance for doubtful accounts	94,500	3,055,500
Inventories—at the lower of cost (first-in, first-out)		
or estimated realizable market		2,800,000
Total current assets		10,241,540
Plant assets (at cost)	3,300,000	
Less accumulated depreciation	1,300,000	2,000,000
Total assets		$12,241,540

Liabilities and Stockholders' Equity

Current liabilities		
Notes payable due within one year		$ 1,000,000
Accounts payable and accrued liabilities		2,091,500
Federal income taxes payable		350,000
Total current liabilities		3,441,500
Notes payable due after one year		4,000,000
Stockholders' equity		
Capital stock—authorized 2,000,000 shares of $1.00 par value;		
issued and outstanding 1,000,000 shares	$1,000,000	
Additional paid-in capital	1,500,000	
Retained earnings	2,300,040	
Total stockholders' equity		4,800,040
Total liabilities and stockholders' equity		$12,241,540

Information concerning the corporation and its activities during 1981 follows:

1. Sales for the year were $15,650,000. The gross profit percentage for the year was 30% of sales. Merchandise purchases and freight-in totaled $10,905,000. Assume that depreciation and other expenses do not enter into cost of goods sold.

2. Administrative, selling, and general expenses (including provision for state taxes) other than interest, depreciation, and provision for doubtful accounts amounted to $2,403,250.

3. The December 31, 1981 accounts receivable were $3,350,000 and the corporation maintains an allowance for doubtful accounts equal to 3% of the accounts receivable outstanding. During the year $50,000 of 1980 receivables were deemed uncollectible and charged off to the allowance account.

4. The rate of depreciation on plant assets is 13% per annum and the corporation consistently follows the policy of taking one-half year's depreciation in the year of acquisition. The depreciation expense for 1981 was $474,500.

5. The notes are payable in 20 equal quarterly installments commencing March 31, 1981 with interest at 5% per annum also payable quarterly.
6. Accounts payable and accrued liabilities at December 31, 1981 were $2,221,000.
7. The balance of the 1980 income tax paid in 1981 was in exact agreement with the amount accrued on the December 31, 1980 balance sheet. (1981 tax rate 52%; first $25,000 taxed at 30%.)
8. For purposes of the 1981 estimated tax payments the controller estimated the total 1981 tax to be $800,000. ($350,000 was paid in 1981.)
9. During the second month of each quarter of the year 1981 dividends of $.10 a share were declared and paid. In addition, in July 1981 a 5% stock dividend was declared and paid.

Instructions

Prepare the following statements in good form, supported by well-organized and detailed computations, at or for the year ended December 31, 1981:

(a) Income statement

(b) Statement of retained earnings

(c) Balance sheet

(AICPA adapted)

P5-7 You have been engaged to examine the financial statements of Warren Corporation for the year 1981. The bookkeeper who maintains the financial records has prepared all the unaudited financial statements for the corporation since its organization on January 2, 1975. The client provides you with the information below.

Warren Corporation
BALANCE SHEET
As of December 31, 1981

Assets		Liabilities	
Current assets	$1,823,130	Current liabilities	$ 951,765
Other assets	6,480,000	Long-term liabilities	1,500,000
		Capital	5,851,365
	$8,303,130		$8,303,130

An analysis of current assets discloses the following:

Cash (restricted in the amount of $480,000 for plant expansion)	$1,113,195
Investments in land	106,500
Accounts receivable less allowance of $48,000	118,710
Inventories (LIFO flow assumption)	484,725
	$1,823,130

Other assets include

Prepaid expenses	$ 47,073
Plant and equipment less accumulated depreciation of $1,506,000	5,123,490
Cash surrender value of life insurance policy	90,198
Unamortized bond discount	47,130
Claim for income tax refund	182,148
Goodwill, at cost less amortization of $4,500	347,100
Land	642,861
	$6,480,000

Current liabilities include

Accounts payable	$ 480,000
Notes payable (due, 1983)	183,513
Estimated income taxes payable	150,000
Premium on common stock	138,252
	$ 951,765

Long-term liabilities include

Unearned income	$ 527,730
Dividends payable (cash)	222,270
6% Serial bonds payable ($150,000 maturing 1982–1986)	750,000
	$1,500,000

Capital includes

Retained earnings (unappropriated)	$2,130,000
Capital stock, par value $10; authorized 200,000 shares, 150,000 shares issued	1,500,000
Reserve for contingencies	2,221,365
	$5,851,365

The supplementary information below is also provided.

1. A major competitor has introduced a line of products that will compete directly with Warren's primary line, now being produced in a specially designed new plant. Because of manufacturing innovations, the competitor's line will be of comparable quality but priced 50% below the client's line. The competitor announced its new line on January 14, 1982. The client indicates that the company will meet the lower prices that are high enough to cover variable manufacturing and selling expenses, but permit recovery of only a portion of fixed costs.

2. You learned on January 28, 1982, prior to completion of the audit, of heavy damage because of a recent fire to one of the client's two plants; the loss will not be reimbursed by insurance. The newspapers described the event in detail.

3. On May 1, 1981, the corporation issued $750,000 of bonds to finance plant expansion. The long-term bond agreement provided for the annual payment of principal and interest over five years. The existing plant was pledged as security for the loan.

4. The bookkeeper made the following mistakes:
   (a) In 1979, the ending inventory was overstated by $183,000. The ending inventories for 1980 and 1981 were correctly computed.
   (b) In 1981, accrued wages in the amount of $330,000 were omitted from the balance sheet and these expenses were not charged on the income statement.
   (c) In 1981, a gain of $150,000 (net of tax) on the sale of certain plant assets was credited directly to retained earnings.

Instructions

Prepare the balance sheet for Warren Corporation in accordance with proper accounting principles. Describe the nature of any footnotes that might need to be prepared.

Compound Interest, Annuities, and Present Value

Importance of the Time Value of Money

Business enterprises both invest and borrow large sums of money. **Investments** are made in the expectation of realizing future benefits through receiving cash returns in future periods. **Borrowing** is performed in full contemplation of repayment, that is, a sum of money is received in return for a promise to repay certain sums of money in the future. The common characteristic in these two transactions is the **time value of the monies** (i.e., the **interest** factor) involved. The timing of the returns on the investment has an important effect on the worth of the investment (asset), and the timing of debt repayments has an effect on the value of the commitment (liability). **Business people have become acutely aware of this timing factor and invest and borrow only after carefully analyzing the relative values of the cash outflows and inflows.**

The accountant also is expected to make value measurements and to understand their implications. To do so, the accountant must understand and be able to measure the present value of future cash inflows and outflows. This measurement requires an understanding of compound interest, annuities, and present value concepts.

Accounting Applications

Compound interest, annuities, and present value concepts and procedures are relevant to accounting and to understanding much of the information in succeeding chapters of this text. Some of the applications involving accounting topics are:

1. **Notes.** Valuing receivables and payables that carry no stated interest rate or a lower than market interest rate.
2. **Leases.** Valuing assets to be capitalized under long-term leases and measuring the amount of the lease payments and annual leasehold amortization.
3. **Amortization of premiums and discounts.** Measuring amortization of premium or discount on both bond investments and bonds payable.
4. **Pensions.** Measuring amortization, accruals, and interest equivalents relative to unfunded past or prior service cost.
5. **Capital assets.** Evaluating alternative investments by discounting cash flows. Determining the value of assets acquired under deferred payment contracts.
6. **Sinking funds.** Determining the contributions necessary to accumulate a fund for debt retirements.
7. **Business combinations.** Determining the value of receivables, payables, liabilities, accruals, and commitments acquired or assumed in a "purchase."
8. **Depreciation.** Measuring depreciation charges under the sinking fund and the annuity methods.
9. **Installment contracts.** Measuring periodic payments on long-term purchase contracts.

This chapter discusses the essentials of compound interest and annuities; a study in greater depth and in special applications of these concepts is usually presented in advanced accounting. This coverage is introduced early in this textbook to provide you with enough knowledge of the subject to understand and to apply present value techniques to topics in Chapters 7, 11, 13, 14, 18, 19, 21, and 22.

Nature of Interest

Interest is the payment for the use of money. It represents an excess in cash exchanged over and above the principal amount lent or borrowed. For example, if the Corner Bank lends you $1,000 with the understanding that you will repay $1,080, the excess over $1,000, or $80, represents interest.

The amount of interest to be paid is generally stated as a rate over a specific period of time. For example, if you used the $1,000 for one year before repaying $1,080, the rate of interest would be 8% per year. That is, the interest is 8% of the principal each year. The custom of expressing interest as a rate is an established business practice.[1] In fact, business managers make investing and borrowing decisions on the basis of the rate of interest involved rather than on the actual dollar amount of interest to be received or paid.

The rate of interest is commonly applied to the time interval of one year. Interest of 6% represents a rate of 6% per year unless stipulated otherwise. The statement that a corporation will pay bond interest of 6%, payable semiannually, means a rate of 3% every six months, not 6% every six months.

Simple Interest

Simple interest is the term used to describe interest that is computed on the amount of the principal only. It is the return on (or growth of) the principal for one time period or for each period in a succession of periods at a given rate per period

---

[1] Federal law requires the disclosure of interest rates on an **annual basis** in all contracts. That is, instead of stating the rate as "1% per month," it must be stated as "12% per year."

applied to the principal at the beginning of the series. For example, if the $1,000 you borrowed in the previous illustration were for a five-year period, with a simple interest rate of 8% per year, the total interest you would pay would be $400 ($80 times five years).

Simple interest[2] is commonly expressed as:

$$\text{Interest} = P \times i \times n$$

where

P = principal
i = rate of interest for a single period
n = number of periods

Compound Interest

Compound interest is the term used to describe interest that is computed on principal *and* on any interest earned that has not been paid. It is the return on (or growth of) the principal for two or more time periods, assuming that the growth (the interest) in each time period is added to the principal at the end of the period and earns a return in all subsequent periods. Compounding calculates interest not only on the principal but also on the interest earned to date on that principal, assuming the interest is left on deposit.[3] To illustrate the difference between simple interest and compound interest, assume that you deposit $1,000 in the Last National Bank, where it will earn simple interest of 6% per year, and you deposit another $1,000 in the First National Bank where it will earn compound interest of 6% per year compounded annually. Also assume that in both cases you receive no interest until you withdraw the proceeds three years from date of deposit. The calculation of interest to be received would be as indicated below.

		Simple Interest Last National	Compound Interest First National
First year	($1,000 × 6%)	$ 60.00	$ 60.00
Second year	($1,000 × 6%)	60.00	60.00
	($60 × 6%)	—0—	3.60
Third year	($1,000 × 6%)	60.00	60.00
	($123.60 × 6%)	—0—	7.42
Total interest, three-year period		$180.00	$191.02

Obviously if you had a choice between investing your money at simple interest or at compound interest, you would choose compound interest, all other things—especially risk—being equal. The interests received from the two banks differ because of the calculation of interest on interest in the case of the compound interest.

[2]Simple interest is traditionally expressed in textbooks in business mathematics or business finance as: i(interest) = P(principal) × R(rate) × T(time).

[3]Here is an illustration of the power of *time* and *compounding* interest on money. In 1626, Peter Minuit bought Manhattan Island from the Manhattoe Indians for $24 worth of trinkets and beads. If the Indians had taken a boat to Holland, invested the $24 in Dutch securities returning 6% per year, and kept the money and interest invested at 6%, they would now have $13 billion, enough to buy back all the land on the island and still have a couple of billion dollars left for doodads (*Forbes*, Vol. 107, #11, June 1, 1971).

For practical purposes in computing compound interest, it may be assumed that unpaid interest earned becomes a part of the principal and is entitled to interest. In the illustration above, the computation of compound interest in the third year—6% times $1,123.60 ($1,000 plus $60 plus $63.60)—is illustrated below.

Year	Annual Amount of Interest	Cumulative Amount of Interest	Principal End of Year
0	—	—	$1,000.00
1 ($1,000 × .06)	$60.00	$ 60.00	1,060.00
2 ($1,060 × .06)	63.60	123.60	1,123.60
3 ($1,123.60 × .06)	67.42	191.02	1,191.02

Compound interest is the typical interest computation applied in business situations, particularly in our economy where large amounts of long-lived capital are used productively and financed over long periods of time. Financial managers view and evaluate their investment opportunities in terms of a series of periodic returns, each of which can be reinvested to yield additional returns. Simple interest is usually applicable only to short-term investments and debts that involve a time span of one year or less.

Compound Interest Tables

Because many people need to know how much a sum invested or borrowed at a certain rate of interest will amount to over a period of time, tables have been constructed to show how much $1.00 invested at various compound rates of interest will amount to at the end of various periods. Compound interest tables are presented at the end of this chapter (see Table 6–1). The excerpt below illustrates the nature of such tables by indicating how much interest a dollar accumulates (the amount of 1) at the end of each of the five periods at different rates of compound interest.

AMOUNT OF 1 AT COMPOUND INTEREST (Excerpt from Table 6-1)			
Period	4%	5%	6%
1	1.04000	1.05000	1.06000
2	1.08160	1.10250	1.12360
3	1.12486	1.15763	1.19102
4	1.16986	1.21551	1.26248
5	1.21665	1.27628	1.33823

Interpreting the table, if $1.00 is invested for three periods at a compound interest rate of 4% per period, the $1.00 will amount to $1.12 (1.12486 × $1.00), the **compound amount;** if the investment were for five periods, it would amount to $1.22. If $1.00 were invested at 6%, at the end of four periods it would amount to $1.26; at the end of five periods it would equal $1.34. If the investment were $1,000 instead of $1.00, the respective amounts would be:

If invested for 3 periods at 4% ($1,000 × 1.12486) = $1,124.86
If invested for 5 periods at 4% ($1,000 × 1.21665) = $1,216.65
If invested for 4 periods at 6% ($1,000 × 1.26248) = $1,262.48
If invested for 5 periods at 6% ($1,000 × 1.33823) = $1,338.23

Throughout the foregoing discussion of "compound interest tables" (and most of the discussion that follows) the use of the term **periods** instead of **years** is intentional. Interest is generally expressed in terms of an annual rate but in many business circumstances the compounding period is less than one year. In such circumstances the annual interest rate must be converted to correspond to the length of the period. The process is to convert the "annual interest rate" into the "compounding period interest rate" by **dividing the annual rate by the number of compounding periods per year.** In addition, the number of periods is determined by **multiplying the number of years involved by the number of compounding periods per year.** To illustrate, assume that $1.00 is invested for six years at 8% annual interest compounded **quarterly.** Using Table 6-1, page 248, we can determine the amount to which this $1.00 will accumulate by reading the factor that appears in the 2% column on the 24th row, namely 1.60844, or approximately $1.61. Thus, the term **periods** not **years** is used in all compound interest tables to express the quantity of n.

As a final point on the frequency of compounding, because interest is theoretically earned (accruing) every second of every day, some savings and loan companies advertise that their interest is **compounded continuously.** Computations involving continuous compounding are facilitated through the use of the natural, or Napierian, system of logarithms. In spite of the soundness of continuous compounding, most business situations involving interest are resolved through discrete compounding techniques as illustrated in this chapter.

Amount of 1 Problems

Computation of Future Amount For any sum invested, the amount to which 1 (one) would accumulate (the compound amount) may be multiplied by the amount invested to determine the amount to which the sum invested would accumulate. For example, if $75,000 is invested for five years at a compound interest rate of 5%, the investment will grow to $95,721.00 ($75,000 × 1.27628) by the end of the fifth year.

The amount to which 1 (one) will accumulate may be expressed as a formula:

$$a = (1 + i)^n$$

where

a = compound amount of 1
i = rate of interest for a single period
n = number of periods

To illustrate, assume that $1.00 is invested at 6% interest for three periods. The amounts to which the $1.00 will accumulate at the end of each period are:

$a = (1 + .06)^1$ for the end of the first period
$a = (1 + .06)^2$ for the end of the second period
$a = (1 + .06)^3$ for the end of the third period

Illustrated diagrammatically, these compound amounts accumulate as follows:

Period	Beginning-of-Period Amount	Multiplier $(1 + i)$	End-of-Period Amount	Formula $(1 + i)^n$
1	1.00000	1.06	1.06000	$(1.06)^1$
2	1.06000	1.06	1.12360	$(1.06)^2$
3	1.12360	1.06	1.19102	$(1.06)^3$
4	1.19102	1.06	1.26248	$(1.06)^4$

When tables are available, there is no need to apply the formula because, as shown above, the formula is the basis for the construction of the table.

Computation of the Number of Periods   If the future amount to which a given investment will accumulate at a given interest rate is known, the number of interest periods involved can be calculated. In other words, three of the four values must be known. For example, assume that the sum to be invested at 5% is $75,000 and the desired future amount is $95,721. The number of interest periods is calculated by dividing the future amount of $95,721 by $75,000 to give 1.27628, the amount $1.00 would accumulate at 5% for the unknown number of interest periods. The factor 1.27628 or its approximate can be located in the amount of 1 table, page 248, by reading down the 5% column **to the 5-period line;** thus 5 is the unknown number of periods.

Investment, Future Amount, and Periods Known—Computation of the Interest Rate   If the future amount to which a given investment will accumulate over a specified number of interest periods is known, the rate of interest can be calculated. For example, again assume that the sum to be invested is $75,000 for five years to accumulate to $95,721. The interest rate required is again calculated by dividing the future amount of $95,721 by $75,000 to give 1.27628, the amount $1.00 would accumulate in five periods at an unknown interest rate. The factor 1.27628 or its approximate can be located in the amount of 1 table, page 248, by reading across the 5-period line **to the 5% column;** thus 5% is the unknown interest rate.

Present Value

The example on page 233 showed that $75,000 invested at a compound interest rate of 5% will be worth $95,721 at the end of five years. It follows then that $95,721 five years from now is worth $75,000 now; that is, $75,000 is the present value of $95,721. The **present value** is the amount that must be invested now to produce the known future value. In the compound amount illustrations, it was the future value of a known present value that was determined; in present-value problems, it is the present value of a known future value that must be determined. The present value is always a smaller amount than the known future amount because interest will be earned and accumulated on the present value to the future date.

The present value of an amount may be computed by dividing 1 by the amount of 1 for a given number of periods and a given rate of interest and then multiplying the result by the known future amount (this process is known as "discounting"). To illustrate, assume that $1,000 is needed in five years and that funds can be invested currently at 6% per year. Using the "amount of 1" table on page 248, we see that

$1.00 invested for five periods at 6% will equal $1.33823. If $1.00 is divided by this amount (1.33823), the result equals the present value of 1 due in five years if invested at 6% per year, or $0.74726. This means that an investment of approximately $0.75 now at 6% compounded annually will equal approximately $1.00 in five years. Because $1,000 is needed, the amount to be invested would be 1,000 times $0.74726 or $747.26.

Present Value of 1 Tables

Quick computations of present values are frequently needed. As a result, tables have been developed showing how much must be invested at various compound interest rates for various periods of time to equal 1 at a future date. A "present value of 1 table" appears at the end of this chapter. The excerpt below illustrates the nature of such a table by indicating the present value of 1 for five different periods at three different rates of interest.

PRESENT VALUE OF 1 AT COMPOUND INTEREST
(Excerpt from Table 6-2)

Period	4%	5%	6%
1	0.96154	0.95238	0.94340
2	0.92456	0.90703	0.89000
3	0.88900	0.86384	0.83962
4	0.85480	0.82270	0.79209
5	0.82193	0.78353	0.74726

"Present value of 1" tables are constructed from the following general formula.

$$p = 1 \div a$$

where

p = present value of 1
a = compound amount of 1

Assume that you need to determine the present value of $1.00 at compound interest of 5% for four periods. Referring to the amount of 1 on page 248, the amount of 1 at 5% compound interest for four periods is 1.21551. To determine the present value, the formula above becomes:

$$p = \frac{1}{1.21551} = \$0.82270$$

or the amount that must be invested now to equal $1.00 in four years at 5% compound interest. A simpler method is to refer to a "present value of 1" table, where this same amount, 0.82270, may be found in the 5% column on the fourth period line.

Computation of Investment   To illustrate the use of the table, assume that your rich uncle proposes to give you $2,000 for a trip to Europe when you graduate from college three years from now. He proposes to finance the trip by investing a sum of money now at 6% compound interest that will provide you with $2,000 upon your graduation. The only conditions are that you graduate and that you tell him how much to invest now. By referring to the "present value of 1" table, 6% column and 3 period row, you find that approximately $0.84 (0.83962) invested now at 6% will yield $1.00 in three years. Because you are promised $2,000 instead of $1.00, you must multiply the 0.83962 by $2,000. The multiplication indicates that your uncle should invest $1,679.24 now to provide you with $2,000 upon graduation. To satisfy his other condition you must pass this course and many more.

If any *three* of the *four* values (amount, rate, periods, and present value) are known, the unknown one can be derived.

Computation of the Number of Periods   Given the present investment, the future amount, and the rate of interest, the number of required periods can be approximated by reference to the appropriate tables. To illustrate, Jerry Kolb has $8,000 to invest now at 6% to pay future obligations of $10,705.80. How many years will it take to accumulate enough to pay the loan? By dividing the future amount of $10,705.80 by the present value of $8,000, the compound amount of $1.00 is computed to be 1.33823 ($10,705.80 ÷ $8,000). The factor 1.33823 or its approximate can be located in the "amount of 1" table (6–1, page 248) in the 6% interest column; and, by reference to the periods row in which it appears, the unknown number of periods can be determined to be 5.

In a similar manner, by dividing the present value of $8,000 by the future amount of $10,705.80, the present value of $1.00 is computed to be .74726 ($8,000 ÷ $10,705.80). The factor .74726 or its approximate can be located in the "present value of 1" table (6–2, page 250) in the 6% interest column; and, by reference to the periods row in which it appears, the unknown number of periods can be determined to be 5.

The exact factors as computed above are not always found in the tables, but for most business decisions the nearest approximate factor suffices. If the situation demands more exact answers, interpolation (as illustrated on page 246) can be used with the tables, or logarithms may be used.

Computation of the Interest Rate   Given the present investment, the future amount, and the number of periods, the required interest rate can be approximated by reference to the appropriate tables. To illustrate, using the data in the preceding illustration, the amount of 1 factor, 1.33823, is similarly computed ($10,705.80 ÷ $8,000) as is the present value of 1 factor, .74726 ($8,000 ÷ $10,705.80). The 1.33823 factor can be found in the "amount of 1" table (6–1, page 248) by reading across the 5-periods (known) row; and, by reference to the interest column in which it appears, the unknown rate of 6% can be determined. Likewise, the .74726 factor can be found in the "present value of 1" table (6–2, page 250) by reading across the 5-periods (known) row; and, by reference to the corresponding interest column, the unknown interest rate of 6% can be determined.

Annuities

The preceding discussion has involved only the accumulation or discounting of a single principal sum. Individuals frequently encounter situations in which a series of dollar amounts are to be paid or received periodically, such as loans or sales to be repaid in installments, invested funds that will be partially recovered at regular intervals, and cost savings that are realized repeatedly. A life insurance contract is probably the most common and most familiar type of transaction involving a series of equal payments made at equal intervals of time. Such a process of periodic saving represents the accumulation of a sum of money through an annuity. An **annuity** by definition requires that the periodic payments or receipts (called **rents**) always be the **same amount** and that **the interval** between such rents always be the same. It is also assumed that **interest is compounded** once each time period.

The **amount of an annuity** is the sum (future value) of all the rents (payments or receipts) plus the accumulated compound interest on them. It should be noted that the rents may occur at either the beginning or the end of the periods (not necessarily January 1 or December 31). To distinguish annuities under these two alternatives, an annuity is classified as an **ordinary annuity** if the rents occur at the end of the period, and as an **annuity due** if the rents occur at the beginning of the period.

To illustrate the difference between an ordinary annuity and an annuity due, assume an annuity of $1,000 a year earning compound interest at 6%.

	Ordinary Annuity	Annuity Due
First year's investment:		
(at the beginning of the year)		$1,000.00
(at the end of the year)	$1,000.00	
First year's interest	—0—	60.00
Balance at end of first year	1,000.00	1,060.00
Second year's investment	1,000.00	1,000.00
Second year's interest:		
$1,000 @ 6%	60.00	
$2,060 @ 6%		123.60
Balance at end of second year	2,060.00	2,183.60
Third year's investment	1,000.00	1,000.00
Third year's interest:		
$2,060 @ 6%	123.60	
$3,183.60 @ 6%		191.02
Balance at end of third year	$3,183.60	$3,374.62

As illustrated above, the amount to which an annuity of $1,000 a year for three years at 6% will accumulate will depend on whether it is an ordinary annuity or an annuity due. The difference is that with an annuity due all deposits receive one more period of compounding.

The amount of an ordinary annuity of 1 may be expressed by the following formula.

$$A_{\overline{n}|i} = \frac{(1 + i)^n - 1}{i}$$

where

$A_{\overline{n}|i}$ = amount of an annuity of 1
n = number of periods
i = rate of interest

The symbol $A_{\overline{n}|i}$ is expressed "capital A angle n at i"; for example, $A_{\overline{5}|.06}$ is expressed "capital A angle 5 at 6%" and refers to the amount to which an annuity of 1 will accumulate in five periods at 6% interest.

Amount of an Ordinary Annuity of 1 Table

One approach to the problem of determining the future amount to which an annuity will accumulate is to compute the amount to which each of the rents in the series will accumulate and then aggregate their individual future amounts. Assuming an interest rate of 6%, the future amount can be computed as follows using the "amount of 1" table:

		End of Period in Which $1.00 Is To Be Invested			
					Amount at End
Present	1	2	3	4	of Year 5
	$1.00 ──→				$1.26245
		$1.00 ─────────────────────────────────→			1.19102
			$1.00 ──────────────────→		1.12360
				$1.00 ─────→	1.06000
					1.00000
Total (amount of an ordinary annuity of $1.00 for 5 periods at 6%)					**$5.63710**

However, tables have been developed similar to those used for the "amount of 1" and the "present value of 1" for both an ordinary annuity and an annuity due. Because annuity due factors are easily converted from an ordinary annuity table, ordinary annuity tables are more commonly found in reference books, textbooks, and in practice. Therefore, we have provided an explanation of the process of converting an ordinary annuity table into annuity due data. The table below is an excerpt from the "amount of an ordinary annuity of 1" table.

AMOUNT OF AN ORDINARY ANNUITY OF 1
(Excerpt from Table 6-3)

Period	4%	5%	6%
1	1.00000	1.00000	1.00000
2	2.04000	2.05000	2.06000
3	3.12160	3.15250	3.18360
4	4.24646	4.31013	4.37462
5	5.41632	5.52563	**5.63709***

*Difference between two bold numbers due to rounding.

Computation of the Future Amount   Interpreting the table, if $1.00 is invested at the end of each year for four years at 5% interest compounded annually, the amount of the annuity at the end of the fourth year will be $4.31 (4.31013 × $1.00). By multiplying the figures from the appropriate line and column of the table above by the dollar amount of the rents involved in an ordinary annuity, the accumulated sum of the rents and the compound interest to the date of the last rent may be determined. For example, if $7,500 is deposited in a bank account at the end of each year for five years at 6% interest compounded annually, the amount on deposit at the end of the fifth year will be $42,278.18 (5.63709 × $7,500).

In the foregoing example three values were known (amount of each annuity, interest rate, and number of periods) and used to determine the fourth value, future amount, which was unknown. Obviously, if any three of these four values are known, the unknown one can be derived.

Computation of Each Rent   The ordinary annuity table (and the formula) may be used to **compute the amount of the periodic rents** when the desired future amount of the annuity is known. To illustrate, assume that you wish to accumulate $14,000 for a down payment on a condominium apartment five years from now; for the next five years you can earn an annual return of 8% compounded semiannually. How much should your deposit at the end of each six-month period be? The amount of each deposit is simply determined by dividing the future amount of $14,000 by the "amount of an ordinary annuity of 1" (Table 6–3) for ten (5 × 2) periods at 4% (8% ÷ 2), or 12.00611. Each six months' deposit must be approximately $1,166 ($14,000 ÷ 12.00611) to accumulate $14,000 in five years.

Computation of the Number of Periodic Rents   If you wish to accumulate $117,332 by making periodic rents of $20,000 at the end of each period that will earn 8% each period while accumulating, how many rent payments must be made? To derive the required number of rents, divide the future amount of $117,332 by the amount of each rent, $20,000, to obtain 5.86660, the "amount of an ordinary annuity of 1" at 8% for the unknown number of periods. By reference to Table 6–3, 8% interest column, we find 5.86660 **at the 5-period line;** thus 5 is the unknown number of periodic rents.

Computation of the Interest Rate   In the example above, if the number of periodic rents were known to be 5 and the interest rate were unknown, the rate would be determined by making the same computation ($117,332 ÷ $20,000 = 5.86660) and reading across the 5-period line of Table 6–3 until we found 5.86660 **in the 8% interest column.**

Relationship of Amount of an Annuity Due to Ordinary Annuity Tables

The preceding analysis of an ordinary annuity was based on the fact that the periodic rents occur at the end of each period. An annuity due is based on the fact that the periodic rents occur at the **beginning** of each period. This means an annuity due will accumulate interest on the first year's rent in the first year, whereas an ordinary annuity rent will earn no interest during the first year because the rent is not received or paid until the end of the period. In other words, the significant difference between the two types of annuities is in the number of interest accumulation periods involved.

If rents occur at the end of a period, in determining the **amount of an annuity,** there will be one less interest period than if the rents occur at the beginning of the period. The distinction is shown graphically at the top of page 240.

The generalization "that the periodic interest earnings under an ordinary annuity will always be lower by one period's interest than the interest earned by an annuity due" suggests the basis for converting an ordinary annuity table to an annuity due table. **If the last rent in an ordinary annuity is deducted from the end-of-**

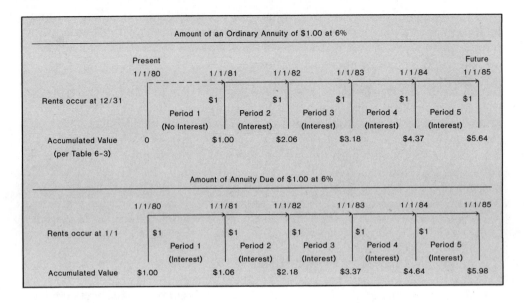

period accumulation, the residual will represent the amount of an annuity due for one less period. For example, if one rent is deducted from the ordinary annuity of three periods at 6%, in the illustration below, the result will be the amount of an annuity due of two periods at 6%.

1.	Amount of ordinary annuity of $1,000 a period for three periods at 6%	$3,183.60
2.	Deduct last payment	−1,000.00
3.	Amount of annuity due of $1,000 per period for two periods at 6%	$2,183.60

In the case of an ordinary annuity, there is one rent (the last) on which no interest is involved. That is the reason for subtracting the last payment as shown above. The annuity due has one more interest period than the ordinary annuity.

To illustrate the use of the ordinary annuity tables in converting to an annuity due, assume that Sue Anderson plans to deposit $800 a year on each birthday of her son Howard, starting with his fifth birthday, at 5% interest compounded annually. Sue wants to know the amount she will have accumulated for college expenses by her son's eighteenth birthday.

If the first deposit is made on her son's fifth birthday, Sue will make a total of 13 deposits over the life of the annuity (assume no deposit on the eighteenth birthday). Because all the deposits will be made at the beginning of the periods, they represent an annuity due. Referring to the "amount of an ordinary annuity of 1" table for 14 periods at 5% and deducting 1, [(factor for n + 1 rents) − 1], to arrive at the annuity due for 13 periods, the solution may be computed as follows.

1.	Amount of an ordinary annuity of 1 for 14 periods at 5%	19.59863
2.	Deduct one rent	−1.00000
3.	Amount of annuity due of 1 for 13 periods at 5%	18.59863
4.	Periodic deposit	× $800
5.	Accumulated amount on son's eighteenth birthday	$14,878.90

The same solution can be arrived at in the following manner.

1.	Amount of an ordinary annuity of $800 per period at 5% for 14 periods (19.59863 × $800)	$15,678.90
2.	Deduct last payment	− 800.00
3.	Amount of an annuity due of $800 a period at 5% for 13 periods	$14,878.90

Present Value of an Ordinary Annuity

The present value of an annuity may be viewed as **the single sum** that, if invested at compound interest now, would provide for an annuity (a series of withdrawals) of a certain amount per period for a certain number of future periods. In other words, the present value of an ordinary annuity is the present value of a series of rents to be made at equal intervals in the future.

One approach to the problem of valuing at the present an annuity consisting of a series of future rents is to determine the present value of each of the rents in the series and then aggregate their individual present values. For example, an annuity of $1.00 to be received at the end of each period for five periods may be viewed as separate amounts and the present value of each computed from the table of present values (see page 250). Assuming an interest rate of 6%, the present value can be computed:

End of Period in Which $1.00 Is To Be Received					
Present Value at Beg. of Year 1	1	2	3	4	5
$0.94340	$1.00				
.89000		$1.00			
.83962			$1.00		
.79209				$1.00	
.74726					$1.00
$4.21237 Total (present value of an annuity of $1.00 for five periods at 6%)					

This computation tells us that if we invest $4.21 at 6% interest for five periods, we will be able to withdraw $1.00 at the end of each period for five periods.

Such a procedure could become quite cumbersome and subject to error if the annuity consisted of 50 or more rents. The formula for which convenient tables of the "present values of annuities of 1" are prepared is expressed:

$$P_{\overline{n}|i} = \frac{1 - \dfrac{1}{(1 + i)^n}}{i}$$

The symbol $P_{\overline{n}|i}$ is expressed "capital P angle n at i"; for example $P_{\overline{5}|.06}$ is expressed "capital P angle 5 at 6%" and refers to the present value of an ordinary annuity of 1 for five periods at 6% interest. An excerpt from a present value of an ordinary annuity of 1 table is illustrated below.

PRESENT VALUE OF AN ORDINARY ANNUITY OF 1 (Excerpt from Table 6-4)			
Period	4%	5%	6%
1	0.96154	0.95238	0.94340
2	1.88609	1.85941	1.83339
3	2.77509	2.72325	2.67301
4	3.62990	3.54595	3.46511
5	4.45182	4.32948	**4.21236***

*Difference between two bold amounts (on page 241, and above) due to rounding.

Computation of the Present Value of the Periodic Rents   Interpreting the table, if $1.00 is due at the end of each period for five periods, compounded annually at 6% interest, the present value of the five rents of $1.00 each is $4.21. The figures in the table above are discount factors that, when multiplied by any series of equal rents due at regular intervals in the future, produce the present equivalent (discounted amount) of that series of rents. For example, to produce $3,000 at the end of each period for the next five periods at 5% interest compounded annually, $3,000 × 4.32948, or $12,988.44, must be deposited now.

Computation of Each Periodic Rent   The "present value of an ordinary annuity table" (and the formula) may be used to **compute each periodic rent** when the present value of the annuity is known. To illustrate, Mary and Ron Bellows have saved $12,000 to finance their daughter's college education. The money has been deposited in the Local Savings and Loan Association and is earning 6% interest compounded semiannually. What equal amounts can their daughter withdraw every six months during the next four years while she attends college and exhaust the fund with the last withdrawal? The amount of each withdrawal is computed by dividing the present investment of $12,000 by the "present value of an ordinary annuity of 1" (Table 6–4) for eight (4 × 2) periods at 3% (6% ÷ 2), or 7.01969. Starting six months from the date of the deposit, she can withdraw $1,709.48 ($12,000 ÷ 7.01969) every six months for four years.

Computation of the Interest Rate or the Number of Periodic Rents   If the present value of an annuity and the amount of the periodic rents are known, the unknown interest rate or the unknown number of periods can be determined either through formula or tables. To illustrate, if Sam Kim wants to invest $57,349.60 today to provide $5,000 payments to his daughter at the end of each year for the next twenty years, what is the **rate of interest** which must be earned on the investment? The present value of $1.00 per period can be calculated by dividing the known present value ($57,349.60) by the known amount of the rents ($5,000).

$57,350 \div \$5,000 = 11.46992$

Referring to the present value of an ordinary annuity table (6–4, page 254), 11.46992 or its approximate can be located in the 20-period row; and, by reference to the column in which it appears, the interest rate is determined to be 6%.

If the interest rate were known but the number of periods unknown, the number of $5,000 annual withdrawals that would be provided Sam Kim's daughter would be determined in a similar manner using the same table.

Present Value of an Annuity Due

In the discussion of the present value of an ordinary annuity, the value now was discounted back one period from the first rent; the number of rents and the number of discount periods were the same. A diagram for finding the present value of an ordinary annuity for five periods follows.

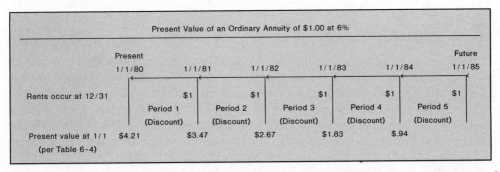

This diagram illustrates that in an ordinary annuity where the rents occur at the end of the period, the first rent can be discounted for one period. In an annuity due where the rents occur at the beginning of the periods, there is no opportunity for discounting the first rent because no time period exists relative to it. In order to see this distinction, compare the following diagram with the one above.

We could compute the present value of an annuity due by simply adding together the present value of each of the periodic rents, but we can use the present value tables for ordinary annuities to simplify the computation. The diagrams in this section illustrate that **in an ordinary annuity the number of discount periods and the number of rents are the same, whereas in an annuity due, the number of**

discount periods is always one less than the number of rents. The basis then for converting a table of present value of an ordinary annuity of 1 to a table of present value of an annuity due of 1 involves adding one rent to the present value of an ordinary annuity **of one less period** $[(n - 1 \text{ rents}) + 1]$ than that of the annuity due. Referring to the table of "present value of an ordinary annuity of 1," this can be illustrated as follows:

1.	Present value of an ordinary annuity of 1 for four rents at 6%	3.46511
2.	Add 1	1.00000
3.	Present value of an annuity due of 1 for five rents at 6%	4.46511

Because the payment and receipt of rentals at the beginning of periods (i.e., leases, insurance, and subscriptions) are as common as those at the end of the periods (referred to as "in arrears"), we have provided annuity due factors in the form of Table 6–5.

Present Value of a Deferred Annuity

A **deferred annuity** is an annuity in which the rents begin a specified number of periods after the arrangement or contract is made. In other words, a deferred annuity does not begin to produce rents until two or more periods have expired. For example, "an **ordinary annuity** of six annual rents deferred four years" means that no rents will occur during the first four years, and that the first of the six rents will occur at the end of the fifth year. "An **annuity due** of six annual rents deferred four years" means that no rents will occur during the first four years, and that the first of six rents will occur at the beginning of the fifth year.

In computing the present value of a deferred annuity, recognition must be given to the interest that accrues on the original investment during the deferral period, which is one period less than the number of periods prior to the first payment, assuming an ordinary annuity.

To compute the present value of a deferred annuity, we compute the difference between the present value of an ordinary annuity of 1 for the total periods and the present value of an ordinary annuity of 1 for the number of deferred periods. This difference is then multiplied by the amount of rent involved each period.

To illustrate, Joe Dumas purchases an ordinary annuity of six annual rents of $5,000 each, the rents deferred four years, with interest accruing at the rate of 8%. What is the present value of the six rents? The present value is $16,989.75 as calculated below:

1.	Each periodic rent		$5,000
2.	Present value of an ordinary annuity of 1 for total periods (10) involved [number of rents (6) plus number of deferred periods (4)] at 8%	6.71008	
3.	Less: Present value of an ordinary annuity of 1 for the number of deferred periods (4) at 8%	−3.31213	
4.	Difference (times amount of periodic rents)		×3.39795
5.	Present value of six rents of $5,000		$16,989.75

The subtraction of the present value of an annuity of 1 for the deferred periods eliminates the nonexistent rents during the deferral period and converts the present value of an ordinary annuity of $1.00 for 10 periods to the present value of 6 rents of $1.00, deferred 4 periods.

Alternatively, the present value of the 6 rents could be computed as follows:

Period of Rent	Present Value of 1 at 8%		Amount of Rent		Present Value
5	.68058	×	$5,000	=	$ 3,402.90
6	.63017	×	5,000	=	3,150.85
7	.58349	×	5,000	=	2,917.45
8	.54027	×	5,000	=	2,701.35
9	.50025	×	5,000	=	2,501.25
10	.46319	×	5,000	=	2,315.95
			Total		$16,989.75

In the case of **the amount of a deferred annuity** there is no accumulation or investment on which interest may accrue, so the amount of a deferred annuity is the same as the amount of an annuity not deferred. The deferral period does not affect the amount.

Summary of Compound Interest Tables

The types of compound interest tables that have been discussed are presented at the end of this chapter. The titles of these tables and their contents follow.

1. **"Amount of 1"** table. Contains the amounts to which 1 will accumulate if deposited now at a specified rate and left for a specified number of periods.
2. **"Present value of 1"** table. Contains the amounts that must be deposited now at a specified rate of interest to amount to 1 at the end of a specified number of periods.
3. **"Amount of an ordinary annuity of 1"** table. Contains the amounts to which periodic rents of 1 will accumulate if the rents are invested at a specified rate of interest and are continued for a specified number of periods. (This table may also be used as a basis for converting to the amount of an annuity due of 1.)
4. **"Present value of an ordinary annuity of 1"** table. Contains the amounts that must be deposited now at a specified rate of interest to permit withdrawals of 1 at regular periodic intervals for the specified number of periods. (This table may also be used as a basis for converting to the present value of an annuity due of 1.)

Careful analysis of problems involving compound interest is necessary to determine which table to use and which procedures to apply. Frequently, problems are encountered that represent a combination of elements. Then each dissimilar element must be identified and separated before deciding which procedure to follow in reaching a solution. Deferred annuities may require the application of a combination of these tables.

Note that present value tables deal with dollars as dollars, without allowance for the likely differences in purchasing power. Therefore, the answers obtained by the use of the tables make no allowance for inflation or deflation. If you need to consider the changes in dollar purchasing power, you have to do so outside the present value framework or by adjusting the interest rate to reflect inflation.

Interpolation of Tables to Derive Interest Rates

Throughout the previous discussion our illustrations were designed to produce interest rates and factors that could be found in the tables. Frequently it is necessary to **interpolate** to derive the exact or required interest rate. Interpolation is useful in finding a particular unknown value that lies between two given table values. The following examples illustrate the method of interpolation using the tables on pages 248–257.

Example 1. If $2,000 accumulates to $5,900 after being invested for 20 years, what is the annual interest rate that the investment paid?

By dividing the future amount of $5,900 by the investment of $2,000 we obtain the amount to which $1.00 would have grown if invested for 20 years, that is, $2.95. Referring to Table 6–1 and reading across the 20-period line, we find that the value under 5% is 2.65330 and the value under 6% is 3.20714. The factor 2.95 is between 5% and 6%, which means that the interest rate is also between 5% and 6%. By interpolation the rate is determined more precisely as follows (i = unknown rate and d = difference between 5% and i):

$$
.01 \left\{ d \left\{ \begin{array}{l} .05 = 2.65330 \\ i = 2.95000 \\ .06 = 3.20714 \end{array} \right. \right.
\begin{array}{l} \\ \left. \right\} .29670 \\ \end{array}
\left. \right\} .55384
$$

$$
\therefore \frac{d}{.01} = \frac{.29670}{.55384} = \frac{.29670}{.55384}(.01) = .00536
$$

$$
\therefore i = .05 + .00536 = .05536
$$

The approximate interest rate is 5.536%, or 5.5% rounded.

Example 2. You are offered an annuity of $1,000 a year beginning one year from now for 25 years for investing $15,000 cash. What rate of interest is your investment earning?

By dividing the investment of $15,000 by the annuity of $1,000 we obtain 15, which is the "present value of an ordinary annuity of 1" for 25 years at an unknown interest rate.

Referring to Table 6–4 and reading across the 25-period line, we find that the value under 4% is 15.62208 and the value under 5% is 14.09394. The factor 15 is between 4% and 5%, which means that the unknown interest rate is also between 4% and 5%. By interpolation the rate is determined more precisely as follows (i = unknown rate and d = difference between 4% and i):

$$
.01 \left\{ d \left\{ \begin{array}{l} .04 = 15.62208 \\ i = 15.00000 \\ .05 = 14.09394 \end{array} \right. \right.
\begin{array}{l} \\ \left. \right\} .62208 \\ \end{array}
\left. \right\} 1.52814
$$

$$
\therefore \frac{d}{.01} = \frac{.62208}{1.52814} = \frac{.62208}{1.52814}(.01) = .00407
$$

$$
\therefore i = .04 + d = .04 + .004 = .04407
$$

The approximate interest rate is 4.407%, or 4.4% rounded.

Interpolation assumes that the change between any two values in the table is linear. Although such an assumption is not correct, if the table value ranges are not too wide, the margin of error is generally insignificant.

FUNDAMENTAL TERMS OR CONCEPTS

1. **Simple interest.** Interest on principal only, regardless of interest that may have accrued in the past.
2. **Compound interest.** Interest accrues on the unpaid interest of past periods as well as on the principal.
3. **Rate of interest.** Interest is usually expressed as an annual rate, but when the interest period is shorter than one year, the interest rate for the shorter period must be determined.
4. **Amount.** Value at a later date of a given sum that is invested at compound interest.
    a. **Amount of 1** (or amount of a given sum). The future value of $1.00 (or a single given sum), P, at the end of n periods at i compound interest rate (Table 6-1).
    b. **Amount of annuity. The amount of a series of rents invested at compound interest; in other words, it is the accumulated total that results from a series of equal deposits at regular intervals invested at compound interest. Both deposits and interest increase the accumulation.**
        (1) Amount of an ordinary annuity. The future value **on** the date of the last rent (hence, there is one less interest period than rents—this is taken into account in the computation of Table 6-3).
        (2) Amount of annuity due. The future value **one period after** the date of the last rent (hence, there are the same number of interest periods as rents). When an annuity due table is not available, use Table 6-3 with the following formula:

        Amount of annuity due of 1 for n rents = Amount of ordinary annuity for $(n + 1$ rents$) - \$1.00$

        Types of Annuities:
        (1) **Ordinary annuity.** Each rent is payable at the **end** of a period.
        (2) **Annuity due.** Each rent is payable at the **beginning** of the period.
5. **Present value.** The value at an earlier date (usually now) of a given sum in the future discounted at compound interest.
    a. **Present value of 1** (or present value of a single sum). The present value (worth) of $1.00 (or a given sum) due n periods hence, discounted at i compound interest (Table 6-2).
    b. **Present value of an annuity.** The present value (worth) of a series of rents discounted at compound interest; in other words, it is the sum when invested at compound interest that will permit a series of equal withdrawals at regular intervals.
        (1) **Present value of an ordinary annuity.** The value now of $1.00 to be received or paid each period (rents) for n periods, discounted at i compound interest (Table 6-4).
        (2) **Present value of an annuity due.** Same as present value of ordinary annuity except that there is no discount back from first rent; thus there is one less discount period than rents. To use Table 6-4 for an annuity due, apply this formula:

        Present value of annuity due of 1 for n rents = Present value of an ordinary annuity of $(n - 1$ rents$) + \$1.00$

TABLE 6-1 AMOUNT OF 1

$$a = (1 + i)^n$$

(n) Periods	2%	2½%	3%	4%	5%	6%
1	1.02000	1.02500	1.03000	1.04000	1.05000	1.06000
2	1.04040	1.05063	1.06090	1.08160	1.10250	1.12360
3	1.06121	1.07689	1.09273	1.12486	1.15763	1.19102
4	1.08243	1.10381	1.12551	1.16986	1.21551	1.26248
5	1.10408	1.13141	1.15927	1.21665	1.27628	1.33823
6	1.12616	1.15969	1.19405	1.26532	1.34010	1.41852
7	1.14869	1.18869	1.22987	1.31593	1.40710	1.50363
8	1.17166	1.21840	1.26677	1.36857	1.47746	1.59385
9	1.19509	1.24886	1.30477	1.42331	1.55133	1.68948
10	1.21899	1.28008	1.34392	1.48024	1.62889	1.79085
11	1.24337	1.31209	1.38423	1.53945	1.71034	1.89830
12	1.26824	1.34489	1.42576	1.60103	1.79586	2.01220
13	1.29361	1.37851	1.46853	1.66507	1.88565	2.13293
14	1.31948	1.41297	1.51259	1.73168	1.97993	2.26090
15	1.34587	1.44830	1.55797	1.80094	2.07893	2.39656
16	1.37279	1.48451	1.60471	1.87298	2.18287	2.54035
17	1.40024	1.52162	1.65285	1.94790	2.29202	2.69277
18	1.42825	1.55966	1.70243	2.02582	2.40662	2.85434
19	1.45681	1.59865	1.75351	2.10685	2.52695	3.02560
20	1.48595	1.63862	1.80611	2.19112	2.65330	3.20714
21	1.51567	1.67958	1.86029	2.27877	2.78596	3.39956
22	1.54598	1.72157	1.91610	2.36992	2.92526	3.60354
23	1.57690	1.76461	1.97359	2.46472	3.07152	3.81975
24	1.60844	1.80873	2.03279	2.56330	3.22510	4.04893
25	1.64061	1.85394	2.09378	2.66584	3.38635	4.29187
26	1.67342	1.90029	2.15659	2.77247	3.55567	4.54938
27	1.70689	1.94780	2.22129	2.88337	3.73346	4.82235
28	1.74102	1.99650	2.28793	2.99870	3.92013	5.11169
29	1.77584	2.04641	2.35657	3.11865	4.11614	5.41839
30	1.81136	2.09757	2.42726	3.24340	4.32194	5.74349
31	1.84759	2.15001	2.50008	3.37313	4.53804	6.08810
32	1.88454	2.20376	2.57508	3.50806	4.76494	6.45339
33	1.92223	2.25885	2.65234	3.64838	5.00319	6.84059
34	1.96068	2.31532	2.73191	3.79432	5.25335	7.25103
35	1.99989	2.37321	2.81386	3.94609	5.51602	7.68609
36	2.03989	2.43254	2.89828	4.10393	5.79182	8.14725
37	2.08069	2.49335	2.98523	4.26809	6.08141	8.63609
38	2.12230	2.55568	3.07478	4.43881	6.38548	9.15425
39	2.16474	2.61957	3.16703	4.61637	6.70475	9.70351
40	2.20804	2.68506	3.26204	4.80102	7.03999	10.28572

8%	9%	10%	12%	15%	*(n)* Periods
1.08000	1.09000	1.10000	1.12000	1.15000	1
1.16640	1.18810	1.21000	1.25440	1.32250	2
1.25971	1.29503	1.33100	1.40493	1.52088	3
1.36049	1.41158	1.46410	1.57352	1.74901	4
1.46933	1.53862	1.61051	1.76234	2.01136	5
1.58687	1.67710	1.77156	1.97382	2.31306	6
1.71382	1.82804	1.94872	2.21068	2.66002	7
1.85093	1.99256	2.14359	2.47596	3.05902	8
1.99900	2.17189	2.35795	2.77308	3.51788	9
2.15892	2.36736	2.59374	3.10585	4.04556	10
2.33164	2.58043	2.85312	3.47855	4.65239	11
2.51817	2.81267	3.13843	3.89598	5.35025	12
2.71962	3.06581	3.45227	4.36349	6.15279	13
2.93719	3.34173	3.79750	4.88711	7.07571	14
3.17217	3.64248	4.17725	5.47357	8.13706	15
3.42594	3.97031	4.59497	6.13039	9.35762	16
3.70002	4.32763	5.05447	6.86604	10.76126	17
3.99602	4.71712	5.55992	7.68997	12.37545	18
4.31570	5.14166	6.11591	8.61276	14.23177	19
4.66096	5.60441	6.72750	9.64629	16.36654	20
5.03383	6.10881	7.40025	10.80385	18.82152	21
5.43654	6.65860	8.14028	12.10031	21.64475	22
5.87146	7.25787	8.95430	13.55235	24.89146	23
6.34118	7.91108	9.84973	15.17863	28.62518	24
6.84847	8.62308	10.83471	17.00000	32.91895	25
7.39635	9.39916	11.91818	19.04007	37.85680	26
7.98806	10.24508	13.10999	21.32488	43.53532	27
8.62711	11.16714	14.42099	23.88387	50.06561	28
9.31727	12.17218	15.86309	26.74993	57.57545	29
10.06266	13.26768	17.44940	29.95992	66.21177	30
10.86767	14.46177	19.19434	33.55511	76.14354	31
11.73708	15.76333	21.11378	37.58173	87.56507	32
12.67605	17.18203	23.22515	42.09153	100.69983	33
13.69013	18.72841	25.54767	47.14252	115.80480	34
14.78534	20.41397	28.10244	52.79962	133.17552	35
15.96817	22.25123	30.91268	59.13557	153.15185	36
17.24563	24.25384	34.00395	66.23184	176.12463	37
18.62528	26.43668	37.40434	74.17966	202.54332	38
20.11530	28.81598	41.14479	83.08122	232.92482	39
21.72452	31.40942	45.25926	93.05097	267.86355	40

TABLE 6-2   PRESENT VALUE OF 1

$$p^n = \frac{1}{(1 + i)^n} = (1 + i)^{-n}$$

(n) Periods	2%	2½%	3%	4%	5%	6%
1	.98039	.97561	.97087	.96154	.95238	.94340
2	.96117	.95181	.94260	.92456	.90703	.89000
3	.94232	.92860	.91514	.88900	.86384	.83962
4	.92385	.90595	.88849	.85480	.82270	.79209
5	.90573	.88385	.86261	.82193	.78353	.74726
6	.88797	.86230	.83748	.79031	.74622	.70496
7	.87056	.84127	.81309	.75992	.71068	.66506
8	.85349	.82075	.78941	.73069	.67684	.62741
9	.83676	.80073	.76642	.70259	.64461	.59190
10	.82035	.78120	.74409	.67556	.61391	.55839
11	.80426	.76214	.72242	.64958	.58468	.52679
12	.78849	.74356	.70138	.62460	.55684	.49697
13	.77303	.72542	.68095	.60057	.53032	.46884
14	.75788	.70773	.66112	.57748	.50507	.44230
15	.74301	.69047	.64186	.55526	.48102	.41727
16	.72845	.67362	.62317	.53391	.45811	.39365
17	.71416	.65720	.60502	.51337	.43630	.37136
18	.70016	.64117	.58739	.49363	.41552	.35034
19	.68643	.62553	.57029	.47464	.39573	.33051
20	.67297	.61027	.55368	.45639	.37689	.31180
21	.65978	.59539	.53755	.43883	.35894	.29416
22	.64684	.58086	.52189	.42196	.34185	.27751
23	.63416	.56670	.50669	.40573	.32557	.26180
24	.62172	.55288	.49193	.39012	.31007	.24698
25	.60953	.53939	.47761	.37512	.29530	.23300
26	.59758	.52623	.46369	.36069	.28124	.21981
27	.58586	.51340	.45019	.34682	.26785	.20737
28	.57437	.50088	.43708	.33348	.25509	.19563
29	.56311	.48866	.42435	.32065	.24295	.18456
30	.55207	.47674	.41199	.30832	.23138	.17411
31	.54125	.46511	.39999	.29646	.22036	.16425
32	.53063	.45377	.38834	.28506	.20987	.15496
33	.52023	.44270	.37703	.27409	.19987	.14619
34	.51003	.43191	.36604	.26355	.19035	.13791
35	.50003	.42137	.35538	.25342	.18129	.13011
36	.49022	.41109	.34503	.24367	.17266	.12274
37	.48061	.40107	.33498	.23430	.16444	.11579
38	.47119	.39128	.32523	.22529	.15661	.10924
39	.46195	.38174	.31575	.21662	.14915	.10306
40	.45289	.37243	.30656	.20829	.14205	.09722

8%	9%	10%	12%	15%	(n) Periods
.92593	.91743	.90909	.89286	.86957	1
.85734	.84168	.82645	.79719	.75614	2
.79383	.77218	.75132	.71178	.65752	3
.73503	.70843	.68301	.63552	.57175	4
.68058	.64993	.62092	.56743	.49718	5
.63017	.59627	.56447	.50663	.43233	6
.58349	.54703	.51316	.45235	.37594	7
.54027	.50187	.46651	.40388	.32690	8
.50025	.46043	.42410	.36061	.28426	9
.46319	.42241	.38554	.32197	.24719	10
.42888	.38753	.35049	.28748	.21494	11
.39711	.35554	.31863	.25668	.18691	12
.36770	.32618	.28966	.22917	.16253	13
.34046	.29925	.26333	.20462	.14133	14
.31524	.27454	.23939	.18270	.12289	15
.29189	.25187	.21763	.16312	.10687	16
.27027	.23107	.19785	.14564	.09293	17
.25025	.21199	.17986	.13004	.08081	18
.23171	.19449	.16351	.11611	.07027	19
.21455	.17843	.14864	.10367	.06110	20
.19866	.16370	.13513	.09256	.05313	21
.18394	.15018	.12285	.08264	.04620	22
.17032	.13778	.11168	.07379	.04017	23
.15770	.12641	.10153	.06588	.03493	24
.14602	.11597	.09230	.05882	.03038	25
.13520	.10639	.08391	.05252	.02642	26
.12519	.09761	.07628	.04689	.02297	27
.11591	.08955	.06934	.04187	.01997	28
.10733	.08216	.06304	.03738	.01737	29
.09938	.07537	.05731	.03338	.01510	30
.09202	.06915	.05210	.02980	.01313	31
.08520	.06344	.04736	.02661	.01142	32
.07889	.05820	.04306	.02376	.00993	33
.07305	.05340	.03914	.02121	.00864	34
.06763	.04899	.03558	.01894	.00751	35
.06262	.04494	.03235	.01691	.00653	36
.05799	.04123	.02941	.01510	.00568	37
.05369	.03783	.02674	.01348	.00494	38
.04971	.03470	.02430	.01204	.00429	39
.04603	.03184	.02210	.01075	.00373	40

TABLE 6-3 AMOUNT OF AN ORDINARY ANNUITY OF 1

$$A_{\overline{n}|i} = \frac{(1 + i)^n - 1}{i}$$

(n) Periods	2%	2½%	3%	4%	5%	6%
1	1.00000	1.00000	1.00000	1.00000	1.00000	1.00000
2	2.02000	2.02500	2.03000	2.04000	2.05000	2.06000
3	3.06040	3.07563	3.09090	3.12160	3.15250	3.18360
4	4.12161	4.15252	4.18363	4.24646	4.31013	4.37462
5	5.20404	5.25633	5.30914	5.41632	5.52563	5.63709
6	6.30812	6.38774	6.46841	6.63298	6.80191	6.97532
7	7.43428	7.54743	7.66246	7.89829	8.14201	8.39384
8	8.58297	8.73612	8.89234	9.21423	9.54911	9.89747
9	9.75463	9.95452	10.15911	10.58280	11.02656	11.49132
10	10.94972	11.20338	11.46338	12.00611	12.57789	13.18079
11	12.16872	12.48347	12.80780	13.48635	14.20679	14.97164
12	13.41209	13.79555	14.19203	15.02581	15.91713	16.86994
13	14.68033	15.14044	15.61779	16.62684	17.71298	18.88214
14	15.97394	16.51895	17.08632	18.29191	19.59863	21.01507
15	17.29342	17.93193	18.59891	20.02359	21.57856	23.27597
16	18.63929	19.38022	20.15688	21.82453	23.65749	25.67253
17	20.01207	20.86473	21.76159	23.69751	25.84037	28.21288
18	21.41231	22.38635	23.41444	25.64541	28.13238	30.90565
19	22.84056	23.94601	25.11687	27.67123	30.53900	33.75999
20	24.29737	25.54466	26.87037	29.77808	33.06595	36.78559
21	25.78332	27.18327	28.67649	31.96920	35.71925	39.99273
22	27.29898	28.86286	30.53678	34.24797	38.50521	43.39229
23	28.84496	30.58443	32.45288	36.61789	41.43048	46.99583
24	30.42186	32.34904	34.42647	39.08260	44.50200	50.81558
25	32.03030	34.15776	36.45926	41.64591	47.72710	54.86451
26	33.67091	36.01171	38.55304	44.31174	51.11345	59.15638
27	35.34432	37.91200	40.70963	47.08421	54.66913	63.70577
28	37.05121	39.85980	42.93092	49.96758	58.40258	68.52811
29	38.79223	41.85630	45.21885	52.96629	62.32271	73.63980
30	40.56808	43.90270	47.57542	56.08494	66.43885	79.05819
31	42.37944	46.00027	50.00268	59.32834	70.76079	84.80168
32	44.22703	48.15028	52.50276	62.70147	75.29883	90.88978
33	46.11157	50.35403	55.07784	66.20953	80.06377	97.34316
34	48.03380	52.61289	57.73018	69.85791	85.06696	104.18376
35	49.99448	54.92821	60.46208	73.65222	90.32031	111.43478
36	51.99437	57.30141	63.27594	77.59831	95.83632	119.12087
37	54.03425	59.73395	66.17422	81.70225	101.62814	127.26812
38	56.11494	62.22730	69.15945	85.97034	107.70955	135.90421
39	58.23724	64.78298	72.23423	90.40915	114.09502	145.05846
40	60.40198	67.40255	75.40126	95.02552	120.79977	154.76197

8%	9%	10%	12%	15%	(n) Periods
1.00000	1.00000	1.00000	1.00000	1.00000	1
2.08000	2.09000	2.10000	2.12000	2.15000	2
3.24640	3.27810	3.31000	3.37440	3.47250	3
4.50611	4.57313	4.64100	4.77933	4.99338	4
5.86660	5.98471	6.10510	6.35285	6.74238	5
7.33592	7.52334	7.71561	8.11519	8.75374	6
8.92280	9.20044	9.48717	10.08901	11.06680	7
10.63663	11.02847	11.43589	12.29969	13.72682	8
12.48756	13.02104	13.57948	14.77566	16.78584	9
14.48656	15.19293	15.93743	17.54874	20.30372	10
16.64549	17.56029	18.53117	20.65458	24.34928	11
18.97713	20.14072	21.38428	24.13313	29.00167	12
21.49530	22.95339	24.52271	28.02911	34.35192	13
24.21492	26.01919	27.97498	32.39260	40.50471	14
27.15211	29.36092	31.77248	37.27972	47.58041	15
30.32428	33.00340	35.94973	42.75328	55.71747	16
33.75023	36.97371	40.54470	48.88367	65.07509	17
37.45024	41.30134	45.59917	55.74972	75.83636	18
41.44626	46.01846	51.15909	63.43968	88.21181	19
45.76196	51.16012	57.27500	72.05244	102.44358	20
50.42292	56.76453	64.00250	81.69874	118.81012	21
55.45676	62.87334	71.40275	92.50258	137.63164	22
60.89330	69.53194	79.54302	104.60289	159.27638	23
66.76476	76.78981	88.49733	118.15524	184.16784	24
73.10594	84.70090	98.34706	133.33387	212.79302	25
79.95442	93.32398	109.18177	150.33393	245.71197	26
87.35077	102.72314	121.09994	169.37401	283.56877	27
95.33883	112.96822	134.20994	190.69889	327.10408	28
103.96594	124.13536	148.63093	214.58275	377.16969	29
113.28321	136.30754	164.49402	241.33268	434.74515	30
123.34587	149.57522	181.94343	271.29261	500.95692	31
134.21354	164.03699	201.13777	304.84772	577.10046	32
145.95062	179.80032	222.25154	342.42945	644.66553	33
158.62667	196.98234	245.47670	384.52098	765.36535	34
172.31680	215.71076	271.02437	431.66350	881.17016	35
187.10215	236.12472	299.12681	484.46312	1014.34568	36
203.07032	258.37595	330.03949	543.59869	1167.49753	37
220.31595	282.62978	364.04343	609.83053	1343.62216	38
238.94122	309.06646	401.44778	684.01020	1546.16549	39
259.05652	337.88245	442.59256	767.09142	1779.09031	40

TABLE 6-4   PRESENT VALUE OF AN ORDINARY ANNUITY OF 1

$$P_{\overline{n}|\,i} = \frac{1 - \dfrac{1}{(1 + i)^n}}{i} = \frac{1 - v^n}{i}$$

(n) Periods	2%	2½%	3%	4%	5%	6%
1	.98039	.97561	.97087	.96154	.95238	.94340
2	1.94156	1.92742	1.91347	1.88609	1.85941	1.83339
3	2.88388	2.85602	2.82861	2.77509	2.72325	2.67301
4	3.80773	3.76197	3.71710	3.62990	3.54595	3.46511
5	4.71346	4.64583	4.57971	4.45182	4.32948	4.21236
6	5.60143	5.50813	5.41719	5.24214	5.07569	4.91732
7	6.47199	6.34939	6.23028	6.00205	5.78637	5.58238
8	7.32548	7.17014	7.01969	6.73274	6.46321	6.20979
9	8.16224	7.97087	7.78611	7.43533	7.10782	6.80169
10	8.98259	8.75206	8.53020	8.11090	7.72173	7.36009
11	9.78685	9.51421	9.25262	8.76048	8.30641	7.88687
12	10.57534	10.25776	9.95400	9.38507	8.86325	8.38384
13	11.34837	10.98319	10.63496	9.98565	9.39357	8.85268
14	12.10625	11.69091	11.29607	10.56312	9.89864	9.29498
15	12.84926	12.38138	11.93794	11.11839	10.37966	9.71225
16	13.57771	13.05500	12.56110	11.65230	10.83777	10.10590
17	14.29187	13.71220	13.16612	12.16567	11.27407	10.47726
18	14.99203	14.35336	13.75351	12.65930	11.68959	10.82760
19	15.67846	14.97889	14.32380	13.13394	12.08532	11.15812
20	16.35143	15.58916	14.87747	13.59033	12.46221	11.46992
21	17.01121	16.18455	15.41502	14.02916	12.82115	11.76408
22	17.65805	16.76541	15.93692	14.45112	13.16300	12.04158
23	18.29220	17.33211	16.44361	14.85684	13.48857	12.30338
24	18.91393	17.88499	16.93554	15.24696	13.79864	12.55036
25	19.52346	18.42438	17.41315	15.62208	14.09394	12.78336
26	20.12104	18.95061	17.87684	15.98277	14.37519	13.00317
27	20.70690	19.46401	18.32703	16.32959	14.64303	13.21053
28	21.28127	19.96489	18.76411	16.66306	14.89813	13.40616
29	21.84438	20.45355	19.18845	16.98371	15.14107	13.59072
30	22.39646	20.93029	19.60044	17.29203	15.37245	13.76483
31	22.93770	21.39541	20.00043	17.58849	15.59281	13.92909
32	23.46833	21.84918	20.38877	17.87355	15.80268	14.08404
33	23.98856	22.29188	20.76579	18.14765	16.00255	14.23023
34	24.49859	22.72379	21.13184	18.41120	16.19290	14.36814
35	24.99862	23.14516	21.48722	18.66461	16.37419	14.49825
36	25.48884	23.55625	21.83225	18.90828	16.54685	14.62099
37	25.96945	23.95732	22.16724	19.14258	16.71129	14.73678
38	26.44064	24.34860	22.49246	19.36786	16.86789	14.84602
39	26.90259	24.73034	22.80822	19.58448	17.01704	14.94907
40	27.35548	25.10278	23.11477	19.79277	17.15909	15.04630

8%	9%	10%	12%	15%	(n) Periods
.92593	.91743	.90909	.89286	.86957	1
1.78326	1.75911	1.73554	1.69005	1.62571	2
2.57710	2.53130	2.48685	2.40183	2.28323	3
3.31213	3.23972	3.16986	3.03735	2.85498	4
3.99271	3.88965	3.79079	3.60478	3.35216	5
4.62288	4.48592	4.35526	4.11141	3.78448	6
5.20637	5.03295	4.86842	4.56376	4.16042	7
5.74664	5.53482	5.33493	4.96764	4.48732	8
6.24689	5.99525	5.75902	5.32825	4.77158	9
6.71008	6.41766	6.14457	5.65022	5.01877	10
7.13896	6.80519	6.49506	5.93770	5.23371	11
7.53608	7.16073	6.81369	6.19437	5.42062	12
7.90378	7.48690	7.10336	6.42355	5.58315	13
8.24424	7.78615	7.36669	6.62817	5.72448	14
8.55948	8.06069	7.60608	6.81086	5.84737	15
8.85137	8.31256	7.82371	6.97399	5.95424	16
9.12164	8.54363	8.02155	7.11963	6.04716	17
9.37189	8.75563	8.20141	7.24967	6.12797	18
9.60360	8.95012	8.36492	7.36578	6.19823	19
9.81815	9.12855	8.51356	7.46944	6.25933	20
10.01680	9.29224	8.64869	7.56200	6.31246	21
10.20074	9.44243	8.77154	7.64465	6.35866	22
10.37106	9.58021	8.88322	7.71843	6.39884	23
10.52876	9.70661	8.98474	7.78432	6.43377	24
10.67478	9.82258	9.07704	7.84314	6.46415	25
10.80998	9.92897	9.16095	7.89566	6.49056	26
10.93516	10.02658	9.23722	7.94255	6.51353	27
11.05108	10.11613	9.30657	7.98442	6.53351	28
11.15841	10.19828	9.36961	8.02181	6.55088	29
11.25778	10.27365	9.42691	8.05518	6.56598	30
11.34980	10.34280	9.47901	8.08499	6.57911	31
11.43500	10.40624	9.52638	8.11159	6.59053	32
11.51389	10.46444	9.56943	8.13535	6.60046	33
11.58693	10.51784	9.60858	8.15656	6.60910	34
11.65457	10.56682	9.64416	8.17550	6.61661	35
11.71719	10.61176	9.67651	8.19241	6.62314	36
11.77518	10.65299	9.70592	8.20751	6.62882	37
11.82887	10.69082	9.73265	8.22099	6.63375	38
11.87858	10.72552	9.75697	8.23303	6.63805	39
11.92461	10.75736	9.77905	8.24378	6.64178	40

TABLE 6-5 PRESENT VALUE OF AN ANNUITY DUE OF 1

$$P_{\overline{n}|i} = 1 + \frac{1 - \dfrac{1}{(1+i)^{n-1}}}{i} = (1+i)\left(\frac{1-v^n}{i}\right) = (1+i)\,(a_{\overline{n}|i})$$

(n) Periods	2%	2½%	3%	4%	5%	6%
1	1.00000	1.00000	1.00000	1.00000	1.00000	1.00000
2	1.98039	1.97561	1.97087	1.96154	1.95238	1.94340
3	2.94156	2.92742	2.91347	2.88609	2.85941	2.83339
4	3.88388	3.85602	3.82861	3.77509	3.72325	3.67301
5	4.80773	4.76197	4.71710	4.62990	4.54595	4.46511
6	5.71346	5.64583	5.57971	5.45182	5.32948	5.21236
7	6.60143	6.50813	6.41719	6.24214	6.07569	5.91732
8	7.47199	7.34939	7.23028	7.00205	6.78637	6.58238
9	8.32548	8.17014	8.01969	7.73274	7.46321	7.20979
10	9.16224	8.97087	8.78611	8.43533	8.10782	7.80169
11	9.98259	9.75206	9.53020	9.11090	8.72173	8.36009
12	10.78685	10.51421	10.25262	9.76048	9.30641	8.88687
13	11.57534	11.25776	10.95400	10.38507	9.86325	9.38384
14	12.34837	11.98319	11.63496	10.98565	10.39357	9.85268
15	13.10625	12.69091	12.29607	11.56312	10.89864	10.29498
16	13.84926	13.38138	12.93794	12.11839	11.37966	10.71225
17	14.57771	14.05500	13.56110	12.65230	11.83777	11.10590
18	15.29187	14.71220	14.16612	13.16567	12.27407	11.47726
19	15.99203	15.35336	14.75351	13.65930	12.68959	11.82760
20	16.67846	15.97889	15.32380	14.13394	13.08532	12.15812
21	17.35143	16.58916	15.87747	14.59033	13.46221	12.46992
22	18.01121	17.18455	16.41502	15.02916	13.82115	12.76408
23	18.65805	17.76541	16.93692	15.45112	14.16300	13.04158
24	19.29220	18.33211	17.44361	15.85684	14.48857	13.30338
25	19.91393	18.88499	17.93554	16.24696	14.79864	13.55036
26	20.52346	19.42438	18.41315	16.62208	15.09394	13.78336
27	21.12104	19.95061	18.87684	16.98277	15.37519	14.00317
28	21.70690	20.46401	19.32703	17.32959	15.64303	14.21053
29	22.28127	20.96489	19.76411	17.66306	15.89813	14.40616
30	22.84438	21.45355	20.18845	17.98371	16.14107	14.59072
31	23.39646	21.93029	20.60044	18.29203	16.37245	14.76483
32	23.93770	22.39541	21.00043	18.58849	16.59281	14.92909
33	24.46833	22.84918	21.38877	18.87355	16.80268	15.08404
34	24.98856	23.29188	21.76579	19.14765	17.00255	15.23023
35	25.49859	23.72379	22.13184	19.41120	17.19290	15.36814
36	25.99862	24.14516	22.48722	19.66461	17.37419	15.49825
37	26.48884	24.55625	22.83225	19.90828	17.54685	15.62099
38	26.96945	24.95732	23.16724	20.14258	17.71129	15.73678
39	27.44064	25.34860	23.49246	20.36786	17.86789	15.84602
40	27.90259	25.73034	23.80822	20.58448	18.01704	15.94907

8%	9%	10%	12%	15%	(n) Periods
1.00000	1.00000	1.00000	1.00000	1.00000	1
1.92593	1.91743	1.90909	1.89286	1.86957	2
2.78326	2.75911	2.73554	2.69005	2.62571	3
3.57710	3.53130	3.48685	3.40183	3.28323	4
4.31213	4.23972	4.16986	4.03735	3.85498	5
4.99271	4.88965	4.79079	4.60478	4.35216	6
5.62288	5.48592	5.35526	5.11141	4.78448	7
6.20637	6.03295	5.86842	5.56376	5.16042	8
6.74664	6.53482	6.33493	5.96764	5.48732	9
7.24689	6.99525	6.75902	6.32825	5.77158	10
7.71008	7.41766	7.14457	6.65022	6.01877	11
8.13896	7.80519	7.49506	6.93770	6.23371	12
8.53608	8.16073	7.81369	7.19437	6.42062	13
8.90378	8.48690	8.10336	7.42355	6.58315	14
9.24424	8.78615	8.36669	7.62817	6.72448	15
9.55948	9.06069	8.60608	7.81086	6.84737	16
9.85137	9.31256	8.82371	7.97399	6.95424	17
10.12164	9.54363	9.02155	8.11963	7.04716	18
10.37189	9.75563	9.20141	8.24967	7.12797	19
10.60360	9.95012	9.36492	8.36578	7.19823	20
10.81815	10.12855	9.51356	8.46944	7.25933	21
11.01680	10.29224	9.64869	8.56200	7.31246	22
11.20074	10.44243	9.77154	8.64465	7.35866	23
11.37106	10.58021	9.88322	8.71843	7.39884	24
11.52876	10.70661	9.98474	8.78432	7.43377	25
11.67478	10.82258	10.07704	8.84314	7.46415	26
11.80998	10.92897	10.16095	8.89566	7.49056	27
11.93518	11.02658	10.23722	8.94255	7.51353	28
12.05108	11.11613	10.30657	8.98442	7.53351	29
12.15841	11.19828	10.36961	9.02181	7.55088	30
12.25778	11.27365	10.42691	9.05518	7.56598	31
12.34980	11.34280	10.47901	9.08499	7.57911	32
12.43500	11.40624	10.52638	9.11159	7.59053	33
12.51389	11.46444	10.56943	9.13535	7.60046	34
12.58693	11.51784	10.60858	9.15656	7.60910	35
12.65457	11.56682	10.64416	9.17550	7.61661	36
12.71719	11.61176	10.67651	9.19241	7.62314	37
12.77518	11.65299	10.70592	9.20751	7.62882	38
12.82887	11.69082	10.73265	9.22099	7.63375	39
12.87858	11.72552	10.75697	9.23303	7.63805	40

Questions

1. What is the "time value" of money?
2. Why should accountants have an understanding of compound interest, annuities, and present value concepts?
3. What is the nature of interest?
4. Distinguish between "simple interest" and "compound interest."
5. Distinguish between "amount" and "present value."
6. Define "discounting" as it applies to measuring receipts and payments.
7. What are the primary characteristics of an annuity?
8. Differentiate between an "ordinary annuity" and an "annuity due."
9. Explain how the amount of an ordinary annuity interest table is converted to the amount of an annuity due interest table.
10. Explain how the present value of an ordinary annuity interest table is converted to the present value of an annuity due interest table.
11. Define a "deferred annuity."

Exercises (Interest rates are per annum unless otherwise indicated.)

E6-1 For each of the following cases, indicate (a) to what rate columns and (b) to what number of periods you would refer in looking up the interest factor.

1. In an amount of 1 table

	Annual Rate	Number of Years Invested	Compounded
a.	5%	15	Annually
b.	10%	5	Quarterly
c.	8%	8	Semiannually

2. In a present value of an annuity of 1 table

	Annual Rate	Number of Years Involved	Number of Rents Involved	Frequency of Rents
a.	8%	20	20	Annually
b.	10%	5	10	Semiannually
c.	8%	4	16	Quarterly

E6-2 Tornado Company recently signed a lease for a new office building, for a lease period of 10 years. Under the lease agreement, a security deposit of $10,000 is made, with the deposit to be returned at the expiration of the lease, with interest compounded at 6% per year.

$1.79085 \times 10,000 = $17,908.50$

Instructions

What amount will the company receive at the time the lease expires?

E6-3 Bonnie Harris invests $1,000 at 8% annual interest, leaving the money invested without withdrawing any of the interest for ten years. At the end of the ten years, Bonnie withdrew the accumulated amount of money.

Instructions

(a) Compute the amount Bonnie would withdraw assuming the investment earns **simple interest.** $1800

(b) Compute the amount Bonnie would withdraw assuming the investment earns **interest compounded annually.** $2158.92

(c) Compute the amount Bonnie would withdraw assuming the investment earns **interest compounded semiannually.**   *2191.12*

E6-4 Under the terms of his salary agreement, President Sassatti has an option of receiving either an immediate bonus of $10,000, or a deferred bonus of $20,000, payable in 20 years. Ignoring tax considerations, and assuming a relevant interest rate of 6%, which form of settlement should President Sassatti accept? *.3118 0 × 20,000 = 6236*
Accept immediate bonus of $10,000

E6-5 Determine the amount that must be deposited now at compound interest to provide the desired sum at the end of the following designated periods at the interest rate specified.

(a) Dollars to be invested and held for 5 years at 8% per year to amount to $1,000. *$680.58 (.68058 × 1000)*

(b) Dollars to be invested and held for 8 years at 10% per year, then invested at 8% per year and held for another 5 years to amount to $10,000. *$3174.97 (.68058 × 10,000)   (6805.8 × .46651)*

(c) Dollars to be invested now at 6% per year and held for 30 years to have $100,000 at retirement. *$17,411   (.17411 × 100,000)*

E6-6 Using the appropriate interest table, compute the amounts to be invested now at compound interest in order to provide the following sums at the end of the designated periods.

(a) Amount invested for 5 periods at 6% to amount to $10,000. *$7472.60*

(b) Amount invested for 15 periods at 10% to amount to $10,000. *$2393.90*

(c) Amount invested for five years at 6%, then at 8% for another five years to amount to $10,000. *$5085.70*

E6-7 Using the appropriate interest table, compute the amounts to which the following periodic investments would accumulate at compound interest by the end of the last period in which an investment is made (end-of-period payments).

(a) $10,000 each period for ten periods at 8%.

(b) $10,000 each period for thirty periods at 6%.

(c) $10,000 each period for ten periods at 8% and then $10,000 each period for the eleventh through the twentieth periods at 10%.

E6-8 Westinghouse Corporation, having recently issued a $20 million, 20-year bond issue, is committed to make annual sinking fund deposits of $600,000. The deposits are made on the last day of each year, and yield a return of 5%. Will the fund at the end of 20 years be sufficient to retire the bonds? If not, what will the deficiency be?
Will not be sufficient. $160,430 short.   (33.06595 × 600,000)

E6-9 Determine the amount that Zaf Iqbal would have at the end of 1988 if investments were made under the following conditions:

(a) $1,000 is to be invested at the end of each year, 1979 through 1988, at 8% interest compounded annually.

(b) $1,000 is to be invested at the beginning of each year, 1979 through 1988, at 8% interest compounded annually.

E6-10 Using the appropriate interest table, answer each of the following questions (each case is independent of the others).

(a) What is the future amount of $1,000 at the end of 10 periods at 8% compounded interest? *$2158.92*

(b) What is the present value of $1,000 due 8 periods hence, discounted at 10%? *$466.56*

(c) What is the future amount of 15 periodic payments of $1,000 each made at the end of each period and compounded at 6%? *$466.16 $23,275.97*

(d) What is the present value of $1,000 to be received at the end of each of 30 periods, discounted at 5% compound interest? *$15,372.45*

E6-11 Using the appropriate interest table, answer the following questions (each case is independent of the others).

(a) What is the future amount of 15 periodic payments of $1,000 each made at the beginning of each period and compounded at 10%?

(b) What is the present value of $1,000 to be received at the beginning of each of thirty periods, discounted at 5% compound interest?

(c) What is the future amount of 10 deposits of $500 each made at the beginning of each period and compounded at 6%? (Future amount as of the end of the tenth period.)

(d) What is the present value of eight receipts of $700 each received at the beginning of each period, discounted at 10% compounded interest?

E6-12 What would you pay for a $10,000 debenture bond that matures in 30 years and pays $500 a year in interest if you wanted to earn a yield of:

(a) 4%? $(10,000 \times .30832) + (500 \times 17.29203)$

(b) 5%? $(10,000 \times .23138) + (500 \times 15.37245)$

(c) 10%? $(10,000 \times .05731) + (500 \times 9.42691)$

E6-13 Mr. Greg Garious, a super salesman contemplating retirement on his fifty-fifth birthday, decides to create a fund on an 8% basis that will enable him to withdraw $5,000 per year on June 30, beginning in 1985, and continuing through 1988. To develop this fund, Greg intends to make equal contributions on June 30 of each of the years 1981–1984.

Instructions

(a) How much must the balance of the fund equal on June 30, 1984, in order for Greg Garious to satisfy his objective?

(b) What are each of Greg's contributions to the fund?

E6-14 Using the appropriate interest table, compute the present values of the following periodic amounts due at the end of the designated periods.

(a) $10,000 receivable at the end of each period for ten periods compounded at 8%.

(b) $10,000 payments to be made at the end of each period for sixteen periods at 10%.

(c) $10,000 payable at the end of the seventh, eighth, ninth, and tenth periods at 8%.

E6-15 Amy Norton wishes to invest $5,000 on July 1, 1980 and have it accumulate to $11,000 by July 1, 1990.

Instructions

At what exact annual rate of interest must Amy invest the $5,000? (Interpolation is required.)

E6-16 On July 17, 1979, Patty Kake borrowed $20,000 from her grandfather to open a boutique. Starting July 17, 1980, Patty has to make five equal annual payments of $5,250 each to repay the loan.

Instructions

What interest rate is Patty Kake paying? (Interpolation is required.)

E6-17 As the purchaser of a new house, Lynn Burch has signed a mortgage note to pay the Honorable National Bank and Trust Co. $2,400 every six months for 15 years, at the end of which time she will own the house. At the date the mortgage is signed the cash value of the house is $40,000. The first payment will be made six months after the date the mortgage is signed.

Instructions

Compute the exact rate of interest earned on the mortgage by the bank. (Interpolate if necessary.)

Problems (Interest rates are per annum unless otherwise indicated.)

P6-1   Becca Diedrich intends to invest $10,000 in a trust on January 10 of every year, 1981 to 1995, inclusive. She anticipates that interest rates will change during that period of time as follows:

1/10/81–1/10/84	5%
1/10/84–1/10/91	6%
1/10/91–1/10/95	8%

Table 6-3

How much will Becca have in trust on January 10, 1995?

P6-2   Using the appropriate interest table, provide the solution to each of the following four questions by computing the unknowns.

(a) Dave Ziebart has $15,000 to invest today at 6% to pay a debt of $25,342.20. How many years will it take him to accumulate enough to liquidate the debt? *9 years*

(b) Liz Rohol has an $8,500 debt which she wishes to repay five years from today; she has $5,784.93 which she intends to invest for the five years. What rate of interest will she need to earn annually in order to accumulate enough to pay the debt?   *8%*

(c) What is the amount of the payments that Vanessa Dailey must make at the end of each of eight years to accumulate a fund of $30,000 by the end of the eighth year, if the fund earns 8% interest, compounded annually? *#2,820.44*

(d) Mary Warden desires to accumulate $200,000 by her fifty-fifth birthday so she can retire to her summer place on Lake Holiday. She wishes to accumulate this amount by equal deposits on each of her next twenty-five birthdays, her thirtieth through her fifty-fourth. What annual deposit must Mary make if the fund will earn 6% interest compounded annually?   *#3439*

P6-3   Mack Aroni, a bank robber, is worried about his retirement. He decides to start a savings account. Mack deposits annually his net share of the "loot," which consists of $50,000 per year, for three years beginning January 1, 1973. Mack is arrested on January 4, 1975 (after making the third deposit) and spends the rest of 1975 and most of 1976 in jail. He escapes in September of 1976. He resumes his savings plan with semiannual deposits of $15,000 each beginning January 1, 1977. Assume that the bank's interest rate was 5% compounded annually from January 1, 1973 through January 1, 1976 and 6% annual rate, compounded semiannually thereafter.

Instructions

When Mack retires on January 1, 1980 (six months after his last deposit), what is the balance in his savings account?

P6-4   Forrest Ranger borrowed $20,000 on March 1, 1979. This amount plus accrued interest at 8% compounded semiannually is to be repaid March 1, 1989. To retire this debt, Forrest plans to contribute to a debt retirement fund five equal amounts starting on March 1, 1984 and for the next four years. The fund is expected to earn 6% per annum.

Instructions

How much must be set aside each year by Forrest Ranger to provide a fund sufficient to retire the debt on March 1, 1989?

P6-5   Your client, Lowrental Leasing Company, is preparing a contract to lease a machine to Neverown Corporation for a period of 20 years. Lowrental has an investment cost of $249,245 in the machine, which has a useful life of 20 years and no salvage value at the end of that time. Your client is interested in earning a 5% return on its investment and has agreed to accept 20 equal rental payments at the end of each of the next 20 years.

Instructions

You are requested to provide Lowrental with the amount of each of the 20 rentals that will render a 5% return on investment.

P6-6 Your client, Conglomerate, Inc., has acquired Brockabrella Manufacturing Company in a business combination that is to be accounted for as a purchase transaction (at fair market value). Along with the assets and business of Brockabrella, Conglomerate assumed an outstanding debenture bond issue having a principal amount of $5,000,000 with interest payable semiannually at a stated rate of 5%. Brockabrella received $4,800,000 in proceeds from the issuance five years ago. The bonds are currently 15 years from maturity. Equivalent securities command an 8% current market rate of interest.

Instructions

Your client requests your advice regarding the amount to record for the acquired bond issue.

P6-7 Cottonco, Inc., has decided to surface and maintain for ten years a vacant lot next to one of its discount retail outlets to serve as a parking lot for customers. Management is considering the following bids involving two different qualities of surfacing for a parking area of 10,000 square yards:

Bid A. A surface that costs $7.00 per square yard to install. This surface has a probable useful life of 10 years and will require annual maintenance in each year except the last year, at an estimated cost of 3 cents per square yard.

Bid B. A surface that costs $4.00 per square yard to install. This surface will have to be replaced at the end of five years. The annual maintenance cost on this surface is estimated at 12 cents per square yard for each year but the last year of its service. The replacement surface will be similar to the initial surface.

Instructions

Prepare computations showing which bid should be accepted by Cottonco, Inc. You may assume that the cost of capital is 10%, that the annual maintenance expenditures are incurred at the end of each year, and that prices are not expected to change during the next ten years.

P6-8 Thomas Robinson Corporation has outstanding a contractual debt. The corporation has available two means of settlement: It can either make immediate payment of $800,000, or it can make annual payments of $115,000 for 10 years, each payment due on the last day of the year. Which method of payment do you recommend, assuming an expected effective interest rate of 8% during the future period? *annual payments*

P6-9 Assuming the same facts as those in Problem 6-8 except that the payments must begin now and be made on the first day of each of the 10 years, what payment method would you recommend? *800,000*

P6-10 Solve for the unknowns in each of the following three situations using the interest tables.

(a) On June 1, 1980, Rick Thompson purchases twenty acres of farm land from his neighbor, Nancy Poole, and agrees to pay the purchase price in five payments of $12,000 each, the first payment to be payable June 1, 1984, with interest compounded annually at the rate of 8%. What is the purchase price of the twenty acres?

(b) Mike Silver wishes to invest $58,881 today to insure $8,000 payments to his wife at the end of each year for the next ten years. At what interest rate must the $58,881 be invested?

(c) Mr. and Mrs. Art Washington have decided to provide for their handicapped son by investing $230,000 today in an annuity at 6% interest, compounded annually. They feel their son should receive approximately $18,000 per year beginning one year from today. The investment of the $230,000 will provide approximately $18,000 per year for how many years before being depleted?

P6-11 Billy Begone died leaving to his wife Renee an insurance policy contract that provides that the beneficiary (Renee) can choose any one of the following four options.

(a) $20,000 immediate cash.

(b) $800 every three months payable at the end of each quarter for 10 years.

(c) $10,000 immediate cash and $400 every three months for eight years, payable at the beginning of each three-month period.

(d) $1,400 every three months for three years and $400 each quarter for the following 25 quarters, all payments payable at the end of each quarter.

Instructions

If money is worth 2% per quarter, compounded quarterly, which option would you recommend that Renee exercise?

P6-12 Provide a solution to each of the following situations by computing the unknowns (use the interest tables).

(a) Jean Isham owes a debt of $7,000 from the purchase of her new sports car. The debt bears interest of 8% payable annually. Jean desires to pay the debt and interest in four annual installments, beginning one year hence. What equal annual installments will pay the debt and interest?

(b) On January 1, 1981, Phil Johnson offers to buy Nadine Sweesy's used combine for $18,000, payable in five equal installments, which are to include 6% interest on the unpaid balance and a portion of the principal with the first payment to be made on January 1, 1981. How much will each payment be?

(c) Missy Mecklenburg invests in a $50,000 annuity insurance policy at 5% compounded annually on February 8, 1981. The first of 20 receipts from the annuity is payable to Missy ten years after the annuity is purchased, or on February 8, 1991. What will be the amount of each of the 20 equal annual receipts?

15.14107
7.10782

P6-13 During the past year Johnny Grapeseed planted a new vineyard on 100 acres of land which he leases for $8,000 a year. He has asked you as his accountant to assist him in determining the value of his vineyard operation.

The vineyard will bear no grapes for the first five years (1–5). In the next five years (6–10), Johnny estimates that the vines will bear grapes that can be sold for $40,000 each year. For the next 20 years (11–30) he expects the harvest will provide annual revenues of $60,000. But during the last 10 years (31–40) of the vineyard's life he estimates that revenues will decline to $50,000 per year.

During the first five years the annual cost of pruning, fertilizing, and caring for the vineyard is estimated at $4,000; during the years of production, 6–40, these costs will rise to $6,000 per year. The relevant market rate of interest for the entire period is 8%. Assume that all receipts and payments are made at the end of each year.

Instructions

Julie Gallo has offered to buy Johnny's vineyard business by assuming the 40-year lease. On the basis of the current value of the business what is the mimimum price Johnny should accept?

P6-14 Laura Kinniry plans to establish an annuity arrangement whereby her three children would each receive $5,000 on December 25 of the years 1983 to 1997, inclusive. Variations in the interest rates during that period of time are estimated as follows:

12/26/82–12/25/87	6%
12/26/87–12/25/93	5%
12/26/93–12/25/97	4%

Instructions

Compute the amount that Mrs. Kinniry must invest on December 26, 1982 to assure these annual payments to her children.

Current Assets and Current Liabilities

Cash, Temporary Investments, and Receivables

The primary liquid assets of most business enterprises are cash, temporary investments, and receivables. Accounting for cash presents few problems because the questions of valuation and classification are easily answered. Accounting for temporary investments and receivables, however, can be somewhat more complex.

SECTION I—CASH

Nature and Composition of Cash

Cash is the standard medium of exchange and provides the basis for measuring and accounting for all other items. It is generally classified as a current asset. To be reported as **"cash,"** it must be readily available for the payment of current obligations, and it must be free from any contractual restriction that limits its use in satisfying debts.

Cash consists of coin, currency, and available funds on deposit at the bank. Negotiable instruments such as money orders, certified checks, cashiers' checks, personal checks, and bank drafts are also viewed as cash.

Savings accounts are usually classified as cash, although the bank has the legal right to demand notice before withdrawal. But the privilege of prior notice is rarely exercised by banks, so savings accounts are considered cash. Certificates of deposit, which may be withdrawn only at certain maturity dates, are more appropriately included in the temporary investment section because of the real restriction on their withdrawal.

Items that present classification problems are postdated checks, I.O.U.'s, travel advances, postage stamps, and special cash funds. **Postdated checks and I.O.U.'s are treated as receivables. Travel advances** are properly treated as receivables if the advances are to be collected from the employees or deducted from their salaries. Otherwise, classification of the travel advance as a prepaid expense is more appropriate. **Postage stamps on hand** are classified as part of office supplies inventory or as a prepaid expense.

Petty cash funds and change funds are included in current assets as cash because these funds are used to meet current operating expenses and to liquidate current liabilities. Generally, the segregation of cash in the current asset section is not made, unless a large fund is established specifically to meet a maturing obligation.

Cash that is restricted or in escrow is segregated from the general cash account. The **restricted cash** is either classified in the current asset or in the long-term asset section, depending on the date of availability or disbursement. If the cash is to be used (within a year or the operating cycle, whichever is longer) for payment of existing or maturing obligations, classification in the current section is appropriate. On the other hand, if the cash is to be held for a longer period of time, the restricted cash is shown in the long-term section of the balance sheet. Generally, cash to be held for long periods is invested and not held in the form of cash.

Cash classified in the long-term section is frequently set aside either for plant expansion or retirement of long-term debt. For example, an annual report of American Can Company contained this item:

American Can Company	
Long-term assets	
Funds held by trustee for construction	$28,157,000

In summary, cash includes the medium of exchange and most negotiable instruments. If the item cannot be converted immediately to coin or currency, it is separately classified as an investment, as a receivable, or as a prepaid expense. Cash that is not available for payment of currently maturing liabilities is segregated and classified in the long-term asset section.

Compensating Balances

In recent years it has become common for banks and other lending institutions to require the maintenance of minimum cash balances on deposit of those customers to whom it lends money or extends credit. These minimum balances, called **compensating balances,** are defined by the SEC as: "that portion of any demand deposit (or any time deposit or certificate of deposit) maintained by a corporation which constitutes support for existing borrowing arrangements of the corporation with a lending institution. Such arrangements would include both outstanding borrowings and the assurance of future credit availability."[1]

The need for the disclosure of compensating balances was highlighted in the early 1970's when a number of companies were involved in a liquidity crisis. Many investors believed that the cash reported on the balance sheet was fully available to meet recurring obligations, but these funds were restricted because of the need for these companies to maintain minimum cash balances at various lending institutions.

The SEC recommends that legally **restricted deposits** held as compensating balances against short-term borrowing arrangements be stated separately among the "cash and cash items" in current assets. Restricted deposits held as compensating balances against long-term borrowing arrangements should be separately classified as noncurrent assets in either the "investments" or "other assets" sections.

In cases where compensating balance arrangements exist but there are not agreements that restrict the use of cash amounts shown on the balance sheet, the arrangements and the amounts involved should be described in footnotes to the financial statements. Compensating balances that are maintained under an agreement to assure future credit availability also must be disclosed separately in the footnotes together with the amount and duration of such agreement.

Cash—Management and Control

Cash presents a special accounting problem not only because it enters into a great many transactions but also for these reasons:

1. Cash is the single asset readily convertible into any other type of asset. It is easily concealed and transported, and it is almost universally desired. Correct accounting for cash transactions therefore requires that controls be established to insure that cash belonging to the enterprise is not improperly converted to personal use by someone in or connected with the enterprise.

2. The amount of cash owned by an enterprise should be regulated carefully so that neither too much nor too little is available at any time. An adequate supply must always be maintained without tying up too much of the firm's resources. As the medium of exchange, cash is required to pay for all assets and services purchased by the company and to meet all its obligations as they mature. The disbursement of cash is thus a daily occurrence, and a sufficient fund of cash must be kept on hand to meet these needs. On the other hand, cash, as such, is not a productive asset; it earns no return. Hence it is undesirable to keep on hand a supply of cash any larger than that necessary to meet day-by-day needs, with a reasonable margin for emergencies. Cash in excess of what is needed should be invested either in income-producing securities or in other productive assets.

Two problems of accounting for cash transactions face the accounting department: (1) proper controls must be established to insure that no unauthorized transactions are entered into by officers or employees; (2) information necessary to the proper management of cash on hand and cash transactions must be provided. Most companies fix the responsibility for obtaining proper record control over cash transactions in the accounting department. Record control, of course, is not possible with-

---

[1]*Accounting Series Release No. 148*, "Amendments to Regulations S-X and Related Interpretations and Guidelines Regarding the Disclosure of Compensating Balances and Short-Term Borrowing Arrangements," Securities and Exchange Commission, November 13, 1973.

out adequate physical control; therefore the accounting department must take an interest in preventing intentional or unintentional mistakes in cash transactions. It should be emphasized that even with sophisticated control devices errors can and do happen. Recently the *Wall Street Journal* ran a story entitled "A 7.8 Million Error Has a Happy Ending for a Horrified Bank" which described how Manufacturers Hanover Trust Co., one of the nation's largest banks, mailed about $7.8 million too much in cash dividends to its stockholders. Happily most of the monies were subsequently returned.

Regulating the amount of cash on hand is primarily a management problem, but accountants must be able to provide the information required by management in regulating cash on hand through the special transactions of borrowing or investing. The accounting aspects of cash are covered in this textbook; the control aspects of cash are adequately treated in auditing and other courses.

The Imprest Petty Cash System   Almost every company finds it necessary to pay small amounts for a great many things such as employees' lunches and carfare, purchases of minor office supply items, and small expense payments. It is obviously impractical to require that such disbursements be made by check, yet some control over them is important. A common method of obtaining reasonable control, simplicity of operation, and general adherence to the rule of disbursement by check is the so-called **imprest system** for petty cash disbursements.

This is how the system works.

(a) Some individual is designated as the petty cash custodian and given a small amount of currency as a fund from which to make small payments.

Petty Cash Fund	200	
Cash		200

(b) As disbursements are made, the petty cash custodian obtains signed receipts from each individual to whom cash is paid. If possible, evidence of the disbursement should be attached to the petty cash receipt.

(Petty cash transactions are not recorded until the fund is reimbursed.)

(c) When the supply of cash runs low, the custodian presents to the general cashier a request for reimbursement supported by a petty cash voucher or memo that has been obtained for all disbursements and receives a company check drawn to "Cash" or "Petty Cash" to replenish the fund.

Office Supplies Expense	22	
Postage Expense	13	
Transportation-In Expense	36	
Cash Over and Short	2	
Cash		73

(d) If it is decided that the amount of cash in the petty cash fund is excessive, an adjustment may be made as follows:

Cash	50	
Petty Cash		50

Entries are made in the Petty Cash account only to increase or decrease the size of the fund or to adjust the petty cash account balance and related expenses if not replenished at year end. The reimbursement entry does not affect the Petty Cash account, but it does affect the amount of petty cash on hand.

A **Cash Over and Short** account is used when the fund fails to prove out. If cash proves out short (i.e., the sum of the vouchers and cash in the fund is less than the imprest amount), the shortage is debited to the Cash Over and Short account. If it proves out over, the overage is credited to Cash Over and Short. This account is left open until the end of the year, when it is closed and generally shown on the income statement as a miscellaneous expense or income.

There are usually expense items in the fund except immediately after reimbursement; therefore, if accurate financial statements are desired, the funds must be reimbursed at the end of each accounting period and also when nearly depleted.

Under the imprest system the petty cash custodian is responsible at all times for the amount of the fund on hand either as cash or in the form of signed vouchers. These vouchers provide the evidence required by the disbursing officer to issue a reimbursement check. Two additional procedures are followed to obtain more complete control over the petty cash fund:

1. Surprise counts of the fund are made from time to time by a superior of the petty cash custodian to determine that the fund is being accounted for satisfactorily.
2. Petty cash vouchers are canceled or mutilated after they have been submitted for reimbursement, so that they cannot be used to secure a second and improper reimbursement.

The imprest system is frequently applied to payroll disbursements through the use of a special payroll account. Separate bank accounts operated under the imprest system are also used to pay dividends, officers' salaries, travel expenses, commissions, bonuses, and confidential expenses.

Cash Balances

Not only must cash receipts and cash disbursements be safeguarded through internal control measures, but also the cash on hand and in banks must be protected. Because receipts become cash on hand and disbursements are made from cash in banks, adequate control of receipts and disbursements is a part of the protection of cash balances. Certain other procedures, however, should be given some consideration.

Physical protection of cash is so elementary a necessity that it requires little discussion. Every effort should be made to hold to a minimum the cash on hand in the office. A petty cash fund, perhaps change funds, and the current day's receipts should be all that is on hand at any one time, and these funds should be kept, insofar as possible, in a vault, safe, or locked cash drawer. Each day's receipts should be transmitted intact to the bank as soon as practicable.

Related to the problem of protecting cash balances is the problem of accurately stating the amount of available cash both in internal reports for management and in financial statements for external use.

Every company has, in its cash books and cash account, a record of all cash received and disbursed and the balance. Because of the many cash transactions, however, errors or omissions may be made in keeping this record. Therefore, it is necessary to prove periodically the balance shown in the general ledger. Cash actually present in the office—petty cash, change funds, and undeposited receipts—can be counted and the amount determined in that way, for comparison with the company records. Cash on deposit with a bank is not available for count and is proved through the **preparation of a bank reconciliation,** that is, a reconciliation of the company's record of cash in the bank and the bank's record of the company's cash that is on deposit.

Reconciliation of Bank Balances   Generally, at the end of each calendar month the bank supplies each customer with a **bank statement** (a copy of the bank's account with the customer) together with the customer's withdrawal checks that have been paid by the bank during the month. If no errors were made by the bank or the customer, if all deposits made and all checks drawn by the customer reached the bank within the same month, and if no other transactions occurred that affected either the company's or the bank's record of cash, the balance of cash reported by the bank to the customer should be the same as that shown in the customer's own records as of the same point in time. Thus, comparison of the balance shown on the bank statement with the balance shown in the customer's own records should verify the latter.

For various reasons this condition seldom occurs. In most cases checks issued by the customer close to the end of the month do not reach the bank within the same month; deposits made by the customer on the last day of the month may not be recorded by the bank until about the first day of the following month; and such items as service charges by the bank are not brought to the attention of the customer until the bank statement is received by the customer. Hence, there regularly are differences between the customer's record of cash and the bank's record, and the two must be reconciled to determine the nature of the differences between the two amounts.

Reconciliation of Bank and Book Balances:

Jersey Company
BANK RECONCILIATION

Memphis National Bank, November 30, 1981

Balance per bank statement, Nov. 30, 1981			$22,365.30
Add			
Bank charge not recorded by the company		$ 8.10	
Receipts of Nov. 30 on hand, not in bank's balance		3,680.43	3,688.53
			26,053.83
Deduct			
Outstanding checks			
#7327	$ 150.47		
#7348	4,820.00		
#7349	30.64	5,001.11	
Interest on Sequoia bonds collected by bank on			
Nov. 30 for the company, not recorded			
by the company		600.00	5,601.11
Balance per books, Nov. 30, 1981			$20,452.72

A **bank reconciliation,** then, is a schedule indicating and explaining any differences between the bank's and the company's records of cash. If the difference results only from transactions with customers not yet recorded by the bank, the company's record of cash is considered correct. But if some part of the difference arises from other items, adjustment of either the bank's or the customer's records is required.

Two general forms of bank reconciliation are in common use. One form starts with the bank balance and, then, by adding or subtracting the various items making up the difference, works to the book balance. This form is entitled **Reconciliation of Bank and Book Balances** or simply "Bank to Books" and is illustrated on page 272.

The other widely used form, entitled **Reconciliation of Bank and Book Balances to Corrected Balance,** is composed of two distinct sections. One section begins with the balance as shown on the bank statement and works to a corrected balance, that is, the balance the bank statement would show if all transactions were recorded. The second section starts with the balance shown by the company records and also works to a corrected balance, the balance that should be shown in the records after all transactions are recorded properly. This form is shown below, with the same facts as those given in the previous illustration.

Reconciliation of Bank and Book Balances to Corrected Balance:

Jersey Company
BANK RECONCILIATION

Memphis National Bank, November 30, 1981

Balance per bank statement, Nov. 30, 1981		$22,365.30
Add		
Receipts of Nov. 30 on hand, not in bank's balance		3,680.43
		26,045.73
Deduct		
Outstanding checks		
#7327	$ 150.47	
#7348	4,820.00	
#7349	30.64	5,001.11
Corrected balance, Nov. 30, 1981		$21,044.62
Balance per books, Nov. 30, 1981		$20,452.72
Add		
Interest on Sequoia bonds collected by bank on Nov. 30		
for the company, not recorded by the company		600.00
		21,052.72
Deduct		
Bank charge not recorded by the company		8.10
Corrected balance, Nov. 30, 1981		$21,044.62

Both forms of reconciliation account for and itemize any differences between the bank and book amounts, but the second form is preferable for the following reasons.

1. It reconciles to the corrected (true) cash balance. The corrected balance of $21,044.62 in the reconciliation above is the amount carried to the balance sheet.
2. All of the reconciling items that require adjusting journal entries for book purposes are grouped in the section devoted to the book balance.

3. The additions and subtractions appear more logical. It avoids adding back items that were properly deducted (note the difference in the handling of the bank charge).

Adjusting entries are required to record items properly recognized by the bank but not yet recorded per the books as illustrated below for the Jersey Company:

	Nov. 30		
Cash		600.00	
Interest Income			600.00
(To record semiannual interest on Sequoia bonds,			
collected by bank)			
	Nov. 30		
Office Expense—Bank Charges		8.10	
Cash			8.10
(To record bank charges for November)			

The corrected cash balance on November 30 is $21,044.62, or $20,452.72 per books increased by $600.00 and decreased by $8.10, as per the entries above. In the second method the correct cash balance is shown as the final figure in each of the two sections. The first method requires a simple calculation to arrive at the corrected cash figure. In general, the second method is favored by internal and industrial accountants, the first method by auditors.

Another widely used form of bank reconciliation is the **four-column reconciliation** ("proof of cash"), which is discussed and illustrated in Appendix F to this chapter.

SECTION II—TEMPORARY INVESTMENTS

Nature of Temporary Investments

Transactions involving investments are infrequent for some enterprises, but for others they occur during every fiscal period. Sound financial management requires not only that cash and other assets be available when needed in the business, but also that cash and near cash assets not immediately needed in the conduct of regular operations be employed advantageously. In many cases, transactions involving investments result in a considerable amount of income in addition to that derived from regular operations.

A distinction is made in accounting between temporary investments and long-term investments. Temporary investments ordinarily consist of **marketable debt securities** (government and corporate bonds) and **marketable equity securities** (preferred and common stock) acquired with cash not immediately needed in operations. The investments are held temporarily in place of cash and can be readily converted to cash when current financing needs make such conversion desirable. A temporary investment must be:

1. Readily marketable.
2. Intended to be converted into cash within one year or the operating cycle, whichever is longer.

Readily marketable means that the stock could be sold quite easily. For example, if the stock is closely held (not publicly traded), there may be no market or a limited market at best for the security and its classification as a long-term investment may be more appropriate. Intent to convert is an extremely difficult principle to apply in practice. Generally, intention to convert is substantiated when the invested cash is considered a contingency fund to be used whenever a need arises or when investment is made from cash temporarily idle because of the seasonality of the business.

Long-term investments, on the other hand, are purchased as a part of some long-range program or plan such as long-term appreciation in the price of the security, ownership for control purposes, or maintaining or increasing supplier or customer relationships. Long-term investments are discussed in Chapter 18.

Marketable Equity Securities

At one time, there was considerable diversity in practice relative to the carrying value of temporary investments. Some enterprises carried marketable securities at cost, some at market, some at lower of cost or market, and some applied more than one of those methods to different classes of securities. Accentuated by severe stock market fluctuations during 1974–1975, this problem of diversity in accounting practice was addressed by the FASB and partially resolved through the issuance of **Statement of Financial Accounting Standards No. 12,** "Accounting for Certain Marketable Securities." The "certain" marketable securities referred to in **Statement No. 12** are **marketable equity securities.**

An **equity security** is "any instrument representing ownership shares (e.g., common, preferred, and other capital stock) or the right to acquire (e.g., warrants, rights, and call options) or dispose of (e.g., put options) ownership shares in an enterprise at fixed or determinable prices."[2] Treasury stock, redeemable preferred stock, and convertible bonds are excluded. **Marketable** means readily tradeable equity securities; restricted stock or "thin market" stock does not qualify.[3]

Acquisition of Marketable Equity Securities

As with other assets, investments in marketable equity securities are recorded at cost when acquired. Cost includes the purchase price and incidental acquisition costs such as brokerage commissions and taxes. According to **Statement No. 12,** "cost refers to the original cost of a marketable equity security unless a new cost basis has been assigned based on recognition of an impairment that was deemed other than temporary or as the result of a transfer between current and noncurrent classifications." In such cases the new cost basis (i.e., after adjustment for impairment of value) shall be the cost.

---

[2]"Accounting for Certain Marketable Securities," *Statement of Financial Accounting Standards No. 12* (Stamford, Conn.: FASB, 1975), par. 7(a).

[3]Investments accounted for by the equity method (as discussed in Chapter 18) are excluded from the requirements of *Statement No. 12.*

Accounting for Changes in Market Value—Marketable Equity Securities

A single share or unit of a marketable equity security has a **market price,** which when multiplied by the number of shares or units of that specific security produces the aggregate market price referred to as the **market value.** The market price generally changes as transactions involving the security occur. The central issue for many years has been: To what extent should the financial statements reflect the changes in market value of marketable securities?

The FASB resolved this issue in relation to marketable equity securities by requiring in **Statement No. 12** that **the carrying amount of a marketable equity securities portfolio be reported at the lower of its aggregate cost or market value determined at the balance sheet date.**[4] (Lower of cost or market is not acceptable for tax purposes.) **Statement No. 12** also stated that the amount by which aggregate cost exceeds market value (the net unrealized loss) of the marketable equity securities portfolio should be accounted for as the "valuation allowance" and the unrealized loss reported in the determination of net income for the period. Further the FASB requires that realized gains and losses and changes in the valuation allowance for a marketable equity securities portfolio included in current assets should be used in the determination of net income of the period in which they occur. In subsequent periods, recoveries of market value are recognized to the extent that the market valuation does not exceed original cost. In substance, the FASB says "adjust to market at each reporting date, down and up, but not in excess of acquired cost." Thus, **unrealized losses and recoveries flow through the income statement.**[5]

The following discussion illustrates application of the lower of cost or market method to marketable equity securities classified as current assets.

Republic Service Corporation made the following purchases of marketable equity securities as temporary investments during the year 1978:

> February 23, 1978—Purchased 20,000 shares of Northwest Industries, Inc. common stock at a market price of $25.75 per share plus brokerage commissions[6] of $4,400 (total cost, $519,400).
>
> April 10, 1978—Purchased 10,000 shares of Campbell Soup Co. common stock at a market price of $31.50 per share plus brokerage commissions of $2,500 (total cost, $317,500).
>
> August 3, 1978—Purchased 5,000 shares of St. Regis Pulp Co. common stock at a market price of $28 per share plus brokerage commissions of $1,350 (total cost, $141,350).

---

[4]The carrying amount of marketable equity securities is the amount at which the portfolio of marketable equity securities is reported in the financial statements of an enterprise.

[5]Specialized industries (investment companies, brokers and dealers in securities, stock life insurance companies, and fire and casualty insurance companies) which carry marketable equity securities at cost do not have to follow lower of cost or market. *Statement No. 12* (like the SEC in *ASR No. 166*) specifically permits the insurance industry (and other specialized industries that have used market) to carry equity securities at market, with unrealized gains and losses being classified in the equity accounts.

If unclassified balance sheets (current assets and noncurrent assets not segregated) are prepared, all marketable equity securities are treated as noncurrent assets. As indicated earlier, the accounting treatment for noncurrent marketable equity securities is different and is discussed in Chapter 18.

[6]Brokerage commissions are incurred both when buying and selling securities; such commissions generally range between 1% and 3% of trade value on lots of 1,000 or less and $12.50 to $30.00 per hundred shares on lots between 1,000 and 100,000 shares. State transfer taxes (New York) and SEC fees are incurred only by the seller of securities.

Each of the purchases above is recorded at total acquisition cost (market price plus commissions) by a debit to "Marketable Equity Securities."

During the year Republic made the following security sale:

> September 23, 1978—Sold 10,000 shares of Northwest Industries, Inc. common stock at a market price of $29 per share less brokerage commissions, taxes, and fees of $2,780 (proceeds, $287,220).

On December 31, 1978, Republic Service Corporation determined the carrying amount of its portfolio in marketable equity securities to be:

	December 31, 1978		
Marketable equity securities—current	Cost	Market	Unrealized Gain (Loss)
Northwest Industries, Inc.	$259,700	$275,000	$ 15,300
Campbell Soup Co.	317,500	304,000	(13,500)
St. Regis Pulp Co.	141,350	104,000	(37,350)
Total of portfolio	$718,550	$683,000	$(35,550)
Balance—valuation allowance			$(35,550)

Applying the lower of cost or market method to Republic's securities portfolio results in a carrying value of $683,000. The net unrealized loss of $35,550 represents the aggregate excess of cost over the market value of Republic's portfolio of marketable equity securities classified as current assets. The unrealized loss of $35,550 is recorded as follows:

December 31, 1978

Unrealized Loss on Valuation of Marketable Equity Securities	35,550	
Allowance for Excess of Cost of Marketable Equity Securities over Market Value		35,550
(To recognize a loss equal to the excess of cost over market value of marketable equity securities)		

The loss account appears on the income statement as an item of "Other Expense" included in income before extraordinary items in Republic's 1978 financial statements. The allowance account appears on the balance sheet among current assets as an asset valuation deducted from the portfolio cost of $718,550 to produce a carrying amount of its portfolio of $683,000.

During 1979, Republic made the following sale and purchase of marketable equity securities:

> March 22, 1979—Sold 5,000 shares of St. Regis Pulp Co. common stock at a market price of $17.50 per share less brokerage commissions, taxes, and fees of $1,590 (proceeds, $85,910).
>
> July 2, 1979—Purchased 10,000 shares of Pacific Gas & Electric common stock at a market price of $20.25 per share plus brokerage commissions of $2,300 (total cost, $204,800).

On December 31, 1979, Republic Service Corporation determined the carrying amount of its portfolio in marketable equity securities to be:

Marketable equity securities—current	December 31, 1979		
	Cost	Market	Unrealized Gain (Loss)
Northwest Industries, Inc.	$259,700	$312,500	$52,800
Campbell Soup Co.	317,500	327,500	10,000
Pacific Gas & Electric	204,800	202,500	(2,300)
Total of portfolio	$782,000	$842,500	$60,500
Balance—valuation allowance			$ -0-

Applying the lower of cost or market method to Republic's portfolio at December 31, 1979, results in a carrying amount of $782,000 and elimination of the balance in the valuation allowance account of $35,550. The adjustment of the valuation allowance is recorded as follows:

December 31, 1979

Allowance for Excess of Cost of Marketable Equity Securities over Market Value	35,550	
Recovery of Unrealized Loss on Valuation of Marketable Equity Securities		35,550

(To record a reduction in the valuation allowance due to the increase in market value of the marketable equity securities portfolio classified as current assets)

The Recovery of Unrealized Loss on Valuation of Marketable Equity Securities of $35,550 is reported as an item of "Other Income" included in income before extraordinary items on Republic's 1979 income statement.

Note that **the recovery is recognized only to the extent that unrealized losses were previously recognized.** That is, the write-down of $35,550 in 1978, representing net unrealized losses, may be reversed but only to the extent that the resulting carrying amount of the portfolio does not exceed original cost or, in other words, to the extent that a balance exists in the valuation allowance account at the date of write-up. Also, note that **the valuation is applied to the total portfolio and not to individual securities.**

The FASB does not regard the reversal of the write-down as representing recognition of an unrealized gain. The unrealized gain is the excess of market value over cost, or the $60,500 net difference between aggregate cost and aggregate market value of Republic's portfolio on December 31, 1979. The FASB views the write-down as establishing a valuation allowance representing the estimated reduction in the realizable value of the portfolio, and it views the subsequent market increase as having reduced or eliminated the requirements for such an allowance. In the Board's view, the reversal of the write-down represents a change in an accounting estimate of an unrealized loss.[7]

If Republic's temporary investments in marketable equity securities had suffered an additional loss of market value during 1979 instead of the increase described above, a loss would have been charged against 1979 income and the valuation allowance would have been increased (credited) by the amount of the additional write-down.

[7]*FASB Statement No. 12*, par. 29(c).

If a marketable equity security is **transferred from the current to the noncurrent portfolio,** or vice versa, the security must be transferred at the lower of its cost or market value at the date of transfer. If market value is less than cost, the market value becomes the new cost basis, and the difference is accounted for as if it were a realized loss and included in the determination of net income.[8] This procedure has the effect of accounting for an unrealized loss at the date of transfer in the same manner as if it had been realized, thus reducing the incentive to manipulate income by transferring securities between the current and noncurrent portfolios.

Disposition of Marketable Equity Securities

Marketable securities are sold when cash needs develop or when good investment management dictates a change in the securities held. The owner who sells the securities incurs costs of brokerage commissions, state transfer taxes, and SEC fees, receiving only the net proceeds for the sale. The difference between the net proceeds from the sale of a marketable equity security and its cost represents the **realized gain or loss.** At the date of sale no regard is given to unrealized losses or recoveries or the amount accumulated in the valuation allowance account because the valuation allowance relates to the total portfolio and not to specific security holdings.

For example, in the previous illustration Republic Service Corporation sold 10,000 shares of Northwest Industries, Inc. common stock on September 23, 1978 for $29 per share, incurring $2,780 in brokerage commissions, taxes, and fees. The gain on the sale is computed as follows:

Gross selling price of 10,000 shares @ $29	$290,000
Less commissions, taxes, and fees	2,780
Net proceeds from sale	287,220
Cost of 10,000 shares ($519,400 ÷ 2)	259,700
Gain on sale	$ 27,520

The sale is recorded as follows:

September 23, 1978

Cash	287,220	
Marketable Equity Securities		259,700
Realized Gain on Sale of Marketable Equity Securities		27,520
(To record sale of 10,000 shares of Northwest Industries common stock held as a temporary investment at a gain)		

Republic Service Corporation also sold 5,000 shares of St. Regis Pulp Co. on March 22, 1979, for $17.50 per share, incurring $1,590 in brokerage commissions, taxes, and fees. The loss on the sale is computed as follows:

[8]*Ibid.,* par. 10.

Cost of 5,000 shares		$141,350
Gross proceeds from sale	$87,500	
Less commissions, taxes, and fees	1,590	
Net proceeds from sale		85,910
Loss on sale		$ 55,440

As in the 1978 security sale, the amount of net proceeds from the 1979 sale of securities is compared with the original cost to determine the gain or loss and recorded as follows:

March 22, 1979		
Cash	85,910	
Realized Loss on Sale of Marketable Equity Securities	55,440	
Marketable Equity Securities		141,350

(To record the sale of 5,000 shares of
St. Regis Pulp Co. common stock held as a
temporary investment)

The presence or absence of realized gains or losses recorded since the last portfolio valuation as a result of sales of marketable equity securities has no effect upon the method of computing the lower of cost or market for the remaining portfolio at the end of the period.

Valuation at Market

The accounting profession's requirement of the use of the lower of cost or market and discontinuance of original cost as the carrying amount of a current asset portfolio of marketable equity securities was long awaited. Using original cost as the basis when the market value of the portfolio is lower has the effect of deferring unrealized losses on the basis of the expectation of a future recovery in market value, which may or may not occur.

However, many accountants are unhappy with **FASB Statement No. 12.** They argue that market value, whether higher or lower than cost, should be recognized in the accounts. It is considered inconsistent to reduce the carrying amount of the securities to an amount below cost without increasing their carrying amount when market value is above cost. **Market value proponents indicate that gains or losses develop when the value of the investments change and not when the investments are sold.** Recognition of losses only is too conservative and does not reflect the underlying economics when prices increase. Because of this situation, management can to some extent manipulate net income by determining when securities are sold to realize gains. For example, an enterprise whose earnings are low in one year might sell some securities that have appreciated in past years to offset the low income figure from current operations.

A major objection to the use of market value is that fluctuations in earnings result as the market price of the equity securities changes. Companies that have substantial amounts invested in short-term securities such as American Express, Sperry & Huchinson, or Leaseway Transportation would have experienced substantial changes in earnings if a market value approach were employed. To illustrate, Leaseway Transportation estimated that in 1974's bear market, the use of market value would have reduced earnings 28%, but that the use of market value in 1975 would have increased earnings approximately 21%. Most companies dislike these types of fluctuations in earnings because they have little control over these changes.

Recognition of impairment as opposed to improvement in the carrying amount of a securities portfolio is still the more dominant attitude of accounting. As a result, it is not surprising that the FASB adopted a compromise position (lower of cost or market). The FASB provided the following rationale for not using market value alone as the determinant of carrying value: "Consideration of that alternative would raise pervasive issues concerning the valuation of other types of assets, including the concept of historic cost versus current or realizable value."[9]

Accounting for Marketable Debt (Nonequity) Securities

Because the FASB in **Statement No. 12** addressed itself only to "marketable equity securities," temporary investments in **marketable debt (nonequity) securities** (securities not qualifying under its definition of marketable equity securities) have continued to be accounted for at cost. **Accounting Research Bulletin No. 43** prescribed cost as the carrying basis for marketable securities except that "where market value is less than cost by a substantial amount and it is evident that the decline in market value is not due to a mere temporary condition, the amount to be included as a current asset should not exceed the market value."[10] Under the cost basis if a permanent decline in the market value of debt securities occurs, the write-down from cost to market is charged to income in the period of recognition but there is no later recognition for subsequent market value increases (no valuation allowance account is utilized).

During the past decade, however, some companies have adopted the **lower of cost or market** method for debt securities that are readily marketable and are classified as current assets. Since the issuance of **Statement No. 12,** this practice has become more acceptable. Marketable debt securities, such as bonds, may be carried at lower of cost or market, and any unrealized loss may be charged to income and a valuation allowance used to carry the credit. The unrealized loss can be recovered and credited to income in the same manner as that accorded the marketable equity securities. Marketable debt securities, therefore, are carried either at cost or at the lower of cost or market bases.

The acquisition of debt securities is recorded at cost. If the debt securities are bonds purchased between interest dates, the accrued interest at the date of purchase is segregated from the acquisition cost and classified appropriately. For example, Western Publishing Company invested some of its excess cash in the bond market. Western purchased at 86 on April 1, 1979, 100 bonds (par value $1,000 and stated interest rate 8%) of Burlington-Northern, Inc., interest payable semiannually on July 1 and January 1. The brokerage commissions associated with this purchase were $1,720. The cash outlay is:

---

[9]*FASB Statement No. 12,* par. 29(a).

[10]Committee on Accounting Procedure, "Restatement and Revision of Accounting Research Bulletins," *ARB No. 43* (New York: AICPA, 1953), Ch. 3A, par. 9; originally adopted as *ARB No. 30* in 1947.

Purchase price of bonds	$86,000
Commission	1,720
Cost of bonds acquired	87,720
Accrued interest (January 1 to April 1)*	2,000
Cash payment	$89,720

*($100,000 × 8% × 3/12)

The journal entry to record this transaction is:

April 1, 1979

Temporary Investment in Bonds	87,720	
Interest Income (or Accrued Interest Receivable)	2,000	
Cash		89,720

Generally, the discount or premium on temporary investments is not recorded in the accounts and not amortized because the investment is ordinarily held for only a short time.

The journal entry to record the receipt of interest as of July 1 is as follows, assuming that interest income was originally debited at the time of purchase:

July 1, 1979

Cash	4,000	
Interest Income		4,000

When marketable debt securities are sold, the difference between the cost (or carrying amount if a permanent type write-down has occurred) and the selling price is recorded as a gain or loss. For example, if Western Publishing Company on November 1, 1979, sold at 98 plus accrued interest the Burlington-Northern, Inc. bonds (purchased above on April 1, 1979), the entry to record the sale would be as follows (assume that commission and taxes associated with the sale are $1,870):

November 6, 1979

Cash*	98,797	
Interest Income**		2,667
Temporary Investment in Bonds		87,720
Gain on Sale of Temporary Investment		8,410

*[(100 × $980) + $2,667 − $1,870]
**($100,000 × 8% × 4/12)

The gain on sale enters into the determination of income before extraordinary items. In cases where there are numerous purchases of similar securities, some flow assumption must be applied to match the proper cost with the proceeds of sale. For financial reporting purposes, specific identification, FIFO, or average cost may be employed. The Internal Revenue Service will accept only specific identification or FIFO for tax purposes.[11]

---

[11]LIFO can be duplicated, however, simply by selling the most recent certificates first and following specific identification.

Presentation in the Financial Statements

Cash, the most liquid asset, is listed first in the current asset section of the balance sheet. All unrestricted cash whether on hand (including petty cash) or on deposit at a financial institution is presented as a single item using the caption "Cash."

Marketable equity securities usually rank next to cash in liquidity and should be listed in the current asset section of the balance sheet (assuming that they are held as temporary investments) immediately after cash. Marketable equity securities that are held for other than liquidity and temporary investment purposes should not be classified as current assets.

As of the date of **each balance sheet** presented, the aggregate cost and the aggregate market value of marketable equity securities must be disclosed either in the body of the financial statements or in the accompanying footnotes. When classified balance sheets are presented, the aggregate cost and the aggregate market value should be disclosed, segregated between current and noncurrent assets.

In addition, for the **latest balance sheet,** disclosures are required of (1) gross unrealized gains and (2) gross unrealized losses. For **each** period for which an **income statement** is presented, disclosures relating to marketable equity securities are required of (1) the net realized gain or loss included in net income, (2) the basis on which cost was determined in computing realized gain or loss, and (3) the change in the valuation allowance included in net income.

Further, **significant** net realized and net unrealized gains and losses arising **after** the date of the financial statements, but prior to their issuance, that are applicable to marketable equity securities in the portfolio at the date of the most recent balance sheet should be disclosed.

To illustrate, we will use the data from Republic Service Corporation's December 31, 1978 and December 31, 1979 portfolio valuations presented on pages 277 and 278, respectively. Republic's marketable equity securities might be presented in the financial statements and the footnotes thereto as shown on page 284.

Temporary investments that do not conform to the criteria of marketable equity securities should be listed after marketable equity securities among the current assets under a classification such as "Debt Securities" or "Other Temporary Investments." If these temporary investments are less liquid than other current asset items such as receivables and inventories, they should be listed as the last item in the current asset section.

United States Treasury Tax Notes or other government securities are purchased by some businesses to facilitate the accumulation of resources with which to pay income taxes and, at the same time, to earn some income on such resources. It is a general principle of accounting that the offsetting of assets and liabilities in the balance sheet is improper except where a right of offset exists. According to **APB Opinion No. 10,** most government securities should not be deducted from taxes payable on the balance sheet. The only exception to this general principle occurs when a purchase of securities (acceptable for the payment of taxes) is in substance an advance payment of taxes that will be payable in the relatively near future, so that the purchase is tantamount to the prepayment of taxes.[12]

---

[12]"Omnibus Opinion—1966," *Opinions of the Accounting Principles Board No. 10* (New York: AICPA, 1966), par. 7.

Unless the purchase of securities is, in fact, an advance payment of taxes, the securities should be shown as temporary investments among the current assets. There is no more justification for offsetting government securities and accrued taxes than there is for offsetting, say, cash and accrued wages.

BALANCE SHEET

	December 31	
	1979	1978
Current assets:		
Marketable equity securities, carried		
at cost in 1979 and at market in 1978	$782,000	$683,000
(Note 2)		

INCOME STATEMENT

	Year Ended December 31	
	1979	1978
Income from operations	$ XXX	$ XXX
Other income		
Realized gain on sale of marketable equity securities		27,520
Recovery of unrealized loss on valuation of		
marketable equity securities	35,550	
Other expense		
Realized loss on sale of marketable equity securities	(55,440)	
Unrealized loss on valuation of marketable equity securities		(35,550)
Income before extraordinary items	$ XXXXX	$ XXXXX

Note 2—*Marketable Equity Securities.* Marketable equity securities are carried at the lower of cost or market at the balance sheet date; that determination is made by aggregating all current marketable equity securities. Marketable equity securities included in current assets had a market value at December 31, 1979 of $842,500 and a cost at December 31, 1978 of $718,550.

At December 31, 1979, there were gross unrealized gains of $62,800 and gross unrealized losses of $2,300 pertaining to the current portfolio.

A net realized loss of $55,440 on the sale of marketable equity securities was included in the determination of net income for 1979. A net realized gain of $27,520 on the sale of marketable equity securities was included in the determination of net income in 1978. The cost of the securities sold was based on the first-in, first-out method in both years. A reduction of $35,550 in the valuation allowance for net unrealized losses was included in income during 1979. The valuation allowance was established in 1978 by a charge against income of $35,550.

SECTION III—RECEIVABLES

SHORT-TERM RECEIVABLES

Short-term receivables are defined as claims held against others for money, goods, or services collectible within a year or the operating cycle, whichever is longer. For financial statement purposes, receivables are generally classified into two categories: (1) trade receivables and (2) nontrade receivables. Trade receivables are amounts owed by customers for goods and services sold as part of the normal operations of the business. They are usually the most significant receivables an enterprise possesses and are commonly called "accounts receivable." Trade receivables are oral as opposed to written commitments by others and are normally collectible within 30 to 60 days. They are represented by "open accounts" resulting from short-term extensions of credit.

Nontrade or special receivables arise from a variety of transactions and are oral or written promises to pay or deliver. Here are some examples of nontrade receivables:

1. Advances to officers and employees.
2. Advances to subsidiaries.
3. Deposits to cover potential damages or losses.
4. Deposits as a guarantee of performance or payment.
5. Dividends and interest receivable.
6. Stock subscriptions receivable.
7. Claims against:
   (a) Insurance companies for casualties sustained.
   (b) Defendants under suit.
   (c) Governmental bodies for tax refunds.
   (d) Common carriers for damaged or lost goods.
   (e) Creditors for returned, damaged, or lost goods.
   (f) Customers for returnable items (crates, containers, etc.).

The basic problems in accounting for receivables relate to (1) their valuation and (2) their classification in the balance sheet.

Valuation Problems

Once the receivable transactions and their dates of occurrence have been identified, the appropriate amount to record must be determined. The accountant must consider (1) the face value of the receivable, (2) the probability of future collection, and (3) the length of time the receivable will be outstanding.

Determination of Face Value

Trade Discount Customers are often quoted prices on the basis of list or catalog prices that may be subject to a trade or quantity discount. Trade discounts are used to avoid frequent changes in catalogs, or to quote different prices for different quantities purchased, or to hide the true invoice price from competitors. They are commonly quoted in percentages. For example, if your textbook has a list price of $18.00 and the publisher sells it to college book stores for list less a 30% trade discount, the receivable recorded by the publisher is $12.60 per textbook. The normal practice is simply to deduct the trade discount from the list price and bill the customer net. Only when a time payment takes on the characteristics of a cash discount is the receivable recorded at gross.

Cash Discounts (Sales Discounts)   Cash discounts (sales discounts) are offered as an inducement for prompt payment and communicated in terms that read 2/10, n/30 (two percent if paid within 10 days, gross amount due in 30 days), or 2/10, E.O.M. (end of month). Companies that fail to take sales discounts are usually not employing their money advantageously. An enterprise that receives a 1% reduction in the sales price for payment within 10 days, total payment due within 30 days, is effectively earning 18.2%, (.01 ÷ 20/365), or at least avoiding that rate of interest cost. For this reason, it is usual for companies to take the discount unless their cash is severely limited.

The easiest and most commonly used method of recording sales and related sales discount transactions is to enter the receivable and sale at the gross amount. Under this method, sales discounts are recognized in the accounts only when payment is received within the discount period. Sales discounts would then be shown in the income statement as a deduction from sales to arrive at net sales.

Some accountants contend that sales discounts are not actually discounts but penalties added to an established price to encourage prompt payment. That is, the seller offers sales on account at a slightly higher price than if selling for cash, and the increase is offset by the cash discount offered. Thus, customers who pay within the discount period purchase at the cash price; those who pay after expiration of the discount period are penalized because they must pay an amount in excess of the cash price.

If this approach is adopted, sales and receivables are recorded net, and any discounts not taken are subsequently debited to Accounts Receivable and credited to Sales Discounts Forfeited. To illustrate the difference between the gross and net methods, assume the following transactions.

ENTRIES UNDER GROSS AND NET METHODS

Gross Method			Net Method		
Sale of $10,000, terms 2/10, n/30:					
Accounts Receivable	10,000		Accounts Receivable	9,800	
Sales		10,000	Sales		9,800
Payment of $4,000 received within discount period:					
Cash	3,920		Cash	3,920	
Sales Discount	80		Accounts Receivable		3,920
Accounts Receivable		4,000			
Payment of $6,000 received after discount period:					
Cash	6,000		Accounts Receivable	120	
Accounts Receivable		6,000	Sales Discounts		
			Forfeited		120
			Cash	6,000	
			Accounts Receivable		6,000

As noted earlier, if the gross method is employed, sales discounts should be reported as a deduction from sales in the income statement. If the net method is used, sales discounted forfeited should be considered as an other income item. Theoretically, the recognition of Sales Discounts Forfeited is correct because the receivable is stated at its realizable value and the net sale figure measures the revenue earned from the sale. As a practical matter, the net method is seldom used because it requires additional analysis and bookkeeping. For example, adjusting entries are required under the net method to record sales discounts forfeited on accounts receivable that have passed the discount period.

Special Allowance Accounts

To properly match expenses against sales revenues, it is sometimes necessary to establish allowance accounts. These allowance accounts are reported as contra accounts to accounts receivable and establish the receivables at net realizable value. The most common allowances are:

1. Allowance for sales returns and allowances.
2. Allowance for freight.
3. Allowance for collection expenses.

Sales Returns and Allowances   Many accountants question the soundness of re-cording returns and allowances in the current period when they are derived from sales made in the preceding period. Normally, however, the amount of mismatched returns and allowances is not material, if such items are handled consistently from year to year. Yet, if a company completes a few special orders involving large amounts near the end of the accounting period, returns and allowances should be anticipated in the period of the sale to avoid distorting the income statement of the current period.

As an example, Astro Turf Corporation recognizes that approximately 5% of its $1,000,000 trade receivables outstanding are returned or some adjustment made to the sale price. Omission of a $50,000 charge could have a material effect on net income for the period.

The entry to reflect this anticipated sales return and allowance is:

Sales Returns and Allowances	50,000	
Allowance for Sales Returns and Allowances		50,000

Sales returns and allowances are reported as an offset to sales revenue in the income statement. Returns and allowances are accumulated separately instead of debited directly to the sales account simply to let the business manager and the statement reader know the magnitude of the returns and allowances. The allowance is an asset valuation account and is deducted from total accounts receivable; the receivable is thereby stated at its realizable value.

In most cases, the inclusion in the income statement of all returns and allowances made during the period, whether or not they resulted from the preceding period's sales, is an acceptable accounting procedure justified on the basis of practicality and immateriality.[13]

Freight   A seller may ship goods f.o.b. destination with the understanding that the purchaser will pay for the freight charges and deduct that amount from the remittance. In such cases, the seller may record the receivable gross with a correspond-

[13]An interesting sidelight to the entire problem of returns and allowances has developed in recent years. Determination of when a sale **is** a sale has become difficult, because in certain circumstances the seller is exposed to such a high risk of ownership through possible return of the property that the entire transaction is nullified and the sale not recognized. Such situations have developed particularly in sales to related parties. This subject is discussed in more detail in Chapters 8 and 19.

ing freight allowance to offset the accounts receivable. This allowance is deducted from accounts receivable with the debit either offsetting sales or being set up as a freight charge (selling expense), the latter treatment being correct.

Collection Expense   A similar concept holds true for collection expense. If a significant handling and service charge is incurred to collect the open accounts receivables at the end of the year, an allowance for collection expenses should be recorded. For example, Sears, Roebuck and Company reports its receivables net, with an attached schedule indicating the types of receivables outstanding. Sears' contra account is entitled "Allowance for Collection Expense and Losses on Customer Accounts" as shown below.

Sears, Roebuck and Company	
Receivables	
Customer installment accounts receivable	
Easy payment accounts	$2,221,017,167
Revolving charge accounts	1,372,874,725
	3,593,891,892
Other customer accounts	101,904,882
Miscellaneous accounts and notes receivable	96,446,334
	3,792,243,108
Less allowance for collection expenses and losses on	
customer accounts	236,826,866
	$3,555,416,242

Probability of Uncollectible Accounts Receivable

As one accountant so aptly noted: "The credit manager's idea of heaven probably would envisage a situation in which everybody (eventually) paid his debts."[14] Sales on any basis other than for cash make subsequent failure to collect the account a real possibility. An uncollectible accounts receivable is a loss of revenue that requires, through proper entry in the accounts, a decrease in the asset accounts receivable and a related decrease in stockholders' equity.

The chief problem in recording uncollectible accounts receivable is establishing the time at which to record the loss. Two general procedures are in use.

1. No entry is made until a specific account has definitely been established as uncollectible. Then the loss is recorded by crediting Accounts Receivable and debiting Bad Debt Expense. This is normally referred to as the "direct write-off" method for receivables.

2. An estimate is made of the expected uncollectible accounts from all sales made on account or from the total of outstanding receivables. This estimate is entered as an expense and a reduction in accounts receivable in the period in which the sale is recorded. This is usually called the "allowance" method.

The direct write-off method records the bad debt in the year it is determined that a specific receivable cannot be collected; the allowance method enters the expense

---

[14]William J. Vatter, *Managerial Accounting* (Englewood Cliffs, N.J.: Prentice-Hall, 1950), p. 60.

on an estimated basis in the accounting period that the sales on account are made. Either method is acceptable for tax purposes as long as it is consistently applied.

Supporters of the **direct write-off method** contend that facts, not estimates, are recorded. It assumes that a good account receivable resulted from each sale, and that later events proved certain accounts to be uncollectible and worthless. From a practical standpoint this method is simple and convenient to apply, although we must recognize that receivables do not generally become worthless at an identifiable moment of time. The direct write-off method is theoretically deficient because it usually does not match costs with revenues of the period, nor does it result in receivables being stated at estimated realizable value on the balance sheet. As a result, its use is not considered appropriate, except when the amount uncollectible is immaterial.

Advocates of the **allowance method** believe that bad debt expense should be recorded in the same period as the sale to obtain a proper matching of expenses and revenues and to achieve a proper carrying value for accounts receivable at the end of a period. They support the position that although estimates are involved, the percentage of receivables that will not be collected can be predicted from past experiences, present market conditions, and an analysis of the outstanding balances.

Because the collectibility of receivables is considered a loss contingency, the allowance method is appropriate only in situations where it is probable that an asset has been impaired and that the amount of the loss can be reasonably estimated.[15] Accountants, for the most part, have accepted the challenge of estimating the proportion of uncollectible accounts. A receivable is a prospective cash inflow, and the probability of its collection must be considered in valuing this inflow. These estimates normally are made either (1) on the basis of percentage of sales or (2) on the basis of outstanding receivables.

Percentage of Sales   When the percentage-of-sales approach is employed, a company's past experience with uncollectible accounts is analyzed. If there is a fairly stable relationship between previous years' charge sales and bad debts, that relationship can be turned into a percentage and used to determine this year's bad debt expense.

The percentage-of-sales method matches costs with revenues because it relates the charge to the period in which the sale is recorded. To illustrate, assume that Kenn's, Inc. estimates from past experience that about 2% of charge sales become uncollectible. If Kenn's, Inc. had charge sales of $400,000 in 1980, the entry to record bad debt expense using the percentage of sales method is as follows:

Bad Debt Expense	8,000	
Allowance for Doubtful Accounts		8,000

The Allowance for Doubtful Accounts is a valuation account and is subtracted from the trade receivables on the balance sheet. The amount of bad debt expense and the related credit to the allowance account is unaffected by any balance currently existing in the allowance account. Because the bad debt expense is related

---

[15]"Accounting for Contingencies," *Statement of the Financial Accounting Standards No. 5* (Stamford, Conn.: FASB, 1975), par. 8.

to a nominal account (Sales), any balance in the allowance is ignored. A proper matching of cost and revenues is therefore achieved.

Percentage of Outstanding Receivables   Using past experience, a company can estimate the percentage of its outstanding receivables that will become uncollectible, without identifying specific accounts. This procedure provides a reasonably accurate estimate of the realizable value of the receivable at any time, but does not fit the concept of matching cost and revenues. Rather, its objective is to report receivables in the balance sheet at net realizable values and it accomplishes that objective reasonably well.

Generally, the percentage of receivables is applied using one **composite rate** that reflects an estimate of the uncollectible receivables. An approach that is more sensitive to the actual status of the accounts receivable is achieved by setting up an **aging schedule.** This schedule indicates which accounts require special attention by providing the age of such accounts receivable. The following schedule of Wilson & Co. is an example.

	Balance Dec. 31	Under 60 days	61–90 days	91–120 days	Over 120 days
Wilson & Co. AGING SCHEDULE					
Name of Customer					
Western Stainless Steel Corp.	$ 98,000	$ 80,000	$18,000	$	$
Brockway Steel Company	320,000	320,000			
Freeport Sheet & Tube Co.	55,000				55,000
Allegheny Iron Works	74,000	60,000		14,000	
	$547,000	$460,000	$18,000	$14,000	$55,000

Summary			
Age	Amount	Percentage	Write-off
Under 60 days old	$460,000	1%	$ 4,600
61–90 days old	18,000	5%	900
91–120 days old	14,000	10%	1,400
Over 120 days	55,000	20%	11,000
Year-end balance of allowance for doubtful accounts			$17,900

The amount $17,900 would be the bad debt expense to be reported for this year, assuming that no balance existed in the allowance account. To change the illustration slightly, assume that the allowance account had a credit balance of $8,000 before adjustment. In this case, the amount to be added to the allowance account is $9,900 ($17,900 − $8,000), and the following entry is made.

Bad Debt Expense	9,900	
Allowance for Doubtful Accounts		9,900

The balance in the Allowance account is therefore correctly stated at $17,900. If the Allowance balance before adjustment had a debit balance of $2,000, then the amount to be recorded for bad debt expense would be $19,900 ($17,900 desired balance + $2,000 negative balance). In the percentage of outstanding receivables method, the balance in the allowance account cannot be ignored because the percentage is related to a real account (accounts receivable).

An aging schedule is usually not prepared to determine the bad debt expense but as a control device to determine the composition of receivables and to identify delinquent accounts. The estimated loss percentage developed for each category is based on previous loss experience and the advice of credit department personnel. Regardless of whether a composite rate or an aging schedule is employed, the primary objective of the percentage of outstanding receivables method for financial statement purposes is to report receivables in the balance sheet at net realizable value. However, it is deficient in that it may not match the bad debt expense to the period in which the sale takes place.

As indicated above, the allowance for doubtful accounts as a percentage of receivables will vary, depending upon the industry and the economic climate. To illustrate, companies such as Eastman Kodak, General Electric, and Monsanto, record allowances of $3 to $6 per $100 of accounts receivable. Others such as CPC International ($1.48), Texaco ($1.23), and U.S. Steel ($.78) are examples of large enterprises that have had debt allowances of less than $1.50 per $100.

In summary, the percentage-of-sales method results in a direct entry to an expense account and the allowance account because the amount calculated is related to the year's sales and not the balance remaining in accounts receivable. Generally, the percentage-of-sales approach provides the best results. If no consistent pattern of uncollectibles to sales is established, other approaches might be desirable. The account description employed for the allowance account is usually "Allowance for Doubtful Accounts" or simply "Allowance."[16]

Collection of Accounts Receivable Written Off

If a collection is made on a receivable that was written off, one procedure is first to reestablish the receivable by debiting Accounts Receivable and crediting Allowance for Doubtful Accounts. An entry is then made to debit Cash and credit the customer's account in the amount of the remittance received.

If the direct write-off approach is employed, the amount collected is debited to Cash and credited to an income account entitled Uncollectible Amounts Recovered, with proper notation in the customer's account.

Timing of Payment

Receivables should be valued in terms of the discounted value of the cash to be received in the future. When expected cash receipts require a waiting period, the receivable currently is not worth the amount that is ultimately received. To illustrate, assume that a company makes a sale on account for $1,000 with payment due in 120 days. Also assume that the applicable rate of interest in this case is 12%

---

[16]*Accounting Trends and Techniques (1978)*, for example, indicates that approximately 73% of the companies surveyed used allowance in their description.

and that payment is made at the end of the 120th day. The present value of that receivable is not $1,000 but $961.54 ($1,000 × present value factor of .96154). In other words, $1,000 to be received 120 days from now is not the same as $1,000 received today.

Any revenue after the period of sale is interest income (actual or implicit). Accountants have chosen to ignore this for the most part in connection with accounts receivable, because the amount of the discount is not usually material in relation to the net income for the period. As recommended by **Opinion No. 6,** however, unearned discounts, finance charges, and interest included in the face amount of a receivable are shown as deductions from the related receivables, whenever they are material.[17] The APB in **Opinion No. 21,** however, specifically excludes from the present value considerations "receivables arising from transactions with customers in the normal course of business which are due in customary trade terms not exceeding approximately one year."[18]

Installment Sales

Unearned interest plays a large role in valuing installment sales and receivables and long-term receivable transactions. The peculiar feature of installment sales is the extended period over which payment of the sales price occurs. Consequently, the receivable recorded is on the books usually from 6 to 36 months.

ARB No. 43 recommends that installment accounts receivable be classified as current assets if they conform to normal trade operations. Even if a receivable is not due for two years, classification as a current asset is appropriate if two years or more is the length of the normal operating cycle. A desirable practice is to indicate the maturity of the receivables.

Normally, installment receivables are stated at their face value less any unrealized income to be received from finance charges or interest income. This example from Oxford Company shows how installment receivables are presented.

Oxford Company	
Current assets	
Installment receivables, including amounts due after one year of $1,682,590	$3,097,061
Less	
Unearned finance charges applicable to installment accounts	(758,266)
	$2,338,795

Other methods of disclosure such as footnotes and parenthetical treatment may be used. "Discounts on Installments Receivable" is another title for unearned finance charges. Chapters 8 and 19 provide further illustration of the unique accounting problems associated with installment sales.

---

[17]"Status of Accounting Research Bulletins," *Opinions of the Accounting Principles Board No. 6* (New York: AICPA, 1965), par. 14.

[18]"Interest on Receivables and Payables," *Opinions of the Accounting Principles Board No. 21* (New York: AICPA, 1971), par. 3(a).

ACCOUNTS RECEIVABLE AND CASH GENERATION

The employment of accounts receivable as an immediate source of cash is a common practice of many small and medium-sized manufacturers and occasionally of retailers. The company that generates cash in this manner either assigns, pledges, factors, or sells its accounts receivable.

Assignment of Accounts Receivable

In an assignment, one party (the assignor) transfers receivable rights under a contract to a third party (the assignee). For example, a company may assign its receivable rights to a bank or finance company to obtain a loan or advance. In most cases, the borrowing company retains physical control of the assigned accounts, collects amounts remitted by the customer, and then forwards the proceeds to the lending agency. Occasionally the accounts are turned over to the lending agency for collection and the assignor has no further contact with the customers concerned (except for additional sales) until the uncollected accounts are returned to the company.

Generally, receivables in excess of the amount borrowed are assigned to insure the assignee against loss. Furthermore, substitution of new accounts is usually guaranteed for receivables remaining unpaid after a certain date. In making a loan or advance of this type, the lending agency customarily charges interest on the unpaid balance of the loan plus a flat fee for accepting the assigned accounts. The flat fee is often deducted from the proceeds of the loan, and only the net proceeds are paid to the borrower.

Assigned accounts are listed separately on the balance sheet, accompanied by an indication of the equity that the assignor has in the assigned accounts.

To illustrate, Chentron Cartridge Company assigns $32,000 of its accounts receivable to a bank. The bank grants an 8% loan for 75% of the accounts receivable assigned and charges $600 for its service. Here are the entries by Chentron.

Cash	23,400	
Commission Expense	600	
Notes Payable		24,000
Accounts Receivable Assigned	32,000	
Accounts Receivable		32,000

The first entry illustrates the receipt of cash from the issuance of the note. The second entry is made to reclassify the accounts receivable assigned. If a balance sheet were prepared at this point, Chentron Cartridge would show:

Current Assets		
Accounts receivable assigned	$32,000	
Less notes payable	(24,000)	
Equity in assigned accounts		$8,000

Note that the Notes Payable is offset against the Accounts Receivable Assigned. This presentation is an exception to the general rule that assets and liabilities should not be netted. Netting is justified in this case because the proceeds from the collection of these receivables are contractually committed to liquidate the note payable.

Pledging of Accounts Receivable

In a pledge, one party (the pledgor) uses accounts receivable accounts as security for a loan from the pledgee. The pledgee has the implied power to sell the security (accounts receivable) if the debt is not paid. When receivables are pledged, the loan is recorded, and information concerning the pledge is disclosed in a footnote or in a parenthetical explanation.

To illustrate, United Air Industries presents its pledges in this manner.

United Air Industries, Inc.

Current Assets

Trade accounts, notes, and other receivables, less allowance of $95,000 in 1978 and $75,000 in 1977 for doubtful accounts (Note B)	$8,695,372

Note B. *Other Notes Payable.* Under the terms of the amended revolving credit agreement with a commercial finance company, the corporation may borrow up to 90% of eligible trade accounts receivable and 60% of certain inventories. The maximum that may be borrowed under this agreement is $7,000,000. The corporation's trade accounts, notes, and other receivables and inventories are pledged as collateral. The long-term portion of these notes, which becomes a current liability in 1982, is reflected in Note C.

Factoring or Sale of Accounts Receivable

Another means of obtaining cash is to sell accounts receivable to factors. Factors are usually finance companies or banks that buy receivables from businesses for a fee and then collect the remittances directly from the customer. Factoring, traditionally associated with the textiles, apparel, footwear, furniture, and home furnishings industries, has now spread to many other types of businesses. For example, recently Sears, Roebuck & Co. arranged to sell $550 million of customer accounts receivable at 99.015% of face value. The sale gives Sears, Roebuck the same advantage as other retailers have in utilizing third-party credit cards, such as Master Charge, BankAmericard, or VISA, which are factoring arrangements.

Factoring arrangements vary widely, but typically the factor charges a commission of from ¾ to 1½% of the net amount of receivables purchased (except for the credit card factoring which costs the retailer or restaurateur 4 to 5 percent). The following chart illustrates in sequential process the basic procedures in factoring.

No loan is created when receivables are sold to factors. No particular problems exist with accounting for such a transaction; the selling of the receivable is handled like any other transaction involving the sale of assets. When receivables are factored, Cash is debited for the proceeds from the sale, the Receivables are credited, and the difference is charged as Factoring Expense. If the factor holds back a portion (5 to 10%) of the agreed upon amounts as a margin of protection against sales returns and allowances, a special Receivable Factor account is set up. When

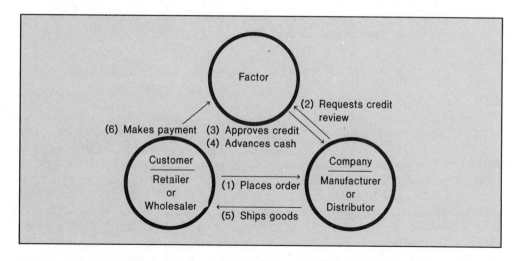

the probability of receiving this withheld amount is small, an allowance for doubt-ful accounts is established.

A special problem develops if receivables are sold on a **"with recourse"** basis. With recourse means that the purchaser of the receivables may demand payment (or replacement with other receivables) from the seller of such receivables if the debtor defaults. The basic issue is whether receivables sold on a with recourse basis should be considered a financing transaction in which the financing costs are amortized over the life of the receivable or a sale transaction in which a gain or loss should be recognized immediately. AcSEC takes the position that the sale of receivables with recourse is in substance a financing transaction and that the cost of financing should be accounted for as an interest cost over the life of the receiv-ables.[19] To illustrate, assume that Selto Enterprises sells receivables on a with re-course basis to Dana Inc. for $86,000, face value $90,000. The following entry might then be recorded

Cash	86,000	
Deferred Financing Expense	4,000	
Accounts Receivable		90,000

The deferred financing expense would then be amortized at a constant rate on the declining balance of the company's obligation to repay on these receivables. Dis-closure of a company's policy with respect to accounting for income or loss on the sale of receivables with recourse should be disclosed in accordance with **APB Opinion No. 22,** "Disclosure of Accounting Policies."

NOTES RECEIVABLE

Technically, a great distinction does not exist between trade accounts receivable and trade notes receivable. A note receivable involves a formal promissory note, whereas an accounts receivable is only an informal promise to pay. In addition, notes frequently carry a provision for interest on the face amount of debt. Except in

[19]"Recognition of Profit on Sales of Receivables with Recourse," *Statement of Position 74–6* (New York: AICPA, 1974).

some businesses that regularly accept notes from customers (installment sales usually require signed installment notes), most companies have relatively few trade notes receivable.

Notes Receivable Discounted

Notes receivable, unlike accounts receivable, are often discounted at the bank before their maturity date. Unless the note is endorsed without recourse, a rare procedure, the company discounting the note guarantees payment of the note to bank at maturity. **"Without recourse"** means that the endorser does not accept liability if the maker of the instrument cannot pay.

If the note is endorsed with recourse, the bank presents the note to the endorser, who is then liable for payment if the maker fails to pay at maturity. The endorser therefore is contingently liable. As most companies are careful to discount with their banks only notes that they are reasonably certain are good, this loss contingency (contingent liability) seldom develops into a real liability. Yet in the interest of full disclosure, any loss contingency of material amounts must be disclosed in the financial statements, and so it is essential that a record be made of the possibility.[20]

There are two satisfactory methods for disclosing a loss contingency for notes receivable. One method requires that when notes are discounted a credit be made to a Notes Receivable Discounted account instead of to Notes Receivable. Notes Receivable Discounted is offset against Notes Receivable on the balance sheet. The second approach requires no entry; disclosure of the contingency is made in a footnote or parenthetically.

To illustrate, assume that Sinclair Micro TV discounts a $500, 90-day, 10% interest-bearing note, 60 days before maturity, at a discount rate of 12% at Shorewood Hills Bank. Note that a discount rate is similar to an interest rate, except that the rate is applied to maturity value rather than the face value of the note. The cash proceeds upon discounting are computed as follows:

Face value of note	$500.00
Interest at 10% for 90 days	12.50
Maturity value	512.50
Discount on $512.50 for 60 days at 12%	10.25
Proceeds	$502.25

In this case note that Sinclair Micro TV is receiving interest income of $12.50 for this transaction, but is paying interest expense of $10.25 for a net effect of $2.25 on income.[21]

---

[20]"Accounting for Contingencies," *op. cit.*, par. 12.

[21]When accounts receivables are sold **with recourse** as indicated in the previous section, a deferred financing expense and a deferred interest income are often shown and amortized separately rather than netted. With short-term notes receivable, however, such a differentiation is not necessary for reasons of materiality.

The entries to record transactions related to this discounting are as follows:

ENTRIES UNDER RECORDING AND DISCLOSURE APPROACHES

Recording Discounted Notes			*Footnote Disclosure*		
The note is discounted at the bank:					
Cash	502.25		Cash	502.25	
Interest Income		2.25	Interest Income		2.25
Notes Rec. Disc.		500.00	Notes Rec.		500.00
If note is paid by maker at maturity date:					
Notes Rec. Disc.	500.00		No entry required		
Notes Rec.		500.00			

If the note is not paid by the maker at maturity date and is, therefore, paid by the endorser:

Notes Rec. Past Due	512.50		Notes Rec. Past Due	512.50	
Cash		512.50	Cash		512.50
Notes Rec. Disc.	500.00				
Notes Rec.		500.00			

Discounted notes that have passed the maturity date by a reasonable time without notice of dishonor from the final holder are considered honored and the loss contingency eliminated from the accounts.

Dishonored Notes

Notes receivable that are not paid at maturity (whether discounted or not) remain notes receivable and are considered notes receivable past due. Defaulted notes should be separately classified on the balance sheet. If all efforts to collect fail, the note is written off as a loss. Whether the loss is charged to the allowance for doubtful accounts or directly to a loss account depends on (1) whether the company has an account for doubtful accounts and (2) whether the periodic provisions cover losses only on accounts receivable or on both accounts and notes receivable.

Determining the Present Value of Notes Receivable

In a transaction involving the receipt of a note, the objective is to record the note at its present value. Establishing the present value permits the determination of the real or effective interest involved irrespective of the stated interest rate or the absence of any stipulated interest rate.

If the note (noninterest-bearing) is received solely for cash, it is presumed to have a present value measured by the cash proceeds received by the borrower. The difference between the face amount and the proceeds (present value) is recorded as a discount or premium. This discount or premium is amortized to interest income or interest expense over the life of the note.

When the note is exchanged for property, goods, or services in a bargained transaction entered into at arm's length, the stated interest rate is presumed to be fair unless:[22]

1. No interest rate is stated, or
2. The stated interest rate is unreasonable, or
3. The stated face amount of the note is materially different from the current cash sales price for the same or similar items or from the current market value of the debt instrument.

In these circumstances the present value of the note is measured by the fair value of the property, goods, or services or by an amount that reasonably approximates the market value of the note.[23]

Imputing an Interest Rate   If the fair value of the property, goods, or services is not determinable and if the note has no ready market, the problem of determining the present value of the note is more difficult. To estimate the present value of a note under such circumstances, an applicable interest rate is approximated that may differ from the stated interest rate. This process of interest-rate approximation is called **imputation,** and the resulting interest rate is called an **imputed interest rate.** The imputed interest rate is used to establish the present value of the note by discounting, at that rate, all future receipts (interest and principal) on the note.

   Opinion No. 21 provides the following general guidelines for imputing the appropriate interest rate:

> "The prevailing rates for similar instruments of issuers with similar credit ratings will normally help determine the appropriate interest rate for determining the present value of a specific note at its date of issuance. In any event, the rate used for valuation purposes will normally be at least equal to the rate at which the debtor can obtain financing of a similar nature from other sources at the date of the transaction. The objective is to approximate the rate which would have resulted if an independent borrower and an independent lender had negotiated a similar transaction under comparable terms and conditions with the option to pay the cash price upon purchase or to give a note for the amount of the purchase which bears the prevailing rate of interest to maturity."[24]

The choice of a rate may be affected specifically by the credit standing of the issuer, restrictive covenants, the collateral, payment, and other terms pertaining to the debt, and the existing prime interest rate. Determination of the imputed interest rate is made when the note is received; any subsequent changes in prevailing interest rates are ignored.

Illustration of Interest Imputation, Recording, and Amortization   On December 31, 1981, Willis, Heide, and Company rendered architectural services and accepted in exchange a promissory note with a face value of $550,000, a due date of December 31, 1986, and a stated interest rate of 2%, receivable at the end of each year. The fair value of the services is not readily determinable and the note is not readily marketable. When the credit rating of the maker of the note, the absence of collat-

---

[22]"Interest on Receivables and Payables," *Opinions of the Accounting Principles Board No. 21* (New York: AICPA, 1971), par. 12.

[23]*Ibid.*

[24]*Ibid.*, par. 13.

eral, the prime interest rate at that date, and the prevailing interest on the maker's outstanding debt are considered, an 8% interest rate is imputed as appropriate in this circumstance. The present value of the note is determined as follows.

Face value of the note		$550,000
Present value of $550,000 due in 5 years at 8%—$550,000 × .6806 (Table 6-2)	$374,330	
Present value of $11,000 ($550,000 × .02) payable annually for 5 years at 8%— $11,000 × 3.9927 (Table 6-4)	43,920	
Present value of the note		418,250
Discount		$131,750

The receipt of the note in exchange for the services is recorded as follows:

Dec. 31, 1981

Notes Receivable	550,000	
Unamortized Discount on Notes Receivable		131,750
Income from Services		418,250

The five-year amortization schedule appears below.

SCHEDULE OF NOTE DISCOUNT AMORTIZATION
EFFECTIVE INTEREST METHOD
2% NOTE DISCOUNTED AT 8% (IMPUTED)

Date	Cash Interest (2%)	Effective Interest (8%)	Discount Amortized	Unamortized Discount Balance	Present Value of Note
12/31/81				$131,750	$418,250
12/31/82	$11,000 (a)	$ 33,460 (b)	$ 22,460 (c)	109,290 (d)	440,710 (e)
12/31/83	11,000	35,257	24,257	85,033	464,967
12/31/84	11,000	37,197	26,197	58,836	491,164
12/31/85	11,000	39,293	28,293	30,543	519,457
12/31/86	11,000	41,543 (f)	30,543	-0-	550,000
	$55,000	$186,750	$131,750		

(a) $550,000 × 2% = $11,000
(b) $418,250 × 8% = $33,460
(c) $33,460 − $11,000 = $22,460
(d) $131,750 − $22,460 = $109,290
(e) $418,250 + $22,460 = $440,710
(f) $13 adjustment to compensate for rounding.

Receipt of the annual interest and amortization of the discount (unearned interest) is recorded as follows:

Dec. 31, 1982

Cash	11,000	
Unamortized Discount on Notes Receivable	22,460	
Interest Income		33,460

In the case of a **noninterest-bearing note** where a reasonable rate must be imputed, the periodic cash receipt for interest would be zero; therefore, the entry would be simply for the imputed interest—debit Unamortized Discount on Notes Receivable and credit Interest Income.

Financial Statement Presentation of Discount or Premium   Any discount or premium resulting from the determination of present value in such transactions is not an asset or a liability separable from the note that gives rise to it. Therefore, the discount or premium is reported in the balance sheet as a direct deduction from or addition to the face amount of the note. It is not classified as a deferred charge or deferred credit. The face amount of the note is disclosed in the balance sheet or in the footnotes, and the description of the note should include the effective interest rate. The balance sheet presentation of discounted notes may assume two different forms: (1) presentation of the discount in caption form and (2) presentation of the discount separately.[25] Using the data from the Willis, Heide, and Company illustration, we see how these two forms would appear, on December 31, 1982, one year after issuance of the note:

Presentation of the Discount in Caption Form		
	12/31/82	12/31/81
Note receivable from services rendered: $550,000 face amount, due December 31, 1986, bearing 2% stated interest (less unamortized discount based on imputed interest rate of 8%—1982, $109,290; 1981, $131,750)	$440,710	$418,250
Presentation of the Discount Separately		
	12/31/82	12/31/81
Note receivable from services rendered: Note due December 31, 1986, bearing stated interest of 2%	$550,000	$550,000
Less unamortized discount based on imputed interest rate of 8%	109,290	131,750
Note receivable less unamortized discount	$440,710	$418,250

If several notes are involved, the principal amount of such notes and the balance of total unamortized discount are presented in the balance sheet with the details of each note disclosed individually in a footnote or separate schedule to the balance sheet.

Amortization of discounts or premiums resulting from imputed interest are reported as interest in the statement of income.

Accounts and Notes Receivable: Balance Sheet Presentation

The general rules in classifying the typical transactions in the receivable section are: (1) segregate the different receivables that an enterprise possesses, if material;

[25]*Ibid.*, par. 16.

(2) insure that the valuation accounts are appropriately offset against the proper receivable accounts; (3) determine that receivables classified in the current asset section will be converted into cash within the year or the operating cycle, whichever is longer; (4) disclose any loss contingencies that exist on the receivables; and (5) disclose any receivables assigned or pledged as collateral.

The following asset sections of Colt Corporation illustrate many of these concepts.

Colt Corporation
As of December 31, 1981

Current Assets

Accounts receivable (Note 1)	$3,767,798		
Less allowance for doubtful accounts	(226,500)		
		$3,541,298	
Installment receivables (including 1,200,000 due after one year)	2,482,331		
Less unearned interest and service charges	(208,021)		
		2,274,310	
Advances to subsidiaries due 9/30/82		980,000	
Dividends receivable		57,000	
Notes receivable (contingently liable for notes discounted at the bank for $200,000)		253,000	
Other receivables and claims (includes debit balances in accounts payable)		120,000	
Total current assets—receivables			$7,225,608

Long-term Receivables

Notes receivable from officers and key employees for purchase of common stock of company			333,000
Claims receivable (refers to litigation settlement to be collected over four years)			125,000
Total receivables			$7,683,608

Note 1. In June 1981, the company arranged with a finance company to refinance a part of their indebtedness. The loans are evidenced by an 8¼ percent note payable. The notes are payable on demand and are secured by substantially all the accounts receivable.

As illustrated, many different types of receivables can arise and are classified in accordance with the definition of current and noncurrent receivables.

APPENDIX

Four-Column Bank Reconciliation

Reconciliation of Receipts and Disbursements

In addition to the forms presented in this chapter, another form of reconciliation, frequently used by auditors and typically illustrated in auditing textbooks, is the so-called **proof of cash** or "four-column bank reconciliation" as shown below.

	Balance October 31	Receipts	Disbursements	Balance Nov. 30
Jersey Company — PROOF OF CASH FOR NOVEMBER 1981 — Memphis National Bank		November		
Per bank statement	$17,520	$96,450	$91,605	$22,365
Deposits in transit				
at Oct. 31	4,200	(4,200)		
at Nov. 30		3,680		3,680
Outstanding checks				
at Oct. 31	(3,700)		(3,700)	
at Nov. 30			5,001	(5,001)
Other reconciling items				
Unrecorded bank charge			(8)	8
Unrecorded interest collected by bank		(600)		(600)
Per books	$18,020	$95,330	$92,898	$20,452

This form of reconciliation is actually four reconciliations in one:

1. Reconciliation of the **beginning** of the period bank balance to the beginning of the period book balance (first column).
2. Reconciliation of **receipts** per the bank statement to receipts per books (second column).
3. Reconciliation of **disbursements** per the bank statement to disbursements per books (third column).
4. Reconciliation of the **end** of the period bank balance to the end of the period book balance (fourth column).

The top line across the four-column reconciliation is a summary of the transactions for the period covered as taken from the bank statement or statements. The beginning and ending bank balances are shown on the bank statement as are the bank receipts (as shown in the "deposits" column) and the bank disbursements (as shown in the "charges" or "checks cashed" column).

The bottom line, "Per books," is a summary of the cash transactions as recorded in the books. These totals should be taken directly from the books, preferably from the Cash account itself, which should, of course, show receipts and disbursements as debit and credit entries and the beginning and ending cash balances.

The left-hand and right-hand columns are simply **end-of-the-prior-period** and **end-of-the-current-period** reconciliations, the preparation of which was illustrated on page 272. The two center columns, receipts and disbursements, tie the left-hand column and right-hand column reconciliations together. With few exceptions, the amounts needed to complete these center columns may be found in the figures included in either the top or bottom lines or in the left- and right-hand columns; no new data need be added. The exceptions consist of such items as a bank error corrected by the bank within the month in which it was made so that bank transactions but not balances are affected. A customer's check deposited, returned N.S.F., and redeposited without entry in the same period would have the same effect. Each of the reconciling items must be analyzed carefully to determine whether an addition or subtraction from the top of the column "Per bank" figure is the logical reconciliation treatment.

The four-column reconciliation is preferred by auditors as a means of identifying differences between the books and the bank statement during the period covered by the reconciliation.

As indicated earlier, an alternative procedure for preparing a bank reconciliation involves reconciling the bank and the book balances to the corrected balance. This same alternative can also be applied to the four-column reconciliation, as illustrated on page 304.

This alternative form of reconciliation is preferable because it (1) reconciles to the correct (true) cash balance, (2) groups all of the reconciling items that require adjusting journal entries in the section devoted to the book balance, and (3) results in a more logical handling of the reconciling items.

Jersey Company
PROOF OF CASH FOR NOVEMBER 1981
Memphis National Bank

	Balance October 31	November Receipts	November Disbursements	Balance Nov. 30
Per bank statement	$17,520	$96,450	$91,605	$22,365
Deposits in transit				
at October 31	4,200	(4,200)		
at November 30		3,680		3,680
Outstanding checks				
at October 31	(3,700)		(3,700)	
at November 30			5,001	(5,001)
Corrected balance	$18,020	$95,930	$92,906	$21,044
Per books	$18,020	$95,330	$92,898	$20,452
Unrecorded bank charge			8	(8)
Unrecorded interest collected by bank		600		600
Corrected balance	$18,020	$95,930	$92,906	$21,044

Note: All **asterisked** questions, cases, or problems relate to material contained in the appendix to each chapter.

Questions

1. What may be included under the heading of "cash"?
2. Define a "compensating balance." How should a compensating balance be reported?
3. In what accounts should the following items be classified?
   (a) Travel advances.
   (b) Cash (to be used for retirement of long-term bonds).
   (c) Three shares of IBM stock (intention is to sell in one year or less).
   (d) Savings and checking accounts.
   (e) Petty cash.
   (f) Cash in a bank that is in receivership.
   (g) Deposits in transit.
   (h) Coin and currency.
   (i) Certificate of deposit.
   (j) U.S. Treasury (Govt.) bonds.
   (k) Postdated checks.
   (l) NSF check (returned with bank statement).
   (m) Deposit in foreign bank (exchangeability limited).
   (n) Stamps.
4. Distinguish between the nature of temporary investments and long-term investments. Give two examples of each type of investment. Is it possible for securities of the same kind to be carried by one company as a temporary investment and to be carried by another company as a long-term investment? Explain.
5. Define "marketable equity securities" and explain how to account for them when they are a current asset.
6. What disclosure is required for current marketable equity securities in either the financial statements or the accompanying footnotes?
7. Why is market value proposed as a substitute for cost in valuing marketable securities?
8. In what way may the accounting treatment of marketable **debt** securities differ from that accorded marketable **equity** securities (both classified as current assets)?
9. The president of the Cajun Company realizes that the ratio of current assets to current liabilities can be rendered more impressive if the company offsets its temporary investments in treasury notes and other government securities against the large accrued

liability for taxes in the balance sheet. He claims that most or all of these notes and other government securities probably will be liquidated to pay the tax liability and, anyway, the investment and the liability are really an account with the same entity, the United States government, and deserve to be offset and netted. As the controller of Cajun Company, how would you advise the president?

10. What is the theoretical justification of the allowance method as contrasted with the direct write-off method of accounting for bad debts?

11. Indicate how well the percentage-of-sales method and the aging method accomplish the objectives of the allowance method of accounting for bad debts.

12. Of what merit is the contention that the allowance method lacks the objectivity of the direct write-off method? Discuss in terms of accounting's measurement function.

13. The Catamaran Shop shows a balance in Accounts Receivable on December 31, 1981 of $135,000. Of this amount $80,000 is assigned to the Security Finance Co. as security for a loan of $60,000. Illustrate three satisfactory methods for showing this information on the balance sheet for December 31, 1981.

14. The Peartree Company includes in its trial balance for December 31 an item for "Accounts Receivable, $477,000." This balance consists of the following items:

Due from regular customers	$301,000
Refund receivable on prior year's income taxes (an established claim)	10,000
Loans to officers	22,000
Loan to wholly owned subsidiary	45,500
Advances to creditors for goods ordered	61,000
Accounts receivable assigned as security for loans payable	31,500
Notes receivable past due plus interest on these notes	6,000
Total	$477,000

Illustrate how these items should be shown in the balance sheet as of December 31.

15. What is the difference between trade receivables and nontrade receivables? Give two examples of each type.

16. What are the basic problems that occur in the valuation of accounts receivable?

17. What are the reasons that a company gives trade discounts? Why are trade discounts not recorded in the accounts like cash discounts?

18. What are two methods of recording accounts receivable transactions when a cash discount situation is involved? Which is the most theoretically correct? Which is used in practice most of the time? Why?

19. Why is the account "Allowance for Sales Returns and Allowances" sometimes used? What other types of allowance accounts (similar to Allowance for Sales Returns and Allowances) are employed? What is their purpose?

20. What is the normal procedure for handling the collection of accounts receivable previously written off using the direct write-off method? The allowance method?

21. The Pacific Company sells a stove for $700 on the installment basis. Part of the terms of the sales agreement reads: "Payments of $70 per month shall be made for 11 months." Pacific therefore records the accounts receivable and sale at $770. Is this the proper procedure? Explain.

22. Because of calamitous earthquake losses the Dain Company, one of your client's oldest and largest customers, suddenly and unexpectedly became bankrupt. Approximately 25% of your client's total sales have been made to the Dain Company during each of the past several years. The amount due from Dain Company—none of which is collectible—equals 20% of total accounts receivable, an amount that is considerably in excess of what was determined to be an adequate provision for doubtful accounts at the close of the preceding year. How would your client record the write-off of the Dain Com-

pany receivable if it is using the allowance method of accounting for bad debts? Justify your suggested treatment.

23. Differentiate between assigning and factoring accounts receivable.

24. Give two methods of disclosing the loss contingency for notes receivable discounted.

25. What is "imputed interest"? In what situations is it necessary to impute an interest rate for notes receivable? What are the considerations in imputing an appropriate interest rate?

26. On January 1, 1981, Hancock, Inc. sells property for which it had paid $500 to Berger Company receiving in return Berger's noninterest-bearing note for $1,000 payable in five years. What entry would Hancock make to record the sale, assuming that Hancock frequently sells similar items of property for a cash sales price of $600?

Cases

C7-1 The president of Leather Luggage Co. is concerned about a proposed accounting change related to investments in marketable securities. The proposal is that all marketable securities be presented at market value on the balance sheet and the changes that occur in market value be reflected in income in the current period. The president agrees that market value on the balance sheet may be more useful to the investor, but he sees no reason why changes in market value should be reflected in income of the current year.

Teresa Chavez, controller of Leather Luggage Co., is also unhappy about the proposal and has recommended the following alternatives.

"Recognize realized gains and losses from changes in market value in income, and report unrealized gains and losses in a special balance sheet account on the equity side of the balance sheet."

"Report realized and unrealized gains and losses from market value changes in a statement separate from the income statement or as direct charges and credits to a stockholders' equity account."

"Recognize gains and losses from changes in market value in income based on long-term yield; for example, use the past performance of the enterprise over several years (a 10-year period has been suggested) to determine an average annual rate of yield because of an increase in value."

To the president of Leather Luggage Co. these recommendations seem more reasonable.

Instructions

(a) Is the use of a market value or fair value basis of accounting for all marketable securities a desirable and feasible practice? Discuss.

(b) Do you believe the president is correct in stating that one of the alternatives is a better approach to recognition of income in accounting for marketable securities?

C7-2 The Walker Company has followed the practice of valuing its temporary investments in marketable equity securities at the lower of cost or market. At December 31, 1980, its account Investment in Marketable Equity Securities had a balance of $40,000, and the account Allowance for Excess of Cost of Temporary Investments over Market had a balance of $2,000. Analysis disclosed that on December 31, 1979, the facts relating to the securities were as follows:

	Cost	Market	Allowance Required
Anna Company Stock	$20,000	$19,000	$1,000
Port Company Stock	10,000	9,000	1,000
Saul Company Stock	20,000	20,400	0
	$50,000		$2,000

During 1980 the Port Company stock was sold for $9,100, the difference between the $9,100 and the "new adjusted basis" of $9,000 being recorded as a "Gain on Sale of Securities." The market price of the stock on December 31, 1980, was: Anna Company stock—$19,900; Saul Company stock—$20,500.

Instructions

(a) What justification is there for the use of the lower of cost or market in valuing marketable equity securities?

(b) Did the Walker Company properly apply this rule on December 31, 1979? Explain.

(c) Did the Walker Company properly account for the sale of the Port Company stock? Explain.

(d) Are there any additional entries necessary for the Walker Company at December 31, 1980, to reflect the facts on the balance sheet and income statement in accordance with generally accepted accounting principles? Explain.

(AICPA adapted)

C7-3 Smalley Supply, Inc. conducts a wholesale merchandising business that sells approximately 5,000 items per month with a total monthly average sales value of $150,000. Its annual bad debt ratio has been approximately 1½% of sales. In recent discussions with his bookkeeper, Mr. Smalley has become confused by all the alternatives apparently available in handling the Allowance for Doubtful Accounts balance. The following information has been shown.

1. An allowance can be set up (a) on the basis of a percentage of sales or (b) on the basis of a valuation of all past due or otherwise questionable accounts receivable—those considered uncollectible being charged to such allowance at the close of the accounting period; or specific items are charged off directly against (c) gross sales, or to (d) bad debt expense in the year in which they are determined to be uncollectible.

2. Collection agency and legal fees, and so on, incurred in connection with the attempted recovery of bad debts can be charged to (a) bad debt expense, (b) allowance for doubtful accounts, (c) legal expense, or (d) general expense.

3. Debts previously written off in whole or in part but currently recovered can be credited to (a) other income, (b) bad debt expense, or (c) allowance for doubtful accounts.

Instructions

Which of the foregoing methods would you recommend to Mr. Smalley in regard to (1) allowances and charge-offs, (2) collection expenses, and (3) recoveries? State briefly and clearly the reasons supporting your recommendations.

C7-4 Surdick, Inc. operates a full-line department store that is dominant in its market area, is easily accessible to public and private transportation, has adequate parking facilities, and is near a large permanent military base. The president of the company seeks your advice on a recently received proposal.

A local bank in which your client has an account recently affiliated with a popular national credit card plan and has extended an invitation to your client to participate in the plan. Under the plan affiliated banks mail credit card applications to persons in the community who have good credit ratings regardless of whether they are bank customers. If the recipients wish to receive a credit card, they complete, sign, and return the application and installment credit agreement. Holders of cards thus activated may charge merchandise or services at any participating establishment throughout the nation.

The bank guarantees payment to all participating merchants on all presented invoices that have been properly completed, signed, and validated with the impression of credit cards that have not expired or been reported stolen or otherwise canceled. Local merchants including your client may turn in all card-validated sales tickets or invoices to their affiliated local bank at any time and receive immediate credits to their checking accounts of 96.5% of the face value of the invoices. If card users pay the bank in full within 30 days for amounts billed, the bank levies no added charges against the customer. If they elect to make their payments under a deferred payment plan, the bank adds a service charge that amounts to an effective interest rate of 18% per annum on unpaid balances. Only the local affiliated banks and the franchiser of the credit card plan share in these revenues.

The 18% service charge approximates what your client has been billing customers who pay their acounts over an extended period on a schedule similar to that offered under the credit card plan. Participation in the plan does not prevent your client from continuing to carry on its credit business as in the past.

Instructions

(a) What are (1) the positive and (2) the negative financial and accounting-related factors that Surdick, Inc. should consider in deciding whether to participate in the described credit card plan? Explain.

(b) If Surdick, Inc. does participate in the plan, which income statement and balance sheet accounts may change materially as the plan becomes fully operative? (Such factors as market position, sales mix, prices, markup, etc., are expected to remain about the same as in the past.) Explain.

(AICPA adapted)

C7-5   Soon after beginning the year-end audit work on March 10 at the Rice Company, the auditor has the following conversation with the controller.

Controller: The year ended March 31st should be our most profitable in history, and, as a consequence, the Board of Directors has just awarded the officers generous bonuses.

Auditor: I thought profits were down this year in the industry, according to your latest interim report.

Controller: Well, they were down but 10 days ago we closed a deal which will give us a substantial increase for the year.

Auditor: Oh, what was it?

Controller: Well, you remember a few years ago our former president bought stock in Hart Enterprises because he had those grandiose ideas about becoming a conglomerate. For six years we have not been able to sell this stock which cost us $1,500,000 and has not paid a nickel in dividends. Thursday we sold this stock to Casino, Inc. for $2,000,000. So, we will have a gain of $350,000 ($500,000 pretax) which will increase our net income for the year to $2,000,000, compared with last year's $1,900,000. As far as I know, we'll be the only company in the industry to register an increase in net income this year. That should help the market value of the stock!

Auditor: Do you expect to receive the $2,000,000 in cash by March 31st, your fiscal year-end?

Controller: No. Although Casino, Inc. is an excellent company, they are a little tight for cash because of their rapid growth. Consequently, they are going to give us a $2,000,000 noninterest-bearing note due $200,000 per year for the next 10 years. The first payment is due on March 31 of next year.

Auditor: Why are the notes noninterest-bearing?

Controller: Because that's what everybody agreed to. Since we don't have any interest-bearing debt, the funds invested in the notes do not cost us anything and besides, we were not getting any dividends on the Hart Enterprises stock.

Instructions

Do you agree with the way the controller has accounted for the transaction? If not, how should the transaction be accounted for?

C7-6 You have just started work for Prescott, Inc. as part of the controller's group involved in current financial reporting problems. The controller for Prescott is interested in your accounting background because the company has experienced a series of financial reporting surprises over the last few years. Recently, the controller has learned from its auditors that an FASB *Statement* may apply to its investment in securities. He assumes that you are familiar with this pronouncement and asks how the following situations should be reported in the financial statements.

Situation I

A marketable equity security, whose market value is currently less than cost, is classified as noncurrent but is to be reclassified as current.

Situation II

A company's current portfolio of marketable equity securities consists of the common stock of one company. At the end of the prior year the market value of the security was fifty percent of original cost, and this reduction in market value was properly reflected in a valuation allowance account. However, at the end of the current year the market value of the security had appreciated to twice the original cost. The security is still considered current at year-end.

Situation III

A marketable equity security whose market value is currently less than cost is classified as current but is to be reclassified as noncurrent.

Situation IV

Marketable debt securities in the current asset section have a market value of $3,000 lower than cost.

Situation V

The company has purchased some convertible debentures that it plans to hold for less than a year. The market value of the convertible debenture is $5,000 below its cost.

Instructions

What is the effect upon classification, carrying value, and earnings for each of the situations above? Assume that these situations are unrelated.

Exercises

E7-1 On July 1, 1980, Pershing Manufacturing Company establishes a petty cash fund in the amount of $400 for the purpose of paying small freight and cartage bills. On July 28, 1980, the receiving clerk, who is custodian of the petty cash fund, requests reimbursement for transportation bills paid in the amount of $378.24; $18.80 of cash is left in petty cash at that time.

Instructions

Prepare the journal entries for establishment of the petty cash fund and for the reimbursement of the fund.

E7-2   The Leonard Company has just received the August 31, 1980, bank statement, which is summarized below:

County National Bank	Disbursements	Receipts	Balance
Balance, August 1			$ 8,600
Deposits during August		$28,000	36,600
Note collected for depositor, including $24 interest		924	37,524
Checks cleared during August	$32,200		5,324
Bank service charges	8		5,316
Balance, August 31			5,316

The general ledger Cash account contained the following entries for the month of August:

Cash			
Balance, August 1	8,200	Disbursements in August	32,500
Receipts during August	31,000		

Deposits in transit at August 31 are $3,000 and checks outstanding at August 31 are determined to total $900. Cash on hand at August 31 is $190. The bookkeeper improperly entered one check in the books at $155.39 which was written for $165.39 for supplies; it cleared the bank during the month of August.

Instructions

(a) Prepare a bank reconciliation dated August 31, 1980, proceeding to a corrected balance.

(b) Prepare any entries necessary to make the books correct and complete.

(c) What amount of cash should be reported in the August 31 balance sheet?

E7-3   The Gaffknee Company desposits all receipts and makes all payments by check. The following information is available from the cash records.

June 30 BANK RECONCILIATION

Balance per bank	$5,510
Add: Deposits in transit	1,200
Deduct: Outstanding checks	(1,500)
Balance per books	$5,210

Month of July Results

	Per Bank	Per Books
Balance July 31	$7,000	$7,700
July deposits	3,200	4,590
July checks	2,500	2,100
July note collected (not included in July deposits)	1,000	-0-
July bank service charge	10	-0-
July NSF check of a customer returned by the bank (recorded by bank as a charge)	200	-0-

Instructions

(a) Prepare a bank reconciliation going from balance per bank and balance per book to corrected cash balance.

(b) Prepare the general journal entry to correct the cash account.

E7-4 Sargent Company has the following securities in its portfolio of marketable equity securities on December 31, 1980:

	Cost	Market
1,000 shares of General Motors, Common	$ 34,250	$ 30,125
5,000 shares of GTE, Common	128,750	128,750
500 shares of AT&T, Preferred	26,250	28,000
	$189,250	$186,875

All of the securities were purchased in 1980.

In 1981, Myers completed the following securities transactions:

March 1   Sold 1,000 shares of General Motors, Common, @ $30 less fees of $875.

April 1   Bought 500 shares of U.S. Steel, Common, @ $45 plus fees of $550.

August 1   Transferred the AT&T, Preferred, from the short-term portfolio to the long-term portfolio when the stock was selling at $50 per share.

The Sargent Company portfolio of marketable equity securities appeared as follows on December 31, 1981:

	Cost	Market
5,000 shares of GTE, Common	$128,750	$145,500
500 shares of U.S. Steel, Common	23,050	20,500
	$151,800	$166,000

Instructions

Prepare the general journal entries for Sargent Company for:
- (a) The 1980 adjusting entry.
- (b) The sale of the GM stock.
- (c) The purchase of the U.S. Steel stock.
- (d) The transfer of the AT&T stock from the short-term to the long-term portfolio.
- (e) The 1981 adjusting entry.

E7-5 Harmon Inc. purchased marketable equity securities at a cost of $250,000 on March 1, 1979. When the securities were purchased, the company intended to hold the investment for more than one year. Therefore, the investment was classified as a noncurrent asset in the company's annual report for the year ended December 31, 1979 and stated at its then market value of $200,000.

On September 30, 1980, when the investment had a market value of $210,000, management reclassified the investment as a current asset because the company intended to sell the securities within the next twelve months. The market value of the investment was $225,000 on December 31, 1980.

Instructions

- (a) The consequence of management's decision to recognize the investment in marketable equity securities as short-term and reclassify it as a current asset was recorded in the accounts. At what amount would the investment be recorded on September 30, 1980, the date of this decision?
- (b) How would the investment in the marketable equity securities be reported in the financial statements of Harmon Inc. as of December 31, 1980 so that the company's financial position and operations for the year 1980 would reflect and report properly the reclassification of the investment from a noncurrent asset to a current asset? Be sure to indicate the affected accounts and the related dollar amounts and the note disclosures, if any.

(CMA adapted)

E7-6   The following information relates to the temporary debt investments of the Pitney Collaters Company.

1. On February 1, the company purchased 8% marketable bonds of Capitol Co. having a par value of $200,000 at 98 plus accrued interest. Interest is payable April 1 and October 1.
2. On April 1, semiannual interest is received.
3. On July 1, 9% marketable bonds of Quincy, Inc. were purchased. These bonds with a par value of $400,000 were purchased at 100 plus accrued interest. Interest dates are June 1 and December 1.
4. On September 1, bonds of a par value of $100,000, purchased on February 1, are sold at 99 plus accrued interest.
5. On October 1, semiannual interest is received.
6. On December 1, semiannual interest is received.
7. On December 31, the market value of the bonds purchased February 1 and July 1 are 94 and 96 respectively.

Instructions

(a) Prepare any journal entries you consider necessary, including year-end entries (Dec. 31), assuming that the cost basis is used.
(b) If Pitney Collaters used the lower of cost or market basis, how would the entries prepared in part (a) differ?

E7-7   Aimless Company frequently invests in marketable debt securities cash that is not immediately needed for operations. These temporary investments are generally held for a period of several months. The company has adopted the lower of cost or market method on an aggregate basis in accounting for its marketable debt securities.

The following transactions occurred over a period of two years.

May 1   6% marketable bonds of a par value of $150,000, with interest payable June 1 and Dec. 1, are purchased at 98 plus accrued interest.

June 1   Semiannual interest is received.

Aug. 1   Bonds of a par value of $20,000, purchased on May 1, are sold at 96½ plus accrued interest.

Dec. 1   Semiannual interest is received.

    31   Entry is made to accrue the proper amount of interest.

    31   The bonds are listed on the market at 95.

June 1   Semiannual interest is received (assume that reversing entries were made on 1/1).

Nov. 15   The remaining bonds of a par value of $130,000 are sold at 97 plus accrued interest.

Dec. 31   The allowance is closed out because no temporary securities are now held.

Instructions

Prepare entries to record the transactions above.

E7-8   The Wingra Stone Company shows a balance of $134,250 in the accounts receivable account on December 31, 1980. The balance consists of the following:

Due from regular customers, of which $30,000 represents accounts pledged as security for a bank loan	$75,000
Advances to employees	1,200
Advance to subsidiary company (made in 1976)	30,000
Installment accounts due in 1981	15,000
Installment accounts due after 1981	12,000
Overpayments to creditors	1,050

Instructions

Illustrate how the information above should be shown on the balance sheet of the Wingra Stone Company on December 31, 1980.

E7-9 Your accounts receivable clerk, Mr. William Voit, to whom you pay a salary of $600 per month, has just purchased a new Cadillac. You decided to test the accuracy of the accounts receivable balance of $52,200 as shown in the ledger.

The following information is available for your *first year* in business:

(1)	Collections from customers	$225,000
(2)	Merchandise purchased	288,000
(3)	Ending merchandise inventory	80,000
(4)	Goods are marked to sell at 40% above cost	

Instructions

Compute an estimate of the ending balance of accounts receivable from customers that should appear in the ledger and any apparent shortages. Assume that all sales are made on account.

E7-10 On June 3, Gilbert Company sold to Mary Scott merchandise having a sale price of $2,000 with terms of 2/10, n/60, f.o.b. shipping point. An invoice totaling $80, terms n/30, was received by Mary Scott on June 8 from the Madsen Transport Service for the freight cost. On receipt of the goods, June 5, Mary Scott notified the Gilbert Company that merchandise costing $200 contained flaws that rendered it worthless; the same day Gilbert Company issued a credit memo covering the worthless merchandise and asked that it be returned at company expense. The freight on the returned merchandise was $10, paid by Gilbert Company on June 7. On June 12, the company received a check for the balance due from Mary Scott.

Instructions

(a) Prepare journal entries on the Gilbert Company books to record all the events noted above under each of the following bases:
  1. Sales and receivables are entered at gross selling price.
  2. Sales and receivables are entered at net of cash discounts.

(b) Prepare the journal entry under basis 2, assuming that Mary Scott did not remit payment until July 29.

E7-11 Presented below is information related to Skelly Corporation.

June 1 Skelly Corp. sold to Moat Co. merchandise having a sales price of $3,000 with terms 2/10, net/60. Skelly records their sales and receivables net.

June 3 Moat Co. returned merchandise having a sales price of $300 which was defective.

June 5 Accounts receivable of $8,000 are factored with Mohr Credit Corp. at a financing charge of 10%. Cash is received for the proceeds; collections are handled by the finance company. (These accounts were all past the discount period.)

June 9 Accounts receivable of $9,000 are assigned to Chase Credit Corp. as security for a loan of $6,000 at a finance charge of 4% of the amount of the loan. The finance company will make the collections. (All the acounts receivable are past the discount period.)

December 30 Moat Co. notifies Skelly that they are bankrupt and will pay only 10% of their account. Give the entry to write off the uncollectible balance using the allowance method. (Note: Skelly increased the receivable by $54 on June 11 when the discount period passed.)

Instructions

Prepare all necessary entries in general journal form for Skelly Corporation.

E7-12 At January 1, 1981, the credit balance in the allowance for doubtful accounts of the Mary Noble Company was $400,000. For 1981, the provision for doubtful accounts is based on a percentage of net sales. Net sales for 1981 were $50,000,000. Based on the latest available facts, the 1981 provision for doubtful accounts is estimated to be 0.7% of net sales. During 1981, uncollectible receivables amounting to $410,000 were written off against the allowance for doubtful accounts.

Instructions

Prepare a schedule computing the balance in Mary Noble's allowance for doubtful accounts at December 31, 1981.

E7-13 The trial balance before adjustment of Johnnie Clark Army-Navy Surplus shows the following balances:

	Dr.	Cr.
Accounts Receivable	60,000	
Allowance for Doubtful Accounts	750	
Sales (all on credit)		581,200
Sales Returns and Allowances	15,000	

Instructions

Give the entry for estimated bad debts assuming that the allowance is to provide for doubtful accounts on the basis of (a) 2% of gross accounts receivable and (b) 1% of net sales.

E7-14 The N. Owens Company includes the following account among its trade receivables.

Eric Grinter

1/1	Balance forward	450	1/28	Cash (#1710)	1,300
1/20	Invoice #1710	1,300	4/2	Cash (#2116)	890
3/14	Invoice #2116	890	4/10	Cash	125
4/12	Invoice #2412	1,420	4/30	Cash (#2412)	1,000
9/5	Invoice #3614	490	9/20	Cash (#3614 and	
10/17	Invoice #4912	860		part of #2412)	790
11/18	Invoice #5681	2,300	10/31	Cash (#4912)	860
12/20	Invoice #6347	630	12/1	Cash (#5681)	1,750
			12/29	Cash (#6347)	630

Instructions

Age the balance and specify any items that apparently require particular attention.

E7-15 The chief accountant for the Sullivan Corporation provides you with the following list of accounts receivable written off in the current year.

Date	Customer	Amount
Mar. 31	GLC Designs	$5,400
June 30	Harley Associates	2,700
Sept. 30	Susan's Dress Shop	4,120
Dec. 31	Drew Corporation	4,800

Sullivan Corporation follows the policy of debiting Bad Debt Expense as accounts are written off. The chief accountant maintains that this procedure is appropriate for financial statement purposes because the Internal Revenue Service will not accept other methods for recognizing bad debts.

All of Sullivan Corporation's sales are on a 30-day credit basis. Sales for the current year total $1,500,000 and research has determined that bad debt losses approximate 1% of sales.

Instructions

(a) Do you agree or disagree with the Sullivan Corporation policy concerning recognition of bad debt expense? Why or why not?

(b) By what amount would net income differ if bad debt expense was computed using the percentage-of-sales approach?

E7-16 Presented below is information related to the Dunn's Supply, Inc.

1. Customers' accounts in the amount of $36,000 are assigned to the Macks Finance Company as security for a loan of $24,000. The finance charge is 2% of the amount borrowed.
2. Cash collections on assigned accounts amount to $12,600.
3. Collections on assigned accounts to date, plus a $300 check for interest, are forwarded to Macks Finance Company.
4. Additional collections on assigned accounts amount to $14,200.
5. The loan is paid in full plus interest of $160.
6. Uncollected balances of the assigned accounts are returned to the regular customers' ledger.

Instructions

Prepare entries in journal form for Dunn's Supply, Inc.

E7-17 Presented below is information related to Lyons Co. and Bell, Inc.

May 1   Lyons Co. gave Bell, Inc. a $5,400, 60-day, 8% note in payment of its account of the same amount.

      16   Bell, Inc. discounted the note at the bank at a 9% discount rate.

June 30 On the maturity date of the note, Lyons Co. paid the amount due.

Instructions

(a) Record the transactions above on both the books of Lyons Co. and the books of Bell, Inc.
(b) Assume that Lyons Co. dishonored its note and the bank notified Bell, Inc., that it had charged the maturity value plus a protest fee of $18 to the Bell, Inc. bank account. What entry(ies) should Bell, Inc. make upon receiving this notification?

E7-18 The trial balance before adjustment for the Cork Sales Company shows the following balances:

	Dr.	Cr.
Accounts Receivable	$64,800	
Allowance for Doubtful Accounts	1,080	
Sales		$369,000
Sales Returns and Allowances	1,800	

Instructions

Using the data above, give the journal entries required to record each of the following cases (each situation is independent):

1. The company wants to maintain the Allowance for Doubtful Accounts at 2% of gross accounts receivable.
2. The company desires to increase the allowance by ½% of net sales.
3. To obtain additional cash, Cork factors $18,000 of Accounts Receivable with Tri-County Finance. The finance charge is 10% of the amount factored.
4. To obtain a one-year loan of $45,000, Cork assigns $54,000 of Accounts Receivable to Blair Accounts. The finance charge is 6% of the loan; the cash is received and the accounts turned over to Blair.

E7-19 Kraus, Inc. sells receivables with a net realizable value of $167,370 to Lisa Company for $135,350 on a with-recourse basis. Lisa Company expects to collect $156,000 over a two-year period to yield an 18% interest rate on the transaction.

Instructions

(a) Should a gain or loss be recognized on this transaction by Kraus, Inc.?

(b) What entry should Kraus, Inc. make for this transaction?

E7-20 On July 1, 1981, S. Robb Company made two sales:

(a) It sold land having a fair market value of $500,000 in exchange for a four-year noninterest-bearing promissory note in the face amount of $680,245. The land is carried on S. Robb Company's books at a cost of $425,000.

(b) It rendered services in exchange for a 3%, eight-year promissory note having a maturity value of $200,000 (interest payable annually).

S. Robb Company recently had to pay 6% interest for monies that it borrowed from Georgia National Bank. The customers in these two transactions have credit ratings that require them to borrow money at 8% interest.

Instructions

Record the two journal entries that should be recorded by S. Robb Company for the sales transactions above that took place on July 1, 1981.

E7-21 On December 31, 1981, Rose Corporation sold some of its product to Three H Company, accepting a $210,000 noninterest-bearing note, receivable in full on December 31, 1984. Rose Corporation enjoys a high credit rating and, therefore, borrows funds from its several lines of credit at 6%. Three H Company, however, pays 8% for its borrowed funds. The product sold is carried on the books of Rose Corporation at a manufactured cost of $150,000. Assume that the effective interest method is used for amortization payments.

Instructions

(a) Prepare the journal entry to record the sale on December 31, 1981, by the Rose Corporation. Assume that a perpetual inventory system is used.

(b) Prepare the journal entries on the books of Rose Corporation for the year 1982 that are necessitated by the sales transaction of December 31, 1981.

(c) Prepare the journal entries on the books of Rose Corporation for the year 1983 that are necessitated by the sale on December 31, 1981.

*E7-22 Following is the general format of a four-column bank reconciliation with the various categories and operations numbered (1) through (8):

	Balance 10/31	November Receipts	November Disbursements	Balance 11/30
Per Bank Statement	$ XXXXX	$ XXXXX	$ XXXXX	$ XXXXX
Items to be *added:*	(1)	(3)	(5)	(7)
Items to be *deducted:*	(2)	(4)	(6)	(8)
Per Books	$ XXXXX	$ XXXXX	$ XXXXX	$ XXXXX

Instructions

(a) For each of the following items indicate in which columns the reconciling items would appear. Question 1 is answered as an example.

6	7	1. November service charge of $10 is included on bank statement.
		2. October service charge of $15 is included in book disbursements for November.
		3. A $6,000 deposit in transit is included in book receipts for November.
		4. All $10,000 of checks written in October, which had not cleared the bank at October 31, cleared the bank in November.
		5. The bank collected a $600 note receivable for the firm in November plus $20 interest. The firm has not yet recorded this receipt.
		6. An "NSF" check in the amount of $200 was returned with the Novem-

ber bank statement. This check will be redeposited in December. The firm has not yet made an entry for this "NSF" check.

_____ _____ 7. The bank, in error, credited the firm's account for $500 in November for another firm's deposit.

_____ _____ 8. A check written in November for $700 was written in the check register in error in the amount of $770. This check cleared the bank in November for $700. Both the debit to Utilities Expense and the credit were overstated as a result of this error in the books.

_____ _____ 9. $10,000 of checks written in November have not cleared the bank by November 30.

_____ _____ 10. The initial $4,500 deposit shown on the November bank statement was included in October's book receipts.

(b) Prepare the entries that should be recorded to make the books complete and accurate at November 30.

Problems

P7-1 The McCoy Foundry closes its books regularly on December 31, but at the end of 1980 it held its cash book open so that a more favorable balance sheet could be prepared for credit purposes. Cash receipts and disbursements for the first 10 days of January were recorded as December transactions. The following information is given.

1. January cash receipts recorded in the December cash book totaled $26,730, of which $12,000 represents cash sales and $14,730 represents collections on account for which cash discounts of $270 were given.

2. January cash disbursements recorded in the December check register liquidated accounts payable of $21,750 on which discounts of $488 were taken.

3. The ledger has not been closed for 1980.

4. The amount shown as inventory was determined by physical count on December 31, 1980.

Instructions

(a) Prepare any entries you consider necesary to correct the McCoy Foundry Company's accounts at December 31.

(b) To what extent was the McCoy Foundry Company able to show a more favorable balance sheet at December 31 by holding its cash book open? Assume that the balance sheet that was prepared by the company showed the following amounts:

	Dr.	Cr.
Cash	$45,000	
Receivables	30,000	
Inventories	75,000	
Accounts payable		$45,000
Other current liabilities		15,000

P7-2 Presented below is information related to Endres Products Company.

Balance per books at October 31, $32,965.58; receipts, $164,834.34; disbursements, $159,225.68. Balance per bank statement November 30, $41,328.44.

The following checks were outstanding at November 30:

1224	$1,600.34
1230	1,335.78
1232	2,285.60
1233	391.18

Included with the November bank statement and not recorded by the company were a bank debit ticket for $33.60 covering bank charges for the month, a debit ticket for $375.60 for a customer's check returned and marked NSF, and a credit ticket for $1,200.00 representing bond interest collected by the bank in the name of the Endres Products Company. Cash on hand at November 30 recorded and awaiting deposit amounted to $3,649.50.

Instructions

(a) Prepare a bank reconciliation (bank balance to book balance) at November 30, 1980, for the Endres Products Company from the information above.

(b) Prepare any journal entries required to adjust the cash account at November 30.

(c) State the amount of cash available for disbursement at November 30.

P7-3   The cash account of Badger Co. showed a ledger balance of $4,112.78 on June 30, 1980. The bank statement as of that date showed a balance of $3,329.13. Upon comparing the statement with the cash records, the following facts were determined:

(a) The bank had charged the Badger Co.'s account for a customer's uncollectible check amounting to $457.20 on June 29.

(b) A 60-day, 6%, $1,000 customer's note dated April 25, and discounted by Badger on June 12, remained unpaid by the customer on the due date. On June 28 the bank charged the Badger Co. for $1,012.90, which included a protest fee of $2.90 (Badger discloses discounted notes receivable by use of a footnote.)

(c) A customer's check for $90 had been entered as $70 in the cash receipts journal by Badger on June 15.

(d) Check no. 742 in the amount of $392 had been entered in the cashbook as $329, and check no. 747 in the amount of $47.10 had been entered as $471. Both checks had been issued to pay for purchases of equipment.

(e) There were bank service charges for June of $19.72.

(f) A bank memo stated that W. W. Briscoe's note for $600 and interest of $18 had been collected on June 29, and the bank had made a charge of $2.50 on the collection. (No entry had been made on Badger's books when Briscoe's note was sent to the bank for collection.)

(g) Receipts for June 30 for $1,735 were not deposited until July 2.

(h) Checks outstanding on June 30 totaled $1,444.77.

Instructions

(a) Prepare a bank reconciliation dated June 30, 1980, proceeding to a corrected cash balance.

(b) Prepare any entries necessary to make the books correct and complete.

P7-4   Presented below is information related to Precision Work Company.

Precision Work Company
BANK RECONCILIATION
May 31, 1980

Balance per bank statement		$20,928.46
Less outstanding checks		
No. 6124	$2,125.00	
No. 6138	932.65	
No. 6139	960.57	
No. 6140	1,420.00	5,438.22
		15,490.24
Add deposit in transit		4,710.56
Balance per books		$20,200.80

Check Register—June

Date		Payee	No.	V. Pay	Discount	Cash
June	1	Lund Mfg.	6141	$ 237.50		$ 237.50
	1	Office Supply Stores	6142	915.00	$ 9.15	905.85
	8	Office Supply Co., Inc.	6143	122.90	2.45	120.45
	9	Lund Mfg.	6144	306.40		306.40
	10	Petty Cash	6145	89.93		89.93
	17	Allservice Photo	6146	706.00	14.12	691.88
	22	Dick Palmer Publishing	6147	447.50		447.50
	23	Payroll Account	6148	4,130.00		4,130.00
	25	Warren Tools, Inc.	6149	390.75	3.91	386.84
	28	American Insurance Agency	6150	1,050.00		1,050.00
	28	Riley Construction	6151	2,250.00		2,250.00
	29	S. Hargrove, Inc.	6152	750.00		750.00
	30	Wixon Bros.	6153	295.25	5.90	289.35
				$11,691.23	$35.53	$11,655.70

STATEMENT
First State Bank of Monona
General Checking Account of Precision Work Co.—June 1980

Debits			Date	Credits	Balance
					$20,928.46
$2,125.00	$237.50	$ 905.85	June 1	$4,710.56	22,370.67
932.65	120.45		12	1,507.06	22,824.63
1,420.00	447.50	306.40	23	1,458.55	22,109.28
4,130.00		11.05 (BC)			17,968.23
89.93	2,250.00	1,050.00	28	4,157.48	18,735.78

Cash received June 29 and 30 and deposited in the mail for the general checking account June 30 amounted to $2,407.96. Because the cash account balance at June 30 is not given, it must be calculated from other information in the problem.

Instructions

From the information above, prepare a bank reconciliation (bank balance to book balance) as of June 30, 1980, for the Precision Work Company.

P7-5   Oregon Corp. invested its excess cash in temporary investments during 1979. As of December 31, 1979, the portfolio of short-term marketable equity securities consisted of the following common stocks:

		Per Share	
Security	Quantity	cost	market
Belden, Inc.	1,000 shares	$12	$17
Dohm Corp.	3,000 shares	25	19
Marco Aircraft	2,000 shares	34	29

Instructions

(a) What descriptions and amounts should be reported on the face of Oregon's December 31, 1979, balance sheet relative to temporary investments?

On December 31, 1980, Oregon's portfolio of short-term marketable equity securities consisted of the following common stocks:

Security	Quantity	Per Share cost	Per Share market
Belden, Inc.	1,000 shares	$12	$19
Belden, Inc.	2,000 shares	18	19
Lakeshore Company	1,000 shares	15	12
Marco Aircraft	2,000 shares	34	18

During the year 1980, Oregon Corp. sold 3,000 shares of Dohm Corp. at a loss of $10,000 and purchased 2,000 more shares of Belden, Inc. and 1,000 shares of Lakeshore Company.

(b) What descriptions and amounts should be reported on the face of Oregon's December 31, 1980, balance sheet? What descriptions and amounts should be reported to reflect the data in Oregon's 1980 income statement?

On December 31, 1981, Oregon's portfolio of short-term marketable equity securities consisted of the following common stocks:

Security	Quantity	Per Share cost	Per Share market
Marco Aircraft	2,000 shares	$34	$45
Lakeshore Company	500 shares	15	13

During the year 1981, Oregon Corp. sold 3,000 shares of Belden, Inc. at a gain of $12,000 and 500 shares of Lakeshore Company at a loss of $2,300.

(c) What descriptions and amounts should be reported on the face of Oregon's December 31, 1981, balance sheet? What descriptions and amounts should be reported to reflect the above in Oregon's 1981 income statement?

(d) Assuming that comparative financial statements for 1980 and 1981 are presented, draft the footnote necessary for full disclosure of Oregon's transactions and position in marketable equity securities.

P7-6 Utah Mining Company invests its excess idle cash on March 2, 1980, in the following short-term marketable securities:

Security	Quantity	Per Share Cost
Mableleen Corporation, preferred stock	800 shares	$90
Seattle Cement Co., common stock	2,500 shares	30
Pacific Electric Co., common stock	1,000 shares	40

The following data related to the years 1980 and 1981:

For year 1980—Cash dividends received: Mableleen, $5.00 per share
Seattle Cement, $.80 per share
Pacific Electric, $2.00 per share

December 31, 1980—Market values per share: Mableleen, $84
Seattle Cement, $32
Pacific Electric, $33

February 12, 1981—Sold all shares of Seattle Cement at $35 per share.

November 30, 1981—Purchased 1,500 shares of Mobil Company common stock for $45 per share.

For year 1981—Cash dividends received: Mableleen $5.00 per share
Seattle Cement, $.20 per share
Pacific Electric, $2.30 per share
Mobil Company, $.40 per share

December 31, 1981—Market values per share: Mableleen, $100
Pacific Electric, $34
Mobil Company, $50

Instructions

(a) Prepare all of the journal entries to reflect the transactions above and data in accordance with professional pronouncements.

(b) Prepare the descriptions and amounts that should be reported on the face of Utah Mining Company's comparative financial statements for 1980 and 1981.

(c) Draft the footnote that should accompany the 1980–81 comparative statements relative to the marketable equity securities.

P7-7 The balance sheet of the Image Builders, Inc. at December 31, 1980 includes the following:

Notes receivable	$ 43,000	
Less: Notes receivable discounted	15,000	$28,000
Accounts receivable	$166,400	
Less: Allowance for doubtful accounts	12,400	154,000

Transactions in 1981 include the following:

1. Notes receivable discounted at 12/31/80 matured and were paid with the exception of a $2,000 note for which the company had to pay $2,050, which included $50 interest and protest fees. Recovery is expected in 1981. (Use Notes Receivable Past Due account.)

2. Cash collected on accounts receivable totaled $135,000 including accounts of $30,000 on which 2% sales discounts were allowed.

3. $2,400 was received in payment of an account which was written off the books as worthless in 1978. (Hint: Reestablish the receivable account.)

4. Customer accounts of $14,400 were written off during the year.

5. At year-end the allowance for doubtful accounts was estimated to need a balance of $16,000. This estimate is based on an analysis of aged accounts receivable.

6. Image Builders, Inc. discounted a $12,000, 90-day note dated Nov. 1, 1981 on Dec. 1, 1981. The note bears an 8% interest rate and was discounted at 7%.

Instructions

Prepare all journal entries necessary to reflect the transactions above.

P7-8 Presented below is information related to the accounts receivable accounts of Custom Creations, Inc. during the current year 1981.

1. The accounts receivable control account has a debit balance of $363,600 on December 31, 1981.

2. Two entries were made in the Bad Debt Expense account during the year: (1) a debit on December 31 for the amount credited to Allowance for Doubtful Accounts, and (2) a credit for $810 on November 3, 1981 because of a bankruptcy.

3. The Allowance for Doubtful Accounts is as follows for 1981:

Allowance for Doubtful Accounts

Nov. 3	Uncollectible accounts written off	810	Jan. 1	Beginning balance	6,660
			Dec. 31	4% of $363,600	14,544

4. An aging schedule of the accounts receivable as of December 31, 1981 is as follows:

Age	Net debit balance	% to be applied after correction made
Under 60 days	$164,664	1%
61–90 days	139,140	3%
91–120 days	39,924*	6%
Over 120 days	19,872	$3,600 definitely
	$363,600	uncollectible; estimated remainder collectible is 75%

*The $810 write-off of receivables is related to the 91 to 120 day category.

5. A credit balance exists in the Accounts Receivable (61–90 days) of $3,960, which represents an advance on a sales contract.

Instructions

Assuming that the books have not been closed for 1981, make the necessary correcting entries.

P7-9 The Dunkin Paper Company has been in business for five years but has never had an audit made of its financial statements. Engaged to make an audit for 1981, you find that the company's balance sheet carries no allowance for doubtful accounts, bad debts having been written off and recoveries credited to income as collected. The company's policy is to write off at December 31 of each year those accounts on which no collections have been received for three months. The installment contracts generally are for two years.

Upon your recommendation the company revises its accounts for 1981 to show the effect of recording bad debt expense on the allowance basis. The allowance is to be based on a percentage of sales that is derived from the experience of prior years.

Here are the statistics for the past five years.

	Charge Sales	Accounts Written Off and Year of Sale			Recoveries and Year of Sale
1977	$100,000	(1977) $ 550			
1978	250,000	(1977) 1,500	(1978) $1,000		(1977) $100
1979	300,000	(1977) 500	(1978) 4,000	(1979) $1,300	(1978) 400
1980	325,000	(1978) 1,200	(1979) 4,500	(1980) 1,500	(1979) 500
1981	275,000	(1979) 2,700	(1980) 5,000	(1981) 1,400	(1980) 600

Accounts receivable at December 31, 1981, were as follows:

1980 sales	$ 15,000
1981 sales	135,000
	$150,000

Instructions

Prepare the adjusting journal entry or entries with appropriate explanations to set up the Allowance for Doubtful Accounts. (Support each item with organized computations; income tax implications should be ignored.)

(AICPA adapted)

P7-10 The Becker Company finances some of its current operations by assigning accounts receivable to a finance company. On July 1, 1981, it assigned, under guarantee, accounts amounting to $40,000, the finance company advancing to them 80% of the accounts assigned (20% of the total to be withheld until the finance company has made its full recovery), less a commission charge of ½% of the total accounts assigned.

On July 31, the Becker Company received a statement that the finance company had collected $18,000 of these accounts, and had made an additional charge of ½% of the total accounts outstanding as of July 31, this charge to be deducted at the time of the first remittance due Becker Company from the finance company. On August 31, 1981, the Becker Company received a second statement from the finance company, together with a check for the amount due. The statement indicated that the finance company had collected an additional $16,000 and had made a further charge of ½% of the balance outstanding as of August 31.

Instructions

(a) Make all entries on the books of the Becker Company that are involved in the transactions above.

(b) Explain how these accounts should be presented in the financial statements of Becker Company at July 31 and at August 31.

(AICPA adapted)

P7-11 Abbot Corporation operates in an industry which has a high rate of bad debts. On December 31, 1980, before any year-end adjustments, the balance in Abbot's accounts receivable account was $500,000 and the allowance for doubtful accounts had a balance of $25,000. The year-end balance reported in the statement of financial position for the allowance for doubtful accounts will be based on the aging schedule shown below.

Days Account Outstanding	Amount	Probability of Collection
Less than 15 days	$300,000	.98
Between 16 and 30 days	100,000	.90
Between 31 and 45 days	50,000	.80
Between 46 and 60 days	30,000	.70
Between 61 and 75 days	10,000	.60
Over 75 days	10,000	.00

Instructions

(a) What is the appropriate balance for the allowance for doubtful accounts on December 31, 1980?

(b) Show how accounts receivable would be presented on the balance sheet prepared on December 31, 1980.

(c) What is the dollar effect of the year-end bad debt adjustment on the before-tax income for 1980?

(CMA adapted)

P7-12 Texas Manufacturing Company produces soccer, football, and track shoes. The treasurer of Texas has recently completed negotiations in which Texas agrees to loan Cederic Company, a leather supplier, $500,000. Cederic Company will issue a noninterest-bearing note due in five years (a 10% interest rate is appropriate), and has agreed to furnish Texas with leather at prices that are 10% lower than those usually charged.

Instructions

(a) Prepare the accounting entry to record this transaction on Texas Manufacturing Company's books.

(b) Determine the balances at the end of each year the note is outstanding for the following accounts for Texas Manufacturing Company:
Notes receivable
Unamortized discount
Interest income

P7-13   On December 31, 1981, Foster Company rendered services to Southern Corporation at an agreed price of $80,000, accepting $20,000 down and agreeing to accept the balance in four equal installments of $15,000 receivable each December 31. An assumed interest of 8% is implicit in the agreed price.

Instructions

Prepare the journal entries that would be recorded by the Foster Company for the sale and for the receipts and interest on the following dates (Assume that the effective interest method is used for amortization purposes.):

(a) December 31, 1981.
(b) December 31, 1982.
(c) December 31, 1983.
(d) December 31, 1984.
(e) December 31, 1985.

P7-14   You are engaged in your fifth annual examination of the financial statements of Jay Corporation. Your examination is for the year ended December 31, 1981. The client prepared the following schedules of Trade Notes Receivable and Interest Receivable for you at December 31, 1981. You have agreed the opening balances to your prior year's audit workpapers.

Jay Corporation
TRADE NOTES RECEIVABLE AND RELATED INTEREST RECEIVABLE
Trade Notes Receivable

Maker	Issue Date	Terms	Interest Rate	Bal. Dec. 31, 1980	1981 Debits	1981 Credits	Bal. Dec. 31, 1981
Heiden Co.	4/1/80	One year	6%	$60,000		$ 60,000	
Eckert Co.	5/1/81	90 days after date	—		$ 20,000	19,750	$ 250
Walsh Ind.	7/1/81	60 days after date	6%		4,000		4,000
R. Jay	8/3/81	Demand	6%		10,000		10,000
Taylor Corp.	10/2/81	60 days after date	6%		40,000 40,000	40,000	40,000
Kanner, Inc.	11/1/81	90 days after date	3%		42,000	35,000	7,000
Lange Co.	11/1/81	90 days after date	6%		24,000		24,000
			Totals	$60,000	$180,000	$154,750	$85,250

Interest Receivable

Due From	Bal. Dec. 31, 1980	1981 Debits	1981 Credits	Bal. Dec. 31, 1981
Heiden Co.	$2,700	$ 900	$3,600	
Walsh Ind.		40		$ 40
R. Jay		200		200
Taylor Corp.		400	198	202
Kanner, Inc.		210		210
Lange Co.		240		240
Totals	$2,700	$1,990	$3,798	$892

Your examination reveals this information.

1. Interest is computed on a 360-day basis. In computing interest, it is the corporation's practice to exclude the first day of the note's term and to include the due date.

2. The Eckert Company's 90-day note was discounted on May 16 at 6%, and the proceeds were credited to the Trade Notes Receivable account. The note was paid at maturity.

3. Walsh Industries became bankrupt on August 31, and the corporation will recover 75 cents on the dollar. The corporation uses the direct write-off method for recording bad debt expense. All of Jay Corporation's notes receivable provide for interest at the legal rate of 6% on the maturity value of a dishonored note.

4. R. Jay, president of Jay Corporation, confirmed that she owed Jay Corporation $10,000 and that she expected to pay the note within six months. You are satisfied that the note is collectible.

5. Taylor Corporation's 60-day note was discounted on November 1 at 6%, and the proceeds were credited to the Trade Notes Receivable and Interest Receivable accounts. On December 2, Jay Corporation received notice from the bank that Taylor Corporation's note was not paid at maturity and that it had been charged against Jay's checking account by the bank. Upon receiving the notice from the bank, the bookkeeper recorded the note and the accrued interest in the Trade Notes Receivable and Interest Receivable accounts. Taylor Corporation paid Jay Corporation the full amount due in January, 1982.

6. The Kanner, Inc., 90-day note was pledged as collateral for $35,000, 60-day, 6% loan from the First National Bank on December 1.

7. On November 1, the corporation received four, $6,000, 90-day notes from Lange Co. On December 1, the corporation received payment from Lange Co. for one of the $6,000 notes with accrued interest. Prepayment of the notes is allowed without penalty. The bookkeeper credited the Lange Company Accounts Receivable account for the cash received.

Instructions

Prepare the adjusting journal entries that you would suggest at December 31, 1981, for the transactions above. Reclassify all past due notes and related carrying costs to accounts receivable.

(AICPA adapted)

P7-15   You are examining Thomas Robinson Corporation's financial statements for the year ended December 31, 1981. Your analysis of the 1981 entries in the Trade Notes Receivable account appears on the next page.

Thomas Robinson Corporation
ANALYSIS OF TRADE NOTES RECEIVABLE
For the Year Ended December 31, 1981

Date 1981		Folio	Trade Notes Receivable Debit	Credit
Jan. 1	Balance forward		$118,000	
Feb. 28	Received $25,000, 6% note due 10/28/81 from Daley, whose trade account was past due.	MEMO		
Feb. 28	Discounted Daley note at 6%.	CR		$ 24,960
Mar. 29	Received noninterest-bearing demand note from Edge, the Corporation's treasurer for a loan.	CD	6,200	
Aug. 30	Received principal and interest due from Allen and, in accordance with agreement, two principal payments in advance.	CR		34,200
Sept. 4	Paid protest fee on note dishonored by Charnes.	CD	5	
Nov. 1	Received check dated 2/1/82 in settlement of Bailey note. The check was included in cash on hand 12/31/81.	CR		8,120
Nov. 4	Paid protest fee and maturity value of Daley note to bank. Note discounted 2/28/81 was dishonored.	CD	26,031	
Dec. 27	Accepted furniture and fixtures with a fair market value of $24,000 in full settlement from Daley.	GJ		24,000
Dec. 31	Received check dated 1/3/82 from Edge in payment of 3/29/81 note. (The check was included in petty cash until 1/2/82, when it was returned to Edge in exchange for a new demand note of the same amount.)	CR		6,200
Dec. 31	Received principal, protest fee, and interest on Charnes note.	CR		42,437
Dec. 31	Accrued interest on Allen note.	GJ	1,200	
	Totals		$151,436	$139,917

The following information is available.

1. Balances at January 1, 1981 were a debit of $1,400 in the Accrued Interest Receivable account (related to Allen note) and a credit of $400 in the Unearned Interest Income account (related to Bailey note). The $118,000 debit balance in the Trade Notes Receivable account consisted of the following three notes:

Allen note dated 8/31/77 payable in annual installments of $10,000 principal plus accrued interest at 6% each August 31	$70,000
Bailey note discounted to Robinson Corp. at 6% on 11/1/80 due 11/1/81	8,000
Charnes note for $40,000 plus 6% interest dated 12/31/80 due on 9/1/81	40,000

2. No entries were made during 1981 to the Accrued Interest Receivable account or the Unearned Interest Income account and only one entry for a credit of $1,200 on December 31 appeared in the Interest Income account.

3. All notes were from trade customers unless otherwise indicated.

4. Debits and credits offsetting Trade Notes Receivable debit and credit entries were correctly recorded unless the facts indicate otherwise.

Instructions

Prepare a work sheet to adjust each entry to correct or properly reclassify it, if necessary. Enter your adjustments in the proper columns to correspond with the date of each entry. Do not combine related entries for different dates. Your completed work sheet provides the basis for one compound journal entry to correct all entries to Trade Notes Receivable and related accounts for 1981. Formal journal entries are not required. In addition to the information shown in the analysis above, these column headings are suggested for your work sheet. Assume that a Note Receivable Past Due account should not be used for this problem.

Adjustment or Reclassification Required

			Other Accounts	
Trade Notes Receivable	Trade Accounts Receivable	Interest Income		Amount
Debit-(Credit)	Debit-(Credit)	Debit-(Credit)	Account Title	Debit-(Credit)

(AICPA adapted)

*P7-16 You have been hired as the new assistant controller of Elbert, Inc. and assigned the task of proving the cash account balance. As of December 31, 1980, you have obtained the following information relative to the December cash operations.

1. Balance per bank

11/30/80	$109,050
12/31/80	100,893

2. Balance per books

11/30/80	77,413
12/31/80	83,800

3. Receipts for the month of December, 1980

per bank	675,925
per books	687,723

4. Outstanding checks

11/30/80	31,762
12/31/80	37,523

5. Dishonored checks are recorded on the books as a reduction of cash receipts and when later redeposited are recorded as a regular cash receipt. Dishonored checks are treated as a disbursement by the bank and when later redeposited treated as a regular deposit. Dishonored checks returned by the bank and recorded by Elbert, Inc. amounted to $3,125 during the month of December 1980; according to the books $2,500 was redeposited. Dishonored checks, recorded on the bank statement but not on the books until the following months, amounted to $125 at November 30, 1980, and $1,150 at December 31, 1980.

6. On December 31, 1980, a $1,162 check of the Northside Company was charged to the Elbert, Inc. account by the bank in error.

7. Proceeds of a note of the Bryant Company collected by the bank on December 10, 1980, were not entered on the books:

Principal	$1,000
Interest	10
	1,010
Less collection charge	3
	$1,007

8. Interest on a bank loan for the month of December charged by the bank but not recorded on the books amounted to $3,070.

9. Deposit in transit:

12/31/80 $16,055

Instructions

Prepare bank reconciliations as of November 30, 1980, and December 31, 1980, using a four-column "proof of cash" with the following column headings for amounts:

11/30/80 Beginning Reconciliation	Receipts	Disbursements	12/31/80 Ending Reconciliation

Proceed from "balance per bank statement" to "balance per books."

*P7-17 Using the data given in Problem 7-16, prepare (a) a four-column bank reconciliation proceeding from "balance per bank statement" to "corrected balance" and "balance per books" to "corrected balance," and (b) accompanying entries to adjust the books.

P7-18 During the year your client, Maxi Bus Company, sold a used bus for $75,000. The purchaser agreed to pay for this bus at the end of three years and gave the bus company a three-year 5% note. When discussing this transaction with the controller, he informed you that the net book value and current cash sales price of the bus was $59,500. The controller's comments are substantiated by a review of published market prices for used buses. You also note that the stated interest rate is well below the prevailing market rate.

Instructions

(a) Does *APB Opinion No. 21* apply to this transaction? If so, why?

(b) What is the present value of the note and the total interest to be received on the transaction?

(c) What is the total effective interest rate on this transaction?

(d) What gain, if any, should be reported by Maxi Bus Company?

Valuation of Inventories: A Cost Basis Approach

Appropriate description and measurement of inventory demand careful attention because inventories are one of the most significant assets of many enterprises. The sale of inventory at a price greater than total cost is the primary source of income for manufacturing and retail business enterprises. Matching inventory cost against revenue is necessary for the proper determination of net income. Inventories are particularly significant because they may materially affect both the income statement and the balance sheet.

Inventories are asset items held for sale in the ordinary course of business or goods that will be used or consumed in the production of goods to be sold. Assets specifically excluded from inventory because they are not normally sold in the course of business include such items as plant and equipment awaiting final disposition and securities being held for sale. The accounting problems associated with inventory valuation are complex; Chapters 8 and 9 discuss the basic issues involved in recording, valuing, and reporting inventoriable items.

Major Classifications of Inventory

Inventories commonly are considered in the context of trading concerns. A **trading concern** ordinarily purchases its merchandise in a form ready for sale to customers and reports the cost assigned to unsold units left on hand at the end of the period as merchandise inventory. Only one inventory account, Merchandise Inventory, appears in the financial statements of a trading concern. Many large businesses however, are manufacturing concerns whose function is to produce goods to be sold to the merchandising firms (either wholesale or retail). A **manufacturing firm** normally has three inventory accounts—raw materials, work in process, and finished goods. The cost assigned to goods and materials on hand but not yet placed into production is reported as **raw materials inventory.** Raw materials include items such as the wood to make a baseball bat or the steel to make a car. These materials ultimately can be traced directly to the end product. At any point in time in a continuous production process some units generally are not completely processed. The cost of the raw material on which production has been started but not completed, plus the cost of direct labor applied specifically to this material and a ratable share of manufacturing overhead costs, constitute the **work in process inventory.** The costs identified with the completed but unsold units on hand at the end of the fiscal period are reported as **finished goods inventory.**

It is, therefore, common to see three inventory accounts on the balance sheet of a manufacturer: (1) raw materials, (2) work in process, and (3) finished goods. A manufacturing or factory supplies inventory account might also be included. This account includes items like machine oils, nails, cleaning materials, and the like that are used in production but are not the primary materials being processed. An annual report of Scott Paper Company illustrates the reporting of these accounts.

Scott Paper Company	
Current assets	(Thousands of dollars)
Inventories	
Finished products	$401,966
Work in process	15,231
Pulp, logs, and pulpwood	22,412
Other materials and supplies	29,836

Management Interest in Accounting for Inventories

From the standpoint of management, inventories constitute an extremely important asset. The investment in inventories is frequently the largest current asset in manufacturing and retail establishments, and also may be a material portion of the company's total assets. If unsaleable items have accumulated in the inventory, a potential loss exists. If products ordered by customers are not available in the desired style, quality, and quantity, sales and customers may be lost. An inefficient purchasing procedure, faulty manufacturing techniques, or inadequate sales efforts all result in excessive and unsaleable inventories.

In many respects inventories are more sensitive to general business fluctuations than are other assets. In periods of prosperity when sales are high, merchandise can be disposed of readily, and quantities on hand may not appear excessive. But with even a slight downward trend in the business cycle, many lines of merchandise begin to move slowly, stocks pile up, and obsolescence becomes a real possibility.

For these and other reasons, management (and therefore the accounting department) is vitally interested in inventory planning and control. One essential of inventory control is an accounting system with accurate, up-to-date records, containing the information needed by management to implement its manufacturing, merchandising, and financial policies. This degree of control usually requires a perpetual inventory system.

Determining Inventory Quantities

As indicated in Chapter 3, inventory records may be maintained on a perpetual or periodic inventory system basis. In a **perpetual inventory system,** purchases and issues of goods are recorded directly in the inventory account as the purchases and issues occur. No Purchases account is used because the purchases are debited directly to the inventory account. A Cost of Goods Sold account is used to accumulate the issuances from inventory. The balance in the inventory account at the end of the year should represent the ending inventory amount. For example, in the case of a manufacturing enterprise, separate inventory accounts may be used for raw materials, work in process, and finished goods. This may be illustrated as follows and contrasted to the inventory account of a trading concern.

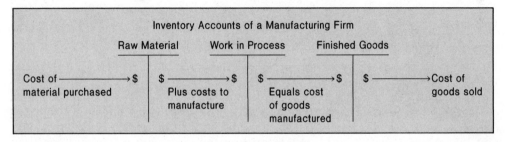

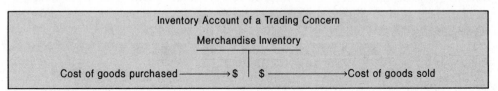

When the inventory records are maintained on a **periodic inventory system,** a Purchases account is used and the beginning inventory is unchanged during the period. At the end of the accounting period the inventory account must be adjusted by closing out the beginning inventory amount and recording the ending inventory amount. Cost of goods sold is therefore determined by adding the beginning inventory together with the net purchases and deducting the ending inventory. To illustrate the difference between a perpetual and a periodic system, assume that Katt, Inc. had the following transactions during the current year:

Sales	600 units at $12 = $7,200
Beginning inventory	100 units at $ 6 = $ 600
Purchases	900 units at $ 6 = $5,400
Ending inventory	400 units at $ 6 = $2,400

The entries to record these transactions during the current year are as follows:

ENTRIES UNDER PERPETUAL AND PERIODIC INVENTORY SYSTEMS

Perpetual Inventory System			*Periodic Inventory System*		
Purchase merchandise for resale:					
Inventory (900 at $6)	5,400		Purchases (900 at $6)	5,400	
Accounts Payable		5,400	Accounts Payable		5,400
Record sale:					
Accounts Receivable	7,200		Accounts Receivable	7,200	
Sales (600 at $12)		7,200	Sales (600 at $12)		7,200
Cost of Goods Sold					
(600 at $6)	3,600				
Inventory		3,600	(no entry necessary)		
Closing entries:					
None required			Cost of Goods Sold	600	
			Inventory (beginning)		600
			Inventory (ending)	2,400	
			Cost of Goods Sold		2,400
			Cost of Goods Sold	5,400	
			Purchases		5,400

Only a couple of decades ago few companies had maintained inventory records in both quantities and dollars. However, with the advent of computers and other electronic data processing equipment, many businesses today maintain perpetual inventories that report more than the quantities and dollars. The additional data might consist of such items as catalogue or reference number, supplier, location, and reorder points. Perpetual inventory systems are used extensively whenever high cost items are involved such as automobiles and appliances. Conversely, enterprises that sell a large variety of low-cost items such as hardware and drug stores rely heavily on the periodic inventory system.

When a periodic system is employed, how is the ending inventory computed? One method is to take a physical inventory count once a year. However, most companies need more current information on the quantities of their inventory items to protect against stockouts, overpurchasing, and to aid in the preparation of monthly or quarterly financial data. As a consequence, many companies use a **modified perpetual inventory system** in which increases and decreases in quantities are kept in a detailed inventory record. The detailed inventory record does not include dollar amounts and is therefore merely an informational memorandum device outside the double entry system which helps in determining the level of inventory at any point in time.

Whether a company maintains a perpetual inventory in quantities and dollars, quantities only, or has no perpetual inventory record at all, it probably takes a physical inventory once a year. No matter what type of inventory records are in use or how well organized the procedures for recording purchases and requisitions, the danger of error is always present. Waste, breakage, theft, improper entry, failure to prepare or record requisitions, and any number of similar possibilities may cause the inventory records to differ from the actual inventory on hand. This requires periodic verification of the inventory records by actual count, weight, or measurement of the inventory items. These counts are compared with the detail inventory records and the records corrected to agree with the quantities actually on hand.

As indicated above, most companies take a **physical inventory count** only once a year.[1] More frequent counts are desirable in businesses that deal in extremely costly merchandise, but in general an annual physical inventory is sufficient to assure reasonable accuracy of the records. Insofar as possible, the physical inventory should be taken close to the end of the concern's fiscal year so that correct inventory quantities are available for use in preparing annual accounting reports and statements. Because this is not always possible, however, physical inventories taken within two or three months of the year's end are quite satisfactory, if the detail inventory records are maintained with a fair degree of accuracy.

BASIC ISSUES IN INVENTORY VALUATION

Because the goods sold or used during an accounting period seldom correspond exactly to the goods bought or produced during that period, the physical inventory either increases or decreases. Accounting for these increases or decreases requires that the cost of all the goods available for sale or use be allocated between the goods that were sold or used and those that are still on hand. The **cost of goods available for sale or use** is the sum of (1) the cost of the goods on hand at the beginning of the period and (2) the cost of the goods acquired or produced during the period. The cost of goods sold is the difference between the cost of goods available for sale during the period and the cost of goods on hand at the end of the period.

Beginning inventory, Jan. 1	$100,000
Cost of goods acquired or produced during the year	800,000
Total cost of goods available for sale	900,000
Ending inventory, Dec. 31	200,000
Cost of goods sold during the year	$700,000

Inventory accounting involves the proper determination of each of the items listed above, but the focus is generally on the valuation of the ending inventory.

The valuation of inventories can be a complex process that requires determination of:

1. the physical goods or items to be included in inventory,
2. the costs to be included in inventory, and
3. the cost flow assumption to be adopted.

[1]In recent years, some companies have developed inventory controls or methods of determining inventories, including statistical sampling, that are highly effective in determining inventory quantities and sufficiently reliable to make unnecessary an annual physical count of each item of inventory. See *Statement on Auditing Procedure No. 43,* "Confirmation of Receivables and Observation of Inventories" (New York: AICPA, 1970).

GOODS OR ITEMS TO BE INCLUDED IN INVENTORY

Goods in Transit

Technically, purchases should be recorded when legal title to the goods passes to the buyer. General practice, however, is to record acquisitions when the goods are received, because it is difficult for the buyer to determine the exact time of legal passage of title for every purchase and because no material error is likely to result from such a practice if it is consistently applied.

Even though the legal rule is not followed in day-to-day transactions, purchased merchandise in transit at the end of a fiscal period, to which legal title has passed, should be recorded as purchases of the fiscal period. This means that ordinarily all goods shipped f.o.b. (free on board) shipping point that are in transit at the end of the period belong to the buyer and should be shown in the buyer's records, because legal title to these goods passed to the buyer when the goods were shipped. To disregard such purchases would result in an understatement of inventories and accounts payable in the balance sheet and an understatement of purchases and ending inventories in the income statement.

The accountant normally prepares a purchase cut-off schedule or worksheet at the end of the period and analyzes the transactions near the end of the year to ensure that the purchases and inventories are recorded in the proper period. Preparation of a purchase cut-off requires application of the "passage of title" rule in the following manner: if the goods are shipped **f.o.b. shipping point,** title passes to the buyer when the seller delivers the goods to the common carrier who acts as an agent for the buyer; if the goods are shipped **f.o.b. destination,** title does not pass until the buyer receives the goods from the common carrier. "Shipping point" and "destination" are designated by a particular location, for example, f.o.b. Denver. When the terms are f.o.b. shipping point, the transportation cost ultimately must be borne by the buyer, and such liability arises when the common carrier completes the delivery. When the terms are f.o.b. destination, the transportation cost is the expense of the seller. It should also be noted that goods produced on special order are ordinarily considered sold as soon as segregated from the regular inventory. In such a case, title is considered to have passed, even though delivery has not taken place.

In cases where there is some question as to whether title has passed, the accountant should exercise judgment, taking into consideration the practices common to the industry, the intent of the sales agreement, the policies of the parties involved, and any other available evidence of intent.

Consigned Goods

A specialized method of marketing certain types of products makes use of a device known as a consignment shipment. Under this arrangement, one party, the consignor, ships merchandise to another, the consignee, who is to act as an agent for the consignor in selling the goods. The consignee agrees to accept the goods without any liability, except to exercise due care and reasonable protection from loss or damage, until the goods are sold to a third party. When the goods are sold by the consignee, the sale price less a selling commission and expenses incurred in accomplishing the sale is remitted to the consignor.

Goods out on consignment remain the property of the consignor and must be included in the consignor's inventory at purchase price or production cost plus the cost of handling and shipping involved in the transfer to the consignee. Occasionally, the inventory out on consignment is shown as a separate item, but unless the amount is large there is little need for this. No ledger entry is made by the consignee for goods received because they are the property of the consignor. The consignee should be extremely careful not to include any of the goods consigned as a part of inventory. Accounting for consignments by both the consignor and the consignee is covered in detail in Chapter 19.

Special Sale Agreements

As indicated earlier, transfer of legal title is the general guideline that accountants follow in determining whether an item should be included in inventory. Unfortunately, transfer of legal title and the underlying economies of the situation often do not match, and therefore considerable professional judgment must be exercised. For example, it is possible that legal title has passed to the purchaser but that the economic substance of the transaction is such that the seller of the good still retains the risks of ownership. Conversely, transfer of legal title may not occur, but the economic substance of the transaction is that the seller no longer retains the risks of ownership. Three special sale situations are illustrated here to indicate the types of problems encountered in practice. These are as follows:

1. Product financing arrangements
2. Sales with high rates of return
3. Installment sales

Product Financing Arrangements   A variety of approaches are used in practice whereby an enterprise finances its inventory without reporting on its balance sheet the liability or the inventory. To illustrate, Hill Enterprises transfers ("sells") inventory to Chase, Inc. and as part of the same transaction agrees to repurchase this merchandise at a specified price over a specified period in the future. Chase, Inc. then uses the inventory as collateral and borrows against the value of the product from a bank and remits the proceeds to Hill Enterprises as "payment" for the inventory. Hill Enterprises then repurchases the inventory in the future and Chase, Inc. employs the proceeds from repayment to meet its loan obligation.

The essence of this transaction is that Hill Enterprises is financing its inventory even though technical legal title to the merchandise was transferred to Chase, Inc. The advantage to Hill Enterprises for structuring a transaction in this manner is the avoidance of personal property taxes in certain states, the removal of the current liability from its balance sheet, and the ability to manipulate income. The advantages to Chase, Inc. are that the purchase of the goods may solve a LIFO liquidation problem (discussed later), or that it may be interested in a reciprocal agreement at a later date.

Legal title has transferred in this situation, but the economic substance of the transaction is that the risks of ownership are retained by Hill Enterprises (seller).

These transactions are often described as **"parking transactions"** in practice, because the seller simply parks the inventory on another enterprise's balance sheet for a short period of time. The profession has taken steps to curtail this practice by requiring that when a repurchase agreement exists at a set price and this price covers all costs of the inventory plus related holding costs, the inventory and related liability remain on the seller's books.[2]

Sales with High Rates of Return   Formal or informal agreements often exist in such industries as publishing, records and tapes, and toys and sporting goods that permit goods to be returned for a full refund or that allow for an adjustment to be made to the amount owed. To illustrate, MEM Publishing Company sells textbooks to University Bookstores with an agreement that any books not sold may be returned for full credit. In the past, approximately 25% of the textbooks sold to University Bookstores were returned. How should MEM Publishing report its sales transactions? One alternative is to record the sale at the full amount and establish an estimated sales returns and allowances account. A second possibility is to not record any sale until circumstances indicate that the buyer will not return the inventory. The key question is: Under what circumstances should the inventory be considered sold and removed from MEM's inventory? According to AcSEC, if a reasonable prediction of the returns can be established, then the goods should be considered sold. Conversely, if returns are unpredictable, then removal of these goods from inventory does not appear warranted.[3]

Installment Sales   "Goods sold on installment" describes any type of sale in which payment is required in periodic installments over an extended period of time. Because the risk of loss from uncollectibles is higher in installment sale situations than in other sale transactions, the seller often asks for protection in the form of a conditional sales contract that withholds legal title to the merchandise until all the payments have been made. The question is whether the inventory should be considered sold, even though legal title has not passed. The economic substance of the transaction is that the goods should be excluded from the seller's inventory if the percentage of bad debts can be reasonably estimated. Chapter 19 covers in detail the accounting for installment sales. Installment sales are discussed here to show that in some cases legal title may not have passed, but the goods should be removed from inventory.

Effect of Inventory Errors

If items are incorrectly included or excluded for inventory purposes, there will be errors in the financial statements. To illustrate, suppose that certain goods in transit that we owned were not recorded either as a purchase or counted in ending inven-

---

[2]"Accounting for Product Financing Arrangements," *AcSEC Statement of Position 78–8* (New York: AICPA, 1978), par. 4.

[3]"Revenue Recognition When Right of Return Exists," *AcSEC Statement of Position 75–1* (New York: AICPA, 1975), par. 11.

tory. To disregard such purchases would result in an understatement of inventories and accounts payable in the balance sheet and an understatement of purchases and ending inventories in the income statement. The net income for the period would not be affected by the omission of such purchases, since purchases and ending inventory would both be understated by the same amount, the error thereby offsetting itself in cost of goods sold. Total working capital would be unchanged, but the **current ratio** would be higher because of the omission of equal amounts from inventory and accounts payable.

To illustrate the effect on working capital items, Barker, Inc. reports the following at the end of a fiscal period:

Current assets		$120,000
Current liabilities		40,000
Current ratio	$\left(\dfrac{\$120,000}{\$\ 40,000}\right)$	3 to 1

If Barker, Inc. should have included goods in transit of $40,000 in ending inventory, then the following would be presented:

Current assets		$160,000
Current liabilities		80,000
Current ratio	$\left(\dfrac{\$160,000}{\$\ 80,000}\right)$	2 to 1

The correct current ratio is 2 to 1 instead of 3 to 1 because the goods in transit should be reported in both the inventory and accounts payable.

What would happen if the beginning inventory and the goods purchased are recorded correctly, but some items on hand are not included in ending inventory? In this situation, ending inventory, net income, current ratio, and working capital are all understated. Net income is understated because cost of goods sold is larger than it should be; the current ratio and working capital are understated because a portion of ending inventory is omitted.

To illustrate the effect on net income, assume that the ending inventory of Antonio, Inc. is understated by $10,000 and that all other items are correctly stated. The effect of this error will be to decrease net income in the current year and to increase net income in the following year. The error will be offset in the next period because the beginning inventory will be understated and net income will be overstated. In other words, both net income figures are misstated, but the total for the two years is correct as illustrated at the top of page 338.

If a purchase is not recorded, but is included in ending inventory, the reverse effect occurs. Net income, the current ratio, and working capital are all overstated. The effect of the error on net income will be offset in the subsequent year (assuming purchases are recorded in the next year), but both years' financial statements will be misstated. These illustrations indicate that an accurate computation of purchases and inventory is needed to assure that proper income and asset figures are presented.

Antonio, Inc.
Effect of Inventory Error on Two Periods
(All figures assumed)

	1980 Correct	1980 Incorrect	1981 Incorrect	1981 Correct
Revenues	$100,000	$100,000	$100,000	$100,000
Cost of goods sold				
Beginning inventory	25,000	25,000	20,000	30,000
Purchased or produced	45,000	45,000	60,000	60,000
Goods available for sale	70,000	70,000	80,000	90,000
Less ending inventory	30,000	20,000	40,000	40,000
Cost of goods sold	40,000	50,000	40,000	50,000
Gross profit	60,000	50,000	60,000	50,000
Administrative and selling expenses	40,000	40,000	40,000	40,000
Net income	$ 20,000	$ 10,000	$ 20,000	$ 10,000

total income for two
years correct

COSTS TO BE INCLUDED IN INVENTORY

One of the most important problems in dealing with inventories concerns the amount at which the inventory should be carried in the accounts and stated in the accounting reports. Inventories, like other assets, are generally accounted for on a basis of cost (other bases are discussed in Chapter 9). In defining cost as it applies to inventories, it becomes necessary to define inventoriable costs (product costs), that is, those costs that are said to attach to the inventory and are considered to be a part of the total inventory valuation. Charges directly connected with the bringing of goods to the place of business of the buyer and converting such goods to a saleable condition are accepted as proper inventoriable costs. Such charges would include freight and hauling charges on goods purchased, other direct costs of acquisition, and labor and other production costs incurred in processing the goods up to the time of sale.

It would seem proper also to allocate to inventories a share of any buying costs or expenses of a purchasing department, storage costs, and other costs incurred in storing or handling the goods before they are sold. Because of the practical difficulties involved in allocating such costs and expenses, however, these items are not ordinarily included in valuing inventories.

Period Expenses

Selling expense and, under ordinary circumstances, **general and administration expenses** are not considered to be directly related to the acquisition or production of goods and, therefore, are not considered to be a part of the inventories. Such costs are period costs rather than product costs. Conceptually, these expenses are as much a cost of the product as the initial purchase price and related freight charges attached to the product. Why then are these costs not considered inventoriable items?

In some industries these charges are not material and no real purpose is served by making an allocation of these costs to inventory. In other cases, especially where selling expenses are significant, the cost is more directly related to the cost of goods sold than to the unsold inventory. In most cases the costs, especially administrative expenses, are so unrelated or indirectly related to the immediate production process that any allocation is purely arbitrary. One guideline that may be followed is to charge to inventory those costs that bear a fairly direct relationship to the quantity produced. If, for example, an increase in administrative expenses occurs, without a subsequent increase in inventories, some justification exists for treating the cost as a period charge on the basis that the inventory quantities were not affected.

Interest costs associated with getting inventories ready for sale usually are expensed as incurred. A major argument for this approach is that interest costs are a cost of financing and should not be considered a cost of the asset. Others have argued, however, that interest costs incurred to finance activities associated with bringing inventories to a condition ready for sale are as much a cost of the asset as materials, labor, and overhead and, therefore, should be capitalized.[4] Recently the FASB indicated that interest cost related to assets constructed for its own use or assets produced as discrete projects (such as ships or real estate projects) for sale or lease should be capitalized.[5] It is emphasized that these discrete projects should take considerable time, entail substantial expenditures, and be likely to involve significant amounts of interest cost. Interest costs should not be capitalized for inventories that are routinely manufactured or otherwise produced in large quantities on a repetitive basis because the informational benefit does not justify the cost of doing so. The interest cost eligible for capitalization is based on the rates on the enterprise's outstanding borrowings or the rate on a specific related new borrowing.

Treatment of Purchase Discounts

In accordance with practice, purchase discounts have been treated in the accounts either as a financial income or as a reduction of purchases. From a theoretical standpoint, the arguments for a reduction of purchases are stronger than those usually presented in support of financial income. If discounts received for prompt payment of purchase invoices are shown as income, this may result in the taking up of income as realized even before the goods have been sold, at least to the extent that such purchases are still in the inventory at the end of the accounting period. It is generally held that a business does not realize income by buying goods and paying bills; it realizes income by selling them, the sale transaction being an essential step in income realization.

---

[4]The reporting rules related to interest cost capitalization have their greatest impact in accounting for long-term assets and, therefore, are discussed in detail in Chapter 11. This brief overview provides the basic issues when inventories are involved.

[5]"Capitalization of Interest Cost," *Statement of Financial Accounting Standards No. 34* (Stamford, Conn.: FASB, 1979).

The treatment of purchase discounts as financial income has been supported by the argument that it is similar to interest earned in that it represents a reduction allowed by the seller so that cash may be obtained promptly. This argument has little merit; it may be countered by the statement that the buyer is not in any sense loaning money to the seller; the buyer is merely paying a bill for purchases, and the amount paid is the cost of such purchases.

The use of a Purchase Discounts account indicates that the company is reporting its purchases and accounts payable at the gross amount. A more thorough approach is to record the purchases and accounts payable at an amount net of the cash discounts. This treatment is often considered more appropriate because the net amount (1) provides a correct reporting of the cost of the asset and related liability and (2) presents the opportunity to measure the inefficiency of financial management if the discount is not taken. In the net approach, the failure to take a purchase discount within the discount period is recorded in a Purchase Discounts Lost account. To illustrate the difference between the gross and net method, assume the following transactions:

ENTRIES UNDER GROSS AND NET METHODS			
Gross Method		*Net Method*	
Purchase cost $10,000, terms 2/10, net 30:			
Purchases	10,000	Purchases	9,800
Accounts Payable	10,000	Accounts Payable	9,800
Invoices of $4,000 are paid within discount period:			
Accounts Payable	4,000	Accounts Payable	3,920
Purchase Discounts	80	Cash	3,920
Cash	3,920		
Invoices of $6,000 are paid after discount period:			
Accounts Payable	6,000	Accounts Payable	5,880
Cash	6,000	Purchase Discounts Lost	120
		Cash	6,000

As indicated earlier, if the gross method is employed, purchase discounts should be reported as a deduction from purchases on the income statement. If the net method is used, purchase discounts lost should be considered a financial expense and reported in the other expense section of the income statement. In addition, when purchases are recorded net, beginning and ending inventories are reported on the same basis. Many believe that the difficulty involved in using the somewhat more complicated net method is not justified by the resulting benefits, which may account for the widespread use of the less logical but simpler gross method illustrated. In addition, some contend that management is reluctant to report the amount of purchase discounts lost in the financial statements.

Manufacturing Costs

As previously indicated, a business that manufactures goods, utilizes three inventory accounts—raw materials, work in process, and finished goods. Work in process and finished goods include raw materials, direct labor, and manufacturing overhead costs. Manufacturing overhead costs include all manufacturing costs except direct materials and direct labor. Items included in manufacturing overhead are indirect material, indirect labor, depreciation, taxes, insurance, heat, electricity, and so on. To illustrate how these different costs affect the inventory accounts, a **cost of goods manufactured statement** is presented below.

The cost of raw materials consumed section is presented in a format similar to that used for reporting cost of goods sold in the income statement. Cost of goods manufactured statements are prepared primarily for internal use; such details are rarely disclosed in published financial statements. The cost of goods sold section in the income statement for a manufacturing firm is similar to the cost of goods sold section for a trading concern. The principal difference is the substitution of cost of goods manufactured during the year for the details related to purchases of merchandise.

Leonard, Inc.
STATEMENT OF COST OF GOODS MANUFACTURED
Year Ended December 31, 1981

Raw materials consumed			
Raw materials inventory, Jan. 1, 1981			$ 14,000
Add net purchases:			
Purchases		$126,000	
Less: Purchase returns and allowances	$1,800		
Purchase discounts	1,200	3,000	123,000
Raw materials available for use		137,000	
Less raw materials inventory, Dec. 31, 1981		17,000	120,000
Direct labor			200,000
Manufacturing overhead			
Supervisors' salaries		52,000	
Indirect labor		20,000	
Factory supplies used		18,000	
Taxes		15,000	
Heat, light, power, and water		13,000	
Depreciation on building and equipment		12,000	
Factory rent		11,000	
Tools expense		2,000	
Patent expense		1,000	
Miscellaneous factory expenses		6,000	150,000
Total manufacturing costs for the period			470,000
Work in process inventory, Jan. 1, 1981			33,000
Total manufacturing costs			503,000
Less work in process inventory, Dec. 31, 1981			28,000
Cost of goods manufactured during the year			$475,000

If the inventory of finished goods was $16,000 at the beginning of the year and $10,000 at the end of the year, the cost of goods sold section of the income statement would appear as follows:

Cost of goods sold	
Finished goods inventory, Jan. 1, 1981	$ 16,000
Cost of goods manufactured during 1981	475,000
Cost of goods available for sale	491,000
Finished goods inventory, Dec. 31, 1981	10,000
Cost of goods sold	$481,000

The principles applied in classifying inventory amounts on the income statement and on the balance sheet are the same for a manufacturing firm as for a trading concern.

Variable Costing Versus Absorption Costing

Fixed manufacturing overhead costs present a special problem in costing inventories because two concepts exist relative to the costs that attach to the product as it flows through the manufacturing process. These two concepts are **variable costing,** frequently called **direct costing,** and **absorption costing,** also called **full costing.**

In a variable cost system all costs must be classified as variable or fixed. **Variable costs** are those that fluctuate in direct proportion to changes in output, and **fixed costs** are those that remain constant in spite of changes in output. Under variable costing only costs that vary directly with the volume of production are charged to products as manufacturing takes place. Only direct material, direct labor, and the variable costs in manufacturing overhead are charged to work in process and finished goods inventories and appear as cost of goods sold. Fixed overhead costs such as property taxes, insurance, depreciation on plant building, and salaries of supervisors are considered to be **period costs.** All fixed costs are charged as expenses to the current period under variable costing. Because the fixed costs are not viewed as costs of the products being manufactured, they are not associated with inventories.

Under **absorption costing,** all manufacturing costs, variable and fixed, direct and indirect, incurred in the factory or production process attach to the product and are included in the cost of inventory. Direct material, direct labor, and all manufacturing overhead—fixed as well as variable—are charged to output and inventories. The AICPA stated its position on inventory costing as follows:

> "As applied to inventories, cost means in principle the sum of the applicable expenditures and charges directly or indirectly incurred in bringing an article to its existing condition and location."[6]

It went on to say that "it should also be recognized that the exclusion of all overhead from inventory costs does not constitute an acceptable accounting procedure."

Proponents of the **variable costing** system believe that it provides data that are more useful to management in formulating pricing policies and in controlling costs than are data prepared under conventional absorption costing methods. Information for marginal income analysis, for fixed and variable expense analysis, and for

---

[6]*Accounting Research Bulletin No. 43*, "Restatement and Revision of Accounting Research Bulletins" (New York: AICPA, 1953), Ch. 4, par. 4.

cost-volume-profit analysis is readily available. Variable costing is not acceptable for income tax purposes or for use in published financial reports (external reporting) because it is claimed that it understates inventories as a reasonable representation of a firm's investment in this asset. In spite of this alleged deficiency, because variable costing is so useful to management in decision making, cost control, and budget preparation, it will continue to be widely used internally. Relatively simple adjustments at the end of each accounting period can be made to convert variable costed inventory and cost of goods sold to a basis acceptable for income tax and financial reporting purposes.

WHAT FLOW ASSUMPTION SHOULD BE ADOPTED?

During any given fiscal period it is very likely that merchandise will be purchased at several different prices. If inventories are to be priced at cost and numerous purchases have been made at different unit costs, the question arises as to which of the various cost prices should be used. In other words, out of many units purchased, which goods remain on hand, and which have been sold? Naturally, a specific identification of the given items sold and unsold seems optimal, but this measure is often not only difficult but impossible to achieve. Consequently, for practical reasons and in the interests of objective financial reporting, the accountant must turn to the consistent application of one of several cost selection methods that are based on differing but systematic inventory flow assumptions. Therefore, the actual physical flow of goods and the cost flow assumption are often quite different. There is no requirement that the cost flow assumption adopted be consistent with the physical movement of goods.

Specific Identification

Specific identification calls for identifying each item sold and each item in inventory. The costs of the specific items sold are included in the cost of goods sold, while the costs of the specific items on hand are included in the inventory. This method may be used only in instances where it is practical to separate physically the different purchases made. Any goods on hand may then be identified as quantities remaining from specific purchases, and the invoice cost of each lot or item may be separately determined. Obviously this method has a very limited application because of the impossibility or impracticability of segregating separate purchases in most instances. It can be successfully applied, however, in situations where a relatively small number of costly, easily distinguishable items are handled. In the retail trade this includes some types of jewelry, fur coats, automobiles, and some furniture. In manufacturing it includes special orders and many products manufactured under a job cost system.

At first glance this method seems to be ideal. On closer observation, however, deficiencies can be found in using this method as a basis for inventory valuation and income measurement. One argument against specific identification is that it makes it possible to manipulate net income. For example, assume that a wholesaler purchases plywood early in the year at three different prices. When the plywood is sold, the wholesaler can, if desired, select either the lowest or the highest price to charge against income simply by selecting the plywood from a specific lot for delivery to the customer. A business manager is, therefore, afforded the opportunity to manipulate net income simply by delivering to the customer the higher- or lower-priced item, depending on whether higher or lower reported earnings are desired for the period.

Another problem relates to the arbitrary allocation of costs that sometimes occurs with specific inventory items. In certain circumstances, it is difficult to relate adequately, for example, shipping charges, storage costs, and discounts directly to a given inventory item. The alternative, then, is to allocate these costs somewhat arbitrarily, which leads to a "breakdown" in the preciseness of the specific identification method.

First-In, First-Out (FIFO)

Under the **FIFO** method, costs are allocated between inventory on hand and goods sold, on the assumption that goods are used in the order in which they are purchased; in other words, the first goods purchased are the first used (in a manufacturing concern) or sold (in a trading concern). The inventory remaining must therefore represent the most recent purchases. An example of this method is shown below, assuming that a perpetual inventory record is kept in units only, and that the amount of the inventory is calculated only at the end of the month (periodic method).

	Perpetual Inventory—Units Only		
Date	Purchases	Sold or Issued	Balance
Mar. 2	(2,000 @ $4.00)		2,000 units
Mar. 15	(6,000 @ 4.40)		8,000 units
Mar. 19		4,000 units	4,000 units
Mar. 30	(2,000 @ 4.15)		6,000 units

The cost of the inventory on hand on March 31 is computed in the following manner, beginning with the most recent purchase and working back until all units in the inventory are accounted for.

	Periodic Inventory—FIFO Method		
Date on Invoice	No. Units	Unit Cost	Total Cost
Mar. 30	2,000	$4.15	$ 8,300
Mar. 15	4,000	4.40	17,600
	6,000		$25,900

If a perpetual inventory record is kept in amounts as well as quantities, a cost figure is attached to each withdrawal. Then the cost of the 4,000 units removed on March 19 would be made up of the items purchased on March 2 and March 15.

Perpetual Inventory—FIFO Method			
Date	Purchased	Sold or Issued	Balance
Mar. 2	(2,000 @ $4.00) $ 8,000		2,000 @ $4.00 $ 8,000
Mar. 15	(6,000 @ 4.40) 26,400		2,000 @ 4.00 ⎱ 6,000 @ 4.40 ⎰ 34,400
Mar. 19		2,000 @ $4.00 ⎱ 2,000 @ 4.40 ⎰	4,000 @ 4.40 17,600
Mar. 30	(2,000 @ 4.15) 8,300		4,000 @ 4.40 ⎱ 2,000 @ 4.15 ⎰ 25,900

In all cases when FIFO is used, the inventory at the end of the month would be shown at the same amount in the perpetual inventory record as if computed on a periodic basis.

One objective of FIFO is to follow an approximation of the physical flow of goods. When the physical flow of goods is actually first-in, first-out, the FIFO method very nearly represents specific identification. At the same time, it does not permit manipulation of income because the enterprise is not free to pick a certain cost item to be charged against revenue.

A major advantage of the FIFO method is that the ending inventory is stated in terms of an approximate current cost figure. Because the first goods in are the first goods out, the ending inventory amount will be composed of the most recent purchases. This is particularly true where the inventory turnover is rapid. This approach generally provides a fairly close approximation of replacement cost, although this is true only where price changes have not occurred since the most recent purchases.

The basic disadvantage of this method is that current costs are not matched against current revenues. The oldest costs are charged against the more current revenue, which can lead to distortions in the operating data.

Last-In, First-Out (LIFO)

The **LIFO** method allocates costs on the assumption that the last goods purchased are used first. If the amount of the inventory is computed at the end of the month and perpetual inventory records are not kept, then it would be assumed that the total quantity sold or issued during the month would have come from the most recent purchases, and ordinarily no attempt would be made to compare the dates

Perpetual Inventory—Units Only			
Date	Purchased	Sold or Issued	Balance
Mar. 2	(2,000 @ $4.00)		2,000 units
Mar. 15	(6,000 @ 4.40)		8,000 units
Mar. 19		4,000 units	4,000 units
Mar. 30	(2,000 @ 4.15)		6,000 units
Total	10,000 units	4,000 units	

of purchases and sales. The purchases and sales are assumed to be as shown at the bottom of page 345.

When the periodic inventory method is used, the ending inventory would be priced by using the total units as a basis of computation and disregarding the exact dates involved. The assumption would be made that the 4,000 units withdrawn absorbed the 2,000 units purchased on March 30 and 2,000 of the 6,000 units purchased on March 15. The inventory would then be computed at the end of the period as follows:

	Periodic Inventory—LIFO Method		
Date of Invoice	No. Units	Unit Cost	Total Cost
Mar. 2	2,000	$4.00	$ 8,000
Mar. 15	4,000	4.40	17,600
	6,000		$25,600

If a perpetual inventory record is kept in dollars, and costs are computed at the time of each withdrawal, application of the last-in, first-out method will result in an ending inventory of a different amount as shown below.

	Perpetual Inventory—LIFO Method				
Date	Purchased		Sold or Issued	Balance	
Mar. 2	(2,000 @ $4.00)	$ 8,000		2,000 @ $4.00	$ 8,000
Mar. 15	(6,000 @ 4.40)	26,400		2,000 @ 4.00 ⎫ 6,000 @ 4.40 ⎭	34,400
Mar. 19			(4,000 @ $4.40) $17,600	2,000 @ 4.00 ⎫ 2,000 @ 4.40 ⎭	16,800
Mar. 30	(2,000 @ 4.15)	8,300		2,000 @ 4.00 ⎫ 2,000 @ 4.40 ⎬ 2,000 @ 4.15 ⎭	25,100

The month-end computation illustrated first shows a different amount from the perpetual inventory computation immediately above because the former matches the total withdrawals for the month with the total purchases for the month in applying the last-in, first-out method, but the latter matches each withdrawal with the immediately preceding purchases. In effect, the first computation assumed that goods that were not purchased until March 30 were included in the sale or issue of March 19.

An adaptation of the LIFO principle and the weighted-average method is the **unit LIFO method,** which eliminates the need for identifying specific unit costs. When a large number of purchase and issue transactions are coupled with a large number of inventory items, this inventory costing method greatly reduces record keeping and the number of computations. Under this method the weighted-average unit cost of the items purchased during the period is used to cost any additions to the inventory for the period. Using the purchase information previously presented, the LIFO inventory at the end of March would be computed as follows:

Unit LIFO Method		
Beginning Inventory not included		
Number of units purchased in March	10,000	
Cost of March purchases	$42,700	
Weighted-average unit price ($42,700 ÷ 10,000)	$4.27	
LIFO cost of ending inventory		
Beginning inventory, Mar. 1,	0 units	$ 0
Increase in March	6,000 units @ $4.27	25,620
Total	6,000	$25,620

Increases in inventory quantities from period to period form successive **"inventory layers."** When the inventory is decreased, the most recently added inventory layer is the first layer eliminated, given the LIFO assumption. If the ending inventory is never lower than the quantity on hand at the beginning of the period, the original unit cost prices remain intact in inventory. For example, in the illustration above if a beginning inventory cost had existed on March 1, the $25,620 increase would have constituted a layer added to the beginning inventory and would be the layer first reduced if a decrease in the number of units on hand took place in the next period. Where there is a net liquidation of inventory, as between the beginning and end of the year, the original cost is lost. That is, if a layer has been eliminated, it cannot be rebuilt in future periods.

Dollar-Value LIFO

The application of the LIFO method as described in the preceding sections, except for the "unit LIFO" procedure, requires a considerable amount of detailed clerical work. It is necessary to keep complete records for each item in the inventory of physical quantities and unit costs at the beginning of each period, and of physical quantities and unit costs of each purchase. The value of each item at the end of the period must be calculated separately, a time-consuming and expensive procedure. Use of this method is therefore confined to industries having a very few basic products.

In addition, the traditional LIFO approach has the following potential weakness. In many business enterprises some inventory items are significantly reduced in quantity while other similar inventory items are increased. Under the traditional LIFO method, the reduction in quantity of one item results in the partial liquidation of its LIFO base and its replacement with current cost, but ignores the effect of an unusually large increase in the quantity of a similar item. Over a long period of time this procedure could effectively replace the LIFO base inventory with current costs and negate the benefit of LIFO. To illustrate, suppose that a business had a significant amount of cotton fabric in its inventory. As synthetic fabrics (dacron, nylon, etc.) begin to replace cotton in the inventory, they cannot be used to preserve the LIFO base. Because these items are not considered identical to cotton, the business will lose much of its LIFO costing benefits.

To overcome this problem, the **dollar-value LIFO** method has been developed. The dollar-value method ordinarily overcomes the fact that substantial changes in the mix of specific goods in the inventory pool have taken place. A broader range of goods may be included in a dollar-value LIFO pool than in the traditional LIFO pool. In the latter case, pooled items must be substantially **identical,** whereas under the dollar-value method the pools must be **similar** as to types of material, similarity in use, or interchangeability.

Under the dollar-value LIFO method, it is possible to have the entire inventory in only one pool, although generally there are several. Once the pools have been defined, the objective of the dollar-value LIFO method is to determine the real change in the number of units on hand and to price these units at the appropriate price. Because the original inventory is the base from which changes take place, each period's ending inventory must be stated in terms of prices of the base year.

Basic Illustration

To determine the real change in the number of units on hand, changes in the price of the inventory must be considered. For example, assume that dollar-value LIFO was first adopted (base period) on December 31, 1979, that the inventory at current prices on that date was $20,000, and that the inventory on December 31, 1980 at current prices is $26,400. We should not conclude that the quantity has increased 32% during the year ($26,400 ÷ $20,000 = 132%). First, we need to ask: What is the value of the ending inventory in terms of beginning of the year prices? Assuming that prices have increased 20% during the year, the ending inventory at beginning of the year prices amounts to $22,000 ($26,400 ÷ 120%). Therefore, the inventory quantity has increased 10%, or from $20,000 to $22,000 in terms of beginning of the year prices.

The next step then is to price this real dollar quantity increase. The dollar quantity increase in quantity of $2,000 valued at year-end prices is $2,400 (120% × 2,000). This increment (layer) of $2,400, when added to the beginning inventory of $20,000, gives a total of $22,400 for the December 31, 1980 inventory, as shown below:

First layer—(beginning inventory) in terms of 100	$20,000
Second layer—(1980 increase) in terms of 120	2,400
Dollar-value LIFO inventory, December 31, 1980	$22,400

It should be emphasized that a layer is formed only when the ending inventory at base-year prices exceeds the beginning inventory at base-year prices.

Complex Illustration

To illustrate the use of the dollar-value LIFO system in a more complex situation, assume that Boston Company develops the following information:

	Dec. 31	Inventory at End-of-Year Prices	÷	Price Index (percentage)	=	End-of-Year Inventory at Base-Year Prices
(Base year)	1977	$200,000		100		$200,000
	1978	299,000		115		260,000
	1979	300,000		120		250,000
	1980	351,000		130		270,000

At December 31, 1977, the ending inventory under dollar-value LIFO is simply the $200,000 computed as follows:

Computation of 1977 Inventory

Ending Inventory at Base-Year Prices	Layer at Base-Year Prices		Price Index (percentage)		Ending Inventory at LIFO Cost
$200,000	$200,000	×	100	=	$200,000

At December 31, 1978, a comparison of the ending inventory at base-year prices ($260,000) with the beginning inventory at base-year prices ($200,000), indicates that the quantity of goods has increased $60,000 ($260,000 − $200,000). This increment (layer) is then priced at 115 to arrive at a new layer of $69,000. Ending inventory for 1978 is $269,000, comprised of the beginning inventory of $200,000 and the new layer of $69,000. The following schedule illustrates these computations:

Computation of 1978 Inventory

Ending Inventory at Base-Year Prices	Layers at Base-Year Prices		Price Index (percentage)		Ending Inventory at LIFO Cost
$260,000	$200,000	×	100		$200,000
	$ 60,000	×	115		69,000
					$269,000

At December 31, 1979, a comparison of the ending inventory at base-year prices ($250,000) with the beginning inventory at base-year prices ($260,000) indicates that the quantity of goods has decreased $10,000 ($250,000 − $260,000). If the ending inventory at base-year prices is less than the beginning inventory at base-year prices, the decrease must be subtracted from the most recently added layer. When a decrease occurs, previous layers must be "peeled off" at the prices in existence when the layers were added. In Boston Company's situation, this means that $10,000 in base year price must be removed from the 1978 layer of $60,000 at base year prices. The balance of $50,000 ($60,000 − $10,000) at base-year prices must be valued at the 1978 price index of 115 so that this 1978 layer now is valued at $57,500 ($50,000 × 115). The ending inventory is therefore computed at $257,500, comprised of the beginning inventory of $200,000 and the second layer, $57,500. The computations are illustrated on page 350.

Computation of 1979 Inventory			
Ending Inventory at Base-Year Price	Layers at Base-Year Prices	Price Index (percentage)	Ending Inventory at LIFO Cost
$250,000 →	$200,000 ×	100 =	$200,000
→	50,000 ×	115 =	57,500
			$257,500

It should be noted that if a layer or base (or portion thereof) has been eliminated, it cannot be rebuilt in future periods, that is, it is gone forever.

At December 31, 1980, a comparison of the ending inventory at base-year prices ($270,000) with the beginning inventory at base-year prices ($250,000) indicates that the dollar quantity of goods has increased $20,000 ($270,000 − $250,000). After converting the $20,000 increase to the 1980 price index, the ending inventory is $283,500, comprised of the beginning layer of $200,000, a 1978 layer of $57,500, and a 1980 layer of $26,000, ($20,000 × 130). This computation is shown below:

Computation of 1980 Inventory			
Ending Inventory at Base-Year Prices	Layers at Base-Year Prices	Price Index (percentage)	Ending Inventory at LIFO Cost
	→ $200,000 ×	100 =	$200,000
$270,000 →	$ 50,000 ×	115 =	57,500
	→ $ 20,000 ×	130 =	26,000
			$283,500

The ending inventory at base-year prices must always equal the total of the layers at base-year prices; checking that this situation exists will help to insure that the dollar value computation is made correctly.

Price Index

One question that has not been answered concerning dollar-value LIFO is: How are the price indexes determined? Although different methods of computation might be used, the general approach is to price the ending inventory at the most current cost. Current cost is ordinarily determined by referring to the actual cost of goods most recently purchased. The price index is then a measurement of the change of price or cost levels between the base year and the current year. An index is computed for each year after the base year. The general formula for computing the index is as follows:

$$\frac{\text{Ending Inventory for the Period at Current-Year Costs}}{\text{Ending Inventory for the Period at Base-Year Costs}} = \text{Price Index for Current Year}$$

Computation of the index becomes difficult where certain goods are only in one of the two inventory figures or where damaged or obsolete merchandise is involved. However, procedures are available to handle these difficulties such as computing the current index on the basis of sample prices at both current and base year costs or using existing indexes that are relevant to the inventories of the enterprise.[7]

In summary, dollar-value LIFO is a method employed by many companies that currently use a LIFO system. Although the approach appears complex, the logic and the computations are deceptively simple, once an appropriate index is determined. Basically the dollar-value method is a more practical way of valuing a complex, multiple-item inventory than the traditional LIFO method.

Evaluation of LIFO

In certain situations the LIFO cost flow may approximate the physical flow of the goods in and out of inventory. For instance, in the case of a coal pile, it can be shown that in some situations the last goods in are the first goods out because the coal remover is not going to take the coal from the bottom of the pile. The goods that are going to be taken first are the goods that were placed on the pile last.

Because the coal pile situation is one of only a few situations where the actual physical flow corresponds to LIFO, most adherents of LIFO use other arguments for its widespread employment, as follows:

Major Advantages of LIFO

Matching In LIFO, the more recent costs are matched against current revenues to provide a better measure of current earnings. With the present inflationary trend, which is expected to continue, many accountants have challenged the quality of non-LIFO earnings, noting that by failing to match current costs against current revenues, transitory or "paper" profits ("inventory profits") are created. Inventory profits occur when the inventory costs matched against sales are less than the replacement cost of the inventory. The cost of goods sold therefore is understated and profit is considered overstated. By using LIFO (rather than some method such as FIFO), current costs are matched against revenues and inventory profits are thereby reduced.

Tax Benefits Tax benefits are the major reason why LIFO has become popular. As long as the price level increases and inventory quantities do not decrease, a deferral of income taxes occurs, because the items most recently purchased at the higher price level are matched against revenues. For example, Fuqua Industries recently decided to switch to LIFO and had a resultant tax savings of $3 to $4 million dollars. Even if the price level later decreases, the company has been given a temporary deferral of its income taxes. It should be noted that if LIFO is used for tax purposes, it must also be used for financial reporting purposes.[8] Other inventory valuation methods do not have that requirement.

---

[7] A more thorough discussion of the development and use of price indexes and other problems related to LIFO are discussed in Appendix G of Chapter 9.

[8] Management often selects an accounting procedure because a lower tax results from its use; an accounting method that is conceptually more appealing therefore is ignored. Throughout this textbook, an effort has been made to identify accounting procedures that provide income tax benefits to the user.

Improved Cash Flow This advantage is related to the tax benefits, because taxes must be paid in cash. As a consequence, some companies are forced to borrow to finance replacement of existing inventory levels, and interest costs can be staggering. Fuqua Industries, for example, expected to save approximately $400,000 in interest costs by switching to LIFO. A side effect of this situation is that given a prolonged period of inflation, the cumulative effect of LIFO cash savings, when reinvested, could increase profit more than is attainable using FIFO inventory.

Future Earnings Hedge With LIFO, a company's future reported earnings will not be affected substantially by future price declines. LIFO eliminates or substantially minimizes write-downs to market as a result of price decreases because the inventory value ordinarily will be much lower than net realizable value, which is in sharp contrast to the FIFO method, which ordinarily has a higher inventory value than LIFO. Inventory costed under FIFO is more vulnerable to price declines, which can reduce net income substantially.

Major Disadvantages of LIFO

Reduced Earnings Many corporate managers view the lower profits reported under the LIFO method as a distinct disadvantage and would rather have higher reported profits than lower taxes. This view assumes that prices are increasing; in some industries where prices are declining, the opposite effect may occur. Some fear that an accounting change to LIFO may be misunderstood and that, as a result of the lower profits, the price of the company's stock will fall. It should be noted that there is some evidence to refute this contention, however, and, in fact, non-LIFO earnings are now highly suspect and may be severely penalized as a result.

Inventory Understated The inventory valuation on the balance sheet is normally outdated because the oldest costs remain in inventory. This understatement presents several problems, but manifests itself most directly in evaluating the working capital position of the company. The magnitude and direction of this variation in the carrying amount of inventory and its current price depend on the degree and direction of the changes in price and the amount of inventory turnover.

Physical Flow LIFO does not approximate the physical flow of the items except in peculiar situations. Originally LIFO could be used only in certain circumstances. This situation has changed over the years to the point where physical flow characteristics no longer play an important role in determining whether LIFO may be employed.

Current Cost Income Not Measured LIFO falls short of measuring current cost (replacement cost) income. In order to measure current cost income, as opposed to monetary income, the cost of goods sold should consist not of the most recently incurred costs but rather of the cost that will be incurred to replace the goods that have been sold. Using replacement cost is referred to as the next-in, first-out method, a method not currently acceptable for purposes of inventory valuation.

Involuntary Liquidation   LIFO also faces the involuntary liquidation problem. If the base or layers of old costs are eliminated, strange results can occur because old, irrelevant costs can be matched against current revenues. A distortion in reported income for a given period may result, as well as consequences that are detrimental from an income tax point of view. The income tax problem is particularly severe when the involuntary liquidation results from a strike or a shortage of materials. In these situations, companies may incur high tax bills when they can least afford to pay taxes.

Poor Buying Habits   LIFO may cause poor buying habits because of this liquidation problem. A company may simply purchase more goods and match these goods against revenue to ensure that these old costs are not charged against revenue. Furthermore, the possibility always exists with LIFO that a company will attempt to manipulate its net income at the end of the year simply by altering its pattern of purchases.

Because price rises have been the way of life in the United States economy during the last four decades, LIFO has provided a tax advantage over FIFO. During periods of continuing price decreases, this tax advantage could become a disadvantage. And during periods of stable prices, FIFO and LIFO methods of inventory costing produce identical results (assuming that at the beginning of the period of price stability the inventory values are equal).

Average Cost

As the name implies, the **average cost method** prices items in the inventory on the basis of the average cost of all similar goods available during the period. If perpetual inventory records are not kept, the cost of the inventory is computed only at the end of the period. The periodic average cost method is often referred to as the **weighted-average method** and is another periodic inventory technique for valuing inventories. The application of the average cost method for periodic inventories is as follows:

Periodic Inventory—Weighted-Average Method				
	Date	No. Units	Unit Cost	Total Cost
Inventory	Mar. 1	—	—	—
Purchases	Mar. 2	2,000	$4.00	$ 8,000
Purchases	Mar. 15	6,000	4.40	26,400
Purchases	Mar. 30	2,000	4.15	8,300
Total goods available		10,000		$42,700

Weighted-average cost per unit $\dfrac{\$42,700}{10,000} = \$4.27$

Inventory Mar. 31   6,000 units

Cost of inventory Mar. 31 $6,000 \times \$4.27 = \$25,620$

As implied in this computation, any beginning inventory is included both in the total units available and in the total cost of goods available in computing the average cost per unit. In the unit LIFO method (page 346), the beginning inventory was not used in computing the average cost per unit.

Another average cost method is the **moving average method,** which is used with perpetual inventory records. The application of the average cost method for perpetual records is shown below.

Date	Purchased	Sold or Issued	Balance
		Perpetual Inventory—Moving Average Method	
Mar. 2	(2,000 @ $4.00) $ 8,000		(2,000 @ $4.00) $ 8,000
Mar. 15	(6,000 @ 4.40) 26,400		(8,000 @ 4.30) 34,400
Mar. 19		(4,000 @ $4.30) $17,200	(4,000 @ 4.30) 17,200
Mar. 30	(2,000 @ 4.15) 8,300		(6,000 @ 4.25) 25,500

As indicated above, a new average unit cost is computed each time a purchase is made. On March 15, after 6,000 units are purchased for $26,400, 8,000 units costing $34,400 ($8,000 plus $26,400) are on hand. The average unit cost is $34,400 divided by 8,000, or $4.30. This unit cost is used in costing withdrawals until another purchase is made, when a new average unit cost is computed. Accordingly, the cost of the 4,000 units withdrawn on March 19 is shown at $4.30, or a total of $17,200, and on March 30 a new unit cost of $4.25 is determined.

The advantages of the average cost methods are usually justified on the basis of practical rather than conceptual reasons. They are simple to apply, objective, and not as subject to income manipulation as some of the other inventory pricing methods. In addition, proponents of the average cost methods argue that it is often impossible to measure a specific physical flow of inventory and therefore it is better to cost items on an average price basis. This argument is particularly persuasive when the inventory involved is relatively homogeneous in nature.

A moving average is probably more representative of the costs to be associated with the product, although a weighted average can give approximately the same results. These methods approximate the FIFO method when the inventory turnover is fairly high and the time interval fairly short. However, if the turnover does not occur frequently, an element of the very oldest cost is often carried forward for an extended period of time.

Base Stock

The **base stock method** is founded on the assumption that a minimum normal stock of goods is required at all times to carry on normal business activity, and that such normal stock should be carried at a long-run "normal" price, which may be, and often is, the lowest cost experienced or likely to be experienced. The lowest cost is used to avoid showing an "unrealized" inventory profit. Proponents of this method contend that the minimum inventory quantity is similar to a fixed asset and should not be affected by fluctuations in purchase prices; the costs of maintaining and replenishing this normal stock are charged to operations. The cost of any excess on hand above the base quantity is considered as a temporary increment and is priced at current costs by the application of the LIFO, FIFO, average cost, or any other suitable method selected. Any shortage in the base stock compared with units on hand is also considered temporary and is charged against revenue at current replacement cost.

If the base stock inventory is assumed to be 5,000 units at $3.80 per unit, then the inventory on hand of 6,000 units on March 31 might be computed as follows (using the data from the prior section and assuming that the excess over the normal stock is to be priced on a first-in, first-out basis):

Base stock (5,000 units @ $3.80)	$19,000
Excess above base quantity (1,000 units @ $4.15)	4,150
Inventory, March 31	$23,150

If the base stock is assumed to be 7,000 units at $3.80 per unit, then the inventory on hand of 6,000 units on March 31 is computed:

Base stock (7,000 units @ $3.80)	$26,600
Temporary deficiency (1,000 units @ $4.15, current replacement cost)	4,150
Inventory, March 31	$22,450

The application of the base stock method represents a departure from the cost principle as applied to assets, because the base stock quantity is carried at an amount that has no necessary relationship to the cost of units now in inventory. Like the LIFO method, the base stock method matches current costs with current revenues. It also is subject to some of the same objections as the LIFO method; in addition, the "normal" quantity is subject to manipulation. It is not a widely used method of inventory pricing because it is difficult to determine a normal quantity, is not acceptable for tax purposes; similar results can be obtained by using LIFO.

Standard Costs

A manufacturing concern that uses a **standard cost system** predetermines the unit costs for material, labor, and manufacturing overhead. Usually the standard costs used are determined on the basis of the costs that should be incurred per unit of finished goods when the plant is operating at normal capacity. The approximate ideal or expected costs are useful to management in its objective of controlling actual costs. Deviations from actual costs are reflected in variance accounts that may be analyzed to determine the reasons for such deviations so that management may take appropriate action to achieve greater control over manufacturing costs.

Under a standard cost system, the raw materials, work in process, and finished goods inventories may be valued at standard costs. For financial reporting purposes the pricing of inventories at standard costs is considered acceptable if there is no significant difference between actual and standard. If there is a significant difference, the inventory amounts should be adjusted to actual cost. Otherwise the net income will be misstated in the income statement, and both the assets and the retained earnings will be misstated in the balance sheet. The profession takes the position that **"standard costs are acceptable if adjusted at reasonable intervals to reflect current conditions so that at the balance sheet date standard costs reasonably approximate costs computed under one of the recognized bases."**[9] The recognized bases are specific identification, FIFO, LIFO, and average cost.

Which Method to Select?

The complex issue of which inventory method to select can be resolved only through careful analysis. Although FIFO has always been the most popular inventory method, a tremendous shift from FIFO and average cost to the LIFO method took place during the 1970s. For example, according to one survey, LIFO users in 1973 numbered 16%, whereas in 1974 this percentage had increased to 28%.[10] During the mid-1970s at least 8 of the largest 100 industrial corporations had changed to LIFO, their change alone reducing reported earnings by approximately $500 million. As noted earlier, the major reason for the shift to LIFO is the tax benefits associated with such a move.

Although no absolute rules can be stated, preferability for LIFO can ordinarily be established if: (1) selling prices and revenues have been increasing, whereas costs have lagged, to such a degree that an unrealistic earnings picture is presented; and (2) in situations where LIFO has been traditional, such as department stores and industries such as refining, chemicals, and glass where a fairly constant "base stock" is present. Conversely, LIFO would probably not be appropriate: (1) where prices tend to lag behind costs; (2) in situations where specific identification is traditional, such as in the sale of automobiles, farm equipment, art, and antique jewelry; and (3) where unit costs tend to decrease as production increases, thereby nullifying the tax benefit that LIFO might provide. Note that where inventory turnover is high, the difference between inventory methods is usually negligible.

It should be noted that switching from FIFO to LIFO usually results in an immediate tax benefit. On the other hand, switching from LIFO to FIFO can result in a substantial tax burden. For example, in 1971 when Chrysler changed from LIFO to FIFO, it became responsible for an additional $53 million in taxes that had been deferred over the preceding 14 years of LIFO inventory valuation. Given that this period (1957-1971) was a period of mild inflation as compared with present inflation rates, it is easy to see the tremendous tax burden a company may face if a switch is made. The major reason why companies like Chrysler changed to FIFO in the late 1960s and early 1970s was the profit crunch of that era. For example, although Chrysler showed a loss of $7.6 million dollars after the switch, the loss would have been $20 million more if the company had not changed its inventory valuation back to FIFO from LIFO.

---

[9]Accounting Research and Terminology Bulletins, Final Edition (New York: AICPA, 1961), Ch. 4, p. 30.

[10]Accounting Trends and Techniques—1978 reports that of 1,066 inventory method disclosures, 392 used FIFO, 332 used LIFO, 227 used average cost, 37 used standard costs, 31 used retail, and 47 used other methods.

Whether companies should switch from LIFO to FIFO for the sole purpose of increasing reported earnings is doubtful. Intuitively one would assume that companies with higher reported earnings would have a higher share (common stock price) valuation. Some studies have indicated, however, that the users of financial data exhibit a much higher sophistication than might be expected and, as a consequence, share prices are the same and, in some cases, even higher under LIFO in spite of lower reported earnings.[11] This difference may result because in the period of change from LIFO to FIFO the differential effect on earnings is clearly disclosed. In subsequent periods, the income difference may not be reported because the IRS believes such a presentation is inappropriate because the company would have the best of both worlds, that is, a lower taxable income but a reconciliation showing a higher income for financial reporting purposes. The valuation of inventories on a FIFO and LIFO basis can be disclosed, however, in a footnote. If a current tax rate is applied to the difference in valuation of the two methods, the net income difference between the two methods can still be determined.[12]

Often the inventory methods are used in combination with other methods. For example, one survey discloses that most industries never used LIFO totally, but often use it in combination with other valuation approaches. The reason for adoption of the average cost method is simply the difficulty of trying to approximate a flow assumption. Some of the other approaches, such as standard costs and base stock, are used infrequently.

The existence of a variety of inventory pricing methods, each of which has a somewhat different effect on net income when prices are increasing or decreasing, points out that the freedom to shift from one pricing method to another at will would permit a wide range of possible net income figures for a given company over a given period. This in turn would make financial statements less meaningful. This variety of methods has been devised to assist accurate computation of net income rather than to permit manipulation. Hence, it is recommended that the pricing method most suitable to a company be selected and, once selected, be applied consistently thereafter. If conditions indicate that the inventory pricing method in use is unsuitable, serious consideration should be given to all other possibilities before selecting another method. If a change is then made, it should be clearly explained and its effect disclosed in the financial statements.

Inventory Valuation Method—Summary Analysis

A number of inventory valuation methods are described in the preceding sections of this chapter. A brief summary of the three major inventory methods is presented on pages 358–359 to show the differing effects these valuation methods have on the financial statements. The first schedule provides selected data for the comparison as follows:

---

[11]See, for example, Shyam Sunder, "Relationship Between Accounting Changes and Stock Prices: Problems of Measurement and Some Empirical Evidence," *Empirical Research in Accounting: Selected Studies, 1973* (Chicago: Univ. of Chicago), pp. 1–40.

[12]The IRS recently proposed to amend its regulations to permit companies using the LIFO method to disclose the profit or loss that would result if other than the LIFO method were used. Such disclosures are to be made as a supplement to or explanation of the taxpayer's primary presentation in financial statements of income.

Selected Data		
Given		
Beginning cash balance		$ 7,000
Beginning retained earnings		$10,000
Beginning inventory	4,000 units @	$ 3
Purchases	6,000 units @	$ 4
Sales	5,000 units @	$ 12
Operating expenses		$10,000
40% tax rate		

The comparative results of using FIFO, LIFO, and average cost on net income are computed as follows:

Comparative Results of FIFO, LIFO, Average Cost			
	FIFO	LIFO	Average Cost
Sales	$60,000	$60,000	$60,000
Cost of goods sold	16,000[a]	20,000[b]	18,000[c]
Gross profit	44,000	40,000	42,000
Operating expenses	10,000	10,000	10,000
Income before taxes	34,000	30,000	32,000
Income taxes (40%)	13,600	12,000	12,800
Net income	$20,400	$18,000	$19,200

[a] 4,000 @ $3 = $14,000
1,000 @ $4 =   4,000
$16,000

[b] 5,000 @ $4 = $20,000

[c] 4,000 @ $3 = $12,000
6,000 @ $4 =   24,000
$36,000

$36,000 ÷ 10,000 = $3.60
$3.60 × 5,000 = $18,000

The table on page 359 then shows the final balances of selected items at the end of the period:

Balances of Selected Items

	Inventory	Gross Profit	Taxes	Net Income	Retained Earnings	Cash
FIFO	$20,000 (5,000 × $4)	$44,000	$13,600	$20,400	$30,400 ($10,000 + $20,400)	$19,400ª
LIFO	$16,000 (4,000 × $3) (1,000 × $4)	$40,000	$12,000	$18,000	$28,000 ($10,000 + $18,000)	$21,000ª
Average Cost	$18,000 (5,000 × $3.60)	$42,000	$12,800	$19,200	$29,200 ($10,000 + $19,200)	$20,200ª

ªCash at year end		=	Beg. balance	+	sales	−	purchases	−	operating expenses	−	taxes
FIFO—$19,400		=	$7,000	+	$60,000	−	$24,000	−	$10,000	−	$13,600
LIFO—$21,000		=	$7,000	+	$60,000	−	$24,000	−	$10,000	−	$12,000
Average cost—$20,200		=	$7,000	+	$60,000	−	$24,000	−	$10,000	−	$12,800

Note that the use of the LIFO inventory valuation method results in the lower net income but the higher cash balance. However, this example assumes that prices are rising; if prices are decreasing, the opposite effect occurs.

Questions

1. In what ways are the inventory accounts of a retailing concern different from those of a manufacturing enterprise?

2. What is the difference between a perpetual inventory and a physical inventory? If a company maintains a perpetual inventory, should its physical inventory at any date be equal to the amount indicated by the perpetual inventory records? Why?

3. Why should inventories be included (a) in a statement of financial position and (b) in the computation of net income?

4. Define "cost" as applied to the valuation of inventories.

5. Where, if at all, should the following items be classified on a balance sheet?
   (a) Raw materials.
   (b) Goods received on consignment.
   (c) Manufacturing supplies.
   (d) Goods out on approval to customers.
   (e) Goods in transit that were recently purchased f.o.b. shipping point.
   (f) Land held by a realty firm for sale.

6. At the balance sheet date the Hartwig Company held title to goods in transit amounting to $7,433. This amount was omitted from the purchases figure for the year and also from the ending inventory. What is the effect of this omission on the net income for the year as calculated when the books are closed? On the company's financial position as shown in its balance sheet? Is materiality a factor in determining whether an adjustment for this item should be made?

7. Briefly indicate the arguments pro and con for variable costing. Indicate how each of the following conditions would affect the amounts of net profit reported under conventional absorption costing and variable costing.
   (a) Sales and production are in balance at a standard volume.
   (b) Sales exceed production.
   (c) Production exceeds sales.

8. What is the difference beween variable costing and conventional absorption costing? Is variable costing acceptable for external financial reporting and for income tax purposes? Why?

9. X purchases 150 units of an item at an invoice cost of $2,700. What is the cost per unit? If the goods are shipped f.o.b. shipping point and the freight bill was $300, what is the cost per unit if X pays the freight charges? If these items were bought on 2/15, n/30 terms and the invoice and the freight bill were paid within the 15-day period, what would be the cost per unit?

10. Specific identification is sometimes said to be the ideal method of assigning cost to inventory and to cost of goods sold. Briefly indicate the arguments for and against this method of inventory valuation.

11. First-in, first-out; weighted average; and last-in, first-out methods are often used instead of specific identification for inventory valuation purposes. Compare these methods with the specific identification method, discussing the theoretical propriety of each method in the determination of income and asset valuation.

12. In what respects is the LIFO method of costing inventories similar to the base stock method? In what respects is it dissimilar? Is the base stock method acceptable for either external financial reporting purposes or income tax purposes?

13. As compared with the FIFO method of costing inventories, does the LIFO method result in a larger or smaller net income in a period of rising prices? What is the comparative effect on net income in a period of falling prices?

14. What is the dollar-value method of LIFO inventory valuation? What advantage does the dollar-value method have over the quantity method of LIFO inventory valuation? Why will the LIFO inventory costing method and the dollar-value LIFO inventory costing method produce different inventory valuations if the composition of the inventory base changes? What are the similarities and differences between the dollar-value LIFO inventory method and the base stock method?

15. On December 31, 1980, the inventory of the Duffy Company amounts to $800,000. During 1981, the company decides to use the dollar-value method of costing inventories. On December 31, 1981, the inventory is $884,000 at December 31, 1981 prices. Using the December 31, 1980, price level of 100 and the December 31, 1981, price level of 104, compute the inventory value at December 31, 1981, under the dollar-value method.

16. Define standard costs. What are the advantages of a standard cost system? Present arguments in support of each of the following three methods of treating standard cost variances (actual costs—standard costs) for purposes of financial reporting:
    (a) They may be carried as deferred charges or credits on the balance sheet.
    (b) They may appear as charges or credits on the income statement.
    (c) They may be allocated between inventories and cost of goods sold.

17. What is a product financing arrangement? How should product financing arrangements be reported in the financial statements?

Cases

C8-1   Salmon Company has been growing rapidly, but during this period of rapid growth the accounting records have not been properly maintained. You were recently employed to correct the accounting records and to assist in the preparation of the financial statements for the fiscal year ended February 28, 1981. One of the accounts you have been analyzing is entitled "Merchandise." That account in summary form follows. Numbers in parentheses following each entry correspond to related numbered explanations and additional information that you have accumulated during your analysis.

Merchandise

Balance, March 1, 1980	(1)	Merchandise sold	(5)
Purchases	(2)	Consigned merchandise	(6)
Freight-in	(3)		
Insurance	(4)		
Freight-out on consigned merchandise	(7)		
Freight-out on merchandise sold	(8)		

Explanations and Additional Information

(1) You have satisfied yourself that the March 1, 1980, inventory balance represents the approximate cost of the few units in inventory at the beginning of the year. Salmon employs the FIFO method of accounting for inventories.

(2) The merchandise purchased was recorded in the account at the sellers' catalog list price, which is the price appearing on the face of each vendor's invoice. All purchased merchandise is subject to a trade (chain) discount of 20%–10%. These discounts have been accounted for as revenue when the merchandise was paid for.

All merchandise purchased was also subject to cash terms of 2/15, n/30. During the fiscal year Salmon recorded $3,500 in purchase discounts as revenue when the merchandise was paid for. Some purchase discounts were lost because payment was made after the discount period ended. All purchases of merchandise were paid for in the fiscal year they were recorded as purchased.

(3) All merchandise is purchased FOB sellers' business locations. The freight-in amount is the cost of transporting the merchandise from the sellers' business locations to Salmon.

(4) The insurance charge is for an all-perils policy to cover merchandise in transit to Salmon from sellers.

(5) The credit to this account for merchandise sold represents the sellers' catalog list price of merchandise sold plus the cost of the beginning inventory; the debit side of the entry was made to the cost of goods sold account.

(6) Consigned merchandise represents goods that were shipped to Mark Company during January 1981, priced at the sellers' catalog list price. The offsetting debit was made to accounts receivable when the merchandise was shipped to Mark.

(7) The freight-out on consigned goods is the cost of trucking the consigned goods to Mark from Salmon.

(8) Freight-out on merchandise sold is the amount paid trucking companies to deliver merchandise sold to Salmon's customers.

Instructions

Consider each of the eight (8) numbered items independently and explain specifically how and why each item should have (if correctly accounted for) affected

(a) The amount of cost of goods sold to be included in Salmon's earnings statement, and

(b) The amount of any other account to be included in Salmon's February 28, 1981, financial statements.

Organize your answer in the following format:

Item Number	How and Why the Amount of Cost of Goods Sold Should Have been Affected	How and Why the Amount of Any Other Account Should Have been Affected

C8-2 The controller for Sutton Enterprises has recently hired you as assistant controller. She wishes to determine your expertise in the area of inventory accounting and therefore requests that you **answer the following unrelated situations:**

(a) A company is involved in the wholesaling and retailing of automobile tires for foreign cars. Most of the inventory is imported, and it is valued on the company's records at the actual inventory cost plus freight-in. At year-end, the warehousing costs are prorated over cost of goods sold and ending inventory. Are warehousing costs considered to be a product cost or a period cost?

(b) A certain portion of a company's "inventory" is composed of obsolete items. Should obsolete items that are not currently consumed in the production of "goods or services to be available for sale" be classified as part of inventory?

(c) A company purchases airplanes for sale to others. However, until they are sold, the company charters and services the planes. What is the proper way to report these airplanes in the company's financial statements?

(d) A competitor uses standard costs for valuing inventory. Is this permissible?

(e) A company wants to buy coal deposits but does not want the financing for the purchase to be reported on its financial statements. The company therefore establishes a trust to acquire the coal deposits. The company agrees to buy the coal over a certain period of time at specified prices. The trust is able to finance the coal purchase and pay off the loan as it is paid by the company for the minerals. How should this transaction be reported?

(f) A company has decided that part of its inventory is similar to a long-term asset in that a portion must always be available for potential stockout problems. The company therefore decides to use the base stock method of inventory valuation. Is this permissible? Discuss.

C8-3   In February, 1981, Forest Products, Inc. requested and secured permission from the Commissioner of Internal Revenue to compute inventories under the last-in, first-out (LIFO) method and elected to determine inventory cost under the dollar-value method. Forest Products, Inc. satisfied the Commissioner that cost could be accurately determined by use of an index number computed from a representative sample selected from the company's single inventory pool.

Instructions

(a) Why should inventories be included in (1) a balance sheet and (2) the computation of net income?

(b) The **Internal Revenue Code** allows some accountable events to be considered differently for income tax reporting purposes and financial accounting purposes, while other accountable events must be reported the same for both purposes. Discuss why it might be desirable to report some accountable events differently for financial accounting purposes than for income tax reporting purposes.

(c) Discuss the ways and conditions under which the FIFO and LIFO inventory costing methods produce different inventory valuations. Do not discuss procedures for computing inventory cost.

(AICPA adapted)

C8-4   You are asked to travel to Seattle to observe and verify the inventory of the Seattle branch of one of your clients. You arrive on Thursday, December 30, and find that the inventory procedures have just been started. You note that there is a railway car spotted on the sidetrack at the unloading door and ask the warehouse superintendent how she plans to inventory the contents of the car. She responds: "We are not going to include the contents in the inventory."

Later in the day, you ask the bookkeeper for the invoice on the carload and the related freight bill. The invoice lists the various items, prices, and extensions of the goods in the car. You note that the carload was shipped December 24 from Chicago f.o.b. Chicago, and that the total invoice price of the goods in the car was $25,300. The freight bill called for a payment of $1,050. Terms were net 30 days. The bookkeeper affirms the fact that this invoice is to be held for recording in January.

Instructions

(a) Does your client have a liability which should be recorded at December 31? Discuss.

(b) Prepare a journal entry(ies), if required, to reflect any audit adjustment required.

(c) For what possible reason(s) might your client wish to postpone recording the transaction?

C8-5 You have a client engaged in a manufacturing business with relatively heavy fixed costs and large inventories of finished goods. These inventories constitute a very material item on the balance sheet. The company has a departmental cost accounting system that assigns all manufacturing costs to the product each period.

The controller of the company has informed you that the management is giving serious consideration to the adoption of direct costing as a method of accounting for plant operations and inventory valuation. The management wishes to have your opinion of the effect, if any, that such a change would have on:

    (1) the year-end financial position,

    (2) the net income for the year.

Instructions

State your reply to the request and the reasons for your conclusions.

(AICPA adapted)

C8-6 Chuck Thomas, president of Mondale, Inc. recently read an article that claimed that at least 100 of the country's largest 500 companies were either adopting or considering adopting the last-in, first-out (LIFO) method for valuing inventories. The article stated that the firms were switching to LIFO to (1) neutralize the effect of inflation in their financial statements, (2) eliminate inventory profits, and (3) reduce income taxes. Thomas wonders if the switch would benefit his company.

Mondale, Inc. currently uses the first-in, first-out (FIFO) method of inventory valuation in its periodic inventory system. The company has a high inventory turnover rate, and inventories represent a significant proportion of the assets.

In discussing this trend toward LIFO inventory with business friends, he has been told that the LIFO system is more costly to operate and will provide little benefit to companies with high turnover. Thomas intends to use the inventory method that is best for the company in the long run rather than selecting a method just because it is the current fad.

Instructions

(a) Explain to Mr. Thomas what "inventory profits" are and how the LIFO method of inventory valuation could reduce them.

(b) Explain to Mr. Thomas the conditions that must exist for Mondale to receive tax benefits from a switch to the LIFO method.

C8-7 Sutro Company is a medium-sized manufacturing company with two divisions and three subsidiaries, all located in the United States. The Gunn Division manufactures metal castings for the automotive industry, and the Dunn Division produces small plastic items for electrical products and other uses. The three subsidiaries manufacture various products for other industrial users.

Sutro Company plans to change from the lower of first-in, first-out (FIFO) cost or market method of inventory valuation to the last-in, first-out (LIFO) method of inventory valuation to obtain tax benefits. To make the method acceptable for tax purposes, the change also will be made for its annual financial statements.

Instructions

(a) Describe the establishment of and subsequent pricing procedures for each of the following LIFO inventory methods:

    1. LIFO applied to units of product when the periodic inventory system is used.

    2. Application of the dollar-value method to LIFO units of product.

(b) Discuss the specific advantages and disadvantages of using the dollar-value LIFO application as compared to traditional LIFO methods. Ignore income tax considerations.

(c) Discuss the general advantages and disadvantages claimed for LIFO methods.

Exercises

E8-1 Two or more items are omitted in each of the following tabulations of income statement data. Fill in the amounts that are missing.

	1979	1980	1981
Sales	$235,000	$300,000	$_____
Sales Returns	_____	7,500	12,500
Net Sales	_____	_____	340,000
Beginning Inventory	_____	15,000	_____
Ending Inventory	_____	_____	22,500
Purchases	119,000	_____	175,000
Purchase Returns and Allowances	4,000	5,000	7,500
Transportation-In	5,000	7,000	5,000
Cost of Goods Sold	125,000	150,000	_____
Gross Profit on Sales	100,000	_____	160,000

E8-2 How would you recommend that the following items be reported on the balance sheet?

(a) An appropriation of retained earnings for possible inventory declines _____

(b) Materials received from a customer for processing _____

(c) Merchandise produced by special order and set aside to be picked up by customer _____

(d) Janitorial supplies _____

(e) Unsold goods in the hands of consignees _____

(f) Raw materials pledged by means of warehouse receipts on notes payable to bank _____

(g) Raw materials in transit from suppliers _____

(h) An allowance to reduce the inventory cost to market _____

E8-3 The net income per books was determined without knowledge of the errors indicated.

Year	Net Income per Books	Error in Ending Inventory
1976	$41,000	Overstated $ 3,000
1977	44,000	Overstated 6,000
1978	42,000	Understated 10,000
1979	44,600	No error
1980	43,800	Understated 2,000
1981	45,000	Overstated 9,000

Instructions

Prepare a work sheet to show the adjusted net income figure for each of the six years after taking into account the inventory errors.

E8-4 Harbor Company has a calendar-year accounting period. The following errors have been discovered in 1981.

1. The December 31, 1979, merchandise inventory had been understated by $10,000.
2. Merchandise purchased on account during 1980 was recorded on the books for the first time in February 1981, when the original invoice for the correct amount of $2,500 arrived. The merchandise had arrived December 28, 1980 and was included in the December 31, 1980 merchandise inventory. The invoice arrived late because of a mixup on the wholesaler's part.
3. Accrued interest of $250 at December 31, 1980, on notes receivable had not been recorded until the cash for the interest was received in March, 1981.

Instructions

(a) Compute the effect each error had on the 1980 net income.
(b) Compute the effect, if any, each error had on the December 31, 1980 balance sheet items.

E8-5 The following purchase transactions occurred during the last few days of the Frank Company's business year, which ends October 31, or in the first few days after that date. A periodic inventory system is used.

1. An invoice for $2,200, terms f.o.b. shipping point, was received and entered November 1. The invoice shows that the material was shipped October 29, but the receiving report indicates receipt of goods on November 3.
2. An invoice for $1,800, terms f.o.b. destination, was received and entered November 2. The receiving report indicates that the goods were received October 29.
3. An invoice for $2,840, terms f.o.b. shipping point, was received October 15 but never entered. Attached to it is a receiving report indicating that the goods were received October 18. Across the face of the receiving report is the following notation: "Merchandise not of same quality as ordered—returned for credit October 19."
4. An invoice for $3,600, terms f.o.b. shipping point, was received and entered October 27. The receiving report attached to the invoice indicates that the shipment was received October 27 in satisfactory condition.
5. An invoice for $1,500, terms f.o.b. destination, was received and entered October 28. The receiving report indicates that the merchandise was received November 2.

Before preparing financial statements for the year, you are instructed to review these transactions and to determine whether any correcting entries are required and whether the inventory of $65,700 determined by physical count should be changed.

Instructions

Complete the following schedule, and state the correct inventory at October 31. Assume that the books have not been closed.

Transaction	Purchase and Related Payable Should be Recognized in (month)	Purchase and Related Payable Were Recognized in (month)	Correcting Journal Entries Needed	Should Inventory Be Included in October Ending Inventory?	Was Inventory Included in October Ending Inventory?	Dollar Adjustments Needed to October Ending Inventory

E8-6 Presented below are the following transactions related to Monona, Inc.

June 10 Purchased goods billed at $14,250 subject to cash discount terms of 2/10, n/60.

11 Purchased goods billed at $7,000 subject to terms of 1/15, n/30.

19   Paid invoice of June 10.

22   Purchased goods billed at $9,000 subject to cash discount terms of 2/10, n/30.

Instructions

(a) Prepare general journal entries for the transactions above under the assumption that purchases are to be recorded at net amounts after cash discounts and that discounts lost are to be treated as financial expense.

(b) Assuming no purchase or payment transactions other than those given above, prepare the adjusting entry required on June 30 if financial statements are to be prepared as of that date.

E8-7   The Bock Manufacturing Company maintains a general ledger account for each class of inventory, debiting such accounts for increases during the period, and crediting them for decreases. The transactions below relate to the Raw Materials inventory account, which is debited for materials purchased and which is credited for materials requisitioned for use.

1. An invoice for $6,000, terms f.o.b. shipping point, was received and entered December 30, 1980. The receiving report shows that the materials were received January 4, 1981, and the bill of lading shows that they were shipped January 2, 1981.

2. Materials costing $15,000 were received December 30, 1980, but no entry was made for them because "they were ordered with a specified delivery of no earlier than January 10, 1981."

3. An invoice for $8,600, terms f.o.b. destination, was received and entered January 2, 1981. The receiving report shows that they were received December 28, 1980.

4. Materials costing $22,000, shipped f.o.b. destination, were not entered by December 31, 1980, "because they were in a railroad car on the company's siding on that date and had not been unloaded."

5. Materials costing $3,600 were returned on December 29, 1980, to the creditor, and were shipped f.o.b. shipping point. They were entered on that date, even though they are not expected to reach the creditor's place of business until January 6, 1981.

Instructions

Prepare correcting general journal entries required December 31, 1980, assuming that the books have not been closed.

E8-8   In an annual audit at December 31, 1981, you find the following transactions near the closing date.

1. A packing case containing a product costing $408 was standing in the shipping room when the physical inventory was taken. It was not included in the inventory because it was marked "Hold for shipping instructions." Your investigation revealed that the customer's order was dated December 18, 1981, but that the case was shipped and the customer billed on January 10, 1982. The product was a stock item of your client.

2. Merchandise received on January 6, 1982, costing $360 was entered in the purchase journal on January 7, 1982. The invoice showed shipment was made f.o.b. supplier's warehouse on December 31, 1981. Because it was not on hand at December 31, it was not included in inventory.

3. A special machine, fabricated to order for a customer, was finished and specifically segregated in the back part of the shipping room on December 31, 1981. The customer was billed on that date and the machine excluded from inventory although it was shipped on January 4, 1982.

4. Merchandise costing $911 was received on January 3, 1982, and the related purchase invoice recorded January 5. The invoice showed the shipment was made on December 29, 1981, f.o.b. destination.

5. Merchandise costing $310 was received on December 28, 1981, and the invoice was not recorded. You located it in the hands of the purchasing agent; it was marked on consignment.

Instructions

Assuming that each of the amounts is material, state whether the merchandise should be included in the client's inventory and give your reason for your decision on each item.

E8-9 The board of directors of the Stanley Calculator Sales Corporation is considering whether or not it should instruct the accounting department to shift from a first-in, first-out (FIFO) basis of pricing inventories to a last-in, first-out (LIFO) basis. The following information is available.

Sales	10,000 units @ $45
Inventory Jan. 1	2,000 units @ 30
Purchases	1,000 units @ 30
	6,000 units @ 33
	4,000 units @ 35
Inventory Dec. 31	3,000 units @ ?
Operating expenses	$100,000

Instructions

Prepare a condensed income statement for the year on both bases for comparative purposes.

E8-10 The following accounts, among others, appear on the trial balance of the San Juan Corporation at the end of the year 1981:

Raw Materials Inventory 1/1/81	$ 20,000
Goods in Process Inventory 1/1/81	40,000
Finished Goods Inventory 1/1/81	50,000
Raw Materials Purchased	66,000
Direct Labor	76,000
Manufacturing Overhead	60,000
Sales	200,000
General and Administrative Expense	50,000

Instructions

Assuming that no other nominal accounts existed, give the adjusting and closing entries that would be made at the end of the year. Inventories on December 31, 1981, are: raw materials, $26,000; goods in process, $36,000; finished goods, $40,000. Ignore income tax effects.

E8-11 The following is a record of transactions for transistor radios for the month of January, 1981:

Jan. 1	Balance 400 units @ $ 9.00	Jan. 10 Sale 300 units @ $14
12	Purchase 200 units @ $10.00	30 Sale 200 units @ $16
28	Purchase 200 units @ $11.00	

(a) Assuming that perpetual inventories are **not** maintained and that a physical count at the end of the month shows 300 units to be on hand, what is the cost of the ending inventory using (1) FIFO? (2) LIFO?

(b) Assuming that perpetual records are maintained and they tie into the general ledger, calculate the ending inventory using (1) FIFO; (2) LIFO.

E8-12 Inventory information for Part 311 discloses the following charges for the month of June:

June 1:	Balance	300 units @ $10
11:	Purchased	500 units @ $8
20:	Purchased	400 units @ $7
June 10:	Sold	200 units @ $12
23:	Sold	400 units @ $11
27:	Sold	200 units @ $11

Instructions

(a) Assuming that the periodic inventory method is used, compute the cost of goods sold and ending inventory under (1) LIFO; (2) FIFO.

(b) Assuming that the perpetual inventory record is kept in dollars, and costs are computed at the time of each withdrawal, what is the value of the ending inventory at LIFO?

(c) Assuming that the perpetual inventory record is kept in dollars, and costs are computed at the time of each withdrawal, what is the gross profit if the inventory is valued at FIFO?

(d) Why is it stated that LIFO usually produces a lower gross profit than FIFO?

E8-13 The Stoughton Sports Shop began operations on January 1, 1981. The following stock record card for footballs was taken from the records at the end of the year.

Date	Voucher	Terms	Units Received	Unit Invoice Cost	Gross Invoice Amount
1/15	10624	Net 30	60	$15.00	$ 900.00
3/15	11437	1/5, net 30	24	14.00	336.00
6/20	21332	1/10, net 30	120	13.00	1,560.00
9/12	27644	1/10, net 30	84	12.00	1,008.00
11/24	31269	1/10, net 30	96	12.00	1,152.00
	Totals		384		$4,956.00

A physical inventory on December 31, 1981 reveals that 150 footballs were in stock. The bookkeeper informs you that all the discounts were taken. Assume that Stoughton uses the invoice price less discount for recording purchases.

Instructions

(a) Compute the 12/31/81 inventory using the FIFO method.

(b) Compute the 1981 cost of goods sold using the LIFO method.

(c) What method would you recommend to the owner to minimize income taxes in 1981, using the inventory information for footballs as a guide?

E8-14 The Stella Pauley Company's record of transactions for the month of May was as follows:

PURCHASES

May	1	(balance on hand)	700 @ $5.00
	4		300 @ 5.20
	8		300 @ 5.20
	13		1,000 @ 5.10
	21		400 @ 5.50
	29		300 @ 5.60
			3,000

SALES

May	3	400 @ $9.00
	9	500 @ 8.50
	11	300 @ 9.20
	23	600 @ 8.60
	27	800 @ 8.70
		2,600

Instructions

(a) Assuming that perpetual inventory records are kept in units only, compute the inventory at May 31 using (1) LIFO; (2) average cost.

(b) Assuming that perpetual inventory records are kept in dollars and costs are computed at the time of each withdrawal, determine the inventory using (1) FIFO; (2) LIFO.

(c) Compute cost of goods sold assuming periodic inventory procedures and inventory priced at FIFO.

(d) In an inflationary period, which of the following inventory methods (FIFO, LIFO, average cost, or base stock) will show the highest net income?

E8-15 The vice president of finance of the Investor Corporation, a retail company, made two different schedules of gross margin for the first quarter ended March 31, 1981. These schedules appear below.

	Sales ($5 per unit)	Cost of Goods Sold	Gross Margin
Schedule 1	$140,000	$118,550	$21,450
Schedule 2	140,000	115,750	24,250

The computation of cost of goods sold in each schedule is based on the following data:

	Units	Cost per Unit	Total Cost
Beginning inventory, January 1	10,000	$4.00	$40,000
Purchase, January 10	8,000	4.20	33,600
Purchase, January 30	5,000	4.16	20,800
Purchase, February 11	7,000	4.30	30,100
Purchase, March 17	12,000	4.25	51,000

The president of the corporation cannot understand how two different gross margins can be computed from the same set of data. As vice president of finance, you have explained to him that the two schedules are based on different assumptions concerning the flow of inventory costs; i.e., first-in, first-out; and last-in, first-out. Schedules 1 and 2 were not necessarily prepared in this sequence of cost-flow assumptions.

Instructions

Prepare two separate schedules computing cost of goods sold and supporting schedules showing the composition of the ending inventory under both cost-flow assumptions.

E8-16 The dollar-value LIFO method was adopted by the Joan Graham Company on January 1, 1981. Its inventory on that date was $150,000. On December 31, 1981, the inventory at prices existing on that date amounted to $143,000. The price level at January 1, 1981, was 100, and the price level at December 31, 1981, was 110.

Instructions

(a) Compute the amount of the inventory at December 31, 1981, under the dollar-value LIFO method.

(b) On December 31, 1982, the inventory at prices existing on that date was $180,000, and the price level was 125. Compute the inventory on that date under the dollar-value LIFO method.

E8-17   Presented below is information related to the Mchan Company.

Date	Ending Inventory (End of Year Prices)	Price Index
December 31, 1978	$ 72,000	100
December 31, 1979	100,000	125
December 31, 1980	150,000	150
December 31, 1981	105,600	120
December 31, 1982	100,000	100
December 31, 1983	81,400	110

Instructions

Compute the ending inventory for Mchan Company for 1978 through 1983 using the dollar-value LIFO method.

Problems

P8-1   The Hill Company is a wholesale distributor of automotive replacement parts. Initial amounts taken from Hill's accounting records are as follows:

Inventory at December 31, 1981 (based on physical count of goods in Hill's warehouse on December 31, 1981) $1,250,000

Accounts payable at December 31, 1981:

Vendor	Terms	Amount
Baker Company	2% 10 days, net 30	$ 265,000
Charlie Company	Net 30	210,000
Dolly Company	Net 30	300,000
Eager Company	Net 30	225,000
Full Company	Net 30	—
Greg Company	Net 30	—
		$1,000,000

Sales in 1981 $9,000,000

Additional information is as follows:

1. Parts received on consignment from Charlie Company by Hill, the consignee, amounting to $155,000, were included in the physical count of goods in Hill's warehouse on December 31, 1981, and in accounts payable at December 31, 1981.

2. $22,000 of parts that were purchased from Full and paid for in December 1981 were sold in the last week of 1981 and appropriately recorded as sales of $28,000. The parts were included in the physical count of goods in Hill's warehouse on December 31, 1981, because the parts were on the loading dock waiting to be picked up by customers.

3. Parts in transit on December 31, 1981, to customers, shipped f.o.b. shipping point, on December 28, 1981, amounted to $34,000. The customers received the parts on January 6, 1982. Sales of $40,000 to the customers for the parts were recorded by Hill on January 2, 1982.

4. Retailers were holding $210,000 at cost ($250,000 at retail), of goods on consignment from Hill, the consignor, at their stores on December 31, 1981.

5. Goods were in transit from Greg to Hill on December 31, 1981. The cost of the goods was $25,000, and they were shipped f.o.b. shipping point on December 29, 1981.

6. A quarterly freight bill in the amount of $2,000 specifically relating to merchandise purchases in December 1981, all of which was still in the inventory at December 31, 1981, was received on January 3, 1982. The freight bill was not included in the inventory or in accounts payable at December 31, 1981.

7. All of the purchases from Baker occurred during the last seven days of the year. These items have been recorded in accounts payable and accounted for in the physical inventory at cost before discount. Hill's policy is to pay invoices in time to take advantage of all cash discounts, adjust inventory accordingly, and record accounts payable, net of cash discounts.

Instructions

Prepare a schedule of adjustments to the initial amounts using the format shown below. Show the effect, if any, of each of the transactions separately and if the transactions would have no effect on the amount shown, state **NONE**.

	Inventory	Accounts Payable	Sales
Initial amounts	$1,250,000	$1,000,000	$9,000,000
Adjustments-increase (decrease)			
1			
2			
3			
4			
5			
6			
7			
Total adjustments			
Adjusted amounts	$	$	$

(AICPA adapted)

P8-2 As manager of a summer resort hotel, you noticed after a few months' operations that the receipts of the cigar counter are less than those in corresponding periods of previous seasons. The receipts from other hotel activities have not decreased, and you determine the following:

1. No stocks are carried over at the counter from the previous season.

2. Cigars and cigarettes are added to the counter from the general storeroom in full boxes and cartons as needed.

3. No inventory records are kept at the counter.

4. The cashier's record shows $1,251.00 received up to date of examination.

5. Four office employees are allowed to serve customers at the counter.

6. All sales are at the established unit selling prices.

7. All cash in excess of a $20 change fund, representing the day's receipts, is to be deposited with the cashier at the close of each day.

An inventory was taken under your supervision and you prepare the following statement.

Boxes of 50 Cigars
Cartons of 10 Packages Cigarettes

Unit Selling Prices	Received from Stockroom	Inventory		Cost per Box or Carton
		Boxes and Cartons	Single Cigars and Packages	
Cigars				
50¢	10 boxes	3	25	$18.00
2/50¢	20 boxes	4	10	9.00
20¢	30 boxes	6	40	7.50
Cigarettes				
60¢	25 cartons	4	6	4.00
50¢	300 cartons	77	5	3.40

Instructions

Prepare a summary of cigar counter transactions, also showing the amount of any shortage.

P8-3 Some of the transactions of the Hartley Company during August are listed below.

August 10 Purchased merchandise on account, $6,000, terms 2/10, n/30.

13 Returned part of the purchase of August 10, $500, and received credit on account.

15 Purchased merchandise on account, $10,000, terms 1/10, n/60.

25 Purchased merchandise on account, $7,500, terms 2/10, n/30.

28 Paid invoice of August 15 in full of account.

Instructions

(a) Assuming that purchases are recorded at gross amounts and that discounts are to be recorded when taken:
1. Prepare general journal entries to record the transactions.
2. Describe how the various items would be shown in the financial statements.

(b) Assuming that purchases are recorded at net amounts and that discounts lost are treated as financial expenses:
1. Prepare general journal entries to enter the transactions.
2. Prepare the adjusting entry necessary on August 31 if financial statements are to be prepared at that time.
3. Describe how the various items would be shown in the financial statements.

(c) Which of the two methods do you prefer and why?

P8-4 The books of Andy Panda Corporation on December 31, 1981, are in agreement with the following balance sheet:

Andy Panda Corporation
BALANCE SHEET AS OF DECEMBER 31, 1981

Assets

Cash	$ 20,000
Accounts and notes receivable	40,000
Inventory	80,000
	$140,000

Liabilities and Capital

Accounts and notes payable	$ 24,000
Common stock	100,000
Retained earnings	16,000
	$140,000

The following errors were made by the corporation and were not corrected: on December 31, 1980, the inventory was overstated $6,000, prepaid expense of $1,600 was omitted, and accrued income of $1,000 was omitted. On December 31, 1981, the inventory was understated $10,000, prepaid expense of $1,200 was omitted, accrued expense of $600 was omitted, and unearned income of $1,400 was omitted.

The net income shown by the books for 1981 was $12,000.

Instructions

(a) Compute the corrected net income for 1981.

(b) Prepare a corrected balance sheet for December 31, 1981.

P8-5 Summarized below are certain quarterly data relative to the Beresford Company. Assume that there was no inventory on hand at the beginning of the first quarter.

	Purchases	Sales
First quarter	10,000 @ $3.00	8,000 @ $3.75
	5,000 @ 3.10	3,000 @ 3.80
Second quarter	8,000 @ 3.10	6,000 @ 3.90
	4,000 @ 3.25	4,000 @ 4.00
Third quarter	9,000 @ 3.30	10,000 @ 4.00
	3,000 @ 3.40	2,000 @ 4.10
Fourth quarter	5,000 @ 3.40	4,000 @ 4.20
	8,000 @ 3.50	5,000 @ 4.25

Instructions

(a) Compute the gross profit for the Beresford Company by quarters under each of the following methods of inventory pricing, assuming that inventory costs are determined only at the end of each quarter.

1. First-in, first-out (FIFO).
2. Last-in, first-out (LIFO).
3. Average cost (carry unit costs to the nearest cent).

(b) Evaluate the effect of each of these three methods on gross profit in a period of rising prices as presented above.

P8-6 The Marlene Manufacturing Company manufactures two products: Mult and Tran. At December 31, 1981, Marlene used the first-in, first-out (FIFO) inventory method. Effective January 1, 1982, Marlene changed to the last-in, first-out (LIFO) inventory method. The cumulative effect of this change is not determinable and, as a result, the ending inventory of 1981 for which the FIFO method was used, is also the beginning inventory for 1982 for the LIFO method. Any layers added during 1982 should be costed by reference to the first acquisitions of 1982 and any layers liquidated during 1982 should be considered a permanent liquidation.

The following information was available from Marlene's inventory records for the two most recent years:

	Mult		Tran	
	Units	Unit Cost	Units	Unit Cost
1981 purchases:				
January 7	5,000	$4.00	22,000	$2.00
April 16	12,000	4.50		
November 8	17,000	5.00	18,500	2.50
December 13	10,000	6.00		

1982 purchases:

February 11	3,000	7.00	23,000	3.00
May 20	8,000	7.50		
October 15	20,000	8.00		
December 23			15,500	3.50

Units on hand:

December 31, 1981	15,000	14,500	
December 31, 1982	16,000	13,000	

Instructions

Compute the effect on income before income taxes for the year ended December 31, 1982, resulting from the change from the FIFO to the LIFO inventory method.

(AICPA adapted)

P8-7 Hoyt Corporation's record of transactions concerning Part 453 for the month of April was as follows:

Purchases

Apr. 1	(balance on hand)	100 @ $4.00
Apr. 4		300 @ 4.10
Apr. 11		400 @ 4.00
Apr. 18		200 @ 3.75
Apr. 26		600 @ 3.50
Apr. 30		300 @ 3.30

Sales

Apr. 5	300
Apr. 12	200
Apr. 27	700
Apr. 28	100

Instructions

(a) Compute the inventory at April 30 on each of the following bases. Assume that perpetual inventory records are kept in units only. Carry unit costs to the nearest cent.

1. First-in, first-out (FIFO).
2. Last-in, first-out (LIFO).
3. Average cost.

(b) If the perpetual inventory record is kept in dollars, and costs are computed at the time of each withdrawal, what amount would be shown as ending inventory in 1, 2, and 3 above? Carry unit costs to the neatest cent.

P8-8 Here is some of the information found on a detail inventory card for S. L. Catlett, Inc. for the first month of operations.

	Received		Issued,	Balance,
Date	No. of Units	Unit Cost	No. of Units	No. of Units
Jan. 2	1,200	$2.00		1,200
7			700	500
10	500	2.10		1,000
13			600	400
18	1,500	2.10	300	1,600
20			1,000	600
23	1,000	2.20		1,600
26			900	700
28	1,500	2.25		2,200
31			1,000	1,200

Instructions

(a) From these data compute the ending inventory on each of the following bases (assume that perpetual inventory records are kept in units only; carry unit costs to the nearest cent):

1. First-in, first-out (FIFO).
2. Last-in, first-out (LIFO).
3. Average cost.
4. Base stock (assume 500 units at $2.00 to be the base stock with receipts and issues over that figure to be priced on a first-in, first-out basis).

(b) If the perpetual inventory record is kept in dollars, and costs are computed at the time of each withdrawal, would the amounts shown as ending inventory in 1, 2, and 3 above be the same? Explain.

P8-9 The management of Logan Products Company has asked its accounting department to describe the effect upon the company's financial position and its financial statements of accounting for inventories on the LIFO rather than the FIFO basis during 1981 and 1982. The accounting department is to assume that the change to LIFO would have been effective on January 1, 1981, and that the initial LIFO base would have been the inventory value on December 31, 1980. Presented below are the company's financial statements and other data for the years 1981 and 1982 when the FIFO method was in fact employed.

Financial Condition as of	12/31/80	12/31/81	12/31/82
Cash	$ 67,700	$121,300	$176,050
Accounts receivable	40,000	54,000	61,750
Inventory	69,000	75,000	84,000
Other assets	114,000	114,000	114,000
Total assets	$290,700	$364,300	$435,800
Accounts payable	$ 23,000	$ 30,000	$ 36,400
Other liabilities	40,000	40,000	40,000
Common stock	140,000	140,000	140,000
Retained earnings	87,700	154,300	219,400
Total equities	$290,700	$364,300	$435,800

Income for Years Ended		12/31/81	12/31/82
Sales		$540,000	$617,500
Less: Cost of goods sold		$294,000	$355,000
Other expenses		135,000	154,000
		$429,000	$509,000
Net income before income taxes		$111,000	$108,500
Income taxes (40%)		44,400	43,400
Net income		$ 66,600	$ 65,100

Other data:

1. Inventory on hand at 12/31/80 consisted of 30,000 units valued at $2.30 each
2. Sales (all units sold at the same price in a given year):
   1981—120,000 units @ $4.50 each
   1982—130,000 units @ $4.75 each
3. Purchases (all units purchased at the same price in given year):
   1981—120,000 units @ $2.50 each
   1982—130,000 units @ $2.80 each
4. Income taxes at the effective rate of 40 percent are paid on December 31 each year.

Instructions

Name the account(s) presented in the financial statement that would have different amounts for 1982 if LIFO rather than FIFO had been used and state the new amount for each account that is named.

(CMA adapted)

P8-10 Presented below is information related to the Orthodont Corporation for the last three years:

Item	Quantities in Ending Inventories	Base-Year Cost		Current Year Cost	
		Unit Cost	Amount	Unit Cost	Amount
December 31, 1979:					
A	10,000	$1.00	$10,000	$1.10	$11,000
B	2,000	2.00	4,000	2.40	4,800
C	1,000	5.00	5,000	5.10	5,100
		TOTALS	$19,000		$20,900
December 31, 1980:					
A	9,200	$1.00	$ 9,200	$1.21	$11,132
B	3,000	2.00	6,000	2.52	7,560
C	800	5.00	4,000	6.00	4,800
		TOTALS	$19,200		$23,492
December 31, 1981:					
A	8,000	$1.00	$ 8,000	$1.30	$10,400
B	2,400	2.00	4,800	2.60	6,240
C	1,600	5.00	8,000	7.00	11,200
		TOTALS	$20,800		$27,840

Instructions

Compute the ending inventories under the dollar-value method as illustrated in the textbook for 1979, 1980, and 1981. The base period is January 1, 1979 and the beginning inventory cost at that date was $18,000. Compute indexes to two decimal places.

P8-11 The controller of Liverpool Leather, Inc., a retail company, made three different schedules of gross margin for the first quarter ended September 30, 1981. These schedules appear below.

	Sales ($10 per Unit)	Cost of Goods Sold	Gross Margin
Schedule A	$560,000	$237,100	$322,900
Schedule B	560,000	233,800	326,200
Schedule C	560,000	231,500	328,500

The computation of cost of goods sold in each schedule is based on the following data:

	Units	Cost per Unit	Total Cost
Beginning inventory, July 1	20,000	$4.00	$ 80,000
Purchase, July 25	16,000	4.20	67,200
Purchase, August 15	10,000	4.13	41,300
Purchase, September 5	14,000	4.30	60,200
Purchase, September 25	24,000	4.25	102,000

The president of the corporation cannot understand how three different gross margins can be computed from the same set of data. As controller, you have explained that the three schedules are based on three different assumptions concerning the flow of inventory costs, i.e., first-in, first-out; last-in, first-out; and weighted average. Schedules A, B, and C were not necessarily prepared in this sequence of cost-flow assumptions.

Instructions

Prepare three separate schedules computing cost of goods sold and supporting schedules showing the composition of the ending inventory under each of the three cost-flow assumptions.

P8-12 Sawtell Company cans two food commodities that it stores at various warehouses. The company employs a perpetual inventory accounting system under which the finished goods inventory is charged with production and credited for sales at standard cost. The detail of the finished goods inventory is maintained on punched cards by the tabulating department in units and dollars for the various warehouses.

Company procedures call for the accounting department to receive copies of daily production reports and sales invoices. Units are then extended at standard cost and a summary of the day's activity is posted to the Finished Goods Inventory general ledger control account. Next the sales invoices and production reports are sent to the tabulating department for processing. Every month the control account and detailed tab records are reconciled and adjustments recorded. The last reconciliation and adjustments were made at November 30, 1981.

Your CPA firm observed the taking of the physical inventory at all locations on December 31, 1981. The inventory count began at 3:00 P.M. and was completed at 8:00 P.M. The company's figure for the physical inventory is $331,400. The general ledger control account balance at December 31 was $373,900 and the final "tab" run of the inventory punched cards showed a total of $392,300.

Unit cost data for the company's two products are as follows:

Product	Standard Cost
A	$2.00
B	3.00

A review of December transactions disclosed the following:

1. Sales invoice #1603, 12/2/81, was priced at standard cost for $11,700 but was listed on the accounting department's daily summary at $11,200. *Acct record incorrect. Sales invoice correct, so Tab dept correct.*
2. A production report for $23,900, 12/15/81, was processed twice in error by the tabulating department.
3. Sales invoice #1481, 12/9/81, for 1,200 units of product A, was priced at a standard cost of $1.50 per unit by the accounting department. The tabulating department noticed and corrected the error but did not notify the accounting department of the error.
4. A shipment of 3,400 units of product A was invoiced by the billing department as 3,000 units on sales invoice #1703, 12/27/81. The error was discovered by your review of transactions.

5. On December 27 the Memphis warehouse notified the tabulating department to re-move 2,200 unsalable units of product A from the finished goods inventory, which it did without receiving a special invoice from the accounting department. The accounting department received a copy of the Memphis warehouse notification on December 29 and made up a special invoice that was processed in the normal manner. The units were not included in the physical inventory.

6. A production report for the production on January 3 of 2,500 units of product B was processed for the Omaha plant as of December 31.

7. A shipment of 300 units of product B was made from the Portland warehouse to Ken's Markets, Inc. at 8:30 P.M. on December 31 as an emergency service. The sales invoice was processed as of December 31. The client prefers to treat the transactions as a sale in 1981.

8. The working papers of the auditor observing the physical count at the Chicago ware-house revealed that 700 units of product B were omitted from the client's physical count. The client concurred that the units were omitted in error.

9. A sales invoice for 600 units of product A shipped from the Newark warehouse was mislaid and was not processed until January 5. The units involved were shipped on December 30.

10. The physical inventory of the St. Louis warehouse excluded 350 units of product A that were marked "reserved." Upon investigation it was ascertained that this merchandise was being stored as a convenience for Steve's Markets, Inc., a customer. This merchan-dise, which has not been recorded as a sale, is billed as it is shipped.

11. A shipment of 10,000 units of product B was made on December 27 from the Newark warehouse to the Chicago warehouse. The shipment arrived on January 6 but had been excluded from the physical inventories.

Instructions

Prepare a work sheet to reconcile the balances for the physical inventory, Finished Goods Inventory general ledger control account, and tabulating department's detail of finished goods inventory ("Tab Run").

The following format is suggested for the work sheet.

	Physical Inventory	General Ledger Control Account	Tabulating Department's Detail of Inventory
Balance per client	$331,400	$373,900	$392,300

(AICPA adapted)

P8-13 You are engaged in an audit of the Underwood Manufacturing Company for the year ended December 31, 1981. To reduce the workload at year-end the company took its annual physical inventory under your observation on November 30, 1981. The company's inventory account, which includes raw material and work-in-process, is on a perpetual basis and the first-in, first-out method of pricing is used. There is no finished goods inventory. The company's physical inventory revealed that the book inventory of $55,570 was understated by $4,000. To avoid distorting the interim financial statements the company decided not to adjust the book inventory until year-end except for obsolete inventory items.

Your audit revealed the following information regarding the November 30 inventory:

1. Pricing tests showed that the physical inventory was overpriced by $2,200.

2. Footing and extension errors resulted in a $150 understatement of the physical inventory.

3. Direct labor included in the physical inventory amounted to $10,000. Overhead was included at the rate of 200% of direct labor. You determined that the amount of direct labor was correct and the overhead rate was proper.

4. The physical inventory included obsolete materials recorded at $400. During December these obsolete materials were removed from the inventory account by a charge to Cost of Sales.

   Your audit also disclosed the following information about the December 31 inventory:

1. Total debits to certain accounts during December are listed below.

	December
Purchases	$26,700
Direct labor	12,100
Manufacturing expense	25,200
Cost of goods sold	68,600

2. The cost of goods sold of $68,600 included direct labor of $13,800.

3. Normal scrap loss on established product lines is negligible. A special order started and completed during December had excessive scrap loss of $800, however, which was charged to Manufacturing Expense.

Instructions

   (a) Compute the correct amount of the physical inventory at November 30, 1981.

   (b) Without prejudice to your solution to part (a), assume that the correct amount of the physical inventory at November 30, 1981, was $59,700. Compute the amount of the inventory at December 31, 1981.

(AICPA adapted)

9

Inventories: Additional
Valuation Problems

In Chapter 8, different methods for computing the unit cost for inventories were explained by examining the various flow assumptions used in accounting. Other possibilities will be explored now. For example, what happens if the value of the inventory increases or decreases after the initial purchase date? Does the accountant recognize these increases or decreases in value before the point of sale? What happens if there is a fire and a physical count cannot be made? How does the accountant determine the ending inventory for insurance purposes? Or, what happens in large department stores where monthly inventory figures are needed, but monthly physical counts are not feasible?

These questions involve the development and use of estimation techniques to value the ending inventory without a physical count. Estimation methods that are widely used are discussed in this chapter.

LOWER OF COST OR MARKET

A major departure from adherence to the historical cost principle is made in the area of inventory valuation. If the inventory declines in value below its original cost for whatever reason (e.g., obsolescence, price level changes, or damaged goods), the inventory should be written down to reflect this loss. **The general rule is that the historical cost principle is abandoned when the future utility (revenue-producing ability) of the asset is no longer as great as its original cost.** A departure from cost is justified on the basis that a loss of utility should be reflected as a charge against the revenues in the period in which it occurs. Inventories are valued therefore on the basis of the lower of cost or market instead of on an original cost basis. The term **"market"** in the phrase "the lower of cost or market" generally means the cost to replace the item (by purchase or reproduction). "Market," however, is limited to an amount that should not exceed the net realizable value (i.e., estimated selling price in the ordinary course of business less reasonably predictable costs of completion and disposal) and "should not be less than net realizable value reduced by an allowance for an approximately normal profit margin."[1]

Basically the accountant determines the replacement cost of the inventory, and when it is lower than cost, uses that valuation for pricing the inventory unless it either exceeds net realizable value or is less than net realizable value less a normal margin. These concepts are illustrated below.

Inventory—sales value	$1,000
Less: Estimated cost of completion and disposal	300
Net realizable value	700
Less: Allowance for normal profit margin (10% of sales)	100
Net realizable value less normal profit margin	$ 600

How Lower of Cost or Market Works

The lower of cost or market rule requires that the inventory be valued at cost unless "market" is lower than cost, in which case the inventory is valued at "market." In retailing, **the term "market" as used in this rule refers to the market in which the goods were purchased, not the market in which they are sold; in manufacturing, the term refers to the cost to reproduce.** Thus the rule really means that goods are to be valued at cost or cost to replace, whichever is lower. For example, material that cost $1.00 a unit when purchased, which can now be sold for $1.15, and which can be replaced for $0.90, should be priced at $0.90 for inventory purposes under the lower of cost or market rule.

To understand the rationale for the use of replacement cost, assume that a buyer and seller are negotiating on the price of a unit of merchandise and agree that the regular selling price should be reduced. It would seem logical that the replacement cost of that unit of merchandise either has decreased or will decrease because the expected revenue-producing ability of that unit has been reduced. In attempting to measure the decrease in value of the unit of merchandise the accountant employs replacement cost, because changes in replacement cost usually reflect or predict a decline in selling price and they are easy to identify. Therefore, to insure that the company continues to obtain the same rate of gross profit margin, the inventory is reduced to replacement cost.

Note that in some cases replacement cost and selling price might not move together; therefore, additional safeguards are needed to insure that a proper inventory value is obtained. Thus **"market" is further limited to an amount that "should not exceed the net realizable value** (i.e., estimated selling price in the ordinary course of business less reasonably predictable costs of completion and disposal)" **and "should not be less than net realizable value reduced by an allowance for an**

---

[1]*Accounting Research Bulletin No. 43*, "Restatement and Revision of Accounting Research Bulletins" (New York: AICPA, 1953), Ch. 4, par. 8.

approximately normal profit margin." These restrictions cover rather unusual circumstances or cases. The first, "not to exceed the net realizable value (ceiling)," covers obsolete, damaged, or shopworn material. For example, an item that costs $1.00 when purchased, and that could be replaced for $0.90, may have a realizable value of only $0.70 because it is becoming obsolete. In this case, the item is priced at $0.70 for inventory purposes because to price the inventory at replacement cost would be an overstatement of the value of that item.

The second limitation, "not be less than net realizable value reduced by an allowance for an approximately normal profit margin," is a deterrent to serious understatement of inventory. In effect, it establishes a floor or minimum below which the inventory should not be priced regardless of replacement costs. For example, assume that an inventory item that originally cost $1.00 has a replacement cost of only $0.75. Because of firm sales contracts at firm prices, this item will be sold at $1.15 per unit; however, the net realizable value after deducting the normal profit margin will be $0.90 per unit. In this case the item would be priced in the inventory at $0.90 per unit.

Note that the appropriate market value (replacement cost, net realizable value, or net realizable value less a normal markup) should first be designated and then the **designated market value** should be compared with cost as determined by an acceptable historical cost method. The following cases illustrate how the inventory value is determined under the lower of cost or market approach.

		ILLUSTRATION OF LOWER OF COST OR MARKET APPROACH			
			Market		
Case	Cost	Replacement Cost	Net Realizable Value	Net Realizable Value Less a Normal Markup	Final Inventory Value
1	$1.00	$1.10	$1.50	$1.20	$1.00
2	1.00	.90	1.00	.70	.90
3	1.00	.95	.80	.56	.80
4	1.00	.40	.80	.56	.56
5	1.00	1.05	.95	.80	.95

Case 1. Cost selected because it is lower than market.

Case 2. Replacement cost selected because it is lower than cost and within the constraints imposed by the rule.

Case 3. Net realizable value (ceiling) selected because replacement cost, while lower than cost, is higher than net realizable value. Future utility is limited to net realizable value.

Case 4. Net realizable value less a normal margin (floor) is selected because replacement cost is below this figure, which is the lower constraint for market.

Case 5. Net realizable value (ceiling) is selected because replacement cost is above this upper constraint. Cost is not selected because it is higher than market.

Only losses in inventory value that occur in the normal course of business from such causes as style changes, shift in demand, or regular shop wear result from the application of the lower of cost or market rule. Damaged and deteriorated goods are reduced to net realizable value; such goods are carried in separate inventory accounts when significant in amount.

Recording "Market" Instead of Cost

In those cases in which "market" rather than cost is used as the inventory price, many accountants consider it undesirable accounting procedure merely to substitute the replacement cost figure for cost when pricing the new inventory. This procedure increases the cost of goods sold by the amount of the loss recognized and thus fails to reflect this loss separately. This objection may be overcome by first determining and recording the inventory at cost at the adjusting or closing process and then making a separate entry to reduce the inventory to market. For a situation in which the inventory cost $82,000 but which must be reduced to $70,000 under the lower of cost or market rule, the entries are:

Inventory	82,000	
Cost of Goods Sold (Revenue and Expense Summary)		82,000
(To record inventory for the year)		
Loss Due to Market Decline of Inventory	12,000	
Inventory		12,000
(To write down inventory to market)		

The loss is then shown as a separate item in the income statement, but not as an extraordinary item, and the cost of the sales for the year is not distorted by its inclusion. Also, the rate of gross profit for the year is not affected by the loss due to market decline.

The advantage of recording a market decline in this manner is indicated in the following comparison.

Inventory Priced at Market		
Sales		$200,000
Cost of goods sold		
Inventory Jan. 1	$ 65,000	
Purchases	125,000	
Goods available	190,000	
Inventory Dec. 31	70,000	
Cost of goods sold		120,000
Gross profit on sales		$ 80,000
Inventory Priced at Cost and Reduced to Market by Separate Journal Entry		
Sales		$200,000
Cost of goods sold		
Inventory Jan. 1	$ 65,000	
Purchases	125,000	
Goods available	190,000	
Inventory Dec. 31	82,000	
Cost of goods sold		108,000
Gross profit on sales		92,000
Loss due to market decline of inventory		12,000
		$ 80,000

The second presentation is preferable, because it clearly discloses the loss resulting from the market decline of inventory prices, which is "buried" in the cost of goods sold figure in the first presentation. Although this presentation is preferred to direct pricing of the inventory at market because the loss due to market decline is shown separately, it does include an inconsistency: the inventory is shown at $82,000 in the income statement but it is included in the balance sheet at only $70,000. In overcoming this inconsistency, some accountants have advocated the use of a special account to receive the credit for such an inventory write-down. Instead of the inventory account being credited directly, the entry to write down the inventory from cost to the lower of cost or market is modified as follows:

Inventory	82,000	
Cost of Goods Sold (Revenue and Expense Summary)		82,000
(To record inventory for the year)		
Loss Due to Market Decline of Inventory	12,000	
Reduction of Inventory to Market		12,000
(To write-down inventory to market)		

The Reduction of Inventory to Market (contra asset) would be shown on the balance sheet as a deduction from the inventory of $82,000, thereby reducing it to the lower of cost or market. This deduction permits both the income statement and the balance sheet to show the amount of $82,000, although the inventory extension in the balance sheet is a net amount of $70,000. It also keeps subsidiary inventory ledgers and records in correspondence with the control account without changing unit prices.

Although this device permits disclosure on the balance sheet of the amount of inventory both at cost and at the lower of cost or market, it raises the additional problem of how to dispose of the balance of the new account in the following period. If the merchandise in question is still on hand, the account may be retained, but, if it is assumed that the goods that suffered the decline have been sold, this account should be removed from the books. Because the inventory account is currently stated at cost, the beginning inventory and thus the cost of goods sold in the next period are overstated if the allowance balance is not closed. **Closing the allowance account against beginning inventory** (or to Cost of Goods Sold if beginning inventory has already been removed from the accounts) **corrects the misstatement.** A "new" allowance account is then established for the decline in inventory value that has taken place in the current period.

Another possibility justified on the basis that the item is immaterial is to close the allowance account to a revenue and expense summary account, either as income or as a reduction of costs and expenses.

Some accountants leave this account on the books and merely adjust the balance at the next year end to agree with the discrepancy between cost and the lower of cost or market at that balance sheet date. Thus, if prices are falling, a loss is recorded and, if prices are increasing, a loss recorded in prior years is recovered, and a gain is recorded, as illustrated in the example on page 385. This "gain" can be thought of as the credit effect of closing the beginning allowance balance exceeding the debit effect of setting up the current year-end allowance account.

Date	Inventory At Cost	Inventory At Market	Amount Required in Valuation Account	Adjustment of Valuation Account Balance	Effect on Net Income
Dec. 31, 1978	$188,000	$176,000	$12,000	$12,000 inc.	Loss
Dec. 31, 1979	194,000	187,000	7,000	5,000 dec.	Gain
Dec. 31, 1980	173,000	174,000	0	7,000 dec.	Gain
Dec. 31, 1981	182,000	180,000	2,000	2,000 inc.	Loss

Recognition of gain or loss has the same effect on net income as closing the allowance balance to beginning inventory or to cost of goods sold.

This discussion indicates some of the basic presentation problems surrounding the lower of cost or market approach. It also illustrates the complications that arise when deviations are made from basic accounting theory. To the alert student of business one conclusion seems inevitable. As long as a number of treatments and practices are followed, real understanding of accounting reports requires some knowledge of all the possibilities and their effect on the reported data.

Methods of Applying Cost or Market

The cost or market rule may be "applied either directly to each item or to the total of the inventory (or, in some cases, to the total of the components of each major category). The method should be the one that most clearly reflects periodic income."[2] Ordinarily the application of the rule to the total of the inventory, or to the total components of each major category, results in an amount that more nearly approaches cost than it would if the rule were applied to each item. Under the first two methods, increases in market prices offset, to some extent, the decreases in market prices, as illustrated below.

	Cost	Market	Lower of Cost or Market by: Individual Items	Lower of Cost or Market by: Major Categories	Lower of Cost or Market by: Total Inventory
Radios					
Type A	$ 800	$ 750	$ 750		
B	1,500	1,600	1,500		
C	900	800	800		
Total	3,200	3,150		$ 3,150	
TV Sets					
Type X	3,000	3,400	3,000		
Y	4,500	4,300	4,300		
Z	2,000	1,900	1,900		
Total	9,500	9,600		9,500	
Total Inventory	$12,700	$12,750	$12,250	$12,650	$12,700

[2]*Ibid.*, par. 10.

If the lower of cost or market rule is applied by individual items, the amount of inventory is $12,250. If applied by major categories, it is $12,650 and, if applied to the total inventory, it is $12,700.

The most common practice is to price the inventory on an item-by-item basis. Companies favor the individual item approach because tax rules require that an individual item basis be used unless it involves practical difficulties. In addition, the individual item approach gives the most conservative valuation for balance sheet purposes.

Whichever method is selected, it should be applied consistently from one period to the next. **As soon as the inventory is written down to market, this new basis is considered to be the cost basis for future periods.** A rise in the market prices of the inventory after it has been written down generally should not be recognized.[3]

Evaluation of Lower of Cost or Market Rule

Conceptually, the lower of cost or market rule has some deficiencies. First, if the inventory is written down because of a loss in utility, does it not seem appropriate to write up the value of the inventory when the utility of the asset increases? Decreases in the value of the asset and the charge to income are recognized in the period in which the loss in utility occurs—not in the period of sale. On the other hand, increases in the value of the asset are recognized only at the point of sale. This situation is inconsistent and can lead to distortions in the presentation of income data.

Even if we accept this inconsistency, another problem arises in defining market. **Basically, three different types of valuation can be used: replacement cost, net realizable value, and net realizable value less a normal markup.** Replacement cost was chosen as the initial value to employ because changes in replacement cost usually reflect or predict declines in the selling price, and changes in replacement cost are easy to identify. Sometimes, however, a reduction in the replacement cost of an item does not indicate a corresponding reduction in the utility of the item. To illustrate, assume that a retailer has several shirts that were bought at $3.00 per shirt. The replacement cost of these shirts falls to $2.50, but the selling price remains the same. Has the retailer suffered a loss? To recognize a loss in this period misstates this year's income and also that of future periods, because when the shirts are subsequently sold, the full price for the shirts is received.

The second valuation approach—net realizable value—is the most logical method for valuing inventory. The net realizable value reflects the future service potential of the asset and, for that reason, it is conceptually sound. Unfortunately, net realizable value cannot often be measured with any certainty. We, therefore, revert to replacement cost, because net realizable value less a normal markup is even more uncertain than net realizable value. With net realizable value less a normal markup, for example, we face the difficult problem of determining a normal profit. In addition, under this approach a large loss occurs in one period, yet part of this loss is booked as profit in a future period. To illustrate, assume that an item costing $10 has a net realizable value of $8.00 and that the normal markup is

---

[3]For tax purposes, the lower of cost or market rule cannot be used with LIFO. There is nothing, however, to prevent the use of lower of cost or market and LIFO for financial reporting purposes.

30% of the selling price. Those who use net realizable value simply indicate that a loss of $2.00 occurs ($10 − $8.00); those who advocate net realizable value less a normal markup show a loss of $5.00 ($10 − $2.00 − $3.00) and then later record a gain of $3.00 ($10 − $5.00 − $2.00). The purpose of the latter approach is to show a normal profit margin in the period of sale.

From the standpoint of accounting theory there is little to justify the lower of cost or market rule. Although conservative from the balance sheet point of view, it permits the income statement to show a larger net income in future periods than would be justified if the inventory were carried forward at cost. The rule is applied only in those cases where strong evidence indicates that market declines in inventory prices have occurred that will result in losses when such inventories are disposed of. Net realizable value and not replacement cost appears to be the appropriate basis of valuation in these circumstances.[4]

Purchase Orders and Contracts

Usually it is neither necessary nor proper for the buyer to make any entries to reflect commitments for purchases of goods that have not been shipped by the seller. Ordinary orders, for which the prices are determined at the time of shipment and **which are subject to cancellation** by the buyer or seller, do not represent either an asset or a liability to the buyer and need not be reflected in the books or in the financial statements.

Formal purchase contracts for which a firm price has been established, however, if of material amount, should be disclosed in the balance sheet of the buyer by means of a footnote. The following is such a footnote.

> Note 1. Contracts for the purchase of raw materials in 1982 have been executed in the amount of $600,000. The market price of such raw materials on December 31, 1981, is $640,000.

In the foregoing illustration we assumed that the contracted price was less than the market price at the date of the balance sheet. If the contracted price is in excess of the purchase market price and it is expected that losses will occur when the purchase is effected, losses should be recognized in the accounts in the period during which such declines in prices take place.[5] For example, if purchase contracts for delivery in 1982 have been executed at a firm price of $800,000 and the market price of the materials on December 31, 1981 is $750,000, the following entry is made:

Loss on Purchase Commitments	50,000	
Accrued Loss on Purchase Commitments		50,000

---

[4]*Accounting Research Study No. 13*, "The Accounting Basis of Inventories" (New York: AICPA, 1973) recommends that net realizable value be adopted. It also should be noted that a literal interpretation of the rules of lower of cost or market is frequently not applied in practice. For example, the lower limit, net realizable value less a normal markup, is rarely computed and applied because it results in an extremely conservative inventory valuation approach. In addition, inventory is often not reduced to market unless its disposition is expected to result in a loss. Furthermore, if the net realizable value of finished goods exceeds cost, it is usually assumed that both work in process and raw materials do as well. In practice, therefore, **ARB No. 43** is considered a guide, and professional judgment is often exercised in lieu of following this pronouncement literally.

[5]*Accounting Research Bulletin No. 43, op. cit.*, par. 16.

This loss would be closed out to Revenue and Expense Summary and shown on the income statement; the Accrued Loss on Purchase Commitments is shown in the liability section of the balance sheet. When the goods are delivered in 1982, the entry will be:

Purchases	750,000	
Accrued Loss on Purchase Commitments	50,000	
Accounts Payable		800,000

This procedure represents a departure from the basic theory that assets should be accounted for on a basis of cost. Those who advocate this procedure contend that the desirability of recognizing the loss in the period during which the price decline takes place justifies departing from the cost principle.

If the price is partially or fully recovered before the inventory is received, the Accrued Loss on Purchase Commitments would be reduced. A resulting gain would then be reported in the period of the price increase for the amount of the partial or full recovery.

Valuation at Selling Price

Under certain circumstances, support exists for **recording inventory at selling price less estimated costs to complete and sell.** For example, an exception to the normal realization rule is permitted where (1) there is a controlled market with a fixed price applicable to all quantities and (2) no significant costs of disposal are involved. Inventories of certain minerals, for example, are ordinarily reflected at selling prices because there is a government-controlled market without significant costs of disposal. A similar treatment is given agricultural products that are immediately marketable at fixed prices.

Another reason for allowing this method of valuation is that often the cost figures are too difficult to obtain. As indicated in Chapter 2, it is difficult to allocate the cost of an animal "on the hoof" into the costs of ribs, chuck, shoulders, and so on. It seems much more useful to determine the market price of the end product less costs of disposal than to make an arbitrary allocation of costs. Recognition of inventories at selling price less cost of disposal means that income is recognized before the goods are transferred to an outside party. If this approach is adopted, the use of such basis should be fully disclosed in the financial statements.

RELATIVE SALES VALUE METHOD

A special problem of pricing inventory items is found when a group of varying units is purchased at a single lump sum price. For example, a lot consisting of 400 melons is purchased at a total cost of $100. These melons are of different weights and grades but can be sorted roughly into three groups graded A, B, and C. As melons are sold, it becomes necessary to apportion the purchase cost of $100 between the melons sold and the melons remaining on hand.

It is unfair to divide 400 melons into the total cost of $100 to get a cost of $0.25 for each melon, because they vary in size and grade. The actual share of the total cost applicable to each melon should also vary. When such a situation is encountered, and it is not at all unusual, the common and most logical practice is to allocate the total cost among the various units on the basis of their relative sales value. For the example given, the allocation works out as follows:

				Allocation of Cost				
Grade	Number of Melons	Sales Price per Melon	Total Sales Price	Relative Sales Price	Total Cost	Cost Allocated To Grade	Cost per Melon
A	100	$1.00	$100.00	100/250	$100	$ 40.00	$.40
B	100	.60	60.00	60/250	100	24.00	.24
C	200	.45	90.00	90/250	100	36.00	.18
			$250.00			$100.00	

The cost of melons sold can be computed by using the amounts given in the column for "Cost per Melon," and the income determined as follows:

		Determination of Gross Income			
Grade	Number of Melons Sold	Cost Per Melon	Cost of Melons Sold	Sales	Gross Profit
A	77	$.40	$30.80	$ 77.00	$ 46.20
B	80	.24	19.20	48.00	28.80
C	100	.18	18.00	45.00	27.00
			$68.00	$170.00	$102.00

This information may be applied in a slightly different way. The ratio of the cost to the selling price of all the melons is $100 divided by $250, or 40%. Accordingly, if the total sales price of melons sold is, say, $170, then the cost of these melons sold is 40% of $170, or $68. The inventory of melons on hand is $100 less $68, or $32.

THE GROSS PROFIT METHOD OF DETERMINING INVENTORY

The basic purpose in taking a physical inventory is to verify the accuracy of the inventory records or, if no records exist, to arrive at an inventory amount. Sometimes substitute measures are used to arrive at the same answer. One substitute method of verifying or determining the inventory amount is called the gross profit method. This method is widely used by auditors in situations where only an estimate of the amount of the company's inventory is needed, or where both inventory and inventory records have been destroyed by fire or other catastrophe.

The **gross profit method** is based on the assumptions that (1) the beginning inventory plus purchases equal total goods to be accounted for; (2) goods not sold must be on hand; and (3) if the sales, reduced to cost, are deducted from the sum of the opening inventory plus purchases, the result is the goods on hand or, in other words, the inventory.

To illustrate, assume that a department has a beginning inventory of $60,000 and purchases of $200,000 both at cost. Sales at selling price amount to $280,000. The average rate of gross margin on selling price for that department is 30%. The gross profit test is applied as follows:

Beginning inventory (at cost)		$ 60,000
Purchases (at cost)		200,000
Goods available (at cost)		260,000
Sales (at selling price)	$280,000	
Less gross margin (30% of $280,000)	84,000	
Sales (at cost)		196,000
Approximate inventory (at cost)		$ 64,000

When the inventory is approximated by this method, care must be taken in applying a blanket rate of gross margin. Frequently a store or department handles merchandise with widely varying rates of gross margin. In these situations the gross profit test may have to be applied by subsections, lines of merchandise, or a similar basis that classifies merchandise according to rates of gross margin.

The gross profit method is not normally acceptable for financial reporting purposes because it is only an estimate, and a physical inventory is needed as additional verification that the inventory indicated in the records is on hand. The gross profit method also uses past percentages for determination of the markup, and although the past can often provide answers to the future, a current rate is more appropriate. The gross profit percentage is an average rate, and whenever several different items are sold, it is best to make separate gross profit calculations for each line of items. If a composite approach is used, a change in the quantity of one line relative to another, or a change in the markup of one line could lead to an inaccurate final inventory value.

Calculation of Gross Margin Percentage

In most situations, the gross margin percentage is given as a percentage of selling price. The previous illustration indicated that a 30% gross margin on sales was used. Gross margin on selling price is the common method for quoting the margin because (1) most goods are stated on a retail basis, not a cost basis, and (2) a margin quoted on selling price is lower than one based on cost, and this lower rate gives a favorable impression to the consumer, and (3) the gross margin based on selling price can never exceed 100%.

To see how gross margin is computed, assume that an article cost $15 and sells for $20, a gross margin of $5.00. This markup is ¼ or 25% of retail and ⅓ or 33⅓% of cost.

$$\frac{\text{markup}}{\text{retail}} = \frac{\$ 5.00}{\$20.00} = 25\% \text{ at retail} \qquad \frac{\text{markup}}{\text{cost}} = \frac{\$ 5.00}{\$15.00} = 33\frac{1}{3}\% \text{ on cost}$$

Although it is normal to compute the gross margin on the basis of selling price, the accountant should understand the basic relationship between markup on cost and markup on selling price. For example, again assume that an item sells for $20 and costs $15, generating a $5 gross margin. As illustrated above, this gross margin is 25% when based on selling price, but is 33⅓% when based on cost. The accountant must be able to convert from one base to another. The following diagram shows these relationships.

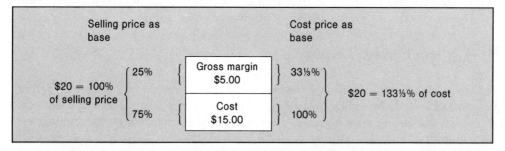

Retailers use the following formulas to express these relationships:

1. Percentage markup on selling price $= \dfrac{\text{percentage markup on cost}}{100\% + \text{percentage markup on cost}}$

2. Percentage markup on cost $= \dfrac{\text{percentage markup on selling price}}{100\% - \text{percentage markup on selling price}}$

To illustrate how these formulas are employed, let us assume that the markup on cost is 25% and that the accountant wishes to determine the markup on the selling price. Using formula (1) we get

$$\frac{25\%}{100\% + 25\%} = 20\%$$

A markup of 50% on selling price is translated to a markup on cost by formula (2):

$$\frac{50\%}{100\% - 50\%} = 100\%$$

The gross margin on cost is naturally higher than the gross margin on selling price. It should be emphasized that sales may not be multiplied by a cost-based gross margin percentage; the gross margin percentage must be converted to a percentage based on selling price.

Appraisal of Gross Profit Method

The gross profit method suffers from the disadvantage that the percentages used are based on data from past periods. When these percentages are fair representations of the current year's gross margin, no problem of valuation occurs. Whenever significant fluctuations have occurred, however, it is the accountant's function to adjust the percentage as appropriate.

Regardless of whether the gross profit test is used for estimating inventory values, a physical inventory should be taken once a year to verify the inventory actually on hand. When a physical inventory is not possible (such as when a catastrophe occurs), the accountant must seriously consider developing a representative gross profit percentage; the accountant must also insure that the goods in inventory are representative of the goods that were available for sale.

RETAIL INVENTORY METHOD

Retailers with certain types of inventory may use the specific identification method for valuation of their ending inventory. When an item is purchased, the cost of the item is coded on the sales tag, and at the end of the accounting period the tags are totaled to determine the ending inventory. An alternative approach is to establish perpetual records for the items purchased and sold during the accounting period. In most retail concerns, however, an observable pattern between cost and sales price lends itself to the computation of inventory on hand without a physical count of items on hand. This method, called **the retail inventory method, requires that a record be kept of (1) the total cost of goods purchased, (2) the total retail value of the goods available for sale, and (3) the sales for the period.** The sales for the period are deducted from the retail value of the goods available for sale to produce an estimated inventory at retail. The ratio of cost to retail for all goods passing through a department or firm is then determined by dividing the total goods available for sale at cost by the total goods available at retail. The inventory valued at retail is reduced to approximate cost by applying the cost to retail ratio. The retail inventory method is illustrated for Marshy Field, Inc.

Marshy Field, Inc. RETAIL INVENTORY METHOD (current period)	Cost	Retail
Beginning inventory	$14,000	$ 20,000
Purchases	63,000	90,000
Goods available	$77,000	110,000
Deduct sales		85,000
Ending inventory, at retail		$ 25,000
Ratio of cost to retail ($77,000 ÷ $110,000)		70%
Ending inventory at cost (70% of $25,000)		$ 17,500

This calculation is based on the equation that the total goods available for sale (at retail) less the goods sold (at retail) equals the goods on hand (at retail). The goods on hand at retail are then converted to goods on hand at cost by application of the cost to retail ratio. To avoid a potential overstatement of the inventory, periodic inventory counts are made, especially in retail operations where loss due to shoplifting and breakage is common.

The retail method is sanctioned by the IRS, various retail associations, and the accounting profession. **One advantage of the retail inventory method is that the**

inventory balance can be approximated without a physical count. This method is particularly useful for any type of interim report, because a fairly quick and reliable measure of the inventory value can be determined. Insurance adjusters often use this approach when estimates of the inventory are needed because of a fire, flood, or other type of casualty. This method also acts as a control device because any deviations from a physical count at the end of the year will have to be explained. In addition, the retail method also expedites the physical inventory count at the end of the year. The inventory crew need only take the retail prices of each item without a careful comparison of each cost invoice, thereby saving time and expense.

Retail Method Terminology

The amounts shown in the Retail column of the preceding illustration represent the original retail prices, assuming no other price changes up or down. Sales prices are frequently changed from the original retail prices, however, that is, marked up or marked down. For retailers, markup is considered in the context of an additional markup on original selling price; normally, we think of markup on the basis of cost. Markup cancellations are decreases in prices of merchandise that had been marked up above the original retail price.

Markdowns below the original sale prices may be necessary because of a decrease in the general level of prices, special sales, soiled and damaged goods, overstocking, and competition, for instance. Markdowns are by far the more common phenomenon. Markdown cancellations occur when the markdowns are partially offset at a later date by increases in the prices of goods that had been marked down below the original sales price. Neither a markup cancellation nor a markdown cancellation can exceed the original markup or markdown.

To illustrate these different concepts, let us assume that the Hub Clothing Store recently purchased 100 high-fashion knit dress shirts from Marroway, Inc. The cost for these shirts was $400 or $4.00 a shirt. Hub Clothing established the selling price on these shirts at $8.50 a shirt. The manager noted that the shirts were selling quickly, so he added a markup of $1.50 per shirt. This markup made the price too high and sales lagged; the manager then reduced the price to $9.00. At this point we would say that Hub Clothing has had a markup of $1.50 and a markup cancellation of $1.00. As soon as the major marketing season passed, the manager marked the remaining shirts down to a sales price of $6.00. At this point, an additional markup cancellation of $.50 has taken place and a $2.50 markdown has occurred. If the shirts are later written up to $7.00, a markdown cancellation of $1.00 will develop.

Retail Inventory Method with Markups and Markdowns

Retailers use these concepts in developing the proper inventory valuation at the end of the accounting period. To obtain the appropriate inventory figures, proper treatment must be given to markups, markup cancellations, markdowns, and markdown cancellations. To illustrate the different possibilities, assume the following conditions for Donovan Stores, Inc.

	Cost	Retail
Beginning inventory	$ 500	$ 1,000
Purchases (net)	20,000	35,000
Markups		3,000
Markup cancellations		1,000
Markdowns		2,500
Markdown cancellations		2,000
Sales (net)		25,000

Donovan Stores, Inc.
RETAIL INVENTORY METHOD

	Cost	Retail	
Beginning inventory	$ 500	$ 1,000	
Purchases (net)	20,000	35,000	
Merchandise available for sale	20,500	36,000	
Cost ratio $\dfrac{\$20,500}{\$36,000} = 56.9\%$			(A)
Add:			
Markups		$3,000	
Less markup cancellations		(1,000)	
Net markups		2,000	
	20,500	38,000	
Cost ratio $\dfrac{\$20,500}{\$38,000} = 53.9\%$			(B)
Deduct:			
Markdowns		2,500	
Less markdown cancellations		(2,000)	
Net markdowns		500	
	$20,500	37,500	
Cost ratio $\dfrac{\$20,500}{\$37,500} = 54.7\%$			(C)
Deduct sales (net)		25,000	
Ending inventory at retail		$12,500	

Computation of ending inventory at cost under different assumptions:

> A $12,500 × 56.9% = $7,112.50
> B 12,500 × 53.9% = 6,737.50
> C 12,500 × 54.7% = 6,837.50

The first percentage considers only the sum of the beginning inventory and net purchases, and represents a cost percentage before markups or markdowns. The second percentage reflects a cost percentage after the additional markups but before the markdowns. Finally, the third percentage is computed after both the markups and the markdowns. Which percentage should be employed to compute the ending inventory valuation?

The conventional retail inventory method is designed to approximate the lower of cost or market. Thus the accountant computes the cost percentage after the markups but before the markdowns. To understand why the markups but not the markdowns are considered in the cost percentage, we must understand how a retail outlet operates. When a company has an additional markup, it normally indicates that the market value of that item has increased. On the other hand, if the company has a net markdown, it means that a decline in the utility of that item has occurred. Therefore, if we attempt to approximate the lower of cost or market, markdowns are considered a current loss and are not involved in the calculation of the cost to retail ratio. For example, two items were purchased for $5 apiece, and the original sales price was established at $10 each. One item was subsequently written down to $2.00. Assuming no sales for the period, if markdowns are considered in the cost to retail ratio, we compute the ending inventory in the following manner.

	Cost	Retail
Cost Method		
Markdowns Considered in Cost Ratio		
Purchases	$10.00	$20.00
Deduct markdowns		8.00
Ending inventory, at retail		$12.00
Cost to retail ratio $\dfrac{\$10.00}{\$12.00} = 83.3\%$		
Ending inventory at cost ($12.00 $\times$ .833) = $10.00		

This approach reflects an average cost of the two items of the commodity without considering the loss on the one item. If a lower of cost or market approach is adopted, the calculation is made in the following manner.

	Cost	Retail
Conventional Method		
Lower of Cost or Market		
Purchases	$10.00	$20.00
Cost to retail ratio $\dfrac{\$10.00}{\$20.00} = 50\%$		
Deduct markdown		8.00
Ending inventory, at retail		$12.00
Ending inventory, at cost ($12 $\times$ .50) = $6.00		

Under the conventional retail inventory method when markdowns are **not** considered in computing the cost to retail ratio, the ratio would be 50% ($10/20) and ending inventory would be $6 ($12 $\times$ .50), the same as lower of cost or market.

The inventory valuation of $6 reflects two inventory items, one inventoried at $5, the other at $1.00. Basically, the sale price was reduced from $10 to $2 and the cost reduced from $5 to $1.00.[6] To approximate the lower of cost or market, therefore,

[6]This figure is really not market (replacement cost), but is net realizable value less the normal margin that is allowed. In other words, the sale price of the goods written down is $2.00, but subtracting a normal margin of 100%, the figure becomes $1.00. The normal margin is 100% based on cost. (A markup of $5.00 on a cost of $5.00.)

the **cost to retail ratio** must be established by dividing the cost of goods available by the sum of the original retail price of these goods plus the net markups; the markdowns and markdown cancellations are excluded. The basic format for the retail inventory method using the lower of cost or market approach is illustrated below using the Donovan Stores information.

Donovan Stores
Retail Method—Lower of Cost or Market Approach

	Cost		Retail
Beginning inventory	$ 500.00		$ 1,000.00
Purchases (net)	20,000.00		35,000.00
Totals	20,500.00		36,000.00
Add net markups—			
Markups		$3,000.00	
Markup cancellations		1,000.00	2,000.00
Totals	$20,500.00		38,000.00
Deduct net markdowns—			
Markdowns		2,500.00	
Markdown cancellations		2,000.00	500.00
Sales price of goods available			37,500.00
Deduct sales			25,000.00
Ending inventory, at retail			$12,500.00

Cost-to-retail ratio $= \dfrac{\text{cost of goods available}}{\text{original retail price of goods available, plus net markups}}$

$= \dfrac{\$20,500}{\$38,000} = 53.9\%$

Ending inventory at lower of cost or market	$ 6,737.50
(53.9% × $12,500.00)	

Because an averaging effect occurs, an exact lower of cost or market inventory valuation is ordinarily not obtained, but an adequate approximation can be achieved. By computing the cost ratio from the totals after adding net markups **and** deducting net markdowns, it is possible to arrive at **approximate cost** instead of approximating the lower of cost or market.

LIFO Retail

Many retailers and accounting theorists have argued that the conventional retail method follows a flow assumption that does not match current cost against current revenues and, therefore, large fluctuations in profit can occur. It is not surprising that many individuals suggest that a LIFO assumption be adopted to obtain a better matching of costs and revenues. In addition, once the LIFO method was accepted for income tax purposes, many retail establishments changed from the more conventional treatment to the LIFO retail approach simply for the tax advantages associated with valuing inventories on a LIFO basis. The application of LIFO retail is made under two assumptions:

1. stable prices,
2. fluctuating prices.

Stable Prices   The computation of the final inventory balance assuming a LIFO flow is much more complex than the calculation related to the conventional retail method. Because the LIFO method is a cost method, not a cost or market approach, both the markups **and** the markdowns must be considered in obtaining the proper cost to retail percentage. Furthermore, since the LIFO method is concerned only with the additional layer that is added, or the amount that should be subtracted from the previous layer, the beginning inventory should be excluded from the cost to retail percentage. **A major assumption of the LIFO retail method is that the markups and markdowns apply only to the goods purchased during the current period and not to the beginning inventory.** In addition, we have assumed that the price level has remained unchanged. The concepts are illustrated below.

Retail LIFO Method (Stable Prices)	Cost	Retail
Beginning inventory	$27,000	$ 45,000
Net purchases during the period	346,500	480,000
Net markups		20,000
Net markdowns		(5,000)
Total (excluding beginning inventory)	346,500	495,000
Total (including beginning inventory)	$373,500	540,000
Net sales during the period		(484,000)
Ending inventory at retail		$ 56,000
Establishment of cost to retail percentage under assumptions of LIFO retail ($346,500 ÷ $495,000)		70%
Ending inventory at cost		
Beginning inventory ($45,000 @ 60%[a])		$27,000
Additional increment		
Ending inventory	$56,000	
Beginning inventory	(45,000)	
	11,000	
Cost to retail percentage	70%	7,700
Ending inventory at LIFO cost (stable prices)		$34,700

[a] $\dfrac{\$27,000}{\$45,000}$ (prior year's cost to retail percentage)

The illustration indicates that the inventory is composed of two layers: the beginning inventory and the additional increase that occurred in the inventory this period. If we start the next period, the beginning inventory will be composed of two layers, and if an increase in inventory occurs again, an additional layer will be added. If, however, the final inventory figure is below the beginning inventory, it is necessary to reduce the beginning inventory starting with the most recent (second) layer. For example, assume that the ending inventory for the next period at retail is $50,000. The computation of the ending inventory at cost is shown on page 398.

When a layer concept is involved, as in a LIFO situation, previous layers must be reduced in a LIFO flow starting with the last layer added, whenever the ending inventory is smaller than the beginning inventory.

Ending inventory at retail	$50,000
Composed of:	
First layer $45,000 × 60%	$27,000
Second layer $ 5,000 × 70%	3,500
Ending inventory at cost	$30,500

Fluctuating Prices   The computation of the LIFO retail method was simplified in the previous illustration because changes in the selling price of the inventory were ignored. Let us now assume that a change in the price level of the inventories occurs (as is usual). If the price level does change, the price change must be eliminated because we are measuring the real increase in inventory, not the dollar increase. To illustrate, assume that the beginning inventory had a retail market value of $10,000 and the ending inventory a retail market value of $15,000. If the price level has risen from 100 to 125, it is inappropriate to suggest that a real increase in inventory of $5,000 has occurred. Instead, the ending inventory should be deflated as indicated by the computation below.

Ending inventory (deflated) $15,000 ÷ 1.25	$12,000	
Beginning inventory	10,000	
Real increase	$ 2,000	
Ending inventory on LIFO basis:		
First layer	$10,000	
Second layer ($2,000 × 1.25)	2,500	$12,500

This approach is essentially the dollar-value method previously discussed in Chapter 8. In computing the LIFO inventory under a dollar-value LIFO approach, the dollar increase in inventory is found and deflated to beginning of the year prices to determine whether actual increases or decreases in quantity have occurred. If an increase in quantities develops, this increase is priced at the new index to find the new layer to be added to the previous layers. If a decrease in quantities develops, it is subtracted from the most recent layers to the extent necessary to find the proper valuation. In deflating the retail inventory figures, an appropriate index representative of the industry involved is employed.

The following computations, taken from our previous illustration, illustrate the differences between the dollar-value LIFO retail method and the regular LIFO retail approach. Assume that the 1980 price index is 112 (1979 = 100) and that the inventory ($56,000) has remained unchanged. (See illustration page 399.)

The inventory is computed as shown on page 399 before adjustment. Note that the computations on page 399 involved in finding the cost to retail percentage are exactly the same as they are under the LIFO approach presented in the preceding section (page 397). At this point the two approaches differ, however, because the dollar-value method, shown on page 399, determines the real increase that has occurred in the inventory.

Dollar-Value LIFO Method (Fluctuating Prices)

	Cost	Retail
Beginning inventory—1980	$ 27,000	$ 45,000
Net purchases during the period	346,500	480,000
Net markups		20,000
Net markdowns		(5,000)
Total (excluding beginning inventory)	346,500	495,000
Total (including beginning inventory)	$373,500	540,000
Net sales during the period at retail		(484,000)
Ending inventory at retail		$ 56,000
Establishment of cost to retail percentage under assumptions of LIFO retail ($346,500 ÷ $495,000)	70%	

A. Ending inventory at retail prices deflated to base year prices

$\qquad$ $56,000 \times \dfrac{100}{112} =$ $\qquad$ $50,000

B. Beginning inventory at base-year prices $\qquad$ 45,000

C. Inventory increase from beginning of period $\qquad$ $ 5,000

D. Increment now priced in terms of end-of-year prices

$\qquad$ $5,000 \times \dfrac{112}{100} =$ $\qquad$ $ 5,600

From this information, we compute the appropriate inventory amount:

First layer—beginning inventory in terms of 100	$27,000
Second layer—(remainder of 1980 increase at new price level times cost to retail percentage) $5,600 × 70% — see (D) above	3,920
Ending inventory at LIFO cost (fluctuating prices)	$30,920

As is illustrated above, layers of a particular year must be restated to the prices in effect in the year when the layer was added before the conversion to cost takes place.

Note the difference between the LIFO approach (stable prices) and the dollar-value LIFO method as indicated below:

	LIFO (stable prices)	LIFO (fluctuating prices)
Beginning inventory	$27,000	$27,000
Increment	7,700	3,920
Ending inventory	$34,700	$30,920

The difference of $3,780 ($34,700 − $30,920) is a result of an increase in the price of goods, but is not representative of an increase in the quantity of goods.

Special Items

The retail inventory method becomes more complicated when such items as freight-in, purchase returns and allowances, and purchase discounts are involved. **Freight costs** are treated as a part of the cost of the purchase; **purchase returns and allowances** are ordinarily considered both as a reduction of the cost price and the retail price; **purchase discounts** usually are considered as a reduction of purchases unless these discounts are recorded as financial income. When the purchase allowance is not reflected by a reduction in the selling price, no adjustment is made to the retail column. In short, the treatment for the items affecting the cost column of the retail inventory approach follow the computation for cost of goods available for sale. Note also that **sales returns and allowances** are considered as proper adjustments to gross sales; **sales discounts,** however, are not recognized when sales are recorded gross. To adjust for the sales discount account in such a situation would provide an ending inventory figure at retail that would be overvalued.

In addition, there are a number of special items that require careful analysis. **Transfers-in** from another department, for example, should be reported similar to purchases. Instead of purchasing from an outside enterprise, a department is purchasing from another department in the same entity. **Normal spoilage** (breakage, damage, theft) should reduce the retail column because these goods are no longer available for use. Because a certain amount of spoilage is considered normal in a retail enterprise, these costs are reflected in the selling price. As a result, this amount is not considered in computing the cost to retail percentage but is shown as a deduction similar to sales to arrive at ending inventory at retail. **Abnormal spoilage** should be deducted from both the cost and retail columns and reported as a special inventory amount or as a loss. To do otherwise, distorts the cost to retail ratio and overstates ending inventory. Finally companies often provide their employees with special discounts to encourage loyalty, better performance, and so on. **Employee discounts** should be deducted from the retail column similar to sales. These discounts should not be considered in the cost to retail percentage because they are not reflective of an overall price change in the selling price.

Appraisal of Retail Inventory Method

The retail inventory method of computing inventory is used widely (1) to permit the computation of net income without the necessity of a physical count of inventory, (2) as a control measure in determining inventory shortages, (3) in regulating quantities of merchandise on hand, and (4) as a basis for information needed for insurance purposes.

The advantages and disadvantages of the lower of cost or market method (conventional retail) versus LIFO (dollar value retail) are the same for retail as for nonretail operations. As a practical matter, the selection of the retail inventory method to be used often involves determining which method provides a lower taxable income. Although it might appear that retail LIFO will provide the lowest taxable income in a period of rising prices, such is not always the case. LIFO will provide an approximate current cost matching, but the ending inventory is stated at cost. The conventional retail method may have a large write-off because of the use of the lower of cost or market approach which may offset the LIFO current cost matching.

One characteristic of the retail inventory method is that it **has an averaging effect on varying rates of gross margin.** When applied to the operations of an entire business where rates of gross margin vary among departments, no allowance is made for possible distortion of results because of the differences in rates of gross margin. Some concerns use a refinement of the retail method under such conditions, by computing the inventory separately by departments or by classes of merchandise with similar rates of gross margin. In addition, the reliability of this method rests on the assumption that the distribution of items in the inventory is roughly the same as the "mix" in the total collection of goods available for sale.

Financial Statement Presentation of Inventories

Inventories are one of the most significant assets of industrial business enterprises; therefore, the accounting profession has adopted standards to be followed in reporting inventory on financial statements. These standards require that information be reported relative to the composition of the inventory, the inventory financing, the inventory costing methods employed, and the consistent application of costing methods from one period to another. Also, in recent years the disclosure of price-level information has become increasingly important.

Manufacturers should report the inventory composition either in the balance sheet or in a separate schedule in the notes, i.e., raw materials, work in process, and finished goods. The relative mix of raw materials, work in process, and finished goods is important in assessing liquidity and in computing the stage of completion of the inventories.

Unusual or significant financing arrangements relating to inventories that may require disclosure are: transactions with related parties, product financing arrangements, firm purchase commitments, involuntary liquidation of LIFO inventories, and pledging of inventories as collateral. Inventories pledged as collateral for a loan should be presented in the current asset section rather than as an offset to the liability.

The basis upon which inventory amounts are stated (lower of cost or market) and the method used in determining cost (LIFO, FIFO, average cost, etc.) should also be reported. A recent annual report of Mumford of Wyoming contains the following disclosures.

Note A—Significant Accounting Policies	
Live feeder cattle and feed—last-in, first-out (LIFO) cost, which is below approximate market	$ 854,800
Live range cattle—lower of principally identified cost or market	$1,240,500
Live sheep and supplies—lower of first-in, first-out, (FIFO) cost or market	$ 674,000
Dressed meat and by-products—principally at market less allowances for distribution and selling expenses	$ 362,630

The illustration on page 401 indicates that a company can use different pricing methods for different elements of its inventory. If Mumford of Wyoming changes the method of pricing any of its inventory elements, a change in accounting principle must be reported. For example, if Mumford changes its method of accounting for live sheep from FIFO to average cost, this change, along with the effect on income, should be separately reported in the financial statements. Changes in accounting principle require a consistency exception in the auditor's report. The methods of reporting accounting changes are discussed in detail in Chapter 23.

The inflation rates of the 1970s have necessitated reporting price-level information related to inventory as supplementary data in the financial statements. The SEC in 1974 took the first step in **ASR No. 151** by requiring the disclosure of **"inventory profits."** "Inventory profits" arise when inventory costs that are matched against current revenues are less than the replacement cost of these inventories. Many accountants believe these profits to be illusory because the company must replace that inventory at a higher price. Disclosure is therefore mandated to provide information to better assess the quality of enterprise earnings.

In 1976 the SEC issued **ASR 190** requiring that inventories and cost of goods sold be disclosed on a replacement cost basis as supplemental information for certain companies. The following disclosure of Koppers Company, Inc. illustrates this type of presentation:

	($ Thousands) Historical Cost From 1976 Balance Sheet	Estimated Replacement Cost
If the Company were to totally replace its year-end 1976 inventories, how much would it cost? Inventories, as of 12/31/76	$157,554	$214,000
What would 1976 cost of sales have been if the replacement cost of the inventory used at the time of sale had been the basis for determining production costs? Cost of sales, (excluding depreciation) for the year ended 12/31/76	$919,954	$921,000

This disclosure requirement has been highly controversial because many companies contend that the high cost of preparing this information is not warranted by the benefits received. The FASB apparently believes that this objection has little merit, however, and now requires even more extensive disclosure of the impact of changing prices. One such requirement is that supplementary information on income from continuing operations on a current cost basis (replacement cost) and on increases (decreases) in specific prices of inventories net of inflation be reported.[7] This means (1) reporting current cost information on inventories and cost of goods sold and (2) computing and disclosing increases (decreases) that arise from the

[7]"Financial Reporting and Changing Prices," *Statement of Financial Accounting Standards No. 33* (Stamford, Conn.: FASB, 1979).

difference between the current cost of inventory and its historical cost adjusted for inflation. These reporting requirements will probably be as controversial as the earlier SEC recommendations. A second requirement is to report inventories on a constant-dollar basis. It should be noted that such price level disclosures are generally required only of certain large publicly held business enterprises. The detailed computational aspects related to reporting changes in prices are discussed in Chapter 25.

APPENDIX

Special LIFO Reporting Problems

The LIFO discussion in the last two chapters has emphasized the basic issues and procedures related to this inventory valuation technique. The purpose of this appendix is to introduce a number of special LIFO reporting problems that may occur. They are generally classified as follows:

1. Initial adoption of LIFO.
2. LIFO reserve.
3. Interim reporting problems.
4. Index determination for dollar-value LIFO.

Initial Adoption of LIFO

The initial adoption of LIFO presents a reporting problem because it is difficult if not impossible to reconstruct the accounting records to determine what net income would have been in prior years had LIFO been used. As a result, **when changing to LIFO neither a cumulative effect nor a retroactive adjustment can be made.** The base-year inventory for all subsequent LIFO computations is the opening inventory of the year the method is adopted. The effect that the change to LIFO has on current net income must be disclosed in a footnote.

Addressograph-Multigraph Corporation's annual report provides a good example of the type of information disclosed:

> **Inventory Pricing**—The company has changed its method of pricing most U.S. inventories from the first-in, first-out method to the last-in, first-out (LIFO) method. This change was made because management believes the LIFO method of pricing these inventories will reflect earnings more realistically by matching the most recent inventory acquisition costs against current sales. The effect of this change was to increase the reported net loss for 1977 by $2,029,000 or $1.25 per share. The cumulative effect of the change could not be determined because assumptions would have to be made that would furnish results different from what they would have been had LIFO been used in prior periods.

Formal journal entries are not required in adopting LIFO except when the inventory is restored to a cost basis from the lower of cost or market approach. Because LIFO is considered a cost approach, the inventory must be restated to a cost basis if market is lower than cost at the time of LIFO adoption. To illustrate, assume that Ramos, Inc. decided to switch **from FIFO to LIFO** for purposes of valuing its inventory. The inventory under FIFO has a cost basis of $100,000 but is reported at $90,000 because market is lower than cost. The following entry is made to restate the inventory to a cost basis (ignoring tax effects):

Inventory	10,000	
Adjustment to Record Inventory at Cost		10,000

The Adjustment to Record Inventory at Cost should be reported on the income statement as other income.

The same type of problem arises when the company changes **from the conventional retail method to LIFO retail.** Because conventional retail is a lower of cost or market approach, the beginning inventory must be restated to a cost basis. The usual approach is to compute the cost basis from the purchases of the prior year, adjusted for both markups and markdowns.[1] To illustrate, assume that Clark Clothing Store employs the conventional retail method but wishes to change to the LIFO retail method beginning in 1981. The amounts shown by the firm's books are as follows:

	At Cost	At Retail
Inventory January 1, 1980	$ 5,210	$ 15,000
Net purchases in 1980	47,250	100,000
Net markups in 1980		7,000
Net markdowns in 1980		2,000
Sales in 1980		95,000

Ending inventory under the **conventional retail method for 1980 is computed as follows:**

Conventional Retail	Cost	Retail
Inventory January 1, 1980	$ 5,210	$ 15,000
Net purchases	47,250	100,000
Net additional markups		7,000
	$52,460	122,000
Net markdowns		(2,000)
Sales		(95,000)
Ending inventory at retail		$ 25,000
Establishment of cost to retail percentage ($52,460 ÷ $122,000)	43%	
December 31, 1980 inventory at cost		
Inventory at retail		$ 25,000
Cost to retail ratio		43%
Inventory at cost under conventional retail		$ 10,750

[1]A logical question to ask is, "Why are only the purchases considered from the prior period and not also the beginning inventory?" Apparently the IRS believes that "the purchases only approach" provides a more reasonable cost basis. The IRS position is debatable and litigation has ensued on this matter. For our purposes, it seems appropriate to use the purchases only approach.

The ending inventory under the **LIFO retail method** can then be quickly computed in the following way.

LIFO Retail
(December 31, 1980 inventory at LIFO cost)

	Retail	Ratio	LIFO
Ending inventory	$25,000 $\times$	45%[a] =	$11,250

[a]The cost-to-retail ratio was computed as follows:

$$\frac{\text{Net purchases at cost}}{\text{Net purchases plus markups less markdowns at retail}} = \frac{\$47,250}{\$100,000 + \$7,000 - \$2,000} = 45\%$$

The difference of $500 ($11,250 − $10,750) between the LIFO retail method and the conventional retail method in the ending inventory for 1980 is the amount by which the beginning inventory for 1981 must be adjusted. The entry to adjust the inventory to a cost basis is a debit to Inventory for $500 and a credit to Adjustment to Record Inventory at Cost for $500.[2] If LIFO is used for tax purposes, the IRS requires that it be used for external reporting purposes also.

LIFO Reserve

Many companies use LIFO for tax and external reporting purposes, but they usually maintain a FIFO, average cost, or standard cost system for internal reporting purposes. The reasons for this procedure are that (1) companies often base their pricing decisions on a FIFO, average, or standard cost assumption, rather than on a LIFO basis; (2) record-keeping is easier because the LIFO assumption usually does not approximate the physical flow of the product; (3) profit-sharing and other bonus arrangements are often not based on a LIFO inventory assumption; and (4) the use of a pure LIFO system is troublesome for interim periods where estimates must be made of year-end quantities and prices.

The difference between the inventory method used for internal reporting purposes and LIFO is referred to as the Allowance to Reduce Inventory to LIFO or the LIFO reserve. The change in the allowance balance from one period to the next is called the **LIFO effect.** The LIFO effect is the adjustment that must be made to the accounting records in a given year. To illustrate, assume that Kroger Company uses the FIFO method for internal reporting purposes and LIFO for external reporting purposes. At January 1, 1981, the Allowance to Reduce Inventory to LIFO balance was $20,000 and the ending balance should be $50,000. The LIFO effect is, therefore, $30,000 and the following entry is made at year-end.

Cost of Goods Sold	30,000	
Allowance to Reduce Inventory to LIFO		30,000

The Allowance to Reduce Inventory to LIFO would be deducted from inventory to insure that the inventory is stated on a LIFO basis at year-end.

[2]It is permissible for an enterprise to use the lower of cost or market approach and LIFO for reporting purposes. To do so, the company establishes a valuation allowance because the inventory account must be reported at cost. Companies are reluctant to use this valuation account because the IRS may void the LIFO method for tax purposes. However, a company faced with obsolete inventories should be required under proper accounting to report this decrease in some manner.

Interim Reporting Problems

The use of LIFO in interim periods is complicated because LIFO is an annual, not an interim computation. **APB Opinion No. 28,** however, specifies that accounting principles must be consistently applied among interim periods and that the same principles used for annual purposes must be used for interim periods.[3] This situation presents difficulties because at an interim period the future prices of the inventory and the quantity on hand at year-end are not known. The accountant, therefore, must estimate the total LIFO effect and allocate this LIFO effect in some reasonable and consistent fashion. Such is not an easy task and it often results in substantial fourth-quarter adjustments. The LIFO effect may be allocated on the basis of estimated sales or estimated production costs, or it may be allocated equally over the four periods.

A special problem develops in interim periods when the temporary liquidation of a LIFO layer occurs. A temporary liquidation occurs when a layer would be liquidated for interim purposes but is expected to be replaced by year-end. In such a situation, the inventory at the interim period should not give effect to the LIFO liquidation. Instead, the cost of goods sold for the interim period affected should include the expected cost of the replacement of the liquidated LIFO layer. To illustrate, assume that in the second quarter Trident Manufacturing Co. experiences a temporary reduction in its LIFO inventory of 1,000 units that cost $40 per unit. Trident expects to replace the entire reduction in the third quarter at a cost of $55 per unit. The entry to record the second-quarter reduction is as follows:

Cost of Goods Sold	55,000	
Inventory		40,000
Excess of Replacement Cost of		
LIFO Temporarily Liquidated		15,000

When the inventory is replenished in the third quarter, the following entry is made:

Inventory	40,000	
Excess of Replacement Cost of		
LIFO Temporarily Liquidated	15,000	
Accounts Payable (Cash)		55,000

The Excess of Replacement Cost of LIFO Temporarily Liquidated is reported as a current liability and **is reported only in interim reports.**

If any part of the LIFO base is liquidated at year-end, it represents a permanent reduction. Because a permanent reduction may have a substantive impact on net income when low-cost items are matched against current revenues, disclosure is required in the annual report. Hershey Foods Corporation recently reported a year-end LIFO liquidation:

> During 1977 the Company reduced inventory quantities, primarily cocoa beans. This reduction resulted in a liquidation of LIFO inventory quantities carried at lower costs prevailing in prior years as compared with the cost of 1977 purchases, the effect of which decreased cost of goods sold by approximately $8,500,000 and increased net income by approximately $4,000,000 or $.29 per share.

---

[3]"Interim Financial Reporting," *APB Opinion No. 28* (New York: AICPA, 1973).

Index Determination for Dollar Value LIFO

In Chapter 8, the development of the indexes used in the dollar-value LIFO method was briefly discussed. The general formula for computing the index is as follows:

$$\frac{\text{Ending Inventory for the Period at Current Cost}}{\text{Ending Inventory for the Period at Base-Year Cost}} = \text{Price Index for Current Year}$$

This approach is generally referred to as the **double-extension method** in that the inventory is extended at both base-year prices and current-year prices. To illustrate this computation, assume that Hartford, Inc.'s base-year inventory (January 1, 1980) was composed of the following:

Items	Quantity	Cost Per Unit	Total Cost
A	1,000	$6	$ 6,000
B	2,000	$20	40,000
(January 1, 1980 inventory at base year costs)			$46,000

Examination of the ending inventory indicates that 3,000 units of Item A and 6,000 units of Item B are held on December 31, 1980. The most recent actual purchases related to these items were as follows:

Items	Purchase Date	Quantity Purchased	Cost Per Unit
A	December 1, 1980	4,000	$ 7
B	December 15, 1980	5,000	25
B	November 16, 1980	1,000	22

We double extend the inventory as follows:

	12/31/80 inventory at base-year costs				12/31/80 inventory at current-year costs		
Items	Units	Cost Per Unit	Total		Units	Cost Per Unit	Total
A	3,000	$6	$ 18,000		3,000	$7	$ 21,000
B	6,000	$20	120,000		5,000	$25	125,000
			$138,000		1,000	$22	22,000
							$168,000

After the inventories are double-extended, the formula above is used to develop the index for the current year as follows:

$$\frac{\text{Ending Inventory for the Period at Current Costs}}{\text{Ending Inventory for the Period at Base-Year Costs}} = \frac{\$168,000}{\$138,000} = 121.74\%$$

This index (121.47%) is then applied to the layer added in 1980. Note in this illustration that Hartford, Inc. used the most recent actual purchases to determine current cost; other approaches such as FIFO and average cost may also be used. Whichever flow assumption is adopted, consistent use from one period to another is required.

Use of the double-extension method is time consuming and is difficult where substantial technological change has occurred or where a large number of items are involved. Another approach, often referred to as the **index method,** is used to simplify the analysis. Under this method, an index is obtained by reference to an outside source or by double-pricing only a sample portion of the inventory. An example of an acceptable outside source for an index is the Bureau of Labor Statistics—Department Store Inventory Price Indexes, published semiannually in the *Internal Revenue Bulletin*. Generally, the IRS frowns on the use of an outside index except by retail department stores. If a sample is employed, statistical methods, judgment, or a combination of the two is utilized to determine the index. Once the index is obtained, the ending inventory at current costs is divided by the index to find the base-year cost.[4]

Note: All **asterisked** questions, cases, exercises, or problems relate to material contained in the appendix to each chapter.

Questions

1. Define "cost" as applied to the valuation of inventories. Define "market" as applied to the valuation of inventories.

2. Why are inventories valued at the lower of cost or market? What are the arguments against the use of the lower of cost or market method of valuing inventories?

3. (a) Determine the ending inventory for the Hat Department of the Michaels Department Store from the following data.

	Cost	Retail
Inventory Jan. 1	$ 94,500	$ 141,750
Purchases	720,000	1,080,000
Freight-in	33,000	
Markups, net		48,000
Markdowns, net		21,000
Sales		1,122,000

   (b) If the results of a physical inventory indicated an inventory at retail of $120,000, what inferences would you draw?

4. In some instances accounting principles require a departure from valuing inventories at cost alone. Determine the proper unit inventory price in the following cases:

	Cases				
	1	2	3	4	5
Cost	$4.00	$4.00	$4.00	$4.00	$4.00
Net realizable value	2.60	4.10	3.60	4.80	3.80
Net realizable value less normal profit	2.20	3.70	3.20	4.40	3.40
Market (replacement cost)	2.40	4.20	3.70	4.30	3.20

5. What method(s) might be used in the accounts to record a loss due to a price decline in the inventories? Discuss.

6. What approaches may the accountant employ in applying the lower of cost or market procedure? Which approach is normally used and why?

7. At December 31, 1981, the Toby Company has outstanding purchase commitments for purchase of 75,000 gallons, at $2.50 per gallon, of a raw material to be used in their manufacturing process. The company prices its raw material inventory at cost or market, whichever is lower. Assuming that the market price as of December 31, 1981 is $2.30, how would you treat this situation in the accounts?

---

[4]Another approach to finding an index is the *link-chain method*. It is not discussed here because it is permitted only in limited circumstances where the double-extension and index methods are impractical.

8. What factors might call for inventory valuation at sales prices?

9. Distinguish between gross profit as a percentage of cost and gross profit as a percentage of sales price. Convert the following gross profit percentages based on cost to gross profit percentages based on sales price: 20% and 33⅓%. Convert the following gross profit percentages based on sales price to gross profit percentages based on cost: 33⅓% and 60%.

10. List the major uses of the gross profit method.

11. A retailer with annual net sales of $3 million maintains a markup of 25% based on cost. Her expenses average 15% of net sales. What is her gross margin and net profit in dollars?

12. What conditions must exist for the retail inventory method to provide valid results?

13. The retail inventory method yields results that are essentially the same as those yielded by the lower of cost or market method. Explain. Prepare an illustration of how the retail inventory method reduces inventory to market.

14. What modifications to the conventional retail method are necessary to approximate a LIFO retail flow?

15. The Madden Corporation provides the following information with respect to its inventories:

Inventories $4,800,000

What additional disclosure is necessary to present the inventory fairly?

*16. Kimberly, Inc. switched from the FIFO to the LIFO method of inventory valuation. As a result, the beginning inventory was increased $4,000 in order to report it on the cost basis. What is the appropriate journal entry to record this adjustment?

*17. Your instructor has noted that some special problems are associated with the use of LIFO. In particular, in interim reports, the allocation of LIFO reserves and the possibility of temporary liquidation present difficulties. Why do these items present difficulties in interim reports?

*18. Suppa Company is considering the use of the dollar-value LIFO method for inventory valuation purposes. The auditor for Suppa Company notes that the double-extension method should be employed. Explain the double-extension method. When might the double-extension method not be appropriate?

Cases

C9-1 You have just been hired as a new accountant for the accounting firm of Jennings and Jones. The manager of the office is interested in your formal education and provides you with the following factual situations that were recently encountered in their practice.

1. One of our client's major business activities is the purchase and resale of used heavy mining and construction equipment, including trucks, cranes, shovels, conveyors, crushers, etc. The company was organized in 1965. In its earlier years it purchased individual items of heavy equipment and resold them to customers throughout the United States. In the early 1970s, the company began negotiating the "package" purchase of all the existing equipment at mine sites, concurrent with the closing down of several of the large iron mines in North Dakota and exhausted coal mines in Illinois. The mine operators preferred to liquidate their mine assets on that basis rather than holding auctions or leaving the mine site open until all of the equipment could be liquidated. As there were numerous pieces of equipment in these package purchases, the client found it difficult to assign costs to each individual item. As a result, the company followed the policy of valuing these "package" purchases by the cost recovery method. Under this method, the company recognized no income until the entire cost had been recovered through sales revenues. This produced a desirable tax answer by deferring income to later periods and represented, for financial reporting purposes, a

"conservative" valuation of inventories in what was essentially a new field for the company where its level of experience had not been demonstrated. **Instruction:** Comment on the propriety of this approach.

2. In December 1979, one of our clients underwent a major management change and a new president was hired. After reviewing the various policies of the company, the president's opinion was that prior systems employed by the company did not allow for adequate testing of obsolescence (including discontinued products) and overstocks in inventories. Accordingly, the president changed the mechanics of the procedures of reviewing for obsolete and excess stock and determining the amount. These reviews resulted in a significant increase between years in the amount of inventory that was written off. You are satisfied that these procedures are accurate and provide reliable results. The amounts charged against operations for excess and obsolete stock for the last three years were: 1979—$440,000; 1978—$114,000; and 1977—$113,000. Net income for 1979 before adjustment for these additional obsolescence charges was $540,000. **Instruction:** How should these charges be reported in the financial statements, if at all?

3. Another of our clients, Mogel Foods, was upset because we forced them to write down their inventory on an item-by-item basis. For example, our computation resulted in a write-down of approximately $300,000 as follows:

	Frozen	Cans
Cut beans	—	25,000
Peas	—	45,000
Mixed vegetables	5,000	15,000
Spinach	183,000	8,000
Carrots	12,000	7,000
	$200,000	$100,000

The company argued that the products are sold on a line basis (frozen or canned) with customers taking all varieties, and only rarely are sales made on an individual product basis. As a result, they argued that the application of the lower of cost or market rule to the total product line would result in the proper determination of income (loss). A pricing of the inventory on this basis would result in a $60,000 write-off. **Instruction:** Why do you believe our accounting firm argued for the item-by-item approach? Which method should be used, given the information in this case?

C9-2 The Michigan Company manufactures and sells four products, the inventories of which are priced at cost or market, whichever is lower. A normal profit margin rate of 30% is usually maintained on each of the four products.

The following information was compiled as of December 31, 1980.

Product	Original Cost	Cost to Replace	Estimated Cost to Dispose	Expected Selling Price[a]
A	$35.00	$42.00	$15.00	$ 80.00
B	47.50	45.00	20.50	95.00
C	17.50	15.00	5.00	30.00
D	45.00	46.00	26.00	100.00

[a]Normal margin is 30% of selling price.

Instructions

(a) Why are expected selling prices important in the application of the lower of cost or market rule?

(b) Prepare a schedule containing unit values (including "floor" and "ceiling") for determining the lower of cost or market on an individual-product basis. The last column of the schedule should contain for each product the unit value for the purpose of inventory valuation resulting from the application of the lower of cost or market rule.

C9-3 The Munz Company, your client, manufactures paint. The company's president, Mr. Munz, has decided to open a retail store to sell Munz paint as well as wallpaper and other supplies that would be purchased from other suppliers. He has asked you for information about the retail method of pricing inventories at the retail store.

Instructions

Prepare a report to the president explaining the retail method of pricing inventories. Your report should include these points:
- (a) Description and accounting features of the method.
- (b) The conditions that may distort the results under the method.
- (c) A comparison of the advantages of using the retail method with those of using cost methods of inventory pricing.
- (d) The accounting theory underlying the treatment of net markdowns and net markups under the method.

(AICPA adapted)

C9-4 Presented below are a number of items that may be encountered in computing the cost to retail percentage when using the conventional retail method or the LIFO retail method.

1. Markdowns
2. Markdown cancellations
3. Cost of items transferred in from other departments
4. Retail value of items transferred in from other departments
5. Sales discounts
6. Purchases discounts (purchases recorded gross)
7. Estimated retail value of goods broken or stolen
8. Cost of beginning inventory
9. Retail value of beginning inventory
10. Cost of purchases
11. Retail value of purchases
12. Markups
13. Markup cancellations
14. Employee discounts (sales recorded net)

Instructions

For each of the items listed above, indicate whether this item would be considered in the cost to retail percentage under (1) conventional retail, (2) LIFO retail.

C9-5 You are in charge of the audit of Manor Nylons, Incorporated. The following items were in Manor's inventory at November 30, 1981 (fiscal year end).

Product number	075936	078310	079104	081111
Selling price per unit November 30, 1981	$15.00	$23.00	$28.00	$13.00
Standard cost, per unit, as included in inventory at November 30, 1981	$ 7.90	$11.25	$14.26	$ 7.40

In discussions with Manor's marketing and sales personnel you were told that there will be a general 7% (rounded to the next highest five cents) increase in selling prices, effective December 1, 1981. This increase will affect all garments except those that have 081 as the first three digits of the product code. The 081 codes are assigned to new apparel introductions, and for product code 081111, the selling price will be $8.00 effective December 1, 1981.

In addition, you were told by the controller that Manor attempts to earn a 50% gross profit in selling price on all their nylons.

From the cost department you obtained the following standards, which will be used for fiscal 1982:

Product number	1982 Standard
075936	$ 8.25
078310	$10.75
079104	$14.71
081111	$ 7.51

Sales commissions and estimates of other costs of disposal approximate 25% of standard costs to manufacture. Assume that standard costs provide an accurate assessment of the replacement cost of the product.

Instructions

(a) Compute the value at which each of the items should be reported in the November 30, 1981, inventory.

(b) Why should inventories be reported at market?

(c) Does the literal interpretation of the rule of lower of cost or market always apply? Could you cite in this case where a possible exception to the lower of cost or market might be employed?

Exercises

E9-1 Bilder Company follows the practice of pricing its inventory at the lower of cost or market, on an individual-item basis.

Item No.	Quantity	Cost per Unit	Cost to Replace	Estimated Selling Price	Cost of Completion and Disposal	Normal Profit
1320	1,000	$3.00	$3.05	$4.50	$.35	$1.25
1333	1,200	2.50	2.40	3.50	.50	.50
1426	600	4.00	3.75	5.00	.40	1.00
1437	2,000	3.60	3.10	3.00	.25	.90
1510	900	2.25	2.00	3.25	.70	.60
1522	400	3.00	2.50	3.50	.40	.35
1573	3,000	1.60	1.50	2.50	.75	.50
1626	1,000	4.50	5.25	6.00	.50	1.00

Instructions

From the information above, determine the amount of Bilder Company inventory.

E9-2 The inventory of the Highland Company on December 31, 1981, consists of these items:

Part No.	Quantity	Cost per Unit	Cost to Replace per Unit
110	200	$100	$106
111	500	60	52
112	1,000	80	76
113	100	160	180
120	300	200	208
121 [a]	2,200	16	14
122	100	240	244

[a]Part No. 121 is obsolete and has a realizable value of $0.20 each as scrap.

Instructions

(a) Determine the inventory as of December 31, 1981, by the method of cost or market, whichever is lower, applying this method directly to each item.

(b) Determine the inventory by cost or market, whichever is lower, applying the method to the total of the inventory.

E9-3   Presented below is information related to Jeter Enterprises.

	Jan. 31	Feb. 28	Mar. 31	Apr. 30
Inventory	$16,000	$15,500	$17,000	$13,000
Inventory at the lower of cost or market	14,500	13,500	16,000	12,500
Purchases for the month		20,000	24,000	22,000
Sales for the month		26,000	33,000	32,000

Instructions

(a) From the information prepare (as far as the data permit) monthly income statements in columnar form for February, March, and April. The inventory is to be shown in the statement at cost, the profit or loss due to market fluctuations is to be shown separately, and a valuation account is to be set up for the difference between cost and the lower of cost or market.

(b) Prepare the journal entry required to establish the valuation account at January 31 and entries to adjust it monthly thereafter.

E9-4   At December 31, 1981, the Ohio Crunch Company has outstanding purchase commitments for 50,000 gallons, at $3.00 per gallon, of raw material to be used in its manufacturing process. The company prices its raw material inventory at cost or market, whichever is lower.

Instructions

(a) Assuming that the market price as of December 31, 1981, is $3.10, how would this matter be treated in the accounts and statements? Explain.

(b) Assuming that the market price as of December 31, 1981, is $2.80, instead of $3.10, how would you treat this situation in the accounts and statements?

(c) Give the entry in January, 1982, when the 50,000-gallon shipment is received, assuming that the situation given in (b) above existed at December 31, 1981. Give an explanation of your treatment.

E9-5   The Cosby Company has been having difficulty obtaining key raw materials for its manufacturing process. The company therefore signed a long-term purchase commitment with its largest supplier of this raw material on November 30, 1981 at an agreed price of $360,000. At December 31, 1981, the raw material had declined in price to $345,000, and it was further anticipated that the price would drop another $20,000, so that at the date of delivery the value of the inventory would be $325,000.

Instructions

What entries would you make on December 31, 1981 to recognize these facts?

E9-6   The Glass Bottle Corporation began business on January 1, 1980. Information about its inventories under different valuation methods is presented below.

		Inventory		
	LIFO Cost	FIFO Cost	Replacement Cost	Lower of Cost or Market
December 31, 1980	$20,400	$20,000	$19,200	$17,800
December 31, 1981	18,200	18,000	17,600	17,000
December 31, 1982	20,600	22,000	24,000	21,800

Instructions

(a) Indicate the inventory basis that will show the highest net income in (1) 1980; and (2) 1981.

(b) Indicate whether the FIFO cost basis would provide a higher or lower profit than the lower of cost or market basis in 1981.

E9-7 The Hastings Furniture Company purchases, during 1981, a carload of wicker chairs at a cost of $34,200. The manufacturer sells the chairs to Hastings for a lump sum of $34,200, because it is discontinuing manufacturing operations and wishes to dispose of its entire stock. Three types of chairs are included in the carload. The three types and the estimated selling price for each are listed below.

Type	No. of Chairs	Estimated Selling Price Each
Lounge chairs	500	$75
Armchairs	300	45
Straight chairs	200	30

During 1981 Hastings sells 150 lounge chairs, 80 armchairs, and 110 straight chairs.

Instructions

What is the amount of gross profit realized during 1981? What is the amount of inventory of unsold wicker chairs on December 31, 1981.

E9-8 The Corner Realty Corporation purchased a tract of unimproved land for $26,560. This land was improved and subdivided into building lots at an additional cost of $15,200. These building lots were all of the same size but owing to differences in location were offered for sale at different prices as follows:

Group	No. of Lots	Price per Lot
1	12	$2,400
2	18	1,800
3	6	1,400

Operating expenses for the year allocated to this project total $17,400. Lots unsold at the year-end were as follows:

Group 1	4 lots
Group 2	6 lots
Group 3	1 lot

Instructions

At the end of the fiscal year the Corner Realty Corporation instructs you to arrive at the net income realized on this operation to date.

E9-9 A fire destroys all of the merchandise of the Sun Devil Company on February 10, 1981. Presented below is information compiled up to the date of the fire.

Inventory January 1, 1981	$ 250,000
Sales to February 10, 1981	1,000,000
Purchases to February 10, 1981	1,050,000
Freight-in to February 10, 1981	40,000
Rate of gross profit on selling price	40%

Instructions

From the information above, compute the approximate inventory on that date.

E9-10 Presented below is information related to Lakeside Machinery Corporation for the current year:

Beginning inventory	$ 300,000	
Purchases	1,050,000	
Total goods available for sale		$1,350,000
Sales		1,800,000

Instructions

Compute the ending inventory, assuming that (1) gross margin is 30% of sales; (2) gross margin is 33⅓% of cost; (3) gross margin is 50% of cost; and (4) gross margin is 25% of sales.

E9-11 R. N. Olson requires an estimate of the cost of goods lost by fire on March 9. Merchandise on hand on January 1 was $30,000. Purchases since January 1 were $22,500; freight-in, $2,500; purchase returns and allowances, $1,500. Sales are made at 20% above cost and totaled $21,000 to March 9. Goods costing $6,125 were left undamaged by the fire; remaining goods were destroyed.

Instructions

(a) Compute the cost of goods destroyed.

(b) Compute the cost of goods destroyed, assuming that the gross profit is 20% of sales.

E9-12 The Fish Lumber Company handles three principal lines of merchandise with these varying rates of gross profit on cost:

Lumber	25%
Millwork	30%
Hardware and fittings	40%

On August 18 a fire destroyed the office, lumber shed, and a considerable portion of the lumber stacked in the yard. To file a report of loss for insurance purposes, the company must know what the inventories were immediately preceding the fire. No detail or perpetual inventory records of any kind were maintained. The only pertinent information you are able to obtain are the following facts from the general ledger, which was kept in a fireproof vault and thus escaped destruction.

	Lumber	Millwork	Hardware
Inventory, Jan. 1, 1981	$ 187,500	$ 67,500	$ 27,750
Purchases to Aug. 18, 1981	1,470,000	375,000	117,750
Sales to Aug. 18, 1981	1,875,000	510,000	180,000

Instructions

Submit your estimate of the inventory amounts immediately preceding the fire.

E9-13 You are called by Rexroad Company on August 16 and asked to prepare a claim for insurance as a result of a theft that took place the night before. You suggest that an inventory be taken immediately. The following data are available:

Inventory, August 1	$28,000
Purchases—goods placed in stock August 1–15	16,400
Sales—goods delivered to customers (gross)	30,000
Sales returns—goods returned to stock	2,400

Your client reports that the goods on hand on August 16 cost $30,000, but you determine that this figure includes goods of $7,000 received on a consignment basis. Your past records show that sales are made at approximately 50% over cost.

Instructions

Compute the claim against the insurance company.

E9-14 Presented below is information related to the M. E. Phillips Company.

	Cost	Retail
Beginning inventory	$ 120,000	$ 180,000
Purchases	1,350,000	2,025,000
Markups		75,000
Markup cancellations		15,000
Markdowns		37,500
Markdown cancellations		7,500
Sales		1,950,000

Instructions

Compute the inventory by the conventional retail inventory method.

E9-15 The records of Simpson Liquor Store show the following data for the month of October.

Sales	$50,000
Sales returns	1,000
Additional markups	19,500
Markup cancellations	2,500
Markdowns	7,500
Markdown cancellations	2,500
Freight on purchases	1,000
Purchases (at cost)	25,000
Purchases (at sales price)	35,000
Purchase returns (at cost)	1,000
Purchase returns (at sales price)	2,000
Beginning inventory (at cost)	35,000
Beginning inventory (at sales price)	50,000

Instructions

Compute the ending inventory by the conventional retail inventory method.

E9-16 Donahue Company began operations on January 1, 1979, adopting the conventional retail inventory system. None of its merchandise was marked down in 1979 and, because there was no beginning inventory, its ending inventory for 1979 of $21,740 would have been the same under either the conventional system or the LIFO system. On December 31, 1980, the store management considers adopting the LIFO system, and desires to know how the December 31, 1980 inventory would appear under both systems. All pertinent data regarding purchases, sales, markups, and markdowns are shown below. There has been no change in the price level.

	Cost	Retail
Inventory, Jan. 1, 1980	$ 21,740	$ 32,000
Markdowns (net)		12,000
Markups (net)		20,000
Purchases (net)	129,540	196,000
Sales (net)		152,000

Instructions

Determine the cost of the 1980 ending inventory under both (1) the conventional retail method and (2) the LIFO method.

E9-17   Presented below is information related to Bennie Enterprises:

	Price Index	LIFO Cost	Retail
Inventory on December 31, 1981 when dollar-value LIFO is adopted	100	$13,080	$45,000
Inventory, December 31, 1982	104	?	49,920

Instructions

Compute the ending inventory under the dollar-value LIFO method at December 31, 1982. The cost to retail ratio for 1982 was 45%.

E9-18   You assemble the following information for the O'Connor Department Store, which computes its inventory under the dollar-value LIFO method.

	Cost	Retail
Inventory on January 1, 1981	$210,600	$270,000
Purchases	360,000	450,000
Increase in price level for year		5%

Instructions

Compute the cost of the inventory on December 31, 1981, assuming that the inventory at retail is (1) $264,600, (2) $302,400.

*E9-19   Oxford Corporation has just experienced a large fire loss to its inventories. Fortunately, the records for the years 1979–1981 have been salvaged. The conventional retail method was in use during 1979. The corporation switched to the LIFO retail method for the year ending 1980. You have been hired to reconstruct the divisional financial statements for the years 1979–1981 and are currently engaged in recomputing the final inventory figures as originally stated in the financial statements of the respective years. The following data are available for your examination.

	1979	1980	1981
Beginning inventory @ retail	$135,000	$225,000	$315,000
Ending inventory @ retail	225,000	315,000	297,000
Ending inventory @ cost (Conventional)	?	223,500	214,500
Ending inventory @ cost (LIFO)	?	?	?
Price index	100	105	110
Cost ratio—conventional retail	72	71	72
Cost ratio—LIFO retail	74	75	76

Instructions

(a) Compute the ending inventory under the (1) conventional retail method for 1979, and (2) the LIFO retail method for the years 1980–1981. Round to the nearest dollar.

(b) Prepare the entry that was necessary when the change was made from the conventional retail to the LIFO retail method.

*E9-20   Futura, Inc., a local retailing concern, has decided to change from the conventional retail inventory method to the LIFO retail method starting on January 1, 1981. The company recomputed its ending inventory for 1980 in accordance with the procedures necessary to switch to LIFO retail. The inventory computed was $178,500.

Instructions

Assuming that Futura's ending inventory for 1980 under the conventional retail inventory method was $175,000, prepare the appropriate journal entry on January 1, 1981.

Problems

P9-1 Casper Company follows the practice of valuing its inventory at the lower of cost or market. The following information is available from the company's inventory records as of December 31, 1981.

Item	On Hand Quantity	Unit Cost	Replacement Cost/Unit	Estimated Unit Selling Price	Completion & Disposal Costs/Unit	Normal Unit Profit
A	1,000	$4.50	$5.00	$ 7.50	$1.50	$1.40
B	1,200	7.00	8.00	8.00	.90	.90
C	1,000	4.20	4.00	6.00	1.10	.60
D	200	8.20	9.00	7.00	.60	2.00
E	800	4.00	7.40	10.00	3.20	3.70

Instructions

(a) Indicate the inventory price that should be used for each item under the lower of cost or market rule.

(b) Casper Company applies the lower of cost or market rule directly to each item in the inventory and uses a perpetual inventory system to account for the items above. Give the adjusting entry, if one is necessary, to write down the ending inventory from cost to market.

(c) If Casper Company applies the lower of cost or market rule to the total of the inventory, what is the proper dollar amount for inventory as of 12/31/81?

P9-2 The Aurora Spartan Company manufactures desks. Most of the company's desks are standard models and are sold on the basis of catalog prices. At December 31, 1981, the following finished desks appear in the company's inventory:

Finished desks	A	B	C	D
1981 catalog selling price	$440	$470	$870	$1,040
FIFO cost per inventory list 12/31/81	440	440	840	950
Estimated current cost to manufacturer (at December 31, 1981 and early 1982)	460	420	710	1,000
Sales commissions and estimated other costs of disposal	80	70	120	160
1982 catalog selling price	480	520	960	1,200

The 1981 catalog was in effect through November, 1981 and the 1982 catalog is effective as of December 1, 1981. All catalog prices are net of the usual discounts. Generally, the company attempts to obtain a 25% gross margin on selling price and has usually been successful in doing so.

Instructions

At what amount should each of the four desks appear in the company's December 31, 1981 inventory, assuming that the company has adopted a lower of FIFO cost or market approach for valuation of inventories on an individual item basis?

P9-3 Franco & Sons, Inc. valued its finished-product inventory on the basis of average yearly production cost and its raw material inventory on the basis of first-in, first-out cost. Because of continuous fluctuation in the market price of the basic raw material used, the management proposes to change its inventory valuations from the cost basis to the basis of lower of FIFO cost or market.

The company inventory data at the beginning and end of 1981 were as follows:

	Jan. 1	Dec. 31
Raw materials:		
Tons on hand	2,000	1,000
Book value on first-in, first-out basis	$53,000	$22,500
Market value, per ton	20	30
Finished product:		
Tons on hand	750	900
Book value at average yearly cost	$38,000	$36,000
Market value, per ton	52	55

Production costs other than those for raw materials have remained constant throughout 1980 at $11 per ton of finished product and 1981 at $11.30 per ton. In 1981, 19,000 tons of raw materials were bought at a total cost of $400,000. Normal shrinkage and waste in the manufacturing process amount to 25% of the materials used, that is, 1 ton of raw material must be used to produce .75 ton of finished product.

Before making a decision, the management requests that you first show the result of changing from one basis to the other.

Instructions

(a) Prepare a comparative statement showing the present and revised values and costs and the effect of the proposed change on the December 31 balance sheet.

(b) Prepare the entry that would bring the books into agreement with the new plan if adopted.

P9-4 The Troy Products Corporation, which began operations in 1978, always values its inventories at the current replacement cost. Its annual inventory figure is arrived at by taking a physical inventory and then pricing each item in the physical inventory at current prices determined from recent vendors' invoices or catalogs. Here is the condensed income statement for this company for the last four years.

	1978	1979	1980	1981
Sales	$800,000	$840,000	$920,000	$900,000
Cost of goods sold	580,000	610,000	650,000	660,000
Gross profit	220,000	230,000	270,000	240,000
Operating expenses	150,000	164,000	180,000	178,000
Income before income taxes	$ 70,000	$ 66,000	$ 90,000	$ 62,000

Instructions

(a) Do you see any objections to their procedure for valuing inventories?

(b) Assuming that the inventory at cost and as determined by the corporation at the end of each of the four years is as follows, restate the condensed income statements, using cost for inventories.

Ending Inventory	At Cost	As Determined By Company
1978	$100,000	$ 84,000
1979	114,000	92,000
1980	104,000	90,000
1981	118,000	100,000

P9-5 Archer, Inc. lost most of its inventory in a fire in December just before the year-end physical inventory was taken. The corporation's books disclosed the following:

Beginning inventory	$102,000	Sales	$418,000
Purchases for the year	346,000	Sales returns	10,000
Purchase returns	32,300	Rate of gross profit on sales	20%

Merchandise with a selling price of $12,000 remained undamaged after the fire. Damaged merchandise with an original selling price of $8,000 had a net realizable value of $1,800.

Instructions

Compute the amount of the loss as a result of the fire, assuming that the corporation had no insurance coverage.

P9-6 Marco Auto Inc. lost most of its inventory in a fire in December just before the year-end physical inventory was taken. Corporate records disclose the following:

Inventory (beginning)	$ 75,000	Sales	$307,500
Purchases	240,000	Sales returns	7,500
Purchase returns	15,000	Gross profit % based on selling price	25%

Merchandise with a selling price of $15,000 remained undamaged after the fire, and damaged merchandise has a salvage value of $3,750. Marco does not carry fire insurance on its inventory. It is estimated that the year-end inventory would have been subject to a normal 10% write-down for obsolescence.

Instructions

Prepare a formal labeled schedule computing the fire loss incurred by Marco Auto Inc. (Do not use the retail inventory method.)

P9-7 On June 30, 1981, a flash flood damaged the warehouse and factory of Spirit Corporation, completely destroying the work-in-process inventory. There was no damage to either the raw materials or finished goods inventories. A physical inventory taken after the flood revealed the following valuations:

Raw materials	$ 62,000
Work-in-process	-0-
Finished goods	119,000

The inventory on January 1, 1981, consisted of the following:

Raw materials	$ 30,000
Work-in-process	100,000
Finished goods	140,000
	$270,000

A review of the books and records disclosed that the gross profit margin historically approximated 25% of sales. The sales for the first six months of 1981 were $340,000. Raw material purchases were $115,000. Direct labor costs for this period were $80,000 and manufacturing overhead has historically been applied at 50% of direct labor.

Instructions

Compute the value of the work-in-process inventory lost at June 30, 1981.

P9-8 The records for the Shoe Department of the Major Department Store are summarized below for the month of January.

Inventory, January 1, at retail, $12,000; at cost, $8,400

Purchases in January, at retail, $83,200; at cost, $52,000

Freight-in, $4,000

Purchase returns, at retail, $3,200; at cost, $2,000

Purchase allowances, $1,200

Transfers in from Department B, at retail, $3,600; at cost, $2,400

Net markups, $4,400

Net markdowns, $3,000

Inventory losses due to normal breakage, etc., at retail, $600

Sales at retail, $60,000

Sales returns, $400

Instructions

Compute the inventory for this department as of January 31, at (1) sales price, and (2) lower of cost or market.

P9-9   Presented below is information related to Rundell's, Inc.

	Cost	Retail
Inventory 12/31/1980	$150,000	$ 225,000
Purchases	900,000	1,290,000
Purchase returns	60,000	90,000
Purchase discounts	15,000	—
Gross sales (after employee discounts)	—	1,275,000
Sales returns	—	97,500
Markups	—	90,000
Markup cancellations	—	15,000
Markdowns	—	30,000
Markdown cancellations	—	15,000
Freight-in	75,000	—
Employee discounts granted	—	6,000
Loss from breakage (normal)	—	1,500

Instructions

Assuming that Rundell's, Inc. uses the conventional retail inventory method, compute the cost of their ending inventory at December 31, 1981.

P9-10   The Almovar Department Store, Inc. uses the retail inventory method to estimate ending inventory for its monthly financial statements. The following data pertain to a single department for the month of October, 1981.

Inventory, October 1, 1981	
At cost	$ 40,000
At retail	60,000
Purchases (exclusive of freight and returns):	
At cost	200,302
At retail	292,990
Freight-in	10,200
Purchase returns	
At cost	4,200
At retail	5,600
Additional markups	5,000
Markup cancellations	530
Markdowns (net)	1,600
Normal spoilage and breakage	9,000
Sales	271,460

Instructions

(a) Using the conventional retail method, prepare a schedule computing estimated lower of cost or market inventory for October 31, 1981.

(b) A department store using the conventional retail inventory method estimates the cost of its ending inventory as $58,000. An accurate physical count reveals only

$44,000 of inventory at lower of cost or market. List the factors that may have caused the difference between the computed inventory and the physical count.

P9-11 As of January 1, 1981, the Downhill Ski Store installed the retail method of accounting for its merchandise inventory.

To prepare the store's financial statements at June 30, 1981, you obtain these data.

	Cost	Selling Price
Inventory, January 1	$26,900	$ 42,000
Markdowns		10,500
Markups		19,500
Markdown cancellations		7,500
Markup cancellations		4,500
Purchases	86,200	109,800
Sales		122,000
Purchase returns and allowances	1,500	1,800
Sales returns and allowances		6,000

Instructions

(a) Prepare a schedule to compute the Downhill Ski Store's June 30, 1981, inventory under the conventional retail method of accounting for inventories.

(b) Without prejudice to your solution to part (a), assume that you computed the June 30, 1981 inventory to be $46,200 at retail and the ratio of cost to retail to be 75%. The general price level has increased from 100 at January 1, 1981 to 105 at June 30, 1981. Prepare a schedule to compute the June 30, 1981 inventory at the June 30 price level under the dollar-value LIFO method.

(AICPA adapted)

*P9-12 Carson-Scott Department Store converted from the conventional retail method to the LIFO retail method on January 1, 1980, and is now considering converting to the dollar-value LIFO inventory method. During your examination of the financial statements for the year ended December 31, 1981, management requested that you furnish a summary showing certain computations of inventory cost for the past three years.

Here is the available information.

1. The inventory at January 1, 1979, had a retail value of $45,000 and cost of $27,500 based on the conventional retail method.

2. Transactions during 1979 were as follows:

	Cost	Retail
Gross purchases	$280,000	$489,000
Purchase returns	4,500	9,000
Purchase discounts	5,000	
Gross sales		492,000
Sales returns		6,000
Employee discounts		4,000
Freight-in	26,500	
Net markups		25,000
Net markdowns		10,000

3. The retail value of the December 31, 1980, inventory was $56,100, the cost ratio for 1980 under the LIFO retail method was 62%, and the regional price index was 102% of the January 1, 1980, price level.

4. The retail value of the December 31, 1981, inventory was $48,300, the cost ratio for 1981 under the LIFO retail method was 61%, and the regional price index was 105% of the January 1, 1980, price level.

Instructions

(a) Prepare a schedule showing the computation of the cost of inventory on hand at December 31, 1979, based on the conventional retail method.

(b) Prepare a schedule showing the recomputation of the inventory on hand on December 31, 1979, in accordance with procedures necessary to convert from the conventional retail method to the LIFO retail method beginning January 1, 1980. Assume that the retail value of the December 31, 1979, inventory was $50,000.

(c) Without prejudice to your solution to part (b) assume that you computed the December 31, 1979, inventory (retail value $50,000) under the LIFO retail method at a cost of $29,000. Prepare a schedule showing the computations of the cost of the store's 1980 and 1981 year-end inventories under the dollar-value LIFO method.

(AICPA adapted)

P9-13 The Dolby Corporation is an importer and wholesaler. Its merchandise is purchased from several suppliers and is warehoused by Dolby Corporation until sold to consumers.

In conducting her audit for the year ended June 30, 1981, the corporation's CPA determined that the system of internal control was good. Accordingly, she observed the physical inventory at an interim date, May 31, 1981, instead of at year-end.

The following information was obtained from the general ledger.

Inventory, July 1, 1980	$ 97,500
Physical inventory, May 31, 1981	95,000
Sales for 11 months ended May 31, 1981	840,000
Sales for year ended June 30, 1981	945,000
Purchases for 11 months ended May 31, 1981 (before audit adjustments)	665,000
Purchases for year ended June 30, 1981 (before audit adjustments)	800,000

The CPA's audit disclosed the following information.

Shipments received in May and included in the physical inventory but recorded as June purchases	7,500
Shipments received in unsalable condition and excluded from physical inventory; credit memos had not been received nor had chargebacks to vendors been recorded:	
Total at May 31, 1981	1,000
Total at June 30, 1981 (including the May unrecorded chargebacks)	1,500
Deposit made with vendor and charged to purchases in April, 1981. Product was shipped in July, 1981.	2,000
Deposit made with vendor and charged to purchases in May, 1981. Product was shipped, f.o.b. destination, on May 29, 1981, and was included in May 31, 1981, physical inventory as goods in transit	5,500
Through the carelessness of the receiving department, a June shipment was damaged by rain. This shipment was later sold in June at its cost of $10,000.	

Instructions

In audit engagements in which interim physical inventories are observed, a frequently used auditing procedure is to test the reasonableness of the year-end inventory by the application of gross profit ratios.

Prepare in good form the following schedules:

(a) Computation of the gross profit ratio for 11 months ended May 31, 1981.

(b) Computation by the gross profit ratio method of cost of goods sold during June, 1981.

(c) Computation by the gross profit ratio method of June 30, 1981, inventory.

(AICPA adapted)

P9-14 On April 15, 1981, fire damaged the office and warehouse of Drummond Electronics Corporation. The only accounting record saved was the general ledger, from which the trial balance below was prepared.

Drummond Electronics Corporation
TRIAL BALANCE
March 31, 1981

Cash	$ 9,000	
Accounts receivable	27,000	
Inventory, December 31, 1980	50,000	
Land	23,000	
Building and equipment	120,000	
Accumulated depreciation		$ 27,200
Other assets	3,600	
Accounts payable		23,700
Other expense accruals		10,200
Capital stock		100,000
Retained earnings		47,700
Sales		90,400
Merchandise	42,000	
Other expenses	24,600	
	$299,200	$299,200

The following data and information have been gathered:

1. The fiscal year of the corporation ends on December 31.

2. An examination of the April bank statement and canceled checks revealed that checks written during the period April 1–15 totaled $11,600: $5,700 paid to accounts payable as of March 31, $2,000 for April merchandise shipments, and $3,900 paid for other expenses. Deposits during the same period amounted to $10,650, which consisted of receipts on account from customers with the exception of a $450 refund from a vendor for merchandise returned in April.

3. Correspondence with suppliers revealed unrecorded obligations at April 15 of $8,500 for April merchandise shipments, including $1,300 for shipments in transit on that date.

4. Customers acknowledged indebtedness of $26,400 at April 15, 1981. It was also estimated that customers owed another $5,000 that will never be acknowledged or recovered. Of the acknowledged indebtedness, $600 will probably be uncollectible.

5. The companies insuring the inventory agreed that the corporation's fire-loss claim should be based on the assumption that the overall gross profit ratio for the past two years was in effect during the current year. The corporation's audited financial statements disclosed this information:

	Year Ended December 31	
	1980	1979
Net sales	$400,000	$300,000
Net purchases	226,000	174,000
Beginning inventory	45,000	35,000
Ending inventory	50,000	45,000

6. Inventory with a cost of $6,500 was salvaged and sold for $3,000. The balance of the inventory was a total loss.

Instructions

Prepare a schedule computing the amount of inventory fire loss. The supporting schedule of the computation of the gross profit margin should be in good form.

(AICPA adapted)

*P9-15   University Book Store uses the conventional retail method and is now considering converting to the retail LIFO method for the period beginning 1/1/1981. Available information consists of the following:

| | 1980 | | 1981 | |
	Cost	Retail	Cost	Retail
Inventory 1/1/1980	$ 12,500	$ 22,500	$?	$?
Purchases (net)	250,000	347,500	245,000	345,000
Net additional markups	—	5,000	—	10,000
Net markdowns	—	2,500	—	5,000
Sales (net)	—	340,000	—	345,450
Loss from breakage	—	1,000	—	-0-
Applicable price index	—	100	—	103

Following is a schedule showing the computation of the cost of inventory on hand at 12/31/1980 based on the conventional retail method.

	Cost	Retail
Inventory 1/1/1980	$ 12,500	$ 22,500
Purchases (net)	250,000	347,500
Net additional markups	—	5,000
Goods available	$262,500	375,000

(Ratio: $262,500 ÷ $375,000 = 70%)

Less:		
Sales		340,000
Net markdowns		2,500
Loss from breakage		1,000
Inventory 12/31/1980 at retail		$ 31,500

Inventory 12/31/1980 at lower of cost or market
Cost ($31,500 × 70%) $ 22,050

Instructions

(a) Prepare a schedule showing the recomputation of the inventory on hand at 12/31/1980 in accordance with the procedures necessary to convert from the conventional retail method to the LIFO retail method beginning January 1, 1981.

(b) Prepare the journal entry necessary to restate the 1/1/81 inventory to LIFO retail.

(c) Prepare a schedule showing the computation of the 12/31/1981 inventory by the LIFO retail method as adjusted for fluctuating prices. Without prejudice to your answers to parts (a) or (b) above, assume that you computed the 12/31/1980 inventory (retail value $31,500) under the LIFO retail method at a cost of $22,500. Round your answer to the nearest dollar.

*P9-16   The Harper Corporation, which uses the conventional retail inventory method, wishes to change to the LIFO retail method beginning with the accounting year ending December 31, 1981.

Amounts as shown below appear on the firm's books before adjustment:

	At Cost	At Retail
Inventory, January 1, 1981	$ 5,700	$ 10,000
Purchases in 1981	78,300	138,000
Markups in 1981		2,000
Markdowns in 1981		5,000
Sales in 1981		115,000

You are to assume that all markups and markdowns apply to 1981 purchases, and that it is appropriate to treat the entire inventory as a single department.

Instructions

Compute the inventory at December 31, 1981, under:

(a) Conventional retail method.

(b) Last-in, first-out retail method, effecting the change in method as of January 1, 1981. Assume that the cost to retail percentage for 1980 was recomputed correctly in accordance with procedures necessary to change to LIFO. This ratio was 65%.

(AICPA adapted)

Current Liabilities

The Concept of Liabilities

In recent years the concept of liabilities has been accorded renewed attention and is apparently undergoing a change. One reason for this attention is that financial statements have become more complicated because of the increase in special financing and sales agreements, new labor contract formulas and provisions, and more complex tax laws. Also, it seems that most accounting thought and analysis have been directed toward the determination of the debit, the valuation of the assets, or the charge to income, with the credit handled as an afterthought and as expediently as possible. Although it is true that all liabilities are "credits," it is debatable whether all credits appearing above the stockholders' equity section in published balance sheets are liabilities, or even that all liabilities have been recorded.

The question of what is a liability is not a simple issue to resolve. It seems clear that liabilities include more than debts arising from borrowings. The acquisition of goods or services on credit terms gives rise to liabilities and is much like borrowing. Less similar are liabilities resulting from the imposition of taxes, withholdings from employees' wages and salaries, dividend declarations, and product warranties.

To illustrate the complexity, a question that might be asked is whether preferred stock is a liability or an ownership claim. The first reaction is to say that preferred stock is in fact an ownership claim and should be reported as part of stockholders' equity. But, assume that the preferred stock is cumulative, non-participating, and callable by the issuer at any time. Now, is it a liability or part of stockholders' equity? Or, go even one step further—assume that the preferred stock is cumulative, non-participating, and is callable by *either* issuer or holder on demand.

Would the preferred stock now be a liability?[1] The answer to this question and others similar to it are difficult to answer without the existence of concise definitions. At the present time, accountants have differing notions as to what constitutes a liability and as a result, the liability section often over or understates the creditorship claims against the business.

Recently, the FASB has attempted to develop a definition of a liability as part of its conceptual framework study. The Board defines liabilities in a proposed exposure draft as **"financial representations of obligations of a particular enterprise to transfer economic resources to other entities in the future as a result of a past transaction or event affecting the enterprise."**[2] The Board states that an obligation must have three characteristics to be reported as a liability: (1) the obligation must involve a future sacrifice of cash, goods, or services; (2) it must be an obligation of the enterprise; and (3) the transaction or event giving rise to the enterprise's obligation must already have occurred. Although this definition may be subject to differing interpretations, it is a welcome addition to the professional literature, especially given past definitions developed by professional bodies.[3] For our purposes, the above definition is sufficiently appropriate to be used as the basis for subsequent discussion.[4]

Because liabilities involve future disbursements of assets or services, one of the most important features is the date on which they are payable. Currently maturing obligations represent a demand on the current assets of the enterprise—a demand that must be satisfied promptly and in the ordinary course of business if operations are to be continued. Liabilities with a more distant due date do not, as a rule, represent a claim on the enterprise's current resources and are in a slightly different category. This feature gives rise to the basic division of liabilities into (1) current liabilities and (2) long-term debt.

---

[1] It should be noted that this illustration is not just a theoretical exercise. In practice, there are a number of preferred stock issues that have all the characteristics of a debt instrument, except that they are called and legally classified preferred stock. In some cases, for example, the IRS has even permitted the dividend payments to be treated as an interest expense for tax purposes. This issue is discussed further in Chapter 15.

[2] "Objectives of Financial Reporting and Elements of Financial Statements of Business Enterprises," *Proposed Statement of Financial Accounting Concepts* (Stamford, Conn.: FASB, 1977), par. 49.

[3] For example, the AICPA, in *Accounting Terminology Bulletins: Review and Resume* (1953) defined liabilities as: "Something represented by a credit balance that is or would be properly carried forward upon the closing of books of account according to the rules or principles of accounting, provided such credit balance is not in effect a negative balance applicable to an asset. Thus the word is used broadly to comprise not only items which constitute liabilities in the popular sense of debts or obligations (including provision for those that are unascertained), but also credit balances to be accounted for which do not involve the debtor and creditor relation."

In 1970, *APB Statement No. 4* defined liabilities as "economic obligations of an enterprise ... and certain deferred credits that are not obligations but that are recognized and measured in conformity with generally accepted accounting principles."

Such definitions are stated in terms of the rules and procedures of accounting and are conceptually unattractive. As a result of these broad definitions, the liability section of the balance sheet has degenerated into a catchall for all leftover and sometimes ill-conceived credit balances.

[4] For definitions that are similar to the proposed FASB definition: see Maurice Moonitz "The Changing Concept of a Liability" *The Journal of Accountancy* (May, 1960), pp. 41–46; Eldon S. Hendricksen, *Accounting Theory*, 3rd edition (Homewood, Illinois: Richard D. Irwin, Inc. 1977), p. 451; and American Accounting Association, *Accounting and Reporting Standards for Corporate Financial Statements* (Sarasota, Fla.: AAA, 1957), p. 16.

Nature of Current Liabilities

For many years payment within one year was the characteristic that distinguished a current liability from a long-term debt. This one-year rule, although simple and easy to follow, produced some unreasonable results when the operating cycle of a business exceeded one year. Under currently acceptable practice, both current liabilities and current assets are defined in terms of the operating cycle of the individual enterprise. The **operating cycle** is the period of time elapsing between the acquisition of goods and services involved in the manufacturing process and the final cash realization resulting from sales and subsequent collections. Industries that manufacture products requiring an aging process and certain capital intensive industries have an operating cycle of considerably more than one year; on the other hand, some processing and most retail establishments have several operating cycles within a year.

Current assets are those assets normally converted into cash or consumed in operations within a single operating cycle or within a year if more than one cycle is completed each year. **Current liabilities are "obligations whose liquidation is reasonably expected to require use of existing resources properly classified as current assets, or the creation of other current liabilities."**[5] This definition has gained wide acceptance because it recognizes operating cycles of varying lengths in different industries and takes into consideration the important relationship between current assets and current liabilities. The FASB has recently affirmed this concept of **"maturity within one year or the operating cycle whichever is longer"** in its definition of short-term obligations in **Statement No. 6.**[6]

Valuation of Current Liabilities

Theoretically, liabilities should be measured by the present value of the future outlay of cash required to liquidate them. But, in practice, current liabilities are usually recorded in accounting records and reported in financial statements at their full maturity amount. Because of the short time periods involved, frequently less than one year, the difference between the present value of a current liability and the maturity value is not usually large. The slight overstatement of liabilities that results from carrying current liabilities at maturity value is justified on the grounds of expediency, conservatism, and immateriality. **APB Opinion No. 21** "Interest on Receivables and Payables" specifically exempts from present value measurements those payables arising from transactions with suppliers in the normal course of business that do not exceed approximately one year.[7]

---

[5]Committee on Accounting Procedure, American Institute of Certified Public Accountants, "Accounting Research and Terminology Bulletins," Final Edition (New York: AICPA, 1961), p. 21.

[6]"Classification of Short-term Obligations Expected to be Refinanced," *Statement of Financial Accounting Standards No. 6* (Stamford, Conn.: FASB, 1975), par. 2.

[7]"Interest on Receivables and Payables," *Opinions of the Accounting Principles Board No. 21* (New York: AICPA, 1971), par. 3.

Differences in Current Liabilities

We have concluded that liabilities are measurable future outlays resulting from past transactions. But within this sphere of similarity, liabilities possess characteristics that lend themselves to categorization. All liabilities, because they are expected future outlays, involve an element of uncertainty. The differences in degrees of uncertainty related to liabilities are the dissimilarities that allow us to discuss current liabilities under the following categories.

1. Determinable current liabilities.
2. Contingent current liabilities.

DETERMINABLE CURRENT LIABILITIES

The types of liabilities discussed in this category are susceptible of precise measurement. The amount of cash that will be needed to discharge the obligation and the date of payment or discharge are reasonably certain. There is nothing uncertain about (1) the fact that the obligation has been incurred and (2) the amount of the obligation. The existence of written or implied contracts or the imposition of legal statutes minimizes the uncertainty in amount, risk, and timing of these liabilities. The primary problem is one of discovery, which arises from the possibility of omitting these liabilities. In contrast to long-term debts, which are normally large in amount and supported by documentary evidence consisting of contracts, authorization, and correspondence, current liabilities may result from unwritten extensions of credit or unrecorded accruals, and may be small. Once these liabilities are discovered, however, the amount is readily determinable.

Accounts Payable

Accounts payable, or **trade accounts payable,** are balances owed to others for goods, supplies, and services purchased on open account. Accounts payable arise because of the time lag between the receipt of services or acquisition of title to assets and the payment for them. This period of extended credit is usually found in the terms of the sale (e.g., 2/10, n/30 or 1/10, E.O.M.) and is commonly 30 to 60 days.

Most accounting systems are designed to record liabilities for purchase of goods when the goods are received or, practically, when the invoices are received. Frequently there is some delay in recording the goods and the related liability on the books. In addition, if title has passed to the purchaser before the goods are received, the transaction should be recorded at the time of title passage. As a result, the accountant must pay particular attention to transactions occurring near the end of one accounting period and at the beginning of the next to ascertain that the record of goods received (the inventory) is in agreement with that of the liability (accounts payable) and that both are recorded in the proper period.

Measuring the amount of an account payable poses no particular difficulty because the invoice received from the creditor specifies the due date and the exact outlay in money that is necessary to settle the account. The only calculation that may be necessary concerns the amount of cash discount. See Chapter 8 for illustrations of entries related to accounts payable and purchase discounts.

Notes Payable

Obligations in the form of written promissory notes that are classified as current liabilities are usually either (1) trade notes, (2) short-term loan notes, or (3) current maturities of long-term debts.

Trade Notes   Trade notes payable represent the unpaid face amount of promissory notes owed to suppliers of goods, services, and equipment. In some industries and for certain classes of customers, promissory notes are required as part of the transaction in lieu of the normal extension of open account or verbal credit. Normally, both the due date and the amount of the outlay necessary to discharge the note are contained on the note. The only calculation that is commonly involved is the calculation of interest if the note is interest bearing.

Short-Term Loan Notes   Short-term promissory notes payable to banks or loan companies represent a current liability, and generally arise from cash loans. When these notes are interest bearing, it is necessary to record and report in financial statements any accrued interest payable and to carry the note payable as a liability in the amount of its **face value** (also called **principal amount**).

   If a **noninterest-bearing note** is issued, the bank or loan company **discounts** the note and remits the proceeds to the borrower. This discounting practice may lead to an inaccurate recording of the transaction. To illustrate, assume that on October 1 the Hull Company has its $100,000 one-year noninterest-bearing note discounted at 9% at the Corner National Bank. The Hull Company would receive the proceeds of $91,000 and would assume the obligation to pay $100,000 to the bank in 12 months. It should be apparent that the Hull Company has borrowed $91,000 for a period of one year at a cost of $9,000. Although the **stated discount rate** was 9%, the **effective interest rate** was 9.89% ($9,000/$91,000), because the full $100,000 is not available to the Hull Company during the year. A loan under these circumstances is frequently recorded on the date the loan is completed in the following manner:

Cash	91,000	
Prepaid Interest Expense	9,000	
Notes Payable		100,000

   The prepaid interest expense balance is subsequently transferred to interest expense over the term of the loan. The above-noted procedure overstates the asset inasmuch as the interest has not been paid in advance. It also overstates the liability because the present value of the obligation at the time of borrowing (October 1) is no greater than the amount borrowed. A more accurate accounting of this situation results from recording the transaction of October 1 as follows:

Cash	91,000	
Discount on Notes Payable	9,000	
Notes Payable		100,000

This procedure avoids the overstatement of the asset and the liability because the balance in the Discount on Notes Payable account would be deducted on the balance sheet from Notes Payable. Interest expense would be recorded in monthly increments of $750 by reducing Discount on Notes Payable through the following entry (assuming straight-line amortization approximates the effective interest method of amortization):

Interest Expense	750	
Discount on Notes Payable		750

Thus, a balance sheet prepared at December 31 would show:

Current liabilities		
Notes payable	$100,000	
Less: Discount on notes payable	6,750	
		$93,250

The interest expense of $2,250 for the three-month period would be reflected in the income statement.

Current Maturities of Long-Term Debts   The portion of bonds, mortgage notes, and other long-term indebtedness that matures within the next fiscal year is reported as a current liability. When only a part of a long-term debt is to be paid within the next 12 months, as in the case of serial bonds that are to be retired through a series of annual installments, the maturing portion of the debt is reported as a current liability, the balance as a long-term debt. Long-term debts maturing currently should not be included as current liabilities if they are (1) to be retired by assets accumulated for this purpose that properly have not been shown as current assets, (2) to be refinanced, or retired from the proceeds of a new debt issue (see next topic below), or (3) to be converted into capital stock. The plan for liquidation of such a debt should be disclosed either parenthetically or by a footnote to the financial statements.

Short-Term Obligations Expected to be Refinanced

Short-term obligations are those debts that are scheduled to mature within one year after the date of an enterprise's balance sheet or within an enterprise's operating cycle, whichever is longer. Some short-term obligations are expected to be refinanced on a long-term basis and, therefore, are not expected to require the use of working capital during the next year (or operating cycle).[8] Prior to 1975 these obligations were presented in balance sheets in a number of ways including (a) classification as current liabilities, (b) classification as long-term liabilities, and (c) presentation as a class of liabilities distinct from both current and long-term liabilities.

---

[8]*Refinancing a short-term obligation on a long-term basis* means either replacing it with a long-term obligation or with equity securities, or renewing, extending, or replacing it with short-term obligations for an uninterrupted period extending beyond one year (or the operating cycle, if longer) from the date of the enterprise's balance sheet.

For many years the accounting profession supported the exclusion of short-term obligations from current liabilities if they were "expected to be refinanced." Because the profession provided no specific guidelines, however, determination of whether a short-term obligation was "expected to be refunded" was usually based solely on management's **intent** to refinance on a long-term basis. A company may sell short-term commercial paper to finance new plant and equipment, intending eventually to refinance it on a long-term basis. Or it may obtain a five-year bank loan but, because the bank prefers it, handle the actual financing with 90-day notes, which it must keep turning over (i.e., renewing). So what is it, long-term debt or current liabilities? To illustrate this problem of classification, the Penn Central Railroad (before it went bankrupt) was deep into short-term debt and commercial paper but classified it as long-term debt. Why? Because the railroad believed it had commitments by lenders to keep refinancing the short-term debt. When those commitments suddenly disappeared, it was good-bye Pennsy. As the Greek philosopher Epictetus once said, "Some things in this world are not and yet appear to be."

In 1975 the FASB issued **Statement No. 6,** in which it set forth authoritative criteria for determining the circumstances under which short-term obligations may properly be excluded from current liabilities.

According to **FASB Statement No. 6,** an enterprise shall exclude a short-term obligation from current liabilities only if both of the following conditions are met:

1. It must **intend to refinance** the obligation on a long-term basis, and
2. It must **demonstrate an ability** to consummate the refinancing.[9]

Intention to refinance on a long-term basis means the enterprise intends to refinance the short-term obligation so that the use of working capital will not be required during the ensuing fiscal year or operating cycle, if longer. The **ability to consummate the refinancing** may be demonstrated by:

a. Actually refinancing the short-term obligation by issuance of a long-term obligation or equity securities after the date of the balance sheet but before it is issued; or
b. Entering into a financing agreement that clearly permits the enterprise to refinance the debt on a long-term basis on terms that are readily determinable.

If an **actual refinancing** occurs, the portion of the short-term obligation to be excluded from current liabilities may not exceed the proceeds from the new obligation or equity securities issued which are applied to retire the short-term obligation. For example, Montavon Winery with $3,000,000 of short-term debt issued 100,000 shares of common stock subsequent to the date of the balance sheet, but before the balance sheet was issued, and intended to use the proceeds to liquidate the short-term debt at its maturity. If the net proceeds from the sale of the 100,000 shares totaled $2,000,000, only that amount of the short-term debt could be excluded from current liabilities.

When a **financing agreement** is relied upon to demonstrate ability to refinance a short-term obligation on a long-term basis, the agreement must meet all of the following conditions:

a. The agreement must be noncancelable as to all parties and must extend beyond the normal operating cycle of the company or one year, whichever is longer.

---

[9]"Classification of Short-term Obligations Expected to be Refinanced," *Statement of Financial Accounting Standards No. 6* (Stamford, Conn.: FASB, 1975), par. 10 and 11.

   b. At the balance sheet date and at the date of its issuance, the company must not be in violation of the agreement.

   c. The lender or investor is expected to be financially capable of honoring the agreement.

The amount of short-term debt that can be excluded from current liabilities:

1. Cannot exceed the amount available for refinancing under the agreement.
2. Must be adjusted for any limitations or restrictions in the agreement which indicate that the full amount obtainable will not be available to retire the short-term obligations.
3. Cannot exceed a reasonable estimate of the minimum amount expected to be available, if the amount available for refinancing will fluctuate (i.e., the most conservative estimate must be used).

If any of these three amounts cannot be reasonably estimated, the entire amount of the short-term debt must be **included** in current liabilities.

As an illustration of a fluctuating amount situation (item 3 above), consider the following:

> Chicago Casket Company enters into an agreement with Continental Bank to borrow up to 80% of the amount of its trade receivables. During the next fiscal year, the receivables are expected to range between a low of $900,000 in the first quarter and a high of $1,700,000 in the third quarter. The minimum amount expected to be available to refinance the short-term obligations that mature during the first quarter of the next year is $720,000 (80% of the expected low for receivables during the first quarter). Consequently, no more than $720,000 of short-term obligations may be excluded from current liabilities at the balance sheet date.

Shortly after the issuance of **FASB Statement No. 6,** the FASB was asked to clarify whether a short-term obligation should be excluded from current liabilities if it is paid-off after the balance sheet date and then subsequently replaced by long-term debt before the balance sheet is issued (e.g., the balance sheet date might be December 31, 1980; the short-term debt repayment date January 17, 1981; the long-term debt issuance date February 3, 1981; and the balance sheet issuance date March 1, 1981). Because the repayment of a short-term obligation **before** funds are obtained through a long-term refinancing requires the use of current assets, the FASB recommends that:

> ...if a short-term obligation is repaid after the balance sheet date and subsequently a long-term obligation or equity securities are issued whose proceeds are used to replenish current assets before the balance sheet is issued, the short-term obligation shall not be excluded from current liabilities at the balance sheet date.[10]

Disclosure of Short-Term Obligations Expected to be Refinanced

FASB Statement No. 6 specifies that "a total of current liabilities shall be presented in classified balance sheets."[11] If a short-term obligation is excluded from current

---

[10]"Classification of a Short-Term Obligation Repaid Prior to Being Replaced by a Long-term Security (an interpretation of *FASB Statement No. 6*), *FASB Interpretation No. 8* (Stamford, Conn.: 1976), par. 3.

[11]A "classified" balance sheet shows separate classifications of current assets and current liabilities permitting ready determination of working capital. *Statement No. 6* does not apply to enterprises in several specialized industries (including broker-dealers and finance, real estate, and stock life insurance companies) for which unclassified balance sheets are prepared because the current/noncurrent distinction is deemed in practice to have little or no relevance.

liabilities because of refinancing, the footnote to the financial statements should include:

1. A general description of the financing agreement.
2. The terms of any new obligation incurred or to be incurred.
3. The terms of any equity security issued or to be issued.

When refinancing on a long-term basis is expected to be accomplished through the issuance of equity securities, it is not appropriate to include the short-term obligation in owners' equity. The obligation is a liability and not owners' equity at the date of the balance sheet.

Short-term obligations expected to be refinanced may be shown in captions distinct from both current liabilities and long-term debt, such as "Interim Debt," "Short-term Debt Expected to be Refinanced," and "Intermediate Debt."

The disclosure requirements of **Statement No. 6** are illustrated below for an actual refinancing situation and on page 437 for a financing agreement situation.

Actual Refinancing	
Current liabilities:	December 31, 1980
Accounts payable	$ 3,600,000
Accrued expenses	2,500,000
Income taxes payable	1,100,000
Current portion of long-term debt	1,000,000
Total current liabilities	$ 8,200,000
Long-term debt:	
Notes payable refinanced in January 1981—Footnote 1	$ 2,000,000
8% bonds due serially through 1996	15,000,000
Total long-term debt	$17,000,000

Footnote 1. On January 19, 1981, the Company issued 50,000 shares of Common Stock and received proceeds totaling $2,385,000 of which $2,000,000 was used to liquidate notes payable that matured on February 1, 1981. Accordingly, such notes payable have been classified as long-term debt at December 31, 1980.

Dividends Payable

A **cash dividend payable** is an amount owed by a corporation to its stockholders as a result of a distribution that the board of directors has formally authorized. At the date of declaration the corporation assumes a liability that places the stockholders in the position of creditors relative to the amount of dividends declared. Because cash dividends are always paid within one year of declaration (generally within three months), they are classified as current liabilities.

Accumulated but undeclared dividends on cumulative preferred stock are not a recognized liability because **preferred dividends in arrears** are not a legal obligation until formal action is taken by the board of directors authorizing the distribution of earnings. Nevertheless, the amount of cumulative dividends unpaid should

---

Financing Agreement

Current liabilities:	December 31, 1980
Accounts payable	$ 3,600,000
Accrued expenses	2,500,000
Income taxes payable	1,100,000
Current portion on long-term debt	1,000,000
Total current liabilities	$ 8,200,000
Long-term debt:	
Notes payable expected to be refinanced in 1981—Footnote 1	$ 2,000,000
8% bonds due serially through 1996	15,000,000
Total long-term debt	$17,000,000

Footnote 1. Under a financing agreement with a major New York bank the Company may borrow up to $4,000,000 at any time through 1982. Amounts borrowed under the agreement bear interest at 1% above the bank's prime interest rate and mature three years from the date of the loan. The agreement requires the Company to maintain a working capital level of $9,000,000 and prohibits the payment of dividends on common stock without prior approval of the bank. The notes have been classified as long-term debt because the Company intends to borrow $2,000,000 under the agreement to liquidate its notes payable which mature on May 1, 1981.

---

be disclosed as a footnote or it may be shown parenthetically in the capital stock section following a description of the stock.

Dividends payable in the form of additional shares of stock are not recognized as a liability because **stock dividends** do not require future outlays of assets or services and they are revocable by the board of directors at any time prior to issuance. Even so, such undistributed stock dividends are generally reported in the stockholders' equity section because they represent retained earnings in the process of transfer to paid-in capital.

Returnable Deposits

Current liabilities of a company may include returnable deposits (monies) received from customers and employees. Deposits may be received from customers to guarantee performance of a contract or service or as guarantees to cover payment of expected future obligations. Deposits may also be received from customers as guarantees for possible damage to property left with the customer. Some companies require their employees to make deposits for the return of keys or other company property or for locker privileges. The classification of these items as current or noncurrent liabilities is dependent on the time involved between the date of the deposit and the termination of the relationship that required the deposit.

Liability on the Advance Sale of Tickets, Tokens, and Certificates

Transportation companies may issue tickets or tokens that can be exchanged or used to pay for future fares, or restaurants may issue meal tickets that can be exchanged or used to pay for future meals, or retail stores may issue gift certificates that are redeemable in merchandise. In such cases, the businesses have received cash in exchange for promises to perform services or to furnish goods at some indefinite future date.

The balance sheet should reflect the obligation for any outstanding instruments that are redeemable in goods or services; the income statement should reflect the revenues earned as a result of performances during the period. The sale of these tickets, tokens, and certificates is recorded by a debit to Cash and a credit to a current liability account usually described as **Deferred** or **Unearned Revenue.** As the claims are redeemed, the liability account is debited and an appropriate revenue account is credited.

Because these advances are usually small in amount and relatively numerous, some are not presented to the issuing company for redemption. If these claims are rendered void by lapse of time or some other reason as defined by the sales agreement, the amount of forfeited claims may be easily measured. If the offer is of indefinite duration, however, it is necessary to reduce the liability balance by an estimate of the claims that will not be redeemed and to credit an appropriate account for the gain that results from forfeitures.

Collections for Third Parties

A common current liability results from a company collecting taxes from customers for a governmental unit and withholding taxes from employees' payrolls.

Sales Taxes   Sales taxes on transfers of tangible personal property and on certain services must be collected from customers and remitted to the proper governmental authority. A liability must be set up to provide for the taxes collected from customers but as yet unremitted to the tax authority. If the actual sales total and the sales tax collections are recorded separately at the time of the sale, the sales tax payable account should reflect the liability for sales taxes due the government. The entry below is the proper one for a sale of $3,000 when a 4% sales tax is in effect.

Cash or Accounts Receivable	3,120	
Sales		3,000
Sales Taxes Payable		120

When the sales tax collections credited to the liability account are not equal to the liability as computed by the governmental formula, an adjustment of the liability account may be made by recognizing a gain or a loss on sales tax collections.

In many companies, however, the sales tax and the amount of the sale are not segregated at the time of sale; both are credited in total in the sales account. To reflect correctly the actual amount of sales and the liability for sales taxes, the sales account must be debited for the amount of the sales taxes due the government on these sales and the sales taxes payable account credited for the same amount. As an illustration, assume that the sales account balance is $150,000 and includes sales taxes of 4%. Because the amount recorded in the sales account is equal to sales plus 0.04 of sales, or 1.04 times the sales total, the sales are $150,000 ÷ 1.04, or $144,230.77. The sales tax liability is $5,769.23 ($144,230.77 × 0.04; or $150,000 − $144,230.77) and the following entry would be made to record the amount due the taxing unit:

Sales   5,769.23
  Sales Taxes Payable   5,769.23

Social Security Taxes Since January 1, 1937, social security legislation has provided federal old-age, survivor, and disability insurance (O.A.S.D.I.) benefits for certain individuals and their families through the imposition of taxes on both the employer and the employee. All employers are required to collect the employee's share of this tax, by deducting it from the employee's gross pay, and to remit it to the government along with the employer's share. Both the employer and the employee are taxed at the same rate, currently 6.13% (1979) based on the employee's gross pay up to a $22,900 annual limit.

In 1965 Congress passed the first federal health insurance program for the aged—popularly known as Medicare. It is a two-part program designed to alleviate the high cost of medical care for those over 65. The Basic Plan, which provides hospital and other institutional services, is financed by a separate Hospital Insurance tax paid by both the employee and the employer on the employee's first $22,900 of annual compensation. The Voluntary Plan takes care of the major part of doctors' bills and other medical and health services and is financed by monthly payments from all who enroll plus matching funds from the federal government.

The combination of the O.A.S.D.I. tax, more commonly called Federal Insurance Contribution Act (F.I.C.A.) tax, and the federal Hospital Insurance is commonly referred to as the **social security tax.** The rates for these taxes are changed intermittently by acts of Congress.

The amount of unremitted employee and employer social security tax on gross wages paid should be reported by the employer as a current liability.

Income Tax Withholding Federal and some state income tax laws require employers to withhold from the pay of each employee an amount approximating the applicable income tax due on those wages. The amount of income tax withheld is computed by the employer according to a government-prescribed formula or a government-provided withholding tax table and is dependent on the length of the pay period and each employee's taxable wages, marital status, and claimed dependents.

If the income tax withheld plus the employee and the employer social security taxes exceeds specified amounts per month, the employer is required to make remittances to the government during the month. Monthly deposits are not required if the employer's liability for the calendar quarter is less than $200. Instead, the tax liability is remitted with the employer's quarterly payroll tax return.

Other Payroll Deductions In addition to the payroll tax deductions, employers frequently deduct insurance premiums, employee savings, and union dues that must be recognized as liabilities to third parties to the extent that the amounts deducted are still among the employer's assets.

Accrued Expenses or Accrued Liabilities

Accrued expenses or accrued liabilities arise through accounting recognition of unpaid costs that come into existence as the result of past contractual commitments, past services received, or by operation of a tax law. The matching principle requires that incurred but unpaid expenses and the related liabilities be estimated as of the financial statement date, recorded in the accounts, and reported in the financial statements on an accrual basis. In published financial statements these accruals, with the exception of accrued taxes, are often conveniently combined under one heading. But, in recording these liabilities, appropriate account titles should be used, such as Wages Payable, Interest Payable, Property Taxes Payable, Payroll Taxes Payable, Bonuses Payable, and Income Taxes Payable. Payroll taxes payable and property taxes payable are two accrued expenses, common to every business, that deserve special mention. Income taxes payable and bonuses payable are accrued liabilities accorded special attention in the discussion of conditional payments that follows this section.

Accrued Payroll Taxes As wages and salaries are earned by employees, the employer's share of F.I.C.A. (social security) tax accrues. The employer incurs a tax expense on each employee's earnings up to an annual maximum (6.13% on $22,900 in 1979). The employer is required to remit to the government its share of F.I.C.A. tax along with the amount of F.I.C.A. tax deducted from each employee's gross compensation. All unremitted employer F.I.C.A. taxes on employee earnings either paid or payable, should be recorded as payroll tax expense and payroll tax payable.

Another payroll tax levied by the federal government in cooperation with state governments provides a system of unemployment insurance. All employers who (1) paid wages of $1,500 or more during any calendar quarter in the year or preceding year or (2) employed at least one individual in each of 20 weeks during the current or preceding calendar year are subject to the Federal Unemployment Tax Act (F.U.T.A.). This tax is levied only on the employer at a rate of 3.4% (1979) on the first $6,000 of compensation paid to each employee during the calendar year. The employer is allowed a tax credit not to exceed 2.7% for contributions paid to a state plan for unemployment compensation. Thus, if an employer is subject to a state unemployment tax of 2.7% or more, only 0.7% tax is due the federal government.

State unemployment compensation laws differ from the federal law and differ among various states. Therefore, employers must be familiar with the unemployment tax laws in each state in which they pay wages and salaries. Although the normal state tax may be 2.7% or higher, all states provide for some form of merit rating under which a reduction in the state contribution rate is allowed. Employers who display by their benefit and contribution experience that they have provided steady employment are entitled to this reduction—if the size of the state fund is adequate to provide the reduction. In order not to penalize an employer who has earned a reduction in the state contribution rate, the federal law allows a credit of 2.7% even though the state contribution rate is less than 2.7%.

To illustrate the application of the federal and state unemployment compensation tax laws, assume that the Ozark Trails Co. has a taxable payroll of $100,000. The federal rate is 3.4% and the state contribution rate is 2.7%, but because of good employment experience, the company's rate has been reduced by the state to 1%. The computation of the federal and state unemployment taxes for Ozark Trails Co. is:

State tax payment (1% of $100,000)			$1,000
Federal tax before credit (3.4% of $100,000)		$3,400	
Less: Credit for state tax payment	$1,000		
Additional credit (difference between $2,700 and $1,000)	1,700	2,700	
Net federal tax			700
Total federal and state tax			$1,700

The federal unemployment tax is paid annually on or before January 31, following the taxable calendar year, and state contributions generally are required to be paid quarterly. Because both the federal and the state unemployment taxes accrue on earned compensation, the amount of accrued but unpaid employer contributions should be recorded as an operating expense and as a current liability as financial statements are prepared at year end.

Accounting for employee payroll deductions and employer's payroll taxes is illustrated below. Assume a weekly payroll of $10,000 entirely subject to F.I.C.A. (6.13%), federal (0.7%) and state (2.7%) unemployment taxes with income tax withholding of $1,320 and union dues of $88 deducted.

The entry to record the wages and salaries paid and the employee payroll deductions would be:

Wages and Salaries	10,000	
Withholding Taxes		1,320
F.I.C.A. Taxes Payable		613
Union Dues Payable to Local No. 257		88
Cash		7,979

The entry to record the employer payroll taxes would be:

Payroll Tax Expense	953	
F.I.C.A. Taxes Payable		613
Federal Unemployment Tax Payable		70
State Unemployment Tax Payable		270

The entries above illustrate the recording of the liabilities associated with withholdings from employees' wages and the employer's share of payroll taxes and fringe benefits. In practice, the cost side of this problem is commonly refined to the extent that all of the payroll costs (wages, payroll taxes, and fringe benefits) are allocated to appropriate cost accounts such as Direct Labor, Indirect Labor, Sales Salaries, Administrative Salaries, and the like.

This abbreviated and somewhat simplified discussion of payroll costs and deductions is not indicative of the volume of records and clerical work that may be involved in maintaining a sound and accurate payroll system or of its importance.

Accrued Property Taxes   Local governmental units generally depend on property taxes as their primary source of revenue. Such taxes are based on the assessed value of both real and personal property and become a lien against the property at a date determined by law, usually the assessment date. This lien is a liability of the property owner and is a cost of the services of such property. The accounting questions that arise from property taxes are: (1) When should the property owner record the liability? (2) To which income period should the cost be charged?

The date that the tax becomes a lien against the property is frequently used as the date to recognize and record the liability. But, the lien date may not coincide with or occur in the period when the taxpayer pays or benefits from the taxes. Therefore, some businesses record the liability as the expense is accrued (up to the date of payment).

The accounting profession in considering the various periods to which property taxes might be charged contends that "generally, the most acceptable basis of providing for property taxes is monthly accrual on the taxpayer's books during the fiscal period of the taxing authority for which the taxes are levied."[12] Charging the taxes to the period subsequent to the levy would relate the expense to the period in which the taxes were used by the governmental unit to provide benefits to the property owner.

Assume that Seaboard Company, which closes its books each year on December 31, receives its property tax bill in May each year. The fiscal year for the city and county in which Seaboard Company is located begins on May 1 and ends on the following April 30. Property taxes of $36,000 are assessed against Seaboard Company property on January 1, and become a lien on May 1. However, tax bills are sent out in May and are payable in equal installments on July 1 and September 1. If the property tax liability is recorded on the lien date of May 1, Seaboard Company would amortize the deferred tax expense monthly throughout the fiscal year of the governmental unit, May 1 to April 30. Entries to record the liability, monthly tax charges, and the tax payments on July 1 and September 1 would be:

May 1

Deferred Property Taxes	36,000	
Property Taxes Payable		36,000
(To record lien)		

May 31 and June 30

Property Tax Expense	3,000	
Deferred Property Taxes		3,000
(To record monthly tax expense)		

July 1

Property Taxes Payable	18,000	
Cash		18,000
(To record payment of first installment)		

July 31 and August 31

Property Tax Expense	3,000	
Deferred Property Taxes		3,000
(To record monthly tax expense)		

September 1

Property Taxes Payable	18,000	
Cash		18,000
(To record payment of second [final] installment)		

---

[12]Possible alternatives are: (a) Year in which paid. (b) Year ending on assessment (or lien) date. (c) Year beginning on assessment (or lien) date. (d) Calendar or fiscal year of taxpayer prior to assessment (or lien) date. (e) Calendar or fiscal year of taxpayer including assessment (or lien) date. (f) Calendar or fiscal year of taxpayer prior to payment date. (g) Fiscal year of governing body levying the tax. (h) Year appearing on tax bill. Committee on Accounting Procedure, American Institute of Certified Public Accountants, *Accounting Research and Terminology Bulletin, Final Edition* (New York: AICPA, 1961), chapter 10, sec. A, par. 10.

September 30, October 31, November 30, and December 31

Property Tax Expense	3,000	
Deferred Property Taxes		3,000
(To record monthly tax expense)		

Deferred property taxes of $12,000 will be reported as a current asset on the December 31 balance sheet, and this amount will be amortized at the rate of $3,000 per month during January, February, March, and April of the following calendar year.

If the property tax liability is not recognized at the lien date of May 1, and instead is accrued monthly by Seaboard Company during the fiscal year of the taxing unit, the entries will be:

May 1

No entry

May 31 and June 30

Property Tax Expense	3,000	
Property Taxes Payable		3,000
(To record monthly tax expense)		

July 1

Property Taxes Payable	6,000	
Deferred Property Taxes	12,000	
Cash		18,000
(To record payment of first installment)		

July 31 and August 31

Property Tax Expense	3,000	
Deferred Property Taxes		3,000
(To record monthly tax expense)		

September 1

Deferred Property Taxes	18,000	
Cash		18,000
(To record payment of second [final] installment)		

September 30, October 31, November 30, and December 31

Property Tax Expense	3,000	
Deferred Property Taxes		3,000
(To record monthly tax expense)		

As in the previous illustration, the Deferred Property Taxes account has a $12,000 balance on December 31 that would be amortized at the rate of $3,000 per month during January, February, March, and April of the following calendar year. Under the first method the deferral is set up when the payable is recorded, whereas under the second method the deferral is set up when the payment is made.

Some accountants advocate accruing property taxes by charges to income during the fiscal year ending on the lien date, rather than during the fiscal year beginning on the lien date or the fiscal year of the tax authority. In such instances the property tax for the coming fiscal year must be estimated and charged monthly to Property Tax Expense and must be credited to Property Tax Payable. Under this method the entire amount of the tax is accrued by the lien date and the expense is charged to the fiscal period preceding payment of the tax. Justification for this method exists when the assessment date precedes the lien date by a year or more, as is the case in some taxing units. Since, in such instances, the amount is estimated and accrued by the property owner before receipt of the tax bill, it is proper theoretically to categorize property taxes as an estimated current liability rather than as a determinable current liability.

Recognizing that special circumstances may suggest the use of alternative accrual periods, the profession supports the view that "consistency of application from year to year is the important consideration and selection of any of the periods mentioned is a matter for individual judgment."[13]

Conditional Payments

The amount of certain liabilities is dependent on annual income, which cannot be known for certain until the end of an accounting period. At the end of the year, items such as income taxes, bonuses, and profit-sharing payments, even though dependent on the results of operations, can be readily measured. For interim monthly or quarterly financial statements, however, the amounts of these obligations must be viewed as estimates in advance of the final determination of annual income.

Income Taxes Payable   Any federal or state income tax is a conditional liability because the amount of this tax varies in proportion to the amount of annual income. Some accountants consider the amount of income tax on annual income as an estimate because the computation of income (and the tax thereon) is subject to the review and the approval of the Internal Revenue Service. The meaning and application of numerous tax rules, especially new ones, are debatable and often dependent on a court's interpretation. Using the best information and advice available, a business must prepare an income tax return and compute the income tax payable resulting from the operations of the current period. The taxes payable on the income of a corporation, as computed per the tax return, should be classified as a current liability. Unlike the corporation, the proprietorship and the partnership are not taxable entities. Because the individual proprietor and the members of a partnership are subject to personal income taxes on their share of the results of the business's operations, income tax liabilities do not appear on the financial statements of proprietorships and partnerships.

Corporations whose tax liability for the tax year is reasonably expected to be $40 or more are required to estimate the amount of annual tax payable. This **estimated tax** is payable in equal installments on the fifteenth day of the fourth, sixth, ninth, and twelfth months of the tax year. A corporation must deposit income taxes in an authorized commercial bank depository or a Federal Reserve bank; failure to make proper payments may result in a penalty ranging from 6% to 9% of the underpayment. If, after computing and making payments of estimated income tax, a corporation determines that the original estimate is substantially too low, or too high, it should recompute the estimated tax before the next installment and increase or decrease the amount of each remaining installment to reflect the change.

If in a later year an additional tax is assessed on the income of an earlier year, Income Taxes Payable should be credited. The related debit should be charged to current operations.

[13]*Ibid.,* par. 13.

Differences between taxable income under the tax laws and accounting income under generally accepted accounting principles have become greater in recent years. Because of these differences and the high income tax rates on corporations, the amount of income tax payable to the government in any given year, based on taxable income, may differ substantially from the amount of income tax that relates to the income before income taxes, as reported on the published financial statements. The accounting procedure recommended by the AICPA to reconcile properly these differences and to reflect business income correctly is called **interperiod income tax allocation.** Chapter 20 is devoted solely to income tax matters and presents an extensive discussion of this complex and controversial problem.

Bonus Agreements   For various reasons, many companies give a bonus to certain or all officers and employees in addition to their regular salary or wage. Frequently the amount of the bonus is dependent on the company's profits for the year so that in effect the employees who are included in the bonus plan participate in the profits of the enterprise.

From the standpoint of the enterprise, **bonus payments to employees** may be considered additional wages and should be included as a deduction in determining the net income for the year.

Because the amount of a bonus to employees is an expense of the business, the problem of computing the amount of bonus to be paid becomes more difficult. To illustrate, assume a situation in which a company has income of $100,000 determined before considering the bonus as an expense. According to the terms of the bonus agreement, 20% of the income is to be set aside for distribution among the employees. Now if the bonus were not itself an expense to be deducted in determining income, the amount of the bonus could be computed very simply as 20% of the net income of $100,000. The bonus is an expense, however, that must be deducted in arriving at the amount of income on which the bonus is to be based. Hence, $100,000 reduced by the amount of the bonus is the figure on which the bonus is to be computed. That is, the bonus is equal to 20% of $100,000 less the bonus. Stated algebraically:

$$B = 0.20 (\$100,000 - B)$$
$$B = \$20,000 - 0.2B$$
$$1.2B = \$20,000$$
$$B = \$16,666.67$$

A similar problem results from the relationship of bonus payments to federal income taxes. Assume the same situation as before with the income of $100,000 computed without subtracting either the employees' bonus or taxes on income. The bonus is to be based on income after deducting income taxes but before deducting the bonus. The rate of income tax is 40% and the bonus of 20% is a deductible expense for tax purposes. The bonus is, therefore, equal to 20% of $100,000 minus the tax, and the tax is equal to 40% of $100,000 minus the bonus. Thus we have two simultaneous equations that, using B as the symbol for the bonus and T for the tax, may be stated algebraically as follows:

$$B = 0.20\ (\$100,000 - T)$$
$$T = 0.40\ (\$100,000 - B)$$

These may be solved by substituting the value of T as indicated in the second equation for T in the first equation.

$$B = 0.20\ (\$100,000 - 0.40\ [\$100,000 - B])$$
$$B = 0.20\ (\$100,000 - \$40,000 + 0.4B)$$
$$B = 0.20\ (\$60,000 + 0.4B)$$
$$B = \$12,000 + 0.08B$$
$$0.92B = \$12,000$$
$$B = \$13,043.48$$

Substituting this value for B into the second equation allows us to solve for T:

$$T = 0.40\ (\$100,000 - \$13,043.48)$$
$$T = 0.40\ (\$86,956.52)$$
$$T = \$34,782.61$$

To prove these amounts, both should be worked back into the original equation.

$$B = 0.20\ (\$100,000 - T)$$
$$\$13,043.48 = 0.20\ (\$100,000 - \$34,782.61)$$
$$\$13,043.48 = 0.20\ (\$65,217.39)$$
$$\$13,043.48 = \$13,043.48$$

If the terms of the agreement provide for deducting both the tax and the bonus to arrive at the income figure on which the bonus is computed, the equations would be:

$$B = 0.20\ (\$100,000 - B - T)$$
$$T = 0.40\ (\$100,000 - B)$$

Substituting the value of T from the second equation into the first equation enables us to solve for B:

$$B = 0.20\ (\$100,000 - B - 0.40\ [\$100,000 - B])$$
$$B = 0.20\ (\$100,000 - B - \$40,000 + 0.4B)$$
$$B = 0.20\ (\$60,000 - 0.6B)$$
$$B = \$12,000 - 0.12B$$
$$1.12B = \$12,000$$
$$B = \$10,714.29$$

The value for B may then be substituted in the second equation above, and that equation solved for T:

$$T = 0.40 \ (\$100,000 - \$10,714.29)$$
$$T = 0.40 \ (\$89,285.71)$$
$$T = \$35,714.28$$

If these values are then substituted back into the original bonus equation, they prove themselves as follows:

$$B = 0.20 \ (\$100,000 - B - T)$$
$$\$10,714.29 = 0.20 \ (\$100,000 - \$10,714.29 - \$35,714.28)$$
$$\$10,714.29 = 0.20 \ (\$53,571.43)$$
$$\$10,714.29 = \$10,714.29$$

Drawing up a legal document such as a bonus agreement is a task for a lawyer, not an accountant, although accountants are frequently called on to express an opinion on the feasibility of the provisions of the agreement. In this respect, one should always insist that the agreement state specifically whether income taxes and the bonus itself are expenses deductible in determining the income for purposes of the bonus computation.

It should be apparent from the preceding paragraphs that no entry can be made for a profit-sharing bonus until all other adjusting entries, except the one for accrued taxes on income, have been made and the income before bonus and tax has been calculated. This calculation can be accomplished through the use of a work sheet or by some other method. Once the income before bonus has been calculated, it is possible to make the bonus calculation and to record it by means of an adjusting entry.

Profit-Sharing Bonus to Employees Expense	10,714.29	
Accrued Profit-Sharing Bonus Payable		10,714.29

Later when the bonus is paid, the journal entry would be:

Accrued Profit-Sharing Bonus Payable	10,714.29	
Cash		10,714.29

The expense account should appear in the income statement as an operating expense. The liability, accrued profit-sharing bonus payable, is usually payable within a short period, and should be included as a current liability in the balance sheet.

Similar to bonus arrangements are contractual agreements covering rents or royalty payments that are conditional on the amount of revenues earned or the quantity of product produced or extracted. Conditional expenses based on revenues or units produced are usually less difficult to compute than the bonus arrangements just illustrated. For example, if a lease calls for a fixed rent payment of $500 per month and 1% of all sales over $300,000 per year, the annual rent obligation would amount to $6,000 plus $.01 of each dollar of revenue over $300,000. Or, a royalty agreement may accrue to the patent owner $1.00 for every ton of product resulting from the patented process, or accrue to the owner of the mineral rights $.50 on every barrel of oil extracted. As each additional unit of product is produced or extracted, an additional obligation, usually of the current liability type, is created.

CONTINGENT LIABILITIES

Contingent liabilities are obligations that are dependent upon the occurrence or nonoccurrence of one or more future events to confirm either the amount payable, or the payee, or the date payable, or its existence; that is, determination of one or more of these factors is dependent upon a contingency. A **contingency** is defined in **FASB Statement No. 5** "as an existing condition, situation, or set of circumstances involving uncertainty as to possible gain (**gain contingency**) or loss (**loss contingency**) to an enterprise that will ultimately be resolved when one or more future events occur or fail to occur."[14] A liability incurred as a result of a "loss contingency" is by definition a **contingent liability.**

When a loss contingency exists, the likelihood that the future event or events will confirm the incurrence of a liability can range from probable to remote. The FASB uses the terms **probable, reasonably possible,** and **remote** to identify three areas within that range and assigns the following meanings:

> **Probable**—the future event or events are likely to occur.
> **Reasonably possible**—the chance of the future event or events occurring is more than remote but less than likely.
> **Remote**—the chance of the future event or events occurring is slight.

An estimated loss from a loss contingency should be accrued by a charge to income and a liability recorded only if both of the following conditions are met:

1. Information available prior to the issuance of the financial statements indicates that it is probable that a liability had been incurred at the date of the financial statements.
2. The amount of the loss can be reasonably estimated.

Only those loss contingencies that result in the incurrence of a liability are relevant to the discussion in this chapter. Loss contingencies that result in the impairment of an asset (e.g., collectibility of receivables or threat of expropriation of assets) are discussed in other appropriate sections of this textbook.

It is implicit in the first condition that it must be **probable** that one or more future events confirming the fact of the loss will occur. Neither the exact payee nor the exact date payable need be known to record a liability. **What must be known is whether it is probable that a liability has been incurred.** The second criterion indicates that an amount for the liability can be reasonably determined; otherwise it should not be accrued as a liability. To determine a reasonable estimate of the liability, such evidence may be based on the company's own experience, experience of other companies in the industry, engineering or research studies, legal advice, or educated guesses of personnel in the best position to know.

Obviously the application of these terms as guidelines for differentiating or classifying economic events or conditions for accounting purposes involves judgment and subjectivity. The following items are examples of loss contingencies and the general accounting treatment accorded them.[15]

---

[14]"Accounting for Contingencies," *Statement of Financial Accounting Standards No. 5* (Stamford, Conn.: FASB, 1975), par. 1.

[15]Adapted from Ernst & Ernst, *Financial Reporting Developments—No. 38353*, August 1975, page 4.

Accounting Treatment of Loss Contingencies			
	Usually Accrued	Not Accrued	Maybe Accrued*
Loss Related to			
1. Collectibility of receivables	X		
2. Obligations related to product warranties and product defects	X		
3. Premiums offered to customers	X		
4. Risk of loss or damage of enterprise property by fire, explosion, or other hazards		X	
5. General or unspecified business risks		X	
6. Risk of loss from catastrophes assumed by property and casualty insurance companies including reinsurance companies		X	
7. Threat of expropriation of assets			X
8. Pending or threatened litigation			X
9. Actual or possible claims and assessments**			X
10. Guarantees of indebtedness of others			X
11. Obligations of commercial banks under "standby letters of credit"			X
12. Agreements to repurchase receivables (or the related property) that have been sold			X

*Should be accrued when both criteria are met (probable and reasonably estimable).
**Estimated amounts of losses incurred prior to the balance sheet date but settled subsequently should be accrued as of the balance sheet date.

The following excerpt from the annual report of Alexander and Baldwin, Inc. is an example of an accrual recorded for a loss contingency.

ALEXANDER & BALDWIN, INC.
Notes to Financial Statements
13. Commitments and Contingent Liabilities

On January 19, 1976, litigation was concluded in two criminal antitrust actions initiated in 1974 by the United States government against California and Hawaiian Sugar Company, approximately 22% owned by the Company. Concurrently, a settlement was reached between C and H and a steering committee of the plaintiffs' counsel in various related private treble damage actions, subject to certain judicial proceedings and various contingencies. C and H has advised that its counsel has expressed the opinion that the settlement ultimately will be carried out and will dispose of substantially all claims likely to be asserted against C and H for alleged antitrust violations to the date of settlement. Pursuant to the settlement agreement, C and H deposited $16,500,000 into an escrow account. About half of this amount was charged to existing reserves by C and H, and the remainder is expected to be withheld in 1976 from sugar proceeds otherwise payable to members. Accordingly, the Company accrued its estimated share of such withholdings, $1,916,000, as a reduction of sugar revenues in 1975, thereby reducing net income by $936,000 or $.10 per share.

The accounting concepts and procedures relating to contingent items is relatively new and unsettled. Practicing accountants express concern over the diversity that now exists in the interpretation of "probable," "reasonably possible," and "remote." Current practice relies heavily on the exact language used in responses received from lawyers (such language is necessarily biased and protective rather than predictive). As a result, accruals and disclosures of contingencies vary considerably in practice.

Guarantee and Warranty Costs

A warranty (product guarantee) is a promise made by a seller to a buyer to make good on a deficiency of quantity, quality, or performance in a product. It is commonly used by manufacturers as a sales promotion technique. For a specified period of time following the date of sale to the consumer, the manufacturer may promise to bear all or part of the cost of replacing defective parts, to perform any necessary repairs or servicing without charge, to refund the purchase price, or even to "double your money back." Warranties and guarantees entail future costs, frequently significant additional costs, which are sometimes called "after costs," or "postsale costs." Although the future cost is indefinite as to amount, due date, and even customer, a liability does exist and should be recognized in the accounts if it can be reasonably estimated. The amount of the liability is an estimate of all the costs that will be incurred after sale and delivery and that are incident to the correction of defects or deficiencies required under the warranty provisions.

There are two basic methods of accounting for warranty costs: (1) the cash basis method and (2) the accrual method. Under the **cash basis method,** warranty costs are charged to expense as they are incurred or, in other words, warranty costs are charged to the period in which the seller or manufacturer performs in compliance with the warranty. No liability is recorded for future costs arising from warranties, nor is the period in which the sale is recorded necessarily charged with the costs of making good on outstanding warranties. This method is the only one recognized for income tax purposes and is frequently justified for accounting on the basis of expediency when warranty costs are immaterial or when the warranty period is relatively short.

Also, the cash basis method is required in accounting for warranty costs when it is not possible to make a reasonable estimate of the amount of a warranty obligation at the time of sale. That is, it must be used whenever either condition stipulated in **Statement No. 5** is not satisfied.

If, on the basis of available information, it is probable that customers will make claims under warranties relating to goods or services that have been sold and a reasonable estimate of the costs involved can be made, the accrual method must be used.

Under the **accrual method,** a provision for warranty costs is made at the time of sale or as the productive activity takes place. The accrual method may be divided further into two different accounting treatments: (1) expensed warranty treatment (accrual method) and (2) sales warranty treatment (deferral method). The expensed warranty treatment charges the estimated future warranty costs to operating expense in the year of sale or manufacture. It is the generally accepted method and should be used whenever the warranty is an integral and inseparable part of the sale and is viewed as a loss contingency. The sales warranty treatment defers a certain percentage of the original sales price until some future time when actual costs are incurred or the warranty expires. The following example illustrates the accrual method of accounting for warranty costs and the difference between the accrual and deferral treatments.

The Denson Machinery Company begins production on a new machine in July, 1980, and sells 100 units at $5,000 each by its year end, December 31, 1980. Each machine is under warranty for one year and the company has estimated, from past experience with a similar machine, that the warranty cost will probably average $200 per unit. Further, as a result of parts replacements and services rendered in compliance with machinery warranties, the company incurs $4,000 in warranty costs in 1980 and $16,000 in 1981.

Under the **expensed warranty treatment** the entries to reflect the foregoing transactions would be recorded as follows:

Sale of 100 machines at $5,000 each, July through December, 1980

Cash or Accounts Receivable	500,000	
Sales of Machinery		500,000

Estimated future warranty costs on July through December machinery sales ($200 × 100)

Warranty Expense	20,000	
Estimated Liability Under Warranties		20,000

Warranty costs incurred July through December 1980

Estimated Liability Under Warranties	4,000	
Cash, or Inventory, or Accrued Payroll		4,000

The December 31, 1980, balance sheet would reflect Estimated Liability Under Warranties as $16,000, and the income statement would show Warranty Expense of $20,000 charged against 1980 revenues. The $16,000 of warranty costs incurred in 1981 on 1980 machinery sales would be recorded in 1981 as a debit to Estimated Liability Under Warranties and a credit to Cash or Inventory or other appropriate account. Differences that result from either over- or under-estimation of actual warranty costs are changes in accounting estimates and are charged to the period of change and future periods, if affected, in accordance with **Opinion No. 20.**

The Estimated Liability Under Warranties is a current liability if the term of the warranty agreement does not exceed a year or an operating cycle. Otherwise, a part of the liability should be classified as a long-term liability.

Under the **sales warranty treatment** the entries to reflect the transactions of Denson Machinery Company might be recorded as follows:

Sale of 100 machines at $5,000 each, July through December, 1980, and estimated advances from customers for warranty services

Cash or Accounts Receivable	500,000	
Sales of Machinery		480,000
Unearned Warranty Revenue		20,000

Warranty revenue earned through December, 1980

Unearned Warranty Revenue	4,000	
Revenue from Warranties		4,000

Warranty expenses incurred in 1980

Warranty Expense	4,000	
Cash, or Inventory, or Accrued Payroll		4,000

The balance of $16,000 in Unearned Warranty Revenue would appear on the December 31, 1980, balance sheet as a current liability. Although the net income for 1980 would be the same as under the expensed warranty treatment, the 1980 income statement would report $16,000 less revenues and $16,000 less operating expenses.

Notice that the sales warranty treatment above assumes that at the time of sale two items are sold, the product and the warranty. Accordingly, a portion of the total sales price is deferred until the warranty revenue is earned through the replacement of parts and the performance of repairs, i.e., as the costs are incurred. For instance, in 1981 when the remaining $16,000 of estimated warranty costs are incurred, the following entry would be recorded:

Unearned Warranty Revenue	16,000	
Revenue from Warranties		16,000

The costs of the warranty repairs and replacements incurred in 1981 to earn the 1981 warranty revenues are mingled on the 1981 income statement with other costs of that year, or the costs may be accumulated and identified as warranty expense and reported as such on the income statement.

The illustration above assumed a zero profit from the sale of the warranty. The deferral of a profit element and its recognition in the periods of warranty coverage might have been assumed instead. This illustration also assumed that the revenue recognition was a function of costs incurred during the period. Other criteria for revenue recognition for "service sales type transactions" similar to this are discussed in Chapter 19.

The sales warranty treatment is applicable to companies that sell warranty contracts separately from the product. For instance, if the Denson Machinery Company had sold each machine for $4,750 and each warranty contract separately for $250, the sales warranty method clearly would be appropriate. A liability in the form of unearned revenue would be recorded at the time of the sale, and the warranty revenues, costs, and any income would be recognized in the periods in which the services, repairs, and replacements under the warranty were performed.

Business managers commonly view warranty costs simply as additional expenses of selling or manufacturing the product rather than as additional sales. It is normally assumed that the selling price of a product covers costs of warranty, not that the warranty is something to be sold separately. Many accountants believe that the deferred warranty revenues must be recognized in the period the sale is made rather than when the cost of repair or replacement is incurred. Neither the expensed warranty nor the sales warranty treatment is allowable for income tax purposes.

If the cash basis method were applied to the facts in the Denson Machinery Company example, $4,000 would be recorded as warranty expense in 1980 and $16,000 as warranty expense in 1981 with all of the sale price being recorded as revenue in 1980. In many instances, application of the cash basis method does not match the warranty costs relating to the products sold during a given period with the revenues derived from such products. Where on-going warranty policies exist year after year, the differences between the cash and the accrual basis would not likely be so great.

Premiums Offered to Customers

Numerous companies offer (either on a limited or on a continuing basis) premiums to customers in return for boxtops, certificates, coupons, labels, or wrappers. The premium may be silverware, dishes, a small appliance, a toy, or other goods. These premium offers are made to stimulate sales, and their costs should be charged to expense in the period of the sale that benefits from the premium plan. At the end of the accounting period many of these premium offers may be outstanding and, when presented in subsequent periods, must be redeemed. The number of outstanding premium offers that will be presented for redemption must be estimated in order to reflect the existing current liability and to match costs with revenues. The cost of premium offers should be charged to Premium Expense, and the outstanding obligations should be credited to an account titled Estimated Premium Claims Outstanding.

Although the FASB did not include premium offers in its list of loss contingencies, the authors believe that premium offers result in the probable existence of a liability at the date of the financial statements, can be reasonably estimated in amount, are contingent upon the occurrence of a future event (redemption) and, therefore, are a loss contingency within the guidelines of **FASB Statement No. 5.**

The following example illustrates the accounting treatment accorded a premium offer. The Fluffy Cakemix Company offered its customers a large nonbreakable mixing bowl in exchange for 25 cents and 10 boxtops. The mixing bowl costs the Fluffy Cakemix Company 75 cents, and the company estimates that 60% of the boxtops will be redeemed. The premium offer began in June 1980 and resulted in the following transactions and entries during 1980.

1. To record purchase of 20,000 mixing bowls

Inventory of Premium Mixing Bowls	15,000	
Cash		15,000

2. To record sales of 300,000 boxes of cake mix at 80 cents

Cash	240,000	
Sales		240,000

3. To record redemption of 60,000 boxtops

Cash [(60,000 ÷ 10) × $0.25]	1,500	
Premium Expense	3,000	
Inventory of Premium Mixing Bowls		4,500
(Computation: [60,000 ÷ 10] × $0.75 = $4,500)		

4. To record estimated liability for outstanding premium offers

Premium Expense	6,000	
Estimated Premium Claims Outstanding		6,000

Computation:

Total boxtops sold in 1980	300,000
Total estimated redemptions (60%)	180,000
Boxtops redeemed in 1980	60,000
Estimated future redemptions	120,000

Cost of estimated claims outstanding
(120,000 ÷ 10) × ($0.75 − $0.25) = $6,000

The December 31, 1980, balance sheet of Fluffy Cakemix Company will report an Inventory of Premium Mixing Bowls of $10,500 as a current asset and Estimated

Premium Claims Outstanding of $6,000 as a current liability. The 1980 income statement will report a $9,000 Premium Expense among the selling expenses.

In the illustration above, the company establishes its own premium plan, issues its own boxtops, and assumes complete redemption responsibilities. Another very common premium plan, also used to stimulate sales, is the issuance of trading stamps. Generally the trading stamp company sells its stamps to consumer-type businesses (commonly grocery stores and gasoline stations) and assumes full responsibility for the redemption of the stamps. The trading stamp company records the sale of stamps, the purchase of premiums (all sorts of consumer articles), the distribution of the premiums at gift centers, and the estimated premium claims outstanding. For instance, the Sperry and Hutchinson Company (licensor of S & H Green Stamps) reported "Liability for Stamp Redemptions—$117,599,000" as a current liability with a like amount as a long-term liability and made the following footnote disclosure:

> *Liability for Stamp Redemptions*—The Company records stamp service revenue and provides for cost of redemptions at the time stamps are furnished to licensees. The liability for stamp redemptions is adjusted each year based upon current operating experience and includes the cost of merchandise and related redemption service expenses required to redeem 95% of the stamps issued.
>
> Company studies have indicated that approximately 50% of the stamps outstanding are not presented for redemption within one year; consequently this portion of the liability for stamp redemptions is classified as a long-term liability.

The businesses that buy the trading stamps merely record the purchase and the issuance of the stamps; stamps on hand are reported as an asset and stamps issued as a selling expense.

Risk of Loss Due to Lack of Insurance Coverage

Uninsured risks may arise in a number of ways, including **noninsurance** of certain risks or **co-insurance** or **deductible clauses** in an insurance contract. But the absence of insurance (frequently referred to as self-insurance) does not mean that a liability has been incurred at the date of the financial statements. For example, fires, explosions, and other similar events that may cause damage to a company's own property are random in occurrence and unrelated to the activities of the company prior to their occurrence. The conditions for accrual stated in **Statement No. 5** are not satisfied prior to the occurrence of the event because until that time there is no diminution in the value of the property. And, unlike an insurance company, which has contractual obligations to reimburse policyholders for losses, a company can have no such obligations to itself and, hence, no liability either before or after the occurrence of damage.[16]

Exposure to risks of loss resulting from uninsured past injury to others, however, is an existing condition involving uncertainty about the amount and timing of losses that may develop, in which case a contingency exists. For example, a company with a fleet of vehicles would have to accrue uninsured losses resulting from injury to others or damage to the property of others that took place prior to the date of the financial statements (if the experience of the company or other information en-

---

[16]"Accounting for Contingencies," *FASB Statement No. 5, op. cit.*, par. 28.

ables it to make a reasonable estimate of the liability). Of course, it should not establish a liability for expected future injury to others or damage to the property of others even if the amount of losses is reasonably estimable.

Litigation, Claims, and Assessments

The following factors, among others, must be considered in determining whether a liability should be recorded with respect to **pending or threatened litigation** and actual or possible claims and assessments:

1. The period in which the underlying cause for action occurred.
2. The degree of probability of an unfavorable outcome.
3. The ability to make a reasonable estimate of the amount of loss.

To report a loss and a liability in the financial statements, the cause for litigation must have occurred on or before the date of the financial statements. It does not matter that the company does not become aware of the existence or possibility of the lawsuit or claims until after the date of the financial statements but before they are issued. Among the factors the FASB recommended be considered in **evaluating the probability of an unfavorable outcome** are: the nature of the litigation; the progress of the case; the opinion of legal counsel; the experience of the company in similar cases; the experience of other companies; and any decision of management as to how the company intends to respond to the lawsuit.

The outcome of pending litigation, however, can seldom be predicted with any assurance. And, even if the evidence available at the balance sheet date does not favor the defendant company, it is hardly reasonable to expect the company to publish in its financial statements a dollar estimate of the probable negative outcome. Such specific disclosures could weaken the company's position in the dispute and encourage the plaintiff to intensify its efforts.

With respect to **unfiled suits** and **unasserted claims and assessments,** a company must determine (1) the degree of **probability** that a suit may be filed or a claim or assessment may be asserted and (2) the **probability** of an unfavorable outcome. For example, assume that Nawtee Company is being investigated by the Federal Trade Commission for practices in restraint of trade and enforcement proceedings have been instituted. Such proceedings are often followed by private claims of triple damages for redress. In this case, Nawtee Company must determine the probability of the claims being asserted **and** the probability of triple damages being awarded. If both are probable, the loss reasonably estimable, and the cause for action dated on or before the date of the financial statements, the liability should be accrued.

Disclosure of Loss Contingencies

If no accrual is made for a loss contingency and a liability is not recorded because one or both conditions necessary for accrual are not met, **Statement No. 5** requires the following disclosure via footnote when there is at least **a reasonable possibility** that a liability may have been incurred:

1. The nature of the contingency.

2. An estimate of the possible loss or range of loss or a statement that an estimate cannot be made.[17]

Presented below is the disclosure of a possible loss contingency as contained in the footnotes to the financial statements of Lynch Corporation:

LYNCH CORPORATION

Note 10: Litigation—During August, 1976, a civil action was filed against the Company by a competitor of the Cox Instrument Division, alleging, among other things, infringement of certain patents and unfair competition by Cox in connection with the design and manufacture of a hot engine test system which was sold to a large automobile manufacturer in 1975. The suit asks for damages of $3,000,000 and punitive damages of an additional $10,000,000.

The Company has engaged special patent counsel to vigorously contest this action and has denied the allegations set forth therein. Management, after taking into consideration information furnished by counsel, is of the opinion that the outcome of this matter will not materially affect the consolidated financial position or results of operations of the Company.

Contingencies involving an unasserted claim or assessment need not be disclosed when there has not been any manifestation by a potential claimant of an awareness of a possible claim or assessment unless (1) it is considered **probable** that a claim will be asserted **and** (2) there is a **reasonable possibility** that the outcome will be unfavorable.

Certain other contingent liabilities which should be disclosed even though the possibility of loss may be remote are as follows:

1. Guarantees of indebtedness of others.
2. Obligations of commercial banks under "stand-by letters of credit."
3. Guarantees to repurchase receivables (or any related property) that have been sold or assigned.

Disclosure should include the nature and amount of the guarantee and, if estimable, the amount that could be recovered from outside parties. Cities Service Company disclosed its guarantees of indebtedness of others in the following footnote:

CITIES SERVICE COMPANY

Note 10: Contingent Liabilities

The Company and certain subsidiaries have guaranteed debt obligations of approximately $62 million of companies in which substantial stock investments are held. Also, under long-term agreements with certain pipeline companies in which stock interests are held, the Company and its subsidiaries have agreed to provide minimum revenue for product shipments. The Company has guaranteed mortgage debt ($80 million) incurred by a 50 percent owned tanker affiliate for construction of tankers which are under long-term charter contracts to the Company and others. It is not anticipated that any loss will result from any of the above described agreements.

---

[17]According to *FASB Interpretation No. 14*, "Reasonable Estimation of the Amount of a Loss" (Stamford, Conn.: FASB, 1976), par. 3, "when some amount within the range appears at the time to be a better estimate than any other amount within the range, that amount shall be accrued. When no amount within the range is a better estimate than any other amount, however, the minimum amount in the range shall be accrued."

CURRENT LIABILITIES IN THE FINANCIAL STATEMENTS

The current liability accounts are commonly presented as the top or first classification in the "liabilities and stockholders' equity" section of the balance sheet. In some instances, current liabilities are presented as a group immediately below current assets with the total of the current liabilities deducted from the total current assets to obtain "working capital" or "current assets in excess of current liabilities."

Within the current liability section the accounts may be listed in order of maturity, according to amount (largest to smallest), or in order of liquidation preference. The authors' review of published financial statements in 1977–78 disclosed that a significant majority of the companies examined listed "notes payable" first, regardless of relative amount, followed most often with "accounts payable," and ended the current liability section with "current portion of long-term debt." However, see Tenneco, Inc.'s current liability section on page 195; it begins with "current maturities of long-term debt."

Detail and supplemental information concerning current liabilities should be sufficient to meet the requirement of full disclosure. Secured liabilities should be identified clearly, and the related assets pledged as collateral indicated. If the due date of any liability can be extended, the details should be disclosed. Current liabilities should not be offset against assets that are to be applied to their liquidation. Current maturities of long-term debt should be classified as current liabilities. A major exception exists when a currently maturing obligation is to be paid from assets classified as long-term. For example, if payments to retire a bond payable are made from a bond sinking fund classified as a long-term asset, the bonds payable should be reported in the long-term liability section. Presentation of this debt in the current liability section would distort the working capital position of the enterprise.

Existing commitments that will result in obligations in succeeding periods that are material in amount may require disclosure. For example, commitments to purchase goods or services, and for the construction, purchase, or lease of equipment or properties may require disclosure in footnotes accompanying the balance sheet.

Presented below is an excerpt of the Dresser Industries, Inc. 1978 published financial statements which is a representative presentation of the current liabilities with appropriate footnotes as found in the reports of large corporations:

Dresser Industries, Inc.

In Millions of Dollars—October 31,	**1978**	1977
Current Liabilities		
Notes payable—Note G	**$ 42.9**	$ 39.2
Accounts payable	**199.8**	150.3
Advances from customers on contracts	**83.4**	135.3
Accrued compensation	**62.9**	57.7
Accrued taxes, interest and other expenses	**146.3**	141.0
Estimated warranty costs	**54.0**	38.4
Federal, state and foreign income taxes	**50.9**	44.8
Current portion of long-term debt	**31.0**	21.2
Total Current Liabilities	**671.2**	627.9

NOTE G—SHORT-TERM NOTES PAYABLE

Summary data pertaining to notes payable during 1978 and 1977 is as follows:

	1978		1977	
	Amount (Millions)	Average Interest Rate	Amount (Millions)	Average Interest Rate
Foreign Bank Loans—				
Outstanding at October 31,	$42.9	14.3%[1]	$39.2	23.0%[1]
Average outstanding during the year	39.3		38.8	
Maximum outstanding during the year	42.9		43.5	
Average interest rate during the year		20.8%[1]		23.7%[1]

[1]The relatively high average interest rates on foreign loans reflect the cost of borrowing in certain foreign countries which presently have significantly higher inflation rates than the United States. Such foreign borrowings serve as protection against translation losses related to currencies that decline in value versus the U.S. dollar. Average interest rates during the years are based on weighted average rates computed quarterly.

At October 31, 1978 the Company had unused lines of credit aggregating $100.0 million for short-term bank borrowings within the United States. Such lines provide for borrowings at the prevailing prime interest rate. The lines of credit may be terminated at the option of the banks or the Company. None of these lines were used during 1978.

Loan arrangements have been established with banks outside the United States under which the Company's foreign subsidiaries may borrow on an overdraft and short-term note basis. At October 31, 1978 the amount available and unused under these arrangements aggregated $27.4 million.

The Company has understandings with certain of the banks regarding deposit balances as compensation for credit arrangements, but the aggregate amount of such compensating balances was not material at October 31, 1978 and 1977. The Company was not legally restricted from withdrawing all or any portion of the compensating balances at any time during the years.

Questions

1. Compare the most recent definition of liabilities as proposed by the FASB in its 1977 Statement of Financial Accounting Concepts (Proposed) with the profession's earlier (1953) definition contained in the AICPA's *Accounting Terminology Bulletins* (see footnote 3 of this chapter).
2. Assume that your friend, who is an engineering major, asks you to define and discuss the nature of a liability. Assist him or her by preparing a definition of a liability and by explaining to him or her what you believe are the elements or factors inherent in the concept of a liability.
3. Distinguish between a current liability and a long-term debt.
4. Why is the liability section of the balance sheet of primary significance to bankers?
5. How are current liabilities related by definition to current assets?
6. How are current liabilities related to a company's operating cycle?
7. How is present value related to the concept of a liability?
8. What is the nature of a "discount" on notes payable?
9. Under what conditions should a short-term obligation be excluded from current liabilities?
10. (a) What evidence is necessary to demonstrate the ability to consummate the refinancing of short-term debt?
    (b) When a financing agreement is relied upon to demonstrate ability to consummate refinancing, what amount of short-term debt may be excluded from current liabilities?

11. Discuss the accounting treatment or disclosure that should be accorded a declared but unpaid cash dividend; an accumulated but undeclared dividend on cumulative preferred stock; a stock dividend payable.

12. How does deferred or unearned revenue arise? Why can it be classified properly as a current liability? Give several examples of business activities that result in unearned revenues.

13. Over which two periods of time is the property tax most commonly allocated? Under what circumstances might each of these periods be justified as the period of expense?

14. What is the nature of a "conditional payment"? How is a conditional payment unlike the other liabilities presented under the classification of determinable current liabilities? List three examples of conditional payment liabilities.

15. Define (a) a contingency and (b) a contingent liability.

16. Under what conditions should a contingent liability be recorded?

17. Distinguish between a "determinable current liability" and a "contingent current liability." Give two examples of each type.

18. How are the terms "probable," "reasonably possible," and "remote" related to contingent liabilities?

19. Contrast the "cash basis method" and the "accrual method" of accounting for warranty costs.

20. How does the "expensed warranty treatment" differ from the "sales warranty method"?

21. Should a liability be recorded for risk of loss due to lack of insurance coverage? Discuss.

22. What factors must be considered in determining whether or not to record a liability for pending litigation? For threatened litigation?

23. Within the current liability section, how do you believe the accounts should be listed? Defend your position.

24. When should liabilities for each of the following items be recorded on the books of an ordinary business corporation?
    (a) Dividends.
    (b) Purchase commitments.
    (c) Acquisition of goods by purchase on credit.
    (d) Officers' salaries.
    (e) Special bonus to employees.

Cases

C10-1 The following items are listed as liabilities on the balance sheet of Porter Industrial Co. on December 31, 1980:

Accounts payable	$ 200,000
Notes payable	300,000
Bonds payable	1,040,000

The accounts payable represent obligations to suppliers that were due in January 1981. The notes payable mature on various dates during 1981. The bonds payable mature on July 1, 1981.

These liabilities must be reported on the balance sheet in accordance with generally accepted accounting principles governing the classification of liabilities as current and noncurrent.

Instructions

(a) What is the general rule for determining whether a liability is classified as current or noncurrent?

(b) Under what conditions may any of Porter Industrial Co.'s liabilities be classified as noncurrent? Explain your answer.

(CMA adapted)

C10-2 May Trix Corporation issued $9,000,000 of short-term commercial paper during the year 1979 to finance construction of a plant. At December 31, 1979, the corporation's year-end, May Trix intends to refinance the commercial paper by issuing long-term debt. However, because the corporation temporarily has excess cash, in January 1980 it liquidates $3,000,000 of the commercial paper as the paper matures. In February 1980, May Trix completes an $18,000,000 long-term debt offering. Later during the month of February, it issues its December 31, 1979, financial statements. The proceeds of the long-term debt offering are to be used to replenish $3,000,000 in working capital, to pay $6,000,000 of commercial paper as it matures in March 1980, and to pay $9,000,000 of construction costs expected to be incurred later that year to complete the plant.

Instructions

(a) How should the $9,000,000 of commercial paper be classified on the December 31, 1979; January 31, 1980; and February 29, 1980, balance sheets? Give support for your answer and also consider the cash element.

(b) What would your answer be if, instead of a completed financing at the date of issuance of the financial statements, a financing agreement existed at that date?

C10-3 (a) What is the meaning of the term "contingency" as used in accounting?

(b) Distinguish between accounting for a "gain contingency" and accounting for a "loss contingency."

(c) How should the following situations be recognized in the calendar year-end financial statements of Abott Labs Inc.? Explain.

1. Pending in a federal district court is a suit against Abott Labs. The suit, which asks for token damages, alleges that Abott has infringed on a 15-year-old patent. Briefs will be heard on March 31. *Token amount immaterial so disregard*

2. The TUF Union, sole bargaining agent of Abott Labs' production employees, has threatened a strike unless Abott agrees to a proposed profit-sharing plan. Negotiations begin on March 1. *in the future disregard*

3. A recently completed (during the calendar year in question) government contract is subject to renegotiation. Although Abbot suspects that a refund of approximately $80,000 may be required by the government, the company does not wish, for obvious reasons, to publicize this fact. *accrue + disclose*

4. Abott has a $100,000, 9% note receivable due next May 1 from Waterhouse Coil Co., its largest customer. Abott discounted the note on December 20, with recourse, at the bank to raise needed cash. Waterhouse Coil Co. has never defaulted on a debt and possesses a high credit rating. *Don't accrue but disclose*

C10-4 On February 1, 1981, one of the huge storage tanks of the Experimental Chemical Company exploded. Windows in houses and other buildings within a one-mile radius of the explosion were severely damaged, and a number of people were injured. As of February 15, 1981 (when the December 31, 1980 financial statements were completed and sent to the publisher for printing and public distribution), no suits had been filed or claims asserted against the company as a consequence of the explosion. The company fully anticipates that suits will be filed and claims asserted for injuries and damages. Because the casualty was uninsured and the company considered at fault, Experimental Chemical will have to cover the damages from its own resources.

Instructions

Discuss fully the accounting treatment and disclosures that should be accorded the casualty and related contingent losses in the financial statements dated December 31, 1980.

C10-5 The following three **independent** sets of facts relate to (1) the possible accrual or (2) the possible disclosure by other means of a loss contingency.

Situation I

A company offers a one-year warranty for the product that it manufactures. A history of warranty claims has been compiled and the probable amount of claims related to sales for a given period can be determined. *accrue + disclose*

Situation II

Subsequent to the date of a set of financial statements, but prior to the issuance of the financial statements, a company enters into a contract that will probably result in a significant loss to the company. The amount of the loss can be reasonably estimated. *disclose but don't accrue*

Situation III

A company has adopted a policy of recording self-insurance for any possible losses resulting from injury to others by the company's vehicles. The premium for an insurance policy for the same risk from an independent insurance company would have an annual cost of $2,000. During the period covered by the financial statements, there were no accidents involving the company's vehicles that resulted in injury to others. *Disclose fact that have no insurance*

Instructions

Discuss the accrual or type of disclosure necessary (if any) and the reason(s) why such disclosure is appropriate for each of the three independent sets of facts above.

Complete your response to each situation before proceeding to the next situation.

(AICPA adapted)

C10-6 The two basic requirements for the accrual of a loss contingency are supported by several basic concepts of accounting. Three of these concepts are: periodicity (time periods), measurement, and objectivity.

Instructions

Discuss how the two basic requirements for the accrual of a loss contingency relate to the three concepts listed above.

(AICPA adapted)

C10-7 RCA Corporation reflects in the current liability section of its balance sheet at December 31, 1980 (its year-end), short-term obligations of $6,000,000, which includes the current portion of 8% long-term debt in the amount of $4,000,000 (mature in March 1981). Management has stated its intention to refinance the 8% debt whereby no portion of it will mature during 1981. The date of issuance of the financial statements is March 25, 1981.

Instructions

(a) Is management's intent enough to support long-term classification of the obligation in this situation?

(b) Assume that RCA Corporation issues $5,000,000 of 10-year debentures to the public in January 1981 and that management intends to use the proceeds to liquidate the $4,000,000 debt maturing in March 1981. Furthermore, assume that the debt maturing in March 1981 is paid from these proceeds prior to the issuance of the financial statements. Will this have any impact on the balance sheet classification at December 31, 1980? Explain your answer.

(c) Assume that RCA Corporation issues common stock to the public in January and that management intends to entirely liquidate the $4,000,000 debt maturing in March 1981 with the proceeds of this equity securities issue. In light of these events, should the $4,000,000 debt maturing in March 1981 be included in current liabilities at December 31, 1980?

(d) Assume that RCA Corporation, on February 15, 1981, entered into a financing agreement with a commercial bank that permits RCA Corporation to borrow at any time through 1982 up to $6,000,000 at the bank's prime rate of interest. Borrowings under the financing agreement mature three years after the date of the loan. The agreement is not cancelable except for violation of a provision with which compliance is objectively determinable. No violation of any provision exists at the date of issuance of the financial statements. Assume further that $4,000,000 representing the current portion of long-term debt does not mature until August 1981. In addition, management intends to refinance the $4,000,000 obligation under the terms of the financial agreement with the bank, which is expected to be financially capable of honoring the agreement.

(1) Given these facts, should the $4,000,000 be classified as current on the balance sheet at December 31, 1980?

(2) Is disclosure of the refinancing method required?

Exercises

E10-1 On December 31, 1980, Curt See Co. had $900,000 of short-term debt in the form of notes payable due February 2, 1981. On January 21, 1981, the company issued 100,000 shares of its common stock for $6 per share, receiving $575,000 proceeds after brokerage fees and other costs of issuance. On February 2, 1981, the proceeds from the stock sale, supplemented by an additional $325,000 cash, are used to liquidate the $900,000 debt. The December 31, 1980, balance sheet is issued on February 23, 1981.   Current Liability 325,000

Instructions   Long term   "   575,000

Show how the $900,000 of short-term debt should be presented on the December 31, 1980, balance sheet, including footnote disclosure.

E10-2 During the month of June, Mexican Imports had cash sales of $142,000 and credit sales of $80,000, both of which include the 4% sales tax that must be remitted to the state by July 15.

Instructions

Prepare the adjusting entry that should be recorded to fairly present the June 30 financial statement.   Sales   8538.47

  Sales Tax payable   8538.47

E10-3 The payroll of the Prozit Company for September 1979 is as follows:

Total payroll was $350,000, of which $225,000 represented amounts paid in excess of $22,900 to certain employees. The amount paid to employees in excess of $6,000 was $250,000. Income taxes in the amount of $58,000 were withheld, as was $9,000 in union dues. The state unemployment tax is 2.7%, but the Prozit Company is allowed a credit of 1.7% by the state for its unemployment experience. Also, assume that the current F.I.C.A. tax is 6% and the federal unemployment tax rate is .5% after state credit.

Instructions

Prepare the necessary journal entries if the wages and salaries paid and the employer payroll taxes are recorded separately.

E10-4 Indian Jewelry Company's payroll for August, 1980, is summarized below.

Payroll	Wages Due	F.I.C.A.	Amount Subject to Payroll Taxes	
			Unemployment Tax	
			Federal	State
Factory	$120,000	$112,000	$40,000	$40,000
Sales	44,000	32,000	4,000	4,000
Administrative	36,000	12,000	—	—
Total	$200,000	$156,000	$44,000	$44,000

At this point in the year some employees have already received wages in excess of those to which payroll taxes apply. Assume that the state unemployment tax is 2.5%. The F.I.C.A. rate is 6% for both employee and employer, and the federal unemployment tax rate is .58% after credits. Income tax withheld amounts to $14,000 for factory, $5,400 for sales, and $5,800 for administrative.

Instructions

(a) Prepare a schedule showing the employer's total cost of wages for August.

(b) Prepare the journal entries to record the factory, sales, and administrative payrolls including the employer's payroll taxes.

E10-5 Lisa Steg, president of the Steg Music Company, has a bonus arrangement with the company under which she receives 20% of the net income (after deducting taxes and bonuses) each year. For the current year, the net income before deducting either the provision for income taxes or the bonus is $128,000. The bonus is deductible for tax purposes, and the effective tax rate may be assumed to be 40%.

Instructions

(a) Compute the amount of Lisa Steg's bonus.

(b) Compute the appropriate provision for federal income taxes for the year.

E10-6 The incomplete income statement of a cement company appears below:

Strong Cement Company
INCOME STATEMENT
For the Year 1980

Revenue		$2,500,000.00
Cost of goods sold		1,700,000.00
Gross profit		800,000.00
Administrative and selling expenses	$250,000.00	
Profit-sharing bonus to employees	?	?
Income before income taxes		?
Income taxes		?
Net income		$?

The employee profit-sharing plan requires that 20% of all profits remaining after the deduction of the bonus and income taxes be distributed to the employees by the first day of the fourth month following each year-end. The federal income tax is 40%, and the bonus is tax-deductible.

Instructions

Complete the condensed income statement of the Strong Cement Company for the year 1980.

E10-7   Malta Manufacturing Company sold 200 copymaking machines in 1980 for $3,000 apiece, together with a one-year warranty. Maintenance on each machine during the warranty period averages $200.

Instructions

(a) Prepare entries to record the sale of the machines and the subsequent expenditure of $38,900 to service the machines during the guarantee period, assuming that the expensed warranty **accural method** is used.

(b) On the basis of the data above, prepare the appropriate entries, assuming that the **cash** basis (i.e., "tax") method is used and that $18,600 was expended to service the machines in 1980.

E10-8   Shout-it-Out Co. includes 1 coupon in each box of soap powder that it packs, and 10 coupons are redeemable for a premium (a kitchen utensil). In 1980, Shout-it-Out Co. purchased 5,000 premiums at 75 cents each and sold 80,000 boxes of soap powder @ $2.00 per box. 20,000 coupons were presented for redemption in 1980. It is estimated that 60% of the coupons will eventually be presented for redemption.

Instructions

Prepare all the entries that would be made relative to sales of soap powder and to the premium plan in 1980.

E10-9   How would each of the following items be reported on the balance sheet? *Current liability*

(a) Current maturities of long-term debts to be paid from current assets. *Current liability*

(b) Discount on notes payable. *Current liability (contra account)*

(c) Notes receivable discounted. *Current Asset (contra account) or contingent liability footnote*

(d) Cash dividends declared but unpaid. *current liability*

(e) Deposit received from customer to guarantee performance of a contract. *current or noncurrent liability*

(f) Dividends in arrears on preferred stock. *Disclose in footnotes*

(g) Loans from officers. *current or long term liability (separate presentation)*

(h) Accommodation endorsement. *Footnote disclosure if material*

(i) Estimated taxes payable. *Current liability*

(j) Employee payroll deductions unremitted. *Current liability (due quarterly)*

(k) Unpaid bonus to officers. *current liability*

(l) Gift certificates sold to customers but not yet redeemed. *current liability*

(m) Accrued vacation pay. *current liability*

(n) Premium offers outstanding. *current liability*

(o) Personal injury claim pending. *Footnote disclosure if material*

(p) Service warranties on appliance sales. *current liability or long term liability*

Problems

P10-1   Described below are certain transactions of Canadian Corporation.

1. On February 2, the corporation purchased goods from Burch Company for $35,000 subject to cash discount terms of 2/10, n/30. Purchases and accounts payable are recorded by the corporation at net amounts after cash discounts. The invoice was paid on February 26.

2. On April 1, the corporation bought a truck for $9,800 from the Tillie Company, paying $1,800 in cash and signing a one-year, 8% note for the balance of the purchase price.

3. On May 1, the corporation borrowed $50,000 from the Hinckley National Bank by signing a $53,600 note due one year from May 1.

4. On June 30 the corporation partially refunded $30,000 of its outstanding 7% note payable made one year ago to the Sycamore State Bank by paying $30,000 plus interest of $2,100, having obtained the $32,100 by using $13,300 of its own cash and signing a new one-year, $20,000 note discounted at 6% by the bank.

5. On August 1, the Board of Directors declared a $100,000 cash dividend that was payable on September 10 to stockholders of record on August 31.

Instructions

    (a) Make all the journal entries necessary to record the transactions above using appropriate dates.

    (b) Canadian Corporation's year-end is December 31. Assuming that no adjusting entries relative to the transactions above have been recorded at year-end, prepare any adjusting journal entries concerning interest that are necessary to present fair financial statements at December 31. Assume straight-line amortization of discounts.

P10-2 Listed below are selected transactions of Halle's Department Store for the current year ending December 31.

1. On December 5, the store received $300 from the Village Stage Players as a deposit to be returned after certain furniture to be used in stage production was returned on January 15.

2. During December, sales totaled $945,000, which includes the 5% sales tax that must be remitted to the state by the fifteenth day of the following month.

3. On December 10, the store purchased for cash three delivery trucks for $24,000. The trucks were purchased in a state that applies no sales tax, but the store is located and must register the trucks in a state that applies a use tax of 5% to nonsalable goods bought outside of its sales tax authority.

4. The store follows the practice of recording its property tax liability on the lien date and amortizing the tax over the subsequent 12 months. Property taxes of $48,000 became a lien on May 1 and were paid in two equal installments on July 1 and October 1.

5. During the year the store estimated that its annual federal income tax would be $680,000. At year-end, income tax expense (for both accounting and tax return purposes) was determined to be $650,000.

Instructions

Prepare all the journal entries necessary to record the transactions noted above as they occurred and any adjusting journal entries relative to the transactions that would be required to present fair financial statements at December 31. Date each entry.

P10-3 On December 31, 1980, Fritos Company has $3,000,000 of short-term debt in the form of notes payable to Chase National Bank due periodically in 1981. On January 28, 1981, Fritos enters into a refinancing agreement with Chase which will permit it to borrow up to 60% of the gross amount of its accounts receivable. Receivables are expected to range between a low of $2,200,000 in May to a high of $3,500,000 in October during the year 1981. The interest cost of the maturing short-term debt is 8%, and the new agreement calls for a fluctuating interest at 1% above the prime rate on notes due in 1985. Fritos' December 31, 1980, balance sheet is issued on February 15, 1981.

Instructions

Prepare a partial balance sheet for Fritos at December 31, 1980, showing how its $3,000,000 of short-term debt should be presented, including footnote disclosures.

P10-4 This is a payroll sheet for Lazy Rocker Company for the month of Sept. 1980. The company is allowed a 1% unemployment compensation rate by the state; the federal unemployment tax rate is .58% and the maximum for both is $6,000. Assume a 10% federal income tax rate for all employees and a 6% F.I.C.A. tax on employee and employer on a maximum of $22,900 per employee.

Name	Earnings to Aug. 31	September Earnings	Income Tax Withholding	F.I.C.A.	State U.C.	Federal U.C.
B. Morris	$ 1,200	$ 600				
H. Remmers	2,800	400				
B. Harris	5,400	900				
V. Odom	12,600	1,700				
A. Scaper	25,600	3,200				
E. Wunder	21,400	2,700				

Instructions

(a) Complete the payroll sheet and make the necessary entry to record the payment of the payroll.

(b) Make the entry to record the payroll tax expenses of Lazy Rocker Company.

(c) Make the entry to pay the payroll liabilities created. Assume that the company pays all payroll liabilities at the end of each month.

P10-5 Reichenbacher Company pays its office employee payroll weekly. Below is a partial list of employees and their payroll data for August. Because August is their vacation period, vacation pay is also listed.

Employee	Earnings to July 31	Weekly Pay	Vacation Pay To Be Received in August
Minnie Sotta	$2,900	$100	—
Brent Grometer	2,465	85	$170
Susan Robinson	4,350	150	300
Wes Konsin	3,770	130	—
Ken Tucki	5,075	175	350

Assume that the federal income tax collected is 10% of wages. Union dues collected are 3% of wages. Vacations are taken the second and third weeks of August by Grometer, Robinson, and Tucki. The state unemployment tax rate is 2.7% and the federal is .58%, both on a $4,200 maximum. The F.I.C.A. rate is 6% on employee and employer on a maximum of $22,900 per employee.

Instructions

Make the journal entries necessary for each of the four August payrolls. The entries for the payroll and for the company's liability are made separately. Also make the entry to record the monthly payment of accrued payroll liabilities.

P10-6 Escalator Company has a contract with its president, Ann Short, to pay her a bonus during each of the years 1979, 1980, 1981, and 1982. The federal income tax rate is 40% during the four years. The profit before deductions for bonus and federal income taxes was $200,000 in 1979, $200,000 in 1980, $400,000 in 1981, and $300,000 in 1982. The president's bonus of 25% is deductible for tax purposes in each year and is to be computed as follows:

(a) In 1979 the bonus is to be based on profit before deductions for bonus and income tax.

(b) In 1980 the bonus is to be based on profit after deduction of bonus but before deduction of income tax.

(c) In 1981 the bonus is to be based on profit before deduction of bonus but after deduction of income tax.

(d) In 1982 the bonus is to be based on profit after deductions for bonus and income tax.

Instructions

Compute the amounts of the bonus and the income tax for each of the four years.

P10-7 Agriculture Fertilizer Company has a profit-sharing agreement with its employees that provides for deposit in a pension trust for the benefit of the employees 20% of the net income after deducting (1) federal taxes on income, (2) the amount of the annual pension contribution, and (3) a return of 8% on the stockholders' equity as of the end of the year 1980.

Instructions

Compute the amount of the pension contribution under the assumption that the stockholders' equity at the end of the year before adding the net income for the year is $1,000,000; that net income for the year before either the pension contribution or tax is $250,000; and that the pension contribution is deductible for tax purposes. Use 40% as the applicable rate of tax.

P10-8 During 1981, Cricket Motor Company sells 40,000 high-compression engines under a three-year warranty that requires the company to replace all defective parts during the warranty period at no cost to the purchaser. These engines constitute nearly all of the company's 1981 business.

Instructions

(a) Name two basic methods of accounting for the warranty costs.

(b) What accounts would be used for each of the two methods?

(c) What effect would each method have on net income during the period of the warranties?

(d) In your opinion, which of the two methods is more appropriate for Cricket Motor Company?

P10-9 The Readyrite Products Company sells electric typewriters for $540 each and offers to each customer a three-year warranty contract for $48 that requires the company to perform periodic services and to replace defective parts. During 1980, the company sold 300 typewriters and 250 warranty contracts for cash. On the basis of past experience, the company has estimated the three-year warranty costs as $12 for parts and $24 for labor. The Readyrite Products Company accounts for warranties on the sales warranty accrual method. (For simplicity, assume that all sales occurred on December 31, 1980.)

Instructions

(a) Record any necessary journal entries in 1980.

(b) What amounts relative to these transactions would appear on the December 31, 1980, balance sheet and how would they be classified?

    In 1981, the Readyrite Company incurred actual costs relative to 1980 typewriter warranty sales of $900 for parts and $1,920 for labor.

(c) Record any necessary journal entries in 1981 relative to 1980 typewriter warranties.

(d) What amounts relative to the 1980 typewriter warranties would appear on the December 31, 1981, balance sheet and how would they be classified?

P10-10 Pewlett-Hackard Corporation sells portable computers under a two-year warranty contract that requires the corporation to replace defective parts and to provide the necessary repair labor. During 1980 the corporation sells for cash 150 computers at a unit price of $6,000. On the basis of past experience, the two-year warranty costs are estimated to be $150 for parts and $105 for labor per unit. (For simplicity, assume that all sales occurred on December 31, 1980.)

Instructions

(a) Record any necessary journal entries in 1980, applying the cash basis method.

(b) Record any necessary journal entries in 1980, applying the expensed warranty accrual method.

(c) What amounts relative to these transactions would appear on the December 31, 1980 balance sheet and how would they be classified if the cash basis method is applied?

(d) What amounts relative to these transactions would appear on the December 31, 1980 balance sheet and how would they be classified if the expensed warranty accrual method is applied?

In 1981 the actual warranty costs to Pewlett-Hackard Corporation were $10,000 for parts and $7,000 for labor.

(e) Record any necessary journal entries in 1981, applying the cash basis method.

(f) Record any necessary journal entries in 1981, applying the expensed warranty accrual method.

P10-11 The Perfecto Gusto Company sells a machine for $3,600 under a 12-month warranty agreement that requires the company to replace all defective parts and to provide the repair labor at no cost to the customers. With sales being made evenly throughout the year, the company sells 1,400 machines in 1981 (warranty expense is incurred ½ in 1981 and ½ in 1982). As a result of product testing, the company estimates that the warranty cost is $120 per machine ($48 parts and $72 labor).

Instructions

Assuming that actual warranty costs are incurred exactly as estimated, what journal entries would be made relative to these facts:

(a) Under application of the expensed warranty accrual method for:
1. sale of machinery in 1981?
2. warranty expense charged against 1981 revenues?
3. warranty costs incurred in 1981?
4. warranty costs incurred in 1982?

(b) Under application of the cash basis method for:
1. sale of machinery in 1981?
2. warranty expense charged against 1981 revenues?
3. warranty costs incurred in 1981?
4. warranty costs incurred in 1982?

(c) What amount, if any, is disclosed in the balance sheet as a liability for future warranty cost as of December 31, 1981, under each method?

(d) Which method best reflects the income in 1981 and 1982 of the Perfecto Gusto Company? Why?

P10-12 To stimulate the sales of its Captain Munch breakfast cereal, the Pilgrim Oats Company places 1 coupon in each box. Four coupons are redeemable for a premium consisting of a children's hand puppet. In 1981, the company purchases 25,000 puppets at 40 cents each and sells 200,000 boxes of Captain Munch at 60 cents a box. From its experience with other similar premium offers, the company estimates that 45% of the coupons issued will be mailed back for redemption. During 1981, 40,000 coupons are presented for redemption.

Instructions

Prepare the journal entries that should be recorded in 1981 relative to the premium plan.

P10-13 The Dandy Candy Company offers a stereo record as a premium for every six candy bar wrappers presented by customers together with 60 cents. The candy bars are sold by the company to distributors for 15 cents each. The purchase price of each record to the company is 80 cents; in addition it costs 15 cents to mail each record. The results of the premium plan for the years 1980 and 1981 are as follows (all purchases and sales are for cash):

	1980	1981
Stereo records purchased	240,000	180,000
Candy bars sold	2,861,420	2,647,500
Wrappers redeemed	924,600	1,350,000
1980 wrappers expected to be redeemed in 1981	360,000	
1981 wrappers expected to be redeemed in 1982		240,000

Instructions

(a) Prepare the journal entries that should be made in 1980 and 1981 to record the transactions related to the premium plan of the Dandy Candy Company.

(b) Indicate the account names, amounts, and classifications of the items related to the premium plan that would appear on the balance sheet and the income statement at the end of 1980 and 1981.

P10-14 Eastinghouse Company must make computations and adjusting entries for the following independent situations at December 31, 1980:

1. Its line of amplifiers carries a three-year warranty against defects. On the basis of past experience the estimated warranty costs related to dollar sales are: first year after sale—1% of sales; second year after sale—2% of sales; and third year after sale—4% of sales. Sales and actual warranty expenditures for the first three years of business were:

	Sales	Warranty Expenditures
1978	$400,000	$ 1,900
1979	520,000	8,700
1980	600,000	23,000

Instructions

Compute the amount that Eastinghouse Company should report as a liability in its December 31, 1980, balance sheet. Assume that all sales are made evenly throughout each year with warranty expenses also evenly spaced relative to the rates above.

2. Eastinghouse Company's profit-sharing plan provides that the company will contribute to a fund an amount equal to one-third of its net income after taxes each year. Income before taxes and before deducting the profit-sharing contribution for 1980 is $600,000. The applicable income tax rate is 40%, and the profit-sharing contribution is deductible for tax purposes.

Instructions

Compute the amount to be contributed to the profit-sharing fund for 1980.

3. With some of its products, Eastinghouse Company includes coupons that are redeemable in merchandise. The coupons have no expiration date and, in the company's experience, 40% of them are redeemed. The liability for unredeemed coupons at December 31, 1979, was $9,000. During 1980, coupons worth $18,000 were issued, and merchandise worth $8,000 was distributed in exchange for coupons redeemed.

Instructions

Compute the amount of the liability that should appear on the December 31, 1980, balance sheet.

(AICPA adapted)

P10-15 On November 24, 1980, 26 passengers on Bluyonder Airlines Flight No. 901 were injured upon landing when the plane skidded off the runway. Personal injury suits for damages totaling $880,000 were filed on January 11, 1981 against the airline by 18 injured passengers. The airline carries no insurance. Legal counsel has studied each suit and advised Bluyonder that it can reasonably expect to pay 50% of the damages claimed. The financial statements for the year ended December 31, 1980 were issued February 27, 1981.

Instructions

(a) Prepare any disclosures and journal entries required by the airline in preparation of the December 31, 1980 financial statements.

(b) Ignoring the Nov. 24, 1980 accident, what liability due to the risk of loss from lack of insurance coverage should Bluyonder Airlines record or disclose? During the past decade the company has experienced at least one accident per year and incurred average damages of $600,000. Discuss fully.

P10-16   Hemisphere, Inc., in preparation of its December 31, 1980 financial statements, is attempting to determine the proper accounting treatment for each of the following situations:

1. As a result of uninsured accidents during the year, personal injury suits for $200,000 and $50,000 have been filed against the company. It is the judgment of Hemisphere's legal counsel that an unfavorable outcome is unlikely in the $50,000 case but that an unfavorable verdict approximating $80,000 will probably result in the $200,000 case.

2. Hemisphere, Inc. owns a subsidiary in a foreign country that has a book value of $6,780,000 and an estimated fair value of $8,500,000. The foreign government has communicated to Hemisphere its intention to expropriate the assets and business of all foreign investors. On the basis of settlements other firms have received from this same country, Hemisphere expects to receive 40% of the fair value of its properties as final settlement.

3. Hemisphere's chemical product division consisting of five plants is uninsurable because of the special risk of injury to employees and losses due to fire and explosion. The year 1980 is considered one of the safest (luckiest) in the division's history because no loss due to injury or casualty was suffered. Having suffered an average of three casualties a year during the rest of the past decade (ranging from $45,000 to $800,000), management is certain that next year the company will probably not be so fortunate.

Instructions

(a) Prepare the journal entries that should be recorded as of December 31, 1980, to recognize each of the situations above.

(b) Indicate what should be reported relative to each situation in the financial statements and accompanying notes. Explain why.

Plant Assets and
Long-Term Liabilities

Acquisition and Disposition of Property, Plant, and Equipment

Almost every business enterprise of any size or activity uses assets of a durable nature in its operations. Such assets, commonly referred to as **property, plant, and equipment; plant assets;** or **fixed assets,** include land, building structures (offices, factories, warehouses), and equipment (machinery, furniture, tools). These terms are used interchangeably throughout this textbook. The major characteristics of property, plant, and equipment are:

1. **They are acquired for use in operations and not for resale.** Only assets used in the normal operations of the business should be classified as property, plant, and equipment. An idle building is more appropriately classified separately as an investment; land held by land developers or subdividers is classified as inventory.

2. **They are long-term in nature and usually subject to depreciation.** Property, plant, and equipment yield services over a number of years. The investment in these assets is assigned to future periods through periodic depreciation charges. The exception is land, which is not depreciated, except where a material erosion in value occurs, such as a loss in fertility of agricultural land because of poor crop rotation, drought, or soil erosion.

3. **They possess physical substance.** Property, plant, and equipment are characterized by physical existence or substance and thus are differentiated from intangible assets, such as patents or goodwill. Unlike raw material, however, property, plant, and equipment do not physically become part of the product held for resale.

This chapter discusses the basic accounting problems associated with (1) the incurrence of costs related to property, plant, and equipment and (2) the accounting methods used to retire or dispose of these costs. The methods of allocating costs of property, plant, and equipment to accounting periods are presented in Chapter 12.

ACQUISITION OF PROPERTY, PLANT, AND EQUIPMENT

Historical cost is the usual basis for valuing property, plant, and equipment. **Historical cost is measured by the cash or cash equivalent price of obtaining the asset and getting it ready for its intended use.** The purchase price, freight costs, and installation costs of a productive asset are considered part of the cost of the asset. These costs are allocated to future periods through the depreciation process. Any costs related to the asset that are incurred after its acquisition, such as additions, improvements, or replacements, are added to the cost of the asset if they provide future service potential; otherwise they are expensed in the period of incurrence.

Accountants agree that cost should be the basis used at the date of acquisition because the cash or cash equivalent price best measures the value of the asset at that time. Disagreement does exist concerning accounting recognition of substantial differences arising subsequent to acquisition between historical cost and other valuation methods such as current replacement cost or fair market value. Current standards as stated in **APB Opinion No. 6** are that "property, plant, and equipment should not be written up by an entity to reflect appraisal, market, or current values which are above cost to the entity." Although minor exceptions are noted, current standards indicate that departures from historical cost should be rare.

The main reasons for the profession's position are: (1) at the date of acquisition, cost reflects fair value; (2) historical cost involves actual, not hypothetical, transactions, and as a result is objective and verifiable; and (3) gains and losses should not be anticipated but should be recognized when the asset is sold. Proponents of the other valuation methods believe that these reasons are not sufficient justification for continuing to retain historical cost. The merits of these alternative valuation concepts are discussed in Chapter 25.

INITIAL COMPONENTS OF COST

Cost of Land

All expenditures made to acquire land and to ready it for use should be considered as part of the land cost. Land costs typically include (1) the purchase price, (2) costs incurred in "closing," such as title to the land, attorney's fees, and recording fees, (3) costs incurred in getting the land in condition for its intended use, such as grading, filling, draining, and clearing, (4) assumption of any liens or mortgages or encumbrances on the property, and (5) any additional land improvements that have an indefinite life.

When land has been purchased for the purpose of constructing a building, all costs incurred up to the excavation for the new building are considered land costs. Removal of old buildings, clearing, grading, and filling are considered costs of the land because these costs are necessary to get the land in condition for its intended purpose. Any proceeds obtained in the process of getting the land ready for its intended use, such as salvage receipts on the demolition of an old building or the sale of timber that has been cleared, are treated as reductions in the price of the land.

In some cases, the purchaser of land has to assume certain obligations on the land such as back taxes or possible liens on the property. In such situations, the cost of the land is the cash paid for it, plus the encumbrances. In other words, if the purchase price of the land is $50,000 cash, but accrued property taxes of $5,000 on the land are assumed, the cost of the land is $55,000.

Special assessments for local improvements, such as pavements, street lights, sewers, and drainage systems, are usually charged to the Land account because they are relatively permanent in nature and are maintained and replaced by the local government body. In addition, if the improvement made by the owner is rather permanent in nature, such as landscaping, then the item is properly chargeable to the Land account. **Improvements with limited lives,** such as private driveways, walks, fences, and parking lots, are best recorded separately as Land Improvements so they can be depreciated over their estimated lives.

Generally, land is considered part of property, plant, and equipment. If the major purpose of acquiring and holding land is speculative, however, it is more appropriately classified as an investment. If the land is held by a real estate concern for resale, it should be classified as part of inventory. In cases where land is held as an investment, a question develops regarding the accounting treatment that should be given taxes incurred while holding the land. Many accounting theorists believe these taxes should be capitalized because the revenue from the investment still has not been received. This approach is reasonable and seems justified except in cases where the asset is currently producing income (such as rental property).

Cost of Buildings

The cost of buildings should include all expenditures related directly to their acquisition or construction. These costs include (1) materials, labor, and overhead costs incurred during construction and (2) fees, such as attorney's and architect's, and building permits. Generally, companies contract to have their buildings constructed. All costs incurred starting with excavation to completion of the building are considered part of the building costs.

One accounting problem in determining building costs is deciding what to do about an old building that is on the site of a newly proposed building. Is the cost of removal of the old building a cost of the land or a cost of the building? Accountants take the position that if land is purchased with an old building on it, the cost of demolition of the old building less its salvage value is a cost of getting the land ready for the intended use and relates to the land rather than to the construction of the new building. As indicated earlier, the general rule is that all costs of getting the asset ready for its intended use are costs of that asset.

Cost of Equipment

The term equipment in accounting includes delivery equipment, office equipment, machinery, furniture and fixtures, furnishings, factory equipment, and similar fixed assets. The cost of such assets includes the purchase price, freight and handling charges incurred, insurance on the equipment while in transit, cost of special foundations if required, assembling and installation costs and costs of conducting trial runs. Costs thus include all expenditures incurred in acquiring the equipment and preparing it for use.

Self-Constructed Assets

Determining the cost of machinery and equipment is a problem when companies (particularly in the railroad and utility industries) construct their own assets. Without a purchase price or contract price, the company must, through proper allocations and distributions of costs and expenses, arrive at the construction cost to be entered in the property records. Materials and direct labor used in construction pose no problem because these costs can be traced directly to work and material orders related to the fixed assets constructed.

The assignment of indirect costs of manufacturing creates special problems, however. These indirect costs, called overhead or burden, consist of such items as power, heat, light, insurance, property taxes on factory buildings and equipment, factory supervisory labor, depreciation of fixed assets, and supplies.

These costs may be handled three ways.

1. **Assign no fixed overhead to the cost of the constructed asset.** The major reason for this treatment is that indirect overhead is generally fixed in nature and does not increase as a result of constructing one's own plant or equipment. This approach assumes that the company will have the same costs regardless of whether the company constructs the asset or not, so to charge a portion of the overhead costs to the equipment will normally relieve current expenses and consequently overstate income of the current period. Variable overhead costs that increase as a result of the construction should be assigned to the cost of the asset.

2. **Assign a portion of all overhead to the construction process.** This approach, a full costing concept, is appropriate if one believes that costs attach to all products and assets manufactured or constructed. This procedure assigns overhead costs to construction as it would to normal production. This method is employed extensively because most accountants believe a better matching of costs with revenues is obtained. Advocates of this approach indicate that failure to allocate overhead costs understates the initial cost of the equipment and results in an inaccurate allocation in the future.

3. **Allocate on basis of lost production.** A third alternative is to allocate to the construction project the cost of any curtailed production that occurs because the asset is built instead of purchased. This method is conceptually appealing, but is based on "what might have occurred," which is essentially an opportunity cost concept. The practicality of this approach is questionable because valuation problems would be extremely difficult.

We prefer the full costing concept indicated above. We believe that in conformance with the historical cost principle developed in Chapter 2, a prorata portion of the fixed overhead should be assigned to the asset to obtain its cost. If the allocated overhead results in recording construction costs in excess of the costs that would be charged by an outside independent producer, the excess overhead should be recorded as a period loss rather than capitalized.

Interest Costs

The proper accounting for interest costs has been a long-standing controversy in accounting. Three approaches have been suggested to account for the interest incurred in financing the construction or acquisition of property, plant, and equipment:

1. **Capitalize no interest charges during construction.** Under this approach interest is considered a cost of financing and not a cost of construction. It is contended that if the company had used stock financing rather than debt financing, this expense would not have developed. The major arguments against this approach are that an implicit interest cost is associated with the use of cash regardless of its source; if stock financing is employed, a real cost exists to the stockholders although a contractual claim does not develop.

2. **Capitalize only the actual interest costs incurred during construction.** This approach relies on the historical cost concept that only actual transactions are recorded. It is argued that interest incurred is as much a cost of acquiring the asset as the cost of the materials, labor, and other resources used. As a result, a company that uses debt financing will have an asset of higher cost than an enterprise that uses stock financing. The results achieved by this approach are held to be unsatisfactory by some because the cost of an asset should be the same whether cash, debt financing, or stock financing is employed.

3. **Charge construction with all costs of funds employed, whether identifiable or not.** This method is an economic cost approach that maintains that one part of the cost of construction is the cost of financing, whether by debt, cash, or stock financing. An asset should be charged with all costs necessary to get it ready for its intended use. Interest, whether actual or imputed, is a cost of building, just as labor, materials, and overhead are costs. A major criticism of this approach is that imputation of a cost of equity capital is subjective and outside the framework of an historical cost system.

Recently, the FASB has established standards for capitalizing interest cost as part of the historical cost of acquiring certain assets.[1] To qualify for interest capitalization, assets must require a period of time to get them ready for their intended use. However, interest capitalization is only required for these assets if its effect, compared with the effect of expensing interest, is material.[2]

Interest costs are capitalized starting with the first expenditure related to the asset and capitalization continues until the asset is substantially completed and ready for its intended use. The amount of interest to be capitalized is the **actual interest incurred** on an enterprises' debt obligations and does not include a **cost of capital charge** for stockholders' equity. Assets that qualify for interest cost capitalization include assets under construction for an enterprise's own use, including buildings, plants, and large machinery; and assets intended for sale or lease that are constructed or otherwise produced as discrete projects (e.g., ships or real estate developments). Examples of assets that do not qualify for interest capitalization are (1) assets that are in use or ready for their intended use in the earnings of the enterprise, and (2) assets that are not being used in the earnings activities of the enterprise and that are not undergoing the activities necessary to get them ready for use (such as land that is not being developed and assets not being used because of obsolescence, excess capacity or need for repair).

[1]*Statement of Financial Accounting Standards No. 34,* "Capitalization of Interest Costs," (Stamford, Conn.: FASB, 1979).

[2]*Ibid.,* summary paragraph.

When interest expense is being allocated to the assets involved, only interest on debt having explicit rates, interest imputed on certain payables in **APB Opinion No. 21,** and interest recognized in accordance with capitalized leases is capitalized. The interest rate used should be based on a weighted average of rates applicable to the debt (borrowings) outstanding during the period. If specific borrowings can be related to the qualifying asset, then the interest on these borrowings may be assigned to the asset for the purpose of capitalization. Judgment must be exercised in the selection of the interest rate to be capitalized. The above requirements are intended to allow the enterprise to determine an appropriate interest rate while minimizing the cost of implementing this requirement.

This FASB Standard could have a substantive impact on the financial statements of business enterprises. To illustrate, public utilities have been permitted to capitalize interest during construction (whether actual or imputed) for many years, and many companies currently follow this practice.[3] For example, at one time it was estimated that Duke Power's net income of $58.5 million would be reduced by more than 85% if interest costs were shown as an expense. In addition, compare the results of different methods of handling interest adopted by two large utilities.

	Comparison of Earnings Between Companies That Follow Different Practices Concerning Capitalization of Interest During Construction	
	Reported Net Income Regulatory	Adjusted for Capitalized Interest
	(In millions)	
Wisconsin Electric Power	$78.1	$78.1
Public Service Company of Colorado	78.3	71.1
Difference	$ (0.2)	$ 7.0
Percentage Differences	(.3%)	9.0%

The difference between the methods of presentation (approximately 9.3%) is significant and illustrates the necessity for appropriate guidelines in this area.

The interest capitalization requirement will be controversial. From a conceptual viewpoint, many believe that either no interest cost should be capitalized or all interest costs, actual or imputed, should be capitalized for the reasons mentioned earlier in this section. In addition, some practical problems exist. For example, capitalization is supposed to take place only when the benefits of the information provided exceed the costs of providing the information; a difficult concept to operationalize. As a result, it appears that this topic will continue to be debated.

---

[3]Non-utility companies traditionally have not capitalized any interest cost during construction, whether actual or imputed. In the early 1970s, however, a number of companies decided to do so. The reason for this switch was to prevent the decline in earnings that resulted when an enterprise expensed these interest costs. In 1974, the SEC in *ASR No. 163* declared a moratorium on the capitalization of interest costs for most non-utility companies, indicating that practices in this area were leading to noncomparability of financial data. The FASB Standard is an attempt to develop guidelines in accounting for interest costs during construction.

THE MEANS OF ACQUISITION AND VALUATION

An asset should be recorded at the fair market value of what is given up to acquire it or at its own fair market value, whichever is more clearly evident. Fair market value, however, is sometimes obscured by the process through which the asset is acquired. As an example, assume that land and buildings are bought together for one price. How are separate values for the land and building computed? A number of accounting problems of this nature are examined in the following sections.

Cash Discount

When plant assets are purchased subject to cash discounts for prompt payment, the question of how the discount should be handled occurs. If the discount is taken, it should be considered a reduction in the purchase price of the asset. What is not clear, however, is whether a reduction in the asset cost should occur if the discount is not taken. Two points of view exist on this matter. Under one approach, the discount, whether taken or not, is considered a reduction in the cost of the asset. The rationale for this approach is that the real cost of the asset is the cash or cash equivalent price of the asset. In addition, some argue that the terms of cash discounts are so attractive that failure to take a discount is a loss because management was inefficient. On the other hand, some argue that the discount should not be considered a loss because the terms may be unfavorable or because it would not be prudent for the company to take the discount. At present, both methods are employed in practice. The former method is generally preferred because it represents the current cash equivalent price to acquire the asset at the date of acquisition.

Deferred Payment Contracts

Plant assets are purchased frequently on long-term credit contracts through the use of notes, mortgages, bonds, or equipment obligations. **Assets purchased on long-term credit contracts should be accounted for at the present value of the consideration exchanged between the contracting parties at the date of the transaction to properly reflect cost.** An asset, therefore, that requires five annual payments of $1,000, with no interest specified in the contract, should not be recorded originally at $5,000. The present value of these payments, assuming an appropriate interest rate, should be used to determine the purchase price of the asset. If the asset in the situation above was purchased on a basis that required the payment of $1,000 per year for five years, including an interest element stated at 8% annually, the cost of the asset would be $3,992.71 ($1,000 × 3.99271 — Table 6–4).

Determining the purchase price becomes more complex when a specific interest rate does not appear on the obligation or if the specified rate is unreasonable. To estimate the present value of a note under such circumstances, an appropriate interest rate is imputed. The objective is to approximate the interest rate that the buyer and seller would negotiate at arms' length in a similar transaction. If an interest rate is not imputed, the asset will be recorded at an amount greater than its fair value. In addition, interest income and expense would be incorrectly projected in future periods. In determining the interest rate, the cash exchange price of the asset acquired might indicate the value.

To illustrate, assume that Menametal, Inc., decides to purchase a specially built metal cutter to help in the preparation of some new molding designs. The company issues a $100,000, 20-year, noninterest-bearing note to T & R Metalcutters for the new equipment when the prevailing market rate of interest for obligations of this nature is 10%. The company will pay off the note in twenty $5,000 installments over the life of the note. The fair market value of this particular metal cutter cannot be established in the market place and is thus approximated by determining the market value of the note. The entries at date of purchase and subsequently are:

At date of purchase:

Equipment ($5,000 × 8.514 — Table 6-4)	42,570	
Discount on Notes Payable	57,430	
Notes Payable		100,000

At end of first year:

Interest Expense	4,257	
Notes Payable	5,000	
Cash		5,000
Discount on Notes Payable		4,257

Interest expense under the effective yield approach is $4,257, ($100,000 — $57,430) × 10%; if straight-line amortization is used, interest expense would be $2,871.50, ($57,430 ÷ 20). The entry at the end of the second year to record interest and to pay off a portion of the note is as follows:

At end of second year:

Interest Expense	4,183	
Notes Payable	5,000	
Cash		5,000
Discount on Notes Payable		4,183

Interest expense in the second year under the effective yield approach is $4,183, [($100,000 — $57,430) — ($5,000 — $4,257)] × 10%

Exchanges of Property, Plant, and Equipment (Nonmonetary Assets)

The proper accounting for exchanges of nonmonetary assets (such as inventories and property, plant, and equipment) is controversial.[4] Some accountants argue that the accounting for these types of exchanges should be based on the fair value of the asset given up with a gain or loss recognized; others believe that the accounting should be based on the recorded amount (book value) of the asset given up with no gain or loss recognized; and still others favor an approach that would recognize losses in all cases, but defer gains in special situations.

Ordinarily accounting for the exchange of nonmonetary assets should be based on **the fair value of the asset given up or the fair value of the asset received, whichever is clearly more evident.**[5] Thus, any gains or losses on the exchange

---

[4]Nonmonetary assets are items whose price in terms of the monetary unit may change over time; monetary assets are in contrast, fixed in terms of units of currency by contract or otherwise; for example, cash and short- or long-term accounts and notes receivable.

[5]"Accounting for Nonmonetary Transactions," *Opinions of the Accounting Principles Board No. 29* (Stamford, Conn.: FASB, 1973), par. 18.

should be recognized immediately. The rationale for this approach is that **the earnings process related to these assets is completed** and, therefore, a gain or loss should be recognized. This approach is always employed when the assets are **dissimilar** in nature, such as the exchange of land for a building, or the exchange of equipment for inventory.

The general rule is modified when exchanges of **similar nonmonetary** assets occurs. For example, when a company exchanges inventory items with inventory of another company because of color, size, etc. to facilitate sale to an outside customer, the earnings process is not considered completed and a **gain** should not be recognized. Likewise if a company swaps **similar productive assets** (assets held for or used in the production of goods or services) such as land for land or equipment for equipment, the enterprise is not considered to have completed the earnings process and, therefore, **a gain should not be recognized.** However, if the exchange transaction involving **similar assets** would result in a loss, **the loss is recognized immediately.**

In certain situations, gains on exchange of similar nonmonetary assets may be involved where **monetary consideration (boot)** is received. When monetary consideration such as cash is received in addition to the nonmonetary asset, it is assumed that a portion of the earnings process is completed and, therefore, a partial gain is recognized.

In summary, losses on nonmonetary transactions are always recognized whether the exchange involves dissimilar or similar assets. Gains on nonmonetary transactions are recognized if the exchange involves dissimilar assets; gains are deferred if the exchange involves similar assets, unless cash or some other form of monetary consideration is received, in which case a partial gain is recognized. Any gain or loss on disposal of nonmonetary assets is computed by comparing the book value of the asset given up with the fair value of the asset given up.

To illustrate the accounting for these different types of transactions, the discussion is divided into three sections as follows:

1. Accounting for dissimilar assets.
2. Accounting for similar assets—loss situation.
3. Accounting for similar assets—gain situations.

Dissimilar Assets   The cost of a nonmonetary asset acquired in exchange for a dissimilar nonmonetary asset is usually recorded at the **fair value of the asset given up,** and a gain or loss is recognized. The **fair value of the asset received** should be used only if it is more clearly evident than the fair value of the asset given up. If the fair value of either asset is not reasonably determinable, the **book value of the asset given up** is used as the basis for recording the nonmonetary exchange.

To illustrate, Newbold Transportation Company exchanged a number of used trucks plus cash for vacant land that might be used for a future plant site. The trucks have a combined book value of $42,000 (cost $64,000 less $22,000 accumulated depreciation). Newbold's purchasing agent, through experience in the second-hand market, indicates that the trucks have a fair market value of $49,000. In addition to the trucks, Newbold must pay $17,000 cash for the land. The cost of the land is $66,000 computed as follows:

	Computation of Land Cost
Fair value of trucks exchanged	$49,000
Cash paid	17,000
Cost of land	$66,000

The journal entry to record the exchange transaction is:

Land	66,000	
Accumulated Depreciation—Trucks	22,000	
Trucks		64,000
Gain on Disposal of Trucks		7,000
Cash		17,000

The gain is the difference between the fair value of the trucks and their book value. It is verified as follows:

	Computation of Gain		
Fair value of trucks			$49,000
Cost of trucks		$64,000	
Less accumulated depreciation		22,000	
Book value of trucks			42,000
Gain on disposal of used trucks			$ 7,000

It follows that if the fair value of the trucks was $39,000 instead of $49,000, a loss on the exchange of $3,000 ($42,000 − $39,000) would be reported. In either case, as a result of the exchange of dissimilar assets, the earnings process on the used trucks has been completed and a gain **or** loss should be recognized.

Similar Assets—Loss Situation   Similar nonmonetary assets are those of the same general type, that perform the same function, or are employed in the same line of business. When similar nonmonetary assets are exchanged and a loss results, the loss should be recognized immediately. For example, Information Processing, Inc. trades its used accounting machine for a new model. The accounting machine given up has a book value of $8,000 (original cost $12,000 less $4,000 accumulated depreciation) and a fair value of $6,000. It is traded for a new model that has a list price of $16,000. In negotiations with the seller, a trade-in allowance of $9,000 is finally agreed on for the used machine. The cash payment that must be made for the new asset and the cost of the new machine are computed as follows:

	Cost of New Machine
List price of new machine	$16,000
Less trade-in allowance for used machine	9,000
Cash payment due	7,000
Fair value of used machine	6,000
Cost of new machine	$13,000

The journal entry to record this transaction is:

Equipment	13,000	
Accumulated Depreciation—Equipment	4,000	
Loss on Disposal of Equipment	2,000	
Equipment		12,000
Cash		7,000

The loss on the disposal of the used machine can be verified as follows:

	Computation of Loss
Fair value of used machine	$6,000
Book value of used machine	8,000
Loss on disposal of used machine	$2,000

Why was the trade-in allowance or the book value of the old asset not used as a basis for the new equipment? The trade-in allowance is not employed because it included a price concession (similar to a price discount) to the purchaser. For example, few individuals pay list price for a new car. Trade-in allowances on the used car are often inflated such that actual selling prices are below list prices. In short, the list price of a new car is usually inflated and to record the car at list price would state it at an amount in excess of its cash equivalent price. Use of book value in this situation would overstate the value of the new accounting machine by $2,000. Because assets should not be maintained at more than their cash equivalent price, the loss should be recognized immediately rather than added to the cost of the newly acquired asset.

Similar Assets—Gain Situation (no cash received)   The accounting treatment for exchanges of **similar** nonmonetary assets when a gain develops is more complex. The APB took the position that if the exchange does not complete the earnings process, then any **gain should be deferred.** The real estate industry provides a good example of why the Board decided not to recognize gains on exchanges of similar nonmonetary assets. In the early 1970s when the real estate business was booming, it was common practice for companies to "swap" real estate holdings. To illustrate, Landmark Company and Hillfarm, Inc. each had undeveloped land on which they intended to build shopping centers. Appraisals indicated that the land of both companies had increased significantly in value. The companies decided to exchange (swap) their undeveloped land, record a gain, and report their new parcels of land at current fair values. But, should income be recognized at this point? The APB stated that the earnings process is not completed because the companies in such situations remain in the same economic position after the swap as before; therefore, the asset acquired should be recorded at book value with no gain recognized. If, however, the book value exceeds fair value, a loss should be recognized.

To illustrate, Davis Rent-A-Car has a rental fleet of automobiles that are primarily Ford Motor Company products. Davis's management is interested in increasing the variety of automobiles in its rental fleet by adding numerous models of General Motors products. During a long delay in delivery from the manufacturer, Davis arranges with Nertz Rent-A-Car to exchange a group of Ford Fairmonts and Futuras with a fair value of $160,000 and a book value of $135,000 (cost $150,000 less accumulated depreciation $15,000) for a number of Chevy Citations and Pontiac Phoenixes. The fair value of the automobiles received from Nertz is $170,000; Davis, therefore, pays $10,000 in cash in addition to the Ford automobiles exchanged. The total gain to Davis Rent-A-Car is computed as follows:

	Computation of Gain
Fair value of Ford automobiles exchanged	$160,000
Book value of Ford automobiles exchanged	135,000
Total gain (unrecognized)	$ 25,000

Because the earnings process is not considered completed in this transaction, the total gain is deferred and the basis of the General Motors automobiles is reduced as illustrated below via two different but acceptable computations:

Basis of New Automobiles to Davis			
Fair value of GM automobiles	$170,000	Book value of Ford automobiles	$135,000
Less gain deferred	(25,000) OR	Cash paid	10,000
Basis of GM automobiles	$145,000	Basis of GM automobiles	$145,000

The entry by Davis to record this transaction is as follows:

Automobiles (GM)	145,000	
Accumulated Depreciation—Automobiles	15,000	
Automobiles (Ford)		150,000
Cash		10,000

The gain that reduced the basis of the new automobiles will be recognized when those automobiles are sold to an outside party. If these automobiles are held for an extended period of time, depreciation charges will be lower and net income higher in subsequent periods because of the reduced basis.

Similar Assets—Gain Situation (some cash received) The accounting issue of gain recognition becomes more difficult if monetary consideration such as cash is **received** in an exchange of similar nonmonetary assets. When cash is received, part of the nonmonetary asset is considered sold and part exchanged; therefore, only a portion of the gain is deferred. The general formula for gain recognition when some cash is received is as follows:

$$\frac{\text{Cash Received (Boot)}}{\text{Cash Received (Boot)} + \text{Fair Value of Asset Received}} \times \text{Total Gain} = \text{Recognized Gain}$$

For example, consider recording the foregoing exchange of automobiles on the books of Nertz Rent-A-Car. If the book value of Nertz's Chevy and Pontiac automobiles exchanged is $136,000 (cost $150,000 less accumulated depreciation $14,000), the total gain on the exchange to Nertz would be computed as follows:

	Computation of Total Gain to Nertz
Fair value of GM automobiles exchanged	$170,000
Book value of GM automobiles exchanged	136,000
Total gain	$ 34,000

But, because Nertz received $10,000 in cash, the recognized gain on this transaction is computed as follows using the formula above:

$$\frac{\$10,000}{\$10,000 + \$160,000} \times \$34,000 = \$2,000$$

The ratio of monetary assets ($10,000) to the total consideration received ($10,000 + $160,000) is the portion of the total gain ($34,000) to be recognized, i.e., $2,000. Because only a gain of $2,000 is recognized on this transaction, the remaining $32,000 ($34,000 − $2,000) is deferred and reduces the basis of the new automobiles. The computation of the basis is as follows:

Basis of New Automobiles to Nertz			
Fair value of Ford automobiles	$160,000	Book value of GM automobiles	$136,000
Less gain deferred	(32,000) OR	Add gain recognized	2,000
Basis of Ford automobiles	$128,000	Less cash received	(10,000)
		Basis of Ford automobiles	$128,000

The entry by Nertz to record this transaction is as follows:

Cash	10,000	
Automobiles (Ford)	128,000	
Accumulated Depreciation—Automobiles	14,000	
Automobiles (GM)		150,000
Gain on Disposal of GM Automobiles		2,000

The APB's rationale for this treatment is as follows: Before the exchange, Nertz Rent-A-Car had an unrecognized gain of $34,000, as evidenced by the difference between the book value ($136,000) and the fair value ($170,000) of its GM automobiles. When the exchange occurred, a portion ($10,000/$170,000 or 1/17) of the fair value was converted to a more liquid asset. The ratio of this liquid asset ($10,000) to the total consideration received ($160,000 + $10,000) is the portion of the gain ($34,000) realized. Thus, a gain of $2,000 (1/17 × $34,000) is realized and recorded.

Presented below in summary form are the accounting requirements for recognizing gains and losses on exchanges of nonmonetary assets.[6]

1. Compute the total gain or loss on the transaction, which is equal to the difference between the fair value of the asset given up and the book value of the asset given up.

2. If a loss is computed in 1, always recognize the entire loss.

[6]Adapted from an article by Robert Capettini and Thomas E. King, "Exchanges of Nonmonetary Assets: Some Changes," *The Accounting Review* (January, 1976).

3. If a gain is computed in 1,
   (a) and the earnings process is considered completed, the entire gain is recognized (dissimilar assets).
   (b) and the earning process is not considered completed (similar assets),
       (1) and no cash is involved, no gain is recognized.
       (2) and some cash is given, no gain is recognized.
       (3) and some cash is received, the following portion of the gain is recognized:

$$\frac{\text{Cash Received (Boot)}}{\text{Cash Received (Boot)} + \text{Fair Value of Assets Received}} \times \text{Total Gain}$$

An enterprise that engages in one or more nonmonetary exchanges during a period should disclose in financial statements for the period the nature of the transactions, the basis of accounting for the assets transferred, and gains or losses recognized on transfers.[7] An algorithm presented below portrays the accounting decision process involved in applying **APB Opinion No. 29.**

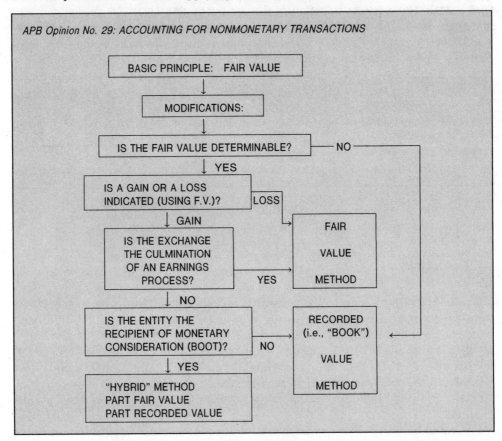

Source: Ronnie J. Burrows, Northern Illinois University.

---

[7]"Accounting for Nonmonetary Transactions," *op. cit.*, par. 28.

Lump Sum Purchase

A special problem of pricing fixed assets arises when a group of plant assets is purchased at a single lump sum price. When such a situation occurs, and it is not at all unusual, the practice is to allocate the total cost among the various assets on the basis of their relative fair market values. The assumption is that costs will vary in direct proportion to sales value.

Although the accountant may not be an expert in this area, responsibility for determining that the valuations associated with the different assets are reasonable and that they can be verified to some degree must be accepted. Generally, an appraisal that was employed for insurance purposes, the assessed valuation for property taxes, or simply an independent appraisal by an engineer or other appraiser might be used. Normally, the seller's book value used should not be employed as a basis for allocation.

To illustrate, Norduct Heating, Inc., decides to purchase several assets of a small heating concern, Harker Heating, for $80,000. Harker Heating is in the process of liquidation, and its assets sold are:

	Book Value	Fair Market Value
Inventory	$30,000	$ 25,000
Land	20,000	25,000
Building	35,000	50,000
	$85,000	$100,000

The $80,000 purchase price would be allocated on the basis of the relative fair market values in the following manner:

$$\text{Inventory} \quad \frac{\$\ 25,000}{\$100,000} \times \$80,000 = \$20,000$$

$$\text{Land} \quad \frac{\$\ 25,000}{\$100,000} \times \$80,000 = \$20,000$$

$$\text{Building} \quad \frac{\$\ 50,000}{\$100,000} \times \$80,000 = \$40,000$$

Issuance of Stock

When property is acquired by issuance of securities, such as common stock, the cost of the property is not properly measured by the par or stated value of such stock. If the stock is being actively traded, **the market value of the stock issued is a fair indication of the cost of the property acquired because the stock is a good measure of the current cash equivalent price.**

For example, Coyle-Lukkin decides to purchase some adjacent land for expansion of its carpeting and cabinet operation. In lieu of paying cash for the land, the company issues to Starret Company 5,000 shares of common stock (par value $10) that have a fair market value of $12 per share. Coyle-Lukkin would make the following entry.

Land (5,000 $\times$ $12)	60,000	
Common Stock		50,000
Additional Paid-In Capital		10,000

If the market value of the common stock exchanged is not determinable, the market value of the property should be established and used as the basis for recording the asset and issuance of the common stock.[8]

Acquisition and Disposition by Donation or Gift

An enterprise may be both the recipient of donations and the maker of donations. Such exchanges are referred to as **nonreciprocal transfers** because they are transfers of assets in one direction. Many agricultural and transportation enterprises, for example, have received substantial donations (in the form of rebates and subsidies) from the federal government. When assets are acquired in this manner, a strict cost concept dictates that the valuation of the asset should be zero. A departure from the cost principle seems justified, however, because the only costs incurred, legal fees and other relatively minor expenditures, do not constitute a reasonable basis of accounting for the assets acquired. To record nothing, we believe, is to ignore the economic realities of an increase in wealth and asset utility. Therefore, **the appraisal or fair market value of the asset should be used to establish a proper basis of asset valuation for purposes of enterprise accountability.**

The classification of the offsetting credit to the asset received, however, is controversial. Some believe that the credit should be to additional paid-in capital[9] because these donations reduce the amount of capital required by the enterprise. Others argue that capital is contributed only by the owners of the business and that donations are benefits to the enterprise which should be reported as income. An issue related to the income approach is whether the income should be reported immediately or over the period that the asset is employed. For example, to attract new industry a city may offer land; but the receiving enterprise may incur additional costs in the future (transportation, higher state income taxes, etc.) because the location is not the most desirable. As a consequence, some argue that the income should be deferred and recognized as these costs are incurred. If known additional costs are to be incurred, an Unrealized Income from Donation account could be established in the liability section and written-off over the life of the asset.

To illustrate, Max Wayer Meat Packing, Inc. has recently accepted donated land with a fair value of $125,000 from the city of Burke in return for a promise to build a packing plant in Burke. Max Wayer's entry is:

Land	125,000	
Unrealized Income on Donation		125,000

The Unrealized Income on Donation would be written off over the life of the plant that would be constructed on this property. It should be emphasized that

---

[8]When the fair market value of the stock is used as the basis of valuation, careful consideration must be given to the effect that the issuance of additional shares will have on the existing market price. Where the effect on market price appears significant, an independent appraisal of the asset received should be made. This valuation should be employed as the basis for valuation of the asset as well as for the stock issued. In the unusual case where the fair market value of the stock or the fair market value of the asset cannot be determined objectively, the board of directors of the corporation may set the value.

[9]The account often used is Donated Capital.

whether the capital approach, the immediate recognition of income approach, or the unrealized income approach is used, if the donation is contingent upon some performance (such as building a plant), this contingency should be reported in the footnotes.

In practice, enterprises permit cash donations in the form of subsidies, rebates, and tax credits from the government to flow through the income statement while cash and noncash donations from stockholders and other nongovernmental entities or individuals are generally credited to additional paid in capital.

When a nonmonetary asset is donated, that is, given away, the amount of the donation should be recorded at the fair market value of the donated asset. If a difference exists between the fair market value of the asset and its book value, a gain or loss should be recognized.[10] To illustrate, Kline Industries donates land which cost $80,000 and has a fair market value of $110,000 to the City of Los Angeles for a city park. The entry to record this donation would be:

Donation	110,000	
Land		80,000
Gain on Disposition of Land		30,000

The donation cost would ordinarily be classified in the other expense section of the income statement.

COSTS SUBSEQUENT TO ACQUISITION

After plant assets are installed and ready for use, additional costs are incurred that range from ordinary repair costs to significant additions. The major problem in this area is allocating these costs to individual periods. Accountants for the most part have adopted the position that costs incurred to achieve greater future benefits should be capitalized (debited to an asset account), whereas expenditures that simply maintain a given level of services should be expensed. In order for costs to be capitalized (capital expenditures), one of three conditions must be present: (1) **the useful life of the asset must be increased; (2) the quantity of units produced from the asset must be increased; or (3) the quality of the units produced must be enhanced.**

Expenditures (revenue expenditures) that do not increase the service benefits of the assets are expensed. Ordinary repairs, for example, are expenditures that maintain the existing condition of the asset or restore it to normal operating efficiency and should be expensed immediately. In addition, most expenditures below an established arbitrary minimum amount are expensed rather than capitalized. For example, many enterprises have adopted the rule that expenditures below a certain arbitrarily selected amount, say, $100 or $500, should always be expensed. Although conceptually this treatment may not be correct, expediency demands that this approach be followed; otherwise, accountants would have to set up depreciation schedules for such things as wastepaper baskets and ash trays.

The distinction between a **capital (asset)** and **revenue (expense)** expenditure is not always clear-cut. For example, determination of the **property unit** with which costs should be associated is critical. If a fully equipped steam ship is considered a property unit, then replacement of the engine might be considered an expense,

---

[10]"Accounting for Nonmonetary Transactions," *op. cit.,* par. 18.

whereas if the ship's engine is considered a property unit, then its replacement would be capitalized. It follows that the disposition and treatment of many items require considerable analysis and judgment before the proper distinction can be made. In many cases, consistent application of a capital/expense policy is justified as more important than attempting to provide general theoretical guidelines.

Generally, four major types of expenditures are incurred relative to existing assets.

1. **Additions.** Increase or extension of existing assets.
2. **Improvements and replacements.** Substitution of an improved asset for an existing one.
3. **Reinstallation and rearrangement.** Movement of assets from one location to another.
4. **Repairs.** Expenditures that maintain assets in condition for operation.

Additions

Additions should present no major accounting problems. By definition, any addition to plant assets is capitalized because a new asset has been created. The addition of a wing to a hospital or the addition of an air conditioning system to an office, for example, increases the service potential of that facility and should be capitalized and matched against the revenues that will result in future periods.

The most difficult problem that develops in this area is accounting for any changes related to the existing structure as a result of the addition. Is the cost that is incurred to tear down a wall of the old structure to make room for the addition a cost of the addition or an expense or loss of the period? The answer is that it depends on the original intent. If the company had anticipated that an addition was going to be added later, then this cost of removal is a proper cost of the addition. But if the company had not anticipated this development, it should properly be reported as a loss in the current period on the basis that the company was inefficient in its planning. Normally, the carrying amount of the old wall remains in the accounts, although theoretically it should be removed.

Improvements and Replacements

Improvements (often referred to as betterments) and replacements are substitutions of one asset for another. The distinguishing feature between an improvement and a replacement is that an improvement is the substitution of a better asset for the one currently used (say, a concrete floor for a wooden floor). A replacement, on the other hand, is the substitution of a similar asset (a wooden floor for a wooden floor).

Many times improvements and replacements occur as the result of a general policy to modernize or rehabilitate an older building or piece of equipment. The problem lies in differentiating these types of expenditure from normal repairs. The accountant should ask: Does the expenditure increase the **future** service potential of the asset, or does it merely maintain the existing level of service? Many times the answer is not clear-cut, and good judgment must be used in order to classify these expenditures properly.

If it is determined that the expenditure increases the future service potential of the asset and, therefore, should be capitalized, this capitalization is handled in one of three ways, depending on the circumstances.

1. **Substitution Approach.** Conceptually, the substitution approach is the correct procedure if the carrying amount of the old asset is available. If the carrying amount of the old asset can be determined, it is a simple matter to remove the cost of the old asset and replace it with the cost of the new asset.

   To illustrate, Instinct Enterprises decides to replace the pipes in its plumbing system. A plumber suggests that in place of the cast iron pipes and copper tubing, a newly developed plastic tubing be used. The old pipe and tubing has a book value of $15,000 (cost of $150,000 less accumulated depreciation of $135,000), and a fair market value of $1,000. The plastic tubing system has a market value of $125,000. Assuming that Instinct has to pay $124,000 for the new tubing after exchanging the old tubing, the entry is:

Plumbing System	125,000	
Accumulated Depreciation	135,000	
Loss on Disposal of Plant Assets	14,000	
Plumbing System		150,000
Cash		124,000

   The problem with this approach is determining the book value of the old asset. Generally, the components of a given asset depreciate at different rates, but no separate accounting is made of each component. As an example, the tires, motor, and body of a truck depreciate at different rates, but most concerns use only one depreciation rate for the truck. Separate depreciation rates could be set for each component, but practicality precludes the use of this approach. If the carrying amount of the old asset cannot be determined, one of two other approaches is adopted.

2. **Capitalizing the New Cost.** The justification for capitalizing the cost of the improvement or replacement is that even though the carrying amount of the old asset is not removed from the accounts, sufficient depreciation was taken on the item to reduce the carrying amount almost to zero. Whether this assumption is true in all cases is unlikely, but in many situations the differences would not be significant. Improvements especially are handled in this manner.

3. **Charging to Accumulated Depreciation.** There are times when there has not been an improvement in the quantity or quality of the asset itself, but the useful life of the asset has been extended. Replacements, particularly, may extend the useful life of the asset, yet they may not improve the quality or quantity of service or product produced in a given period. In these circumstances, the expenditure may be debited to Accumulated Depreciation rather than to an asset account on the theory that the replacement extends the useful life of the asset and thereby recaptures some or all of the past depreciation. The main justification for this approach is that it is a recovery of past depreciation charges. The carrying amount of the asset is the same whether the asset is charged or the accumulated depreciation is charged—it is only in the manner of presentation that a difference arises. Many people question this approach because the replacement cost of an asset changes over time, and to charge accumulated depreciation ignores this possibility entirely.

Reinstallation and Rearrangement

Reinstallation and rearrangement costs are expenditures that will benefit future periods but do not represent either additions, replacements, or improvements. An example is the reinstallation or rearrangement of a group of machines to facilitate future production. If the original installation cost can be estimated along with the accumulated depreciation taken to date, the reinstallation cost might properly be handled as a replacement. If not, which is generally the case, the new costs should be carried forward as an asset (deferred charge) to be amortized against future income.[11]

Repairs

Ordinary repairs are expenditures made to maintain plant assets in operating condition; they are charged to an expense account in the period in which they are incurred on the basis that it is the only period benefited. Replacement of minor parts, lubricating and adjusting of equipment, repainting, and cleaning are examples of the type of maintenance charges that occur regularly and are treated as ordinary operating expenses. It is often difficult to distinguish a repair from an improvement or replacement. The major consideration is whether the expenditure increases the future service potential. If a **major repair,** such as an overhaul, occurs, several periods will benefit and the cost should be handled as an addition, improvement, or replacement, depending on the type of repair made.

If operating and income statements are prepared for short periods of time, say, monthly or quarterly, the same principles must be applied to accounting for repair costs. Ordinary repairs and other regular maintenance charges for an annual period may benefit several quarters, and allocation of the cost among the periods concerned might be required. For example, a concern will often find it advantageous to concentrate its repair program at a certain time of the year, perhaps during the period of least activity or when the plant is shut down for vacation. Short-term comparative statements might be misleading if such expenditures are shown as expenses of the quarter in which they were incurred. To give comparability to monthly or quarterly income statements, an account such as Allowance for Repairs might be used so that repair costs are better assigned to periods benefited.

To illustrate, Cricket Tractor Company estimated that its total repair expense for the year would be $720,000. It decided to charge each quarter for a portion of the repair cost even though the total cost for the year would occur only in two quarters.

End of first quarter (zero repair costs incurred)

Repair Expense	180,000	
Allowance for Repairs (¼ × $720,000)		180,000

End of second quarter ($344,000 repair costs incurred)

Allowance for Repairs	344,000	
Cash, Wages Payable, Inventory, etc.		344,000
Repair Expense	180,000	
Allowance for Repairs (¼ × $720,000)		180,000

---

[11]Another cost of this nature is relocation costs. For example, when Shell Oil moved its headquarters from New York to Houston, it amortized the cost of relocating over four years. Conversely, estimated relocation costs of $15 million were charged to income at GAF Corp. The point is that no definitive guidelines have been established in this area, and generally costs are deferred over some arbitrary period in the future. Recently, some writers have argued that these costs should generally be expensed as incurred. See, for example, Charles W. Lamden, Dale L. Gerboth, and Thomas W. McRae, "Accounting for Depreciable Assets" *Accounting Research Monograph No. 1* (New York: AICPA, 1975), pp. 54–61.

End of third quarter (zero repair costs incurred)

Repair Expense	180,000	
Allowance for Repairs (¼ × $720,000)		180,000

End of fourth quarter ($380,800 repair costs incurred)

Allowance for Repairs	380,800	
Cash, Wages Payable, Inventory, etc.		380,800
Repair Expense	184,800	
Allowance for Repairs		184,800
($344,000 + $380,800 − $180,000 − $180,000 − $180,000)		

Ordinarily, no balance should be carried over to the following year in the Allowance for Repairs account, and the fourth quarter would normally absorb the variation from estimates. If balance sheets are prepared during the year, the allowance account should be added to or subtracted from the property, plant, and equipment section to obtain a proper valuation during the year.

Some accountants advocate the accrual of estimated repair costs beyond one year. This approach is based on the assumption that the allocation of asset cost via depreciation charges does not take into consideration the incurrence of repair costs. For example, in aircraft overhaul and steel furnace rebuilding, an allowance for repairs is sometimes established because the amount of repairs can be established with a high degree of certainty. Although conceptually this approach may be appealing, there are many drawbacks. First, it is difficult to justify the Allowance for Repairs account as a liability because one might ask, Whom do you owe? Placement in the stockholders' equity section is also illogical because no addition to the stockholders' investment has taken place. One possibility might be to treat allowance for repairs as an addition to or subtraction from the asset on the basis that the value has increased or decreased, depending on when the repairs were made. The fact is that expenses should not be anticipated before they arise unless estimates of the future are predictable within a reasonable range.

DISPOSITIONS OF PLANT ASSETS

Plant assets may be retired voluntarily or disposed of by sale, exchange, involuntary conversion, or abandonment. Regardless of the time of disposal, depreciation must be taken up to the date of disposition, and all accounts related to the retired asset should be removed from the accounts. Ideally, the book value of the specific plant asset would be equal to its disposal value. This is generally not the case, however, and a resulting gain or loss occurs.

This gain or loss develops because depreciation is a process of cost allocation and not a process of valuation. The gain or loss in most situations is in reality a correction of net income for the years during which the fixed asset was used. If it had been possible at the time of acquisition to forecast the exact date of disposal and the amount to be realized at disposition, then a more accurate estimate of depreciation could have been recorded and no gain or loss would have developed.

In accordance with **APB Opinion No. 30,** gains or losses on the retirement of plant assets should be shown in the income statement along with other items that arise from customary business activities. If, however, the "operations of a segment of a business" are sold, abandoned, spun off, or otherwise disposed of, the APB in **Opinion No. 30** concluded that the results of "continuing operations" should be reported separately from "discontinued operations" and that any gain or loss from disposal of a segment of a business should be reported in conjunction with the related results of discontinued operations and not as an extraordinary item. To be reported as discontinued operations, however, the segment of a business must represent a separate line of business or class of customers. Reporting requirements were discussed in Chapter 4.

Sale of Plant Assets

The problems related to the outright sale of a plant asset are relatively simple. Depreciation must be recorded for the period of time between the date of the last depreciation entry and the date of retirement. To illustrate, assume that depreciation on a machine costing $18,000 has been recorded for nine years at the rate of $1,200 per year. If the machine is sold in the middle of the tenth year for $7,000, the entry to record depreciation to the date of sale is:

Depreciation Expense	600	
Accumulated Depreciation of Machinery		600

This separate entry ordinarily is not made because most companies enter all depreciation, including this amount, in one entry at the end of the year. In either case the entry for the sale of the asset is:

Cash	7,000	
Accumulated Depreciation of Machinery	11,400	
($1,200 × 9 plus $600)		
Machinery		18,000
Gain on Disposal of Plant Assets		400

The book value of the machinery at the time of the sale is $6,600 ($18,000 − $11,400); because it is sold for $7,000, the amount of the gain on the sale is $400.

Involuntary Conversion

Sometimes, an asset's service is terminated through some type of involuntary conversion such as fire, flood, theft, condemnation, and so on. The accounting problems in this area are not difficult, inasmuch as the gains or losses are no different from those in any other type of disposition.

To illustrate, Camel Transport Corp. was forced to sell a plant located on company property that stood directly in the path of an interstate highway. For a number of years the state had sought to purchase the land on which the plant stood but the company resisted. The state ultimately exercised its right of eminent domain and was upheld by the courts. In settlement, Camel received $500,000, which was substantially in excess of the $200,000 book value of the plant and land (cost of $400,000 less accumulated depreciation of $200,000). The following entry was made:

Cash	500,000	
Accumulated Depreciation of Plant Assets	200,000	
Plant Assets		400,000
Gain on Disposal of Plant Assets		300,000

Recently, there has been some objection to the recognition of a gain or loss in certain involuntary conversion situations. For example, the federal government is continually condemning forests for national parks; as a result, the paper companies who owned these forests are required to report a gain or loss on the condemnation. However, companies such as Georgia Pacific contend that because they must replace this condemned forest land immediately, they are in the same economic position as they were before and no gain or loss should be reported. The issue is whether the condemnation and subsequent purchase should be viewed as one or two transactions. **FASB Interpretation No. 30** requires "that gain or loss be recognized when a nonmonetary asset is involuntarily converted to monetary assets even though an enterprise reinvests or is obligated to reinvest the monetary assets in replacement nonmonetary assets."[12]

The gain or loss that develops on these types of unusual, nonrecurring transactions should normally be shown as an extraordinary item in the income statement. Similar treatment would be given to other types of involuntary conversions such as those resulting from a major casualty (such as an earthquake) or an expropriation, assuming that it meets the conditions for extraordinary item treatment. The difference between the amount recovered (condemnation award or insurance recovery), if any, and the book value of the asset would be reflected as a gain or loss. The determination of the insurance proceeds to be received in a casualty situation is sometimes quite complex; it is discussed in the appendix to this chapter.

Miscellaneous Problems

If an asset is scrapped or abandoned without any cash recovery, a loss should be recognized in the amount of the asset's book value. If scrap value exists, the gain or loss that occurs is the difference between the asset's scrap value and its book value. If an asset still can be used even though it is fully depreciated, either the asset may be kept on the books at historical cost less its related depreciation or the asset may be carried at scrap value. If the asset is written up or down to scrap value, the gain or loss could be recognized, although many accountants believe that recognition of the gain or loss violates the realization principle. Footnote disclosure of the amount of fully depreciated assets in service should be made in the financial statements.

OTHER ASSET VALUATION METHODS

We have generally assumed that accountants have used cost as the basis for valuing assets at acquisition. The major exception has been the acquisition of plant assets through donation. Another approach that is sometimes allowed and not considered a violation of historical cost is a concept often referred to as **prudent cost.**

---

[12]"Accounting for Involuntary Conversions of Nonmonetary Assets to Monetary Assets," *FASB Interpretation No. 30* (Stamford, Conn.: FASB, 1979), summary paragraph.

This concept states that if for some reason you were ignorant about a certain price and paid too much for the asset originally, it is theoretically preferable to charge a loss immediately. As an example, assume that a company constructs an asset at a cost substantially in excess of its present economic usefulness. In this case, an appropriate procedure would be to charge these excess costs as a loss to the current period, rather than capitalize them as part of the cost of the asset. This problem seldom develops because at the outset individuals either use good reasoning in paying a given price or fail to recognize any such errors. On the other hand, a purchase that is obtained at a bargain, or a piece of equipment internally constructed at what amounts to a cost savings, should not result in immediate recognition of income under any circumstances. Although conceptually immediate recognition of income is appealing, the implications of such a treatment would be to change completely the entire basis of accounting.

There are several concepts of valuation other than historical cost that might be used to value property, plant, and equipment such as: (1) constant dollar accounting (adjustments for general price-level changes), (2) current cost accounting (adjustments for specific price-level changes), (3) fair market value, or (4) a combination of constant dollar accounting and one of these other methods. These valuation methods are discussed in Chapter 25.

The general accounting rule of lower of cost or market does not apply to property, plant, and equipment. And, even when property, plant, and equipment has suffered partial obsolescence, accountants are reluctant to write it down to net realizable value. This reluctance stems from the fact that it is difficult to arrive at a net realizable value that is not subjective and arbitrary for property, plant, and equipment, unlike inventories, for which values can be more easily obtained. In addition, many argue that depreciation is a method of cost allocation and, therefore, should not be concerned with valuation. Finally, there is some concern that permitting write-offs of this type may lead companies to make unreasonable write-offs in bad years to insure that future periods will be relieved of these costs (the "big bath" phenomenon). We are not sympathetic with these arguments and believe that whenever a permanent impairment in the revenue-producing ability of property, plant, and equipment occurs, a loss should be recognized.

APPENDIX

Casualty Insurance

Business enterprises constantly face the risk of loss of assets by fire, storm, theft, accident, or other casualties. Generally companies shift the burden of such losses by entering into a casualty insurance contract whereby an insurance company in consideration for a premium payment assumes the risk of all or a portion of these losses. The premium, a charge per $100 of insurance carried, is paid in advance. Because a premium discount is given when the term of the policy exceeds one year, many companies pay insurance premiums in advance for periods of three to five years, creating the asset (deferred charge) **prepaid insurance.**

When an insured asset is damaged, destroyed, or lost, the relevant accounts must be adjusted and settlement with the insurance company must be completed. The maximum amount recoverable is the **fair market value** of the property at the date of loss and is referred to as the **insurable value.** Although the book value is irrelevant in determining the amount recoverable from the insurance company, it is used for accounting purposes to measure the loss (or gain) resulting from the casualty and any insurance settlement. For example, if $40,000 is recovered under an insurance policy after the complete destruction of an asset having a book value of $34,000, a gain of $6,000 would be recognized. In some instances the amount recoverable is limited by some special feature such as a **deductible clause** in the case of automobile insurance ($50 or $100 deductible) or a **coinsurance clause** in the case of fire insurance.

Coinsurance

Because most assets are only partially destroyed by any casualty, companies would take out only enough insurance to cover a fraction of the value of the asset and receive full reimbursement of most losses if they were not encouraged through a coinsurance clause to do otherwise. Most casualty insurance policies therefore contain a **coinsurance clause** which provides that if the property is insured for less than a certain percentage (frequently 80%) of its fair market value (insurable value) at the time of the loss, the insurance company will be liable for only a portion of any loss, that is, the owner becomes a **coinsurer** with the insurance company.

Stated proportionately, coinsurance means that the amount recoverable is to the loss as the face value of the policy (amount of insurance carried) is to the coinsurance requirement (amount of insurance that should be carried). As a formula, coinsurance may be stated as follows:

$$\frac{\text{Face value of policy}}{\text{Coinsurance requirement}} \times \text{Loss} = \text{Amount Recoverable}$$

The following examples illustrate the use of the formula in determining the amount recoverable using an 80% coinsurance clause.

Amount Recoverable Under Coinsurance				
	Case 1	Case 2	Case 3	Case 4
Fair market value	$10,000	$10,000	$10,000	$10,000
Face value of policy	7,000	5,000	9,000	8,000
Coinsurance requirement	8,000	8,000	8,000	8,000
Amount of loss	6,000	6,000	6,000	9,000
Amount recoverable	5,250[a]	3,750[b]	6,000[c]	8,000[d]

[a] $\dfrac{\$7,000}{\$8,000} \times \$6,000 = \$5,250$

[b] $\dfrac{\$5,000}{\$8,000} \times \$6,000 = \$3,750$

[c] $\dfrac{\$9,000}{\$8,000} \times \$6,000 = \$6,750$*

[d] $\dfrac{\$8,000}{\$8,000} \times \$9,000 = \$9,000$**

*Amount recoverable limited to amount of loss.
**Amount recoverable limited to face value of policy.

As illustrated above, the amount recoverable from the insurance company is the lowest of (1) the amount of the loss, (2) the face value of the policy, or (3) the coinsurance formula amount.

Recovery from Multiple Policies

If an asset is insured under two or more insurance policies, all of which have the same or **no coinsurance** requirement, recovery of a loss is obtained from the different policies in proportion to the face value of each policy. If the policies have **different coinsurance** requirements, the amount recoverable under each of the policies is computed by multiplying the loss by a fraction, the numerator of which is the face value of the individual policy, and the denominator of which is the higher of (1) the total face value of all policies, or (2) the amount required under the coinsurance requirement of the particular policy. To illustrate, assume that an asset having a fair market value of $100,000 is insured under policies presented on the next page, and that a fire loss of $72,000 is suffered.

If the policies contain the same (90%) coinsurance requirement, recovery from each policy would be as follows:

Amount Recoverable Under Multiple Policies with Identical Coinsurance

Policy	Face Value	Coinsurance Requirement	Fraction	Loss	Amount Collectible
A	$30,000	$90,000	30/90	$72,000	$24,000
B	40,000	90,000	40/90	72,000	32,000
C	10,000	90,000	10/90	72,000	8,000
	$80,000				$64,000

If the policies contain different (70%, 85%, and 90%) coinsurance requirements, recovery from each policy would be as follows:

Amount Recoverable Under Multiple Policies with Different Coinsurance

Policy	Face Value	Coinsurance Requirement	Fraction	Loss	Amount Collectible
A	$30,000	$70,000	30/80	$72,000	$27,000
B	40,000	85,000	40/85	72,000	33,882
C	10,000	90,000	10/90	72,000	8,000
	$80,000				$68,882

Accounting for Casualty Losses

In the event of a casualty loss the accounting records as maintained or as reconstructed (if destroyed in the casualty) must be adjusted as of the date of the casualty. The loss may be summarized in a casualty loss account, charging such account for the book value of the assets destroyed or damaged and crediting it for amounts recoverable from salvage and from insurance companies. The total amount recoverable (receivable) from the insurance companies would be classified as a current asset if current settlement is anticipated. If the casualty loss is material and the consequence of an unusual and infrequent event or circumstance, it would be classified as an extraordinary item.

Because the amount recovered under insurance policies is based upon fair market and appraised values, the insurance proceeds may exceed the book value of the assets destroyed or damaged. The excess of insurance proceeds over the book value should be presented as a book gain.

Questions

1. What are the major characteristics of plant assets?
2. What are the principal types of items that should be included in the cost of a purchased machine? Would merchandise bought for resale be valued initially on the same basis?

3. Indicate where the following items would be shown on a balance sheet.
   (a) Attorney's fees and recording fees related to purchasing land.
   (b) Variable overhead related to construction of machinery.
   (c) Cost of temporary building for workers during construction of building.
   (d) Interest expense on bonds payable incurred during construction of a building.
   (e) Sidewalks that are maintained by the city.
   (f) A parking lot servicing employees in the building.
   (g) The cost of demolishing an old building that was on the land when purchased.
   (h) A lien that was attached to the land when purchased.
   (i) Landscaping costs.

4. Once equipment has been installed and placed in operation, subsequent expenditures relating to this equipment are frequently thought of as being in the nature of repairs or general maintenance and, hence, chargeable to operations in the period in which the expenditure is made. Actually, determination of whether such an expenditure should be charged to operations or capitalized involves a much more careful analysis of the character of the expenditure. What are the factors that should be considered in making such a decision? Discuss fully.

5. What accounting treatment is normally given to the following items in accounting for plant assets?
   (a) Major repairs.
   (b) Improvements and replacements.
   (c) Additions.

6. Name the items, in addition to the amount paid to the former owner or contractor, that may be properly included as part of the acquisition cost of the following plant assets:
   (a) Buildings.
   (b) Machinery and equipment.
   (c) Land.

7. Three positions have normally been taken with respect to the recording of fixed manufacturing overhead as an element of the cost of plant assets constructed by a company for its own use:
   (a) It should be excluded completely.
   (b) It should be included at the same rate as is charged to normal operations.
   (c) It should be allocated on the basis of the lost production that occurs from normal operations.
   What are the circumstances or rationale that support or deny the application of these methods?

8. Expenditures may be divided into two general categories: (1) capital expenditures and (2) revenue expenditures.
   (a) Distinguish between these two categories of expenditures and between their treatments in the accounts.
   (b) Discuss the impact on both present and future balance sheets and income statements of improperly distinguishing between capital and revenue expenditures.
   (c) What criteria do accountants generally use in establishing a policy for classifying expenditures under these two general categories?

9. The Hunt Trucking Company purchased a heavy-duty truck on July 1, 1977, for $30,000. It was estimated that it would have a useful life of 10 years and then would have a trade-in value of $6,000. It was traded on October 1, 1981, for a similar truck costing $38,000; $14,000 was allowed as trade-in value on the old truck and $24,000 was paid in cash. What is the entry to record the trade-in? The company uses the straight-line method.

10. The Buildings account of a corporation includes the following items that were used in determining the basis for depreciating the cost of a building:
    (a) Organization and promotion expenses.
    (b) Architect's fees.
    (c) Interest and taxes during construction.
    (d) Commission paid on the sale of capital stock.

(e) Bond discount and expenses.

Do you agree with these charges? If not, how would you deal with each of the items above in the corporation's books and in its annual financial statements?

11. New machinery, which replaced a number of employees, was installed and put in operation in the last month of the fiscal year. The employees had been dismissed after payment of an extra month's wages and this amount was added to the cost of the machinery. Discuss the propriety of the charge and, if it was improper, describe the proper treatment.

12. To what extent do you consider the following items to be proper costs of the fixed asset? Give reasons for your opinions.
    (a) Freight on equipment returned before installation, for replacement by other equipment of greater capacity.
    (b) Cost of moving machinery to a new location.
    (c) Cost of plywood partitions erected as part of the remodeling of the office.
    (d) Replastering of a section of the building.
    (e) Cost of a new motor for one of the trucks.
    (f) Overhead of a business that builds its own equipment.
    (g) Cost of constructing new models of machinery.
    (h) Cash discounts on purchases of equipment.
    (i) Interest paid during construction of a building.
    (j) Cost of a safety device installed on a machine.

13. Discuss the basic accounting problem that arises in handling each of the following situations.
    (a) Assets purchased by issuance of capital stock.
    (b) Acquisition of plant assets by gift or donation.
    (c) Purchase of a plant asset subject to a cash discount.
    (d) Assets purchased on a long-term credit basis.
    (e) A group of assets acquired for a lump sum.
    (f) An asset traded in or exchanged for another asset.

14. Recently, a large manufacturing enterprise presented the account "Allowance for Repairs" in the long-term liability section. Evaluate this procedure.

15. Cole Enterprises has a number of fully depreciated assets that are still being used in the main operations of the business. Because the assets are fully depreciated, the president of the company decides not to show them on the balance sheet or disclose this information in the footnotes. Evaluate this procedure.

16. Recently, Morrow, Inc. decided to discontinue production of one of its product lines because demand for it had fallen substantially. Although it is highly unlikely that the plant may be used for this type of production in the future, the controller is reluctant to write the plant down to its net realizable value. Why might the controller be reluctant to write the asset down?

*17. What is the objective of a coinsurance clause in a casualty insurance policy?

Note: All **asterisked** questions, cases, exercises, or problems relate to material contained in the appendix to each chapter.

Cases

C11-1 You have recently been hired as a junior accountant in the firm of Hargrove, Tick, and Check. Mr. Hargrove is an alumnus of the same school from which you graduated and, therefore, is quite interested in your accounting training. He therefore presents the following situations and asks for your response.

Situation I

Recently a construction company agreed to construct a new hospital for its client at the construction company's cost; that is, the contractor was to realize no profit. The construction company was interested in performing this service because it had substantial interests in the community and wanted to make the community more attractive. The building was completed in 1980, and the costs of the hospital were $7,000,000. An appraisal firm indicated, however, that the fair market value of the properties was $8,500,000, the difference due to the $1,500,000 that the company did not charge the hospital. **Instructions** At what amount should the hospital value the asset? A related question is whether the donated property should be reported as income or as a capital contribution. What is your answer to this question?

Situation II

Recently, one of our clients asked whether it would be appropriate to capitalize a portion of the salaries of the corporate officers for time spent on construction activities. During construction, one of the officers devotes full time to the supervision of construction projects. His activities are similar to those of a construction superintendent for a general contractor. During periods of heavy construction activity, this officer also employs several assistants to help with administrative matters related to construction. All other officers are general corporate officers.

The compensation and other costs related to the construction officer are not dependent upon the level of construction activity in a particular period (except to the extent that additional assistants are employed on a short-term basis). These expenses would continue to be incurred even if there was no construction activity unless the company decided to discontinue permanently, or for the foreseeable future, all construction activity. In that case, it could well reach the decision to terminate the construction officer. The company has, however, aggressive expansion plans which anticipate continuing construction of shopping center properties. **Instructions** What salary costs, if any, should be capitalized to the cost of properties?

Situation III

Every few years one of our clients publishes a new catalog for distribution to its sales outlets and customers. The latest catalog was published in 1976. Periodically, current price lists and new product brochures are issued. The company is now contemplating the issue of a new catalog during the latter part of 1979. The cost of the new catalog has been accounted for as follows:

(a) Estimated total cost of the catalog is accounted for over a period beginning with the initial planning (1977) and is expected to end at time of publication.

(b) Estimated costs are accumulated in an accrued liability account through monthly charges to selling expenses.

(c) Monthly charges were based upon the estimated total cost of the guide and the estimated number of months remaining before publication; periodic revisions were made to the estimates as current information became available.

(d) Actual costs were recorded as charges to the accrued liability account as they were accrued.

In summary, the company accrues the entire estimated cost (including anticipated costs to be incurred) of a contemplated catalog through charges to operations prior to the expected publication date. **Instructions** Comment on the propriety of this treatment.

C11-2   Warren Manufacturing, Inc. began operations five years ago producing stetrics, a new type of instrument it hoped to sell to doctors, dentists, and hospitals. The demand for stetrics far exeeded initial expectations, and the company was unable to produce enough stetrics to meet demand.

The company was manufacturing its product on equipment that it built at the start of its operations. To meet demand, more efficient equipment was needed. The company decided to design and build the equipment since the equipment currently available on the market was unsuitable for producing stetrics.

In 1980 a section of the plant was devoted to development of the new equipment and a special staff of personnel was hired. Within six months a machine was developed at a cost of $210,000 which successfully increased production and reduced labor costs substantially. Sparked by the success of the new machine, the company built three more machines of the same type at a cost of $130,000 each.

Instructions

(a) In general, what costs should be capitalized for self-constructed plant?

(b) Discuss the propriety of including in the capitalized cost of self-constructed assets:
1. The increase in overhead caused by the self-construction of fixed assets.
2. A proportionate share of overhead on the same basis as that applied to goods manufactured for sale.

(c) Discuss the proper accounting treatment of the $80,000 ($210,000 − $130,000) by which the cost of the first machine exceeded the cost of the subsequent machines. This additional cost should not be considered research and development costs.

C11-3 Your client, Shirtsleeve Co., found three suitable sites, each having certain unique advantages, for a new plant facility. In order to thoroughly investigate the advantages and disadvantages of each site, one-year options were purchased for an amount equal to 6% of the contract price of each site. The costs of the options cannot be applied against the contracts. Before the options expired, one of the sites was purchased at the contract price of $110,000. The option on this site had cost $6,600. The two options not exercised had cost $4,000 each.

Instructions

Present arguments in support of recording the cost of the land at each of the following amounts.

1. $110,000.
2. $116,600.
3. $124,600.

(AICPA adapted)

C11-4 You have been engaged to examine the financial statements of Goldman Corporation for the year ending December 31, 1981. Goldman Corporation was organized in January, 1981, by Messrs. Moses and Price, original owners of options to acquire oil leases on 5,000 acres of land for $350,000. They expected that first the oil leases would be acquired by the corporation and subsequently 180,000 shares of the corporation's common stock would be sold to the public at $6 per share. In February 1981, they exchanged their options, $150,000 cash, and $50,000 of other assets for 75,000 shares of common stock of the corporation. The corporation's board of directors appraised the leases at $600,000, basing its appraisal on the price of other acreage recently leased in the same area. The options were therefore recorded at $250,000 ($600,000 − $350,000 option price).

The options were exercised by the corporation in March, 1981, prior to the sale of common stock to the public in April, 1981. Leases on approximately 500 acres of land were abandoned as worthless during the year.

Instructions

(a) Why is the valuation of assets acquired by a corporation in exchange for its own common stock sometimes difficult?

(b) 1. What reasoning might Goldman Corporation use to support valuing the leases at $600,000, the amount of the appraisal by the board of directors?
2. Assuming that the board's appraisal was sincere, what steps might Goldman Corporation have taken to strengthen its position to use the $600,000 value and to provide additional information if questions were raised about possible overvaluation of the leases?

(c) Discuss the propriety of charging one-tenth of the recorded value of the leases against income at December 31, 1981, because leases on 500 acres of land were abandoned during the year.

(AICPA adapted)

C11-5 Senbet Airline is converting from piston-type planes to jets. Delivery time for the jets is three years, during which period substantial progress payments must be made. The multimillion-dollar cost of the planes cannot be financed from working capital; Senbet must borrow funds for the payments.

Because of high interest rates and the large sum to be borrowed, management estimates that interest costs in the second year of the period will be equal to one-third of income before interest and taxes, and one-half of such income in the third year.

After conversion, Senbet's passenger-carrying capacity will be doubled with no increase in the number of planes, although the investment in planes would be substantially increased. The jet planes have a seven-year service life.

Instructions

Give your recommendation concerning the proper accounting for interest during the conversion period. Support your recommendation with reasons **and** suggested accounting treatment. (Disregard income tax implications.)

(AICPA adapted)

C11-6 The invoice price of a machine is $20,000. Various other costs relating to the acquisition and installation of the machine including transportation, electrical wiring, special base, and so on amount to $4,500. The machine has an estimated life of 10 years, with no residual value at the end of that period.

The owner of the business suggests that the incidental costs of $4,500 be charged to expense immediately for the following reasons:

1. If the machine should be sold, these costs cannot be recovered in the sales price;

2. The inclusion of the $4,500 in the machinery account on the books will not necessarily result in a closer approximation of the market price of this asset over the years, because of the possibility of changing demand and supply levels; and

3. Charging the $4,500 to expense immediately will reduce federal income taxes.

Instructions

Discuss **each** of the points raised by the owner of the business.

(AICPA adapted)

Exercises

E11-1 Amcord Company, a newly formed corporation, incurred the following expenditures related to Land, to Buildings, and to Machinery and Equipment.

Architect's fees		$ 2,000
Cash paid for land and dilapidated building thereon		60,000
Removal of old building	$8,000	
Less salvage	1,000	7,000
Abstract company's fee for title search		240
Surveying before construction		400
Interest on short-term loans during construction		6,000
Excavation before construction for basement		12,400
Machinery purchased (subject to 3% cash discount, which was not taken); record net		40,000
Freight on machinery purchased		680
Storage charges on machinery, necessitated by noncompletion of building when machinery was delivered		970
New building constructed (building construction took 6 months from date of purchase of land and old building)		360,000
Assessment by city for drainage project		790

Hauling charges for delivery of machinery from storage to new building	260
Trees, shrubs, and other landscaping after completion of building (permanent in nature)	4,000
Installation of machinery	1,240

Instructions

Determine the amounts that should be debited to Land, to Buildings, and to Machinery and Equipment accounts. Assume the benefits of capitalizing interest during construction exceed the cost of implementation.

E11-2 The Bateman Co. purchased land as a factory site for $150,000. Two old buildings were standing on the site. The process of tearing down the old buildings and constructing the factory required six months.

  The company paid $6,000 to raze the old buildings and sold salvaged lumber and brick for $1,050. Legal fees of $780 were paid for title investigation and drawing the purchase contract. Payment to an engineering firm was made for a land survey, $900, and for drawing the factory plans, $30,000. The land survey had to be made before definitive plans could be drawn. Title insurance on the property cost $750, and a liability insurance premium paid during construction was $300. The contractor's charge for construction was $1,125,000. The company paid the contractor in two installments: $600,000 at the end of three months and $525,000 upon completion. Interest costs of $22,500 were incurred to finance the construction.

Instructions

Determine the cost of the land and the cost of the building as they should be recorded on the books of the Bateman Co. Assume that the land survey was for the building.

E11-3 The following property control account is shown on the books of the Keenguy Company.

Balance Dec. 31, 1980 (Property)			$586,000
Additions			
Feb. 28	Transfer from construction work in progress— building completed	$120,000	
28	Interest cost on construction in progress	15,000	
June 30	1981 taxes on real estate (Valuations: land, $50,000; building, $100,000—Rate, $3 per $100)	4,500	
July 31	Legal and other expenses re title search of property not acquired	300	
Oct. 31	Purchase of two machines, including freight, $79, and installation, $100	1,079	
31	Cost of removing used machines replaced by machines just purchased	243	
Nov. 30	Cost of moving the two machines to third floor to effect more economical operation	173	141,295
			$727,295
Credits			
Mar. 31	Removal of the cost of the old machine		2,000
Balance Dec. 31, 1981			$725,295

Instructions

What adjustments would you suggest and why? Assume the benefits of capitalizing interest during construction exceed the cost of implementation.

E11-4   Chem Systems, Inc. constructed some machinery for its own use, and expended the following amounts:

Direct labor	$24,000
Materials and supplies	42,000
Total	$66,000

In the manufacture of furniture the company regularly uses a predetermined factory overhead rate of 50% of direct labor cost in applying factory overhead to production.

It is estimated that factory overhead costs increased in the amount of $6,000 for the year because of the manufacture of the above-mentioned machinery.

If the company had purchased the machinery that it constructed from an outside firm, it would have cost $84,000.

Instructions

For what amount should the company debit its Machinery account? Justify your answer.

E11-5   Surely Co. machine shop builds machines for its regular manufacturing department. During 1980, the company built a machine that had the following costs associated with it:

	Machinery Cost
Material and purchased parts	$ 6,000
Freight on material and parts	600
Insurance in transit	75
Implicit interest on tied-up	
working capital	60
Labor to build	9,000
Labor to test	1,500
Overhead	4,500
	$21,735

The machine immediately after construction has a fair market value of $28,000.

Instructions

What dollar amount should appear in Surely's balance sheet for this machinery?

E11-6   Rockwell, Inc. has decided to purchase equipment from IDS Industries on January 2, 1980, to expand its production capacity to meet customers' demand for its product. Rockwell issues a $600,000, five-year, noninterest-bearing note to IDS for the new equipment when the prevailing market rate of interest for obligations of this nature is 8%. The company will pay off the note in five $120,000 installments due at the end of each year over the life of the note.

Instructions

(a) Prepare the journal entry(ies) at the date of purchase. (Round to nearest dollar in all computations.)

(b) Prepare the journal entry(ies) at the end of the first year to record the payment and interest, assuming that the company employs the effective interest method.

(c) Prepare the journal entry(ies) at the end of the second year to record the payment and interest.

(d) Assuming that the equipment had a 10-year life and no salvage value, prepare the journal entry necessary to record depreciation in the first year. (Straight-line depreciation is employed.)

E11-7 Ross, Inc. purchased a computer on December 31, 1979, at a price of $40,000, paying $10,000 down and agreeing to pay the balance in four equal installments of $7,500 payable each December 31 beginning in 1980. An assumed interest of 8% is implicit in the purchase price.

Instructions

(a) Prepare the journal entry(ies) at the date of purchase.

(b) Prepare the journal entry(ies) at December 31, 1980, to record the payment and interest (effective interest method employed).

(c) Prepare the journal entry(ies) at December 31, 1981, to record the payment and interest (effective interest method employed).

E11-8 The Kitefly Corporation, which manufactures shoes, hired a recent college graduate to work in their accounting department. On the first day of work, the accountant was assigned to total a batch of invoices with the use of an adding machine. Before long, the accountant, who had never before seen such a machine, managed to break the machine. The Kitefly Corporation gave the machine plus $620 to the Lear Business Machine Company in exchange for a new machine. Assume the following information about the machines:

	Kitefly Corp. (Old Machine)	Lear Co. (New Machine)
Machine cost	$500	$600
Accumulated depreciation	250	-0-
Fair value	100	720

Instructions

For each company, prepare the necessary journal entry to record the exchange.

E11-9 The Republic Company exchanged equipment used in its manufacturing operations plus $2,000 in cash for similar equipment used in the operations of the Tyler Company. The following information pertains to the exchange:

	Republic Co.	Tyler Co.
Equipment (cost)	$24,000	$22,000
Accumulated depreciation	20,000	5,000
Fair value of equipment	12,000	14,000
Cash given up	2,000	

Instructions

Prepare the journal entries to record the exchange on the books of both companies.

E11-10 Union Company has negotiated the purchase of a new piece of automatic equipment at a price of $36,000, f.o.b. factory. Union paid $7,500 cash, gave an installment note calling for monthly payments of $2,100 for 10 months plus interest at 8% on the unpaid balance, and traded in used equipment. The used equipment had originally cost $27,000; it had a book value of $9,000 and a second-hand market value of $5,250, as indicated by recent transactions involving similar equipment. Freight and installation charges for the new equipment amounted to $1,500.

Instructions

(a) Prepare the general journal entry to record this transaction, assuming that the assets Union exchanged are similar in nature.

(b) Assuming the same facts as in (a) except that the asset traded in has a fair market value of $10,500, prepare the general journal entry to record this transaction.

E11-11 Sperry Company purchased an electric wax melter on 6/30/81 by trading in their old gas model and paying the balance in cash. The following data relate to the purchase:

List price of new melter	$12,000
Cash paid	6,960
Cost of old melter (eight-year life, no residual value)	9,600
Accumulated depreciation—old melter (straight-line)	5,400
Second-hand market value of old melter	4,320

Instructions

Prepare the journal entry(ies) necessary to record this exchange, assuming that the melters exchanged are (1) similar in nature; (2) dissimilar in nature. Sperry's fiscal year ends on 12/31 and depreciation has been recorded through 12/31/80.

E11-12 On October 1, Bell's, a local entertainment establishment, acquired a new piano that had a list price of $1,700. Bell received a trade-in allowance of $1,200 on its old piano, which had a book value of $900 (original cost $1,400). The fair market value of the old piano was $700. The remainder owed by Bell was paid in cash.

Instructions

(a) Prepare the journal entry to record this transaction.

(b) What significance does the list price have for this computation?

E11-13 Presented below is information related to the National Company.

1. On July 6 the National Company acquired the plant assets of the Sem Company, which had discontinued operations. The appraised value of the property is:

Land	$ 200,000
Building	1,400,000
Machinery and Equipment	400,000
Total	$2,000,000

The National Company gave 12,000 shares of its $100 par value common stock in exchange. The stock had a market value of $150 per share on the date of the purchase of the property.

2. The National Company expended the following amounts in cash between July 6 and December 15, the date when it first occupied the building.

Repairs to building	$ 70,000
Construction of bases for machinery to be installed later	120,000
Driveways and parking lots	100,000
Remodeling of office space in building, including new partitions and walls	160,000
Special assessment by city	10,400

3. On December 20, the company paid cash for machinery, $180,000, subject to a 2% cash discount, and freight on machinery of $7,000.

Instructions

Prepare entries on the books of the National Company for these transactions.

E11-14 Below are transactions related to Ronald Manufacturing Company.

1. On March 10, 1981, Ronald Manufacturing Company purchases land with an appraised value of $12,000 and buildings with an appraised value of $30,000 for $36,000.

2. Between March 10, 1981, and September 1, 1981, the date of occupancy, the company expends the following amounts in cash.

Additional wing constructed	$21,600
Replastering	3,600
Additional windows and doors	2,160
Repairs to roof	2,640
Brick pointing and masonry repairs	4,380
Painting and decorating	4,920

Instructions

(a) Prepare entries on the books of the Ronald Manufacturing Company to reflect the information given above.

(b) Prepare entries to record depreciation on a straight-line basis at December 31, 1981, assuming a 20-year life.

E11-15   Below are transactions related to Emhart Company.

(a) The City of Belleville gives the company five acres of land as a plant site. The market value of this land is determined to be $40,000.

(b) 10,000 shares of common stock with a par value of $50 per share are issued in exchange for land and buildings. The property has been appraised at a fair market value of $560,000, of which $200,000 has been allocated to land and $360,000 to buildings. The stock of the Emhart Company is not listed on any exchange, but a block of 100 shares was sold by a stockholder 12 months ago at $60 per share, and a block of 200 shares was sold by another stockholder 18 months ago at $55 per share.

(c) No entry has been made to remove from the accounts for Materials, Factory Supplies, Direct Labor, and Overhead the amounts properly chargeable to plant asset accounts for machinery constructed during the year. The following information is given relative to costs of the machinery constructed.

Materials used	$ 8,000
Factory supplies used	800
Direct labor incurred	9,300
Additional overhead (over regular) caused by construction of machinery	1,800
Fixed overhead rate applied to regular manufacturing operations	50% of direct labor cost
Cost of similar machinery if it had been purchased from outside suppliers	$29,000

Instructions

Prepare journal entries on the books of the Emhart Company to record these transactions.

E11-16   The following transactions occurred during 1981. Assume that depreciation of 10% per year is charged on all machinery and 4% per year on buildings, on a straight-line basis, with no estimated salvage value. Depreciation is charged for a full year on all fixed assets acquired during the year, and no depreciation is charged on fixed assets disposed of during the year.

Jan. 30   A building that cost $45,000 in 1958 is torn down to make room for a new building. The wrecking contractor was paid $3,000 and was permitted to keep all materials salvaged.

Mar. 10   Machinery that was purchased in 1972 for $12,000 is sold for $1,350 cash, f.o.b. purchaser's plant. Freight of $300 is paid on this machinery.

Mar. 20   A gear breaks on a machine that cost $9,000 in 1975 and the gear is replaced at a cost of $500.

May 18   A special base installed for a machine in 1976 when the machine was purchased has to be replaced at a cost of $4,500 because of defective workmanship on the original base. The cost of the machinery was $10,500 in 1976; the cost of the base was $3,300, and this amount was charged to the Machinery account in 1976.

June 23   One of the buildings is repainted at a cost of $4,000. It had not been painted since it was constructed in 1977.

Instructions

Prepare general journal entries for the transactions.

E11-17 Presented below is information related to the United Company.

1. In January, 1977, the United Company built a loading dock to accommodate heavy tractor- and trailer-type trucks at a cost of $19,000 as follows:

Labor	$10,000
Materials	6,000
Estimated overhead	3,000

It is estimated that this structure will have a useful life of 20 years.

2. During 1979 several planks in the loading platform split and were weakened to such an extent that they had to be replaced at a cost of $120.

3. In July, 1980, the entire dock was repainted at a cost of $300.

4. An inexperienced driver backed into the end of the dock and caused considerable damage in February, 1981. The company for which he worked was insured against such accidents, and a settlement of $1,800 was obtained. Cost to the United Company of repairing the damage was: labor, $700, and materials, $500 and overhead, $200.

5. In June, 1981, a hailstorm damaged the roof. A settlement of $1,400 was obtained from the insurance company. It was decided, however, that a new roof would soon be needed and repairs were not worthwhile. Therefore nothing was done until October, when a roofing contractor was engaged to reroof the loading dock at a price of $3,600.

Instructions

State how each of the items above should be recorded in the accounts and support your conclusions.

E11-18 Able Corporation purchased conveyor equipment with a list price of $5,000. The vendor's credit terms were 2/10, n/30. Presented below are three independent cases related to the equipment. Assume that the purchases of equipment are recorded gross.

(a) Able paid cash for the equipment eight days after the purchase.

(b) Able traded in equipment with a book value of $300, and paid $4,700 in cash one month after the purchase. The old equipment could have been sold for $300 at the date of trade.

(c) Able gave the vendor a $4,100 noninterest-bearing note for the equipment on the date of purchase. The note was due in one year and was paid on time. Assume that the effective interest rate in the market was 10%. (Round to the nearest dollar.)

Instructions

Prepare the general journal entries required to record the acquisition and payment in each of the independent cases above.

*E11-19 Presented below are data for three independent cases involving coinsurance coverage.

	Case 1	Case 2	Case 3
Fair market value at date of loss	$60,000	$45,000	$120,000
Face value of policy	36,000	39,600	72,000
Coinsurance requirement (80%)	48,000	36,000	96,000
Amount of loss	30,000	27,000	120,000

Instructions

For each of the cases above compute the amount recoverable.

Problems

P11-1 At December 31, 1979, certain accounts included in the property, plant, and equipment section of the Townsand Company's balance sheet had the following balances:

Land	$100,000
Buildings	800,000
Leasehold improvements	500,000
Machinery and equipment	700,000

During 1980 the following transactions occurred:

Land site number 621 was acquired for $1,000,000. In addition, to acquire the land Townsand paid a $60,000 commission to a real estate agent. Costs of $15,000 were incurred to clear the land. During the course of clearing the land, timber and gravel were recovered and sold for $5,000.

A second tract of land (site number 622) with a building was acquired for $300,000. The closing statement indicated that the land value was $200,000 and the building value was $100,000. Shortly after acquisition, the building was demolished at a cost of $30,000. A new building was constructed for $150,000 plus the following costs:

Excavation fees	$11,000
Architectural design fees	8,000
Building permit fee	1,000
Imputed interest on funds used	
during construction (stock financing)	6,000

The building was completed and occupied on September 30, 1980.

A third tract of land (site number 623) was acquired for $600,000 and was put on the market for resale.

During December 1980 costs of $65,000 were incurred to improve leased office space. The related lease will terminate on December 31, 1982, and is not expected to be renewed. (Hint: Leasehold improvements should be handled in the same manner as land improvements.)

A group of new machines was purchased under a royalty agreement which provides for payment of royalties based on units of production for the machines. The invoice price of the machines was $75,000, freight costs were $2,000, unloading charges were $1,500, and royalty payments for 1980 were $13,000.

Instructions

(a) Prepare a detailed analysis of the changes in each of the following balance sheet accounts for 1980:

  Land
  Buildings
  Leasehold improvements
  Machinery and equipment

Disregard the related accumulated depreciation accounts.

(b) List the items in the fact situation that were not used to determine the answer to (a) above, and indicate where, or if, these items should be included in Townsand's financial statements.

(AICPA adapted)

P11-2   Presented below is a schedule of property dispositions for Hanner Corporation

Schedule of Property Dispositions

	Cost	Accumulated Depreciation	Cash Proceeds	Fair Market Value	Nature of Disposition
Land	$22,000	—	$20,000	$20,000	Condemnation
Building	6,800	—	2,100	—	Demolition
Warehouse	60,000	$7,978	58,000	58,000	Destruction by fire
Machine	4,000	1,700	600	3,300	Trade-in
Furniture	8,200	6,560	—	1,900	Contribution
Automobile	6,000	2,250	3,000	3,000	Sale

The following additional information is available

Land—On February 15, a condemnation award was received as consideration for unimproved land held primarily as an investment, and on March 31, another parcel of unimproved land to be held as an investment was purchased at a cost of $21,500.

Building—On April 2, land and building were purchased at a total cost of $34,000, of which 20% was allocated to the building on the corporate books. The real estate was acquired with the intention of demolishing the building, and this was accomplished during the month of November. Cash proceeds received in November represent the net proceeds from demolition of the building.

Warehouse—On June 30, the warehouse was destroyed by fire. The warehouse was purchased January 2, 1970, and had depreciated $7,978. On December 27, part of the insurance proceeds was used to purchase a replacement warehouse at a cost of $53,000.

Machine—On December 26, the machine was exchanged for another machine having a fair market value of $2,700 and cash of $600 was received. (Round to nearest dollar.)

Furniture—On August 15, furniture was contributed to a qualified charitable organization. No other contributions were made or pledged during the year.

Automobile—On November 3, the automobile was sold to Fred Bates, a stockholder.

Instructions

Indicate how these items would be reported on the income statement of Hanner Corporation.

(AICPA adapted)

P11-3   During 1981, Norlin Company manufactured a machine for its own use. At December 31, 1981, the account related to that machine is as follows:

Machinery

Machine cost	$ 4,800	Old machine—cost	$4,800
Cost of dismantling old machine	1,200	Cash proceeds from sale of old machine	480
Raw materials used in construction of new machine	18,000	Depreciation for 1981, 10% of $45,120	4,512
Labor in construction of new machine	12,600		
Cost of installation	2,040		
Materials used in trial runs	960		
Profit on construction	10,800		

An analysis of the detail in the account discloses the following:

1. The old machine, which was removed during installation of the new one, has been fully depreciated.

2. Cash discounts received on the payments for materials used in construction totaled $600 and were reported in the "purchases discount" account.

3. The factory overhead account shows a balance of $300,000, which includes variable overhead and total fixed overhead, for the year ended December 31, 1981. $3,600 of the variable overhead is attributable to the production of the machine. Fixed overhead is normally priced to operations at $2 per man-hour of labor. 1,000 man-hours of labor were consumed in the production of the machine.

4. A profit was recognized on construction for the difference between costs incurred and the price at which the machine could have been purchased. The profit was credited to "self-construction gains."

5. Machinery has an estimated life of 10 years with no salvage value. The new machine was used for production beginning July 1, 1981.

Instructions

Prepare the entries necessary to correct the Machinery account as of December 31, 1981, and to record depreciation expense for the year 1981.

P11-4 The Berkey Manufacturing Company was incorporated on January 2, 1981, but was unable to begin manufacturing activities until July 1, 1981, because new factory facilities were not completed until that date.

The Land and Building account at December 31, 1981, was as follows:

January 31, 1981	Land and building	$ 98,000
February 28, 1981	Cost of removal of building	1,500
May 1, 1981	Partial payment of new construction	35,000
May 1, 1981	Legal fees paid	2,000
June 1, 1981	Second payment on new construction	30,000
June 1, 1981	Insurance premium	1,800
June 1, 1981	Special tax assessment	2,500
June 30, 1981	General expenses	12,000
July 1, 1981	Final payment on new construction	35,000
December 31, 1981	Asset write-up	12,500
		$230,300
December 31, 1981	Depreciation—1981 at 1%	2,300
	Account balance	$228,000

The following additional information is to be considered.

1. To acquire land and building the company paid $48,000 cash and 500 shares of its 5% cumulative preferred stock, par value $100 per share. Fair market value of the stock is $100 per share.

2. Cost of removal of old buildings amounted to $1,500, and the demolition company retained all materials of the building.

3. Legal fees covered the following:

Cost of organization	$ 500
Examination of title covering purchase of land	1,000
Legal work in connection with construction contract	500
	$2,000

4. Insurance premium covered the building for three-year term beginning May 1, 1981.

5. General expenses covered the following for the period from January 2, 1981, to June 30, 1981.

President's salary	$ 6,000
Plant superintendent covering supervision of new building	5,000
Office salaries	1,000
	$12,000

6. The special tax assessment covered street improvements that are permanent in nature.

7. Because of a general increase in construction costs after entering into the building contract, the board of directors increased the value of the building $12,500, believing that such an increase was justified to reflect the current market at the time the building was completed. Retained earnings was credited for this amount.

8. Estimated life of building—50 years.
   Write-off for 1981—1% of asset value (1% of $230,000, or $2,300).

Instructions

(a) Prepare entries to reflect correct land, building, and depreciation allowance accounts at December 31, 1981.

(b) Show the proper presentation of land, building, and depreciation on the balance sheet at December 31, 1981.

(AICPA adapted)

P11-5   Martin Corporation wishes to exchange a machine used in its operations. Martin has received the following offers from other companies in the industry:

1. The Alt Company offered to exchange a similar machine plus $22,500.

2. The Dart Company offered to exchange a similar machine.

3. The El Paso Company offered to exchange a similar machine, but wanted $15,000 in addition to Martin's machine.

In addition, Martin contacted the Time Corporation, a dealer in machines. To obtain a new machine, Martin must pay $150,000 in addition to trading in its old machine.

	Martin	Alt	Dart	El Paso	Time
Machine cost	$150,000	$112,500	$262,500	$180,000	$190,000
Accumulated depreciation	60,000	37,500	225,000	108,000	-0-
Fair value	75,000	52,500	75,000	90,000	225,000

Instructions

For each of the four independent situations, prepare the journal entries to record the exchange on the books of each company.

P11-6   On August 1, 1981, Hamilton, Inc. exchanged productive assets with Crowe, Inc. Hamilton's asset is referred to below as "Asset X" and Crowe's is referred to as "Asset Y." The following facts pertain to these assets:

	Asset X	Asset Y
Original cost	$80,000	$100,000
Accumulated depreciation (to date of exchange)	40,000	52,000
Fair market value at date of exchange	50,000	60,000
Cash paid by Hamilton, Inc.	10,000	
Cash received by Crowe, Inc.		10,000

Instructions

(a) Assume that Assets X and Y are similar, and record the exchange for both Hamilton, Inc. and Crowe, Inc. in accordance with generally accepted accounting principles.

(b) Assume that Assets X and Y are dissimilar, and record the exchange for both Hamilton, Inc. and Crowe, Inc. in accordance with generally accepted accounting principles.

P11-7 Presented below are unrelated transactions related to the acquisition of plant assets for Sunset Corp. for the current year.

1. Sunset Corp. acquired a machine with a list price of $130,000 on May 1 of the current year. To acquire this machine, Sunset Corp. exchanged 5,000 shares of its $1.00 par common stock, and paid cash of $40,000. The stock of Sunset Corp. was selling for $13 per share on May 1.

2. A used truck costing $11,000 with a book value of $4,000 is exchanged for a new truck with a fair market value of $8,000 and $6,000 cash is given. Assume that the assets exchanged are similar productive assets.

3. Used machinery having a fair market value of $9,000 and cash of $3,000 is received in exchange for a newer piece of machinery having a book value of $10,000 (original cost $10,500 less accumulated depreciation of $500). Assume that the assets exchanged are similar productive assets.

4. Sunset Corporation purchased plant assets which included land and building for cash of $90,000. Sunset Corp. borrowed $40,000 in cash at 11% interest (principal and interest are due in one year) to finance part of the purchase. The property was appraised for tax purposes as follows: land, $27,000, and building, $54,000. It is decided to use the tax appraisals to allocate cost between the land and the building because the relative tax values appear reasonable.

5. An old computer has a book value of $41,000 (original cost $100,000 less $59,000 accumulated depreciation), and a fair market value of $56,000. A new computer having a fair market value of $130,000 is obtained by paying $74,000 cash and trading in the old computer. Assume that the assets exchanged are considered similar in nature.

Instructions

(a) Prepare the general journal entries necessary to record these transactions during the current year.

(b) Assume that the assets exchanged in the foregoing transactions were dissimilar in nature, and prepare the general journal entries necessary to record these transactions during the current year.

P11-8 During the current year, Clark Construction trades an old crane that has a book value of $84,000 (original cost $108,000 less accumulated depreciation $24,000) for a new crane from Britain Manufacturing Co. The new crane cost Britain $132,000 to manufacture. The following information is also available.

	Clark Const.	Britain Mfg. Co.
Fair market value of old crane	$ 72,000	
Fair market value of new crane		$180,000
Cash paid	108,000	
Cash received		108,000

Instructions

(a) Assume that this exchange is considered to involve dissimilar assets (culmination of the earnings process), and prepare the journal entries on the books of (1) Clark Construction, and (2) Britain Manufacturing.

(b) Assume that this exchange is considered to involve similar assets (no culmination of the earnings process), and prepare the journal entries on the books of (1) Clark Construction, and (2) Britain Manufacturing.

(c) Assuming the same facts as those in (a), except that the fair market value of the old crane is $90,000 and the cash paid $90,000, prepare the journal entries on the books of (1) Clark Construction, and (2) Britain Manufacturing.

(d) Assuming the same facts as those in (b), except that the fair market value of the old crane is $96,000 and the cash paid $84,000, prepare the journal entries on the books of (1) Clark Construction, and (2) Britain Manufacturing.

P11-9   You are engaged in the examination of the financial statements of Goblin Mfg. Company and are auditing the Machinery and Equipment account and the related depreciation accounts for the year ended December 31, 1981.

Your permanent file contains the following schedules.

Machinery and Equipment

	Balance 12/31/79	1980 Retirements	1980 Additions	Balance 12/31/80
1967-70	$ 8,000	$2,100	—	$ 5,900
1971	400	—	—	400
1972	—	—	—	—
1973	—	—	—	—
1974	3,900	—	—	3,900
1975	—	—	—	—
1976	5,300	—	—	5,300
1977	—	—	—	—
1978	4,200	—	—	4,200
1979	—	—	—	—
1980	—	—	$5,700	5,700
	$21,800	$2,100	$5,700	$25,400

Accumulated Depreciation

	Balance 12/31/79	1980 Retirements	1980 Provision	Balance 12/31/80
1967-70	$ 7,840	$2,100	$ 160	$ 5,900
1971	340	—	40	380
1972	—	—	—	—
1973	—	—	—	—
1974	2,145	—	390	2,535
1975	—	—	—	—
1976	1,855	—	530	2,385
1977	—	—	—	—
1978	630	—	420	1,050
1979	—	—	—	—
1980	—	—	285	285
	$12,810	$2,100	$1,825	$12,535

Here is a transcript of the Machinery and Equipment for 1981.

1981	Machinery and Equipment	Ref.	Debit	Credit
Jan. 1	Balance forward		$25,400	
Mar. 1	—Burnham grinder	VR	1,200 *add*	
May 1	—Air compressor	VR	4,500	
June 1	—Power lawnmower	VR	600	
June 1	—Lift truck battery	VR	320	
Aug. 1	—Rockwood saw	CR		$ 150
Nov. 1	—Electric spot welder	VR	4,500	
Nov. 1	—Baking oven	VR	2,800	
Dec. 1	—Baking oven	VR	236	
			39,556	150
Dec. 31	Balance forward			39,406
			$39,556	$39,556

Your examination reveals the following information:

1. The company uses a 10-year life for all machinery and equipment for depreciation purposes. Depreciation is computed by the straight-line method. Six months' depreciation is recorded in the year of acquisition or retirement. For 1981 the company recorded depreciation of $2,800 on machinery and equipment.

2. The Burnham grinder was purchased for cash from a firm in financial distress. The chief engineer and a used machinery dealer agreed that the machine, which was practically new, was worth $2,300 in the open market. *No gain unless sell*

3. For production reasons the new air compressor was installed in a small building that was erected in 1981 to house the machine. The building will also be used for general storage. The cost of the building, which has a 25-year life, was $2,000 and is included in the $4,500 voucher for the air compressor.

4. The power lawnmower was delivered to the home of the company president for personal use.

5. On June 1, the battery in a battery-powered lift truck was accidentally damaged beyond repair. The damaged battery was included at a price of $600 in the $4,200 cost of the lift truck purchased on July 1, 1978. The company decided to rent a replacement battery instead of buying a new battery. The $320 expenditure is the annual rental for the battery paid in advance, net of a $40 allowance for the scrap value of the damaged battery that was returned to the battery company.

6. The Rockwood saw sold on August 1 had been purchased on August 1, 1968, for $1,500. The saw was in use until it was sold.

7. On September 1, the company determined that a production casting machine was no longer needed and advertised it for sale for $1,800 after determining from a used machinery dealer that this was its market value. The casting machine had been purchased for $5,000 on September 1, 1976. *No exchange transaction yet. record loss though*

8. The company elected to exercise an option under a lease-purchase agreement to buy the electric spot welder. The welder had been installed on February 1, 1981, at a monthy rental of $100. Monthly rental payments had been charged as an expense as incurred. (Hint: Capitalize monthly rental payments to Machinery and Equipment.)

9. On November 1, a baking oven was purchased for $10,000. A $2,800 down payment was made, and the balance will be paid in monthly installments over a three-year period. The December 1 payment includes interest charges of $36. Legal title to the oven will not pass to the company until the payments are completed.

Instructions

Prepare the auditor's adjusting journal entries required at December 31, 1981, for machinery and equipment, and the related depreciation. Prepare schedules for detailing the effects of additions and retirements on the assets and related accumulated depreciation balances.

(AICPA adapted)

P11-10 Gremlin Corporation received a $435,000 low bid from a reputable manufacturer for the construction of special production equipment needed by Gremlin in an expansion program. Because the company's own plant was not operating at capacity, Gremlin decided to construct the equipment there and recorded the following production costs related to the construction:

Services of consulting engineer	$ 15,000
Work subcontracted	25,000
Materials	220,000
Plant labor normally assigned to production	65,000
Plant labor normally assigned to maintenance	100,000
Total	$425,000

Management prefers to record the cost of the equipment under the incremental cost method. Approximately 40% of the corporation's production is devoted to government supply contracts which are all based in some way on cost. The contracts require that any self-constructed equipment be allocated its full share of all costs related to the construction.

The following information is also available:

(a) The production labor was for partial fabrication of the equipment in the plant. Skilled personnel were required and were assigned from other projects. The maintenance labor would have been idle time of nonproduction plant employees who would have been retained on the payroll whether or not their services were utilized.

(b) Payroll taxes and employee fringe benefits are approximately 30% of labor cost and are included in manufacturing overhead cost. Total manufacturing overhead for the year was $5,630,000, including the $100,000 maintenance labor used to construct the equipment.

(c) Manufacturing overhead is approximately 50% variable and is applied on the basis of production labor cost. Production labor cost for the year for the corporation's normal products totaled $6,810,000.

(d) General and administrative expenses include $22,500 of allocated executive salary cost and $10,500 of postage, telephone, supplies, and miscellaneous expenses identifiable with this equipment construction.

Instructions

(a) Prepare a schedule computing the amount that should be reported as the full cost of the constructed equipment to meet the requirements of the government contracts. Any supporting computations should be in good form.

(b) Prepare a schedule computing the incremental cost of the constructed equipment.

(c) What is the greatest amount that should be capitalized as the cost of the equipment? Why?

(AICPA adapted)

*P11-11 Sue Kendall, Inc. has two fire insurance policies. Policy A covers the office building at a face value of $360,000 and the furniture and fixtures at a face value of $108,000. Policy B covers only the office building at an additional face value of $140,000. Each policy is with a different insurance company. A fire caused losses to the office building and the furniture and fixtures. The relevant data are summarized below:

	Furniture and Fixtures	Office Building	
Insurance policy	A	A	B
Fair market value of the property **before** fire	$120,000	$720,000	$720,000
Fair market value of the property **after** fire	$ 10,000	$440,000	$440,000
Face of insurance policy	$ 91,200	$360,000	$172,800
Co-insurance requirement	80%	80%	80%

Instructions

Compute the amount due from **each** insurance company for the loss on **each** asset category. Show computations in good form.

(AICPA adapted)

Depreciation and Depletion

Accountants, engineers, lawyers, and economists all define depreciation differently, and probably will continue to do so because each group uses depreciation in a different context.

All agree, however, that most assets are on an inevitable "march to the rubbish heap," and some type of write-down or write-off of cost is needed to indicate that the usefulness of an asset has declined. **Depreciation** is the term most often employed to indicate that tangible plant assets have declined in service potential. Where natural resources, such as timber, oil, and coal, are involved, the term **depletion** is employed. The expiration of intangible assets, such as patents or goodwill, is called **amortization.**

A Method of Cost Allocation

Most individuals at one time or another are party to the trade-in and purchase of an automobile. In discussions with the automobile dealer, depreciation is a consideration on two points. First, how much has the old car "depreciated"? That is, how much is the trade-in value? Second, how fast will the new car depreciate? That is, what will its trade-in value be? In both cases the concept of depreciation is viewed as a valuation approach; depreciation is thought of as a loss in value.

To accountants, depreciation is not a matter of valuation but a means of cost allocation. Assets are not depreciated on the basis of a decline in their fair market value, but on the basis of systematic charges of cost to income.

This approach is employed because between the time the asset is purchased and the time it is sold or junked, fluctuations in the value of the asset may take place. Attempts to measure these interim value changes have not been well received by accountants because values are difficult to measure objectively. Therefore, accountants charge the cost of the asset to depreciation expense over its estimated life, making no attempts at valuation of the asset between acquisition and disposition. The cost allocation approach is justified because a matching of costs with revenues occurs and because fluctuations in market value are tenuous and difficult to measure.

Factors Involved in the Depreciation Process

Before a pattern of charges to revenue can be established, three basic questions must be answered:

1. What depreciation base is to be used for the asset?
2. What is the asset's useful life?
3. What method of cost apportionment is best for this asset?

The answer to these questions involves the distillation of several estimates into one single figure. Keep in mind that the depreciation charge is not a measurement of value changes; **it is an allocation of the cost of the asset.** The calculations on which it is based assume perfect knowledge of the future, which is never attainable.

Depreciation Base for the Asset

The base established for depreciation is a function of two factors: the original cost and salvage or disposal value. In the previous chapter, the procedures used in establishing a cost basis for plant assets were illustrated; little attention was given to salvage value. Salvage value is the estimated amount that will be received at the time the asset is sold or removed from service. The salvage value is the amount to which the asset must be written down or depreciated during its useful life. To illustrate, if an asset has a cost of $10,000 and a salvage value of $1,000, the depreciation base is $9,000.

Original cost	$10,000
Less salvage value	1,000
Depreciation base	$ 9,000

From a practical standpoint, salvage value is often considered to be zero because the valuation is small. Some long-lived assets, however, have substantial residual values.

Companies also differ as to their estimate of salvage value. For example, Leasco, Greyhound Corp., and Boothe Computer all depreciated their IBM 360 equipment on a straight-line basis, but Leasco and Greyhound assumed a 10% salvage value, whereas Boothe assumed zero.

Estimation of Service Lives

There is a basic difference between the service life of an asset and its physical life. A piece of machinery may be physically capable of producing a given product for many years beyond its service life, but the equipment is not used for all of those years because the cost of producing the product in later years may be too high. For example, the old Slater cotton mill in Pawtucket, Rhode Island is preserved in remarkable physical condition as an historic landmark in American industrial development, although its service life was terminated many years ago.[1]

Assets are retired for two reasons: **physical factors** (such as casualty or expiration of physical life) and **economic factors** (obsolescence).

Physical factors are the wear and tear, decay, and casualties that make it difficult for the asset to perform indefinitely. These physical factors set the outside limit for the service life of an asset.

Economic or functional factors are other constraints that develop to shorten the service life of an asset. The reasons why an asset is scrapped before its physical life expires are varied. New processes or techniques or improved machines, for example, may provide the same service at lower costs and with higher quality. Changes in the product may also shorten the service life of the asset. Public requirements may also demand that the asset be retired. Ecological factors, for instance, often play a role in a decision to retire a given asset.

The economic or functional factors can be classified into three categories: inadequacy, supersession, and obsolescence. **Inadequacy** results when an asset ceases to be useful to a given enterprise because the demands of the firm have increased: for example, the need for a larger building to handle increased production. Although the old building may still be sound, it may have become inadequate for that enterprise's purposes. **Supersession** is the replacement of one asset with another more efficient and economical asset: for example, the replacement of a second-generation computer (transistor type) with a third-generation computer (integrated circuit type) or the replacement of the Boeing 727 with the Boeing 747. **Obsolescence** is the catchall for situations not involving inadequacy and supersession. Because the distinction between these categories appears artificial, it is probably best to consider economic factors totally instead of trying to make distinctions that are not clear-cut.

To illustrate the above mentioned concepts, consider a new nuclear power plant. What do you think would be the most important factors in determining its useful life: physical factors or economic factors? An answer may not be possible on the basis of the limited data provided, but some observations seem valid. The limiting factors seem to be (1) ecological considerations, (2) competition from other power sources (nonnuclear), and (3) safety concerns.

In this situation, the physical life does not appear to be the primary factor affecting useful life. Although the plant's physical life may be far from over, the plant may become obsolete in 10 years. For a house, physical factors undoubtedly supersede the economic or functional factors relative to useful life. Whenever the physical nature of the asset is the primary determinant of useful life, maintenance plays an extremely vital role. The better the maintenance, the longer the life of the asset.[2]

---

[1]Taken from J. D. Coughlan and W. K. Strand, *Depreciation Accounting*, Taxes and Business Decisions (New York: The Ronald Press, 1969), pp. 10–12.

[2]The airline industry also illustrates the type of problem involved in estimation. In the past, aircraft were assumed not to wear out—they just became obsolete. However, some jets have been in service as long as seventeen years, and maintenance costs on these aircraft have become increasingly expensive. As a result, some airlines are finding it necessary to replace aircraft not because of obsolescence but because of their physical deterioration.

The problem of estimating service life is difficult; yet estimation and judgment are the primary means of developing service lives. In some cases, arbitrary lives are selected; in others, fairly sophisticated statistical methods are employed to establish a useful life for accounting purposes. In many cases, the primary basis for estimating the useful life of an asset is the enterprise's past experience with the same or similar assets. In a highly industrial economy such as that of the United States, where research and innovation are so prominent, economic and technological factors have as much, if not more, effect on the service lives of tangible plant assets as physical factors do.

METHODS OF COST APPORTIONMENT (DEPRECIATION)

The determination of the depreciation charge also is dependent on the selection of an appropriate method. The AICPA's professional standards recommend that the depreciation method employed be "systematic and rational." The arbitrary assignment of cost to accounting periods without regard to the probable pattern of losses in an asset's services is not acceptable.

Depreciation methods may be classified as follows:

1. Activity methods (units of use or production)
2. Straight-line methods
3. Decreasing charge methods
   (a) Sum-of-the-years'-digits
   (b) Double-declining balance
4. Special depreciation methods
   (a) Inventory method
   (b) Retirement and replacement methods
   (c) Group and composite-life methods
   (d) Compound interest methods

To illustrate, Barek Coal Mines recently purchased an additional crane for digging purposes. Pertinent data concerning the purchase of the crane are:

Cost of crane	$500,000
Estimated useful life	5 years
Estimated salvage value	$ 50,000
Productive life in hours	30,000 hours

Activity Method

The activity method (often called the variable charge approach) assumes that depreciation is a function of use or productivity instead of the passage of time. The life of the asset is considered in terms of either the output it provides (units it produces), or the number of hours it works. Conceptually, the proper cost association is established in terms of output instead of hours used, but often the output is not homogeneous and is difficult to measure.

The crane poses no particular problem because the usage (hours) is relatively easy to measure. If we assume that the crane is used 4,000 hours the first year, the depreciation charge is:

$$\frac{(\text{cost less salvage}) \times \text{hours this year}}{\text{Total estimated hours}} = \text{depreciation charge}$$

$$\frac{(\$500,000 - \$50,000) \times 4,000}{30,000} = \$60,000$$

The major limitation of this method is that it is not appropriate in situations in which depreciation is a function of time instead of activity. For example, a building is subject to a great deal of steady deterioration from the elements (a function of time) regardless of its use. In addition, where an asset is subject to economic or functional factors, independent of its use, the activity method loses much of its significance. For example, if a company is expanding rapidly, a particular building may soon become obsolete for its intended purposes, without activity playing any role in its loss of utility.

Another problem in using an activity method is that the units of output or service hours received are often difficult to estimate. Data are more frequently available concerning estimated lives of given assets in relation to time than on the number of units of output that will be achieved. Finally, many theoreticians question activity methods because the cost per unit is the same for each unit of output. If a time factor is considered, revenue earned in future periods should be discounted using a present value approach, and the cost per unit also should be discounted.

Straight-Line Method

The straight-line approach overcomes some objections directed at the activity method, because depreciation is considered a function of time instead of a function of usage. This method is widely employed in practice because of its simplicity. The straight-line procedure is often justified on a more theoretical basis as well. When creeping obsolescence is the primary reason for a limited service life, a decline in usefulness may be constant from period to period. In this situation, the straight-line approach is appropriate. The depreciation charge for the crane is computed as follows:

$$\frac{\text{Cost less salvage}}{\text{Estimated service life}} = \text{depreciation charge}$$

$$\frac{\$500,000 - \$50,000}{5} = \$90,000$$

The major objection to the straight-line approach is that it rests on tenuous assumptions that in most situations are not realistic. The major assumptions are that (1) the asset's economic usefulness is the same each year, and (2) the repair and maintenance expense is essentially the same each period (given constant revenue flows).

One additional problem that occurs in using the straight-line method is that distortions in the rate of return analysis (income/assets) develop. For example, Table 12–1 indicates how the rate of return increases, given constant revenue flows.

TABLE 12-1 DEPRECIATION AND RATE OF RETURN ANALYSIS—CRANE EXAMPLE

Year	Depreciation Expense	Undepreciated Asset Balance (book value)	Income Flow (after depreciation expense)	Rate of Return (income ÷ book value)
0	$	$500,000	$	
1	90,000	410,000	100,000	24.4%
2	90,000	320,000	100,000	31.2%
3	90,000	230,000	100,000	43.5%
4	90,000	140,000	100,000	71.4%
5	90,000	50,000	100,000	200.0%

This illustration indicates that the rate of return analysis can be misleading when the straight-line method is employed because the income flow remains the same, whereas the book value of the asset decreases. A student of accounting soon realizes that any cost allocation procedure has several limiting assumptions and that simplicity and ease of understanding are valid considerations in making the final selection.

Decreasing Charge Methods

The decreasing charge methods (often called accelerated depreciation) provide for a higher depreciation cost in the earlier years and lower charges in later periods. The main justification for this approach is that inasmuch as the asset is more efficient or suffers the greatest loss of services in the earlier years, more depreciation should be charged in those years. Another argument presented is that repair and maintenance costs are often higher in the later periods, and the accelerated methods thus provide a constant cost because the depreciation charge is lower in the later periods. Generally, one of two approaches is employed in the decreasing charge approach: the sum-of-the-years'-digits method or the double-declining balance method.

Sum-of-the-Years'-Digits The sum-of-the-years'-digits method results in a decreasing depreciation charge based on a decreasing fraction of depreciable cost (original cost less salvage value). Each fraction uses the sum of the years as a denominator (5 + 4 + 3 + 2 + 1 = 15) and the number of years of estimated life remaining as of the beginning of the year as a numerator. In this method, the numerator decreases year by year although the denominator remains constant (5/15, 4/15, 3/15, 2/15, and 1/15). At the end of the asset's useful life, the balance remaining should be equal to the salvage value. The example (Table 12-2) involving a crane shows this method of computation.[3]

[3]What happens if the estimated service life of the asset is, let us say, 51 years? How then would you calculate the sum-of-the-years'-digits? Fortunately the mathematicians have developed a formula that permits easy computation as follows. It is:

$$\frac{n(n+1)}{2} = \frac{51(51+1)}{2} = 1326.$$

TABLE 12-2 SUM-OF-THE-YEARS'-DIGITS
DEPRECIATION SCHEDULE—CRANE EXAMPLE

Year	Depreciation Base	Remaining Life in Years	Depreciation Fraction	Depreciation Expense	Book Value, End of Year
1	$450,000	5	5/15	$150,000	$350,000
2	450,000	4	4/15	120,000	230,000
3	450,000	3	3/15	90,000	140,000
4	450,000	2	2/15	60,000	80,000
5	450,000	1	1/15	30,000	50,000[a]
		15	15/15	$450,000	

[a]Salvage value.

Double-Declining Balance   Another decreasing charge method is the double-declining balance approach that utilizes a depreciation rate that is twice the straight-line approach. Unlike other methods, salvage value is ignored in computing the depreciation base. The double-declining balance rate is multiplied by the book value of the asset at the beginning of each period. In addition, the book value of the asset is reduced each period by the depreciation charge so that each year the constant double-declining balance rate is applied to a successively lower book value. On the basis of the crane example, Barek Coal Mines would have the depreciation charges shown in Table 12-3.

TABLE 12-3 DOUBLE-DECLINING DEPRECIATION SCHEDULE—CRANE EXAMPLE

Year	Book Value of Asset First of Year	Rate on Declining Balance[a]	Debit Depreciation Expense	Balance Accumulated Depreciation	Book Value, End of Year
1	$500,000	40%	$200,000	$200,000	$300,000
2	300,000	40%	120,000	320,000	180,000
3	180,000	40%	72,000	392,000	108,000
4	108,000	40%	43,200	435,200	64,800
5	64,800	40%	14,800[b]	450,000	50,000

[a]Based on twice the straight-line rate of 20% ($90,000/$450,000 = 20%; 20% $\times$ 2 = 40%).
[b]Limited to $14,800 because book value should not be less than salvage value.

Enterprises often switch from the double-declining to the straight-line method near the end of the asset's useful life to insure that the asset is depreciated only to salvage value. For tax purposes, the double-declining balance method can be used only on new assets (with some exceptions). For used assets, 150% of straight line is permitted; the same computational assumptions are applied as in the double-declining approach.

A pure form of the declining-balance method (sometimes appropriately called the "fixed percentage of book-value method") has also been suggested as a possibility. This approach finds a rate that depreciates the asset exactly to salvage value at the end of its expected useful life. The formula for determination of this rate is as follows:

$$\text{Depreciation rate} = 1 - \sqrt[n]{\frac{\text{salvage value}}{\text{acquisition cost}}}$$

The life in years is n. Once the depreciation rate is computed, it is applied on the declining book value of the asset from period to period, which means that depreciation expense will be successively lower period by period. The rate for the crane is approximated at 36.9%, as computed below.

$$\text{Depreciation rate} = 1 - \sqrt[5]{\frac{50,000}{500,000}} = 36.9\%$$

This method is not used extensively in practice, because the computations are cumbersome, and it is not permitted for tax purposes.

Selection of Depreciation Method

Which method should be selected and why? Conceptually, the answer depends on many factors such as the effects of usage and obsolescence, the pattern of revenue flows, the timing of repair costs, the interest factor, and the uncertainty of revenue receipts. When one of these features predominates, as is generally the case, choice of one particular depreciation method is dictated.[4]

Conceptually, the selection of a depreciation method results in the adoption of the method that most clearly reflects net income. The reasons for selecting a depreciation method are usually more practical. For example, many companies adopt some type of accelerated depreciation method for tax purposes, but use the straight-line method for book purposes. This practice provides the best of both sides: a lower tax and usually a higher net income for financial reporting purposes. Straight-line depreciation results in a smaller charge and a higher reported net income in the earlier years of an asset's life. An expanding company that is continually acquiring and replacing assets is apt to seek the advantages associated with this dual methodology. Some companies adopt the accelerated method for book purposes so that additional depreciation records are not necessary.

SPECIAL DEPRECIATION SYSTEMS

Sometimes an enterprise does not select one of the more popular depreciation methods because the assets involved have unique characteristics, or the nature of

---

[4]*Accounting Trends and Techniques—1978* reports that of its 600 surveyed companies various depreciation methods were used for financial reporting purposes by the following number of companies: straight-line, 559; declining balance, 67; sum-of-the-years'-digits, 34; accelerated method (not specified), 60; units of production, 40; sinking fund, 1. No utility or transportation companies (the ones that use the "special depreciation methods") are included in the AICPA's survey.

the industry dictates that a special depreciation method be adopted. Generally, these systems can be classified into four groups:

1. Inventory systems.
2. Retirement and replacement systems.
3. Group and composite methods.
4. Compound interest methods.

Inventory Systems

The inventory method (often called the appraisal system) is used to value small tangible assets such as hand tools or utensils. A tool inventory, for example, might be taken at the beginning and the end of the year; the value of the beginning inventory plus the cost of tools acquired for the year less the value of the ending inventory provides the amount of depreciation expense for the year. Separate depreciation schedules for the assets in use are impractical; consequently, this method is appealing.

The major objection to this depreciation method is that it is not "systematic and rational." No set formula is involved, and a great deal of subjectivity may be involved in the valuations presented. In many situations, a market or liquidation value is used as the basis for valuation, a practice that is criticized as a violation of the realization principle.

Retirement and Replacement Systems

The retirement and replacement methods are used principally by public utilities and railroads that own many similar units of small value such as poles, ties, conductors, telephones, and so on. The purpose of these approaches is to avoid elaborate depreciation schedules for the individual assets. The distinction between the two methods is that **the retirement system charges the cost of the retired asset (less salvage value) to depreciation expense,** and **the replacement system charges the cost of units purchased as replacements less salvage value from the units replaced to depreciation expense.** In the replacement method the original cost (sometimes called aboriginal cost) of the old asset is maintained in the accounts indefinitely.

To illustrate these two methods, let us assume that the transmission lines of Hi-Test Utility, Inc. originally cost $1,000,000 and that eight years later lines costing $150,000 are replaced with lines having a cost of $200,000.

Entries Under Retirement and Replacement System

Retirement System		Replacement System	

Record installation of lines—1980

Plant Assets—Lines	1,000,000		Plant Assets	1,000,000	
Cash		1,000,000	Cash		1,000,000

Record retirement of old asset as depreciation expense—1988

Depreciation Expense	150,000		(no entry)		
Plant Assets—Lines		150,000			

Record cost of new asset as depreciation expense—1988

(no entry)	Depreciation Expense 200,000
	Cash 200,000

Record cost of new asset—1988

Plant Assets—Lines 200,000	(no entry)
Cash 200,000	

Any salvage value from the old transmission lines is considered a reduction of the depreciation expense in the period of retirement or replacement under both methods. Note that neither makes use of an accumulated depreciation account.

Both systems are subject to the criticism that a proper allocation of costs to all periods does not occur, particularly in the early years. To overcome this objection, a special allowance account may be established in the earlier years so that an assumed depreciation charge can be provided. The probability of retirements or replacements being fairly constant is essential to the validity of this concept; otherwise, depreciation is simply a function of when retirement and replacement occur.

Group and Composite Systems

Depreciation methods are usually applied to a single asset. In certain circumstances, however, multiple-asset accounts are depreciated using one rate. For example, an enterprise such as American Telephone and Telegraph Co. might depreciate by equipment groups, such as telephone poles, microwave systems, or switchboards. Two methods of depreciating multiple-asset accounts are employed: the group method and the composite method. The term **group refers to a collection of assets that are similar in nature; composite refers to a collection of assets that are dissimilar in nature.** The group method is frequently used where the assets are fairly homogeneous and have approximately the same useful lives. The composite approach is used when the assets are heterogeneous and have different lives. The group method more closely approximates a single-unit cost procedure because the dispersion from the average is not as great. The method of computation for either group or composite is essentially the same: find an average and depreciate on that basis.

To illustrate, Smart Motors depreciates its fleet of cars, trucks, and campers on a composite basis. The depreciation rate is established in this manner:

Asset	Original Cost	Residual Value	Depreciable Cost	Estimated Life (yrs.)	Depreciation Per Year (straight line)
Cars	$145,000	$25,000	$120,000	3	$40,000
Trucks	44,000	4,000	40,000	4	10,000
Campers	35,000	5,000	30,000	5	6,000
	$224,000	$34,000	$190,000		$56,000

$$\text{Depreciation or composite rate} = \frac{\$56,000}{\$224,000} = 25\%$$

$$\text{Composite life} = 3.39 \text{ years } (\$190,000 \div \$56,000)$$

If there are no changes in the asset account, the group will be depreciated to the residual or salvage value at the rate of $56,000 ($224,000 × .25) a year for 3.39 years. This system simplifies the procedure for keeping depreciation records when there are a multitude of assets.

The differences between the group or composite method and the single-unit depreciation methods become accentuated in the area of asset retirements. If an asset is retired before the average service life of the group is reached, the resulting gain or loss is buried in the accumulated depreciation account. This practice is justified because some assets will be retired before the average service life and others after the average life. For this reason, the debit to Accumulated Depreciation is the difference between original cost and cash received. No gain or loss on disposition is recorded. To illustrate, suppose that one of the campers with a cost of $5,000 was sold for $2,600 at the end of the third year. The entry is:

Accumulated Depreciation	2,400	
Cash	2,600	
Cars, Trucks, and Campers		5,000

If additional assets are purchased (mopeds, for example), a new depreciation rate must be computed and applied in subsequent periods.

Compound Interest Methods

The compound interest methods are not discussed in this chapter. Conceptually, the interest methods have much to offer, but they have found limited acceptance. The compound interest methods are discussed in advanced accounting for the student who is interested in pursuing this type of depreciation adjustment.

SPECIAL DEPRECIATION PROBLEMS

Several special problems develop in accounting for matters related to depreciation. Although it is difficult to classify these problems in special categories, the major issues are:

1. How should depreciation be computed for partial periods?
2. Does depreciation provide for the replacement of assets?
3. How are revisions in depreciation rates handled?

Depreciation and Partial Periods

Plant assets are seldom purchased on the first day of a fiscal period and are seldom disposed of on the last day of a fiscal period. A practical question is: How much depreciation should be charged for the partial periods involved? Assume, for example, that an asset with a five-year life is purchased for $4,500 (no salvage value) on June 10 and the company's fiscal year ends December 31; depreciation is charged for 6⅔ months during that year. In other words, the total depreciation for a full year (assuming straight-line depreciation) is $900 ($4,500/5), and the depreciation for the fraction of the year is:

$$\frac{6\frac{2}{3}}{12} \times \$900 = \$500$$

In some cases, the previous method is modified to handle acquisitions and disposals of plant assets more simply. For example, depreciation is computed for the full period on the opening balance in the asset account and no depreciation is charged on acquisitions during the year. Another variation is to charge a full year's depreciation on assets used for a full year and to charge one-half year's depreciation in the year of acquisition and in the year of disposal.

These are examples of modifications that are acceptable if they are applied consistently. Depreciation, however, is normally computed on the basis of the nearest whole month unless otherwise stipulated.

What happens when an accelerated method such as sum-of-the-years'-digits or double-declining balance is used when partial periods are involved? As an illustration, assume that an asset was purchased for $10,000 on July 1, 1980, with an estimated useful life of five years; the depreciation figures for 1980, 1981, and 1982 are as below.

	Sum-of-the-Years'-Digits	Double-Declining Balance
1st Full Year	(5/15 × $10,000) = $3,333.33	(40% × $10,000) = $4,000
2nd Full Year	(4/15 × 10,000) = 2,666.67	(40% × 6,000) = 2,400
3rd Full Year	(3/15 × 10,000) = 2,000.00	(40% × 3,600) = 1,440
	Depreciation from July 1, 1980 to December 31, 1980	
1/2 × $3,333.33 =	$1,666.67	1/2 × $4,000 = $2,000
	Depreciation for 1981	
1/2 × $3,333.33 =	$1,666.67	1/2 × $4,000 = $2,000
1/2 × 2,666.67 =	1,333.33	1/2 × 2,400 = 1,200
	$3,000.00	$3,200
		or ($10,000 − $2,000) × 40% = $3,200
	Depreciation for 1982	
1/2 × $2,666.67 =	$1,333.33	1/2 × $2,400 = $1,200
1/2 × 2,000.00 =	1,000.00	1/2 × 1,440 = 720
	$2,333.33	$1,920
		or ($10,000 − $5,200) × 40% = $1,920

In computing depreciation expense for partial periods, it is necessary to determine the depreciation expense for the full year and then to prorate this depreciation expense between the two periods involved. This process should continue throughout the useful life of the asset.

Depreciation and Replacement of Fixed Assets

A common misconception about depreciation is that it provides funds for the replacement of fixed assets. Depreciation is similar to any other expense, in that it reduces net income, and differs from most other expenses, in that it does not involve a current cash outflow.

To illustrate why depreciation does not provide funds for replacement of plant assets, assume that a business starts operating with plant assets of $500,000, which have a useful life of five years. The company's balance sheet at the beginning of the period is:

Plant Assets	$500,000		Owner's Equity	$500,000

Now if we assume that the enterprise earned no revenue over the five years, the income statements are:

	Year 1	Year 2	Year 3	Year 4	Year 5
Revenue	-0-	-0-	-0-	-0-	-0-
Depreciation	(100,000)	(100,000)	(100,000)	(100,000)	(100,000)
Loss	(100,000)	(100,000)	(100,000)	(100,000)	(100,000)

The balance sheet at the end of the five years is:

Plant Assets	-0-		Owner's Equity	-0-

This extreme illustration points out that depreciation in no way provides funds for the replacement of assets. The funds for the replacement of the assets come from the revenues; without the revenues no income materializes and no cash inflow results.

Revision of Depreciation Rates

When a plant asset is purchased, depreciation rates are determined as accurately as possible; the necessary estimates are based on past experience with similar assets and all other pertinent information available. The provisions for depreciation are only estimates, however, and it may be necessary to effect revisions during the life of the asset. Unexpected physical deterioration or unforeseen obsolescence may indicate that the useful life of the asset is less than originally estimated. Improved maintenance procedures, revision of operating procedures, or similar developments may prolong the life of the asset beyond the expected period.

For example, assume that machinery costing $90,000 and originally estimated to have a life of 20 years with no salvage value at the end of that time has been used for 10 years when it is estimated that it will be used an additional 20 years. It, therefore, will have a total life of 30 years instead of 20 years. Depreciation has been recorded at the rate of 1/20 of $90,000, or $4,500 per year by the straight-line method. On the basis of a 30-year life, depreciation should have been 1/30 of $90,000, or $3,000 per year. Depreciation, therefore, has been over estimated, and net income has been less in the amount of $1,500 for each of the past 10 years, or a total amount of $15,000. The amount of the difference can be computed as follows:

	Per Year	For 10 Years
Depreciation charged per books (1/20 × $90,000)	$4,500	$45,000
Depreciation based on a 30-year life (1/30 × $90,000)	3,000	30,000
Excess depreciation charged	$1,500	$15,000

APB Opinion No. 20, "Accounting Changes," requires that changes in estimate be handled in the current and prospective periods; that is, no changes are to be made in previously reported results. Opening balances are not adjusted and no attempt is made to "catch up" for prior periods. The reason for this requirement is that changes in estimates are a continual process, an inherent part of any estimation process, and continual restatement would occur for revisions of estimates unless they are handled prospectively. Therefore, no entry is made at the time the change in estimate occurs, and charges for depreciation in subsequent periods are based on dividing the remaining book value less any salvage value by the remaining estimated life:

Machinery	$90,000
Less: Accumulated depreciation	45,000
Book value of machinery at end of 10th year	$45,000

The entry to record depreciation for the following year is:

Depreciation Expense	2,250	
Accumulated Depreciation—Machinery		2,250
($45,000 ÷ 20 years)		

Disclosure of Property, Plant and Equipment, and Depreciation

The basis of valuation for property, plant and equipment should be stated; it is usually historical cost. Pledges, liens, and other commitments related to these assets should be disclosed also. Any liability secured by property, plant and equipment should not be offset against these assets, but should be reported in the liability section. Property, plant and equipment not currently employed as producing assets in the business, such as idle facilities and land held as an investment, should be segregated from assets being used in operations. When assets are depreciated, a valuation account normally called Accumulated Depreciation or Allowance for Depreciation results. The employment of an Accumulated Depreciation account permits the reader of the financial statements to determine the original cost of the asset and provides the reader with information concerning the amount of depreciation that has been charged to income in past years.

The APB required the presentation of depreciation indicating that the following disclosures should be made in the financial statements or in notes thereto:

(a) Depreciation expense for the period.
(b) Balances of major classes of depreciable assets, by nature and function, at the balance sheet date.

(c) Accumulated depreciation, either by major classes of depreciable assets or in total, at the balance sheet date, and

(d) A general description of the method or methods used in computing depreciation with respect to major classes of depreciable assets.[5]

The financial report of Campbell Soup Company below illustrates an acceptable disclosure.

Campbell Soup Company
CONSOLIDATED BALANCE SHEET

	1977	1976
	($000)	
Plant assets, less depreciation	$438,142	$402,004

SUMMARY OF SIGNIFICANT ACCOUNTING POLICIES
Depreciation—Depreciation provided in costs and expenses is on the straight-line method. The United States, Canadian and certain other foreign companies use accelerated methods of depreciation for income tax purposes.

NOTES TO CONSOLIDATED FINANCIAL STATEMENTS
(000 omitted from dollars amounts)

Plant assets, at cost		
Land	$ 21,567	$ 19,700
Buildings	295,885	274,894
Machinery and equipment	529,142	491,414
Projects in progress	26,682	25,633
	873,276	811,641
Accumulated depreciation	435,134	409,637
	$438,142	$402,004

Depreciation provided in costs and expenses was $42,079 in 1977 and $40,697 in 1976. Approximately $49,800 is required to complete projects in progress at July 31, 1977.

Many individuals argue that the disclosure requirements are still not sufficient. For example, some accountants believe that the average useful life of the assets or the range of years for asset life is significant information that should be disclosed.[6]

As with inventories, but even more so for property, plant and equipment the effects of inflation are substantial. The Commerce Department recently noted that if depreciation based on the replacement cost of aging assets were correctly measured, corporate net income for U.S. companies would decrease $18 billion. The FASB recognizing the need for price-level information now requires the disclosure of this type of information for certain companies. One such requirement is that supplementary information on income from continuing operations on a current cost basis (replacement cost) and on increases (decreases) in specific prices of property, plant and equipment net of inflation be reported. This means (1) reporting current cost information on property, plant and equipment and depreciation expense and

---

[5]"Omnibus Opinion—1967," *Opinions of the Accounting Principles Board No. 12* (New York: AICPA, 1967), par. 5.

[6]Charles W. Lamden, Dale L. Gerboth, and Thomas W. McRae, "Accounting for Depreciable Assets," *Accounting Research Monograph No. 1* (New York: AICPA, 1975), p. 111. Also, one writer found that variances in useful life had a greater impact on the variation among companies than the depreciation methods selected. See Robert R. Sterling, "A Test of the Uniformity Hypothesis," *Abacus* (September 1969), pp. 39–47.

(2) computing and disclosing increases (decreases) that arise from the difference between the current cost of property, plant and equipment and its historical cost adjusted for inflation. The detailed computational aspects related to price-level information are discussed in Chapter 25.

Investment Credit

In recent years, Congress has attempted to stimulate the economy by permitting special tax advantages to enterprises that invest in capital assets. One special tax advantage that has occurred intermittently over the past 15 years is the investment credit. The investment credit allows a taxpayer to reduce taxes payable by an amount up to 10% of the cost of qualified depreciable property purchased. For example, suppose that an enterprise purchases an asset for $100,000 in 1981 that qualifies for the investment credit. If the company has a tax liability of $30,000 before the credit, the company's final tax liability is:

Taxes payable for 1981 prior to investment credit	$30,000
Less: investment credit ($100,000 × 10%)	10,000
Final tax liability	$20,000

A vigorous controversy has developed within the accounting profession about how the investment credit should be reported for financial reporting purposes. Many believe that the investment credit is a government reduction in the cost of qualified property similar to a purchase discount and should be accounted for over the same period as that of the related asset (cost reduction or deferred approach). Others believe that the investment credit is a selective reduction in the taxes payable for the year of the purchase and should be handled similarly for financial reporting purposes (tax reduction or flow-through approach). The arguments for the two approaches are presented below.

Cost Reduction or Deferral Method Advocates for this position argue that earnings (or reduction in tax expense) do not arise from the purchase of qualified property. Instead, the use of the asset creates the benefits to be received from the investment credit. Additional support is given to this argument on the basis that if the property is not kept a given number of years, part or all of the investment credit must be refunded to the government.

Another position taken is that the true cost of the asset is not the invoice cost but the invoice cost less the investment credit. Many believe that a company would not buy the property unless the credit were available, and the invoice cost of the asset should be reduced accordingly.

Tax Reduction or Flow-Through Method In the tax-reduction method the investment credit is a selective tax reduction in the period of the purchase and, therefore, tax expense for that period should be reduced by the credit. Advocates of this approach indicate that realization of the credit is not dependent on future use of the property, and the benefits of the credit should therefore not be deferred. The investment credit is earned by the act of investment. Except for a minimum holding period the credit is not affected by the use or nonuse, retention or nonretention, of the asset.

The following illustration indicates how the investment credit is handled under the two approaches.

Illustration. Kane, Inc. purchases a small computer on January 1, 1981 for $100,000 that qualifies for the 10% investment credit. The computer has a useful life of 10 years and no salvage value. The company intends to use straight-line depreciation for both book and tax purposes, and net taxable income before income taxes, but after depreciation is $25,000. The tax rate is 50%. Assume that yearly revenues are $35,000 for the next 10 years.

Entries Under Cost Reduction and Tax Reduction Bases				
Cost Reduction (Deferral)			**Tax Reduction (Flow through)**	
At time of purchase				
Machinery	100,000		Machinery	100,000	
Cash		100,000	Cash		100,000
Recognition and Payment of Taxes				
Income Tax Expense	12,500		Income Tax Expense	2,500	
Cash		2,500	Cash		2,500
Deferred Investment Credit		10,000			
Deferred Investment Credit	1,000				
Income Tax Expense		1,000			
Recognition of Depreciation				
Depreciation Expense	10,000		Depreciation Expense	10,000	
Accumulated Depr.		10,000	Accumulated Depr.		10,000
Annual Entries in Subsequent Periods, Assuming Revenues of $35,000				
Income Tax Expense	11,500		Income Tax Expense	12,500	
Deferred Investment Credit	1,000		Cash		12,500
Cash		12,500			
Depr. Expense	10,000		Depr. Expense	10,000	
Accumulated Depr.		10,000	Accumulated Depr.		10,000

The effect on the income statement and the balance sheet for 1981 and the 10 years combined are illustrated on the bottom of page 536.

Given a choice, most companies prefer the tax reduction or flow-through method for financial reporting purposes because the earnings in the year of the purchase of qualified property can be substantially increased.[7] Currently either method is acceptable for financial reporting purposes. The APB attempted to resolve the controversy but was unsuccessful. In 1962, the APB issued **Opinion No. 2,** "Accounting for the Investment Credit," which permitted only the cost reduction method to be used.[8] Such strong resistance to this Opinion resulted that **APB Opinion No. 4**

[7]*Accounting Trends and Techniques—1978* reports that 84% of the companies surveyed used the flow-through method.

[8]"Accounting for the Investment Credit," *Opinions of the Accounting Principles Board No. 2* (New York: AICPA, 1962).

(amended No. 2), "Accounting for the Investment Credit" was issued. **Opinion No. 4** indicated that the cost reduction method was the preferred approach but that the tax reduction method could be used.[9]

In 1971 the APB considered the matter again, but the question became academic when the Treasury Department, with the support of Congress, included a provision in tax legislation that no taxpayer is required to use any particular method of accounting for the credit in reports subject to the jurisdiction of any federal agency. This pronouncement permits complete flexibility in accounting for the investment credit.

The accounting profession is concerned about this legislation because the establishment of accounting principles for financial reports to investors has been largely the responsibility of the accounting profession and the Securities and Exchange Commission. This action by Congress sets a dangerous precedent, one that is particularly disconcerting because Congress and others have complained about the numerous alternatives existing in financial reporting, and yet they have chosen to continue one themselves.

INCOME STATEMENT AND BALANCE SHEET UNDER COST REDUCTION AND TAX REDUCTION METHODS OF RECORDING INVESTMENT CREDIT

Income Statement

	1981 Cost Reduction	1981 Tax Reduction	Ten Years Combined Cost Reduction	Ten Years Combined Tax Reduction
Sales	$35,000	$35,000	$350,000	$350,000
Depreciation expense	10,000	10,000	100,000	100,000
Income before income taxes	25,000	25,000	250,000	250,000
Income taxes	11,500	2,500	115,000	115,000
Net income	$13,500	$22,500	$135,000	$135,000

Balance Sheet

	1981 Cost Reduction	1981 Tax Reduction	At End of Ten Years Cost Reduction	At End of Ten Years Tax Reduction
Machinery	$100,000	$100,000	$100,000	$100,000
Accumulated depreciation	(10,000)	(10,000)	(100,000)	(100,000)
	$ 90,000	$ 90,000	-0-	-0-
Deferred investment credit (liability)	$ 9,000	-0-	-0-	-0-

---

[9]"Accounting for the Investment Credit," *Opinions of the Accounting Principles Board No. 4* (Amended No. 2) (New York: AICPA, 1964).

DEPLETION

Natural resources, often called wasting assets, include petroleum, minerals, and timber. Natural resources are characterized by two main features: (1) the complete removal (consumption) of the asset, and (2) replacement of the asset only by an act of nature. Unlike plant and equipment, natural resources are consumed physically over the period of use and do not maintain their physical characteristics. For the most part, the accounting problems associated with natural resources are similar to those encountered in the plant asset area. The questions to be answered are:

1. How is the cost basis for write-off (depletion) established?
2. What pattern of allocation should be employed?

Establishment of Depletion Base

How do we determine the proper cost for an oil well? Rather large expenditures are needed to find these natural resources, and for every successful discovery there are many "dry holes." Furthermore, long delays are encountered between the time the costs are initially incurred and the benefits are obtained from the extracted resources. As a result, a conservative policy frequently is adopted in accounting for the expenditures incurred in finding and extracting natural resources.

The **costs of natural resources** can be divided into three categories: (1) acquisition cost of deposit, (2) exploration costs, and (3) development costs. The **acquisition cost of the deposit** is the price paid to obtain the property right to search and find an undiscovered natural resource or the price paid for an already discovered resource. In some cases, property is leased and special royalty payments paid to the lessor if a productive natural resource is found and is commercially profitable. Generally, the acquisition cost is placed in an account titled Undeveloped Property and assigned to the natural resource if exploration efforts are successful. If they are unsuccessful, the cost is written off as a loss.

As soon as the enterprise has the right to use the property, considerable **exploration costs** are entailed in finding the resource. The accounting treatment for these costs varies: some firms expense all exploration costs; others capitalize only those costs that are directly related to successful projects **(successful efforts approach)**; and others adopt a **full-cost approach** (capitalization of all costs whether related to successful or unsuccessful projects).

Conceptually, the question is whether the unsuccessful exploration costs are a cost of those that are successful. At first glance, the full-cost approach appears to have much validity, but at present most companies have not adopted it. The prevalent practice is to capitalize all exploration costs that result in the discovery of profitable natural resources and to expense all other costs. The large international oil companies such as Exxon, Mobil, and Gulf use such an approach. Full-cost accounting is used by most of the smaller, exploration-oriented companies. The differences in net income figures under the two methods can be staggering. For example, until Texaco switched to the successful efforts approach in 1975, it was estimated that full-cost accounting increased Texaco's reported profits by $500 million over the past 10 years.

Proponents of the full-cost concept believe that unsuccessful ventures are a cost of those that are successful, because the cost of drilling a dry hole is a cost that is needed to find the commercially profitable wells. Those who believe that only the costs of successful projects should be capitalized contend that the unsuccessful companies will end up capitalizing many costs that will make an unsuccessful company over a short period of time show no less income than does one that is successful. In addition, it is contended that to measure accurately cost and effort for a single property unit, the only measure is in terms of the cost directly related to that unit. The remainder of the costs should be allocated as period charges similar to such period costs as advertising, which at present are not assigned to inventory.

The final costs that are incurred in finding natural resources are **development costs** which are classified in two ways: (1) tangible equipment, and (2) intangible development costs. Tangible equipment includes all of the transportation and other heavy equipment necessary to extract the resource and get it ready for production or shipment. **Tangible equipment costs are normally not considered in the depletion base;** instead, separate depreciation charges are employed because the asset can be moved from one drilling or mining site to another. Depreciation expense is, therefore, based on a service life relevant to its total usefulness. Tangible assets that cannot be moved should be depreciated over their useful life or the life of the resource, whichever is shorter. **Intangible development costs, on the other hand, are considered part of the depletion base.** These costs are for such items as the drilling costs, tunnels, shafts, and wells, which have no tangible characteristics, but are needed for the production of the natural resource.

Write-off of Resource Cost

As soon as the depletion base is established, the next problem is determining how the natural resource cost should be allocated to accounting periods. Normally, depletion is computed on the unit of production method (activity approach), which means that depletion is a function of the number of units withdrawn during the period. In adopting this approach, the total cost of the natural resource is divided by the number of units estimated to be in the resource deposit to obtain a cost per unit of product. This cost per unit is multiplied by the number of units extracted to compute the depletion.

For example, MaClede Oil Co. has acquired the right to use 1,000 acres of land in northern Texas to explore for oil. The lease cost is $50,000; the related exploration costs for a discovered oil deposit on the property is $100,000; and intangible development costs incurred in erecting and drilling the well are $850,000. Total costs related to the oil deposit before the first gallon is extracted are, therefore, $1,000,000. It is estimated that the well will provide approximately 1,000,000 barrels of oil. The depletion rate established is computed in the following manner:

$$\frac{\text{total cost}}{\text{total estimated units available}} = \text{depletion charge per unit}$$

$$\frac{\$1,000,000}{1,000,000} = \$1.00 \text{ per barrel}$$

If 250,000 barrels are withdrawn in the first year, then the depletion charge for the year is $250,000 (250,000 barrels at $1.00). The entry to record the depletion is:

Depletion Expense	250,000	
Accumulated Depletion		250,000

In some instances an Accumulated Depletion account is not used, and the credit goes directly to the natural resources asset account. In the income statement the depletion cost is part of the cost of producing the product. The balance sheet presents the cost of the property and the amount of depletion entered to date as follows:

Oil deposit (at cost)	$1,000,000	
Less accumulated depletion	250,000	$750,000

The tangible equipment used in extracting the oil may also be depreciated on a unit of production basis, especially if the estimated lives of the equipment can be directly assigned to one given resource deposit. If the equipment is utilized in more than one job, other cost allocation methods such as straight-line or accelerated depreciation methods would be more appropriate.

Controversy Concerning Oil and Gas Accounting

As indicated, either the successful efforts approach or the full costing approach is permitted in accounting for costs in the oil and gas industry. The FASB recently attempted to narrow the available accounting alternatives but met with little success. In 1977, the FASB issued **Statement No. 19,** which would have required oil and gas companies to follow a form of successful efforts accounting.[10] However, as soon as this standard was issued, the smaller oil and gas producers voiced strong objections and lobbied extensively in Congress for relief from this type of accounting. As a result, governmental agencies assessed the implications of **FASB Statement No. 19** from a public interest standpoint and reacted contrary to the FASB's position.[11] For example, the Department of Energy indicated that companies now using the full cost method would reduce their exploration activities because of the unfavorable earnings impact associated with successful efforts accounting. The Justice Department asked the SEC to postpone adoption of one uniform method of accounting in the oil and gas industry until the SEC could determine whether the information reported to investors would be enhanced and whether competition would be constrained by adoption of the successful efforts method.

In response, the SEC in 1978 issued three **Accounting Series Releases** on the subject of oil and gas accounting in which it (1) adopted the form of successful efforts approach recommended by **FASB Statement No. 19,** (2) adopted a unique

[10]"Financial Accounting and Reporting by Oil and Gas Producing Companies," *FASB Statement No. 19* (Stamford, Conn.: FASB, 1977).

[11]The recent concern for economic consequences of a proposed accounting alternative is an added dimension to accounting standard setting. One group believes that because accounting standards affect the public, standard setting should take into consideration the economic effects of any proposed standards. Others believe that such an approach is inappropriate for accountants and view the standard-setting role less pragmatically.

form of full costing, and (3) stated that it found both successful efforts and full cost accounting inadequate because neither reflects the economic substance of oil and gas exploration in a meaningful way.[12] As a substitute, the SEC argues in favor of a yet-to-be developed method, **Reserve Recognition Accounting (RRA),** which it believes would provide more useful information.

Under RRA, as soon as a company discovered oil, its value would be reported on the balance sheet and in the income statement. Thus, RRA is a current value approach as opposed to full costing and successful efforts, which are historical cost approaches. To illustrate the differences in these methods, assume that Allied Oil Company has spent $2,000,000 on each of two oil fields. On the one field Allied discovers oil; the other is a dry hole. Under successful efforts accounting, the $2,000,000 associated with the producing well is capitalized, while the $2,000,000 related to the dry hole is expensed. Under full costing, the entire $4,000,000 is capitalized and amortized over the life of the reserves because the cost of the unsuccessful wells is considered a cost of the successful wells. Once RRA is in effect, the fair value of the reserves will have to be determined and reported as assets. If the value of the oil reserve is $15,000,000, an asset ("oil deposits") is reported on the balance sheet at $15,000,000. On the income statement, income of $11,000,000 ($15,000,000 − $4,000,000) would be reported.

The use of RRA would make a substantial difference in the balance sheets and income statements of oil companies. For example, Atlantic Richfield Co. recently reported net producing property of $2.6 billion. If RRA were adopted, the same properties would be valued at $11.8 billion. Similarly, Standard Oil of Ohio, which reported net producing properties of $1.7 billion, would report approximately $10.7 billion under RRA.

Conceptually there is merit for writing the asset upward, particularly where a significant disparity exists. For example, assume that $50,000 was paid for land on which an oil deposit worth $10 million is discovered. Should the oil deposit not be reported or at least disclosed in the financial statements? In the past, the accounting treatment has ranged from complete silence to actual reporting in the financial statements. However, **there are numerous practical problems, in estimating (1) the amount of the reserves, (2) the future production costs, (3) the periods of expected disposal, (4) the discount rate, and (5) the selling price.** An estimate for each of these elements is necessary to arrive at an accurate valuation of the existing oil or gas reserve. If the oil or gas reserve is not to be extracted and sold for several years, estimating the future selling price, the appropriate discount rate, and the future costs of extraction and delivery can each be a formidable task.

Because RRA involves numerous estimates, the SEC needs time (at least three years) to develop the method. In the interim either the full cost approach or the successful efforts approach is acceptable. As a result of SEC interest in the area, in 1979 the FASB issued **Statement No. 25,** which suspended **FASB Statement No. 19,** except for certain disclosure provisions.[13]

---

[12]"Adoption of Requirements for Financial Accounting and Reporting Practices for Oil and Gas Producing Activities," *Accounting Series Release No. 253* (Washington, D.C.: SEC, August 1978); "Requirements for Financial Accounting and Reporting Practices for Oil and Gas Producing Activities," *Accounting Series Release No. 257* (Washington, D.C.: SEC, December 1978); and "Oil and Gas Producers—Full Cost Accounting Practices," *Accounting Series Release No. 258* (Washington, D.C.: SEC, 1978).

[13]"Suspension of Certain Accounting Requirements for Oil and Gas Producing Companies," *Statement of Financial Accounting Standards No. 25* (Stamford, Conn.: FASB, 1979).

What the accepted accounting method for the oil and gas industry will be eventually is difficult to predict. The SEC contends that RRA will work; others are skeptical. It does seem ironic that Congress mandated that the FASB develop one method of accounting for the oil and gas industry, and when it did so, the government chose not to accept it. As a result, alternatives still exist in the oil and gas industry that hinder financial comparability between companies and limit the usefulness of financial statement information.

The investment credit situation and the oil and gas controversy demonstrate the strong influence that federal agencies have in financial reporting matters.

Special Problems in Depletion Accounting

Accounting for natural resources has some interesting problems that are uncommon to most other types of assets. For purposes of discussion we have divided these problems into four categories:

1. Difficulty of estimating recoverable reserves.
2. Problems of discovery value.
3. Tax aspects of natural resources.
4. Accounting for liquidating dividends.

Estimating Recoverable Reserves   Not infrequently the estimate of recoverable reserves has to be changed either because new information has become available or because production processes have become more sophisticated.

Natural resources such as oil and gas deposits and some rare metals have recently provided the greatest challenges. Estimates of these reserves are in large measure "knowledgeable guesses." And these estimates change frequently in today's environment where marginal projects are undertaken because of price escalations.

This problem is the same as that faced in accounting for changes in estimates of the useful lives of plant and equipment. The procedure is to revise the depletion rate on a prospective basis by dividing the remaining cost into an estimate of the new recoverable reserves. This approach has much merit in this field because the required estimates are quite tenuous.

Discovery Value   Discovery value accounting and reserve recognition accounting are essentially similar. RRA is specifically related to the oil and gas industry, whereas discovery value is a broader term associated with the whole natural resources area. As indicated earlier, general practice has not recognized discovery values in the general ledger accounts. If discovery value is recorded, an asset account would be debited and usually an Unrealized Appreciation account would be credited. Unrealized Appreciation is part of stockholders' equity. Unrealized Appreciation would then be transferred to revenue (realized income) as the natural resources are sold. It is possible, for example, that the SEC may adopt this approach in applying RRA.

A similar problem arises with resources such as growing timber, aging liquor, and maturing livestock that increase in value over time. One method is to record the increase in value as the accretion occurs as a debit to the asset account and as a credit to income or to an unrealized income account. Accountants have been hesitant to record these increases because of the uncertainty regarding the final sales price and the problem of estimating the costs involved in getting the resources ready for sale.

Tax Aspects of Natural Resources   The tax aspects of accounting for most natural resources have comprised some of the most controversial provisions of the Internal Revenue Code (IRC). The tax law has long provided a deduction for the greater of **cost** or **percentage** depletion against income from oil, gas, and most minerals. The percentage or statutory depletion allows a write-off ranging from 5% to 22% (depending on the natural resource) as a percentage of gross income received instead of as a percentage of cost. As a result, the amount of depletion may exceed the investment cost that is assigned to a given natural resource. For example, the asset may have a zero valuation, but a depletion deduction may be taken if the enterprise has gross income, subject to certain constraints. The significance of the percentage depletion allowance is now greatly reduced because it has been repealed for most oil and gas companies and is of only limited use in most other situations.

Note that the taxpayer may use the cost-depletion method for tax purposes if it is more favorable. For tax purposes the cost-depletion method does not have to coincide with the cost depletion taken for financial reporting purposes. For example, the IRC permits expensing certain intangible development costs that are capitalized for financial reporting purposes.[14]

Liquidating Dividend   A company often owns as its only major asset a certain property from which it intends to extract natural resources. If the company does not expect to purchase additional properties, it distributes gradually to stockholders their capital investments by paying dividends equal to the amount of accumulated net income (after depletion) plus the amount of depletion charged. The major accounting problem is to distinguish between dividends that are a return of capital and those that are not. The company in issuing a liquidating dividend should debit Additional Paid-in Capital for that portion related to the original investment instead of Retained Earnings, because the dividend is a return of part of the investor's original contribution.

Financial Reporting of Depletion

The reporting of natural resources in a balance sheet is similar to the reporting for other assets. The following classification might be adopted:

Properties and mineral rights	
Undeveloped mineral properties and rights	xx
Producing mineral properties and rights, less accumulated depletion of xx	xx

---

[14]The FASB has recently issued a standard requiring certain tax allocation procedures in such circumstances. "Accounting for Income Taxes—Oil and Gas Producing Companies," *Statement of the Financial Accounting Standards Board No. 9* (Stamford, Conn.: FASB, 1975).

Some companies do not record depletion because the number of recoverable units is considered not determinable with enough certainty to avoid distortions. In addition, it is argued that as long as resources are being discovered, there is no need for depletion. This approach has no validity in theory and should not be condoned.

In the oil and gas industry, required disclosure includes the classification and amount of costs incurred for property acquisition, exploration, development, and production. The method of accounting for these costs (successful efforts or full costing) should also be disclosed. A controversy surrounds the disclosure related to recoverable reserves. Because the most important component in assessing the future profitability of an oil and gas enterprise is its recoverable reserves, many argue that this information should be provided. Others contend that determination of these reserves is so difficult that presentation in the financial statements will only lead to confusion and distortion. **FASB Statement No. 25,** issued in 1979, recommends that the disclosure of reserve data be made **outside** the financial statements. This insures its presentation without the necessity of incurring substantive costs in obtaining independent verification of this information.[15] The following excerpt taken from the 1978 annual report of NICOR Inc. illustrates the typical brief disclosures about reserves that are being made to investors and stockholders.

NICOR Inc.
Naperville, Illinois

NICOR, through its subsidiaries, increased energy reserves to approximately 2.5 million barrels of oil and 61 Bcf of gas by the end of 1978. This compares with reserves of 1.8 million barrels of oil and 37 Bcf of gas at December 31, 1977. Reserves are expected to increase even more significantly in 1979.

The current level of oil and gas exploration expenditures places NICOR among the larger independent operators. In 1978 alone the Company had interests in 379 new wells, of which 67 were producing oil, 119 producing gas, 12 producing oil and gas and 181 were dry holes. NICOR produced approximately 457,000 barrels of oil and 5.2 Bcf of gas in 1978. We have oil and gas interests in 24 states, Canada and Central America.

Questions

1. What is accounting for depreciation, and what is its objective? Are the decreasing-charge methods of depreciation consistent with this objective? Discuss.

2. Distinguish between depreciation, depletion, and amortization.

3. The plant manager of a manufacturing firm suggested in a conference of the company's executives that accountants should speed up depreciation on the machinery in the finishing department because improvements were rapidly making those machines obsolete, and a depreciation fund big enough to cover their replacement is needed. Discuss the accounting concept of depreciation and the effect on a business concern of the depreciation recorded for plant assets, paying particular attention to the issues raised by the plant manager.

---

[15]It should be noted that FASB *Statement of Financial Accounting Concepts No. 1,* "Objectives of Financial Reporting by Business Enterprises," indicates that the FASB intends to establish standards in the area of disclosure outside the financial statements. The Board's requirement on disclosure of price-level information outside the financial statements is another example of its interest in developing guidelines in this area.

4. What basic questions must be answered before the amount of the depreciation charge can be computed?

5. For what reasons are plant assets retired? Define inadequacy, supersession, and obsolescence.

6. Marvel Company purchased machinery for $120,000 on January 1, 1981. It is estimated that the machinery will have a useful life of 20 years, scrap value of $16,000, production of 84,000 units, and working hours of 42,000. During 1981 the company uses the machinery for 14,300 hours, and the machinery produces 20,000 units. Compute depreciation under the straight-line, units-of-output, working-hours, sum-of-the-years'-digits, and declining-balance (use 10% as the annual rate) methods.

7. What are the major factors considered in determining what depreciation method to use?

8. It has been suggested that plant and equipment could be replaced more quickly if depreciation rates for income tax and accounting purposes were substantially increased. As a result, business operations would receive the benefit of more modern and more efficient plant facilities. Discuss the merits of this proposition.

9. A building that was purchased December 31, 1956, for $300,000 was originally estimated to have a life of 50 years with no salvage value at the end of that time. Depreciation has been recorded through 1980. During 1980 an examination of the building by an engineering firm discloses that its estimated useful life is 15 years after 1980. What should be the amount of depreciation for 1981?

10. Discuss the accounting justification for recording on the books (a) plant assets received as a gift and (b) their depreciation or depletion.

11. Under what conditions is it appropriate for a concern to use the retirement method of depreciation for plant assets? What are the advantages of this method?

12. If a business that uses the retirement method sells for $9,000 plant assets originally costing $30,000 five years ago, what entry should be made? The assets sold consist of 500 small motors, which usually last about seven years.

13. Under what conditions is it appropriate for a business to use the composite method of depreciation for its plant assets? What are the advantages and disadvantages of this method?

14. If a concern uses the composite method and its composite rate is 7.2% per year, what entry should it make when plant assets that originally cost $40,000 and have been used for 10 years are sold for $9,000?

15. List (a) the similarities and (b) the differences in the accounting treatments of depreciation and cost depletion.

16. Describe cost depletion and percentage depletion. Why is the percentage depletion method permitted?

17. In what way may the use of percentage depletion violate sound accounting theory?

18. In the extractive industries, businesses may pay dividends in excess of net income. What is the maximum permissible? How can this practice be justified?

19. Neither depreciation on replacement cost nor depreciation adjusted for changes in the purchasing power of the dollar has been recognized as generally accepted accounting practice for inclusion in the primary financial statements. Briefly present the accounting treatment that might be used to assist in the maintenance of the ability of a company to replace its productive capacity.

20. Recently the following statement appeared in a financial magazine: "RRA—or Rah-Rah, as it's sometimes dubbed—has kicked up quite a storm. Oil companies, for example, are convinced that the approach is misleading. Major accounting firms agree." What is RRA? Why might oil companies believe that this approach is misleading?

Cases

C12-1   Franklin Manufacturing Company was organized January 1, 1981. During 1981, it has used in its reports to management the straight-line method of depreciating its plant assets.

On November 8 you are having a conference with Franklin's officers to discuss the depreciation method to be used for income tax and stockholder reporting. The president of Franklin has suggested the use of a new method, which he feels is more suitable than the straight-line method for the needs of the company during the period of rapid expansion of production and capacity that he foresees. Following is an example in which the proposed method is applied to a fixed asset with an original cost of $32,000, an estimated useful life of 5 years, and a scrap value of approximately $2,000.

Year	Years of Life Used	Fraction Rate	Depreciation Expense	Accumulated Depreciation at End of Year	Book Value at End of Year
1	1	1/15	$ 2,000	$ 2,000	$30,000
2	2	2/15	4,000	6,000	26,000
3	3	3/15	6,000	12,000	20,000
4	4	4/15	8,000	20,000	12,000
5	5	5/15	10,000	30,000	2,000

The president favors the new method because he has heard that

1. It will increase the funds recovered during the years near the end of the assets' useful lives when maintenance and replacement disbursements are high.

2. It will result in increased write-offs in later years and thereby will reduce taxes.

Instructions

(a) What is the purpose of accounting for depreciation?

(b) Is the president's proposal within the scope of generally accepted accounting principles? In making your decision discuss the circumstances, if any, under which use of the method would be reasonable and those, if any, under which it would not be reasonable.

(c) The president wants your advice.

   1. Do depreciation charges recover or create funds? Explain.

   2. Assume that the Internal Revenue Service accepts the proposed depreciation method in this case. If the proposed method were used for stockholder and tax reporting purposes, how would it affect the availability of funds generated by operations?

C12-2   Presented below are three different and unrelated situations involving depreciation accounting. Answer the question(s) at the end of each case situation.

Situation I

Morgan Paper Company, a subsidiary of Scott Paper Company, operates a 300-ton-per-day kraft pulp mill and four sawmills in Wisconsin. The company is in the process of expanding its pulp mill facilities to a capacity of 1,000 tons per day and plans to replace three of its older, less efficient sawmills with an expanded facility. One of the mills to be replaced did not operate for most of 1980 (current year), and there are no plans to reopen it before the new sawmill facility becomes operational.

In reviewing the depreciation rates and in discussing the residual values of the sawmills that were to be replaced, it was noted that if present depreciation rates were not adjusted, substantial amounts of plant costs on these three mills would not be depreciated by the time the new mill came on stream.

Instruction

What is the proper accounting for the four sawmills at the end of 1980?

Situation II

Recently, Arkansas Company experienced a strike that affected a number of its operating plants. The controller of this company indicated that it was not appropriate to report depreciation expense during this period because the equipment did not depreciate and an improper matching of costs and revenues would result. He based his position on the following points:

1. It is inappropriate to charge the period with costs for which there are no related revenues arising from production.
2. The basic factor of depreciation in this instance is wear and tear, and because equipment was idle no wear and tear occurred.

Instruction

Comment on the appropriateness of the controller's comments.

Situation III

The Norvell Company manufactures electrical appliances, most of which are used in homes. Company engineers have designed a new type of blender which, through the use of a few attachments, will perform more functions than any blender currently on the market. Demand for the new blender can be projected with reasonable probability. In order to make the blenders, Norvell needs a specialized machine that is not available from outside sources. It has been decided to make such a machine in Norvell's own plant.

Instructions

(a) Discuss the effect of projected demand in units for the new blenders (which may be steady, decreasing, or increasing) on the determination of a depreciation method for the machine.

(b) What other matters should be considered in determining the depreciation method? Ignore income tax considerations.

C12-3 The certified public accountant is frequently called upon by management for advice regarding methods of computing depreciation. Of comparable importance, although it arises less frequently, is the question of whether the depreciation method should be based on consideration of the assets as units, as a group, or as having a composite life.

Instructions

(a) Briefly describe the depreciation methods based on treating assets as:
1. Units.
2. A group or as having a composite life.
(b) Present the arguments for and against the use of each of the two methods.
(c) Describe how retirements are recorded under each of the two methods.

(AICPA adapted)

C12-4 Recently, the following comments appeared in the financial press:

"RRA goes too far too fast. It leads to a high degree of imprecision and uncertainty in the income statement and balance sheet."

"Companies using full-cost tend to show higher earnings and accumulate assets faster than do companies using the successful-efforts approach."

"Congress put the problem to the SEC, which put it to the FASB, which solved it in a way the SEC didn't like. So the SEC came up with its own oil and gas industry accounting rules."

Instructions

    (a) What is meant by the terms RRA, full-cost, and successful-efforts accounting?

    (b) Why might RRA lead to imprecision and uncertainty?

    (c) Why do companies show higher earnings and accumulate assets faster under full-cost accounting under successful efforts accounting?

    (d) Should Congress be directly involved in the establishment of accounting principles?

Exercises

E12-1   The Huffy Corp. purchased machinery for $60,000 on July 1, 1980. It is estimated that it will have a useful life of 10 years, scrap value of $8,000, production of 273,000 units, and working hours of 63,000. During 1981 the Huffy Corp. uses the machinery for 7,150 hours, and the machinery produces 32,300 units.

Instructions

From the information given below, compute the depreciation charge for 1981 under each of the following methods:

    (a) Straight-line.

    (b) Units of output.

    (c) Working hours.

    (d) Sum-of-the-years'-digits.

    (e) Declining-balance (use 20% as the annual rate).

E12-2   The Shale Oil Company purchased equipment for $105,000 on October 1, 1979. It is estimated that the equipment will have a useful life of 10 years and a salvage value of $6,000. Estimated production is 40,000 units and estimated working hours 60,000. During 1979 the Shale Oil Company uses the equipment for 1,500 hours and the equipment produces 2,000 units.

Instructions

Compute depreciation expense under each of the following methods. Shale Oil is on a calendar-year basis ending December 31.

    (a) Straight-line method for 1979.

    (b) Activity method (units of output) for 1979.

    (c) Activity method (working hours) for 1979.

    (d) Sum-of-the-years'-digits method for 1981.

    (e) Double-declining balance method for 1980.

E12-3   The Marion Corporation purchased a new machine for its assembly process on October 1, 1980. The cost of this machine was $57,600. The company estimated that the machine would have a trade-in value of $3,600 at the end of its service life. Its life is estimated at 5 years and its working hours are estimated at 20,000 hours. Year-end is December 31.

Instructions

Compute the depreciation expense under the following methods: (1) straight-line depreciation for 1980, (2) activity method for 1980, assuming that machine usage was 800 hours, (3) sum-of-the-years'-digits for 1981, and (4) double-declining balance for 1981. Each of the foregoing should be considered unrelated.

E12-4 The Datapoint Company shows the following entries in its Equipment account for 1981; all amounts are based on historical cost.

Equipment

1981			1981		
Jan. 1	Balance	80,000	June 30	Cost of equipment sold	
Aug. 10	Purchases	16,000		(purchased prior	
12	Freight on equipment			to 1981)	8,000
	purchased	320			
25	Installation costs	800			
Nov. 10	Repairs	240			

Instructions

(a) Prepare any correcting entries necessary.

(b) Assuming that depreciation is to be charged for a full year on the ending balance in the asset account, compute the proper depreciation charge for 1981 under each of the methods listed below. Assume an estimated life of 10 years, with no salvage value. The machinery included in the January 1, 1981, balance was purchased in 1979.
  1. Straight line.
  2. Sum-of-the-years'-digits.
  3. Declining balance (assume twice the straight-line rate).

E12-5 The account for Machinery and Equipment on the books of the Danly Wire Company for 1981 shows the information given below. All amounts shown in the account represent original cost of assets.

Machinery and Equipment

1981			1981		
Jan. 1	Balance	184,500	Apr. 25	Scrapped (purchased	
Mar. 20	Purchased	21,600		prior to 1981)	22,800
Aug. 11	Purchased	9,000	Dec. 31	Balance	192,300
		215,100			215,100
1982					
Jan. 1	Balance	192,300			

Instructions

(a) Compute the depreciation for the year, assuming that the company uses the straight-line method and that the estimated life of machinery and equipment is 10 years, with no scrap value. Depreciation is computed on acquisitions from the date of purchase to the end of the period and on disposals from the beginning of the period to the date of disposal. (Use 365 days for base.)

(b) Compute the depreciation for the year, assuming that it is computed for the full period on the beginning balance in the asset account.

(c) Compute the depreciation for the year, assuming that depreciation is charged on additions from the beginning of the month following acquisition, and on disposals to the beginning of the month following disposal.

(d) Which of the three methods above is the best method? Discuss briefly.

E12-6 On April 10, 1981, the Sanders Company sells equipment that it purchased for $36,000 on September 25, 1967. It was originally estimated that the equipment would have a life of 15 years and a scrap value of $3,600 at the end of that time, and depreciation has been computed on that basis. The company uses the straight-line method of depreciation.

1. Depreciation is computed for the exact period of time during which the asset is owned. (Use 365 days for base.)

2. Depreciation is computed for the full year on the January 1 balance in the asset account.

3. Depreciation is computed for the full year on the December 31 balance in the asset account.

4. Depreciation for one-half year is charged on plant assets acquired or disposed of during the year.

5. Depreciation is computed on additions from the beginning of the month following acquisition and on disposals to the beginning of the month following disposal.

6. Depreciation is computed for a full period on all assets in use for over one-half year, and no depreciation is charged on assets in use for less than one-half year. (Use 365 days for base.)

Instructions

(a) Compute the depreciation charge on this equipment for 1967, for 1981, and the total charge for the period from 1967 to 1981, inclusive, under each of the six assumptions above with respect to partial periods.

(b) Briefly evaluate the methods above, considering them from the point of view of basic accounting theory as well as simplicity of application.

E12-7 Joanie Kreidle Corporation bought a machine on June 1, 1978, for $6,000, f.o.b. the place of manufacture. Freight to the point where it was set up was $200, and $125 was expended to install it. The machine's useful life was estimated at 10 years, with a scrap value of $50. In June, 1979, an essential part of the machine is replaced, at a cost of $700, with one designed to reduce the cost of operating the machine. On June 1, 1982, the company buys a new machine of greater capacity for $9,000, delivered, being allowed a trade-in value on the old machine of $2,000. To prepare the old machine for removal from the plant cost $75, and expenditures to install the new one were $225. It is estimated that the new machine has a useful life of 10 years, with a scrap value of $100 at the end of that time.

Instructions

Assuming that depreciation is to be computed on the straight-line basis, prepare schedules showing the amount of depreciation on this equipment that should be provided during the year beginning June 1, 1982. (Round to the nearest dollar.)

E12-8 Presented below is information related to the Tappan Corporation:

Asset	Cost	Estimated Scrap	Estimated Life (in years)
A	$24,000	$2,400	9
B	32,000	4,000	10
C	12,000	2,400	8
D	20,000	3,200	10
E	4,000	640	7

Instructions

(a) Compute the rate of depreciation per year to be applied to the plant assets under the composite method.

(b) Prepare the adjusting entry necessary at the end of the year to record depreciation for the year.

(c) Prepare the entry to record the sale of fixed asset C for cash of $5,040. It was used for six years, and depreciation was entered under the composite method.

E12-9 In 1981, Varlen Power Co. replaced 20,000 utility poles at a cost of $100 each. The old poles originally cost $75 apiece.

Instructions

(a) Prepare the entry(ies) assuming that Varlen Power Co. uses the retirement method for depreciating their utility poles.

(b) Prepare the entry(ies) assuming that Varlen Power Co. uses the replacement method for depreciating their utility poles.

E12-10 The Pacific Power Company decides to use the retirement method in accounting for house meters that it installs, because they are of small value and replaced frequently. The life of the meters is from 1 to 15 years, with the average life about 12 years.

Below are the transactions related to the house meters for 1981.

Jan. 10, 1981　Purchases 10,000 meters at $300 each.
Apr. 15, 1981　Discards 20 of the meters purchased January 10, 1980, as worthless.
June 20, 1981　Sells 50 of the meters purchased January 10, 1980, for $500.
Dec. 12, 1981　Replaces 500 meters at $320 each.

Instructions

Using the retirement method, prepare entries to record the transactions for 1981.

E12-11 Fairmont Manufacturing Company has approximately 3,000 hand tools, which it uses in its operations. Each is of relatively small value and is frequently replaced. The total cost of such tools is approximately $30,000.

Because of the characteristics of this asset, the company prefers not to keep detailed records of each tool and depreciate it. You are asked to suggest some reasonably simple method of accounting for these tools so that the asset is carried at a fair amount and operating expenses are charged with a fair amount. What do you suggest?

Instructions

Illustrate your suggestion with pro forma entries for the various types of transactions that might occur.

E12-12 Machinery purchased for $30,000 was originally estimated to have a life of 8 years with a salvage value of $6,000 at the end of that time. Depreciation has been entered for 6 years on this basis. In 1981, it is determined that the total estimated life (including 1981) should be 12 years with a salvage value of $7,500 at the end of that time. Assume straight-line depreciation.

Instructions

(a) Prepare the entry to correct the prior years' depreciation, if necessary.

(b) Prepare the entry to record depreciation for 1981.

E12-13 In 1951, Tinkerbell Company completed the construction of a building at a cost of $960,000 and first occupied it in January, 1952. It is estimated that the building will have a useful life of 50 years, and a salvage value of $60,000 at the end of that time.

Early in 1962, an addition to the building was constructed at a cost of $96,000. At that time it was estimated that the remaining life of the building would be, as originally estimated, an additional 40 years, and that the addition would have a life of 40 years, and a salvage value of $6,000.

In 1982, it is determined that the probable life of the building will extend to the end of 2011, or 10 years beyond the original estimate.

Instructions

(a) Compute the annual depreciation that would have been charged from 1952 to 1961.

(b) Compute the annual depreciation that would have been charged from 1962 to 1981.

(c) Prepare the entry, if necessary, to adjust the account balances because of the revision of the estimated life in 1982.

(d) Compute the annual depreciation to be charged beginning with 1982.

E12-14   A. C. Littleton Company constructed a building at a cost of $1,000,000 and occupied it beginning in January, 1961. It was estimated at that time that its life would be 40 years, with no salvage value.

In January, 1981, a new roof was installed at a cost of $120,000, and it was estimated then that the building would have a useful life of 30 years from that date. The cost of the old roof was $60,000.

Instructions

(a) What amount of depreciation should have been charged annually from the years 1961 to 1980? (Assume straight-line depreciation.)

(b) What entry should be made in 1981 to record the replacement of the roof?

(c) Prepare the entry in January, 1981, to record the revision in the estimated life of the building, if necessary.

(d) What amount of depreciation should be charged for the year 1981?

E12-15   Wm. Paton, Inc. bought a number of machines at a total cost of $80,000 during 1981. All of them qualify for the 10% investment credit. Wm. Paton, Inc. had income before taxes of $600,000 (tax rate 40%).

Instructions

(a) Prepare the entry(ies) required at December 31, 1981 to account for the investment credit. Assume that the cost reduction (deferral) method is used and that the credit is amortized over a seven-year life.

(b) Prepare the entry(ies) at December 31, 1981 for the investment credit if the tax reduction (flow-through) method is used by Wm. Paton, Inc.

E12-16   Geo. O. May, Inc. purchased machinery and equipment during 1981 amounting to $160,000, and all of these acquisitions qualify for the investment credit. Geo. O. May, Inc. has decided to record the investment credit in a deferred income account and amortize it over the productive life of the acquired property (seven years). The company's income before taxes was $500,000 (tax rate 45%). Assume a 10% rate for the investment credit.

Instructions

(a) Prepare the entry(ies) required at December 31, 1981, to account for the income tax expense and investment credit, assuming that a full year's amortization is taken in the first year.

(b) Prepare the entry(ies) required at December 31, 1981, to account for the income tax expense and investment credit, assuming that the tax reduction (flow-through) method was used.

(c) How would the journal entries under these two approaches be different in future periods?

E12-17   You are the assistant controller for H. R. Hatfield & Associates. On January 1, 1981, Hatfield purchased heavy machinery with an estimated service life of 20 years. The machinery cost $390,000. This machinery qualified for a 10% investment credit. The controller believed that the cost reduction (deferral) method would be the most appropriate method for handling this transaction. Accordingly, the following entry was made:

Jan. 1	Machinery	351,000	
	Reserve for Investment Credit	39,000	
	Accounts Payable		390,000

Income tax expense for the year prior to any allowable credits was correctly determined to be $110,550. The controller therefore made the following entry on December 31, 1981:

Dec. 31 Income Tax Expense	71,550	
Deferred Investment Credit	39,000	
Income Taxes Payable		71,550
Reserve for Investment Credit		39,000

The controller, however, is unsure of the entries above and asks your opinion. Amortize investment credit over 20 years.

Instructions

If you believe that the cost reduction method has not been applied correctly, prepare the entry(ies) that will correct the books and bring them into proper adjustment for 1981. (Ignore any depreciation considerations.)

E12-18   The R. H. Montgomery Mining Company purchased land on February 1, 1980, at a cost of $660,000. It estimated that a total of 60,000 tons of mineral was available for mining. After it has removed all the natural resources, the company will be required to restore the property to its previous state because of strict environmental protection laws. It estimates the cost of this restoration at $40,000. It believes it will be able to sell the property afterwards for $50,000. It incurred developmental costs of $100,000 before it was able to do any mining. In 1980, resources removed totaled 15,000 tons. It sold 10,000 tons.

Instructions

Compute the following information for 1980: (1) per unit material cost; (2) total material cost of 12/31/80 inventory; and (3) total material cost in cost of goods sold at 12/31/80.

E12-19   The Eric Koehler Drilling Company has leased property on which oil has been discovered. Wells on this property produced 8,000 barrels of oil during the past year that sold at an average sales price of $15.30 per barrel. Total oil resources of this property are estimated to be 100,000 barrels.

    The lease provided for an outright payment of $400,000 to the lessor before drilling could be commenced and an annual rental of $5,000. A premium of 5% of the sales price of every barrel of oil removed is to be paid annually to the lessor. In addition, the lessee is to clean up all the waste and debris from drilling and to bear the costs of reconditioning the land for farming when the wells are abandoned. It is estimated that this clean-up and reconditioning will cost no more than $3,000.

Instructions

From the provisions of the lease agreement, you are to compute the cost per barrel, exclusive of operating costs, to the Eric Koehler Drilling Company. (Round to three decimal places.)

Problems

P12-1   The cost of equipment purchased by A. Lowes Dickinson, Inc. on April 1, 1980 is $30,000. It is estimated that the machine will have a $2,000 salvage value at the end of its service life. Its service life is estimated at eight years; its total working hours are estimated at 32,000 and its total production is estimated at 480,000 units. During 1980, the machine was operated 3,000 hours and produced 46,000 units. During 1981, the machine was operated 4,000 hours and produced 62,000 units. (Round per hour and unit costs to three decimal places.)

Instructions

Compute depreciation expense on the machine for the year ending December 31, 1980, and the year ending December 31, 1981, using the following methods: (1) Straight-line; (2) units-of-output; (3) working hours; (4) sum-of-the-years'-digits; and (5) declining balance (twice the straight-line rate).

P12-2 Niven & Bailey, Inc. purchased Machine #201 on April 1, 1980. The following information relating to Machine #201 was gathered at the end of April.

Price	$60,000
Credit terms	2/10, n/30
Freight-in costs	$ 2,400
Preparation and installation costs	$ 7,800
Labor costs during regular production operations	$ 9,600

It was expected that the machine could be used for 10 years, after which the salvage value would be zero. Niven & Bailey, Inc. intends to use the machine for only 8 years, however, after which it expects to be able to sell it for $9,600. The invoice for Machine #201 was paid April 5, 1980. Niven & Bailey uses the calendar year as the basis for the preparation of financial statements.

Instructions

(a) Compute the depreciation expense for the years indicated using the following methods. (Round to the nearest cent.)
  1. Straight-line method for 1980.
  2. Sum-of-the-years'-digits method for 1981.
  3. Double-declining balance method for 1980.

(b) Suppose the president of Niven & Bailey, Inc. tells you that because the company is a new organization, she expects it will be several years before production and sales are at optimum levels. She asks you to recommend a depreciation method that will allocate less of the company's depreciation expense to the early years and more to later years of the assets' lives. What method would you recommend?

P12-3 The following data relate to the Plant Asset account of Pacioli Company at December 31, 1980:

	Plant Asset			
	A	**B**	**C**	**D**
Original cost	$30,000	$30,000	$60,000	$50,000
Year purchased	1975	1976	1977	1979
Useful life	10 years	15,000 hours	10 years	40 years
Salvage value	$ 5,250	-0-	$ 5,000	$ 5,000
Depreciation method	Sum-of-the-years'-digits	Activity	Straight-line	Double-declining balance
Accum. Depr. through 1980*	$18,000	$20,000	$16,500	$ 2,500

*In the year an asset is purchased, Pacioli Company does not record any depreciation expense on the asset. In the year an asset is retired or traded in, Pacioli Company takes a full year's depreciation on the asset.

The following transactions occurred during 1981:

(a) On May 5, Asset A was sold for $22,500 cash. The company's bookkeeper recorded this retirement in the following manner in the cash receipts journal:

Cash	22,500	
Asset A		22,500

(b) On December 31, it was determined that Asset B had been used 3,000 hours during 1981.

(c) On December 31, before computing depreciation expense on Asset C, the management of Pacioli Company decided the useful life remaining from 1/1/81 was 10 years.

(d) On December 31, it was discovered that a plant asset purchased in 1980 had been expensed completely in that year. This asset cost $7,000 and has a useful life of 10 years and no salvage value. Management has decided to use the double-declining balance method for this asset, which can be referred to as "Asset E."

Instructions

Prepare the necessary correcting entries for the year 1981. Record the appropriate depreciation expense on the above-mentioned assets.

P12-4 On January 1, 1978, Barth Company, a small machine-tool manufacturer, acquired for $1,000,000 a piece of new industrial equipment. The new equipment was eligible for the investment tax credit and Barth took full advantage of the credit and accounted for the amount using the flow-through method. The new equipment had a useful life of 5 years and the salvage value was estimated to be $100,000. Barth estimates that the new equipment can produce 10,000 machine tools in its first year. It estimates that production will decline by 1,000 units per year over the remaining useful life of the equipment.

The following depreciation methods may be used:

Double-declining balance Sum-of-the-years'-digits
Straight-line Units-of-output

Instructions

Which depreciation method would result in the maximization of net income for financial statement reporting for the three-year period ending December 31, 1980? Prepare a schedule showing the amount of accumulated depreciation at December 31, 1980, under the method selected. Ignore present value, income tax, and deferred income tax considerations in your answer.

Which depreciation method would result in the minimization of net income for income tax reporting for the three-year period ending December 31, 1980? Prepare a schedule showing the amount of accumulated depreciation at December 31, 1980, under the method selected. Ignore present value considerations in your answer.

(AICPA adapted)

P12-5 A depreciation schedule for semitrucks of the A. Barr Manufacturing Company was requested by your auditor soon after December 31, 1981, showing the additions, retirements, depreciation, and other data affecting the taxable income of the company in the four-year period 1978 to 1981, inclusive. The following data were ascertained:

Balance of Semitrucks account, Jan. 1, 1978:	
Truck No. 1 purchased Jan. 1, 1975, cost	$ 4,000
Truck No. 2 purchased July 1, 1975, cost	3,600
Truck No. 3 purchased Jan. 1, 1977, cost	2,400
Truck No. 4 purchased July 1, 1977, cost	2,000
Balance, Jan. 1, 1978	$12,000

The Semitrucks-Accumulated Depreciation account previously adjusted to January 1, 1978, and duly entered in the ledger, had a balance on that date of $4,880 (depreciation on the four trucks from the respective dates of purchase, based on a 5-year life). No charges had been made against the account before January 1, 1978.

Transactions between January 1, 1978, and December 31, 1981, and their record in the ledger were as follows:

July 1, 1978 Truck No. 3 was traded for a larger one (No. 5), the agreed purchase price of which was $3,200. The A. Barr Mfg. Co. paid the automobile dealer $1,560 cash on the transaction. The entry was a debit to Semitrucks and a credit to Cash, $1,560.

Jan. 1, 1979 Truck No. 1 was sold for $1,200 cash; entry debited Cash and credited Semitrucks, $1,200.

July 1, 1980   Truck No. 4 was damaged in a wreck to such an extent that it was sold as junk for $100 cash. A. Barr Mfg. Co. received $600 from the insurance company. The entry made by the bookkeeper was a debit to Cash, $700, and credits to Miscellaneous Income, $100, and Semitrucks, $600.

July 1, 1980   A new truck (No. 6) was acquired for $2,400 cash and was charged at that amount to the Semitrucks account. (Assume truck No. 2 was not retired.)

Entries for depreciation had been made at the close of each year as follows: 1978, $2,400; 1979, $2,152; 1980, $2,152; 1981, $2,492.

Instructions

(a) For each of the four years compute separately the increase or decrease in net income arising from the company's errors in determining or entering depreciation or in recording transactions affecting trucks, ignoring income tax considerations.

(b) Prepare one compound journal entry as of December 31, 1981, for adjustment of the Semitrucks account to reflect the correct balances as revealed by your schedule, assuming that the books have not been closed for 1981.

P12-6   The J. L. Carey Tool Company records depreciation annually at the end of the year. Its policy is to take a full year's depreciation on all assets used throughout the year and depreciation for one-half a year on all machines acquired or disposed of during the year. The depreciation rate for the machinery is 10% applied on a straight-line basis, with no estimated scrap value.

The balance of the Machinery account at the beginning of 1981 was $135,420; the Accumulated Depreciation on Machinery account had a balance of $51,240. The following transactions affecting the machinery accounts took place during the year.

Jan. 15   Machine No. 38, which cost $3,270 when acquired June 3, 1973, was retired and sold as scrap metal for $54.

Feb. 27   Machine No. 81 was purchased. The fair market value of this machine was $5,160. It replaces Machines No. 12 and No. 27, which were traded in on the new machine. Machine No. 12 was acquired Feb. 4, 1968, at a cost of $1,800 and is still carried in the accounts although fully depreciated and not in use; Machine No. 27 was acquired June 11, 1973, at a cost of $1,500. In addition to these two used machines, $4,620 was paid in cash. (Assume exchange of similar assets.)

Apr. 7   Machine No. 54 was equipped with electric control equipment at a cost of $210. This machine, originally equipped with simple hand controls, was purchased Dec. 11, 1977, for $540. The new electric controls can be attached to any one of several machines in the shop.

12   Machine No. 24 was repaired at a cost of $330 after a fire caused by a short circuit in the wiring burned out the motor and damaged certain essential parts.

July 22   Machines No. 25, 26, and 41 are sold for $1,250 cash. The purchase dates and cost of these machines are:

No. 25	$1,400	May 8, 1972
No. 26	1,400	May 8, 1972
No. 41	1,800	June 1, 1976

Nov. 17   Rearrangement and reinstallation of several machines to facilitate material handling and to speed up production are completed at a cost of $8,200.

Instructions

(a) Record each transaction in general journal entry form.

(b) Compute and record depreciation for the year. No machines now included in the balance of the account were acquired before Jan. 1, 1972.

P12-7   The C. Blough Mining Company has purchased a tract of mineral land for $120,000. It is estimated that this tract will yield 100,000 tons of ore with sufficient mineral content to make mining and processing profitable. It is further estimated that 5,000 tons of ore will be mined the first year and 10,000 tons each year thereafter. The land will have no residual value.

The company builds necessary structures and sheds on the site at a cost of $21,600. It is estimated that these structures can serve 15 years but, because they must be dismantled if they are to be moved, they have no scrap value. The company does not intend to use the buildings elsewhere. Mining machinery installed at the mine was purchased second-hand at a cost of $34,200. This machinery cost the former owner $38,000 and was 40% depreciated when purchased. The C. Blough Mining Company estimates that about half of this machinery will still be useful when the present mineral resources have been exhausted but that dismantling and removal costs will just about offset its value at that time. The company does not intend to use the machinery elsewhere. The remaining machinery will last until about one-half the present estimated mineral ore has been removed and will then be worthless. Cost is to be allocated equally between these two classes of machinery.

Instructions

(a) As chief accountant for the company, you are to prepare a schedule showing estimated depletion and depreciation costs for each year of the expected life of the mine.

(b) Also draft entries in general journal entry form to record depreciation and depletion for the first year assuming actual production of 4,800 tons. Nothing occurred during the year to cause the company engineers to change their estimates of either the mineral resources or the life of the structures and equipment.

P12-8   The Pacific Lumber Company purchased an L-shaped tract of timber land at a cost of $300,000. Once cleared of the natural growth, the land is to be planted with small evergreens for Christmas trees. The worth of the land for this purpose is judged to be $96,000. To remove the timber now on the land, a railroad spur must be constructed at an estimated cost of $33,600 including rolling stock. This railroad will be of some use in the proposed evergreen planting and harvesting operations of the company but, because of the heavy use it will receive during the logging operations, its residual value at the close of the logging operations will be only about 30% of original cost.

Present plans call for working the logging operation in two parts. The most accessible one-third of the tract will be worked first; the remainder of the timber is to await further development of the evergreen project. The entire stand of timber is estimated at 50,000 M board feet of lumber. When it is sawed, three grades will result, having relative sales values approximately as follows:

Grade	Estimated Board Feet	Relative Sales Value
1	5,000 M	1.5
2	33,000	1.0
3	12,000	0.5

The activities of the company during the first year of operations are summarized below.

1. 12,000 M board feet of lumber was cut, 8,000 M board feet of which was sawed and sold at a gross sales price of $360,000. Relative sales prices of the three grades of lumber were about as estimated.

2. Sawing costs paid to an affiliated company on a contract basis amounted to $7.00 per M board feet sawed.

3. Wages and salaries applicable to the logging operations totaled $164,400.

4. Administrative expenses amounted to $69,600.

5. Costs of $23,500 were incurred in connection with preparing cleared land and planting it with evergreens.

6. At a cost of $33,600, the railroad spur was completed, rolling stock acquired, and terminal facilities constructed.

Instructions

Assume that the railroad spur should be depreciated using an activity method of depreciation.

(a) Compute the cost of ending inventory of lumber (4,000 M board feet).

(b) Compute the net income for the first year of operations.

P12-9 You are engaged in the examination of the financial statements of the Asia Corporation for the year ended December 31, 1981. The schedules below for the property, plant and equipment, and related accumulated depreciation accounts have been prepared by the client. You have checked the opening balances to your prior year's audit workpapers.

Your examination reveals the following information:

1. All equipment is depreciated on the straight-line basis (no salvage value taken into consideration) using the following estimated lives: buildings, 25 years; all other items, 10 years. The company's policy is to take one-half year's depreciation on all asset acquisitions and disposals during the year.

2. On April 1, the company entered into a 10-year lease contract for a die-casting machine with annual rentals of $5,000 payable in advance every April 1. The lease can be canceled by either party (60 days written notice is required) and there is no option to renew the lease or buy the equipment at the end of the lease. The estimated useful life of the machine is 10 years with no salvage value. The company recorded the die-casting machine in the Machinery and Equipment account at $40,400, the present discounted value at the date of the lease, and $2,020, applicable to the machine, has been included in depreciation expense for the year. (**Hint:** leases with these conditions should not be capitalized nor should a liability be recognized.)

3. The company completed the construction of a wing on the plant building on June 30. The useful life of the building was not extended by this addition. The lowest construction bid received was $17,500, the amount recorded in the Buildings account. Company personnel were used to construct the addition at a cost of $16,000 (materials, $7,500; labor, $5,500; and overhead, $3,000).

4. On August 18, $10,000 was paid for paving and fencing a portion of land owned by the company and used as a parking lot for employees. The expenditure was charged to the Land account.

5. The amount shown in the machinery and equipment asset retirement column represents cash received on September 5 upon disposal of a machine purchased in July, 1977, for $48,000. The bookkeeper recorded depreciation expense of $3,500 on this machine in 1981.

6. Indiana City donated land and building appraised at $10,000 and $40,000, respectively, to the Asia Corporation for a plant. On September 1, the company began operating the plant. Because no costs were involved, the bookkeeper made no entry to record the transaction.

Asia Corp.
ANALYSIS OF PROPERTY, PLANT AND EQUIPMENT, AND
RELATED ACCUMULATED DEPRECIATION ACCOUNTS
Year Ended December 31, 1981

Description	Final 12/31/80	Additions	Retirements	Per Books 12/31/81
	Assets			
Land	$ 32,500	$10,000		$ 42,500
Buildings	120,000	17,500		137,500
Machinery and equipment	385,000	40,400	$26,000	399,400
	$537,500	$67,900	$26,000	$579,400

| | | Accumulated Depreciation | | |
Description	Final 12/31/80	Additions[a]	Retirements	Per Books 12/31/81
Buildings	$ 60,000	$ 5,150		$ 65,150
Machinery and equipment	173,250	39,220		212,470
	$233,250	$44,370		$277,620

[a]Depreciation expense for the year.

Instructions

Prepare the formal journal entries that you would suggest at December 31, 1981, to adjust the accounts for the transactions noted above. Disregard income tax implications. The books have not been closed. Computations should be rounded off to the nearest dollar.

(AICPA adapted)

P12-10 Heritage Corporation, a manufacturer of steel products, began operations on October 1, 1979. The accounting department of Heritage has started the fixed-asset and depreciation schedule presented below. You have been asked to assist in completing this schedule. In addition to ascertaining that the data already on the schedule are correct, you have obtained the following information from the company's records and personnel:

1. Depreciation is computed from the first of the month of acquisition to the first of the month of disposition.

2. Land A and Building A were acquired from a predecessor corporation. Heritage paid $812,500 for the land and building together. At the time of acquisition, the land had an appraised value of $72,000, and the building had an appraised value of $828,000.

3. Land B was acquired on October 2, 1979, in exchange for 3,000 newly issued shares of Heritage's common stock. At the date of acquisition, the stock had a par value of $5 per share and a fair value of $25 per share. During October 1979, Heritage paid $10,400 to demolish an existing building on this land so it could construct a new building.

4. Construction of Building B on the newly acquired land began on October 1, 1980. By September 30, 1981, Heritage had paid $210,000 of the estimated total construction costs of $300,000. It is estimated that the building will be completed and occupied by July, 1982.

5. Certain equipment was donated to the corporation by a local university. An independent appraisal of the equipment when donated placed the fair value at $16,000 and the salvage value at $2,000.

6. Machinery A's total cost of $110,000 includes installation expense of $550 and normal repairs and maintenance of $11,000. Salvage value is estimated as $5,500. Machinery A was sold on February 1, 1981.

7. On October 1, 1979, Machinery B was acquired with a down payment of $4,000 and the $55,000 balance to be paid in 11 annual installments of $5,000 each beginning October 1, 1980. The prevailing interest rate was 8%. The following data were abstracted from present-value tables (rounded):

Present value of $1.00 at 8%

10 years	.463
11 years	.429
15 years	.315

Present value of an ordinary annuity of $1.00 at 8%

10 years	6.710	+	= 7.710 annuity due 12 periods
11 years	7.139
15 years	8.559

Heritage Corporation
FIXED ASSET AND DEPRECIATION SCHEDULE
For Fiscal Years Ended September 30, 1980, and September 30, 1981

Assets	Acquisition Date	Cost	Salvage	Depreciation Method	Estimated Life in Years	Depreciation Expense Year Ended September 30,	
						1980	1981
Land A	October 1, 1979	$ (1)	N/A	N/A	N/A	N/A	N/A
Building A	October 1, 1979	(2)	$47,500	Straight-Line	(3)	$14,000	(4)
Land B	October 2, 1979	(5)	N/A	N/A	N/A	N/A	N/A
Building B	Under Construction	210,000 to date	—	Straight-Line	30	—	(6)
Donated Equipment	October 2, 1979	(7)	2,000	150% Declining Balance	10	(8)	(9)
Machinery A	October 2, 1979	(10)	5,500	Sum-of-the-Years'-Digits	10	(11)	(12)
Machinery B	October 1, 1980	(13)	—	Straight-Line	15	—	(14)

N/A—Not applicable

Instructions

For each numbered item on the foregoing schedule, supply the correct amount. Round each answer to the nearest dollar.

(AICPA adapted)

Intangible Assets

Nature of Intangible Assets

Intangible assets are generally characterized by a lack of physical existence, and a high degree of uncertainty concerning future benefits. These criteria are not so clear-cut as they may seem. The following discussion by a well-noted accountant typifies some of the major problems encountered in attempting to define intangibles.

Q. I infer, Mr. May, from your experience . . . that you know what in ordinary speech the word tangible means, don't you?
A. Yes.
Q. Well, what do you understand it to mean in ordinary speech?
A. Something that can be touched, I imagine.
Q. Like merchandise?
A. Yes.
Q. You can touch merchandise or horses?
A. Yes.
Q. Can you touch an account receivable?
A. You can touch the debtor.
Q. Is that the basis on which you include the debtor's debt as tangible?
A. It had not occurred to me before, but possibly it is.[1]

This discussion indicates that the lack of physical existence is not by itself a satisfactory criterion for distinguishing a tangible from an intangible asset. Such assets as bank deposits, accounts receivable, and long-term investments lack physical substance, yet accountants classify them as tangible assets.

[1]From testimony given to referee, *In the Matter of the Estate of E. P. Hatch Deceased (1912)*. Reprinted in Bishop Carleton Hunt, ed., *Twenty-five Years of Accounting Responsibility, 1911–1936* (New York: Price Waterhouse and Company, 1936), I, p. 246. Selected essays and discussions of George O. May.

Some accountants believe that the major characteristic of an intangible asset is the high degree of uncertainty concerning the future benefits that are to be received from its employment. For example, many intangibles (1) have value only to a given enterprise, (2) have indeterminate lives, and (3) are subject to large fluctuations in value because their benefits are based on a competitive advantage. The determination and timing of future benefits are extremely difficult and pose serious valuation problems. Tangible assets possess similar characteristics but they are not so pronounced.

Other accountants, finding the problem of defining intangibles insurmountable, prefer simply to present them in financial statements on the basis of tradition. The more common types of intangibles are patents, copyrights, franchises, goodwill, organization costs, and trademarks or trade names. These intangibles may be further subdivided on the basis of the following characteristics.

1. **Identifiability.** Separately identifiable or lacking specific identification.
2. **Manner of acquisition.** Acquired singly, in groups, or in business combinations, or developed internally.
3. **Expected period of benefit.** Limited by law or contract, related to human or economic factors, or indefinite or indeterminate duration.
4. **Separability from an entire enterprise.** Rights transferable without title, salable, or inseparable from the enterprise or a substantial part of it.[2]

Valuation of Purchased Intangibles

Intangibles, like tangible assets, should be **recorded at cost.** Cost includes all costs of acquisition and expenditures necessary to make the intangible asset ready for its intended use. These costs are normally purchase price, legal fees, and other incidental expenses incurred in obtaining the asset.

If intangibles are acquired for stock or in exchange for other assets, the cost of the intangible is the fair market value of the consideration given or the fair market value of the intangible received, whichever is more clearly evident. Sometimes both the value of what is given and the value of what is received are difficult to estimate: at this point, exercise of professional judgment is required to establish an appropriate valuation. Essentially the accounting treatment closely parallels that followed for tangible assets. For example, when several intangibles, or a combination of intangibles and tangibles, are bought in a "basket purchase," the cost should be allocated on the basis of fair market values or on the basis of relative sales values.

There is little sentiment for employment of some other basis of valuation, such as current replacement costs or appraisal value for these types of assets. The basic attributes of intangibles, their uncertainty as to future benefits, and their uniqueness, do not lend themselves to valuation in excess of cost.[3]

---

[2]"Intangible Assets," *Opinions of the Accounting Principles Board No. 17* (New York: AICPA, 1970), par. 10.

[3]For example, Sprouse and Moonitz in *AICPA Accounting Research Study No. 3*, "A Tentative Set of Broad Accounting Principles for a Business Enterprise," advocate abandonment of historical cost in favor of replacement cost for most asset items, but suggest that intangibles should normally be carried at acquisition cost less amortization because valuation problems are so difficult.

Amortization of Intangible Assets

Intangible assets should be amortized by systematic charges to revenue over their useful lives. **APB Opinion No. 17** enumerates the factors that might be considered in determining useful life.

1. Legal, regulatory, or contractual provisions may limit the maximum useful life.
2. Provisions for renewal or extension may alter a specified limit on useful life.
3. Effects of obsolescence, demand, competition, and other economic factors may reduce a useful life.
4. A useful life may parallel the service life expectancies of individuals or groups of employees.
5. Expected actions of competitors and others may restrict present competitive advantages.
6. An apparently unlimited useful life may in fact be indefinite and benefits cannot be reasonably projected.
7. An intangible asset may be a composite of many individual factors with varying effective lives.[4]

One problem relating to the amortization of intangibles is that some intangibles have indeterminable useful lives. In this case, the APB concluded that the value of an intangible asset eventually disappears and that the recorded costs of intangible assets should be amortized by systematic charges to income over the periods estimated to be benefited. **APB Opinion No. 17** requires that intangible assets be amortized over a period not exceeding 40 years.[5] The 40-year requirement is based on the premise that only a few, if any, intangibles last for a lifetime. Sometimes, because it is difficult to determine useful life, a 40-year period is practical, although admittedly it is an arbitrary solution. Another reason for this 40-year limitation is simply that it ensures that companies start to write off their intangibles. There was evidence that some companies retained their intangibles (notably goodwill) indefinitely on their balance sheet for only one reason—to avoid the charge against income that occurs when goodwill is written off.

Intangible assets acquired from other enterprises (notably goodwill) should not be written off at acquisition. Some accountants contend that certain intangibles should not be carried as assets on the balance sheet under any circumstances but should be written off directly to retained earnings or additional paid-in capital. The position of the profession is that the immediate write-off to retained earnings and additional paid-in capital is not acceptable because this approach denies the existence of an asset that has just been purchased.

Intangible assets are generally amortized on a straight-line basis (tax practice requires a straight-line approach), although there is no reason why another systematic approach might not be employed if the firm demonstrates that another method is more appropriate. In any case the method and period of amortization should be disclosed.

When intangible assets are amortized, the charges should be shown as expenses, deductions from income, of the years benefited, and the credits should be made either to the appropriate asset accounts or to separate accumulated amortization accounts.

[4]*APB Opinion No. 17, op. cit.,* par. 27.
[5]*Ibid.,* par. 10.

SPECIFICALLY IDENTIFIABLE INTANGIBLE ASSETS

As indicated earlier, a number of bases may be employed to differentiate one group of intangible assets from another. Originally, the accounting profession recognized two types of classification for intangibles: type (a) intangibles that had a limited life and type (b) intangibles that had an unlimited life.

The classification framework was changed by the APB in 1970 to intangibles that are specifically identifiable as contrasted to "goodwill type" intangible assets (unidentifiable values). **Specifically identifiable** means that costs associated with obtaining a given intangible asset can be identified as a part of the cost of that intangible asset. In contrast, **goodwill type** intangibles may create some right or privilege, but it is not specifically identifiable, has an indeterminable life, and its cost is inherent in a continuing business. The major identifiable assets and goodwill are discussed below.

Patents

Patents are granted by the U.S. Patent Office. A patent gives the holder exclusive right to use, manufacture, and sell a product or process **for a period of 17 years** without interference or infringement by others. If a patent is purchased from an inventor (or other owner), the purchase price represents its cost. Other costs incurred in connection with securing a patent, and attorneys' fees and other unrecovered costs of a successful legal suit to protect the patent, can be capitalized as part of the patent cost. **Research and development costs** related to the development of the product, process, or idea that is subsequently patented must be expensed as incurred, however. See pages 567–569 for a more complete presentation of accounting for research and development costs.

The cost of a patent should be amortized over its legal life or its useful life (i.e., over the period benefits are received), whichever is shorter. If a patent is owned from the date it is granted, and it is expected to be useful during its entire legal life, it should be amortized over 17 years. If it appears that the patent will be useful for a shorter period of time, say, for five years, its cost should be amortized against income over five years. Changing demand, new inventions superseding old ones, inadequacy, and other factors often limit the useful life of a patent to less than the legal life.

Legal fees and other costs incurred in successfully defending a patent suit may properly be charged to the Patents account because such a suit establishes the legal rights of the holder of the patent. Such costs should be amortized along with acquisition cost over the remaining useful life of the patent.

Amortization of patents may be computed on a time basis or on a basis of units produced and may be credited directly to the Patents account; it is acceptable also, although less common in practice, to credit an Accumulated Patent Amortization account. Assuming that the cost of a patent is $102,000, that it will be useful for 17 years, and that it is being amortized on a straight-line basis, the entry at the end of each year would be:

Patent Amortization Expense	6,000	
Patents (Or Accumulated Patent Amortization)		6,000

Amortization on a units of production basis would be computed in a manner similar to that described for depreciation on property, plant, and equipment.

Royalties received from the assignment of patents to other enterprises represent income of the period in which the royalties are earned and should be accrued as income.

Although a patent's useful life should not extend beyond its legal life of 17 years, small modifications or additions may lead to a new patent. The effect may be to extend the life of the old patent, in which case it is permissible to apply the unamortized costs of the old patent to the new patent if the new patent provides essentially the same benefits. Alternatively, if a patent becomes worthless because demand drops for the product produced, the asset should be written off immediately to operations.

Copyrights

Prior to January 1, 1978, a copyright was granted by the federal government for 28 years, subject to renewal for another 28 years; subsequent to January 1, 1978 a copyright is granted for the **life of the creator plus 50 years,** and gives the owner, or heirs, the exclusive right to reproduce and sell an artistic or published work. Copyrights, like patents, may be assigned or sold to other individuals. The costs of acquiring and defending a copyright may be capitalized but the research and development costs involved must be expensed as incurred.

Generally, the useful life of the copyright is less than the legal life (life in being plus 50 years). The costs of the copyright should be allocated to the years in which the benefits are expected to be received, not to exceed 40 years. The difficulty of determining the number of years over which benefits will be received normally encourages the company to write these costs off over a fairly short period of time.

Leaseholds

A leasehold is a contractual understanding between a lessor and a lessee that grants the lessee the right to use specific property, owned by the lessor, for a specific period of time in return for stipulated, and generally periodic, cash payments. Most lease agreements provide simply for the right of the lessee to use property of the lessor for stipulated periods. In such a case the rent is included as an expense on the books of the lessee. Special problems, however, develop in the following situations.

Lease Prepayments If the rent for the period of the lease is paid in advance, or if a lump sum payment is made in advance in addition to periodic rental payments, it is necessary to allocate this prepaid rent to the proper periods. The lessee, by payment of the amount agreed upon, has purchased the exclusive right to use the property for an extended period of time. Some accountants advocate presenting this prepayment as an intangible asset; in many published financial statements, prepayments on long-term leases are classified as deferred charges.

Capitalization of Leases In some cases, the lease agreement transfers substantially all of the benefits and risks incident to ownership of the property so that the economic effect on the parties is similar to that of an installment purchase. As a result, the asset value recognized when a lease is capitalized is classified as a tangible rather than an intangible asset. Such a lease is referred to as a **capital lease.** And, according to **FASB Statement No. 13,** the lessee must record a capital lease as an asset and an obligation at an amount equal to the present value of the minimum lease payments required during the lease term, excluding that portion of the payments representing executory costs such as insurance, maintenance, and taxes to be paid by the lessor.[6] Further, in such cases, it is appropriate for the lessee to depreciate the capitalized asset in a manner consistent with the lessee's normal depreciation policy for owned assets.

The FASB requires that if the lessee is party to a lease that meets one or more of the following four criteria, the lessee must classify the transaction as a capital lease and record an asset and a liability at an amount equal to the present value of the future lease payments:

1. The lease transfers ownership of the property to the lessee.
2. The lease contains a bargain purchase option.
3. The lease term (including any bargain renewal options) is equal to 75% or more of the economic life of the leased property.
4. The present value of the lease payments (excluding executory costs) equals or exceeds 90% of the fair value of the leased property.[7]

Significant provisions of material leases should be disclosed in the financial statements or in notes to the financial statements, in order that the reader may have knowledge of the financial effect of lease commitments. Chapter 22 is devoted entirely to accounting for leases.

Leasehold Improvements Long-term leases ordinarily provide that any improvements made to the leased property revert to the lessor at the end of the life of the lease. If the lessee constructs new buildings on leased land or reconstructs and improves existing buildings, the lessee has the right to use such facilities during the life of the lease, but they become the property of the lessor when the lease expires.

The lessee should charge the cost of the facilities to the Leasehold Improvements account and **depreciate the cost as operating expense over the remaining life of the lease, or the useful life of the improvements, whichever is shorter.** If a building with an estimated useful life of 25 years is constructed on land leased for 35 years, the cost of the building should be depreciated over 25 years. On the other hand, if the building has an estimated life of 50 years, it should be depreciated over 35 years, the life of the lease.

If the lease contains an option to renew for a period of additional years and the likelihood of renewal is too uncertain to warrant apportioning the cost over the longer period of time, the leasehold improvements are generally written off over the original term of the lease (assuming that the life of the lease is shorter than the useful life of the improvements). Leasehold improvements are generally shown in

---

[6]"Accounting for Leases," *Statement of Financial Accounting Standards No. 13* (Stamford, Conn.: FASB, 1976), par. 10.

[7]*Ibid.,* par. 7.

the property, plant, and equipment section, although some accountants classify them as intangible assets.

Trademarks and Trade Names

The right to use a trademark or trade name under common law rests exclusively with the original user as long as the original user continues to use it, whether it is registered or not. The registration system provides for an indefinite number of renewals for periods of 20 years each, so a business that uses an established trademark or trade name may properly consider it to have an unlimited life. The trademark or trade name, however, must be amortized for accounting purposes over a period not to exceed 40 years.

Cost is the purchase price or, if the trademark or trade name is developed by the concern itself, cost should include attorney's fee, registration fees, design costs, and other expenditures incurred in securing it. Where the total costs of a trade name are insignificant, they are sometimes charged to expense as incurred.

Organization Costs

Costs incurred in the formation of a corporation such as fees to underwriters for handling stock or bond issues, legal fees, state fees of various sorts, and promotional expenditures involving the organization of a business are classified as **organization costs.**

These items are usually charged to an account called Organization Costs or Organization Expense, and may be carried as an asset on the balance sheet as expenditures that will benefit the company over its life. Many companies amortize these costs over an arbitrary period of time (maximum 40 years), since the life of the corporation is indeterminable. Income tax regulations permit the amortization of organization costs over a period of five years or more.

It is difficult to draw a line between organization costs, normal operating expenses, and losses. Some accountants contend that **operating losses incurred in the start-up of a business** should be capitalized, since they are unavoidable and are a cost of starting a business. This approach is not sound, since this expenditure of cost has no future service potential and cannot be considered an asset.

Our position that operating losses should not be capitalized during the early years is supported by the FASB in **Statement of Financial Accounting Standards No. 7,** which clarifies the accounting and reporting practices for **development stage enterprises.** The FASB concludes that the accounting practices and reporting standards should be no different for a development stage enterprise trying to establish a new business than they are for other enterprises. Except for some unique notations and disclosures, the same "generally accepted accounting principles that apply to established operating enterprises shall govern the recognition of revenue by a development stage enterprise and shall determine whether a cost incurred by a development stage enterprise is to be charged to expense when incurred or is to be capitalized or deferred."[8]

Franchises

Franchise agreements are commonly entered into by a municipality or other governmental body and a utility or other business concern that uses public property. In such cases a privately owned enterprise is permitted to use public property in performing its services. Examples are the use of public waterways for a ferry service, the use of public land for telephone or electric lines, or the use of city streets for a bus line. Franchises may be for a definite period of time, for an indefinite period of time, or perpetual. The company securing the franchise from the governmental unit carries a Franchise account in its records only when there are costs such as a lump sum payment in advance, or legal fees and other expenditures that are identifiable with the acquisition of the franchise. **The cost of a franchise for a limited period should be amortized as operating expense over the life of the franchise.** A franchise with an indefinite life or a perpetual franchise should be carried at cost and amortized over a reasonable period not to exceed 40 years.

Annual payments made under a franchise agreement should be entered as operating expenses in the period in which they are incurred. They do not represent an asset to the concern since they do not relate to future rights to use public property.

Businesses frequently enter into similar agreements among themselves that relate to the manufacture or sale of a specific product; payments made under such agreements are properly handled as described above. Examples are the right to operate a hamburger drive-in under a particular trade name (like McDonald's or Burger King) or the exclusive right to sell a particular name brand product in an area (like Omega timepieces or Sunbeam appliances).

Research and Development Costs

Many businesses expend considerable sums of money on research and development to develop new products or processes, to improve present products, and to discover new knowledge that may be valuable at some future date. The difficulties in accounting for these research and development (R & D) expenditures are (1) identifying the costs associated with particular activities, projects, or achievements and (2) determining the magnitude of the future benefits and the length of time over which such benefits may be realized. Because of these latter uncertainties the accounting profession (through **FASB Statement No. 2**) has greatly standardized and simplified accounting practice in this area by requiring that **all research and development costs be charged to expense when incurred.**[9]

To differentiate research and development costs from **other similar costs,** the FASB issued the following definitions:

[8]"Accounting and Reporting by Development Stage Enterprises," *Statement of Financial Accounting Standards No. 7* (Stamford, Conn.: FASB, 1975), par. 10. A company is considered to be in the developing stages when its efforts are directed towards establishing a new business and either the principal operations have not started or no significant revenue has been achieved.

[9]"Accounting for Research and Development Costs," *Statement of Financial Accounting Standards No. 2* (Stamford, Conn.: FASB, 1974), par. 12.

Research is planned search or critical investigation aimed at discovery of new knowledge with the hope that such knowledge will be useful in developing a new product or service . . . or a new process or technique . . . or in bringing about a significant improvement to an existing product or process.

Development is the translation of research findings or other knowledge into a plan or design for a new product or process or for a significant improvement to an existing product or process whether intended for sale or use. It includes the conceptual formulation, design, and testing of product alternatives, construction of prototypes, and operation of pilot plants. It does not include routine or periodic alterations to existing products, production lines, manufacturing processes, and other on-going operations even though those alterations may represent improvements and it does not include market research or market testing activities.[10]

Many costs have characteristics similar to those of research and development costs, for instance, costs of relocation and rearrangement of facilities, start-up costs for a new plant or new retail outlet, marketing research costs, promotion costs of a new product or service, and costs of training new personnel. To further distinguish between R & D and these other similar costs, the following schedule provides (1) examples of activities that typically would be **included** in research and development, and (2) examples of activities that typically would be **excluded** from research and development.[11]

1. R & D Activities	2. Activities Not Considered R & D
(a) Laboratory research aimed at discovery of a new knowledge.	(a) Engineering follow-through in an early phase of commercial production.
(b) Searching for applications of new research findings.	(b) Quality control during commercial production including routine testing.
(c) Conceptual formulation and design of possible product or process alternatives.	(c) Trouble-shooting break-downs during production.
(d) Testing in search for or evaluation of product or process alternatives.	(d) Routine, on-going efforts to refine, enrich, or improve the qualities of an existing product.
(e) Modification of the design of a product or process.	(e) Adaptation of an existing capability to a particular requirement or customer's need.
(f) Design, construction, and testing of preproduction prototypes and models.	(f) Periodic design changes to existing products.
(g) Design of tools, jigs, molds, and dies involving new technology.	(g) Routine design of tools, jigs, molds, and dies.
(h) Design, construction, and operation of a pilot plant not useful for commercial production.	(h) Activity, including design and construction engineering related to the construction, relocation, rearrangement, or start-up of facilities or equipment.
(i) Engineering activity required to advance the design of a product to the manufacturing stage.	(i) Legal work on patent applications, sale, licensing, or litigation.

According to **FASB Interpretation No. 6,** the Board's intent was that the acquisition, development, or improvement of a product or process by an enterprise **for use in its selling or administrative activities** be excluded from the definition of research and development activities. For example, the costs of software incurred by an airline in acquiring, developing, or improving its computerized reservation sys-

---

[10]*Ibid.,* par. 8.
[11]*Ibid.,* par. 9 and 10.

tem or for development of a general management information system are not research and development costs.[12]

The costs associated with R & D activities and the accounting treatment accorded them are as follows:[13]

(a) **Materials, equipment, and facilities.** Expense the entire costs, **unless the items have alternative future uses** (in other R & D projects or otherwise), then carry as inventory and allocate as consumed or capitalize and depreciate as used.

(b) **Personnel.** Salaries, wages, and other related costs of personnel engaged in R & D should be expensed as incurred.

(c) **Purchased intangibles.** Expense the entire cost, **unless the items have alternative future uses** (in other R & D projects or otherwise), then capitalize and amortize.

(d) **Contract services.** The costs of services performed by others in connection with the reporting company's R & D should be expensed as incurred.

(e) **Indirect costs.** A reasonable allocation of indirect costs shall be included in R & D costs, except for general and administrative cost, which must be clearly related to be included and expensed.

Costs of R & D activities conducted for other entities under a **contractual arrangement** are not covered by **FASB Statement No. 2** and, therefore, may be capitalized and deferred rather than expensed when incurred; projects under government contract are included under this provision. Therefore, companies whose production is devoted partly to government or other contract work and partly to noncontract work are capitalizing some R & D costs and deferring them as part of construction in process while simultaneously expensing other R & D costs as they are incurred as period costs.

Costs of research and development activities that are unique to companies in the **extractive industries** (e.g., prospecting, acquisition of mineral rights, exploration, drilling, mining, and related mineral development) and those costs discussed above which are similar to but not classified as R & D costs may be: (1) expensed as incurred, (2) capitalized and either depreciated or amortized over an appropriate period of time, or (3) accumulated as part of inventoriable costs. Choice of the appropriate accounting treatment for such costs should be guided by the degree of certainty of future benefits and the principle of matching revenues and expenses.

Acceptable accounting practice requires that disclosure be made in the financial statements (generally in the footnotes) of the total R & D costs charged to expense in each period for which an income statement is presented.

The requirement that all R & D costs incurred internally be expensed immediately is a conservative, practical solution which insures consistency in practice and comparability between companies. The practice, however, of writing off against revenues of the present period expenditures made in the expectation of benefiting future periods cannot be justified on the grounds that it is good accounting theory.

Defendants of immediate expensing contend that from an income statement standpoint long-run application of this standard frequently makes little difference. The amount of R & D cost charged against income each accounting period would be about the same whether there is immediate expensing or capitalization and subsequent amortization because of the on-going nature of most companies' R & D

---

[12]"Applicability of FASB Statement No. 2 to Computer Software," *FASB Interpretation No. 6* (Stamford, Conn.: FASB, 1975), par. 4 (also see Interpretation Nos. 4 and 5).

[13]FASB Statement No. 2, *op. cit.*, par. 11.

activities. Aside from the revenue/expense mismatching, which may be minimal, critics of this practice argue that the balance sheet should report an intangible asset related to expenditures that have future benefit. To preclude capitalization of all R & D expenditures removes from the balance sheet what may be a company's most valuable asset. This standard represents one of the many trade-offs made between good theory and uniformity and expediency.

Deferred Charges and Long-Term Prepayments

Deferred charges is a classification often used to describe a number of different items that have debit balances, among them certain types of intangibles. Intangibles sometimes classified as deferred charges include plant rearrangement costs, preoperating and start-up costs, and organization costs. How do these items happen to be classified in this section and not in a separate intangible section? Probably the major reason is that this section often serves as a "dumping ground" for a number of small items.

Deferred charges also include such items as long-term prepayments for insurance, rent, taxes and other down payments. The deferred charge classification probably should be abolished because it cannot be clearly differentiated from other amortizable and depreciable assets (which also are deferred charges) and a more informative disclosure could be made of the smaller items often found in this section of the balance sheet.

GOODWILL

Goodwill is undoubtedly one of the most complex and controversial assets presented in financial statements; it is often referred to as the most "intangible" of the intangibles. Goodwill is unique because unlike receivables, inventories, and patents that can be sold or exchanged individually in the marketplace, goodwill can be identified only with the business as a whole. For example, a substantial list of regular customers and an established reputation are unrecorded assets that give the enterprise a valuation greater than the sum of the fair market value of the individual identifiable assets. **Accounting Research Study No. 10** cites numerous advantageous factors and conditions that might contribute to the value and the earning power of an enterprise; in the aggregate they represent goodwill:

1. Superior management team
2. Outstanding sales organization
3. Weakness in management of a competitor
4. Effective advertising
5. Secret process or formula
6. Good labor relations
7. Outstanding credit rating
8. Top-flight training program
9. High standing in the community
10. Unfavorable developments in the operations of a competitor
11. Favorable association with another company
12. Strategic location
13. Discovery of talents or resources
14. Favorable tax conditions
15. Favorable government regulation[14]

---

[14]George R. Catlett and Norman O. Olson, "Accounting for Goodwill," *Accounting Research Study No. 10* (New York: AICPA, 1968), pp. 17–18.

Goodwill is recorded only when an entire business is purchased because goodwill is a "going concern" valuation and cannot be separated from the business as a whole.[15] Goodwill generated internally should **not** be capitalized in the accounts, because measuring the components of goodwill (as listed on page 570) is simply too complex and associating any costs with future benefits is too difficult. The future benefits of goodwill may have no relationship to the costs incurred in the development of that goodwill. To add to the mystery, goodwill may exist in the absence of specific costs to develop it. In addition, no objective transaction with outside parties is present, so that a great deal of subjectivity and possible misrepresentation might occur.

Methods of Measuring Goodwill

The following discussion on the valuation of goodwill and of the related methods of estimation is provided not so much as the solution to an accounting problem as it is a basis for developing an acquisition price for a business enterprise. The accountant is frequently called upon to provide this information as part of the purchase negotiations.

How does one determine the value of goodwill? Conceptually, the answer is to identify the individual attributes that comprise goodwill and attempt to value them individually. This procedure is impossible at present because our measurement techniques are not sophisticated enough to measure accurately the value of a superior management team, the value of a good reputation, and so on. The methods of measuring goodwill are somewhat related to the **two basic views of the nature of goodwill:**

1. Goodwill represents intangible resources and conditions attributable to an enterprise's above-average strength in areas such as technical skill and knowledge, management, and marketing research and promotion that cannot be separately identified and valued.
2. Goodwill represents expected earnings in excess of anticipated normal earnings.[16]

One method, in accordance with the first view of goodwill, simply compares the fair market value of the net tangible and identifiable intangible assets with the bargained purchase price of the acquired business. The difference is considered goodwill, which is why goodwill is sometimes referred to as a "plug" or "gap filler" or **"master valuation"** account. Goodwill is the residual or the excess of the cost over the fair value of the identifiable net assets acquired.

Another view of goodwill is reflected in the second method, one that determines the earnings in excess of those that normally could be earned by the tangible and identifiable intangible assets. These excess earnings are discounted to determine the present value of this extra inflow, which is considered the amount of goodwill.

---

[15]See "Conceptual Framework for Financial Accounting and Reporting: Elements of Financial Statements and Their Measurement," *FASB Discussion Memorandum* (Stamford, Conn.: FASB, 1976), p. 235.

[16]"Accounting for Business Combinations and Purchased Intangibles," *FASB Discussion Memorandum* (Stamford, Conn.: FASB, 1976), p. 48.

Excess of Cost over the Fair Value of Net Assets Acquired

To illustrate what is meant by the "excess of cost over fair value of net assets acquired (master valuation account) approach," the sequence followed in a possible merger is illustrated. Multi-Diversified, Inc. decides that it needs a parts division to supplement its existing tractor distributorship. The president of Multi-Diversified is interested in a small concern in Chicago (Tractorling Company) that has an established reputation and is seeking a merger candidate. The balance sheet of Tractorling Company is presented below.

Tractorling Co.
BALANCE SHEET
as of Dec. 31, 1981

Assets		Equities	
Cash	$ 25,000	Current liabilities	$ 55,000
Receivables	35,000	Capital stock	100,000
Inventories	42,000	Retained earnings	100,000
Property, plant, and equipment	153,000		
Total assets	$255,000	Total equities	$255,000

Serious negotiations ensue, and Tractorling Company finally decides to accept Multi-Diversified's offer of $400,000. What then is the value of the goodwill, if any?

The answer is not quite so obvious, because the fair market values of the identifiable assets of Tractorling are not disclosed in the cost-based balance sheet above. Suppose, for example, that as the negotiations progressed, an investigation of the underlying assets of Tractorling was conducted to determine the fair market value of the assets. Such an investigation may be accomplished either through a purchase audit undertaken by Multi-Diversified's auditors in order to estimate the values of the seller's assets, or an independent appraisal from some other source. The following valuations are determined.

FAIR MARKET VALUES

Cash	$ 25,000
Receivables	35,000
Inventories	122,000
Property, plant, and equipment	205,000
Patents	18,000
Liabilities	55,000

Normally, differences between current fair market value and book value are more common among the long-term assets, although significant differences can also develop in the current asset category. Cash obviously poses no problems, and receivables normally are fairly close to current valuation, although at times certain adjustments need to be made because of inadequate prior provisions for uncollectible accounts. Liabilities usually are stated at their book value, although if interest rates have changed since the liabilities were incurred, a different valuation might be appropriate. Careful analysis must be made in this area to determine that no unrecorded liabilities are present.

It is not surprising to find large variances in most of the other asset areas. The difference in inventories of $80,000 ($122,000 − $42,000) could result from a number of factors, the most likely being that Tractorling Company has followed a LIFO inventory valuation. If prices have been rising for a number of years and the company is expanding, a large difference in valuation could occur. In addition, the company may not have a full cost accounting system and many of the costs of operations may not be embodied in the inventory valuation.

In many cases, the values of long-term assets such as property, plant, and equipment, and intangibles may have increased substantially over the years. This differential may be caused by inaccurate estimates of useful lives, continual expensing of small expenditures (say, less than $300), inaccurate estimates of salvage values, the discovery of some unrecorded assets, or increases in replacement cost.

Given that the fair market value of the net assets is now determined to be $350,000, how was a purchase price of $400,000 determined? Undoubtedly, the seller pointed to an established reputation, good credit rating, top management team, and so on, as factors that make the value of the business greater than $350,000. On the other hand, Multi-Diversified probably was attempting to assess the future earning power of these attributes as well as the basic asset structure of the enterprise today. At this point in the negotiations, price can be a function of many factors: the most important is probably sheer skill at the bargaining table. Finally, a price of $400,000 is agreed upon. The difference between the purchase price of $400,000 and the fair market value of $350,000 is labeled goodwill. Goodwill is viewed as one or a group of unidentifiable values (intangible assets) the cost of which "is measured by the difference between the cost of the group of assets or enterprise acquired and the sum of the assigned costs of individual tangible and identifiable intangible assets acquired less liabilities assumed."[17] This procedure for valuation is referred to as a master valuation approach because goodwill is assumed to cover all the values that cannot be specifically identified with any identifiable tangible or intangible asset.

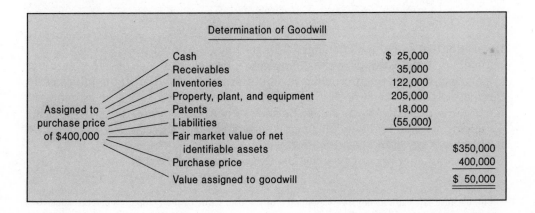

Determination of Goodwill

Assigned to purchase price of $400,000	Cash	$ 25,000
	Receivables	35,000
	Inventories	122,000
	Property, plant, and equipment	205,000
	Patents	18,000
	Liabilities	(55,000)
	Fair market value of net identifiable assets	$350,000
	Purchase price	400,000
	Value assigned to goodwill	$ 50,000

Excess Earning Power

Conceptually, a more appealing and direct approach to valuing goodwill is to determine the total earning power that a company commands. By determining what a normal rate of return is on the tangible and identifiable intangibles in that industry, the typical earnings are computed. **The difference between what the firm earns and what is normal in the industry is referred to as the excess earning power.** This extra earning power indicates that there are unidentifiable values (intangible assets) that provide this increased earning power. Finding the value of goodwill then is a matter of discounting these excess earnings over their estimated lives.

This approach appears to be a systematic and logical way of attacking the problems for determining goodwill. Each factor necessary to compute a value under this approach is subject to question, however. Generally, the problems relate to getting answers to the following questions:

1. What is a normal rate of return?
2. How does one determine the future earnings?
3. What discount rate should be applied to the excess earnings?
4. Over what period should the excess earnings be discounted?

Normal Rate of Return Determination of the normal rate of return for tangible and identifiable intangible assets means that companies similar to the enterprise in question must be analyzed. An industry average may be determined by examination of annual reports, financial services, or other related financial data. The problem with this approach is that the rate normally employed is based on the historical value of the other firms' assets, not on their fair value. Suppose, however, that a rate of 15% is decided as normal for a concern such as Tractorling. In this case, the normal earnings are calculated in the following manner.[18]

Fair market value of Tractorling's net identifiable assets	$350,000
Normal rate of return	15%
Normal earnings	$ 52,500

Determination of Future Earnings The starting point for this type of analysis is normally the past earnings of the enterprise. Although estimates of future earnings are needed, the past often provides useful information concerning the future earnings potential of a concern. The past earnings are also useful because estimates of the future are usually overly optimistic and the hard facts of previous periods bring a sobering sense of reality to the negotiations. Generally a three- to six-year period is examined to develop past earnings data.

Tractorling's net earnings for the last five years is as follows:

[18]The fair value of Tractorling's assets (rather than historical cost) is used to compute the normal profit, because fair value is more representative of the true value of the company's assets exclusive of goodwill. To use historical cost may result in a misstatement of normal profit and an overstatement of goodwill. This illustration assumes that no significant change in assets has occurred over the past five years, that is, the current fair value of the assets approximates the average fair value for the past five years.

Earnings History—Tractorling

1977	$ 60,000	Average Earnings
1978	55,000	$\dfrac{\$375,000}{5} = \$75,000$
1979	110,000[a]	
1980	70,000	
1981	80,000	
	$375,000	

[a]Includes extraordinary gain of $25,000.

The average net earnings for the last five years is $75,000 or a rate of return of approximately 21.4% on the current value of the assets excluding goodwill ($75,000 ÷ $350,000). Before we go further, a question that needs answering is whether $75,000 is representative of the future earnings of this enterprise.

Often past earnings of a company to be acquired need to be adjusted because the acquirer tends to evaluate the average earnings on the basis of its own accounting procedures. Suppose, for example, that in determining earning power, Multi-Diversified measured earnings in relation to a FIFO inventory valuation figure rather than LIFO, which Tractorling employs, and that the use of LIFO reduced Tractorling's net income by $2,000 per year. In addition, Tractorling used accelerated depreciation although Multi-Diversified used a straight-line approach to estimate its earnings; the resulting earnings were lower therefore in the amount of $3,000.

Also, assets discovered on examination that might affect the earning flow should be considered. For example, the patent costs not previously recorded should be amortized, say, at the rate of $1,000 per period. Finally because the estimate of the future earnings is what we are attempting to determine, some items, like the extraordinary gain of $25,000, probably should not be considered. An analysis can now be made.

Average net earnings per Tractorling computation		$75,000
Add		
Adjustment for switch from LIFO to FIFO	$2,000	
Adjustment for change from accelerated to straight-line approach	3,000	5,000
		80,000
Deduct		
Extraordinary gain ($25,000 ÷ 5)	5,000	
Patent amortization on straight-line basis	1,000	6,000
Adjusted average net earnings of Tractorling		$74,000

The $74,000 is then evaluated to determine whether it represents a realistic figure for the projected earnings. Assuming that it does, the excess earnings would be determined to be $74,000 − $52,500 or $21,500.

Choosing a Discount Rate to Apply to Excess Earnings Determination of the discount rate is a fairly subjective estimate. The lower the discount rate, the higher the value of the goodwill. To illustrate, assume that the excess earnings are $21,500 and that these earnings will continue indefinitely. If the excess earnings are capitalized at, say, a rate of 25% in perpetuity, the results are:

Capitalization at 25%
Excess earnings $21,500
Capitalization rate   .25 = $86,000

If the excess earnings are capitalized in perpetuity at a somewhat lower rate, say 15%, a much higher goodwill figure results.

Capitalization at 15%
Excess earnings $21,500
Capitalization rate   .15 = $143,333

The higher the discount rate, the lower the value of the goodwill. Normally, a rate somewhat higher than the normal rate is employed because the continuance of excess profits is uncertain. Factors that can be considered in this analysis are the stability of past earnings figures along with the speculative nature of the business. Although these factors are often difficult to crystallize into a discount rate, they do provide a basis on which a rate may be established.

Discounting Period for Excess Earnings   Determination of the period over which the excess earnings will exist is perhaps the most difficult problem associated with computing a value for goodwill. If, for example, it is assumed that the excess earnings will last indefinitely, the superior earnings may be capitalized by the discount rate selected. If the discount rate employed is the same as the normal return (15%), then goodwill is $143,333 as computed in the previous section.

Another method of computing goodwill that gives the same answer, using the normal return of 15%, is to discount the total average earnings of the company and subtract the fair market value of the assets as illustrated below.

Average earnings capitalized at 15% in perpetuity	
($74,000 ÷ 15%)	$493,333
Less fair market value of assets	350,000
Present value of estimated earnings (goodwill)	$143,333

Frequently, however, the excess earnings are assumed to last a limited number of years, say 10, and then it is necessary to discount these earnings only over that time at a given discount rate.

To illustrate this approach, assume that Multi-Diversified believes that the excess earnings of Tractorling will last 10 years and, because of the uncertainty surrounding this earning power, 25% is considered an appropriate rate of return. The present value of an annuity of $21,500 ($74,000 − $52,500) discounted at 25% for ten years is $78,941.55.[19]

Some accountants fail to discount but simply multiply the excess earnings by the number of years they believe the excess earnings will continue. This approach, often referred to as the **number of years method,** is used to provide a rough measure for what the goodwill factor should be. The approach has only the advantage of simplicity; it is sounder to recognize the discount factor.

It seems safe to say that the valuation of goodwill is at best a highly uncertain process. As the illustration shows, the estimated value of goodwill depends on a number of factors all of which are highly tenuous and subject to bargaining.

Amortization of Goodwill

Once goodwill has been recognized in the accounts, the next question is: What is the proper accounting at this point? Three basic approaches have been suggested.

1. **Charge goodwill off immediately to stockholders' equity. Accounting Research Study No. 10, Accounting for Goodwill,**[20] takes the position that goodwill differs from other types of assets and demands special attention. This argument is based on the proposition that goodwill, unlike other assets, is not separable and distinct from the business as a whole and therefore is not an asset in the same sense as cash, receivables, or plant assets. In other words, goodwill cannot be sold without selling the business. Furthermore, **ARS No. 10** notes that the accounting treatment for purchased goodwill and goodwill internally created should be consistent. Goodwill created internally is immediately expensed and does not appear as an asset: the same treatment should be accorded purchased goodwill. It is also contended that amortization of purchased goodwill leads to double counting, because net income is reduced by amortization of the purchased goodwill as well as by the internal expenditure made to maintain or enhance the value of the assets. Perhaps the best rationale for direct write-off is that determination of the periods over which the future benefits are to be received is so difficult that immediate charging to stockholders' equity is justified.

2. **Retain goodwill indefinitely unless reduction in value occurs.** Many accountants believe that goodwill can have an indefinite life and should be maintained as an asset until a decline in value occurs. They contend that inasmuch as internal goodwill is being expensed to maintain or enhance the purchased goodwill, some form of goodwill should always be an asset. In addition, without sufficient evidence that a decline in value has occurred, a write-off of goodwill is both arbitrary and capricious and will lead to distortions in net income.

3. **Amortize goodwill over useful life.** Still other accountants believe that goodwill as service potential eventually disappears and it is proper that the asset be charged to income over the periods affected. This procedure provides a better matching of costs and revenues in that amortization over its useful life provides the appropriate charge against income.

APB Opinion No. 17 takes the position that goodwill should be written off over its useful life, its useful life being dependent on a myriad of factors such as regulatory restrictions, demand, competition, and obsolescence. **The APB did note that (1) goodwill should never be written off at the date of acquisition and (2) the period of amortization should not exceed 40 years.**

---

[19]The present value of an annuity of one dollar received in a steady stream for 10 years in the future discounted at 25% is 3.6717 × $21,500 = $78,941.55.

[20]Catlett and Olson, *op. cit.,* pp. 89–95.

Immediate write-off was not considered proper, because it would lead to the untenable conclusion that all noncurrent assets should be charged off immediately. It might be noted that **APB Opinion No. 17** merely prohibits the writing off of goodwill in the period of purchase and over a period exceeding forty years; no other mention is made regarding another period. Some believe that a five-year period for amortization would be appropriate unless, depending on the specific circumstances, such as continued loss of profitability or loss of managerial talent, a shorter period is obviously justified. A single loss year or a combination of loss years does not automatically necessitate a charge-off of the goodwill.

The amortization of the goodwill should be computed using the straight-line method unless another method is deemed more appropriate, and it should be treated as a regular operating expense. Where the amortization is material, a disclosure of the charge is necessary, as well as the method and period of amortization. Goodwill amortization is not deductible for tax purposes.

Negative Goodwill—Badwill

Negative goodwill, often appropriately dubbed badwill, or fortunate purchase, arises when the fair market value of the assets acquired is higher than the purchase price of the asset. This situation is a result of market imperfection because the seller would be better off to sell the assets individually than in total. Situations do occur where the purchase price is less than the value of the identifiable assets and therefore a credit develops that is referred to as negative goodwill or excess of fair value over the cost of assets acquired. Companies that have negative goodwill are in a very interesting position because the amortization of this negative goodwill to income increases earnings.

APB Opinion No. 16 takes the position that an excess of fair value over purchase price should be allocated to reduce proportionately the values assigned to noncurrent assets (except long-term investments in marketable securities) in determining their fair values. If the allocation reduces the noncurrent assets to zero value, the remainder of the excess over cost should be classified as a deferred credit and should be amortized systematically to income over the period estimated to be benefited but not in excess of 40 years. The method and period of amortization should be disclosed.[21]

Negative goodwill most frequently develops in a depressed securities market when the market value of a company's stock sells at less than book value. For example, Emhart Corp. offered $23 a share (a premium over market) for U.S.M. Corp. stock which had a per-share book value of $53. Emhart Corp. (in consolidation) was able to write down its plant assets by more than $49 million and thereby effect a reduction in annual depreciation charges of $5.8 million and add 50 cents annually to its earnings per share (on top of the $2 a share it would gain from consolidating U.S.M.'s reported profits—a 90% increase in Emhart's prior year earnings).

---

[21]"Business Combinations," *Opinions of the Accounting Principles Board No. 16* (New York: AICPA, 1970), par. 91.

Reporting of Intangibles

The reporting of intangibles differs from the reporting of property, plant and equipment in that contra accounts are not normally shown for the intangibles. The amortization of intangibles is generally credited directly to the intangible asset.[22]

The financial statements should disclose the method and period of amortization. Intangible assets might appear on the balance sheet as follows:

Intangible assets (Note 3)		
Patents	$ 18,000	
Franchises	115,000	
Goodwill	342,000	$475,000

Note 3. The patents are amortized on a unit-of-production approach over a period of six years. The franchises are perpetual in nature, but in accordance with **APB Opinion No. 17** are being written off over the maximum period allowable (40 years) on a straight-line basis. The goodwill arose from the purchase of Multi-Media and is being amortized over a 10-year period on a straight-line basis.

The following example, taken from the 1977 annual report of Purolator, Inc., illustrates the amortization of intangibles using a contra valuation account:

PUROLATOR, INC.	1977	1976
Intangible assets (Note 7)	$16,685,521	$18,782,174
Less accumulated amortization	1,614,333	1,758,321
Net intangible assets	$15,071,188	$17,023,853

Note 7: *Intangible Assets*—Intangible assets consist of the following:		
December 31	1977	1976
Excess of cost over underlying value of net assets of companies acquired	$13,029,985	$14,985,445
Franchise costs and other intangibles	3,655,536	3,823,729
	$16,685,521	$18,782,174

The excess of cost over the underlying value of the net assets of companies acquired prior to November 1, 1970 is not being amortized as, in the opinion of management, there has been no diminution in the value of the investments. The excess of cost over the underlying value of the net assets of companies acquired after October 31, 1970 is being amortized on a straight-line basis over its estimated life, not exceeding forty years, in accordance with accounting principles related to acquisitions subsequent to such date.

Franchise costs and other intangibles are being amortized on a straight-line basis over their estimated lives.

At December 31, 1977, approximately $6,990,000 of the excess of cost over the underlying value of net assets of companies acquired is being amortized.

Some companies follow the practice of writing their intangibles down to $1.00 to indicate that they have intangibles of which the values are uncertain. This practice is not in accord with good accounting. It would be much better to disclose the nature of the intangible, its original cost, and other relevant information such as competition, danger of obsolescence, and so on.

[22]*Accounting Trends and Techniques—1978* reports that the most common type of intangible is goodwill followed by patents, trademarks, brand names, copyrights; and then licenses, franchises, and memberships.

Questions

1. Intangible assets may be classified on a number of different bases. Indicate three different bases and illustrate how intangibles could be subdivided into these groupings.

2. Many accountants advocate the abandonment of historical cost for plant assets but argue that historical cost should be used in accounting for intangible assets. Are the two viewpoints inconsistent?

3. What are the major accounting problems related to accounting for intangibles?

4. Accounting practitioners, accounting authors, and this course have proposed various solutions to the problems of accounting in terms of historical cost for goodwill and similar intangibles. What problems of accounting for goodwill and similar intangibles are comparable to those of accounting for plant assets? What problems are different?

5. What are some examples of internally created intangibles? Why does the accounting profession make a distinction between internally created "goodwill type" intangibles and other intangibles?

6. State the generally accepted accounting procedures for the amortization and write-down or write-off of capitalized intangible assets.

7. It has been argued, on the grounds of conservatism, that all intangible assets should be written off immediately after acquisition. Give the accounting arguments against this treatment.

8. Indicate the period of time over which each of the following should be amortized.
   (a) Franchises.
   (b) Patents.
   (c) Leasehold improvements.
   (d) Copyrights.
   (e) Research and development costs.
   (f) Trademarks.
   (g) Goodwill.
   (h) A 20-year lease with payments of $40,000 per year on property with an estimated useful life of 50 years. The lessee has the option to renew the lease for 30 additional years at $10,000 per year.

9. What is a lease prepayment? What are property rights capitalized by the lessee? What are leasehold improvements? Should any of these items be classified as an intangible asset?

10. Recently Moluf Corporation entered into a lease agreement with Mountain Developers, Inc., to lease some land for 20 years in southwest Colorado. Moluf Corporation as lessee then built on this site a number of apartment buildings having a useful life of 35 years. The lease agreement states that the lessee has the option to renew the lease for another 20 years. Over what period should the apartments be depreciated?

11. Recently, a group of university students decided to incorporate for the purposes of selling light bulbs. Some of the initial costs involved were legal fees and office expenses incurred in starting the business, state incorporation fees, and stamp taxes. One student wishes to charge these costs against income in the current period; another wishes to defer these costs and amortize them in the future; and another believes these costs should be netted against common stock. Which student is correct?

12. What is the nature of research and development costs? What other costs have similar characteristics?

13. Research and development activities may include (a) personnel costs, (b) materials and equipment costs, and (c) indirect costs. What is the recommended accounting treatment for these three types of R & D costs?

14. During the current year Burlington Western Railroad spent $500,000 to develop a computer program that will assist in identifying and locating all of its rolling equipment; the railroad also spent $230,000 to develop a unique software package that will be offered on a lease basis to other railroads. How should Burlington account for these two expenditures?

15. What is goodwill? What is negative goodwill?

16. Under what circumstances is it appropriate to record goodwill in the accounts? How should goodwill, properly recorded on the books, be amortized in order to conform with generally accepted accounting principles?

17. Explain how "average excess earnings" are determined. What is the justification for the use of this method of estimating goodwill?

18. In examining financial statements, financial analysts often write off goodwill immediately. Evaluate this procedure.

19. Discuss two methods for estimating the value of goodwill in determining the amount that should properly be paid for it.

20. Although the FASB in *Statement No. 2* precludes the capitalization of R & D costs even when the future benefit is estimable, explain how probability analysis might be employed in estimating the unexpired portion of research and development costs to be carried as an asset in the statement of financial condition.

Cases

C13-1   In examining the books of Cuisinart Mfg. Company, you find on the December 31, 1980, balance sheet, the item, "Costs of patents, $308,440."

Referring to the ledger accounts, you note the following items regarding one patent acquired in 1977.

1977 Legal costs incurred in defending the validity of the patent	$6,300
1979 Legal costs in prosecuting an infringement suit	8,600
1979 Legal costs (additional expenses) in the infringement suit	3,100
1979 Cost of improvements (unpatented) on the patented device	14,800

There are no credits in the account, and no allowance for amortization has been set up on the books for any of the patents. There are three other patents issued in 1974, 1976, and 1977; all were developed by the staff of the client. The patented articles are currently very marketable, but it is estimated that they will be in demand only for the next few years.

Instructions

Discuss the items included in the Patent account from an accounting standpoint.

(AICPA adapted)

C13-2   On June 30, 1980, your client, Creative Corporation, was granted two patents covering plastic cartons that it has been producing and marketing profitably for the past three years. One patent covers the manufacturing process and the other covers the related products.

Creative executives tell you that these patents represent the most significant breakthrough in the industry in the past 30 years. The products have been marketed under the registered trademarks Safetainer, Duratainer, and Sealrite. Licenses under the patents have already been granted by your client to other manufacturers in the United States and abroad and are producing substantial royalties.

On July 1, Creative commenced patent infringement actions against several companies whose names you recognize as those of substantial and prominent competitors. Creative's management is optimistic that these suits will result in a permanent injunction against the manufacture and sale of the infringing products and collection of damages for loss of profits caused by the alleged infringement.

The financial vice-president has suggested that the patents be recorded at the discounted value of expected net royalty receipts.

Instructions

(a) What is the meaning of "discounted value of expected net receipts"? Explain.

(b) How would such a value be calculated for net royalty receipts?

(c) What basis of valuation for Creative's patents would be generally accepted in accounting? Give supporting reasons for this basis.

(d) Assuming no practical problems of implementation and ignoring generally accepted accounting principles, what is the preferable basis of valuation for patents? Explain.

(e) What would be the preferable theoretical basis of amortization? Explain.

(f) What recognition, if any, should be made of the infringement litigation in the financial statements for the year ending September 30, 1980? Discuss.

(AICPA adapted)

C13-3 During the examination of the financial statements of the Bombeck Company, your assistant calls attention to significant costs incurred in the development of EDP programs (i.e., software) for major segments of the sales and inventory scheduling systems.

The EDP program development costs will benefit future periods to the extent that the systems change slowly and the program instructions are compatible with new equipment acquired at three- to six-year intervals. The service value of the EDP programs is affected almost entirely by changes in the technology of systems and EDP equipment and does not decline with the number of times the program is used. Because many system changes are minor, program instructions frequently can be modified with only minor losses in program efficiency. The frequency of such changes tends to increase with the passage of time.

Instructions

(a) Discuss the propriety of classifying the unamortized EDP program development costs as
1. A prepaid expense.
2. An intangible asset.
3. A tangible fixed asset.

(b) Discuss the propriety of amortizing the EDP program development costs by means of
1. The straight-line method.
2. A decreasing-charge method (e.g., the sum-of-the-years'-digits method).
3. A variable-charge method (e.g., the units-of-production method).

(AICPA adapted)

C13-4 After securing lease commitments from several major stores, Cherry Valley Shopping Center, Inc. was organized and built a shopping center in a growing suburb.

The shopping center would have opened on schedule on January 1, 1981, if it had not been struck by a severe tornado in December; it opened for business on October 1, 1981. All of the additional construction costs that were incurred as a result of the tornado were covered by insurance.

In July, 1980, in anticipation of the scheduled January opening, a permanent staff had been hired to promote the shopping center, obtain tenants for the uncommitted space, and manage the property.

A summary of some of the costs incurred in 1980 and the first nine months of 1981 follows.

	1980	January 1, 1981, through September 30, 1981
Interest on mortgage bonds	$50,000	$65,000
Cost of obtaining tenants	22,000	40,000
Promotional advertising	29,000	31,000

The promotional advertising campaign was designed to familiarize shoppers with the Center. Had it been known in time that the Center would not open until October, 1981, the 1980 expenditure for promotional advertising would not have been made. The advertising had to be repeated in 1981.

All of the tenants who had leased space in the shopping center at the time of the tornado accepted the October occupancy date on condition that the monthly rental charges for the first nine months of 1981 be canceled.

Instructions

Explain how each of the costs for 1980 and the first nine months of 1981 should be treated in the accounts of the shopping center corporation. Give the reasons for each treatment.

(AICPA adapted)

C13-5 The Metamorphosis Company is in the process of developing a revolutionary new product. A new division of the company was formed to develop, manufacture, and market this new product. As of year-end (December 31, 1981) the new product has not been manufactured for resale; however, a prototype unit was built and is in operation.

Throughout 1981 the new division incurred certain costs. These costs include design and engineering studies, prototype manufacturing costs, administrative expenses (including salaries of administrative personnel), and market research costs. In addition, approximately $500,000 in equipment (estimated useful life—10 years) was purchased for use in developing and manufacturing the new product. Approximately $200,000 of this equipment was built specifically for the design development of the new product; the remaining $300,000 of equipment was used to manufacture the pre-production prototype and will be used to manufacture the new product once it is in commercial production.

Instructions

(a) How are "research" and "development" defined in *Statement of Financial Accounting Standards No. 2*?

(b) Briefly indicate the practical and conceptual reasons for the conclusion reached by the Financial Accounting Standards Board on accounting and reporting practices for research and development costs.

(c) In accordance with *Statement of Financial Accounting Standards No. 2*, how should the various costs of Metamorphosis described above be recorded on the financial statements for the year ended December 31, 1981?

(AICPA adapted)

C13-6 After extended negotiations Elbert Corporation bought from Robinson Company most of the latter's assets on June 30, 1981. At the time of the sale Robinson's accounts (adjusted to June 30, 1981) reflected the following descriptions and amounts for the assets transferred.

	Cost	Contra (Valuation) Account	Book Value
Receivables	$ 83,600	$ 3,000	$ 80,600
Inventory	107,000	5,200	101,800
Land	20,000	—	20,000
Buildings	207,500	73,000	134,500
Fixtures and equipment	205,000	41,700	163,300
Goodwill	50,000	—	50,000
	$673,100	$122,900	$550,200

You ascertain that the contra (valuation) accounts were allowance for doubtful accounts, allowance to reduce inventory to market, and accumulated depreciation.

During the extended negotiations Robinson held out for a consideration of approximately $600,000 (depending on the level of the receivables and inventory). As of June 30, 1981, however, Robinson agreed to accept Elbert's offer of $450,000 cash plus 1% of the net sales (as defined in the contract) of the next five years with payments at the end of each year. Robinson expects that Elbert's total net sales during this period will exceed $15,000,000.

Instructions

(a) How should Elbert Corporation record this transaction? Explain.

(b) Discuss the propriety of recording goodwill in the accounts of Elbert Corporation for this transaction.

(AICPA adapted)

C13-7 Brayfield Corporation, a retail fuel oil distributor, has increased its annual sales volume to a level three times greater than the annual sales of a dealer it purchased in 1980 in order to begin operations.

The board of directors of Brayfield Corporation recently received an offer to negotiate the sale of Brayfield Corporation to a large competitor. As a result, the majority of the board wants to increase the stated value of goodwill on the balance sheet to reflect the larger sales volume developed through intensive promotion and the current market price of sales gallonage. A few of the board members, however, would prefer to eliminate goodwill altogether from the balance sheet in order to prevent "possible misinterpretations." Goodwill was recorded properly in 1980.

Instructions

(a) Discuss the meaning of the term "goodwill."

(b) List the techniques used to calculate the tentative value of goodwill in negotiations to purchase a going concern.

(c) Why are the book and market values of the goodwill of Brayfield Corporation different?

(d) Discuss the propriety of
1. Increasing the stated value of goodwill prior to the negotiations.
2. Eliminating goodwill completely from the balance sheet prior to negotiations.

(AICPA adapted)

C13-8 Hallam Company operates several plants at which limestone is processed into quicklime and hydrated lime. The Batavia Plant, where most of the equipment was installed many years ago, continually deposits a dusty white substance over the surrounding countryside. Citing the unsanitary condition of the neighboring community of Geneva, the pollution of the Fox River, and the high incidence of lung disease among workers at Batavia, the state's Pollution Control Agency has ordered the installation of air pollution control equipment. Also, the Agency has assessed a substantial penalty, which will be used to clean up Geneva. After considering the costs involved (which could not have been reasonably estimated prior to the Agency's action), Hallam decides to comply with the Agency's orders, the alternative being to cease operations at Batavia at the end of the current fiscal year. The officers of Hallam agree that the air pollution control equipment should be capitalized and depreciated over its useful life, but they disagree over the period(s) to which the penalty should be charged.

Instructions

Discuss the conceptual merits and reporting requirements of accounting for the penalty as a
1. Charge to the current period.
2. Correction of prior periods.
3. Capitalizable item to be amortized over future periods.

(AICPA adapted)

Exercises

E13-1 The Rickety Company has provided information on intangible assets as follows:

A patent was purchased from the Doug Company for $1,500,000 on January 1, 1980. Rickety estimated the remaining useful life of the patent to be 10 years. The patent was carried in Doug's accounting records at a net book value of $1,250,000 when Doug sold it to Rickety.

During 1981, a franchise was purchased from the Debbie Company for $500,000. In addition, 5% of revenue from the franchise must be paid to Debbie. Revenue from the franchise for 1981 was $2,000,000. Rickety estimates the useful life of the franchise to be 10 years and takes a full year's amortization in the year of purchase.

Rickety incurred research and development costs in 1981 as follows:

Materials and equipment	$120,000
Personnel	140,000
Indirect costs	60,000
	$320,000

Rickety estimates that these costs will be recouped by December 31, 1984.

On January 1, 1981, Rickety, because of recent events in the field, estimates that the remaining life of the patent purchased on January 1, 1980, is only 5 years from January 1, 1981.

Instructions

(a) Prepare a schedule showing the intangibles section of Rickety's balance sheet at December 31, 1981. Show supporting computations in good form.

(b) Prepare a schedule showing the income statement effect for the year ended December 31, 1981, as a result of the facts above. Show supporting computations in good form.

(AICPA adapted)

E13-2 As the recently appointed auditor for Denise L. Rode Corporation, you have been asked to examine selected accounts before the six-month financial statements of June 30, 1980, are prepared. The controller for Denise L. Rode Corporation mentions that only one account (shown below) is kept for Intangible Assets.

Intangible Assets

		Debit	Credit	Balance
January 4	Research and development costs	960,000		960,000
January 5	Legal costs to obtain patent	40,000		1,000,000
January 31	Payment of seven months rent on property leased by Rode	70,000		1,070,000
February 1	Stock issue costs	60,000		1,130,000
February 11	Premium on common stock		300,000	830,000
March 31	Unamortized bond discount on bonds due March 31, 1990	100,000		930,000
April 30	Promotional expenses related to start-up of business	300,000		1,230,000
June 30	Operating losses for first six months	270,000		1,500,000

Instructions

Prepare the entry or entries necessary to correct this account. Assume that the patent has a useful life of 10 years, and that organization costs are being amortized over a 5-year period.

E13-3 Flypaper Airlines leases an old building which it intends to improve and use as a warehouse. To obtain the lease, the company pays a bonus of $25,000. Annual rental for the 10-year lease period is $90,000. No option to renew the lease or right to purchase the property is given.

After the lease is obtained, improvements costing $139,000 are made. The building has an estimated remaining useful life of 16 years.

Instructions

(a) What is the annual cost of this lease to Flypaper Airlines?

(b) What amount of annual depreciation, if any, on a straight-line basis should Flypaper record?

(c) How would the annual charges stated above be changed if Flypaper had been granted as part of the lease agreement the right to purchase the building for a nominal sum at the end of the lease period?

E13-4 The net worth of Ecumenical Company excluding goodwill totals $610,000 and earnings for the last five years total $330,000. Included in the latter figure are extraordinary gains of $60,000, nonrecurring losses of $40,000, and sales commissions of $15,000. An 8% return on net worth is considered normal for the industry, and annual excess earnings are to be capitalized at 15% in arriving at goodwill in developing a sales price for the business.

Instructions

Compute estimated goodwill.

E13-5 Smolinski Corporation's pretax accounting income for the year 1980 was $600,000 and included the following items:

Amortization of goodwill	$ 30,000
Amortization of identifiable intangibles	35,000
Depreciation on building	88,000
Extraordinary losses	70,000
Extraordinary gains	160,000
Profit-sharing payments to employees	50,000

Brenner Industries is seeking to purchase Smolinski Corporation. In attempting to measure Smolinski's normal earnings for 1980, Brenner determines that the fair value of the building is triple the book value and that the remaining economic life is double that used by Smolinski. Brenner would continue the profit-sharing payments to employees; such payments are based on income before depreciation and amortization.

Instructions

Compute the normal earnings of Smolinski Corporation for the year 1980.

E13-6 As the president of AMC Records Corp., you are considering purchasing Eagles Corp., whose balance sheet is summarized as follows:

Current assets	$ 200,000	Current liabilities	$ 200,000
Fixed assets (net of depreciation)	800,000	Long-term liabilities	600,000
Other assets	200,000	Common stock	300,000
		Retained earnings	100,000
Total	$1,200,000	Total	$1,200,000

The fair market value of current assets is $400,000 because of the undervaluation of inventory. The normal rate of return on net assets for the industry is 8%. The average expected annual earnings projected for Eagles Corp. is $60,000.

Instructions

Assuming that the excess earnings continue for four years, how much would you be willing to pay for goodwill? (Estimate goodwill by the present-value method.)

E13-7   Aggressive Corporation is interested in acquiring Shy Company. It has determined that Shy Company's excess earnings have averaged approximately $90,000 annually over the last six years. Shy Company agrees with the computation of $90,000 as the approximate excess earnings and feels that such amount should be capitalized over an unlimited period at a 10% rate. Aggressive Corporation feels that because of increased competition the excess earnings of Shy Company will continue for eight more years at best and that an 8% discount rate is appropriate.

Instructions

(a) How far apart are the positions of these two parties?

(b) Is there really any difference in the two approaches used by the two parties in evaluating Shy Company's goodwill? Explain.

E13-8   John Birkett Corporation is contemplating the purchase of Jon Axelson Industries and evaluating the amount of goodwill to be recognized in the purchase.

Axelson reported the following net incomes:

1975	—	$ 90,000
1976	—	96,000
1977	—	144,000
1978	—	150,000
1979	—	240,000

Axelson has indicated that 1979 net income included the sale of one of its warehouses at a gain of $120,000 (net of tax). Net identifiable assets of Axelson have a total fair market value of $600,000.

Instructions

Calculate goodwill in the following cases, assuming that expected income is to be a simple average of **normal income** for the past 5 years.

(a) Goodwill is determined by capitalizing average net earnings at 10%.

(b) Goodwill is determined by presuming a 10% return on identifiable net assets and capitalizing excess earnings at 20%.

E13-9   Allan Nilsson Company bought a business that would yield exactly a 20% annual rate of return on its investment. Of the total amount paid for the business, $27,000 was deemed to be goodwill, and the remaining value was attributable to the identifiable net assets.

Allan Nilsson Company projected that the estimated annual future earnings of the new business would be equal to its average annual ordinary earnings over the past four years. The total net income over the past four years was $144,000, which included an extraordinary loss of $18,000 in one year and an extraordinary gain of $54,000 in one of the other four years.

Instructions

Compute the fair market value of the **identifiable** net assets that Allan Nilsson Company purchased in this transaction.

E13-10   Swineheart Co. has averaged its income for the past three years and finds that its average income equals $78,000. Its net assets have a fair market value of $600,000 exclusive of goodwill. The company is considering a sale of its net assets and wishes to determine an asking price that would include goodwill. Average earnings should be 10% of net assets, and earnings in excess of that amount should be capitalized at 25%.

Instructions

(a) What is the amount of goodwill?

(b) Compute the total value of net assets.

E13-11 Mike "the Millionaire" Michaelson is considering acquiring Kroos Company in total as a going concern. He makes the following computations and conclusions:

The fair value of the individual assets of Kroos Company is	$678,000
The liabilities of Kroos Company are	366,000
A fair estimate of annual earnings for the indefinite future is	72,000 per year
Considering the risk and potential of Kroos Company, Mike feels that he must earn a 20% return on his investment	

Instructions

(a) How much should Mike be willing to pay for Kroos Company?

(b) How much (if any) of the above-noted estimates would be goodwill?

E13-12 Net income figures for Juan Garcia Company are as follows:

1976—$54,000	1977—$30,000	1978—$66,000
	1979—$48,000	1980—$36,000

Tangible net assets of this company are appraised at $480,000 on December 31, 1980. This business is to be acquired by Amy Odom Co. early in 1981.

Instructions

What amount should be paid for goodwill if:

(a) 8% is assumed to be a normal rate of return on net tangible assets, and average excess earnings for the last five years are to be capitalized at 20%?

(b) 6% is assumed to be a normal rate of return on net tangible assets, and payment is to be made for excess earnings for the last four years?

Problems

P13-1 Meteoric Products Company from time to time embarks on a research program when a special project seems to offer possibilities. In 1980 the company expends $200,000 on a research project, but by the end of 1980 it is impossible to determine whether any benefit will be derived from it.

Instructions

(a) What account should be charged for the $200,000, and how should it be shown in the financial statements?

(b) The project is completed in 1981, and a successful patent is obtained. The R & D costs to complete the project are $90,000. The administrative and legal expenses incurred in obtaining patent number 381-1003-81 in 1981 total $11,000. The patent has an expected useful life of 5 years. Record these costs in journal entry form. Also, record patent amortization (full year) in 1981.

(c) In 1982 the company successfully defends the patent in extended litigation at a cost of $32,000, thereby extending the patent life to 12/31/89. What is the proper way to account for this cost? Also, record patent amortization (full year) in 1982.

(d) Additional engineering and consulting costs incurred in 1982 to improve the quality of the patented product total $40,000. The improvements enhance the salability of the product considerably. Discuss the proper accounting treatment for this cost.

P13-2 Patriot Products, Inc. has its own research department. In addition, the company purchases patents from time to time. The following statements summarize the transactions involving all patents now owned by the company.

During 1974 and 1975, $109,200 was spent developing a new process that was patented (No. 1) on March 18, 1976 at additional legal and other costs of $12,240. A patent (No. 2) developed by Philip Remmers, an inventor, was purchased for $133,500 on November 30, 1977, on which date it had 12½ years yet to run.

During 1976, 1977, and 1978, research and development activities cost $230,000. No additional patents resulted from these activities.

A patent infringement suit brought by the company against a competitor because of the manufacture of articles infringing on Patent No. 2 was successfully prosecuted at a cost of $4,800. A decision in the case was rendered in July, 1978.

A competing patent (No. 3) was purchased for $32,000 in August, 1979. This patent had 16 years yet to run. During 1980, $45,500 has been expended on patent development: $22,000 of this amount represents the cost of a device for which a patent application has been filed, but no notification of acceptance or rejection by the Patent Office has been received. The other $23,500 represents costs incurred on uncompleted development projects.

Instructions

(a) Compute the carrying value of these patents as of December 31, 1980, assuming that the legal life and useful life of each patent is the same and that each patent is to be amortized from the first day of the month following its acquisition.

(b) Prepare a journal entry to record amortization for 1980.

P13-3 The following information relates to the intangible assets of S. L. Denson Company:

	Organization Costs	Goodwill	Purchased Patent Costs
Original cost at 1/1/1980	$72,000	$360,000	$36,000
Useful life at 1/1/1980 (estimated)	Indefinite*	50 years	8 years

*The company has decided to write off for accounting and tax purposes the organization costs as quickly as the tax law allows.

Instructions

(a) Assuming straight-line amortization, compute the amount of the amortization of **each** item for 1980 in accordance with generally accepted accounting principles.

(b) Prepare the journal entries for the amortization of organization costs and goodwill for 1980.

(c) Assume that at January 1, 1981, S. L. Denson Company incurred $3,500 of legal fees in defending the rights to the patents. Prepare the entry for the year 1981 to amortize the patents.

(d) Assume that at the beginning of year 1982 the company decided that the patent costs would be applicable only for the years 1982 and 1983. (A competitor has developed a product that will eventually make Denson's obsolete.) Record the amortization of the patent costs at the end of 1982.

P13-4 Environmental Laboratories holds a valuable patent (No. 248-1212-73) on a precipitator that prevents certain types of air pollution. Environmental does not manufacture or sell the products and processes it develops; it conducts research and develops products and processes which it patents, and then assigns the patents to manufacturers on a royalty basis. Occasionally it sells a patent. The history of Environmental's patent number 248-1212-73 is as follows:

Date	Activity	Cost
1970–1971	Research conducted to develop precipitator	$585,000
Jan. 1972	Design and construction of a prototype	110,000
March 1972	Testing of models	43,000
Jan. 1973	Fees paid engineers and lawyers to prepare patent application; patent granted July 1, 1973	51,000
Nov. 1974	Engineering activity necessary to advance the design of the precipitator to the manufacturing stage	60,000

Dec. 1975	Legal fees paid to successfully defend precipitator patent	21,000
April 1977	Research aimed at modifying the design of the patented precipitator	50,000
July 1980	Legal fees paid in unsuccessful patent infringement suit against a competitor	30,000

Environmental assumed a useful life of 17 years when it received the initial precipitator patent. In December 1978 it revised its useful life estimate downward to 5 remaining years. Amortization is computed for a full year if the cost is incurred prior to July 1, and no amortization for the year if the cost is incurred after June 30. The company's year ends December 31.

Instructions

Compute the carrying value of patent No. 248-1212-73 on each of the following dates (assume that *FASB Statement No. 2* applies to all years involved):

(a) December 31, 1973.

(b) December 31, 1977.

(c) December 31, 1980.

P13-5 The following situations relate to accounting for intangible assets and research and development costs.

1. American Company purchased two patents directly from the inventors. Patent No. 1 can be used only in its bicycle frame development research project. Patent No. 2 can be used in many different projects and currently is being used in a research project.

2. Shirt Sleeve Company deferred all of its 1979 R & D costs, which totaled $380,000. In November 1980, you are hired as controller and informed that an additional $450,000 has been deferred thus far in 1980. The company wants to issue comparative financial statements in accordance with generally accepted accounting principles for the first time this year.

3. Upstart Corporation, a development stage company, deferred all its preoperating and R & D costs. Its 1980 financial statements consisted only of statements of cash receipts and disbursements, capital shares, and assets and unrecovered preoperating costs and liabilities. The officers indicate that operations should start June 30, 1981 and complete financials will be issued December 31, 1981.

4. Digital Components Corp. develops computer software to be sold to interested users. The corporation incurred $175,000 in developing a new software package to control the energy use in high-rise buildings.

5. Talent Research Company is developing a new lightweight tennis racquet under contract for Sports & Games Corp. The contract, signed January 4, requires payments to Talent Research of $200,000 on December 31 and $300,000 at the completion of the project. At December 31, Talent has recorded an account receivable of $200,000 and has deferred R & D costs of $113,000.

Instructions

For each of the situations above discuss the accounting treatment you recommend or the propriety of the accounting treatment applied with reference to *FASB Statement No. 2* and related interpretations and *FASB Statement No. 7*.

P13-6 During 1978 Innovative Company purchased a building site for its proposed research and development laboratory at a cost of $60,000. Construction of the building was started in 1978. The building was completed on December 31, 1979, at a cost of $200,000 and was placed in service on January 2, 1980. The estimated useful life of the building for depreciation purposes was 20 years; the straight-line method of depreciation was to be employed and there was no estimated net salvage value.

Management estimates that about 50% of the projects of the research and development group will result in long-term benefits (i.e., at least 10 years) to the corporation. The remaining projects either benefit the current period or are abandoned before completion. A summary of the number of projects and the direct costs incurred in conjunction with the research and development activities for 1980 appears in the next column.

Upon recommendation of the research and development group Innovative Company acquired a patent for manufacturing rights at a cost of $100,000. The patent was acquired on April 1, 1979 and has an economic life of 5 years.

	Number of Projects	Salaries and Employee Benefits	Other Expenses (excluding Building Depreciation Charges)
Completed projects with long-term benefits	15	$ 75,000	$35,000
Abandoned projects or projects that benefit the current period	10	20,000	10,000
Projects in process—results indeterminate	5	25,000	10,000
Total	30	$120,000	$55,000

Instructions

If generally accepted accounting principles were followed, how would the items above relating to research and development activities be reported on the company's

1. income statement for 1980?
2. balance sheet as of December 31, 1980?

Be sure to give account titles and amounts, and briefly justify your presentation.

(CMA adapted)

P13-7 Sierra Timber Products Co., organized in 1979, has set up a single account for all intangible assets. The following summary discloses the debit entries that have been recorded during 1979 and 1980.

Intangible Assets

7/ 1/79	10-year franchise; expiration date 6/30/89	$ 36,000
10/ 1/79	Advance payment on leasehold (5-year lease)	20,000
12/31/79	Net loss for 1979 including state incorporation fee, $1,000, and related legal fees of organizing, $7,000 (all fees incurred in 1979)	16,000
1/2/80	Patent purchased (8-year life)	68,000
3/1/80	Cost of developing a secret formula (indefinite life)	100,000
4/1/80	Goodwill purchased (indefinite life)	220,000
6/1/80	Legal fee for successful defense of patent	14,400
9/1/80	Research and development costs	178,000

Instructions

Prepare the necessary entries to clear the Intangible Assets account and to set up separate accounts for distinct types of intangibles. Make the entries as of December 31, 1980, recording any necessary amortization and reflecting all balances accurately as of that date.

P13-8 Louisiana Associates, Inc. has recently become interested in acquiring an Alaskan plant to handle many of its production functions in that market. One possible candidate is Arctic, Inc., a closely held corporation, whose owners have decided to sell their business if a proper settlement can be obtained. Arctic's balance sheet appears as follows:

Current assets	$150,000		Current liabilities	$ 80,000
Investments	50,000		Long-term debt	100,000
Plant assets (net)	400,000		Capital stock	50,000
Total assets	$600,000		Additional paid-in capital	170,000
			Retained earnings	200,000
			Total equities	$600,000

Louisiana Associates has hired Accurate Appraisal Corporation to determine the proper price to pay for Arctic, Inc. The appraisal firm finds that the investments have a fair market value of $125,000 and that inventory is understated by $50,000. All other assets and equities are properly stated. An examination of the company's income for the last four years indicates that the net income has steadily increased. In 1980 the company had a net operating income of $100,000, and this income should increase 20% each year over the next four years. Louisiana Associates believes that a normal return in this type of business is 15% on net assets. The asset investment in the Alaskan plant is expected to stay the same for the next four years.

Instructions

(a) Accurate Appraisal Corporation has indicated that the fair value of the company can be estimated in a number of ways. Prepare an estimate of the value of the firm, assuming that any goodwill will be computed as:
1. The capitalization of the average excess earnings of Arctic, Inc. at 15%.
2. The purchase of average excess earnings over the next four years.
3. The capitalization of average excess earnings of Arctic, Inc. at 20%.
4. The present value of the average excess earnings over the next four years discounted at 8%.

(b) Arctic, Inc. is willing to sell the business for $1,000,000. How do you believe Accurate Appraisal should advise Louisiana Associates?

(c) If Louisiana Associates were to pay $750,000 to purchase the assets and assume the liabilities of Arctic, Inc., how would this transaction be reflected on Louisiana's books?

P13-9 Presented below are financial forecasts related to Earl Schultz Company for the next 10 years.

Forecasted average earnings (per year)	$ 24,000
Forecasted market value of net assets, exclusive of goodwill (per year)	144,000

Instructions

You have been asked to compute goodwill under the following methods. The normal rate of return on net assets for the industry is 10%.

(a) Goodwill is equal to 5 years' excess earnings.

(b) Goodwill is equal to the present value of 5 years' excess earnings discounted at 8%.

(c) Goodwill is equal to the average excess earnings capitalized at 15%.

(d) Goodwill is equal to average excess earnings capitalized at the normal rate of return for the industry of 10%.

P13-10 Presented below is information related to Typhoon Manufacturing Company for 1981, its first year of operation.

Revenue and Expense Summary

Raw Material Purchased	$123,300	Sales	$474,000
Productive Labor	37,650	Closing Inventories	
Factory Overhead	28,350	Raw Material	32,250
Selling Expenses	37,050	Goods in Process	27,000
Adm. Expenses	27,300	Finished Goods	39,000
Interest Expense	8,250	Appreciation of Land	9,000
Opening Inventories		Profit on Sale of Forfeited Stock	3,000
Raw Material	29,100		
Goods in Process	24,000		
Finished Goods	30,000		
Extraordinary Loss (net)	6,900		
Income Taxes	81,000		
Net Income	151,350		
	$584,250		$584,250

Instructions

Typhoon is negotiating to sell the business after one full year of operation. Compute the amount of goodwill as 200% of the income before extraordinary items and before taxes that is in excess of $135,000; $135,000 is considered to be a normal return on investment.

P13-11 Gulf & Eastern, a high-flying conglomerate, has recently been involved in discussions with Redwing, Inc. As its CPA, you have been instructed by Gulf & Eastern to conduct a purchase audit of Redwing's books to determine a possible purchase price for Redwing's net assets. The following information is found.

Total identifiable assets of Redwing's (fair market value)	$224,000
Liabilities	32,000
Average rate of return on net assets for Redwing's industry	8%
Forecasted earnings per year based on past earnings figures	20,000

Instructions

(a) Gulf & Eastern asked you to determine the purchase price on the basis of the following assumptions:
1. Goodwill is equal to 3 years' excess earnings.
2. Goodwill is equal to the present value of excess earnings discounted at 8% for 3 years.
3. Goodwill is equal to the capitalization of excess earnings at 8%.
4. Goodwill is equal to the capitalization of excess earnings at 25%.

(b) Gulf & Eastern asks you which of the methods above is the most theoretically sound. Justify your answer. Any assumptions made should be clearly indicated.

P13-12 Almaden Stores, Inc. has contracted to purchase the Riesling Company including the goodwill of the latter company. The agreement between purchaser and seller on the price to be paid for goodwill is as follows: "The value of the goodwill to be paid for is to be determined by capitalizing at 7% the average annual earnings from ordinary operations for the last five years in excess of 8% on the net worth, which, for purposes of this computation, is to be considered to be $540,000."

The net income per books for the last five years is:

1977	$45,840
1978	47,280
1979	68,040
1980	39,960
1981	51,360

As assistant to the treasurer of Almaden Stores, you are instructed to review the accounts of the Riesling Company and determine the amount to be paid for goodwill in accordance with the terms of the contract. In your review of the accounts you discover the following:

1. An additional assessment of federal income taxes in the amount of $15,120 for the year 1979 was made and paid in 1981. The amount was charged against Retained Earnings.
2. In 1977 the company reviewed its accounts receivable and wrote off as an expense of that year $10,440 of accounts receivable that had been carried for years and appeared very unlikely to be collected.
3. In 1978 an account for $1,080 included in the 1977 write-off above was collected and credited to "Miscellaneous Income."
4. A fire in 1980 caused a loss, charged to Income, as follows:

Book value of property destroyed	$15,360
Recovery from insurance company	9,000
Net loss	$ 6,360

5. Expropriation of property in 1980 resulted in a gain of $5,760 credited to income.

6. Amounts paid out under the company's product guarantee plan and charged to expense in each of the five years were as follows:

1977	$ 800
1978	1,150
1979	970
1980	1,200
1981	850

7. In 1981 the president of the company died, and the company realized $60,000 on an insurance policy on his life. The cash surrender value of this policy had been carried on the books as an investment in the amount of $50,400. The excess of proceeds over cash surrender value was credited to income.

Instructions

What is the price to be paid for the goodwill in accordance with the contract agreement? Prepare your computations in good form so that you can answer any specific questions asked by the treasurer in regard to your conclusions.

P13-13 Nadia Machine Tool Corporation was incorporated on January 3, 1979. The corporation's financial statements for its first year's operations were not examined by a CPA. You have been engaged to examine the financial statements for the year ended December 31, 1980, and your examination is substantially completed. The corporation's trial balance appears below.

Nadia Machine Tool Corporation
TRIAL BALANCE
December 31, 1980

	Debit	Credit
Cash	$ 11,000	
Accounts receivable	42,500	
Allowance for doubtful accounts		$ 500
Inventories	38,500	
Machinery	75,000	
Equipment	29,000	
Accumulated depreciation		10,000
Patents	85,000	
Leasehold improvements	26,000	
Prepaid expenses	10,500	
Organization expenses	29,000	
Goodwill	24,000	
Licensing agreement No. 1	50,000	
Licensing agreement No. 2	49,000	
Accounts payable		147,500
Unearned revenue		12,500
Capital stock		300,000
Retained earnings, January 1, 1980	27,000	
Sales		668,500
Cost of goods sold	454,000	
Selling and general expenses	173,000	
Interest expense	3,500	
Extraordinary losses	12,000	
Totals	$1,139,000	$1,139,000

The following information relates to accounts that may yet require adjustment.

1. Patents for Nadia's manufacturing process were acquired January 2, 1980, at a cost of $68,000. An additional $17,000 was spent in December, 1980, to improve machinery covered by the patents and charged to the Patents account. Depreciation on fixed assets has been properly recorded for 1980 in accordance with Nadia's practice, which provides a full year's depreciation for property on hand June 30 and no depreciation otherwise. Nadia uses the straight-line method for all depreciation and amortization and the legal life on its patents.

2. On January 3, 1979, Nadia purchased licensing agreement No. 1, which was believed to have an unlimited useful life. The balance in the Licensing Agreement No. 1 account includes its purchase price of $48,000 and expenses of $2,000 related to the acquisition. On January 1, 1980, Nadia purchases licensing agreement No. 2, which has a life expectancy of 10 years. The balance in the Licensing Agreement No. 2 account includes its $48,000 purchase price and $2,000 in acquisition expenses, but it has been reduced by a credit of $1,000 for the advance collection of 1981 revenue from the agreement.

   In late December 1979 an explosion caused a permanent 60% reduction in the expected revenue-producing value of licensing agreement No. 1 and in January, 1981, a flood caused additional damage that rendered the agreement worthless.

3. The balance in the Goodwill account includes (a) $8,000 paid December 30, 1979, for an advertising program it is estimated will assist in increasing Nadia's sales over a period of 4 years following the disbursement, and (b) legal expenses of $16,000 incurred for Nadia's incorporation on January 3, 1979.

4. The Leasehold Improvements account includes (a) the $15,000 cost of improvements with a total estimated useful life of 12 years, which Nadia, as tenant, made to leased premises in January, 1979, (b) movable assembly line equipment costing $8,500 that was installed in the leased premises in December, 1980, and (c) real estate taxes of $2,500 paid by Nadia in 1980, which under the terms of the lease should have been paid by the landlord. Nadia paid its rent in full during 1980. A 10-year nonrenewable lease was signed January 3, 1979, for the leased building that Nadia used in manufacturing operations.

5. The balance in the Organization Expenses account properly includes costs incurred during the organizational period. The corporation has exercised its option to amortize organization costs over a 60-month period for federal income tax purposes and wishes to amortize these for accounting purposes on the same basis.

Instructions

Prepare an eight-column worksheet to adjust accounts that require adjustment and include columns for an income statement and a balance sheet.

A separate account should be used for the accumulation of each type of amortization and for each prior period adjustment. Formal adjusting journal entries and financial statements are **not** required. (**Hint:** Make sure that Licensing Agreement No. 1 is amortized over the maximum life required in **APB Opinion No. 17** before the explosion damage loss is determined.)

(AICPA adapted)

Long-Term Liabilities

Nature of Long-Term Debt

Long-term debt consists of present obligations, arising out of past actions or transactions, that are not payable within the operating cycle of the business, or within a year if there are several operating cycles within one year. Mortgages payable, bonds payable, long-term notes payable, lease obligations, pension obligations, and long-term contracts for the purchase of land or other plant assets are examples of long-term liabilities. Pension and lease obligations are discussed in Chapters 21 and 22, respectively.

Long-term debt is ordinarily used by an enterprise as a more or less permanent means of financing growth and to increase the earnings available to stockholders. If a larger rate of return can be earned on the borrowed funds than is paid as interest, the excess will represent income to the stockholders. **Long-term creditors have no vote in management affairs and receive a stated rate of interest whether the earnings of the firm are low or high.** Incurring long-term debt is often accompanied by considerable formality. The bylaws of corporations usually require approval by the board of directors and the stockholders before bonds can be issued or other long-term debt can be created.

Generally, long-term debt, in whatever form, is issued subject to various **covenants or restrictions** for the protection of the lenders. The covenants and other terms of the agreement between the borrower and the lender are stated in the **bond indenture or note agreement** and may be printed on (or referred to in) the formal instrument that is evidence of the debt. Items that might be mentioned in the indenture or agreement include the amounts authorized to be issued, interest rate, due date or dates, property pledged as security, sinking fund, working capital and dividends restrictions, and assumptions of additional debt. Whenever these stipulations are important to a complete understanding of the financial position and the results of operations, they should be described in the body of the financial statements or the notes thereto. In many cases, the loan instrument or contract is held by a trustee, usually a bank or trust company, who acts as an independent third party to protect the interests of the lender(s) and the borrower.

Mortgages Payable

A **mortgage payable** is a promissory note secured by a document called a mortgage that pledges title to property as security for the loan. Mortgage notes payable are used more frequently by proprietorships and partnerships than by corporations, as corporations usually find that bond issues offer advantages in obtaining large loans.

Mortgages may be payable in full at maturity date or in installments over the life of the loan. If payable in full at maturity date, a mortgage payable is shown as a long-term liability on the balance sheet until such time as the approaching maturity date warrants showing it as a current liability. If it is payable in installments, the current installments due would properly be shown as current liabilities, with the remainder shown as a long-term liability.

Short-Term Obligations Expected to be Refinanced

Some short-term obligations are expected to be refinanced on a long-term basis and may be excluded from current liabilities and classified as long-term debt. Such classification is permitted if an enterprise (1) **intends** to refinance the obligations on a long-term basis, and (2) **demonstrates an ability** to consummate the refinancing. The particulars of refinancing and financial agreements related to short-term obligations that may be classified as long-term debt have been discussed in Chapter 10, as have the disclosure requirements pertaining to such situations.

BONDS PAYABLE

A bond arises from a contract known as an **indenture** and represents a promise to pay a sum of money at a designated maturity date plus periodic interest at a specified rate on the face value. Individual bonds typically have a $1,000 maturity amount (face value), although some bond issues are in denominations of $50, $100, and $10,000. Bond interest payments usually are made semiannually, although the interest rate is generally expressed as an annual rate. Bonds are assumed to have a $1,000 face value unless otherwise indicated.

Bond issues that mature on a single date are called **term bonds,** and issues that mature in installments are called **serial bonds.** To attract different types of investors, bonds of differing characteristics are available in the marketplace. Bonds may be **secured**—mortgage bonds, having a claim on real estate, and collateral trust bonds, having securities of other corporations as security—or **unsecured** as to principal, such as debenture bonds. Bonds may be **convertible** into equity securities; they may be **guaranteed** by another party; or they may be **income bonds** on which interest payments depend on the existence of operating income in the issuing company. If the issuer reserves the right to call and retire the bonds prior to maturity, they are **callable bonds.** Bonds issued in the name of the owner are **registered bonds** and require surrender of the certificate and issuance of a new certificate for the investor to complete a sale. A **bearer or coupon bond,** however, is not recorded in the name of the owner and may be transferred from one investor to another by mere delivery.

Bonds are used to borrow from the general public or from institutional investors for the long term when the amount of capital funds needed is too large for one lender to supply. By issuing bonds in $100, $1,000, or $10,000 denominations, a large amount of long-term indebtedness can be divided into many small investing units, thus enabling more than one lender to participate in the loan.

Accounting for the Issuance of Bonds

An entire bond issue may be sold to an investment banker, who acts as a selling agent in the process of marketing the bonds. The investment bankers often underwrite the entire issue by guaranteeing a certain sum to the corporation, taking the risk of selling the bonds for whatever price they can get, or they may sell the bond issue for a commission to be deducted from the proceeds of the sale. Alternatively, the issuing company may choose to place privately a bond issue by selling the bonds directly to a large institution, financial or otherwise, without the aid of an underwriter.

If an entire bond issue is sold to an underwriter or another institution at par (face value), the journal entry is:

Cash	800,000	
Bonds Payable		800,000

If a company takes subscriptions for its bond issue and sells its own bonds, entries may be made similar to those made for capital stock sold under the subscription plan. Assume that a company authorizes a $600,000 bond issuance consisting of 600 bonds, each having a $1,000 maturity value. The entries to record the subscription, collection of cash, and issuance of bonds are:

Subscriptions Receivable on Bonds Payable	600,000	
Bonds Payable Subscribed		600,000
(Subscriptions received on 600 bonds, at par)		
Cash	400,000	
Subscriptions Receivable on Bonds Payable		400,000
(Cash received in full from subscribers to 400 bonds)		
Bonds Payable Subscribed	400,000	
Bonds Payable		400,000
(Bonds are issued to subscribers who have paid subscription price in full)		

The Subscriptions Receivable account now has a debit balance of $200,000. If this amount is to be collected in the near future, it is shown as a current asset in the balance sheet. The other accounts relating to the bonds are shown as follows:

Long-term liabilities		
10% First mortgage bonds payable due Jan. 1, 1990:		
Issued and outstanding	$400,000	
Subscribed	200,000	
Total amount outstanding and subscribed		$600,000

If the entire bond issue is not sold at one time, both the amount of the bonds authorized and the bonds issued should be disclosed on the balance sheet or in the footnotes. This disclosure is important because unissued bonds represent a source of working capital and potential indebtedness that may be incurred without securing further authorization or without pledging additional assets.

Bonds Issued Between Interest Dates

Bond interest payments are usually made semiannually on dates specified in the bond indenture. When bonds are issued at other than the interest payment dates, buyers of the bonds will pay the seller the interest accrued from the last interest payment date to the date of issue. The purchasers of the bond, in effect, pay the bond issuer for the portion of the full six-month interest payment to which they are not entitled because they did not hold the bonds during this period. The purchasers will receive the full six-month interest payment on the next semiannual interest payment date.

To illustrate, if bonds of a par value of $800,000, dated January 1, 1980, and bearing interest at an annual rate of 10% payable semiannually on January 1 and July 1, are issued at par plus accrued interest on March 1, 1980, the entry on the books of the issuing corporation is:

Cash	813,333	
Bonds Payable		800,000
Bond Interest Expense (or Interest Payable)		13,333
($800,000 $\times$ .10 $\times$ $^{2}/_{12}$)		

The purchaser pays for two months' interest, because on July 1, 1980, four months after the date of purchase, six months' interest will be received from the issuing company. The company makes the following entry on July 1, 1980:

Bond Interest Expense	40,000	
Cash		40,000

The expense account now contains a debit balance of $26,666.67, which represents the proper amount of expense, or interest, for four months at 10% on $800,000.

Discount and Premium on Bonds Payable (Influences of the Market)

Several different terms are frequently applied to the interest element of bonds. The interest rate written in the terms of the bond issue and ordinarily appearing on the bond instrument is known as the **stated,** or **nominal,** rate. This rate is set by the party issuing the bonds and is expressed as a percentage of the **par value**, also called **face value** or **maturity value**, of the bonds. If bonds are sold for more than par value (at a **premium**) or less than par value (at a **discount**), the actual interest yield to the bondholder is less than or greater than the stated rate. This rate of interest actually earned by the bondholders is called the **effective, yield,** or **market rate** and is set by the investment market. If bonds are sold at a discount, the effective rate is higher than the stated rate. Conversely, if the bonds are sold at a premium, the stated rate is higher than the effective rate or yield rate.

If bonds are sold below par, it means that investors demand a rate of interest higher than the rate stated on the bonds. The investors are not satisfied with the nominal interest rate because they can earn a greater rate on alternative investments of equal risk. They cannot change the nominal rate, and so they refuse to pay par for the bond and, thus, by changing the amount invested alter the effective rate of interest. Inasmuch as the investors receive interest at the stated rate computed on the par value of the bonds, they are earning at an effective rate that is higher than the stated rate because they paid less than par for the bonds. When the issuing corporation sells bonds of a par value of $800,000 at 97, the entry is:

Cash ($800,000 × .97)	776,000	
Discount on Bonds Payable	24,000	
Bonds Payable		800,000

Bond discount does not represent prepaid interest, but because of its relation to the interest described above **the discount is amortized over the period of time that the bonds are outstanding** and charged to interest expense. If the amounts involved are not material, the discount may be amortized by the straight-line method instead of the effective interest method to be described later. Assume that the bonds are due in 20 years and bear interest at the rate of 8%, payable semiannually. An entry is made at the end of each fiscal year to amortize the discount on a straight-line basis as follows:

Bond Interest Expense	1,200	
Discount on Bonds Payable		1,200
($24,000 ÷ 20 years = $1,200)		

Discount on Bonds Payable is credited for 1/20 of the original amount of the discount because one year represents 1/20 of the life of the bonds. If the bonds were dated and sold on October 1 and the fiscal year of the company ended on December 31, the discount amortized on December 31 of the first year is only 3/12 of 1/20 of $24,000, or $300. The $1,200 per year is amortized in each of the next 19 years, and $900 is amortized in the year in which the bonds mature.

In practice, the unamortized portion of Discount on Bonds Payable has frequently been shown on the balance sheet under Deferred Charges. Because the **effective liability** of bonds issued at a discount is the difference beween the par of the bonds and the unamortized discount on issuance, the unamortized bond discount should be deducted from bonds payable in the liability section of the balance sheet. **APB Opinion No. 21** requires that bond discount be reported on the balance sheet as a direct deduction from the face amount of the bond.[1]

---

[1]"Interest on Receivables and Payables," *Opinions of the Accounting Principles Board No. 21* (New York: AICPA, 1971), par. 16.

Premium on Bonds Payable is treated in a manner similar to that described for Discount on Bonds Payable. If 20-year bonds of a par value of $800,000 are sold at 103, then the cash proceeds are $824,000 ($800,000 × 1.03) and Bonds Payable is credited for $800,000 and Premium on Bonds Payable is credited for $24,000. At the end of each year the entry to amortize premium on a straight-line basis is:

Premium on Bonds Payable	1,200	
Bond Interest Expense		1,200

The unamortized portion of Premium on Bonds Payable has frequently been shown on the balance sheet as a deferred credit. The effective liability of bonds issued at a premium, however, is the total of the par of the bonds and the unamortized premium and, therefore, any premium should be added to bonds payable. **APB Opinion No. 21** requires that bond premium be reported on the balance sheet as a direct addition to the face amount of the bond.

Effective Interest Method

The straight-line method, as illustrated, results in an even or average allocation of the interest expense over the life of the bonds. This assumption, that the interest cost for each year is equal, is not realistic when a premium or discount is involved. A more accurate procedure is the **effective interest method** (also called **present value amortization**), because for interest allocation, including bond discount or premium amortization, it should be recognized that bond interest expense is computed at the effective rate at which the bonds are issued. **Under this method the interest cost for each period is the effective interest rate multiplied by the carrying amount (book value) of the bonds at the start of that period (the carrying amount changing each period by the amount of the amortized discount or premium).** The amount of amortization of bond discount or premium is the difference between the effective interest expense for the period and the actual interest payments.

To illustrate, Grometer Corporation issued $100,000 of 8% bonds on January 1, 1980, due on January 1, 1985, with interest payable each July 1 and January 1. Because the investors wished to earn effective interest of 10%, they paid $92,278 for the $100,000 of bonds, creating a $7,722 discount. The $7,722 discount is a result of the considerations noted below.

Maturity value of bonds payable		$100,000
Present value of $100,000 due in 5 years at 10%, interest payable semiannually (Table 6-2)	$61,391[2]	
Present value of $4,000 interest payable semiannually for 5 years at 10% annually (Table 6-4)	30,887[2]	
Proceeds from sale of bonds		92,278
Discount on bonds payable		$ 7,722

[2]As determined from present value tables using 5% rate for 10 periods: ($100,000 × .61391) and ($4,000 × 7.72173).

The five-year amortization schedule appears below.

		SCHEDULE OF BOND DISCOUNT AMORTIZATION EFFECTIVE INTEREST METHOD—SEMIANNUAL INTEREST PAYMENTS 8% BONDS SOLD TO YIELD 10%		
Date	Credit Cash	Debit Interest Expense	Credit Bond Discount	Carrying Value of Bonds
1/1/80				$ 92,278
7/1/80	$ 4,000ᵃ	$ 4,614ᵇ	$ 614ᶜ	92,892ᵈ
1/1/81	4,000	4,645	645	93,537
7/1/81	4,000	4,677	677	94,214
1/1/82	4,000	4,711	711	94,925
7/1/82	4,000	4,746	746	95,671
1/1/83	4,000	4,783	783	96,454
7/1/83	4,000	4,823	823	97,277
1/1/84	4,000	4,864	864	98,141
7/1/84	4,000	4,907	907	99,048
1/1/85	4,000	4,952	952	100,000
	$40,000	$47,722	$7,722	

ᵃ$4,000 = $100,000 × .08 × 6/12   ᶜ$614 = $4,614 − $4,000
ᵇ$4,614 = $92,278 × .10 × 6/12   ᵈ$92,892 = $92,278 + $614

The journal entry to record the first interest payment on July 1, 1980, is:

Bond Interest Expense	4,614	
Discount on Bonds Payable		614
Cash		4,000

If the market had been such that the investors were willing to earn an effective interest of 6% on the bond issue described above, they would have paid $108,530 or a premium of $8,530, computed as follows:

Maturity value of bonds payable		$100,000
Present value of $100,000 due in 5 years at 6%, interest payable semiannually (Table 6–2)	$74,409³	
Present value of $4,000 interest payable semiannually for 5 years at 6% annually (Table 6–4)	34,121³	
Proceeds from sale of bonds		108,530
Premium on bonds payable		$ 8,530

³As determined from present value tables using 3% rate for 10 periods: ($100,000 × .74409) and ($4,000 × 8.53020).

The five-year amortization schedule appears below.

		SCHEDULE OF BOND PREMIUM AMORTIZATION EFFECTIVE INTEREST METHOD—SEMIANNUAL INTEREST PAYMENTS 8% BONDS SOLD TO YIELD 6%		
Date	Credit Cash	Debit Interest Expense	Debit Bond Premium	Carrying Value of Bonds
1/1/80				$108,530
7/1/80	$ 4,000[a]	$ 3,256[b]	$ 744[c]	107,786[d]
1/1/81	4,000	3,234	766	107,020
7/1/81	4,000	3,211	789	106,231
1/1/82	4,000	3,187	813	105,418
7/1/82	4,000	3,162	838	104,580
1/1/83	4,000	3,137	863	103,717
7/1/83	4,000	3,112	888	102,829
1/1/84	4,000	3,085	915	101,914
7/1/84	4,000	3,057	943	100,971
1/1/85	4,000	3,029	971	100,000
	$40,000	$31,470	$8,530	

[a]$4,000 = $100,000 \times .08 \times 6/12 \qquad$ [c]$744 = $4,000 - $3,256$

[b]$3,256 = $108,530 \times .06 \times 6/12 \qquad$ [d]$107,786 = $108,530 - 744

The journal entry to record the first interest payment on July 1, 1980, is:

Bond Interest Expense	3,256	
Premium on Bonds Payable	744	
Cash		4,000

Discount or premium should be amortized "as interest expense or income over the life of the note in such a way as to result in a constant rate of interest when applied to the amount outstanding at the beginning of any given period."[4] Although the effective interest method is recommended, other methods are permitted if the results obtained are not materially different from those produced by the effective interest method.

Expenses of Issuing Bonds

The issuance of bonds involves engraving and printing costs, legal and accounting fees, commissions, promotion expenses, and other similar charges. According to **APB Opinion No. 21,** these items should be debited to a **deferred charge** account for Unamortized Expenses of Bond Issue and amortized over the life of the issue, in a manner similar to that used for discount on bonds.[5] Prior to the issuance of **Opinion No. 21** the common practice was to merge these items with the discount or premium on bonds, increasing the balance of the discount account or decreasing the balance of the premium account. Unlike discounts, issuance costs are a true

[4]"Interest on Receivables and Payables," *op. cit.,* par. 15.

[5]*Ibid.*

deferred charge. Lumping these costs with discounts or premiums should be avoided; appropriate treatment calls for the use of separate accounts and classification in different sections of the balance sheet.

To illustrate the accounting for expenses of issuing bonds, assume that Wren Corporation sold $20,000,000 of 10-year debenture bonds for $20,795,000 on January 1, 1981 (also the date of the bonds). Expenses of issuing the bonds were $245,000. The entries at January 1, 1981 and December 31, 1981 for issuance of the bonds and amortization of the bond issue costs would be as follows:

Cash	20,550,000	
Unamortized Expenses of Bond Issue	245,000	
Premium on Bonds Payable		795,000
Bonds Payable		20,000,000
(To record issuance of bonds)		
Bond Issue Expense	24,500	
Unamortized Expenses of Bond Issue		24,500
(To amortize one year of bond issue expenses—straight-line method)		

While the expenses of issuing bonds should be amortized using the effective interest method, the straight-line method is generally used in practice because it is easier and the results are not materially different.

Bond Interest Paid by Agent or Trustee

The issuing corporation frequently arranges to have an agent or trustee handle the payment of interest to individual bondholders. Payment to the agent or trustee does not constitute payment of the liability for bond interest, and accounts should be kept that will reflect the full facts. Illustrative entries are given below.

Semiannual accrual of interest at 10% (per annum) on $700,000 bonds payable:

Bond Interest Expense	35,000	
Bond Interest Payable		35,000

Cash for interest is transferred to trustee:

Bond Interest Fund Cash (X Trust Co.)	35,000	
Cash		35,000

Trustee returns canceled interest coupons paid:

Bond Interest Payable	30,000	
Bond Interest Fund Cash (X Trust Co.)		30,000

After the entries above, the Bond Interest Payable account has a credit balance of $5,000 representing the amount of coupons due but unpaid. The Bond Interest Fund Cash account has a debit balance of $5,000 representing cash in the hands of the trustee with which to pay the coupons when they are presented.

If Bond Interest Payable is shown on the balance sheet as a current liability, Bond Interest Fund Cash is shown as a current asset, but separately from the general cash.

The canceled interest coupons should be retained under an appropriate filing system as documentary evidence of the payment of interest on the bonds.

Early Extinguishment of Debt

Computing Gain or Loss   The reacquisition of bonds (or any form of debt security or instrument) before their scheduled maturity, except through conversion by the holder, is termed **early extinguishment.** Early extinguishment occurs regardless of whether the bonds are considered to be terminated or to be held as so-called "treasury bonds." The amount paid on early extinguishment or redemption before maturity, including any call premium and expense of reacquisition is called the **reacquisition price.** The **net carrying amount** of the bonds on any specified date is the amount payable at maturity, adjusted for unamortized premium, discount, and expense of issuance. The excess of the net carrying amount over the acquisition price is the **gain** from early extinguishment while the excess of the reacquisition price over the net carrying amount is the **loss.**

Bonds may be issued that are **callable** by the issuer after a certain date at a stated price, so that the issuing corporation may have the opportunity to reduce its bonded indebtedness or take advantage of lower interest rates. **Noncallable** bonds may be extinguished early through purchase on the market by the issuing corporation for the same reasons. **Whether callable or noncallable, any premium or discount should be amortized over the life to maturity date** because early redemption or extinguishment is not a certainty. If the prevailing interest rates decrease after the issuance of the bonds, it is often advantageous for the issuing corporation to acquire the entire bond issue outstanding and replace it with a new bond issue bearing a lower rate of interest. The replacement of an existing issuance with a new one is called **refunding.**

Whether the early redemption or extinguishment of outstanding bonds is a nonrefunding or a refunding situation, the difference between the reacquisition price and the net carrying amount of the redeemed bonds should be recognized currently in income of the period of redemption.[6] In accordance with **APB Opinion No. 26,** gain or loss resulting from early extinguishment of a debt is not amortized to future periods. Differing reasons for early redemption or differing means by which the bonds are redeemed have no bearing on how to account for the loss or gain. "All extinguishments of debt before scheduled maturities are fundamentally alike."[7]

At the time of redemption, the unamortized premium or discount, and expenses of issue applicable to the bonds canceled should be amortized up to the acquisition date and removed from the accounts and the liability for bonds reduced in the proper amount. For example, assume that bonds of a par value of $800,000 due in 20 years, are issued on January 1, 1980, at 97. Ten years after the issue date, the entire issue is redeemed at 101 and canceled. The loss on redemption is computed as follows (straight-line amortization is used for simplicity):

---

[6]Amortization of a refunding loss over the remaining life of the old issue being canceled or over the life of the new issue is no longer acceptable practice.

[7]"Early Extinguishment of Debt," *Opinions of the Accounting Principles Board No. 26* (New York: AICPA, 1972), par. 20.

Reacquisition price		$808,000
Net carrying amount of bonds redeemed:		
Par value	$800,000	
Unamortized discount—straight-line basis		
($24,000 × 10/20)	12,000	788,000
Loss on redemption		$ 20,000

The entry to record the reacquisition and cancellation of the bonds is:

Bonds Payable	800,000	
Loss (Extraordinary) on Redemption of Bonds	20,000	
Discount on Bonds Payable		12,000
Cash		808,000

The issuer of callable bonds is generally required to exercise the call on an interest date. Therefore, the amortization of any discount or premium will be up to date and there will be no accrued interest. However, early extinguishment through purchases of bonds in the open market are more likely to be on other than an interest date. If the purchase is not on an interest date, the discount or premium must be amortized and the interest payable must be accrued from the last interest date to the date of purchase.

Reporting Gains and Losses   In October, 1972 the Accounting Principles Board in **Opinion No. 26** required that gains and losses from debt extinguishment be included in income before extraordinary items. Because of money market conditions in 1973–1974, however, many companies were able to buy back long-term debt securities issued in the 1960s at prices well below face value. For instance, in 1973 United Brands extinguished $125 million (face value) of 5½% convertible subordinate debentures due in 1994 (having a market value of $75 million in 1973) by exchanging $12.5 million in cash and $75 million in 9⅛% debenture bonds (nonconvertible) and realized a gain of approximately $37.5 million which was taken entirely into 1973 pretax earnings. At the urging of the SEC the FASB issued **Statement No. 4** in 1975.

In accordance with FASB Statement No. 4, gains or losses from extinguishment of debt should be aggregated and, if material, classified in the income statement as an extraordinary item, net of related income tax effect.[8] That treatment shall apply whether an extinguishment is early or at scheduled maturity date or later without regard to the criteria of "unusual nature" and "infrequency of occurrence."

The following types of extinguishment result in classification of the gains or losses as extraordinary items:

1.   Early extinguishment of debt at a discount (at less than the net carrying amount).
2.   Early extinguishment of debt at a premium (at more than the net carrying amount).
3.   Refinancing existing debt with new debt.
4.   Retirement of debt maturing serially.

Only gains and losses from cash purchases of debt made to satisfy current or future

---

[8]"Reporting Gains and Losses from Extinguishment of Debt," *Statement of Financial Accounting Standards No. 4* (Stamford, Conn.: FASB, 1975), par. 8.

sinking fund requirements are not required to be classified as extraordinary items.[9]

Gains or losses from extinguishment of debt that are reported as extraordinary items should be described in such a way that readers of the financial statements can evaluate their significance. The following disclosures are required by **Statement No. 4:**

1. A description of the extinguishment transactions, including the sources of any funds used to extinguish debt if it is practicable to identify the sources.
2. The income tax effect in the period of extinguishment.
3. The per share amount of the aggregate gain or loss net of related tax effect.[10]

The preceding information, to the extent that it is not shown separately on the face of the income statement, must be disclosed in a single footnote or adequately cross-referenced if in more than one footnote. The following illustration presents disclosure on the face of the income statement and in a footnote to the financial statements.

Digital Computer Corp. purchased for $5,000,000 cash its outstanding 5% debenture bonds having a face or maturity value, as well as net carrying amount, of $6,000,000. Disclosure was appropriately made in its annual report as follows:

Income before extraordinary item	$4,200,000
Extraordinary item—gain from liquidation of debt, net of income tax effect of $480,000—Note 3	520,000
Net income	$4,720,000
Per share of common stock:	
Income before extraordinary item	$1.62
Extraordinary item, net of tax	.20
Net income	$1.82

Note 3. *Extraordinary Item.* The extraordinary item represents a gain of $1,000,000 less related income tax effect from the redemption and retirement of the company's outstanding 5% debenture bonds due in 1995 pursuant to an offer made by the company. The funds used to purchase the debentures represent a portion of the proceeds from the sale of 300,000 shares of the company's common stock.

Treasury Bonds

Bonds payable that have been reacquired by the issuing corporation or its agent or trustee and have not been canceled are known as treasury bonds. They should be shown on the balance sheet at their par value as a deduction from the bonds payable issued to arrive at a net figure representing bonds payable outstanding. When they are sold or canceled, the Treasury Bonds account should be credited.

---

[9]Some debt agreements require that the debtor periodically set aside cash in a sinking fund for the purpose of systematically accumulating funds for the eventual redemption of the debt; sinking fund accounting is presented in Chapter 18.

[10]Disclosure of earnings per share applicable to extraordinary items is optional under the provisions of *APB Opinion No. 15;* however, *FASB Statement No. 4* requires disclosure of the per share effect of gains and losses from extinguishment of debt.

Convertible Bonds

If bonds may be converted into other securities of the corporation during some specified time after issuance, they are called convertible bonds. If convertible bonds are issued at a discount or premium, it is necessary to amortize the discount or premium on the basis of the maturity date of the issue instead of the conversion date, because it is impossible to predict when, if at all, the conversion privilege will be exercised. Accounting for bond conversions is discussed in Chapter 17.

Serial Bonds

An entire bond issue may be due at one maturity date, or the bonds may mature serially, that is, in a series of installments with some bonds maturing each year over a period of years. Serially maturing bonds are frequently issued by school or sanitary districts or other taxing bodies that borrow money that will be paid off in installments through a specially levied tax.

A serial bond issue may be sold as though each series is a separate bond issue or it may be sold as a package. Whether sold separately or as a package, one account for the total premium or discount is used in the general ledger for that serial issue. The total premium or discount to be amortized, whether computed for each series separately or for the entire issue, is entered as one amount in the Premium (or Discount) on Bonds Payable account. **The straight-line, bonds outstanding, or effective interest methods may be used to amortize the premium or discount.**

Both the amortization of premium or discount on serial bond issues and the accounting for the redemption of serial bonds before maturity are illustrated under all three methods of amortization in Appendix J of this chapter.

IMPUTED INTEREST ON LONG-TERM DEBT

Business transactions often involve the exchange of notes or similar instruments for cash or property, goods, or services. If the note is not currently receivable, the transaction is in effect a long-term loan with interest as an inherent and natural ingredient. It is unrealistic and improbable for any business to lend money interest-free. Yet during the 1960s numerous business transactions material in amount were consummated either with no apparent interest or with a very low interest cost.

APB Opinion No. 21 was issued to insure proper accounting for transactions where the form does not reflect the economic substance of the arrangement because of failure to provide for a realistic interest rate on monies payable or receivable in the future. Whenever the face amount of the instrument (notes, bonds, mortgage notes, equipment obligations, and long-term accounts payable) does not reasonably represent the present value of the consideration given or received in the exchange, the accountant must evaluate the entire arrangement to determine the amounts involved for properly recording the exchange and subsequent related interest. This circumstance is most apparent when the note is noninterest-bearing or has a stated interest rate that is different from the rate of interest appropriate for the transaction at the date of issuance. Unless such notes are recorded at present value, the purchase price and cost of property to the buyer (issuing the note) and the sales price and profit to the seller (accepting the note) in the year of the transaction are misstated. In addition, the interest expense and interest income in subsequent periods are also misstated.

Entries for Noninterest-Bearing Long-Term Debt

For example, assume that Scenic Development Company sells land having a cash sale price of $200,000 to Laural Contracting, Inc., in exchange for Laural's five-year noninterest-bearing note in the amount of $293,860. The $200,000 cash sale price represents the present value of the $293,860 note discounted at 8% for five years. If the transaction is recorded on the sale date at the face amount of the note, $293,860, by both parties, Laural's land account and Scenic's sales would be overstated by $93,860, because the $93,860 represents the interest for five years at an effective rate of 8%. Interest income to Scenic and interest expense to Laural for the five-year period would be understated by $93,860.

Because the difference beween the cash sale price of $200,000 and the face amount of the note, $293,860, represents interest at an effective rate of 8%, the transaction is recorded at the exchange date as follows:

Laural Contracting, Inc., books		
Land	200,000	
Discount on Notes Payable	93,860	
Notes Payable		293,860

Scenic Development Company books		
Notes Receivable	293,860	
Discount on Notes Receivable		93,860
Sales		200,000

During the five-year life of the note, Laural Contracting amortizes annually the discount of $93,860 against income as a charge to interest expense. Scenic Development records interest income totaling $93,860 over the five-year period by also amortizing the discount. The effective interest method is recommended although other approaches to amortization may be used if the results obtained are not materially different from those that result from the effective interest method.

Application of Opinion No. 21

All payables that represent commitments to pay money at a determinable future date are considered under **Opinion No. 21,** although certain exceptions do exist. This opinion does not apply to obligations that will be settled in property or services (e.g., deposits on construction in progress), instead of in money. Also, it does not apply to obligations that are payable at some indeterminable date.

The following types of payables are specifically excluded from the provisions of **APB Opinion No. 21:**

1. Payables arising from transactions with suppliers in the normal course of business that are due on customary trade terms not exceeding approximately one year.
2. Amounts that do not require repayment in cash but, instead, will be applied to the

purchase price of property, goods, or services: for example, deposits or progress payments on construction contracts, advance payments for raw materials, and advances to encourage exploration in the extractive industries.

3. Amounts intended to provide security for one party to an agreement: for instance, security deposits and retainages on contracts.

4. The customary cash lending activities and demand- or savings-deposit activities of financial institutions whose primary business is lending money.

5. Transactions where interest rates are affected by tax attributes or legal restrictions prescribed by a governmental agency: for example, industrial revenue bonds, tax-exempt obligations, government-guaranteed obligations, income tax settlements.

6. Transactions between parent and subsidiary companies and between subsidiaries of a common parent.

7. Contractual or other obligations assumed in connection with sales of property, goods, or services: for example, a warranty for product performance.

8. Convertible debt securities.

In discussing the appropriate accounting for long-term payables, the following categories are important:

1. Notes issued solely for cash.

2. Notes issued for cash, but with some right or privilege also being exchanged. For example, a corporation may lend a supplier cash that is receivable five years hence with no stated interest, in exchange for which the supplier agrees to make products available to the lender at lower than prevailing market prices.

3. Notes issued in a noncash exchange for property, goods, or services.

Notes Issued Solely for Cash

When the effective interest on a note is equal to its stated rate, the note sells at its face value. When the stated rate is different from the effective interest, the cash proceeds will be different from the face value of the note. As indicated earlier, the difference between the face value and the cash proceeds received is a discount or a premium that should be amortized over the life of a note to approximate the effective interest rate.

When a note is issued solely for cash, the interest factor is assumed to be the stated or coupon rate plus or minus the amortization of the discount or premium. Because the note issued for cash has a present value equal to the cash proceeds, interest other than that provided by the coupon or stated rate plus or minus amortization of the discount or premium should not be imputed.

Notes Exchanged for Cash and Some Right or Privilege

Sometimes when a note is issued, additional rights or privileges are given to the recipient of the note. For example, a corporation issues a noninterest-bearing note that is to be repaid over five years with no stated interest and in exchange agrees to sell merchandise to the lender at less than the prevailing prices of their merchandise. In this circumstance, the difference between the present value of the payable and the amount of cash loaned should be regarded as a discount on the note. This discount should be amortized as a charge to interest expense over the life of the note. At the same time, the supplier credits an unearned income account in an amount equal to the discount. This unearned income reflects a partial prepayment for sales transactions that will occur over the next five years. This unearned income should be recognized as income while sales are made to the lender over the next five years.

For example, assume that the face or maturity value of a five-year interest-free note is $100,000 and that the appropriate rate at which to impute interest is 10%. The conditions of the note provide that the recipient of the note can purchase $500,000 of merchandise from the debtor corporation (borrower) at 90% of regular selling price over the next five years. To record the loan, the borrower (supplier) recognizes a discount of $37,908, the difference between the $100,000 face amount of the loan and its present value of $62,092. The borrower also records a credit to unearned income of $37,908. The borrower's journal entry is:

Cash	100,000	
Discount on Notes Payable	37,908	
Notes Payable		100,000
Unearned Income		37,908

The Discount on Notes Payable is subsequently amortized to interest expense using the effective interest method. The Unearned Income is recognized as revenue from sales and prorated on the same basis that each period's sales to the lender-customer bear to the total sales to that customer for the term of the note. In this situation the write-off of the discount and the recognition of the unearned income are at different rates.

Noncash Transactions

The third type of situation involves the issuance of a note for some noncash consideration such as property, goods, or services. When the debt instrument is exchanged for property, goods, or services in a bargained transaction entered into at arm's length, the stated interest rate is presumed to be fair unless:

1. No interest rate is stated, or
2. The stated interest rate is unreasonable, or
3. The stated face amount of the debt instrument is materially different from the current cash sales price for the same or similar items or from current market value of the debt instrument.

In these circumstances the present value of the debt instrument is measured by the fair value of the property, goods, or services or by an amount that reasonably approximates the market value of the note.[11] The interest element plus any stated rate of interest is evidenced by the difference between the face amount of the note and the fair value of the property.

Imputing an Interest Rate

If the fair value of the property, goods, or services is not determinable and if the debt instrument has no ready market, the problem of determining the present value of the debt instrument is more difficult. To estimate the present value of a

---

[11]"Interest on Receivables and Payables," *op. cit.*, par. 12.

debt instrument under such circumstances, an applicable interest rate is approximated that may differ from the stated interest rate. This process of interest rate approximation is called **imputation,** and the resulting interest rate is called an **imputed interest rate.** The imputed interest rate is used to establish the present value of the debt instrument by discounting, at that rate, all future payments on the debt instrument.

Opinion No. 21 provides the following general guidelines for imputing the appropriate interest rate:

> The prevailing rates for similar instruments of issuers with similar credit ratings will normally help determine the appropriate interest rate for determining the present value of a specific note at its date of issuance. In any event, the rate used for valuation purposes will normally be at least equal to the rate at which the debtor can obtain financing of a similar nature from other sources at the date of the transaction. The objective is to approximate the rate which would have resulted if an independent borrower and an independent lender had negotiated a similar transaction under comparable terms and conditions with the option to pay the cash price upon purchase or to give a note for the amount of the purchase which bears the prevailing rate of interest to maturity.[12]

The choice of a rate may be affected specifically by the credit standing of the issuer, restrictive covenants, the collateral, payments and other terms pertaining to the debt, and the existing prime interest rate. Determination of the imputed interest rate is made at the time the debt instrument is issued; **any subsequent changes in prevailing interest rates are ignored.**

Illustration of Interest Imputation, Recording, and Amortization

On December 31, 1980, Wunderlich Company issued for architectural services a promissory note with a face value of $550,000, a due date of December 31, 1985, and bearing a stated interest rate of 2%, payable at the end of each year. The fair value of the services is not readily determinable nor is the note readily marketable. On the basis of the credit rating of Wunderlich Company, the absence of collateral, the prime interest rate at that date, and the prevailing interest on the company's other outstanding debt, an 8% interest rate is imputed as appropriate in this circumstance. The imputed interest portion of the note is determined as follows:

Maturity value of the note		$550,000
Present value of $550,000 due in 5 years at 8%—		
$550,000 × .6806 (Table 6-2)	$374,330	
Present value of $11,000 payable annually for		
5 years at 8% annually—		
$11,000 × 3.9927 (Table 6-4)	43,920	
Present value of the note		418,250
Discount		$131,750

---

[12]*Ibid.*, par. 13.

The issuance of the note and receipt of the services is recorded as follows:

Dec. 31, 1980

Building (or Construction in Process)	418,250	
Discount on Notes Payable	131,750	
Notes Payable		550,000

The five-year amortization schedule appears below.

SCHEDULE OF NOTE DISCOUNT AMORTIZATION
EFFECTIVE INTEREST METHOD
2% NOTE DISCOUNTED AT 8% (IMPUTED)

Date	Credit Cash	Debit Interest Expense	Credit Unamortized Discount	Present Value of Note
12/31/80				$418,250
12/31/81	$11,000	$ 33,460[a]	$ 22,460[b]	440,710[c]
12/31/82	11,000	35,257	24,257	464,967
12/31/83	11,000	37,197	26,197	491,164
12/31/84	11,000	39,293	28,293	519,457
12/31/85	11,000	41,543[d]	30,543[d]	550,000
	$55,000	$186,750	$131,750	

[a]$418,250 × .08 = $33,460.
[b]$33,460 − $11,000 = $22,460.
[c]$418,250 + $22,460 = $440,710.
[d]$13 adjustment to compensate for rounding.

Payment of the first year's interest and amortization of the discount is recorded as follows:

Dec. 31, 1981

Interest Expense	33,460	
Discount on Notes Payable		22,460
Cash		11,000

Financial Statement Presentation of Discount or Premium

Any discount or premium resulting from the determination of present value in these transactions is not an asset or a liability separable from the note that produces it. Therefore, the discount or premium is reported in the balance sheet as a direct deduction from or addition to the face amount of the debt instrument. It is not classified as a deferred charge or deferred credit. The face amount of the note is disclosed in the balance sheet or in the footnotes, and the description of the note includes the effective interest rate. The balance sheet presentation of discounted notes may assume two different forms: (1) presentation of the discount in caption form and (2) presentation of the discount separately.[13] If we use the data from the

[13]*Ibid.*, par. 16.

Wunderlich Company illustration, these two forms appear as follows on December 31, 1981, one year after issuance of the note:

Presentation of the Discount in Caption Form		
	12/31/81	12/31/80
Note payable issued for services:		
$550,000 face amount, due December 31, 1985, bearing 2% stated interest (less unamortized discount based on imputed interest rate of 8%— 1981, $109,290; 1980, $131,750)	$440,710	$418,250
Presentation of the Discount Separately		
	12/31/81	12/31/80
Note payable issued for services:		
Note due December 31, 1985, bearing stated interest of 2%	$550,000	$550,000
Less unamortized discount based on imputed interest rate of 8%	109,290	131,750
Note payable less unamortized discount	$440,710	$418,250

If several notes are involved, the principal amount of such notes and the balance of total unamortized discount is presented in the balance sheet with the details of each note disclosed individually in a footnote or separate schedule to the balance sheet.

Amortization of discounts or premiums resulting from imputed interest is reported as interest in the statement of income. Any costs of issue are reported in the balance sheet as deferred charges and are amortized to expense over the life of the debt issue.

Reporting Long-Term Debt

Companies that have large amounts and numerous issues of long-term debt frequently report only one amount in the balance sheet and support this with comments and schedules in the accompanying notes. The supplementary disclosures generally indicate the nature of the liabilities, maturity dates, interest rates, call provisions, conversion privileges, restrictions imposed by the borrower, and assets pledged as security. Any assets pledged as security for the debt should be shown in the asset section of the balance sheet. Long-term debt that matures within one year should be reported as a current liability, unless retirement is to be accomplished with other than current assets. If the debt is to be refinanced, converted into stock, or is to be retired from a bond retirement fund, it should continue to be reported as noncurrent and accompanied with a footnote explaining the method to be used in its liquidation.[14] See pages 200–201 for Tenneco's footnote disclosure and detail of its long-term debt.

---

[14]"Balance Sheet Classification of Short-Term Obligations Expected to be Refinanced," *FASB Statement of Financial Accounting Standards No. 6* (Stamford, Conn.: FASB, 1975), par. 15.

APPENDIX

Illustration of Serial Bond Amortization and Redemption Before Maturity

The following comprehensive illustration demonstrates (1) the amortization of premium or discount on serial bonds using the straight-line, bonds outstanding, and effective interest methods; and (2) the accounting for redemption of serial bonds before maturity under all three methods of amortization.

Amortization of Premium or Discount on Serial Bonds

A serial bond issue in the amount of $1,000,000, dated January 1, 1979, bearing 8% interest payable at December 31 each year, is sold by Yorkville School Products to yield 9% per annum; the bonds mature in the amount of $200,000 on January 1 of each year beginning in 1980. The bond price and discount are computed as follows:

			Selling Price	Discount
Bonds due 1/1/80 (1 year away):				
Principal: $200,000 × .91743 (Table 6-2)		$183,486		
Interest: $ 16,000 × .91743 (Table 6-4)		14,679		
			198,165	$ 1,835*
Bonds due 1/1/81 (2 years away)	Computations		196,482	3,518
Bonds due 1/1/82 (3 years away)	similar to		194,937	5,063
Bonds due 1/1/83 (4 years away)	those for		193,522	6,478
Bonds due 1/1/84 (5 years away)	1/1/80 bonds.		192,220	7,780
Total price for all series			$975,326	
Total discount on all series				$24,674

*$1,835 = $200,000 minus $198,165

Straight-line Amortization   The straight-line method of amortization may be used if the results are not materially different from those resulting from use of the effective interest method. The total discount for the Yorkville School Products issue described on page 615 would be apportioned for each series over the five years as shown in the following schedule:

		Amortization Schedule—Straight-line Method				
				Apportioned to		
Series Due Jan. 1	Total Discount	1979	1980	1981	1982	1983
1980	$ 1,835	$1,835				
1981	3,518	1,759	$1,759			
1982	5,063	1,688	1,688	$1,687		
1983	6,478	1,619	1,619	1,620	$1,620	
1984	7,780	1,556	1,556	1,556	1,556	$1,556
	$24,674	$8,457	$6,622	$4,863	$3,176	$1,556

Bonds Outstanding Method   If the entire issue of serial bonds is sold to underwriters at a stated price, however, the discount or premium is frequently amortized by the **bonds outstanding method,** since the discount or premium on each series is not definitely determinable. The bonds outstanding method is an application of the straight-line method to serial bonds and assumes that the discount applicable to each bond of the issue is the same dollar amount per bond per year.

The total discount for the Yorkville School Products issue, would be apportioned over the five years as shown in the following schedule:

		Amortization Schedule—Bonds Outstanding Method		
Year Ending Dec. 31	Bonds Outstanding During the Year	Bonds Outstanding During the Year ÷ Total of Bonds Outstanding Column	Total Discount to be Amortized	Discount to be Amortized During Each Year
1979	$1,000,000	10/30	$24,674	$ 8,224
1980	800,000	8/30	24,674	6,580
1981	600,000	6/30	24,674	4,935
1982	400,000	4/30	24,674	3,290
1983	200,000	2/30	24,674	1,645
	$3,000,000	30/30		$24,674

The effect of the column for "Bonds Outstanding During the Year" is to convert all the bonds into terms of bonds outstanding for one year, or a total of $3,000,000 for five years. Accordingly, during 1979 the premium to be amortized would be $1,000,000/$3,000,000 × $24,674, or $8,224. Similarly, during 1982 the premium to be amortized would be $400,000/$3,000,000 × $24,674, or $3,290.

An amortization schedule should be prepared for serial bonds in the same manner as the amortization schedule for single-maturity bonds, except that the maturity value of each serial must be deducted from the total carrying amount of the bonds when the serial is paid. The schedule shown below illustrates the amortization of the discount and the reduction in carrying amount for the serial bond issue described above using the bonds outstanding method.

Date	Credit Cash	Credit Bond Discount	Debit Interest Expense	Debit Bonds Payable	Carrying Amount of Bonds
		Schedule of Bond Discount Amortization—Serial Bonds Bonds Outstanding Method			
1/1/79					$975,326
12/31/79	$ 80,000ª	$ 8,224ᵇ	$ 88,224ᶜ	—	983,550ᵈ
1/1/80	200,000	—	—	$ 200,000	783,550
12/31/80	64,000	6,580	70,580	—	790,130
1/1/81	200,000	—	—	200,000	590,130
12/31/81	48,000	4,935	52,935	—	595,065
1/1/82	200,000	—	—	200,000	395,065
12/31/82	32,000	3,290	35,290	—	398,355
1/1/83	200,000	—	—	200,000	198,355
12/31/83	16,000	1,645	17,645	—	200,000
1/1/84	200,000	—	—	200,000	—
	$1,240,000	$24,674	$264,674	$1,000,000	

ª$80,000 = $1,000,000 × .08
ᵇ$8,224 = $1,000,000/$3,000,000 × $24,674
ᶜ$88,224 = $80,000 + $8,224
ᵈ$983,550 = $975,326 + $8,224

A schedule with similar debit and credit columns could be prepared using the data from the straight-line amortization schedule. The credit to Bond Discount on December 31, 1979 would be $8,457 using the straight-line data on page 616.

Effective Interest Method   Application of the effective interest method to serial bonds is similar to that illustrated in the section concerned with single-maturity bonds. Interest expense for the period is computed by multiplying the effective interest rate times the carrying amount of bonds outstanding during that period. The amount of amortization of bond discount or premium is the difference between the effective interest expense for the period and the actual interest payments. Under this method, the interest is at a constant rate relative to the carrying amount of the bonds outstanding. The schedule shown on page 618 illustrates the amortization of discount and the reduction in carrying amount for the Yorkville serial bond issue using the effective interest method.

The journal entries that would be recorded for the payment of the interest, amortization of the discount, and retirement of each series of bonds can be determined from the column headings in the amortization schedule.

		Schedule of Bond Discount Amortization—Serial Bonds			
		Effective Interest Method			
		8% Bonds Sold to Yield 9%			
	Credit Cash	Debit Interest Expense	Credit Bond Discount	Debit Bonds Payable	Carrying Amount of Bonds
Date					
1/1/79					$975,326
12/31/79	$ 80,000ᵃ	$ 87,779ᵇ	$ 7,779ᶜ	—	983,105ᵈ
1/1/80	200,000	—	—	$ 200,000	783,105
12/31/80	64,000	70,479	6,479	—	789,584
1/1/81	200,000	—	—	200,000	589,584
12/31/81	48,000	53,063	5,063	—	594,647
1/1/82	200,000	—	—	200,000	394,647
12/31/82	32,000	35,518	3,518	—	398,165
1/1/83	200,000	—	—	200,000	198,165
12/31/83	16,000	17,835	1,835	—	200,000
1/1/84	200,000	—	—	200,000	—
	$1,240,000	$264,674	$24,674	$1,000,000	

ᵃ$80,000 = $1,000,000 × .08   ᶜ$7,779 = $87,779 − $80,000
ᵇ$87,779 = $975,326 × .09   ᵈ$983,105 = $975,326 + $7,779

Redemption of Serial Bonds Before Maturity

If bonds of a certain series are redeemed before maturity date, it is necessary to compute the amount of unamortized discount or premium applicable to those bonds and to remove it from the Discount (or Premium) on Bonds Payable account.

Straight-Line Method   Assume that on January 1, 1981, $200,000 of the Yorkville School Products serial bonds due January 1, 1984 are redeemed for $201,000. The unamortized discount on the $200,000 of bonds due on January 1, 1984 is $4,668 ($1,556 + $1,556 + $1,556; the discount apportioned to 1981, 1982, and 1983, respectively) as determined from the straight-line amortization schedule on page 616. The loss on early redemption of these bonds is computed as follows:

Purchase price of bonds redeemed	$201,000
Carrying amount of 1/1/84 series bonds:	
($200,000 − $7,780 + $1,556 + $1,556) or	
($200,000 − $4,668)	195,332
Loss (extraordinary) on bond redemption	$ 5,668

Bonds Outstanding Method   Using the same data, the computation of the applicable unamortized discount under the bonds outstanding method is as follows:

$$\frac{3 \text{ (number of years before maturity)} \times \$200,000 \text{ (par of bonds)} \times \$24,674 \text{ (total discount)}}{\$3,000,000 \text{ (total of bonds outstanding column)}} = \$4,935$$

Expressed a little differently, the discount to be amortized each year for each $200,000 of bonds is $200,000/$3,000,000 $\times$ $24,674, or $1,645. Therefore, if $200,000 of bonds are retired three years before maturity, the discount to be eliminated is 3 $\times$ $1,645, or $4,935.

Under the bonds outstanding method of amortization, the loss on early retirement of these bonds is computed as follows:

Purchase price of bonds redeemed	$201,000
Carrying amount of 1/1/84 series bonds:	
($200,000 − $4,935)	195,065
Loss (extraordinary) on bond redemption	$ 5,935

Effective Interest Method   Under the effective interest method the carrying amount of all the serial bonds outstanding at the time of an early retirement must be reduced by the present value of the bonds being retired. Reference to the effective interest amortization schedule shows that the carrying amount of all the Yorkville bonds still outstanding at January 1, 1981 is $589,584. The present value of the bonds being retired is computed as follows (3 years at 9%):

Present value of principal ($200,000 $\times$ .77218)	$154,436
Present value of interest payments ($16,000 $\times$ 2.53130)	40,501
Present value of bonds to be retired	$194,937

The entry to record the early redemption using the effective interest method would be as follows on January 1, 1981.

Bonds Payable	200,000	
Loss (Extraordinary) on Redemption of Bonds	6,063	
Discount on Bonds Payable ($200,000 − $194,937)		5,063
Cash		201,000

The gain or loss on redemption is the difference between the present value of the bonds ($194,937) and the cost to retire the bonds ($201,000); in this example the loss is $6,063.

APPENDIX

Accounting for Troubled Debt
Restructurings

During periods of depressed economic conditions or other financial hardship, some debtors have difficulty meeting their financial obligations because of serious cash flow problems. For example, New York City has had a difficult time paying its interest and principal obligations on debt issued to finance its municipal operations. In addition, many real estate investment trusts, referred to as REITs (enterprises established to invest in real estate), have experienced financial problems because of the general downturn in the economy in the mid-1970s, coupled with poor investment selection on their part. As a result, debt obligations are often restructured to permit the debtor either to defer or to reduce the interest or the principal obligation.

FASB Statement No. 15, "Accounting by Debtors and Creditors for Troubled Debt Restructurings," was issued in 1977 to clarify the proper accounting for these types of transactions. According to this statement, a troubled debt restructuring occurs when ". . . the creditor for economic or legal reasons related to the debtor's financial difficulties grants a concession to the debtor that it would not otherwise consider."[1] For example, a financial institution such as a bank recognizes that granting some concessions (that is, restructuring of the debt in a troubled loan situation), is a more likely way to maximize recovery than forcing the debtor into bankruptcy.

FASB Statement No. 15 applies only to **troubled** debt restructurings in which the creditor grants some concessions; it does not apply to modifications of a debt obli-

---

[1]"Accounting by Debtors and Creditors for Troubled Debt Restructurings," *FASB Statement of Financial Accounting Standards No. 15* (Stamford, Conn.: FASB, 1977), par. 1.

gation that reflect general economic conditions that dictate a reduction in interest rates. Nor does it apply to the refunding of an old debt with new debt having an effective interest rate approximately equal to that of similar debt issued by nontroubled debtors.

A troubled debt restructuring involves one of two basic types of transactions:

1. Settlement of debt at less than its recorded amount.
2. Continuation of debt with a modification in terms.

Whether the troubled debt restructuring is a "settlement of the debt" or a "continuation of the debt with modification in terms," the concessions granted the debtor (borrower) by the creditor (lender) generally will result in a **gain to the debtor** and a **loss to the creditor.**[2] **The gain and the loss are measured by both the debtor and creditor as the difference between the carrying amount (book value) of the obligation immediately prior to restructuring (prerestructuring value) and the undiscounted total future cash flows required after restructuring (post restructure value).** Therefore, if the carrying amount of the obligation is greater than the total future cash flows, the difference is recorded at the date of restructure as a gain to the debtor and as a loss to the creditor. And, if the carrying amount of the obligation is less than the total future cash flows, no restructure gain or loss is recognized. These are the basic principles set forth in **FASB Statement No. 15,** which attempts to achieve "accounting symmetry" between the debtor and the creditor.

Settlement of Debt at Less than Carrying Amount

A transfer of noncash assets (real estate, receivables, or other assets) or the issuance of the debtor's stock can be used to settle a debt obligation in a troubled debt restructuring. In these situations, **the noncash assets or equity interest given should be accounted for at their fair market value.** The debtor is required to determine the excess of the carrying amount of the payable over the fair value of the assets or equity transferred (gain), and, likewise, the creditor is required to determine the excess of the recorded investment in the receivable over the fair value of those same assets or equity interests transferred (loss). The debtor recognizes an extraordinary gain equal to the amount of the excess and the creditor normally would charge the excess (loss) against an appropriate allowance account. In addition, the debtor recognizes a gain or loss on disposition of assets to the extent that the fair value of those assets differs from their carrying amount (book value).

To illustrate a transfer of assets, assume that American City Bank has loaned $20,000,000 to Union Mortgage Company, a real estate investment trust. Union Mortgage Company in turn has invested these monies in residential apartment

---

[2]While the restructuring may result in the recognition of no gains or losses by either debtor or creditor, it is the nature of a troubled debt situation that the creditor cannot have a gain and the debtor cannot have a loss from restructuring.

buildings, but because of low occupancy rates it cannot meet its loan obligations. American City Bank, therefore, agrees to accept from Union Mortgage Company real estate with a fair market value of $16,000,000 in full settlement of the $20,000,000 loan obligation. The real estate has a recorded value of $21,000,000 on the books of Union Mortgage Company. The entry to record this transaction on the books of American City Bank (creditor) is as follows:

Real Estate	16,000,000	
Allowance for Doubtful Accounts	4,000,000	
Note Receivable from Union Mortgage Co.		20,000,000

The real estate is recorded at fair market value, and a charge is made to the Allowance for Doubtful Accounts to reflect the bad debt write-off. If no allowance were available to absorb the charge of $4,000,000, the debit would be to a loss (ordinary) account.

The entry to record this transaction on the books of Union Mortgage Company (debtor) is as follows:

Note Payable to American City Bank	20,000,000	
Loss on Disposition of Real Estate	5,000,000	
Real Estate		21,000,000
Gain on Restructuring of Debt		4,000,000

Union Mortgage Company has a loss on the disposition of real estate in the amount of $5,000,000, the difference between the $21,000,000 book value and the $16,000,000 fair market value, which should be shown as an ordinary loss on the income statement in accordance with **APB Opinion No. 30.** In addition, it has a gain on restructuring of debt of $4,000,000, the difference between the $20,000,000 carrying amount of the note payable and the $16,000,000 fair market value of the real estate. The gain on restructuring should be shown as an extraordinary item in accordance with **FASB Statement No. 4.**

To illustrate the granting of an equity interest, assume that American City Bank had agreed to accept from Union Mortgage Company 320,000 shares of Union's common stock ($10 par) that has a fair market value of $16,000,000 in full settlement of the $20,000,000 loan obligation. The entry to record this transaction on the books of American City Bank (creditor) is as follows:

Investment in Marketable Equity Securities	16,000,000	
Allowance for Doubtful Accounts	4,000,000	
Note Receivable from Union Mortgage Co.		20,000,000

The stock received by American City Bank is recorded as an investment at the fair market value at the date of restructure.

The entry to record this transaction on the books of Union Mortgage Company (debtor) is as follows:

Note Payable to American City Bank	20,000,000	
Common Stock		3,200,000
Additional Paid-in Capital		12,800,000
Gain on Restructuring of Debt		4,000,000

The stock issued by Union Mortgage Company is recorded in the normal manner with the difference between the par value and the fair market value of the stock recorded as additional paid-in capital.

Continuation of Debt With Modification of Terms

In some cases, a debtor will have serious short-run cash flow problems that lead the debtor to request one or a combination of the following modifications:

1. Reduction of the stated interest rate.
2. Extension of the maturity date of the face amount of the debt.
3. Reduction of the face amount of the debt.
4. Reduction or deferral of any accrued interest.

The FASB takes the position that a troubled debt restructuring involving any of these modifications of terms is a continuation of an existing debt arrangement and does not transfer economic resources on the restructure date. **FASB Statement No. 15 specifies that the effects from these types of restructurings should be accounted for prospectively (over future years) by both the debtor and the creditor.** Unless the carrying amount at the time of restructure exceeds the undiscounted total future cash flows, the debtor will not change the carrying amount of the payable and the creditor will not change the recorded investment in the receivable.[3] In other words, **neither the debtor nor the creditor makes any entries at the date of restructuring except when the carrying amount of the debt is greater than the total future cash flows.**

The Board also specifies that the effective interest method (as prescribed in **APB Opinion No. 21**) be used to compute the future interest expense of the debtor and the future interest income of the creditor. The new effective interest rate to be used is the discount rate that makes the present value of the future cash flows specified by the new terms equal to the carrying amount of the debt.[4]

No Gain or Loss Recognized   The following example illustrates a restructuring in which no gain or loss is recorded. On December 31, 1980, the Morgan National Bank enters into a debt restructuring agreement with Resorts Development Company, which is experiencing financial difficulties. The bank restructures a $10,000,000 note receivable by:

1. Reducing the principal obligation from $10,000,000 to $9,000,000.
2. Forgiving $500,000 of accrued interest.
3. Extending the maturity date from December 31, 1980 to December 31, 1984, and
4. Reducing the interest rate from 12% to 8%.

The total future cash flow after restructuring of $11,880,000 ($9,000,000 of principal plus $2,880,000 of interest payments) exceeds the total pre-restructure carrying amount of the debt of $10,500,000 ($10,000,000 of principal plus $500,000 of accrued interest). Consequently, no gain or loss is recorded and no adjustment is made by the debtor to the carrying amount of the payable or by the creditor to the carrying amount of the investment in the receivable.

A new effective interest rate must be computed by the debtor and the creditor in order to record interest expense and income in future periods. The new rate is computed by relating the pre-restructure carrying amount ($10,500,000) to the total future cash flow ($11,880,000). By trial and error and by interpolation or formula we are able to derive the rate necessary to discount the total future cash flow

[3]"Accounting by Debtors and Creditors for Troubled Debt Restructurings," *op. cit.*, pars. 16 and 30.
[4]*Ibid.*

($11,880,000) to a present value equal to the remaining balance ($9,000,000). The desired rate is 3.46613.[5]

On the basis of the effective rate of 3.46613%, the following interest schedule can be prepared:

Date	Cash	Interest at Effective Rate	Reduction in Carrying Amount	Carrying Amount
12/31/80				$10,500,000
12/31/81	$ 720,000	$ 363,944[a]	$ 356,056	10,143,944
12/31/82	720,000	351,602	368,398	9,775,546
12/31/83	720,000	338,833	381,167	9,394,379
12/31/84	720,000	325,621	394,379	9,000,000
	$2,880,000	$1,380,000	$1,500,000	

[a]$363,944 = $10,500,000 × 3.46613%

Using the data above, the entries on the debtor's and creditor's books would be as follows:

Resorts Development Co. (Debtor)
December 31, 1980 (date of restructure):

Notes Payable to Bank	1,000,000
Interest Payable	500,000
Premium on	
Notes Payable	1,500,000

Morgan National Bank (Creditor)

Discount on Notes	
Receivable	1,500,000
Notes Receivable	
from Resorts	1,000,000
Interest Receivable	500,000

[5]Only by trial and error using present value Tables 6–2 and 6–4 can we determine the rate:

	Present value at		
	3%	?%	4%
Principal (n = 4)			
3%—.88849 × $9,000,000	$ 7,996,410		
?%—(Factor from Table 6–2) × $9,000,000		?	
4%—.85480 × $9,000,000			$ 7,693,200
Interest (n = 4)			
3%—3.71710 × $720,000	2,676,312		
?%—(Factor from Table 6–4) × $720,000		?	
4%—3.62990 × $720,000			2,613,528
Total present value	$10,672,722	$10,500,000	$10,306,278

Once we know that the rate is between 3% and 4%, we can interpolate to obtain an approximation of the desired rate:

$$\left(\frac{\$10,672,722 - \$10,500,000}{\$10,672,722 - \$10,306,728}\right) \times (4\% - 3\%) = .4719\%$$

$$3\% + .4719\% = 3.4719\%$$

A more accurate interest rate i can be found by using the formulas given at the tops of Tables 6–2 and 6–4 to set up the following equation:

$$\$10,500,000 = \underbrace{\frac{1}{(1+i)^4}}_{\text{(from Table 6–2)}} \times \$9,000,000 + \underbrace{\frac{1 - \dfrac{1}{(1+i)^4}}{i}}_{\text{(from Table 6–4)}} \times \$720,000$$

Solving algebraically for i, it can be found that $i = 3.46613\%$.

A computer program is frequently used in practice to find the implicit interest rate.

December 31, 1981 (date of first interest payment following restructure):

Premium on Notes Payable	356,056	Cash	720,000
Interest Expense	363,944	Discount on	
Cash	720,000	Notes Receivable	356,056
		Interest Income	363,944

December 31, 1982, 1983, and 1984 (dates of 2nd, 3rd, and last interest payment):
(Same accounts as 12/31/81 entry using applicable amounts from the interest schedule)

December 31, 1984 (date of principal payment):

Note Payable to Bank	9,000,000	Cash	9,000,000
Cash	9,000,000	Note Receivable	
		from Resorts	9,000,000

Recognition of Gain and Loss   If the pre-restructure carrying amount exceeds the total future cash flows as a result of a modification of the terms, the debtor records a gain and the creditor records a loss at the date of restructure. To illustrate, assume the facts in the previous example except that Morgan National Bank **reduced the principal to $7,000,000** (and forgave the accrued interest of $500,000, extended the maturity date to December 31, 1984, and reduced the interest from 12% to 8%). The total future cash flow is now $9,240,000 ($7,000,000 of principal plus $2,240,000 of interest), which is $1,260,000 less than the pre-restructure carrying amount of $10,500,000. Under these circumstances, Resorts Development Company (debtor) would reduce the carrying amount of the payable and Morgan National Bank (creditor) would reduce the carrying amount of the receivable by $760,000 and both would write-off the accrued interest of $500,000. Resorts would recognize an extraordinary gain and Morgan Bank would recognize an ordinary loss (or debit the allowance account) in the same amount of $1,260,000. Because the effective interest rate is 0%, all of the future cash flows reduce the new principal balance and no interest expense or interest income is recognized by either the debtor or the creditor. The following journal entries illustrate the accounting by the debtor and the creditor.

Resorts Development Corps. (Debtor)

December 31, 1980 (Restructure date):

Interest Payable	500,000		
Note Payable to			
Morgan	760,000		
Gain on Restructured			
Debt		1,260,000	

Morgan National Bank (Creditor)

Loss on Restructured Debt			
(or Allowance for			
Doubtful Accts.)	1,260,000		
Note Receivable from			
Resorts		760,000	
Interest Receivable		500,000	

December 31, 1981, 1982, 1983, and 1984 (Interest payment dates):

Note Payable to Morgan	560,000		
Cash		560,000	

Cash	560,000		
Note Receivable from			
Resorts		560,000	

December 31, 1984 (Principal payment date):

Note Payable to Morgan	7,000,000		
Cash		7,000,000	

Cash	7,000,000		
Note Receivable			
from Resorts		7,000,000	

FASB Justification for Not Recognizing Gain or Loss   The FASB reasoned that a troubled debt restructuring involving a modification of terms is a continuation of an existing debt and is not a business transaction involving transfers of resources and obligations. Therefore, the restructured debt should continue to be accounted for on the basis of the carrying amounts before restructuring. Some accountants challenge this approach; if a company has a $1,000,000 loan receivable earning interest at 10% and the interest rate is lowered to 5% because the debtor has financial problems, they believe that a loss should be recorded immediately. The Board contends that the creditor's primary objective of modifying the terms is to recover its investment, which is carried at the principal amount and not at principal plus future interest. The Board concluded that the effect on cash flows is essentially the same whether the modifications involve changes in amounts designated as principal amount or interest. Furthermore, accounting for restructured debt should be based on the substance of the modification—the effect on cash flows— not on the labels chosen to describe those cash flows. Therefore, to the extent that recoverability of the investment itself is not affected, no gain or loss should be recognized.[6]

The authors believe that nonrecognition of a loss in modification of terms situations is unsound accounting. In our opinion, if an item such as the interest rate is reduced, an economic loss has resulted and an accounting loss should be reported. The FASB has failed to recognize the change that has taken place in the present value of the receivable (obligation).

Disclosures Required   **FASB Statement No. 15** prescribes the following disclosures for troubled debt restructurings as of the date of each balance sheet presented:

Debtor

1. A description of the changes in terms or major features of settlement.
2. The aggregate gain on restructuring and the related tax effect.
3. The per share amount of the aggregate gain on restructuring.
4. The aggregate gain or loss on transfers of assets.
5. Information on any contingent payments.

Creditor

1. The aggregate recorded investment (receivable).
2. The gross interest income that would have been recorded in the period ignoring restructure.
3. The gross interest income on those receivables that was recorded in the period.
4. The amount of commitments to lend additional funds to debtors whose terms have been modified.

---

[6]"Accounting by Debtors and Creditors for Troubled Debt Restructurings," *op. cit.*, pars. 140–155. The restructuring does not preclude the necessity for the creditor to make appropriate allowance for doubtful accounts in relation to the future collectibility of amounts from the troubled debtor.

Summary of Accounting for Troubled Debt Restructurings

Summary of Accounting Procedures
for Troubled Debt Restructurings

Form of Restructure	Accounting Procedure
Settlement of Debt	
1. Transfer of noncash assets.	1. Recognize gain (debtor) or loss (creditor) on restructure. Debtor—Recognize gain or loss on asset transfer.
2. Granting of equity interest.	2. Recognize gain (debtor) or loss (creditor) on restructure.
Continuation of Debt with	
Modified Terms	
1. Carrying amount of debt is less than total future cash flows.	1. Recognize no gain (loss) on restructure. Determine new effective interest rate to be used in amortizing carrying amount.
2. Carrying amount of debt is greater than total future cash flows.	2. Recognize gain (loss) on restructure.* Recognize no interest expense or income over remaining life of debt.

*Recognition of gain or loss here implies that the pre-restructure carrying amount will be *reduced* to an amount equal to the total future cash flows.

Note: All **asterisked** questions, cases, exercises, or problems relate to material contained in the appendix to each chapter.

Questions

1. (a) From what sources might a corporation obtain funds through long-term debt?
   (b) What is a bond indenture? What does it contain?
2. Under what conditions may a short-term obligation be classified as a long-term debt?
3. (a) What is the typical denomination of corporate bonds?
   (b) How often is bond interest typically payable?
4. Differentiate among term bonds, mortgage bonds, collateral trust bonds, debenture bonds, income bonds, callable bonds, registered bonds, bearer or coupon bonds.
5. In what different ways may bonds be issued?
6. Distinguish between the following interest rates for bonds payable:
   (a) yield rate;
   (b) nominal rate;
   (c) stated rate;
   (d) market rate;
   (e) effective rate.

7. Distinguish between the following values relative to bonds payable:
   (a) par value;
   (b) face value;
   (c) market value;
   (d) maturity value.

8. Under what conditions of bond issuance does a discount on bonds payable arise? Under what conditions of bond issuance does a premium on bonds payable arise?

9. How should unamortized discount on bonds payable be reported on the financial statements? Unamortized premium on bonds payable?

10. What are the two methods of amortizing discount and premium on bonds payable? Explain each.

11. Benson Company sells its bonds at a premium and applies the effective interest method in amortizing the premium. Will the annual interest expense increase or decrease over the life of the bonds? Explain.

12. How should the expenses of issuing bonds be accounted for and classified in the financial statements?

13. Where should treasury bonds be shown on the balance sheet? Should treasury bonds be carried at par or at reacquisition cost?

14. What is the "call" feature of a bond issue? How does the call feature affect the amortization of bond premium or discount?

15. Why would a company wish to reduce its bond indebtedness before its bonds reach maturity? Indicate how this can be done and the correct accounting treatment for such a transaction.

16. How are gains and losses from extinguishment of debt classified in the income statement? What disclosures are required of such transactions by **FASB Statement No. 4?**

17. What are convertible bonds? How does the convertible feature of a bond issue affect the amortization of premium or discount on bonds payable?

18. What entries should be made on a corporation's books for:
   (a) Transfers of cash to the agent or trustee for interest and principal payments.
   (b) Recognition of accrued interest.
   (c) Notification of payment of interest and principal amounts by the agent or trustee?

19. What must the accountant do to record properly a transaction involving the issuance of a noninterest-bearing long-term note in exchange for property?

20. How is the present value of a noninterest-bearing note computed?

21. When is the stated interest rate of a debt instrument presumed not to be fair?

22. What types of payables are exempted from the provisions of **APB Opinion No. 21?**

23. What are the considerations in computing an appropriate interest rate?

*24. (a) Describe the bonds-outstanding method of premium or discount amortization.
   (b) Describe the effective interest method of bond premium or discount amortization for serial bonds.

*25. (a) In a troubled debt situation, why might the creditor grant concessions to the debtor?
   (b) What type of concessions might a creditor grant the debtor in a troubled debt situation?

*26. What are the general rules for measuring and recognizing gain or loss by both the debtor and the creditor in a troubled debt restructuring?

*27. Sautern National Bank agrees to restructure Chablis Company's troubled debt situation by reducing the interest rate from 14% to 8% and extending the maturity date of the debt five additional years. Explain how Chablis Company should account for this modification of terms in the restructuring of its debt to Sautern National Bank.

Cases

C14-1   The following article appeared in the June 19, 1979 issue of the *Wall Street Journal:*

Bond Markets
Giant Commonwealth Edison Issue Hits Resale Market With $70 Million Left Over
NEW YORK—Commonwealth Edison Co.'s slow-selling new 9¼% bonds were tossed onto the resale market at a reduced price with about $70 million still available from the $200 million offered Thursday, dealers said.

The Chicago utility's bonds, rated double-A by Moody's and double-A-minus by Standard & Poor's, originally had been priced at 99.803, to yield 9.3% in five years. They were marked down yesterday the equivalent of about $5.50 for each $1,000 face amount, to about 99.25, where their yield jumped to 9.45%.

Instructions

(a) How will the above development affect the accounting for Commonwealth Edison's bond issue?

(b) Provide several possible explanations for the mark down and the slow sale of Commonwealth Edison's bonds.

C14-2   On January 1, 1977, Chavez Company issued for $1,106,775 its 20-year, 8% bonds that have a maturity value of $1,000,000 and pay interest semiannually on January 1 and July 1. Bond-issue costs were not material in amount. Below are three presentations of the long-term liability section of the balance sheet that might be used for these bonds at the issue date:

1. Bonds payable (maturing January 1, 1997)		$1,000,000
Unamortized premium on bonds payable		106,775
Total bond liability		$1,106,775
2. Bonds payable—principal (face value $1,000,000 maturing January 1, 1997)		$ 252,572ᵃ
Bonds payable—interest (semiannual payment $40,000)		854,203ᵇ
Total bond liability		$1,106,775
3. Bonds payable—principal (maturing January 1, 1997)		$1,000,000
Bonds payable—interest ($40,000 per period for 40 periods)		1,600,000
Total bond liability		$2,600,000

ᵃThe present value of $1,000,000 due at the end of 40 (six-month) periods at the yield rate of 3½% per period.
ᵇThe present value of $40,000 per period for 40 (six-month) periods at the yield rate of 3½% per period.

Instructions

(a) Discuss the conceptual merit(s) of each of the date-of-issue balance sheet presentations shown above for these bonds.

(b) Explain why investors would pay $1,106,775 for bonds that have a maturity value of only $1,000,000.

(c) Assuming that a discount rate is needed to compute the carrying value of the obligations arising from a bond issue at any date during the life of the bonds, discuss the conceptual merit(s) of using for this purpose:
1. The coupon or nominal rate.
2. The effective or yield rate at date of issue.

(d) If the obligations arising from these bonds are to be carried at their present value computed by means of the current market rate of interest, how would the bond valuation at dates subsequent to the date of issue be affected by an increase or a decrease in the market rate of interest?

(AICPA adapted)

C14-3 As the accountant for Goodwealth Tire Company, you have prepared the balance sheet and have presented it to the president of the company. You are asked the following questions about it:

1. Why has depreciation been charged on equipment being purchased under contract? Title has not passed to the company as yet and, therefore, they are not our assets. Why should the company not show on the left side of the balance sheet only the amount paid to date instead of showing the full contract price on the left side and the unpaid portion on the right side?

2. What is bond discount? As a debit balance, why is it not classified among the assets?

3. Bond interest payable is shown as a current liability. Did we not pay our trustee, County Trust Company, the full amount of interest due this period?

4. Treasury bonds are shown as a deduction from bonds payable issued. Why should they not be shown as an asset, since they can be sold again? Are they the same as bonds of other companies that we hold as investments?

Instructions

Outline your answers to these questions by writing a brief paragraph that will justify your treatment.

C14-4 Part I. The appropriate method of amortizing a premium or discount on issuance of bonds is the effective interest method.

Instructions

(a) What is the effective interest method of amortization and how is it different from and similar to the straight-line method of amortization?

(b) How is amortization computed using the effective interest method, and why and how do amounts obtained using the effective interest method differ from amounts computed under the straight-line method?

Part II. Gains or losses from the early extinguishment of debt that is refunded can theoretically be accounted for in three ways:

1. Amortized over remaining life of old debt.
2. Amortized over the life of the new debt issue.
3. Recognized in the period of extinguishment.

Instructions

(a) Develop supporting arguments for each of the three theoretical methods of accounting for gains and losses from the early extinguishment of debt.

(b) Which of the above methods is generally accepted and how should the appropriate amount of gain or loss be shown in a company's financial statements?

(AICPA adapted)

Exercises

E14-1 Presented below are various account balances of Christian Sisters Winery:

1. Notes payable due January 15, 1983.
2. Credit balances in customers' accounts arising from returns and allowances after collection in full of account.
3. Bonds payable of $500,000 maturing June 30, 1982.
4. Overdraft of $300 in a bank account. (Debit balances are carried in two other accounts.)
5. Deposits made by customers who have ordered goods.
6. Unamortized premium of bonds payable, of which $1,400 will be amortized during the next year.

7. Bank loans payable of a winery, due March 10, 1984. (The product requires aging for five years before sale.)

8. Serial bonds payable, $800,000, of which $200,000 are due each July 31.

9. Dividends payable in shares of stock on January 20, 1982.

10. Amounts withheld from employees' wages for income taxes.

Instructions

Indicate whether each of the items above should be classified on December 31, 1981, as a current liability, a long-term liability, or under some other classification. Consider each one independently from all others; that is, do not assume that all of them relate to one particular business. If the classification of some of the items is doubtful, explain why in each case.

E14-2 Connecticut United Company authorized the issuance of 9% coupon bonds in the amount of $1,000,000, with interest coupons payable semiannually, and the bonds to be dated January 1, 1981. The financial events are as follows:

1. The authorization of 1,000 bonds of $1,000 each.

2. Subscriptions received for 700 bonds, at par.

3. Cash received in full on January 1, 1981, from subscribers to 500 bonds; bonds are issued.

4. On April 1, 1981, cash is received from subscribers to 200 bonds in the amount of the par value of the bonds plus accrued interest. The bonds are issued.

5. On July 1, 1981, six months' interest is paid on the bonds outstanding.

Instructions

Prepare entries to record the events listed above.

E14-3 In each of the following cases indicate whether the bond is sold at a premium or a discount and explain.

1. The stated interest rate for the bond is 8% and the effective rate is 7.5%.

2. The bond carries a coupon rate of 6% and is sold to yield 7%.

3. The market rate is 8.75% and the nominal rate of the bond is 8.75%.

E14-4 On June 30, 1970, Steve Robinson Company issued 10% bonds with a par value of $600,000 due in 20 years. They were issued at 99 and were callable at 103 at any date after June 30, 1980. Because of lower interest rates and a significant change in the company's credit rating, it was decided to call the entire issue on June 30, 1981, and to issue new bonds. New 8% bonds were sold in the amount of $750,000 at 101; they mature in 20 years. Steve Robinson Company uses straight-line amortization. Interest payment dates are December 31 and June 30.

Instructions

(a) Prepare journal entries to record the retirement of the old issue and the sale of the new issue on June 30, 1981.

(b) Prepare the entry required on December 31, 1981, to record the payment of the first six months' interest and the amortization of premium on the bonds.

E14-5 Heublein Company had bonds outstanding with a maturity value of $100,000. On April 30, 1981, when these bonds had an unamortized discount of $4,000, they were called in at 106. To pay for these bonds, Heublein had issued other bonds a month earlier bearing a lower interest rate. The newly issued bonds had a life of 10 years. The new bonds were issued at 102 (face value $100,000). Issue costs related to the new bonds were $3,000.

Instructions

Ignoring interest, compute the gain or loss and record this refunding transaction.

(AICPA adapted)

E14-6   On January 2, 1975, Drambuie Corporation issued $1,000,000 of 8% bonds at 98 due December 31, 1984. Legal and other costs of $30,000 were incurred in connection with the issue. Interest on the bonds is payable annually each December 31. The $30,000 issue costs are being deferred and amortized on a straight-line basis over the 10-year term of the bonds. The discount on the bonds is also being amortized on a straight-line basis over the 10 years (straight-line is not materially different in effect from the preferable "interest method").

The bonds are callable at 101 (that is, at 101% of face amount), and on January 2, 1980, Drambuie called $500,000 face amount of the bonds and retired them.

Instructions

Ignoring income taxes, compute the amount of loss, if any, to be recognized by Drambuie as a result of retiring the $500,000 of bonds in 1980 and prepare the journal entry to record the retirement.

(AICPA adapted)

E14-7   Schwinn Cycle, Inc. had $5,000,000 of 8% bonds (interest payable July 9 and January 9) due in 10 years outstanding. On July 1, it issued $8,000,000 of 6% 15-year bonds (interest payable July 1 and January 1) at 99. A portion of the proceeds was used to call the 8% bonds at 103 on July 10. Unamortized bond discount and issue cost applicable to the 8% bonds were $50,000 and $25,000, respectively.

Instructions

Prepare the journal entries necessary to record the refunding of the bonds.

E14-8   Under the terms of its 9% bonds (interest payable June 30 and December 31), Drexel Furniture Company must pay $1,000,000 to a trustee each year. The funds are to be used to retire as many bonds as possible in the open market.

On July 1, 1980, the company paid $1,000,000 to the trustee, who purchased $1,100,000 par value of bonds. Unamortized bond discount applicable to the bonds purchased was $25,000.

Instructions

Record the payment and purchase of the bonds on the Drexel Furniture Company books.

E14-9   On July 1, 1981, Ernstmeyer Company makes the two following acquisitions:

1.   Purchases land having a fair market value of $100,000 by issuing a four-year noninterest-bearing promissory note in the face amount of $146,411.
2.   Purchases equipment by issuing a 3%, eight-year promissory note having a maturity value of $80,000 (interest payable annually).

Ernstmeyer Company has to pay 10% interest for funds from its bank.

Instructions

(a)   Record the two journal entries that should be recorded by Ernstmeyer Company for the two purchases on July 1, 1981.

(b)   Record the interest at the end of the first year (July 1, 1982) on both notes using the effective interest method.

*E14-10   Harker Pen Company sells 8% bonds of a serial bond issue in the amount of $2,000,000 to underwriters for $2,060,000. The bonds are dated January 1, 1977, and mature in the amount of $400,000 on January 1 of each year beginning January 1, 1979.

Instructions

Compute the premium to be amortized during each of the years in which any of the bonds are outstanding, using the "bonds-outstanding method."

*E14-11   Debtor owes $100,000 plus $10,000 of accrued interest to Creditor. The debt is a 10-year 5% note. Because Debtor is in financial trouble, Creditor agrees to accept some property and cancel the entire debt. The property has a cost of $50,000 and a fair market value of $70,000.

Instructions

(a) Prepare the journal entry on Debtor's books for debt restructure.

(b) Prepare the journal entry on Creditor's books for restructure.

*E14-12 Lassie Corp. owes $100,000 plus $10,000 of accrued interest to Dumbo Trust Co. The debt is a 10-year 5% note due today 12/31/80. Because Lassie Corp. is in financial trouble, Dumbo agrees to extend the maturity date to 12/31/82, reduce the interest rate to 3%, payable annually on 12/31 and forgive the accrued interest.

Instructions

(a) Prepare the journal entries on Lassie's books on 12/31/80, 81, 82.

(b) Prepare the journal entries on Dumbo's books on 12/31/80, 81, 82.

Problems

P14-1 The following amortization and interest schedule reflects the issuance of 10-year bonds by Burgundy Corporation on January 1, 1973, and the subsequent interest payments and charges. The company's year end is December 31, and financial statements are prepared once yearly.

AMORTIZATION SCHEDULE

Year	Cash	Interest	Amount Unamortized	Book Value
1/1/73			$7,361	$ 92,639
1973	$5,000	$5,558	6,803	93,197
1974	5,000	5,592	6,211	93,789
1975	5,000	5,627	5,584	94,416
1976	5,000	5,665	4,919	95,081
1977	5,000	5,705	4,214	95,786
1978	5,000	5,747	3,467	96,533
1979	5,000	5,792	2,675	97,325
1980	5,000	5,840	1,835	98,165
1981	5,000	5,890	945	99,055
1982	5,000	5,945		100,000

Instructions

(a) Indicate whether the bonds were issued at a premium or a discount and how you can determine this fact from the schedule.

(b) Indicate whether the amortization schedule is based on the straight-line method or the effective interest method and how you can determine which method is used.

(c) On the basis of the schedule above, prepare the journal entry to record the issuance of the bonds on January 1, 1973.

(d) On the basis of the schedule above, prepare the journal entries to reflect the bond transactions and accruals for 1973.

(e) On the basis of the schedule above, prepare the journal entries to reflect the bond transactions and accruals for 1981.

P14-2 On January 1, 1980, McGinnis Company sold 9% bonds having a maturity value of $100,000 for $103,992, which provides the bondholders with an 8% yield. The bonds are dated January 1, 1980, and mature January 1, 1985 with interest payable December 31 of each year. McGinnis Company allocates interest and unamortized discount or premium on the effective interest basis.

Instructions

(a) Prepare the journal entry at the date of the bond issuance.

(b) Prepare the journal entry to record the interest payment and the amortization for 1980. Preparation of a partial schedule of interest expense and bond amortization will aid in the solution.

(c) Prepare the journal entry to record the interest payment and the amortization for 1982.

P14-3 Carolina Company sells 5% bonds having a maturity value of $100,000 for $95,787. The bonds are dated January 1, 1980, and mature January 1, 1985. Interest is payable annually on January 1. (**Hint:** The effective interest or yield rate must be computed.)

Instructions

(a) Set up a schedule of interest expense and discount amortization under the straight-line method.

(b) Set up a schedule of interest expense and discount amortization under the effective interest method.

P14-4 In 1980, Adelaine Corporation was considering the issuance of bonds as of January 1, 1981, as follows:

Plan 1: $1,000,000 par value 7%, 1st mortgage, 20-year bonds, due Dec. 31, 2001, at 96, with interest payable annually, or

Plan 2: $1,000,000 par value 7%, 1st mortgage, 20-year bonds, due Dec. 31, 2001, at 100, with provision for payment of a 4% ($40,000) premium at maturity, interest payable annually.

Costs of issue such as printing and lawyers' fees may be ignored for the purpose of answering this question. Discount and premium are to be allocated to accounting periods on a straight-line basis.

Instructions

Give two separate sets of journal entries with appropriate explanations showing the accounting treatment that the foregoing bond issues would necessitate, respectively:

(a) At time of issue. (c) On payment at date of maturity.

(b) Yearly thereafter.

P14-5 In each of the following independent cases the company closes its books on December 31 (PV of 1 for 7 periods at 3½% is .78599; PV of an ordinary annuity of 1 for 7 periods at 3½% is 6.11454).

1. Heather Co. sells $200,000 of 6% bonds on February 1, 1980. The bonds pay interest on February 1 and August 1. The due date of the bonds is August 1, 1983. The bonds yield 7%. Give entries through December 31, 1981.

2. Dawna Co. sells $200,000 of 8% bonds on June 1, 1980. The bonds pay interest on June 1 and December 1. The due date of the bonds is June 1, 1984. The bonds yield 5%. On September 1, 1981, Dawna buys back $40,000 worth of bonds for $41,000 (includes accrued interest). Give entries through December 1, 1982.

Instructions (Round to the nearest dollar.)

For the two cases above prepare all of the relevant journal entries from the time of sale until the date indicated. Use the effective interest method for discount and premium amortization (construct amortization tables where applicable). Amortize premium or discount on interest dates and at year end. (Assume that no reversing entries were made.)

P14-6 Presented below are selected transactions on the books of Barbara Hamsmith Corporation.

July 1, 1980   Bonds payable with a par value of $900,000, which are dated January 1, 1980, are sold at 103 plus accrued interest. They are coupon bonds, bear interest at 6% (payable annually at January 1), and mature January 1, 1990.

Dec. 31   Adjusting entries are made to record the accrued interest on the bonds, and the amortization of the proper amount of premium. (Use straight-line amortization.)

Jan. 1, 1981   Interest on the bonds is paid.

April 1   Bonds of par value of $450,000 are purchased at 101 plus accrued interest, and retired. (Bond premium is to be amortized only at the end of each year.)

Dec. 31   Adjusting entries are made to record the accrued interest on the bonds, and the proper amount of premium amortized.

Instructions

Prepare journal entries for the transactions above.

P14-7 Cardinal Company issued its 9% 30-year mortgage bonds in the principal amount of $5,000,000 on January 2, 1966, at a discount of $100,000, which it proceeded to amortize by charges against income over the life of the issue on a straight-line basis. The indenture securing the issue provided that the bonds could be called for redemption in total but not in part at any time before maturity at 105% of the principal amount, but it did not provide for any sinking fund.

On December 18, 1980, the company issued its 7% 25-year debenture bonds in the principal amount of $6,000,000 at par, and the proceeds were used to redeem the 9% 30-year mortgage bonds on January 2, 1981. The indenture securing the new issue did not provide for any sinking fund or for retirement before maturity.

Instructions

(a) Prepare journal entries to record the issuance of the 7% bonds and the retirement of the 9% bonds.

(b) Indicate the income statement treatment of the gain or loss from retirement and the footnote disclosure required. Assume 1981 income before extraordinary items of $3,460,000, a weighted number of shares outstanding of 1,500,000, and an income tax rate of 40%.

P14-8 On January 1, 1978, Revlon Products Company sold $150,000 (face value) of bonds. The bonds are dated January 1, 1978 and will mature on January 1, 1983. Interest is paid annually on December 31. The bonds are callable after December 31, 1980 at 102. Issue costs related to these bonds amounted to $1,500, and these costs are being amortized by the straight-line method. The following amortization schedule was prepared by the accountant for the first two years of the life of the bonds:

Date	Cash	Interest	Amortization	Net Carrying Value of Bonds
1/ 1/78				$138,021
12/31/78	$9,000	$11,041	$2,041	140,062
12/31/79	9,000	11,205	2,205	142,267

Instructions

On the basis of the information above, answer the following questions (round your answers to the nearest dollar or percent):

(a) What is the nominal or stated rate of interest for this bond issue?

(b) What is the effective or market rate of interest for this bond issue?

(c) Present the journal entry to record the sale of the bond issue, including the issue costs.

(d) Present the appropriate entry(ies) at December 31, 1980.

(e) Present the disclosure of this bond issue on the December 31, 1980, balance sheet. Proper balance sheet subheadings must be indicated.

(f) On June 30, 1981, $75,000 of the bond issue was redeemed at the call price. Present the journal entry for this redemption. Amortization of the discount is recorded only at the end of the year.

(g) Present the effects of the bond redemption on the 1981 income statement and proper footnote disclosure. Proper income statement subheadings must be indicated. The income tax rate is 20%; 1981 income before extraordinary items is $31,023 with a weighted number of common shares outstanding during the year of 18,000. Working capital funds were used to redeem the bonds.

P14-9 Payton Company issued 10-year coupon bonds in the amount of $1,000,000 on July 1, 1979. They were issued at par and bear interest at 8%, payable semiannually on July 1 and January 1. The Sayers Bank is to act as trustee to handle the payment of interest.

On December 10, 1979, the Payton Company sent the Sayers Bank a check for the interest due January 1, 1980, none of which was paid to bondholders before January 1, 1980.

Instructions

(a) What balances will be shown in the ledger of the Payton Company on December 31, 1979, relating to the bonds and the interest on the bonds? How will these balances be shown in the financial statements?

(b) Assume that in 1980 the Payton Company sends the Sayers Bank checks for the interest due July 1, 1980, and January 1, 1981, and that the Sayers Bank returns to the company canceled interest coupons in the amount of $76,000. The Payton Company sent the Sayers Bank a check for $940 to cover the trustee expenses.

What balances will be shown in the ledger of the Payton Company on December 31, 1980, relating to the bonds and the interest on the bonds? How will these balances be shown in financial statements?

P14-10 Here are transactions of Baker Company:

Jan. 1, 1980   Bonds payable (coupon bonds) in the amount of $1,000,000, and bearing interest at the rate of 8% payable semiannually on January 1 and July 1, due January 1, 2000, are issued at 98.

June 15   The First Bank and Trust Co. has been engaged as trustee to handle the payment of interest to individual bondholders. A check for the interest due July 1, 1980, is sent to the trustee.

30   Record the interest expense for the first six months of 1980. Bond discount is to be amortized only at the end of each year and by the straight-line method.

July 20   The trustee returns to the company canceled interest coupons paid in the amount of $16,800 and reports that trustee's expenses charged against the account amounted to $280.

Dec. 15   A check for the interest due January 1, 1981, and for reported expenses is sent to the trustee.

31   Record the interest expense for the six months ended December 31, and amortize the proper amount of discount for the year.

Jan. 21, 1981   The trustee returns to the company canceled interest coupons paid in the amount of $21,600.

Mar. 1   Bonds of par value of $20,000 are bought on the market at 97 plus accrued interest, and retired. All interest coupons dated before July 1, 1981, have been removed.

Instructions

(a) Prepare entries in journal form on the books of Baker Company for the transactions given above.

(b) What will be the amount of the check to the trustee for the interest for the first six months of 1981?

(c) What will be the amount of the discount amortized on December 31, 1981?

P14-11 Danish Inc. has been producing quality children's apparel for over 25 years. The company's fiscal year runs from April 1 to March 31. The following information relates to the obligations of Danish as of March 31, 1981.

Bonds Payable

Danish issued $4,000,000 of 7% bonds on July 1, 1975 at 98 which yielded proceeds of $3,920,000. The bonds will mature on July 1, 1985. Interest is paid semi-annually on July 1 and January 1. Danish uses the straight-line method to amortize the bond discount.

Lease Obligations

Some of Danish's computer equipment is obtained under an operating lease agreement signed on April 1, 1980. The company has agreed to lease the equipment for three years at an annual rental of $500,000 payable at the beginning of each year.

Notes Payable

Danish has signed several long-term notes with financial institutions and insurance companies. The maturities of these notes are given in the schedule below. The total unpaid interest for all of these notes amounts to $90,000 on March 31, 1981.

Due Date	Amount Due
April 1, 1981	$ 100,000
July 1, 1981	200,000
October 1, 1981	100,000
January 1, 1982	200,000
April 1, 1982–March 31, 1983	600,000
April 1, 1983–March 31, 1984	400,000
April 1, 1984–March 31, 1985	400,000
April 1, 1985–March 31, 1986	500,000
April 1, 1986–March 31, 1987	500,000
	$3,000,000

Estimated Warranties

Danish has a one-year product warranty on some selected items in its product line. The estimated warranty liability on sales made during the 1979–80 fiscal year and still outstanding as of March 31, 1980 amounted to $55,000. The warranty costs on sales made from April 1, 1980 through March 31, 1981 are estimated at $145,000. The actual warranty costs incurred during the current 1980–81 fiscal year are as follows

Warranty claims honored on 1979–80 sales	$ 55,000
Warranty claims honored on 1980–81 sales	75,000
Total warranty claims honored	$130,000

Other Information

1. *Trade payables.* Accounts payable for supplies, goods and services purchased on open account amount to $325,000 as of March 31, 1981.

2. *Payroll related items.* Outstanding obligations related to Danish's payroll as of March 31, 1981 are:

Accrued salaries and wages	$145,000
FICA taxes	15,000
State and federal income taxes withheld from employees	30,000
Other payroll deductions	3,000

3. *Taxes.* The following taxes incurred but not due until the next fiscal year are:

State and federal income taxes	$300,000
Property taxes	125,000
Sales and use taxes	185,000

4. *Miscellaneous accruals.* Other accruals not separately classified amount to $50,000 as of March 31, 1981.

5. *Dividends.* On March 15, 1981 Danish's Board of Directors declared a cash dividend of $.40 per common share and a 10 percent common stock dividend. Both dividends were to be distributed on April 12, 1981 to the common stockholders of record at the close of business on March 31, 1981. Data regarding Danish common stock are as follows:

Par value	$5 per share
Number of shares issued and outstanding	2,500,000 shares
Market values of common stock:	
March 15, 1981	$22.00 per share
March 31, 1981	21.50 per share
April 12, 1981	22.50 per share

Instructions

Prepare the liability section of the balance sheet and appropriate notes to the statement for Danish Inc. as of March 31, 1981, as they should appear in its annual report to the stockholders.

(CMA adapted)

P14-12   On December 31, 1980, Harvester Company acquired a computer from IBMX Corporation by issuing a $350,000 noninterest-bearing note, payable in full on December 31, 1983. Harvester Company's credit rating permits it to borrow funds from its several lines of credit at 8%. The computer is expected to have a six-year life and a $50,000 salvage value.

Instructions

(a) Prepare the journal entry for the purchase on December 31, 1980.

(b) Prepare any necessary adjusting entries relative to depreciation (use straight-line) and amortization (use effective interest method) on December 31, 1981.

(c) Prepare any necessary adjusting entries relative to depreciation and amortization on December 31, 1982.

P14-13   Dick Nofftz and Associates, Inc. purchased machinery on December 31, 1979, at a price of $80,000, paying $20,000 down and agreeing to pay the balance in four equal installments of $15,000 payable each December 31. An assumed interest of 8% is implicit in the purchase price.

Instructions

Prepare the journal entries that would be recorded for the purchase and for the payments and interest on the following dates:

(a) December 31, 1979.

(b) December 31, 1980.

(c) December 31, 1981.

(d) December 31, 1982.

(e) December 31, 1983.

*P14-14   On May 1, 1980, Nebraska Company sold a new serial bond issue with $600,000 par value for $636,000. The nominal interest rate on these bonds is 8% and the interest is payable annually on May 1. One-half of the bonds will be retired on May 1 each year for two years, beginning in 1981. Nebraska Company closes its books on December 31 each year.

Instructions

Prepare all of the journal entries required over the life of these bonds to record the issuance, amortization, interest accruals and payments, and retirements (assume that the reversing entries are made at the beginning of each period). Use the bonds outstanding method.

*P14-15   On December 31, 1976, Flatt Company sold a 9% serial bond issue in the amount of $1,400,000 for $1,397,200. The bonds mature in the amount of $200,000 on December 31 of each year, beginning December 31, 1977 and interest is payable annually.

On December 31, 1979, the company retired the $200,000 of bonds due on that date and in addition purchased at 99 and retired bonds in the amount of $100,000 which were due on December 31, 1981.

Instructions

(a) Prepare entries to record the payment of interest for 1977, and to record the amortization of discount for the year using the bonds outstanding method.

(b) Prepare entries to record the redemption of the bonds of $300,000 which were retired on December 31, 1979.

(c) Discuss the disclosures that are required relative to the bond transactions in 1979.

(d) What amount of discount would be amortized for the year 1981?

*P14-16   On January 1, 1978, Happy Products Corporation issued $1,000,000 in five-year, 5% serial bonds to be repaid in the amount of $200,000 on January 1, of 1979, 1980, 1981, 1982, and 1983. Interest is payable at the end of each year. The bonds were sold to yield a rate of 6%.

Instructions

1. Prepare a schedule showing the computation of the total amount received from the issuance of the serial bonds. Show supporting computations in good form.

2. Assume the bonds were originally sold at a discount of $26,254. Prepare a schedule of amortization of the bond discount for the first three years after issuance, using the interest (effective rate) method. Show supporting computations in good form.

(AICPA adapted)

*P14-17   Irish, Inc. owes English Bank a 10-year, 19% note in the amount of $110,000 plus $11,000 of accrued interest. The note is due today 12/31/81. Because Irish, Inc. is in financial trouble, English agrees to accept 40,000 shares of Irish's $1.00 par value common stock which is selling for $1.25, forgive the accrued interest, reduce the face amount of the note to $60,000, extend the maturity date to 12/31/84, and reduce the interest rate to 5%. Interest will continue to be due on 12/31 each year.

Instructions

(a) Prepare all the necessary journal entries on the books of Irish, Inc. from restructure through maturity.

(b) Prepare all the necessary journal entries on the books of English Bank from restructure through maturity.

*P14-18   Union Corp. owes Confederate Corp. a 10-year, 10% note in the amount of $110,000 plus $11,000 of accrued interest. The note is due today, 12/31/81. Because Union Corp. is in financial trouble, Confederate Corp. agrees to forgive the accrued interest, $10,000 of the principal, and to extend the maturity date to 12/31/84. Interest will continue to be due on 12/31 each year.

Assume the following present value factors for 3 periods:

	2¼%	2⅜%	2½%	2⅝%	2¾%	3%
Amt. of 1	.935	.932	.929	.925	.922	.915
Ord. Ann. of 1	2.869	2.863	2.856	2.850	2.842	2.829

Instructions

(a) Compute the new effective interest rate following restructure. (**Hint:** Find the interest rate which establishes $121,000 as the present value of the total future cash flows.)

(b) Prepare a schedule of debt (receivable) reduction and interest expense (income) for the years 1981 through 1984.

(c) Prepare all the necessary journal entries on the books of Union Corp. for the years 1981, 1982, and 1983.

(d) Prepare all the necessary journal entries on the books of Confederate Corp. for the years 1981, 1982, and 1983.

Stockholders' Equity, Dilutive Securities, and Investments

Stockholders' Equity: Issuance and Reacquisition of Capital Stock

In your first exposure to financial statements you were probably taught that the credit side of the balance sheet represents the sources of enterprise assets. Liabilities represent the amount of assets that were borrowed, and stockholders' equity represents (1) the amount that was contributed by the stockholders and (2) the portion that was earned and retained by the enterprise. While this explanation is accurate and may seem simple enough, stockholders' equity is generally the least understood section of the financial statements because of its distinctive accounting terminology and its legalistic nature.

The Nature of Stockholders' Equity

The owners of an enterprise bear the ultimate risks and uncertainties and receive the benefits of enterprise operations. Their interest in the enterprise is measured by the difference between the assets and the liabilities of the enterprise. Therefore, **the owners' or stockholders' interest in a business enterprise is a residual interest.**[1] As an amount, stockholders' equity represents the cumulative net contributions by stockholders plus recorded earnings that have been retained. As a residual interest, stockholders' equity has no existence apart from the assets and liabilities of the enterprise—stockholders' equity equals net assets. Stockholders' equity is not

[1]"Conceptual Framework for Financial Accounting and Reporting: Elements of Financial Statements and Their Measurement," *FASB Discussion Memorandum* (Stamford, Conn.: FASB, December 2, 1976), p. 90–92.

a claim to specific assets but a claim against a portion of the total assets. Its amount is not specified or fixed; it depends on the enterprise's profitability. Stockholders' equity grows if the enterprise is profitable and shrinks or may disappear entirely if the enterprise is unprofitable.

Accounting for stockholders' equity is greatly influenced by tradition and by corporate law.[2] Although the legal aspects of equity must be respected and disclosed, legal requirements need not be the accounting basis for classifying and reporting the components of equity.[3] **The two primary sources from which equity is derived are (1) contributions by stockholders and (2) earnings retained by a corporation,** and these two components should be accounted for and reported by every corporation.

We have chosen, therefore, to divide our coverage of stockholders' equity by discussing the accounting matters relating to contributions by stockholders in Chapter 15 and the other component, retained earnings, in Chapter 16. Other securities that may be reported in stockholders' equity (convertible debt, stock purchase warrants, and stock options) are covered in Chapter 17, "Dilutive Securities." But first, in order to account for stockholders' equity, one must understand the corporate form of entity.

The Corporate Form of Entity

Of the three **primary forms of business organization—the proprietorship, the partnership, and the corporation,** the dominant form of business is the corporate form. In terms of the aggregate amount of resources controlled, goods and services produced, and people employed, the corporation is by far the leader. Nearly all, if not all, of the "500" largest industrial firms are corporations. Although the corporate form has a number of advantages (as well as disadvantages) over the other two forms, the principal attribute that has helped it to reach its present dominant role is its facility for attracting and accumulating large amounts of capital.

Corporations may be classified by the nature of ownership as follows:

1. **Public corporations:** governmental units or business operations owned by governmental units (such as the Federal Deposit Insurance Corporation).
2. **Private corporations.**
    a. **Nonstock:** nonprofit in nature and no stock issued (such as churches, charities, and colleges).
    b. **Stock:** companies that operate for profit and issue stock.
        (i) **Closed corporations:** stock held by a few stockholders (perhaps a family) and not available for public purchase.
        (ii) **Open corporations:** stock widely held and available for purchase by the public.
            (a) **Listed corporation:** stock traded on an organized stock exchange.
            (b) **Unlisted or over-the-counter corporation:** stock traded in a market in which securities dealers buy from and sell to the public.

The owners' equity accounts in a corporation are considerably different from those in a partnership or proprietorship. It is not necessary to enter into a detailed

[2]"Objectives of Financial Reporting and Elements of Financial Statements of Business Enterprises," *FASB Exposure Draft* (Stamford, Conn.: FASB, December 29, 1977).

[3]Beatrice Melcher, "Stockholders' Equity," *Accounting Research Study No. 15* (New York: AICPA, 1973), p. 2. Ms. Melcher's study is the most comprehensive pronouncement published on this topic.

discussion of the advantages or disadvantages of the corporate form of business enterprise at this point. However, certain characteristics of the corporation do have a direct effect on what may be termed proprietorship, owners' equity, or net worth accounting, and it is helpful if these are clearly understood.

Among those special characteristics of the corporate form that affect accounting are:

1. Influence of state corporate law.
2. Use of the capital stock or share system.
3. Development of a variety of ownership interests.
4. Limited liability of stockholders.
5. Formality of profit distribution.

State Corporate Law

Anyone desiring to establish a corporation must submit **articles of incorporation** to the proper department of the government of the state in which incorporation is desired. If the requirements are fulfilled, the corporation charter is issued, and the corporation is recognized as a legal entity subject to the laws of the state of incorporation. To some extent its actions are circumscribed by the laws of any state in which it seeks to carry on business, but, insofar as stockholders' equity accounting is concerned, the business corporation act of the state of incorporation governs.

The importance of this condition to accountants lies in the fact that **each of the 50 states has its own business corporation act.** Some of these laws are quite uniform; others vary considerably, which means that permissible transactions may vary from state to state and that accounting must reflect the difference. State laws usually prescribe the requirements for issuing stock, the treatment of proceeds of issued stock, the distributions permitted to stockholders, the effects of retiring stock, the regulations for and restrictions on acquiring treasury stock, and other procedures and restrictions.

Many states have adopted in their corporation laws the principles contained in the Model Business Corporation Act that was prepared in 1959 by the Committee of Corporate Laws of the American Bar Association. But other states have enacted corporate legislation with contrary features, often including elaborate and unusual provisions. The state laws are complex and vary not only in their provisions but also in their definitions of certain terms. Some laws fail to define technical terms, terms that often mean one thing in one state and another in a different state. And the problems are compounded because legal authorities often interpret the effects and restrictions of the laws differently.[4]

The laws are so diverse that there are exceptions to most generalizations we can make in regard to statutory provisions or meanings of terms. This situation somewhat complicates a discussion of stockholders' equity, but it cannot be avoided. While it is neither practical nor necessary for us to tabulate the provisions of all 50 states, we shall point out those matters on which state laws are most likely to differ.

[4]*Ibid.*, p. 8.

Capital Stock or Share System

The stockholders' equity in a corporation is generally made up of a large number of units or shares. Within a given class of stock each share is exactly equal to every other share. Each owner's interest is determined by the number of shares possessed. If a company has but one class of stock divided into 1,000 shares, a person owning 500 shares controls one-half the ownership interest of the corporation; one holding 10 shares has a one-hundredth interest.

Each share of stock has certain rights and privileges that can be restricted only by special contract at the time the shares are issued. One must examine the articles of incorporation, stock certificates, and the provisions of the state law to ascertain such restrictions on or variations from the standard rights and privileges. In the absence of restrictive provisions, each share carries the following rights:

1. To share proportionately in profits.
2. To share proportionately in management (the right to vote for directors).
3. To share proportionately in corporate assets upon liquidation.
4. To share proportionately in any new issues of stock of the same class (called the preemptive right).

The first three rights are to be expected in the ownership of any business; the last may be used in a corporation to protect each stockholder's proportional interest in the enterprise. **The preemptive right protects an existing stockholder from involuntary dilution of ownership interest.** Without this right stockholders with a given percentage interest might find their interest reduced by the issuance of additional stock without their knowledge and at prices that were not favorable to them. Because the preemptive right attached to existing shares makes it inconvenient for a corporation to make large issuances of additional stock, as frequently takes place in acquiring other companies, it has been eliminated by many corporations.

The great advantage of the share system is the ease with which an interest in the business may be transferred from one individual to another. **Individuals owning shares in a corporation may sell them to others at any time and at any price without obtaining the consent of the company or other stockholders.** Each share is personal property of the owner and may be disposed of at will. All that is required of the corporation is that it maintain a list or subsidiary ledger of stockholders as a guide to dividend payments, issuance of stock rights, voting proxies, and the like. Because shares are freely and frequently transferred, it is necessary for the corporation to revise the subsidiary ledger of stockholders periodically, generally in advance of every dividend payment or stockholders' meeting. As the number of stockholders grows, the need may develop for a more efficient system that can handle large numbers of stock transactions. Also, the major stock exchanges require controls that the typical corporation finds uneconomic to provide. Thus **registrars and transfer agents** who specialize in providing services for recording and transferring stock are usually used. The negotiability of stock certificates is governed by the Uniform Stock Transfer Act and the Uniform Commercial Code.

Variety of Ownership Interests

In every corporation one class of stock must represent the basic ownership interest. That class is called common stock. **Common stock** is the residual corporate interest that bears the ultimate risks of loss and receives the benefits of success. It is guaranteed neither dividends nor assets upon dissolution. But common stockholders generally control the management of the corporation and tend to profit most if the company is successful. In the event that a corporation has only one authorized issue of capital stock, that issue is by definition common stock, whether so designated in the charter or not.

In an effort to appeal to all types of investors, corporations may offer two or more classes of stock with different rights or privileges attached to each class. In the preceding section it was pointed out that each share of stock of a given issue has the same rights as other shares of the same issue and that there are four rights inherent in every share. By special stock contracts between the corporation and its stockholders, certain of these rights may be sacrificed by the stockholder in return for other special rights or privileges. Thus special classes of stock are created. Because they have certain preferential rights, they are usually called **preferred stock.** In return for any special preference, the preferred stockholder is always called on to sacrifice some of the inherent rights of capital stock interests.

A common type of preference is to give the preferred stockholders a prior claim on earnings. They are assured a dividend, usually at a stated rate, before any amount may be distributed to the common stockholders. In return for this preference the preferred stock may sacrifice its right to a voice in management or its right to share in profits beyond the stated rate.

A company may accomplish much the same thing by issuing two classes of common stock, Class A stock and Class B stock. In this case one of the issues is the common stock and the other issue has some preference or restriction of basic rights. For example, DeKalb Agresearch, Inc. created two classes of common stock, Class A and Class B, when it decided to issue shares to the public several years ago. Both Class A and Class B participate equally (per share) in all dividend payments and have the same claim on assets in dissolution. The differences are that Class A is voting and Class B is not; Class B is traded publicly over the counter while Class A, which is "family owned," must be sold privately (Class A shares are convertible, one for one, into Class B shares but not vice versa). By issuing two classes of common stock, the Class A owners of DeKalb Agresearch have obtained a ready market for the company's stock and yet provided an effective shield against outside takeover.

Limited Liability of Stockholders

Those who "own" a corporation, that is the stockholders, contribute either property or services to the enterprise in return for ownership shares. The property or service invested in the enterprise is the extent of a stockholder's possible loss. That is, if the corporation sustains losses to such an extent that remaining assets are insufficient to pay creditors, no recourse can be had by the creditors against personal assets of the individual stockholders. In a partnership or proprietorship, personal assets of the owners can be attached to satisfy unpaid claims against the enterprise. Ownership interests in a corporation are legally protected against such a contingency; **the stockholders may lose their investment but they cannot lose more than their investment.**

Stock that has a fixed per share amount printed on each stock certificate is called **par value stock.** Par value has but one real significance; it establishes the maximum responsibility of a stockholder in the event of insolvency or other involuntary dissolution. Par value is thus not "value" in the ordinary sense of the word. It is merely an amount per share determined by the incorporators of the company and stated in the corporation charter or certificate of incorporation. Par value establishes the nominal value per share and is the minimum amount that must be paid in by each stockholder if the stock is to be fully paid when issued. In most states, a corporation may, however, issue its capital stock either above or below par, in which case the stock is said to be issued at a **premium or a discount,** respectively.[5]

If par value stock is issued at par or at a price above par and the corporation subsequently suffers losses so that assets to repay stockholders upon dissolution are insufficient, stockholders may lose their entire investment. If, however, the stock is issued at a price below par and the losses prove to be of such magnitude as to consume not only the stockholders' investments but also a portion of the assets required to repay creditors, the creditors can force the stockholders to pay in to the corporation the amount of the discount on their capital shares. Thus the original purchasers of stock issued at a price below par are contingently liable to creditors of the corporation. In other words, stockholders may lose their entire investment in a corporation if the investments are equal to or in excess of the par value of the shares they own, or, if the investments are less than their par value, they may lose the amount of their investment plus an additional amount equal to the discount at which they purchased the stock. The limited liability feature of corporate capital stock prevents them from losing any more than the par value of their stock plus any premium paid upon purchase.

It should be emphasized that **the contingent liability of a stockholder for stock purchased at a price below par:**

1. Is an obligation to the corporation's creditors, not to the corporation itself.
2. Becomes a real liability only if the amount below par must be collected in order to pay the creditors upon dissolution of the company.
3. Is the responsibility of the original certificate holder at the time of dissolution unless by contract such responsibility is transferred to a subsequent holder.

While the corporate form of organization grants the protective feature of limited liability to the stockholders, it must guarantee not to withdraw the amount of stockholders' investment unless all prior claims on corporate assets have been paid. The corporation must maintain the corporate capital until dissolution and upon dissolution it must satisfy all prior claims before distributing any amounts to the stockholders.

In a proprietorship or partnership the owners can withdraw amounts at will because all their personal assets may be called on to protect creditors from loss. In a corporation, however, the owners cannot withdraw any amounts paid in because

---

[5]In some states capital stock may not be issued below par.

the only protection creditors have against loss is the amount paid in plus any discount below par.

Formality of Profit Distribution

Essentially the owners of an enterprise may determine what is to be done with profits realized through operations. Profits may be left in the business to permit expansion or merely to provide a margin of safety, or they may be withdrawn and divided among the owners. In a proprietorship or partnership this decision is made by the owner or owners informally and requires no specific action. In a corporation, however, profit distribution is controlled by certain legal restrictions.

First of all, **no amounts may be distributed among the owners unless the corporate capital is maintained intact,** as discussed in the preceding section. State laws vary in the manner in which this specific restriction is worded and interpreted, but in general profits determined under generally accepted accounting principles or standards are legally available for distribution. Some states require a cumulative profit from the inception of the corporation, that is, profits from the date of organization of the corporation must exceed the sum of any losses plus dividends already paid; others require a profit only for the period for which the dividend is to be declared.

Second, **distributions to stockholders must be formally approved by the board of directors** and recorded in the minutes of their meetings. As the top executive body in the corporation, the board of directors must make certain that no distributions are made to stockholders that are not justified by profits, and directors are generally held liable to creditors if liabilities cannot be paid because company assets have been illegally paid out to stockholders.

Third, **dividends must be in full agreement with the capital stock contracts as to preferences, participation, and the like.** Once the corporation has entered into contracts with various classes of stockholders, the stipulations of such contracts must be observed.

Characteristics of Preferred Stock

Preferred stock is a special class of shares that is designated "preferred" because it possesses certain preferences or features not possessed by the common stock. The following features are those most associated with preferred stock issues:

1. Preference as to dividends.
2. Preference as to assets in the event of liquidation.
3. Convertible into common stock.
4. Callable at the option of the corporation.

The features that distinguish between preferred and common stock may be of a more restrictive and negative nature than preferences; for example, the preferred stock may be nonvoting, noncumulative, and nonparticipating. Unless specifically prohibited though, all of the basic rights of stock ownership apply to preferred stock.

Preferred stock is usually issued with a par value, and the dividend preference is expressed as a **percentage of the par value.** Thus, holders of 8% preferred stock with a $100 par value are entitled to an annual dividend of $8 per share. In the case of no-par preferred stock a dividend preference is expressed as a **specific dollar amount** per share. A preference as to dividends is not assurance that dividends will be paid; it is merely assurance that the stated dividend rate or amount applicable to the preferred stock must be paid before any dividends can be paid on the common stock.

A corporation may attach whatever preferences or restrictions in whatever combination it desires to a preferred stock issue so long as it does not specifically violate its state incorporation law, and it may issue more than one class of preferred stock. For example, Bird & Son, Inc. reported the following:

5% cumulative preferred stock, par value $100 per share, callable at $110 per share.

$2.75 convertible preference stock without par value, stated at $65 per share.

The most common features attributed to preferred stock are discussed below:

1. **Cumulative.** Dividends not paid in any year must be made up in a later year before any profits can be distributed to common stockholders. If the directors fail to declare a dividend at the normal date for dividend action, the dividend is said to have been "passed." Any passed dividend on cumulative preferred stock constitutes a **dividend in arrears.** Because no liability exists until the board of directors declares a dividend, a dividend in arrears is not recorded as a liability but is disclosed in a footnote to the financial statements. (At common law, if the corporate charter is silent about the cumulative feature, the preferred stock is considered to be cumulative.) Noncumulative preferred stock is seldom issued because a passed dividend is lost forever to the preferred stockholder.

2. **Participating.** Holders of participating preferred stock share ratably with the common stockholders in any profit distributions beyond the prescribed rate. That is, 5% preferred stock, if fully participating, will receive not only its 5% return, but also, if amounts in excess of 5% are paid to common stockholders, dividends at the same rates as those paid to common stockholders. Also, participating preferred stock may not always be fully participating as described, but partially participating. For example, provision may be made that 5% preferred stock will be participating up to a maximum total rate of 10%, after which it ceases to participate in additional profit distributions; or 5% preferred stock may participate only in additional profit distributions that are in excess of a 9% dividend rate on the common stock. Participating preferred stocks, popular in the early 1900s, have seldom been issued in the past few decades.

3. **Convertible.** The stockholders may at their option exchange their preferred shares for common stock at a predetermined ratio. The convertible preferred stockholder not only enjoys a preferred claim on dividends but also has the option of converting into a common stockholder with unlimited participation in earnings. Convertible preferred stock has been widely used in the past two decades, especially in consummating business combinations, and is favored by investors. The accounting problems related to convertible securities are discussed in Chapter 17.

4. **Callable.** The issuing corporation can call or redeem at its option the outstanding preferred shares at specified future dates and at stipulated prices. Many preferred issues are callable. The call or redemption price is ordinarily set slightly above the original issuance price and is commonly stated in terms related to the par value. The callable feature permits the corporation to use the capital obtained through the issuance of such stock until the need has passed or it is no longer advantageous. The existence of a call price or prices tends to set a ceiling on the market value of the preferred shares unless

they are convertible into common stock. When a preferred stock is called for redemption, any dividends in arrears must be paid.

For many decades some preferred stock issues have contained provisions for redemption at some future date, through sinking funds or other means. More recently, some preferred stock issues have provided for mandatory redemption within five or ten years of issuance. In some instances, the motivation for issuance of preferred stock instead of debt lies in the existing debt to equity ratio of the issuer. As the ratio weakens because of increasing debt, an issuance of preferred stock may be used to improve upon that ratio. In other instances, issuances are made through private placements with other corporations at a lower than market dividend rate because the acquiring corporation receives dividends that are largely tax free (due to an 85% dividends received deduction).

Debt Characteristics of Preferred Stock   With the right combination of features (i.e., fixed return, no vote, redeemable), a preferred stockholder may possess more of the characteristics of a creditor than of an owner. Preferred shares generally have no maturity date, but the preferred stockholder's relationship with the company may be terminated if the corporation exercises its call privilege. Despite these creditorship characteristics, preferred stock is usually accounted for as an equity security and is reported in the stockholders' equity section of the balance sheet.

In 1979, however, the SEC issued a rule that prohibits companies from combining preferred stock with common stock in financial statements. Amounts have to be separately presented for redeemable preferred stock,[6] nonredeemable preferred stock, and common stock. The amounts applicable to these three categories of equity items cannot be totaled or combined for SEC reporting purposes. The general heading, stockholders' equity, is not to include **redeemable preferred stock.**

The proposal was triggered by an SEC concern about the increasing issuance of preferred stock specifying redemption over relatively short periods such as 5 to 10 years, therefore called transient preferreds. According to the SEC, such stock involves a commitment to use future resources of the company to redeem the issue, giving the holder a claim against prospective cash flows and hence a unique status different from that of holders of equity securities that represent permanent capital investments. This new type of preferred is nothing but debt thinly disguised. The roster of issuers includes Eastern Airlines, National Distillers, Occidental Petroleum, TWA, and Tenneco (see page 202).

The rule also requires disclosure of the redemption feature of the preferred stock issued and a schedule of redemptions required within the next 5 years. For example, Reliance Group, Inc., which might otherwise report only the $4 million par value of its preferred issue, is now required to disclose (to the SEC) the $116 million redemption price due in 5 years.

At present GAAP does not distinguish between redeemable preferred stock and

---

[6]*Redeemable preferred stock* is subject to mandatory redemption requirements or has a redemption feature that is outside the control of the issuer. It includes preferred stock that (1) has a fixed or determinable redemption date, (2) is redeemable at the option of the holder, or (3) has conditions for redemption that are not solely within the control of the issuer.

Nonredeemable preferred stock is not redeemable or is redeemable solely at the option of the issuer. *Securities and Exchange Commission Release No. 33-6097,* (Washington, D.C.: SEC, July 27, 1979).

other classes of capital stock for balance sheet reporting purposes.[7] The redemption features of such stocks are usually disclosed in footnotes to the financial statements.

ACCOUNTING FOR THE ISSUANCE OF STOCK

From the preceding discussion of the special features of the corporate system it may be seen that a corporation obtains funds from its stockholders through a series of transactions that may vary considerably. First, the stock must be authorized by the state, generally in a certificate of incorporation or charter; next, shares are offered for sale and contracts to sell stock are entered into; then, amounts to be received for the stock are collected and the shares issued. The accounting problems involved in the issuance of stock are discussed under the following topics:

1. Accounting for par value stock.
2. Accounting for no-par stock.
3. Accounting for stock sold on a subscription basis.
4. Accounting for stock issued in combination with other securities.
5. Accounting for additional assessments.
6. Accounting for expenses related to issuance.

Accounting for Par Value Stock

As indicated earlier, the par value of a stock has no relationship to the fair market value of the stock. At present, the par value associated with most capital stock issuances is very low ($1, $5, $10), which contrasts dramatically with the situation in the early 1900s when practically all stock issued had a par value of $100. The reason for this change is to permit the original sale of stock at low amounts per share and at the same time to avoid the contingent liability associated with stock sold below par. Stock with a low par value is rarely, if ever, sold below par value. In addition, some states charge a transfer tax based on the par value of the stock, so a low par value may result in lower taxes.

To show the required information for issuance of par value stock, accounts must be kept for each class of stock as follows:

1. **Preferred Stock or Common Stock.** Reflects the par value of the corporation's issued shares. These accounts are credited when the shares are originally issued. No additional entries are made in this account unless additional shares are issued or shares are retired.
2. **Paid-in Capital in Excess of Par or Additional Paid-in Capital.** Indicates any excess over par value paid in by stockholders in return for the shares issued to them. Once paid in, the excess over par becomes a part of the corporation's additional paid-in capital and the individual stockholder has no greater claim on the excess paid in than all other holders of the same class of shares.

[7]Several accounting standards, however, recognize the difference between redeemable and nonredeemable preferred stock (not necessarily using those terms). These include *FASB Statement No. 12* (it excludes redeemable preferred stock from the definition of "equity security"), *FASB Statement No. 8* (redeemable preferred stock is translated at the current rate rather than the historical rate), and *APB Opinion No. 16* (the cost of a company acquired by issuing senior equity securities having characteristics of redeemable preferred stock is determined on the same basis as in the case of debt securities).

3. **Discount on Stock.** Indicates that the stock has been issued at less than par. The holder of shares issued below par may be called on to pay in the amount of the discount if necessary to prevent creditors from sustaining loss upon liquidation of the corporation.

To illustrate how these accounts are used, assume that Colonial Corporation sold, for $1,100, one hundred shares of stock with a par value of $5 per share. The entry to record the issuance is:

Cash	1,100	
Common Stock		500
Paid-in Capital in Excess of Par		600
(Premium on Common Stock)		

If the stock had been issued in return for $300, the entry would have been recorded as follows:

Cash	300	
Paid-in Capital in Excess of Par	200	
(Discount on Common Stock)		
Common Stock		500

The use of only these capital accounts assumes that no entry would be made in the general ledger accounts at the time the corporation receives its stock authorization from the state of incorporation. In case a formal journal entry is to be made for the authorization of stock, the following separate accounts would be used for authorized stock and for unissued stock:

1. **Authorized Preferred or Common Stock.** Shows the total amount of capital stock authorized. This account is credited at the time authorization from the state is received. No additional entries are made in this account unless the charter is amended to authorize the issuance of additional shares or to reduce the present authorized shares.

2. **Unissued Preferred or Common Stock.** Shows the total authorized shares not yet issued. When subtracted from the amount authorized, the stock already issued is obtained. This account is debited at the time of recording the stock authorized, and is credited for the par value of stock issued. When these accounts are kept, the amount of stock issued is determined by subtracting the balance of the unissued stock account from the balance of the authorized stock account.

Accounting for No-Par Stock

Many states permit the issuance of capital stock without par value. Shares are issued that have no per share amount printed on the stock certificate. **The reasons for issuance of no-par stock are twofold.** First, issuance of no-par stock avoids the contingent liability that might occur if par value stock were issued at a discount. Second, some confusion still exists over the relationship (or rather the absence of a relationship) between the par value and fair market value. If shares have no par value, the questionable treatment of using par value as a basis for value never arises. This circumstance is particularly advantageous whenever stock is issued for property items such as tangible or intangible fixed assets. The major disadvantages of no-par stock are that some states levy a high tax on these issues and the total may be considered legal capital.

No-par stock, like par value shares, are sold for what they will bring, but unlike par value shares, neither a premium nor a discount is associated with the issuance and, therefore, no contingent liability accrues to the stockholders. The exact amount received represents the credit to common or preferred stock. For example, Video Electronics Corporation is organized with authorized common stock of 10,000 shares without par value. No entry, other than a memorandum entry, need be made for the authorization inasmuch as no amount is involved. If 500 shares are then issued for cash at $10 per share, the entry should be:

Cash	5,000	
Common Stock—No-Par Value		5,000

If another 500 shares are issued for $11 per share the entry should be:

Cash	5,500	
Common Stock—No-Par Value		5,500

True no-par stock should be carried in the accounts at issue price without any complications due to additional paid-in capital or discount. But some states permit the issuance of no-par stock and then proceed either to require or, in some cases, to permit such stock to have a **stated value** or minimum value below which it cannot be issued. Thus, instead of becoming no-par stock it becomes, in effect, stock with a very low par value, open to all the criticisms and abuses that first encouraged the development of no-par stock.[8]

If no-par stock is required to have a minimum issue price of $5 per share and no provision is made as to how amounts in excess of $5 per share are to be handled, the inclination is for the board of directors to declare all such amounts to be additional paid-in capital which in many states is fully or partially available for dividends. Thus, no-par value stock with either a minimum stated value or a stated value assigned by the board of directors permits a new corporation to commence its operations with additional paid-in capital that may be in excess of its stated capital. For example, if 1,000 of the shares described above ($5 stated value) were issued at $15 per share for cash, the entry could be either

Cash	15,000	
Common Stock		15,000

or

Cash	15,000	
Common Stock		5,000
Paid-in Capital in Excess of Stated Value		10,000

In most instances the obvious advantages to the corporation of setting up an initial additional paid-in capital account will influence the board of directors to require the latter entry. Whether for this or for other reasons, the prevailing tendency is to account for no-par stock with stated value as if it were par value stock with a par equal to the stated value.

Stock Sold on a Subscription Basis

The preceding discussion assumed that the stock was sold for cash, but stock may also be sold on a subscription basis. Sale on a subscription basis generally occurs when new, small companies "go public" or when stock is offered to employees by

[8]*Accounting Trends and Techniques—1978* indicates that its 600 surveyed companies reported 622 issues of outstanding common stock, 546 par value issues, and 76 no-par issues; all of the no-par issues were shown at their stated (assigned) values.

corporations to obtain employee participation in the ownership of the business. When stock is sold on a subscription basis, the full price of the stock is not received initially. Normally only a partial payment is made originally and the stock is not issued until the full subscription price is received.

Accounting for Subscribed Stock   Two new accounts are used when stock is sold on a subscription basis. The first, **Common or Preferred Stock Subscribed,** indicates the corporation's obligation to issue shares of its stock upon payment of final subscription balances by those who have subscribed for stock. This account thus signifies a commitment against the unissued capital stock. Once the subscription price is fully paid, the Common or Preferred Stock Subscribed account is debited and the Common or Preferred Stock account is credited. Common or Preferred Stock Subscribed is presented in the stockholders' equity section below Common or Preferred Stock.

The second account, **Subscriptions Receivable,** indicates the amount to be collected in full before stock is issued; therefore, this account indicates the amount yet to be collected before subscribed stock will be issued. It is a receivable just as ordinary trade accounts are receivable, but it differs in inception. Trade accounts receivable grow out of sales transactions in the ordinary course of business; subscriptions receivable relate to the issuance of a concern's own stock and in a sense represent capital contributions not yet paid in to the corporation.

Some controversy exists concerning the presentation of Subscriptions Receivable on the balance sheet. Most accountants place Subscriptions Receivable in the current asset section (assuming of course that payment on the receivable will be received within the operating cycle). In some cases, Subscriptions Receivable is shown as a deduction from Common or Preferred Stock Subscribed in the stockholders' equity section, rather than as an asset, as, for example, when there is no intention to collect the balance due from subscribers in the near future, or when the receivable hinges on some event or performance related to the subscriber, or where the subscription approach is used to circumvent a state law that may prohibit the sale of capital stock at a discount.

Most states consider common or preferred stock subscribed to be similar to outstanding common or preferred stock, which means that **individuals who have signed a valid subscription contract normally have the same rights and privileges as a stockholder who holds outstanding shares of stock.**

The journal entries for handling stock sold on a subscription basis are illustrated by the following example. Pennzoil Corp. offers stock on a subscription basis to selected individuals giving them the right to purchase 10 shares of stock (par value $5) at a price of $20 per share. Fifty individuals accept the company's offer and agree to pay 50% down in cash and the remaining 50% at the end of six months.

At date of issuance—

Subscriptions Receivable	10,000	
Common Stock Subscribed		2,500
Paid-in Capital in Excess of Par		7,500
(To record receipt of subscriptions for 500 shares)		
Cash	5,000	
Subscriptions Receivable		5,000
(To record receipt of first installment representing 50% of total due on subscribed stock)		

When the final payment is received and the stock is issued, the entries are:

Six months later—

Cash	5,000	
Subscriptions Receivable		5,000
(To record receipt of final installment on		
subscribed stock)		
Common Stock Subscribed	2,500	
Common Stock		2,500
(To record issuance of 500 shares upon receipt of		
final installment from subscribers)		

Defaulted Subscription Accounts Sometimes a subscriber is unable to pay all installments and defaults on the agreement. The question is then raised of what to do with the balance of the subscription account as well as the amount already paid in. The solution to this problem is a function of the applicable state law. Some states permit the corporation to retain any amounts paid in on defaulted subscription accounts; other states require that any amount realized on the resale in excess of the amount due from the original subscriber be returned.

Lump-Sum Sales of Stock

Generally, corporations sell classes of stock separately from one another so that the proceeds relative to each class, and ordinarily even relative to each lot, are known. Occasionally, two or more classes of securities are issued for a single payment or lump sum. It is not uncommon for more than one type or class of security to be issued in the acquisition of another company. The accounting problem in a lump-sum issuance is the allocation of the proceeds between the several classes of securities. The two methods of allocation available for accountants are (1) the proportional method and (2) the incremental method.

If the fair market value or other sound basis for determining relative value is available for each class of security, the **lump sum received is best allocated between the classes of securities on a proportional basis,** that is, the ratio that each is to the total. For instance, if 1,000 shares of $10 stated value common stock having a market value of $20 a share and 1,000 shares of $10 par value preferred stock having a market value of $12 a share are issued for a lump sum of $30,000, the allocation of the $30,000 to the two classes would be as follows:

Fair market value of common	(1,000 × $20) =	$20,000
Fair market value of preferred	(1,000 × $12) =	12,000
Aggregate fair market value		$32,000
Allocated to common:	$\frac{\$20,000}{\$32,000} \times \$30,000 =$	$18,750
Allocated to preferred:	$\frac{\$12,000}{\$32,000} \times \$30,000 =$	$11,250
Total allocation		$30,000

In instances **where the fair market value of all classes of securities is not deter-**

minable, the incremental method may be used. The market value of the securities is used as a basis for those classes that are known and the remainder of the lump-sum is allocated to the class for which the market value is not known. For instance, if 1,000 shares of $10 stated value common stock having a market value of $20 and 1,000 shares of $10 par value preferred stock having no established market value are issued for a lump-sum of $30,000, the allocation of the $30,000 to the two classes would be as follows:

Lump-sum receipt	$30,000
Allocated to common (1,000 shs. × $20 fair mkt. value)	20,000
Balance allocated to preferred	$10,000

   If no fair market value is determinable for any of the classes of stock involved in a lump-sum exchange, the allocation may have to be arbitrary. If it is known that one or more of the classes of securities issued will have a determinable market value in the near future, the arbitrary basis may be used with the intent to make an adjustment when the future market value is established.

Noncash Stock Transactions

It is not uncommon for some paid-in capital of a corporation to be the result of stock issued in exchange for property, services, or any form of asset other than cash. Accounting for the issuance of shares of stock for property or services may involve a problem of valuation. **The general rule to be applied when stock is issued for services or property other than cash is that the property or services be recorded at either its fair market value or the fair market value of the stock issued, whichever is more clearly determinable.**
   If the fair market value of the property or services is readily determinable, it is used as a basis for recording the exchange. If it is not readily determinable but the fair market value of the stock issued is, the transaction is recorded at the fair market value of the stock. If both are readily determinable and the transaction is the result of an arm's-length exchange, there will probably be little difference in their fair market values. In such cases it should not matter which value is regarded as the basis for valuing the exchange. If the fair market value of the stock being issued and the property or services being received are not readily determinable, the value to be assigned is generally established by the board of directors, usually through independent appraisals. The use of the book, par, or stated values as a basis of valuation for these transactions should be avoided.
   When stock is issued for personal services by employees or outsiders, the fair value of the services as of the date of the contract for such services, rather than the date of issuance of the shares (even though the date of issuance is prescribed for income tax purposes), should be the basis for valuation because the contract is viewed in an accounting sense as a subscription. In these exchanges, however, the fair market value of the shares issued is usually more readily determinable.
   Unissued stock or treasury stock (issued shares that have been reacquired but not retired) may be exchanged for the property or services. If treasury shares are used,

their cost should not be regarded as the decisive factor in establishing the fair market value of the property or services. The current value of the property or services, if determinable, is a better basis of valuation.

The following series of transactions illustrates the procedure for recording the issuance of 10,000 shares of $10 par value common stock for a patent:

1. The fair market value of the patent is not readily determinable but the fair market value of the stock is known to be $140,000.

Patent	140,000	
Common Stock		100,000
Paid-in Capital in Excess of Par		40,000

2. The fair market value of the stock is not readily determinable, but the fair market value of the patent is determined to be $150,000.

Patent	150,000	
Common Stock		100,000
Paid-in Capital in Excess of Par		50,000

3. Neither the fair market value of the stock nor the fair market value of the patent is readily determinable. An independent consultant values the patent at $125,000, and the board of directors agrees with that valuation.

Patent	125,000	
Common Stock		100,000
Paid-in Capital in Excess of Par		25,000

In corporate law, the board of directors is granted the power to set the value of noncash transactions. This power has been abused. The issuance of stock for property or services has resulted in cases of overstated corporate capital through intentional overvaluation of the property or services received. The overvaluation of the stockholders' equity resulting from inflated asset values creates what is referred to as **watered stock.** The "water" can be eliminated from the corporate structure either by simply writing down the overvalued assets or by having the stockholders donate some shares, selling the donated shares, and crediting the overvalued assets for the proceeds of the resold shares.

If as a result of the issuance of stock for property or services the recorded assets are undervalued, **secret reserves** are created. An understated corporate structure or secret reserve may also be achieved by excessive depreciation or amortization charges, by expensing capital expenditures, excessive write-downs of inventories or receivables, or any other understatement of assets or overstatement of liabilities.

Assessments on Capital Stock

The laws of some states provide that a corporation may assess stockholders an additional amount above their original contribution. Although this situation occurs rather infrequently, when stockholders are assessed they must either pay or possibly forfeit their existing shares. Upon receiving the assessments from the stockholders, the corporation should determine whether the original stock was sold at a discount or a premium. If the stock was originally sold at a discount, the additional proceeds should be credited to the discount account. If the stock was originally issued at a premium, the account Additional Paid-in Capital Arising from Assessments should be credited.

Costs of Issuing Stock

The costs associated with the acquisition of corporate capital resulting from the issuance of securities include the following:

1. Attorneys' fees.
2. Certified public accountants' fees.
3. Underwriters' fees and commissions.
4. Expenses of printing and mailing certificates and registration statements.
5. Expenses of filing with the SEC.
6. Clerical and administrative expenses of preparation.
7. Costs of advertising the issue.

In practice there are two primary methods of accounting for initial issue costs. **The first method treats issue costs as a reduction of the amounts paid in.** In effect, such costs are debited to the Paid-in Capital in Excess of Par or Stated Value. This treatment is based on the premise that issue costs are unrelated to corporate operations and thus are not properly chargeable against earnings from operations; issue costs are viewed as a reduction of proceeds of the financing activity.

The second method treats issue costs as an organization cost that is charged neither to current earnings nor to corporate capital; such costs are capitalized and classified as an intangible asset and written off over an arbitrary time period not to exceed 40 years. This treatment is based on the premise that amounts paid in as invested capital should not be violated, and that issue costs benefit the corporation over a long period of time or so long as the invested capital is utilized.

Although both treatments are applied in practice, the first method of charging issue costs to paid-in capital predominates. The Securities and Exchange Commission permits the use of either method. In addition to the costs of initial issuance of stock, corporations annually incur costs of maintaining the stockholders' records and handling ownership transfers. These recurring costs, primarily registrar and transfer agents' fees, should be charged as expense to the period in which incurred.

Definitions of Capital

To this point, we have used the term stockholders' or owners' equity to denote the total capital of the enterprise. It is important to understand the many different meanings that are attached to the word capital, because the word often is construed differently by various user groups.

In corporation finance, for example, **capital** commonly represents the gross assets of the enterprise. In a **legal context,** capital is considered that portion of stockholders' equity that is required by statute to be retained in the business for the protection of creditors. Generally **legal capital (stated capital)** is the par value of all capital stock issued, but when shares without par value are issued, it may be:

1. Total consideration paid in for the shares.
2. A minimum amount stated in the applicable law.
3. An arbitrary amount established by the board of directors at its discretion.

Accountants for the most part define capital more broadly than legal capital but more narrowly than total assets. When accountants refer to capital they mean stockholders' equity or owners' equity. They then classify stockholders' or owners' equity into two further categories—contributed capital and earned capital. **Contributed capital** (paid-in capital) is the term used to describe the total amount paid in on capital stock at any given time, or stated another way, it is the amount advanced by stockholders to the corporation for use in the business. Contributed capital includes the par value of all outstanding capital stock plus any premiums less any discounts on issuance plus the amount paid in on any subscription agreements and additional assessments. **Earned capital** is the capital that develops if the business operates profitably; it consists of all undistributed income that remains invested in the enterprise.

REACQUISITION OF SHARES

It is not unusual to find comments in the financial media similar to the following quotations:

> Bluebird Incorporated, a Pennsylvania corporation, is offering to purchase for cash 750,000 shares of its outstanding common stock, par value $.25 per share, at $10.00 net per share to the seller. Such shares represent approximately 13% of the outstanding Common Shares.[9]
>
> Continental Oil Co. joined the growing list of companies buying their own shares in the stock market, announcing its directors have authorized purchases of up to 400,000 shares of common stock.[10]

Corporations purchase their outstanding stock for a variety of reasons. The major factors are (1) to have enough stock on hand to meet employee stock option contracts, (2) to reduce the shares outstanding in hopes of increasing earnings per share, (3) to buy out a particular ownership interest, (4) to attempt to make a market in the company's stock, (5) to contract the operations of the business, or (6) to meet the stock needs of a potential merger.

Once shares are reacquired, they may either be retired or held in the treasury for reissue. If not retired, such shares are referred to as treasury shares or treasury stock. Technically treasury stock is a corporation's own stock that has been reacquired after having been issued and fully paid. Stock originally issued at a discount and then reacquired is not properly treasury stock, but the distinction is of such little practical importance that it is commonly ignored.

Treasury stock is not an asset. It is absurd to imply that a corporation can own a part of itself. Treasury stock may be sold to obtain funds, but that possibility does not make treasury stock a balance sheet asset. When a corporation buys back some of its own outstanding stock, it has reduced its capitalization but has not acquired an asset.[11]

[9]*The Wall Street Journal,* June 11, 1979, p. 19.

[10]*The Wall Street Journal,* May 27, 1970, p. 4.

[11]In special circumstances treasury stock is presented as an asset in the balance sheet. For example, in 1977, Dresser Industries, Inc. reported among its "Investments and Other Assets" 460,399 treasury shares that had been designated for the purpose of future issuance to satisfy an accrued deferred compensation liability (Dresser discontinued this classification in 1978, although it still had treasury stock designated for that purpose). *Accounting Trends and Techniques—1978* reported that 8 of 461 companies having treasury stock classified it among the noncurrent assets.

Methods of Accounting for Treasury Stock

Two general methods of handling treasury stock in the accounts are the cost method and the par value method. Both methods are considered generally acceptable and are applied in practice. The **cost method,** which enjoys more widespread use,[12] results in debiting the Treasury Stock account for the reacquisition cost and in reporting this account as a deduction from contributed capital **and** retained earnings on the balance sheet. The **par** or **stated value method,** which is theoretically more justifiable, records all transactions in treasury shares at the par value of the shares and reports the treasury stock as a reduction of outstanding capital stock.

Treasury Shares Accounted for at Cost Under the cost method, acquisition of treasury stock is viewed as the initial step in a two-part transaction; the reissuance of the treasury stock, the second step, completes the transaction. The acquisition is a temporary contraction of total capital, and reissuance is an expansion of the total capital. Between acquisition and reissuance, treasury shares are held in suspense by the corporation. To some extent the fiction that treasury shares are an asset is followed. **The Treasury Stock account is debited for the cost of the shares acquired and is credited upon reissuance for this same cost** in a manner similar to an inventory account. In fact, if numerous acquisitions of blocks of treasury shares are made at different prices, inventory costing methods, such as specific identification, average, or FIFO, may be used to identify the cost at date of reissuance. **Under the cost method, the price received for the stock when originally issued does not affect the entries to record the acquisition and reissuance of the treasury stock.**

If the treasury shares are reissued at a price in excess of the acquisition cost (at a "gain"), that excess is credited to an account titled Paid-in Capital from Treasury Stock. If the treasury shares are reissued at less than acquisition cost (at a "loss"), the "loss" may be charged first against any previous "gains" from reissuance or retirement of the same class of stock, and second if the "gains" are insufficient to absorb such "loss," the remainder is charged against retained earnings.[13]

For example, if 1,000 shares of common stock of $100 par value are originally issued at 110, the entry would be:

Cash	110,000	
Common Stock		100,000
Paid-in Capital in Excess of Par		10,000
(To record sale of common stock)		

The acquisition of 10 shares of common stock at 112 would be recorded as follows:

Treasury Stock	1,120	
Cash		1,120
(To record purchase of treasury stock at cost)		

---

[12]*Accounting Trends and Techniques*—1978 indicates that of its selected list of 600 companies, 364 carried common stock in treasury at cost and only 45 at par or stated value.

[13]"Status of Accounting Research Bulletins," *Opinions of the Accounting Principles Board No. 6* (New York: AICPA, 1965), par. 12.

Reissue Assumption #1

If the treasury stock is subsequently sold at 112, the entry is simply as follows:

```
Cash                                              1,120
   Treasury Stock                                          1,120
      (To record sale of treasury stock at cost)
```

Reissue Assumption #2

If the treasury stock were subsequently sold instead at 115, the entry would be as follows:

```
Cash                                              1,150
   Treasury Stock                                          1,120
   Paid-in Capital from Treasury Stock                        30
      (To record sale of treasury stock above cost)
```

Reissue Assumption #3

If the treasury stock were subsequently sold instead at 98 and an assumed "gain" (Paid-in Capital from Treasury Shares) of $50 were carried on the books from previous treasury stock transactions, the entry would be as follows:

```
Cash                                               980
Paid-in Capital from Treasury Stock                 50
Retained Earnings                                   90
   Treasury Stock                                          1,120
```

Notice that in each of the reissuing transactions assumed above the Treasury Stock account was credited for its acquisition cost regardless of the reissuance price.

Accounting practice frequently applies a slight variation to the foregoing cost treatment of the reissuance transaction. The "loss" on reissuance is charged to Paid-in Capital with a pro rata amount per share of any premium (or discount) on the original sale of the stock, and any remaining loss is charged to Retained Earnings. Under the third assumption of reissuance at 98, the alternative entry therefore would be:

```
Cash                                               980
Paid-in Capital in Excess of Par                   100
   (10 shares at original premium of $10 per share)
Retained Earnings                                   40
   Treasury Stock                                          1,120
```

In its most recent pronouncement on treasury stock, the profession takes the position that the cost method is acceptable when a corporation acquires its own stock for purposes other than retirement (formal or constructive), or when ultimate disposition has not yet been decided.[14]

Treasury Shares Accounted for at Par Those who advocate accounting for treasury shares at par adhere to the theory that **the purchase or other acquisition of treasury shares is, in effect, a constructive retirement of those shares.** Inasmuch as the shares cannot be an asset, they must represent a retirement or at least a reduction of outstanding stock. Because shares outstanding are shown at par, the

---

[14]*Ibid.*

reacquired shares must be carried at par to indicate the proper reduction in stock outstanding.

Under the par value method, **the acquisition cost of treasury shares is compared with the amount received at the time of their original issue.** The Treasury Stock account is debited for the par value of the shares, and a pro rata amount of any excess over par on original issuance is charged to the appropriate Paid-in Capital account. **Any "loss" or excess of the acquisition cost over the original issue price is charged to Retained Earnings.** The amount charged to Retained Earnings may be viewed as a dividend to the retiring stockholder. **Any "gain" or excess of the par or stated value over the acquisition price of the treasury stock is credited to Paid-in Capital from Treasury Stock** (Paid-in Capital in Excess of Par); the credit to Paid-in Capital may be viewed as a capital contribution from the retiring stockholder. This accounting treatment removes all original capital balances identifiable with the treasury shares. If the treasury shares are reissued, the accounting treatment is similar to that accorded any original issuance of stock. A series of transactions with suggested entries illustrates the par value method.

1. One thousand shares of common stock of $100 par value are originally issued at 110.

Cash	110,000	
Common Stock		100,000
Paid-in Capital in Excess of Par		10,000

2. Ten of these shares are reacquired at 100.

Treasury Stock	1,000	
Paid-in Capital in Excess of Par	100	
Cash		1,000
Paid-in Capital from Treasury Stock		100

The debit to Paid-in Capital in Excess of Par and the credit to Paid-in Capital from Treasury Stock in equal amounts constitute a reclassification of the original premium on the shares when issued.

3. Ten additional shares are reacquired at 112.

Treasury Stock	1,000	
Paid-in Capital in Excess of Par	100	
Retained Earnings	20	
Cash		1,120

4. Ten additional shares are reacquired at 98.

Treasury Stock	1,000	
Paid-in Capital in Excess of Par	100	
Cash		980
Paid-in Capital from Treasury Stock		120

5. Ten shares of treasury stock are reissued at 105.

Cash	1,050	
Treasury Stock		1,000
Paid-in Capital in Excess of Par		50

If stock was originally issued at 95, the discount of $5 per share should be eliminated if such stock is acquired later as treasury shares. For example, if 10 shares of stock originally issued at 95 are acquired at 97, the entry would be:

Treasury Stock	1,000	
Retained Earnings	20	
Cash		970
Discount on Common Stock		50

In this entry, Treasury Stock is debited for par value, Cash is credited for the acquisition cost, and Discount on Common Stock is credited for the amount of the discount originally charged to this account when the 10 shares were issued. The charge to Retained Earnings represents the difference between the acquisition cost of $970 and the original issue price of $950 and is a form of dividend to the retiring stockholder. The contingent liability for the discount continues for the original stockholder.

The cost method avoids identifying and accounting for the premiums, discounts, and other amounts related to the original issue of the specific shares acquired and is the simpler, more popular method. The par method, however, maintains the integrity of the sources of the various components of capital. Thus, the par method, although more complex in application, is the conceptually superior method.

Other Methods of Accounting for Treasury Stock   In some states the purchase of treasury stock must be handled by methods other than the two previously described. For example, the applicable state law may require a permanent reduction of retained earnings, in which case the total cost of the shares purchased (other than stated or par value) would be charged against retained earnings. Many companies use the balance in "additional paid-in capital," regardless of its source, to absorb "losses" on treasury stock transactions. Although not theoretically sound, this method is acceptable under **APB Opinion No. 6,** and it avoids reclassification of premiums and discounts because only one "additional paid-in capital" account is used. Care should always be exercised in recording treasury stock transactions because of the considerable variety of possible requirements. The advice of an attorney is frequently desirable in this connection.

Donated Treasury Stock

Those who advocate recording treasury stock in the accounts at cost price would make no formal entry for treasury stock donated to the corporation by stockholders; instead only a memorandum record would be made. Under this method, the entire proceeds from reissuance of the shares would be considered to be the amount of the "gain," that is, the credit to Paid-in Capital from ~~Treasury Stock.~~ Donation

If treasury shares are accounted for at par, the donated stock should be recorded at par, and the difference between original issue price and reacquisition cost (zero) taken up as donated capital, as follows:

Treasury Stock	1,000	
Donated Capital		1,000

If part of these shares is later reissued at a premium or a discount, the Donated Capital balance should probably be adjusted upward for any premium or downward for any discount. Some accountants, however, favor establishing a separate premium or discount account if the amount is material or, if not material, merging the treasury discount or premium with the original issue premium or discount, as illustrated in the previous section. Theoretically, the establishment of separate premium or discount accounts is preferable.

If the treasury shares donated were originally issued for noncash items, attention should be directed to the original transaction, because, as was often the case in the early 1900s, an assumption of implicit discount might apply. In other words, issuance of stock for property with a donation by the stockholders was a convenient way to avoid the discount liability associated with issuing stock at a discount. Essentially the property, as well as the stockholders' equity, was overvalued initially. In this case, the proceeds received from the sale of donated shares should be credited to the overvalued assets. The approach used to avoid the discount liability is referred to as the **treasury stock subterfuge approach.** With par values so low today, this type of problem should rarely occur.

Treasury Stock in the Balance Sheet

There are three possible methods of showing treasury stock in the balance sheet, but only two of them are acceptable. The first method, which at one time was common but should no longer be considered acceptable, includes the treasury stock on the left side of the balance sheet as if it were an asset. As discussed in this chapter, treasury stock may be a possible source of assets, but it is not an asset and should not be shown as such.[15]

The other two methods are related to the two bases of accounting for treasury stock. If the treasury stock is accounted for **at cost,** it is customary to report the cost as an unallocated reduction of the stockholders' equity. The cost of the treasury stock is subtracted from the total of capital stock, additional paid-in capital, and retained earnings, as shown below by Zenith Radio Corporation in its 1978 annual report:

Cost Method of Reporting Treasury Stock

Stockholders' equity:
Capital stock, $1.00 par value per share; authorized	
24,000,000 shares; issued 19,045,870 shares	$ 19,046,000
Additional paid-in capital	8,640,000
Retained earnings	253,265,000
Total capital and retained earnings	280,951,000
Less—Treasury 209,970 shares, at cost	(7,527,000)
Total stockholders' equity	$273,424,000

Under the par value method, treasury stock is reported in the balance sheet as a deduction from issued shares of the same class in order to show those outstanding. The following illustration is from the annual report of Dan River, Inc.:

---

[15]If treasury stock is held to retire a liability classified as current, some accountants maintain that there is logical justification and authoritative support for classifying such treasury stock as an asset. (See footnote 11 on page 660.)

Par Value Method of Reporting Treasury Stock	
Stockholders' equity:	
Preferred stock of $5 par value per share; authorized	
2,000,000 shares; $1.10 cumulative convertible,	
issued and outstanding 288,115 shares	$ 1,441,000
Common stock of $5 par value per share; authorized	
10,000,000 shares; outstanding 5,607,935 after	
deducting 44,175 shares held in treasury	28,040,000
Capital in excess of par value	28,758,000
Retained earnings	100,272,000
Total stockholders' equity	$158,511,000

The foregoing presentation which deducts treasury shares from issued shares of the same class is more predominant in practice than the alternative form of presentation that (1) deducts the dollar value attributable to the treasury shares from the dollar value attributable to the issued stock of the same class and (2) separately discloses any excess of issue price over cost (see the next illustration for this alternative form).

State corporation laws frequently restrict the amount of a corporation's retained earnings available for dividends by cost of any treasury shares acquired. Under either of the methods of presentation described above, a restriction of this kind should be indicated:

DISCLOSURE OF RESTRICTION (Par Method)		
Stockholders' Equity		
Capital stock—authorized 1,000 shares of $50 par value;		
issued 800 shares	$40,000	
Less 100 shares reacquired and held in treasury	5,000	$35,000
Excess of issue price over cost of treasury shares		1,000
Retained earnings (restricted in the amount of $4,000		
by the acquisition of treasury stock)	18,520	$54,520

In the case above, if Paid-in Capital in Excess of Par had existed at the time of the treasury stock transaction, the excess of the reissue price over cost of treasury stock probably would have been merged with the original issue premiums.

Financial statement form under the par method has the merit of presenting the amount of additional paid-in capital and retained earnings after the treasury stock par amount. But because many state statutes do not permit a reduction in legal capital by the acquisition of treasury stock, the cost method presentation avoids misinterpretation of the net amount of capital stock ($35,000 under the par method) as legal capital.

Retirement of Treasury Stock

A corporation may retire treasury stock held if it complies with all legal requirements that apply to it. Retired treasury shares have the status of authorized and unissued shares. The accounting treatment for retired treasury stock is dependent on whether the cost or the par value method was used to record the acquisition and whether or not retained earnings have been appropriated in the amount of the cost. Using data from the previous cost method and par value method illustrations, the following entries would be made for the retirement of 10 shares of common stock of $100 par value issued at 110.

Retirement Under the Cost Method

1. If the treasury shares were acquired at 112:

Common Stock	1,000	
Paid-in Capital in Excess of Par	100	
Retained Earnings	20	
Treasury Stock		1,120

2. If the treasury shares were acquired at 98:

Common Stock	1,000	
Paid-in Capital in Excess of Par	100	
Paid-in Capital from Retirement of Common Stock		120
Treasury Stock		980

In both instances, if retained earnings had been appropriated in the amount of the cost of the treasury shares, a properly titled account such as Appropriated Retained Earnings—Treasury Stock would be debited and Retained Earnings credited. The debit and credit amount would be $1,120 in the first case and $980 in the second.

Retirement Under the Par Value Method

1. If the treasury shares were acquired at 112:

Common Stock	1,000	
Treasury Stock		1,000

2. If the treasury shares were acquired at 98:

Common Stock	1,000	
Treasury Stock		1,000

Because the Treasury Stock account is carried at the par value of the shares held in the treasury, the entry to record the retirement is at par. In both instances, if retained earnings had been appropriated in the amount of the cost of the treasury shares, as under the cost method, Appropriated Retained Earnings—Treasury Stock would be debited and Retained Earnings credited, again in the same amounts—$1,120 in the first case and $980 in the second.

Basic Records Related to Stock

A stock certificate book and a stock transfer book are included among the special corporate records involved in accounting for stock. A stock certificate book is similar to a checkbook in that printed stock certificates are enclosed. A stock transfer book simply tells who owns the stock at a given point in time. Obviously the corporation must be able to obtain at any time a list of the current stockholders so that dividend payments, notices of annual stockholder meetings, and voting proxies may be sent to the proper persons.

Many corporations avoid the problems concerned with handling capital stock sales and transfers by engaging some organization that specializes in this type of work to serve as **registrar and transfer agent.** Banks and trust companies frequently serve in this capacity, keeping all the necessary records. The corporation is provided upon request with a registered list of stockholders for such purposes as mailing dividend checks or voting proxies.

As might be expected, certain accounts act as controlling accounts in the general ledger with subsidiary ledgers to supply necessary detail. These are:

General Ledger Account	Subsidiary Ledger
Common or Preferred Stock	Stockholders' Ledger
Subscriptions Receivable	Subscriptions Receivable Ledger
Common or Preferred Stock Subscribed	Subscribed Stock Ledger

Questions

1. Distinguish between the following types of corporations:
   (a) Public vs. private.
   (b) Nonstock vs. stock.
   (c) Closed vs. open.
   (d) Listed vs. unlisted.
2. Discuss the special characteristics of the corporate form of business that have a direct effect on proprietorship or owners' equity accounting.
3. In the absence of restrictive provisions, what are the basic rights of stockholders of a corporation?
4. Distinguish between common and preferred stock.
5. What features or rights may alter the character of preferred stock?
6. What is the difference between non-participating, partially participating, and fully participating stock?
7. (a) In what ways may preferred stock be more like a debt security than an equity security?
   (b) How should preferred stock be classified in the financial statements?
8. What is meant by par value, and what is its significance to stockholders?
9. What are the legal restrictions that control the distribution of profit of a corporation?
10. Explain each of the following terms: authorized capital stock, unissued capital stock, issued capital stock, outstanding capital stock, subscribed stock, and treasury stock.
11. Distinguish between paid-in capital and stated capital.
12. When might the Stock Subscription Receivable account be classified as a current asset? As a noncurrent asset? As a deduction in stockholders' equity section?
13. How are premiums and discounts on issued stocks accounted for and reported?
14. Explain the difference between the proportional method and the incremental method of allocating the proceeds of lump-sum sales of capital stock.
15. What are the different bases for stock valuation when assets other than cash are received for issued shares of stock?
16. Discuss the two methods of accounting for initial issue costs. Which do you support and why?
17. Differentiate between capital in a legal sense, capital in a corporate finance sense, and capital in an accounting sense.
18. For what reasons might a corporation purchase its own stock?
19. Distinguish between the cost method and the par value method of accounting for treasury stock.

20. How is stockholders' equity affected differently by using the cost method instead of the par method for treasury stock purchases?

21. Discuss the propriety of showing
    (a) treasury stock as an asset,
    (b) "gain" or "loss" on sale of treasury stock as additions to or deductions from income, and
    (c) dividends received on treasury stock as income.

22. Although under most circumstances subscriptions receivable are traditionally regarded as an asset, the theoretical propriety of this treatment has been questioned. The alternative is to treat them as a contra to stockholders' equity.
    (a) Discuss and justify the traditional treatment of subscriptions receivable.
    (b) Present arguments that question the theoretical propriety of the traditional treatment, and, instead, lend support to the view that subscriptions receivable should be treated as a contra to stockholders' equity.

Cases

C15-1 The Hock Pencil Company is a small closely held corporation. Eighty percent of the stock is held by Clay Hock, President; of the remainder, 10% is held by members of his family and 10% by Phyllis Barker, a former officer who is now retired. The balance sheet of the company at June 30, 1980 was substantially as shown below:

Assets		Liabilities and Capital	
Cash	$ 11,000	Current liabilities	$ 75,000
Other	285,000	Capital stock	150,000
		Retained earnings	71,000
	$296,000		$296,000

Additional authorized capital stock of $150,000 par value had never been issued. To strengthen the cash position of the company, Mr. Hock issued capital stock of a par value of $50,000 to himself at par for cash. At the next stockholders' meeting, Ms. Barker objected and claimed that her interests had been injured.

Instructions
(a) Which stockholders' right was ignored in the issue of shares to Mr. Hock?
(b) How may the damage to Ms. Barker's interests be repaired most simply?
(c) If Mr. Hock offered Ms. Barker a personal cash settlement and they agreed to employ you as an impartial arbitrator to determine the amount, what settlement would you propose? Present your calculations with sufficient explanation to satisfy both parties.

C15-2 Medical Equipment Corporation purchased $144,000 worth of equipment in 1981 for $90,000 cash and a promise to deliver an indeterminate number of treasury shares of its $5 par common stock, with a market value of $15,000 on January 1 of each year for the next four years. Hence $60,000 in "market value" of treasury shares will be required to discharge the $54,000 balance due on the equipment.
   The corporation then acquired 5,000 shares of its own stock in the expectation that the market value of the stock would increase substantially before the delivery dates.

Instructions
(a) Discuss the propriety of recording the equipment at
   1. $90,000 (the cash payment).
   2. $144,000 (the cash price of the equipment).
   3. $150,000 (the $90,000 cash payment + the $60,000 market value of treasury stock that must be transferred to the vendor in order to settle the obligation according to the terms of the agreement).

(b) Discuss the arguments for treating the balance due as
  1. A liability.
  2. Treasury stock subscribed.

(c) Assuming that legal requirements do not affect the decision, discuss the arguments for treating the corporation's treasury shares as
  1. An asset awaiting ultimate disposition.
  2. A capital element awaiting ultimate disposition.

(AICPA adapted)

C15-3 In connection with your first audit of Happy Jack Mining Company, you note the following facts concerning its capital stock transactions:

1. Authorized capital consists of 5,000,000 shares of $1.00 par value common stock.
2. All 5,000,000 shares were issued initially in exchange for certain mineral properties, which were recorded at an amount equal to twice the par value of the shares issued.
3. Soon thereafter, owing to the need for additional working capital, 3,000,000 of the shares were donated to the company and immediately sold for $4,500,000 cash, which resulted in a credit to paid-in capital of this amount.

Instructions

(a) Describe in order of preference alternative methods of accounting for the receipt and immediate disposition of donated treasury stock that was originally issued at its fair market value and had no aspect of a "treasury stock subterfuge."

(b) 1. What values should be assigned to the mineral properties and the stockholders' equity? Discuss.
  2. What adjustment, if any, would you recommend?

(AICPA adapted)

C15-4 It has been said that (1) the use of the LIFO inventory method during an extended period of rising prices and (2) the expensing of all human-resource costs are among the accepted accounting practices that help create "secret reserves."

Instructions

(a) What is a "secret reserve"? How can "secret reserves" be created or enlarged?

(b) What is the basis for saying that the two specific practices cited above tend to create "secret reserves"?

(c) Is it possible to create a "secret reserve" in connection with accounting for a liability? If so, explain or give an example.

(d) What are the objections to the creation of "secret reserves"?

(e) It has also been said that "watered stock" is the opposite of a "secret reserve." What is "watered stock"?

(f) Describe the general circumstances in which "watered stock" can arise.

(g) What steps can be taken to eliminate "water" from a capital structure?

(AICPA adapted)

Exercises

E15-1 The management of Thomas Barton Contractors, Inc. has decided to sell capital stock to raise additional capital to allow for expansion in the rapidly growing construction industry. The corporation decides to sell this stock through a subscription basis and publicly notifies the investment world. The stock is a $5 par value issue and 15,000 shares are offered at $20 a share. The terms of the subscription are 40% down and the balance at the end of six months. All shares are subscribed for during the offering period.

Instructions

Give the journal entry for the original subscription, the collection of the down payments, the collection of the balance of the subscription price, and the issuance of the common stock.

E15-2 Cascade Redwood Corp. is authorized to issue 500,000 shares of $10 par common stock. On November 30, 1981, 60,000 shares were subscribed at $12 per share. A 30% down payment was made on the subscribed stock. On January 30, 1982, the balance due on the subscribed shares was collected except for a subscriber of 8,000 shares who defaulted on his subscription. The 8,000 shares were sold on February 10, 1982, at $13 per share and the defaulting subscriber's down payment was returned.

Instructions

Prepare the required journal entries for the transactions above.

E15-3 On January 1, 1980, Wanda Wallace, Inc. received authorization to issue an additional 200,000 shares of $10 par value common stock. Subscribers have contracted to purchase the shares at the subscription price of $40 per share with terms of 50% down in cash and the remaining 50% at the end of six months.

Instructions

(a) Give Wallace's journal entry for the situation above on the date of issuance.

(b) Assume that Will Galliart has subscribed to 600 of the shares but defaults after paying his 50% down payment. Assume also that the applicable state law affords the subscriber stock on a pro rata basis. Give Wallace's journal entry for the disposition of the balances in the accounts related to Mr. Galliart.

E15-4 Bubbly Aircraft, Inc. issues 500 shares of $5 par value common stock and 100 shares of $100 par value preferred stock for a lump sum of $80,000.

Instructions

(a) Prepare the journal entry for the issuance when the market value of the common shares is $150 each and market value of the preferred is $200 each.

(b) Prepare the journal entry for the issuance when only the market value of the common stock is known and it is $120 per share.

E15-5 The Peggy Graham Company was organized with 50,000 shares of $100 par value 9% preferred stock and 100,000 shares of common stock without par value. During the first year, 1,000 shares of preferred and 1,000 shares of common were issued for a lump-sum price of $140,000.

Instructions

What entry should be made to record this transaction under each of the following independent conditions:

(a) Shortly after the transaction described above, 500 shares of preferred stock were sold at $104.

(b) The directors have established a stated value of $60 a share for the common stock.

(c) At the date of issuance, the preferred stock had a market price of $108 per share and the common stock had a market price of $36 per share.

E15-6 Sumptuous Furniture, Inc. has outstanding 50,000 shares of $10 par common stock which has been issued at $30 per share. On July 5, 1980, Sumptuous repurchased 1,000 of these shares at $48 per share. Sumptuous then retires the treasury shares.

Instructions

Give the appropriate journal entries for the acquisition and retirement of the treasury stock under:

(a) the cost method.

(b) the par value method.

E15-7 On November 15, 1980, Robert Skabo, a wealthy shareholder of Beta Publishing Company, donates 2,000 shares of Beta's $10 par common stock to the corporation. The stock was originally issued at $24 per share and is now selling for $20 in the marketplace.

Instructions

(a) Prepare Beta's journal entry to record the donation under (1) the cost method, (2) the par value method.

(b) Assume that Beta resells the stock on December 20, 1980, when the market value is $26 per share. Prepare Beta's journal entries for the resale under (1) the cost method, (2) the par value method.

E15-8 M. M. Yanker Corporation's charter authorized 100,000 shares of $10 par value common stock, and 25,000 shares of 8% cumulative and non-participating preferred stock, par value $100 per share. Yanker engaged in the following stock transactions through December 31, 1980: 30,000 shares of common stock were issued for $350,000 and 5,000 shares of preferred stock for machinery valued at $600,000. Subscriptions for 3,000 shares of common have been taken, and 40% of the subscription price of $18 per share has been collected. The stock will be issued upon collection of the subscription price in full. Treasury stock of 500 shares of common has been purchased for $14 and accounted for under the cost method. The Retained Earnings balance is $85,000.

Instructions

Prepare the stockholders' equity section of the balance sheet in good form. Assume that state law requires that the amount of retained earnings available for dividends be restricted by an amount equal to the cost of treasury shares acquired.

Problems

P15-1 Stock transactions of Pentex Camera Company are as follows:

Apr. 1 Subscriptions to 600 shares of its $100 par value capital stock are received, together with checks from the various subscribers to cover a 25% down payment. The stock was subscribed at 108. The remainder of the subscription price is to be paid in three equal monthly installments.

May 1 First installments are collected from all subscribers.

June 1 Second installments are received from all subscribers except Lyle McGinnis, who had subscribed for 60 shares.

5 In reply to correspondence, Mr. McGinnis states that he is unable to complete his installment payments and authorizes the company to dispose of the shares subscribed for by him.

17 The shares subscribed for by Mr. McGinnis are sold for cash at 98. Expenses of $90 were incurred in disposing of this stock. (**Hint:** Expenses and deficiencies are charged against the amount due to the subscriber.)

25 A check is mailed to Mr. McGinnis equal to the refund due him.

July 1 The final installments are collected on all open subscription accounts, and the stock is issued.

Instructions

Prepare entries in general journal form for the transactions above. Assume that defaulting subscribers are to receive refunds; any premium subscribed is refunded only if it is collected on resale.

P15-2 Galloping Enterprises, Inc. (GEI) is a closely held toy manufacturer in the northeast. You have been engaged as the independent public accountant to perform the first audit of GEI. It is agreed that only current-year (1981) financial statements will be prepared.

The following sotckholders' equity information has been developed from GEI records on December 31, 1980:

Common stock, no par value; no stated value;
    authorized 10,000 shares; issued 2,000 shares $70,000
    Retained earnings   38,000

The following stock transactions took place during 1981:
(1) On March 15, GEI issued 1,200 shares of common stock to Kathy Norton for $54 per share.
(2) On March 31, GEI reacquired 800 shares of common stock from Floyd Beams (GEI's founder) for $60 per share. These shares were canceled and retired upon receipt.

For the year 1981, GEI reported net income of $28,000.

Instructions

(a) How should the stockholders' equity information be reported in the GEI financial statements for the year ended December 31, 1981 (1) assuming specific identification of the shares is impossible and (2) assuming application of the FIFO method?
(b) How would your answer in part (a) have been altered if GEI had treated the reacquired shares as treasury stock carried at cost rather than retired?
(c) On December 30, 1982, GEI's Board of Directors changed the common stock from no par, no stated value to no par with a $10 stated value per share. How will the stockholders' equity section be affected if comparative financial statements are prepared at December 31, 1982? (Apply the method used in (a)(1).)

P15-3   On January 5, 1980, Citrus Products Corporation received a charter granting the right to issue 5,000 shares of $100 par value, 6% cumulative and non-participating preferred stock and 50,000 shares of $5 par value common stock. It then completed these transactions:

Jan. 11   Accepted subscriptions to 20,000 shares of common stock at $10 per share; 20% down payments accompanied the subscription.

Feb. 1   Issued Thomas J. Nessinger Corp. 2,800 shares of preferred stock for the following assets: machinery with a fair market value of $35,000; a factory building with a fair market value of $85,000; and land with an appraised value of $175,000.

Mar. 16   Other machinery, with a fair market value of $80,000 was donated to the company.

Apr. 15   Collected the balance of the subscription price on the common shares and issued the stock.

July 29   Purchased 1,200 shares of common stock at $8 per share (use cost method).

Aug. 10   Sold 1,200 of the treasury shares at $6 per share.

Aug. 26   Declared a 10% stock dividend on the common shares. The stock was selling at $6 per share on the day of the declaration.

Sept. 15   Distributed the stock dividend.

Dec. 31   Declared a $0.10 per share cash dividend on the common stock and declared the preferred dividend.

Dec. 31   Closed the Revenue and Expense Summary account. There was a $54,000 net income.

Instructions

(a) Record the journal entries for the transactions listed above.
(b) Prepare the stockholders' equity section of Citrus Products' balance sheet as of December 31, 1980.

P15-4   Transactions of Mankato Manufacturing Company are as follows:
1. The company is granted a charter that authorizes issuance of 12,000 shares of $100 par value preferred stock and 12,000 shares of common stock without par value.

2. 9,600 shares of common stock are issued to founders of the corporation for land valued by the board of directors at $336,000. The board establishes a par value of $20 a share for the common stock.
3. 6,000 shares of preferred stock are sold for cash at 105.
4. 600 shares of common stock are sold to an officer of the corporation for $40 a share.
5. 240 shares of outstanding preferred stock are purchased for cash at par.
6. 360 shares of outstanding preferred stock are purchased for cash at 98.
7. 600 shares of the outstanding common stock issued in No. 2 above are purchased at $41 a share.
8. 120 shares of repurchased preferred stock are reissued at 102.
9. 2,400 shares of preferred stock are issued at 98.
10. 300 shares of reacquired common stock are reissued for $38 a share.
11. 120 shares of the common stock sold in No. 10 above are repurchased for $35 a share.

Instructions

(a) Prepare entries in journal form to record the transactions listed above. No other transactions affecting the capital stock accounts have occurred. Treasury stock is to be entered in the Treasury Stock accounts at par.

(b) Assuming that the company has retained earnings from operations of $65,000, prepare the stockholders' equity section of its balance sheet after considering all the transactions given.

P15-5 Before Buckeye Communications Corporation engages in the treasury stock transactions listed below, its general ledger reflects, among others, the following account balances (par value of its stock is $50 per share).

Paid-in Capital in Excess of Par	Common Stock	Retained Earnings
Balance $36,000	Balance $120,000	Balance $30,000

Instructions

Record the treasury stock transactions (given below) under the two generally accepted methods of handling treasury stock; use the FIFO method for purchase-sale purposes.

(a) Bought 300 shares of treasury stock at $63 per share.
(b) Bought 150 shares of treasury stock at $67 per share.
(c) Sold 225 shares of treasury stock at $66 per share.
(d) Sold 120 shares of treasury stock at $62 per share.
(e) Retired the remaining shares in the treasury.

P15-6 The accounts shown below appear in the December 31 trial balance of the Mary Beth VanBuer Company:

Preferred stock authorized ($100 par value)	$500,000
Common stock authorized ($10 par value)	200,000
Unissued preferred stock	180,000
Unissued common stock	100,000
Subscriptions receivable, common	18,000
Subscriptions receivable, preferred	19,000
Preferred stock subscribed	30,000
Common stock subscribed	22,500
Treasury stock, preferred (700 shares at cost)	68,600
Paid-in capital (excess of amount paid in over par value of common stock)	87,500

Instructions

(a) Assuming it is reasonably assured that the subscriptions will be collected, use the above accounts to determine the following:
1. Total authorized capital stock.
2. Total unissued capital stock.
3. Total issued capital stock.
4. Capital stock subscribed.
5. Capital stock available for subscription.
6. Total stockholders' equity.

(b) What changes would occur in these six items if there is evidence that collection of the subscriptions is uncertain?

P15-7   Austermiller Company has the following owners' equity accounts at December 31, 1980:

Common stock—$100 par value, authorized 4,000 shares	$320,000
Retained earnings	200,000

Instructions

(a) Prepare entries in journal form to record the following transactions, which took place during 1980.
1. 160 shares of outstanding stock were purchased at 97. (These are to be accounted for using the cost method.)
2. A 5% cash dividend was declared.
3. The dividend declared in No. 2 above was paid.
4. The treasury shares purchased in No. 1 above were resold at 101.
5. 400 shares of outstanding stock were purchased at 103.
6. 80 shares of outstanding stock were purchased at 104 and retired.
7. 240 of the shares purchased in No. 5 above were resold at 100.

(b) Prepare the stockholders' equity section of Austermiller Company's balance sheet after giving effect to these transactions, assuming that the net income for 1980 was $24,000.

P15-8   The stockholders' equity section of Pinehurst-Denson Company's balance sheet at December 31, 1981, was as follows:

Common stock—$100 par (authorized 50,000 shares, issued and outstanding 12,000 shares)	$1,200,000
Paid-in capital in excess of par	240,000
Retained earnings	120,000
	$1,560,000

On January 2, 1982, having idle cash, the company repurchased 480 shares of its stock for $60,000. During the year it sold 120 of the reacquired shares at $135 per share, another 120 at $122.50 per share, and legally retired the remaining 240 shares.

Instructions

(a) Discuss the possible alternatives in handling these transactions.

(b) Prepare journal entries for each transaction in accordance with the method that you believe should be applied.

P15-9   The Danegeld Corporation charter authorized issuance of 10,000 shares of $100 par value common stock and 10,000 shares of $50 preferred stock. The following transactions involving the issuance of shares of stock were completed. Each transaction is independent of the others.

1. Issued a $1,000, 5% bond payable at par and gave as a bonus one share of preferred stock, which at that time was selling for $70 a share.

2. Issued 40 shares of common stock for machinery. The machinery had been appraised at $5,000; the seller's book value was $6,000. The most recent market price of the common stock is $120 a share.

3. Voted a 10% assessment on both the 1,000 shares of outstanding common and the 500 shares of outstanding preferred. The assessment was paid in full.

4. Issued 60 shares of common and 40 shares of preferred for a lump-sum amounting to $12,600. The common had been selling at $120 and the preferred at $60.

5. Issued 20 shares of common and 10 shares of preferred for furniture and fixtures. The common had a fair market value of $140 per share and the furniture and fixtures were appraised at $3,500.

Instructions

Record the transactions listed above in journal entry form.

P15-10 Galactica Corporation is a publicly-owned company whose shares are traded on a national stock exchange. At December 31, 1979, Galactica had 25,000,000 shares of $10 par value common stock authorized, of which 15,000,000 shares were issued and 14,000,000 shares were outstanding.

The stockholders' equity accounts at December 31, 1979, had the following balances:

Common stock	$150,000,000
Additional paid-in capital	80,000,000
Retained earnings	50,000,000
Treasury stock	18,000,000

During 1980, Galactica had the following transactions:

On February 1, 1980, a secondary distribution of 2,000,000 shares of $10 par value common stock was completed. The stock was sold to the public at $18 per share, net of offering costs.

On February 15, 1980, Galactica issued at $110 per share, 100,000 shares of $100 par value, 8% cumulative preferred stock.

On March 1, 1980, Galactica reacquired 20,000 shares of its common stock for $18.50 per share. Galactica uses the cost method to account for treasury stock.

On March 15, 1980, when the common stock was trading for $21 per share, a major stockholder donated 10,000 shares which are appropriately recorded as treasury stock. (Hint: use cost as a basis for donation.)

On March 31, 1980, Galactica declared a semiannual cash dividend on common stock of $0.10 per share, payable on April 30, 1980, to stockholders of record on April 10, 1980. The appropriate state law prohibits cash dividends on treasury stock.

On April 30, 1980, employees exercised 100,000 options that were granted in 1978 under a noncompensatory stock option plan. When the options were granted, each option had a preemptive right and entitled the employee to purchase one share of common stock for $20 per share. On April 30, 1980, the market price of the common stock was $20 per share. Galactica issued new shares to settle the transaction.

On May 31, 1980, when the market price of the common stock was $20 per share, Galactica declared a 5% stock dividend distributable on July 1, 1980, to stockholders of record on June 1, 1980. The appropriate state law prohibits stock dividends on treasury stock. The stock dividend is recorded using the market price.

On June 30, 1980, Galactica sold the 20,000 treasury shares reacquired on March 1, 1980, and an additional 280,000 treasury shares costing $5,600,000 that were on hand at the beginning of the year. The selling price was $25 per share.

On September 30, 1980, Galactica declared a semiannual cash dividend on common stock of $0.10 per share and the yearly dividend on preferred stock, both payable on October 30, 1980, to stockholders of record on October 10, 1980. The appropriate state law prohibits cash dividends on treasury stock.

Net income for 1980 was $25,000,000.

Instructions

Prepare a work sheet to be used to summarize, for each transaction, the changes in Galactica's stockholders' equity accounts for 1980. The columns on this work sheet should have the following headings:

Date of transaction (or beginning date)
Common stock—number of shares
Common stock—amount
Preferred stock—number of shares
Preferred stock—amount
Additional paid-in capital
Retained earnings
Treasury stock—number of shares
Treasury stock—amount

Show supporting computations in good form.

(AICPA adapted)

Stockholders' Equity: Additional Paid-in Capital and Retained Earnings

ADDITIONAL STOCKHOLDERS' EQUITY ACCOUNTS

One source of the stockholders' interest in a business—capital stock—was discussed in Chapter 15. Other sources are of a very diverse nature and require careful analysis. The following three categories normally appear as part of stockholders' equity:

1. Capital stock (legal capital)
2. Additional paid-in capital (capital in excess of par or stated value)
3. Retained earnings or deficit

The first two categories, capital stock and additional paid-in capital, comprise **contributed capital;** retained earnings represents the **earned capital** of the enterprise. The distinction between contributed capital and earned capital has a legal origin, but at present it serves the useful purpose of indicating the different sources from which the corporation has obtained its **equity capital.**

Trends in Terminology

As far back as 1941, the Committee on Terminology of the AICPA suggested discontinuance of the use of the term "surplus" in corporate accounting, particularly in financial statements. The accounting profession has recommended substitute terminology for the various types of surplus because it believes that the term "surplus" connotes to many readers of the financial statements a residue or "something not needed."

The use of the term is gradually decreasing. "Retained earnings" or some modification of this term has generally replaced the term "earned surplus." Apparently, widely accepted terminology to replace "capital surplus" and "paid-in surplus" has not yet been found, inasmuch as these two terms still appear in many financial statements. "Capital in excess of par (or stated value)" or "additional paid-in capital" are gaining favor over the term "paid-in surplus." But, no term having the broad connotation of "capital surplus" (all owners' equity exclusive of capital stock and retained earnings) has emerged.[1]

The persistent use of these "surplus" terms by many leading corporations can be attributed to the numerous state incorporation acts that still contain antiquated terminology in their provisions regulating the issuance of stock and other equity transactions.

The AICPA recommendations relating to changes in terminology have been directed primarily to the balance sheet presentation of stockholders' equity so that words or phrases used will more accurately and more adequately describe the nature of the amounts shown. The term paid-in surplus is still used by many concerns in their accounts and, unfortunately, it appears frequently in the professional literature.

Additional Paid-in Capital

Additional paid-in capital is derived from a considerable variety of transactions. The basic transactions affecting additional paid-in capital are expressed in T-account form below.

Additional Paid-in Capital	
1. Discounts on capital stock issued.	1. Premiums on capital stock issued.
2. Sale of treasury stock below cost.	2. Sale of treasury stock above cost.
3. Absorption of a deficit in a recapitalization (quasi reorganization).	3. Additional capital arising in recapitalizations or revisions in the capital structure (quasi reorganizations).
4. Distribution of a liquidating dividend.	4. Additional assessments on stockholders.
	5. Conversion of convertible bonds or preferred stock.

In balance sheet presentation, only one amount need appear, Additional Paid-in Capital, to summarize all of these possible transactions. A subsidiary ledger or separate general ledger accounts may be kept of the different sources of additional paid-in capital because certain state laws permit dividend distributions out of additional paid-in capital that occurs from specific transactions.

If transactions in treasury stock result in a decrease in additional paid-in capital

---

[1]*Accounting Trends and Techniques—1978* reports that the use of the term surplus is gradually declining. In its survey of 600 companies, 95 out of 529 companies reporting additional paid-in capital used either "capital surplus" or "paid-in surplus" for the caption. Only six companies used the term "earned surplus," while 465 used the caption "retained earnings."

and no additional paid-in capital exists against which additional decreases may be charged, retained earnings should absorb any additional charges.

No operating gains or losses or extraordinary gains and losses may be debited or credited to additional paid-in capital. The profession has long discouraged by-passing net income and retained earnings through the write-off of losses (e.g., write-offs of bond discount, goodwill, or obsolete plant and equipment) to additional paid-in capital accounts or other capital accounts.

Other Capital Items

Two other items that may be reported in the stockholders' equity section as a form of additional capital are **donated capital** and **revaluation or unrealized appreciation capital.** Donated capital results from donations to the company by stockholders, creditors, and so on. Revaluation capital results from the write-up or write-down of assets from cost. Because of adherence to the cost principle and the concept of conservatism, assets are generally not written up from cost. (The write-up of discovery value is one exception.) Therefore, revaluation or unrealized appreciation capital having a credit balance rarely appears on financial statements.

Because donated capital and revaluation capital (write-ups or write-downs not reported in the income statement) are such unique items, they warrant special attention when they occur. For this reason, the following classifications should be set out separately as part of stockholders' equity:

> Capital Stock
> Additional Paid-in Capital
> Donated Capital
> Revaluation Capital

One recent development in asset revaluation has resulted in a new item for inclusion at the bottom of the stockholders' equity section. It is, however, an asset write-down rather than a write-up. **FASB Statement No. 12** ("Accounting for Certain Marketable Securities") requires that the "net unrealized loss on noncurrent marketable equity securities" be reported separately as a deduction (contra item) from stockholders' equity (see Chapter 18 for a more complete discussion of this topic).

Retained Earnings

The basic source of retained earnings consists of income from operations. Stockholders assume the greatest risk in enterprise operations and stand any losses or share in any profits resulting from enterprise activities. Thus any income not distributed among the stockholders becomes additional stockholders' equity. Income from operations, if operations are interpreted in the broad sense, includes a considerable variety of gains. The main operation of the enterprise, such as manufacturing and selling a given product, plus any ancillary activities, such as disposing of scrap or renting out unused space, plus the results of extraordinary and unusual items all give rise to net income that increases Retained Earnings. The more common items that either increase or decrease retained earnings are expressed in T-account form below.

Retained Earnings	
1. Net loss 2. Prior period adjustments, error corrections, and changes in accounting principle 3. Cash dividends 4. Stock dividends 5. Property dividends 6. Treasury stock transactions	1. Net income 2. Prior period adjustments, error corrections, and changes in accounting principle

The reader may recall that Chapter 4 pointed out that the results of unusual and extraordinary transactions should be placed in the income statement, not the retained earnings statement, under the all-inclusive concept of income reporting. Prior period adjustments and error corrections should be handled as adjustments to beginning retained earnings, bypassing completely the current income statement.

DIVIDEND POLICY

As soon as retained earnings is recorded, two alternatives exist: (1) the credit balance can be reduced by a distribution of assets (a dividend) to the stockholders, or (2) it can be left intact and the offsetting assets used in the operations of the business. Further decisions are required under each of these alternatives, but the original decision must be whether to distribute the increase in net assets generated by profitable operations (the retained earnings) in the form of dividends to the stockholders or to retain the net assets (earnings) in the enterprise and use them for business purposes.

Very few companies pay dividends in amounts equal to their retained earnings legally available for dividends. The reasons for this are varied and include at least the following:

1. Agreements (bond covenants) with specific creditors to retain all or a portion of the earnings (in the form of assets) to build up additional protection against possible loss for those creditors.
2. Requirements of some state corporation laws requiring that earnings equivalent to the cost of treasury shares purchased be restricted against dividend declarations.
3. Desire to retain in the business the assets that would otherwise be paid out as dividends. This is sometimes called internal financing, reinvesting earnings, or "plowing" the profits back into the business.
4. Desire to smooth out dividend payments from year to year by accumulating earnings in good years and using such accumulated earnings as a basis for dividends in bad years.
5. Desire to build up a cushion or buffer against possible losses or errors in the calculation of profits.

No particular explanation is required for any of these except the second. The laws of most states require that the corporation's stated capital (legal capital) be restricted from distribution to stockholders so that it may serve as a protection against loss to creditors. If the corporation buys its own outstanding stock, it has reduced its stated capital and distributed assets to stockholders. If this were permitted, the corporation could, by purchasing treasury stock at any price desired, return to the stockholders their investments and leave creditors with little or no protection against loss.

If a company is considering declaring a dividend, two preliminary questions must be asked:

1. Is the condition of the corporation such that a dividend is permissible legally?
2. Is the condition of the corporation such that a dividend is economically sound?

Legality of Dividend

The legality of a dividend can be determined only by reviewing the applicable state law. Even then the law may not be clear, and eventually a decision may require recourse to courts of law. Frequently, the company's lawyer may provide an opinion on a dividend problem to reduce the possibility of misinterpretation of the law. For most general dividend declarations the following summary is adequate:

1. Retained earnings, unless legally encumbered in some manner, is usually the correct basis for dividend distributions.
2. Revaluation capital is seldom the correct basis for dividends (except possibly stock dividends).
3. In some states, additional paid-in capital and donated capital may be used for dividends, although such dividends may be limited to preferred stock.
4. Deficits in retained earnings and debits in paid-in capital accounts must be restored before payment of any dividends.
5. Dividends in most states may not reduce retained earnings below the cost of treasury stock held.

Financial Condition and Dividend Distributions

Legally, about all that is required to distribute a dividend is that the corporation have a credit balance in retained earnings. From the standpoint of good management attention must be given to other conditions as well. If we assume an extreme situation such as the following, these considerations become more apparent.

BALANCE SHEET			
Plant assets	$500,000	Capital stock	$400,000
		Retained earnings	100,000
	$500,000		$500,000

This company has a retained earnings credit balance and, unless it is encumbered, legally can declare a dividend of $100,000. As all its assets are plant assets and used in operations, payment of a cash dividend of $100,000 requires the sale of plant assets or borrowing.

If we assume a balance sheet showing current assets, there is still the further question of whether those assets are needed for other purposes.

BALANCE SHEET				
Cash	$100,000	Current liabilities		$ 40,000
Plant assets	440,000	Capital stock	$400,000	
		Retained earnings	100,000	500,000
	$540,000			$540,000

The existence of current liabilities implies very strongly that some of the cash is needed to meet current debts as they mature. Furthermore, day-by-day cash requirements for payrolls and other expenditures not included in current liabilities will require additional cash.

Thus, before a dividend is declared, the question of **availability of funds to pay the dividend must be considered.** Availability of funds includes more than possession of a cash balance sufficiently large to pay the dividend. Other demands for cash such as those considered in preparing a cash forecast must be investigated, and a dividend should not be paid unless both the present and future financial position appear to warrant the distribution. In regard to dividends there is an important relationship between retained earnings and current assets. No corporate director should ever recommend a dividend based on the existence of retained earnings alone. The present and expected future current position must also be considered.

Types of Dividends

Dividend distributions are based either on accumulated profits, that is, retained earnings, or on some other capital item such as donated or additional capital paid-in. The natural expectation of any stockholder who receives a dividend is that the corporation has operated successfully and that the stockholder is receiving a share of its profits. Any dividend not based on retained earnings should be adequately described in the accompanying message to the stockholders so that there will be no misunderstanding of its source. Dividends are of the following types:

1. Cash dividends.
2. Property dividends.
3. Scrip dividends.
4. Liquidating dividends.
5. Stock dividends.

Dividends are commonly paid in cash but occasionally in stock, scrip, or some other asset. **Any dividend other than a stock dividend reduces the stockholders' equity in the corporation,** because a portion of the equity is reduced either through an immediate or promised future distribution of assets. When a stock dividend is declared, the corporation does not pay out assets or incur a liability. It merely issues additional shares of stock to each stockholder. The individual stockholder receives nothing more than additional shares of stock.

Cash Dividends   The board of directors votes on the declaration of dividends, and if the resolution is properly approved, the dividend is declared. It cannot be paid immediately, however, because transfers of stock from one holder to another requires that a current list of stockholders be prepared. For this reason the dividend resolution generally allows a short period of time before payment. A resolution approved at the January 10 (date of declaration) meeting of the board of directors might be declared payable February 5 (date of payment) to all stockholders of record January 25 (date of record).

The period from January 10 to January 25 gives time for any transfers in process to be completed and registered with the transfer agent. The time from January 25 to February 5 provides an opportunity for the transfer agent or accounting department, depending on who does this work, to prepare a list of stockholders as of January 25 and to prepare and mail dividend checks.

A declared dividend, except a stock dividend, is a liability and, because payment is generally required very soon, it is usually a current liability. The following entries are required to record the declaration and payment of an ordinary dividend payable in cash.

At date of declaration:

Retained Earnings (Cash Dividends Declared)	5,000	
Dividends Payable		5,000

At date of record:

No entry

At date of payment:

Dividends Payable	5,000	
Cash		5,000

At the time of declaration an account called Cash Dividends Declared might be debited instead of Retained Earnings, to set up in the ledger an account that shows the amount of dividends declared during the year. This account is then closed to Retained Earnings at the end of the year.

Dividends are usually declared either as a certain percent of par, such as a 6% dividend on preferred stock, or as an amount per share, such as $0.60 per share on no-par common stock. In the first case, the rate is multiplied by the par value of the outstanding shares to get the total dividend; in the second, the amount per share is multiplied by the number of shares outstanding. **Dividends should not be declared and paid on treasury stock.**

Dividend policies of boards of directors vary among corporations. Some older, well-established firms take pride in a long, unbroken string of quarterly dividend payments and would lower or pass the dividend only if forced to do so by a sustained decline in earnings or a critical shortage of cash. The percentage of annual earnings distributed as cash dividends ("payout ratio") is somewhat dependent on the stability and trend of earnings, with 25 to 75% of earnings being paid out by many well-established corporations. "Growth companies," on the other hand, pay little or no cash dividends because their policy is to expand as rapidly as internal and external financing permit.

Property Dividends   Dividends payable in assets of the corporation other than cash are called property dividends or dividends in kind. Property dividends may be in whatever form the board of directors designates, for example, merchandise, real estate, or investments. Because of the obvious difficulties of divisibility of units and delivery to the stockholders, the usual property dividend is in the form of securities of other companies that the distributing corporation held as an investment.

A property dividend is a nonreciprocal transfer[2] **of nonmonetary assets between an enterprise and its owners.** Prior to the issuance of **APB Opinion No. 29** in 1973, the accounting for such transfers was based on the carrying amount (book value) of the nonmonetary assets transferred. This practice was based on the rationale that there is no sale or arm's-length transaction on which to base a gain or loss and that only this method is consistent with the historical cost basis of accounting. The profession's current position is quite clear on this matter:

> A transfer of a nonmonetary asset to a stockholder or to another entity in a nonreciprocal transfer should be recorded at the fair value of the asset transferred, and a gain or loss should be recognized on the disposition of the asset.[3]

The **fair value** of the nonmonetary asset distributed is measured by the amount that would be realizable in an outright sale at or near the time of the distribution. Such amount should be determined by referring to estimated realizable values in cash transactions of the same or similar assets, quoted market prices, independent appraisals, and other available evidence.

The distribution of a nonmonetary asset as an ordinary dividend (not as a liquidating dividend or in a spin-off or reorganization) may be regarded as equivalent to an exchange with owners and, therefore, recorded at the fair value of the nonmonetary asset distributed. The failure to recognize the fair value of nonmonetary assets transferred may both misstate the dividend and fail to recognize gains and losses on nonmonetary assets that have already been earned or incurred by the enterprise. Recording the dividend at fair value permits future comparisons of dividend rates and if cash must be distributed to stockholders in place of the nonmonetary asset, determination of the amount to be distributed is simplified. Recording fair value is especially appropriate when property dividends are given to a class of stock other than common stock. For example, preferred stock should not profit by property dividends, the market value of which exceeds the fixed dividend rate.

When the property dividend is declared, the corporation should restate at fair value the property to be distributed, recognizing any gain or loss as the difference between the fair value and carrying value of the property at date of declaration. The declared dividend may then be recorded as a debit to Retained Earnings (or Property Dividends Declared) and a credit to Property Dividends Payable at an amount equal to the fair value of the property to be distributed. Upon distribution of the dividend, Property Dividends Payable is debited, and the account containing the distributed asset (restated at fair value) is credited.

For example, Melanie, Inc., transferred some of its investments in marketable securities costing $1,250,000 to shareholders by declaring a property dividend on December 28, 1980, to be distributed on January 30, 1981, to stockholders of record

---

[2]A nonreciprocal transfer is a transfer of assets or services in one direction, either from an enterprise to its owners or another entity or from owners or another entity to the enterprise.

[3]"Accounting for Nonmonetary Transaction," *Opinions of the Accounting Principles Board No. 29* (New York: AICPA, 1973), par. 18.

on January 15, 1981. At the date of declaration the securities have a market value of $2,000,000. The entries are as below.

December 28, 1980 (Date of declaration)

Investments in Securities	750,000	
Gain on Appreciation of Securities		750,000
Retained Earnings (Property Dividends Declared)	2,000,000	
Property Dividends Payable		2,000,000

January 30, 1981 (Date of distribution)

Property Dividends Payable	2,000,000	
Investments in Securities		2,000,000

Scrip Dividend   A dividend payable in scrip means that the corporation, instead of paying the dividend now, has elected to pay it at some later date. **The scrip issued to stockholders as a dividend is merely a special form of note payable.** Scrip dividends may be declared when the corporation has a sufficient retained earnings balance but is short of cash. The recipient of the scrip dividend may hold it until the due date, if one is specified, and collect the dividend, or possibly, may discount it to obtain immediate cash. When a scrip dividend is declared, the corporation debits Retained Earnings (or Scrip Dividend Declared) and credits Scrip Dividend Payable, reporting the payable as a liability on the balance sheet. Upon payment, Scrip Dividend Payable is debited and Cash credited. If the scrip bears interest, the interest portion of the cash payment should be debited to Interest Expense and not treated as part of the dividend.

Liquidating Dividend   Examples exist of corporations that have used paid-in capital in the early years as a basis for dividends. Without proper disclosure of this fact, stockholders may believe the corporation has been operating at a profit. A further result could be subsequent sale of additional shares at a higher price than is warranted. This type of deception, intentional or unintentional, can be avoided by requiring that a clear statement of the basis of every dividend accompany the dividend check.

Dividends based on other than retained earnings are sometimes described as liquidating dividends, thus implying that they are a return of the stockholder's investment rather than of profits. In fact, the distribution may be based on capital that resulted from donations by outsiders or other stockholders and not be a return of the given stockholder's contribution. But, in a more general sense, **any dividend not based on earnings must be a reduction of corporate capital and, to that extent, it is a liquidating dividend.** We noted in an earlier chapter that companies in the extractive industries may pay dividends equal to the total of accumulated income and depletion. The portion of these dividends in excess of accumulated income represents a return of part of the stockholder's investment.

For example, McChesney Mines, Inc., recently issued a "dividend" to its common stockholders of $100,000. The cash dividend announcement noted that $70,000 should be considered income and the remainder a return of capital. The entries are:

At date of declaration:

Retained Earnings	70,000	
Additional Paid-in Capital	30,000	
Dividend Payable		100,000

At date of payment:

Dividend Payable	100,000	
Cash		100,000

According to **Opinion No. 29,** accounting for the distribution of nonmonetary assets to owners of an enterprise in a spin-off or other form of reorganization or liquidation should be based on the **book value** (after reduction, if appropriate, for an indicated impairment of value) of the nonmonetary assets distributed.[4]

Stock Dividends[5]   If the management wishes to capitalize part of the earnings, and thus retain earnings in the business on a permanent basis, it may issue a stock dividend. In this case, **no assets are distributed,** and each stockholder has exactly the same proportionate interest in the corporation and the same total book value after the stock dividend as before the dividend was declared. Of course, the book value per share is lower because an increased number of shares is held.

Accountants do not agree about the proper entries to be made at the time of a stock dividend. Some believe that the par value of the stock issued as a dividend should be transferred from retained earnings to capital stock. Others believe that the fair value of the stock issued should be transferred from retained earnings to capital stock and additional paid-in capital. Ordinarily fair value is measured by the market price of the stock on the dividend date of declaration.

According to the Committee on Accounting Procedure of the AICPA, the **fair value** of the stock issued should be transferred from retained earnings.[6] This method of handling stock dividends is justified on the grounds that "many recipients of stock dividends look upon them as distributions of corporate earnings and usually in an amount equivalent to the fair value of the additional shares received."[7] We do not consider this a convincing argument. It is generally agreed that stock dividends are not income to the recipients, and, therefore, sound accounting should not recommend procedures simply because some recipients think they are income. Nonetheless, **the position of the Committee on Accounting Procedure was supported by the APB and is the generally accepted accounting procedure for recording stock dividends.**[8]

The case against treating an ordinary stock dividend as income is supported under either an entity or proprietory assumption regarding the business enterprise. If the corporation is considered an entity separate from the stockholders, the in-

[4]"Accounting for Nonmonetary Transaction," *op. cit.*, par. 23.

[5]*Accounting Trends and Techniques—1978* reported that of 600 companies surveyed, 39 issued stock dividends.

[6]American Institute of Certified Public Accountants, *Accounting Research and Terminology Bulletins,* No. 43 (New York: AICPA, 1961), Ch. 7, par. 10.

[7]*Ibid.,* par. 10.

[8]A recent study has concluded that *small* stock dividends do not always produce significant amounts of extra value on the date after issuance (ex date) and that *large* stock dividends almost always fail to generate extra value on the ex-dividend date. Taylor W. Foster III and Don Vickrey, "The Information Content of Stock Dividend Announcements," *The Accounting Review,* Vol. LIII, No. 2, April, 1978, pp. 360–370.

come of the corporation is corporate income and not income to the stockholders, although the equity of the stockholders in the corporation increases. This position argues that a dividend is not income to the recipients until it is realized by them as a result of a division or severance of corporate assets. The stock dividend merely distributes the "recipient's" equity over a larger number of shares. Under this interpretation, selling the stock received as a dividend has the effect of reducing the recipient's proportionate share of the corporation's equity. Under a "proprietary" assumption, income of the corporation is considered income to the owners, and, hence, a stock dividend represents only a reclassification of equity, inasmuch as there is no change in total proprietorship.

Entries for Stock Dividends   Assume that a corporation has outstanding 1,000 shares of $100 par-value capital stock, and a retained earnings balance of $50,000. If it declares a 10% stock dividend, it issues 100 additional shares of stock to present stockholders. If it is assumed that the fair value of the stock at the time of the stock dividend was $130 per share, the entry is:

Retained Earnings (Stock Dividend Declared)	13,000	
Common Stock Dividend Distributable		10,000
Paid-in Capital in Excess of Par		3,000

If a balance sheet is prepared between the dates of declaration and distribution, the common stock dividend distributable should be shown in the stockholders' equity section as an addition to capital stock (whereas cash or property dividends payable are shown as current liabilities).

When the stock is issued the entry is:

Common Stock Dividend Distributable	10,000	
Common Stock		10,000

No matter what the fair value is at the time of the stock dividend, each stockholder retains the same proportionate interest in the corporation.

Note from the detail on page 689 that the total net worth has not changed as a result of the stock dividend, and that each stockholder owns the same proportion of the total shares outstanding after as before the stock dividend.

Stock Split and Stock Dividend Differentiated   If a company operates successfully over a long period of time, so that a sizable balance in retained earnings has accumulated, the market value of its outstanding shares may increase considerably. Stock that was issued at prices less than $50 a share not infrequently attains a market value in excess of $200 a share. The higher the market price of a stock, the less readily it can be traded in by most people. The managements of many corporations believe that for better public relations, wider ownership of the corporation stock is desirable. Therefore, they wish to have a market price sufficiently low to be within range of the majority of potential investors. To reduce the market value of shares, the common device of a **stock split** is employed. For example in 1979 when IBM's stock was selling at $304 a share, the company split its common stock four for one. The day after IBM's split (involving 583,268,480 shares) was effective, the stock sold for $76 a share, exactly one quarter of its price per share before the split. IBM's intent was to obtain a wider distribution of its stock by improving the marketability of the shares.

Before dividend:

Capital stock, 1,000 shares of $100 par	$100,000
Retained earnings	50,000
Total stockholders' equity	$150,000

Stockholders' interests:

A 400 shares, 40% interest, book value	$ 60,000
B 500 shares, 50% interest, book value	75,000
C 100 shares, 10% interest, book value	15,000
	$150,000

After declaration but before payment of 10% stock dividend:

If fair value ($130) is used as basis for entry

Capital stock, 1,000 shares at $100 par	$100,000
Common stock distributable 100 shares at $100 par	10,000
Paid-in capital in excess of par	3,000
Retained earnings, $50,000 − $13,000	37,000
Total stockholders' equity	$150,000

After declaration and payment of 10% stock dividend:

If fair value ($130) is used as basis for entry

Capital stock 1,100 shares at $100 par	$110,000
Paid-in capital in excess of par	3,000
Retained earnings, $50,000 − $13,000	37,000
Total stockholders' equity	$150,000

Stockholders' interest:

A 440 shares, 40% interest, book value	$ 60,000
B 550 shares, 50% interest, book value	75,000
C 110 shares, 10% interest, book value	15,000
	$150,000

From a legal standpoint a stock split is distinguished from a stock dividend, because a stock split results in an increase or decrease in the number of shares outstanding and a corresponding decrease or increase in the par or stated value per share. A stock dividend, although it results in an increase in the number of shares outstanding, does not result in a decrease in the par value of the shares and thus it increases the total par value of outstanding shares. From an accounting standpoint, no entry is recorded for a stock split; a memorandum note, however, is made to indicate that the par value of the shares has changed.

The reasons for issuing a **stock dividend** are numerous and varied. Stock dividends can be more of a publicity gesture, because they are considered by many as dividends and, consequently, the corporation is not criticized for retention of profits. In addition, the corporation may simply wish to retain profits in the business by capitalizing a part of retained earnings. In such a situation, a transfer is made on declaration of a stock dividend from earned capital to contributed or permanent capital.

A stock dividend, like a stock split, also may be used to increase the marketability of the stock, although marketability is often a secondary consideration. If the stock dividend is so large that the principal consideration appears to be a desire to reduce the price of the stock, the action results in a stock split, regardless of the form it may take. The Committee on Accounting Procedure states that **whenever additional shares are issued for the purpose of reducing the unit market price, then the distribution more closely resembles a stock split than a stock dividend. This effect usually results only if the number of shares issued is more than 20 or 25% of the number of shares previously outstanding.**[9] The Committee recommends that such a distribution not be called a stock dividend, but it might properly be called "a split-up effected in the form of a dividend" or "stock split." Also, in this case the par value of the outstanding shares would not be altered, and the transfer from retained earnings need be only in the amount required by statute. Ordinarily this means a transfer from retained earnings to capital stock for the amount of the par value of the stock issued.

To illustrate, on December 18, 1980, Rockland Steel, Inc., declares a 30% stock dividend, payable December 29, 1980. At present 100,000 shares, par value $100, are outstanding and at the date of declaration, the stock had a fair market value of $200 per share.

The entries are:

At date of declaration:

Retained Earnings	3,000,000	
Common Stock Dividend Distributable		3,000,00

(Computation: 100,000 shares	30,000 Additional shares
× 30%	× $100 Par value
30,000	$3,000,000)

At date of payment:

Common Stock Dividend Distributable	3,000,000	
Common Stock		3,000,000

Illustrations of the Effects of Dividend Preferences

The examples given below illustrate the effect of some provisions on dividend distributions to common and preferred stockholders. If, in a given year, $50,000 is to be distributed as cash dividends, outstanding common stock has a par value of $400,000, and 6% preferred stock has a par value of $100,000, dividends would be distributed to each class as shown below, under each of the assumptions given.

(1) If the preferred stock is noncumulative, nonparticipating:

	Preferred	Common	Total
6% of $100,000	$6,000		$ 6,000
The remainder to common		$44,000	44,000
Totals	$6,000	$44,000	$50,000

---

[9] *Accounting Research and Terminology Bulletin No. 43, par. 13.*

(2) If the preferred stock is cumulative and nonparticipating, and dividends were not paid on the preferred stock in the preceding two years:

	Preferred	Common	Total
Dividends in arrears, 6% of $100,000 for two years	$12,000		$12,000
Current year's dividend, 6% of $100,000	6,000		6,000
The remainder to common		$32,000	32,000
Totals	$18,000	$32,000	$50,000

(3) If the preferred stock is noncumulative and is fully participating:

	Preferred	Common	Total
Current year's dividend, 6%	$ 6,000	$24,000	$30,000
Participating dividend of 4%	4,000	16,000	20,000
Totals	$10,000	$40,000	$50,000

The participating dividend was determined as follows:

Current year's dividend: Preferred, 6% of $100,000 = $ 6,000 Common, 6% of $400,000 = 24,000	$ 30,000
Amount available for participation ($50,000 − $30,000)	$ 20,000
Par value of stock that is to participate ($100,000 + $400,000)	$500,000
Rate of participation ($20,000 ÷ $500,000)	4%
Participating dividend: Preferred, 4% of $100,000 Common, 4% of $400,000	$ 4,000 16,000
	$ 20,000

(4) If the preferred stock is cumulative and is fully participating, and if dividends were not paid on the preferred stock in the preceding two years:

	Preferred	Common	Total
Dividends in arrears, 6% of $100,000 for two years	$12,000		$12,000
Current year's dividend, 6%	6,000	$24,000	30,000
Participating dividend, 1.6% ($8,000 ÷ $500,000)	1,600	6,400	8,000
Totals	$19,600	$30,400	$50,000

APPROPRIATIONS OF RETAINED EARNINGS

The act of appropriating retained earnings is a policy matter requiring approval by the board of directors. As soon as the action is taken by the board, the accounting department records the appropriation as approved. According to **FASB Statement No. 5,** the appropriation of retained earnings is acceptable practice, "provided that it is shown within the stockholders' equity section of the balance sheet and is clearly identified as an appropriation of retained earnings."[10]

Appropriations of retained earnings are regarded as nothing more than segregations of retained earnings, temporarily or perhaps even permanently established for a given purpose. When the appropriation is no longer necessary, either because the loss has accrued or because it no longer appears as a possibility, the appropriation should be returned to retained earnings. In accordance with **FASB Statement No. 5,** "costs or losses shall not be charged to an appropriation of retained earnings, and no part of the appropriation shall be transferred to income."[11]

Any improper use of such appropriations or failure to disclose properly their nature calls for comment by the independent accountant even though the retained earnings appropriation is basically a management problem.

Reasons for Retained Earnings Appropriations

Various reasons are advanced for appropriation of retained earnings. These include:

1. **Legal restrictions.** As indicated earlier, some state laws prohibit the purchase of treasury stock by the corporation unless earnings available for dividends are present. They then restrict the retained earnings in an amount equal to the cost of any treasury stock acquired. Such laws actually require that stated capital be maintained by requiring that earnings be retained to substitute for capital stock temporarily acquired as treasury stock.

2. **Contractual restrictions.** Bond indentures frequently contain a requirement that retained earnings in specified amounts be appropriated each year during the life of bonds. The appropriation created under such a provision is commonly called Appropriation for Sinking Fund or Appropriation for Bonded Indebtedness.

3. **Existence of possible or expected loss.** Some companies establish Appropriations for Anticipated Future Inventory Declines to reflect expected losses should a general decline in prices occur. Similar appropriations might be established for estimated losses due to lawsuits, unfavorable contractual obligations, and other contingencies.

4. **Protection of working capital position.** The board of directors may authorize the creation of an "Appropriation for Working Capital" out of retained earnings in order to indicate that the amount specified is not available for dividends because it is desirable to maintain a strong current position. Another example involves a decision made to finance a building program by internal financing. An "Appropriation for Plant Expansion" is created to indicate that retained earnings in the amount appropriated will not be considered by the directors as available for dividends.

Some corporations establish appropriations for general contingencies, or appropriate retained earnings for unspecified purposes. The real reason for the restriction may be any of those given above. The essence of the action is that the board

---

[10]"Accounting for Contingencies," *Statement of Financial Accounting Standards No. 5* (Stamford, Conn.: FASB, March, 1975), par. 15.

[11]*Ibid.,* par. 15.

of directors desires to reduce the amount of retained earnings apparently available for dividends without explaining to the stockholders exactly why. In some cases this is justified by statutory or contractual restrictions. In other cases no adequate explanation for such actions is possible. The FASB does not encourage the establishment of general or unspecified appropriations.

Recording Appropriations of Retained Earnings

As soon as the board of directors has approved an appropriation of retained earnings, it becomes necessary to record the appropriation in the accounts. First, the unappropriated retained earnings must be reduced by the amount of the appropriation and, second, a new account must be established to receive the amount transferred. If the appropriation merely augments a previously established segregation, the account already in use should receive the credit. The appropriation is recorded as a debit to Retained Earnings and a credit to an appropriately named account that itself is really a subdivision of retained earnings. For example:

(a) An Appropriation for Plant Expansion is to be created by transfer from Retained Earnings of $40,000 a year for 10 years. The entry for each year would be:

Retained Earnings	40,000	
Appropriation for Plant Expansion		40,000

(b) At the end of 10 years the appropriation would have a balance of $400,000. If we assume that the expansion plan has been completed, the appropriation is no longer required and can be returned to retained earnings.

Appropriation for Plant Expansion	400,000	
Retained Earnings		400,000

Return of such an appropriation to retained earnings has the effect of increasing unappropriated retained earnings considerably without affecting the assets or current position. In effect, over the 10 years the company has expanded by reinvesting earnings.

Formerly, the term "reserve" was used in accounting to describe such diverse items as accumulated depreciation, accumulated allowances for doubtful accounts, current liabilities, and segregations of retained earnings. The AICPA as early as 1941 recommended that use of the word "reserve" be confined to appropriations of retained earnings if it is to be used at all. The general adoption of this recommendation would help to clear up one of the most troublesome terminology areas in accounting.[12]

Disclosure of Restrictions on Retained Earnings

In many corporations restrictions on retained earnings or dividends exist, but no appropriation resulting in a debit to Retained Earnings and a credit to an appropriation account is recorded. In such cases the accountant must weigh the significance of the restriction, and decide whether to disclose it in some manner other than through debits and credits in the equity accounts. Some bond indentures and loan

[12]*Accounting Trends and Techniques—1978* indicates that of its list of 600 selected companies, 139 continued incorrectly to use the term reserve in the asset or liability section of the balance sheet.

agreements make appropriations of retained earnings mandatory. In recent years, however, the use of appropriations to give effect to retained earnings restrictions has declined. In its 1950 survey of the annual report of 600 companies, the AICPA noted approximately 100 appropriations of various types; a similar survey in 1971 revealed that only 10 balance sheets contained such appropriations; and, in 1975 the AICPA ceased tabulating this bit of data.

Most restrictions for which journal entries are not made are of a contractual nature resulting from agreements with creditors and are best disclosed by footnote. Parenthetical notations are sometimes used, but restrictions imposed by bond indentures and loan agreements commonly require an extended explanation; footnotes provide a medium for more complete explanations and free the financial statements from abbreviated notations. The footnote disclosure should reveal the source of the restriction, pertinent provisions, and the amount of retained earnings subject to restriction, or the amount not so restricted. The following examples from annual reports illustrate some of the various forms of footnote disclosures relating to restrictions on retained earnings and dividends.

The BF Goodrich Company

NOTES TO FINANCIAL STATEMENTS

Income Retained in the Business and Dividend Restrictions—Dividends on outstanding Series Preferred Stock must be declared and paid or set apart for payment, and funds required for sinking fund payments on the Series Preferred Stock must be paid or set apart for payment, before any dividends may be paid or set apart for payment on the Common Stock.

Agreements pertaining to certain of the Company's funded debt include, among other things, limitations on the payments of cash dividends on capital stock of the Company and amounts that can be expended to acquire or retire capital stock of the Company. Under the most restrictive of these agreements, income retained in the business in the amount of $124,394,000 was free from such limitations at December 31, 1977.

The May Department Stores Company (Jan)

NOTES TO CONSOLIDATED FINANCIAL STATEMENTS

Note 4 (in part): Long-Term Debt—Under the most restrictive covenants of the various debt agreements with all of which the Company was in compliance: 1) stockholders' investment must exceed $261,259,000; 2) accumulated earnings retained in the business of approximately $280,522,000 at January 28, 1978, are subject to dividend restrictions; 3) additional long-term borrowing by the Company and its subsidiaries (excluding designated finance and real estate subsidiaries) is limited to approximately $55,861,000 at January 28, 1978; 4) working capital must be at least $120,000,000 for the company and its subsidiaries (excluding designated finance and real estate subsidiaries); and 5) rentals under long-term leases are limited to 2% of net retail sales.

As noted in the illustrations above, restrictions may be based on the retention of a certain amount of retained earnings, on the corporation's ability to observe certain working capital requirements, upon additional borrowing, and on other considerations. When there is more than one type of restriction, disclosure of the amount of retained earnings, so restricted, may be based on the most restrictive covenants likely to be effective in the immediate future. This is sufficient because restrictions seldom, if ever, pyramid in amount.

Appropriations or Disclosures for Contingencies and for Self-Insurance

A **contingency** is defined as an existing condition, situation, or set of circumstances involving uncertainty as to possible gain or loss to an enterprise that will ultimately be resolved when one or more future events occur or fail to occur.[13]

At its discretion, the board of directors of a corporation may give recognition to possible future losses by directing that a portion of retained earnings be restricted, or that an appropriation of retained earnings be made for a specific amount in the accounts. Disclosing the existence of contingencies in the notes to the financial statements is more common than appropriating a specific portion of retained earnings.[14] Shown below is an example of one taken from a 1977 annual report.

Wheeling-Pittsburgh Steel Corporation

NOTES TO FINANCIAL STATEMENTS
Note G (in part): Commitments and Contingencies—On December 6, 1977, coal mines owned in whole or in part by the Corporation discontinued operations due to the United Mine Workers of America strike, which has not yet been settled.

Although the Corporation's steel-mining operations have not been curtailed as of this date due to the strike, the strike has adversely affected profits and will continue to have an adverse effect. Management believes there are adequate coal and coke supplies to maintain steel-making operations through mid-March, 1978.

Utility companies supplying electricity to the Corporation have indicated that they may curtail electricity supplied and/or increase the price of electricity if their coal supplies continue to liquidate. An extended period of curtailment and/or increased electricity cost would adversely affect the Corporation's operations, employment and profitability.

A company may insure against many contingencies such as fire, flood, storm, and accident by taking out insurance policies and paying premiums to insurance companies. But some contingencies are not insurable or the rates are prohibitive (e.g., earthquakes and riots). Some businesses, even though insurance is available, may adopt a policy of **self-insurance.**[15] Self-insurance appears especially valid when a company's physical or operating characteristics permit application of the law of large numbers as utilized by insurance companies. Whenever the risk of loss can be spread over a large number of possible loss events that individually would be small in relation to the total potential loss, self-insurance is a temptation. It is based on the belief that the losses will be less over an extended period of time than the premiums that would be paid to insure against such losses, that is, the company avoids the insurance company's overhead costs including the insurance agent's commission. Examples of such situations are an airline with hundreds of planes always in different locations, or a grocery chain with hundreds of stores scattered

---

[13]"Accounting for Contingencies," *op. cit.,* par. 1.

[14]*Accounting Trends and Techniques—1978* indicates just how common the disclosure of contingencies is: of the 600 companies surveyed, 690 loss contingency disclosures of varying types were reported, a total of 330 devoted to litigation alone.

[15]The American Management Association advertises its popular 2½-day course on "Self-insurance and Risk Retention" (offered several times a year) as follows: "There comes a point where sky-high insurance rates no longer make sense. The dollars you're investing in premiums could be building your corporate assets. Find out how more and more companies are using self-insurance to cut down premium costs."

geographically. For instance, Shell Oil Company decided in 1971 that it was paying a large amount for insurance while incurring few losses. Therefore, it decided against insuring its offshore drilling rigs and many of its onshore facilities as well; instead, it set up a self-insurance appropriation classified as a liability.

The accounting treatment for self-insurance takes three forms:

1. Make no entries in the accounts except for losses incurred as they arise,
2. Appropriate retained earnings annually and when losses occur, reverse the entry appropriating retained earnings and charge losses against revenues of the period in which the losses occur, and
3. Accrue annually as an expense a portion of the anticipated losses.

Methods 1 and 2 are acceptable accounting treatments; method 3 is no longer acceptable for accounting or tax purposes.[16] Under the **first method** no accounting recognition is given to the fact that self-insurance is the mode of operation and that uninsured losses may have to be absorbed in some future period. Losses are charged against revenues of the period in which "it is probable that an asset has been impaired or a liability has been incurred at the date of the financial statements" and "the amount of loss can be reasonably estimated."[17]

The **second method** treats uninsured losses in the same manner, that is, they are charged entirely against revenues of the period in which they are sustained. Recognition is given to contingent losses in periods other than their incurrence, however, by appropriations of retained earnings. The amount of the annual appropriation may approximate the premium cost of adequate insurance covering the risk, or it may be a prorated allocation of an estimated and anticipated future loss. The balance of the appropriation account normally does not exceed the maximum expected loss at any one time and is never charged with actual losses. The effect of this and the first method is a varying charge for actual losses instead of a stable charge to expense that would result from premium payments of an insurance policy. The annual appropriation is a debit to Retained Earnings and a credit to Appropriation for Self-Insurance or other appropriately titled equity accounts. When the casualty loss occurs, a loss account is debited, the appropriate asset account credited for the book value of the loss, and the entry creating the appropriation is reversed.

The **third method** avoids the irregular effects on net income resulting from nonrecurring uninsured losses and makes the income statement of a company that does not insure appear to be comparable to those of firms carrying insurance. This method accrues the estimated losses by having the self-insurance company charge operations each year with a hypothetical amount of insurance expense, crediting a similar amount to a liability account entitled Accumulated Provision for Self-Insured Risks or Allowance for Uninsured Losses. A liability account is credited instead of an appropriation of retained earnings as in the second method. The amount of the annual charge to Insurance Expense is based on an estimate of the expected future losses or it approximates the premiums that would be paid if insurance were in force. When the casualty losses occur, they are charged against the liability account. The liability account absorbs the impact of the loss; each year's income statement absorbs only a portion of the loss. Under this method there is no

---

[16]Although unacceptable today, this method is presented because of its previous widespread usage and appeal.

[17]*Ibid.*, par. 8.

specific appropriation of retained earnings. Of course, unappropriated retained earnings is affected each year by the hypothetical insurance expense. Before 1975 the liability for self-insurance was acceptable and widely used by many large companies, especially in the airlines, insurance, and oil industries.

Self-insurance is no insurance, and any company that assumes its own risks puts itself in the position of incurring expenses or losses as the casualties occur. **The improper application of the accrual method to self-insurance obscures a fundamental difference in circumstances between companies that transfers risks to others through insurance and those that do not.** There is little theoretical justification for the establishment of a liability based on a hypothetical charge to insurance expense. This is "as if" accounting.[18] Can there be an expense, in advance of the actual occurrence of a casualty, or a liability to incur a casualty loss in the future? The FASB's recent answer to that question is:

> Fires, explosions, and other similar events that may cause loss or damage of an enterprise's property are random in their occurrence. With respect to events of that type, the condition for accrual is not satisfied prior to the occurrence of the event because until that time there is no diminution in the value of the property. There is no relationship of those events to the activities of the enterprise prior to their occurrence, and no asset is impaired prior to their occurrence. Further, unlike an insurance company, which has a contractual obligation under policies in force to reimburse insureds for losses, an enterprise can have no such obligation to itself, and, hence, no liability.[19]

With respect to uninsured losses that may result from injury to others, damage to the property of others, or business interruptions that may occur after the balance sheet date, premature accrual is similarly objectionable.

Are Appropriations of Retained Earnings Necessary?

If all reasons for establishing appropriations of Retained Earnings are examined critically, it appears that they are somewhat superficial and that there is really one fundamental reason for retained earnings appropriations. The creation of appropriations reduces the amount of retained earnings that appears to be available for dividends.

To anyone well trained in accounting it seems unrealistic to contend that a mere journal entry transferring an amount from Retained Earnings to an appropriation account can prevent dividends and protect working capital. The procedure is often used to prevent pressure from stockholders and other interests to distribute or share retained earnings. A footnote is much more informative and less confusing.

Statements Presenting Changes in Retained Earnings and Paid-in Capital

Statements of retained earnings and statements of additional paid-in capital are frequently presented in the following basic format:

---

[18]A commentary in *Forbes* (June 15, 1974, p. 42) stated its position on this matter quite succinctly: "The simple and unquestionable fact of life is this: Business is cyclical and full of unexpected surprises. Is it the role of accounting to disguise this unpleasant fact and create a fairyland of smoothly rising earnings? Or, should accounting reflect reality, warts and all—floods, expropriations and all manner of rude shocks?"

[19]"Accounting for Contingencies," *op. cit.,* par. 28.

1. Balance at the beginning of the period.
2. Additions.
3. Deductions.
4. Balance at the end of the period.

Although a large segment of the general public (investors and creditors) has gained an elementary understanding of an appreciation for the balance sheet and income statement and, to some degree, the statement of retained earnings, only a small minority comprehend the items appearing in the statement of additional paid-in capital. **APB Opinion No. 12** indicated that disclosure of changes in the separate accounts comprising stockholders' equity (in addition to retained earnings) is required to make the financial statements sufficiently informative. Disclosure of such changes may take the form of separate statements or may be made in the basic financial statements or notes thereto.

A **columnar format** for the presentation of changes in stockholders' equity items in published annual reports is gaining in popularity; an example is St. Regis Paper Company's Statements of Shareholders' Equity reproduced on page 699.

The annual report of Tenneco Inc. in Appendix E of Chapter 5, page 196 includes a comprehensive illustration of the various items that commonly appear as either additions or deductions in a "Statement of Changes in Stockholders' Equity."

Illustration of a Comprehensive Stockholders' Equity Section

The following presentation is an example of a comprehensive stockholders' equity section taken from a balance sheet that includes most of the equity items discussed in Chapters 15 and 16.

Model Corporation Stockholders' Equity December 31, 1981		
Capital stock:		
Preferred stock, $100 par value, 7%		
cumulative, 30,000 shares issued and outstanding		$3,000,000
Common stock, no par, stated value		
$10 per share 400,000 shares issued		4,000,000
Common stock dividend distributable, 20,000 shares		200,000
Total capital stock		7,200,000
Additional paid-in capital:		
Excess over par—preferred	$ 150,000	
Excess over stated value—common	840,000	990,000
Total paid-in capital		8,190,000
Donated capital		100,000
Retained earnings		
Appropriated for plant expansion	2,100,000	
Unappropriated	2,160,000	4,260,000
Total capital and retained earnings		12,550,000
Less cost of treasury stock (2,000 shares, common)		(80,000)
Total stockholders' equity		$12,470,000

St. Regis Paper Company and Consolidated Subsidiaries
STATEMENT OF SHAREHOLDERS' EQUITY

	Preferred Stock	Common Stock	Common Treasury Stock	Capital Surplus	Retained Earnings
Balance at January 1, 1977[1]	$113,000	$155,638,000	$(1,000)	$204,067,000	$616,324,000
Net earnings					106,786,000
Cash dividends:					
Preferred stock, $5.50 per share					(619,000)
Common stock, $1.66 per share					(39,548,000)
Pooled company—Southland Paper Mills, Inc.					(4,568,000)
Purchase of common stock, 16 shares			—		
Issuance of common stock:					
Conversion of 4⅞% debentures, 117,028 shares		585,000		2,920,000	
Stock option plan, 19,138 shares		96,000		370,000	
Management incentive compensation plan, 28,678 shares		143,000		647,000	
Balance at December 31, 1977[2]	113,000	156,462,000	(1,000)	208,004,000	678,375,000
Cumulative effect of change in accounting for leases					(1,114,000)
Pooling of interests—					
Power Materials Handling Company, 134,984 shares		675,000		(910,000)	1,510,000
Restated balance, January 1, 1978	113,000	157,137,000	(1,000)	207,094,000	678,771,000
Net earnings					126,514,000
Cash dividends:					
Preferred stock, $5.50 per share					(619,000)
Common stock, $1.74 per share					(54,936,000)
Purchase of common stock, 23 shares			(1,000)		
Issuance of common stock:					
Conversion of 4⅞% debentures, 397,097 shares		1,986,000		9,919,000	
Stock option plan, 16,864 shares		84,000		307,000	
Management incentive compensation plan, 26,897 shares		134,000		579,000	
Balance at December 31, 1978[3]	$113,000	$159,341,000	$(2,000)	$217,899,000	$749,730,000

[1]Stock balances at January 1, 1977: preferred stock, 112,500 shares; common stock, 31,127,575 shares; and treasury stock 17 shares.
[2]Stock balances at December 31, 1977: preferred stock, 112,500 shares; common stock, 31,292,419 shares; and treasury stock, 33 shares.
[3]Stock balances at December 31, 1978: preferred stock, 112,500 shares; common stock, 31,868,261 shares; and treasury stock, 56 shares.

QUASI REORGANIZATION

A corporation that consistently suffers net losses accumulates negative retained earnings, or a deficit. The laws of many states provide that no dividends may be declared and paid so long as a corporation's paid-in capital has been reduced by a deficit. In these states, a corporation with a debit balance of retained earnings must accumulate sufficient profits to offset the deficit before dividends may be paid.

This situation may be a real hardship on a corporation and its stockholders. For example, a company that has operated unsuccessfully for several years and accumulated a deficit may attain a position that gives promise of successful operation in the future. Development of new products and new markets, a new management group placed in control, or merely improved economic conditions may point to much improved operating results. But, if the state law prohibits dividends until the deficit has been replaced by earnings, the stockholders must wait until such profits have been earned, which may take a considerable period of time. Furthermore, future success may depend on obtaining additional funds through the sale of stock. If no dividends can be paid for some time, however, the market price of any new stock issue is likely to be low, if such stock can be marketed at all.

Thus, a company with every prospect of a successful future may be prevented from accomplishing its plans because of a deficit, although present management may have had nothing whatever to do with the years over which the deficit was accumulated. To permit the corporation to proceed with its plans might well be to the advantage of all interests in the enterprise; to require it to make up the deficit out of profits might actually force it to liquidate to the possible injury of all parties at interest.

A procedure provided for in some state laws eliminates an accumulated deficit and permits the company to proceed on much the same basis as if it had been legally reorganized, without the difficulty and expenses generally connected with a legal reorganization. This procedure, known as a "quasi reorganization," consists of the following steps:

1. All assets are revalued at appropriate current values so the company will not be burdened with excessive inventory or plant asset valuations in following years. Any loss on revaluation of course increases the deficit.

2. Paid-in or other types of capital must be available or must be created, at least equal in amount to the deficit. If no such capital exists, it is created through donation of stock to the corporation by stockholders, by reduction of the par value of shares outstanding, or by some similar means.

3. The deficit is then charged against the paid-in capital and thus eliminated.

A series of entries given below illustrates the steps taken in a quasi reorganization. We assume that the concern shows a deficit of $20,000 before the quasi reorganization is effected.

Retained Earnings	80,000	
Inventory		30,000
Plant Assets		50,000
(To revalue assets to recognize unrecorded losses)		
Common Stock	150,000	
Additional Paid-in Capital		150,000
(To reduce par value of 3,000 shares of		
common stock outstanding from $100		
per share to $50 per share)		
Additional Paid-in Capital	100,000	
Retained Earnings		100,000
(To charge deficit against additional		
paid-in capital)		

The paid-in capital created at the time of the quasi reorganization may be called Reorganization Capital, Capital from Reduction in Par Value of Capital Stock, or other appropriate titles, depending on its source.

In connection with the foregoing steps, certain requirements must be fulfilled. (a) The proposed quasi-reorganization procedure should be submitted to and receive the approval of the corporation stockholders before it is put into effect. (b) The new asset valuations should be fair and not deliberately understate or overstate assets, liabilities, and future earnings. (c) After the reorganization the corporation must have a zero balance of retained earnings, although it may have additional paid-in capital arising from the reorganization. (d) In subsequent reports the retained earnings must be "dated" for a period of approximately 10 years to show the fact and the date of the quasi reorganization, as illustrated in the following example of a balance sheet presentation.

Stockholders' equity		
Common stock of par value of $5 per share authorized and issued, 30,000 shares	$150,000	
Capital arising from reduction in par value of common stock	50,000	
Earnings retained in the business (after quasi reorganization on June 30, 1977)	33,500	$233,500

Questions

1. Distinguish among: contributed capital, earned capital, and equity capital.
2. List the possible sources of "additional paid-in capital."
3. What equity accounts might conceivably have debit balances? Discuss.
4. Indicate the ways in which revaluation and donated capital originate.
5. What are some of the common items that increase or decrease retained earnings?
6. Very few companies pay dividends in amounts equal to their retained earnings legally available for dividends. Why?
7. What are the principal considerations of a board of directors in making decisions involving dividend declarations? Discuss briefly.
8. Distinguish among: cash dividends, property dividends, scrip dividends, liquidating dividends, and stock dividends.
9. What factors influence the dividend policy of a company?
10. Describe the accounting entry for a stock dividend. Describe the accounting entry for a stock split.
11. Stock splits and stock dividends may be used by a corporation to change the number of shares of its stock outstanding.
    (a) What is meant by a stock split effected in the form of a dividend?
    (b) From an accounting viewpoint, explain how the stock split effected in the form of a dividend differs from an ordinary stock dividend.
    (c) How should a stock dividend which has been declared but not yet issued be classified in a statement of financial position? Why?
12. For what reasons might a company appropriate a portion of its retained earnings?
13. How should appropriations of retained earnings be created and written off?
14. Indicate the misuse and the proper use of the term "reserve."
15. What are some of the ways in which retained earnings may be restricted?

16. What is self-insurance? What are the two acceptable forms that the accounting treatment for self-insurance may take?

17. Dividends are sometimes said to have been paid "out of retained earnings." What is the error in that statement?

18. Under what circumstances would a corporation consider submitting itself to a quasi reorganization?

19. Outline the accounting steps involved in accomplishing a quasi reorganization.

20. What objections do you have to the use of revaluation capital (a) to absorb operating losses, (b) as a basis for cash dividends, and (c) as a basis for stock dividends?

21. Is there a duplication of charges to current year's costs or expenses where a sinking-fund appropriation is created for the retirement of bonds, as well as accumulated depreciation with respect to the capital assets by which such bonds are secured? Discuss briefly the point raised by this question.

22. (a) **APB Opinion No. 9** recommends that net income include all items of profit and loss recognized in the period except prior period adjustments and capital transactions involving equity accounts, and that extraordinary items be shown separately as an element of net income of the period.
    1. List the advantages of the recommendation.
    2. List the disadvantages of the recommendation.
    (b) The recommendation described above is based on the premise that capital transactions should be distinguished from income.
    1. Why should capital transactions be distinguished from income?
    2. In what way does the income expected to be generated by an asset relate to its acquisition cost and valuation in financial statements?

Cases

C16-1 Airfoil Boat Corporation, a client, is considering the authorization of a 5% common stock dividend to common stockholders. The financial vice-president of Airfoil wishes to discuss the accounting implications of such an authorization with you before the next meeting of the board of directors.

Instructions

(a) The first topic the vice-president wishes to discuss is the nature of the stock dividend to the recipient. Discuss the case **against** considering the stock dividend as income to the recipient.

(b) The other topic for discussion is the propriety of issuing the stock dividend to all "stockholders of record" or to "stockholders of record exclusive of shares held in the name of the corporation as treasury stock." Discuss the case **against** issuing stock dividends on treasury shares.

(AICPA adapted)

C16-2 The directors of Aromatic Spray Corporation are considering the issuance of a stock dividend. They have asked you to discuss the proposed action by answering the following questions.

Instructions

(a) What is a stock dividend? How is a stock dividend distinguished from a stock split-up (1) from a legal standpoint? (2) from an accounting standpoint?

(b) For what reasons does a corporation usually declare a stock dividend? A stock split-up?

(c) Discuss the amount, if any, of retained earnings to be capitalized in connection with a stock dividend.

(AICPA adapted)

C16-3 Stack and Sell, a large retail chain store company, has stores throughout the United States. Due to the stores' many different locations, Stack and Sell's president thinks it would be advantageous to self-insure the company's stores against the risk of any future loss or damage from fire or other natural causes. From past experience and by applying appropriate statistical and actuarial techniques, the president feels the amount of future losses can be predicted with reasonable accuracy.

Instructions

The president has asked you how Stack and Sell should record this type of contingency and on what basis the current period should be allocated a portion of the estimated losses. What would you tell the president?

C16-4 Sportique Company, a medium-sized manufacturer, has been experiencing losses for the five years that it has been doing business. Although the operations for the year just ended resulted in a loss, several important changes resulted in a profitable fourth quarter, and the future operations of the company are expected to be profitable.

The treasurer suggests that there be a quasi reorganization to: (1) eliminate the accumulated deficit of $423,620, (2) write-up the $493,100 cost of operating land and buildings to their fair value, and (3) set up an asset of $203,337 representing the estimated future tax benefit of the losses accumulated to date.

Instructions

(a) What are the characteristics of a quasi reorganization? In other words, of what does it consist?

(b) List the conditions under which a quasi reorganization generally is justified.

(c) Discuss the propriety of the treasurer's proposals to:
   1. Eliminate the deficit of $423,620.
   2. Write up the $493,100 cost of the operating land and buildings to their fair value.
   3. Set up an asset of $203,337 representing the estimated future tax benefit of the losses accumulated to date.

(AICPA adapted)

C16-5 After operating several years, Melanie Elbert Fashions, Inc. showed a net worth of $500,000, of which $100,000 was represented by 1,000 shares of $100 each, and $400,000 was retained earnings. Subsequently, three additional shares were issued for each share held, which made the capital stock $400,000 and retained earnings $100,000. The operations of later years showed an aggregate loss of $280,000, leaving a deficit of $180,000.

The corporation then reduced the par value of each share of stock to 25% of its former value, thus restoring the capital to the original amount of $100,000. The deficit was absorbed and the retained earnings shown as $120,000. It is argued that this amount represents the net operating results since organization and is, therefore, retained earnings.

Instructions

Give your opinion of these transactions; disregard their legal aspects.

Exercises

E16-1 Stockholders' equity on the balance sheet is composed of four major sections. They are: A. Capital stock; B. Additional paid-in capital; C. Donated capital; and D. Retained earnings.

Instructions

Classify each of the following items as affecting one of the four sections above or as E. an item not to be included in stockholders' equity.

1. Cash dividends declared
2. Preferred stock
3. Retained earnings appropriated
4. Allowance for Doubtful Accounts
5. Sinking fund
6. Common stock

7. Paid-in capital in excess of par—common
8. Net income
9. Preferred stock subscribed
10. Goodwill
11. Donated land

E16-2 The following information has been taken from the ledger accounts of Georgia Peanut Corporation:

Total income since incorporation	$100,000
Total cash dividends paid	40,000
Proceeds from sale of donated stock	20,000
Total value of stock dividends distributed	12,000
Gains on treasury stock transactions	14,000
Unamortized discount on bonds payable	30,000
Appropriated for plant expansion	20,000

Instructions

Determine the current balance of unappropriated retained earnings.

E16-3 The stockholders' equity accounts of the Bailey Company have the following balances on December 31, 1981:

Common stock, $10 par, 400,000 shares issued and outstanding	$4,000,000
Paid-in capital in excess of par	1,600,000
Retained earnings	7,200,000

Shares of Bailey Company stock are currently selling on the Northwest Stock Exchange at $40.

Instructions

Prepare the appropriate journal entries for each of the following cases:

1. A stock dividend of 10% is declared and issued.
2. A stock dividend of 100% is declared and issued.
3. A 4 for 1 stock split is declared and issued.

E16-4 The following data were taken from the balance sheet accounts of Spartan-Aurora Corporation on December 31, 1980:

Current Assets	$495,000
Investments	308,250
Capital Stock (par value $25)	450,000
Paid-in Capital in Excess of Par	72,000
Retained Earnings	780,000

Instructions

Prepare the required journal entries for the following unrelated items:

1. A 10% stock dividend is declared and distributed at a time when the market value of the shares is $30 per share.
2. A scrip dividend of $22,500 is declared.
3. The par value of the capital stock is reduced to $5 and the stock is split 5 for 1.
4. A dividend is declared January 5, 1981, and paid January 25, 1981 in bonds held as an investment; the bonds have a book value of $25,000 and a fair market value of $37,500.

E16-5   Dominiak Corporation, which has suffered losses for several years, has the following stockholders' equity on December 31, 1980:

Common stock, $10 par value, 10,000 shares authorized and issued	$100,000
Discount on common stock	(6,000)
Retained earnings (deficit)	(20,000)
	$ 74,000

Instructions

Assume that, to supply badly needed cash, the company assesses the stockholders $1 per share on the shares they own.

(a) Compute: (1) The book value per share before the assessment, (2) The book value per share after the assessment.

(b) Prepare the revised stockholders' equity after the assessment.

E16-6   The outstanding capital stock of Comfortable Sleepwear Corporation consists of 1,000 shares of $100 par value, 8% preferred, and 2,000 shares of $100 par value common.

Instructions

Assuming that the company has retained earnings of $52,000, all of which is to be paid out in dividends, and that preferred dividends were not paid during the two years preceding the current year, state how much each class of stock should receive under each of the following conditions:

1. The preferred stock is non-cumulative and non-participating.
2. The preferred stock is cumulative and non-participating.
3. The preferred stock is cumulative and participating.

E16-7   Entertainment Company's ledger shows the following balances on December 31, 1981:

7% Preferred stock—$10 par value, outstanding 20,000 shares	$ 200,000
Common stock—$50 par value, outstanding 20,000 shares	1,000,000
Retained earnings	360,000

Instructions

Assuming that the directors decide to declare total dividends in the amount of $130,000, determine how much each class of stock should receive under each of the conditions stated below. One year's dividends are in arrears on the preferred stock.

(a) The preferred stock is cumulative and fully participating.

(b) The preferred stock is non-cumulative and non-participating.

(c) The preferred stock is non-cumulative and is participating in distributions in excess of a 10% dividend rate on the common stock.

E16-8   Rick Murdock, as president of Golf Cart, Inc., has decided against purchasing casualty insurance to cover the company's four plants. Recognizing the possibility of casualty losses, he has $12,000 a year appropriated as a reserve for such contingencies; the first appropriation is made in 1980. In 1983 a fire destroys one of his plants. The plant had a 20-year life, no salvage value, and an original cost of $160,000 when it was constructed 12 years ago. After the fire in 1983, Murdock changes his mind, buys insurance and pays an annual premium of $14,000 on January 2, 1984, and eliminates his casualty reserve.

Instructions

Prepare the entries to journalize the insurance and casualty transactions of 1980, 1983, and 1984.

E16-9 The following account balances are available from the ledger of Rejuvenated Corporation on December 31, 1980:

Capital Stock—$50 par value, 15,000 shares authorized and outstanding	$750,000
Retained Earnings (deficit)	(225,000)

As of January 2, 1981, the corporation gave effect to a stockholder-approved quasi reorganization by reducing the par value of the stock to $30 a share, writing down plant assets by $37,500, and eliminating the deficit.

Instructions

Prepare the required journal entries for the quasi reorganization of Rejuvenated.

E16-10 The condensed balance sheets of the Turnaround Company immediately before and one year after it had completed a quasi reorganization appear below:

	Before Quasi	One Year After		Before Quasi	One Year After
Current assets	$ 600,000	$ 840,000	Common stock	$4,500,000	$2,700,000
Plant assets (net)	3,000,000	2,100,000	Premium on common	300,000	
			Retained earnings	(1,200,000)	240,000
	$3,600,000	$2,940,000		$3,600,000	$2,940,000

For the year following the quasi reorganization, the Turnaround Company reported net income of $300,000, depreciation expense of $150,000, and paid a cash dividend of $60,000. As part of the quasi reorganization, the company wrote down inventories by $150,000. No purchases or sales of plant assets and no stock transactions occurred in the year following the quasi reorganization.

Instructions

Prepare all the journal entries made at the time of the quasi reorganization.

Problems

P16-1 As the newly appointed controller in 1981 for Ethical Drug Company, you are interested in analyzing the "Additional Capital" account of the company in order to present an accurate balance sheet. Your assistant, who has analyzed the account from the inception of the company, submits the following summary:

	Debits	Credits
Excess of amount paid in over par value of common stock		$ 280,000
Discount on preferred stock	$ 60,000	
Net income		600,000
Cash dividends—preferred	90,000	
Cash dividends—common	220,000	
Contra to appraisal increase of land		200,000
Additional assessments of prior years' income taxes	87,000	
Extraordinary gain		15,000
Donated treasury stock, preferred; issued and reacquired, at par		130,000
Extraordinary loss	115,000	
Correction of a prior period error	45,000	
	617,000	1,225,000
Credit balance of additional capital account	608,000	
	$1,225,000	$1,225,000

Instructions

    (a) Prepare a journal entry to close the single "Additional Capital" account now used and to establish appropriately classified accounts. Indicate how you derive the balance of each new account.

    (b) If generally accepted accounting principles had been followed, what amount should have been shown as total net income?

P16-2 The balance sheet of Prep-Frat, Inc. shows $200,000 capital stock, consisting of 2,000 shares of $100 each, and retained earnings of $150,000. As controller of the company, you find that the assistant treasurer is $40,000 short in his accounts and had concealed this shortage by adding the amount to the inventory. He owns 300 shares of the company's stock and, in settlement of the shortage, offers this stock at its book value. The offer is accepted; the company pays him the excess value and distributes the 300 shares thus acquired to the other shareholders.

Instructions

    (a) What amount should Prep-Frat, Inc. pay the assistant treasurer?

    (b) By what journal entries should the foregoing transactions be recorded? (Treasury stock is recorded using the cost method.)

    (c) What is the total stockholders' equity after the distribution noted above?

    (d) What would have been done if Prep-Frat, Inc. had had a deficit of $50,000 and the 300 shares had been accepted at par?

P16-3 The Board of Directors of Oak Corporation on December 1, 1981, declared a 2% stock dividend on the common stock of the corporation, payable on December 28, 1981, only to the holders of record at the close of business December 15, 1981. They stipulated that cash dividends were to be paid in lieu of issuing any fractional shares. They also directed that the amount to be charged against Retained Earnings should be an amount equal to the market value of the stock on the record date multiplied by the total of (a) the number of shares issued as a stock dividend, and (b) the number of shares on which cash is paid in place of the issuance of fractional shares. The following facts are given:

1. At the dividend record date—

(a) Shares of Oak common issued	2,771,600
(b) Shares of Oak common held in treasury	1,000
(c) Shares of Oak common included in (a) above held by persons who will receive cash in lieu of fractional shares	202,500
(d) Shares of predecessor company stock that are exchangeable for Oak common at the rate of 1¼ shares of Oak common for each share of predecessor company stock (necessary number of shares of Oak common have been reserved but not issued)	600
Provision was made for a cash dividend in lieu of fractional shares to holders of 240 of these 600 shares.	

2. Values of Oak common were:

Par value	$ 5
Market value at December 1st and 15th	$22
Book value at December 1st and 15th	$16

Instructions

Prepare entries and explanations to record the payment of the dividend.

                                                              (AICPA adapted)

P16-4 The books of Fantasy Clothes Corporation carried the following account balances as of December 31, 1980:

Cash	$113,250
Preferred stock, 6% cumulative, nonparticipating, $10 par	150,000
Common stock, no par value, 75,000 shares issued	375,000
Paid-in capital in excess of par (preferred)	22,500
Treasury stock (common 1,800 shares at cost)	10,800
Retained earnings	52,500

The preferred stock has dividends in arrears for the past year (1980).

The board of directors, at their annual meeting on December 21, 1981, declared the following: "The current year dividends shall be 6% on the preferred and $.50 per share on the common; the dividends in arrears shall be paid by issuing one share of treasury stock for each ten shares of preferred held."

The preferred is currently selling at $110 per share and the common at $6 per share. Net income for 1981 is estimated at $18,000.

Instructions

(a) Prepare the journal entries required for the dividend declaration and payment, assuming that they occur simultaneously.

(b) Could Fantasy Clothes Corporation give the preferred shareholders two year's dividends and common shareholders a $.50 per share dividend, all in cash?

P16-5 Subscription TV, Inc. has outstanding 1,500 shares of $100 par, 7% preferred stock and 4,500 shares of $10 par value common. The schedule below shows the amount of dividends **paid out** over the last four years.

Instructions

Allocate the dividends to each type of stock under assumptions (a) and (b). Express your answers in **per share** amounts using the following format.

		Assumptions			
		(a) Preferred, non-cumulative, and non-participating		(b) Preferred, cumulative, and fully participating	
Year	Paid-out	Preferred	Common	Preferred	Common
1978	$ 6,000				
1979	$18,000				
1980	$29,500				
1981	$39,000				

P16-6 Pontiff Products, Inc., began operations in January 1977 and had the following reported net income or loss for each of its five years of operations:

1977	$ 150,000 loss
1978	130,000 loss
1979	120,000 loss
1980	250,000 income
1981	1,000,000 income

At December 31, 1981, the Pontiff capital accounts were as follows:

Common stock, par value $10 per share; authorized 100,000 shares; issued and outstanding 50,000 shares	$ 500,000
4% nonparticipating noncumulative preferred stock, par value $100 per share; authorized, issued and outstanding 1,000 shares	100,000
8% fully participating cumulative preferred stock, par value $100 per share; authorized, issued and outstanding 10,000 shares	1,000,000

Pontiff has never paid a cash or stock dividend. There has been no change in the capital accounts since Pontiff began operations. The appropriate state law permits dividends only from retained earnings.

Instructions

Prepare a work sheet showing the **maximum** amount available for cash dividends on December 31, 1981, and how it would be distributable to the holders of the common shares and each of the preferred shares. Show supporting computations in good form.

(AICPA adapted)

P16-7 Some of the account balances of Varsity Company at December 31, 1980, are shown below:

Retained Earnings Appropriated for Contingencies	$ 75,000
Retained Earnings Appropriated for Fire Insurance	65,000
6% Preferred Stock ($100 par, 1,000 shares authorized)	10,000
Paid-in Capital in Excess of Par—Preferred Stock	300
Common Stock ($10 par, 100,000 shares authorized)	500,000
Paid-in Capital in Excess of Par—Common Stock	50,000
Unappropriated Retained Earnings	340,500
Treasury Stock—Preferred (50 shares at cost)	5,500
Treasury Stock—Common (1,000 shares at cost)	15,000

The price of the company's common stock has been increasing steadily on the market; it was $23 on January 1, 1981, advanced to $28 by July 1, and to $30 at the end of the year 1981. The preferred stock is not openly traded but was appraised at $105 per share during 1981.

Instructions

Give the proper journal entries for each of the following:

1. The company incurred a fire loss of $60,000 to its warehouse.
2. The company declared a property dividend on April 1. Each common stockholder was to receive one share of Akes & Panes for every 10 shares outstanding. Varsity had 8,000 shares of Akes & Panes (2% of total outstanding stock) which was purchased in 1978 for $64,000. The market value of Akes & Panes stock was $15 per share on April 1. Record appreciation only on the shares distributed.
3. The company resold the 50 shares of preferred stock held in the treasury for $115 per share.
4. On July 1, the company declared a 4% stock dividend to the common shareholders.
5. The city of Yorktown, in an effort to persuade the company to expand into that city, donated to Varsity Company a plot of land with an appraised value of $20,000.
6. At the annual board of directors meeting, the board decided to "Set up an appropriation in retained earnings for the future construction of a new plant. Such appropriation to be for $50,000 per year. Also, to increase the appropriation for possible contingencies by $20,000 and to eliminate the appropriation for fire insurance and begin purchasing such insurance from Prude Insurance Company."

P16-8 The following accounts and balances appear in Ocean Resources Company's ledger after closing but before any entries resulting from the following resolutions:

Land Held for Investment	$ 76,000 dr.
Retained Earnings Appropriated for Possible Decline of Inventory Prices	118,000 cr.
Retained Earnings Appropriated for Contingencies	200,000 cr.
Retained Earnings	540,000 cr.
Revenue and Expense Summary	250,000 cr.

The following resolutions were passed by the board of directors of the Ocean Resources Company at their last meeting for the year 1980:

1. A Retained Earnings Appropriated for Possible Additional Federal Income Tax Assessments of Prior Years is to be created in the amount of $25,000.
2. An amount equal to 20% of the net income for the year is to be transferred to the Retained Earnings Appropriated for Contingencies.
3. The present Retained Earnings Appropriated for Possible Decline of Inventory Prices that was set up as a charge against Retained Earnings in 1979 is to be written off as no longer required.
4. A decline in the value of land purchased for investment is to be recorded. As measured by the sales value of other property in the area, the value of the Ocean Resources Company's land has decreased 50% since date of purchase, and an equivalent write-down is to be made in the carrying value of the property.
5. A Retained Earnings Appropriated for Future Plant Expansion is to be established equal to 50% of the balance of the Retained Earnings account, after all transactions for the year noted above have been recorded.
6. A stock dividend of 10% on the capital stock (par value $100) of $500,000 is declared and issued. The market price of the stock on the date of declaration was $120 per share.

Instructions

(a) Prepare entries in general journal form to record the board of directors' resolutions above.
(b) What is the amount of retained earnings apparently available for dividends?
(c) What is the amount of retained earnings actually (legally) available for dividends?

P16-9   Tiptoe Shoe Company has these stockholders' equity accounts:

	Issued Shares	Amount
Preferred stock, $100 par value	1,200	$120,000
Treasury shares, preferred (at cost)	80	12,000
Common stock without par value (at issue price)	1,800	59,400
Retained earnings		247,320

In view of the large retained earnings, the board of directors resolves: (1) "to pay a 100% stock dividend on all shares outstanding, capitalizing amounts of retained earnings equal to the par value and the issue price of the preferred and common stock outstanding," respectively, and thereafter (2) "to pay a cash dividend of 6% on preferred stock and a cash dividend of $3 a share on common stock."

Instructions

(a) Prepare entries in journal form to record declaration of these dividends.
(b) Prepare the stockholders' equity section of a balance sheet for Tiptoe Shoe Company after declaration but before distribution of these dividends.

P16-10   The following is a summary of all relevant transactions of the Beauty Cream Corporation since it was organized in 1978:

In 1978, 10,000 shares were authorized and 5,000 shares of common stock ($50 par value) were issued at a price of $55. In 1979, 1,000 shares were issued as a stock dividend when the stock was selling for $62. Two hundred shares of common stock were bought in 1980 at a cost of $66 per share. These 200 shares are still in the company treasury. (State law requires an appropriation of retained earnings equal to cost of treasury stock.)

In 1979, 5,000 preferred shares were authorized and the company issued 2,000 of them ($100 par value) at $104. Some of the preferred stock was reacquired by the company and later reissued for $2,500 more than it cost the company. In 1980 a block of preferred stock was donated to the company and immediately resold for $12,600.

The corporation has earned a total of $400,000 in net income after income taxes and paid out a total of $235,000 in cash dividends since incorporation. An appropriation was made in 1980 by the board of directors from retained earnings in the amount of $50,000 for Fixed Asset Replacements.

Instructions

Prepare the stockholders' equity section of the balance sheet in proper form for the Beauty Cream Corporation as of December 31, 1980. Account for treasury stock using the cost method.

P16-11 Anderson Tank Corp. has outstanding 1,000,000 shares of common stock of a par value of $10 each. The balance in its retained earnings account at January 1, 1980, was $12,000,000, and it then had Additional Paid-in Capital of $2,500,000. During 1980 the company's net income was $2,700,000. A cash dividend of 40¢ a share was paid June 30, 1980, and a 10% stock dividend was distributed to stockholders of record at the close of business on December 31, 1980. You have been asked to advise on the proper accounting treatment of the stock dividend.

The existing stock of the company is quoted on a national stock exchange. The market price of the stock has been as follows:

October 31, 1980	$22
November 30, 1980	24
December 31, 1980	29
Average price over the two-month period	26

Instructions

(a) Prepare a journal entry to record the cash dividend.

(b) Prepare a journal entry to record the stock dividend.

(c) Prepare the stockholders' equity section (including schedules of retained earnings and additional paid-in capital) of the balance sheet of the Anderson Tank Corp. for the year 1980 on the basis of the foregoing information. Draft a note to the financial statements setting forth the basis of the accounting for the stock dividend and add separately appropriate comments or explanations regarding the basis chosen.

P16-12 On December 15, 1980, the directors of Jan Felver Corporation voted to appropriate $50,000 of retained earnings and to retain in the business assets equal to the appropriation for use in expanding the corporation's factory building. This was the fourth of such appropriations; after it was recorded, the stockholders' equity section of Felver's balance sheet appeared as follows:

Stockholders' equity:		
Common stock, $10 par value, 250,000 shares authorized,		
200,000 shares issued and outstanding		$2,000,000
Paid-in capital in excess of par		3,400,000
Total paid-in capital		5,400,000
Retained earnings—		
Unappropriated	$1,300,000	
Appropriated for plant expansion	200,000	
Total retained earnings		1,500,000
Total stockholders' equity		$6,900,000

On January 9, 1981, the corporation entered into a contract for the construction of the factory addition for which the retained earnings were appropriated. On November 1, 1981, the addition was completed and the contractor paid the contract price of $187,500.

On December 14, 1981, the board of directors voted to return the balance of the Retained Earnings Appropriated for Plant Expansion account to Unappropriated Retained Earnings. They also voted a 25,000 share stock dividend distributable on January 23, 1982 to the January 15, 1982 stockholders of record. The corporation's stock was selling at $32 in the market on December 14, 1981. Felver reported net income for 1980 of $300,000 and for 1981 of $400,000.

Instructions

(a) Prepare the appropriate journal entries for Felver Corporation for the information above (December 15, 1980 to January 23, 1982, inclusive).

(b) Prepare the stockholders' equity section of the balance sheet for Felver at December 31, 1981 in proper accounting form.

P16-13 The stockholders' equity section of Sjolund Manufacturing Company balance sheet on January 1 of the current year is as follows:

Paid-in Capital

Common stock, par $50, 20,000 shares authorized,		
15,000 shares issued	$750,000	
Paid-in capital in excess of par	225,000	
Total paid-in capital		$ 975,000
Retained Earnings:		
Unappropriated	$300,000	
Appropriated for plant expansion	150,000	
Appropriated for treasury stock	70,000	
Total retained earnings		520,000
		$1,495,000
Less cost of treasury stock (1,000 shares)		70,000
Total stockholders' equity		$1,425,000

The following selected transactions occurred during the year:

1. Paid cash dividends of $1.20 per share on the common stock. The dividend had been properly recorded when declared last year. (State law prohibits cash or stock dividends on treasury shares.)

2. Declared a 5% stock dividend on the common stock when the shares were selling at $80 each in the market.

3. Made a prior period adjustment to correct an error of $60,000 (net of tax) which overstated net income in the previous year. The error was the result of an overstatement of ending inventory. The applicable tax rate was 40%.

4. Sold all of the treasury shares for $85,000.

5. Issued the certificates for the stock dividend.

6. The board appropriated $50,000 of retained earnings for plant expansion, eliminated the appropriation for treasury stock, and declared a cash dividend of $1.50 per share on the common stock.

7. The company reported net income of $150,000 for the year.

Instructions

(a) Prepare journal entries for the selected transactions above (ignore income taxes).

(b) Prepare a retained earnings statement for the current year.

P16-14 On June 30, 1980, the stockholders' equity section of the balance sheet of Marvelous Equipment Company, Inc., appears as follows:

Stockholders' equity

6% cumulative preferred stock			
Authorized and issued, 1,000 shares			
of $100 par value	$100,000		
Common stock			
Authorized 10,000 shares of $50 par value,			
issued, 5,200 shares	260,000	$360,000	
Retained earnings (deficit)		(70,000)	$290,000

A footnote to the balance sheet points out that preferred stock dividends are in arrears in the amount of $24,000.

At a stockholders' meeting, a new group of officers was voted into power, and a quasi reorganization plan proposed by the new officers was accepted by the stockholders. The terms of this plan are as follows:

1. Preferred stockholders to cancel their claim against the corporation for accrued dividends.
2. The par value of the common stock to be reduced from $50 a share to $20 in order to create "capital in excess of par."
3. Certain depreciable properties and inventories owned by the company to be revalued downward $50,000 and $15,000, respectively.
4. The deficit to be written off against capital in excess of par created by reduction of the par value of common stock.

Instructions

(a) Assuming that the various steps in the reorganization plan are carried out as of June 30, prepare journal entries to record the effect of the reorganization.
(b) Assuming that the company earns a net income of $25,000 for the year ended June 30, 1981, prepare the net worth section of the balance sheet as of that date.

P16-15   The controller of High Gloss Paint Company presents the owners' equity section of the company's December 31, 1980 balance sheet in the following form:

Net Worth

Common stock	$ 80,000
Preferred stock	214,000
Retained earnings	366,200
Appraisal capital	20,000
Total net worth	$680,200

A study of the company records revealed the following facts:

1. The company sold 8,000 shares of no-par common stock for $12 per share at the time the firm was organized. The common stock has a stated value of $10 per share. The firm was incorporated in 1973.
2. In 1975 the company issued 2,000 shares of $100 par value, cumulative and non-participating, 6%, preferred stock at a price of $107 per share.
3. A common stock dividend of 800 shares was issued but not recorded in 1978, when the market value of the common stock was $20 per share.
4. The company has bought and sold its own common stock on several occasions. It has received $4,300 in excess of cost from the resale of its own common stock, which was purchased in the market.
5. At the end of 1980 the company holds 100 shares of common stock, which was acquired at a cost of $25 per share, in the treasury. The state law does not permit stated capital to be impaired as a result of treasury stock purchases. (Treasury stock recorded at cost.)
6. In 1979, certain shareholders donated 200 shares of common stock to the company; this stock was immediately sold for $22 per share.
7. The $20,000, which is shown as appraisal capital, represents the appraised value of land given to the firm by the local government.
8. From 1973 to the end of 1980, the company earned net income of $544,000, and distributed $200,000 of this net income in cash dividends to stockholders.
9. The total amount of the owner's equity was correctly computed by the company's accountants at the end of 1980.

Instructions

Prepare a revised stockholders' equity section of the balance sheet of High Gloss Paint Company as of December 31, 1980. (Accompany with a schedule indicating how the retained earnings balance of $366,200 was achieved.)

Dilutive Securities and Earnings Per Share Calculations

The urge to merge that predominated the business scene in the 1960s created a number of headaches for accountants, but probably the most notable was the rapid increase in the use of dilutive securities such as convertible bonds, convertible preferred stocks, warrants, and contingent shares.[1] **Dilutive securities** are defined as securities which are not common stock in form but which enable their holders to obtain common stock upon exercise or conversion. A reduction in earnings per share often arises when these securities become common stock. During the sixties, corporate officers recognized that the issuance of these types of securities in a merger did not have the same immediate adverse effect on earnings per share as the issuance of common stock. In addition, many companies found that issuance of convertible securities did not seem to upset common stockholders, even though when these securities were later converted or exercised, the common stockholders' interest was substantially diluted. For these reasons, such terms as "funny money" and "Chinese money" were coined to indicate the peculiar nature of these types of securities and the unusual tricks that could be played on the uninformed investor.

Coupled with this dilutive phenomenon was the increasing use of certain forms of compensation packages, such as stock option plans. These plans were introduced mainly to attract and retain executive talent and to provide tax relief for executives in high tax brackets.

---

[1]Companies merge for a variety of reasons. Some merge for the diversification potential, others believe that the chance of successful expansion is less risky in a merger situation, and others believe that certain companies are simply undervalued. The late 1960s and the late 1970s appear to be heavy merger periods. For example, in 1977 there were over 2,224 mergers.

The widespread use of different types of dilutive securities led the accounting profession to reexamine many of its earlier positions in this area. Specifically, the profession has directed its attention to accounting for these securities at date of issuance and to the presentation of earnings per share figures that recognize the effect of these dilutive securities. The following discussion includes consideration of convertible securities, warrants, stock options, and contingent shares.

Section I Dilutive Securities

Accounting for Convertible Debt

If bonds may be converted into other securities of the corporation during some specified period of time after issuance, they are called convertible bonds. A **convertible bond** combines the benefits of a bond with the privilege of exchanging it for stock at the holder's option. This security is purchased by investors who desire the security of a bond holding, but want the added option of conversion if the value of the stock appreciates significantly.

Corporations issue convertibles for two main reasons. One is the desire to raise equity capital that, assuming conversion, will arise when the original debt is converted. To illustrate, assume that a company wants to raise $1,000,000 at a time when its common stock is selling at $45 per share. Such an issue would require sale of approximately 22,222 shares (ignoring issue costs). By selling 1,000 bonds at $1,000 par, each convertible into 20 shares of common stock, the enterprise may raise $1,000,000 by committing only 20,000 shares of its common stock. The convertible bonds sell at a higher price because the investor is entitled to fixed income in the form of interest and is entitled to a fixed maturity value at a stipulated date if conversion never materializes. Most studies of convertible bonds indicate that the main purpose of issuing these securities has been to obtain common stock financing at cheaper rates.[2]

A second reason why companies issue convertible securities is that many enterprises could issue debt only at high interest rates unless a convertible covenant were attached. The conversion privilege entices the investor to accept a lower interest rate than would normally be the case on a straight debt issue.

The method for recording convertible bonds follows that used in recording straight debt issues. Any discount or premium resulting from the issuance of convertible bonds is amortized on the basis of the maturity date, because it is difficult to predict when, if at all, conversion will occur.

If bonds are converted into other securities, the principal accounting problem is the determination of the amount at which to record the securities exchanged for the bond. For example, Hilton, Inc., issued a $1,000 bond convertible into 10 shares of common stock (par value $10) at a premium of $60. At the time of conversion the unamortized premium is $50, the market value of the bond is $1,200, and the stock is quoted on the market at $120. Two possible methods of determining the issue price of the stock might be used.

1. The market price of the stocks or bonds, $1,200.
2. The book value of the bonds, $1,050.

[2]See, for example, James C. Pilcher, *Raising Capital with Convertible Debentures*, Michigan Business Studies (Ann Arbor: University of Michigan, Bureau of Business Research, 1955), pp. 60–61.

Market Value Approach Recording the stock issued at the **market price** of the stock or bond offers a theoretically sound way to measure the price at which to record the transaction. If 10 shares of common stock could be sold for $1,200, paid-in capital in excess of par of $1,100 should be recorded. Since at the time of sale bonds having a book value of $1,050 are converted, a loss on the conversion of the bonds of $150 occurs. The entry would be:

Bonds Payable	1,000	
Premium on Bonds Payable	50	
Loss on Redemption of Bonds Payable	150	
Common Stock		100
Paid-in Capital in Excess of Par		1,100

The use of the market price of the bonds can be supported on similar grounds. If the market price of the stock is not determinable, but the bonds can be purchased at $1,200, a good argument can be made that the stock has an issue price of $1,200.

The weakness in using the fair market value of the stock or bonds is the assumption that a gain or loss can be incurred by the corporation as a result of an equity investment in that corporation. The conversion may be favorable or unfavorable to the existing stockholder group, because an increase or decrease in their equity might occur, but the corporate entity, as a whole, is unaffected.

Book Value Approach The **book value** method of recording convertible bonds has received the most widespread acceptance among practitioners. From a practical point of view, if the market price of the stock or the market price of the bonds is not determinable, the book value of the bonds offers the best available measurement of the issue price. Also, many accountants contend that even if market quotations are available, they should not be used, inasmuch as the common stock is merely substituted for the bonds and should be recorded at the carrying amount of the bonds that were converted. Under this method, no gain or loss is recorded and the entry for the foregoing transaction of Hilton, Inc. would be:

Bonds Payable	1,000	
Premium on Bonds Payable	50	
Common Stock		100
Paid-in Capital in Excess of Par		950

The book value method represents a conversion transaction between the stockholders and bondholders that does not give rise to gain or loss recognition. Because the conversion described above is initiated by the holder of the debt instrument (rather than the issuer), it is not classified as an "early extinguishment of debt."

Retirement of Convertible Debt

A special problem relates to the retirement of convertible debt for cash. The question is whether the retirement of convertible debt is a debt transaction or an equity transaction. If it is a debt transaction, the difference between the carrying amount of the retired convertible debt and the cash paid should result in a charge or credit to income; if it is an equity transaction, the difference would presumably go to additional paid-in capital.

Because the method for recording convertible bonds follows that used in recording straight debt issues, no portion of the proceeds should be attributable to the conversion feature and credited to Additional Paid-in Capital. Although theoretical objections to this approach can be raised, to be consistent, a gain or loss on retiring convertible debt needs to be recognized in the same way as a gain or loss on retiring debt that is not convertible. For this reason, **APB Opinion No. 26**, "Early Extinguishment of Debt," concluded that differences between the cash acquisition price of debt and its carrying amount should be reflected currently in income as a gain or loss. As indicated in Chapter 14, gains or losses on extinguishment of debt are considered extraordinary items.

Failure to recognize the equity feature of convertible debt when issued creates problems upon early extinguishment. To illustrate, assume that URL issues convertible debt at a time when the investment community attaches value to the convertible feature. Subsequently the price of URL stock decreases so sharply that the conversion feature has little or no value. If URL extinguishes their convertible debt early, a large gain develops because the book value of the debt will exceed the retirement price. Many accountants consider this treatment incorrect, because the reduction in value of the convertible debt relates to its equity features, not its debt features, and therefore an adjustment to Additional Paid-in Capital is made. As indicated earlier, present practice requires that a gain or loss be recognized.

Convertible Preferred Stock

Convertible preferred stock is handled at acquisition and conversion in the same manner as convertible debt. The major difference in accounting for a convertible bond and a convertible preferred stock is in the initial recording of the security investment. Convertible bonds are considered liabilities; convertible preferreds are considered a part of stockholders' equity.

In addition, when convertible preferred stocks are exercised, there is no theoretical justification for recognition of a gain or loss. The book value method is employed and, the Preferred Stock, along with any related Additional Paid-in Capital, is debited; Common Stock and Additional Paid-in Capital (if an excess exists) are credited. A different treatment develops when the par value of the common stock issued exceeds the book value of the preferred stock. In that case, Retained Earnings is usually debited for the difference.

To illustrate, Host Enterprises issued 1,000 shares of common stock (par value $2.00) for 1,000 shares of preferred stock (par value $1.00). The premium on the preferred stock is $200. The entry would be:

Convertible Preferred Stock	1,000	
Paid-in Capital in Excess of Par	200	
Retained Earnings	800	
Common Stock		2,000

The rationale for the debit to retained earnings is that the preferred stockholders are offered an additional return to facilitate their conversion to common stock. The additional return should be charged to retained earnings. In many states, however, it is required that this charge simply reduce additional paid-in capital from other sources.

Stock Warrants

Warrants are certificates entitling the holder to acquire shares of stock at a certain price within a stated period. This option is similar to the conversion privilege because warrants, if exercised, become common stock and have a dilutive effect (reduce earnings per share) similar to that of the conversion of convertible securities. There are two substantial differences between convertible securities and stock warrants: (1) upon exercise of the warrants, the holder has to pay a certain amount of money to obtain the shares; and (2) debt still remains after warrants are exercised, provided, of course, that warrants are separable from the debt (in other words, the warranty may be sold independently of the debt).

The issuance of warrants or options to buy additional shares normally arises under three situations.

1. When issuing different types of securities, such as bonds or preferred stock, warrants are often included to make the security more attractive, to provide an "equity kicker."
2. Upon the sale of additional common stock, existing stockholders have a preemptive right to purchase common stock first. Warrants may be issued to evidence that right.
3. Warrants, often referred to as stock options, are given as compensation to executives and employees.

The problems in accounting for stock warrants are complex and present many difficulties. Many of the problems remain unresolved.

Stock Warrants Issued with Other Securities

Warrants issued with other securities are basically long-term options to buy common stock at a fixed price. Although some perpetual warrants are traded, generally their life is five years, with a few up to 10 years.

Here is an illustration of the way a warrant works: Tenneco offered a **unit** comprised of one share of stock and one detachable warrant exercisable at $24.25 per share and good for five years. The unit sold for 22¾ ($22.75) and, since the price of the common the day before the sale was 19⅞ ($19.88), it suggests a price of 2⅞ ($2.87) for the warrants.

In this situation, the warrants had an apparent value of 2⅞ ($2.87), even though it would not be profitable at present for the purchaser to exercise the warrant and buy the stock, because the price of the stock is much below the exercise price of $24.25.[3] The investor pays for the warrant to receive a possible future call on the stock at a fixed price when the price is expected to rise significantly. For example, if the price of the stock rises to $30, the investor has gained $2.88 ($30 − $24.25 − $2.87) on an investment of $2.87, a 100% increase! Obviously, if the price does not rise, the investor loses the full $2.87.[4]

APB Opinion No. 14 recommended that the proceeds from the sale of debt with

---

[3]Later in this discussion it will be shown that the value of the warrant is normally determined on the basis of a relative market value approach because of the difficulty of imputing a warrant value in any other manner.

[4]Trading in warrants is often referred to as licensed gambling. From the illustration, it is apparent that buying warrants can be an "all or nothing" proposition.

detachable stock warrants should be allocated between the two securities.[5] The Board took the position that two separable instruments are involved, that is, (1) a bond and (2) a warrant giving the holder the right to purchase common stock at a certain price. Warrants that are detachable can be traded separately from the debt and, therefore, a market value can be determined. The allocation of the sale's proceeds between the two securities would be made on the basis of their fair market values at the date of issuance.

To illustrate, AT & T's offering of five-year warrants to buy common stock (par value $5) at $25 (at a time when a share was selling for approximately $50) enabled it to price its offering of bonds at par with a competitive 8¾% yield. In this situation, to place a value on the two securities one would determine (1) the value of the bonds without the warrants and (2) the value of the warrants. For example, assume that AT & T's bonds (par $1,000) would sell for 99 without the warrants. The market value of the warrants at that time was $30. Prior to sale the warrants will not have a market value. The allocation is based on an estimate of market value, generally as established by an investment banker. The price paid for the bonds with the warrants attached was par or $1,000. The allocation between the bonds and warrants would be made in this manner:

$$\frac{\text{Value of bonds without warrants}}{\text{Value of bonds without warrants} + \text{value of warrants}} \times \text{Purchase price} = \text{Value assigned to bonds}$$

$$\frac{\$990}{\$990 + \$30} \times \$1,000 = \$970.59$$

$$\frac{\text{Value of warrants}}{\text{Value of bonds without warrants} + \text{value of warrants}} \times \text{Purchase price} = \text{Value assigned to warrants}$$

$$\frac{\$30}{\$990 + \$30} \times \$1,000 = \$ 29.41$$

In this situation, assuming the issuance of one bond, the entries are:

Cash	971	
Discount on Bonds Payable	29	
Bonds Payable		1,000
Cash	29	
Paid-in Capital—Stock Warrant		29

(The entries may be combined if desired; they are shown separately here to indicate that the purchaser of the bond is buying not only a bond, but also a possible claim on common stock in the future.)

Assuming that the warrants are exercised one warrant per one share of stock, the following entry would be made:

Cash	25	
Paid-in Capital—Stock Warrant	29	
Common Stock		5
Paid-in Capital in Excess of Par		49

[5]A detachable warrant means that the warrant can sell separately from the bond. *APB Opinion No. 14* makes a distinction between detachable and nondetachable warrants because nondetachable warrants must be sold with the security as a complete package; thus, no allocation is permitted.

If we assume, however, that the warrants are not exercised, Paid-in Capital—Stock Warrants is debited and Paid-in Capital from Expired Warrants is credited. The additional paid-in capital reverts to the old stockholders.

The question arises whether this treatment is consistent with the handling accorded convertible debt. The Board stated that the features of a convertible security are **inseparable** in the sense that choices are mutually exclusive; the holder either converts or redeems the bonds for cash, but cannot do both. No basis, therefore, exists for recognizing the conversion value in the accounts. The Board, however, indicated that the issuance of bonds with **detachable warrants** involves two securities, one a debt investment, which will remain outstanding until maturity, and the other a warrant to purchase common stock. At the time of issuance, separable instruments exist, and therefore separate treatment is justified.

Many argue that the conversion feature is not significantly different in nature from the call represented by a warrant. The question is whether, although the legal forms are different, sufficient similarities of substance exist to support the same accounting treatment. Some contend that inseparability per se is not a valid basis for restricting allocation between identifiable components of a transaction. Examples of allocation between assets of value in a single transaction are not uncommon to the accountant's experience. To illustrate, such transactions as allocation of values in basket purchases, separation of principal and interest in capitalizing long-term leases, and so on, indicate that the accountant has attempted to allocate values in a single transaction. **To deny recognition of value to the conversion feature appears to be a recourse only to the form of the instrument and does not deal with the substance of the transaction.** For example, debt with stock purchase warrants can have the essential attributes of a convertible bond—warrants can be subject to a call and the debentures can be used as consideration for the exercise price.

In both situations (convertible debt and debt issued with warrants), the investor has made a payment to the firm for an equity feature, that is, the right to acquire an equity instrument in the future. The only real distinction between them is that the additional payment made when the equity instrument is formally acquired takes different forms. The warrant holder pays additional cash to the issuing firm; the convertible debt holder pays for stock by foregoing the receipt of interest from conversion date until maturity date and by foregoing the receipt of the maturity value itself. Thus, it is argued that the difference is one of method or form of payment only, rather than one of substance. **Until the profession officially reverses its stand in regard to accounting for convertible debt, however, only bonds issued with detachable stock warrants will result in accounting recognition of the equity feature.**

Rights to Subscribe to Additional Shares

If the directors of a corporation decide to issue new shares of stock, the old stockholders generally have the right (preemptive privilege) to purchase newly issued shares in proportion to their holdings. The privilege, referred to as a stock right, saves existing stockholders from suffering a dilution of voting rights without their consent, and it may allow them to purchase stock somewhat below its market value. The warrants issued in these situations are of short duration, unlike the warrants issued with other securities.

The certificate representing the stock right states the number of shares the holder of the right may purchase, as well as the price at which the new shares may be purchased. Each share owned ordinarily gives the owner one stock right. The price is normally less than the current market value of such shares, thereby giving the rights a value in themselves. From the time they are issued until they expire, they may be purchased and sold like any other security.

No entry is required when rights are issued to existing stockholders. Only a memorandum entry is needed to indicate the number of rights issued to existing stockholders and to insure that the company has additional unissued stock registered for issuance in case exercise of the rights occurs.

If the rights are exercised, usually a cash payment of some type is involved. If the cash received is equal to the par value, an entry crediting Capital Stock at par value is made. If it is in excess of par value, a credit to Paid-in Capital in Excess of Par develops; if it is less than par value, a charge to Paid-in Capital is appropriate.

Stock Compensation Plans

Another form of the warrant is the stock option plan, which is employed to compensate employees. For accounting purposes, stock option plans or stock purchase plans may be classified as **noncompensatory or compensatory plans** (a plan is any arrangement to issue stock to officers and employees, as a group or individually).[6] **APB Opinion No. 25** concluded that noncompensatory plans have the following characteristics: (1) participation by all employees who meet limited employment qualifications, (2) equal offers of stock to all eligible employees, (3) limitation of time permitted for exercise of an option or purchase right to a reasonable period, and (4) discount from the market price of the stock no greater than would be reasonable in an offer of stock to stockholders or others.[7] For example, IBM has a stock purchase plan under which employees who meet minimal employment qualifications are entitled to purchase IBM stock at a 15% reduction from market price for a short period of time. Such a reduction from market price is not considered compensatory because the employer's objectives appear to be either to raise additional equity capital or to expand ownership of the enterprise's stock among the employees as a means of enhancing loyalty to the enterprise. This position is debatable because the employee is receiving a valuable fringe benefit. However, because it is difficult to determine the company's objectives, in practice, if the discount is in the amount of 10–15% of the market price, the foregoing type of stock purchase plan is considered noncompensatory. **It should be emphasized that plans**

---

[6]Plans in which employees pay cash, either directly or through payroll withholding, as all or a significant part of the consideration for stock they receive, are commonly referred to as stock option, stock purchase, or stock thrift or savings plans. Plans in which employees receive stock for current or future services without paying cash (or with a nominal payment) are commonly referred to as stock bonus or stock award plans. Stock bonus and award plans are invariably compensatory. Stock thrift and savings plans are compensatory to the extent of contributions of an employer corporation. Stock option and purchase plans may be either compensatory or noncompensatory.

[7]"Accounting for Stock Issued to Employees," *Opinions of the Accounting Principles Board No. 25* (New York: AICPA, 1972), par. 7.

that do not possess all of the above mentioned four characteristics are classified as compensatory.

Accounting for Stock Compensation Plans

Accounting for noncompensatory plans poses no practical difficulties for accountants because compensation expense is not recorded by the employer corporation. The exercise of the option is simply accounted for as the normal issue of stock with stockholders' equity increased by the amount of the option price. Compensatory plans, however, present more difficulties. The three questions to be resolved are as follows:

1. How should compensation expense be determined?
2. Over what periods should compensation expense be allocated?
3. What types of plans are used to compensate officers and key executives?

Determination of Compensation Expense   **APB Opinion No. 25** requires that total compensation expense should be computed as the difference between the market price of the stock and the option price on the **measurement date.** The measurement date is the first date on which are known both (1) the number of shares that an individual employee is entitled to receive and (2) the option or purchase price, if any. That date for practically all plans is the date an **option is granted** or **stock is awarded** to an employee. The date of grant or award was chosen because at this date the corporation forgoes the principal alternative use of the shares optioned and a cost is measurable by the employer. The measurement date may be later than the date of grant or award in plans with variable terms that depend on events after date of grant or award.

If the number of shares or the option price or both are not known, compensation expense may have to be estimated on the basis of assumptions as to what will be the final number of shares and the option price.

Allocation of Compensation Expense   Compensation expense is recognized in the period(s) in which the **employee performs the services.** The total compensation expense is determined (ordinarily at the date of grant) and then allocated to the appropriate periods benefited by the employee's services. In practice, it is often difficult to specify the period of service, and considerable judgment is exercised in this determination. The general rule followed is that any method that is systematic and rational is appropriate, if the periods of service cannot be clearly defined. As a result, many enterprises recognize the compensation expense over an arbitrary period; others amortize it from the grant date to the date the option may be first exercised; and others record it as a current expense.

If the measurement date is later than the date of grant or award, the employer corporation should record the compensation expense each period from date of grant or award to the measurement date based on the market price of the stock at the end of each period. **APB Opinion No. 25** also states that "if stock is issued in a plan before some or all of 'he services are performed, part of the consideration recorded for the stock issued is unearned compensation and should be shown as a separate reduction of stockholders' equity."[8] The unearned compensation is expensed in the period or periods in which the employee performs service.

Types of Plans   Many different types of plans are used to compensate key executives. The popularity of a given plan usually depends on prospects in the stock market and tax considerations. For example, if it appears that appreciation will occur in a company's stock, a plan that offers the option to purchase stock is attractive to an executive. Conversely, if it appears that price appreciation is unlikely, then compensation might be tied to some performance measure such as an increase in book value or earnings per share. A good illustration of this type of plan is that of Atlantic Richfield, which recently offered performance units valued in excess of $700,000 to the chairman of the board. These performance units are payable in five years, contingent upon the company's meeting certain conditions regarding return on stockholders' equity and cash dividends. Three common plans that illustrate different accounting issues are:

1. Qualified or nonqualified stock option plans.
2. Stock appreciation rights.
3. Restricted stock plans.

Qualified or Nonqualified Stock Option Plans

A stock option plan can either be a **qualified** or **nonqualified** (or nonstatutory) plan. The distinction between qualified and nonqualified is based on the IRS Code and relates to the tax treatment afforded the plan. **Qualified option plans** are being phased out by the IRS and by the end of 1981 will no longer be permitted. The major differences between a qualified stock option plan and a nonqualified option plan relate to the holding period for the option, the tax treatment at exercise, and the spread between the market price and the option price at the date of grant. For example, in a qualified stock option plan the market price of the stock and the option price at the date of grant must be equal. This equality is not necessary in nonqualified plans. It should be noted that **no compensation expense is recorded for a qualified stock option plan** because no excess of market price over the option price exists at the date of grant.

Nonqualified option plans usually involve compensation expense because the market price exceeds the option price **at the date of grant.** Total compensation cost is measured by this difference and then allocated to the periods benefited. The option price is set by the terms of the grant and generally remains the same throughout the option period. The market price of the shares under option, however, may vary materially in the extended period during which the option is outstanding. A number of dates had been considered but the date of grant came closest to determining the value the corporation had in mind.[9]

---

[8]*Ibid.*, par. 14. The acceptability of issuing stock for future services is governed by state laws.

[9]Committee on Accounting Procedure, American Institute of Certified Public Accountants, *Accounting Research and Terminology Bulletin,* Final edition (New York: 1961), p. 122.

Accounting for Nonqualified Stock Option Plans

To illustrate the accounting for a nonqualified plan, assume that on November 1, 1979, the stockholders of Scott Company approve a plan that grants the company's executives options to purchase 10,000 shares of the company's $1.00 par value common stock. The options are granted on January 1, 1980, and may be exercised at any time within the next ten years. The option price per share is $60, and the market price of the stock at the date of grant is $70 per share. The total compensation expense is computed as follows:

Market value of 10,000 shares at date of grant ($70 per share)	$700,000
Option price of 10,000 shares at date of grant ($60 per share)	600,000
Total compensation expense	$100,000

As indicated earlier, **APB Opinion No. 25** recommends that the value of the option be recognized as an expense in the period(s) in which the employee performs services. In the case of Scott Company, assume that documents associated with issuance of the options indicate that the expected period of benefit is two years, starting with the grant date. The entry to record the total compensation expense at the date of grant is as follows:

Deferred Compensation Expense	100,000	
Paid-in Capital—Stock Options		100,000

The deferred compensation expense (a contra stockholders' equity account) then is amortized to income over the period of service involved (two years). The credit balance in the Paid-in Capital—Stock Options account is treated as an element of stockholders' equity (additional paid-in capital). An alternative to the entry above would be to record no formal entry at the date of grant, but accrue compensation expense at the end of each period as incurred. We will use the former approach for problem material because this method formalizes in the records the compensation element of these plans. On December 31, 1980, and on December 31, 1981, the following journal entry is recorded to recognize the compensation cost for the year attributable to the stock option plan.

Compensation Expense	50,000	
Deferred Compensation Expense		50,000

At December 31, 1980, the stockholders' equity section would be presented as follows, assuming that 1,000,000 shares were issued at $1.00 par value.

Stockholders' Equity		
Common stock, $1.00 par, 1,000,000 shares		
issued and outstanding		$1,000,000
Paid-in capital—stock options	$100,000	
Less deferred compensation expense	50,000	50,000
Total stockholders' equity		$1,050,000

If 20% or 2,000 of the 10,000 options were exercised on June 1, 1983 (three years and five months after date of grant), the following journal entry would be recorded:

Cash (2,000 × $60)	120,000	
Paid-in Capital—Stock Options (20% of $100,000)	20,000	
Common Stock (2,000 × $1.00)		2,000
Paid-in Capital in Excess of Par		138,000

If the remaining stock options are not exercised before their expiration date, the balance in Paid-in Capital—Stock Options account should be transferred to a more properly titled paid-in capital account, such as Paid-in Capital from Expired Stock Options. The entry to record this transaction at the date of cancellation would be as follows:

Paid-in Capital—Stock Options (80% of $100,000)	80,000	
Paid-in Capital from Expired Stock Options		80,000

The fact that a stock option is not exercised does not nullify the propriety of recording the costs of services received from the executives and attributable to the stock option plan. Under GAAP, compensation expense is, therefore, not adjusted upon expiration of the options. However, **APB Opinion No. 25** states that if a stock option is not exercised because **an employee fails to fulfill an obligation,** the estimate of compensation expense recorded in previous periods should be adjusted (as a change in estimate) by decreasing compensation expense in the period of forfeiture.

Stock Appreciation Rights

don't worry about

One of the main advantages of a nonqualified stock option plan is that an executive may receive shares of stock in the future having a market price substantially above the option price. A major disadvantage is that an executive must pay income tax on the difference between the market price of the stock and the option price at the **date of exercise.** This can be a big financial hardship for an executive who wishes to keep the stock (rather than sell it immediately) because the executive would have to pay not only income tax but the option price as well.

One solution to this problem was the creation of **stock appreciation rights (SARs).** In this type of plan, the executive is given the right to receive **share appreciation,** which is defined as the excess of the market price of the stock at the date of exercise over a pre-established price. This share appreciation may be paid in cash, shares, or a combination of both. The major advantage of SARs is that the executive often does not have to make a cash outlay at the date of exercise, but receives a payment for the share appreciation which may be used to pay any related income taxes.

Until the issuance of **FASB Interpretation No. 28** in December 1978, the accounting for SARs was undefined. As indicated earlier, the usual date for measuring compensation related to stock compensation plans is the date of grant. However, with SARs, the final amount of cash or shares (or a combination of the two) to be distributed is not known until the date of exercise and therefore total compensation cannot be measured until this date. Thus, the measurement date is the **date of exercise.** How then should compensation expense be recorded during the interim periods from the date of grant to the date of exercise? "An enterprise shall measure compensation expense as the amount by which the quoted market value of the shares of the enterprise's stock covered by the grant exceeds the option price or value specified."[10] Changes, either up or down, in the market value of those shares between the date of grant and the measurement date result in a change in the measure of compensation for the SARs. In this situation, it is entirely possible that some periods may have credits to compensation expense if the quoted market price of the stock falls from one period to the next, although the credit to compensation expense may not exceed previously recognized compensation expense.

To illustrate, assume that American Hotels, Inc. establishes a SAR program which entitles executives to receive cash at the date of issue for the difference between the market price of the stock and the pre-established price of $10 on 10,000 SARs; the current market price of the stock is $13, and the service period runs for two years (1980–81). The following schedule indicates the amount of compensation expense to be recorded each period, assuming that the executive holds the SARs for three years.

Stock Appreciation Rights
Schedule of Compensation Expense

(1) Date	(2) Market Price	(3) Pre-established Price (10,000 SARs)	(4) Cumulative Compensation Recognizable[a]	(5) Percentage Accrued[b]	(6) Compensation Accrued to Date	Expense 1980	Expense 1981	Expense 1982
12/31/80	$13	$10	$30,000	50%	$ 15,000	$15,000		
					55,000		$55,000	
12/31/81	17	10	70,000	100%	70,000			
					(70,000)			$(70,000)
12/31/82	9	10	-0-	100%	-0-			

[a]Cumulative compensation for unexercised SAR's to be allocated to periods of service.
[b]The percentage accrued is based upon a two-year service period (1980–1981).

In 1980, American Hotels would record compensation expense of $15,000 because 50% of the $30,000 of compensation expense recognizable at December 31, 1980 is allocable to 1980. In 1981, the market price increased to $17 per share; therefore, the additional compensation expense of $55,000 ($70,000 − $15,000) was recorded. The SARs were held through 1981 during which time the stock decreased substantially. The decrease is recognized by recording a $70,000 credit to compensation expense. Any such credit to compensation expense cannot exceed previous charges to expense attributable to that program.

As the compensation expense is recorded each period, the corresponding credit should be to a liability account if the stock appreciation is to be paid in cash. If stock is to be issued, then a more appropriate credit would be to Paid-in Capital. The entry to record compensation expense in the first year, assuming that the SAR ultimately will be paid in cash, is as follows:

Compensation Expense	15,000	
Liability Under Stock Appreciation Plan		15,000

---

[10]"Accounting for Stock Appreciation Rights and Other Variable Stock Option or Award Plans," *FASB Interpretation No. 28.* (Stamford, Conn.: FASB, 1978), par. 2.

The liability account would be credited in 1982 and debited in 1983 when the negative compensation expense is recorded. Because compensation expense is measured by the difference between market prices of the stock from period to period, multiplied by the number of SARs, compensation expense can increase or decrease substantially from one period to the next.

Many accountants are disturbed about the accounting for SARs because the amount of compensation expense to be reported each period is subject to fluctuations in the stock market. As some accountants have questioned, "Shouldn't earnings determine stock prices, rather than stock prices determine earnings?"[11] Even with this drawback, this type of plan is gaining in popularity because executives are required to make little, if any, cash outlay under these programs. For example, in 1974 only about 20 top industrial companies were using SARs; now well in excess of 100 are employing these plans, and many more companies are asking stockholders to approve SAR plans.

Compensation measured as shown above for SARs is accrued as a charge to expense over the periods the employee performs the related services, referred to as the **service period.** If the service period is not defined in the plan, it is presumed to be the **vesting period,** which frequently is the period from the date of grant to the date the SARs become exercisable. Rights are vested when continued employment is no longer required for the employee to retain or receive the rights.

SARs are often issued in combination with compensatory stock options (referred to as **tandem** or **combination plans**) and the executive may then select which of the two sets of terms to exercise, thereby canceling the other. The existence of alternative plans running concurrently poses additional problems from an accounting standpoint because according to **Opinion No. 25** the accountant must determine, on the basis of the facts available each period, which of the two plans has the higher probability of exercise and then account for this plan, and ignore the other.

Restricted Stock Plans

Accounting for a restricted stock plan is similar to accounting for a nonqualified stock option plan. The main difference between the two types of plans is that in a restricted stock purchase plan, shares of stock are **physically issued** to the executive at a price (which may be as low as zero) at the grant date. In a stock option plan, no shares are issued until the options are exercised. Restricted stock plans usually carry a restriction as to transferability, requiring that during a specified period of time the shares not be sold or pledged, except that they may be sold to the issuing company at the original purchase price if the employee leaves the firm within that period. It should be noted that if the market price has fallen below the original issue price, the company does not have to repurchase the shares.

The advantage of this plan is that an executive **may elect** to be taxed for the difference between the fair market value and the option price at the date of grant or at the time the restrictions lapse. If the individual pays the tax at the date of the

---

[11]For this reason, companies are reluctant to measure compensation expense other than at the date of grant for nonqualified option plans, because a very high compensation cost can develop that must be reported as an expense on the income statement. Few nonqualified option plans are, therefore, adopted where the measurement date is other than the date of the grant.

grant, and the stock's price goes up, the employee pays a minimal tax. If the stock goes down, however, the tax paid is not refundable. If the employee waits to be taxed at the time the restrictions lapse, the stock may have skyrocketed, leaving the executive with a higher tax bill. The restricted stock plan affords the executive some flexibility in tax planning.

If a company does adopt a restricted stock bonus plan, a number of interesting accounting problems develop. For example, International Telephone and Telegraph adopted a Career Executive Incentive Stock Purchase Plan whereby key employees could purchase a designated number of ITT shares, subject to numerous restrictions, at 50% of the fair market value. The restrictions on the stock were lifted on a partial basis over a period of years (5% each year for the fifth through the twenty-fifth year). The company reserved the right to repurchase the shares if the employee left before the restrictions lapsed.

The problem in accounting for such a plan is measuring the compensation involved. Generally, the compensation is measured by the difference between the fair market value of the stock and the option price. But, if it is appropriate to base the compensation expense on the value of the securities issued less option price, how should the value of the restricted shares be determined in the absence of an available market price? One solution is to use the market price of regularly traded shares, ignoring the restrictions. The other approach is to compute a discount based on statements from officers and investment bankers. Because a method for determining a value for the effect of the restrictions at this time cannot be measured objectively or realistically, the fair value of the stock ignoring restrictions should be used.

As an example, suppose that ITT issued 100,000 shares, subject to various restrictions, to its key personnel at $1.00 per share on January 1, 1981, when the market value of the stock on that date was $5.00. Investment bankers indicate that the value of the stock subject to the restrictions is $3.00. The amount recorded for compensation is $400,000 (100,000 × [$5.00 − $1.00]). The entry at date of purchase is (for the compensation only):

Deferred Compensation Expense	400,000	
Paid-in Capital—Stock Purchase Plan		400,000

At the end of 1981, the company would make the following entry, assuming a 20-year amortization period:

Compensation Expense	20,000	
Deferred Compensation Expense		20,000

The nature of the plan and its significant provisions are to be disclosed in footnotes to the financial statements, like those of other option plans.

Alternative Methods of Measuring Compensation Expense

Valuing compensation plans such as stock options, stock appreciation rights, and restricted stock plans is a difficult problem. In general, most accountants agree that the value of the compensation should be determined on the grant date because the company forgoes an alternative use of the shares on that date. They differ, however, as to how the value at the grant date should be determined.

One group believes that an attempt should be made to value the **option** itself.[12] They note that an option to buy stock at a price equal to or below the market price has value and cannot be considered worthless. In addition, because there is no risk of loss to the executive and a possibility, if not a probability, of great gain, the option may possess value that is greater than the spread between the option price and the market price at the date of the grant. Similarly, others argue that although services are normally valued at the cost of the assets given in exchange for them, the **fair value of the services received** is also a proper and acceptable basis of valuation. Using this approach, an attempt is made to determine what type of cash trade-off the executives make when receiving an option for stock in lieu of a straight cash distribution. By imputing this cash trade-off, the total amount of compensation may be determined.

Others stress that the approaches described above are too subjective and argue for the approach adopted by **APB Opinion No. 25,** namely, that compensation expense be measured by the difference between the market price and the option price at the **date of grant.** This argument is based on the premise that the only objective and verifiable amount that can be determined at the date of grant is the spread between the market and option price.

Others believe that the spread between the market price and the option price should be used, but at other dates. For example, the **date the option becomes exercisable** by the executive is submitted by some accountants as the most reasonable basis of valuing the compensation represented by the stock option. At that date, the employee has performed the option contract, and the company is obligated to issue shares at the option price.

In addition, some accountants state that the excess of the market price over the option price at the date the option becomes exercisable is still an incomplete valuation that understates the value of the option, particularly when this option may be held for several years before expiring. They believe that only at the **date that the option is exercised** is the final value of the employee's services recognizable. It is questionable whether compensation cost to the company, however, should be based on the speculative activity of its employees.

Finally, it is sometimes argued that **no compensation expense should be shown at all** because no cost to the entity results from the issuance of additional shares of stock; the cost is to the stockholders in the possible dilution of their interest in the entity, and accountants should ignore this factor in their accounting. This does not appear to be a reasonable approach because a cost is involved to the existing stockholders which should be considered a cost of operating the enterprise.

Measuring compensation cost in stock option and stock purchase plans is an extremely important and controversial issue. The measurement problem becomes even more difficult as additional considerations are introduced, such as when either the option price or the number of shares into which the option is exercised is not known at the date of the grant. With increased scrutiny being given compensation plans by stockholders, the IRS, and management, it appears that this area will be under continued evaluation and discussion.

---

[12]For an interesting discussion of an attempt to value options, see Clifford W. Smith, Jr. and Jerold L. Zimmerman, "Valuing Employee Stock Option Plans Using Option Pricing Models," *Journal of Accounting Research* (Autumn, 1976), pp. 357–364.

Disclosure of Stock Options and Stock Appreciation Rights

Regardless of the basis used in valuing stock options, rights, or plans, full disclosure should be made as to the status of the options, rights, or plan at the end of the period, including the number of shares as to which options or rights were exercisable. In regard to options exercised during the period, disclosure should be made of the number of shares involved and the option price involved. An example taken from Bell & Howell Company's 1978 annual report presented on page 731 is illustrative of how these plans are often disclosed in the financial statements.

Section II Computing Earnings Per Share

The practice of reporting earnings per share on outstanding common stock prior to the mid-1960s, while commonplace, was left to management's discretion. In 1966, the profession strongly recommended that earnings per share be disclosed in the statement of income.[13]

The APB subsequently changed its recommendation to a requirement through the issuance of **Opinion No. 15.** In addition, **Opinion No. 15** greatly complicated the computation of earnings per share by requiring two presentations of earnings per share on the income statement of companies with dilutive securities: (1) earnings per common and common equivalent shares and (2) fully diluted earnings per share.[14] **Opinion No. 15** is a complex, 60-page document containing new definitions, new concepts, and a bevy of rules. So complex is **No. 15** that within one year of its issuance the AICPA supplemented it with an interpretative publication of 116 pages devoted to explanations and clarifications.

Also, as an additional consequence of this complexity, the reporting requirements of **APB Opinion No. 15** have been recently suspended for nonpublic enterprises through issuance of **FASB Statement No. 21.**[15] A **nonpublic enterprise** is an enterprise other than one (1) whose debt or equity securities are traded in a public market on a foreign or domestic stock exchange or in the over-the-counter market (including securities quoted locally or regionally) or (2) that is required to file financial statements with the SEC. An enterprise is no longer considered a nonpublic enterprise when its financial statements are issued in preparation for the sale of any class of securities in a public market.

Whether there should be differential disclosure between public and nonpublic companies (so-called two-tier disclosure) is controversial. On the one side, nonpublic business enterprises (generally small or closely held) are critical of the added paperwork and auditing expense that is associated with the increase in financial reporting requirements. Others believe that the development of a possible "two-tier" reporting system with financial statements differing between public and nonpublic companies may lead to confusion and inferior accounting practices for the nonpublic enterprises. The FASB is currently studying the question of whether

---

[13]"Reporting the Results of Operations," *Opinions of the Accounting Principles Board No. 9* (New York: AICPA, 1966).

[14]"Earnings per Share," *Opinions of the Accounting Principles Board No. 15* (New York: AICPA, 1969).

[15]"Suspension of the Reporting of Earnings per Share and Segment Information by Nonpublic Enterprises," *Statements of the Financial Accounting Standards Board No. 21* (Stamford, Conn.: FASB, 1978).

Note H—Common Stock and Incentive Stock Plans:
Changes in Common Stock were as follows:

BELL & HOWELL

	1978		1977	
	Shares	Amount	Shares	Amount
Issued at beginning of year	5,758,451	$39,189,000	5,744,821	$38,959,000
Held in treasury	(32,795)	(990,000)	(32,795)	(990,000)
Outstanding at beginning of year	5,725,656	38,199,000	5,712,026	37,969,000
Additional Treasury Stock acquired	(200,000)	(3,240,000)	—	—
Issued under Incentive Stock Plans:				
Options exercised	10,868	168,000	13,630	182,000
Restricted stock transactions and federal income tax benefits	—	1,000	—	48,000
	(189,132)	(3,071,000)	13,630	230,000
Outstanding at end of year	5,536,524	$35,128,000	5,725,656	$38,199,000

At December 30, 1978, a total of 355,905 shares of authorized and unissued Common Stock were reserved for conversion of Preferred Stock or issuance under Incentive Stock Plans.

The Company's Incentive Stock Plans provide for stock appreciation rights along with related stock options. The rights are granted to senior executives and permit the holder, upon surrendering all or part of his related stock option, to receive cash, Common Stock, or both, of up to 100% of the difference between the market price and the option price, but not in excess of 50% of the option price. Shares covered by such surrendered stock option or portion thereof are not available for the grant of further stock options.

Proceeds from the sale of Common Stock issued under stock options granted and related federal tax benefits are credited to Common Stock at the time the option is exercised, and no charge is made against operations with respect to stock options. Stock appreciation rights granted require a charge to operations based upon the amount, if any, by which the fair market value of the Common Stock subject to related stock options exceeds the option price of such shares. The charges to operations in 1978 and 1977 with respect to such rights were $69,000 and $122,000, respectively. The value of restricted stock (which was issued in prior years) is charged to operations over periods ranging up to ten years, depending upon the restrictions related to the stock.

Transactions during 1978 and 1977 under Incentive Stock Plans were as follows:

	1978	1977
Shares under option at beginning of year	272,154	209,514
Options granted	13,900	107,790
Options and stock appreciation rights exercised	(10,868)	(13,630)
Surrendered upon exercise of stock appreciation rights	(12,779)	(5,625)
Canceled or expired	(25,653)	(25,895)
Shares under option at end of year	236,754	272,154
Shares available for future grants at end of year (6,365 may be used for restricted stock)	111,423	99,670
Price range of shares under option at end of year (market value at date of grant)	$11.25 to $20.94	$11.25 to $20.94

Of the shares under option at the end of the year, 90,250 with option prices ranging from $12.69 to $20.94 had related stock appreciation rights.

all enterprises should be required to report the same information or if a certain amount of differential disclosure should be permitted. Until this study is completed, the Board has chosen to suspend the reporting requirements of **APB Opinion No. 15** for nonpublic companies.

Weighted Average Number of Shares

In all computations of earnings per share, the weighted average of shares outstanding during the period constitutes the basis for the per-share amounts reported. Shares issued or retired during a period are weighted by the fraction of the period in which they were outstanding. The weighted number of these shares is added to the number of shares outstanding for the entire period to obtain the weighted average number of shares outstanding during the period.

For example, assume that a corporation had 100,000 common shares outstanding on January 1 and issued 6,000 additional common shares on March 1. The weighted average computed at different dates of the year would be as follows:

> For quarter ended March 31
>   100,000 + 1/3 (6,000)   = 102,000 shares
> For six months ended June 30
>   100,000 + 4/6 (6,000)   = 104,000 shares
> For nine months ended September 30
>   100,000 + 7/9 (6,000)   = 104,667 shares
> For the year ended December 31
>   100,000 + 10/12 (6,000) = 105,000 shares

Reacquired shares are included in the weighted average only for the time they were outstanding. For example, assume that a corporation had 100,000 shares outstanding on January 1 and reacquired 6,000 shares on March 1. The weighted average at different dates of the year could be computed as follows:

> For quarter ended March 31
>   94,000[a] + 2/3 (6,000) = 98,000 shares
> For six months ended June 30
>   94,000 + 2/6 (6,000) = 96,000 shares
> For nine months ended September 30
>   94,000 + 2/9 (6,000) = 95,333 shares
> For the year ended December 31
>   94,000 + 2/12 (6,000) = 95,000 shares
>
> [a]100,000 − 6,000 = 94,000 shares outstanding for the full period

More complex methods of computing a weighted average may be used if the number of shares involved changes frequently. The sum of the shares outstanding each day divided by the number of days in the period would produce a precise average. The schedule on page 733 illustrates computation of a weighted average on a share-day basis. Ordinarily computations reflect outstanding shares to the nearest month.

When stock dividends, stock splits, or reverse splits occur, computation of the weighted average number of shares requires restatement of the shares outstanding before the stock dividend or split. Stock dividends or splits are retroactive adjust-

COMPUTATION OF WEIGHTED AVERAGE NUMBER OF SHARES

Date	Number of Shares Increase (Decrease)	Outstanding	Days Outstanding	Share-days
January 1		25,000	15[a]	375,000
January 16	1,000	26,000	78[b]	2,028,000
April 4	2,700	28,700	151	4,333,700
September 2	(1,500)	27,200	47	1,278,400
October 19	5,000	32,200	74	2,382,800
			365	10,397,900
			A	B

Weighted average number of shares outstanding (B ÷ A) = 28,487

[a]Days between 1/1 and 1/16 that 25,000 shares were outstanding.
[b]Days between 1/16 and 4/4 that 26,000 shares were outstanding.

ments rather than transactions to be weighted by the number of days a stock dividend or split was outstanding. For example, assume that a corporation had 100,000 shares outstanding on January 1 and issued a 25% stock dividend on June 30. For purposes of computing a weighted average for the current year, the additional 25,000 shares outstanding as a result of the stock dividend are assumed to have been outstanding since the beginning of the year; the weighted average for the year would be 125,000 shares. On a months outstanding basis a restatement due to a stock dividend is illustrated in the schedule below.

COMPUTATION OF WEIGHTED AVERAGE NUMBER OF SHARES WITH RESTATEMENT FOR STOCK DIVIDEND
1980

Date	Transaction	Number of Shares Increase (Decrease)	Outstanding	Months Outstanding	Share Months Original	Restated
January 1	—	—	25,000	1	25,000	
January 29	Issued for cash	1,000	26,000	2	52,000	
April 1	10% stock dividend	2,600	28,600	5		143,000[a]
	Restatement of 25,000 and 52,000 amounts by 10%;					
	25,000 + .10(25,000) =		27,500	1	27,500	
	26,000 + .10(26,000) =		28,600	2	57,200	84,700
September 2	Purchase of common stock	(1,500)	27,100	2		54,200
October 31	Issued for cash	5,000	32,100	2		64,200
				12		346,100
				A		B

[a]5 × 28,600 = 143,000

Weighted average number of shares outstanding (B ÷ A) = 28,842 (rounded)

If a stock dividend or stock split occurs after the end of the year, but before the financial statements are issued, the weighted average number of shares outstanding for the prior year (and any other years presented in comparative form) must be restated. The illustration at the bottom of page 733, for example, indicates 28,842 shares outstanding on a weighted average basis for 1980; if a 2 for 1 stock split (100% stock dividend) occurred January 10, 1981 (the next year), the shares outstanding on a weighted average basis for 1980 would be 57,684 (2 × 28,842). It should be noted that all problems in the textbook assume use of the months basis for computing weighted average unless stated otherwise.

Earnings Per Share and Dilutive Securities

The merger movement of the sixties, the increased demand by executives for noncash compensation packages, and differing capital-seeking transactions resulted in the issuance of new and unique securities, many of which were dilutive or potentially dilutive from an earnings per share viewpoint. Dilutive securities present a serious problem in determining the proper earnings per share because upon conversion or exercise an adverse effect on earnings per share occurs. This adverse effect can be significant and, more importantly, unexpected unless the financial statements call attention to the potential dilutive effect in some manner.

For this reason, the APB issued **Opinion No. 15** dealing specifically with the manner in which these securities should be handled in earnings per share computations.

Simple and Complex Capital Structures

A corporation's capital structure is regarded as **simple** if it consists only of common stock or includes no potentially dilutive convertible securities, options, warrants, or other rights that upon conversion or exercise could in the aggregate dilute earnings per common share. A capital structure is regarded as **complex** if it includes securities that could have a dilutive effect on earnings per common share.

The appropriate presentation of earnings per share data for corporations having a simple capital structure is a **single presentation** expressed in terms such as "earnings per common share" on the face of the income statement. The computation of earnings per common share is simply the net income reported for the period (less any preferred dividends) divided by the weighted number of actual shares outstanding during the period.

A complex capital structure requires a **dual presentation** of earnings per share, each with equal prominence on the face of the income statement. In accounting jargon these two presentations are referred to as "primary earnings per share" and "fully diluted earnings per share." **Primary earnings per share** is based on the number of common shares outstanding plus the shares referred to as common stock equivalents—securities that are in substance equivalent to common shares. **Fully diluted earnings per share** is a pro forma presentation that reflects the dilution of earnings per share that would have occurred if **all** contingent issuances of common stock that would have reduced earnings per share had taken place.

Opinion No. 15 involves the computation and presentation of dual earnings per share amounts for complex capital structures, and the computation and presentation of a single earnings per share amount for a simple capital structure.

To provide relief from complex computations to corporations that have insignificant potential dilution, the profession adopted a **3% materiality test.** Any corporation whose capital structure has potential dilution of less than 3% of earnings per common share outstanding is considered to have a simple capital structure. Apparently, dilution of less than 3% is not considered to be material. To illustrate, Streeter Company has earnings per share of $2.00, ignoring all dilutive securities in its capital structure. If the possible conversion or exercise of the dilutive securities in the aggregate would reduce earnings per share to $1.94 or below (97% $\times$ $2.00), a presentation involving dilutive securities would be required. Otherwise the company reports earnings per share at $2.00 and no additional disclosure is required. It is to be assumed that the weighted average number of shares is the basis and that potential dilution, if any exists, is less than 3%. In computing the 3% dilution factor, the aggregate of all dilutive securities must be considered. The dilutive securities are not considered individually, but in total.

Whether the capital structure is simple or complex, where applicable, earnings per share data should be shown before and after extraordinary items. In addition, when the income statement includes a disposal of a segment of a business, "Income from Continuing Operations" must also be shown per share. Also, earnings per share amounts must be shown for all periods presented; and all prior period earnings per share amounts presented should be restated for stock dividends and stock splits. When results of operations of a prior period have been restated as a result of a prior period adjustment, the earnings per share data shown for the prior period should also be restated. The effect of the restatement, expressed in per share terms, should be disclosed in the year of the restatement.

Primary Earnings Per Share

A primary earnings per share amount must be computed and presented for corporations having a complex capital structure. The basis for primary earnings per share is the outstanding common shares plus the common equivalent shares. If **no** common stock equivalents exist in a complex capital structure, the primary earnings per share is the same as the basic earnings per share for a simple capital structure; that is, net income less preferred dividends is divided by the number of common shares outstanding. For complex capital structures **with** common stock equivalents, however, **Opinion No. 15** does not provide for the presentation of an earnings per share figure that is based solely on common shares issued and outstanding. Many accountants believe that in spite of the increased number of earnings per share amounts presented for a complex capital structure, the omission of actual earnings per common shares outstanding is a failure to report the one real fact available.

Common Stock Equivalents

A common stock equivalent is a security that, although not a common stock, gives its holder the right through conversion or exercise to acquire shares of common stock. Its value tends to change with changes in the value of the common stock to which it is related. Only if common stock equivalents are dilutive, as opposed to antidilutive, are they added to common shares in computing primary earnings per share. Antidilutive securities are securities that would create an increase in earnings per share (or a reduction in net loss per share). Once a security is classified as a common stock equivalent, it is always a common stock equivalent; it enters into the computation of primary earnings per share, however, only if it is dilutive. That is, a common stock equivalent may enter into the computation in one period and not in another depending on whether it is dilutive or antidilutive.

Convertible Securities

Convertible securities should be considered common stock equivalents if the cash yield to the holder at the time of issuance is significantly below what would be a comparable yield for a similar security of the issuer without the conversion option.[16] After giving consideration to various approaches, the Board concluded that a convertible security, whether bonds or preferred stock, is a common stock equivalent if, at the time of issuance and on the basis of its market price, it has a **cash yield of less than 66⅔%** of the then current bank prime rate of interest. The term "cash yield" refers to the ratio of cash received annually to the market price of the related security. The prime rate is the rate of interest charged to the best creditors of banks. The rationale for the cash yield test is that **the investor would not be willing to accept a cash yield less than ⅔ of the prime rate unless the convertible security contains significant common stock characteristics.** To illustrate this test, assume that Clayton Corp. had a convertible bond (par $1,000) with a coupon rate of 8% and a market price of $1,200. It would have a cash yield at **time of issuance** of 6.67% ($80/$1,200). If the prime rate were 12% at the **date of issuance,** this security would be considered a common stock equivalent because the cash yield is less than ⅔ of the prime rate:

$$\text{⅔ of bank prime rate of } 12\% = 8\%$$
$$\text{Cash yield} \qquad\qquad\quad = 6.67\%$$

The cash yield test is an arbitrary rule but it provides a simple and objective criterion that is easily applied. There are certain weaknesses in this approach, however. If market conditions change, the convertible may lose much of its apparent initial conversion value. This means that a company may have outstanding a convertible bond that has little possibility of conversion; yet, it may be classified as a common stock equivalent because at the date of issuance the investors placed a high value on the conversion option.

Also, the use of the prime rate is questionable. The prime rate is a short-term rate and the cash yield is a long-term rate. In a sense, some argue that we are comparing apples and oranges when the cash yield test is applied. For example, in the last few years, the prime rate has been so volatile that at times it was higher than the cash yield on most long-term bonds. When the cash yield test was adopted, it was assumed that the prime rate would be lower than the cash yield.

To be included in the computation of primary earnings per share, the conversion feature must be exercisable within five years of the date of the financial statement.

---

[16]APB *Opinion No. 15,* par. 33.

Convertible securities initially exercisable only beyond five years but within ten years of the financial statement date and all other convertible securities not included in primary earnings per share computations are included in fully diluted earnings per share.

"If Converted" Method

In computing earnings per share amounts for both the primary and the fully diluted earnings per share with convertible securities, the "if converted" method is used. The "if converted" approach computes earnings per share by assuming (1) the conversion of convertible securities at the beginning of the period (or time of issuance of the security, if issued during the period), and (2) the elimination of the related interest charges net of tax or preferred dividends from the net income available for common stockholders.

As an example, Marshy Field Corporation has net income for the year of $210,000 and an average number of shares outstanding during the period of 100,000 shares. The company has two convertible debenture bond issues outstanding. One is a 6% issue sold at 100 (total $1,000,000) in a prior year when the prime rate was 11% and convertible into 20,000 common shares. The other is a 10% issue sold at 100 (total $1,000,000) on April 1 of the current year when the prime rate was 11% and convertible into 32,000 common shares. Assume that the tax rate at present is 50%.

COMPUTATION OF PRIMARY EARNINGS PER SHARE			
Net income for the year	$210,000	Average number of shares outstanding	100,000
Add: Adjustment for interest (net of tax) on 6% debentures	30,000	Add: Shares assumed to be issued upon conversion of 6% debentures as of the beginning of	
Adjusted net income	$240,000	the year	20,000
	A		
		Average number of common and common equivalent shares	120,000
			B
PRIMARY EARNINGS PER SHARE (A ÷ B) $2.00			

The primary earnings per share calculation includes only one dilutive security—the 6% convertible debentures. The 6% yield rate at date of issue is less than ⅔ of the prime rate of 11%. The 10% convertible is not considered in the primary earnings per share calculation because the cash yield (10%) at date of issue was higher than ⅔ of the prime rate (⅔ × 11% = 7⅓%). To determine the adjusted net income, interest on the "if converted" securities less the related tax effect must be added back. Because the "if converted" method assumes conversion as of the beginning of the year, it is only logical and consistent to assume that the related interest or dividends on the convertibles would not have been paid during the year. The elimination of $60,000 tax deductible interest expense would result in a $30,000 increase in income taxes, and only the net addition to income of $30,000 would have been available to common stockholders.

Fully diluted earnings per share includes not only the 6% debentures but also the 10% debentures. The interest charges (net of tax) for both issuances are added back to arrive at adjusted net income. Note also that a weighted average determination is made of the number of shares outstanding. Because the date of issuance is subsequent to the beginning of the year in the case of the 10% convertibles, the shares assumed to have been issued on that date, April 1, are weighted as outstanding from then to the end of the period.

COMPUTATION OF FULLY DILUTED EARNINGS PER SHARE			
Net income for the year	$210,000	Average number of common shares outstanding	100,000
Add: Adjustment for interest (net of tax) — 6% debentures (previously computed)	30,000	Add: Shares assumed to be issued upon conversion of debentures	
10% debentures ($1,000,000 × 10% × ¾ year × 50% tax rate)	37,500	6% (as of beginning of year) 10% (as of date of issue, Apr. 1; ¾ × 32,000)	20,000 24,000
Adjusted net income	$277,500	Average number of common and common equivalent shares	144,000
	A		B
FULLY DILUTED EARNINGS PER SHARE (A ÷ B) $1.93			

Marshy Field Corporation would present the per-share earnings as computed above in the following manner:

PRESENTATION OF EARNINGS PER SHARE[a]	
(Bottom of income statement) Net income	$210,000
Earnings per share: On common and common equivalent shares (Note X)	$2.00
On a fully diluted basis (Note X)	$1.93

Note X. Earnings per common share and common equivalent share was computed by dividing net income by the weighted number of shares of common stock and common stock equivalents outstanding during the year. The 6% convertible debentures have been considered to be common stock equivalents. Consequently, the number of shares issuable assuming full conversion of these debentures as of the beginning of the year was added to the number of common shares, and net income was adjusted to eliminate the interest on these debentures, net of the applicable tax effect. Fully diluted earnings per share was computed assuming conversion of all debentures.

[a]A dual presentation is required because $1.93 is less than 97% of $2.10 ($210,000 ÷ 100,000 shares).

When the "if converted" method is employed, the conversion rate in effect during the period is used in computing primary earnings per share. It is not uncommon, however, in bond agreements for conversion to be disallowed for at least two years after issuance followed by a conversion rate that changes over the period **the bond is outstanding.** In this situation, the **earliest conversion rate** is used for computation of primary earnings per share. For fully diluted earnings per share the

most advantageous conversion rate available to the holder within 10 years is used. To illustrate, assume that a convertible bond was issued January 1, 1979, with a conversion rate of 10 common shares for each bond starting January 1, 1981; beginning January 1, 1984, the conversion rate is 12 common shares for each bond, and beginning January 1, 1988, it is 15 common shares for each bond. In computing primary EPS the conversion rate of 10 shares to one bond is used; in computing fully diluted EPS the conversion rate of 15 shares to one bond is used.

Options and Warrants

Stock options and warrants outstanding and their equivalents (whether or not exercisable) are considered common stock equivalents and are included in earnings per share computations unless they are antidilutive or exercise cannot take place within five years. Stock purchase contracts, stock subscriptions not fully paid, deferred compensation packages providing for the issuance of common stock, and convertible securities that allow or require the payment of cash at issuance are treated as options and warrants. Options, warrants, and their equivalents are included in earnings per share computations through the **treasury stock method.**

The treasury stock method assumes that the options and/or warrants are exercised at the beginning of the year (or date of issue if later) and the proceeds from the exercise of options and warrants are used to purchase common stock for the treasury. The treasury stock method will increase the number of shares outstanding whenever the exercise price of an option or warrant is below the market price of the common stock.[17] For example, if the exercise price of a warrant is $5.00 and the fair market value of the stock is $15, it follows that using the treasury stock method would increase the shares outstanding. Exercise of the warrant would result in one additional share outstanding, but the $5.00 received for the one share issued is not sufficient to purchase one share in the market at $15. Three warrants would have to be exercised (and three additional shares issued) to produce enough money ($15) to acquire one share in the market. Thus, an increase of two shares outstanding would result.

In terms of larger numbers, assume 1,500 options outstanding at an exercise price of $30 a common share and a common stock market price per share of $50. Through application of the treasury stock method it can be seen that there would be 600 **incremental shares** outstanding computed as follows:

COMPUTATION OF INCREMENTAL SHARES	
Proceeds from exercise of 1,500 options (1,500 $\times$ $30)	$45,000
Shares issued upon exercise of options	1,500
Treasury shares purchasable with proceeds ($45,000 $\div$ $50)	900
Incremental shares outstanding (considered common stock equivalents)	600

[17]The opposite effect develops when the exercise price is greater than the market value of the common stock; the security is then antidilutive. The treatment accorded antidilutive securities is discussed later in this chapter.

For both options and warrants,[18] exercise may not be assumed until the market price of the stock is above the exercise price for substantially[19] all of three consecutive months, with the latest month being the last month of the period to which earnings per share data relate. Once this three-month criterion has been satisfied, the **average market price** of the common stock for the period should be used in computing primary earnings per share. In computing fully diluted earnings per share, it is assumed that the **closing market price** (if it is higher than the average price) is used in computing the incremental shares.

To illustrate application of the treasury stock method, assume that Pauley Industries, Inc., has net income for the period of $220,000. The average number of shares

	Pauley Industries, Inc. COMPUTATION OF EARNINGS PER SHARE (Treasury Stock Method) Options	
	Primary Earnings Per Share	Fully Diluted Earnings Per Share
Average number of shares under options outstanding	5,000	5,000
Option price per share	× $20	× $20
Proceeds upon exercise of options	$100,000	$100,000
Market price of common stock:		
Average	$24	
Closing		$28
Treasury shares that could be repurchased with proceeds ($100,000 ÷ $24)	4,166	
($100,000 ÷ $28)		3,571
Excess of shares under option over treasury shares that could be repurchased (5,000 − 4,166);	834	
(5,000 − 3,571)		1,429
Common stock equivalent shares (Incremental shares)	834	1,429
Average number of common shares outstanding	100,000	100,000
Total average number of common and common equivalent shares	100,834	101,429
	A	C
Net income for the year	$220,000	$220,000
	B	D
Earnings per share	$2.18 (B ÷ A)	$2.17 (D ÷ C)

---

[18]It might be noted that options and warrants have essentially the same assumptions and computational problems, although the warrants allow or require the tendering of some other security such as debt in lieu of cash upon exercise. In such situations, the accounting becomes quite complex, and the reader should refer to *Opinion No. 15* for its proper disposition.

[19]"Substantially" is assumed to mean 11 of 13 weeks.

outstanding for the period was 100,000 shares. The average number of shares under outstanding options (although not exercisable at this time), at an option price of $20 per share, is 5,000 shares. The average market price of the common stock during the year was $24 and the closing price at the end of the year is $28 (see illustrated computations on page 740).

In this example potential dilution is less than 3% for both primary and fully diluted, and, therefore, the options can be ignored. In other words, if both primary and fully diluted earnings per share are more than 97% of earnings per common share outstanding, earnings per share need be based only on the weighted average of the common shares outstanding, which would be $220,000 ÷ 100,000 shares or $2.20. In this illustration, either the primary or fully diluted would have to be $2.13 or below ($2.20 × 97%) before a dual presentation would be required. Primary

---

Pauley Industries, Inc.
COMPUTATION OF EARNINGS PER SHARE
(Treasury Stock Method)

Options and Warrants

	Primary Earnings Per Share	Fully Diluted Earnings Per Share
Proceeds upon exercise of options and warrants outstanding		
Options (5,000 shares @ $20)	$100,000	$100,000
Warrants (46,000 shares @ $10)	460,000	460,000
	$560,000	$560,000
Average number of shares outstanding	100,000	100,000
Assumed use of proceeds:		
Shares from exercise of options	5,000	5,000
Shares from exercise of warrants	46,000	46,000
Shares assumed to be repurchased with proceeds from exercise (subject to 20% maximum)	(20,000)[a]	(20,000)[a]
Total common and common equivalent shares	131,000	131,000
Net income for the year	$220,000	$220,000
Add: interest income from purchase of government securities ($560,000 − $480,000) × 6% × 50% tax rate	2,400	—
Adjusted net income	$222,400	$220,000
	A	C
Total average number of common and common equivalent shares	131,000	131,000
	B	D
Earnings per share	$1.70 (A ÷ B)	$1.68 (C ÷ D)

[a]20,000 shares were repurchased under both the primary and fully diluted earnings per share. It took only $480,000 ($24 × 20,000) to purchase the shares under the primary earnings per share calculation, but it took $560,000 ($28 × 20,000) to purchase the shares under the fully diluted earnings per share calculation.

earnings per share was $2.18 ($220,000 ÷ 100,834 shares) and fully diluted earnings per share was $2.17 ($220,000 ÷ 101,429 shares); therefore, a simple capital structure is assumed and a single presentation of $2.20 per share is appropriate.

If upon exercise of the options and warrants, the number of shares assumed to be repurchased would exceed 20% of the already outstanding common stock, the treasury stock approach is modified. Once the proceeds have been applied to purchase common stock up to 20% of the outstanding common stock, the balance of the proceeds is assumed to be used to reduce first short-term debt and then long-term borrowings, with any remaining funds invested in government securities. The rationale for the 20% cutoff is that the purchase of this amount of stock would have a significant impact on the market price of the stock, and make the use of the treasury stock method questionable.

For example, assume the same facts as in the previous illustration, except that there are also warrants outstanding to purchase 46,000 shares of common stock at $10 per share (see illustrated computations on page 741).

In this case, primary and fully diluted earnings per share should be reported because dilution is 3% or more ($2.20 − $1.68 = dilution of 23.6%). Because there was no outstanding debt to be repurchased, it is assumed that the excess proceeds are used to purchase government securities yielding 6%. Also the ending market price was used for fully diluted earnings per share, whereas the average price was employed for primary earnings per share. Acquisition of the 20% maximum treasury shares at the ending market price (fully diluted computation) would utilize all the assumed proceeds from exercise; therefore, only the primary earnings per share computation resulted in the assumed purchase of governmental securities in this example.

Contingent Issuance Agreement

If shares are issuable upon the mere passage of time, they should be considered as outstanding for the computation of primary earnings per share. If attainment or maintenance of a level of earnings is the condition, and if that level is currently being attained, the additional shares should be considered as outstanding for the purpose of computing both primary and fully diluted earnings per share.

For example, assume that Walz Corporation purchased Cardella Company and agreed to pay the stockholders of Cardella Company 20,000 additional shares in 1982 if Cardella Company's net income in 1981 is $90,000; in 1980 Cardella Company's net income is $100,000. Both primary and fully diluted earnings per share for 1980 would reflect the 20,000 contingent shares because the 1981 stipulated earnings of $90,000 are already being attained.

If attainment of increased earnings above the present level is the condition, the additional shares should be considered as outstanding only for the purpose of computing fully diluted earnings per share (but only if dilution results). For this computation, current earnings should be adjusted to give effect to the increase in earnings necessary to reach the specified level. To illustrate, assume the same facts as those above for Walz and Cardella except that the 20,000 shares are contingent upon Cardella Company's attaining a net income of $110,000 in 1981. Inasmuch as the earnings level is not being attained currently in 1980, no computation for primary earnings per share other than the traditional one need be made. In computing fully diluted earnings per share, however, the 20,000 shares would be considered outstanding. In addition, in computing fully diluted earnings per share, the 1980 net income of $100,000 would be increased by $10,000 to achieve an earnings level of $110,000.

To illustrate this point further, assume that TRS Industries has $220,000 of net income for 1980 and net income of $150,000 for 1981. An examination of TRS's capital structure indicates that it has an average number of common shares outstanding of 100,000 shares in both 1980 and 1981. In addition, the company has a number of contingent shares, with terms that indicate that one share is issuable for each $20 of net income if average net income for 1980 and 1981 exceeds $200,000 — maximum issuable is 20,000 shares. The earnings per share figures would be computed as illustrated below.

TRS Industries
Computation of Earnings Per Share
Contingent Shares—1980

	1980 Primary EPS	1980 Fully Diluted EPS
Average number of common shares outstanding	100,000	100,000
Add: Contingent shares issued		
Assuming average net income will equal 1980 net income ($220,000 ÷ 20)	11,000	
Assuming maximum shares possible		20,000
Adjusted average number of common shares outstanding	111,000	120,000
Net income for the year	$220,000	$220,000
Add: Additional income required if maximum contingent shares are issued (20,000 shares × $20 less $220,000)		180,000
	$220,000	$400,000
	A	C
Adjusted average number of common shares outstanding	111,000	120,000
	B	D
Earnings per share	$1.98 (A ÷ B)	~~$3.33~~ (C ÷ D)
		$1.98 (A ÷ B)

In 1980, the primary earnings per share and fully diluted earnings per share would both be reported as $1.98 in spite of C ÷ D being $3.33. Fully diluted earnings per share should never be reported higher than primary earnings per share. A computation for primary earnings per share had to be made in this illustration because the company was meeting future levels of earnings currently.

In 1981 the computation of earnings per share would be relatively simplified.

TRS Industries	
Computation of Earnings Per Share	
Contingent Shares—1981	
Net income	$150,000
	A
Average number of common shares outstanding	100,000 shares
	B
Earnings per share (A ÷ B)	$1.50

In 1981, $150,000 did not bring the average for the two years up to $200,000, so no consideration of the contingency was necessary for the primary earnings per share calculation. Fully diluted earnings per share was much higher than the basic computation for earnings per share, so that only one earnings per share figure need be presented. In essence, no dilution exists at the end of 1981.

Antidilution

In computing the 3% dilution factor, the aggregate of **all** dilutive securities must be considered. The dilutive securities are not considered individually, but in total. In addition, any security that is antidilutive should be excluded and cannot be used to offset dilutive securities. **Antidilutive** securities are securities that would create an increase in earnings per share (or a reduction in net loss per share). For example, convertible debt is antidilutive whenever interest (net of tax) on the debt expressed in per common share terms to be received upon conversion is higher than earnings per share calculated assuming no conversion. With options or warrants, whenever the exercise price is higher than the market price, the security is antidilutive. **Antidilutive securities should be ignored in all calculations and should not be considered in computing either primary or fully diluted earnings per share.** This approach is reasonable because the profession's intent was to inform the investor of the possible dilution that might occur in reported earnings per share and not to be concerned with securities that, if converted or exercised, would result in an increase in earnings per share.

Earnings Per Share Presentations and Disclosures

If a corporation's capital structure is complex but contains no securities classified as common stock equivalents, the earnings per share presentation would be as follows:

Earnings per common share	
Assuming no dilution	$3.30
Assuming full dilution	$2.70

If common stock equivalents are present and dilutive, the earnings per share presentation should be as follows:

Earnings per share	
On common and common equivalent share	$3.00
On a fully diluted basis	$2.70

When the earnings of a period include special transactions, per share amounts (where applicable) should be shown for income from continuing operations, income before extraordinary items, cumulative effect of changes in accounting principles, and net income. Reporting per share amounts for gain or loss on discontinued operations and gain or loss on extraordinary items is optional. A presentation reporting extraordinary items only is presented below.

Earnings per common and common equivalent share	
Income before extraordinary item	$3.80
Extraordinary item	.80
Net income	$3.00
Earnings per common share—assuming full dilution	
Income before extraordinary item	$3.35
Extraordinary item	.65
Net income	$2.70

Earnings per share amounts must be shown for all periods presented and all prior period earnings per share amounts presented should be restated for stock dividends and stock splits. When results of operations of a prior period have been restated as a result of a prior period adjustment, the earnings per share data shown for the prior periods should also be restated. The effect of the restatement should be disclosed in the year of the restatement.

Complex capital structures and dual presentation of earnings require the following additional disclosures in footnote form.

1. Description of pertinent rights and privileges of the various securities outstanding.
2. Bases on which both primary and fully diluted earnings per share were computed.
   a. Identify issues included in common stock equivalents.
   b. Identify securities included in fully diluted earnings per share computation.
   c. Describe all assumptions made.
   d. Disclose the number of shares issued upon conversion, exercise, or satisfaction of required conditions.
3. Effect of conversions subsequent to year end.

The footnote presented at the top of page 746 illustrates the use of the columnar format for disclosing the required information clearly and concisely (this is an excerpt from notes to the financial statements of Marcor, Inc.).

EARNINGS PER SHARE

Earnings per share for the year have been calculated as follows:

	Common and Common Equivalent Shares	Assuming Full Dilution
Average number of common shares outstanding	12,692,190	12,692,190
Common stock equivalents due to assumed exercise of options	99,636	114,612
Average number of Series A preferred shares outstanding	—	6,513,378
Series A preferred stock equivalents due to assumed exercise of options	—	175,154
Total shares	12,791,826	19,495,334
Net earnings	$66,950,000	$66,950,000
Less: Preferred dividend requirements based on average number of preferred shares and preferred equivalent shares outstanding during year	13,372,000	—
Net earnings used in per share calculations	$53,578,000	$66,950,000
Net earnings per share	$4.19	$3.43

Net earnings per common share and common equivalent share and net earnings per common share assuming full dilution comply with an opinion of the Accounting Principles Board of the American Institute of Certified Public Accountants issued in May 1969.

Dividends on nonconvertible preferred stock should be subtracted from income from continuing operations, income before extraordinary items, and net income to arrive at income available to common stockholders. Income available to common stockholders should be divided by the weighted average number of shares outstanding to arrive at earnings per share. If the preferred is cumulative and the dividend is not paid in the current year, an amount equal to the dividend that should have been paid for the **current year** only should be subtracted from net income. Dividends in arrears for previous years should have been included in the **previous years'** computations. If the preferred stock is convertible, and dilutive, however, then the preferred stock dividend ordinarily should be added back to income available to common stockholders because it is assumed that the convertible preferred has been converted and is considered outstanding common stock for purposes of computing earnings per share.

Summary

Computation of earnings per share has become a complex issue. Many accountants take strong exception to some of the arbitrary rules contained in **Opinion No. 15.** It is doubtful that **Opinion No. 15** will be the final pronouncement on this topic. The situation facing accountants in this area is a difficult one, because many securities, although technically not common stock, have many of the basic characteristics of common stock. In addition, many companies have issued these types of securities rather than common stock in order to avoid an adverse effect on the earnings per share figure. **APB Opinion No. 15** was issued as an attempt to develop credibility in reporting earnings per share data.

The following schematic diagram displays graphically the elementary points of calculating earnings per share in a complex capital structure.

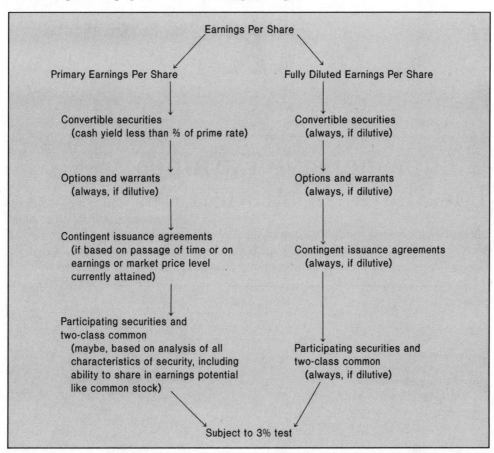

APPENDIX

Comprehensive Earnings
Per Share Illustration

The following comprehensive illustration demonstrates how the methods for computing earnings per share would be handled in a complex situation. The following section of the balance sheet of Rode Corporation is presented for analysis; assumptions related to the capital structure follow.

Rode Corporation BALANCE SHEET—DECEMBER 31, 1981 Liabilities and Net Worth			
Long-term debt:			
Notes payable, 7.2%		$ 500,000	
4% convertible debentures		2,500,000	
5% convertible debentures		2,500,000	5,500,000
Stockholders' investment:			
5% cumulative convertible preferred, par value			
$100, authorized 100,000 shares, issued			
25,000 shares		2,500,000	
Common stock, $1.00 par value authorized			
5,000,000 shares issued 500,000 shares		500,000	
Paid-in capital		2,500,000	
Retained earnings			
Beginning of year	$8,000,000		
Net income	1,000,000	9,000,000	14,500,000
			$20,000,000

---

[1]If an enterprise has a number of dilutive securities, a question arises as to which security should be handled first for purposes of computing earnings per share. The approach is to rank order the securities for maximum possible dilution in terms of one share of stock. Starting with the most dilutive, earnings per share is reduced until one of the securities increases earnings per share. When an increase in earnings per share occurs, the security that causes the increase in earnings per share should be excluded. The previous computation therefore provided the maximum dilution. See for example Sidney Davidson and Roman L. Weil, "A Short-Cut in Computing Earnings Per Share," *Journal of Accountancy*, December, 1975. Assume in this illustration that such a procedure was performed.

Notes and Assumptions[1]

Dec. 31, 1981

1. Options have been granted to purchase 50,000 shares of common stock at $20 per share.
2. Warrants have been issued to purchase 100,000 shares of common stock at $25 per share.
3. The average market price of the company's common stock was $30 per share during the year. The price at the close of the period was $35 per share.
4. 4% and 5% convertible debentures are convertible into common stock at $25 per share.
5. 5% cumulative convertible preferred stock is convertible at the rate of four shares of common stock for each share of preferred stock ($25 conversion price).
6. All debt was issued at face value and all preferred stock was issued at par value.
7. All debt and securities were outstanding at the beginning and end of the year.
8. The bank prime interest rate was 7% at all times.
9. The average applicable income tax rate is 50%.

The computation of earnings per share before issuance of **APB Opinion No. 15** would have been as follows:

Computation of Earnings Per Share	
Prior to APB 15	
Net income	$1,000,000
Less: 5% convertible preferred stock dividend requirements	125,000
Net income applicable to common stock	$ 875,000
Average number of common shares outstanding	500,000
Earnings per common share	$1.75

   The computation of earnings per share after issuance of **APB Opinion No. 15** is as follows:

Computation of Earnings Per Share		
After APB 15		
Earnings per share before APB 15		$1.75
Effect on primary earnings per share of items covered by APB 15:		
5% convertible preferred stock (Exhibit 1)	$—	
4% convertible debentures (Exhibits 2 and 3)	.21	
5% convertible debentures (Exhibit 4)	—	
Stock options and warrants (Exhibit 7)	.09	.30
Primary earnings per share		$1.45
Additional effect of the items above on fully diluted earnings per share:		
5% convertible preferred stock (Exhibit 8)	$ .03	
4% convertible debentures	—	
5% convertible debentures (Exhibit 9)	.09	
Stock options and warrants (Exhibit 11)	.02	.14
Fully diluted earnings per share		$1.31

Presentation of Exhibits

The following exhibits illustrate the computations for arriving at primary and fully diluted earnings per share. Exhibit 1 shows that the 5% convertible preferred stock does not meet the cash-yield test and is not a common stock equivalent.

Exhibit 1 5% Convertible Preferred Stock	
Bank prime interest rate at time of issuance	7%
Cash yield on issue	5%
Cash yield as a percent of bank prime interest rate at time of issuance	71%

Exhibit 2 indicates that the 4% convertible debentures are a common stock equivalent because the cash yield at the time of issuance is less than 66⅔% of the prime rate.

Exhibit 2 4% Convertible Debentures	
Bank prime interest rate at time of issuance	7%
Cash yield on issue	4%
Cash yield as a percent of bank prime interest rate at time of issuance	57%

Exhibit 3 illustrates how the "if converted" method is applied to determine the effect of the 4% convertible debenture on earnings per share.

Exhibit 3 Effect of 4% Convertible Debentures On Primary Earnings Per Share		
Net income applicable to common stock		$875,000
Add: Increase in net income arising from reduction of interest expense on assumed conversion of 4% convertible debentures, net of tax ($100,000 − $50,000)		50,000
Adjusted net income		$925,000
Number of shares for computation:		
Average number of outstanding common shares	500,000	
Number of shares applicable to assumed conversion of 4% debentures	100,000	600,000
Primary earnings per share ($925,000 ÷ 600,000)		$1.54
Earnings per share prior to assumed conversion of 4% debentures		1.75
Effect of including 4% convertible debentures		$ .21

Exhibit 4 discloses that the 5% convertible debentures are not common stock equivalents because they do not meet the cash-yield test.

Exhibit 4	
5% Convertible Debentures	
Bank prime interest rate at time of issuance	7%
Cash yield on issue	5%
Cash yield as a percent of bank prime interest rate at time of issuance	71%

Exhibit 5 illustrates the use of the treasury stock method for computing the increase in net income resulting from the assumed exercise of the stock options and stock warrants.

Exhibit 5	
Use of Proceeds—Treasury Stock Method	
Primary Earnings Per Share	
Proceeds arising from exercise of outstanding stock options and warrants	
Options (50,000 @ $20)	$1,000,000
Warrants (100,000 @ $25)	2,500,000
	$3,500,000
Funds to be used to purchase treasury stock (maximum 100,000 shares, 20% of outstanding common stock)	
Average market price ($30 × 100,000)	3,000,000
Funds remaining	$ 500,000
Funds remaining are applied as follows:	
$500,000 to reduce 7.2% long-term debt—reduction of interest expense	$ 36,000
Tax provision of 50% applicable to increased income	(18,000)
Increase in net income	$ 18,000

The increase in common equivalent shares for the options and warrants then can be computed as follows:

Exhibit 6	
Increase in Common Equivalent Shares	
Treasury Stock Method	
Total shares assumed issued	
Options	50,000
Warrants	100,000
	150,000
Total treasury shares repurchased	(100,000)[a]
Increase in common equivalent shares	50,000

[a]Maximum shares purchasable with the proceeds of $3,500,000 is 20% of the outstanding common stock or 100,000 shares at the average market price of $30 per share.

The effect of the options and warrants on primary earnings per share is then computed as follows:

Exhibit 7
Effect of Options and Warrants on
Primary Earnings Per Share

Adjusted net income (Exhibit 3)		$925,000
Add: Adjustment to reflect the effect on net income of the assumed reduction of $500,000 of 7.2% long-term debt (Exhibit 5)		18,000
Adjusted net income		$943,000
Number of shares for computation:		
From Exhibit 3	600,000	
Number of common equivalent shares arising from assumed conversion of outstanding stock options and warrants (Exhibit 6)	50,000	650,000
Primary earnings per share ($943,000 ÷ 650,000)		$1.45
Primary earnings per share prior to assumed conversion of options and warrants (Exhibit 3)		1.54
Effect of including options and warrants		$ .09

The full effect of the common stock equivalents has now been considered and primary earnings per share properly calculated. Computation of fully diluted earnings per share is still necessary, however, and must also include those convertible securities that were not common stock equivalents. The effect of the 5% convertible preferred stock on fully diluted earnings per share is computed as follows:

Exhibit 8
Effect of 5% Convertible Preferred Stock
on Fully Diluted Earnings Per Share

Adjusted net income (Exhibit 7)		$ 943,000
Add: Preferred stock dividends previously deducted		125,000
Adjusted net income		$1,068,000
Number of shares for computation:		
From Exhibit 7	650,000	
Number of shares applicable to assumed conversion of 5% preferred stock	100,000	750,000
Fully diluted earnings per share ($1,068,000 ÷ 750,000)		$1.42
Primary earnings per share (Exhibit 7)		1.45
Effect of including convertible preferred stock		$ .03

The 4% convertible debentures were considered common stock equivalents and entered into the computation of primary earnings per share, so no further dilution need be considered. The 5% convertible debentures, on the other hand, were not in the computation of primary earnings per share, but should be considered in fully diluted earnings per share as follows:

Exhibit 9
Effect of 5% Convertible Debentures
on Fully Diluted Earnings Per Share

Adjusted net income (Exhibit 8)		$1,068,000
Add: Increase in net income arising from reduction of interest expense on assumed conversion of 5% convertible debentures, net of tax		62,500
Adjusted net income		$1,130,500
Number of shares for computation:		
From Exhibit 8	750,000	
Number of shares applicable to assumed conversion of 5% debentures	100,000	850,000
Fully diluted earnings per share ($1,130,500 ÷ 850,000)		$1.33
Fully diluted earnings per share prior to assumed conversion of 5% debentures (Exhibit 8)		1.42
Effect of including 5% convertible debentures		$ .09

Finally, the treasury stock method was applied to the options and warrants to compute primary earnings per share, but the price used to purchase common stock was the average price for the year, $30. In computing fully diluted earnings per share, the closing price of $35 should be used because it is greater than the option price, as indicated below:

Exhibit 10
Use of Proceeds—Treasury Stock Method
Fully Diluted Earnings Per Share

Proceeds arising from exercise of outstanding stock options and warrants:	
Options (50,000 @ $20)	$1,000,000
Warrants (100,000 @ $25)	2,500,000
	$3,500,000
Funds to be used to purchase treasury stock (maximum 100,000 shares, 20% of outstanding common stock)	
Closing market price ($35 × 100,000)	3,500,000
Funds remaining	$ -0-

The effect on fully diluted earnings per share is:

Exhibit 11 Effect of Options and Warrants on Fully Diluted Earnings Per Share	
Adjusted net income (Exhibit 9)	$1,130,500
Less: Assumed income from use of excess proceeds on conversion of options and warrants (Exhibits 5 and 10)	(18,000)
Adjusted net income	$1,112,500
Number of shares for computation, no change from Exhibit 9	850,000
Fully diluted earnings per share ($1,112,500 ÷ 850,000)	$1.31
Fully diluted earnings per share prior to assumed conversion of options and warrants (Exhibit 9)	1.33
Effect of including options and warrants	$ .02

The income statement and related footnote presentation can now be given.

Income Statement Presentation	
Net income	$1,000,000
Earnings per common share and common equivalent share (Note X)	$1.45
Earnings per common share, assuming full dilution	$1.31

NOTE X: Earnings per common share and common equivalent share was computed by dividing net income by the weighted average number of shares of common stock and common stock equivalents outstanding during the year. The 4% convertible debentures have been considered to be common stock equivalents. Consequently, the number of shares issuable assuming full conversion of these debentures as of the beginning of the year was added to the number of common shares, and net income was adjusted to eliminate the interest on these debentures, net of the applicable tax effect. Options and warrants were also considered in the computation of earnings per common and common equivalent shares.

   Fully diluted earnings per share was computed assuming conversion of all debentures and exercise of all options and warrants.

Questions

1. Define the terms "convertible debt" and "debt issued with stock purchase warrants."
2. Discuss the similarities and the differences between convertible debt and debt issued with stock purchase warrants.
3. What accounting treatment is required for convertible debt? What accounting treatment is required for debt issued with stock purchase warrants?
4. Explain how the conversion feature of convertible debt has a value (a) to the issuer, and (b) to the purchaser.
5. What are the arguments for giving separate accounting recognition to the conversion feature of debentures?

6. Assume that no value is assigned to the conversion feature upon issue of the debentures. Assume further that four years after issue, debentures with a face value of $100,000 and book value of $96,000 are tendered for conversion into 8,000 shares of common stock on an interest payment date when the market price of the debentures is 104 and the common stock is selling at $14 per share (par value $10) and that the company records the conversion as follows:

Bonds Payable	100,000	
Discount on Bonds Payable		4,000
Common Stock		80,000
Paid-in Capital in Excess of Par		16,000

Discuss the propriety of this accounting treatment.

7. On July 1, 1981, Salem Corporation issued $2,000,000 of 7% bonds payable in ten years. The bonds include detachable warrants giving the bondholder the right to purchase for $30 one share of $1.00 par value common stock at any time during the next ten years. The bonds were sold for $2,000,000. The value of the warrants at the time of issuance was $100,000. Prepare the journal entry to record this transaction.

8. For what reasons might a company adopt an employee stock option plan? What is the principal accounting problem related to employee stock option plans?

9. Sample Corporation has an employee stock purchase plan which permits all full-time employees to purchase 10 shares of common stock on the third anniversary of their employment and an additional 10 shares on each subsequent anniversary date. The purchase price is set at the market price on the date purchased and no commission is charged. Discuss whether this plan would be considered compensatory.

10. What date or event does the AICPA believe should be used in determining the value of the stock option? What arguments support the AICPA position? What criticism may be brought against the date or event advocated by the AICPA?

11. What support can be offered for dates other than the date of grant in order to determine the value of a stock option?

12. What are the basic accounting problems related to restricted stock bonus plans? What is the recommendation of the AICPA in regard to the accounting for restricted stock bonus plans?

13. What is the advantage to an executive of a stock appreciation right (SAR) plan? How is compensation expense measured in a SAR plan?

14. Define the following terms.
    (a) 3% test for dilution.
    (b) Complex capital structure.
    (c) Primary earnings per share.
    (d) Common stock equivalent.
    (e) Potentially dilutive security.
    (f) Fully diluted earnings per share.

15. What are the computational guidelines for determining whether a convertible security is a common stock equivalent?

16. Discuss the reasons why securities other than common stock may be considered common stock equivalents for the computation of primary earnings per share.

17. Explain how convertible securities are determined to be common stock equivalents and how those convertible senior securities that are not considered to be common stock equivalents enter into the determination of earnings per share data.

18. Explain the treasury stock method as it applies to options and warrants in computing primary earnings per share data.

19. Earnings per share can affect market prices. Can market prices affect earnings per share? Explain.

20. What is meant by the term anti-dilution? Give an example.

Cases

C17-1 For various reasons a corporation may issue warrants to purchase shares of its common stock at specified prices that, depending on the circumstances, may be less than, equal to, or greater than the current market price. For example, warrants may be issued:

1. To existing stockholders on a pro rata basis.
2. To certain key employees under a qualified stock option plan.
3. To purchasers of the corporation's bonds.

Instructions

For each of the three examples of how stock warrants are used:

(a) Explain why they are used.

(b) Discuss the significance of the price (or prices) at which the warrants are issued (or granted) in relation to (1) the current market price of the company's stock, and (2) the length of time over which they can be exercised.

(c) Describe the information that should be disclosed in financial statements, or notes thereto, which are prepared when stock warrants are outstanding in the hands of the three groups listed above.

(AICPA adapted)

C17-2 Incurring long-term debt with an arrangement whereby lenders receive an option to buy common stock during all or a portion of the time the debt is outstanding is a frequently used corporate financing practice. In some situations the result is achieved through the issuance of convertible bonds; in others the debt instruments and the warrants to buy stock are separate.

Instructions

(a) 1. Describe the differences that exist in current accounting for original proceeds of the issuance of convertible bonds and of debt instruments with separate warrants to purchase common stock.
   2. Discuss the underlying rationale for the differences described in (a) 1. above.
   3. Summarize the arguments that have been presented in favor of accounting for convertible bonds in the same manner as for debt with separate warrants.

(b) At the start of the year Locust Company issued $6,000,000 of 7% notes along with warrants to buy 400,000 shares of its $10 par value common stock at $18 per share. The notes mature over the next ten years starting one year from date of issuance with annual maturities of $600,000. At the time, Locust had 3,200,000 shares of common stock outstanding and the market price was $23 per share. The company received $6,680,000 for the notes and the warrants. For Locust Company, 7% was a relatively low borrowing rate. If offered alone, at this time, the notes would have been issued at a 22 percent discount. Prepare journal entries for the issuance of the notes and warrants for the cash consideration received.

(AICPA adapted)

C17-3 The "Highlights . . . in Review" section of the 1981 Annual Report of Hargrove Manufacturing Company included these items:

	1981	1980
Net earnings after taxes	$2,100,000	$2,300,000
Net earnings per share of common stock	$6.35	$7.01
Net earnings per share assuming full conversion of convertible notes	$5.03	$5.81

Excerpts from the December 31, 1981, balance sheet were as follows:

Long-Term Debt		
5% Note due December 31, 1987		$1,500,000
6% subordinated convertible note due December 31, 1993		2,000,000
Stockholders' Investment		
Common stock ($2 par) shares outstanding— at Jan. 1, 302,000; at Dec. 31, 316,000		632,000
Additional paid-in capital		2,000,000
Retained earnings		
Balance—January 1	$3,500,000	
Dividends	(500,000)	
Net income	2,000,000	5,000,000

Note A. The 6% subordinated convertible note is subordinated to the 5% note and short-term bank borrowings. The note is convertible into common stock at $16 a share and 125,000 shares of authorized common stock are reserved for conversion.

To reduce the threat of a take-over by a larger company, the Hargrove management began to negotiate the retirement of the $2 million convertible note. In February, 1982, agreement was reached to retire $1 million of the note for payment of $3 million, an amount that was approximately equal to the $48 per share market value of the 62,500 shares into which that portion of the original note was then convertible.

Hargrove naturally intended to take the $2 million difference as a tax deduction, claiming the discharge of the liability as a necessary business expense. The company's tax attorney stated, however, that its deductibility was not completely assured, and that treatment of the item as a charge against earnings in the financial statements could prove crucial in any contest with the Internal Revenue Service.

Instructions

How should the transaction be treated?

C17-4 On December 12, 1978, the board of directors of the Weyland Company authorized a grant of nonqualified options to company executives for the purchase of 10,000 shares of common stock at 52 any time during 1981 if the executives still were employed by the company. The closing price of Weyland common stock was 55 on December 12, 1978, 51 on January 2, 1981, and 49⅛ on December 31, 1981. None of the options were exercised.

Instructions

(a) Prepare a schedule presenting the computation of the compensation cost that should be attributed to the options of Weyland Company.

(b) Assume that the market price of Weyland common stock rose to 58 (instead of declining to 51) on January 2, 1981, and that all options were exercised on that date. Would the company incur a cost for executive compensation? Why?

(c) Discuss the arguments for measuring compensation from executive stock options in terms of the spread between the
1. Market price and option price when the grant is made.
2. Market price and option price when the options are first exercisable.
3. Market price and option price when the options are exercised.
4. Cash value of the executives' services estimated at date of grant and the amount of their salaries.

(AICPA adapted)

C17-5 In 1978 Union Technologies adopted a plan to give additional incentive compensation to its dealers to sell its principal product, fire extinguishers. Under the plan Union transferred 6,000 shares of its $1.00 par value stock to a trust with the provision that Union would have to forfeit interest in the trust and no part of the trust fund could ever revert to Union. Shares were to be distributed to dealers on the basis of their shares of fire extinguisher purchases from Union (above certain minimum levels) over the three-year period ending June 30, 1981.

In 1978 the stock was closely held. The book value of the stock was $6.90 per share as of June 30, 1978, and in 1978 additional shares were sold to existing shareholders for $7 per share. On the basis of this information, market value of the stock was determined to be $7 per share.

In 1978 when the shares were transferred to the trust, Union charged prepaid expenses for $42,000 ($7 per share market value) and credited capital stock for $6,000 and additional paid-in capital for $36,000. The prepaid expense was charged to operations over a three-year period ended June 30, 1981.

Union sold a substantial number of shares of its stock to the public in 1980 at $60 per share.

In July 1981 all shares of the stock in the trust were distributed to the dealers. The market value of the shares at date of distribution of the stock from the trust had risen to $120 per share. Union obtained a tax deduction equal to that market value for the tax year ended June 30, 1982.

Instructions

(a) How much should be reported as selling expense in each of the years noted above?

(b) Union is also considering other types of option plans. One such plan is a stock appreciation right (SAR) plan. What is a stock appreciation right plan? What is a potential disadvantage of a SAR plan from the viewpoint of the company?

C17-6   Warren Corporation, a new audit client of yours, has not reported earnings per share data in its annual reports to stockholders in the past. The treasurer requested that you furnish information about the reporting of earnings per share data in the current year's annual report in accordance with generally accepted accounting principles.

Instructions

(a) Define the term "earnings per share" as it applies to a corporation with a capitalization structure composed of only one class of common stock and explain how earnings per share should be computed and how the information should be disclosed in the corporation's financial statements.

(b) Discuss the treatment, if any, that should be given to each of the following items in computing earnings per share of common stock for financial statement reporting.
 1. The declaration of current dividends on cumulative preferred stock.
 2. The acquisition of some of the corporation's outstanding common stock during the current fiscal year. The stock was classified as treasury stock.
 3. A 2-for-1 stock split of common stock during the current fiscal year.
 4. A provision created out of retained earnings for a contingent liability from a possible lawsuit.
 5. Outstanding preferred stock issued at a premium with a par value liquidation right.
 6. The exercise at a price below market value but above book value of a common stock option issued during the current fiscal year to officers of the corporation.
 7. The replacement of a machine immediately prior to the close of the current fiscal year at a cost 20 percent above the original cost of the replaced machine. The new machine will perform the same function as the old machine that was sold for its book value.

C17-7   "Earnings per share" (EPS) is the most featured single financial statistic about modern corporations. Daily published quotations of stock prices have recently been expanded to include for many securities a "times earnings" figure which is based on EPS. Stock analysts often focus their discussions on the EPS of the corporations they study.

Instructions

(a) Explain how dividends or dividend requirements on any class of preferred stock that may be outstanding affect the computation of EPS.

(b) One of the technical procedures applicable in EPS computations is the "treasury-stock method."

    1. Briefly describe the circumstances under which it might be appropriate to apply the treasury-stock method.

    2. There is a limit to the extent to which the treasury-stock method is applicable. Indicate what this limit is and give a succinct summary of the procedures that should be followed beyond the treasury-stock limits.

(c) Under some circumstances, convertible debentures would be considered "common stock equivalents"; under other circumstances they would not.

    1. When is it proper to treat convertible debentures as common stock equivalents? What is the effect on computation of EPS in such cases?

    2. In case convertible debentures are not considered as common stock equivalents, explain how they are handled for purposes of EPS computations.

(AICPA adapted)

Exercises

E17-1 The Foley Company has bonds payable outstanding in the amount of $300,000 and carries in its account Premium on Bonds Payable in the amount of $4,500. Each $1,000 bond is convertible into 20 shares of preferred stock of par value of $50 per share.

Instructions

(a) Assuming that the bonds are quoted on the market at 102 and that the preferred stock may be sold on the market at $50⅞, make the entry to record the conversion of the bonds to preferred stock. (Use the market value approach.)

(b) Assuming that the book value method was used, what entry would be made?

E17-2 For each of the unrelated transactions described below, present the entry(ies) required to record each transaction.

1. The Jolinda Company issued $20,000,000 par value 7% convertible bonds at 99½. If the bonds had not been convertible, the company's investment banker estimates they would have been sold at 95. Expenses of issuing the bonds were $100,000.

2. The Finns Company issued $20,000,000 par value 8% bonds at 98. One detachable stock purchase warrant was issued with each $100 par value bond. At the time of issuance, the warrants were selling for $3.

3. On July 1, 1980, the Schmidt Company called its 5½% convertible debentures for conversion. The $10,000,000 par value bonds were converted into 1,000,000 shares of $2 par value common stock. On July 1, there was $200,000 of unamortized discount applicable to the bonds, and the company incurred expenses of $100,000 in connection with the conversion of all the bonds. The company records the conversion using the book value method.

E17-3 Crestwood, Inc. issued $4,000,000 of 6%, 10-year convertible bonds on June 1, 1980, at 98 plus accrued interest. The bonds were dated April 1, 1980, with interest payable April 1 and October 1. Bond discount is amortized semiannually on a straight-line basis.

    On April 1, 1981, $1,000,000 of these bonds were converted into 1,000 shares of $20 par value common stock. Accrued interest was paid in cash at the time of conversion.

Instructions

(a) Prepare the entry to record the interest expense at October 1, 1980. Assume that accrued interest payable was credited when the bonds were issued. (Round to nearest dollar.)

(b) Prepare the entry(ies) to record the conversion on April 1, 1981. (Book value method is used.) Assume that the entry to record amortization of the bond discount and interest payment has been made.

E17-4   On January 1, 1979, when its $30 par value common stock was selling for $80 per share, a corporation issued $10,000,000 of 4% convertible debentures due in 10 years. The conversion option allowed the holder of each $1,000 bond to convert the bond into five shares of the corporation's $30 par value common stock. The debentures were issued for $11,000,000. The present value of the bond payments at the time of issuance was $8,500,000 and the corporation believes the difference between the present value and the amount paid is attributable to the conversion feature. On January 1, 1980, the corporation's $30 par value common stock was split 3 for 1. On January 1, 1981, when the corporation's $10 par value common stock was selling for $90 per share, holders of 40% of the convertible debentures exercised their conversion options. The corporation uses the straight-line method for amortizing any bond discounts or premiums.

Instructions

(a) Prepare in general journal form the entry to record the original issuance of the convertible debentures.

(b) Prepare in general journal form the entry to record the exercise of the conversion option, using the book value method. Show supporting computations in good form.

E17-5   The December 31, 1980 balance sheet of Santana Corp. is as follows:

5% callable, Convertible Bonds Payable (semiannual interest dates April 30 and October 31; convertible into 25 shares of $5 par value common stock per $1,000 of bond principal; maturity date April 30, 1986)	$400,000	
Discount on Bonds Payable	4,800	$395,200

On March 5, 1981, Santana Corp. called all of the bonds as of April 30 for the principal plus interest through April 30. By April 30 all bondholders had exercised their conversion to common stock as of the interest payment date. Consequently, on April 30, Santana Corp. paid the semiannual interest and issued shares of common stock for the bonds. The discount is amortized on a straight-line basis.

Instructions

Prepare the entry(ies) to record the interest expense and conversion on April 30, 1981. Reversing entries were made on January 1, 1981. (Round to the nearest dollar.)

E17-6   Benes, Inc. has decided to raise additional capital by issuing $100,000 face value of bonds with a coupon rate of 7%. In discussions with their investment bankers, it was determined that to help the sale of the bonds, detachable stock warrants should be issued at the rate of one warrant for each $100 bond sold. The value of the bonds without the warrants is considered to be $88,000, and the value of the warrants in the market is $16,000. The bonds sold in the market at issuance for $98,000.

Instructions

(a) What entry should be made at the time of the issuance of the bonds and warrants?

(b) If the warrants were nondetachable, would the entries be different? Discuss.

E17-7   On January 1, 1980, the Boyd Corporation issues $2,000,000 of 10-year, 5% convertible debentures at 102. Interest is to be paid semiannually on June 30 and December

31. Each $1,000 debenture can be converted into eight shares of the Boyd Corporation $100 par value common stock after December 31, 1981.

On January 1, 1982, $200,000 of debentures are converted into common stock, which is then selling at $112. An additional $200,000 of debentures is converted on March 31, 1982. The market price of the common stock is then $115.

Bond premium is amortized on a straight-line basis.

Instructions

Make the necessary journal entries for:

(a) December 31, 1981.

(b) January 1, 1982.

(c) March 31, 1982.

(d) June 30, 1982.

Record the conversions under both the fair market value method and the book value method.

E17-8 On November 1, 1978, the Danow Company adopted a stock option plan that granted options to key executives to purchase 30,000 shares of the company's $10 par value common stock. The options were granted on January 2, 1979, and were exercisable two years after date of grant if the grantee was still an employee of the company; the options expired six years from date of grant. The option price was set at $35; market price at the date of the grant was $47 a share.

All of the options were exercised during the year 1981; 20,000 on January 3 when the market price was $67, and 10,000 on May 1 when the market price was $77 a share.

Instructions

(a) Compute the value of the stock option and the corresponding amount of executive compensation.

(b) Prepare journal entries relating to the stock option plan for the years 1979, 1980, and 1981. Assume that the employee performs services equally in 1979 and 1980.

E17-9 On November 2, 1977, the stockholders of Moore Company voted to adopt a stock option plan for Moore's key officers. According to terms of the option agreement, the officers of the company can purchase 20,000 shares of common stock during 1980 and 36,000 shares during 1981. The shares that are purchasable during 1980 represent executive compensation for 1978 and 1979, and those purchasable during 1981 represent such compensation for 1978, 1979, and 1980. If options for shares are not exercised during either year, they lapse as of the end of that year.

Options were granted to the officers of Moore on January 1, 1978, and at that time the option price was set for all shares at $30. During 1980, all options were exercised. During 1981, however, options for only 18,000 shares were exercised. The remaining options lapsed because the executives decided not to exercise. Par value of the stock is $10. The market prices of Moore common at various dates follows:

Dates	Market Price of Moore's Common
Option agreement accepted by stockholders	$32
Options granted	35
Options exercised in 1980	37
Options exercised in 1981	33

Instructions

Make any necessary journal entries related to this stock option for the following years: 1977, 1978, 1980, and 1981 (Moore closes its books on December 31).

E17-10 Mr. James Colt has recently been elected president of Ray-lite Company. As an incentive for Mr. Colt to become president, the company offered him the following pay package: (1) a salary of $85,000 per year, (2) an expense allowance of $16,000 per year, and (3) the right to purchase 6,000 shares of common stock at $10 per share; the current market price is $16 per share.

Instructions

(a) What entry is needed to record the granting of these stock options to Mr. Colt?

(b) Assume that the stock options had the following restriction attached: Mr. Colt must remain an employee of the company for three years before he is entitled to the stock. Consultation with investment bankers suggests that the value of these restricted shares is $14. What entry is needed to record the granting of these stock options to Mr. Colt?

E17-11 Futuristic Products Company establishes a stock appreciation rights program which entitles its new president Jill Castleberry to receive cash for the difference between the market price of the stock and a preestablished price of $30 (also market price) on December 31, 1980 on 20,000 SARs. The date of grant is December 31, 1980 and the required employment (service) period is three years. President Castleberry exercises all of the SARs in 1986. The market value of the stock fluctuates as follows: 12/31/81—$36; 12/31/82—$39; 12/31/83—$45; 12/31/84—$36; 12/31/85—$48.

Instructions

(a) Prepare a five-year (1981-1985) schedule of compensation expense pertaining the 20,000 SARs granted President Castleberry.

(b) Prepare the journal entry for compensation expense in 1981, 1984, and 1985 relative to the 20,000 SARs.

E17-12 On December 31, 1979, Bubley Soap Company issues 100,000 stock appreciation rights to its officers entitling them to receive cash for the difference between the market price of its stock and a preestablished price of $10. The date of exercise is December 31, 1983. The market price fluctuates as follows: 12/31/80—$14; 12/31/81—$8; 12/31/82—$20; 12/31/83—$18. Rights are exercisable only if the officer is employed by the company at the date of exercise.

Instructions

(a) Prepare a schedule that shows the amount of compensation expense allocable to each year affected by the stock appreciation rights plan.

(b) Prepare the entry at 12/31/83 to record compensation expense, if any, in 1983.

(c) Prepare the entry on 12/31/83 assuming that all 100,000 SARs are exercised by all of the eligible officers.

E17-13 Hallmark Corporation had 100,000 shares outstanding on January 1 and reacquired 12,000 shares on March 1.

Instructions

What is the weighted average number of shares outstanding:

1. For the quarter ending March 31?
2. For the six months ending June 30?
3. For the year ending December 31?

E17-14 The Kieth Company had 120,000 shares of common stock outstanding on December 31, 1981. During the year 1982 the company issued 12,000 shares on May 1 and retired 24,000 shares on October 31. For the year 1982 the Kieth Company reported net income of $372,000 after a casualty loss of $62,000 (net of tax).

Instructions

What earnings per share data should be reported at the bottom of its income statement, assuming that the casualty loss is extraordinary?

E17-15 Hanley, Inc. presented the following data:

Net income	$5,700,000
Preferred stock: 100,000 shares outstanding,	
$100 par, 6% cumulative, not convertible	10,000,000
Common stock: Shares outstanding 1/1	2,000,000
Issued for cash, 5/1	900,000
Acquired treasury stock for cash, 8/1	240,000
2-for-1 stock split, 10/1	

Instructions

Compute earnings per share.

E17-16 A portion of the combined statement of income and retained earnings of Rochelle Corporation for the current year follows:

Income before extraordinary item		$ 17,175,000
Extraordinary loss, net of applicable		
income tax (Note 1)		1,687,500
Net income		15,487,500
Retained earnings at the beginning of the year		99,162,700
		114,650,200
Dividends declared:		
On preferred stock—$6.00 per share	$ 300,000	
On common stock—$2.00 per share	14,000,000	14,300,000
Retained earnings at the end of the year		$100,350,200

Note 1. During the year, the Rochelle Corporation suffered a major casualty loss of $1,687,500 after applicable income tax reduction of $1,755,000.

    At the end of the current year, the Rochelle Corporation has outstanding 7,000,000 shares of $10 par common stock and 50,000 shares of 6% preferred.

    On April 1 of the current year, the Rochelle Corporation issued 1,000,000 shares of common stock for $32 per share to help finance the casualty.

Instructions

Compute the earnings per share on common stock for the current year as it should be reported to stockholders.

E17-17 On January 1, 1981, Castle Industries had stock outstanding as follows:

5% Cumulative preferred stock, $100 par value,	
issued and outstanding 6,000 shares.	$ 600,000
Common stock, $10 par value, issued and	
outstanding 200,000 shares.	2,000,000

    To acquire the net assets of three smaller companies, Castle authorized the issuance of an additional 160,000 common shares. The acquisitions took place as follows:

	Date of Acquisition	Shares Issued
Company A	April 1, 1981	100,000
Company B	July 1, 1981	40,000
Company C	October 1, 1981	20,000

    On May 14, 1981, Castle realized a $90,000 insurance gain on the expropriation of investments originally purchased in 1970.

    On December 31, 1981, Castle recorded net income of $300,000 before tax and exclusive of the gain.

Instructions

Assuming a 50% tax rate, compute the earnings per share data that should appear on the financial statements of Castle Industries as of December 31, 1981. Assume that the expropriation is extraordinary.

E17-18 At January 1, 1981 the Indiana Cement Company's outstanding shares included:

> 100,000 shares of $100 par value, 6% cumulative preferred stock
> 1,000,000 shares of $1.00 par value common stock

Net income for 1981 was $2,584,500. No cash dividends were declared or paid during 1981. On February 15, 1982, however, all preferred dividends in arrears were paid, together with a 5% stock dividend on common shares. There were no dividends in arrears prior to 1981.

On April 1, 1981, 400,000 shares of common stock were sold for $10 per share and on October 1, 1981, 160,000 shares of common stock were purchased for $20 per share and held as treasury stock.

Instructions

Compute earnings per share for 1981. Assume that financial statements for 1981 were issued in March, 1982.

E17-19 In 1980, Saunders Enterprises issued, at par, 20, $500, 8% bonds, each convertible into 100 shares of common stock. At the time the bonds were issued, the prime rate was 11%. Saunders had revenues of $10,000 and expenses other than interest and taxes of $7,600 for 1981 (assume that the tax rate is 40%). Throughout 1981, 1,000 shares of common stock were outstanding; none of the bonds were converted or redeemed.

Instructions

(a) Compute earnings per share for 1981.

(b) Assume the same facts as those assumed for Part (a), except that the 20 bonds were issued on October 1, 1981 (rather than in 1980), and none have been converted or redeemed.

(c) Assume the same facts as assumed for Part (a), except that 10 of the 20 bonds were actually converted on July 1, 1981.

E17-20 On June 1, 1978, Harden Company and Lower Company merged to form MHL Inc. A total of 450,000 shares were issued to complete the merger. The new corporation reports on a calendar-year basis.

On April 1, 1980, the company issued an additional 200,000 shares of stock for cash. All 650,000 shares were outstanding on December 31, 1980.

MHL Inc. also issued $500,000 of 20-year, 6 percent convertible bonds at par on July 1, 1980, when the bank prime rate was 8 percent. Each $1,000 bond converts to 40 shares of common at any interest date. None of the bonds have been converted to date.

MHL Inc. is preparing its annual report for the fiscal year ending December 31, 1980. The annual report will show earnings per share figures based upon a reported after-tax net income of $840,000 (the tax rate is 40 percent).

Instructions

(a) Should the MHL Inc. convertible bonds be treated as common stock equivalents for the calculation of earnings per share? Explain your answer.

(b) Without prejudice to your answer in Part a, assume that the convertible bonds are not to be treated as common stock equivalents. Determine for 1980:
  1. the number of shares to be used for calculating
     (a) primary earnings per share.
     (b) fully diluted earnings per share.

2. the earnings figures to be used for calculating
   (a) primary earnings per share.
   (b) fully diluted earnings per share.

(CMA adapted)

E17-21 Plunger's net income for 1981 is $20,000. The only potentially dilutive securities outstanding were 2,000 options issued during 1980, each exercisable for one share at $5. None have been exercised, and 10,000 shares of common were outstanding during 1981. The average market price of Plunger's stock during all quarters of 1981 was $11.08; the December 31, 1981, price was $20.

Instructions

(a) Compute the earnings per share (round to nearest cent).

(b) Assume the same facts as those assumed for Part (a), except that the 2,000 options were issued on November 1, 1981 (rather than in 1980). The average market price during the last two months of 1981 was $17.67.

E17-22 Ardent Steel indicates that its net income for 1978 is $10,050,000, which includes a gain on casualty (net of tax) of $900,000. Its capital structure includes some common stock reserved under employee stock options (57,000 shares). The common shares outstanding for the year remained at 3,300,000. The controller asks your advice concerning the earnings per share figure that they should present. The common stock price has remained fairly stable during the year at $38 per share and the option price for the stock options is $32 per share.

Instructions

What would you tell the controller? (Assume that the gain is extraordinary.)

E17-23 Amaro Corporation earned $125,000 during a period when it had an average of 60,000 shares of common stock outstanding. The common stock sold at an average market price of $20 per share during the period and sold at $25 at the end of the period. Also outstanding were 10,000 warrants that could be exercised to purchase one share of common stock for $15 for each warrant exercised.

Instructions

(a) Are the warrants dilutive?

(b) Compute primary earnings per share.

(c) Compute fully diluted earnings per share.

E17-24 Carol Roper, Inc., recently purchased International Homes, a large midwestern prefabricated-home manufacturer. One of the terms of the merger was that if International Homes' income for 1981 was $9,000 or more, 2,000 additional shares would be paid to International Homes' stockholders in 1980. International's income for 1980 was $10,000.

Instructions

(a) Would the contingent shares have to be considered in 1980 earnings per share computations?

(b) Assume the same facts, except that the 2,000 shares are contingent on International Homes' achieving a net income of $11,000 in 1981. Would the contingent shares have to be considered in earnings per share computations?

Problems

P17-1 The Goodman Company issued $1,000,000 of convertible 10-year bonds on July 1, 1980. The bonds provide for 6% interest payable semiannually on January 1 and July

1. Expense and discount in connection with the issue was $19,500, which is being amortized monthly on a straight-line basis.

The bonds are convertible after one year into 8 shares of the Goodman Company's $100 par value common stock for each $1,000 of bonds.

On August 1, 1981, $100,000 of bonds were turned in for conversion into common. Interest has been accrued monthly and paid as due. At the time of conversion any accrued interest on bonds being converted is paid in cash.

Instructions

Prepare the journal entries to record the conversion, amortization, and interest in connection with the bonds as of:

(a) August 1, 1981.

(b) August 31, 1981.

(c) December 31, 1981, including closing entries for end of year.

(AICPA adapted)

 P17-2 The Haas Company adopted a stock option plan on November 30, 1979, that provided that 40,000 shares of $5 par value stock be designated as available for the granting of options to officers of the corporation at a price of $8 a share. The market value was $12 a share on November 30, 1979.

On January 2, 1980, options to purchase 12,000 shares were granted to President Steven Elbert—6,000 for services to be rendered in 1980 and 6,000 for services to be rendered in 1981. Also on that date, options to purchase 6,000 shares were granted to Vice-President Alan Donahue—2,000 for services to be rendered in 1980 and 4,000 for services to be rendered in 1981. The market value of the stock was $14 a share on January 2, 1980. The options were exercisable for a period of one year following the year in which the services were rendered.

In 1981 neither the president nor the vice-president exercised their options because the market price of the stock was below the exercise price. The market value of the stock was $6 a share on December 31, 1981, when the options for 1980 services lapsed.

On December 31, 1982, both President Elbert and Vice-President Donahue exercised their options for 6,000 and 4,000 shares, respectively, when the market price was $14 a share.

Instructions

(a) Prepare the necessary journal entries in 1979 when the stock option plan was adopted, in 1980 when options were granted, in 1981 when options lapsed and in 1982 when options were exercised.

(b) What disclosure of the stock option plan should appear in the financial statements at December 31, 1979? At December 31, 1980? Assume that the stock options outstanding or exercised at any time are a significant financial item.

P17-3 The stockholders' equity section of Stach, Inc. at the beginning of the current year appears below:

Common stock, $10 par value, authorized 500,000 shares, 100,000 shares issued and outstanding	$1,000,000
Premium on common stock	200,000
Retained earnings	190,000

During the current year the following transactions occurred:

1. The company issued to the stockholders 100,000 rights. Ten rights are needed to buy one share of stock at $16. The rights were void after 30 days. The market price of the stock at this time was $17 per share.

2. The company sold to the public a $200,000, 7% bond issue at par. The company also issued with each $100 bond one detachable stock purchase warrant, which provided for

the purchase of common stock at $14 per share. Shortly after issuance, similar bonds without warrants were selling at 96 and the warrants at $4.

3. All but 10,000 of the rights issued in (1) were exercised in 30 days.

4. At the end of the year, 50% of the warrants in (2) had been exercised, and the remaining were outstanding and in good standing.

5. During the current year, the company granted stock options for 3,000 shares of common stock to company executives. The market price of the stock on that date was $20 and the option price was $15. The options were to expire at year-end and were considered compensation for the current year.

6. All but 500 shares related to the stock option plan were exercised by year-end. The expiration resulted because one of the executives failed to fulfill an obligation related to the employment contract.

Instructions

(a) Prepare general journal entries for the current year to record the transactions listed above.

(b) Prepare the stockholders' equity section of the balance sheet at the end of the current year. Assume that retained earnings at the end of the current year is $340,000.

P17-4 As auditor for Hamler and Peabody, you have been assigned to check the Atkins Corporation's computation of earnings per share for the current year. The controller has supplied you with the following computations:

Net income	$3,119,286
Common shares issued and outstanding:	
Beginning of year	1,106,417
End of year	906,557
Average	1,006,487

Earnings per share

$$\frac{\$3,119,286}{1,006,487} = \qquad \$3.09 \text{ per share}$$

You have developed the following additional information:

1. There are no other equity securities in addition to the common shares.

2. There are no options or warrants outstanding to purchase common shares.

3. There are no convertible debt securities.

4. Activity in common shares during the year was as follows:

Outstanding, Jan. 1	1,106,417
Treasury shares acquired, Oct. 1	(300,000)
	806,417
Shares reissued, Dec. 1	100,140
Outstanding, Dec. 31	906,557

Instructions

(a) On the basis of the information above, do you agree with the controller's computation of earnings per share for the year? If you disagree, prepare a revised computation of earnings per share.

(b) Assume the same facts as those in (a), except that options had been issued to purchase 100,000 shares of common stock at $10 per share. These options were outstanding at the beginning of the year and none had been exercised or canceled during the year. The average market price of the common shares during the year was $25 and the ending market price was $35. Prepare a computation of earnings per share.

P17-5 Forster Company had the following account titles on its December 31, 1981, trial balance:

7% cumulative convertible preferred stock, $100 par value

Paid-in Capital in Excess of Par—Preferred Stock

Common stock, $1.00 stated value

Paid-in Capital in Excess of Par—Common Stock

Retained Earnings

The following additional information about the Forster Company was available for the year ended December 31, 1981:

1,500,000 shares of preferred stock were authorized, of which 1,000,000 were outstanding. All 1,000,000 shares outstanding were issued on January 2, 1978, for $110 a share. The bank prime interest rate was 8.5% on January 2, 1978, and was 10% on December 31, 1981. The preferred stock is convertible into common stock on a one-for-one basis until December 31, 1987; thereafter the preferred stock ceases to be convertible and is callable at par value by the company. No preferred stock has been converted into common stock, and there were no dividends in arrears at December 31, 1981.

The common stock has been issued at amounts above stated value per share since incorporation in 1963. Of the 5,500,000 shares authorized, there were 3,600,000 shares outstanding at January 1, 1981. The market price of the outstanding common stock has increased slowly, but consistently, for the last five years.

The company has an employee stock option plan under which certain key employees and officers may purchase shares of common stock at 100% of the market price at the date of the option grant. All options are exercisable in installments of one-third each year, commencing one year after the date of the grant, and expire if not exercised within four years of the grant date. On January 1, 1981, options for 70,000 shares were outstanding at prices ranging from $47 to $83 a share. Options for 20,000 shares were exercised at $47 to $79 a share during 1981. No options expired during 1981 and additional options for 15,000 shares were granted at $86 a share during the year. The 65,000 options outstanding at December 31, 1981, were exercisable at $54 to $86 a share; of these, 30,000 were exercisable at that date at prices ranging from $54 to $79 a share.

The company also has an employee stock purchase plan under which the company pays one-half and the employee pays one-half of the market price of the stock at the date of the subscription. During 1981, employees subscribed to 60,000 shares at an average price of $87 a share. All 60,000 shares were paid for and issued late in September 1981.

On December 31, 1981, a total of 370,000 shares of common stock was set aside for the granting of future stock options and for future purchases under the employee stock purchase plan. The only changes in the stockholders' equity for 1981 were those described above, 1981 net income, and cash dividends paid.

Instructions

(a) Prepare the stockholders' equity section of the balance sheet of Forster Company at December 31, 1981; substitute, where appropriate, Xs for unknown dollar amounts. Use good form and provide full disclosure. Write appropriate footnotes as they should appear in the published financial statements.

(b) Explain how the amount of the denominator should be determined to compute **primary** earnings per share for presentation in the financial statements. Be specific as to the handling of each item. If additional information is needed to determine whether an item should be included or excluded or the extent to which an item should be included, identify the information needed and how the item would be handled if the information were known. Assume Forster Company had substantial net income for the year ended December 31, 1981.

(AICPA adapted)

P17-6 The controller of Braun Corporation has requested assistance in determining income, primary earnings per share, and fully diluted earnings per share for presentation in the company's income statement for the year ended September 30, 1982. As currently calculated, the company's net income is $500,000 for fiscal year 1981–1982. The controller has indicated that the income figure might be adjusted for the following transactions that were recorded by charges or credits directly to retained earnings (the amounts are net of applicable income taxes):

1. The sum of $280,000, applicable to a breached 1978 contract, was received as a result of a lawsuit. Prior to the award, legal counsel was uncertain about the outcome of the suit.
2. A gain of $250,000 was realized from condemnation sale (extraordinary).
3. A "gain" of $110,000 was realized on the sale of treasury stock. *contributed capital*
4. A special inventory write-off of $160,000 was made, of which $120,000 applied to goods manufactured prior to October 1, 1981. *loss*

Your working papers disclose the following opening balances and transactions in the company's capital stock accounts during the year:

1. Common stock (at October 1, 1981, stated value $10, authorized 300,000 shares; effective December 1, 1981, stated value $5, authorized 600,000 shares):

Balance, October 1, 1981—issued and outstanding 60,000 shares.
December 1, 1981—60,000 shares issued in a 2 for 1 stock split.
December 1, 1981—280,000 shares (stated value $5) issued at $39 per share.

2. Treasury stock—common:

March 1, 1982—purchased 40,000 shares at $37.25 per share.
April 1, 1982—sold 40,000 shares at $40 per share.

3. Stock purchase warrants, Series A (initially, each warrant was exchangeable with $60 for one common share; effective December 1, 1981, each warrant became exchangeable for two common shares at $30 per share):

October 1, 1981—25,000 warrants issued at $6 each.

4. Stock purchase warrants, Series B (each warrant is exchangeable with $40 for one common share): *antidilutive*

April 1, 1982—20,000 warrants authorized and issued at $10 each.

5. First mortgage bonds, 5½%, due 1997 (nonconvertible; priced to yield 5% when issued):

Balance, October 1, 1981—authorized, issued, and outstanding—the face value of $1,400,000.

6. Convertible debentures, 7%, due 2001 (initially, each $1,000 bond was convertible at any time until maturity into 12½ common shares; effective December 1, 1981, the *not primary* conversion rate became 25 shares for each bond):

October 1, 1981—authorized and issued at their face value (no premium or discount) of $2,400,000.

The following table shows market prices for the company's securities and the assumed bank prime interest rate during 1981–1982:

	Price (or Rate) at			Average for Year
	10/1/81	4/1/82	9/30/82	Ended 9/30/82
Common stock	66	40	36¼	37½[a]
First mortgage bonds	88½	87	86	87
Convertible debentures	100	120	119	115
Series A Warrants	6	22	19½	15
Series B Warrants	—	10	9	9½
Bank prime interest rate	8%	7¾%	7½%	7¾%

[a]Adjusted for stock split

Instructions

    (a) Prepare a schedule computing net income as it should be presented in the company's income statement for the year ended September 30, 1982.

    (b) Assuming that net income after income taxes for the year was $543,600 and that there were no extraordinary items, prepare a schedule computing (1) the primary earnings per share and (2) the fully diluted earnings per share that should be presented in the company's income statement for the year ended September 30, 1982. A supporting schedule computing the numbers of shares to be used in these computations should also be prepared. (Because of the relative stability of the market price for its common shares, the annual average market price may be used where appropriate in your calculations. Assume an income tax rate of 48% with no surcharge.)

(AICPA adapted)

P17-7 On February 1, 1981, when your audit and report are nearly complete, the president of the Nevin Corporation asks you to prepare statistical schedules of comparative financial data for the past five years for inclusion in the company's annual report. Your working papers reveal the following information.

1. Income statements show net income amounts as follows:

> 1976—$19,000
> 1977— (20,000) (loss)
> 1978— 25,000
> 1979— 38,000
> 1980— 49,000

2. On January 1, 1976, there were outstanding 1,000 shares of common stock, par value $100, and 500 shares of 6% cumulative preferred stock, par value $50.

3. A 5% dividend was paid in common stock to common stockholders on December 31, 1977. The fair market value of the stock was $145 per share at the time.

4. Four hundred shares of common stock were issued on March 31, 1978, to purchase another company. (The transaction was accounted for as a purchase, not a pooling of interests: use weighted average approach for purchase of a business.)

5. A dividend of cumulative preferred stock was distributed to common stockholders on July 1, 1978. One share of preferred stock was distributed for every five shares of common stock held. The fair market value of the preferred stock was $56 per share before the distribution and $54 per share immediately after the distribution.

6. The common stock was split 2-for-1 on December 31, 1979, and again on December 31, 1980.

7. Cash dividends are paid on the preferred stock on June 30 and December 31. Preferred stock dividends were paid in each year except 1977; the 1977 and 1978 dividends were paid in 1978.

8. Cash dividends on common stock are paid on June 30 and December 31. Dividends paid per share of stock outstanding at the respective dates were:

1976	$ .50	$ .50
1977	None	None
1978	.75	.75
1979	1.00	.50[a]
1980	.75	.75[b]

[a]After 2-for-1 split.
[b]Before 2-for-1 split.

Instructions

    (a) In connection with your preparation of the statistical schedule of comparative financial data for the past five years:

1. Prepare a schedule computing the number of shares of common stock and preferred stock outstanding as of the respective year-end dates.
2. Prepare a schedule computing the current equivalent number of shares of common stock outstanding as of the respective year-end dates. The current equivalent shares means the weighted average number of shares outstanding in the respective prior periods after restatement for stock splits and stock dividends.
3. Compute the total cash dividends paid to holders of preferred stock and to holders of common stock for each of the five years.

(b) Prepare a five-year summary of financial statistics to be included in the annual report. The summary should show by years "Net Income (or Loss)," "Earnings Per Share of Common Stock," and "Dividends Per Share of Common Stock." The per share figures should be computed on the basis of current equivalent shares.

(AICPA adapted)

P17-8 The stockholders' equity section of Makay Company's balance sheet as of December 31, 1981, contains the following:

$1.00 cumulative convertible preferred stock (par value $25 a share; authorized 1,600,000 shares, issued 1,400,000, converted to common 750,000, and outstanding 650,000 shares; involuntary liquidation value, $30 a share, aggregating $19,500,000)	$16,250,000
Common stock (par value $.25 a share; authorized 15,000,000 shares, issued and outstanding 8,800,000 shares)	2,200,000
Additional paid-in capital	30,500,000
Retained earnings	41,650,000
Total stockholders' equity	$90,600,000

On April 1, 1981, Makay Company acquired the business and assets and assumed the liabilities of Lockhart Corporation in a transaction accounted for as a pooling of interests. For each of Lockhart Corporation's 2,400,000 shares of $.25 par value common stock outstanding, the owner received one share of common stock of the Makay Company. (**Hint:** In a pooling of interests, shares are considered outstanding for the entire year.)

Included in the liabilities of Makay Company are 7% convertible subordinated debentures issued at their face value of $20,000,000 in 1980. The debentures are due in 2000 and until then are convertible into the common stock of Makay Company at the rate of five shares of common stock for each $100 debenture. To date none of these have been converted.

On April 2, 1981, Makay Company issued 1,400,000 shares of convertible preferred stock at $40 per share. Quarterly dividends to December 31, 1981, have been paid on these shares. The preferred stock is convertible into common stock at the rate of two shares of common for each share of preferred. On October 1, 1981, 150,000 shares and on November 1, 1981, 600,000 shares of the preferred stock were converted into common stock.

During July, 1980, Makay Company granted options to its officers and key employees to purchase 500,000 shares of the company's common stock at a price of $20 a share. The options do not become exercisable until 1982.

During 1981, dividend payments and average market prices of the Makay common stock were:

	Dividend Per Share	Average Market Price Per Share
First quarter	$.11	$25
Second quarter	.13	30
Third quarter	.15	20
Fourth quarter	.12	25
Average for the year		25

The December 31, 1981 closing price of the common stock was $25 a share.

Assume that the bank prime interest rate was 10% throughout 1980 and 1981. Makay Company's consolidated net income for the year ended December 31, 1981, was $9,200,000. The provision for income taxes was computed at a rate of 48%.

Instructions

(a) Prepare a schedule that shows the evaluation of the common stock equivalency status of the (1) convertible debentures, (2) convertible preferred stock, and (3) employee stock options.

(b) Prepare a schedule that shows for 1981 the computation of:
   1. The weighted average number of shares for computing primary earnings per share.
   2. The weighted average number of shares for computing fully diluted earnings per share.

(c) Prepare a schedule that shows for 1981 the computation to the nearest cent of:
   1. Primary earnings per share.
   2. Fully diluted earnings per share.

(AICPA adapted)

Investments in Securities and Funds

In order to engage in the production and sale of goods or services, a business enterprise must invest funds in many types of assets: monetary assets—cash and receivables; productive tangible assets—inventories, plant and equipment, and land; and intangible assets—patents, licenses, trademarks, and goodwill. In addition, some funds may be applied to the acquisition of securities of other companies. Such investments are classified as either temporary or long-term. **Temporary investments,** as discussed in Chapter 7, must be (1) readily marketable, and (2) intended to be converted into cash within one year or within the operating cycle, whichever is longer. Investments not meeting these two criteria are classified as **long-term** or **permanent.**

This chapter is devoted primarily to long-term investments in corporate securities: bonds of various types, preferred stocks, and common stocks. Numerous other items are commonly classified as long-term investments: funds for bond retirement, stock redemption, and other special purposes; investments in notes receivable, mortgages and similar debt instruments; and miscellaneous items such as advances to affiliates, cash surrender value of life insurance policies, interests in estates and trusts, equity in joint ventures and partnerships, and real estate held for appreciation or future use. Some of these items are also discussed. Long-term investments are usually presented on the balance sheet just below current assets in a separate section called Long-Term Investments, Investments and Funds, or just Investments.

Although many reasons prompt a corporation to invest in the securities of another corporation, **the primary motive is to enhance its own income.** A corporation may thus enhance its income (1) directly through the receipt of dividends or interest from the investment or through appreciation in the market value of the securities, or (2) indirectly by creating and insuring desirable operating relationships between companies to improve income performance. Frequently the most permanent of investments are those in the latter category: those for improving income performance. Benefits to the investors are derived from the influence or control that may be exercised over a major supplier, customer, or otherwise related company.

INVESTMENTS IN BONDS

Accounting for bonds as a long-term liability was presented in Chapter 14. In this chapter our attention is on accounting for these same securities from the investor's viewpoint. The types and characteristics of bonds that may be purchased are presented on pages 597–598; you should reread that discussion as background for this chapter. The variety in these features, along with the variability in interest rates, permits investors to shop for exactly the investment that satisfies their safety, yield, and marketability preferences.

Accounting for Bond Acquisitions

Investments in bonds should be recorded on the date of acquisition at cost, which includes brokerage fees and any other costs incident to the purchase. **The cost or purchase price of a bond investment is its market value, which is the product of the market's appraisal of the risk involved and consideration of the stated interest rate in comparison with the prevailing market (yield) rate of interest for that type of security.** The cash amount of interest to be received periodically is fixed by the stated rate of interest on the face value (also, called principal, par, or maturity value). If the rate of return desired by the investors is exactly equal to the stated rate, **the bond will sell at its face amount.** If investors demand a higher yield than the stated rate offers, **the bond will sell at a discount.** Purchasing the bond at an amount below the face amount, or at a discount, is the method of equating the yield on the bond with the market rate of interest. If the market rate of interest is below the stated rate, **investors will pay a premium,** more than maturity value, for the bond. The relationship between bond market values and interest rates is similar to that discussed under the heading of bonds payable, pages 599–600.

If bonds are **purchased between interest payment dates,** the investor must pay the owner the market price plus the interest accrued since the last interest payment date. The investor will collect this interest plus the additional interest earned by holding the bond to the next interest date. For example, assume the purchase on June 1 of bonds having a $100,000 face value and paying 6% interest on April 1 and October 1, for 98. The entry to record purchase of the bonds and accrued interest is as follows:

Investments in Bonds	98,000	
Interest Income on Bonds ($100,000 × .06 × 2 / 12)	1,000	
(Interest Receivable might be debited instead)		
Cash		99,000

On October 1 the investor will receive interest of $3,000 consisting of $1,000 paid at date of acquisition and $2,000 earned for holding the bond for four months.

Investments acquired at par, at a discount, or at a premium are generally recorded in the accounts at cost, including brokerage and other fees but excluding the accrued interest; generally they are not recorded at maturity value. The use of a separate discount or premium account as a valuation account is acceptable procedure, but in practice it has not been widely used. This traditional exclusion of a separate discount or premium account has not yet changed even though **APB Opinion No. 21 recommends the disclosure of unamortized discount or premium on notes and bonds receivable.**

If the discount of $2,000 were recorded separately and the bond recorded at maturity value, the entry to record the investment in bonds would be as follows:

Investments in Bonds	100,000	
Interest Income	1,000	
Discount on Investment in Bonds		2,000
Cash		99,000

When the investment is recorded net of the discount, at $98,000 as in the first example, the discount is amortized by debit entries recorded directly to the Investment in Bonds account. When the investment is recorded at maturity value, at $100,000 as in the second example, the discount is amortized by debiting the Discount on Investments in Bonds account. Both methods produce exactly the same net results on the financial statements. The following illustrations record the investment at net of discount or premium.

Computing Bond Prices

Theoretically the market price of a bond is the present value of its maturity amount plus the present value of its interest payments, both discounted at the market rate of interest. Using this as a basis, determine the price that should be paid for $10,000 of 8% bonds, interest payable semiannually, and maturing in six years, if a 10% yield is desired. The computation is as follows:

$$
\begin{aligned}
\text{Purchase price} &= \text{PV of maturity amount plus PV of interest payments} \\
&= \$10,000 \times \text{PV of 1 for 12 periods at 5\%} \\
&\quad + \$400 \times \text{PV of annuity of 1 for 12 periods at 5\%} \\
&= (\$10,000 \times .55684, \text{Table 6-2}) + (\$400 \times 8.86325, \text{Table 6-4}) \\
&= \$5,568.40 + \$3,545.30 \\
&= \$9,113.70
\end{aligned}
$$

Amortization of Bond Premium and Bond Discount

As previously discussed in Chapter 14, there are two widely used methods of amortizing bond premium and bond discount: (1) **the straight-line method,** and (2) **the effective interest method** (also called the present value or compound interest or effective yield method).

Both methods of amortizing bond discount and premium on long-term investments are illustrated below. The write-off of discount on bond investments is sometimes referred to as discount "accumulation" instead of "amortization."

Straight-line Amortization of Premium   Assume that on March 1, 1981, bonds of a par value of $50,000, bearing 8% interest payable January 1 and July 1, are purchased for $53,008 plus accrued interest. The bonds mature January 1, 1989. The entry on March 1, 1981, is:

Investments in Bonds	53,008.00	
Interest Income on Bonds	666.67	
Cash		53,674.67

The accrued interest of $666.67 represents interest at 8% for two months on $50,000, the par value of the bonds purchased.

When six months' interest is received on July 1, 1981, premium allocable to four months is written off by a credit to the Investments account, and the income is reduced accordingly. The premium amortized would be 4/94 of $3,008, or $128, because the bonds have been held for four months and because there are 94 months from the date of purchase to maturity date. The entry on July 1, 1981, therefore, is:

Cash	2,000	
Investments in Bonds		128
Interest Income on Bonds		1,872

The Interest Income account now has a balance of $1,872 less $666.67, or $1,205.33. This represents the income earned on the bonds during the four months from March 1 to July 1. This amount is analyzed as follows:

Interest received on July 1, 1981, 8% $\times$ $50,000 $\times$ 6/12	$2,000.00
Deduct interest accrued on Mar. 1, 1981, date of purchase of bonds, 8% $\times$ $50,000 $\times$ 2/12	666.67
Interest received that is applicable to the 4 months from Mar. 1 to July 1	1,333.33
Deduct premium amortized for 4 months, 4/94 $\times$ $3,008	128.00
Income earned during the 4 months	$1,205.33

On December 31, 1981, an adjusting entry would be made to accrue six months' interest and to amortize the premium applicable to six months.

Interest Receivable on Bonds	2,000	
Investments in Bonds		192
Interest Income on Bonds		1,808

The $192 credit to the Investments account, represents the premium amortization for the six months from July 1 to December 31, or 6/94 of $3,008. The credit to Interest Income, $1,808, represents the difference between the interest receivable of $2,000 and the premium amortized of $192, or the net amount taken up as income for the six months ended December 31, 1981.

During the next year and during each succeeding year, a premium of $384, representing 12/94 of the total premium paid, will be amortized. Thus, by maturity date the entire amount of the premium will have been removed from the Investments account, and the bonds will be carried on the books at par at that time. The entry to record the redemption of the bonds will therefore be:

Cash	50,000	
Investments in Bonds		50,000

In the entries given on page 776, the premium was amortized simultaneously with the interest received or accrued. They do not have to be combined in one entry, however, or entered at the same time. The entries for interest received or receivable are made at the proper times independently of the entries for premium amortization. The proper amount of premium may be amortized at the end of each fiscal year or any other designated time by debiting Interest Income on Bonds and crediting Investments in Bonds. In the example above, the recognition of accrued interest and amortization of premium in separate entries would be as follows:

Interest Receivable on Bonds	2,000	
Interest Income on Bonds		2,000
Interest Income on Bonds	192	
Investments in Bonds		192

Separate entries are convenient when reversing entries are used because the entry for accrued interest would be reversed but no reversing entry is needed for premium amortization.

Amortization (Accumulation) of Discount   If bonds are purchased below par, the straight-line method of amortization is the same as that illustrated above for amortization of premium. For discount, however, the amount of discount amortized is added to the interest income.

Assume that bonds with a par value of $50,000, bearing 8% interest payable January 1 and July 1, and maturing January 1, 1989, are purchased on March 1, 1981, for $46,992 plus accrued interest. In other words, assume that they are purchased at a discount of $3,008 instead of a premium of $3,008, as above. Because they have 94 months yet to run, the discount to be amortized for each month is 1/94 of $3,008, or $32. The entry to record the purchase is:

Investments in Bonds	46,992.00	
Interest Income on Bonds	666.67	
Cash		47,658.67

When six months' interest is received on July 1, 1981, the entry is:

Cash	2,000	
Investments in Bonds	128	
Interest Income on Bonds		2,128

In this case the Investments account is debited, and the credit to Interest Income is the total of the interest received and the discount amortized. If bonds are purchased at a discount, the discount amortized is debited to the asset account; by maturity date the book value of the bonds will be at par.

Thus, bonds purchased at a premium are written down to par through amortization of premium, and bonds purchased at a discount are written up to par through amortization of the discount.

Effective Interest Method   As discussed previously under long-term debt, Chapter 14, when a premium or discount is amortized under the straight-line method, the rate of return is not the same year after year. Although the interest received is constant from period to period, the carrying amount of the bond is either increasing or decreasing by the amount of the discount or premium amortization. The straight-line method produces a constant revenue, but produces a variable rate of return on the book value of the investment. Although the effective interest method results in a varying amount being recorded as interest income from period to period, its virtue is that it produces a constant rate of return on the investment from period to period.

The straight-line method is the more popular method because (1) it is simple to apply; (2) it avoids the computation of the effective interest rate; and (3) it produces a close approximation of the effective interest earned, unless the maturity date is many years distant or the premium or discount is exceptionally large. **APB Opinion No. 21** specifies a preference for the effective interest method when interest is imputed and permits other methods if the results obtained are not significantly different from those produced by the effective interest method. If interest is not imputed, the effective interest method of amortization is not required.

The effective interest method is applied to bond investments in a fashion similar to that described for bonds payable. The effective interest rate or yield is computed at the time of investment and is applied to the beginning book value of the investment for each interest period. In each period the book value of the investment is increased by the amortized discount or decreased by the amortized premium.

To illustrate, the Robinson Company is the purchaser of the Grometer Corporation bonds discussed in Chapter 14, page 601. To restate the situation, Robinson Company purchased $100,000 of 8% bonds of Grometer Corporation on January 1, 1980, paying $92,278. The bonds mature January 1, 1985; interest is payable each July 1 and January 1. The discount of $7,722 ($100,000 − $92,278) provided an effective interest yield of 10%. The schedule below discloses the effect of the dis-

SCHEDULE OF INTEREST INCOME AND BOND DISCOUNT
AMORTIZATION—EFFECTIVE INTEREST METHOD
8% BONDS PURCHASED TO YIELD 10%

Date	Debit Cash	Credit Interest Income	Debit Bond Investment[e]	Book Value of Bonds
1/1/80				$ 92,278
7/1/80	$ 4,000[a]	$ 4,614[b]	$ 614[c]	92,892[d]
1/1/81	4,000	4,645	645	93,537
7/1/81	4,000	4,677	677	94,214
1/1/82	4,000	4,711	711	94,925
7/1/82	4,000	4,746	746	95,671
1/1/83	4,000	4,783	783	96,454
7/1/83	4,000	4,823	823	97,277
1/1/84	4,000	4,864	864	98,141
7/1/84	4,000	4,907	907	99,048
1/1/85	4,000	4,952	952	100,000
	$40,000	$47,722	$7,722	

[a]$4,000 = $100,000 × .08 × 6/12
[b]$4,614 = $92,278 × .10 × 6/12
[c]$614 = $4,614 − $4,000
[d]$92,892 = $92,278 + $614
[e]Or, debit Discount on Investment in Bonds if the investment is carried at maturity value.

count amortization on the interest income recorded each period using the effective interest method of amortization if the bonds are held to maturity. The investment is carried in the accounts net of the unamortized discount.

The journal entry to record the receipt of the first semiannual interest payment on July 1, 1980 (as shown on the schedule) is:

Cash	4,000	
Investments in Bonds	614	
Interest Income on Bonds		4,614

Sale of Bonds Before Maturity Date

If bonds carried as long-term investments are sold before maturity date, entries must be made to amortize the discount or premium to the date of sale and to remove from the Investments account the book value of bonds sold.

For example, assume that the bonds described on page 776 are sold on April 1, 1987, at 99½ plus accrued interest. Discount has been amortized at the rate of $32 per month from the date of purchase, March 1, 1981, through the last closing date, December 31, 1986. An entry is made to amortize discount for the three months that have expired in 1987:

Investments in Bonds	96	
Interest Income on Bonds		96

The entry to record the sale is:

Cash	50,750	
Interest Income on Bonds		1,000
Investments in Bonds		49,328
Gain on Sale of Bonds		422

The credit to Interest Income represents accrued interest for three months, for which the purchaser pays cash. The debit to Cash represents the selling price of the bonds, $49,750, plus the accrued interest of $1,000. The credit to the Investments account represents the book value of the bonds on the date of the sale, and the credit to Gain on Sale of Bonds represents the excess of the selling price over the book value of the bonds. The computation of the latter two credits is shown below:

Selling price of bonds (exclusive of accrued interest)		$49,750
Deduct book value of bonds on April 1, 1987:		
Cost	$46,992	
Add discount amortized for the period from March 1, 1981,		
to April 1, 1987, 73/94 × $3,008	2,336	49,328
Gain on sale		$ 422

INVESTMENTS IN STOCKS

Stock Acquisitions

Shares of stock may be acquired in the market through security exchanges or "over the counter" through stockbrokers. Stock may also be acquired directly from an issuing company or from a private investor. When stock is purchased outright for cash, the full cost includes the purchase price of the security plus brokers' commissions and other fees incidental to the purchase. If stock is **acquired "on margin"** (the margin representing borrowings from the broker), the stock purchase should be recorded at its full cost, and a liability recognized for the unpaid balance. A stock **subscription** or agreement to buy the stock of a corporation is recognized by a charge to an asset account for the security to be received and a credit to a liability account for the amount to be paid. Any interest on an obligation arising from a stock purchase should be recognized as expense. Stock acquired in **exchange for noncash consideration** (property or services) should be recorded at (1) the fair market value of the consideration given or (2) the fair market value of the stock received, whichever is more clearly determinable.

The absence of clearly determinable values for the property or services or a market price for the security acquired may force the use of appraisals or estimates to arrive at a cost.

The purchase of two or more classes of securities for a **lump sum price** calls for the allocation of the cost to the different classes in some equitable manner. If market prices are available for each class of security, the lump sum cost may be apportioned on the basis of the **relative market values.** If the market price is available for one security but not for the other, the market price may be assigned to the one and the cost excess to the other. If market prices are not available at the date of acquisition of several securities, it may be necessary to defer cost apportionment until evidence of at least one value becomes available. In some instances cost apportionment may have to wait until one of the securities is sold. In such cases, the proceeds from the sale of the one security may be subtracted from the lump sum cost, leaving the residual cost to be assigned as the cost of the other.

Accounting for numerous purchases of securities requires that information regarding the cost of individual purchases be preserved as well as the dates of purchases and sales. If specific identification is not possible, the use of an average cost may be used for multiple purchases in close proximity to the same class of security. The first-in, first-out method of assigning costs to investments at the time of sale is acceptable and is normally employed.

Effect of Ownership Interest

The extent to which one corporation **(investor)** acquires an equity interest in another corporation **(investee),** i.e., the degree of ownership interest, generally determines the accounting treatment for the investment. Long-term investments by one corporation in the common stock of another can be classified according to the percentage of the common stock of the investee held by the investor:

1. Holdings of more than 50%.
2. Holdings between 20% and 50%.
3. Holdings of less than 20%.

When one corporation acquires an interest of more than 50% **(controlling interest)** in another corporation, the investor corporation is referred to as the **parent** and the investee corporation as the **subsidiary.** The investment in the common stock of the subsidiary is presented as a long-term investment on the separate financial statements of the parent.

Instead of separate financial statements for the parent and the subsidiary in which the parent treats the subsidiary as an investment, **consolidated financial statements** are generally prepared. Consolidated financial statements disregard the distinction between separate legal entities and treat the parent and subsidiary corporations as a single economic entity. When and how to prepare consolidated financial statements are discussed extensively in advanced accounting. Whether or not consolidated financial statements are prepared, the investment in the subsidiary is generally accounted for on the parent's books using the **equity method** as explained in this chapter.

Although an investor corporation may hold an interest of less than 50% in an investee corporation and thus not possess legal control, its "investment in voting stock gives it the ability to exercise significant influence over operating and financial policies of an investee."[1] To provide a guide for accounting for investors when 50% or less of the common of voting stock is held and to develop an operational definition of "significant influence," the APB submitted this statement:

> Ability to exercise that influence may be indicated in several ways, such as representation on the board of directors, participation in policy making processes, material intercompany transactions, interchange of managerial personnel, or technological dependency. Another important consideration is the extent of ownership by an investor in relation to the concentration of other shareholdings, but substantial or majority ownership of the voting stock of an investee by another investor does not necessarily preclude the ability to exercise significant influence by the investor. The Board recognizes that determining the ability of an investor to exercise such influence is not always clear and applying judgment is necessary to assess the status of each investment.[2]

To achieve a reasonable degree of uniformity in application of the "significant influence" criterion, the APB concluded that:

> An investment (direct or indirect) of 20% or more of the voting stock of an investee should lead to a presumption that in the absence of evidence to the contrary an investor has the ability to exercise significant influence over an investee. Conversely, an investment of less than 20% of the voting stock of an investee should lead to a presumption that an investor does not have the ability to exercise significant influence unless such ability can be demonstrated.[3]

In instances of "significant influence" (generally an investment of 20% or more) the investor is required under **Opinion No. 18** to account for the investment using the **equity method.** When the investor lacks significant influence over the investee, presumably less than a 20% interest, the investment is to be accounted for using either (1) **the cost method** or (2) **the lower of cost or market method,** depending upon the character of the securities as discussed later. In specialized industries, investments in certain securities of others are accounted for using the **market value method.** The following pages discuss and illustrate the four methods of accounting for long-term investments, namely, (1) the cost method, (2) the equity method,

---

[1]"The Equity Method of Accounting for Investments in Common Stock," *Opinions of the Accounting Principles Board No. 18* (New York: AICPA, 1971), par. 17.

[2]*Ibid.*

[3]*Ibid.*

(3) the lower of cost or market method, and (4) the market value method, and their applicability.[4]

Cost Method

Under the **cost method** a long-term investment is originally recorded and reported at cost, and it continues to be carried and reported at cost in the investment account until it is either partially or entirely disposed of, or until some fundamental change in conditions makes it clear that the value originally assigned can no longer be justified. Write-downs from cost are appropriate (1) when the dividends received represent a distribution of earnings retained in the business prior to the acquisition of the stock by the investor (liquidating dividend), and (2) when operating losses of the investee significantly reduce the net assets and greatly impair its earning potential. The cost method recognizes as income to the investor only what is received in the form of assets distributed by the investee. Ordinary cash dividends received from the investee are recorded as investment income.

To illustrate the cost method, assume the following four transactions:

1. On January 2, 1980, Maxi Company acquired 48,000 shares (12% of Mini Company common stock) at a cost of $10 a share.

Investment in Mini Company	480,000	
Cash		480,000

2. For the year 1980, Mini Company reported net income of $200,000; Maxi Company's share is 12% or $24,000.

[No entry recorded by Maxi Company.]

3. On January 28, 1981, Mini Company announced and paid a cash dividend of $100,000; Maxi Company received 12% or $12,000.

Cash	12,000	
Investment Income		12,000

4. For the year 1981 Mini Company reported a net loss of $50,000; Maxi Company's share is 12% or $6,000.

[No entry recorded by Maxi Company.]

Equity Method

Under the **equity method** a substantive economic relationship is acknowledged between the investor and the investee. The investment is originally recorded at the cost of the shares acquired but is subsequently adjusted each period for changes in the net assets of the investee. That is, the **investment carrying amount is periodically increased (decreased) by the investor's proportionate share of the earnings (losses) of the investee and decreased by all dividends received by the investor from the investee.** The equity method gives recognition to the fact that investee

---

[4]*Accounting Trends and Techniques—1978* reports that in 1977 of its 600 surveyed companies 330 employed the equity method, 136 the cost method, 27 the cost less allowances for decline in value method, and 19 the lower of cost or market method as the basis for valuing investments in equity securities of other companies. The different methods resulted from differing circumstances and percentages of interest.

earnings increase investee net assets that underlie the investment, and that investee losses and dividends decrease these net assets.

Further, under the equity method, **periodic investor income** consists of the investor's proportionate share of investee earnings (adjusted to eliminate inter-company gains and losses) and amortization of the difference between the investor's initial costs and the investor's proportionate share of the underlying book value of the investee at date of acquisition. And, if the investee's net income includes extraordinary items, the investor treats a proportionate share of the extraordinary items as an extraordinary item rather than as ordinary investment income before extraordinary items.

Illustration of the Equity Method   On January 1, 1980, I. N. Vestor Company purchased 250,000 shares of Investee Company's 1,000,000 shares of outstanding common stock for $8,500,000. The book value of Investee Company's total net worth was $30,000,000 at the date of I. N. Vestor Company's 25% investment. I. N. Vestor Company thereby paid $1,000,000 [$8,500,000 − .25($30,000,000)] in excess of book value. It was determined that $600,000 of this is attributable to its share of **undervalued depreciable assets** of Investee Company and $400,000 to **unrecorded goodwill.** I. N. Vestor Company estimated the average remaining life of the under-valued assets to be 10 years and decided upon a 40-year amortization period for goodwill (the maximum length of time allowed by **APB No. 17**). For the year 1980, Investee Company reported net income of $2,800,000 including an extraordinary loss of $400,000, and paid dividends at June 30, 1980 of $600,000 and at December 31, 1980 of $800,000. The following entries would be recorded on the books of I. N. Vestor Company to reflect its long-term investment using the equity method:

January 1, 1980

Investment in Investee Company Stock	8,500,000	
Cash		8,500,000
(To record the acquisition of 250,000		
shares of Investee Company common stock)		

June 30, 1980

Cash	150,000	
Investment in Investee Company Stock		150,000
[To record dividend received		
($600,000 × .25) from Investee Company]		

December 31, 1980

Investment in Investee Company Stock	700,000	
Loss from Investment (extraordinary)	100,000	
Income from Investment (ordinary)		800,000
[To record share of Investee Company		
ordinary income ($3,200,000 × .25)		
and extraordinary loss ($400,000 × .25)]		

December 31, 1980

Cash	200,000	
Investment in Investee Company Stock		200,000
[To record dividend received ($800,000 × .25)		
from Investee Company]		

December 31, 1980

Income from Investment (ordinary)	70,000	
Investment in Investee Company Stock		70,000

(To record amortization of investment cost
in excess of book value represented by:

Undervalued depreciable assets—$600,000 ÷ 10	=$60,000	
Unrecorded goodwill—$400,000 ÷ 40	= 10,000	
Total	$70,000)	

The investment in Investee Company is presented in the balance sheet of I. N. Vestor Company at a carrying amount of $8,780,000 computed as follows:

Investment in Investee Company		
Acquisition cost, 1/1/80	$8,500,000	
Plus: Share of 1980 net income	800,000	$9,300,000
Less: Share of extraordinary loss	100,000	
Dividends received 6/30 and 12/31	350,000	
Amortization of undervalued depreciable assets	60,000	
Amortization of unrecorded goodwill	10,000	520,000
Carrying amount, 12/31/80		$8,780,000

In the illustration above the investment cost exceeded the underlying book value. In some cases, an investor may acquire an investment at a **cost less than the underlying book value.** In such cases specific assets are assumed to be overvalued and, if depreciable, the excess of the investee's book value over the investor's acquisition cost is amortized into investment income over the remaining lives of the assets. Investment income is increased under the presumption that the investee's net income as reported is actually understated because the investee is charging depreciation on overstated asset values.

Investee Losses Exceed Carrying Amount   If an investor's share of losses of an investee exceeds the carrying amount of the investment, the question arises as to whether the investor should provide for additional losses. Ordinarily the investor should discontinue applying the equity method and not provide additional losses. If the investor's potential loss is not limited to the amount of its original investment (by guarantee of the investee's obligations or other commitment to provide further financial support), however, or if imminent return to profitable operations by the investee appears to be assured, it is appropriate for the investor to provide for additional losses.[5]

Change in Method *from* the Equity Method   If the investor level of influence or ownership falls below that necessary for continued use of the equity method, a change must be made to either the lower of cost or market method or the cost method, whichever is appropriate. The earnings or losses that relate to the stock retained by the investor and that were previously recognized by the investor should remain as part of the carrying amount of the investment with no retroactive restatement to the new method.

[5]"The Equity Method of Accounting for Investments in Common Stock," op. cit., par. 19(i).

To the extent that dividends received by the investor in subsequent periods exceed its share of the investee's earnings for such periods, they should be accounted for as a reduction of the investment carrying amount, rather than as income. For example, using the data from the previous illustration, assume that on January 2, 1981, Investee Company sold 1,500,000 additional shares of its common stock to the public, thereby reducing I. N. Vestor Company's ownership from 25% to 10% and that the net income (or loss) and dividends of Investee Company for the years 1981 through 1983 were as follows:

Year	Investor's Share of Investee Income (Loss)	Investee Dividends Received by Investor
1981	$600,000	$400,000
1982	350,000	400,000
1983	(200,000)	300,000

Assuming a change from the equity method to the cost method as of January 2, 1981, I. N. Vestor Company's reported investment in Investee Company and its reported income would be as follows:

Year	Dividend Income Recognized	Cumulative Excess of Share of Earnings Over Dividends Received	Investment at December 31
1981	$400,000	$200,000[a]	$8,780,000
1982	400,000	150,000[b]	8,780,000
1983	-0-	(350,000)[c]	8,780,000 − $350,000 = $8,430,000

[a]$600,000 − $400,000 = $200,000
[b]($350,000 − $400,000) + $200,000 = $150,000
[c]$150,000 − ($200,000 + $300,000) = ($350,000)

Note from the illustration above that when a change is made from the equity method to the cost method, the cost basis for accounting purposes is the carrying amount of the investment at the date of the change. Also, note the cessation of the amortization of the excess of acquisition price over the proportionate share of book value acquired attributable to undervalued depreciable assets and unrecorded goodwill when the change of methods occurs. In other words, the new method is applied in its entirety once the equity method is no longer appropriate.

Change in Method *to* the Equity Method   An investment in common stock of an investee that has been accounted for by other than the equity method may become qualified for use of the equity method by an increase in the level of ownership. At the time that an investment qualifies for use of the equity method, the investor should adopt the equity method of accounting. Such a change involves **adjusting retroactively** the carrying amount of the investment, results of operations (current and prior periods presented), and retained earnings of the investor in a step-by-step acquisition manner as if the equity method has been in effect during all of the previous periods in which this investment was held.[6]

[6]*Ibid.*, par. 19(m).

For example, on January 2, 1977, Amsted Corp. purchased for $500,000 cash 10 percent of the outstanding shares of Cable Company common stock. On that date, the net assets of Cable Company had a book value of $3,000,000. The excess of cost over the underlying equity in net assets of Cable Company is attributed to goodwill, which is amortized over 40 years. On January 2, 1979, Amsted Corp. purchased an additional 20% of Cable Company's stock for $1,200,000 cash when the book value of Cable's net assets was $4,000,000. Now having a 30% interest, Amsted Corp. must use the equity method. The net income reported by Cable Company and the Cable Company dividends received by Amsted during the period 1977 through 1979 were as follows:

Year	Cable Company Net Income	Cable Co. Dividends Paid to Amsted
1977	$ 500,000	$ 20,000
1978	1,000,000	30,000
1979	1,200,000	120,000

The journal entries recorded from January 2, 1977, through December 31, 1979, relative to Amsted Corp's. investment in Cable Company reflecting the data above and a change from the cost method to the equity method are as follows:[7]

January 2, 1977

Investment in Cable Company Stock	500,000	
Cash		500,000
(To record the purchase of a 10% interest in Cable Company)		

December 31, 1977

Cash	20,000	
Dividend Income		20,000
(To record the receipt of cash dividends from Cable Company)		

December 31, 1978

Cash	30,000	
Dividend Income		30,000
(To record the receipt of cash dividends from Cable Company)		

January 2, 1979

Investment in Cable Company Stock	1,290,000	
Cash		1,200,000
Retained Earnings		90,000
(To record the purchase of an additional interest in Cable Company and to reflect retroactively a change from the cost method to the equity method of accounting for the investment. The $90,000 adjustment is computed as follows:		

[7]Adapted from Paul A. Pacter, "Applying APB Opinion No. 18—Equity Method," *Journal of Accountancy* (September, 1971), pp. 59-60.

	1977	1978	Total
Amsted Corp. equity in earnings of Cable Company 10%	$50,000	$100,000	$150,000

Amortization of excess of acquisition
    price over underlying equity
    [$500,000 − (10% × $3,000,00)] ÷ 40
    years = $5,000 per year.
	(5,000)	(5,000)	(10,000)

Dividend received	(20,000)	(30,000)	(50,000)
Prior period adjustment	$25,000	$ 65,000	$ 90,000

December 31, 1979

Investment in Cable Company Stock	345,000	
Income from Investment		345,000

[To record equity in earnings of Cable
Company (30% of $1,200,000) less $15,000
amortization of goodwill[a]]

[a]Goodwill amortization includes $5,000 [$500,000 − (10% × $3,000,000) ÷ 40 years] from 1977 purchase of 10% interest plus $10,000 [$1,200,000 − (20% × $4,000,000) ÷ 40 years] from 1979 purchase of 20% interest.

Cash	120,000	
Investment in Cable Company Stock		120,000

(To record the receipt of cash
dividends from Cable Company)

Changing to the equity method is accomplished by placing the accounts related to and affected by the investment on the same basis as if the equity method has always been the basis of accounting for that investment.

Disclosures Required Under the Equity Method   The significance of an investment to the investor's financial position and operating results should be considered in evaluating the extent of disclosures about the investment and the investee company. According to **APB Opinion No. 18,** the following disclosures in the investor's financial statements are generally applicable to the equity method:

1. The name of each investee and the percentage of ownership of common stock.
2. The accounting policies of the investor with respect to investments in common stock.
3. The difference, if any, between the amount in the investment account and the amount of underlying equity in the net assets of the investee.
4. The aggregate value of each identified investment based on quoted market price (if available).
5. When investments of 20% or more interest are in the aggregate material in relation to the financial position and operating results of an investor, it may be necessary to present summarized information concerning assets, liabilities, and results of operations of the investees, either individually or in groups, as appropriate.

In addition, the investor is expected to disclose the reasons for **not** using the equity method in cases of 20% or more ownership interest and **for** using the equity method in cases of less than 20% ownership interest. See page 792 for examples of such disclosures from the financial statements of Borg-Warner Corporation and Insilco Corporation.

Lower of Cost or Market Method

Whenever the investment is in "marketable equity securities" and the equity method is not appropriate (less than 20% interest or "lack of significant influence"), the investor is required to use the **lower of cost or market method** in accounting for the investment. The application of lower of cost or market to investments in marketable equity securities classified as current assets was discussed in considerable detail in Chapter 7. Securities qualify as "marketable equity securities" if they represent ownership shares or the right to acquire or dispose of ownership shares in an enterprise at fixed or determinable prices and there are currently available for such securities sales prices or bid and ask prices in the securities market.[8]

Under the lower of cost or market method all noncurrent marketable equity securities are grouped in a separate noncurrent portfolio for purposes of comparing the **aggregate** cost and the **aggregate** market value to determine the carrying amount at the balance sheet date. Accounting for noncurrent marketable equity securities is both similar to and different from accounting for marketable equity securities classified as current assets. Similarity: **FASB Statement No. 12** requires that the amount by which aggregate cost of the noncurrent portfolio exceeds market value (unrealized loss) be accounted for as the **valuation allowance.** Difference: whereas changes in the valuation allowance for equity securities classified as current assets are included in the determination of income, **accumulated changes in the valuation allowance for a marketable equity securities portfolio included in noncurrent assets are included in the equity section of the balance sheet and shown separately.** In substance, the FASB says "mark to market" at each reporting date, down and up, but not in excess of original cost, and report unrealized losses and recoveries in the equity section of the balance sheet (so long as the decline in the market value is viewed as temporary).

Illustration of Lower of Cost or Market Method   Bolex Company made the following long-term investments in marketable equity securities during 1980:

> January 15, 1980—Purchased 20,000 shares of Witco, Inc. common stock (a 6% interest) for $1,446,000 including brokerage commissions.
>
> July 22, 1980—Purchased 52,000 shares of Cuneo Tool Company common stock (an 11% interest) for $2,340,000 including brokerage commissions.

On December 31, 1980, Bolex determined the carrying amount of its portfolio in marketable equity securities classified as a long-term investment to be:

---

[8]"Accounting for Certain Marketable Securities," *Statement of Financial Accounting Standards No. 12* (Stamford, Conn.: FASB, December, 1975), par. 7.

Long-Term Investments—	December 31, 1980		
	Cost	Market	Unrealized Gain (Loss)
Witco, Inc.	$1,446,000	$1,478,000	$ 32,000
Cuneo Tool Company	2,340,000	1,900,000	(440,000)
Total of portfolio	$3,786,000	$3,378,000	$(408,000)
Balance—valuation allowance			$(408,000)

Applying the lower of cost or market method to the Bolex portfolio at December 31, 1980, results in a carrying amount of $3,378,000. The net unrealized loss of $408,000 represents the aggregate excess of cost over the market value of the portfolio of marketable equity securities classified as noncurrent assets and is recorded in the accounts as follows:

December 31, 1980

Net Unrealized Loss on Noncurrent Marketable Equity Securities	408,000	
Allowance for Excess of Cost of Long-Term Equity Securities over Market Value		408,000
(To record excess of cost over market value of marketable equity securities portfolio classified as noncurrent assets)		

If the market value of the Bolex portfolio subsequently rises, the write-down would be reversed to the extent that the resulting carrying amount does not exceed cost.

Disclosure in the Financial Statements   The following information with respect to marketable equity securities classified as noncurrent assets should be disclosed in the body of the financial statements or in the accompanying footnotes:

(1) For each balance sheet presented—the aggregate cost and aggregate market value.
(2) For the latest balance sheet presented—gross unrealized gains and gross unrealized losses.
(3) For each income statement presented:
    (a) Net realized gain or loss included in the determination of net income.
    (b) The basis on which cost was determined in computing realized gain or loss.
    (c) The change in the valuation allowance that has been included in the equity section of the balance sheet during the period.[9]

The data from the Bolex Company investment discussed above would be presented in the December 31, 1980, financial statements as follows:

[9]*Ibid.*, par. 12.

BALANCE SHEET

Long-Term Investments—
Marketable equity securities, carried at market (Note 1) $ 3,378,000

Stockholders' Equity—
Common stock $ 9,000,000
Additional paid-in capital 2,500,000
Retained earnings 7,349,000

  18,849,000

Net unrealized loss on noncurrent marketable
equity securities (Note 1) (408,000)

Total stockholders' equity $18,441,000

Note 1. *Marketable Equity Securities.* Marketable equity securities are carried at the lower of cost or market at the balance sheet date, with that determination made by aggregating all noncurrent marketable equity securities. Marketable equity securities included in long-term investments had a cost of $3,786,000.

At December 31, 1980, there were gross unrealized gains of $32,000 and gross unrealized losses of $440,000 pertaining to the long-term portfolio. Because no sale of such securities occurred during the period, no gains or losses have been included in the determination of net income.

To reduce the carrying amount of the long-term marketable equity securities portfolio to market, which was lower than cost at December 31, 1980, a valuation allowance in the amount of $408,000 was established by a charge to stockholders' equity representing the net unrealized loss.

Note that the charge to equity for net unrealized losses is treated as a reduction from the total equity in much the same manner as treasury stock is accounted for under the cost method.

Decline in Market Value Other Than Temporary Occasionally a long-term investment in an individual marketable equity security suffers a decline in market value below cost that is other than temporary. If the decline is judged to be other than temporary, the cost basis of the individual security is written down to a new cost basis. Although the security is one for which the effect of a change in carrying amount is included in stockholders' equity, the amount of a nontemporary writedown is accounted for as a **realized loss.** The new cost basis is not changed for subsequent recoveries in market value.

In judging whether a decline in market value below cost at the balance sheet date is other than temporary, a gain or loss realized on subsequent disposition or changes in market price occurring after the date of the financial statements but prior to their issuance should be taken into consideration along with other factors.[10]

Change in Classification of a Marketable Equity Security If there is a change in the classification of a marketable equity security between current and noncurrent, the individual security is transferred between the portfolios at the lower of its cost or market value at the date of transfer. If market value is lower than cost, the market value becomes the new cost basis, and the difference is accounted for **as if**

---

[10]"Changes in Market Value after the Balance Sheet Date," *FASB Interpretation No. 11* (Stamford, Conn.: FASB, Sept. 1976), par. 3.

it were a **realized loss** and is included in the determination of net income.[11] The FASB prescribed this treatment to reduce the incentive to change the classification of securities in order to effect changes in income.

Market Value Method

Although not sanctioning the market value method of accounting for long-term investments, the APB did give credence to it by discussing it at considerable length in **Opinion No. 18.** Under the market value method, the investor recognizes both dividends received and changes in market prices of the stock of the investee company as earnings or losses from the investment. Dividends received are accounted for as part of income from the investment. In addition, the investment account is adjusted for changes in the market value of the investee's stock. The change in market value since the preceding reporting date is included in the results of operations of the investor.

Reporting of investments in common stock at market value is considered by some accountants to meet most closely the objective of reporting the economic consequences of holding the investment. Although the APB believed that the market value method provides the best presentation of investments in some situations, it concluded that further study will be necessary before the market value method is used as the sole basis.

APB Opinion No. 18 recommends that where a 20% to 50% interest exists, a market price is available, and the equity method is employed, "the aggregate value of each identified investment based on the quoted market price usually should be disclosed."

Applicability of Methods

In summary, application of the cost, equity, and lower of cost or market methods for long-term stock investments is as follows:

Nature of Investment	Method
Investment in excess of 50% equity interest	Equity
Investment in excess of 20% equity interest, except when evidence exists of an inability to exercise significant influence	Equity
Investment less than a 20% interest in the form of marketable equity securities, with no ability to exercise significant influence	Lower of Cost or Market
Investment in nonequity or nonmarketable securities	Cost

Even in cases of investments in excess of 50% interest, certain conditions may militate against the use of the equity method, for example, foreign subsidiaries operating under conditions of exchange restrictions, governmental controls, or other uncertainties. Shown on the next page are two examples of such cases.

---

[11]FASB Statement No. 12, *op. cit.*, par. 10. Also see "Clarification of Definitions and Accounting for Marketable Equity Securities That Become Nonmarketable," *FASB Interpretation No. 16* (Stamford, Conn.: FASB, 1977), pars. 9 & 10.

Borg-Warner Corporation

Principles of Consolidation—The consolidated financial statements include all subsidiaries except those in Mexico and South America, which are carried at cost due to political and economic uncertainty, and the financial services companies. Investments in the financial services companies and in affiliated companies, at least 20% owned by Borg-Warner, are carried at equity in underlying net assets.

Insilco Corporation

Principles of Consolidation—The consolidated financial statements include the accounts of the Company and its significant majority owned subsidiaries except its wholly-owned finance subsidiary and Times Fiber Communications, Inc., a joint venture in which the Company's 51% control is expected to be temporary. Investments in the finance subsidiary, joint ventures and other associated companies are accounted for using the equity method.

The following schedule compares the various methods of accounting for long-term investments in terms of their effects upon the financial statements.

COMPARISON OF THE EFFECTS OF METHODS OF ACCOUNTING FOR LONG-TERM INVESTMENTS IN STOCK[12]

	Balance Sheet	Income Statement
Cost Method	Investments are carried at acquisition cost.	Dividends are recognized as income.
Equity Method	Investments are carried at cost, are periodically adjusted by the investor's share of the investee's earnings or losses, and are decreased by all dividends received from the investee.	Income is recognized to the extent of the investee's earnings or losses reported subsequent to the date of investment (adjusted by amortization of the difference between cost and underlying book value).
Lower of Cost or Market	Investments (current and noncurrent) are carried at cost or market value, whichever is lower at the balance sheet date, through use of a valuation allowance.	*Current*—excess of cost over market value and recoveries thereof are included in the determination of income. *Noncurrent*—excess of cost over market value are included in the equity section.
Market Value Method	Investments are carried at market value.	Cash dividends received plus or minus the changes in market price during the period are recognized as income.

Income from Investments in Stocks

Income recognized from investments, whether under the cost, lower of cost or market, or the equity methods, should be included in the income statement of the investor. Under the cost and the lower of cost or market methods, the dividends received (or receivable if declared but unpaid) are reported as investment income.

---

[12]Adapted and updated from Copeland, Strawser, and Binns, "Accounting for Investments in Common Stock," *Financial Executive* (February, 1972), p. 37.

Under the equity method, if the investee has extraordinary and prior period items reported during the period, the investor should report in a similar manner its proportionate share of the ordinary income, of the extraordinary items, and prior period adjustments unless separation into these components is considered immaterial.

The gains or losses on sales of investments also are factors in determining the net income for the period. The gain or loss resulting from the sale of long-term investments, unless it is the result of a major casualty, an expropriation, or the introduction of a new law prohibiting its ownership (which may be viewed as unusual and nonrecurring), is reported as part of current income from operations and is not an extraordinary item.

Dividends that are paid in some form of assets other than cash are called **property dividends.** In such instances, the fair market value of the property received becomes the basis for debiting an appropriate asset account and crediting Dividend Income.

Occasionally an investor receives a dividend that is in part, or entirely, a **liquidating dividend.** The investor should reduce the Investment account for that amount of the liquidating portion of the dividend and credit Dividend Income for the balance.

Dividends Received in Stock

If the investee corporation declares a dividend payable in its own stock of the same class as that upon which it is declared, instead of in cash, each stockholder retains the same proportionate interest in the firm, but owns a larger number of shares than before. The issuing corporation has distributed no assets; it has merely transferred a specified amount of retained earnings to capital stock, thus indicating that this amount is not available in the future for cash dividends. Shares received as a result of a stock dividend or stock split-up do not constitute income to the recipients, because their interest in the issuing corporation is unchanged and because the issuing corporation has not distributed any of its assets to them.

The recipient of such additional shares would make no formal entry, but should make a memorandum entry and record a notation in the Investments account to show that additional shares have been received.

Although no dollar amount is entered at the time of the receipt of these shares, the fact that additional shares have been received must be considered in computing the carrying amount of any shares sold. The cost of the original shares purchased (plus the effect of any adjustments under the equity method) now constitutes the total carrying amount of those shares plus the additional shares received, because no price was paid for the additional shares. The carrying amount per share is computed by dividing the total shares into the carrying amount of the original shares purchased.

To illustrate, assume that 100 shares of Flemal Company common stock are purchased for $9,600, and that two years later the company issues to stockholders one additional share for every two shares held; 150 shares of stock that cost a total of $9,600 are then held. Therefore, if 60 shares are sold for $4,300, the carrying amount of the 60 shares would be computed as on the top of page 794, assuming that the investment has been accounted for under the cost method.

Cost of 100 shares originally purchased	$9,600
Cost of 50 shares received as stock dividend	0
Carrying amount of 150 shares held	$9,600
Carrying amount per share is $9,600/150, or $64	
Carrying amount of 60 shares sold is 60 × $64, or $3,840.	

The entry to record the sale is:

Cash	4,300	
Investments in Stocks		3,840
Gain on Sale of Investments		460

A total of 90 shares is still retained, and they are carried in the Investments account at $9,600 minus $3,840, or $5,760. Thus the carrying amount for those shares remaining is also $64 per share, or a total of $5,760 for the 90 shares.

Stock Rights

When a corporation is about to offer for sale additional shares of an issue already outstanding, it may forward to present holders of that issue certificates permitting them to purchase additional shares in proportion to their present holdings. These certificates represent rights to purchase additional shares and are called **stock rights.** In rights offerings, rights generally are issued on the basis of one right per share, but it may take one or many rights to purchase one new share.

The certificate representing the stock rights, called a **warrant,** states the number of shares that the holder of the right may purchase and also the price at which they may be purchased. If this price is less than the current market value of such shares, the rights have a value in themselves, and from the time they are issued until they expire they may be purchased and sold like any other security.

Three dates are important to a proper understanding of stock rights: (1) the date the rights offering is announced, (2) the date as of which the certificates or rights are issued, and (3) the date the rights expire. From the date the right is announced until it is issued, the share of stock and the right are not separable, and the share is described as **rights-on;** after the certificate or right is received and up to the time it expires, the share and right can be sold separately. A share sold separately from an effective stock right is sold **ex-rights.**

When a right is received, the stockholders have actually received nothing that they did not have before, because the share already owned brought them the right; they have received no distribution of the corporation assets. The carrying amount of the original shares held is now the carrying amount of those shares plus the rights and should be allocated between the two on the basis of their total market values at the time the rights are received.

Disposition of Rights   The investor who receives rights to purchase additional shares has three alternatives:

1. To exercise the rights by purchasing additional stock.
2. To sell the rights.
3. To permit them to expire without selling or using them.

If the investor buys additional stock, the carrying amount of the original shares allocated to the rights becomes a part of the carrying amount of the new shares purchased; if the investor sells the rights, the allocated carrying amount compared with the selling price determines the gain or loss on sale; and, if the investor permits the rights to expire, a loss is suffered, and the investment should be reduced accordingly. The following example illustrates the problem involved.

Shares owned before issuance of rights—100.
Cost of shares owned—$50 a share for a total cost of $5,000.
Rights received—one right for every share owned, or 100 rights; two
  rights are required to purchase one new share at $50.
Market values at date rights issued:

Shares $60 a share
Rights $ 3 a right

Total market value of shares (100 × $60)	$6,000
Total market value of rights (100 × $3)	300
Combined market value	$6,300

Cost allocated to stock: $\dfrac{\$6,000}{\$6,300} \times \$5,000 = \$4,761.90$

Cost allocated to rights: $\dfrac{\$300}{\$6,300} \times \$5,000 = \quad 238.10$

$$\underline{\$5,000.00}$$

Cost allocated to each share of stock: $\dfrac{\$4,761.90}{100} = \$47.62$

Cost allocated to each right: $\dfrac{\$238.10}{100} = \$2.38$

Note that the total cost of the stock and the rights is still $5,000 and, therefore, no entry is made in the Investments account in the general ledger at this time. The subsidiary records should reflect, however, the reduction in the carrying amount of the stock from $5,000 to $4,761.90 and the acquisition of the rights, with an allocated cost of $238.10. The general ledger account is not affected until the stock is sold, or the rights are sold or used or permitted to expire, as described below.

Entries for Stock Rights   If some of the original shares are later sold, their cost for purposes of determining gain or loss on sale is $47.62 per share, as computed above. If 10 of the original shares are sold at $58 per share, the entry would be:

Cash	580.00	
Investments in Stocks		476.20
Gain on Sale of Investments		103.80

Rights may be sold, or used to purchase additional stock, or permitted to expire. The carrying amount allocated to the rights is a part of the Long-Term Investments account in the general ledger and, therefore, any entries made that are related to the rights are reflected in the Long-Term Investments account. For example, let us assume that part of the rights are sold, part are used to purchase additional stock, and part are allowed to expire.

If 40 rights to purchase 20 shares of stock are sold at $3 each, the entry is:

Cash	120.00	
Investments in Stocks		95.20
Gain on Sale of Investments		24.80

The amount removed from the Long-Term Investments account is the amount allocated to 40 rights, 40 × $2.381.

If rights to purchase 20 shares of stock are exercised, and 20 additional shares are purchased at the offer price of $50, the entry is:

Investments in Stock	1,000.00	
Cash		1,000.00

If these shares are sold in the future, their cost should be considered to be $1,095.20, or $54.76 per share. The price paid of $50 per share and the amount allocated to two rights of $4.76 is already in the long-term investments account.

If the remaining 20 rights are permitted to expire, the amount allocated to these rights should be removed from the general ledger account by this entry:

Loss on Expiration of Stock Rights	47.60	
Investments in Stocks		47.60

The balance of the general ledger account is now $5,381.00, as shown below.

Investments in Stocks				
Purchase of original 100 shares @ $50 per share	5,000.00	Sale of 10 shares of original purchase		476.20
Purchase of 20 shares by exercise of rights	1,000.00	Sale of 40 rights		95.20
		Loss on expiration of 20 rights		47.60
		Balance		5,381.00
	6,000.00			6,000.00
Balance	5,381.00[a]			

[a]**Analysis of Balance**	
90 shares of original purchase, at allocated cost of $47.62 per share	$4,285.80
20 shares purchased through exercise of rights, carried at $54.76 per share (cash paid of $50.00, plus $4.76 for allocated cost of two rights)	1,095.20
Balance of account, as above	$5,381.00

The balance represents 110 shares of stock, of which 90 are of the original purchase, and 20 are shares purchased through the exercise of stock rights.

Cash Surrender Value of Life Insurance

There are many different kinds of insurance. The kinds usually carried by businesses include (a) casualty insurance, (b) liability insurance, and (c) life insurance. Accounting for casualty insurance is discussed in Appendix H of Chapter 11. Certain types of **life insurance** constitute an investment whereas casualty insurance and liability insurance do not. The three common types of life insurance policies that companies often carry on the lives of their principal officers are (a) **ordinary life,** (b) **limited payment,** and (c) **term insurance.** During the period that ordinary life and limited payment policies are in force, there is a cash surrender value and a loan value. Term insurance has no cash surrender value or loan value.

If the insured officers or their heirs are the beneficiaries of the policy, the premiums paid by the company represent expense to the company and, for income tax purposes, represent income to the officer insured. In that case the cash surrender value of the policy does not represent an asset to the company.

If the company is the beneficiary, however, and has the right to cancel the policy at its own option, the cash surrender value of the policy or policies is an asset of the company. Accordingly, part of the premiums paid is not expense, because the cash surrender value increases each year. Only the difference between the premium paid and the increase in cash surrender value represents expense to the company.

For example, if McGinnis Corporation pays an insurance premium of $2,300 on a $100,000 policy covering its president and, as a result, the cash surrender value of the policy increases from $15,000 to $16,400 during the period, the entry to record the premium payment is:

Life Insurance Expense	900	
Cash Surrender Value of Life Insurance	1,400	
Cash		2,300

The cash surrender value of such life insurance policies should be shown in the balance sheet as a long-term investment, inasmuch as it is unlikely that the policies will be surrendered and canceled in the immediate future. The premium is not deductible for tax purposes, however, and the proceeds of such policies are not taxable as income.

If the insured officer died half-way through the most recent period of coverage for which the $2,300 premium payment was made, the following entry would be made (assuming cash surrender value of $15,700 and refund of the premium paid beyond the date of death):

Cash [$100,000 + (1/2 of $2,300)]	101,150	
Cash Surrender Value of Life Insurance		16,400
Life Insurance Expense		450
[(1/2 × $2,300) − (1/2 × $1,400)]		
Gain on Life Insurance Coverage		84,300
($100,000 − $15,700)		

The gain on life insurance coverage is not reported as an extraordinary item because it is considered to be a "normal" business transaction.

FUNDS

Purpose of Funds

Assets may be set aside in special funds for specific purposes and, therefore, become unavailable for ordinary operations of the business. In this way the assets segregated in the special funds are available when needed for the intended purposes.

There are two general types of funds: (1) those in which cash is set aside to meet specific current obligations, and (2) those that are not directly related to current operations and therefore are in the nature of long-term investments.

Several funds of the first type discussed in preceding chapters include the following:

Fund	Purpose
Petty Cash Fund	Payment of small expenditures, in currency
Payroll Cash Account	Payment of salaries and wages
Dividend Cash Account	Payment of dividends
Interest Fund	Payment of interest on long-term debt

In general, these funds are used to handle more conveniently and more expeditiously the payments of certain current obligations, to maintain better control over such expenditures, and to divide adequately the responsibility for cash disbursements. These funds are ordinarily shown as current assets in the balance sheet, because the obligations to which they relate are ordinarily current liabilities.

As mentioned above, funds of the second type are similar to long-term investments, as they do not relate directly to current operations. The more common funds of this type and the purpose of each are listed below:

Fund	Purpose
Sinking Fund	Payment of long-term indebtedness
Plant Expansion Fund	Purchase or construction of additional plant
Stock Redemption Fund	Retirement of capital stock (usually preferred stock)
Contingency Fund	Payment of unforeseen obligations

Because the cash set aside for purposes such as those listed above will not be needed until some time in the future, it is usually invested in securities so that an income may be earned on the assets of the fund. The assets of a fund may or may not be placed in the hands of a trustee. If appointed, the trustee becomes the custodian of the assets, accounts to the company for them and reports incomes and expenses of the fund. Funds of this second type are ordinarily shown in the long-term investments section of the balance sheet or in a separate section if relatively large in amount.

Entries for Funds

To account for the assets, incomes, and expenses of funds, it is desirable to keep separate accounts to accumulate such information. For example, if a fund is kept for the redemption of a preferred stock issue that was issued with a redemption provision at par after a certain date, the following accounts might be kept:

> Stock Redemption Fund Cash
> Stock Redemption Fund Investments
> Stock Redemption Fund Income
> Stock Redemption Fund Expense
> Gain on Sale of Stock Redemption Fund Investments
> Loss on Sale of Stock Redemption Fund Investments

When cash is transferred from the regular cash account, perhaps periodically, the entry is:

Stock Redemption Fund Cash	30,000	
Cash		30,000

Securities purchased by the fund are recorded at cost:

Stock Redemption Fund Investments	27,000	
Stock Redemption Fund Cash		27,000

If securities purchased for the fund are to be held temporarily, they would be treated in the accounts in the same manner as temporary investments, described in Chapter 7. If they are to be held for a long period of time, they are treated in accordance with the entries described for long-term investments earlier in this chapter. In both cases the securities purchased are recorded at cost when acquired, but in the case of bonds purchased as long-term investments for the fund, premium or discount should be amortized. If we assume that the entry above records the purchase at a premium of 10-year bonds of a par value of $25,000 on April 1, the issue date, and that the bonds bear interest at 8%, the entry for the receipt of semiannual interest on October 1 is:

Stock Redemption Fund Cash	1,000	
Stock Redemption Fund Income		1,000

At December 31, entries are made to record amortization of premium for nine months and to accrue interest on the bonds for three months:

Stock Redemption Fund Income	150	
Stock Redemption Fund Investments		150
(To record amortization of premium for 9 months, 9/12 of 1/10 of $2,000)		
Accrued Interest on Stock Redemption Fund Investments	500	
Stock Redemption Fund Income		500
(To record accrued interest for 3 months, 3/12 of 8% of $25,000)		

Expenses of the fund paid are recorded by debiting Stock Redemption Fund Expenses and crediting Stock Redemption Fund Cash.

When the investments held by the fund are disposed of, the entries to record the sale are in accord with the entries illustrated earlier in the chapter, using the accounts designated as relating to the redemption fund. Any income and expense accounts set up to record fund transactions should be closed to Revenue and Expense Summary at the end of the accounting period and reflected in earnings of the current period.

The entry for retirement of the preferred stock is:

Preferred Capital Stock	500,000	
Stock Redemption Fund Cash		500,000

Any balance remaining in the Stock Redemption Fund Cash account is transferred back to a general cash account.

Company's Own Preferred Stock in Fund

If there is a trustee of the redemption fund, the trustee may acquire some of the company's own preferred stock on the market at a favorable price, several years before the redemption date. If this stock is canceled and retired, no special problem arises, but, if it is held by the trustee until redemption date, a question arises about the proper accounting treatment of dividends. The declaration and payment of dividends on stock held by the trustee and the recording of such dividends as income on the fund investments result in an overstatement of net income for the period. The dividends declared are charged to Retained Earnings and do not appear in the income statement, yet the dividends received by the trustee are recorded as Stock Redemption Fund Income and, therefore, would be included as income in the income statement. The result of this procedure is that the company would take up as income dividends declared on its own stock, a practice that cannot be justified. The trustee who holds the stock is an agent of the company and not an independent party, and no income can be realized by a company paying dividends to itself.

This objection can be overcome, however, by declaring dividends only on the stock outstanding in the hands of the public and, at the same time, transferring to the fund an amount of cash equivalent to the dividend on the stock held. For example, if 6% preferred stock of a par value of $500,000 was originally issued and the fund holds stock of a par value of $20,000, the entries to record transactions as described are:

Retained Earnings	28,800	
Dividends Payable		28,800
(To record 6% dividends declared on		
preferred stock of $480,000)		
Stock Redemption Fund Cash	1,200	
Cash		1,200
(To transfer to the redemption fund an		
amount of cash equivalent to 6% of the par		
value of the preferred stock held by the fund)		

As a result of these two entries, dividends were declared only on preferred stock in the hands of the public and, at the same time, the redemption fund was increased by the amount that would have been received as dividends on the stock held.

In the balance sheet it is preferable to exclude the company's own preferred stock from the assets of the redemption fund, as follows:

Investments	
Stock redemption fund assets (excluding 200 shares of the company's own	
preferred stock, held by the trustee, deducted from preferred stock issued)	$32,000

In the stockholders' equity section these shares are deducted from the preferred stock issued:

Stockholders' Equity		
6% preferred stock:		
Authorized and issued, 5,000 shares of $100 par value	$500,000	
Less 200 shares held by trustee of stock redemption fund	20,000	$480,000

Another method of presentation often followed is to include the company's own preferred stock as an asset of the redemption fund. Although this method does not seem as realistic as that described above, there appear to be no serious objections to it if the facts are clearly indicated parenthetically or by footnote.

Company's Own Bonds in Sinking Fund

A similar situation arises when the trustee of a sinking fund being accumulated to retire bonds at maturity date invests cash in some of the company's own bonds. There is one difference, however; the net income will not be misstated as a result of recording the interest received on such bonds as income. Disregarding discount or premium on issuance and purchase, the expense recorded for payment of interest is identical in amount to the income received by the trustee. For this reason some accountants regard this method as acceptable. In our opinion, however, this method results in an overstatement of both revenue and expense and, therefore, the treatment of this item should be similar to that accorded dividends above. In other words, interest expense should be debited only for the interest paid to outsiders. At the same time the company should transfer from general cash to sinking fund cash an amount equivalent to the interest on bonds held in the sinking fund.

Similarly, the company's own bonds should be shown as a deduction from bonds payable, although many companies will show the bonds as an asset of the sinking fund. We believe that the former approach is preferable, as long as adequate disclosure of the facts is made in the balance sheet, no serious objection should exist.

Funds and Reserves Distinguished

Although funds and reserves (appropriations) are not similar, they are sometimes confused because they may be related and often have similar titles. **A simple distinction may be drawn: a fund is always an asset and always has a debit balance; a reserve (if used only in the limited sense recommended) is an appropriation of retained earnings, always has a credit balance, and is never an asset.**

This distinction is illustrated by reconsidering the entries made in connection with a stock redemption fund on the preceding pages.

The fund was originally established by the entry:

Stock Redemption Fund Cash	30,000	
Cash		30,000

Some of this cash was used to purchase investments; the assets of the fund were then cash and investments. Ultimately the investments were sold, and the stock redemption fund cash was used to retire the preferred stock.

If the company chose to do so, it could establish an appropriation for stock redemption at the same time to reduce the retained earnings apparently available for dividends. Appropriated retained earnings is established by periodic transfers from retained earnings, as follows:

Retained Earnings	30,000	
Appropriation for Stock Redemption		30,000

It will have a credit balance and will be shown in the stockholders' equity section of the balance sheet. When the stock is retired by payment of cash from the stock redemption fund, the appropriation is transferred back to retained earnings:

Appropriation for Stock Redemption	500,000	
Retained Earnings		500,000

The foregoing discussion indicates that the fund was an asset accumulated to retire stock and had a debit balance; the appropriation was a subdivision of retained earnings and had a credit balance. The fund was used to purchase the stock; the appropriation was transferred back to retained earnings.

Questions

1. Where on the balance sheet are long-term investments customarily presented? Identify six items customarily classified as long-term investments.
2. Distinguish between the nature of temporary investments and long-term investments. Give two examples of each type. Is it possible for securities of the same kind to be carried by one company as a long-term investment and by the other as a short-term investment? Explain.
3. What purpose does the variety in bond features (types and characteristics) serve?
4. Distinguish between bond maturity value, bond market value, bond face value, bond par value, and bond principal value.
5. What factors cause a difference between the stated interest rate and the yield interest rate?
6. What are the problems of accounting for bond investments between interest dates?
7. Theoretically, what is the price of a bond?
8. Distinguish between the effective-interest method and the straight-line method relative to their effect on net income over the life of a bond investment. What are the merits of each method?
9. What is the cost of a long-term investment in bonds? What is the cost of a long-term investment in stock?
10. Contrast the accounting treatment of a premium or discount on long-term bond investments with the treatment of a premium or discount on a long-term bond debt. How is the premium or discount handled relative to a temporary investment?
11. On what basis should stock acquired in exchange for non-cash consideration be recorded?
12. How should the purchase of two or more classes of securities for a lump-sum price be accounted for if the market price of each class is known? If the market price of only one class is known? If no market prices are known?
13. Name four methods of accounting for long-term investments in stocks subsequent to the date of acquisition. When is each method applicable?
14. What constitutes "significant influence" when an investor's financial interest is below the 50% level?
15. Distinguish between the cost and equity method of accounting for long-term investments in stocks subsequent to the date of acquisition.
16. When the equity method is applied, what disclosures should be made in the investor's financial statements?
17. Distinguish between the accounting treatment for "marketable equity securities—current" and marketable "equity securities—noncurrent."
18. University, Inc. gradually acquired stock in College Corp. (a nonsubsidiary) until its ownership exceeded 20%. How is this investment recorded and reported after the last purchase?
19. In applying the equity method what recognition, if any, does the investor give to the excess of its investment cost over its proportionate share of the investee book value at the date of acquisition? What recognition, if any, is given if the investment cost is less than the underlying book value?

20. Shark Corp. has an investment carrying value (equity method) on its books of $170,000 representing a 40% interest in Poquito Company, which suffered a $600,000 loss this year. How should Shark Corp. handle its proportionate share of Poquito's loss?
21. How is a stock dividend accounted for by the recipient? How is a stock split accounted for by the recipient?
22. What three dates are significant in relation to stock rights? What are the alternatives available to the recipient of stock rights?
23. What are the two general types of funds? Give three examples of each type of fund.
24. Distinguish between a fund and a reserve.

Cases

C18-1 The Financial Accounting Standards Board issued its Statement No. 12 to clarify accounting methods and procedures with respect to certain marketable securities. An important part of the statement concerns the distinction between noncurrent and current classification of marketable securities.

Instructions

(a) Why does a company maintain an investment portfolio of current and noncurrent securities?

(b) What factors should be considered in determining whether investments in marketable equity securities should be classified as current or noncurrent, and how do these factors affect the accounting treatment for unrealized losses?

C18-2 For the past five years Copley, Inc. has maintained an investment (properly accounted for and reported upon) in Trumbo Co. amounting to a 10% interest in the voting common stock of Trumbo Co. The purchase price was $700,000 and the underlying net equity in Trumbo at the date of purchase was $620,000. On January 2 of the current year, Copley purchased an additional 15% of the voting common stock of Trumbo for $1,200,000; the underlying net equity of the additional investment at January 2 was $1,000,000. Trumbo has been profitable and has paid dividends annually since Copley's initial acquisition.

Instructions

Discuss how this increase in ownership affects the accounting for and reporting upon the investment in Trumbo Co. Include in your discussion adjustments, if any, to the amount shown prior to the increase in investment to bring the amount into conformity with generally accepted accounting principles. Also include how current and subsequent periods would be reported upon.

(AICPA adapted)

C18-3 Presented below are four **unrelated** situations involving marketable equity securities:

Situation I
A noncurrent portfolio with an aggregate market value in excess of cost includes one particular security whose market value has declined to less than one-half of the original cost. The decline in value is considered to be other than temporary.

Situation II
The statement of financial position of a company does not classify assets and liabilities as current and noncurrent. The portfolio of marketable equity securities includes securities normally considered current that have a net cost in excess of market value of $2,000. The remainder of the portfolio has a net market value in excess of cost of $5,000.

Situation III
A marketable equity security, whose market value is currently less than cost, is classified as noncurrent but is to be reclassified as current.

Situation IV

A company's noncurrent portfolio of marketable equity securities consists of the common stock of one company. At the end of the prior year the market value of the security was **fifty percent** of original cost, and this effect was properly reflected in a valuation allowance account. However, at the end of the current year the market value of the security had appreciated to **twice** the original cost. The security is still considered noncurrent at year-end.

Instructions

What is the effect upon classification, carrying value, and earnings for each of the situations above? Complete your response to each situation before proceeding to the next situation.

C18-4   Shoestring Inc. purchased marketable equity securities at a cost of $250,000 on March 1, 1980. When the securities were purchased, the company intended to hold the investment for more than one year. Therefore, the investment was classified as a noncurrent asset in the company's annual report for the year ended December 31, 1980 and stated at its then market value of $200,000.

On September 30, 1981 when the investment had a market value of $210,000, management reclassified the investment as a current asset because the company intended to sell the securities within the next twelve months. The market value of the investment was $225,000 on December 31, 1981.

The presentation of investments in marketable equity securities on a company's financial statement is affected by management's intentions regarding how long the investment is to be held and by the reporting requirements specified in *FASB Statement No. 12*, "Accounting for Certain Marketable Securities."

Instructions

(a) Explain how the difference between cost and market value of the investment in the marketable equity securities would be reflected in the financial statements of Shoestring Inc. prepared for the fiscal year ending December 31, 1980, when the investment was classified as a noncurrent asset.

(b) The consequence of management's decision to recognize the investment in marketable equity securities as short-term and reclassify it as a current asset was recorded in the accounts. At what amount would the investment be recorded on September 30, 1981, the date of this decision?

(c) How would the investment in the marketable equity securities be reported in the financial statements of Shoestring Inc. as of December 31, 1981 so that the company's financial position and operations for the year 1981 would reflect and report properly the reclassification of the investment from a noncurrent asset to a current asset. Be sure to indicate the affected accounts and the related dollar amounts and the note disclosures, if any.

(CMA adapted)

C18-5   In the course of your examination of the financial statements of the Taylor Corporation as of December 31, 1980, the following entry came to your attention.

January 4, 1980

Receivable from Insurance Company	$100,000	
Cash Surrender Value of Life Insurance Policies		$13,600
Retained Earnings		15,900
Donated Capital from Life Insurance Proceeds		70,500
(Disposition of the proceeds of the life insurance policy on Mr. Taylor's life. Mr. Taylor died on January 1, 1980.)		

You are aware that Mr. Greg Taylor, an officer-stockholder in the small manufacturing firm, insisted that the corporation's board of directors authorize the purchase of an insurance policy to compensate for any loss of earning potential upon his death. The corporation paid $29,500 in premiums prior to Mr. Taylor's death, and was the sole beneficiary of the policy. At the date of death there had been no premium prepayment and no rebate was due. In prior years cash surrender value in the amount of $13,600 had been recorded in the accounts.

Instructions

(a) What is the "cash surrender value" of a life insurance policy?

(b) How should the cash surrender value of a life insurance policy be classified in the financial statements while the policy is in force? Why?

(c) Comment on the propriety of the entry recording the insurance receivable.

C18-6 Part A. To manufacture and sell its products a company must invest in inventories, plant and equipment, and other operating assets. In addition, a manufacturing company often finds it desirable or necessary to invest a portion of its available resources, either directly or through the operation of special funds, in stocks, bonds, and other securities.

Instructions

1. List the reasons why a manufacturing company might invest funds in stocks, bonds, and other securities.

2. What are the criteria for classifying investments as current or noncurrent assets?

Part B. Because of favorable market prices, the trustee of Walker Company's bond sinking fund invested the current year's contribution to the fund in the company's own bonds. The bonds are being held in the fund without cancellation. The fund also includes cash and securities of other companies.

Instructions

Describe three methods of classifying the bond sinking fund on the balance sheet of Walker Company. Include a discussion of the propriety of using each method.

C18-7 A company administers the sinking fund applicable to its own outstanding long-term bonds. The following four proposals relate to the accounting treatment of sinking-fund cash and securities.

(a) To mingle sinking-fund cash with general cash and sinking-fund securities with other securities, and to show both as current assets on the balance sheet.

(b) To keep sinking-fund cash in a separate bank account and sinking-fund securities separate from other securities, but on the balance sheet to treat cash as a part of the general cash and the securities as part of general investments, both being shown as current assets.

(c) To keep sinking-fund cash in a separate bank account and sinking-fund securities separate from other securities, but to combine the two accounts on the balance sheet under one caption, such as "Sinking-Fund Cash and Investments," to be listed as a noncurrent asset.

(d) To keep sinking-fund cash in a separate bank account and sinking-fund securities separate from other securities, and to identify each separately on the balance sheet among the current assets.

Instructions

Identify with reasons for your selection, the proposal that is most appropriate.

Exercises

E18-1 The transactions given below relate to bonds purchased by Jacques Company:

Apr. 1, 1981   Bonds of the SLK Company of a par value of $20,000 are purchased as a long-term investment at 95 plus accrued interest. The bonds bear interest at 6% payable annually on Dec. 1, and they mature Dec. 1, 1987.

Dec.   1   Interest of $1,200 is received on the SLK Company bonds. (Do not amortize
                discount at this time.)

Dec. 31   The proper amount of interest is accrued, and the entry is made to amortize
                the proper amount of discount for 1981.

June   1, 1982 Bonds of a par value of $5,000 are sold at 97 plus accrued interest. Assume
                that reversing entries are made January 1.

Instructions

Prepare journal entries required by Jacques Company to record the transactions above using
straight-line amortization.

E18-2   The following data show the long-term investments of Discorama Company on June
30, 1980, the end of its fiscal year. These investments were purchased on the dates
and at the costs shown.

February 1	Penwell Company $1,000, 9% bonds.	
	Interest payable April 1 and Oct. 1.	
	50 bonds. Due March 1, 1982.	$ 52,500
March 30	Brook Company common stock, $10 par	
	4,000 shares (5% of the outstanding shares)	45,000
May 1	Teddieo, Inc., $1,000, 7% bonds.	
	Interest payable June 1 and Dec. 1.	
	25 bonds. Due September 1, 1983.	23,000
		$120,500

Instructions

(a) If amortization of premium or discount is recorded once a year on June 30, what
    entry would be necessary? (Apply the straight-line method.)

(b) What entry (if any) would be necessary if the market value of the investments was as
    follows on June 30:

Penwell Company	$ 51,200
Brook Company	41,000
Teddieo, Inc.	25,400
	$117,600

E18-3   On December 31, 1981, Tumbleweed Company owns long-term investments purchased on dates and at costs shown below:

Jan. 10, 1980	A Company common stock, no par, 1,000 shares	$ 23,000
Mar. 20	B Company preferred stock, $100 par, 3,000 shares	30,300
Apr. 1	C Company $1,000, 8% bonds due Apr. 1, 1990, interest payable	
	Apr. 1 and Oct. 1, 25 bonds	28,000
June 1, 1981	D Company $1,000, 9% bonds due June 1, 1985, interest payable	
	Jan. 1 and June 1, 22 bonds	20,560
		$101,860

Instructions

(a) Prepare the entry to record amortization of discount or premium on December 31,
    1980. Assume that the company records amortization of discount and premium only
    at the end of each year using the straight-line method and records its debt securities
    at net cost.

(b) Prepare the entry to record amortization of discount or premium on December 31,
    1981.

(c) The market value of the securities as of December 31, 1981, is as follows:

A Company common stock (representing a 2% interest)	$24,000
B Company preferred stock (representing a 5% interest)	26,300
C Company bonds	26,000
D Company bonds	23,000
	$98,200

What entry, if any, would you recommend be made with respect to this information, and what disclosures, if any, should be made to the financial statements?

E18-4 On January 1, 1981, Dandelion Company purchases $200,000 of Charmglo Company 5% bonds for $159,230. The interest is payable semiannually on June 30 and December 31 and the bonds mature in 10 years. The purchase price provides a yield of 8% on the investment.

Instructions

(a) Prepare the journal entry on January 1, 1981, to record the purchase of the investment (record the investment at gross or maturity value).

(b) Prepare the journal entry on June 30, 1981, to record the receipt of the first interest payment and any amortization using the straight-line method.

(c) Prepare the journal entry on June 30, 1981, to record the receipt of the first interest payment and any amortization using the effective interest method.

E18-5 Boat Corp. was a 30% owner of Ski Company, holding 300,000 shares of Ski's common stock on December 31, 1979. The investment account had the following entries:

Investment in Ski

1/1/78 Cost	$2,700,000	12/6/78 Dividend received	$100,000
12/31/78 Share of income	400,000	12/31/78 Amortization of under-	
12/31/79 Share of income	500,000	valued assets	30,000
		12/5/79 Dividend received	200,000
		12/31/79 Amortization of under-	
		valued assets	30,000

On January 2, 1980, Boat sold 150,000 shares of Ski for $2,500,000, thereby losing its significant influence. During the years 1980 and 1981 Ski experienced the following results of operations and paid the following dividends to Boat.

	Ski Income (Loss)	Dividends Paid to Boat
1980	$300,000	$40,000
1981	(200,000)	10,000

Instructions

(a) What effect does the January 2, 1980 transaction have upon Boat's accounting treatment for its investment in Ski?

(b) Compute the carrying value of the investment in Ski as of December 31, 1981, assuming a market value of $1,500,000.

E18-6 Monterey Company purchased 30,000 shares (a 40% interest) of common stock of Naval Company at $18 per share on January 2, 1980. During 1980, Naval Company reported net income of $200,000 and paid dividends of $50,000. On January 2, 1981, Monterey received 10,000 shares of common stock as a result of a stock split by Naval Company.

Instructions

    (a) Prepare the entry to record the sale of 1,000 shares at $14 per share by Monterey Company on January 3, 1981, applying the lower of cost or market method in accounting for the investment (owing to lack of significant influence).

    (b) Prepare the entry to record the sale of 1,000 shares at $14 per share on January 3, 1981, applying the equity method in accounting for the investment. Assume the acquisition cost approximated the book value acquired on January 2, 1980.

E18-7   Ryan Company pays the premiums on two insurance policies on the life of its president, Sylvia Ryan. Information concerning premiums paid in 1981 is given below.

| | | | | | Cash Surrender Value | |
Beneficiary	Face	Prem.	Dividends Cr. to Prem.	Net Prem.	1/1/81	12/31/81
1. Ryan Co.	$160,000	$5,200	$1,840	$3,360	$20,000	$21,600
2. President's husband	50,000	2,100		2,100	6,000	6,500

Instructions

    (a) Prepare entries in journal form to record the payment of premiums in 1981.

    (b) If the president died in January, 1982, and the beneficiaries are paid the face amounts of the policies, what entry would the Ryan Company make?

E18-8   The transactions given below relate to a fund being accumulated by the Dumore Tool Company over a period of 20 years for the construction of additional buildings.

  1. Cash is transferred from the general cash account to the fund.

  2. Preferred stock of Pinkowski Company is purchased as an investment of the fund.

  3. Bonds of H. Castle Corporation are purchased between interest dates at a discount as an investment of the fund.

  4. Expenses of the fund are paid from the fund cash.

  5. Interest is collected on H. Castle Corporation bonds.

  6. Bonds held in the fund are sold at a gain between interest dates.

  7. Dividends are received on Pinkowski Company preferred stock.

  8. Common stocks held in the fund are sold at a loss.

  9. Cash is paid from the fund for building construction.

  10. The cash balance remaining in the fund is transferred to general cash.

Instructions

Prepare journal entries to record the miscellaneous transactions listed above with amounts omitted.

E18-9   Gary Angotti Inc., has $100,000 in its bonds payable account at the beginning of 1980. Interest at 9% is payable April 1 and Oct. 1. On July 17, the sinking-fund trustee for Gary Angotti Inc., purchases at par $20,000 of the bonds.

Instructions

    (a) Prepare the journal entries necessary on April 1 and October 1.

    (b) What two methods may be used to disclose the holding on the balance sheet?

E18-10   The general ledger of Poland Company shows an account for Bonds Payable with a balance of $1,000,000. Interest is payable on these bonds semiannually. Of the $1,000,000, bonds in the amount of $200,000 were recently purchased at par by the sinking-fund trustee and are held in the sinking fund as an investment of the fund. The annual rate of interest is 8%.

Instructions

(a) What entry or entries should be made by Poland Company to record payment of the semiannual interest? (The company makes interest payments directly to bond-holders.)

(b) Illustrate how the bonds payable and the sinking-fund accounts should be shown in the balance sheet. Assume that the sinking-fund investments other than Poland Company's bonds amount to $233,000, and that the sinking-fund cash amounts to $8,200.

Problems

P18-1 On January 1, 1978, Dallas Company acquires $100,000 of Cheerleader Stores, Inc., 6% bonds at a price of $94,846. The interest is payable each December 31, and the bonds mature January 1, 1981. The investment will provide Dallas Company an 8% yield.

Instructions

(a) Prepare a three-year schedule of interest income and bond discount amortization, applying the straight-line method.

(b) Prepare a three-year schedule of interest income and bond discount amortization, applying the effective interest method.

(c) Prepare the journal entry for the interest receipt of December 31, 1980, and the discount amortization under the straight-line method.

(d) Prepare the journal entry for the interest receipt of December 31, 1980, and the discount amortization under the effective interest method.

P18-2 On December 31, 1979, Celebration Company acquired 50,000 shares of the Vrana Corporation common stock at a cost of $28 a share; the purchase represented 25% of the Vrana Corporation's outstanding stock.

On May 1, 1980, Vrana Corporation paid a cash dividend of $1.50 a common share. For the year 1980, the Vrana Corporation reported net income of $400,000; the market value of the investment was $1,200,000 at December 31, 1980.

On May 1, 1981, the Vrana Corporation paid a dividend of $0.50 a share. For the year 1981, the Vrana Corporation reported a net income of $600,000; the market value of the investment was $1,350,000 at December 31, 1981.

Instructions

(a) Prepare the journal entries necessary to record the transactions listed above on Celebration Company's books, assuming that the investment in the Vrana Corporation does not represent a significant influence and, therefore, is carried on the lower of cost or market basis. December 31 is Celebration Company's year-end.

(b) Prepare the journal entries necessary to record the transactions listed above on Celebration Company's books, assuming that the investment in the Vrana Corporation is carried on the equity basis.

(c) What is the carrying value of the investment in the Vrana Corporation stock on January 1, 1982 (1) under the lower of cost or market basis, and (2) under the equity method?

P18-3 On January 1, 1980, Cat Corp. bought 4,000 shares of Mouse Company common stock at $12 per share. At that time Mouse Company's balance sheet showed total assets of $200,000, liabilities of $20,000, common stock ($10 par value) of $100,000, and retained earnings of $80,000. The difference between book value acquired and the purchase price is attributable to assets having a remaining life of 10 years.

At the end of 1980, Mouse Company reported net income of $25,000 and paid cash dividends of $7,500 on December 31, 1980. The market value of Mouse Company stock was $13 per share at December 31, 1980.

On January 1, 1981, Cat Corp. sold 1,000 shares of Mouse Company stock at the market price of $14 per share.

Instructions

    (a) Prepare journal entries to record the events noted above and data on the books of Cat Corp., assuming that it is unable to exercise significant influence over Mouse Company during 1980 and, therefore, applies the lower of cost or market method.

    (b) Prepare journal entries to record the events above and data on the books of Cat Corp., applying the equity method.

P18-4   On January 3, 1978, Rio Grande Company purchased for $400,000 cash a 10% interest in Summerset Corp. On that date the net assets of Summerset had a book value of $3,000,000. The excess of cost over the underlying equity in net assets is attributable to undervalued depreciable assets having a remaining life of 10 years from date of Rio Grande purchase.

On January 2, 1980, Rio Grande purchased an additional 30% of Summerset's stock for $1,520,000 cash when the book value of Summerset's net assets was $4,000,000. The excess was attributable to depreciable assets having a remaining life of 8 years.

During 1978, 1979, and 1980 the following occurred:

	Summerset Net Income	Dividends Paid by Summerset to Rio Grande
1978	$300,000	$10,000
1979	360,000	15,000
1980	400,000	30,000

Instructions

On the books of Rio Grande Company prepare all journal entries in 1978, 1979, and 1980 which relate to its investment in Summerset Corp., reflecting the data above and a change from the cost method to the equity method.

P18-5   Pawelko Company has the following portfolio of long-term marketable equity securities at December 31, 1980.

			Per Share	
Security	Quantity	Percent Interest	Cost	Market
Microtape, Inc.	2,000 shares	8%	$10	$15
Karkow Corp.	6,000 shares	14%	22	16
Strueck Company	4,000 shares	2%	30	25

Instructions

    (a) What descriptions and amounts should be reported on the face of Pawelko's December 31, 1980 balance sheet relative to long-term investments?

On December 31, 1981, Pawelko's portfolio of long-term marketable equity securities consisted of the following common stocks.

			Per Share	
Security	Quantity	Percent Interest	Cost	Market
Karkow Corp.	6,000 shares	14%	$22	$29
Strueck Company	4,000 shares	2%	30	24
Strueck Company	2,000 shares	1%	24	24

During the year 1981, Pawelko Company changed its intent relative to its investment in Microtape, Inc. and reclassified the shares to current asset status when the shares were selling for $8 per share.

(b) What descriptions and amounts should be reported on the face of Pawelko's December 31, 1981 balance sheet relative to long-term investments? What descriptions and amounts should be reported to reflect the transactions above in Pawelko's 1981 income statement?

(c) Assuming that comparative financial statements for 1980 and 1981 are presented, draft the footnote necessary for full disclosure of Pawelko's transactions and position in marketable equity securities.

P18-6 Purdue Boiler Corp. makes the following long-term investments during 1980:

Security	Quantity	Percent Interest	Per Share Cost
Ohio Forms Company	1,600 shares	2%	$80
Lexington Grader Corp.	5,000 shares	16%	20
Knoblett Development Inc.	2,000 shares	4%	35

The following information concerning these investments relates to 1980 and 1981:

1. For the year 1980—Cash dividends received:
   Ohio Forms $4.00 per share
   Lexington Grader $ .60 per share
   Knoblett Development $1.50 per share

2. Market values per share, 12/31/80:
   Ohio Forms $74
   Lexington Grader $22
   Knoblett Development $28

3. For the year 1981—Cash dividends received:
   Ohio Forms $4.00 per share
   Lexington Grader $ .15 per share
   Knoblett Development $1.70 per share

4. On Sept. 30, 1981, the investment in Lexington Grader was reclassified to current asset status when its market value per share was $15.

5. Market value per share, 12/31/81:
   Ohio Forms $68
   Knoblett Development $46

Instructions

(a) Prepare all of the journal entries to reflect the transactions above and data in accordance with **FASB Statement No. 12**.

(b) Prepare the descriptions and amounts that should be reported on the face of Purdue Boiler Corp.'s comparative financial statements for 1980 and 1981 relative to these long-term investments.

(c) Draft the footnote that should accompany the 1980–81 comparative statements relative to the noncurrent marketable equity securities.

P18-7 Maxipump Corporation carries an account in its general ledger called "Investments," which contained the following debits for investment purchases, and no credits.

Feb. 1, 1980	RC Company common stock, $100 par, 200 shares	$32,000
April 1	U.S. Government bonds, 8%, due April 1, 1990, interest payable April 1 and October 1, 100 bonds of $1,000 par each (current asset)	106,000
July 1	Bar Steel Company 9% bonds, par $50,000, dated March 1, 1980 purchased at 103 plus accrued interest, interest payable annually on March 1, due March 1, 2000 (noncurrent asset)	53,000

Instructions

(a) Prepare entries necessary to classify the amounts into proper accounts, assuming that, of the securities held, the U.S. Government bonds are the only temporary investments.

(b) Prepare the entry to record the accrued interest and amortization of premium on December 31, 1980, using the straight-line method.

(c) The market values of the securities on December 31, 1980, were:

RC Company common stock	$ 30,000 (1% interest)
U.S. Government bonds	108,000
Bar Steel Company bonds	54,000

What entry or entries, if any, would you recommend be made?

(d) The U.S. Government bonds were sold on July 1, 1981, for $107,000 plus accrued interest. Give the proper entry.

(e) Twenty additional shares of RC Company common stock were received on July 15, 1981, as a stock dividend, and on July 31, 1981, 30 shares of RC Company common stock were sold at $160 per share. What entries would be made for these two transactions?

P18-8   On January 10, 1980, Copper Clapper Company purchased 200 shares, $100 par value (a 3% interest), of common stock of the Valley Corporation for $24,000 as a long-term investment. On July 12, 1980, the Valley Corporation announced that one right would be issued for every two shares of stock held.

July 30, 1980   Rights to purchase 100 shares of stock at par value of $100 per share are received. The market value of the stock is $150 per share and the market value of the rights is $20 per right.

Aug. 10   The rights to purchase 40 shares of stock are sold at $20 per right.

Aug. 11   The additional 60 rights are exercised, and 60 shares of stock are purchased at $100 per share.

Nov. 15   50 shares of those purchased on January 10, 1980, are sold at $130 per share.

Instructions

Prepare general journal entries on the books of Copper Clapper Company for the foregoing transactions.

P18-9   The Hillcrest Company purchases 200 shares of common stock of Watson, Inc., on February 17. The $100 par stock, costing $25,000, is to be a long-term investment for the Hillcrest Company.

1. On June 30, Watson, Inc., announces that rights are to be issued. One right will be received for every two shares owned.

2. The rights mentioned in (1) are received on July 15. 100 shares of $100 par stock may be purchased with these rights at par. The stock is currently selling for $118 per share. Market value of the stock rights is $15 per right.

3. On August 5, 70 rights are exercised, and 70 shares of stock are purchased at par.

4. On August 12, the remaining stock rights are sold at $17 per right.

5. On September 28, the Hillcrest Company sells 50 shares of those purchased February 17, at $130 a share.

Instructions

Prepare necessary journal entries for the five numbered items above.

P18-10   Autumn Company holds 300 shares of common stock of Mountainview Company that it purchased for $33,000 as a long-term investment. On January 15, 1981, it is announced that one right will be issued for every 4 shares of Mountainview Company stock held.

Instructions

(a) Prepare entries on Autumn Company's books for the transactions below that occurred after the date of this announcement. Show all computations in good form.
1. 100 shares of stock are sold "rights-on" for $12,300.
2. Rights to purchase 50 additional shares of stock at par value of $100 per share are received. The market value of the stock on this date is $105 per share and the market value of the rights is $6 per right.
3. The rights are exercised, and 50 additional shares are purchased at $100 per share.
4. 100 shares of the stock originally held are sold at $107 per share.

(b) If the rights had not been exercised but instead had been sold at $6 per right, what would have been the amount of the gain or loss on the sale of the rights?

(c) If the stock purchased through the exercise of the rights is later sold at $107 per share, what is the amount of the gain or loss on the sale?

(d) If the rights had not been exercised, but had been allowed to expire, what would be the proper entry?

P18-11   The transactions given below relate to a sinking fund for retirement of long-term bonds of Montazuma Corp.

1. In accordance with the terms of the bond indenture, cash in the amount of $100,000 is transferred at the end of the first year, from the regular cash account to the sinking fund.
2. NIU Company 4% bonds of a par value of $40,000, maturing in five years, are purchased for $36,000.
3. 400 shares of UW Company 6% preferred stock ($50 par value) are purchased at $53 per share.
4. Annual interest of $1,600 is received on NIU Company bonds. (Amortize the proper amount of discount using straight-line amortization.)
5. Sinking-fund expenses of $380 are paid from sinking-fund cash.
6. ISU Company 5% bonds with interest payable February 1 and August 1 are purchased on April 15 at par value of $20,000 plus accrued interest.
7. Dividends of $1,200 are received on UW Company preferred stock.
8. All the ISU Company bonds are sold on September 1 at 101 plus accrued interest. Assume interest collected August 1 was properly recorded.
9. Investments carried in the fund at $1,604,000 are sold for $1,576,000.
10. The fund contains cash of $1,607,000 after disposing of all investments and paying all expenses. $1,600,000 of this amount is used to retire the bonds payable at maturity date.
11. The remaining cash balance is returned to the general account.

Instructions

Prepare the journal entries required by Montazuma Corp. for the transactions above.

P18-12   Temperance Corporation has various long-term investments and maintains its books on the accrual basis. The books for the year ended December 31, 1981, have not been closed. Here is an analysis of the Investment account for the year.

Temperance Corporation
ANALYSIS OF INVESTMENT ACCOUNT
Year Ended December 31, 1981

1981	Transactions	Fol.	Account Per Books Debit	Account Per Books Credit
Jan. 1	5,000 shares Backand Oil Co.		$ 5,000	
	1,000 shares General Corp.		33,500	
	50 shares, 6% Pfd. Grey Steel		6,000	
	$10,000, 4% bonds, Martin Co.		10,225	
Feb. 10	Purchased 5,000 shares, Wash Motors	CD	15,000	
Mar. 1	Cash dividend, Grey Steel	CR		$ 300
April 1	Interest, Martin Co. bonds	CR		200
May 15	Sold 800 rights, General Corp.	CR		1,200
May 16	Exercised 200 rights, General Corp. to purchase 50 shares, General Corp.	CD	2,250	
Aug. 5	Sold 200 shares, Wash Motors	CR		2,500
Sept. 18	Sold 100 shares, General Corp.	CR		3,350
Oct. 1	Interest, Martin Co. bonds	CR		200
			$71,975	$7,750

Your work sheets for the year ended December 31, 1980, show these securities in the Investment account.

Date of Acquisition	Number of Shares or Face Value of Bonds	Type of Security	Name of Issuer	Amount
Jan. 2, 1973	5,000	Common stock, no par value	Backand Oil Co.	$ 5,000
April 1, 1974	1,000	Common stock, $100 par value	General Corp.	33,500
Nov. 15, 1974	50	6% preferred stock, par value $100	Grey Steel	6,000
Oct. 1, 1979	$10,000	4% bonds	Martin Co.	10,225
				$54,725

After inquiry the following additional data were obtained:

1. The General Corporation on May 12 issued warrants representing the right to purchase, at $45 per share, one share for every four shares held. On May 12, the market value of the stock rights-on was $50 and ex-rights was $49. Temperance Corporation sold 800 rights on May 15, when the market price of the stock was $51. On May 16, 200 rights were exercised.

2. On June 30, Wash Motors declared a reverse stock split of 1 for 5. One share of new $.50 par value common was exchanged for five shares of old $.10 par value common.

3. Temperance Corporation acquired the Martin Company bonds, which are due September 30, 1984, for $10,300. Interest is payable April 1 and October 1.

4. The sale of 100 shares of General Corporation stock was part of the 1,000 shares purchased on April 1, 1974. The stock was sold for $65 per share.

5. The government of Backand in early 1981 confiscated the assets of the Backand Oil Company and nationalized the company. Despite the protest of the United States government, the Backand government has refused to recognize any claims of the stockholders or management of the Backand Oil Company.

Instructions

Prepare a work sheet showing the adjustments to arrive at the correct balance at December 31, 1981, in the Investment account. The work sheet should include the names of other accounts affected by the adjustments or reclassifications. (Formal journal entries are not required but may be prepared to expedite and support the work sheet.)

(AICPA adapted)

P18-13 Hawkes Systems, Inc., a chemical processing company, has been operating profitably for many years. On March 1, 1980, Hawkes purchased 50,000 shares of Diversified Insurance Company stock for $2,000,000. The 50,000 shares represented 25% of Diversified's outstanding stock. Both Hawkes and Diversified operate on a fiscal year ending August 31.

For the fiscal year ended August 31, 1980, Diversified reported net income of $800,000 earned ratably throughout the year. During November, 1979, February, May, and August, 1980, Diversified paid its regular quarterly cash dividend of $100,000.

Instructions

(a) What criteria should Hawkes consider in determining whether its investment in Diversified should be classified as (1) a current asset (marketable security) or (2) a noncurrent asset (investment) in Hawkes' August 31, 1980, balance sheet? Confine your discussion to the decision criteria for determining the balance sheet classification of the investment.

(b) Assume that the investment should be classified as a long-term investment in the noncurrent asset section of Hawkes' balance sheet. The cost of Hawkes' investment equaled its equity in the recorded values of Diversified's net assets; recorded values were not materially different from fair values (individually or collectively). For the fiscal year ended August 31, 1980, how did the net income reported and dividends paid by Diversified affect the accounts of Hawkes (including Hawkes' income tax accounts)? Indicate each account affected, whether it increased or decreased, and explain the reason for the change in the account balance (such as Cash, Investment in Diversified, etc.). Organize your answer in the following format.

Account Name	Increase or Decrease	Reason for Change in Account Balance

(AICPA adapted)

P18-14 Pacemaker, Inc., a domestic corporation having a fiscal year ending June 30, has purchased common stock in several other domestic corporations. As of June 30, 1981, the balance in Pacemaker's Investments account was $870,600, the total cost of stock purchased less the cost of stock sold. Pacemaker wishes to restate the Investments account to reflect the provisions of **APB Opinion No. 18, "The Equity Method of Accounting for Investments in Common Stock."**

Data concerning the investments follow:

	Turner, Inc.	Grotex, Inc.	Scott, Inc.
Shares of common stock outstanding	3,000	32,000	100,000
Shares purchased by Pacemaker	(a) 300 (b) 810	8,000	30,000
Date of purchase	(a) July 1, 1978 (b) July 1, 1980	June 30, 1979	June 30, 1980
Cost of shares purchased	(a) $ 49,400 (b) $ 142,000	$ 46,000	$ 670,000
Balance sheet at date indicated: **Assets**	July 1, 1980	June 30, 1979	June 30, 1980
Current assets	$ 362,000	$ 39,600	$ 994,500
Fixed assets, net of depreciation	1,638,000	716,400	3,300,000
Patent, net of amortization			148,500
	$2,000,000	$756,000	$4,443,000
Liabilities and Capital			
Liabilities	$1,500,000	$572,000	$2,494,500
Common stock	260,000	80,000	1,400,000
Retained earnings	240,000	104,000	548,500
	$2,000,000	$756,000	$4,443,000
Changes in common stock since July 1, 1978	None	None	None
Average remaining life of fixed assets at date of balance sheet (above)	12 years	9 years	22 years
Analysis of retained earnings:			
Balance, July 1, 1978	$ 234,000		
Net income, July 1, 1978 to June 30, 1979	53,400		
Dividend paid—April 1, 1979	(51,000)		
Balance, June 30, 1979	236,400	$104,000	
Net income (loss), July 1, 1979 to June 30, 1980	55,600	(2,000)	
Dividend paid—April 1, 1980	(52,000)		
Balance, June 30, 1980	240,000	102,000	$548,500
Net income, July 1, 1980 to June 30, 1981	25,000	18,000	330,000
Dividends paid: December 28, 1980			(150,000)
June 1, 1981		(5,600)	
Balance, June 30, 1981	$ 265,000	$114,400	$ 728,500

Pacemaker's first purchase of Turner's stock was made because of the high rate of return expected on the investment. All later purchases of stock have been made to gain substantial influence over the operations of the various companies.

In December 1980, changing market conditions caused Pacemaker to reevaluate its relation to Grotex. On December 31, 1980, Pacemaker sold 6,400 shares of Grotex for $54,400.

For Turner and Grotex, the fair values of the net assets did not differ materially from the book values as shown in the balance sheets above. For Scott, fair values exceeded book values only with respect to the patent, which had a fair value of $300,000 and a remaining life of 15 years as of June 30, 1980.

Instructions

Prepare a work sheet to restate Pacemaker's Investments account as of June 30, 1981, and its investment income by year for the three years then ended. Transactions should be listed in chronological order and supporting computations should be in good form. **Ignore income taxes.** Amortization of goodwill, if any, is to be over a 40-year period. Use the following columnar headings for your work sheet:

		Investments			Investment Income, Year Ended June 30			Other Accounts	
		Turner	Grotex	Scott	1979	1980	1981	Amount	Name
Date	Description	Dr. (Cr.)	Dr. (Cr.)	Dr. (Cr.)	Cr. (Dr.)	Cr. (Dr.)	Cr. (Dr.)	Dr. (Cr.)	

(AICPA adapted)

Issues Related to
Income Determination

19

Revenue Recognition

Revenue recognition is one of the most difficult and pressing problems facing the accounting profession. Although the profession has general guidelines to determine when revenue should be recognized, the many methods of marketing and selling products and services make it extremely difficult for the accountant to develop guidelines that will apply to all situations. Significant lawsuits involving revenue recognition problems, such as those involving U.S. Financial (related party transactions), National Student Marketing (revenue that did not materialize), and Equity Funding (sales that never were) illustrate the complexity of determining when and at what amount revenue should be recognized.

As a result, there has been a significant increase in the number of professional pronouncements on accounting for revenue transactions. For example, the AICPA has published a number of industry accounting guides that deal specifically with revenue recognition problems in such areas as retail land sales, sales of real estate, franchises, and the motion picture industry. The AICPA's Accounting Standards Executive Committee (AcSEC) has issued Statements of Position on such issues as accounting for sales of personal property where right of return exists, recognition of profit on sales of receivables with recourse, sales of real estate, and on other specific industry revenue recognition problems in such areas as broadcasting, construction, mortgage banking, and records and music. The APB provided guidance in **APB Opinion No. 29** in handling revenue recognition problems involving nonmonetary transactions where goods and services were exchanged for other goods and services. And the FASB has established guidelines in **FASB No. 13** "Accounting for Leases," to determine when a lease transaction should be considered a sale. In addition, in late 1978, the FASB issued an Invitation to Comment on "Accounting for Service Transactions" which deals primarily with revenue recognition problems in such diverse areas as health spas, mortuaries, advertising agencies, and travel agencies. Determination of when a sale is a sale is a complex question that is being examined continually.[1]

Guidelines for Revenue Recognition

Revenues are gross increases in assets or gross decreases in liabilities (or a combination of both) from delivering or producing goods, rendering services, or other earning activities of an enterprise during a period.[2] As an element in the income measurement process, the revenue for a period is generally determined independent of expenses by applying the revenue realization principle. The **revenue realization principle provides that revenue is recognized when (1) the earning process is complete or virtually complete and (2) an exchange transaction has taken place.**[3] In accordance with this principle: (a) revenue from selling products is recognized at the date of sale, usually interpreted to mean the date of delivery to customers; (b) revenue from services rendered is recognized when services have been performed and are billable; (c) revenue from permitting others to use enterprise assets, such as interest, rent, and royalties, is recognized as time passes or as the assets are used; (d) revenue from disposing of assets other than products is recognized at the date of sale.

These statements describe the conceptual nature of revenue and are the basis of accounting for revenue transactions. Yet, in practice, there are departures from the realization rule, and other points in the earning process are sometimes used in recognizing revenue, owing in great measure to the considerable variety of revenue transactions. For example, many revenue recognition problems develop because the ultimate collection of the selling price is not reasonably assured or because it is difficult to determine when the earning process is complete. Real estate land sales provide a good example. To illustrate, in the early 1970s General Development recognized the entire sales price of real estate as revenue as soon as it received 5% of the purchase price or a minimum down payment and two monthly payments. Cavanaugh Industries indicated that the percentage collected need only be 3%. Dart Industries required a 10% down payment, as did Boise Cascade, yet McCulloch demanded 15%. Subsequently an industry accounting guide was issued that specified the proper percentage to be used (see Appendix J to this chapter). However, the point is that although accountants have attempted to develop a closely defined framework in which to judge when revenue should be recognized, new problems present themselves every day, and new approaches and new solutions must be developed.

This chapter is devoted exclusively to the discussion and illustration of two of the four general types of revenue transactions described earlier, namely, (1) selling products and (2) rendering services—both of which are **sales transactions.** Ac-

---

[1]Recently, as part of its conceptual framework study, the FASB indicated that it is going to study the appropriate display of information about earnings, focusing on the kinds of revenues, gains, expenses, and losses that should be displayed in the context of objectives of financial reporting. The relationship of net income to cash and working capital flows will also be examined.

[2]"Objectives of Financial Reporting and Elements of Financial Statements of Business Enterprises," *Proposed Statements of Financial Accounting Concepts,* (Stamford, Conn.: FASB, 1977), par. 54.

[3]"Basic Concepts and Accounting Principles Underlying Financial Statements of Business Enterprises," *Statement of the Accounting Principles Board No. 4,* (New York: AICPA, 1970), pars. 148 and 150.

counting for the other two types of revenue transactions, (3) revenue from permitting others to use enterprise assets, and (4) revenue from disposing of assets other than products, is discussed in several other sections of the textbook.

Sales Transactions

Many business enterprises are interested in marketing one or more products or services: retail stores have many different articles they have purchased and wish to sell; manufacturers market the products they have fabricated or processed; transportation companies offer to transport freight or persons; public accounting firms offer the services of their expert accountants; and so on with many kinds of business ventures. In return for the product or service sold, the enterprise usually receives cash or a promise of cash at some date in the future (credit sales). Thus sales transactions have two sides; on the one hand, a product or service is given; on the other, cash or a promise of cash in the future is received.

Inherent in any sales transaction is the element of gain or loss. Therefore, instead of merely recording an increase in one asset and a decrease in another, the transaction is recognized as involving both revenue and cost elements, each of which is recorded separately. Net income is determined later when expenses are matched against revenues.

Cash sales differ from credit sales in that once made they are complete in themselves; no additional steps are necessary to collect cash from the customer. In a **credit sale** (sales on account) the seller receives not cash, but a promise by the purchaser to pay cash in the future. The consideration obtained by the seller is a receivable rather than cash in hand. The accounting treatment accorded receivable transactions and related allowance for bad debts was discussed in Chapter 7.

Whether cash or credit sales are involved, a special problem arises with claims for returns and allowances. In Chapter 7, the accounting treatment for normal returns and allowances was presented. However, certain companies experience such a **high ratio of returned merchandise** to sales that they find it necessary to postpone reporting sales until the return privilege has substantially expired. For example, in the publishing industry the rate of return runs up to 25% for hardcover books and 65% for some magazines. Other types of companies that experience high return rates are: perishable food dealers; rack jobbers or distributors who sell to retail outlets; record and tape companies; and some toy and sporting goods manufacturers. Returns in these industries frequently are made either through a right of contract or as a matter of practice involving "guaranteed sales" agreements or consignments.

Three alternative methods are available when the seller is exposed to continued risks of ownership through return of the product. These are: (1) not recording a sale until nonreturn of the property is assured; (2) recording the sale, but reducing sales by an estimate of future returns; and (3) recording the sale and accounting for the returns as they occur in future periods. AcSEC concluded that realization has not occurred if the sale does not have any economic significance. AcSEC, therefore, recommends that transactions not be recognized currently as sales unless **all** of the following six conditions have been met:

1. The seller's price to the buyer is substantially fixed or determinable at the date of exchange.
2. Payment from the buyer to the seller has been made, or the indebtedness will not be excused until the product is resold.
3. The buyer's obligation to the seller would not be changed in the event of theft, damage, or destruction of the product.
4. The buyer has economic substance apart from that of the seller; that is, the buyer is not a "straw party" or a conduit set up for the purpose of recognizing sales.
5. The seller does not retain significant future performance obligations to bring about the resale of the product.
6. The amount of future returns can be reasonably predicted.[4]

Generally, the choice between the recognition and nonrecognition of sales in these situations is dependent on whether the returns can be reasonably predicted. If the amount of future returns can be reasonably predicted, then it seems appropriate to recognize revenue, because no material uncertainties exist to cause postponement (assuming that the other five conditions above have been met). The last alternative of not recording returns and allowances until they occur has little theoretical justification and is acceptable only if expected future returns and losses are insignificant.

Product Sales Transactions vs. Service Sales Transactions

Since the mid-1800s when the industrial revolution was in full swing in the United States, the production and sale of capital goods has comprised the main thrust of our economy. Only in the past decade has the proportion of Gross National Product (GNP) attributable to payments for **labor and services** surpassed the amount attributable to **capital goods and materials.** In like fashion, the accounting profession throughout most of its modern history has devoted a greater proportion of its attention to the proper capitalization of property and accounting for the manufacture and sale of goods. Only recently have accountants experimented with capitalization of human resources and accounting for service transactions. For example, the FASB recently issued "Accounting for Service Transactions" in the form of an "Invitation to Comment." This pronouncement represents the profession's attempt to develop **accounting theory and methodology related to "service transactions" as distinct from "product transactions."**

The balance of this chapter is divided as follows:

1. Accounting for product sales transactions.
    a. Sales made in advance of delivery.
    b. Cash collection methods.
    c. Consignment sales.
2. Accounting for service sales transactions.

The three topics presented under "Accounting for Product Sales Transactions" involve accounting principles and methods that have been acceptable for years. The accounting principles and methods presented later under "Accounting for Service Sales Transactions" are more illustrative than authoritative. Appendix **L** pro-

---

[4]"Revenue Recognition When Right of Return Exists," *AcSEC Statement of Position 75-1* (New York: AICPA, 1975), pp. 4-5.

vides discussion and illustrations of revenue recognition issues related to specific industries to provide insight into the types of problems and the variety of revenue recognition approaches that have been developed by the profession.

Section I—Accounting for Product Sales Transactions

SALES MADE IN ADVANCE OF DELIVERY

Sometimes questions arise as to whether revenue should be recognized before the actual delivery of the product. For instance, revenue might be recognized:

1. Prior to completion of production.
2. At completion of production.
3. During the production phase on a percentage basis.

Revenue Recognition Prior to Completion

In certain types of manufacturing and in some phases of agriculture, contracting for the sale of goods well in advance of delivery is a common practice. Heavy machinery of a specialized type may be "sold" before it is even in existence; fruit, vegetable, and grain crops may be sold before maturity, with provisions for continued cultivation and harvesting by the seller; fashion goods and clothing are sometimes sold in advance of completion and delivery. Sales of this type may or may not be accompanied by deposits or advance payments, depending on trade practice in the given industry.

Proper accounting here as elsewhere requires suitable recording of the facts. The terms of the sales agreement or contract must be analyzed and then observed in recording the transaction. In general, the business community does not recognize a sale until the transaction is completed and the title passed. The Uniform Sales Act distinguishes between a **contract of sale,** whereby property is transferred from a seller to a buyer in return for a consideration called the price, and a **contract to sell,** whereby the seller and buyer agree to a future exchange of property for a price. Accountants generally record only completed transactions as sales; delivery of the product or service sold normally completes the sale. No entry, other than perhaps a memorandum record, is made for contracts to sell. Advances made by the purchaser are recorded by the seller as a liability when received. When all conditions of the contract have been fulfilled, the sale is recorded as revenue by the seller.

For example, if $3,000 is received from a customer as an advance under a contract to sell machinery made to order at a price of $10,000, the entry should be made as follows:

Cash	3,000	
Customers' Advances		3,000

When the machinery is manufactured and delivered, an entry should be made to record the sale:

Accounts Receivable	7,000	
Customers' Advances	3,000	
Sales		10,000

The account for Customers' Advances represents a liability, and any balance appearing in that account at the time of preparation of financial statements should ordinarily be shown in the balance sheet as a current liability. This approach is sometimes referred to as the **deposit method** of accounting for revenue recognition.

Revenue Recognition At Completion of Production

In certain cases revenue is recognized at the completion of production even though no sale has been made. Examples of such situations involve precious metals or agricultural products with assured prices. Revenue is recognized when these metals are mined or agricultural crops harvested because the sales price is reasonably assured, the units are interchangeable, and no significant costs are involved in distributing the product.

Revenue Recognition During the Production Phase on a Percentage Basis

Long-term contracts such as construction-type contracts, contracts for development of military and commercial aircraft, weapons delivery systems, and space exploration hardware frequently provide that the seller (builder) may bill the purchaser at intervals as various points in the project are reached. When the project to be constructed consists of separable units such as a group of buildings or many miles of roadway, provision may be made for passage of title as well as billing at stated stages of completion, such as, with the completion of each building unit or every 10 miles of road. Such contract provisions in effect provide for delivery in installments, and the accounting records should report this by taking up sales as "delivered."

The accounting measurements associated with long-term projects are difficult because events and amounts must be estimated for a period of years. Construction companies, for example, often invest capital and labor over a considerable time. Production on one contract or job may extend over two or more accounting periods, and progress billings and collections for work performed at predetermined intervals are commonplace. Two basic methods of accounting for long-term construction contracts are recognized by the accounting profession: (1) the percentage-of-completion method, and (2) the completed-contract method. The selection of one method over the other can affect greatly the timing of income among periods.

Percentage-of-Completion Method

Under the percentage-of-completion method, income (in the form of gross profit) is recognized periodically on the basis of the percentage of the job that is complete rather than when the entire job is completed. The rationale for this approach is that under most of these contracts the buyer and seller have obtained enforceable rights. The buyer has the legal right to require specific performance on the contract; the seller has the right to require progress payments that provide evidence of the buyer's ownership interest. As a result, the economics of the situation suggest that a continuous sale occurs as the work progresses, and income should be recognized accordingly.

The accounting profession considers the percentage-of-completion method preferable "when estimates of costs to complete and extent of progress toward completion of long-term contracts are reasonably dependable."[5] A recent AcSEC proposal contains much the same criteria for application of the percentage-of-completion method.[6]

It follows that most contractors can develop reliable estimates of work completed and that only in extraordinary situations, such as those in which litigation is involved, the enforcement of contract rights is in question, or the condemnation of properties is involved, should the income measurement be deferred.

Various methods are used in practice to determine the **extent of progress toward completion;** the most common are "cost to cost method," "efforts expended methods," and "units of work performed method." The objective of all the methods is to measure the extent of progress in terms of costs, units, or value added. The various measures (costs incurred, labor hours worked, tons produced, stories completed, etc.) are identified and classified as input and output measures. **Input measures** (costs incurred, labor hours worked) are made in terms of efforts devoted to a contract. **Output measures** (tons produced, stories of a building completed, miles of a highway completed) are made in terms of results. Neither are universally applicable to all long-term projects; their use requires careful tailoring to the circumstances and the exercise of judgment.

Illustration of the Percentage-of-Completion Method (Cost to Cost Basis). To illustrate the percentage-of-completion method, assume that the Pfeifer Construction Company has a contract starting July, 1980, to construct a $4,500,000 bridge that is expected to be completed in October, 1982, at a total cost of $4,000,000. The following data pertain to the construction period:

	1980	1981	1982
Costs to date	$1,000,000	$3,000,000	$4,050,000
Estimated costs to complete	3,000,000	1,050,000	—
Progress billings to date	900,000	2,750,000	4,500,000
Cash collected to date	750,000	2,500,000	4,500,000

In this illustration, the costs incurred to date as a proportion of the estimated total costs to be incurred on the project is a measure of the extent of progress toward completion. The estimated income (gross profit) to be recognized for each year is calculated as follows:

---

[5]Committee on Accounting Procedure, "Long-Term Construction-Type Contracts" *Accounting Research Bulletin No. 45* (New York: AICPA, 1955), p. 7.

[6]"Accounting for Performance of Construction-Type and Certain Production-Type Contracts" *Proposed Statement of Position* (New York: AICPA, 1979), par. 21.

	Calculation of Income Earned		
	1980	1981	1982
Contract price	$4,500,000	$4,500,000	$4,500,000
Less estimated cost:			
Cost to date	1,000,000	3,000,000	4,050,000
Estimated cost to complete	3,000,000	1,050,000	—
Estimated total cost	4,000,000	4,050,000	4,050,000
Estimated total income (gross profit)	$ 500,000	$ 450,000	450,000
Income recognized in:			
1980 $\frac{\$1,000,000}{\$4,000,000} \times \$500,000$	$ 125,000		
1981 $\frac{\$3,000,000}{\$4,050,000} \times \$450,000$		$ 333,333	
Less 1980 recognized income		125,000	
Income in 1981		$ 208,333	
1982 Less 1980–1981 recognized income			333,333
Income in 1982			$ 116,667

The following entries would be recorded under the percentage-of-completion method from the start of construction to its completion:

	1980	1981	1982
To record cost of construction			
Construction in Process	1,000,000	2,000,000	1,050,000
Materials, cash, payable, etc.	1,000,000	2,000,000	1,050,000
To record progress billings			
Accounts Receivable (Construction in Process)	900,000	1,850,000	1,750,000
Billings on Construction in Process	900,000	1,850,000	1,750,000
To record collections			
Cash	750,000	1,750,000	2,000,000
Accounts Receivable (Construction in Process)	750,000	1,750,000	2,000,000
To recognize income (per computations above)			
Construction in Process	125,000	208,333	116,667
Income on Long-Term Contract	125,000	208,333	116,667
Final approval of project			
Billings on Construction in Process			4,500,000
Construction in Process			4,500,000

Generally when a receivable from a sale is recorded, the inventory account is reduced. But in this case both the receivable and the inventory continue to be carried. By subtracting the balance in the "Billings" account from Construction in Process, double counting the inventory is avoided.

Balance Sheet Presentation During the life of the contract the difference between the Construction in Process and the Billings On Construction in Process accounts is reported in the balance sheet as a current asset if a debit, and as a current liability if a credit. For example, the 1980 balance sheet would appear as follows:

Current assets: (12/31/80)	
Receivables—construction in process	$150,000
Inventories—construction in process totaling	
$1,125,000 less billings of $900,000	225,000

Similar balance sheet disclosures with differing amounts would be made in 1981. The billings are subtracted from the construction in process to indicate to the reader of the financial statements the amount of cost plus income (gross profit) that has not yet been billed. The unbilled portion of a contract price can be calculated at any time by subtracting the billings to date from the revenue earned to date as illustrated below.

Calculation of Unbilled Contract Price at 12/31/80	
Contract price earned to date	
$4,500,000 \times \dfrac{\$1,000,000}{\$4,000,000} = \$1,125,000$	
Billings to date	900,000
Unbilled	$ 225,000

The $225,000 is the excess of construction costs plus estimated income earned over billings. The Construction in Process account would include the following summarized entries over the term of the construction project.

Construction in Process				
1980 construction costs	$1,000,000	12/31/82	to close	
1980 recognized income	125,000		completed	
1981 construction costs	2,000,000		project	$4,500,000
1981 recognized income	208,333			
1982 construction costs	1,050,000			
1982 recognized income	116,667			
Total	$4,500,000		Total	$4,500,000

It should be noted that if billings exceed costs incurred and income to date, this excess would be reported as a current liability entitled "Billings in Excess of Construction in Process." When a company has a number of projects, and costs exceed billings on some contracts, and billings exceed costs on others, the contracts should be segregated so that the asset side includes only those contracts on which costs exceed billings, and the liability side includes only those on which billings exceed costs. Separate disclosures of the dollar volume of billings and costs are preferable to a presentation of the net difference only.

Completed-Contract Method Under the completed-contract method, income (gross profit) is recognized only at point of sale, i.e., when the contract is completed. Costs of long-term contracts in process and current billings are accumulated, but there are no interim charges or credits to income. The profession has taken the position for many years that the completed-contract method is preferable "when lack of dependable estimates or inherent hazards cause forecasts to be doubtful."[7] Only in extraordinary situations should the completed-contract method be used for financial reporting purposes. The presumption is that dependable estimates can be made in most circumstances and only where significant uncertainties exist is the completed-contract method considered appropriate.

The principal advantage of the completed-contract method is that reported income is based on final results rather than on estimates of unperformed work. Its major disadvantage is that a distortion of earnings may occur; it does not reflect current performance when the period of a contract extends into more than one accounting period. Although operations may be fairly uniform during the period of the contract, income is not reported until the year of completion.

The **annual entries** to record costs of construction, progress billings, and collections from customers would be identical to those illustrated under the percentage-of-completion method with the significant exclusion of the recognition of income. For the bridge project illustrated on the preceding pages, the final entry to record completion of the contract in 1982 is as follows:

Billings on Construction in Process	4,500,000	
Construction in Process		4,050,000
Income on Long-Term Contracts		450,000

Comparing the two methods relative to the same bridge project, the Pfeifer Construction Company would have recognized income as follows:

	Percentage-of-Completion	Completed Contract
1980	$125,000	$ 0
1981	208,333	0
1982	116,667	450,000

The completed-contract method and the percentage-of-completion method produce similar results when there are foreseeable losses on a contract. Although the completed-contract method does not permit the recording of any income prior to completion, provision is made under both methods for expected total losses in accordance with the well-established practice of making provision for foreseeable losses.

---

[7]Committee on Accounting Procedure, *op. cit.*

To illustrate, assume that Sanford, Inc. obtained a contract for $2,000,000 to do underground construction work. Profit was estimated at $300,000. During the first year of the three-year project, the company incurred $600,000 in costs and it is now estimated that total costs for the project will be $2,100,000 because of unanticipated soil condition problems. Because a loss is expected to be incurred on the project, the entire amount of the loss should be recognized in the period that the probable loss becomes known, as follows:

Provision for Loss on Construction in Process	100,000	
Esimated Loss on Construction in Process		100,000

The provision for the loss should be shown on the income statement for that contract. The Estimated Loss on Construction in Process should be classified as current liability if it is expected to require the use of assets classified as current.

When the completed-contract method is employed, there is some justification for deferring general and administrative expenses related to the contract rather than charging them as period charges. It is hoped that the deferral would produce a better matching of costs and revenues, although where numerous projects are involved it may be preferable to charge these expenses as incurred. Federal income tax laws permit the application of either the percentage-of-completion method or the completed-contract method to long-term construction contracts. Consistent application of the method used is required.[8]

Disclosures in Financial Statements   In addition to making the financial statement disclosures required of all businesses, construction contractors usually make some unique disclosures. Generally these additional disclosures are made in the notes to the financial statements. For example, a construction contractor could disclose the method of recognizing revenue, the basis used to classify assets and liabilities as current (the nature and length of the operating cycle), the basis for recording inventory, the effects of any revision of estimates, the amount of backlog on incompleted contracts, and the details about receivables (billed and unbilled, maturity, interest rates, and retainage provisions).[9]

In 1974, the SEC issued **ASR No. 164,** in which it set forth its own comprehensive guidelines for disclosure of all contracts for which gross profits are recognized on a percentage-of-completion method and any contracts that "have been or are expected to be performed over a period of more than twelve months."[10]

An illustration of footnote disclosures relating to long-term construction contracts as presented in a recent annual report is shown at the top of page 832.

---

[8]*Accounting Trends and Techniques—1978* reports that in 1977, of the 97 of its 600 sample companies that referred to long-term construction contracts, 75 used the percentage-of-completion method and 14 used the completed-contract method (8 were not determinable).

[9]"Working Draft of an AICPA Audit and Accounting Guide for Construction Contractors," prepared by the Construction Contractors Guide Committee, Accounting Standards Division (New York: AICPA, August 28, 1979).

[10]"Improved Disclosure Related to Defense and Other Long-term Contract Activities," *ASR No. 164,* (Washington: SEC, November 21, 1974). Relative to **long-term contract receivables** the SEC requires disclosure of: (1) the amount expected to be collected after one year, (2) amounts retained, and (3) amounts not yet billed and prerequisites for billing such amounts. Relative to **long-term contract inventories** the SEC requires disclosure of: (1) total inventoried costs relating to long-term contracts, (2) the nature of cost elements inventoried, (3) assumptions used where an estimate of costs or units was made, (4) amount of general and administrative costs charged to inventory, (5) "learning curve" costs deferred to future units and periods, and (6) amounts of progress payments netted against inventory.

PULLMAN INCORPORATED
NOTES TO CONSOLIDATED FINANCIAL STATEMENTS

Note 1 (in part): *Significant Accounting Policies*

Long-Term Contracts: Revenues on engineering and construction contracts are recognized on the percentage of completion method based generally on the ratio of costs incurred to date on the contract to total estimated contract costs. Revenues on passenger car contracts are recognized as cars are delivered and accepted by the customer. Estimates of total contract costs are reviewed periodically during each year and the cumulative effects of changes in total estimated contract costs are recognized in the period determined and losses, if any, are recognized fully when identified. For engineering and construction contracts, revenues recognized or costs incurred in excess of amounts billed are classified under current assets as costs and earnings on uncompleted contracts not yet billed. Amounts billed in excess of revenue recognized to date for both enginering and construction and passenger car contracts are classified under current liabilities as advance billings on uncompleted contracts.

Note 5: *Long-Term Engineering and Construction Contracts*—Accounts receivable at December 31, 1977 include $65,653,000 ($102,242,000 at December 31, 1976) relating to long-term engineering and construction contracts. Except for retainage of $7,376,000 ($30,097,000 in 1976), these amounts are billed.

The amounts by which billings exceed total costs and earnings recognized to date under uncompleted engineering and construction contracts at December 31 consist of:

	1977	1976
	(Thousands of dollars)	
Project costs and earnings	$4,300,104	$3,376,589
Less billings to date	4,445,215	3,547,484
	$ (145,111)	$ (170,895)
Included in current assets as costs and earnings on uncompleted contracts not yet billed	$ 17,741	$ 8,194
Included in current liabilities as advance billings on uncompleted contracts	(162,852)	(179,089)
	$ (145,111)	$ (170,895)

CASH COLLECTION METHODS

In some cases, the collection of the sales price is not reasonably assured and revenue recognition is deferred. One of three methods is generally employed to account for the cash received, i.e., **the deposit method, the cost recovery method,** or **the installment method.** As indicated earlier, sometimes cash is received prior to delivery of the goods and is recorded as a deposit (customer advance) because the sale transaction is incomplete. In such cases, the seller has not performed under the contract and has no claim against the purchaser. Cash received represents advances and should not be reported as revenue until the contract is performed by delivery of the product.

Under the cost recovery method, equal amounts of revenue and expense are recognized as collections are made until all costs have been recovered. After all costs have been recovered, any additional cash receipts are included in income. This method is used where a high degree of uncertainty exists related to collection of receivables. The major difference between this approach and the deposit method is that in the cost recovery method it is assumed that the seller has performed on the contract, but cash collection is highly uncertain. In the deposit method, the seller has not performed and no legitimate claim exists. **Under the installment method, emphasis is placed on collection rather than on sale, and installment sales lead to income realization in the periods of collection rather than in the period of sale.** The installment basis of accounting is justified on the basis that when there is no reasonable basis for estimating the degree of collectibility, revenue should not be recognized until cash is collected. The exercise of professional judgment is necessary in selecting between the installment method and the cost recovery method. The resolution revolves around the degree of uncertainty in the collection of the receivable. The cost recovery method is adopted when there is a greater degree of uncertainty. Because the installment method is used extensively in certain industries, this subject is discussed in more detail in the following sections.

Installment Sales Accounting

The expression "installment sales" is generally used by accountants and others to describe any type of sale for which payment is required in periodic installments over an extended period of time. It is used in the retail field where all types of farm and home equipment and furnishings are sold on an installment basis. It is also used to a limited degree in the heavy equipment industry where machine installations are sometimes paid for over a long period. A more recent application of the method is in the area of realty or land development sales. Because payment for the product or property sold is spread over a relatively long period, the risk of loss resulting from uncollectible accounts is greater in installment sales transactions than in ordinary sales. Consequently, various devices are used to protect the seller. In the area of merchandise, the two most common are (1) the use of a conditional sales contract that provides that title to the item sold does not pass to the purchaser until all payments have been made, and (2) use of notes secured by a chattel (personal property) mortgage on the article sold. Either of these permits the seller to "repossess" the goods sold if the purchaser defaults on one or more payments. The repossessed merchandise is then resold at whatever price it will bring to compensate the seller for the uncollected installments and the expense of repossession.

Under the installment method of accounting income recognition is deferred until the period of cash collection. Both revenues and cost of sales are recognized in the period of sale but the related gross profit is deferred to those periods in which cash is collected. Thus, instead of the sale being deferred to the future periods of anticipated collection and then related costs and expenses being deferred, only the proportional gross profit is deferred, which is equivalent to deferring both sales and cost of sales. Other expenses, that is, selling expense, administrative expense, and so on, are not deferred. **The cost of the goods sold is deferred proportionally to the deferred sales (by deferring gross profit),** but operating or financial expenses are considered as expenses in the period incurred.

Thus, the theory that cost and expenses should be matched against sales is applied in installment sales transactions through the gross profit figure but no further.

Concerns operating under the installment sales method of accounting generally record operating expenses without regard to the fact that some portion of the year's gross profit is to be deferred. This practice is often justified on the basis that (1) these expenses do not follow sales as closely as does the cost of goods sold, and (2) accurate apportionment among periods would be so difficult that it could not be justified by the benefits gained.

Acceptability of Installment Sales

The use of the installment method as a method for revenue recognition has fluctuated widely over the last twenty years. Until the early 1960s the installment method of accounting was widely used and accepted for installment sales transactions. As installment sales transactions increased during the sixties, somewhat paradoxically, acceptance and application of the installment method for financial accounting purposes decreased. In 1966 the APB concluded that except in special circumstances, "the installment method of recognizing revenue is not acceptable."[11]

The rationale for this position is that because the installment method of accounting recognizes no revenue until cash is collected, it is not exactly in accordance with the concept of accrual accounting. The installment method is frequently justified on the grounds that the risk of not collecting an accounts receivable may be so great that the sale itself is not sufficient evidence that realization has taken place. In some cases, this reasoning may be valid but not in a majority of cases. The general approach is that if a sale has been completed, it should be recognized; and if bad debts are expected, they should be recorded as separate estimates of uncollectibles. Current accounting practices indicate that although collection expenses, repossession expenses, and bad debts are an unavoidable part of installment sales activities, the incurrence of these costs and the collectibility of the receivables are reasonably predictable.

The study of this topic is justified by its widespread use as a tax accounting method and the method's acceptability in cases where a reasonable basis of estimating the degree of collectibility is deemed not to exist. In addition, weaknesses in the sales method of revenue recognition became very apparent in the late sixties when the franchise and land development booms produced many failures and disillusioned investors. Application of the sales method to **franchise and license operations** resulted in an abuse called **"front-end loading"** (recognizing revenue prematurely, that is, when the franchise is granted or the license issued rather than as it is earned or as the cash is received). Many **"land development"** ventures were susceptible to the same abuses. As a result, accounting for these transactions is now in the direction of revenue recognition on a cash basis.[12]

Procedure for Deferring Revenue and Cost of Sales of Merchandise

One could easily work out a procedure that deferred both the uncollected portion of the sales price and the proportionate part of the cost of the goods sold. Instead of

---

[11]"Omnibus Opinion," *Opinions of the Accounting Principles Board No. 10* (New York: AICPA, 1966), par. 12.

[12]See Appendix **L** for additional information on these reporting problems.

apportioning both sales price and cost over the period of collection, however, **only the gross profit is deferred.** This procedure has exactly the same effect as deferring both sales and cost of sales but requires only one deferred account rather than two.

The steps to be used are described as follows:

For the sales in any one year—

1. During the year, record both sales and cost of sales in the regular way, using the special accounts described later, and compute the rate of gross profit on installment sales transactions.
2. At the end of the year, apply the rate of gross profit to the cash collections of the current year's installment sales to arrive at the realized gross profit.
3. The gross profit not realized should be deferred to future years.

For sales made in prior years—

1. The gross profit rate of each year's sales must be applied against cash collections of accounts receivable resulting from that year's sales to arrive at the realized gross profit.

From the preceding discussion of the general practice followed in taking up income from installment sales, it is apparent that special accounts must be used to provide certain special information required to determine the realized and unrealized gross profit in each year of operations. The requirements are as follows:

1. Installment sales transactions must be kept separate in the accounts from all other sales.
2. Gross profit on sales sold on installment must be determinable.
3. The amount of cash collected on installment sales accounts receivable must be known, and, further, the total collected on the current year's and on each preceding year's sales must be determinable.
4. Provision must be made for carrying forward each year's deferred gross profit.

In each year, the ordinary operating expenses are charged to expense accounts as under customary accounting procedure and are closed to the Revenue and Expense Summary account. Thus, the only peculiarity in computing net income under the installment sales method as generally applied is the deferment of gross profit until realized by collection of the accounts receivable.

To illustrate, assume the following:

	1980	1981	1982
Sales (on installment)	$200,000	$250,000	$240,000
Cost of sales	150,000	190,000	168,000
Gross profit	$ 50,000	$ 60,000	$ 72,000
Rate of gross profit on sales	25%	24%	30%
Cash receipts			
1980 sales	$ 60,000	$100,000	$ 40,000
1981 sales		100,000	125,000
1982 sales			80,000

Summary entries in general journal form have been prepared for the transactions in the illustration. In reviewing these entries it must be remembered that as a practical matter they would not appear as summary entries, but the transactions would be entered individually as they occur. The entries as given are for purposes of illustration only. All transactions not concerned with the installment sales problem have been omitted.

1980

Installment Accounts Receivable, 1980	200,000	
Installment Sales		200,000
(To record sales made on installment in 1980)		
Cash	60,000	
Installment Accounts Receivable, 1980		60,000
(To record cash collected on installment receivables)		
Cost of Installment Sales	150,000	
Inventory (or Purchases)		150,000
(To record cost of goods sold on installment in 1980 on either a perpetual or a periodic inventory basis)		
Installment Sales	200,000	
Cost of Installment Sales		150,000
Deferred Gross Profit, 1980		50,000
(To close installment sales and cost of installment sales for the year)		
Deferred Gross Profit, 1980	15,000	
Realized Gross Profit on Installment Sales		15,000
(To remove from deferred gross profit the profit realized through collections)		
Realized Gross Profit on Installment Sales	15,000	
Revenue and Expense Summary		15,000
(To close profits realized by collections)		

The realized and deferred gross profit is computed for the year 1980 as follows:

1980	
Rate of gross profit current year	25%
Cash collected on current year's sales	$ 60,000
Realized gross profit (25% of $60,000)	15,000
Gross profit to be deferred ($50,000 − $15,000)	35,000

1981

Installment Accounts Receivable, 1981	250,000	
Installment Sales		250,000
(To record sales per account sales)		
Cash	200,000	
Installment Accounts Receivable, 1980		100,000
Installment Accounts Receivable, 1981		100,000
(To record cash collected on installment receivables)		
Cost of Installment Sales	190,000	
Inventory (or Purchases)		190,000
(To record cost of goods sold on installment in 1981)		

Installment Sales	250,000	
Cost of Installment Sales		190,000
Deferred Gross Profit, 1981		60,000
(To close installment sales and cost of		
installment sales for the year)		
Deferred Gross Profit, 1980	25,000	
Deferred Gross Profit, 1981	24,000	
Realized Gross Profit on Installment Sales		49,000
(To remove from deferred gross profit the		
profit realized through collections)		
Realized Gross Profit on Installment Sales	49,000	
Revenue and Expense Summary		49,000
(To close profits realized by collections)		

The realized and deferred gross profit is computed for the year 1981 as follows:

1981	
Current year's sales	
Rate of gross profit	24%
Cash collected on current year's sales	$100,000
Realized gross profit (24% of $100,000)	24,000
Gross profit to be deferred ($60,000 − $24,000)	36,000
Prior year's sales	
Rate of gross profit—1980	25%
Cash collected on 1980 sales	$100,000
Gross profit realized in 1981 on 1980 sales (25% of $100,000)	25,000
Total gross profit realized in 1981	
Realized on collections of 1980 sales	$ 25,000
Realized on collections of 1981 sales	24,000
Total	$ 49,000

The entries in 1982 would be similar to those of 1981, and the total gross profit taken up or realized would be $64,000, as shown by the computations below.

1982	
Current year's sales	
Rate of gross profit	30%
Cash collected on current year's sales	$ 80,000
Gross profit realized on 1982 sales (30% of $80,000)	24,000
Gross profit to be deferred ($72,000 − $24,000)	48,000
Prior year's sales	
1980 sales	
Rate of gross profit	25%
Cash collected	$ 40,000
Gross profit realized in 1982 on 1980 sales	10,000
1981 sales	
Rate of gross profit	24%
Cash collected	$125,000
Gross profit realized in 1982 on 1981 sales	30,000
Total gross profit realized in 1982	
Realized on collections of 1980 sales	$ 10,000
Realized on collections of 1981 sales	30,000
Realized on collections of 1982 sales	24,000
Total	$ 64,000

Additional Problems of Installment Sales Accounting

In addition to computing realized and deferred gross profit currently, other problems are involved in accounting for installment sales transactions. These problems are related to:

1. Interest on installment contracts.
2. Uncollectible accounts.
3. Defaults and repossessions.

Interest on Installment Contracts Because the collection of installment receivables is spread over a long period, it is customary to charge the buyer interest on the unpaid balance. Interest charges are generally provided for in setting up the schedule of payments required by the sales contract; that is, each installment payment consists of interest and principal. Generally, each payment is equal (level payment pattern) in amount to each successive payment. However, a smaller portion of each successive payment is attributable to interest and a correspondingly larger amount attributable to principal, as shown in the following schedule:

		Installment Payment Schedule		
Date	Cash (Debit)	Interest Earned (Credit)	Installment Receivables (Credit)	Unpaid Balance
1/2/80	—	—	—	$3,000.00
1/2/81	$1,164.10*	$240.00**	$ 924.10	2,075.90
1/2/82	1,164.10	166.07	998.03	1,077.87
1/2/83	1,164.10	86.23	1,077.87	-0-

*Periodic payment = Original unpaid balance ÷ PV of an annuity of $1.00 for three periods at 8%; $1,164.10 = $3,000 ÷ 2.57710.
**$3,000 × .08 = $240

When interest is involved in installment sales, it should be separately accounted for as interest income distinct from the gross profit recognized on the installment sales collections during the period. The interest is recognized as interest income at the time of the cash receipt. Also, interest accrued since the last collection date on the installment receivables should be recorded as an adjusting entry at year end.

Uncollectible Accounts The problem of bad debts or uncollectible accounts receivable is somewhat different for concerns selling on an installment basis because of a repossession feature commonly incorporated in the sales agreement. This feature gives the selling company an opportunity to recoup any uncollectible accounts through repossession and resale of repossessed merchandise. If the experience of the company indicates that repossessions do not, as a rule, compensate for uncollectible balances, it may be advisable to provide for such losses through charges to a special bad debts expense account just as is done for other credit sales. This matter was covered in detail in Chapter 7.

Defaults and Repossessions Depending on the terms of the sales contract and the policy of the credit department, the seller can repossess merchandise sold under an installment arrangement if the purchaser fails to meet payment requirements. Repossessed merchandise may be reconditioned before it is offered for sale, and it may be resold for cash or under a plan for installment payments.

Repossession of merchandise sold is a recognition that the related installment receivable account is not collectible and that it should be written off. Along with the account receivable, the applicable deferred gross profit must be removed from the ledger in any entry similar to the following:

Repossessed Merchandise (an inventory account)	xx	
Deferred Gross Profit	xx	
Installment Accounts Receivable		xx

The entry above assumes that the repossessed merchandise is to be recorded on the books at exactly the amount of the uncollected account less the deferred gross profit applicable. This assumption may or may not be proper. The condition of the merchandise repossessed, the cost of reconditioning, and the market for second-hand merchandise of that particular type must all be considered. **The objective should be to put any asset acquired on the books at its fair value or, when fair value is not ascertainable, at the best possible approximation of fair value.** And, if the fair value of the merchandise repossessed is less than the uncollected balance less the deferred gross profit, a "loss on repossession" should be recorded at the date of repossession.

Some accountants contend that repossessed merchandise should be entered at a valuation that will permit the company to make its regular rate of gross profit on resale. If it is entered at its approximated cost to purchase, the regular rate of gross profit is provided for, but that is completely a secondary consideration. It is more important that the asset acquired by repossession be recorded at fair value in accordance with the general practice of carrying assets at acquisition price as represented by the fair market value at the date of acquisition.

To illustrate the required entry, assume that a refrigerator was sold to Jay Hirsch for $500 on September 1, 1980. Terms require a down payment of $200 and $20 on the first of every month thereafter. It is further assumed that the refrigerator cost $300, and is sold to provide a 40% rate of gross profit on selling price. At the year-end, December 31, 1980, a total of $60 should have been collected in addition to the original down payment.

Now if Hirsch makes his January and February payments in 1981 and then defaults, the account balances applicable to Hirsch at time of default would be:

Installment Account Receivable	200 (dr.)
Deferred Gross Profit (40% × $240)	96 (cr.)

The deferred gross profit applicable to the Hirsch account still has the December 31, 1980, balance because no entry has been made to take up gross profit realized by cash collections in 1981. The regular entry at the end of 1981, however, will take up the gross profit realized by all cash collections including amounts received from Hirsch. Hence, the balance of deferred gross profit applicable to Hirsch's account may be computed by applying the gross profit rate for the year of sale to the balance of Hirsch's account receivable, 40% of $200, or $80. The account balances should therefore be considered as:

Installment Account Receivable (Hirsch)	200 (dr.)
Deferred Gross Profit (applicable to Hirsch after	
recognition of $16 of profit in January and February)	80 (cr.)

If the estimated fair value of the article repossessed is set at $70, the following entry would be required to record the repossession:

Deferred Gross Profit	80	
Repossessed Merchandise	70	
Loss on Repossession	50	
Installment Account Receivable (Hirsch)		200

The amount of the loss is determined by (1) subtracting the deferred gross profit from the amount of the account receivable to determine the unrecovered cost (or book value) of the merchandise repossessed, and (2) subtracting the estimated fair value of the merchandise repossessed from the unrecovered cost to get the amount of the loss on repossession.

Balance of account receivable (representing uncollected selling price)	$200
Less deferred gross profit	80
Unrecovered cost	120
Less estimated fair value of merchandise repossessed	70
Gain (or loss) on repossession	($ 50)

As pointed out earlier, the loss on repossession may be charged to allowance for doubtful accounts if such an account is carried.

Financial Statement Presentation of Installment Sales Transactions If install-ment sales transactions represent a significant part of total sales, full disclosure of installment sales, the cost of installment sales, and any expenses allocable to in-stallment sales is desirable. If, however, installment sales transactions constitute an insignificant part of total sales, it may be satisfactory to include only the realized gross profit in the income statement as a special item following the gross profit on sales as follows:

HEALTH MACHINE COMPANY	
Statement of Income	
For the Year Ended December 31, 1981	
Sales	$620,000
Cost of goods sold	490,000
Gross profit on sales	130,000
Gross profit realized on installment sales	51,000
Total gross profit on sales	$181,000

If more complete disclosure of installment sales transactions is desired, a presen-tation similar to the following may be used:

HEALTH MACHINE COMPANY

Statement of Income
For the Year Ended December 31, 1981

	Installment Sales	Other Sales	Total
Sales	$248,000	$620,000	$868,000
Cost of goods sold	182,000	490,000	672,000
Gross margin on sales	66,000	130,000	196,000
Less deferred gross profit on installment sales of this year	47,000		47,000
Realized gross profit on this year's sales	19,000	130,000	149,000
Add gross profit realized on installment sales of prior years	32,000		32,000
Gross profit realized this year	$ 51,000	$130,000	$181,000

The apparent awkwardness of this method of presentation is difficult to avoid if full disclosure of installment sales transactions is to be provided in the income statement. One solution, of course, is to prepare a separate schedule showing installment sales transactions with only the final figure carried into the income statement.

In the balance sheet it is generally considered desirable to classify installment accounts receivable by year of collectibility. There is some question as to whether installment accounts that are not collectible for two or more years should be included in current assets. If installment sales are part of normal operations, they may be considered as current assets because they are collectible within the operating cycle of the business. Little confusion should result from this practice if maturity dates are fully disclosed as illustrated in the following example:

CURRENT ASSETS		
Notes and accounts receivable		
Trade customers	$78,800	
Less allowance for doubtful accounts	3,700	
	75,100	
Installment accounts collectible in 1981	22,600	
Installment accounts collectible in 1982	47,200	$144,900

On the other hand, receivables from an installment contract, or contracts, resulting from a transaction **not** related to normal operations should be reported in the "other assets" section if due beyond the normal operating cycle.

Financial statement presentation of Repossessed Merchandise and of Gain or Loss on Repossessions is based on the nature of each of these items. Repossessed merchandise is a part of inventory and should be included as such in the current asset section of the balance sheet; any gain or loss on repossessions should be included in the income statement.

Deferred gross profit on installment sales is generally treated as consisting entirely of unearned revenue and classified as a current liability. Theoretically, deferred gross profit consists of three elements: (1) income tax liability to be paid when the sales are reported as realized revenue (current liability); (2) allowance for collection expense, bad debts, and repossession losses (deduction from installment accounts receivable); and (3) net income (retained earnings, restricted as to dividend availability). Because of the difficulty in allocating deferred gross profit among these three elements, however, the whole amount is treated as unearned revenue.

CONSIGNMENT SALES ACCOUNTING

A specialized method of marketing certain types of products makes use of a device known as a consignment shipment. Under this arrangement, one party, the **consignor,** ships merchandise to another, the **consignee,** who is to act as an agent for the consignor in selling the goods. Both consignor and consignee are interested in selling, the former to make a profit or develop a market, the latter to make a commission on the sales. Subject to special provisions of the consignment contract, the following legal rules govern the transaction:

1. The merchandise shipped on consignment remains the property of the consignor until sold. Although physically and geographically separated from the remainder of the inventory, it is part of the consignor's inventory.
2. The consignee is entitled to reimbursement from the consignor for expenses paid in connection with handling the shipment and selling the goods and is generally entitled to a commission at an agreed rate on sales actually made.
3. Normally, sales made by the consignee on account result in a credit risk to the consignor. Special terms of the agreement, however, may state that the consignee is responsible for any losses due to uncollectible accounts, in which case the consignee is called a **del credere agent.**
4. Because the merchandise shipped remains the property of the consignor, certain legal principles of bailment govern the relations of the parties. These principles require, in general, that the consignee use proper diligence in caring for the property as agent of the consignor, as principal. This provision is an important part of the contract but has little effect on accounting for the transactions.

The steps in a consignment shipment and sale may be many, because the arrangement may continue over a long period. To analyze the activities, however, we can reduce them to the few typical types listed below.

1. **The consignment agreement is made.** This requires no entry by either party as it is merely an agreement governing transactions to be effected in the future.
2. **Goods are shipped on consignment.** The consignor must record the fact that part of the inventory has been shipped to the consignee for attempted sale. The consignor does **not** record a sale because no sale has been made as yet.
   The consignee must record the receipt of merchandise that is not owned property but for which the consignee is responsible (within certain special legal limits). The consignee does **not** record a purchase because the goods are not purchased.
3. **Expenses are paid by the consignor.** If the consignor wishes to know the total cost of consignment shipments, these expenses must be charged to a special account or accounts; otherwise, the consignor may use regular expense accounts.
4. **Expenses are paid by the consignee.** Under the terms of the agreement, these expenses are chargeable to the consignor and are so recorded by the consignee. The consignor can make no entry for such expenses until notice of their payment is received from the consignee.

5. **Sales are made by the consignee.** The consignee must record the sale (cash or account) and the obligation to the consignor for any cash collected less expenses. The consignee may also record any commission earned, which normally is deductible from the cash to be remitted.

6. **An "account sales."** This statement shows goods received, goods sold, expenses chargeable to the consignment, and other related information; it is prepared by the consignee and forwarded to the consignor. Any cash owing to the consignor should also be forwarded at this time. The consignee need enter only cash remitted inasmuch as sales, expenses, and commissions have been recorded already.

The consignor determines from the account sales the amount of sales that have been made and the expenses paid by the consignee. The consignor must record these facts together with the amount of the commission. Cash remitted must also be entered, or, if due and not remitted, an account receivable must be set up.

Special Accounts of the Consignor

From the foregoing discussion it is apparent that the consignor must have a record of goods shipped, expenses incurred, and sales made in connection with each consignment shipment. To prepare accurate financial statements the consignor must know what profit or loss has been made on each shipment, and the cost of any goods still out on consignment and unsold so that it can be included in inventory. A special account for each consignment shipment is used by the consignor to provide almost all this information. This account is commonly titled **Consignment Out** and includes the name of the consignee. It is charged with the cost of goods shipped out on consignment, all expenses incurred, either by consignee or consignor, and the consignee's commissions, and is credited with sales as reported in the account sales.

If the entire consignment shipment has been sold by the consignee, the Consignment Out account not only is a complete record of the consignment transactions, but also provides all information necessary to compute gain or loss on that consignment. If balanced and ruled, the result is profit or loss on the consignment. If all goods shipped have not been sold, the cost of those remaining unsold must be left in the Consignment Out account; **it then serves as a combination revenue and expense summary account and inventory account.**

Consignment Out—Best Value Stores			
Cost of merchandise shipped	360.00	Sales as reported in account sales	400.00
Expenses incurred by consignor	37.50	Inventory of consigned goods (carried down)	140.00
Expenses incurred by consignee per account sales	22.50		
Commission charged by consignee per account sales	40.00		
Profit on consignment	80.00		
	540.00		540.00
Inventory of consigned goods (brought down)	140.00		

Goods out on consignment remain the property of the consignor and should be included in the consignor's inventory when financial statements are prepared. Of course, the alternatives of carrying inventory at either cost or the lower of cost or market extend to consignment inventories. Cost includes purchase price plus legitimate costs of getting the merchandise in position and condition for sale. In consignment transactions this includes such costs as transportation and handling but excludes advertising, commission on sales made, and similar items. Inventoriable costs incurred must be prorated over total units concerned as illustrated below.

12 units shipped at cost	$360.00
Freight	37.50
Handling and local hauling	22.50
Total inventoriable cost	$420.00
4 units on hand (1/3)	$140.00
8 units sold (2/3)	280.00
Total, as shown	$420.00

This computation indicates that the cost of the units sold is $280 and that $140 represents the inventoriable cost of the four units remaining unsold. Observe that the commission is not included in the computation above. Because the commission is based on the sales made, it is not related to goods unsold and, therefore, should not be included as an inventoriable cost.

After the inventory amount has been calculated as illustrated, the gross profit on consignment operations is computed as follows:

Computation of Consignment Gross Profit		
Consignment sales		$400
Cost of 8 units sold	$280	
Commission charged by consignee	40	320
Gross profit on consignment sales		$ 80

This gross profit can be recorded by an entry as follows:

Consignment Out—Best Value Stores	80	
Gross Profit on Consignment Sales		80

The balance of the Consignment Out account, after this entry is posted, represents the consignment inventory.

The profit determined by balancing and ruling the Consignment Out account is a gross profit instead of a net profit. Direct expenses have been deducted from sales along with the cost of the goods sold, but proportionate parts of many of the company's other expenses also could be charged against the consignment. In practice, this procedure is seldom desirable. Instead, the consignment profit is included in the statement of income immediately following gross profit on sales to arrive at total gross profit from which all other expenses are deducted.

In addition to a Consignment Out account for each consignee, the consignor frequently has an account receivable with each; this is essential if the consignee does not remit all cash due with the account sales, but it is advisable in any case to provide a ledger record of amounts remitted by each consignee. The entries made by the consignor are as follows:

ENTRIES BY THE CONSIGNOR
(Nelba Manufacturing Company)

Shipment of merchandise—based on shipping orders
and shipping room reports:

Consignment Out—Best Value Stores	360.00	
Inventory (or Purchases)		360.00
(To record merchandise shipped on consignment)		

Payment of expenses—based on expense vouchers:

Consignment Out—Best Value Stores	37.50	
Cash (or Accounts Payable)		37.50
(To record freight paid on consignment shipment)		

Account sales received—based on information in account sales:

Accounts Receivable—Best Value Stores	400.00	
Consignment Out—Best Value Stores		400.00
(To record sales per account sales)		
Consignment Out—Best Value Stores	62.50	
Accounts Receivable—Best Value Stores		62.50
(To record consignee's expenses and commission		
per account sales; handling and local hauling, $22.50;		
commission, 10% of $400.00, $40.00)		

Cash or check received from consignee:

Cash	337.50	
Accounts Receivable—Best Value Stores		337.50
(To record cash received on account)		

Gross profit on consignment to date entered preparatory
to closing:

Consignment Out—Best Value Stores	80.00	
Gross Profit on Consignment Sales		80.00
(To record gross profit on consignment)		

Special Accounts of the Consignee

The consignee also finds it practicable to record most of the transactions arising out of each consignment in a special account. A record must be kept of goods received from each consignor, expenses incurred, sales made, and commissions charged.

No ledger entry is made by the consignee for goods received because the consignee's responsibility is only for adequate care of the merchandise received. The payment of expenses or completion of sales results in a financial obligation running between the parties to the consignment contract, and this the consignee must record. A special account called a **Consignment In** account is used to record any amounts due from or to the consignor. This account on the books of Best Value Stores appears at the top of page 846.

Consignment In—Nelba Manufacturing Company			
Expenses paid in connection with the consignment	22.50	Sales made	400.00
Commission on sales made	40.00		
Remittance to Nelba	337.50		
	400.00		400.00

The balance of this account represents the amount due to or due from the consignor. Normally, after sales have been made, the consignee has a liability to the consignor that is paid in cash when the account sale is rendered, or shortly thereafter, and after such payment the account would have no balance (even though the consignee may still have some units on hand). The entries made by the consignee are as follows:

ENTRIES BY THE CONSIGNEE
(Best Value Stores)

Receipt of goods on consignment shipment—based on copies of consignor's shipping reports after comparison with merchandise received:

(Entry in memorandum record of consignment shipments received)

Payment of expenses—based on expense vouchers:

Consignment In—Nelba Mfg. Co.	22.50	
Cash (or Accounts Payable)		22.50
(To record expenses on consignment in)		

Sales made—based on sales tickets:

Cash (or Accounts Receivable)	400.00	
Consignment In—Nelba Mfg. Co.		400.00
(To record consignment sales made)		

Commissission earned—calculated before or in preparation of account sales:

Consignment In—Nelba Mfg. Co.	40.00	
Commission Earned		40.00
(To record commission on consignment sales)		

Remittances to consignor—based on check stub or check copy:

Consignment In—Nelba Mfg. Co.	337.50	
Cash		337.50
(To record remittance to consignor)		

Presenting Consignment Data in the Financial Statements

The results of consignment transactions can be reported in the income statement merged with other sales and expense items, or they can be presented separately. If they are presented separately, the gross profit from consignment sales can be shown as a special item immediately following the amount of gross profit on sales, or a columnar presentation may be used to give additional consignment data.

Illustration 1. Consignment profit shown separately.

Nelba Manufacturing Company
STATEMENT OF INCOME
For the Year Ended December 31, 1980

Sales		$680,000
Cost of goods sold		450,000
Gross profit on sales		230,000
Gross profit on consignment sales		30,000
Total		260,000
Operating epenses		
Selling expenses	$83,000	
Administrative expenses	70,000	153,000
Net income		$107,000

Illustration 2. Consignment sales and cost of consignment sales shown separately.

Nelba Manufacturing Company
STATEMENT OF INCOME
For the Year Ended December 31, 1980

	Consignment Sales	Other Sales	Total
Sales	$140,000	$680,000	$820,000
Cost of goods sold	110,000	450,000	560,000
Gross profit on sales	30,000	230,000	260,000
Operating expenses			
Selling expenses	3,000	80,000	83,000
Administrative expenses		70,000	70,000
Total operating expenses	3,000	150,000	153,000
Net income	$ 27,000	$ 80,000	$107,000

The method of presentation shown in the second illustration has the advantage of giving more complete information about consignment transactions entered into by the company. However, unless administrative expenses are prorated between consignment and other operations, as was not done in this example, a false impression of the net income on consignment operations may be given.

Any consigned goods not sold are part of the consignor's inventory and should be included in the inventory quantity in the balance sheet. Occasionally the inventory out on consignment is shown as a separate item, but unless the amount is large, there is little need for this. Consignment accounts receivable may be included with other trade accounts receivable in the current asset section of the balance sheet.

The consignees do not have the same problems of statement presentation of consignment operations that the consignors have. The consignees must include commissions on consignment sales in their income statement, generally added to gross profit on sales, in much the same manner as the consignor shows gross profit on consignment sales. Because part of the consignee's selling and administrative expenses are incurred in selling goods received on consignment, it seems appropriate that the commission income should be shown on the income statement above these expenses. Also, the consignees should be extremely careful not to include any of the goods consigned to them as a part of their own inventories.

Section II—Accounting for Service Sales Transactions

To the student—

This short section is more illustrative than authoritative because the concepts and methods presented are not official GAAP. Service sales represent a significant portion of all sales made in our economy and they are obviously being accounted for in some manner. Yet, no written official pronouncement provides specific standards of accounting for service sales transactions. Some of the methods presented on the following pages are being applied uniformly and properly in practice and to that extent (and because they do not violate any existing accounting standard) they are GAAP. But, because the profession has not issued specific guidelines, considerable variation exists in practice in accounting for revenue from service sales, even between firms in the same industry.

This section is based on the recent combined effort of the FASB and the AICPA to establish standards of accounting for certain service transactions through their issuance in 1978 of an *Invitation to Comment*. Like many attempts to achieve uniformity in accounting practice, this effort is being resisted and criticized by special interest groups. We present this material (1) because of its instructional value and practical applicability, (2) because it fills an area long in need of standards, and (3) because it complements so well the subject matter of this chapter.

The number and variety of businesses that offer services to the public are increasing and the range of services they offer is broadening. Examples of the types of industries that offer services are listed below.

Advertising agencies	Accounting
Cemetery associations	Architecture
Computer service organizations	Garbage and waste removal
Correspondence schools	Interior design or decoration
Electronic security	Legal services
Employment agencies	Management consulting
Entertainment	Medical
Modeling agencies	Moving and storage
Engineering firms	Placement agencies
Equipment and office maintenance	Private and social clubs
Health spas	Public relations
Mortgage banking	Real estate brokerage
Perpetual care societies	Research and development labs
Retirement homes	Travel agencies
Transportation	

The list above is only representative of service industries; an all-inclusive list cannot be provided because the range of services is so wide.

The major accounting questions facing the types of service organizations listed above relate to when revenue should be recognized as being earned and when costs should be charged to income. Because diverse accounting methods were being used to account for similar service transactions, the profession recently moved to narrow the range of alternative methods. The following discussion represents newly developed concepts and methods that are still in the initial stages of reception and implementation.

Nature of Service Transactions

Service transactions are defined as transactions

> between a seller and a purchaser in which, for a mutually agreed price, the seller performs, agrees to perform at a later date, or agrees to maintain readiness to perform an act or acts, including permitting others to use enterprise resources that do not alone produce a tangible commodity or product as the principal intended result.[13]

Although this definition does not require that the act or acts to be performed be specified by a contract, in practice most service transactions performed over a period of time or requiring performance in the future are formalized by a contract. However, agreements to perform at a later date and agreements to maintain a readiness to perform an act are often only commitments or executory contracts, and commitments and executory contracts are not currently viewed as transactions to be recorded in accrual-based transaction-oriented financial statements.

Some transactions may involve both services and products. **When the sale of a product is incidental to the rendering of a service, the transaction would be accounted for as a service transaction.** For example, a fixed price equipment maintenance contract that includes parts would be considered a service transaction. Conversely, **if a service is incidental to the sale of a product, the transaction would be accounted for as a product transaction.** For example, the inclusion of a warranty or guarantee in the sale of a product is considered incidental.

Determining when a service or a product is incidental to a transaction can be difficult. An incidental nature may be indicated, however, in one of the following two ways:

1. The inclusion of a product or a service does not result in a variance in the total transaction price from what would be charged excluding that product or service.
2. A product is not sold or a service is not rendered separately in the seller's normal business.[14]

If both the product and the service are stated separately and the total transaction price would vary because the product or the service is included or excluded, the transaction would be accounted for as both a product and a service transaction. For example, equipment maintenance contracts in which parts are charged separately would qualify for separable product and service transaction accounting.

Revenue and Expense Recognition

Revenue from service transactions should be recognized on the basis of the seller's performance of the transaction. **Performance** is "the execution of a defined act or acts or occurs with the passage of time."[15]

---

[13]"Accounting for Certain Service Transactions," *FASB Invitation to Comment*, (Stamford, Conn.: FASB, 1978), page 1.

[14]*Ibid.*, pages 10–11.

[15]*Ibid.*, page 11.

Authoritative professional literature generally specifies that costs should be charged to expense in the period in which the revenue with which they are associated is recognized as earned. And costs should not be deferred unless they are expected to be recoverable from future revenue.[16]

Three Types of Service Costs   For purposes of accounting for service transactions, related costs are identified as follows:[17]

1. **Initial direct costs** are costs that are directly associated with negotiating and consummating service agreements. They include, but are not necessarily limited to commissions, legal fees, costs of credit investigations, and installment paper processing fees. No portion of supervisory and administration expenses or other indirect expenses, such as rent and facilities costs, is included in initial direct costs.
2. **Direct costs** are costs that have a clearly identifiable beneficial or causal relationship (i) to the services performed or (ii) to the level of services performed for a group of customers, for example, servicemen's labor and repair parts included as part of a service agreement.
3. **Indirect costs** are all costs other than initial direct costs and direct costs. They include provisions for uncollectible accounts, general and administrative expenses, advertising expenses, and general selling expenses.

Indirect costs should be charged to expense as incurred regardless of the revenue recognition method applied to the transaction. The method of accounting for initial direct costs and direct costs is dependent upon the revenue recognition method applied to the transaction.

Methods of Service Revenue Recognition

Four different methods of accounting for revenues on service transactions have been proposed. The major determinant of each method's applicability is the nature and extent of performance. The four recommended methods are:

1. Specific performance method.
2. Completed performance method.
3. Proportional performance method.
4. Collection method.

Specific Performance Method   The specific performance method is appropriate when a service transaction consists of **a single act.** Revenue should be recognized at the time the act takes place. Initial direct costs and direct costs should be charged to expense at the time revenues are recognized. Thus, initial direct costs and direct costs incurred before the service is performed should be deferred until the revenue is recognized.

This method can be used by a real estate broker who would record sales commissions as revenue when the real estate transaction is consummated at the "closing." This method might also be applicable to an employment agency whose fee is contingent upon the new employee remaining at a job for a specified time period. Because the agency has rendered its services in locating and placing an employee

---

[16]"Basic Concepts and Accounting Principles Underlying Financial Statements of Business Enterprises," *APB Statement No. 4* (New York: AICPA, 1970), par. 155.

[17]"Accounting for Certain Service Transactions," pages 13 and 14.

for its client, the fee would be recorded at the time the employee is placed. However, if experience shows that there is a reasonable possibility of having to refund the fee because of the employment period contingency, it is appropriate to record an allowance based on estimates of fees that will never be collected.

Completed Performance Method   The completed performance method is appropriate when services are performed in **more than one act** and the proportion of services to be performed in the last of a series of acts is so significant in relation to the entire service transaction that **performance cannot be deemed to have occurred until the last act occurs.** For example, for a moving company that packs, loads, and delivers goods to various locations, the act of delivery is so significant to its completing the earning process that revenue should not be recognized until delivery occurs.

Under the completed performance method, initial direct and direct costs would be expensed when revenue is recognized. Costs incurred before the service is performed should be deferred until the revenue is recognized.

Proportional Performance Method   The proportional performance method is appropriate when services are performed in **more than one act** and revenue should be recognized as the various acts that make up the entire transaction occur, that is, in proportion to the performance of each act.[18] This method can be applied in a slightly different manner to three differing sets of circumstances:

1. **Specified number of identical or similar acts.** An equal amount of revenue would be recorded for each act expected to be performed.

    The processing of monthly mortgage payments by a mortgage banker is an appropriate application of this method.

2. **Specified number of defined but not identical acts.** Revenue is recognized in the ratio that the direct costs of performing each act have to the total estimated direct cost of the entire transaction.

    A correspondence school that provides progress evaluations, lessons, examinations, and grading might appropriately use this method.

    If the direct cost ratio is impractical or not objectively determinable as a measurement basis, a systematic and rational basis that reasonably relates revenue recognition to performance should be used. As a last resort, the straight-line method should be used.

3. **Unspecified number of identical or similar acts with a fixed period for performance.** Revenue is recognized on the straight-line method over the specified period unless there is evidence that another method is more representative of the pattern of performance.

    A two-year club membership in which the club's facilities are available for the member's usage throughout that period is an example of appropriate application of the straight-line method.

Under the proportional performance method, **initial direct costs** are recorded as expenses in the same manner as revenue is recorded. Because there generally is a close correlation between the incurrence of **direct costs** and the extent of performance achieved, direct costs are recorded as expenses as they are incurred.

---

[18]Proportional measurement is necessary only if the acts are performed in more than one financial accounting period.

Collection Method   If there is a significant degree of uncertainty surrounding the collectibility of service revenue, revenue should be recorded as cash is collected. Under this method, initial direct and direct costs should be recorded as expenses as incurred. The collection method is appropriate when a service is being provided to a customer whose ability to pay for those services is questionable.

APPENDIX

Accounting for Specialized Revenue Recognition Transactions: Franchise, Real Estate, and Retail Land Sales

To the student—

We have included this material not only because of its practical applicability but also because of its instructional value. Accounting for franchises, real estate, and retail land sales provides a good summarization and review of the several methods of revenue recognition presented earlier in this chapter, because nearly all of them have applicability to these special industry problems. Also these problems demonstrate clearly the challenge that the accountant faces in properly accounting for complex, yet common, business transactions. For example, the accountant must:

1. Understand and be fully acquainted with the economic substance of the transactions.
2. Apply skilled judgment in selecting the proper method of accounting.
3. Monitor the situation over a long period of time.
4. If necessary, change the method of accounting to conform to new circumstances.

FRANCHISE SALES

As indicated earlier, the accountant determines when revenue is realized, essentially on the basis of two criteria: (1) completion or virtual completion of the earning process, and (2) occurrence of an exchange. These criteria are appropriate for most business activities, but for some sales transactions they simply are not adequate in defining when revenue should be realized. In some situations, the accountant is forced to look to the circumstances surrounding the contract to ascertain when to recognize revenue and income. Sales transactions in some industries (e.g., land development, leasing, and franchising) require closer scrutiny. The fast-growing franchise industry has given accountants special concern and challenge.

Four types of franchising arrangements have evolved: (1) manufacturer-retailer, (2) manufacturer-wholesaler, (3) service sponsor-retailer, and (4) wholesaler-retailer. The fastest growing category of franchising, and the one that caused a reexamination of appropriate accounting, has been the third category, **service sponsor-retailer.** Included in this category are such industries and businesses as:

Soft ice cream drive-ins (Tastee Freez, Dairy Queen)
Food drive-ins (McDonald's, Kentucky Fried Chicken, Burger King)
Restaurants (Lums, Pizza Hut, Denney's)
Motels (Holiday Inns, Howard Johnson, Best Western)
Auto rentals (Avis, Hertz, National)
Part-time help (Manpower, Kelly Girl)
Others (H. R. Block, Arthur Murray Studios, Seven-Eleven Stores)

Franchise companies derive their income from one or both of two sources: (1) from the sale of initial franchises and related assets or services, and (2) from continuing fees based on the operations of franchises. The **franchisor** (the party who grants business rights under the franchise) normally provides the **franchisee** (the party who operates the franchised business) with the following services:

1. Assistance in site selection.
   (a) Analyzing location.
   (b) Negotiating lease.
2. Evaluation of potential income.
3. Supervision of construction activity.
   (a) Obtaining financing.
   (b) Designing building.
   (c) Supervising contractor while building.
4. Assistance in the acquisition of signs, fixtures, and equipment.
5. Provision of bookkeeping and advisory services.
   (a) Setting up franchisee's records.
   (b) Advising on income, real estate, and other taxes.
   (c) Advising on local regulations of the franchisee's business.
6. Provision of employee and management training.
7. Provision of quality control.
8. Provision of advertising and promotion.[1]

During the sixties and early seventies it was standard practice for franchisors to recognize the entire franchise fee at the date of sale whether the fee was received then or was collectible over a long period of time as represented by a long-term note. Frequently, franchisors recorded the entire amount as revenue in the year of sale even though many of the services were yet to be performed and uncertainty

---

[1]Archibald E. MacKay, "Accounting for Initial Franchise Fee Revenue," *The Journal of Accountancy* (January, 1970), pp. 66–67.

existed regarding the collection of the entire fee. For example, a **franchise agreement** may provide for refunds to the franchisee if certain conditions are not met, and franchise fee profit can be reduced sharply by future costs of obligations and services to be rendered by the franchisor.

Conditions such as these made it necessary for the accounting profession to examine the old rules for realization and develop new guidelines for revenue recognition. As a result, **initial franchise fees** are to be recorded as revenue only when and as the franchisor makes "substantial performance" of the services it is obligated to perform and collection of the fee is reasonably assured. **Substantial performance** occurs when the franchisor has no remaining obligation to refund any cash received or excuse any nonpayment of a note and has performed all the initial services required under the contract. "Nevertheless, conservatism justifies the presumption that commencement of operations by the franchisee is the earliest point at which substantial performance has occurred."[2]

To illustrate, assume that Tum's Pizza, Inc., charges an initial franchise fee of $50,000 for the right to operate as a franchisee of Tum's Pizza. Of this amount, $10,000 is payable when the agreement is signed and the balance is payable in five annual payments of $8,000 each. In return for the initial franchise fee the franchisor will help in locating the site, negotiate the lease or purchase of the site, supervise the construction activity, and provide the bookkeeping services. The credit rating of the franchisee indicates that money can be borrowed at 8%. The present value of an ordinary annuity of five annual receipts of $8,000 each discounted at 8% is $31,941.60. The discount of $8,058.40 represents the interest income to be accrued by the franchisor over the payment period.

1. If there is reasonable expectation that the down payment may be refunded and if substantial future services remain to be performed by Tum's Pizza, Inc., the entry should be:

Cash	10,000.00	
Notes Receivable	40,000.00	
Discount on Notes Receivable		8,058.40
Unearned Franchise Fees		41,941.60

2. If the probability of refunding the initial franchise fee is extremely low, the amount of future services to be provided to the franchisee is minimal, and collectibility of the note is reasonably assured and substantial performance has occurred, the entry should be:

Cash	10,000.00	
Notes Receivable	40,000.00	
Discount on Notes Receivable		8,058.40
Revenue from Franchise Fees		41,941.60

3. If the initial down payment is not refundable, represents a fair measure of the services already provided, with a significant amount of services still to be performed by the franchisor in future periods, and collectibility of the note is reasonably assured, the entry should be:

Cash	10,000.00	
Notes Receivable	40,000.00	
Discount on Notes Receivable		8,058.40
Revenue from Franchise Fees		10,000.00
Unearned Franchise Fees		31,941.60

---

[2]"Accounting for Franchise Fee Revenue," *Industry Accounting Guide* (New York: AICPA, 1973), p. 8.

4. If the initial down payment is not refundable and no future services are required by the franchisor, but collection of the note is so uncertain that recognition of the note as an asset is unwarranted, the entry should be:

Cash	10,000	
Revenue from Franchise Fees		10,000

5. Under the same conditions as those listed under 4 except that the down payment is refundable or substantial services are yet to be performed, the entry should be:

Cash	10,000	
Unearned Franchise Fees		10,000

In cases 4 and 5 above where collection of the note is extremely uncertain, cash collections may be recognized using the installment method or the cost recovery method.[3]

Franchise accounting also involves proper accounting for the **franchisor's costs.** The objective is to match related costs and revenues by reporting them as components of income in the same accounting period. Franchisors should ordinarily defer **direct costs** (usually incremental costs) relating to specific franchise sales for which revenue has not yet been recognized. **Indirect costs** of a regular and recurring nature which are incurred irrespective of the level of franchise sales such as selling and administrative expenses (and other fixed costs) should be expensed as incurred. Costs should not be deferred, however, without reference to anticipated revenue and its realizability.[4]

The divergent entries presented above suggest that the accounting for franchise revenue is far from standardized. The revenue recognition problem related to franchise arrangements illustrates the complexity of modern-day business transactions.

REAL ESTATE SALES

In recent years, real estate transactions have become highly complex, and their legal form often obscures their economic substance. As demonstrated in the following discussion, the casual or single sale of real estate (including the sale of lots to builders and the sale of homes, buildings, and parcels of land to builders and others but not including retail lot sales on a volume basis) may require application of the whole range of revenue recognition methods used in accounting.

Profit Recognition on Realty Sales

Revenue is conventionally recognized at the time real estate is sold provided (1) **the amount of the revenue is reasonably measurable,** that is, the collectibility of the sales price is reasonably assured or the amount uncollectible can be estimated reasonably, and (2) **the earning process is complete** or virtually complete, that is, the seller is not obliged to perform significant activities after the sale to earn the

---

[3]A study which compared four revenue recognition procedures—installment sales basis, spreading recognition over the contract life, percentage-of-completion basis, and substantial performance—for franchise sales concluded that the percentage-of-completion method is the most acceptable revenue recognition method; the substantial performance method was found sometimes to yield ultra-conservative results. (Charles H. Calhoun III, "Accounting for Initial Franchise Fees: Is It a Dead Issue?" *The Journal of Accountancy* (February, 1975), pp. 60–67.)

[4]"Accounting for Franchise Fee Revenue," p. 17.

revenue. Unless **both** conditions exist, recognition of all or part of the revenue and income (profit) on a real estate sale transaction is postponed.

When the substance of a real estate transaction indicates that a sale has occurred for accounting purposes, but collectibility of the sales price cannot be estimated reasonably, the **installment method** or the **cost recovery method** of accounting is appropriate. Because default on loans secured by real estate usually results in recovery of the real estate, the installment method is usually appropriate. The cost recovery method is more appropriate "where there is (a) uncertainty as to whether all or even a portion of cost will be recovered upon default by the purchaser or (b) cost has already been recovered in the sale and collection of further proceeds is uncertain."[5]

The installment and cost recovery methods defer recognition of profit until collections are received. Under the cost recovery method, all cash received is accounted for as recovery of cost with no recognition of deferred profit until cost is fully recovered; thereafter all cash received is recognized as profit. Under the installment method, each cash receipt is apportioned between cost recovered and profit recognized in the same ratio as cost and profit constitute the sales value. In other words, profit under the installment method is based on the percentage of total profit to total sales value (including any first mortgage debt assumed by the buyer).[6] To illustrate, assume the following data:

Cash down payment	$ 150,000
Second mortgage payable by buyer to seller	350,000
Total cash to be received by seller	500,000
First mortgage assumed by buyer	500,000
Total sales price and sales value	1,000,000
Cost of seller	600,000
Total profit	$ 400,000
Additional current period payments by buyer subsequent to down payment: $25,000 of principal on first mortgage $35,000 of principal on second mortgage	

Total profit is equal to 40% of total sales value ($400,000 ÷ $1,000,000). Therefore, the profit recognition attributable to the $150,000 down payment is $60,000, and the profit attributable to the principal payments is $24,000, representing 40% of $60,000 ($25,000 + $35,000).

Some kinds of uncertainty about collectibility of the realty sales price may lead to use of the **deposit method**[7] of accounting, in which the effective date of a sale is

---

[5]"Profit Recognition on Sales of Real Estate," *Industry Accounting Guide* (New York: AICPA, 1973), par. 36.

[6]"Application of the Deposit, Installment, and Cost Recovery Methods in Accounting for Sales of Real Estate," *AcSEC Statement of Position 78-4* (New York: AICPA, 1978), par. 11.

[7]The **deposit method** postpones recognizing a sale until a determination can be made as to whether a sale has occurred for accounting purposes. Pending recognition of the sale, the seller records no receivable but continues to show in the financial statements the property and related existing debt, and discloses the status of the property. Cash received from the buyer is reported as a deposit on the contract except that portions of cash received that are designated by the contract as interest and are not subject to refund may appropriately offset interest on existing debt on the property.

deferred until the uncertainty is reasonably resolved. No revenue or income is recognized before the date the sale is considered to be effective, and all cash received before then is accounted for as a deposit (i.e., a liability) on the sales price.

If the earning process is incomplete, the emphasis of income recognition shifts from the time of sale to the seller's performance that is an integral part of earning the revenue. A sale has occurred when the seller performs those acts that earn the revenue. Under rigid conditions, revenue may be recognized by a **percentage-of-completion method** before the earning process is complete. Cash collected before the related revenue is earned results in unearned revenue (i.e., a liability) to be recognized as revenue when it is earned.[8]

Analyzing Real Estate Transactions

Economic substance usually should determine the timing of recognition, amount, and designation of revenue if the economic substance of a realty transaction differs from its legal form. For example, a real estate transaction that is in the legal form of a sale (that is, title to or possession of a product or other asset is transferred in exchange for cash or a promise to pay cash) may be in substance (1) a construction contract, (2) a lease for use of the property, (3) an agreement to loan or borrow funds, (4) an agreement establishing a joint venture, (5) a deposit on or an option to purchase the property, (6) a contract for services for a fee, or (7) a sale of something other than the property that is the apparent object of the "sale" (for example, depreciation or other deductions for income taxes or a right to participate in profits from operating the asset). Thus, instead of recognizing revenue and income on the sale of the real estate the appropriate accounting may be the **percentage-of-completion** or **completed contracts method** during or after sale and construction, as services are rendered, as rent accrues, as interest accrues, by the **equity method** when earnings are reported, or by some other method that reflects the essence of the transaction. The substance of a single real estate transaction may contain elements of two or more types of transactions.

Careful analysis is necessary when a realty sale transaction is deemed not to be a sale for accounting purposes. To be accounted for as a sale certain conditions should be met:

1. The transaction should transfer from the seller to the buyer the usual risks of ownership (e.g., obsolescence, unprofitable operation, unsatisfactory performance, idle capacity, and dubious residual value) and the rewards of ownership (e.g., profitable operation and gain from appreciation in value).

2. The interest that is retained by the seller in the realty sold should be limited essentially to that of a secured creditor. Examining the rights and obligations of the parties under the contract, the patterns of cash flows, the nature of the interest retained by the "seller," and the like should indicate the substance of the transaction and the method of accounting that should be applied.

---

[8]"Profit Recognition on Sales of Real Estate," *Industry Accounting Guide* (New York: AICPA, 1973).

Criteria for a Sale

A real estate transaction differs from most business exchanges because a significant portion of the consideration is often a receivable collectible over relatively long periods, and the receivable is normally not supported by the full faith and credit of the buyer. Thus, often the only recourse of the seller on default by the buyer is to recover the property. Because uncertainty about collectibility of a receivable may be greater in a real estate sale than in other commercial transactions, recognizing profit at the time of sale depends on finding additional assurance that the sales price will be collected from the buyer.

The AICPA's Committee on Real Estate Accounting in 1973 concluded "that to recognize revenue and profit on a sale of real estate, a buyer's initial investment and his continuing investment should both be adequate to demonstrate his commitment to pay for the property."[9]

Initial Investment   The factors to be evaluated in determining whether a buyer's initial financial investment to purchase real estate is sufficient to indicate a reasonable likelihood of the seller's collecting the receivable from the buyer are (1) **the relative size of the buyer's down payment compared with the sales value of the property, and** (2) **the composition of the down payment.**[10] In most instances a **down payment of 25%** of the sales value of the property is an initial financial investment that is adequate to support recognizing profit at the time of sale. Generally, the down payment should consist of **cash,** not notes of the buyer.

Continuing Investment   In order to satisfy the Committee's criterion for continuing investment, the buyer's payments on the total indebtedness for the purchase price of the property must be by contract at least equal each year to the level annual payment that would be needed to pay the total indebtedness, including interest on the unpaid balance, **over a maximum period of 20 years** (the customary term of a first mortgage loan).

Failure of the buyer's initial and continuing investment in the property to conform to the foregoing requirements leads to application either of methods that defer recognizing a sale until the uncertainty about collectibility is resolved (deposit method) or methods that recognize income as cash is collected (installment or cost recovery methods).

In addition, the following provisions in a contract for sale of real estate dictate accounting for it as a **financing, leasing,** or **profit-sharing** transaction:

1. The seller has an obligation or an option to repurchase the property.
2. The buyer has an option to compel the seller to repurchase the property.
3. The seller guarantees the return of the buyer's investment.

If the transaction is in substance a financing, leasing, or profit-sharing agreement, no sale is recognized. Payments from "buyer" to "seller" are accounted for as (1) funds loaned, or (2) rental payments, or (3) transfers needed to effect a division of profits.

[9]*Ibid.*
[10]Sales value is a stated sales price adjusted for other consideration that clearly constitutes additional proceeds on the sale, services without compensation, imputed interest, etc.

The various accounting methods that may be applicable to real estate transactions either have been illustrated earlier in this chapter (accrual or sale method, percentage-of-completion method, completed-contract method, cost recovery method, deposit method, and installment method) or are illustrated in later chapters (financing and lease methods).

RETAIL LAND SALES

Nature of Retail Land Sales

During the last two decades the retail land sales industry, consisting of "land development companies," has gained prominence. The basic characteristic of the industry is the acquisition by a sales company of large tracts of unimproved land for subdivision into lots for sale to widely dispersed retail customers through intensive marketing programs. In some instances, retail land sellers market lots in a totally unimproved state; frequently, however, the lots are improved, or are intended to be improved, through the addition of roads, utilities, and offsite "amenities" such as golf courses, recreation centers, and lakes.

The primary difference between "retail land sales" and "retail real estate sales" (discussed in the previous section) is **volume.** Retail land sales applies to sales of real estate on a volume basis with down payments that are less than those required to evaluate the collectibility of casual sales of real estate.

Typically, a retail land sales company acquires land, prepares a master plan for subdivision and improvement, obtains requisite governmental and regulatory approvals, undertakes to sell the lots, and performs (or contracts with others to perform) the necessary improvement work. Although financing is sometimes provided to the purchaser by financial institutions and the purchaser takes title at the time of sale, in most instances a substantial portion of the purchase price is financed by a receivable accepted by the seller as part of the consideration. The receivable is usually a land sales contract. The receivable is typically collectible with interest over a number of years; unless the purchaser cancels the contract within a specified refund period, default in payments results in loss of the lot and of all payments made. Receivables from retail land sales are sometimes based on the purchasers' personal credit but frequently involve no credit investigation or personal credit obligation, and the seller cannot require performance or seek deficiency judgments by operation of law or contract.[11]

Accounting for Retail Land Sales The characteristics of "sales" in the retail land sales industry—**small down payment, unenforceability of the sales contract by the seller,** and **customer refunds** within an established cancellation period—have resulted in the establishment of special criteria to determine when a sale should be recorded for accounting purposes. In 1973 the AICPA Committee on Land Development Companies issued, with the approval of the APB, an industry accounting guide entitled "Accounting for Retail Land Sales." The Committee recommends

---

[11]AICPA Committee on Land Development Companies, "Accounting for Retail Land Sales" (New York: AICPA, 1973), pp. 1–3.

that recognition of a sale be deferred until certain conditions are met that indicate that (1) the customer seriously intends to complete the contract, and (2) the company is capable of fulfilling its obligations under the contract so that customers cannot later demand and receive refunds for failure to deliver. Retail land contracts should be recorded as sales only when **all** the following conditions have been met:

1. The customer has made the down payment and each regularly required subsequent payment until the period of cancellation with refund has expired.
2. The aggregate payments (including interest) equal or exceed 10% of the contract sales price.
3. The selling company is clearly capable of providing both land improvements and offsite facilities promised in the contract and of meeting all other representations it has made.[12]

Until all three conditions are met, monies collected should be recorded as deposits and the transactions accounted for under the "deposit method."

Under the **deposit method,** all collections (including interest) should be recorded as deposits until the contracts qualify to be recorded as sales. No amounts should be reflected in revenue until the period has expired during which the customer may cancel and receive a full refund. Selling costs directly associated with the project, including commissions paid to sales personnel, should be proportionately deferred until the sale is recorded. When a contract qualifies as a sale under the **accrual method,** all applicable deferred selling costs should be charged to expense; under the **installment method** such sales costs are either charged along with other costs of sales to income of the period of sale or deferred and recognized in income as payments of principal are received on the sales contract receivable.[13] When a contract is cancelled (with or without refund), unrecoverable deferred selling costs should be charged to expense and deposits forfeited credited to income.

If the conditions noted above are met, the contracts may be accounted for as a sale applying either the accrual method of sale accounting or the installment sales method of accounting. The **accrual method** of accounting should be applied to those projects in which collections on contracts are reasonably assured and **all** of the following conditions are met (the installment method must be followed for all other projects):

1. The properties clearly will be useful for residential or recreational purposes at the end of the normal payment period.
2. The project's improvements have progressed beyond preliminary stages, and there is evidence that the work will be completed according to plan.
3. The receivable is not subject to subordination to new loans.
4. Collection experience for the project indicates that collectibility of receivable balances are reasonably predictable and that 90% of the contracts in force six months after sales are recorded will be collected in full.[14]

---

[12]*Ibid.,* p. 6.

[13]A recent analysis of the Industry Accounting Guide "Accounting for Retail Land Sales" indicates that the accrual method of accounting for retail land sales is "sufficiently reliable." In addition, the study disclosed, "it is superior in respect to the criteria of relevance, understandability, comparability, neutrality, and timeliness to the installment method." From Alan Cerf, "Accounting for Retail Land Sales," *The Accounting Review* (July, 1975), pp. 451–465.

[14]"Accounting for Retail Land Sales," *op. cit.,* pp. 7–8.

Thus, income should be recorded under the accrual method if the company's collection experience can provide information that supports a reasonable prediction of whether the required percentage of contracts will pay out to maturity **and** all other conditions are met. **Unless all conditions for use of the accrual method are met for the entire project, the installment method should be applied to all recorded sales.** When all four of the conditions listed on the preceding page are satisfied on a project originally recorded under the installment method, the accrual method of accounting should be adopted for the entire project (current and prior sales) and the effort accounted for as a change in accounting estimate due to changed circumstances (described in Chapter 23).

The conditions listed above indicate the extent to which rule making and the establishment of precise criteria can complicate accounting. The necessity and applicability of such specificity are being challenged by many accountants who feel that the development of general principles or standards and the application of sound judgment are sufficient to render useful financial statements.

Note: All **asterisked** questions, cases, exercises, or problems relate to material contained in the appendix to each chapter.

Questions

1. What is revenue? When is revenue realized in a theoretical sense? According to the "realization principle," when is revenue realized?

2. When is revenue recognized in the following situations:
   (a) Revenue from selling products? (b) Revenue from services rendered? (c) Revenue from permitting others to use enterprise assets? (d) Revenue from disposing of assets other than products?

3. Identify several types of sales transactions and indicate the types of business for which that type of transaction is common.

4. What are the three alternative accounting methods available to a seller that is exposed to continued risks of ownership through return of the product?

5. Under what conditions may a seller who is exposed to continued risks of a high rate of return of the product sold recognize sales transactions as current revenue?

6. How does the accounting for a "contract of sale" differ from the accounting for a "contract to sell"?

7. What are the two basic methods of accounting for long-term construction contracts? Indicate the circumstances that determine when one or the other of these methods should be used.

8. For what reasons should the percentage-of-completion method be used over the completed-contract method whenever possible?

9. What methods are used in practice to determine the extent of progress toward completion? Identify some "input measures" and some "output measures" that might be used to determine the extent of progress.

10. What disclosures does the SEC require for long-term contract receivables? What disclosures does it require for long-term contract inventories?

11. Identify and briefly describe the three methods generally employed to account for the cash received in situations where the collection of the sales price is not reasonably assured.

12. What is the nature of an installment sale? How do installment sales differ from ordinary credit sales?

13. Describe the installment sales method of accounting.

14. How are operating expenses (not included in cost of goods sold) handled under the installment method of accounting? What is the justification for such treatment?

15. When interest is involved in installment sales transactions, how should it be treated for accounting purposes?

16. How should the results of installment sales be reported on the income statement?

17. What legal rules govern a consignment sales transaction?

18. What is a "del credere agent"? What is an "account sales"?

19. When should revenue from service transactions be recognized?

20. Identify and differentiate between the three types of service costs. What is the guideline for expensing costs in general? What are the general guidelines for recognizing the three types of service costs?

21. At what time is it proper to recognize income in the following cases: (a) installment sales with no reasonable basis for estimating the degree of collectibility; (b) sales for future delivery; (c) merchandise shipped on consignment; (d) profit on incomplete construction contracts; and (e) subscriptions to publications?

22. When is revenue conventionally recognized? What conditions should exist for the recognition at date of sale of all or part of the revenue and income of any sale transaction?

*23. Why in franchise arrangements may it not be proper to recognize the entire franchise fee as revenue at the date of sale?

*24. How does the concept of "substantial performance" apply to accounting for franchise sales?

*25. Describe the "deposit method" of accounting as it relates to revenue recognition in realty sales.

*26. In what ways is a real estate sales transaction different from other sale transactions? What conditions should be present in a real estate transaction to justify the recognition of revenue and profit at the date of sale?

*27. Differentiate between a "real estate sale transaction" and a "retail land sale transaction." How does the accounting differ for these two different types of realty transactions?

*28. What conditions should be met in order to account for retail land contracts as a sale?

*29. What conditions should be met in order to apply the accrual method of accounting to a land development project?

*30. Indicate when each of the following accounting methods is applicable to accounting for retail land sale projects: (a) deposit method, (b) accrual method, (c) installment method.

Cases

C19-1 The earning of revenue by a business enterprise is recognized for accounting purposes when the transaction is recorded. In some situations, revenue is recognized approximately as it is earned in the economic sense. In other situations, however, accountants have developed guidelines for recognizing revenue by other criteria, for example, such as, at the point of sale.

Instructions

(Ignore income taxes.)

(a) Explain and justify why revenue is often recognized as earned at time of sale.

(b) Explain in what situations it would be appropriate to recognize revenue as the productive activity takes place.

(c) At what times, other than those included in (a) and (b) above, may it be appropriate to recognize revenue? Explain.

C19-2 Revenue is usually recognized at the point of sale. Under special circumstances, however, bases other than the point of sale are used for the timing of revenue recognition.

Instructions

(a) Why is the point of sale usually used as the basis for the timing of revenue recognition?

(b) Disregarding the special circumstances when bases other than the point of sale are used, discuss the merits of each of the following objections to the sales basis of revenue recognition:
1. It is too conservative because revenue is earned throughout the entire process of production.
2. It is not conservative enough because accounts receivable do not represent disposable funds, sales returns and allowances may be made, and collection and bad debt expenses may be incurred in a later period.

(c) Revenue may also be recognized (1) during production and (2) when cash is received. For each of these two bases of timing revenue recognition give an example of the circumstances in which it is properly used and discuss the accounting merits of its use in lieu of the sales basis.

(AICPA adapted)

C19-3 S & M Trading Stamps, Inc., was formed early this year to sell trading stamps throughout the Southwest to retailers who distribute the stamps gratuitously to their customers. Books for accumulating the stamps and catalogs illustrating the merchandise for which the stamps may be exchanged are given free to retailers for distribution to stamp recipients. Centers with inventories of merchandise premiums have been established for redemption of the stamps. Retailers may not return unused stamps to S & M.

The following schedule expresses S & M's expectations as to percentages of a normal month's activity that will be attained. For this purpose, a "normal month's activity" is defined as the level of operations expected when expansion of activities ceases or tapers off to a stable rate. The company expects that this level will be attained in the third year and that sales of stamps will average $2,000,000 per month throughout the third year.

Month	Actual Stamp Sales Percent	Merchandise Premium Purchases Percent	Stamp Redemptions Percent
6th	30%	40%	10%
12th	60	60	45
18th	80	80	70
24th	90	90	80
30th	100	100	95

S & M plans to adopt an annual closing date at the end of each 12 months of operation.

Instructions

(a) Discuss the factors to be considered in determining when revenue should be recognized in measuring the income of a business enterprise.

(b) Discuss the accounting alternatives that should be considered by S & M Trading Stamps, Inc., for the recognition of its revenues and related expenses.

(c) For each accounting alternative discussed in (b), give balance sheet accounts that should be used and indicate how each should be classified.

(AICPA adapted)

C19-4 Universal Products Company is a large conglomerate consisting of forty-four subsidiary companies with plants and offices throughout the United States and the world. Arthur Ross, Pricewhinney, Coopersells, and Peat Co. is the international public accounting firm engaged to design and install a computerized total information, accounting, and cost control system in each of Universal's subsidiaries. The CPA firm is given three years to complete the engagement; it intends to work continuously on the project but will assign the largest number of its staff to the project during its least busy period each year (May to October). Arthur Ross, Pricewhinney, Coopersells, and Peat Co. obtained this consulting engagement after much study, planning, an elaborate presentation, and a bid of $2,950,000.

Instructions

(a) Name and describe four different methods of accounting for the revenues from service-type engagements, indicating when revenue is recognized.

(b) For each of the four types of methods of accounting for revenues from a service type engagement, describe how initial direct costs and direct costs should be expensed.

(c) Discuss the manner or method of revenue recognition and expensing of initial indirect costs and direct costs that you believe is appropriate for the CPA firm in its performance of the engagement described above.

(d) How does the receipt of cash for payment of services affect revenue recognition in this and other service transactions?

C19-5 Southern Fried Shrimp sells franchises to independent operators throughout the southeastern part of the United States. The contract with the franchisee includes the following provisions:

1. The franchisee is charged an initial fee of $25,000. Of this amount $5,000 is payable when the agreement is signed and a $4,000 noninterest-bearing note is payable at the end of each of the five subsequent years.

2. All of the initial franchise fee collected by Southern Fried Shrimp is to be refunded and the remaining obligation canceled if, for any reason, the franchisee fails to open his franchise.

3. In return for the initial franchise fee Southern Fried Shrimp agrees to (a) assist the franchisee in selecting the location for his business, (b) negotiate the lease for the land, (c) obtain financing and assist with building design, (d) supervise construction, (e) establish accounting and tax records, and (f) provide expert advice over a five-year period relating to such matters as employee and management training, quality control, and promotion.

4. In addition to the initial franchise fee the franchisee is required to pay to Southern Fried Shrimp a monthly fee of 2% of sales for menu planning, recipe innovations, and the privilege of purchasing ingredients from Southern Fried Shrimp at or below prevailing market prices.

   Management of Southern Fried Shrimp estimates that the value of the services rendered to the franchisee at the time the contract is signed amounts to at least $5,000. All franchisees to date have opened their locations at the scheduled time and none has defaulted on any of the notes receivable.

   The credit ratings of all franchisees would entitle them to borrow at the current interest rate of 10%. The present value of an ordinary annuity of five annual receipts of $4,000 each discounted at 10% is $15,163.

Instructions

(a) Discuss the alternatives that Southern Fried Shrimp might use to account for the initial franchise fee, evaluate each by applying generally accepted accounting principles to this situation, and give illustrative entries for each alternative.

(b) Given the nature of Southern Fried Shrimp's agreement with its franchisees, when should revenue be recognized? Discuss the question of revenue recognition for both the initial franchise fee and the additional monthly fee of 2% of sales and give illustrative entries for both types of revenue.

(c) Assuming that Southern Fried Shrimp sells some franchises for $35,000, which includes a charge of $10,000 for the rental of equipment for its useful life of 10 years, that $15,000 of the fee is payable immediately and the balance on noninterest-bearing notes at $4,000 per year, that no portion of the $10,000 rental payment is refundable in case the franchisee goes out of business, and that title to the equipment remains with the franchisor, what would be the preferable method of accounting for the rental portion of the initial franchise fee? Explain.

(AICPA adapted)

*C19-6 Bunny Hutch, Inc., acquired land and acted as the prime contractor for the construction of a "swingles" apartment complex on Lake Shore Drive in Chicago. Total land and construction cost to Bunny Hutch, Inc., is $3,200,000. Charlie Livealot, a local investor, signs a contract for $3,600,000 on May 1, 1975, makes a down payment of $900,000, and agrees to pay $350,000 a year for 15 years. Bunny Hutch, Inc., retains an option to repurchase the complex until May 2, 1985, and guarantees Livealot the return of the down payment of $900,000, but not the annual payments of $350,000, upon the exercise of the option. The option is included in the contract because Livealot's financial condition is not highly regarded.

Instructions

How and when should revenue and profit from this transaction be recognized by Bunny Hutch, Inc.? Discuss fully.

*C19-7 Gotcha Developers, Inc., purchased a 2,000-acre swamp in southern Georgia for $100,000 and has begun an intensified hard-sell marketing program in several northern states. The development is divided into 2,000 one-acre lots having retail prices of $1,500 to $5,000. Gotcha Developers promises to drain the acreage and make such improvements as access roads, water supply, sewage treatment plant, two lakes, and a club house when sufficient cash is generated. Buyers must make a down payment of $200 upon signing the purchase agreement and promise to pay the balance in 60 equal monthly payments plus interest at 1½% a month on the unpaid balance. During the first year 560 contracts were issued, of which 308 are still in force at year end.

Instructions

You have been hired as accounting consultant for Gotcha Developers. How do you recommend that the company account for the revenues from the development project?

*C19-8 Livealittle, Inc., is a developer of commercial real estate. In the summer of 1980, Livealittle had completed an apartment complex near Detroit at a cost of $750,000. In July, Livealittle was able to sell the property to Edsel Motor Industries for a contract price of $875,000. The terms of the purchase agreement require Edsel Motor to make a down payment of $105,000 and annual payments to Livealittle of $55,940 (includes a 6% interest factor) for the next 30 years.

Instructions

In accordance with recommended accounting practice, how and when should revenue and profit be recognized by Livealittle, Inc.? Discuss fully.

*C19-9 Dizzy Corporation purchased an 18-hole operating golf course near Orlando, Florida for $8,000,000 on September 5, 1980. It planned to reduce this to a 9-hole golf course and sell the remaining acreage as half-acre lots, fully developed exclusive of homes. By February 10, 1981, the improvements (roads, sewers, water, and other amenities) are completed and in place; marketing of the 600 lots at $40,000 each is then begun. No cancellation privileges are granted to the buyers, and down payments of $8,000 per lot are required. For the first year, collections have continued for 96% of the contracts sold.

Instructions

At what point should sales be recognized and under what accounting method should revenue and profit be recognized?

Exercises

E19-1 On June 3, Hyperopia Company sold to Barbara Morris merchandise having a sale price of $3,000 with terms of 2/10, n/60, f.o.b. shipping point. An invoice totaling $90, terms n/30, was received by Barbara Morris on June 8 from the Messenger Transport Service for the freight cost. Upon receipt of the goods, June 5, Barbara Morris notified Hyperopia Company that merchandise costing $200 contained flaws that rendered it worthless; the same day Hyperopia Company issued a credit memo covering the worthless merchandise and asked that it be returned at company expense. The freight on the returned merchandise was $16, paid by Hyperopia Company on June 7. On June 12, the company received a check for the balance due from Barbara Morris.

Instructions

(a) Prepare journal entries on Hyperopia Company books to record all the events noted above under each of the following bases:
1. Sales and receivables are entered at gross selling price.
2. Sales and receivables are entered net of cash discounts.

(b) Prepare the journal entry under basis 2, assuming that Barbara Morris did not remit payment until July 29.

E19-2 Rascal Construction Company uses the percentage-of-completion method of accounting. In 1980, Rascal began work under contract #E2-D2, which provided for a contract price of $2,000,000. Other details follow:

	1980	1981
Costs incurred during the year	$ 300,000	$1,375,000
Estimated costs to complete, as of December 31	1,200,000	-0-
Billings during the year	360,000	1,640,000
Collections during the year	250,000	1,550,000

Instructions

(a) What portion of the total contract price would be recognized as revenue in 1980? 1981?

(b) Assuming the same facts as those above except that Rascal uses the completed-contract method of accounting, what portion of the total contract price would be recognized as revenue in 1981?

(AICPA adapted)

E19-3 In 1980, Underland Tunnel Corp. began construction work under a three-year contract. The contract price was $800,000. Underland uses the percentage-of-completion method for financial-accounting purposes. The income to be recognized each year is based on the proportion of cost incurred to total estimated costs for completing the contract. The financial-statement presentations relating to this contract at December 31, 1980, follow:

Balance Sheet

Accounts receivable—construction contract billings		$15,000
Construction in progress	$50,000	
Less contract billings	47,000	
Cost of uncompleted contract in excess of billings		3,000

Income Statement

Income (before tax) on the contract recognized in 1980	$10,000

Instructions

(a) How much cash was collected in 1980 on this contract?

(b) What was the initial estimated total income before tax on this contract?

(AICPA adapted)

E19-4 In 1980, Complete Construction Company agreed to construct an apartment building at a price of $1,000,000. The information relating to the costs and billings for this contract is as follows:

	1980	1981	1982
Costs incurred to date	$240,000	$440,000	$ 840,000
Estimated costs yet to be incurred	560,000	360,000	-0-
Customer billings to date	100,000	360,000	1,000,000
Collection of billings to date	80,000	300,000	900,000

Instructions

(a) Assuming that the percentage-of-completion method is used, compute the amount of income to be recognized in 1980 and 1981.

(b) For 1981, show how the details related to this construction contract would be disclosed on the balance sheet and on the income statement.

E19-5 The Dainty Construction Company began operations January 1, 1980. During the year, Dainty entered into a contract with Redbeard Razor Corporation to construct a manufacturing facility. At that time, Dainty estimated that it would take five years to complete the facility at a total cost of $4,800,000. The total contract price for construction of the facility is $6,000,000. During the year, Dainty incurred $1,250,000 in construction costs related to the construction project. The estimated cost to complete the contract is $3,750,000. Redbeard was billed and paid 30% of the contract price.

Instructions

Prepare schedules to compute the amount of gross profit to be recognized for the year ended December 31, 1980, and the amount to be shown as "cost of uncompleted contract in excess of related billings" or "billings on uncompleted contract in excess of related costs" at December 31, 1980, under each of the following methods:

(a) Completed-contract method.

(b) Percentage-of-completion method.

Show supporting computations in good form.

(AICPA adapted)

E19-6 Nemesis Company appropriately uses the installment-sales method of accounting. On December 31, 1982, the books show balances as follows:

Installment Receivables		Deferred Gross Profit			Gross Profit on Sales	
1980	$10,000	1980	$	7,000	1980	40%
1981	40,000	1981		26,000	1981	30%
1982	90,000	1982		105,000	1982	35%

Instructions

(a) Prepare the adjusting entry or entries required on December 31, 1982 to recognize 1982 realized gross profit. (Cash receipts entries have already been made.)

(b) Compute the amount of cash collected in 1982 on accounts receivable of each year.

E19-7 Wiggley Gum Corporation, which began business on January 1, 1980, appropriately uses the installment-sales method of accounting. The following data were obtained for the years 1980 and 1981:

	1980	1981
Installment sales	$350,000	$420,000
Cost of installment sales	280,000	315,000
General & administrative expenses	35,000	42,000
Cash collections on sales of 1980	150,000	125,000
Cash collections on sales of 1981	-0-	200,000

Instructions

(a) Compute the balance in the deferred gross profit accounts on December 31, 1980 and on December 31, 1981.

(b) A 1980 sale resulted in default in 1982. At the date of default, the balance on the installment receivable was $6,000, and the repossessed merchandise had a fair value of $4,100. Prepare the entry to record the repossession.

(AICPA adapted)

E19-8 Discount Outlet, Inc. was involved in two default and repossession cases during the year:

1. A refrigerator was sold to Ms. Alice Congdon for $900, including a 40% markup on selling price. Ms. Congdon made a down payment of 20%, four of the remaining 24 equal payments, and then defaulted on further payments. The refrigerator was repossessed, at which time the fair value was determined to be $400.

Instructions

Prepare the journal entry to record the repossession.

2. An oven which cost $600 was sold to Mr. Robb Russell for $800 on the installment basis. Mr. Russell made a down payment of $120 and paid $40 a month for six months, after which he defaulted. The oven was repossessed and the estimated value at time of repossession was determined to be $360.

Instructions

Prepare the journal entry to record the repossession.

E19-9 Disco Stereo Company uses the installment sales method in accounting for its installment sales. On January 1, 1981, Disco Company had an installment account receivable from Ellen Odom with a balance of $1,250. During 1981, $250 was collected from Odom. When no further collection could be made, the merchandise sold to Odom was repossessed. The merchandise, when repossessed, had a fair market value of $400. The company spent $50 for reconditioning of the merchandise. The merchandise was originally sold with a gross profit rate of 40%.

Instructions

Prepare the entries on the books of Disco Company to record all transactions related to Odom during 1981.

E19-10   On May 3, 1980, Shortstuff Company consigned 60 trunks, costing $400 each to Terrier Company. The cost of shipping the trunks amounted to $600, and was paid by Shortstuff Company. On December 30, 1980, an account sales was received from the consignee, reporting that 40 trunks had been sold for $500 each. Remittance was made by the consignee for the amount due, after deducting a commission of 10%, advertising of $100, and total installation costs of $200 on the trunks sold.

Instructions

(a) Compute the inventory value of the units unsold in the hands of the consignee.

(b) Compute the profit for the consignor for the units sold.

(c) Compute the amount of cash that will be remitted by the consignee.

E19-11   The Cardinal Company has a consignment agreement with Walmark Retailers. The agreement provides that Walmark is to sell the desks of the Cardinal Company at a price of $300. In return, Walmark is to receive a commission of 10% of sales, and is to be reimbursed for other expenses. On April 24, Cardinal ships 100 desks to Walmark; each desk has a cost of $225. Cardinal pays the freight charge of $1,200. On December 31, Cardinal receives an account sales from Walmark, indicating that 60 desks were sold, and that freight costs of $300 were paid on goods delivered on consignment for local hauling. Walmark also remitted a check of $9,750.

Instructions

Prepare the journal entries for the consignor to record the transactions noted above and to record the profit on consignment sales.

E19-12   Presented below is information related to The Appalachian Company.

1. Merchandise that cost $3,120 was shipped on consignment to a retailer in Chicago on July 29. Shipping charges of $264 were incurred and paid in advance. Through an oversight, the cost of this merchandise was not included in the July 31 inventory.

2. On June 8, merchandise which cost $6,480 was shipped to Gary Fish, freight collect, on consignment. On August 2, 1981, an account sales was received from Gary Fish as follows:

Gary Fish		
ACCOUNT SALES TO THE APPALACHIAN COMPANY		
July 31, 1981		
Sales (120 of 180 units received)		$7,200
Less:		
Freight in	$432	
Commissions (at 5%)	360	792
Remitted herewith		$6,408

The account sales was entered on August 3 under that date and did not affect the statements as of July 31. The merchandise out on consignment was included in the July 31 inventory at $6,480.

3. Thirteen cases of electric lamps received on consignment July 24 were included in the July 31 inventory at $80 a case.

4. Five invoices for sales on account made August 1 were inadvertently dated July 31 and entered under that date in the July sales register.

5. The July 31 physical inventory omitted consideration of merchandise shipped to customers on a C.O.D. basis. The selling price of the total amount involved was $2,580. Of this amount, merchandise sold for $1,950 was accepted by customers and was recorded as sold under date of July 31. The remaining merchandise, which has been marked up 33⅓% on selling price, was returned to stock on August 2 after the physical inventory had been completed.

Instructions

Describe the complete effect of each of the errors above if made by The Appalachian Company in preparing financial statements for the year ended July 31, 1981. Assume no errors other than those specified.

*E19-13   Herb Huskie Hamburgers, Inc., charges an initial franchise fee of $30,000. Upon the signing of the agreement, a payment of $15,000 is due; thereafter, three annual payments of $5,000 are required. The credit rating of the franchisee is such that it would have to pay interest at 10% to borrow money.

Instructions

Prepare the entries to record the initial franchise fee on the books of the franchisor under the following assumptions:

(a) The down payment is not refundable, no future services are required by the franchisor, and collection of the note is reasonably assured.

(b) The franchisor has substantial services to perform, and the collection of the note is very uncertain.

(c) The down payment is not refundable, collection of the note is reasonably certain, the franchisor has yet to perform a substantial amount of services, and the down payment represents a fair measure of the services already performed.

Problems

P19-1   Hardhat Construction Company has entered into a contract beginning January 1, 1980, to build a parking complex. It has been estimated that the complex will cost $700,000 and will take three years to construct. The complex will be billed to the purchasing company at $950,000. The following data pertain to the construction period.

	1980	1981	1982
Costs to date	$350,000	$490,000	$700,000
Estimated costs to complete	350,000	210,000	—
Progress billings to date	300,000	650,000	950,000
Cash collected to date	250,000	600,000	950,000

Instructions

(a) Using the percentage-of-completion method, compute the estimated income that would be recognized during each year of the construction period.

(b) Using the completed-contract method, compute the estimated income that would be recognized during each year of the construction period.

P19-2   Husky Construction Company has contracted to build an office building. The construction is scheduled to begin on January 1, 1980, and the estimated time of completion is July 1, 1983. The building cost is estimated to be $50,000,000 and will be billed at $55,000,000. The following data relate to the construction period.

	1980	1981	1982	1983
Costs to date	$15,000,000	$25,000,000	$35,000,000	$50,000,000
Estimated cost to complete	35,000,000	25,000,000	15,000,000	—
Progress billings to date	7,000,000	20,000,000	35,000,000	55,000,000
Cash collected to date	7,000,000	18,000,000	30,000,000	55,000,000

Instructions

(a) Compute the estimated income for 1980, 1981, 1982, and 1983, assuming that the percentage-of-completion method is used. (Ignore income taxes.)

(b) Prepare the necessary journal entries for Husky Construction Company for the years 1982 and 1983.

P19-3   On February 1, 1980, Delicate Construction Company obtained a contract to build an athletic stadium. The stadium was to be built at a total cost of $4,500,000 and was scheduled for completion by September 1, 1982. One clause of the contract stated that Delicate was to deduct $10,000 from the $6,000,000 billing price for each week that completion was delayed. Completion was delayed five weeks, which resulted in a $50,000 penalty. Below are the data pertaining to the construction period.

	1980	1981	1982
Costs to date	$1,500,000	$3,220,000	$4,600,000
Estimated costs to complete	3,000,000	1,380,000	—
Progress billings to date	1,000,000	2,500,000	5,950,000
Cash collected to date	800,000	2,300,000	5,950,000

Instructions

(a) Using the percentage-of-completion method, compute the estimated income realized in the years 1980–1981.

(b) Prepare a partial balance sheet for December 31, 1981, showing the balances in the receivable and inventory accounts.

P19-4   Presented below is summarized information for New Rosis Company, which sells merchandise on the installment basis:

	1980	1981	1982
Sales (on installment plan)	$200,000	$240,000	$200,000
Cost of sales	140,000	180,000	160,000
Gross profit	$ 60,000	$ 60,000	$ 40,000
Collections from customers on:			
1980 installment sales	$ 60,000	$110,000	$ 20,000
1981 installment sales		80,000	120,000
1982 installment sales			70,000

Instructions

(a) Compute the realized gross profit for each of the years 1980, 1981, and 1982.

(b) Prepare in journal form all entries required in 1982, applying the installment method of accounting.

P19-5   Cutrate Appliance Company sells merchandise on open account as well as on installment terms.

	1980	1981	1982
Sales on account	$417,000	$389,000	$510,000
Installment sales	240,000	320,000	380,000
Collections on installment sales			
Made in 1980	80,000	120,000	40,000
Made in 1981		110,000	160,000
Made in 1982			125,000
Cost of sales			
Sold on account	305,000	280,000	362,000
Sold on installment	144,000	188,800	235,600
Selling expenses	87,000	84,500	110,000
Administrative expenses	42,000	48,000	54,000

Instructions

From the data above, which cover the three years since the Cutrate Appliance Company commenced operations, determine the net income for each year, applying the installment method of accounting.

P19-6 Wheeler-Dealer Company sells appliances for cash and also on the installment plan. Entries to record cost of sales are made monthly.

Wheeler-Dealer Company
TRIAL BALANCE
December 31, 1982

Cash	$ 72,600	
Installment Accounts Receivable, 1981	24,000	
Installment Accounts Receivable, 1982	76,000	
Inventory—New Merchandise	62,000	
Inventory—Repossessed Merchandise	12,000	
Accounts Payable		$ 48,300
Deferred Gross Profit, 1981		22,800
Capital Stock		100,000
Retained Earnings		42,400
Sales		212,000
Installment Sales		150,000
Cost of Sales	165,000	
Cost of Installment Sales	97,500	
Gain or Loss on Repossessions	400	
Selling and Administrative Expenses	66,000	
	$575,500	$575,500

The accounting department has prepared the following analysis of cash receipts for the year:

Cash sales (including repossessed merchandise)	$212,000
Installment accounts receivable, 1981	52,000
Installment accounts receivable, 1982	74,000
Other	18,000
Total	$356,000

Repossessions recorded during the year are summarized as follows:

	1981
Uncollected balance	$4,000
Loss on repossession	400
Repossessed merchandise	2,400

Instructions

From the trial balance and accompanying information:
  (a) Compute the rate of gross profit for 1981 and 1982.
  (b) Prepare closing entries as of December 31, 1982 under the installment method of accounting.
  (c) Prepare a statement of income for the year ended December 31, 1982. Include only the realized gross profit in the income statement.

P19-7 Selected transactions of Widescreen TV Sales Company are presented below:

1. A television set costing $560 is sold to C. E. Kingston on November 1, 1981 for $700. Kingston makes a down payment of $200 and agrees to pay $25 on the first of each month for twenty months thereafter.
2. Kingston pays the $25 installment due December 1, 1981.
3. On December 31, 1981, the appropriate entries are made to record profit realized on the installment sales.
4. The first seven 1982 installments of $25 each are paid by Kingston. (Make one entry.)
5. In August 1982 the set is repossessed, after Kingston fails to pay the August 1 installment and indicates that he will be unable to continue the payments. The estimated fair value of the repossessed set is $130.

Instructions

Prepare journal entries to record on the books of Widescreen TV Sales Company the transactions above.

P19-8 The following summarized information relates to the installment sales activity of Neeman Markus Stores, Inc. for the year 1980:

Installment sales during 1980	$600,000
Cost of goods sold on installment basis	360,000
Collections from customers	170,000
Unpaid balances on merchandise repossessed	20,000
Estimated value of merchandise repossessed	6,600

Instructions

(a) Prepare journal entries at the end of 1980 to record on the books of Neeman Markus Stores, Inc. the summarized data above.

(b) Prepare the entry to record the gross profit realized during 1980.

P19-9 Kay-Mart Discount Centers, Inc. sells merchandise for cash and also on the installment plan. Entries to record cost of goods sold are made at the end of each year.

TRIAL BALANCE, DECEMBER 31, 1982

	Dr.	Cr.
Cash	$ 50,700	
Installment Accounts Receivable, 1981	36,000	
Installment Accounts Receivable, 1982	55,000	
Inventory, Jan. 1, 1982	60,000	
Repossessed Merchandise	3,000	
Accounts Payable		$ 12,000
Deferred Gross Profit, 1981		26,600
Capital Stock, Common		100,000
Retained Earnings		20,000
Sales		200,000
Installment Sales		80,000
Purchases	180,000	
Loss on Repossessions	900	
Operating Expenses	53,000	
	$438,600	$438,600

Repossessions of merchandise (sold in 1981) were made in 1982 and were recorded correctly as follows:

Deferred Gross Profit, 1981	2,100	
Repossessed Merchandise	3,000	
Loss on Repossessions	900	
Installment Accounts Receivable, 1981		6,000

Part of this repossessed merchandise was sold for cash during 1982, and the sale was recorded by a debit to Cash and a credit to Sales.

The inventory of repossessed merchandise on hand December 31, 1982, is $2,000; of new merchandise, $50,000. There was no repossessed merchandise on hand January 1, 1982.

Collections on accounts receivable during 1982 were:

Installment Accounts Receivable, 1981	$40,000
Installment Accounts Receivable, 1982	25,000

The cost of the merchandise sold under the installment plan during 1982 was $54,400.

The rate of gross profit on 1981 and on 1982 installment sales can be computed from the information given above.

Instructions

(a) From the trial balance and other information given above, prepare adjusting and closing entries as of December 31, 1982.

(b) Prepare an income statement for the year ended December 31, 1982. Include only the realized gross profit in the income statement.

P19-10 Listed below are selected transactions of Ambiquity Company, consignor.

Dec. 8 Ships 500 units, costing $24 each, to Jim Nast to be sold on consignment.

  8 Pays $360 freight on the shipment above.

  31 Receives an account sales from Nast that shows:

Units received	500	
Units on hand	200	
Units sold @ $36 each	300	$10,800
Expenses deducted:		
Freight-in (local)	$ 144	
Commission—10% of sales	1,080	1,224
Amount remitted		$ 9,576

Instructions

(a) From the information given above, prepare entries in general journal form on the books of Ambiguity Company.

(b) Compute the inventory as of December 31, and make the proper entry to record the profit on the consignment, preparatory to closing.

(c) Construct the Consignment In account that appears on the books of Jim Nast and show therein the debits and credits indicated by this information.

P19-11 Presented below is information related to L. T. Grant Company.

Dec. 10 Ships goods costing $12,000 to Paul Bearer, a **del credere** agent, on consignment.

  10 Pays trucking charges of $180 on the goods shipped.

  31 Receives an account sales from Bearer that shows the following:

Sales (⅔ of the shipment)		$10,400
Deduct:		
Repairs to defective goods (abnormal)	$ 160	
Commission, 10% of sales	1,040	1,200
Net amount remitted to L. T. Grant Co.		$ 9,200

  31 The consignment inventory is computed, and the entry is made to take up the profit earned on the consignment to date.

Jan.   15   Receives an account sales from Bearer that shows the following:

Sales (remainder of shipment)	$ 5,200
Deduct:	
Commission, 10% of sales	520
Net amount remitted	$ 4,680

15   The Consignment Out account for Bearer is closed, and an entry is made to take up the profit earned on the remainder of the consignment.

Instructions

(a) From the information given above, prepare entries in general journal form on the books of L. T. Grant Company. Ledger accounts are not required, but it may prove helpful if T-accounts are used.

(b) Explain how the balance of each account relating to the consignment is shown in the financial statements of L. T. Grant Company prepared at the end of December.

(c) Prepare entries in general journal form on the books of Paul Bearer for the transactions listed below.

Dec.   10   Receives the consignment of goods from L. T. Grant Co.

11   Discovers that some items were damaged because of faulty packing and has the necessary repairs made at the R. W. Machine Shop at a cost of $160 on account.

30   Cash sales to date $7,000; sales on account to L. C. Warren, $3,400; collections from L. C. Warren, $2,000.

30   Sends an account sales to L. T. Grant Co., showing therein the information indicated above in part (a). Makes an entry to record the commission earned to date.

Jan.   8   Sells the remainder of the consigned goods on account to Harry Wright, for $5,200.

10   Wright returns goods and receives credit, $800.

11   The goods returned by Wright are sold for cash, $800.

13   Wright pays his account in full, $4,400.

14   An account sales is sent to L. T. Grant Co., and the commission earned during January is entered.

(d) Explain how the balance of each account relating to the consignment is shown in the financial statements of Paul Bearer, prepared at the end of December.

(e) If Paul Bearer had not been a **del credere** agent, which of the entries in (a) and (c) would be different and in what amount?

P19-12   Listed below are selected transactions of Burt & Reynolds, consignor.

Nov.   1   Shipped merchandise costing $2,100 to Poe Company on consignment.

1   Shipped merchandise costing $1,800 to Clarence Hankes Company on consignment.

1   Paid freight as follows:

Shipment to Poe	$70
Shipment to Hankes	60

24   Received an account sales from Hankes with this information:

Sales (45 of 60 units)		$1,800
Less expenses:		
Local advertising	$ 25	
Commissions	180	205
		1,595
Less cash herewith		900
Accounts yet to be collected		$ 695

28 Received an account sales from Poe:

Sales (50 of 70 units)		$2,000
Less expenses:		
Freight-in (local)	$ 14	
Commissions	200	214
Our check will follow		$1,786

Instructions

Prepare entries in journal form on the books of Burt & Reynolds for the transactions above. Record the profit on the consignment sales at the time the account sales is received.

P19-13 Vertigo Contractors, Inc. undertakes long-term, large-scale construction projects and began operations on October 15, 1981 with contract No. 1, its only job during 1981. A trial balance of the company's general ledger at December 31, 1982 follows:

Vertigo Contractors, Inc.
TRIAL BALANCE
December 31, 1982

Cash	$ 68,090	
Accounts receivable	136,480	
Costs of contracts in progress	469,120	
Plant and equipment	35,500	
Accumulated depreciation		$ 8,000
Accounts payable		70,820
Deferred income taxes		1,908
Billings on contracts in progress		507,200
Capital stock		139,000
Retained earnings		2,862
Selling and administrative expenses	20,600	
	$729,790	$729,790

The following information is available:

1. The company has the approval of the Internal Revenue Service to determine income on the completed contract basis for federal income tax reporting and on the percentage-of-completion basis for accounting and financial statements.

2. At December 31, 1982 there were three jobs in progress, the contract prices of which had been computed as follows:

	Contract 1	Contract 2	Contract 3
Labor and material costs	$169,000	$34,500	$265,700
Indirect costs	30,000	5,500	48,000
Total costs	$199,000	$40,000	$313,700
Add: Profit in contract	40,000	3,000	30,300
Total	$239,000	$43,000	$344,000

3. All job costs are charged to cost of contracts in progress. Cost estimates are carefully derived by engineers and architects and are considered reliable. Data on costs to December 31, 1982 follow:

Contract	Original Estimate	Incurred to Date Total	Incurred to Date Labor & Materials	Incurred to Date Indirect
1	$199,000	$115,420	$ 92,620	$22,800
2	40,000	32,000	26,950	5,050
3	313,700	313,700	265,700	48,000
Totals	$552,700	$461,120	$385,270	$75,850

4. At December 31, 1981 accumulated costs on contract 1 were $39,800; no costs had accumulated on contracts 2 and 3.

Instructions

(a) Prepare a schedule computing the percentage of completion of contracts in progress at December 31, 1982.

(b) Prepare a schedule computing the amounts of revenue, related costs, and net income to be recognized in 1982 from contracts in progress at December 31, 1982.

(AICPA adapted)

P19-14 Coolcat Company, on January 2, 1980, entered into a contract with a manufacturing company to purchase room-size air conditioners and to sell the units on an installment plan with collections over approximately 30 months with no carrying charge.

For income tax purposes Coolcat elected to report income from its sales of air conditioners according to the installment method.

Purchases and sales of new units were as follows:

Year	Units Purchased Quantity	Units Purchased Price Each	Units Sold Quantity	Units Sold Price Each
1980	1,200	$100	1,000	$150
1981	1,800	90	2,000	140
1982	800	105	700	143

Collections on installment sales were as follows:

	Collections Received 1980	Collections Received 1981	Collections Received 1982
1980 sales	$30,000	$60,000	$ 60,000
1981 sales		70,000	115,000
1982 sales			21,000

In 1982, 40 units from the 1981 sales were repossessed and sold for $72.50 each on the installment plan. At the time of repossession $1,200 had been collected from the original purchasers and the units had a fair value of $2,520.

General and administrative expenses for 1982 were $50,000. No charge has been made against current income for the applicable insurance expense from a three-year policy expiring June 30, 1983 costing $3,000, and for an advance payment of $10,000 on a new contract to purchase air conditioners beginning January 2, 1983.

Instructions

Assuming that the weighted-average method is used for determining the inventory cost, including repossessed merchandise, prepare schedules computing for 1980, 1981 and 1982:

- (a) (1) The cost of goods sold on installments.
    - (2) The average unit cost of goods sold on installments for each year.
- (b) The gross profit percentages for 1980, 1981 and 1982.
- (c) The gain or loss on repossessions in 1982.
- (d) The net income from installment sales for 1982 (ignore income taxes).

(AICPA adapted)

Accounting for Income Taxes

Business income is generally subject to federal, state, and local income taxes. In computing income taxes payable to governmental units, businesses must complete tax returns including a statement showing the amount of net income subject to tax. In general, the form and content of the tax return income statement are similar to the form and content of the accounting income statement. **Taxable income** in the tax return, however, is computed in accordance with prescribed tax regulations and rules, while **accounting income** in the income statement is measured in accordance with generally accepted accounting principles and standards. And, because the basic objectives of measuring taxable income are different from the objectives of measuring accounting income, tax rules are frequently different from accounting principles. Therefore, differences between taxable income and accounting income exist.

The differences between taxable income and accounting income give rise to **tax differences,** some of which must be recognized in the accounting records and in the resultant financial statements. The accounting presentation for tax allocation within a period **(intraperiod tax allocation)** was discussed in Chapter 4. This chapter is about the accounting for tax differences between periods **(interperiod tax allocation).**

Major Differences Between Taxable Income and Pretax Accounting Income

The income tax on corporations is a tax on income. Hence any specific features of the law that increase income also increase the amount of tax; any features of the tax law that decrease the amount of income decrease the amount of tax. The major differences between income for tax and for general accounting purposes then can be grouped as follows:

1. Differences causing taxable income to exceed accounting income:
   a. Items not considered to be income in general accounting that are taxed as income under the tax law.
   b. Items considered as business expenses in general accounting that are not allowed as deductions for tax purposes.
2. Differences causing accounting income to exceed taxable income:
   a. Items generally considered to be income that are exempted from tax under the law.
   b. Items not generally considered to be expenses that are deductible for tax purposes.

Some of the specific items that constitute differences between accounting (book) income and tax income are discussed in the following paragraphs.

Non-income Items Subject to Tax   The items under this heading are not particularly common. They include income collected in advance of being earned such as rent, interest, or royalties, which are considered to be income for tax purposes when received instead of when earned. This provision does not apply to subscription income received by publishing companies.

Expenses Not Allowed as Deductions for Tax Purposes   Certain items that are normally considered expense for accounting purposes are not allowed as deductions for tax purposes. These items are discussed below.

1. Charitable contributions in excess of 5% of the taxable income of a corporation are not currently deductible even if made for business purposes (a five-year carryover does exist).
2. Premiums paid on insurance carried by the corporation on the lives of its officers or employees are not deductible if the corporation is the beneficiary. (For general accounting purposes the part of the premium that does not increase the cash surrender value of the policy is ordinarily considered to be an expense.)
3. Interest on indebtedness incurred to purchase tax-exempt securities is not deductible.
4. Losses on wash sales are not deductible. A "wash sale" is a transaction in which securities are sold and the effect of the sale offset within 30 days by a purchase of identical or substantially identical securities. Tax regulations require that the new securities be disposed of before any loss is recognized.
5. Fines and expenses resulting from a violation of law are not deductible for tax purposes.
6. Federal income taxes themselves are not an expense for tax purposes.
7. Any amortization of goodwill is not deductible for tax purposes.
8. Estimated guarantee and warranty costs are not deductible for tax purposes until paid.

In addition, there are various other situations in which a portion of what is considered to be a business expense is not really allowed as a deduction for tax purposes. Amounts provided for depreciation and for bad debts are frequently reduced by the IRS, thereby increasing income for tax purposes. Expenditures made for fixed asset repair and maintenance are often difficult to allocate between asset or expense accounts. Disallowance of such items for income tax purposes when they have been charged to expense accounts also increases income and the tax thereon.

Income Items Exempt from Taxation   For many reasons ranging from social desirability to administrative expediency, certain items commonly included in accounting income are exempted from taxation under the Internal Revenue Code. These exempt items are discussed below.

1. Life insurance proceeds received on the death of the insured are not taxed. (Notice that premiums paid by a company on life insurance policies of which it is the beneficiary are not deductible because any proceeds received are not taxed.)
2. Improvements made to leased property by a lessee that revert to the lessor on expiration of the lease are not taxed as income to the lessor when received.
3. Interest received on state and municipal obligations is not taxed.
4. Profits arising from involuntary conversion, that is, loss by fire or storm, and so on, or through condemnation proceedings, are not taxed if the entire proceeds of the involuntary conversion are reinvested in similar assets or property of the same general nature within a specific time period.

Allowable Deductions Not Considered Expenses   Included in this category are:

1. Depletion in excess of cost.
2. Net operating loss deduction. This special feature of tax law is designed to give taxpayers who suffer a loss in a bad year some relief from taxes paid in the three years immediately preceding and/or the seven years following the loss year.

Permanent Differences Versus Timing Differences

Although all of the items listed above create differences between taxable income and accounting income, for purposes of accounting recognition these differences are of two types: (1) permanent differences and (2) timing differences. **Permanent differences** are (1) items that enter into accounting income but **never** into taxable income and (2) items that enter into taxable income but **never** into accounting income. Examples of permanent differences are:

Permanent Differences
1. Statutory depletion in excess of cost of assets depleted.
2. Interest received on state and municipal obligations.
3. Premiums paid on insurance carried by the company on its officers or employees.
4. Life insurance proceeds.
5. Fines and expenses resulting from a violation of law.
6. Amortized goodwill.

These differences and some others will not be offset by corresponding differences or "turn around" in other periods; the difference continues during the life of the enterprise as between taxable income and accounting income. The APB concluded that "since permanent differences do not affect other periods, interperiod tax allocation is not appropriate to account for such differences."[1]

A corporation that has tax-free income, nondeductible expenses, or allowable deductions in excess of accounting cost has an effective tax rate that is different from the statutory tax rate. The apparent discrepancy between the reported tax and what is "normal" tax does not require tax allocation. Full reporting, however, re-

---

[1]"Accounting for Income Taxes," *Opinions of the Accounting Principles Board No. 11* (New York: AICPA, 1967), par. 34.

quires that the "discrepancy" be explained in the financial statements or in related notes if it is material.

Timing differences arise when (1) the time of including items of revenue and expense in the computation of accounting income and (2) the time of including them in the computation of taxable income do not coincide. Timing differences originate in one period and reverse or turn around in one or more subsequent periods. Some timing differences reduce income taxes that would otherwise be payable currently; others increase current income taxes that would otherwise not have been payable until the future. Examples of items that result in timing differences are classified as follows:

Timing Differences

1. Revenues or gains included in taxable income **later** than in accounting income (gross profits on installment sales).
2. Revenues or gains included in taxable income **earlier** than in accounting income (rents collected in advance).
3. Expenses or losses deducted for taxable income determination **later** than for accounting income (estimated costs of guarantees and warranties).
4. Expenses or losses deducted for taxable income determination **earlier** than for accounting income (accelerated depreciation for tax versus straight-line depreciation for accounting).[2]

To illustrate timing differences further, let us assume that an asset purchased January 1, 1977 with a cost of $100,000 is being depreciated for tax purposes over a 5-year life and for accounting purposes over a 10-year life. Depreciation year by year is as follows:

	Amount of Depreciation	
Year	For Tax Purposes	For Accounting Purposes
1977	$ 20,000	$ 10,000
1978	20,000	10,000
1979	20,000	10,000
1980	20,000	10,000
1981	20,000	10,000
1982		10,000
1983		10,000
1984		10,000
1985		10,000
1986		10,000
Total	$100,000	$100,000

Notice that total depreciation is the same in each case, although for tax purposes it is taken in the first 5 years, whereas for book purposes it is spread over 10 years.

[2]In addition to the typical types of problems associated with deferred income taxes, a number of professional pronouncements have been issued involving special areas. See "Accounting for Income Taxes—Investments in Common Stock Accounted for by the Equity Method," *Opinions of the Accounting Principles Board No. 23* (New York: AICPA, 1972); "Accounting for Income Taxes—Special Areas" (New York: AICPA, 1972); "Accounting for Income Taxes—Oil and Gas," *Statement of Financial Accounting Standards No. 9* (Stamford, Conn.: FASB, 1974); "Applicability of Indefinite Reversal Criteria to Timing Differences," *FASB Interpretation No. 22* (Stamford, Conn.: FASB, 1978); "Accounting for Unused Investment Credit," *FASB Interpretation No. 25* (Stamford, Conn.: FASB, 1978); "Accounting for Tax Benefits Related to U. K. Tax Legislation Concerning Stock Relief," Statement of Financial Accounting Standards No. 31 (Stamford, Conn.: FASB, 1979).

Under special conditions, the tax laws permit just such rapid write-offs or accelerated depreciation. To induce companies to expand their plants in certain ways, the tax law permits them to deduct "accelerated depreciation" in their income tax returns, thereby paying less taxes in the early years of the life of the asset but, if income remains constant, paying more taxes in the later years. If we carry the preceding illustration a step further, the results of this practice become clearer. Assume that the company owning the asset described in the preceding paragraph has gross revenue of $300,000, that it has costs and expenses other than depreciation of $250,000, and that it is subject to an income tax at the rate of 50% of its income before tax. Its income statements for tax purposes and for accounting purposes appear below.

	For Tax Purposes	For Accounting Purposes
Partial Income Statement		
(WITHOUT INTERPERIOD TAX ALLOCATION)		
EACH OF THE FIRST 5 YEARS:		
Gross income	$300,000	$300,000
Costs and expenses	250,000	250,000
	50,000	50,000
Depreciation	20,000	10,000
Income before income tax	30,000	40,000
Income tax	15,000	15,000
Net income for the year	$ 15,000	$ 25,000
EACH OF THE REMAINING 5 YEARS:		
Gross income	$300,000	$300,000
Costs and expenses	250,000	250,000
	50,000	50,000
Depreciation	0	10,000
Income before income tax	50,000	40,000
Income tax	25,000	25,000
Net income for the year	$ 25,000	$ 15,000

Owners and prospective investors acquainted only with the information found in the "accounting" income statement, might get an erroneous impression of the company's profitability. During the first 5 years, the business income statement indicates that the company is making an income of $25,000 a year after taxes and is paying taxes of only 37½% of its income before taxes. This favorable position results from the fact that the company is temporarily enjoying a substantial tax advantage. After the 5-year period of accelerated depreciation has expired, the company will continue to depreciate the asset for accounting purposes but will not be entitled to depreciation on it for taxation purposes. The result will be an increase in income taxes and a decrease in net income, so that the effective tax rate is 62½%.

Reasons for Interperiod Tax Allocation

Most accountants believe that an income presentation such as the one shown above gives an unrealistic view of the company's activities, is misleading to readers, and should be adjusted to relate income tax expense to income before taxes for accounting purposes. **Interperiod tax allocation** has become recognized as the accepted and required adjustment process that reflects tax expense based on pretax accounting income where such tax expense is different from actual taxes paid primarily because of timing differences. Using accelerated depreciation as the example, this position is supported by the following reasoning:

1. The provisions of the IRS Code give companies using accelerated depreciation only a temporary "postponement" of tax, not a permanent tax reduction.

2. This postponement of tax should not influence the reported income of a company over the period during which the asset subject to accelerated depreciation is being depreciated because, other things being equal, the aggregate tax paid over that period by the company is the same whether it uses accelerated depreciation for tax purposes or not.

3. To avoid a misleading income statement, a company enjoying this temporary tax advantage should show in its income statement an amount for income tax expense that is related to its reported income before taxes. The difference between this amount and the tax actually due and payable for the year is credited (or debited) to an account entitled "Deferred Income Taxes."

4. When the period of accelerated depreciation has ended, the amount accumulated in the Deferred Income Taxes account absorbs the difference between the tax on the reported income and the tax actually payable for those later years. The income tax expense will then bear a constant relationship to income before taxes year by year, and the temporary tax advantage will have no significant influence on the income statement.

Tax Expense Greater Than Tax Payable   For the example given, the income tax expense reported in the income statement each year would be $20,000, the amount obtained if the $40,000 (pretax accounting income) is multiplied by the tax rate of 50%. The difference between this amount and the $15,000 of tax actually payable in each of the first five years is $5,000, which would be credited to Deferred Income Taxes. This could be accomplished with the following entry:

Income Tax Expense	20,000	
Income Tax Payable		15,000
Deferred Income Taxes		5,000

At the end of the five years the Deferred Income Taxes account would have five credits of $5,000 each as follows:

Deferred Income Taxes	
1977	5,000
1978	5,000
1979	5,000
1980	5,000
1981	5,000

The Deferred Income Taxes account balance is presented on the balance sheet in the liability section.

During the next five years, the income tax actually payable each year, as shown in the tax return computations, will be $25,000. The income statement for business purposes will continue to show income of $40,000 before taxes. The appropriate tax on this amount is $20,000, and the difference between this amount and the tax payable is $5,000. Thus, for each of the last five years of the asset's life, a charge of $5,000 to the Deferred Income Taxes account should be made as follows:

Income Tax Expense	20,000	
Deferred Income Taxes	5,000	
Income Tax Payable		25,000

If at the end of 1981 we divide the balance of the Deferred Income Taxes account, $25,000, by the remaining five years of life of the asset, we get an amount of $5,000 a year, the difference between the actual tax paid each year and the apparent tax on the company's income statement. At the end of the asset's life, the Deferred Income Taxes account would appear as follows:

Deferred Income Taxes			
1982	5,000	1977	5,000
1983	5,000	1978	5,000
1984	5,000	1979	5,000
1985	5,000	1980	5,000
1986	5,000	1981	5,000

Partial Income Statement
(WITH INTERPERIOD TAX ALLOCATION)

	For Tax Purposes	For Accounting Purposes
EACH OF THE FIRST 5 YEARS:		
Gross income	$300,000	$300,000
Costs and expenses	250,000	250,000
	50,000	50,000
Depreciation	20,000	10,000
Income before income tax	30,000	40,000
Income tax payable	15,000	
Income tax expense		20,000
Net income for the year	$ 15,000	$ 20,000
EACH OF THE REMAINING 5 YEARS:		
Gross income	$300,000	$300,000
Costs and expenses	250,000	250,000
	50,000	50,000
Depreciation	0	10,000
Income before income tax	50,000	40,000
Income tax payable	25,000	
Income tax expense		20,000
Net income for the year	$ 25,000	$ 20,000

Thus, by this allocation of income taxes, the income tax expense during each period in which the asset is used is unaffected by the decision to use accelerated depreciation for income tax purposes. The temporary tax advantage, although of real significance for financial purposes, has no influence on reported net income. The tax return calculations and the income statements appear on the lower half of page 886. Note that the business purpose income statements indicate the same net income for each of the first five years as for each of the following five; the income tax return, however, is not affected by the allocation of taxes to periods based on accounting income.

The income statements for accounting purposes with tax allocation on page 886 should be compared with the accounting income statements without tax allocation as presented on page 884. Note that the **tax effect of a timing difference** in any year is found by computing income taxes both with and without the timing difference. The difference in the computations is the amount charged or credited to the deferred income tax account.

Tax Payable Greater Than Tax Expense   To illustrate a timing difference that results in a greater tax payable in the first year than is recorded as tax expense, the following data are taken from the tax returns of Cardella Corporation:

Income Tax Return			
	Years Ended December 31		
	1980	1981	1982
Revenue from sales	$140,000	$190,000	$160,000
Rent	180,000		
Total revenues	320,000	190,000	160,000
Deductible expenses	120,000	150,000	130,000
Taxable income	$200,000	$ 40,000	$ 30,000

The income statements of Cardella Corporation before tax computations appear below:

Income Statement			
	Years Ended December 31		
	1980	1981	1982
Revenue from sales	$140,000	$190,000	$160,000
Rent	20,000	120,000	40,000
Total revenues	160,000	310,000	200,000
Operating expenses	120,000	150,000	130,000
Income before federal taxes	$ 40,000	$160,000	$ 70,000

The only differences between the tax returns and the income statements relate to rent. For tax purposes, $180,000 of rent collected November 1, 1980, relating to the 18-month period ending April 30, 1982, was included entirely in 1980 taxable income. For book purposes, the rent was recognized as income earned ratably over the 18 months. Assuming an average income tax rate of 40% in effect for each year, the tax payable and the tax expense are computed as follows:

	1980	1981	1982
Income tax payable:			
($200,000 × 40%)	$80,000		
($ 40,000 × 40%)		$16,000	
($ 30,000 × 40%)			$12,000
Income tax expense:			
($ 40,000 × 40%)	$16,000		
($160,000 × 40%)		$64,000	
($ 70,000 × 40%)			$28,000

Note that over the three-year period the total income tax payable of $108,000 ($80,000 + $16,000 + $12,000) in the tax returns is equal to the income tax expense of $108,000 ($16,000 + $64,000 + $28,000) in the income statements. The difference is in the timing of revenue recognition.

The interperiod income tax allocations are recorded in the accounts at each year end as follows:

December 31, 1980		
Income Tax Expense	16,000	
Deferred Income Taxes ($160,000 × 40%)	64,000	
Income Taxes Payable		80,000

December 31, 1981		
Income Tax Expense	64,000	
Deferred Income Taxes ($120,000 × 40%)		48,000
Income Taxes Payable		16,000

December 31, 1982		
Income Tax Expense	28,000	
Deferred Income Taxes ($40,000 × 40%)		16,000
Income Taxes Payable		12,000

In the example above Deferred Income Taxes has a debit balance and would be classified as a deferred charge.

METHODS OF INTERPERIOD TAX ALLOCATION

The foregoing discussion and illustrations have assumed that the tax rate did not change during the life of the assets involved. Tax rates do change, however. Therefore, should the tax rate in effect when the "timing difference" originated be used to measure the tax effect, or should the tax rates expected to be in effect in the relevant future years be used to measure the tax effect? The first alternative, an integral part of the **deferred method,** has been adopted by the profession and is used almost universally in practice. The second alternative, an integral part of the **liability method,** is not acceptable practice and not in common usage, although it is advocated by some accountants. These two methods, along with the **net of tax method,** constitute the three different methods or concepts of accounting for the tax effects of timing differences.

Deferred Method

Under the deferred method the tax effects of timing differences that reduce taxes currently payable are treated as deferred credits, while the tax effects of timing differences that increase taxes currently payable are treated as deferred charges. **The amount of the deferred tax is based on the tax rate in effect when the timing difference originates, and is not adjusted to reflect subsequent changes in the rate or the imposition of new taxes.** Advocates of the deferred method are divided about whether the deferred credit is a liability and whether the expectation of future taxable income is a prerequisite to recognition of the deferred charge or credit.

Liability Method

Under the liability method the differences between income tax expense and income taxes payable in the periods in which the timing differences originate are either liabilities for taxes payable in the future or assets for prepaid taxes. **The amounts of the estimated future tax liabilities or prepaid taxes are computed at the tax rates expected to be in effect during the periods in which the timing differences reverse.** Advocates of this method believe that the initial computation is an estimate, is tentative, and is subject to future adjustment if the tax rate changes or new taxes are imposed. Ordinarily, the most reasonable assumption about future tax rates is that the current tax rate will continue. If a rate change is known or reasonably certain at the time of the initial computation, however, the anticipated rate would be used under the liability method.[3]

Net of Tax Method

Different from and yet related to the deferred and liability methods is the **net of tax method.** Under the net of tax method it is assumed that taxability and tax deductibility are factors in the valuation of individual assets and liabilities, that is, **the tax effects are applied to adjust the carrying amounts of specific assets or liabilities and the related revenues and expenses.** For example, depreciation is said to reduce the value of an asset both because of a decline in economic usefulness and because of a loss of a portion of future tax deductibility; accelerated tax depreciation uses up a portion of the asset value more rapidly than does straight-line depreciation. Therefore, depreciation in the financial statements should include, in addition to an amount for straight-line depreciation, an amount equal to

---

[3]Recently, the use of the liability method to account for deferred income taxes has been receiving increased attention. Some individuals are expressing concern that the deferred credit treatment currently required is not well understood by financial statement users. In addition, some companies are contending that if these taxes are effectively postponed for a period of time, deferred income taxes should be discounted. Such an approach is consistent with the liability method of accounting for deferred income taxes. Finally, the FASB appears sympathetic to the liability approach. For example, in a recent pronouncement involving the presentation of supplementary price-level data, the board indicated that deferred income taxes should be treated as a liability in computing certain price-level information. The conceptual framework study on the elements of financial reporting may provide the answer to the FASB's long-term position on this subject.

the tax effect of the excess of tax depreciation over book depreciation. Because it is customary to adjust the asset, liability, revenue, or expense directly, these items are presented "net of tax" amounts. In theory the net of tax method, like the liability method, applies the anticipated future tax rates in effect during the life of the asset. But, in practice, the amortization of cost attributed to the loss of tax deductibility is recorded, as it is under the deferred method, at the rate in effect when the timing difference originates.[4]

Desirability of Income Tax Allocation

The desirability of using the deferred income tax procedure is not unanimously agreed upon. Some accountants and others believe that the appropriate tax to be shown in the income statement is the tax actually levied in that year, not the amount of tax that would have been payable if the company had not enjoyed certain special tax benefits. Some also believe that the nature of the Deferred Income Taxes account (credit balance) itself is not clear. They believe that at the time the account is established it is not really a liability, because at that time it is not payable to anyone. Only if the company continues to make a profit and if tax rates remain the same will the company be required to pay additional tax in the future.

In **Opinion No. 11** the APB submitted the following rationale as theoretical justification for the propriety of interperiod tax allocation:

(a) The operations of an entity subject to income taxes are expected to continue on a going concern basis, in the absence of evidence to the contrary, and income taxes are expected to continue to be assessed in the future.

(b) Income taxes are an expense of business enterprises earning income subject to tax.

(c) Accounting for income tax expense requires measurement and identification with the appropriate time period and therefore involves accrual, deferral and estimation concepts in the same manner as these concepts are applied in the measurement and time period identification of other expenses.

(d) Matching is one of the basic processes of income determination; essentially it is a process of determining relationships between costs (including reductions of costs) and (1) specific revenues or (2) specific accounting periods. Expenses of the current period consist of those costs which are identified with the revenues of the current period and those costs which are identified with the current period on some basis other than revenue. Costs identifiable with future revenues or otherwise identifiable with future periods should be deferred to those future periods. When a cost cannot be related to future revenues or to future periods on some basis other than revenues, or it cannot reasonably be expected to be recovered from future revenues, it becomes, by necessity, an expense of the current period (or of a prior period).[5]

Although the predominant view holds that interperiod tax allocation is appropriate, there are two concepts about the extent to which it should be applied: (1) partial allocation and (2) comprehensive allocation.

---

[4]Homer A. Black, "Interperiod Allocation of Corporate Income Taxes," *Accounting Research Study No. 9* (New York: AICPA, 1966).

[5]"Accounting for Income Taxes," *Opinions of the Accounting Principles Board No. 11* (New York: AICPA, 1967), par. 14.

Partial Allocation Versus Comprehensive Allocation

Under **partial allocation** the general assumption is that the income tax expense for financial statement purposes is the income tax payable for the period covered by the income statement, with the major exception that specific nonrecurring differences between taxable income and pretax accounting income that could lead to a **material** misstatement of income tax expense and net income should be treated as an interperiod allocation. Accountants who hold this view believe that **only nonrecurring, material differences between tax payable and financial accounting tax expense should be allocated between periods,** and then only if such a difference is reasonably expected to be paid as income tax (or recovered as a reduction of income taxes) within a relatively short period of time not exceeding, for example, five years. An example is an **isolated** installment sale in which the gross profit is reported for financial accounting purposes at the date of sale and for tax purposes when collected later.

Under **comprehensive allocation,** income tax expense includes the tax effects of all transactions entering into the determination of pretax accounting income for the period, even though some transactions affect the amount of taxes payable in a different period. In other words, the current accounting period should be charged with all income taxes arising from the current accounting income, regardless of when the taxes are paid. This view recognizes that the amount of income taxes payable for a particular period is not necessarily indicative of the income tax expense relating to the transactions of that period. **Income tax expense encompasses any accrual, deferral, or estimation necessary to adjust the income tax payable to reflect the tax effects of the transactions included in pretax accounting income.** The supporters of this view believe that there is a need to recognize the tax effects of initial differences (both timing and permanent differences) because only by doing so will the income tax expense in the period of initial differences include the tax effects of transactions of those periods. They also contend that the partial allocation concept is a departure from accrual accounting because it emphasizes cash outlays, whereas comprehensive allocation results in a more thorough and consistent approach to the matching of revenues and expenses.

> These differences in viewpoint become most significant with respect to the tax effects of transactions of a recurring nature—for example, depreciation of machinery and equipment using the straight-line method for financial accounting purposes and an accelerated method for income tax purposes. Under partial allocation the tax effects of these timing differences would not be recognized under many circumstances; under comprehensive allocation the tax effects would be recognized beginning in the periods of the initial timing differences. Under partial allocation, the tax effects of these timing differences would not be recognized so long as it is assumed that similar timing differences would arise in the future creating tax effects at least equal to the reversing tax effects of the previous timing differences. Thus, under partial allocation, so long as the amount of deferred taxes is estimated to remain fixed or to increase, no need exists to recognize the tax effects of the initial differences because they probably will not "reverse" in the foreseeable future. Under comprehensive allocation tax effects are recognized as they occur.[6]

---

[6]*Ibid.,* par. 32.

Official Position

The APB adopted comprehensive interperiod tax allocation under the deferred method as the acceptable accounting method, considering it "an integral part of the determination of income tax expense." The Board believed that the tax effects of transactions that determine pretax accounting income either earlier or later than they enter into the computation of taxable income should be recognized both in the periods in which the differences between accounting income and tax income arise and in the periods in which the differences reverse. And, because permanent differences do not affect other periods, the Board contended that interperiod tax allocation is not appropriate to account for such differences.

A significant minority of the Board supported partial allocation; they believed that to the extent that comprehensive allocation deviates from accrual of income tax reasonably expected to be paid or recovered, it results in (1) accounts carried as assets that have no demonstrable value and that are never expected to be realized, (2) amounts carried as liabilities that are mere contigencies, and (3) corresponding charges or credits to income for contingent amounts.

Financial Statement Presentation

Deferred income tax credit is the excess of the accounting income tax expense relative to certain transactions over the income tax payable applicable to those same transactions, and **deferred income tax debit** is the excess of the income tax payable applicable to certain transactions over the accounting income tax expense relative to those same transactions. Classification of deferred income tax credits on the balance sheet as a liability is seriously questioned by some accountants on the grounds that no present debt exists. Other accountants believe that the term "deferred" is a misnomer when used in relation to tax effect credits resulting from tax allocation, because these items have the characteristics of accruals instead of deferrals. Deferred income tax credits are usually reported in the liability section while some companies report them on the balance sheet between the long-term debt and the stockholders' equity sections.

We believe that if income taxes are subject to the basic theory submitted by the APB on page 890, which justifies interperiod tax allocation, then the unpaid tax accrued during a period should be classified as a liability. If it cannot be reasonably established that the tax in question is payable at some future date, no charge against income can be made validly during the period. Denial of the liability aspect of interperiod tax allocation invalidates the incurrence of a current cost.

GAAP Disclosures   Relative to these problems, the APB gave the following interpretation and recommendations for balance sheet treatment:

> Deferred charges and deferred credits relating to timing differences represent the cumulative recognition given to their tax effects and as such do not represent receivables or payables in the usual sense. They should be classified in two categories—one for the net current amount and the other for the net noncurrent amount. This presentation is consistent with the customary distinction between current and noncurrent categories and also recognizes the close relationship among the various deferred tax accounts, all of which bear on the determination of income tax expense. **The current portions of**

such deferred charges and credits should be those amounts which relate to assets and liabilities classified as current. Thus, if installment receivables are a current asset, the deferred credits representing the tax effects of uncollected installment sales should be a current item; if an estimated provision for warranties is a current liability, the deferred charge representing the tax effect of such provision should be a current item.

Deferred taxes represent tax effects recognized in the determination of income tax expense in current and prior periods, and they should, therefore, be excluded from retained earnings or from any other account in the stockholders' equity section of the balance sheet.[7]

SEC Disclosures   For companies reporting the results of operations in form 10-K, the SEC requires that the components of **income tax expense** be segregated into (1) the current and noncurrent components, (2) the tax effects of current period timing differences, and (3) a reconciliation between the effective tax rate indicated by the book income and the statutory income tax rate.

The reason for this disclosure is twofold: first, when the oil companies in the mid seventies were considered to have earned excess profits, many politicians and other interested parties attempted to determine the effective tax rates of these companies. Because this information was not available in published financial reports, pressure was exerted on the SEC to require this type of disclosure. Second, many investors are interested in the reconciliation of the book income to taxable income to assess the quality of the company's earnings. Earnings that are enhanced by a favorable tax effect should be examined carefully, particularly if the tax effect is nonrecurring. For example, Wang Laboratories reported net income of $3.3 million, or 82 cents a share, versus $3.1 million, or 77 cents, in the preceding period. All of the increase in net income and then some resulted from a tax rate that was lower in the current year than in the preceding year (32.6% versus 39%). The difference in the rates was due primarily to the investment credit.

In compliance with the SEC's disclosure requirements, Armco Steel Corporation presented the components of income tax expense in its 1977 annual report as follows:

ARMCO STEEL CORPORATION ($000)	
	1977
Income Taxes (Note 6)	
Currently Paid or Payable	
Federal (after Investment Tax Credits of $16,727 for 1977 and $17,370 for 1976)	$23,651
State and Foreign	29,629
Total	53,180
Deferred (to be recovered in future years)	(51,917)
Total	$ 1,263

Armco's effective tax rate was 1% in 1977, whereas the federal statutory rate was 48%. A reconciliation of the major components causing such a difference was reported as shown at the top of page 894.

---

[7]*Ibid.,* par. 57.

ARMCO STEEL CORPORATION
Tax Rate Reconciliation

	1977	
	Amount	Percent
Tax at statutory rate	$58,126	48.0
Investment tax credits	(45,249)	(37.4)
Equity in net income of Armco Financial		
Corporation and associated companies	(9,983)	(8.3)
Percentage depletion allowance	(6,186)	(5.1)
Other	4,555	3.8
Total	$ 1,263	1.0

For another example refer to the Tenneco Inc. annual report (see pages 199 and 200) footnotes which contain a comprehensive presentation of the components of income tax expense and the variation in tax rates.

Practical Approaches to Application of the Deferred Method

In each of the preceding illustrations of interperiod tax allocation only one item caused the difference between taxable income and accounting income. It was relatively easy to determine the exact tax effect, the build-up of the deferral, and the turn around. This method is called the "individual item basis." The **individual item basis** as an interperiod tax allocation method requires:

1. Determining for each transaction causing a timing difference the initial tax effect and the subsequent reversal.
2. "Drawing down" an equivalent portion of deferred taxes previously provided as a particular timing difference reverses.

If many items cause timing differences, a considerable amount of record keeping is required under this method. As a result it is applied mostly in situations where a few large differences constitute the basis for allocation.

In practice, however, it is typical for a corporation to have a multitude of transactions handled differently for tax purposes than for accounting purposes. Although some items are originating, effecting increases to deferred income taxes, others are reversing, effecting decreases. When it becomes impractical to identify, follow, and account for each individual transaction, one of two acceptable alternatives may be applied to simplify computation of the tax effect. These two methods are called (1) the "group-of-similar-items, gross change basis" and (2) the "group-of-similar-items, net change basis" or simply the "gross change method" and the "net change method."

Gross Change Method

Under the **gross change method** the net change in deferred income taxes is determined by a combination of amounts representing (1) the tax effects arising from timing differences originating in the period at the current tax rates, and (2) reversals of tax effects arising from timing differences originating in prior periods at the prior tax rates. The following steps outline the gross change method:

1. Group similar timing differences, that is, all installment method transactions, or all accelerated depreciation items.
2. Calculate the tax effects arising from timing differences originating in the current period at the current tax rate.
3. Determine the tax effects on reversals of timing differences that originated in prior periods using the applicable prior-period tax rates.
4. The difference between (2) and (3) constitutes the net change in deferred taxes for the period.

Under this method, computation of the write-down (amortization) of deferred taxes during the period when the timing difference is reversed is at the tax rates that were in effect when the timing difference originated. If the balance in deferred income taxes consists of layers of accumulated balances at different tax rates, a FIFO or an average rate may be used for selecting the tax rates to be applied to the reversing timing differences. If the FIFO basis is employed, a record must be maintained of all the originating differences and the rate at which they originated. As these timing differences reverse, the first-in differences are the amounts first reversed. If an average rate basis is used, the amount of the reduction in deferred taxes is determined by multiplying the reversing amount by the weighted average tax rate in effect in prior periods. This weighted average tax rate is equal to the ratio of (a) aggregate deferred taxes at the beginning of the period to (b) aggregate timing differences at the beginning of the period.

The gross change basis is similar to the individual-item basis in that the tax effects of timing differences are reversed (drawn down) at the same tax rate at which they originated. The two bases are different in that **the gross change basis groups similar timing differences and the individual-item basis does not.** The gross change basis is a practical extension of the individual-item basis.

Net Change Method

Under the **net change method,** the net change in deferred income taxes for a period is calculated by a differential calculation of taxes with and without the net change in timing differences. The tax effects are not applied to specific timing differences as they arise and reverse but, instead, are **associated with net changes in the aggregate** of such differences. In other words, similar types of timing differences can be grouped together even though some of the differences within the group may be originating while others are reversing.

Illustration of Gross Change and Net Change Methods

To illustrate the differing effect of the gross change method and the net change method on the deferred taxes account, assume that Higgins Corporation had the following timing differences and deferred taxes for the last four years:

Year	Timing Difference	Tax Rate	Deferred Taxes
1977	$ 5,000	50%	$2,500
1978	4,000	45%	1,800
1979	6,000	45%	2,700
1980	2,000	40%	800
	$17,000		$7,800

The average rate for the four preceding periods is approximately 45.9% $\left(\dfrac{\$7,800}{\$17,000}\right)$. In 1981, the company reported taxable income of $103,000 and pretax accounting income of $106,000. The difference resulted because the company has a current excess of depreciation for tax purposes over depreciation for book purposes of $10,000 (originating difference).[8] In addition, the company currently reports $7,000 of gross profit on installment sales for tax purposes; this had been recognized in prior years for accounting purposes (reversing difference). The net effect is a $3,000 excess of pretax accounting income over taxable income. The tax rate for 1981 is 42%. A reconciliation of taxable income to pretax accounting income and the computation of income taxes payable is provided below:

Reconciliation and Computation of Taxes Payable	
Taxable income	$103,000
Originating difference	
Tax depreciation in excess of book depreciation	**10,000**
Reversing difference	
Tax gross profit on installment sales in excess of book gross profit on installment sales	(7,000)
Pretax accounting income	$106,000
Taxable income $103,000	
1981 tax rate $\times$ 42%	
Taxes payable $ 43,260	

Computation of the taxes payable, deferred income taxes, and taxes expense under the gross change method and the net change method would be as follows:

Gross change—Average method	
Taxes payable	$43,260
Originating difference $10,000 $\times$ 42% = $ 4,200	
Reversing difference ($ 7,000) $\times$ 45.9% = ($3,213)	
Deferred income taxes change	987
Taxes expense	$44,247

[8]An originating difference is the initial difference between pretax accounting income and taxable income, whether the pretax accounting income exceeds, or is exceeded by, tax income. In this illustration, for example, in the early years when the depreciation expense for tax purposes exceeds the depreciation expense for book purposes, the differences are "originating differences." (In the later years when the depreciation expense for book purposes exceeds the depreciation expense for tax purposes, the differences would be "reversing differences.") The reversing difference in this illustration relates to current recognition for tax purposes of gross profit on installment sales which had been recognized in prior periods for accounting purposes. In this illustration the originating differences are credits to Deferred Income Taxes and the reversing differences are debits to Deferred Income Taxes. Under different circumstances, the originating differences may be debits and the reversing differences credits to Deferred Income Taxes.

Gross change—FIFO method

Taxes payable			$43,260
Originating difference	$10,000 × 42%	= $ 4,200	
Reversing difference	**($ 5,000)** × 50%	= **($2,500)**	
	($ 2,000) × 45%	= ($900)	
Deferred income taxes change			800
Taxes expense			$44,060

Net change method

Taxes payable			$43,260
Originating difference	$10,000 × 42%	= $ 4,200	
Reversing difference	**($ 7,000)** × 42%	= **($2,940)** *	
Deferred income taxes change			1,260
Taxes expense			$44,520

*The originating and reversing differences of $10,000 and ($7,000), respectively, are shown above for purposes of comparison with the gross change method. When the net change method is applied in practice, the originating and reversing differences are not separately identified; only the net change of $3,000 is identified.

The **taxes payable** is unaffected whether the gross change or net change method is employed. If the tax rate was the same in all periods, the tax expense and the deferred income tax amounts would be the same under both methods. But, because of tax rate changes, the methods produce different results. Under the gross change method the reversing differences are reversed (amortized) at a tax rate applicable to a prior period(s) in which the timing difference(s) originated. Under the net change method, the reversing differences are reversed at the tax rate applicable to the period of the reversal.

Depending on whether taxable income exceeds pretax accounting income or vice versa in the year of origination, the originating difference may be either a debit or credit; likewise, the reversing difference may be a debit or credit depending upon what the originating difference was. That is, the originating and reversing differences may be in either direction depending on the circumstances.

Under the net change method no amortization of deferred taxes is recorded for periods in which the aggregate timing differences **increase.** Instead an amount equal to the tax effect of the aggregate increase in timing differences will be added to the deferred tax account. In each period in which the aggregate timing differences **decrease** deferred taxes are amortized, but never in excess of the amounts previously provided. In a period when reversal of all timing differences of a particular type occurs, the entire related deferred tax account should be amortized regardless of the amount determined under the current computation. For example, if a company that has been using the installment method for tax purposes abandons that method by selling all installment receivables, then the entire amount of deferred tax credits relative to installment sales which was carried over from the preceding period should be amortized.[9]

[9]Donald J. Bevis and Raymond E. Perry, "Accounting for Income Taxes," *An Interpretation of APB Opinion No. 11* (New York: AICPA, 1969), p. 20.

Criteria for Choosing Between Methods

The illustrative cases above were based on simple nonrecurring timing differences where reversals of specific or similar items could be readily identified. In practice, many timing differences are self-perpetuating; new ones replace old ones. Furthermore, the net change method of providing deferred taxes does not require that deferred taxes be identified with specific timing differences. When timing differences originate at one rate and reverse at another, credits or debits will accumulate in the balance sheet which have no relationship to the cumulative timing differences at the balance sheet date.

Because of these problems, both the short-run and the long-run effects of the alternative methods of income tax allocation must be reviewed. Where cumulative timing differences are expected to increase continuously over a number of years, or level off after a period of time, tax rate changes will have no significant impact on net income as a result of adopting the net change method of allocation. Accordingly, the net change method, which is the easiest to apply, appears most desirable in these circumstances.

On the other hand, where cumulative timing differences are expected to reverse, rate changes during periods of reversal can result in the reporting of tax expense that is considerably in excess of (or less than) the statutory rate. In these cases, the gross change method (or individual-item basis) appears more appropriate.

When individual groupings of originating differences can be identified by year, the FIFO method is usually considered most appropriate. An example would be the establishment of a liability for warranties with losses recognized in subsequent periods. When it is difficult to identify individual items or groupings, as it is with a great number of depreciable assets, the average basis is generally selected.

Although the net change method is the more popular method in practice, the gross change method is considered theoretically more accurate.

THE WITH AND WITHOUT TECHNIQUE

The presentation thus far in this chapter has illustrated the deferred tax computation as simply the current tax rate times the timing differential. This is referred to as the **"short-cut method."** In practice, however, owing to the interplay of such items as the surtax exemption, special tax rates, investment credits, foreign tax credits, and operating losses, the deferred tax is frequently computed using the **"with and without timing differences technique."** The following steps are involved in applying this technique:

1. Compute the income tax that would have been paid on pretax accounting income (adjusted for any permanent differences). All special tax rates and credits are applied to pretax accounting income **as if it were taxable income** on which tax would be paid. This represents the without portion of the computation (i.e., **without** the timing differences involved).

2. Compute the income tax on **pretax accounting income** after **all originating** timing differences have been included, again applying the same special tax rates and credits as in the first computation. This represents the with portion of the computation (i.e., **with** timing differences involved).

3. The difference between (1) the pro forma tax based on pretax accounting income **without** the timing differences and (2) the pro forma tax based on pretax accounting income

with the originating timing differences represents the current year's income statement deferred tax provision. (Note that the reversing differences are amortized using either the gross or net change method. The differences between the originating and reversing differences provide the net change in the deferred income tax balance.)

The following example illustrates one application of the with and without technique. Assume that the tax rate is 22% on the first $25,000 and 48% thereafter.

Computation of Taxes Payable		
	1980	1981
Pretax accounting income	$50,000	$35,000
Timing difference—		
Excess of tax over book depreciation	(20,000)	(15,000)
Taxable income	$30,000	$20,000
Taxes currently payable (computed on taxable income)—	$ 5,500[a]	$ 4,400[b]
	2,400[c]	
Taxes payable	$ 7,900	$ 4,400

[a]$25,000 × 22%
[b]$20,000 × 22%
[c]$ 5,000 × 48%

On the basis of the data above the deferred tax provisions for 1980 and 1981 are computed as follows using the with and without technique.

(1) Tax computed on pretax accounting income **without** timing difference:

	1980		1981	
Tax Bracket	Income (Without)	Tax Expense	Income (Without)	Tax Expense
$0–$25,000	$25,000 × 22% =	$ 5,500	$25,000 × 22% =	$ 5,500
Over $25,000	25,000 × 48% =	12,000	10,000 × 48% =	4,800
	$50,000	$17,500	$35,000	$10,300

(2) Tax computed on pretax accounting income **with** timing difference:

	1980		1981	
Tax Bracket	Income (With)	Tax Payable	Income (With)	Tax Payable
$0–$25,000	$25,000 × 22% =	$5,500	$20,000 × 22% =	$4,400
Over $25,000	5,000 × 48% =	2,400	-0- × 48% =	-0-
	$30,000	$7,900	$20,000	$4,400

(3) Deferred tax provision:

	1980	1981
$17,500–$7,900 (tax expense minus tax payable)	$ 9,600	
$10,300–$4,400 (tax expense minus tax payable)		$ 5,900

Under the short-cut method the deferred tax would have been computed in 1980 as $9,600 ($20,000 × 48%) and in 1981 as $7,200 ($15,000 × 48%); 1980 would be correct but not 1981. The amount deferred in 1981 is not 48% times the timing difference, as happened to be the case in 1980, but owing to the interplay of the surtax exemption the deferral is at an effective rate somewhere between 22% and 48%. This illustrates that the "short-cut method" of applying the current tax rate to the amount of timing differences should be used only when there is no possibility that special tax rates or credits will apply.

ACCOUNTING FOR NET OPERATING LOSSES

The federal tax laws permit corporations that experience alternate periods of income and loss to equalize their tax burden through carryback and carryforward provisions. Under these provisions a corporation that has been profitable but has a current-year loss has one of two options. One option is **to carry the loss back three years** (receiving refunds for income taxes paid in those years) and the remaining unused loss forward seven years. The other option is not to carry the loss back but **to carry it forward for seven years** as a reduction of income taxes that would otherwise be paid on income of those future years.[10] Once an option is selected, it is irrevocable.

Operating losses can be substantial. Penn Central's loss carryforward is estimated to be $1 billion. Companies that have suffered substantial losses are often attractive merger candidates because in certain cases the acquirer may use these losses to reduce its income taxes.

Loss Carryback

If a corporation suffers a loss in a period following periods of net income, a refund of prior-period taxes may be claimed. In such cases the accounting treatment as stated in **APB Opinion No. 11** is quite clear:

> The tax effects of any realizable loss carrybacks should be recognized in the determination of net income (loss) of the loss periods. The tax loss gives rise to a refund (or claim for refund) of past taxes, which is both measurable and currently realizable; therefore the tax effect of the loss is properly recognizable in the determination of net income (loss) for the loss period.[11]

---

[10]The election to forego the three-year carryback period might be advantageous where a taxpayer had investment credit carryovers that might be wiped out and lost because of the carryback of the net operating loss.

[11]APB Opinion No. 11, par. 44.

To illustrate, Remmers Corporation reports a net operating loss for the year 1980 of $100,000 after having reported profits in the three preceding years of $50,000 in 1977, $40,000 in 1978, and $35,000 in 1979; the average tax rates were 40% in 1977, 40% in 1978, and 50% in 1979, and is 50% in 1980. The total income tax paid in 1977, 1978, and 1979 was $53,500. The accounting and taxable income (or loss) coincide for all years, and the entire $100,000 is available without reduction for carryback purposes. The claim for tax refund amounts to $41,000, computed as follows (carryback to the earliest year first):

Year	Income	Rate	Tax Refund
1977	$50,000 × 40%		$20,000
1978	$40,000 × 40%		16,000
1979	$10,000 × 50%		5,000
Total			$41,000

The following journal entry is appropriate in 1980:

Income Tax Refund Receivable	41,000	
Refund of Income Taxes Due to Loss Carryback		41,000

The refund is reported on the income statement in the year of the loss as follows:

Operating loss before income tax effect	$(100,000)
Less: refund of prior year's income taxes due to loss carryback	41,000
Net loss	$ (59,000)

The refund receivable should be reflected in the balance sheet as a current asset.

Note that if the loss is carried back, the loss must be applied to the earliest year first. If the loss in the current year exceeds the total income from the three preceding years, the remainder of the loss is be carried forward.

Loss Carryforward

If it is decided not to carry the operating loss back, or the operating loss is not fully absorbed through a carryback, it can be carried forward for seven succeeding years. As with the carryback provision, the operating loss must be applied to the earliest year in which income is reported. Because the value of the loss carryforward is dependent on future earnings to provide the income tax offset, the realization of a future tax savings is not assured and the proper accounting treatment in the loss year is not obvious. The APB rendered the following conclusion:

> The tax effects of **loss carryforwards** also relate to the determination of net income (loss) of the loss periods. However, a significant question generally exists as to realization of the tax effects of the carryforwards, since realization is dependent upon future taxable income. Accordingly, the Board has concluded that the tax benefits of loss carryforwards should not be recognized until they are actually realized, except in unusual circumstances when realization is **assured beyond any reasonable doubt** at the time the loss carryforwards arise. When the tax benefits of loss carryforwards are not

recognized until realized in full or in part in subsequent periods, the tax benefits should be reported in the results of operations of those periods as extraordinary items.

In those rare cases in which realization of the tax benefits of loss carryforwards is assured beyond any reasonable doubt, the potential benefits should be associated with the periods of loss and should be recognized in the determination of results of operations for those periods.[12]

To illustrate the two possible accounting treatments, assume that Norton Corporation suffered a $200,000 net operating loss in 1980, its first year of operations, when the tax rate was 40%. The tax savings value of the 1980 loss is dependent on future taxable income.

If realization of the future tax savings is "assured beyond any reasonable doubt," Norton Corporation may recognize the tax carryforward as an **asset** (future tax benefit) and reduce the current operating loss by the amount of the tax carryforward. The tax carryforward of $80,000 ($200,000 × 40%) is recorded in 1980 through this journal entry:

Estimated Future Tax Benefits—Loss Carryforward	80,000	
Reduction of Loss Due to Tax Carryforward		80,000

The lower portion of the income statement in 1980 would appear as follows:

Operating loss before income tax effect	$200,000
Less: reduction of loss due to tax carryforward	80,000
Net loss	$120,000

If in 1981 the Norton Corporation experiences $600,000 income before taxes, the following entry is recorded in 1981 assuming a 40% tax rate:

Income Tax Expense	240,000	
Estimated Future Tax Benefits—Loss Carryforward		80,000
Income Taxes Payable		160,000

The 1981 income statement would appear as follows:

Income before taxes	$600,000
Less: income tax expense	240,000
Net income	$360,000

If the Norton Corporation is not assured of future earnings against which to offset its 1980 loss, the tax carryforward should not be recognized in the loss year. Instead, it should be recognized as an **extraordinary item** in the future periods when the tax saving is realized. Therefore, in 1980 Norton Corporation would make no entry for income tax, and would report a net operating loss of $200,000 on its income statement.

If in this situation the Norton Corporation experiences a $600,000 pretax accounting income in 1981, the following entry would be recorded:

---

[12]*Ibid.*, par. 45 and 46.

Income Tax Expense	240,000	
Tax Reduction Due to Loss Carryforward—Extraordinary Item		80,000
Income Taxes Payable		160,000

The lower portion of the income statement in 1981 would appear as follows:

Income before income taxes	$600,000
Income taxes	240,000
Income before extraordinary item	360,000
Extraordinary item:	
Tax reduction due to loss carryforward	80,000
Net income	$440,000

The APB provided the following insight into situations where realization is assured beyond any reasonable doubt:

> Realization of the tax benefit of a loss carryforward would appear to be assured beyond any reasonable doubt when **both** of the following conditions exist: (a) the loss results from an identifiable, isolated and nonrecurring cause and the company either has been continuously profitable over a long period or has suffered occasional losses which were more than offset by taxable income in subsequent years, and (b) future taxable income is virtually certain to be large enough to offset the loss carryforward and will occur soon enough to provide realization during the carryforward period.[13]

Summary

Interperiod tax allocation represents one of the most challenging and complex areas in accounting practice. The presentation in this chapter has been kept purposely uncomplicated in the hope that comprehension of the basic theory along with some of the mechanics may be readily obtained. For example, the tax and accounting losses from operations were assumed to be the same in amount as were the taxable income and pretax accounting income for all years involved in our illustrations; that is, there were no timing differences that further complicated implementation of any carryback and carryforward provisions. In practice, however, it is common for a loss carryback to occur when net deferred tax debits or credits exist. Under these circumstances it may be necessary in the loss period to adjust the net deferred tax balance.

Questions

1. In what basic ways do the objectives of determining taxable income differ from the objectives of measuring accounting income?
2. It is sometimes contended that the federal income tax is not an expense but a sharing of profits with the government. Do you agree? Why or why not?
3. As controller for Genuine Products Company, you are asked to meet with the board of directors to discuss the company's income tax situation. Several members of the board express concern over the fact that the company is reporting a larger amount of income

[13]*Ibid.*, par. 47.

tax expense on its published income statements than is to be paid to the federal government with the company's income tax return for that same year.
(a) Explain to the board members the accounting rationale for this discrepancy.
(b) How might this difference between tax paid and tax expense have arisen?

4. Describe two items that account for taxable income being higher than accounting income.

5. Describe two items that account for accounting income being higher than taxable income.

6. Explain what a permanent difference is in the interperiod allocation of income taxes. Give three examples.

7. Explain what a timing difference is in the interperiod allocation of income taxes. Give three examples.

8. What are the various methods of interperiod tax allocation? Explain each and identify the one adopted by the APB.

9. What is the theoretical rationale for allocating income taxes between periods?

10. What two concepts exist about the extent to which interperiod tax allocation should be applied? Elaborate briefly on each concept.

11. What method of interperiod income tax allocation has the accounting profession adopted and why?

12. How are deferred charges and deferred credits, arising from income tax allocation, treated on the balance sheet?

13. Explain the "individual-item basis" of interperiod tax allocation.

14. What are the steps that are involved in applying the "gross-change method"?

15. Explain the "net-change method" of applying interperiod income tax allocation.

16. What is the basic difference between the "gross-change method" and the "net-change method"?

17. In what circumstances is application of the "gross-change method" more desirable than application of the "net-change method"? In what circumstances is it less desirable?

18. What is the tax effect of a sustained large operating loss to a corporation after it has operated profitably for several consecutive years?

19. Differentiate between "carrybacks" and "carryforwards." Which can be accounted for with the greater certainty when they arise? Why?

20. What are the alternatives in accounting for a loss carryforward? What are the circumstances that determine the alternative to be applied?

Cases

C20-1 Income tax allocation is an integral part of generally accepted accounting principles. The applications of intraperiod tax allocation (within a period) and interperiod tax allocation (among periods) are both required.

Instructions

(a) Explain the need for **intraperiod** tax allocation (covered in Chapter 4).

(b) Accountants who favor **interperiod** tax allocation argue that income taxes are an expense rather than a distribution of earnings. Explain the significance of this argument. **Do not explain the definitions of expense or distribution of earnings.**

(c) Indicate and explain whether each of the following **independent** situations should be treated as a timing difference or a permanent difference.
1. Estimated warranty costs (covering a three-year warranty) are expensed for accounting purposes at the time of sale but deducted for income tax purposes when incurred.

2. Depreciation for accounting and income tax purposes differs because of different bases of carrying the related property. The different bases are a result of a business combination treated as a purchase for accounting purposes and as a tax-free exchange for income tax purposes.
3. A company properly uses the equity method to account for its 30% investment in another company. The investee pays dividends that are about 10% of its annual earnings.

(d) Discuss the nature of the deferred income tax accounts and possible classifications in a company's statement of financial position.

C20-2   Listed below are 19 of the more common items that are treated differently for accounting and tax purposes.

1. Charitable contributions—excess of book cost over tax limitation. T
2. Fine for polluting. P
3. Income discovered after closing but included in the tax return. T
4. Excess of tax depreciation over book depreciation. T
5. Tax-exempt interest income. P   _____   based on % of revenue (tax) 20% revenue
6. Percentage depletion over cost depletion. P   financial accounting
7. Excess of charge to tax return over charge to books for estimated uncollectibles. T
8. Excess of accrued pension expense over amount paid. T
9. Excess of fair market value of a charitable contribution (deductible for taxes) over cost T (charged to expense).
10. Installment sales income for book purposes exceeds tax income. T
11. Expenses incurred in obtaining tax-exempt income. P
12. A trademark acquired directly from the government is amortized for tax purposes and expensed per the books in this period. T
13. Prepaid advertising expense deferred on the books and deducted as an expense for tax purposes. T
14. Premiums paid on life insurance of officers (corporation beneficiary). P
15. Amortization of goodwill. P
16. Proceeds of life insurance policies on lives of officers. P
17. Estimated future warranty costs. T
18. Excess of research and development cost per tax return over book. T
19. Carryover from prior years of excess charitable contribution over limitation. T

Instructions

Indicate whether the items are **permanent** differences or **timing** differences and whether the **originating** difference will result in a debit to deferred taxes or a credit to deferred taxes.

C20-3   In its financial statements for 1980 the Clear Glass Company reports an item—Deferred Federal Income Tax, $351,000. The president in his letter to stockholders states that this is in connection with a five-year accelerated amortization allowed by the federal government.

Instructions

(a) Explain the nature of this item on the financial statement, and the accounting theory involved in this procedure.
(b) Assuming straight-line depreciation with no salvage value, give the journal entries that were probably made to record this item, and the entries that will affect this account in future years. Entries that will be repeated over a number of years may be so labeled. (Assume a 20-year life, a cost of $4,500,000 for the assets involved, and a flat 52% corporation tax rate.)

Exercises

E20-1 The pretax accounting income of Costumes Company has differed from that of its taxable income throughout each of the last four years as follows:

Year	Pretax Accounting Income	Taxable Income	Tax Rate
1979	$270,000	$180,000	50%
1980	300,000	225,000	40%
1981	330,000	270,000	40%
1982	360,000	480,000	40%

Pretax accounting income for each year includes an expense of $10,000 from the amortization of goodwill, which is not deductible for tax purposes.

Instructions

Prepare journal entries to reflect income tax allocation in all four years using the deferred method. Assume that the reversing differences in 1982 originated in 1979.

E20-2 Because of a timing difference in an expense item, Executone, Inc., reported the following tax and accounting income:

	1979	1980	1981
Taxable income	$ 90,000	$135,000	$225,000
Pretax accounting income	150,000	120,000	180,000

The company's income is taxed at a 48% rate.

Instructions

Prepare the year-end journal entries to accrue its income tax liability and to reflect tax allocation at the end of each of the three years. All differences between taxable income and pretax accounting income are the result of timing differences.

E20-3 The income statements of Airport Limo, Inc. for a three-year period provide the following data:

	1980	1981	1982
Income before depreciation	150,000	170,000	190,000
Depreciation (asset with 3-year life)	30,000	30,000	30,000
Pretax income after depreciation	120,000	140,000	160,000

A 45% tax rate is applicable to all three years. The sum-of-the-years'-digits method is used for tax-depreciation purposes.

Instructions

Prepare the journal entry for each year to record the income tax expense and the income tax payable.

E20-4 Dingbat Manufacturing Company has recently completed a $1,800,000 plant that it is permitted to depreciate, for purposes of income taxation, over a period of 60 months from the date the plant became operational, October 31, 1980. Dingbat Company plans to use this favorable procedure but wishes to charge depreciation for book purposes on the basis of a 20-year life.

Instructions

(a) Prepare entries in journal form to record depreciation (straight-line depreciation with no salvage value) of plant and to record income taxes at the close of the first complete year of operations. Assume that taxable income was $580,000 and that the applicable tax rate is 52%.

(b) Reproduce the deferred income taxes account as it should appear in the general ledger of Dingbat Manufacturing Company after closing October 31, 1990.

E20-5 The following information about Carla Collin Co. is provided:

	1980	1981	1982
Pretax Accounting Income	$80,000	$95,000	$60,000
Taxable Income	60,000	65,000	75,000

Instructions

(a) Assuming a tax rate of 40% and that the differences in income are entirely the result of timing differences, prepare the journal entries at the end of each year to reflect income tax allocation.

(b) Assume the same facts as in (a) except that in 1981, $10,000 of the income reflected in pretax accounting income is from interest on municipal bonds (tax exempt). Prepare any journal entries that would change from what they were in part (a).

E20-6 Summit Co., an installment seller of furniture, records sales on the accrual basis for financial-reporting purposes but on the installment method for tax purposes. As a result, $50,000 of deferred income taxes have been accrued at December 31, 1981. In accordance with trade practice, installment accounts receivable from customers are shown as current assets, although the average collection period is approximately three years.

At December 31, 1981, Summit Co. has recorded a $20,000 deferred income tax debit arising from a book accrual of noncurrent deferred compensation expense which is **not** currently tax deductible.

Also, at December 31, 1981, Summit has accrued $15,000 of deferred income taxes resulting from the use of accelerated depreciation for tax purposes and straight-line depreciation for financial-reporting purposes.

Instructions

How should the deferred income taxes be classified on Summit's December 31, 1981, balance sheet?

(AICPA adapted)

E20-7 Pockets and Cuffs Corporation has an item costing $90,000 that is expensed for tax purposes but is amortized over three years for book purposes. The tax rate is 40% in the year of origination, 1980, and 30% in the years of "turn around," 1981 and 1982. The accounting and tax data for the three years is shown below.

	Financial Accounting	Tax Return
1980 (40% tax rate)		
Income before timing difference	$100,000	$100,000
Timing difference	30,000	90,000
Income after timing difference	$ 70,000	$ 10,000
1981 (30% tax rate)		
Income before timing difference	$100,000	$100,000
Timing difference	30,000	-0-
Income after timing difference	$ 70,000	$100,000
1982 (30% tax rate)		
Income before timing difference	$100,000	$100,000
Timing difference	30,000	-0-
Income after timing difference	$ 70,000	$100,000

Instructions

Prepare the journal entries to record the income tax expense and the income tax payable at the end of each year applying the deferred method.

E20-8   Bouquet Perfume Company uses accelerated depreciation for tax purposes and straight-line depreciation for book purposes. In the current year 1981 the tax rate increased to 55%. The tax rate in all prior years was 35%. Pretax accounting income is $750,000 in 1981 while originating timing differences are $110,000 and reversing timing differences are $84,000.

Instructions

    (a) Compute the change in deferred taxes under (1) the gross change method and (2) the net change method.

    (b) Prepare the journal entry to record the taxes payable, the tax expense, and the deferred taxes for 1981 under (1) the gross change method and (2) the net change method.

E20-9   During your audit of Aroma Wine Company, the following information was disclosed:

    (a)

Year	Amount due per Tax Return
1980	$70,000
1981	64,000

    (b) On January 1, 1980, equipment costing $100,000 was purchased. The equipment has a life of five years and a salvage value of $10,000. The sum-of-the-years'-digits method of depreciation is used for income tax purposes and the straight-line method is used for book purposes.

    (c) In January 1981, $90,000 was collected in advance rental of a building for a three-year period. The entire $90,000 was reported as taxable income in 1981, but $60,000 of the $90,000 was reported as unearned revenue in 1981 for book purposes.

    (d) The tax rate is 40% in both 1980 and 1981.

    (e) The client company used the accepted deferred method of income tax allocation.

Instructions

    (a) Determine the balance in the deferred income tax account at the end of 1980 and whether it is a debit or a credit balance.

    (b) Determine the balance in the deferred income tax account at the end of 1981 and whether it is a debit or a credit balance.

E20-10   Moustafa Rug Company purchased fixed assets that cost $1,200,000 on January 1, 1979. For tax purposes the company is permitted to completely depreciate the assets over three years. For book purposes the company will depreciate the assets over six years. The tax rates for the years involved are 1979, 40%; 1980, 40%; 1981, 50%; 1982, 50%; 1983, 50%; 1984, 50%. The straight-line method of depreciation is applied for both book and tax purposes with zero salvage value estimated.

Instructions

Determine the amount entered in the Deferred Tax account for each year and whether the amount is a debit or a credit to the Deferred Tax account. Assume that depreciation is the only variable involved and that the deferred method on the gross change basis is applied.

    (a) Use the FIFO method to determine the tax rate applicable to reversing differences.

    (b) Use the average method to determine the tax rate applicable to reversing differences.

E20-11 Mike Moluf Taxi Company leases equipment under five-year leases, which require each year's rent to be paid in advance.

At the beginning of the year, there was $300,000 of deferred rental income which for accounting purposes was earned during the year. During the year, $500,000 of taxable rent was collected, of which $250,000 was earned, leaving a balance of $250,000 in the deferred rental income account.

The tax rate in the current year was 40%; in prior years it had been 50%.

Instructions

Compute the income tax expense for the current year and the ending balance in deferred taxes using (a) the gross change method, and (b) the net change method. Book income before taxes was $1,000,000.

E20-12 Taxable income and pretax accounting income would be identical for Great America Co. except for its treatments of rents collected in advance and estimated costs of warranties. The following income computations have been prepared:

Taxable Income	1980	1981	1982
Excess of Revenues over Expenses	$50,000	$70,000	$25,000
Rent Collected	24,000	-0-	-0-
Cost of Warranties	5,000	5,000	5,000
Taxable Income	$69,000	$65,000	$20,000

Pretax Accounting Income	1980	1981	1982
Excess of Revenues over Expenses	$50,000	$70,000	$25,000
Rent Earned	8,000	8,000	8,000
Estimated Cost of Warranties	15,000	-0-	-0-
Income Before Taxes	$43,000	$78,000	$33,000

The tax rates in effect were: 1980—40%; 1981–1982—50%.

Instructions

Prepare the journal entries to reflect income tax expense and payable for each of the years under:
   (a) the net change method.
   (b) the gross change method (FIFO basis).

E20-13 Assume the following for Motts Fruit Company:

Pretax accounting income	$120,000
Taxable income	60,000

Tax rates:	
$0–$25,000	22%
Over $25,000	48%

Pretax accounting income includes $10,000 of interest on tax exempt municipal bonds. Depreciation expense computed under the double-declining balance method (used for tax purposes) exceeds the amount computed under the straight-line method (used for financial accounting purposes) by $50,000.

During the year, the company purchased equipment for $20,000. This equipment qualifies for the investment tax credit of 10%. The company uses the flow-through method to account for the investment tax credit, that is, the current tax payable is reduced by the amount of the investment credit.

Instructions

Compute the amount of income tax expense that will be reported on the income statement, differentiating between the portion that is current and that which is deferred. (Compute the tax using the "with and without" method.)

E20-14   The income of the Cola-Pepsi Company for the year is as follows:

Pretax accounting income	$40,000
Taxable income	68,000

The income figures above include an $18,000 gain on the sale of land; this gain is taxed as a capital gain. The difference between pretax accounting income and taxable income is a result of accruing warranty expense for book purposes, but recording the expense when paid for tax purposes.

The following tax rates are in effect:

$0–$25,000	22%
Over $25,000	48%
Capital gains	30%

Instructions

(a) Prepare the journal entry to record the tax payable, tax expense, and tax deferral for the year using the "with and without method."

(b) What is the amount of the deferral that would have been arrived at applying the short-cut method?

E20-15   The pretax income or (loss) figures for the Suntan Lotion Company are as follows:

1976	$100,000
1977	60,000
1978	30,000
1979	(50,000)
1980	(100,000)
1981	40,000
1982	40,000

Pretax accounting income and taxable income were the same for all years involved. Assume a 50% tax rate for 1976 and 1977, and a 40% rate for the remaining years. In 1979 and 1980, the company is not assured of future earnings against which to offset the loss.

Instructions

Prepare the journal entries for the years 1978 to 1982 to reflect income tax expense and the effects of the loss carrybacks and carryforwards assuming Suntan Lotion Company elects the carryback and the carryforward.

E20-16   Pretzel-Chip Corporation experienced pretax accounting income and taxable income from 1973 through 1981 as follows:

	Income (Loss)	Tax Rate
1973	$10,000	20%
1974	20,000	40%
1975	8,000	40%
1976	32,000	50%
1977	(80,000)	30%
1978	40,000	30%
1979	20,000	40%
1980	70,000	50%
1981	(40,000)	46%

Instructions

(a) What entry for income taxes should have been recorded in 1977 if there was no assurance at that time that taxable income would be reported in the next seven years?

(b) What entry for income taxes should have been recorded in 1977 if taxable income was assured beyond any reasonable doubt in the next seven years?

(c) Indicate what the bottom portion of the income statement in 1978 would look like, assuming that the situation as stated in part (b) above existed in 1977.

E20-17 Taco Still Company reports the following pretax income (loss) for both accounting purposes and tax purposes:

Year	Pretax Income (Loss)	Tax Rate
1979	$40,000	50%
1980	20,000	50%
1981	(80,000)	40%
1982	60,000	40%

Instructions

(a) Prepare the journal entries for the years 1979 to 1982 to reflect tax expense and the allocation of loss carrybacks and carryforwards, assuming that in 1981 Taco Still Company is not assured of future earnings against which to offset the loss.

(b) Prepare the journal entries for 1981 and 1982, assuming that Taco Still Company is assured beyond any reasonable doubt of future earnings against which to offset the loss.

Problems

P20-1 The Rhino Company has fixed assets that cost $400,000 in December 1979, which it is permitted to depreciate for federal income tax purposes over 60 months, beginning January 1, 1980. The net income subject to federal income taxes exceeds $150,000 each year and is taxed at the rate of 52%.

Instructions

What should be the balance of the Deferred Federal Income Tax account in the ledger of the Rhino Company after closing on December 31, 1980, 1984, 1994, and 2000, assuming for book purposes that (a) the fixed assets are to be depreciated over a 20-year life, (b) over a 10-year life, (c) over a 5-year life?

P20-2 The following facts apply to the Camel Fur Company, for the calendar year 1980 (all figures in thousands).

1. Assets are purchased at the beginning of 1980 at a cost of $20,000, 8-year life, double-declining balance depreciation for tax purposes, straight-line in books (assume that no investment credit is permitted); there is no salvage value.

2. Warranty liability of $2,800 provided for book purposes is not deductible for tax purposes until warranty costs are incurred.

3. Income before taxes includes $4,000 related to construction-type contracts still in process which are accounted for on the percentage-of-completion method for book purposes and on the completed contract method for tax purposes.

4. Amortization of goodwill of $800 is not deductible for tax purposes.

5. Investments sold during the year resulted in a gain of $1,000, which is taxed at capital gain rates of 30%.

6. Included in book income is $1,500 of interest on tax-exempt municipal bonds.

7. Pretax accounting income is $24,400.

Instructions

Calculate the income taxes payable and the income tax expense for the year 1980. Assume that the federal income tax rate on ordinary income is 48%.

P20-3 The following information is obtained from the records of Pine Oaks Company:

Year	Pretax Accounting Income	Tax Depr. over (under) Book Depr.	Taxable Income	Tax Paid at 48%
1976	$ 20,000	$ 20,000	-0-	-0-
1977	60,000	20,000	$ 40,000	$ 19,200
1978	120,000	100,000	20,000	9,600
1979	180,000	120,000	60,000	28,800
1980	80,000	(60,000)	140,000	67,200
1981	20,000	(200,000)	220,000	105,600
	$480,000	$ -0-	$480,000	$230,400

Instructions

Prepare a schedule that provides for each of the years above the amount for each of the following column heads:

Income Tax Expense	Income Tax Payable	Increase (Decrease) in Deferred Tax	Balance in Deferred Tax

P20-4 Crop-Keep Corp. manufactures, sells and constructs huge silos. The company was organized and began operations on January 1, 1976. The silo sells for a gross profit of $60,000. One-third of the total sale is collected in the first year and ⅓ in each of the following two years. Twelve silos were sold in 1979, 18 in 1980, and 20 in 1981. There have been no bad debts and none are expected. Gross profit is recognized **in the year of sale for book purposes but is recognized in the year cash is received for tax purposes.** Installment accounts receivable are considered a current asset.

The company's plant and equipment, acquired on January 1, 1979, cost $1,800,000 and is depreciated over a 9-year life with no salvage value. Sum-of-the-years'-digits depreciation is used for tax purposes, and straight-line is used for book purposes. The company owns $100,000 of 5% municipal bonds, the interest on which is nontaxable.

A partial 1981 income statement follows:

Gross profit	$1,200,000
Operating expense (except depreciation)	(600,000)
Depreciation	(200,000)
Operating income	400,000
Interest income	5,000
Income before taxes	$ 405,000

Instructions

(a) Prepare the necessary journal entry to record the tax accrual and allocation of income taxes under the deferred method for 1981. The tax rate has been 40% since the company was organized.

(b) State the amount of the Deferred Income Taxes account arising from the 1981 transactions and indicate the section(s) of the balance sheet where it would be shown. The cumulative deferred income tax account balance should not be calculated.

(c) Prepare the necessary journal entry to record the tax accrual and allocation under the deferred method for 1981, assuming that the tax rate changed to 30% for 1981. The gross-change method should be used.

P20-5 The following data represent the differences between accounting and tax income for Asian Import, Inc., whose pretax accounting income is $688,000 for the current year.

1. The company uses accelerated methods of computing depreciation for tax purposes, and the straight-line method for book purposes. Tax depreciation expense exceeded book depreciation expense by $82,000.

2. Officer life insurance expense was $4,200 for the year and you have determined that this expense is not deductible for tax purposes. The expense amount represents the difference between the premium paid ($5,900) and the increase in the cash value of the policy ($1,700).

3. Rents of $4,000, applicable to next year, had been collected in December and deferred for financial statement purposes.

4. In a previous year, the company established an allowance for product warranty expense. A summary of the current year's transactions appears below:

Balance at January 1	$ 77,100
Provision for the year	28,500
	105,600
Payments made on product warranties	20,000
Balance at December 31	$ 85,600

Instructions

(a) Compute the current and deferred, if any, federal income tax provision. (Assume a 40% tax rate and apply the net-change method.)

(b) Draft the income statement for the current year, beginning with "income before federal income taxes" and identifying "taxes currently payable" and "deferred" (net tax effect of timing differences).

P20-6 Refrigfry Products, Inc. recognizes gross margin on installment sales for accounting purposes at the time of sale and defers such gross margin for tax purposes until subsequent periods when the receivables arising from the installment sales are collected. For accounting purposes, Refrigfry Products, Inc. uses the straight-line method for depreciation, and an accelerated method for tax purposes.

Additional information:

Property	
1980 tax depreciation in excess of accounting depreciation	$ 70,000
All depreciable property acquired in 1978; estimated useful life	10 years
Installment sales	
Gross margin on 1980 installment sales uncollected at year end	$120,000
Gross margin on prior-years' installment sales collected during 1980	$100,000
Taxes	
Pretax accounting income for 1980	$200,000
Tax rate for 1980	50%
Average rate for all prior deferred income taxes	48%
Ignore surtax exemptions and surcharge and assume no investment credit	

Instructions

Compute taxable income and the tax payable in 1980, and summarize the 1980 changes in the deferred income tax account balance.

(a) Using the gross-change method.

(b) Using the net-change method.

P20-7 The following information about the Oak Haven Company is provided to you:

1. In 1980, $40,000 was collected in rent; for book purposes the entire amount was reported as revenue in 1981. In 1981, $50,000 was collected in rent; of this amount, $20,000 was reported as unearned revenue in 1981. For tax purposes, the rent is reported as revenue in the year of collection.

2. On January 1, 1977, the company purchased a machine costing $80,000. The machine

has a salvage value of $5,000, and has a useful life of 5 years. The straight-line method of depreciation is used for book purposes, and the sum-of-the-years'-digits method is used for income tax purposes.

3. On January 1, 1981, equipment was purchased which had a cost of $120,000. The equipment has no salvage value, and has a useful life of 4 years. The straight-line method of depreciation is used for book purposes, and the double-declining balance method for tax purposes.

4. The tax rate for years prior to 1981 is 40%; for 1981, the tax rate is 50%.

5. Pretax accounting income of $215,000 for 1981 includes interest revenue of $15,000 from tax-exempt municipal obligations.

6. On the 1981 tax return, the company reported $30,000 of gross profit from installment sales. This profit was reported in 1980 for book purposes.

7. The balance (credit) in the Deferred Tax account as of December 31, 1980 is $60,000.

Instructions

(a) Using the gross-change method, compute the tax expense for 1981, and the balance in the Deferred Tax account at December 31, 1981.

(b) Using the net-change method, compute the tax expense for 1981, and the balance in the Deferred Tax account at December 31, 1981.

P20-8 You have been assigned to make a computation of Oakwood Company's provision for income taxes for 1980 and 1981. On the basis of your review of the working papers, you have developed the following information.

Reconciliation of Book Income to Taxable Income	1980	1981
(dollars in thousands)		
Pretax book income	$120	$ 920
Permanent book/tax differentials:		
Amortization of goodwill	80	80
Pretax book income after adjustment for permanent tax differentials	200	1,000
Book/tax timing differences:		
Excess for tax depreciation over book	(400)	(200)
Provision for loss on sale of plant—booked in 1980 but sold in 1981	200	(200)
Provision for warranties:		
Provided during year	500	
Paid during year		(300)
Taxable income	$500	$ 300
Federal income tax rates	40%	50%

Instructions

Assuming that only federal income taxes are payable, compute the provision for income taxes and net income for both years by drafting the lower portion of the comparative income statement beginning with "income before taxes" and presenting the portion of the tax "currently payable" and the amount due to increase or decrease in the deferral (net tax effect of timing differences). Apply the gross-change method and compute the tax on pretax accounting income "with and without" originating timing differences.

P20-9 Rozanna Dana, Inc. sustained a $105,000 net operating loss during the first year of operations when the applicable tax rate was 40%.

Instructions

(a) Assuming that the corporation is not confident it will have future earnings against which it can offset the loss carryforward, prepare the entries for income taxes in the year of loss and in the succeeding year (assume a $135,000 pretax income and a 40% rate in the succeeding year).

(b) Assuming that the corporation is assured beyond a reasonable doubt of earnings in the succeeding periods to cover the loss, prepare the entries for income taxes in the year of the loss and in the succeeding year (assume a $135,000 pretax income and a 40% tax rate in the succeeding year).

(c) For both the loss year and the succeeding year, present the lower portion of the income (pretax accounting income or loss and below) for both assumptions (a) and (b).

P20-10 On January 2, 1980, Oak Waters Company commenced operations. The company had a book loss of $600,000 for that year. There were no timing differences during 1980. The loss carryforward cannot be assured beyond a reasonable doubt, because 1980 was the company's first year of operations. During 1981, the company had taxable income (equal to its book income) of $800,000. Assume the tax rate for 1980 and 1981 was 50%.

Instructions

(a) Prepare the comparative partial statement of income (loss) for Oak Waters Company for the year ended December 31, 1981, with comparative figures for 1980. The statement will start with "Income (loss) before income taxes and extraordinary item."

(b) Assume that Oak Waters Company has been in existence since January 1, 1975, and had taxable income (loss) as follows (use the carryback elective):

Year ended December 31	Taxable income (loss)
1975	$ (50,000)
1976	60,000
1977	(10,000)
1978	70,000
1979	190,000

Instructions

Prepare the partial statement of income (loss) for the years ended December 31, 1980 and 1981. Explain how the tax refund, if any, should be treated. Assume the tax rate for all previous periods is 50%.

P20-11 The Mikis Company has supplied you with information regarding its 1980 income tax expense for financial statement reporting as follows:

1. The provision for current income taxes (exclusive of investment tax credits) was $600,000 for the year ended December 31, 1980. Mikis made estimated tax payments of $550,000 during 1980.

2. Investment tax credits of $100,000 arising from fixed assets put into service in 1980 were taken for income tax reporting in 1980. Mikis defers investment tax credits and amortizes them to income over the productive life of the related assets for financial statement reporting. Investment tax credits recognized for financial statement purposes is $25,000 in 1980.

3. Mikis generally depreciates fixed assets using the straight-line method for financial statement reporting and various accelerated methods for income tax reporting. During 1980, depreciation on fixed assets amounted to $900,000 for financial statement reporting and $950,000 for income tax reporting. Commitments for the purchase of fixed assets amounted to $450,000 at December 31, 1980. Such fixed assets will be subject to an investment tax credit of 10%.

4. For financial statement reporting, Mikis has accrued estimated losses from product warranty contracts prior to their occurrence. For income tax reporting, no deduction is taken until payments are made. At December 31, 1979, accrued estimated losses of $200,000 were included in the liability section of Mikis' balance sheet. Based on the

latest available information, Mikis estimates that this figure should be 30% higher at December 31, 1980. Payments of $250,000 were made in 1980.

5. In 1975, Mikis acquired another company for cash. Goodwill resulting from this transaction was $800,000 and is being amortized over a forty-year period for financial statement reporting. The amortization is not deductible for income tax reporting.

6. Premiums paid on officers' life insurance amounted to $80,000 in 1980. These premiums are not deductible for income tax reporting.

7. Assume that the United States income tax rate was 48%.

Instructions

(a) What amounts should be shown for (1) provision for current income taxes; (2) provision for deferred income taxes; and (3) investment tax credits recognized in Mikis' income statement for the year ended December 31, 1980? Show supporting computations in good form.

(b) Identify any information in the fact situation which was not used to determine the answer to (a) above and explain why this information was not used.

(AICPA adapted)

P20-12 Your firm has been appointed to examine the financial statements of Cimple Energy, Inc. (CEI) for the two years ended December 31, 1981 in conjunction with an application for a bank loan. CEI was formed on January 2, 1970 by the nontaxable incorporation of the Cimple family partnership.

Early in the engagement you learned that the controller was unfamiliar with income tax accounting and that no tax allocations had been recorded.

During the examination, considerable information was gathered from the accounting records and client employees regarding interperiod tax allocation. This information, which has been audited, is as follows (with dollar amounts rounded to the nearest $100):

1. CEI uses a bad debt write-off method for tax purposes and a full accrual method for book purposes. The balance of the Allowance for Doubtful Receivables account at December 31, 1979 was $62,000. Following is a schedule of accounts written off and the corresponding year(s) in which the related sales were made.

Year(s) in Which Sales Were Made	Year in Which Accounts Written Off	
	1981	1980
1979 and prior	$19,800	$29,000
1980	7,200	
1981		
	$27,000	$29,000

The following is a schedule of changes in the Allowance for Doubtful Receivables account for the two years ended December 31, 1981:

	Year Ended December 31	
	1981	1980
Balance at beginning of year	$66,000	$62,000
Accounts written off during the year	(27,000)	(29,000)
Bad debt expense for the year	38,000	33,000
Balance at end of year	$77,000	$66,000

2. Following is a reconciliation between net income per books and taxable income:

	Year Ended December 31	
	1981	1980
1. Net income per books	$333,100	$262,800
2. Federal income tax payable during year	182,300	236,800
3. Taxable income not recorded on the books this year:		
Deferred sales commissions	10,000	
4. Expenses recorded on the books this year not deducted on the tax return:		
(a) Allowance for doubtful receivables	11,000	4,000
(b) Amortization of goodwill	8,000	8,000
5. Total of lines 1 through 4	544,400	511,600
6. Income recorded on the books this year not included on the tax return:		
Tax exempt interest—Watertown 5% Municipal Bonds	5,000	
7. Deductions on the tax return not charged against book income this year:		
Depreciation	83,700	38,000
8. Total of lines 6 and 7	88,700	38,000
9. Taxable income (line 5 less line 8)	$455,700	$473,600

3. Assume that the effective tax rates are as follows:

    1979 and prior years: 60%
    1980:   50%
    1981:   40%

4. In December 1981 CEI entered into a contract to serve as distributor for Brown Manufacturer, Inc.'s engineering products. The contract became effective December 31, 1981, and $10,000 of advance commissions on the contract were received and deposited on December 31, 1981. Because the commissions had not been earned, they were accounted for as a deferred credit to income on the balance sheet at December 31, 1981.

5. Goodwill represents the excess of cost over fair value of the net tangible assets of a retiring competitor that were acquired for cash on January 2, 1976. The original balance was $80,000.

6. Depreciation on plant assets transferred at incorporation and acquisitions through December 31, 1979 have been accounted for on a straight-line basis for both financial and tax reporting. Beginning in 1980 all additions of machinery and equipment have been depreciated using the declining-balance method for tax reporting but the straight-line method for financial reporting. Company policy is to take a full year's depreciation in the year of acquisition and none in the year of retirement. There have been no sales, trade-ins, or retirements since incorporation. Following is a schedule disclosing significant information about depreciable property and related depreciation:

Asset	Cost	Life	Annual Straight-line Amount*	Declining-balance Depreciation 1981	Declining-balance Depreciation 1980	Depreciation Taken Through December 31, 1979
Buildings	$1,190,000	20 & 50 yrs.	$31,000			$380,000
Machinery and equipment:						
Transferred at incorporation or acquired through December 31, 1979	834,000	Various	45,900			495,800
Acquisitions since December 31, 1979:						
1980	267,000	6 yrs.	38,000	$ 63,700	$ 76,000	
1981	395,000	6 yrs.	58,000	116,000		
Total asset cost	$2,686,000					

	Total Depreciation Expense 1981	Total Depreciation Expense 1980	Through December 31, 1979
For book purposes	$172,900	$114,900	$875,800
For tax purposes	$256,600	$152,900	$875,800

*After giving appropriate consideration to salvage value.

Instructions

(a) Prepare a schedule calculating (1) the balance of deferred income taxes at December 31, 1980 and 1981, and (2) the amount of the timing differences between actual income tax payable and financial income tax expense for 1980 and 1981. Round all calculations to the nearest $100. (Use the gross change technique.)

(b) Independently of your solution to part (a) and assuming data shown below, prepare the section of the income statement beginning with pretax accounting income to disclose properly income tax expense for the years ended December 31, 1981 and 1980.

	1981	1980
Pretax accounting income	$480,400	$465,600
Taxes payable currently	182,300	236,800
Deferred tax account change—Dr. (Cr.)	(28,100)	24,500
Balance of deferred tax at end of year—Dr. (Cr.)	(44,200)	(16,100)

(AICPA adapted)

Accounting for Pension Costs

Business organizations have been concerned with providing for the retirement of employees since the late 1800s. During recent decades a marked increase in this concern has resulted in the establishment of private pension plans in most large companies and in many medium- and small-sized ones.

The substantial growth of these plans, both in numbers of employees covered and in amounts of retirement benefits, has increased the significance of pension cost in relation to the financial position and the results of operations of many companies. Widely divergent practices in accounting for the cost of pension plans have persisted until recent years. The complex array of social concepts, legal considerations, actuarial techniques, income tax regulations, and varying business philosophies that characterize the environment in which pension plans have developed were partly responsible for the accounting profession's inability to standardize practice in this area. Since 1965 the variation of accounting practices considered acceptable for pension plans has narrowed greatly.

This development in accounting for pension plans is the result of the AICPA's 1965 publication of **Research Study No. 8** and the APB's issuance of **Opinion No. 8** in 1966, both entitled, "Accounting for the Cost of Pension Plans."[1] Recently, the administration of pensions has been significantly influenced by ERISA (Employee Retirement Income Security Act), commonly referred to as the Pension Reform Act of 1974.

---

[1]Ernest L. Hicks, "Accounting for the Cost of Pension Plans," *Accounting Research Study No. 8* (New York: AICPA, 1965), and "Accounting for the Cost of Pension Plans," *Opinions of the Accounting Principles Board No. 8* (New York: AICPA, 1966).

The Nature of Pension Plans

A **private pension plan** is an arrangement under which a company undertakes to provide its retired employees with benefits (ordinarily, monthly payments) that can be determined or estimated in advance from the provisions of a document or from the company's practices (commonly called a **defined-benefit plan**). Some pension plans are **funded,** that is, the company sets funds aside for future pension benefits by making payments to a funding agency that is responsible for accumulating the assets of the pension fund and for making payments to the recipients as the benefits become due. In an insured plan, the funding agency is an insurance company; in a trust-fund plan, the funding agency is a trustee. The process of making the cash payments to a funding agency is called **funding.** Some plans are **unfunded,** that is, the fund is under the control of the company instead of an independent funding agency; pension payments to retired employees are made directly by the company as they become due.

Some plans are **contributory;** the employees bear part of the cost of the stated benefits or voluntarily make payments to increase their benefits. Other plans are **noncontributory,** because the employer bears the entire cost. Companies generally design **qualified pension plans** in accord with federal income tax requirements that permit deductibility of the employer's contributions to the pension fund (within certain limits) and tax-free status of the earnings of the pension fund assets.

The above-mentioned differences, together with differences in eligibility requirements, specified retirement ages, levels of benefits, and disability options, result in an almost infinite variety of plans. In all pension plans, however, the three primary accounting problems are (1) **measuring the amount** of pension obligation resulting from the plan, (2) **allocating the cost** of the plan to the proper accounting periods, and (3) **disclosing the status and effects** of the plan in the financial statements and the accompanying footnotes. Because the first problem involves complicated actuarial considerations, **actuaries** are engaged to measure the amount of the pension obligation. Actuaries also play a leading role in allocating pension costs to accounting periods.

Employer Versus Plan (Fund) Accounting

The subject of pension accounting may be divided and separately treated as **accounting for the employer** and **accounting for the pension fund.** The company or employer is the organization sponsoring the pension plan; the employer incurs

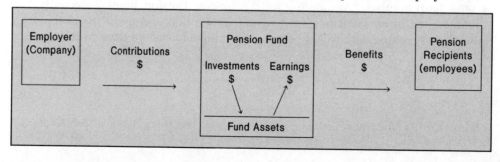

the cost and makes contributions to the pension fund. The fund or plan is the entity that receives the contributions from the employer, administers the pension assets, and makes the benefit payments to the pension recipients (retired employees). The diagram at the bottom of page 920 shows the three distinct entities involved in a pension plan and indicates the flow of cash between them.

The need for proper administration of and sound accounting for pension funds becomes apparent when one appreciates the absolute as well as the relative size of these funds. For example, the following companies recently had pension funds that had assets as follows:

Company	Size of the Pension Fund
General Motors Corp.	$8,446,000,000
duPont deNemours	2,570,000,000
Sears, Roebuck & Co.	2,919,000,000
Eastman Kodak	682,000,000

In addition, pension expense as a percent of pretax income is substantial for many companies. For example, General Motors' pension expense was recently 20% of its pretax accounting income.

An unfunded pension plan is administered by the employer, while a funded plan is administered by a trustee. In either case, however, the fund should have separate legal and accounting identity for which a set of books is maintained and financial statements are prepared. Maintaining books and records and preparing financial statements for the fund, known as "accounting for employee benefit plans," is not the subject of this chapter.[2] This chapter (with the exception of the last section) is devoted to the pension accounting and reporting problems of the employer as the sponsor of a pension plan.

The company as the employer records pension cost on its books in accordance with management policy within the standards prescribed by **APB Opinion No. 8** and any subsequent statements of the FASB. Contributions in the form of cash payments are made by the company to the pension fund in accordance with policies established jointly by the company and the trustees of the pension plan and the Pension Reform Act of 1974. Measurement of the pension cost and determination of the amount to be funded are separate, independent functions. If the recorded pension expense exceeds the cash contributions to the pension fund, the excess is reported as a pension liability on the company's balance sheet. Correspondingly, if the payments exceed the expense, the excess is reported as a prepaid asset.

The pension fund administrator invests the contributions received from the employer, reinvests earnings therefrom, and pays pension benefits to retired employees. At any time the expected present value of future pension payments (the pension liability) may be actuarially computed. This liability represents the amount that the pension fund must equal now (assuming no further contributions by the employer) in order for earnings from the fund and the gradual reductions in the

---

[2]The FASB has issued an exposure draft covering the accounting standards to be employed in accounting and reporting for employee benefit plans. "Accounting and Reporting by Defined Benefit Plans," *Proposed Statement of Financial Accounting Standards* (Stamford, Conn.: FASB, 1979).

fund itself to exactly cover all expected future payments to present and expected future retirees over their expected lifetimes for employment services rendered to date. If the pension fund assets equal or exceed the expected pension liability, the plan is **fully funded**.[3]

Pension liability has one meaning in reference to the pension fund and another in reference to the employer company. The expected pension liability of the pension fund is an actuarial concept representing an economic liability under the pension plan for future cash payments to retirees. The pension liability that frequently appears on company balance sheets represents an accounting credit that results from an excess of amounts expensed over amounts contributed to the pension fund; it does not represent the economic obligations under the plan and usually does not represent amounts legally owed to the pension fund.

Cash Basis Versus Accrual Basis

Until 1965, with few exceptions, companies applied the **cash basis** of accounting to pension plans by recognizing the amount paid in a particular accounting period for pension benefits as the pension expense for the period. The amount paid or funded in a fiscal period is dependent upon financial management and may be discretionary; however, funding may be based on the availability of cash, the level of earnings, or other factors unrelated to accounting considerations. Application of the cash basis permits the manipulation of the amount of pension cost appearing in the income statement simply by varying the cash paid to the pension fund. Two once-common funding methods, **"pay-as-you-go"** (recognize pension costs only when benefits are paid directly to the retired employee) and **"terminal funding"** (recognize pension costs when annuity is purchased or contribution is made to the trust for retired employees), are no longer considered acceptable because they are cash basis oriented and do not recognize pension costs prior to the retirement of employees.

There is now broad agreement that pension cost should be accounted for on the **accrual basis.** Most accountants and an increasing number of business managers recognize that **accounting for pension plans requires measurement of the cost and its identification with the appropriate time periods,** which involves application of accrual, deferral, and estimation concepts in the same manner that they are applied in the measurement and the time-period identification of other costs and expenses. The going-concern, matching, and consistency assumptions are all applicable and relevant to pension plan accounting.

Past Service Cost and Normal Pension Cost

In determining future retirement benefits, many pension plans give employees credit for their years of service prior to adoption of the plan. For example, if on January 1, 1978, a company adopted a pension plan that granted benefits to em-

---

[3]As used in this context, the term "funding" refers to the relationship between pension fund assets and the present value of expected future pension benefit payments. This usage is in contrast to the use of "funding" to mean the contributions made by the employer to the pension fund. Thus, it is possible, and generally accurate, to say that a company is "fully funding" its accrued pension expense as recorded on the books and yet state that the pension fund is "under funded" in an actuarial sense.

ployees on the basis of their total years of service to the company, an employee who had been an employee since January 1, 1968, would already have 10 years of service toward pension credit. Some of the actuarial methods frequently used to determine pension cost compute separately the cost associated with the years prior to the date of adoption (this is called **past service cost**) and the cost associated with the years after the date of adoption or amendment (this is called **normal cost**). The diagram below identifies past service cost and normal cost as they relate to the adoption date of a pension plan.

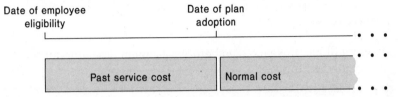

Past service cost arises from the granting of service credits to employees for years of service prior to adoption of a pension plan. The amount of past service cost is an actuarial estimate derived from a complicated actuarial method that takes into consideration such factors as life expectancy of employees, retirement age, employee turnover, future salary levels, interest rates, gains and losses of the fund, administrative costs, and pension benefits.

Normal pension cost is the cost assigned annually for the service credits earned by the employees during a given year. Normal cost also involves a complicated determination based on service credits for the current year with a separate determination made annually because of changes in the number of employees, salaries, and terms of the plan.

If a pension plan is initiated when a company is organized, no past service cost is recognized; only normal pension cost is incurred. Similarly, if no credits are given for service prior to inception of a pension plan, no past service cost arises.

Accountants generally agree that, although past service cost results from consideration given to years of service prior to adoption of the pension plan, this cost is related to periods subsequent to the adoption. Therefore, it should be treated as an expense of the years following adoption of the plan and should not be charged against retained earnings as something applicable to the past.

To illustrate these points, assume that the actuarial firm of Rowe and Satter Co. is hired by Boston Corp. to prepare a report on a proposed pension plan that Boston Corp. is considering. Boston Corp. wishes to determine the past service cost and the normal cost that would be incurred for the typical employee. The following basic assumptions have been made by the actuary:

1. The plan is noncontributory and plan assets will earn 6% interest.
2. The typical employee will receive at retirement $200 per year for each year employed by Boston Corp.
3. Mortality table—1975 is used.
4. The typical employee is 50 years old, will retire at age 65, and has worked for the company for 10 years.

Boston Corp. indicates that it will give credit for past service prior to adoption of the plan. **To compute the past service cost** the actuary first determines the expected life of the employee subsequent to retirement; the mortality table indicate that it is 13 years. Because the employee has already worked 10 years, the company has a future obligation of $2,000 ($200 × 10) for 13 years. The computation to determine the amount of monies the pension fund must have on hand at the date of this employee's retirement to meet the pension cost attributable to the period of past service is as follows:

(Attributable to 10 Years of Past Service)

Amount to be paid each period	$ 2,000
Present value of ordinary annuity for 13 periods at 6% (Table 6-4)	× 8.85268
Amount needed at retirement	$17,705

Because the employee still has 15 years to go before retirement, the amount needed at retirement is discounted as follows:

Amount needed at retirement	$17,705
Present value of $17,705 for 15 periods at 6% interest (Table 6-2)	× .41727
Past service cost	$ 7,388

The present value of the past service cost pension obligation of $2,000 per year beginning in fifteen years and continuing for 13 years is $7,388. The past service cost of $7,388 may be funded immediately or over some period of years that may or may not coincide with the amortization period.

To compute the normal cost, the actuary must determine the cost of the pension plan at the date of the employee's retirement for the service credits earned by the employee subsequent to adoption of the plan. This employee will work for 15 more years before retirement and will be entitled to receive $3,000 ($200 × 15) for each year of expected life subsequent to the age of 65, which in this case is 13 years. The following computation is made to determine the amount that the pension fund must have on hand at the date of the employee's retirement:

(Attributable to 15 Years of Future Service)

Amount to be paid each period	$ 3,000
Present value of ordinary annuity for 13 periods at 6% (Table 6-4)	× 8.85268
Amount needed at retirement	$26,558

Assuming that Boston Corp. desires a constant normal cost from year to year, the amount needed at retirement is divided by the amount of an ordinary annuity of 1 for 15 years at 6% to arrive at the normal cost per year, as follows:

$$\$26,558 \div 23.27597 = \$1,141[4]$$

On the basis of the facts and assumptions given, normal cost each period is $1,141 for Boston Corp. As illustrated later, other patterns for allocating the normal cost to each year may have been employed. This decision usually depends on the pref-

[4]An alternative computation is to find the amount needed at the date of the adoption of the plan to fund the normal cost. This value then should be divided by the present value of an ordinary annuity to arrive at the normal cost, as indicated below:

$$\$26,558 \times .41727 = \$11,082$$
$$\$11,082 \div 9.71225 = \$1,141$$

erences of the company as to the earnings and funding patterns it wishes to fol-low. Also, to keep the illustration simple, we used data for one typical employee, whereas in practice pension costs are computed for groups of employees.

Amendments to Pension Plans and Prior Service Cost

Pension plans are frequently amended to increase retirement benefits. A change in benefits requires an actuarial valuation of the plan. Ordinarily, these amendments recognize service prior to the date of the amendment and also the years thereafter. The period of service prior to the date of the amendment, or any actuarial valu-ation of the plan, is labeled the prior service period. Similarly, **prior service cost** refers to the portion of the total pension cost that, under the actuarial cost method in use, is identified with all periods prior to the date of an actuarial valuation of the plan (date of amendment). Therefore, as of the date of its computation, prior ser-vice cost includes (1) the past service cost, (2) the normal cost for years prior to that date, and (3) the increases in pension cost arising from any amendment and attrib-utable to years prior to that date. **Essentially, prior service cost is computed at any time in the same way that past service cost would be computed if the plan were being put into effect for the first time.** The diagram below identifies the prior service period.

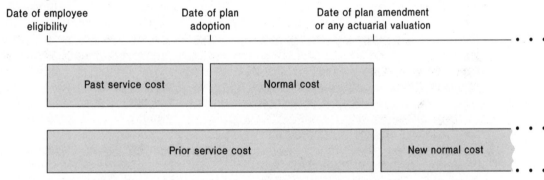

APB Opinion No. 8 makes reference to a **specific part** of prior service cost, that is, any increases or decreases in prior service cost arising as a result of an amend-ment to the plan. Because this cost is accounted for in a manner similar to that used for past service cost, the term past service cost is used to refer to both types of cost.

Past and Prior Service Cost—Financial Statement Presentation

One question that arises is whether a liability should be reported on the balance sheet for unfunded past service cost. The APB took the position that unfunded past service cost is not a liability that should be reported on the balance because the liability will be created in the future as the employee performs services.

Others contend that an obligation to pay these costs arises immediately and, therefore, the balance sheet should report a liability with a related debit to a de-ferred charge account. This argument has gained support recently because ERISA requires that past service cost be funded over a period not to exceed 40 years.

Unfunded past service costs can be quite substantial, as indicated by the following table:

Company	Amount of Unfunded Past Service Cost
Ford Motor	$3,400,000,000
Monsanto	388,000,000
International Harvester	1,097,000,000
Goodyear Tire and Rubber	679,000,000

If Ford Motor Company's unfunded past service costs were capitalized, its long-term debt to stockholders' equity ratio would increase from 14% to 24%; Goodyear Tire & Rubber would change from 36% to 44%. At present, the FASB does not require companies to disclose unfunded past service costs; however, companies are required by the SEC to do so in reports filed with that agency.

Vested Benefits

The expected pension liability may be divided in terms of vested and unvested benefits. **Vested benefits** are earned pension benefits that are not contingent upon the employee continuing in the service of the employer. Thus, to the extent that benefits vest, a present employee is entitled at some specified future date (normally retirement age) to benefits earned, even if the employee leaves the company before retirement. The actuarially computed value of vested benefits at any given date is the present value of the sum of (1) the expected future payments to employees who have retired, left, or been terminated with vested rights; and (2) the expected future payments to active employees for benefits already earned (without regard to future job history). If payments for benefits already earned are contingent on staying with the same employer until retirement, the plan is "nonvesting." According to **Opinion No. 8,** as long as prior service costs are being funded, vested benefits need not be accrued and recorded, but the amount must be disclosed. If prior service costs are not being funded, a provision for vested benefits may be required. Because the Pension Reform Act of 1974 (ERISA) significantly increased the vesting requirements of company pension plans, this area is receiving increased attention from accountants.

Actuarial Cost Methods

The major difficulties in estimating pension cost are in selecting the pertinent data relating to the employee group (employee age, years of service, compensation, etc.), designing the actuarial computations, and formulating the assumptions regarding future events (employee turnover and mortality, and pension fund earnings). Having made the necessary assumptions, the actuary would make a valuation using one of several actuarial cost methods to determine the periodic contributions the employer is to make to the pension fund. Although the actuarial methods are used primarily to determine the amounts to be funded, they may also be used to measure periodic pension expense. According to **APB Opinion No. 8,** five actuarial cost methods are acceptable for assigning pension costs to accounting periods; the five are:

1. Accrued benefit cost method (unit credit method)[5]
   Projected benefit cost methods:
   Individual level cost methods:
2. Without supplemental liability (individual level premium method)
3. With supplemental liability (entry age normal method—individual basis)
   Aggregate level cost methods:
4. Without supplemental liability (aggregate method)
5. With supplemental liability (attained age normal method; entry age normal method—aggregate basis)

Just as different depreciation methods result in different amounts of periodic depreciation expense, so do the actuarial cost methods above produce different amounts of periodic pension expense. The diagrams[6] below illustrate the annual cost patterns produced by these five actuarial cost methods.

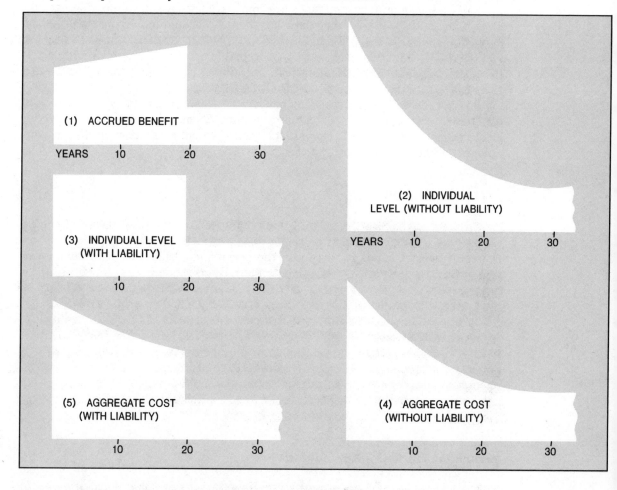

[5]The terms in parentheses are the related terms that were most commonly employed in practice until 1966, when the new terminology was proposed by the actuarial profession. "Supplemental liability" means past service cost or prior service cost.

[6]Source: William A. Dreher, "Alternatives Available Under APB Opinion No. 8: An Actuary's View," *Journal of Accountancy* (September, 1967), p. 41.

The **two major reasons why these actuarial cost methods differ relate to how the past service cost is handled and whether present or future salary levels are employed to determine the normal cost.** For example, the individual level premium method *without* supplemental liability includes the amortization of past service cost in its computation of normal cost. Conversely, the individual level premium method *with* supplemental liability does not include past service cost in its computation. In addition the accrued benefit cost method accrues normal cost on the basis of today's employee salary level. Under this approach, assuming that salary levels increase, more cost will be reported in later years than in earlier years. Conversely, the projected benefit cost methods attempt to allocate the normal cost more evenly over the periods involved by projecting the future salary levels and normalizing these costs over the entire period affected.

All of these actuarial cost methods are considered acceptable to provide pension costs consistent with the objectives of accrual accounting. The actuarial cost method chosen for accounting purposes does not have to be the same as the method used to fund the pension plan. Acceptable accounting merely requires that the method be rational and systematic, be applied consistently, and result in a reasonable measure of pension cost from year to year.

Although the technical aspects of pension cost determination require the skill, experience, and judgment of an actuary, accountants must be familiar enough with actuarial methods and concepts to reach their own conclusions about the reasonableness of the estimated provision.

Interest Equivalents

A pension fund is established and maintained for the purpose of accumulating the amounts necessary to pay retirement benefits as they come due. The primary source of pension funds is, of course, the periodic contributions of the employer. Another source of funds assumed in actuarially determining the amount of the employer's contributions and expense is the **earnings** on the pension fund assets. If the employer does not fund or underfunds the pension plan, earnings do not materialize in the amount actuarially assumed or necessary to meet the expected benefit payments. Therefore, when the amounts of the actuarially determined pension expense vary from the amounts funded, the annual accounting pension provision is adjusted by "an amount equivalent to interest" on the accumulated difference. The annual pension expense is **increased** by an amount equivalent to interest on the prior years' expense provisions not funded, or it is **decreased** by an amount equivalent to interest on prior years' funding in excess of expense provisions.

Accounting Entries for Pension Costs

The amount of pension expense recognized during a particular accounting period depends on the factors listed below.

1. **The amount of past or prior service cost.** The amount of past or prior service cost is determined by an actuary and represents the present value of the future obligations resulting from the cost of credits for employee services rendered prior to the adoption or amendment of the pension plan.

2. **The funding or nonfunding of past or prior service cost.** The funding or nonfunding of the past or prior service cost is a financial decision of the employer subject to laws such as ERISA. As a minimum, the annual pension expense should include an amount equivalent to interest on any unfunded past or prior service cost.

3. **The periods over which past or prior service cost is amortized.**[7] The amortization of past or prior service cost is also the decision of the employer. The acceptable rate of amortization may range from no amortization at all to a maximum of 10% a year.

4. **The amount of normal cost.** The amount of normal cost is determined by an actuary on the basis of employee service credits for the current year.

5. **The interest rate appropriate to the pension fund.** The interest rate determined by the actuary to be appropriate to the pension fund operation affects all computations of pension cost. Interest is an integral part of pension cost because time and annuity factors are inherent in pension concepts.

6. **The amounts funded annually.** The amounts funded annually are frequently a financial decision of the employer and need not parallel the amounts expensed annually. Interest equivalents on the difference between the amounts expensed and the amounts funded can increase or decrease the periodic pension expense.

7. **The amount of vested benefits.** Pension expenses must include a provision for vested benefits only if prior service costs are not being amortized over 40 years or less. Even then a provision may not be required except in limited circumstances.[8]

Each of the foregoing factors must be considered and resolved before an accounting entry can be recorded to recognize annual pension cost.

To illustrate the accounting entries that result under different circumstances, assume that on January 1, 1977, the Odom Corporation, in business since 1963, adopts a funded pension plan for the benefit of its employees. The plan is noncontributory and provides for vesting after 15 years of service by each eligible employee. A local bank is engaged to be the trustee of the pension fund. An actuarial consulting firm recommends a 5% interest rate as appropriate and, applying an acceptable actuarial method, determines that the past service cost at the date of adoption (January 1, 1977) is $240,000 and that the normal (current) pension cost for the year 1977 is $50,000, which is to be funded fully each year.

The management of Odom Corporation must now formulate an **amortization** policy and a **funding** policy for past service cost.

Case A—**Amortization and Funding Periods the Same.** Management decides to amortize and fund the past service cost of $240,000 over 15 years; equal payments are to be made to the pension fund trustee at the end of each year. The annual amortization of past service cost and the annual payment to the pension fund trustee are identical and computed as follows:

$$\$240,000 \div \frac{\text{PV of an ordinary annuity}}{\text{of 1 for 15 periods at 5\%}} = \frac{\text{Periodic amortization}}{\text{and funding payment}}$$

$$\$240,000 \div 10.37966 \text{ (Table 6-4)} = \$23,122$$

---

[7]The 1978 issue of *Accounting Trends and Techniques*, p. 255, reported that of 472 pension plans, 467 amortize prior service costs; only 5 do not amortize these costs.

[8]The amount of the vested benefit provision would be the lesser of (1) the amount, if any, by which 5% of such excess of vested benefits at the beginning of the year exceeds any reduction in vested benefits during the year, or (2) the amount needed to amortize all prior service costs over 40 years.

The entry on December 31, 1977 to recognize the annual pension expense and to record the Odom Corporation contributions to the pension fund trustee would appear as follows:

Pension Expense (normal cost)	50,000	
Pension Expense (past service cost)	23,122	
Cash		73,122

(Normal and past service costs are recorded separately merely for illustration purposes. These two amounts are generally combined and recorded in one pension expense account.)

The following schedule (first three years only) shows the relationship of the past service cost amortization and funding policies to the amount charged annually to pension expense.

Odom Corporation—Case A
Schedule of Amortization and Funding of Past Service Cost

Year	Amortization—15 Years			Funding 15 Years	Balance Sheet Deferred Expense/Liability	
	15-Year Annual Amount	Interest Reduction/ Addition	Pension Expense Debit	Cash Credit	Debit/ (Credit)	12/31 Balance
	(a)	(b)	(c)	(d)	(e)	(f)
1977	$23,122	-0-	$23,122	$23,122	-0-	-0-
1978	23,122	-0-	23,122	23,122	-0-	-0-
1979	23,122	-0-	23,122	23,122	-0-	-0-

(a) $240,000 ÷ 10.37966.
(b) 5% of the preceding balance of (f).
(c) (a) plus (or minus) (b).
(d) $240,000 ÷ 10.37966.
(e) (d) minus (c).
(f) Preceding balance plus (or minus) (e).

Because the current provisions for pension expense, normal cost, and past service cost are fully funded each year, the balance sheet would contain neither a debit for deferred pension cost nor a credit for pension liability. At the end of 15 years when the past service cost is fully amortized and funded, only the normal pension cost would be expensed and funded each year.

It should be noted that it is difficult to understand what is being amortized because the principal amount to be amortized is **unrecorded**. Generally, amortization involves the write-off of an amount that has been recorded on the books as a debit or a credit. The past or prior service cost that is amortized may be likened to an unrecorded deferred charge. In fact, if all past service costs were funded at the initiation of the pension plan, they might be recorded as a deferred charge, and the amortization could then be related to the write-off of the unamortized amount which would appear on the balance sheet.

Case B—**Amortization Period Longer than Funding Period.** Management decides to amortize past service cost of $240,000 over 15 years and to fund this cost by making equal payments at the end of each of the first 10 years. The annual amortization and funding payments are computed as follows:

Amortization:

$$\$240,000 \div \frac{\text{PV of an ordinary annuity}}{\text{of 1 for 15 periods at 5\%}} = \text{Periodic amortization}$$

$$\$240,000 \div 10.37966 \text{ (Table 6-4)} \quad = \$23,122$$

Funding:

$$\$240,000 \div \frac{\text{PV of an ordinary annuity}}{\text{of 1 for 10 periods at 5\%}} = \text{Periodic funding payment}$$

$$\$240,000 \div 7.72173 \text{ (Table 6-4)} \quad = \$31,081$$

The following schedule shows the results from funding past service cost over a shorter period than the period of amortizing that cost. A deferred charge accumulates during the first 10 years and is depleted during the next 5 years. Also, the periodic amortization is reduced by the interest on the cumulative amount funded in excess of the amounts amortized.

Odom Corporation—Case B
Schedule of Amortization and Funding of Past Service Cost

	Amortization—15 Years			Funding 10 Years	Balance Sheet Deferred Charge	
Year	15-Year Annual Amount	Interest Reduction	Pension Expense Debit	Cash Credit	Debit/ (Credit)	12/31 Balance
	(a)	(b)	(c)	(d)	(e)	(f)
1977	$23,122	-0-	$ 23,122	$ 31,081	$ 7,959	$ 7,959
1978	23,122	$ 398	22,724	31,081	8,357	16,316
1979	23,122	816	22,306	31,081	8,775	25,091
1980	23,122	1,255	21,867	31,081	9,214	34,305
1981	23,122	1,715	21,407	31,081	9,674	43,979
1982	23,122	2,199	20,923	31,081	10,158	54,137
1983	23,122	2,707	20,415	31,081	10,666	64,803
1984	23,122	3,240	19,882	31,081	11,199	76,002
1985	23,122	3,800	19,322	31,081	11,759	87,761
1986	23,122	4,388	18,734	31,081	12,347	100,108
1987	23,122	5,005	18,117	-0-	(18,117)	81,991
1988	23,122	4,100	19,022	-0-	(19,022)	62,969
1989	23,122	3,148	19,974	-0-	(19,974)	42,995
1990	23,122	2,150	20,972	-0-	(20,972)	22,023
1991	23,122	1,099*	22,023	-0-	(22,023)	-0-
1992	-0-	-0-	-0-	-0-	-0-	-0-
			$310,810	$310,810		

* Adjusted for $2 discrepancy due to rounding of computations.
(a) $240,000 ÷ 10.37966.
(b) 5% of the preceding balance of (f).
(c) (a) minus (b).
(d) $240,000 ÷ 7.72173.
(e) (d) minus (c).
(f) Preceding balance plus (e).

Using data from the schedule on page 931, the entries to recognize the annual pension expense (normal cost assumed to be $50,000 for all years, although it generally changes from year to year in actual practice) and to record Odom Corporation's annual contribution to the pension fund trustee would appear as follows for 1977, 1988, and 1992:

December 31, 1977

Pension Expense (normal cost)	50,000	
Pension Expense (past service cost)	23,122	
Deferred Pension Expense	7,959	
Cash ($50,000 + $31,081)		81,081

December 31, 1988

Pension Expense (normal cost)	50,000	
Pension Expense (past service cost)	19,022	
Deferred Pension Expense		19,022
Cash		50,000

December 31, 1992

Pension Expense (normal cost)	50,000	
Cash		50,000

Case C—Amortization Period Shorter than Funding Period. Management decides to amortize past service cost of $240,000 over 15 years and to fund past service cost by making equal payments at the end of each of the first 20 years. The annual amortization and funding payments are computed as follows:

$$\text{Amortization} = \$240,000 \div 10.37966 = \$23,122$$
$$\text{Funding} \quad = \$240,000 \div 12.46221 = \$19,258$$

The schedule at the top of page 933 shows the results from funding past service cost over a longer period than the period of amortizing that cost. A liability for the excess of the annual pension cost over the amount funded accumulates during the first 15 years and is eliminated during the next 5 years. Also, the periodic amortization is increased by the interest on the cumulative amount amortized in excess of the amounts funded.

Using data from the schedule at the top of page 933, the entries to recognize the annual pension expense (normal cost assumed to be $50,000 for all years) and to record Odom Corporation's annual contribution to the pension fund trustee would appear as follows for 1977, 1991, 1992, and 1997:

December 31, 1977

Pension Expense (normal cost)	50,000	
Pension Expense (past service cost)	23,122	
Liability for Pension Expense Not Funded		3,864
Cash		69,258

December 31, 1991

Pension Expense (normal cost)	50,000	
Pension Expense (past service cost)	26,907	
Liability for Pension Expense Not Funded		7,649
Cash		69,258

Odom Corporation—Case C
Schedule of Amortization and Funding of Past Service Cost

Year	Amortization—15 Years			Funding 20 Years	12/31 Balance Sheet Pension Liability	
	15-Year Annual Amount	Addition Due To Interest	Pension Expense Debit	Cash Credit	(Debit)/ Credit	Credit Balance
	(a)	(b)	(c)	(d)	(e)	(f)
1977	$23,122	-0-	$ 23,122	$ 19,258	$ 3,864	$ 3,864
1978	23,122	193	23,315	19,258	4,057	7,921
1979	23,122	396	23,518	19,258	4,260	12,181
⎰	⎱	⎰	⎱	⎰	⎱	⎰
1991	23,122	3,785	26,907	19,258	7,649	83,346
1992	-0-	4,167	4,167	19,258	(15,091)	68,255
⎱	⎰	⎱	⎰	⎱	⎰	⎱
1996	-0-	915	915	19,258	(18,343)	-0-
1997	-0-	-0-	-0-	-0-	-0-	-0-
			$385,160	$385,160		

(a) $240,000 ÷ 10.37966.
(b) 5% of preceding balance of (f).
(c) (a) plus (b).
(d) $240,000 ÷ 12.46221.
(e) (c) minus (d).
(f) Preceding balance plus (e).

December 31, 1992

Pension Expense (normal cost)	50,000	
Pension Expense (past service cost)	4,167	
Liability for Pension Expense Not Funded	15,091	
Cash		69,258

December 31, 1997

Pension Expense (normal cost)	50,000	
Cash		50,000

As indicated in the foregoing illustrations, the typical elements of periodic pension expense are (1) normal cost, (2) an amortized amount of past service cost, and (3) an amount equivalent to interest on the difference between amounts recorded for accounting purposes and the amounts funded.

The amortization and funding schedules above were presented to illustrate the effect on the annual expense provisions of differences in the amounts funded and the amounts amortized for past service cost. These differences occur in practice and are justifiable because the amortization or write-off of the past or prior service cost is independent of the funding of that same amount, just as the depreciation of an asset is separate from the retirement of the liability incurred when the asset was acquired.

The preceding schedules are unrealistic in that the real world pension situation seldom remains so constant and unaltered for such long periods of time. It is not uncommon for pension plans to be amended as frequently as every three years. Therefore, computations for pension expense and minimum and maximum provisions (explained in the following section) are made on a year-to-year basis and are dependent upon the amounts funded and accrued in the previous year.

Two Views of Pension Cost

Adoption of the accrual basis of accounting does not resolve a major controversy that exists relating to pension plan accounting. The question that still must be resolved is: What cost must be accounted for? And that question begs the question: What is the nature of pension cost? Two opposing views of the nature of pension cost exist among accountants.

Some accountants argue that pension cost is related to **the plan or the continuing employee group as a whole.** They believe that it is unnecessary to make specific expense charges for prior service cost if all future benefit payments can be met by annual provisions representing normal cost plus an amount equivalent to interest[9] on the unfunded prior service cost. The justification given for this treatment is that actuarial assumptions are a function of the mass of employees moving through the pension plan over the years and are not based on particular people at a particular time. In addition, they claim that an employer obtains diverse advantages of indefinite duration as a result of granting past service credits under a pension plan. The past service cost is, therefore, an intangible that does not diminish in value and thus does not need to be amortized.[10]

This approach, often referred to as the **minimum method,** holds that pension cost should not be less than the total of:

1. Normal cost.
2. An amount equivalent to interest on any unfunded prior service cost.
3. A provision for vested benefits, if any is indicated.

Other accountants believe that the annual expense of a pension plan is related to **the cost of specific pension benefits payable in the future to specific persons.** Proponents of this view advocate recognition of the past service cost over a period related to the remaining years of service of the employee group that is to receive credit for working years before adoption of the plan. Their argument is supported by the fact that past service cost is part of the cost of providing pensions for the employees initially covered. And, although it may be true that the future periods benefited by the past service element of the plan are indefinite in length, by far the greatest part of the benefit is related to the service lives of the employees who will receive pensions measured in part by past service. Therefore, past service cost should be charged to expense over the remaining service lives of such employees.[11]

---

[9]Such interest is necessary to keep the unfunded cost from growing, that is, to maintain the original size of unfunded past service cost stated at present value relative to the future benefits applicable to that past period.

[10]Hicks, *op. cit.,* pp. 31–55.

[11]Hicks, *op. cit.,* pp. 31–55.

This approach, often referred to as the **maximum method,** holds that pension cost should not be more than the total of:

1. Normal cost.
2. Ten percent (10%) of the past service cost (until fully amortized).
3. Ten percent (10%) of any increase or decrease in prior service cost arising from amendments of the plan (until fully amortized).
4. Interest equivalents on any differences between the amounts expensed and the amounts funded.

The major difference between these two approaches is essentially in the accounting for prior service cost. Under the minimum method, only interest on the unfunded prior service cost is considered. Under the maximum, 10% of the past service cost and 10% of any increase or decrease in prior service cost arising from amendments of the plan are included in current pension expense.

In examining the elements of the minimum computation, note that a provision for vested benefits may be needed. This provision is generally required under the minimum method when the present value of the vested benefits exceeds the value of the assets in the fund plus any accrued pension liability currently reported on the balance sheet. For example, assume that Sloan Inc. has $2 million of net assets in a pension fund and an accrued pension liability of $500,000. If the present value of the vested benefits payable are $2,800,000, should $300,000 [$2,800,000 — ($2,000,000 + $500,000)] be reported on the balance sheet as a liability with a related expense? Under the minimum method, the general approach is to recognize this amount as additional pension expense by means of a complex formula. The formula essentially limits the amount to be added to expense by spreading these costs over future periods. In many cases the vested liability is not recognized because the normal cost allocation covers this liability. This problem does not arise under the maximum approach because the normal cost plus the rapid write-off of past or prior service costs more than offsets the vested liability.

Additional Points on Minimum-Maximum Computations

The minimum and maximum computations represent the floor and the ceiling for periodic charges of pension costs against income. **APB Opinion No. 8** does not specify the method to be used in computing pension expense. It merely advocates the consistent application of any accounting method that uses an acceptable actuarial cost method and that results in an expense provision that falls between the defined minimum and maximum.

The minimum and the maximum do not exist per se; rather, they relate to the particular policies adopted by the employer. In other words, you can only test for a minimum and a maximum if given a particular amortization and funding policy. That is, each year should be tested because the minimum and maximum depend upon the actual amortization and funding practices that have occurred prior to and during the year.

Under actuarial cost methods that do not recognize past service cost separately, the maximum and the minimum are the same. In the maximum, the 10% limitation applies separately to **past** service cost on the initiation of a pension plan and to changes in **prior** service cost resulting from plan amendments. For example, if the initial past service cost is $1,000,000 and an amendment at the end of the fifth year results in an additional $500,000 of prior service cost, the amortization amounts might be as follows:

Years 1- 5	$100,000
Years 6-10	150,000
Years 11-15	50,000

Minimum and Maximum Illustrated

Using the data from Case A (pages 929–930), in which the amortization and funding periods are the same, results in the following minimum computations (below) and the maximum computations (top of page 937) for selected years.

Computation of Minimum Provision—Case A

Year	Normal Cost	Past Service Cost Funded 12/31	Past Service Cost Unfunded Bal. 1/1	5% Interest on Unfunded PSC	Vested Benefits Charge	Minimum Pension Provision
	(a)	(b)	(c)	(d)	(e)	(f)
1977	$50,000	$11,122	$240,000	$12,000	-0-	$62,000
1978	50,000	11,678	228,878	11,444	-0-	61,444
1979	50,000	12,262	217,200	10,860	-0-	60,860
〜	〜	〜	〜	〜	〜	〜
1988	50,000	19,022	81,991	4,100	-0-	54,100
〜	〜	〜	〜	〜	〜	〜
1992	50,000	-0-	-0-	-0-	-0-	50,000

(a) Actuarially determined.
(b) $23,122 (PSC funding payments) minus (d), the interest portion.
(c) Preceding balance minus (b) in preceding year.
(d) 5% of (c).
(e) No charge assumed necessary.
(f) (a) plus (d) plus (e).

A comparison of Odom Corporation's practice in Case A of amortizing and funding past service cost over 15 years with the computed minimum and maximum provisions indicates that the amounts expensed are acceptable because they fall between the minimum and maximum each year.

Using the data from Case B (pages 930–931), in which the amortization period is longer than the funding period, results in the following minimum computations (bottom of page 937) and the maximum computations (top of page 938).

Computation of Maximum Provision—Case A

Year	Normal Cost	PSC Amortization 10%	Def. Charge or Liability Bal. 1/1	Interest Equivalent at 5%	Maximum Pension Provision
	(a)	(b)	(c)	(d)	(e)
1977	$50,000	$24,000	-0-	-0-	$74,000
1978	50,000	24,000	-0-	-0-	74,000
1979	50,000	24,000	-0-	-0-	74,000
⎰	⎰	⎰	⎰	⎰	⎰
1990	50,000	24,000	-0-	-0-	74,000
1991	50,000	24,000	-0-	-0-	74,000
1992	50,000	-0-	-0-	-0-	50,000

(a) Actuarially determined.
(b) 10% of past service cost (until fully amortized).
(c) Cumulative difference between expense accrued and amounts funded.
(d) 5% of (c).
(e) (a) plus (b) minus (d), if deferred charge, or plus (d), if liability.

Computation of Minimum Provision—Case B

Year	Normal Cost	Past Service Cost Funded 12/31	Past Service Cost Unfunded 1/1	5% Interest on Unfunded PSC	Vested Benefits Charge	Minimum Pension Provision
	(a)	(b)	(c)	(d)	(e)	(f)
1977	$50,000	$19,081	$240,000	$12,000	-0-	$62,000
1978	50,000	20,035	220,919	11,046	-0-	61,046
1979	50,000	21,037	200,884	10,044	-0-	60,044
⎰	⎰	⎰	⎰	⎰	⎰	⎰
1988	50,000	-0-	-0-	-0-	-0-	50,000
⎰	⎰	⎰	⎰	⎰	⎰	⎰
1992	50,000	-0-	-0-	-0-	-0-	50,000

(a) Actuarially determined.
(b) $31,081 (past service cost funding payment) minus (d), the interest portion.
(c) Preceding balance minus (b) in preceding year.
(d) 5% of (c).
(e) No charge assumed necessary.
(f) (a) plus (d) plus (e).

Computation of Minimum Expense—1978

Normal cost	$50,000
Interest on unfunded PSC (5% $\times$ $220,919)	11,046
Vested benefits provision	-0-
Minimum expense, 1978	$61,046

Computation of Maximum Provision—Case B

Year	Normal Cost	PSC Amortization 10%	Deferred Charge Bal. 1/1	Interest Equivalent at 5%	Maximum Pension Provision
	(a)	(b)	(c)	(d)	(e)
1977	$50,000	$24,000	-0-	-0-	$74,000
1978	50,000	24,000	$ 7,959	$ 398	73,602
1979	50,000	24,000	16,316	816	73,184
{	}	}	{	}	{
1988	50,000	24,000	81,991	4,100	69,900
1989	50,000	24,000	62,969	3,148	70,852
1990	50,000	24,000	42,995	2,150	71,850
1991	50,000	24,000	22,023	1,099	72,901
1992	50,000	-0-	-0-	-0-	50,000

(a) Actuarially determined.
(b) 10% of past service cost (until fully amortized).
(c) Cumulative difference between expense accrued and amounts funded.
(d) 5% of (c).
(e) (a) plus (b) minus (d).

Computation of Maximum Expense—1978

Normal cost	$50,000
Amortization of PSC (10% × $240,000)	24,000
Interest equivalent—deduction (5% × $7,959)	(398)
Maximum expense, 1978	$73,602

A comparison of Odom Corporation's practice in Case B of amortizing the past service cost over 15 years and funding it over 10 years with the computed minimum and maximum provisions indicates that the amounts expensed are acceptable because they fall between the minimum and maximum each year.

Using the data from Case C (pages 932–933), in which the amortization period is shorter than the funding period, results in the following minimum and maximum computations as shown on page 939.

A comparison of Odom Corporation's practice in Case C of amortizing the past service cost over 15 years and funding it over 20 years with the computed minimum and maximum provisions indicates that the amounts expensed are acceptable because they fall between the minimum and maximum each year.

In all of the three cases above the periodic pension expense fell between the minimum and maximum limits and, therefore, was an acceptable provision. **If the pension expense falls outside the minimum and maximum limits, the closest limit would be recorded as pension expense;** an adjustment in the deferred balance would be required, together with a recomputation of the defined maximum in succeeding years.[12]

[12]Also, in all of the illustrations the defined maximum exceeded the defined minimum in amount. **It is possible for the minimum to exceed the maximum,** generally in cases when prior service cost is unfunded and the interest rate (used in computing the interest equivalents for both the minimum and the maximum) exceeds the rate of prior service cost amortization under the maximum. When the minimum exceeds the maximum, the minimum should be used as the basis for recognizing the accrued pension expense. The fact that the minimum can exceed the maximum (as both are defined in **Opinion No. 8**) is a result of the deficiencies in the maximum concept approved by the APB. Because of the mandatory funding now required under ERISA, this situation is unlikely to occur.

Computation of Minimum Provision—Case C

Year	Normal Cost	Past Service Cost Principal Funded 12/31	Past Service Cost Unfunded 1/1	5% Interest on Unfunded PSC	Vested Benefits Charge	Minimum Pension Provision
	(a)	(b)	(c)	(d)	(e)	(f)
1977	$50,000	$ 7,258	$240,000	$12,000	-0-	$62,000
1978	50,000	7,621	232,742	11,637	-0-	61,637
1979	50,000	8,002	225,121	11,256	-0-	61,256
⟨	⟩	⟨	⟩	⟩	⟨	⟨
1992	50,000	15,089	83,371	4,169	-0-	54,169
⟩	⟩	⟩	⟨	⟩	⟩	⟩
1996	50,000	18,341	18,341	917	-0-	50,917
1997	50,000	-0-	-0-	-0-	-0-	50,000

(a) Actuarially determined.
(b) $19,258 (PSC funding payment) minus (d), the interest portion.
(c) Preceding balance minus (b) in preceding year.
(d) 5% of (c).
(e) No charge assumed necessary.
(f) (a) plus (d) plus (e).

Computation of Maximum Provision—Case C

Year	Normal Cost	PSC Amortization 10%	Liability Balance 1/1	Interest Equivalent at 5%	Maximum Pension Provision
	(a)	(b)	(c)	(d)	(e)
1977	$50,000	$24,000	-0-	-0-	$74,000
1978	50,000	24,000	$ 3,864	$ 193	74,193
1979	50,000	24,000	7,921	396	74,396
⟨	⟩	⟨	⟨	⟨	⟨
1991	50,000	24,000	75,697	3,785	77,785
1992	50,000	-0-	83,346	4,167	54,167
⟩		⟩	⟨	⟩	⟩
1996	50,000	-0-	18,304	915	50,915
1997	50,000	-0-	-0-	-0-	50,000

(a) Actuarially determined.
(b) 10% of past service cost (until fully amortized).
(c) Cumulative difference between expense accrued and amounts funded.
(d) 5% of (c).
(e) (a) plus (b) plus (d).

In these illustrations the minimum and maximum did not change over the 15 years. As long as the company's pension expense falls between these two constraints, these lower and upper boundaries may not be affected. It is sometimes difficult to understand why the maximum can be applied for 15 years, when the past service cost and prior service cost increments should be amortized over 10 years. However, it should be remembered that in the cases illustrated here the maximum is not being used as the amount of the pension expense; rather, it is being used only as an upper boundary.

Experience (Actuarial) Gains or Losses

As discussed earlier, actuaries deal with several uncertainties in estimating the cost of a pension plan. In tentatively resolving these uncertainties, actuaries make assumptions. Assumptions, for example, usually have to be made about such items as the interest rate, mortality rate, retirement rate, turnover rate, disability rate, and salary amounts. Seldom does actual experience coincide with estimated results. Consequently, **adjustments may need to be made to reflect (1) deviations between estimated conditions and actual experience, and (2) revisions in the underlying assumptions.** These adjustments are referred to as "experience gains and losses" in the Pension Reform Act of 1974 and as "actuarial gains and losses" in **APB Opinion No. 8.** If the experience is favorable (actual earnings rate exceeds assumed earnings rate) or if the new assumptions are more optimistic, the adjustments that result are gains; if experience has been unfavorable (actual salary rates of employees higher than assumed salary rates) or if the new assumptions are less optimistic, the adjustments are losses. The net effect of the gains and losses determined in a particular valuation is ordinarily dealt with as a single amount.

Once the gains and losses have been identified and measured, the problem becomes one of timing their recognition in providing for pension expense: the familiar problem of allocating gains and losses to accounting periods. To eliminate wide fluctuations in pension costs caused by these gains and losses, the APB concluded that **these gains and losses usually should be spread or averaged over the current and future periods.** The time period considered reasonable for spreading or averaging is from 10 to 20 years. In practice, therefore, one of the following methods is usually applied:

1. **Spreading method.** Net gains and losses are applied to current and future cost, either through the normal cost or through the past service cost (or prior service cost on amendment); a future period of 10 to 20 years is considered reasonable.
2. **Averaging method.** An average of annual net gains and losses, developed from knowledge of those that occurred in the past and consideration of those expected to occur in the future, is applied either to the normal cost or through the past service cost (or prior service cost on amendment).

The accountant must be careful to determine whether normal cost has already been adjusted for the actuarial gain or loss. For example, some actuarial cost methods, such as the entry age normal method, automatically spread the actuarial gains or losses and therefore double accounting might occur if a separate adjustment were made. Other actuarial cost methods, such as the unit credit method, recognize the actuarial gain immediately but spread or average the loss.

Note also that there is a major exception to the two approaches mentioned above. Actuarial gains and losses should be recognized immediately if they arise from a single occurrence not directly related to the operation of the pension plan and not in the ordinary course of the employer's business. Examples of **single occurrence gains or losses** are effects of a plant closing and a merger or acquisition of another whole business. To illustrate, Bethlehem Steel recently reported a third-quarter loss of $477 million, one of the largest quarterly deficit ever recorded by a U.S. corporation. A great part of this loss was attributable to future estimated benefits payable to workers who were permanently laid off. In this situation, the actuarial loss should be treated as an adjustment to the gain or loss on the plant closing, and should not affect pension cost for the current or future periods.

To illustrate the spreading method assume that Harden Co.'s actuarial reports indicate that actuarial gains and losses are computed separately, are not a part of normal cost, and are spread over 10 years. The information relative to normal cost and actuarial gains and losses for Harden Co. is as follows:

Year	Normal Cost	Actuarial Gain or (Loss)	Cumulative Actuarial Gain or (Loss)
1970	$83,000	$ 7,000	$ 7,000
1971	85,000	32,000	39,000
1972	86,000	(7,000)	32,000
1973	86,000	(21,000)[a]	11,000
1974	87,000	18,000	29,000
1975	88,000	(73,000)[b]	(44,000)
1976	90,000	6,000	(38,000)
1977	91,000	9,000	(29,000)
1978	90,000	15,000	(14,000)
1979	92,000	(8,000)	(22,000)
1980	94,000	12,000	(10,000)

[a]Changed interest rate assumption from 7% to 6½%.
[b]Plant closing resulted in a $69,000 actuarial loss.

The total pension cost for 1979 and 1980, assuming that actuarial gains and losses (excluding single occurrence loss of $69,000 due to plant closing) are spread, is as follows:

Computation of Pension Expense—1979

Normal cost	$92,000
Adjustment for actuarial gain	4,700[a]
Total pension expense	$87,300

[a][($22,000) + $69,000] ÷ 10 = $4,700 Gain

Computation of Pension Expense—1980

Normal cost	$94,000
Adjustment for actuarial gain	5,200[a]
Total pension expense	$88,800

[a][($10,000) + $69,000 − $7,000] ÷ 10 = $5,200 Gain

In 1980, the computation of the cumulative actuarial gain or loss is again adjusted for the single occurrence actuarial loss and the actuarial gain of $7,000 related to 1970 (now outside the 10-year period) is eliminated because it is fully amortized.

The profession further recommends recognizing **unrealized appreciation and depreciation** on investments to determine annual pension expense on a rational and systematic basis that avoids giving unjustified weight to short-term market fluctuations. Appreciation and depreciation ordinarily need not be recognized, however, for debt securities expected to be held to maturity and redeemed at face value.

The Pension Reform Act of 1974 requires that actuarial gains and losses be amortized over a period not to exceed 15 years for a single employer plan and 20 years for a multi-employer plan. Actuarial gains decrease the contributions of the employer, whereas losses increase the amount the employer must contribute to meet funding requirements.

Disclosure of Pensions in Financial Statements

Within the Financial Statements The existence of a pension plan may result in recording not only an annual provision for pension expense, which is charged against revenue appearing on the income statement, but also accrued or deferred pension costs that are reported in the body of the balance sheet. As already indicated, if the amount paid (credit to Cash) by the employer to the pension trust is less than the annual provision (debit to Pension Expense), a credit balance accrual in the amount of the difference arises. This accrued pension cost usually appears in the long-term liability section and might be described as Liability for Pension Expense Not Funded, Provisions for Pension Cost in Excess of Payments, or Pension Costs Charged to Expense But Not Funded, or Due to Pension Fund. Classification as a current liability occurs when the liability requires the disbursement of cash within the next year.

If the cash paid (amount funded) to the pension trust during the period is greater than the amount charged to expense, a deferred charge equal to the difference arises. This deferral should be reported as Prepaid Pension Expense in the current asset section if it is current in nature, and as Deferred Pension Expense in the other assets section if it is long-term in nature.

Unfunded prior service cost and past service cost do not represent liabilities in either a legal or an accounting sense and, therefore, are not reported as such in the employer's balance sheet. Prior service cost in general and past service cost in particular, although measured by employee service in years prior to incurrence of the cost, are an expense of subsequent years. Neither prior nor past service have accounting significance until recognized as expense under appropriate accrual accounting. Only if the prior or past service cost is a part of the accrual or the deferral discussed in the two preceding paragraphs would this cost appear in the employer's balance sheet.

If employees have legally enforceable claims against the employer, **vested pension rights** exist, and any excess of the actuarial present value of such rights over the amount funded or accrued might be reported as a liability. This circumstance arises occasionally in the early years of a pension plan that creates significant unfunded vested pension obligations. The unfunded vested pension right is a legal obligation that would be reported as a long-term liability (unless payment within the year appears likely) with other pension cost accruals but should be described as Pension Benefits Payable But Not Funded or Expensed. The debit side of this entry should not be charged to expense but should be carried forward as a deferred charge to the operations of future years and reported in the other assets section as Deferred Pension Expense.[13]

Footnote Disclosure   Because company pension plans are frequently important to an understanding of financial position and the results of operations, the following information, if not disclosed in the body of the financial statements, should be disclosed in footnotes:[14]

1. A brief statement that a pension plan exists, identifying the employee groups covered.
2. A brief statement of the company's accounting and funding policies.
3. The provision for pension cost for the period.
4. The excess, if any, of vested benefits over the amount funded or accrued.
5. The nature and effect of significant matters affecting comparability for all periods presented, such as changes in accounting methods, changes in circumstances, or significant amendments.

This is an example of what the profession considers appropriate disclosure:

> The company and its subsidiaries have several pension plans covering substantially all of their employees, including certain employees in foreign countries. The total pension expense for the year was $. . . . , which includes, as to certain of the plans, amortization of prior service cost over periods ranging from 25 to 40 years. The company's policy is to fund pension cost accrued. The actuarially computed value of vested benefits for all plans as of December 31, 19. ., exceeded the total of the pension fund and balance-sheet accruals less pension prepayments and deferred charges by approximately $. . . . . . A change during the year in the actuarial cost method used in computing pension cost had the effect of reducing net income for the year by approximately $. . . . .

Tenneco's footnote to its financial statements on pages 201 and 202 discloses details of its several pension plans.

Effects of the Pension Reform Act of 1974

The Employee Retirement Income Security Act of 1974 (ERISA) affects virtually every private retirement plan in the United States. It attempts to safeguard employees' pension rights by mandating many pension plan requirements, including mini-

---

[13]In December 1974, IBM transferred $150 million to its pension trust because the vested benefits exceeded the market value of the fund and balance sheet accruals by $340 million. IBM classified the transfer as a prepaid expense.

[14]As of the date of this writing the FASB has outstanding a Proposed Statement of Financial Accounting Standards, "Disclosure of Pension and Other Post-Retirement Benefit Information" (July 12, 1979) as an amendment to *APB Opinion No. 8*. The FASB would substitute for disclosure 4 above the following for an employer having a single defined benefit pension plan:
1. The actuarial present value of accumulated plan benefits.
2. The actuarial present value of vested plan benefits.
3. The plan's net assets available for benefits.
4. A description of significant actuarial assumptions and asset valuation methods used to determine 1, 2, and 3.

The reasons for the recent modification are many and varied. However, recent sales of some companies at below book value provide a clue as to why accumulated plan benefits should be disclosed. Recently, for example, Wisconsin Steel Co. stock sold substantially below book value per share because it had a large amount of unfunded pension cost. In addition, disclosure of the net assets available and of the significant actuarial assumptions employed is badly needed. For example, it is estimated that a ¼% change in the interest rate assumption generally affects the annual pension cost by 6 percent. At present this type of information is generally not available.

mum funding, participation, and vesting. These requirements can influence the employers' costs significantly. An important part of this legislation is that annual funding is no longer discretionary; an employer must fund the plan in accordance with an actuarial cost method which over time will be sufficient to pay for all pension obligations. If funding does not occur in a reasonable manner, fines may be imposed and tax deductions denied. Plan administrators are required to publish a comprehensive description and summary of the plan and detailed annual reports accompanied by many supplementary schedules and statements relating to the plan. ERISA further mandates that the required reports, statements, and supplementary schedules be subjected to audit by qualified independent public accountants.

Another important part of the Act is the creation of the Pension Benefit Guaranty Corporation (PBGC). **The PBGC's purpose is to administer terminated plans** and to impose liens on the employer's assets for certain unfunded pension liabilities. If a plan is terminated, the PBGC can effectively impose a lien against the employer's assets for the excess of the present value of guaranteed vested benefits over the pension fund assets. This lien has the status of a tax lien and, therefore, takes priority over most other creditorship claims. An interesting aspect of this section of the Act is that the PBGC has the power to force an involuntary termination of a pension plan whenever the risks related to nonpayment of the pension obligation seem unreasonable. Because ERISA restricts the lien that the PBGC can impose to 30% of net worth, the PBGC must monitor all plans to insure that net worth is sufficient to meet the pension benefit obligations. The PBGC is now trustee for approximately 280 private pension plans that have been terminated since 1974.[15] In addition, the PBGC estimates that another 160 plans are so weak financially that they are potential candidates for termination over the next decade. If these plans were terminated in the next ten years, an unfunded liability of approximately $8.3 billion would be left.

An interesting accounting problem relates to the manner of disclosing the possible termination of a plan. When, for example, should a contingent liability be disclosed, given that the company is experiencing financial difficulty and may have difficulty meeting its pension obligations if its plan is terminated. At present this issue is unresolved, and considerable judgment would have to be exercised in assessing the proper accounting for these contingent liabilities.

In response to the 1974 Pension Reform Act, the FASB issued **Interpretation No. 3** and placed the overall subject of pension accounting on its technical agenda. **The FASB concluded that as a result of the 1974 Act, no change is required in the minimum and maximum limits for the annual pension provision for pension cost as set forth in APB Opinion No. 8.** (Because the provisions of the 1974 Act support the maximum amount as pension cost, however, the maximum and minimum distinction loses some of its significance.) If a change in pension cost results from compliance with the 1974 Act, it must enter into the determination of periodic

---

[15]Case law in this area is extremely sketchy at the present time. Recently, however, a case was settled indicating that liability extends beyond subsidiary companies and reaches to parent companies and other subsidiary units as well. The case involved Avon Sole Co. and Tenn.-ERO Corp., both units of Ouimet Corp. When these two companies went bankrupt, PBGC attempted to obtain payment from the parent and other related subsidiaries. The court held that when one member of a controlled group terminates an underfunded pension plan, the entire group may be liable.

provisions for pension expense **subsequent** to the date the plan becomes subject to the Act.

Also, on the basis of its analysis of the 1974 Act, the Board does not believe that the Act creates a legal obligation for unfunded pension costs that warrants accounting recognition as a liability except in the following two respects: (1) In the event of the termination of a pension plan, the Act imposes a liability on an enterprise. When there is convincing evidence that a plan will be terminated, and the liability on termination will exceed fund assets and related prior accruals, the excess liability must be accrued. If the amount of the excess liability cannot be reasonably determined, disclosure of the circumstances and an estimate of the possible range of the liability must be disclosed in notes to the financial statements. (2) The employer must fund a minimum amount annually unless a waiver is obtained from the government; without a waiver, the amount currently required to be funded must be recognized as a liability by a charge to pension expense for the period, by a deferred charge, or by a combination of the two as appropriate.[16]

Questions

1. Define a private pension plan. Differentiate between a **funded** and an **unfunded** pension plan. How does a **contributory** pension plan differ from a **noncontributory plan**?
2. Differentiate between "accounting for the employer" and "accounting for the pension fund."
3. Explain the term "funded" as it relates to (1) the pension fund and (2) the employer. Explain the meaning of "pension liability" as it relates to (1) the pension fund and (2) the employer.
4. Explain how cash basis accounting for pension plans differs from accrual basis accounting for pension plans.
5. Why is cash basis accounting generally considered unacceptable for pension-plan accounting?
6. Distinguish among (a) normal cost, (b) past service cost, and (c) prior service cost as they relate to pension plans.
7. This footnote to the financial statement of the Dryer Soap Company discloses the existence of the company's employee pension plan:
   Pension Plan. The company has a pension plan covering all employees. Total pension expense for the year was $528,400, which includes normal cost, and the amortization of "past service cost," which originally totaled $1,400,000 (unamortized balance at year end being $1,033,826), over a 20-year period at 6%. The company's policy is to fund the pension cost accrued with the trustee of the pension plan.
   (a) What is meant by "past service cost"?
   (b) Of the total annual pension expense, what amount is normal cost?
   (c) What amount was paid to the pension fund trustee during the year?
   (d) On the basis of the footnote above, what amounts appear in the body of the balance sheet relative to the pension plan?
8. What are "vested benefits" and under what circumstances must they be accrued?
9. Upon what factors is the amount of pension expense recognized during a particular accounting period dependent?

---

[16]"Accounting for the Cost of Pension Plans Subject to the Employee Retirement Income Security Act of 1974," *FASB Interpretation No. 3* (Stamford, Conn.: FASB, 1974), par. 3 and 5.

10. What is the nature of "interest equivalents" and what is the justification for including them in the determination of pension cost?

11. Accountants currently are divided in their opinions of the nature of pension cost. Two primary views are supported.
    (a) What are these two views?
    (b) Indicate which of these views you support and explain your view.

12. What is the minimum annual provision for pension cost that may be provided under **APB Opinion No. 8**?

13. What is the maximum annual provision for pension cost that may be provided under **APB Opinion No. 8**?

14. Which method results in the more appropriate pension cost provision: the minimum provision or the maximum provision? Support your view.

15. Why is "interest on unfunded past service cost" considered as a necessary inclusion in the computation of the minimum pension provision?

16. If accounting charges for past service costs exceed funding payments, what kind of account arises and how should it be reported in the financial statements? If the reverse occurs, that is, payments exceed charges, what kind of account arises and how should it be reported?

17. Discuss the probable effect of a pension plan amendment to the annual pension provision (a) if the accounting method in use results in the minimum provision, and (b) if the accounting method in use results in the maximum provision.

18. What are actuarial gains and losses as related to pension plans?

19. What methods are applied in practice to account for actuarial gains or losses? In what situations should actuarial gains and losses be recognized immediately?

20. What disclosures should be made in financial statements or their related footnotes for pension plans?

21. (a) What are the arguments in favor of accruing past service cost only to the extent funded?
    (b) What are the arguments in favor of accruing past service cost regardless of the amount funded?

Cases

C21-1 In examining the costs of pension plans, a CPA encounters certain terms. The elements of pension costs that the terms represent must be dealt with appropriately if generally accepted accounting principles are to be reflected in the financial statements of entities with pension plans.

Instructions

(a) 1. Discuss the theoretical justification for accrual recognition of pension costs.
    2. Discuss the relative objectivity of the measurement process of accrual versus cash (pay-as-you-go) accounting for annual pension costs.

(b) Explain the following terms as they apply to accounting for pension plans:
    1. Actuarial valuations.
    2. Actuarial cost methods.
    3. Vested benefits.

(c) What information should be disclosed about a company's pension plans in its financial statements and their notes?

(AICPA adapted)

C21-2 The following items frequently appear on financial statements.
- (a) Under the caption Deferred Charges:
       Deferred Pension Cost (attributable to Funding of Past Service Liability).
- (b) Under the caption Retained Earnings Appropriated:
       Reserve for Past Service Pension Cost (after deducting the related anticipated tax reduction).
- (c) On the Income Statement:
       Current Service Cost (Normal Cost)
       Past Service Cost
       Trustee's Fees.

Instructions

With regard to "accounting for pension cost," explain the significance of each of the items above on corporate financial statements. Show how each is consistent with generally accepted accounting principles. (**Note:** all items set forth above are **not** necessarily to be found on the statements of a single company.)

(AICPA adapted)

C21-3 Moluf, Inc. has just acquired all of the capital stock of Beltline Railway Corporation and has asked you to audit the balance sheet of the latter as of the date of acquisition. In the course of your examination you determine that the company has a noncontributory pension plan and has charged to income all payments made to the pension trust. There is no special provision in the pension plan that limits the company liability to an amount equal to assets in trust. The independent actuaries employed by the company have furnished you with the following summary of past service liability as of the audit date.

	Accrued Liability	Assets in Trust	Net Liability
For employees already retired	$1,189,000	$425,000	$ 764,000
For employees eligible to retire at their own option	477,000		477,000
For employees under retirement age	1,569,000		1,569,000
	$3,235,000	$425,000	$2,810,000

Instructions

Discuss the factors to be considered in making adjustments to properly set forth the financial position disclosed by the statements under audit. Moluf, Inc. is in the 48% tax bracket.

(AICPA adapted)

C21-4 Delta & Sigma Phototype, Inc., was organized in 1960 and established a formal pension plan on January 1, 1976, to provide retirement benefits for all employees. The plan is noncontributory and is funded through a trustee, the Corner National Bank, which invests all funds and pays all benefits as they become due. Vesting occurs when the employee retires at age sixty-five. Original past service cost of $110,000 is being amortized over 15 years and funded over 10 years. The company also funds an amount equal to current normal cost net of actuarial gains and losses. There have been no amendments to the plan since its inception. Portions of the independent actuary's report follows:

Delta & Sigma Phototype, Inc.
BASIC NONCONTRIBUTORY PENSION PLAN
Actuarial Report as of June 30, 1980

I. Current Year's Funding and Pension Cost

Normal cost (before adjustment for actuarial gains) computed under the entry-age-normal method		$ 34,150
Actuarial gains:		
Investment gains (losses):		
Excess of expected dividend income over actual dividend income		(350)
Gain on sale of investments		4,050
Gains in actuarial assumptions for:		
Mortality		3,400
Employee turnover		5,050
Reduction in pension cost from closing of plant		8,000
Net actuarial gains		20,150
Normal cost (funded currently)	$14,000	14,000
Past service costs:		
Funding	14,245	
Amortization		10,597
Total funded	$28,245	
Total pension cost for financial-statement purposes		$ 24,597

II. Fund Assets

Cash		$ 4,200
Dividends receivable		1,525
Investment in common stocks, at cost (market value, $177,800)		162,750
		$168,475

III. Actuarial Liabilities

Number of employees	46
Number of employees retired	0
Yearly earnings of employees	$598,000
Actuarial liability	$145,000

Instructions

(a) What interest rate is being used in the amortization and funding of the past service cost?

(b) On the basis of requirements for accounting for the cost of pension plans, evaluate the (1) treatment of actuarial gains and losses and (2) computation of pension cost for financial-statement purposes. **Ignore income tax considerations.**

(c) Independently of your answer to part (a), assume that the total amount to be funded is $32,663, the total pension cost for financial-statement purposes is $29,015, and all amounts presented in the actuary's report are correct. In accordance with **APB No. 8,** write a footnote for the financial statements of Delta & Sigma Phototype, Inc., for the year ended June 30, 1980.

(AICPA adapted)

Exercises

E21-1 On January 2, 1980, Duplex Corp. adopted a pension plan covering all its employees. The plan's actuary estimated past service costs at $300,000. Duplex funds the entire amount of past service cost plus interest at the end of the first year of the plan, and each year funds normal cost in full at the end of the year. For accounting purposes, Duplex has chosen to record as annual pension expense 10% of past service cost, plus normal cost, plus (or minus) interest on any differences between amounts expensed and amounts funded. Normal cost is as follows: 1980, $60,000; 1981, $60,000; 1982, $70,000; and 1983, $80,000. The actuary recommends the use of a 7% rate for discounting.

Instructions

(Round to the nearest dollar.)

 (a) Prepare the journal entry to record the pension expense and the amount funded in 1980.

 (b) Prepare the journal entry to record the pension expense and the amount funded in 1983.

E21-2 On January 1, 1980, the Caboose Railway Company adopts an employee pension plan. The following data relate to the operation of the plan for the year 1980:

 1. Normal pension cost was actuarially computed to be $84,000 for 1980 and $89,000 for 1981 and is being funded annually.

 2. The past service cost of $360,000 is to be amortized over 10 years.

 3. It is estimated that investments of the pension fund will earn 6%.

 4. The past service cost is being funded over 15 years with end-of-year payments.

Instructions

(Round to the nearest dollar and ignore the minimum and maximum limits.)

 (a) Prepare the journal entry to record the payment to the pension trust and the provision for pension cost for 1980.

 (b) Assuming that the same facts exist in 1981, prepare the journal entry to record the payment to the pension trust and the provision for pension cost for 1981.

E21-3 On January 1, 1980, Wingtip Airlines adopted a noncontributory pension plan. An actuary determined that the past service cost at the date of adoption was $650,000, and that the normal pension cost is $200,000. The actuary also indicated that the appropriate interest rate was 5%.

 Management plans to fund the normal cost fully each year, and to fund the past service cost by making equal payments at the end of each of the first 5 years. The past service cost is to be amortized over 20 years.

Instructions

(Round to the nearest dollar and ignore the minimum and maximum limits.)

Prepare the journal entries to recognize the annual pension expense and to record the annual contribution to the pension fund for the years 1980, 1981, and 1982.

E21-4 Susan Robinson Bakeries, Inc. adopted a pension plan for its employees on January 1, 1979. The pertinent data relative to the cost of the plan are as follows:

 1. Cost allocated to past service, $700,000.

 2. Period of past service cost amortization: 20 years.

 3. Normal cost, $75,000.

 4. Amount funded annually, $100,000.

 5. Rate of earnings on pension-fund investments, 5%.

Instructions

 (a) Prepare a five-year schedule that discloses for each year, beginning with the year of adoption, the amounts of (1) normal cost, (2) amortized past service cost, (3) interest equivalent on difference between prior years' provisions and amounts funded, (4) total annual charge to expense, (5) amount funded, and (6) cumulative difference between provisions and amounts funded (round to the nearest dollar and ignore the minimum and maximum limits).

(b) Using the data from part (a), prepare the journal entry to record the amount funded in the fifth year and the provision for pension expense.

E21-5 As a result of labor negotiations, 21st Century Films Co. adopts a pension plan for its employees. An actuarial firm estimates past service cost at $400,000 and normal cost for the first year of $50,000. Films Co. will amortize the past service cost at the rate of 10% per year and fund it over 20 years with end-of-the-year payments. Only half of each year's normal cost will be funded during the first three years. The company's intent is to expense the maximum allowable for acceptable accounting purposes. The actuary recommends the use of a 6% discounting rate.

Instructions

(Round to the nearest dollar.)

(a) Prepare the journal entry to record the pension provision and the amount funded during the first year.

(b) Prepare the journal entry to record the pension provision and the amount funded during the third year. Normal cost is $60,000 in the second year and $80,000 in the third year.

(c) What is reported on Films' balance sheet at the end of the third year?

E21-6 Advanced Concepts Corp. adopts a pension plan on January 1, 1980. The following information relates to the operation of the plan for 1980 and 1981:

1. Normal pension cost was actuarially computed to be $44,000 for both years. Normal cost is funded annually.
2. The past service cost of $270,000 is to be funded by making equal payments at the end of each of the first 20 years, and is to be amortized over 10 years.
3. It is estimated that investments of the pension fund will earn a 5% return.

Instructions

Compute the minimum provision allowed under **APB Opinion No. 8** for the years 1980 and 1981.

E21-7 As part of your 1981 audit of the Dairy Products Company, you are to determine if the pension expense computed by the client falls within the maximum and minimum limits. After the actuary has been questioned and the company's records examined, the following relevant data have been established:

1.	Pension expense computed by the client and recorded in 1981	$105,000
2.	Pension fund balance—1/1/81	750,000
3.	Pension fund balance—12/31/81	865,000
4.	Accrued pension liability—1/1/81 (Same as costs in excess of payments)	250,000
5.	Past service cost (initial total in 1973)	600,000
6.	Normal cost	50,000
7.	Cash paid into fund during 1981	75,000
8.	Unfunded past service cost—1/1/81	400,000
9.	Rate of return earned on pension fund investments	5%

Instructions

(a) Determine the minimum and maximum pension expense provisions for 1981 in accordance with **APB Opinion No. 8.**

(b) On the basis of the data above, indicate the entry (accounts debited and credited) the company most likely recorded for pension cost in 1981.

E21-8 Denson Originals, Inc. adopts a pension plan on January 1, 1980. According to actuarial computations, the past service cost is $1,350,000, and the normal cost for 1980 and 1981 is $400,000. The past service cost is completely funded in 1980; normal cost is funded each year. The pension fund is able to earn 9% on its investments.

Instructions

Assuming that the defined maximum limit is recognized as pension expense, prepare the journal entries for 1980 and 1981 to record pension expense and to record the payment to the pension fund. Support your entries with labeled computations.

E21-9 Current pronouncements on pension accounting advocate the consistent application of an accounting method that uses an acceptable actuarial cost method and that results in annual pension provisions that lie between the minimum and maximum. Interest equivalents are a part of both minimum and maximum annual pension provisions.

Presented below are data related to the employee's pension plan of the S. Louise Woolen Corporation:

Past service cost	$800,000
Normal cost	65,000
Cash deposited in the fund during 1981	100,000
Pension expense not funded, 1/1/81	280,000
Funded portion of past service cost, 1/1/81	200,000
Pension expense for 1981 as computed by the firm's accountants	125,000
Rate of return earned on pension fund investment	8%

Instructions

(a) What would the 1981 interest equivalent be under the **minimum** annual provision for the case above?

(b) What would the 1981 interest equivalent be under the **maximum** annual provision for the case above?

E21-10 Glo-Coat Paint Co., a calendar-year corporation, adopted a company pension plan at the beginning of 1980. This plan is to be funded and noncontributory. Glo-Coat used an appropriate actuarial cost method to determine its normal annual pension cost for 1980 and 1981 as $15,000 and $16,000, respectively, which was paid in the same year.

Glo-Coat's actuarially determined past service costs were funded on December 31, 1980, at an amount properly computed as $106,000. These past service costs are to be amortized at the maximum amount permitted by generally accepted accounting principles. The interest factor assumed by the actuary is 6%.

Instructions

Prepare journal entries to record the funding of past service costs on December 31, 1980, and the pension expenses for the years 1980 and 1981. Under each journal entry give the explanation or computation to support your entry. Round to the nearest dollar.

(AICPA adapted)

Problems

P21-1 The notes to the financial statements of Elbert Cheese Products Company, for the year ended December 31, 1980, include the following:

Retirement Plan: The charge to operations for pension expense of $2,306,609 includes normal cost of $2,000,000, past service cost amortization of $296,856, and interest (6%) equivalents of $9,753 on the excess of provisions over amounts funded. Normal cost is funded annually and, although the company's plan (adopted January 1, 1978) does not require funding of past service cost, this cost is currently being funded over 30 years. For accounting purposes the past service cost is being amortized over a 16-year period. As of the balance sheet date the unamortized past service cost allocable to future periods was $2,627,978.

Instructions

(Round all amounts to the nearest dollar.)

(a) Differentiate "normal cost" from "past service cost."

(b) What justification is there for allocating past service cost to future periods?

(c) What amounts relative to the company's pension plan appear in the body of the balance sheet at December 31, 1980? Assume normal cost is $2,000,000 each year.

(d) Prepare the journal entry, with explanation, to record the amount funded in 1980 and the pension provision for the year.

P21-2   Helen Buggert Company initiated a funded, noncontributory pension plan and gave employees credit for prior employment. The actuary estimated the past service cost at date of inception of the plan to be $120,000. Management decides to amortize past service cost over three years and to fund past service cost over four years using a 6% interest rate. (A less than 10-year amortization period is assumed only to keep the problem short.) Normal cost is actuarially determined to be $18,000 for year 1, $22,000 for year 2, $25,000 for year 3, and $27,000 for year 4; normal cost is fully funded each year.

Instructions

(Round all amounts to the nearest dollar and ignore the minimum and maximum limits.)

(a) Prepare an amortization, funding, and expense schedule for the first four years.

(b) Prepare the entries for each of the first four years of the plan.

(c) Indicate the amounts that would be reflected on the income statement and the balance sheet for the first four years.

P21-3   Ginny Brown Hospital Corp. initiated a funded, noncontributory pension plan and gave employees credit for prior employment (assume no vested benefits). The past service cost was actuarially estimated at the date of inception of the plan to be $840,000. To keep the problem short, assume the past service cost is to be amortized over four years and funded over three years in equal amounts. Normal cost is actuarially determined to be $300,000 each year for the first two years and $380,000 for the next two years; normal cost is fully funded each year. The actuary recommends an 8% interest rate.

Instructions

(Round amounts to the nearest dollar and ignore the minimum and maximum limits.)

(a) Prepare an amortization, funding, and expense schedule for the first four years.

(b) Prepare the entries for each of the first four years of the pension plan.

(c) Indicate the amounts that are reflected on the income statement and the balance sheet for the first four years.

P21-4   Paul Steg Piano Company is contemplating the adoption of a pension plan for its employees. President Steg wishes to know the effect such a plan might have on the company's earnings. An actuarial consulting firm has indicated that the cost of the proposed plan allocated to past service would be $800,000 and that normal cost would be $120,000. President Steg had indicated that the company will not fund the past service cost, but each year the company will pay to the pension trustee an amount equal to normal cost and interest at 4% on the unfunded past service cost.

Instructions

(a) Compute for President Steg (1) the minimum provision and (2) the maximum provision allowable **in the first year** under the stipulations and data relative to the company's pension plan.

(b) Compute for President Steg (1) the minimum provision and (2) the maximum provision allowable **in the fifth year** of the plan assuming no change in actuarial method or the funding policies of the company (round computations to the nearest dollar).

P21-5 Several years after incorporation Fresno Canning Company initiated a funded, noncontributory pension plan. The past service cost at the date of inception of the plan was actuarially estimated to be $354,595.00. The past service cost is to be amortized over four years and funded over three years.

Instructions

(Ignore the minimum and maximum limits.)

(a) Prepare a schedule that reflects the amortization and funding of the past service cost using a 5% interest rate.

(b) Assuming the actuary determined the normal pension cost to be $75,000 for year one and $80,000 for year two, prepare the entries with respect to the pension plan for both years.

(c) Indicate the amounts that are reflected on the income statement and the balance sheet for each of the first two years.

P21-6 Melissa Porter Model Agency initiated a funded, noncontributory pension plan several years after incorporation. The actuary estimated the past service cost at the date of inception of the plan to be $188,609.00. To keep the problem short, assume the company decides to amortize the past service over three years and to fund past service cost over two years.

Instructions

(Ignore the minimum and maximum limits.)

(a) Prepare a schedule that reflects the amortization and funding of the past service cost using a 4% interest rate.

(b) Assuming that the actuary determined the normal pension cost to be $70,000 for year one and $73,000 for year two, prepare the entries with respect to the pension plan for both years.

(c) Indicate the amounts that are reflected on the income statement and the balance sheet for each of the first two years.

P21-7 Allservice Enterprises, which started operations in 1975, instituted a pension plan on January 1, 1980. The insurance company which is administering the pension plan has computed the present value of past service costs at $100,000 for the five years of operations through December 31, 1979. The pension plan provides for fully vested benefits when employees have completed ten years of service. Therefore, there will be no vested benefits until December 31, 1984.

The insurance company proposed that Allservice Enterprises fund the past service cost in equal installments over 15 years calculated by the present value method. Using an interest rate of 5 percent, the annual payment for past service cost would be $9,634. The company's treasurer agreed to this payment schedule. In addition, the controller concluded that a 15-year period was a reasonable period for amortizing the past service costs for book purposes. Consequently, the past service costs will also be amortized at the annual rate of $9,634 for 15 years.

The normal cost for the pension fund is estimated to be $30,000 each year for the next four years. The annual payment to the insurance company covering the current year's normal cost and the annual installment on the past service cost is payable on December 31 each year, the end of Allservice Enterprises' fiscal year. The insurance company was paid $39,634 ($30,000 + $9,634) on December 31, 1980, to cover the company's pension obligations for 1980.

Instructions

(a) Calculate and label the components which comprise the maximum and minimum 1980 financial statement pension expense limits in accordance with generally accepted accounting principles for Allservice Enterprises.

(b) Assume Allservice Enterprises will be unable to remit the full pension payment ($39,634) in 1981 and will only submit $30,000 (the normal cost) to the insurance company. If Allservice Enterprises can recognize $39,634 as pension expense in 1981, show the entry required. If the company cannot recognize the $39,634 as pension expense in 1981, explain why not.

(CMA adapted)

P21-8 The Forest Products Company adopts a pension plan on January 1, 1980. An actuarial firm advises that a 5% interest rate is appropriate, and determines that the past service cost as of January 1, 1980 is $525,000, and the normal cost for 1980 is $76,000. The plan provides for vesting after 25 years of service by employees.

Management decides to fund the normal cost fully each year and to fund the past service cost over 25 years. Past service cost is to be amortized over 15 years.

Instructions

Assuming that the normal cost remains the same for 1981 and 1982, prepare the following for the years 1980, 1981, and 1982.

(a) A schedule that reflects the amortization and funding of past service cost, and the amounts to be reflected in the balance sheet.

(b) A schedule showing the computation of the minimum provision.

(c) A schedule showing the computation of the maximum provision.

(d) Journal entries at each year end to recognize the annual pension expense and to record the contribution to the pension fund.

P21-9 Mary Noble Ad Agency initiated a pension plan several years after incorporation. The amount of the past service cost was computed at the date of adoption of the plan to be $730,000. Management decides to amortize the past service cost over four years and to fund it each year end over three years. The normal cost is computed to be $40,000 for the first four years of the plan; normal cost is completely funded each year. An interest rate of 5% is appropriate for the pension fund. Assume that there are no vested benefits.

Instructions

(a) Prepare a schedule that reflects the amortization and funding of past service cost and the amounts reflected on the balance sheet at the end of the first four years.

(b) Prepare a schedule showing the computation of the minimum provision.

(c) Prepare a schedule showing the computation of the maximum provision.

(d) For financial accounting reporting purposes, will the company be allowed to amortize past service cost over four years?

P21-10 On January 1, 1980, Sherolyn Baker Publishing Co. adopts a funded, noncontributory pension plan. An actuarial firm computes the normal cost to be $54,000 for 1980 and 1981 and determines that the past service cost amounts to $440,000 at the date of the plan adoption. An interest rate of 5% is appropriate to the pension fund. Normal cost is fully funded each year. Past service cost is to be funded by equal payments at the end of each of the first 20 years.

Instructions

(a) Assuming that management decides to amortize past service costs over 20 years, prepare a schedule to reflect the amortization and funding of past service cost for 1980 and 1981. Also compute the maximum and minimum provisions under these policies.

(b) Prepare the journal entries to record the pension expense and the contribution to the pension fund for the years 1980 and 1981 under each of the following situations using the funding information above:
1. Past service cost is amortized over 20 years.
2. Management desires to record the minimum acceptable pension expense.
3. Management desires to record the maximum acceptable pension expense.

P21-11 Coquillette Corporation, which has been in operation for the past 23 years, decided late in 1980 to adopt, beginning on January 1, 1981, a funded pension plan for its employees. The pension plan is to be noncontributory and will provide for vesting after 5 years of service by each eligible employee. A trust agreement has been entered into whereby a large national insurance company will receive the yearly pension fund contributions and administer the fund.

Management, through extended consultation with the fund trustee, internal accountants, and independent actuaries, arrived at the following conclusions:

1. The normal pension cost for 1981 will be $30,000.
2. The present value of the past service cost at date of inception of the pension plan (January 1, 1981) is $200,000.
3. Because of the large sum of money involved, the past service costs will be funded at a rate of $23,365 per year for the next 15 years. The first payment will not be due until January 1, 1982.
4. In accordance with **APB Opinion No. 8,** the "unit credit method" of accounting for the pension costs will be followed. Pension costs will be amortized over a 10-year period. The 10-year accrual factor is $29,805 per year. Neither the maximum or minimum amortization amounts as prescribed by **APB Opinion No. 8** will be violated.
5. Where applicable, an 8% interest rate was assumed.

Instructions
(a) Define: Normal pension costs, past service costs.
(b) What amounts (use xxx if amount can't be calculated) will be reported in the company's
1. income statement for 1981?
2. balance sheet as of December 31, 1981?
3. notes to the statements?
Give account titles with the amounts.
(c) What amounts (use xxx if amount can't be calculated) will be reported in the company's
1. income statement for 1982?
2. balance sheet as of December 31, 1982?
3. notes to the statements?
Give account titles with the amounts.

(CMA adapted)

P21-12 Michelle Mattress Co., through labor negotiations has been encouraged to amend as of January 1, 1981, its employee pension plan, which has been in operation for 4 years, having been adopted on January 1, 1977. At the time the plan was adopted, the past service cost was actuarially computed to be $800,000 with normal cost set at $100,000 annually. Since the inception of the plan, the company has been funding in amounts equal to the annual provisions. The annual provisions for pension costs have included normal cost and amortization of past service cost over 20 years at a 5% interest rate.

As a result of the amendment, retirement benefits are to be increased. And, because credit has been given for years of service prior to the date of amendment, prior service cost has increased $420,000, and normal cost has increased to $145,000. The increase in prior service cost is to be amortized over 14 years, but the company will continue to fund annually the same amount it funded during the first 4 years of the plan.

Annual provisions for pension cost from January 1, 1981, include normal cost, amortization of past service cost (until fully amortized), amortization of the increase in prior service cost, and interest equivalents at 5% on any difference between prior years' provisions and amounts funded.

Instructions

(a) Compute the amount of prior service cost as of the amendment date, January 1, 1981.

(b) What amounts relative to the pension plan appeared in the body of the December 31, 1980, balance sheet?

(c) Prepare the journal entry that was recorded in 1980 for the amount funded and the provision for pension cost. Show computations in your explanation.

(d) Prepare the journal entry, with explanation, to record the amount funded in 1981 and the provision for pension cost for that year.

(e) What amounts relative to the pension plan would appear in the body of the December 31, 1981, balance sheet?

(f) Prepare the journal entry, with explanation, to record the amount funded in 1982 (assume no change in actuarial method or funding policy from 1981) and the provision for pension cost for 1982.

P21-13 In December 1970 a noncontributory employee group-retirement plan was adopted by the Yummy Candy Company. Assume that the market value of the securities in the fund is equal to book value. The following information has been obtained from the actuary's reports.

Year	Current Cost	Actuarial Gains (Losses)	Net Contribution
1971	$133,064	$ 3,994	$129,070
1972	156,452	26,438	130,014
1973	167,078	43,306	123,772
1974	206,192	(720)	206,912
1975	232,404	22,614	209,790
1976	203,758	203,758[a]	-0-
1977	256,250	114,806[b]	141,444
1978	279,794	110,210	169,584
1979	346,078	77,764	268,314
1980	394,222	102,498	291,724
1981	395,602	282,178[c]	113,424

Additional Information:

[a] Includes $170,112 gain from change in interest assumption from 5 to 5½%.

[b] Includes $24,084 of gain carried over from 1976.

[c] Includes $85,000 gain due to withdrawal of 2 officers of the company.

Instructions

Yummy Candy Company uses the spreading method to allocate actuarial gains and losses. The company has adopted a 10-year period for allocation.

(a) Compute the pension expense for 1980 and 1981.

(b) What alternative methods could be used to allocate the actuarial gains and losses?

P21-14 The following information has been obtained from the actuarial reports for the Lucky Oil Company. Assume that the market value of the securities in the pension fund is equal to book value, and that there is no past- or prior-service cost.

Year	Current Cost	Actuarial Gains (Losses)	Net Contribution
1971	$ 33,266	$ 998	$32,268
1972	39,113	6,609	32,504
1973	41,770	10,827	30,943
1974	51,548	(180)	51,728
1975	58,101	5,654	52,447
1976	50,940	50,940[a]	-0-
1977	64,063	28,701[b]	35,362
1978	69,948	27,552	42,396
1979	86,520	19,441	67,079
1980	98,955	25,624	73,331
1981	109,200	173,542[c]	-0-

Additional Information:

[a] Includes $35,025 gain as a result of change in interest assumption from 6% to 6½%.

[b] Includes $6,021 of gain carried over from 1976. —

[c] Includes:

1. $27,000 gain due to withdrawal of 2 officers of the Company.
2. $65,600 gain as result of change in interest assumption from 6½% to 7½%.
3. $48,900 gain from withdrawals in connection with a plant closing 2/20/81.— *unusual*

Instructions

Lucky Oil Company uses the spreading method to allocate its actuarial gains and losses over a period of 10 years. Compute the amount of pension expense for the years 1980 and 1981 giving proper consideration to the separately noted items in a, b, and c.

Accounting for
Leases

A **lease** is a contractual agreement between a **lessor** and a **lessee** that conveys to the lessee the right to use specific property (real or personal), owned by the lessor, for a specific period of time in return for stipulated, and generally periodic, cash payments (rents). An essential element of the lease agreement is that the lessor conveys less than the total interest in the property. Because of the financial, operating, and risk advantages that the lease arrangement provides, many businesses lease substantial amounts of property, both real and personal, as an alternative to ownership.

Prior to 1960, leasing chiefly affected retailing companies, which frequently lease their premises. Over the past two decades, leasing has grown tremendously in popularity; instead of borrowing money to buy an airplane, a computer, a nuclear core, or a satellite, a company leases it. Even the gambling casinos lease their slot machines. Airlines and railroads lease huge amounts of equipment; many hotel and motel chains lease their facilities; and most retail chains lease the bulk of their retail premises and warehouses. Increasingly, utilities have turned to leasing, as it has become harder for them to borrow money. It is estimated that $150 billion of assets was leased by American industry in 1979.[1] The increased significance and prevalence of lease arrangements in recent years have intensified the need for uniform accounting and complete informative reporting of these transactions.[2]

---

[1] Sidney R. Rose, "Leasing: The Creative Force of Asset Financing," *Fortune*, Vol. 100, No. 4, August 27, 1979, pp. 55–79. This same article contains the estimate "that by 1985, 75 per cent of the railcars operating in the United States will be owned by leasing companies and non-rail firms."

[2] The popularity and general applicability of leasing are evidenced by the fact that 527 of 600 companies surveyed by the AICPA in 1977 disclosed either capitalized or noncapitalized lease data (*Accounting Trends and Techniques—1978*).

Advantages of Leasing

Although the lease arrangement is not without its disadvantages, the growth in its use suggests that leasing often has a genuine advantage over owning property. Some of the commonly discussed advantages of leasing are:

1. Leasing permits 100% financing versus 60 to 80% under purchasing, thus conserving cash and working capital.
2. Leasing permits rapid changes in equipment, reduces risk of obsolescence, and in many cases passes the risk in residual value to the lessor.
3. Leasing permits write-off of the full cost of the asset (including land and residual values) and provides additional tax advantages through acceleration of deductions.
4. Leasing may be more flexible, because lease agreements may contain less restrictive provisions than other debt agreements.
5. Leasing in a certain manner leads to junior claims, does not add debt on a balance sheet, and does not affect financial ratios; hence it may add to borrowing capacity.[3]

The last point, commonly referred to as "off balance sheet financing," is critical to some companies. For instance, the 1977 balance sheet of UAL, Inc., a major United States airline, showed long-term debt of $978 million and total stockholders' equity of $777 million. Therefore, UAL's debt-to-equity ratio was a high but manageable 1.26 to 1. But the company also was obligated under leases, chiefly for airplanes and terminals; the future rental payments related to those noncancelable operating leases was $1.28 billion. Add the capitalized value of these payments to the long-term debt and UAL's debt-to-equity ratio climbs well over 2 to 1. In 1977, Safeway Stores was first required to capitalize lease commitments with a present value of $748 million on a balance sheet showing only $131 million in long-term debt. Or, consider what the situation of Glosser Bros., Inc., a retail department store chain, would be if it had to capitalize its future minimum lease commitments on noncancelable leases of $47.7 million on its 1979 balance sheet showing less than $1 million of long-term debt.

The existence or nonexistence of these advantages depends a great deal on the type and use required of the asset, the period of time involved, the financial condition of the company, and the future tax and economic conditions. Therefore, the decision to lease or to purchase deserves thorough individual analysis.

Lease Provisions

Because a lease is a contract, the provisions agreed to by the lessor and lessee may vary widely and be limited only by their ingenuity and the peculiarities of the asset. The **duration** (lease term) of the lease may be from a few moments to the entire expected economic life of the asset. The **rental payments** may be level from year to year, increasing in amount, or decreasing; the rents may be predetermined or may vary with sales, the prime interest rate, the consumer price index or some other factor; in most cases the rent is set to enable the lessor to recover the

---

[3]As demonstrated later in this chapter, certain types of lease arrangements need not be capitalized on the balance sheet. The liability section is frequently relieved of large future lease commitments which if recorded would adversely affect the debt-to-equity ratio. The reluctance to record lease obligations as liabilities is one of the primary reasons capitalized lease accounting is resisted and circumvented by lessees.

cost of the asset plus a fair return over the life of the lease. The **obligations for taxes, insurance, and maintenance** (executory costs) may be assumed by either the lessor or the lessee, or they may be divided between the lessor and the lessee. **Restrictions** somewhat comparable to those in bond indentures may limit the lessee's activities relative to dividend payments, or incurrence of further debt and lease obligation. The lease contract may be **noncancelable** or may grant the right to **early termination** on payment of a set scale of prices (prices often representing the unrecovered cost of the lessor) plus a penalty. In case of **default** the lessee may be liable for all future payments at once, receiving title to the property in exchange; or the lessor may enjoy the prerogative to sell and to collect from the lessee all or a portion of the difference between the sale price and the lessor's unrecovered cost. **Alternatives of the lessee at termination** of the lease may range from none, to the right to purchase the leased asset at the fair market value, or the right to renew or buy at a nominal price.[4]

In practice, any combination of provisions on these different points may be used, ranging from provisions that approach the purchase of a current service through the traditional short-term rental lease to those that seem to be purely financing devices for purchase/sale transactions. These different transactions call for different accounting methods to portray properly the substance of each situation.

Accounting for Leases—A Brief Background

Prior to 1965, leases, irrespective of their duration or other character, were not capitalized and little about them was disclosed by the lessee or the lessor in the notes to the financial statements. Accounting for all leases was simply a matter of debiting rent expense by the lessee and crediting rent income by the lessor as lease payments were made or accrued. In 1964 and 1965 the APB in **Opinion No. 5** (lessee accounting) and **Opinion No. 7** (lessor accounting), required that leases that were in substance "installment purchases" be capitalized by the lessee as asset purchases with a related obligation. However, the accounting criteria set forth for capitalization or noncapitalization of lease arrangements were readily and generally circumvented by lessees. Furthermore, **Opinions No. 5 and No. 7** did not require that there be symmetry in the classification of and accounting for the lease by both the lessee and the lessor as parties to the same lease. The later issuance of **APB Opinion No. 27** (1972) and **Opinion No. 31** (1973) on lease accounting did little to eliminate these inconsistencies in lease accounting practices.

In 1976 the FASB issued **Statement No. 13,** "Accounting for Leases," which superseded all previous official pronouncements on lease accounting. It was the final product of a three-year project that involved a Discussion Memorandum, two successive exposure drafts, and numerous hearings. The Board believed that **Statement No. 13** would remove "most, if not all, of the conceptual differences in lease classification as between lessors and lessees and that it provides criteria for such classification that are more explicit and less susceptible to varied interpretation than those in previous literature."[5]

---

[4]John H. Myers, "Reporting of Leases in Financial Statements," *Accounting Research Study No. 4* (New York: AICPA, 1964), pp. 10–11.

[5]"Accounting for Leases," *Statement of Financial Accounting Standards No. 13* (Stamford, Conn.: FASB, 1976), par. 62.

Despite the attention that the accounting profession has given to lease accounting and the special effort put forth in **Statement No. 13,** uniformity of treatment has not been achieved, and the assertion of "less susceptibility to varied interpretation" has not been reached. As of late 1979, the FASB had amended **Statement No. 13** seven times, had issued six interpretations, and had additional amendments and interpretations in exposure draft or development stages. Lease accounting now ranks high among the seemingly insoluble and frustrating problem areas for the accounting profession. The causes for abusing and the methods of circumventing GAAP for leases are discussed in the concluding section of this chapter. The following material, illustrating acceptable accounting and reporting for leases by lessees and lessors, is based on **FASB Statement No. 13** and its amendments and interpretations. Keep in mind throughout this presentation the **objective of Statement No. 13** is as follows:

> A lease that transfers substantially all of the benefits and risks incident to the ownership of property should be accounted for as the acquisition of an asset and the incurrence of an obligation by the lessee and as a sale or financing by the lessor.[6]

ACCOUNTING BY LESSEES

Classification of Leases by the Lessee

From the standpoint of the **lessee** all leases may be classified for accounting purposes as follows:

A. Operating leases.
B. Capital leases.

If at the date of the lease agreement (inception of the lease[7]) the lessee is party to a noncancelable lease that meets **one or more** of the following four criteria, the lessee shall classify and account for the arrangement as a **capital lease:**

1. The lease transfers ownership of the property to the lessee.
2. The lease contains a bargain purchase option.[8]
3. The lease term is equal to 75% or more of the estimated economic life of the leased property.[9]
4. The present value of the minimum lease payments (excluding executory costs) equals or exceeds 90% of the fair value of the leased property.[10]

Leases that do not meet any of the four criteria above are classified and accounted for by the lessee as **operating leases.**

[6]*Ibid.*, par. 60.

[7]For purposes of classifying the lease transaction, inception is the date of the lease agreement or commitment, if earlier. See "Inception of the Lease," *Statement of Financial Accounting Standards No. 23* (Stamford, Conn.: FASB, 1978), par. 7.

[8]A **bargain purchase option** is a provision allowing the lessee to purchase the leased property for a price that is lower than the expected fair value of the property at the date the option becomes exercisable; the difference between the purchase price and the expected fair market value must be large enough to make exercise of the option reasonably assured at the inception of the lease.

[9]However, this criterion cannot be used for a lease that begins within the last 25% of the total estimated economic life of the leased property, including earlier years of use.

[10]"Accounting for Leases," *Statement of Financial Accounting Standards No. 13* (Stamford, Conn.: FASB, 1976), par. 7.

Lessee Accounting Methods

The acceptable accounting methods available to the lessee as related to the type of lease are as follows:

Type of Lease	Lessee Accounting Method
Operating lease	Operating (noncapitalization) method
Capital lease	Capital lease (capitalization) method

Operating Method (Lessee)

Under the **operating method,** rent expense (and a compensating liability) accrues day by day to the lessee as the property is used. The lessee assigns rent to the periods benefiting from the use of the asset and ignores, in the accounting, any commitments to make future payments. Appropriate accruals are made if the accounting period ends between cash payment dates. For example, if on January 1, 1981, a company leases an asset for four years at an annual rental of $80,000

Operating Lease Disclosures

Glosser Bros., Inc. (Lessee)

NOTE D—LEASING ARRANGEMENTS

The company conducts all of its retail store operations from leased facilities comprised of six combined food / department store units, nine shopping center or mall integrated department store units, and three free-standing food stores. All leases are classifiable as operating leases.

The following is a schedule by years of future minimum rental payments required under operating leases that have a remaining noncancellable lease term in excess of one year as of January 27, 1979:

Year ending 1980	$ 2,552,628
1981	2,552,628
1982	2,552,628
1983	2,533,506
1984	2,437,896
Later years	35,090,315
Total minimum payments required	$47,719,601

Total rent expense amounted to approximately $2,967,000 and $2,694,000 for the fiscal years ended January 27, 1979 and January 28, 1978, respectively.

Substantially all leases contain multiple renewal options which extend the lease terms from 5 to 30 years at approximately the same rental rates.

The leases also require the payment of real estate taxes and certain other expenses and require additional rental amounts based on percentages of gross sales. Additional rents of approximately $251,000 and $189,000, based on percentages of gross sales, were paid or payable for the fiscal years ended January 27, 1979 and January 28, 1978, respectively.

During the fiscal years ended January 27, 1979 and January 28, 1978, approximately $516,000 and $491,000, respectively was paid or payable to affiliated persons for rental of real property.

payable at the beginning of each year, the following journal entry is recorded annually for four years:

Rent Expense	80,000	
Cash (or Rent Payable)		80,000

The rented asset does not appear within the body of the balance sheet but lessees must make the following footnote disclosure of all operating leases having noncancelable lease terms in excess of one year:

1. **Minimum future rental payments,** in total and for each of the next five years.
2. **Minimum sublease income,** total receivable in the future under noncancelable subleases.
3. **Total rental expense,** showing separately the minimum rentals, contingent rentals, and sublease income.

Presented on page 962 is the footnote disclosure made by Glosser Bros., Inc. in its 1979 annual report; the disclosure covers all of the three requirements above for operating leases and more.

Capital Lease Method (Lessee)

Under the **capital lease method** the lessee treats the lease transaction as if an asset were being purchased on time, that is, like a financing transaction in which an asset is acquired and an obligation is created. **The lessee records a capital lease as an asset and a liability at the lower of (1) the present value of the minimum lease payments (excluding executory costs) during the lease term[11] or (2) the fair market value of the leased asset at the inception of the lease.[12]**

The special terms related to accounting for capital leases are discussed below:

Minimum Lease Payments The amount of minimum lease payments for the lessee is the sum of:

1. The minimum rental payments required during the lease term.
2. The amount of any bargain purchase option, or if there is no such option:
   a. The amount of any guarantee by the lessee of the residual value.
   b. The amount payable for failure to renew or extend the lease.

Contingent rentals and executory costs (defined on page 964) are not included in the lessee's computation of the present value of the minimum lease payments.

---

[11]The **lease term** is the sum of all the following periods, but not beyond the date a bargain purchase option becomes exercisable:
1. The fixed noncancelable term.
2. Any periods covered by a bargain renewal option.*
3. Renewal periods in which penalties are imposed in an amount that reasonably assures the renewal of the lease.
4. Renewal periods during which a lessee's guarantee of the lessor's debt is expected to be in effect.
5. Renewal periods preceding the date a bargain purchase becomes exercisable.
6. Periods for which the *lessor* has the option to renew or extend the lease term.
* A **bargain renewal option** is a provision allowing the lessee to renew the lease for a rental that is lower than the expected fair rental of the property at the date the option becomes exercisable; the difference between the renewal rental and the expected fair rental must be great enough to make exercise of the option to renew reasonably assured at the inception of the lease.
[12]"Accounting for Leases," *op. cit.,* par. 10.

Residual Value The residual value is the estimated fair value of the leased property at the end of the lease term.[13] The lessor often transfers to the lessee or to a third party the risk of loss through a guaranteed residual value. The amount of a **guaranteed residual value** is (1) the certain or determinable amount at which the lessor has the right to require the lessee to purchase the asset, or (2) the amount the lessee or the third-party guarantor guarantees will be realized. According to **FASB Interpretation No. 19,** a lease provision requiring the lessee to make up a residual value deficiency that is attributable to damage, extraordinary wear and tear, or excessive usage is not included in the minimum lease payments. Such costs are similar to contingent rentals in that the amount is not determinable at the inception of the lease. Like **contingent rentals,** such costs are recognized as period costs when incurred.[14]

Discount Rate The lessee computes the present value of the minimum lease payments using the **lessee's incremental borrowing rate,** which is defined as: "The rate that, at the inception of the lease, the lessee would have incurred to borrow the funds necessary to buy the leased asset on a secured loan with repayment terms similar to the payment schedule called for in the lease."[15]

If, however, the lessee (1) knows the **implicit rate computed by the lessor** and (2) the implicit rate computed by the lessor is less than the lessee's incremental borrowing rate, then the lessee must use the implicit rate. The interest rate implicit in the lease is the discount rate that, when applied to the minimum lease payments and the residual value accruing to the lessor, causes the aggregate present value to be equal to the fair value of the leased property to the lessor.[16] In practice, the lessee frequently does not know the implicit rate. Because the lessee may not capitalize the leased property at more than its fair value, the lessee is prevented from using an excessively low discount rate.

In a capital lease transaction the lessee is using the lease as a source of financing. The lessor finances the transaction (provides the investment capital) through the leased asset and the lessee makes rent payments which actually are installment payments. Therefore, over the life of the property rented, the rental payments to the lessor constitute a payment of principal plus interest.

Executory Costs Like most assets, leased tangible assets require the incurrence of insurance, maintenance, and tax expenses (called **executory costs**) during their economic life. If the lessor retains responsibility for the payment of these "ownership-type costs," a portion of each lease payment that represents executory costs should be excluded in computing the present value of the minimum lease payments because it does not represent payment on or reduction of the obligation. If the portion of the minimum lease payments representing executory costs is not determinable from the provisions of the lease, an estimate of such amount must be made. Many lease agreements, however, specify that these executory costs be as-

---

[13]"Lessee Guarantee of the Residual Value of Leased Property," *FASB Interpretation No. 19* (Stamford, Conn.: FASB, 1977), par. 3.

[14]For a discussion of contingent rentals, see *FASB Statement No. 29*, "Determining Contingent Rentals" (Stamford, Conn.: FASB, 1979).

[15]*Ibid.*, par. 5 (l).

[16]*Ibid.*, par. 5 (k).

sumed by the lessee; in these cases the rental payment can be used without adjustment in the present value computation.

Accounting Separately for the Asset and the Liability If the lease agreement satisfies either criterion (1) or (2), that is, transfers ownership of the asset to the lessee or contains a bargain purchase option, the leased asset is depreciated in a manner consistent with the lessee's normal depreciation policy for owned assets, using the economic life of the asset and any estimated salvage value. If the lease does not transfer ownership of the asset to the lessee, or if it does not contain a bargain purchase option, the leased asset is amortized over the term of the lease.

Throughout the term of the lease, **the effective interest method** is used to allocate each lease payment between a reduction of the lease obligation and interest expense. This method produces a constant rate of interest in each period on the outstanding balance of the obligation.

Whichever discount rate is used by the lessee in determining the present value of the minimum lease payments, that rate usually must be used by the lessee in applying the effective interest method to capital leases.

Although the amount capitalized as an asset and the amount recorded as an obligation at the inception of the lease are computed at the same present value, the amortization of the asset and the discharge of the obligation are **independent accounting processes** during the term of the lease. The lessee should amortize the leased asset by applying the conventional depreciation methods: straight-line, sum-of-the-years'-digits, declining balance, units of production, etc. It may be tempting to apply the effective interest method because the asset is related to a lease financing arrangement and because the effective interest calculations are readily available from the lease obligation amortization schedule. The selection of a depreciation method should be more in line with the objectives of income measurement and asset valuation, however, than with the liquidation of liabilities.

The FASB uses the term "amortization" more frequently than the term "depreciation" in recognition of intangible leased property rights. The authors prefer the term "depreciation" as a description of the write-off of the costs of the expired services of a tangible asset.

Capitalized Lease Method Illustrated (Lessee)

The preceding section was a discussion of the theory and rules underlying the accounting treatment used by the lessee in recording capitalized lease transactions. The following presentation illustrates the accounting involved in applying the capitalized lease method.

Lessor Company and Lessee Company sign a lease agreement dated January 1, 1981, that calls for Lessor Company to lease equipment to Lessee Company beginning January 1, 1981. The lease agreement contains the following terms and provisions:

1. The term of the lease is five years, and the lease agreement is noncancelable, requiring equal rental payments of $25,981.62 at the beginning of each year.
2. The equipment has a fair value at the inception of the lease of $100,000, an estimated economic life of five years, and no residual value.

3. Lessee Company pays all of the executory costs except for the property taxes of $2,000 per year, which are included in the annual payments.
4. The lease contains no renewal options and the equipment reverts to Lessor Company at the termination of the lease.
5. Lessee Company's incremental borrowing rate is 11% per year.
6. Lessee Company depreciates similar equipment that it owns on a straight-line basis.
7. Lessor Company set the annual rental to insure a rate of return on its investment of 10% per year; this fact is known to Lessee Company.

The lease meets the criteria for classification as a capital lease because (1) the lease term of five years, being equal to the equipment's estimated economic life of five years, satisfies the 75% test, and (2) the present value of the minimum lease payments ($100,000 as computed below) exceeds 90% of the fair value of the property ($100,000).

The minimum lease payments are $119,908.10 ($23,981.62 × 5) and the amount capitalized as leased assets is computed as the present value of the minimum lease payments (excluding executory costs) as follows:

> Capitalized amount = ($25,981.62 − $2,000) × present value of an annuity due of 1
> for 5 periods at 10% (Table 6-5)
>
> = $23,981.62 × 4.16986
> = $100,000

The lessor's implicit interest rate of 10% is used instead of the lessee's incremental borrowing rate of 11%, because (1) it is lower, and (2) the lessee has knowledge of it.

The entry to record the signing of the lease and the capitalization of the present value of the minimum lease payments net of executory costs (i.e., the recorded value of the asset and the liability) on Lessee Company's books on January 1, 1981, is:

Leased Equipment Under Capital Leases	100,000	
Obligations Under Capital Leases		100,000

Note that the preceding entry records the obligation at the net amount of $100,000 (the present value of the future rental payments) rather than at the gross amount of $119,908.10 ($23,981.62 × 5).

The journal entry to record the **first lease payment on January 1, 1981** is as follows:

Property Tax Expense	2,000.00	
Obligations Under Capital Leases	23,981.62	
Cash		25,981.62

Recording the annual lease payment in subsequent periods results in the recognition of additional expenses relative to the leased equipment, because in this case each lease payment of $25,981.62 consists of three elements: (1) a reduction in the lease obligation, (2) a financing cost (interest expense), and (3) executory costs (property taxes). The total financing cost (interest expense), over the term of the lease, is the difference between the present value ($100,000) of the lease payments and the actual cash disbursed, net of executory costs, ($119,908.10), or $19,908.10. The FASB requires that the annual interest be computed by applying the effective interest method. Therefore, the annual interest expense is a function of the outstanding obligation, as illustrated in the following schedule:

LESSEE COMPANY

Lease Amortization Schedule
(Annuity due basis)

Date	Annual Lease Payment	Executory Costs	Interest (10%) on Unpaid Obligation	Reduction of Lease Obligation	Balance of Lease Obligation
	(a)	(b)	(c)	(d)	(e)
1/1/81					$100,000.00
1/1/81	$ 25,981.62	$ 2,000	$ -0-	$ 23,981.62	76,018.38
1/1/82	25,981.62	2,000	7,601.84	16,379.78	59,638.60
1/1/83	25,981.62	2,000	5,963.86	18,017.76	41,620.84
1/1/84	25,981.62	2,000	4,162.08	19,819.54	21,801.30
1/1/85	25,981.62	2,000	2,180.32*	21,801.30	-0-
	$129,908.10	$10,000	$19,908.10	$100,000.00	

(a) Lease payment as required by lessor.
(b) Executory costs included in rental payment.
(c) Ten percent of the preceding balance of (e) except for 1/1/81; since this is an annuity due, no time has elapsed at the date of the first payment and no interest has accrued.
(d) (a) minus (b) and (c).
(e) Preceding balance minus (d).
  *Rounded by 19 cents.

At December 31, 1981, Lessee Company's fiscal year-end, **accrued interest** is recorded as follows (if reversing entries are used, this entry would be reversed at 1/1/82):

Interest Expense	7,601.84	
Interest Payable		7,601.84

Depreciation of the leased equipment over its lease term of five years applying Lessee Company's normal depreciation policy (straight-line method) results in the following entry on December 31, 1981:

Depreciation Expense—Capital Leases	20,000	
Accumulated Depreciation—Capital Leases		20,000
($100,000 ÷ 5 years)		

It is acceptable accounting practice to make the credit above directly to the account Leased Equipment Under Capital Leases, in the manner accorded intangible assets. Because the FASB recommends financial statement disclosure of the accumulated depreciation on capital leases, we have chosen to utilize the accumulated account.

The journal entry to record the **lease payment of January 1, 1982,** is as follows:

Property Tax Expense	2,000.00	
Interest Expense (or Interest Payable)	7,601.84	
Obligations Under Capital Leases	16,379.78	
Cash		25,981.62

Entries through 1985 would follow the pattern above. Other executory costs (insurance and maintenance) assumed by Lessee Company would be recorded in a manner similar to that used to record any other operating costs incurred on assets owned by Lessee Company.

Upon expiration of the lease, the amount capitalized as leased equipment is fully amortized and the lease obligation is fully discharged. If not purchased, the equipment would be returned to the lessor, and the leased equipment and related accumulated depreciation accounts would be removed from the books.[17] If the equipment is purchased at termination of the lease at a price of $5,000, and the estimated life of the equipment is changed from five to seven years, the following entry might be made:

Equipment ($100,000 + $5,000)	105,000	
Accumulated Depreciation—Capital Leases	100,000	
Leased Equipment Under Capital Leases		100,000
Accumulated Depreciation—Equipment		100,000
Cash		5,000

Comparison of Capital Lease with Operating Lease

If the lease illustrated above had been accounted for as an operating lease, the first-year charge to operations would have been $25,981.62, the amount of the rental payment. Treating the transaction as a capital lease, however, resulted in a first-year charge of $29,601.84: depreciation of $20,000 (assuming straight-line), interest expense of $7,601.84 (per schedule on page 967), and executory costs of $2,000. The following schedule shows that while the total charges to operations are the same over the lease term whether the lease is accounted for as a capital lease or as an operating lease, under the capital lease treatment the charges are higher in the earlier years and lower in the later years.[18]

<table>
<tr><td colspan="7" align="center">Lessee Company
Schedule of Charges to Operations
Capital Lease Versus Operating Lease</td></tr>
<tr><td></td><td colspan="4" align="center">Capital Lease</td><td>Operating
Lease</td><td></td></tr>
<tr><td>Year</td><td>Depreciation</td><td>Executory
Costs</td><td>Interest</td><td>Total
Charge</td><td>Charge</td><td>Difference</td></tr>
<tr><td>1981</td><td>$ 20,000</td><td>$ 2,000</td><td>$ 7,601.84</td><td>$ 29,601.84</td><td>$ 25,981.62</td><td>$ 3,620.22</td></tr>
<tr><td>1982</td><td>20,000</td><td>2,000</td><td>5,963.86</td><td>27,963.86</td><td>25,981.62</td><td>1,982.24</td></tr>
<tr><td>1983</td><td>20,000</td><td>2,000</td><td>4,162.08</td><td>26,162.08</td><td>25,981.62</td><td>180.46</td></tr>
<tr><td>1984</td><td>20,000</td><td>2,000</td><td>2,180.32</td><td>24,180.32</td><td>25,981.62</td><td>(1,801.30)</td></tr>
<tr><td>1985</td><td>20,000</td><td>2,000</td><td>—</td><td>22,000.00</td><td>25,981.62</td><td>(3,981.62)</td></tr>
<tr><td></td><td>$100,000</td><td>$10,000</td><td>$19,908.10</td><td>$129,908.10</td><td>$129,908.10</td><td>$ –0–</td></tr>
</table>

[17]If the lessee purchases a leased asset *during the term of a* "*capital lease,*" it is accounted for like a renewal or extension of a capital lease, that is, "any difference between the purchase price and the carrying amount of the lease obligation shall be recorded as an adjustment of the carrying amount of the asset." See "Accounting for Purchase of a Leased Asset by the Lessee During the Term of the Lease," *FASB Interpretation No. 26* (Stamford, Conn.: FASB, 1978), par. 5.

[18]The higher charges in the early years is one reason lessees are reluctant to adopt the capital lease accounting method. Lessees (especially those of real estate) claim that it is really no more costly to operate the leased asset in the early years than in the later years; thus, they advocate an even charge similar to that produced by the operating method.

If an accelerated method of depreciation is used, the differences between the amount charged to operations under the two methods would be even larger in the earlier and later years.

Classification in Lessee's Balance Sheet

During the term of the lease, assets recorded under capital leases are separately identified in the lessee's balance sheet. Similarly, the related obligations are separately identified with the portion due within one year or the operating cycle, whichever is longer, classified with current liabilities and the balance with noncurrent liabilities. For instance, the current portion of the 12/31/81 total obligation of $76,018.38 in the Lessee's Amortization Schedule at 1/1/81 (page 967) is the amount of the reduction in the obligation in 1982, or $16,379.78.

ACCOUNTING BY LESSORS

Classification of Leases by the Lessor

From the standpoint of the **lessor,** all leases may be classified for accounting purposes as follows:

A. Operating leases.
B. Direct financing leases.
C. Sales-type leases.

If at the date of the lease agreement (inception) the lessor is party to a lease that meets **one or more** of the following Group I criteria (1, 2, 3, and 4) and **both** of the following Group II criteria (1 and 2), the lessor shall classify and account for the arrangement as a **direct financing lease** or a **sales-type lease.**[19] (Note that the Group I criteria are identical to the criteria that must be met for a lease to be classified as a capital lease by a lessee, per page 961.)

GROUP I

1. The lease transfers ownership of the property to the lessee.
2. The lease contains a bargain purchase option.
3. The lease term is equal to 75% or more of the estimated economic life of the leased property.
4. The present value of the minimum lease payments (excluding executory costs) equals or exceeds 90% of the fair value of the leased property.

GROUP II

1. Collectibility of the payments required from the lessee is reasonably predictable.
2. No important uncertainties surround the amount of unreimbursable costs yet to be incurred by the lessor under the lease.

All leases that do not qualify as a direct financing lease or a sales-type lease are classified and accounted for by the lessor as **operating leases.**

[19]*Ibid.*, pars. 6, 7, and 8.

Lessor Accounting Methods

The acceptable accounting methods available to the lessor as related to the type of lease are as follows:

Type of Lease	Lessor Accounting Method
Operating lease	Operating method
Direct financing lease	Financing method
Sales-type lease	Sales-financing method

The distinction for the lessor between a direct financing lease and a sales-type lease is the presence or absence of a manufacturer's or dealer's profit (or loss). A sales-type lease involves a manufacturer's or dealer's profit, and a direct financing lease does not. The profit (or loss) to the lessor is evidenced by the difference between the fair value of the leased property at the inception of the lease and the lessor's cost or carrying amount. Normally, sales-type leases arise when manufacturers or dealers use leasing as a means of marketing their products. For example, a computer manufacturer will lease its computer equipment to businesses and institutions. Direct financing leases generally result from arrangements with lessors that are primarily engaged in financing operations, such as lease-finance companies, banks, insurance companies, and pension trusts. However, a lessor need not be a manufacturer or dealer to realize a profit (or loss) at the inception of the lease that requires application of the sales-type lease accounting.

The primary difference between applying the financing method to a direct financing lease and applying the sales-financing method to a sales-type lease is the recognition of the manufacturer's or dealer's profit at the inception of the lease.

Operating Method (Lessor)   Under the **operating method** each rental receipt of the lessor is recorded as rental revenue on the use of an item carried as a plant asset. The plant asset is depreciated in the normal manner, with the depreciation expense of the period matched against the rental revenue. The amount of revenue recognized in each accounting period is a level amount (straight-line basis) regardless of the lease provisions, unless another systematic and rational basis is more representative of the time pattern in which the benefit is derived from the leased asset. In addition to the depreciation charge, maintenance costs and the cost of any other services rendered under the provisions of the lease that pertain to the current accounting period are charged against the recognized revenue. To illustrate the operating method, assume that Mayo, Inc., as owner-operator of a medical arts building having a cost of $2,000,000 and a depreciable life of 40 years (no salvage value), earned gross rentals of $460,000 during the year from its three-year leases with various doctors and dentists. The earned gross rentals of $460,000 are recorded in a straightforward manner:

Cash (or Rent Receivable)	460,000	
Rental Revenue		460,000

Depreciation is simply recorded (using the straight-line method) as follows:

Depreciation Expense—Leased Buildings	50,000	
Accumulated Depreciation—Leased Buildings		50,000

If $240,000 in real estate taxes, insurance, maintenance, and other operating costs during the year are the obligation of the lessor, they are recorded as expenses chargeable against the gross rental revenues. All the revenues and expenses of the leased building would be conventionally recorded by Mayo, Inc., with income before interest and taxes of $170,000 resulting from the rental activity (revenue of $460,000 less expenses of $290,000).

If Mayo, Inc., owned plant assets that it used in addition to those leased to others, the leased building would be separately classified with or near property, plant, and equipment in an appropriately titled account such as Building Leased to Others or Investment in Leased Property; Accumulated Depreciation is conventionally shown as a deduction from the investment. If significant in amount or in terms of activity, the rental revenues and accompanying expenses are separated in the income statement from sales revenue and cost of goods sold.

Rent is reported as revenue over the lease term as it becomes receivable according to the provisions of the lease. Generally, rentals under an operating lease are receivable on a straight-line basis, i.e., in equal amounts at equal intervals. However, if the rentals depart from a straight-line basis, the revenue still should be recognized on a straight-line basis unless another basis more accurately reflects a decline in the service potential of the asset.

Financing Method Applied to Direct Financing Leases   Leases that are in substance the financing of an asset purchase by a lessee require the lessor to substitute a "lease payments receivable" for the leased asset. The information necessary to record a direct financing lease is as follows:

1. **Gross investment ("lease payments receivable").** The minimum lease payments plus the unguaranteed residual value.[20]
2. **Unearned interest income.** The difference between the gross investment (the receivable) and the cost or carrying amount (book value) of the property.
3. **Net investment.** The gross investment (the receivable) less the unearned interest income.

The minimum lease payments (net of executory costs paid by lessor) plus the unguaranteed residual value accruing to the benefit of the lessor (labeled "gross investment" by the FASB) are recorded as the "lease payments receivable." The unearned income is amortized to income over the lease term by applying the effective interest method. Thus, a constant rate of return is produced on the net investment in the lease. Any **contingent rentals,** including rentals based on variables such as machine hours of use or sales volume, are credited to revenue when they become receivable.[21]

The following presentation, utilizing the data from the preceding Lessor Company/Lessee Company illustration on pages 965 and 966, illustrates the accounting treatment accorded a direct financing lease. The information relevant to Lessor Company in accounting for this lease transaction is repeated here (top of page 972).

---

[20]*Ibid.,* par. 17. Initially the unguaranteed residual value could be classified in a separate account. If the unguaranteed residual value is included in the lease payments receivable account, it would be reclassified by the lessor at the end of the lease term if not purchased by the lessee.

[21]See amendment of *FASB Statement No. 13:* "Determining Contingent Rentals," *Statement of Financial Accounting Standards No. 29* (Stamford, Conn.: FASB, 1979).

1. The term of the lease is five years beginning January 1, 1981, noncancelable, and requires equal rental payments of $25,981.62 at the beginning of each year; payments include $2,000 of executory costs (property taxes).
2. The equipment has a cost of $100,000 to Lessor Company, a fair value at the inception of the lease of $100,000, an estimated economic life of five years, and no residual value.
3. No initial direct costs were incurred in negotiating and closing the lease transaction.
4. The lease contains no renewable options and the equipment reverts to Lessor Company at the termination of the lease.
5. Collectibility is reasonably assured and no additional costs (with the exception of the property taxes being collected from the lessee) are to be incurred by Lessor Company.
6. Lessor Company set the annual rentals to insure a rate of return of 10% (implicit rate) on its investment as follows:

Amount of rentals = $100,000 ÷ Present value of an annuity due of 1 for five years at 10% (Table 6-5)
= $100,000 ÷ 4.16986
= $23,981.62

The lease meets the criteria for classification as a direct financing lease because (1) the lease term exceeds 75% of the equipment's estimated economic life, (2) the present value of the minimum lease payments exceeds 90% of the equipment's fair value, (3) collectibility of the payments is reasonably assured, and (4) there are no further costs to be incurred by Lessor Company. It is not a sales-type lease because there is no difference between the fair value ($100,000) of the equipment and the lessor's cost ($100,000).

The lease payments receivable (*gross investment*) is calculated as follows:

Lease payments receivable = Minimum lease payments minus executory costs paid by lessor plus unguaranteed residual value
= ($25,981.62 − $2,000) × 5
= $119,908.10

The unearned interest income is computed as the difference between the lease payments receivable and the lessor's cost or carrying amount of the leased asset:

Unearned interest income = Lease payments receivable minus asset cost or carrying amount
= $119,908.10 − $100,000
= $19,908.10

The net investment in direct financing leases is $100,000, i.e., the gross investment of $119,908.10 minus the unearned interest income of $19,908.10.

The lease of the asset, the resulting receivable, and the unearned interest income are recorded January 1, 1981 (the inception of the lease) as follows:

Lease Payments Receivable	119,908.10	
Equipment		100,000.00
Unearned Interest Income—Leases		19,908.10

The unearned interest income is classified on the balance sheet as a deduction from the lease payments receivable if the receivable is reported gross. Generally, the lease payments receivable, although **recorded** at the gross investment amount, is **reported** at the "net investment" amount (gross investment less unearned interest income) and entitled "Net investment in direct financing leases," classified between its current and noncurrent portions.

The leased equipment with a cost of $100,000, which represents Lessor Company's investment, is replaced with a lease receivable that includes the interest receivable. In a manner similar to the lessee's treatment of interest, Lessor Company applies the effective interest method and recognizes interest income as a function of the unrecovered net investment, as illustrated in the following schedule:

	LESSOR COMPANY Lease Amortization Schedule (Annuity due basis)				
Date	Annual Lease Payment	Executory Costs	Interest (10%) on Net Investment	Net Investment Recovery	Net Investment
	(a)	(b)	(c)	(d)	(e)
1/1/81					$100,000.00
1/1/81	$ 25,981.62	$ 2,000.00	-0-	$ 23,981.62	76,018.38
1/1/82	25,981.62	2,000.00	$ 7,601.84	16,379.78	59,638.60
1/1/83	25,981.62	2,000.00	5,963.86	18,017.76	41,620.84
1/1/84	25,981.62	2,000.00	4,162.08	19,819.54	21,801.30
1/1/85	25,981.62	2,000.00	2,180.32*	21,801.30	—
	$129,908.10	$10,000.00	$19,908.10	$100,000.00	

(a) Annual rental that provides a 10% return on net investment.
(b) Executory costs included in rental payment.
(c) Ten percent of the preceding balance of (e) except for 1/1/81.
(d) (a) minus (b) and (c).
(e) Preceding balance minus (d).   *Rounded by 2 cents.

On January 1, 1981, the journal entry to record receipt of the first year's lease payment is as follows:

Cash	25,981.62	
Lease Payments Receivable		23,981.62
Property Tax Expense		2,000.00

On 12/31/81 the interest income earned during the first year and included in the receipt above is recognized through the following entry

Unearned Interest Income—Leases	7,601.84	
Interest Income—Leases		7,601.84

The following entries record receipt of the second year's lease payment and accrual of the interest earned:

1/1/82

Cash	25,981.62	
Lease Payments Receivable		23,981.62
Property Tax Expense		2,000.00

12/31/82

Unearned Interest Income—Leases	5,963.86	
Interest Income—Leases		5,963.86

Journal entries through 1985 would follow the same pattern except that no entry would be recorded in 1985 (the last year) for accrued interest. Because the receivable is fully collected by 1/1/85, no balance (investment) is outstanding during 1985 to which Lessor Company could attribute any interest. Upon expiration of the lease (whether an ordinary annuity or an annuity due situation), the gross receivable and the unearned interest income would be fully written-off. **Lessor Company recorded no depreciation.** If the equipment is sold to Lessee Company for $5,000 upon expiration of the lease, Lessor Company would recognize disposition of the equipment as follows:

Cash	5,000	
Gain on Sale of Equipment Leased		5,000

Sales-Financing Method Applied to Sales-Type Lease   As already indicated, the primary difference between a direct financing lease and a sales-type lease is the manufacturer's or dealer's profit (or loss). The information necessary to record the sales-type lease is as follows:

1. **Gross investment** (also "lease payments receivable"). The minimum lease payments plus the unguaranteed residual value.
2. **Unearned interest income.** The gross investment less the sum of the present values of the two components of gross investment.
3. **Sales price of the asset.** The present value of the minimum lease payments.
4. **Cost of goods sold.** The cost of the asset to the lessor, less the present value of any unguaranteed residual value.

For example, in the Lessor Company/Lessee Company illustration, assume all information is the same except that the equipment had a cost of $85,000 to Lessor Company. The information used to record that sales-type lease is as follows:

1. Gross investment is $119,908.10 (five annual lease payments of $23,981.62 each excluding executory costs, plus the unguaranteed residual value, 0).
2. Unearned interest income is $19,908.10 (gross investment of $119,908.10 less $100,000, the sum of the present values of the lease payments and the residual value).
3. Sales price is $100,000 (the present value of the lease payments).
4. Cost of goods sold is $85,000 (the cost of the asset to the lessor; no unguaranteed residual value exists).

Using this information, the sales-type lease is recorded by Lessor Company as follows:

Lease Payments Receivable	119,908.10	
Cost of Goods Sold	85,000.00	
Sales Revenue		100,000.00
Equipment		85,000.00
Unearned Interest Income—Leases		19,908.10

The manufacturer's or dealer's profit of $15,000 is the difference between the cost of goods sold ($85,000) and the present value of the lease payments ($100,000). This illustration is somewhat simplified because there is no residual value.

In this situation the same lease amortization schedule (page 973) can be used as was used under the direct financing method to recognize annually the interest earned. With the exception of the initial entry, Lessor Company would make the same entries as those recorded under the direct financing lease. (The lessee's entries are not affected by the lessor's classification of the lease as direct financing or sales-type.)

SPECIAL ACCOUNTING PROBLEMS CHARACTERISTIC OF LEASES

The unique features of lease arrangements that provide unique accounting problems are:

1. Residual values.
2. Bargain purchase options.
3. Initial direct costs.
4. Leased real estate.
5. Sale leasebacks.

Accounting for Residual Values

Frequently, a significant residual value exists at the end of the lease term, especially when the economic life of the leased asset exceeds the lease term. The residual value may be unguaranteed or guaranteed by the lessee. If the lessee, for example, agrees to make up any deficiency below a stated amount that the lessor realizes in residual value at the end of the lease term, that stated amount is the guaranteed residual value. The lessee may recognize a gain or a loss at the end of the lease term as a result of this guarantee.

The guaranteed residual value is employed in lease arrangements for two reasons. One is a business reason: it protects the lessor against any loss in estimated residual value, thereby insuring the lessor of the desired rate of return on investment. The second is an accounting reason that has given added significance to the guaranteed residual value: as you will learn from the discussion at the end of this chapter, the guaranteed residual value is one of the devices frequently used to circumvent certain accounting rules.

Guaranteed Residual Value (Lessee Accounting)   A guaranteed residual value affects the lessee's computation of the minimum lease payments and of the capitalized amount of the leased asset and the lease obligation. For example, assume that Lessee Company in the direct financing lease illustration had guaranteed a residual value of $5,000 at the end of the five-year lease term. With a residual value of $5,000 and an objective of earning a 10% return, Lessor Company would compute the amount of the lease payments as follows:

Lessor's Computation of Lease Payments (10%) (Annuity due basis, including residual value)	
Cost of leased asset	$100,000.00
Less: Present value of residual value ($5,000 × .62092, Table 6-2)	3,104.60
Amount to be recovered by lessor through lease payments	$ 96,895.40
Five periodic lease payments: $96,895.40 ÷ 4.16984 (Table 6-5)	$ 23,237.20

The foregoing lease payment amount should be contrasted to the lease payments of $23,981.62 as computed on page 972 where no residual value existed. The payments are less because the lessor's recoverable amount is less by the present value of the residual value.

The minimum lease payments are $121,186 [($23,237.20 × 5) + $5,000]. The capitalized present value of the minimum lease payments (excluding executory costs) is computed as follows:

Lessee's Capitalized Amount (10% Rate) (Annuity due basis; including **guaranteed** residual value)	
Present value of five annual rental payments of $23,237.20 × 4.16984 (Table 6-5)	$ 96,895.40
Present value of guaranteed residual value of $5,000 due five years after date of inception: $5,000 × .62092	3,104.60
Lessee's capitalized amount	$100,000.00

A schedule of interest expense and amortization of the lease obligation of $100,000 that produces a guaranteed residual value of $5,000 at the end of five years is prepared by Lessee Company as follows:

	Rental Payments 1/1	Obligation Outstanding During Year	Interest 10% for the Year	Reduction of Lease Obligation	Obligation at End of Year
Date	(a)	(b)	(c)	(d)	(e)
1/1/81					$100,000.00
1981	$ 23,237.20	$76,762.80	$ 7,676.28	$15,560.92	84,439.08
1982	23,237.20	61,201.88	6,120.19	17,117.01	67,322.07
1983	23,237.20	44,084.87	4,408.49	18,828.71	48,493.36
1984	23,237.20	25,256.16	2,525.62	20,711.58	27,781.78
1985	23,237.20	4,544.58	455.42*	22,781.78	5,000.00**
	$116,186.00		$21,186.00	$95,000.00	

Lessee Company
Lease Amortization Schedule
(Annuity due basis, guaranteed residual value)

(a) Annual rental payment made on January 1 (excluding executory costs of $2,000).
(b) Preceding balance of (e) minus (a).
(c) (b) × 10%.
(d) (a) minus (c).
(e) Preceding balance minus (d).
*Rounded by 96 cents.
**Represents guaranteed residual value.

If the residual value of the leased property is less than $5,000, Lessee Company may have to record a loss at the end of the lease.[22] Or, it may realize a gain if the

[22] A loss could result only if Lessee Company assumed that a residual value of $5,000 would exist at the end of the lease term to settle the $5,000 guarantee and, therefore, depreciated the capitalized asset only down to a $5,000 residual value. An alternative would be to assume a zero residual value and to depreciate the entire capitalized amount. The FASB has not indicated the exact accounting treatment that should be followed relative to depreciation or nondepreciation of the residual value.

residual value exceeds $5,000. Gains on guaranteed residual values may be apportioned in whatever ratio the lessee and lessor initially agree.

Unguaranteed Residual Value (Lessee Accounting) An unguaranteed residual value from the lessee's viewpoint is the same as no residual value in terms of its effect upon the lessee's method of computing the minimum lease payments and the capitalization of the leased asset and the lease obligation. For example, assume the same facts as those above except that the $5,000 residual value is **unguaranteed instead of guaranteed.** The amount of the annual lease payments would be the same, $23,237.20, because whether the residual value is guaranteed or unguaranteed, Lessor Company's amount to be recovered though lease rentals is the same, i.e., $96,895.40. The minimum lease payments are $116,186 ($23,237.20 × 5). Lessee Company would capitalize the following amount:

Lessee's Capitalized Amount (10% Rate)	
(Annuity due basis, including **unguaranteed** residual value)	
Present value of five annual rental payments of $23,237.20 × 4.16984	
(Table 6-5)	$96,895.40
Unguaranteed residual value of $5,000 (Not capitalized by lessee)	–0–
Lessee's capitalized amount	$96,895.40

If we continue the assumption that the fair value of the leased asset is $100,000, this lease still satisfies the 90% of fair value criterion. Note that if the unguaranteed residual value is sufficiently large, the present value of the minimum lease payments can be less than 90% of the fair value of the leased asset, thereby disqualifying the transaction from capital lease status for the lessee **and the lessor** (assuming that the transaction did not qualify under any of the other three criteria). If **the residual value is guaranteed by a third party,** it is treated by the lessee as an unguaranteed residual value but by the lessor as a guaranteed residual value. This anomaly in lease accounting has been used extensively in the business world to undermine the FASB's intent to maintain accounting *symmetry* between the lessee and the lessor (see the last section of this chapter for a more extended discussion of these attempts at circumvention).

Guaranteed and Unguaranteed Residual Value (Lessor) The net investment to be recovered by the lessor is the same whether the residual value is guaranteed or unguaranteed. Therefore, the amount of the periodic lease payments as set by the lessor is the same whether the residual value is guaranteed or unguaranteed. The schedule on page 975 showing the "Lessor's Computation of Lease Payments (10%)" is applicable.

Direct Financing Lease. Using the Lessee Company/Lessor Company data and assuming a residual value (either guaranteed or unguaranteed) of $5,000 and classification of the lease as a direct financing lease, the following necessary amounts are computed:

> Gross investment = ($23,237.20 $\times$ 5) + $5,000 = $121,186
> Unearned income = $121,186 - $100,000 = $21,186
> Net investment = $121,186 - $21,186 = $100,000

The same lease amortization schedule (on page 976) that shows a $5,000 residual value in 1985 and is used by Lessee Company can be used by Lessor Company merely by adopting the column headings to fit the lessor.

Sales-Type Lease. A **guaranteed** residual value in a sales-type lease is accounted for in much the same way that it is in the direct financing lease as shown above. An **unguaranteed** residual value in a sales-type lease affects the computation of the manufacturer's or dealer's profit because the present value of the unguaranteed residual value must be deducted from cost of the asset; the profit recognized at the date of sale is increased by the present value of the residual value. Thus, the manufacturer's or dealer's profit margin is maintained.

The **estimated residual value** in either financing or sales-type leases must be periodically reviewed. If the estimate of the unguaranteed residual value declines, the accounting for the transaction must be revised using the changed estimate. The decline, which represents a reduction in the lessor's net investment, is recognized as a loss in the period in which the residual estimate is changed. Upward adjustments in estimated residual value are not recognized.

Bargain Purchase Option (Lessee)

A bargain purchase option allows the lessee to purchase the leased property for a future price that is so much lower than the expected future fair value of the property that at the inception of the lease the future exercise of the option appears to be reasonably assured. If a bargain purchase option exists, **the lessee must increase the present value of the minimum lease payments by the present value of the option price.**

For example, assume that Lessee Company in the illustration on page 976 had an option to buy the leased equipment for $5,000 at the end of the five-year lease term when the fair value is expected to be $19,000. The significant difference between the option price and the fair value creates a bargain purchase option, the exercise of which is reasonably assured. The computations of (1) the amount of the five lease payments necessary for the lessor to earn a 10% return on net investment, (2) the amount of the minimum lease payments, (3) the amount capitalized as leased assets and lease obligation, and (4) the amortization of the lease obligation are affected by a bargain purchase option in the same manner that they are by a guaranteed residual value. Therefore, the computations and amortization schedule that would be prepared for this $5,000 bargain purchase option are identical to those shown on page 975–976 for the $5,000 guaranteed residual value.

The only difference between the accounting treatment given a bargain purchase option and a guaranteed residual value of identical amounts and circumstances is in the computation of the annual depreciation. In the case of a guaranteed residual value the lessee depreciates the asset over the lease life while in the case of a bargain purchase option the lessee uses the economic life of the asset. To illustrate (assume a lease life of 5 years and an economic life of 6 years) using the capitalized value of $100,000, Lessee Company's annual depreciation (straight-line method) in the case of the $5,000 guaranteed residual value would be $20,000 per year for five years ($100,000 ÷ 5); in the case of the $5,000 bargain purchase option, depreciation per year would be $16,667 for six years ($100,000 ÷ 6).

If Lessee Company allows the bargain purchase option to lapse on January 1, 1985, it will be necessary to remove from the accounts all remaining balances related to the leased property and to recognize a loss in the amount of the undepreciated asset valuation less any remaining obligation. In this case the loss is $11,665 computed as follows: [$100,000 − ($16,667 × 5)] − $5,000. The lease obligation is $5,000 at January 1, 1985, the $5,000 being the expected bargain purchase option price.

Initial Direct Costs (Lessor)

The incremental costs incurred by the lessor that are directly associated with negotiating, consummating, and initially processing leasing transactions are called **initial direct costs.** Examples of initial direct costs are: commissions, legal fees, costs of investigating the lessee's financial status, costs of preparing and processing documents, and that portion of salespersons' and other employees' compensation that is applicable to time spent on **completed** lease transactions.[23]

For **operating leases,** the lessor should defer initial direct costs and allocate them over the lease term in proportion to the recognition of rental income. In a **sales-type lease** transaction, the lessor expenses the initial direct costs in the year of incurrence, i.e., the period in which the profit on the sale is recognized. In a **direct financing lease,** however, initial direct costs should be allocated over the term of the lease by charging any initial direct costs against income as incurred and recognized as income in the same period a portion of the unearned income equal to the initial direct costs. To illustrate, if Lessor Corp. incurred $4,900 of initial direct costs in consummating the lease with Lessee Corp., Lessor would make the following two entries:

Various natural expenses, i.e., Sales Commissions, Legal Expense, Office Salaries, Travel Expense, etc.	4,900	
Cash and Accounts Payable		4,900
Unearned Interest Income	4,900	
Lease Income		4,900

The remaining unearned income is amortized over the lease term applying the effective interest method. Because the unearned income is reduced by the amount of the initial direct costs, a new implicit interest rate must be computed to amortize the remaining unearned income. This dual entry method of allocating initial direct costs over the lease term is recommended by the FASB because it is the method that has been used for some years throughout the leasing industry.

[23]"Accounting for Leases—Initial Direct Costs," *Statement of Financial Accounting Standards No. 17* (Stamford, Conn.: FASB, 1977), par. 8.

Leases Involving Real Estate[24]

Special problems can arise when leases involve land, or land and buildings, or equipment as well as real estate. **If land** is the sole item of property leased, the **lessee** should account for the lease as a capital lease only if criteria (1) or (2) are met, that is, if the lease transfers ownership of the property or contains a bargain purchase option; otherwise it is accounted for as an operating lease. Because ownership of the land is expected to pass to the lessee when the lease is classified as a capital lease, the asset is not normally depreciated. The **lessor** accounts for a land lease either as a sales-type or direct financing lease, whichever is appropriate, if the lease transfers ownership or contains a bargain purchase option and meets both the collectibility and uncertainties tests; otherwise the operating method is used.

If both **land and building** are involved and the lease transfers ownership or contains a bargain purchase option, the land and the building should be separately classified by the **lessee.** The present value of the minimum lease payments is allocated between land and building in proportion to their fair values at the inception of the lease. The **lessor** accounts for the lease as a single unit either as a sales-type, direct financing, or operating lease, as appropriate.

When both land and building are involved and the lease does not transfer ownership or contain a bargain purchase option, the accounting treatment is dependent upon the proportion of land to building. If the fair value of the land is less than 25% of the total fair value of the leased property, both the lessee and the lessor consider the land and the building as a single unit. The land is then amortized along with the building by the lessee. If the fair value of the land is 25% or more of the total fair value, the land and building are considered separately by both the lessee and the lessor. The lessee accounts for the building as a capital lease and the land as an operating lease if one of the two remaining criteria (3 or 4) is met. If none of the criteria is met, the lessee uses the operating method on the land and building. The lessor accounts for the building as a sales-type or direct financing lease as appropriate and the land element separately as an operating lease.

If a lease involves both **real estate and equipment,** the portion of the lease payments applicable to the equipment should be estimated by whatever means are appropriate and reasonable. The equipment then should be treated separately for purposes of applying the criteria and accounted for separately according to its classification by both lessees and lessors.

When the leased property is part of a larger whole, e.g., an office or a floor of a building or a store in a shopping center, "reasonable estimates of the leased property's fair value might be objectively determined by referring to an independent appraisal of the leased property or to estimated replacement cost information."[25]

---

[24]*Ibid.*, pars. 24–26.

[25]"Leases Involving Only Part of a Building," *FASB Interpretation No. 24* (Stamford, Conn.: FASB, 1978), par. 6.

SALE-LEASEBACK

Nature of a Sale-Leaseback Transaction

The term "sale-leaseback" describes a transaction in which the owner of property (seller-lessee) sells the property to another and simultaneously leases it back from the new owner. The use of the property is continued without interruption. For example, a company buys land, constructs a building to its specifications, sells the property to an investor, and then immediately leases it.

Generally, in such a transaction the property is sold at a price equal to or greater than current market value and is leased back for a term approximating the property's useful life and for lease payments sufficient to repay the buyer for the cash invested plus a reasonable return on investment. In addition, the lessee pays all executory costs (maintenance, insurance, and taxes), just as if title had passed. The sale price and the amount of the rents are related. The tax advantage for the seller-lessee is the deductibility of the entire lease payment, which may include interest and amortization of the cost of land and already partially depreciated other real property. Thus, the tax deduction under the lease arrangement may exceed allowable depreciation had title been retained. The sale-leaseback mechanism is used frequently where financing is a problem.

Lessee   If the lease meets one of the four criteria for treatment as a capital lease (see page 961), the **seller-lessee accounts for the lease as a capital lease.** If none of the criteria is satisfied, the seller-lessee accounts for the lease as an operating lease. Any profit or loss experienced by the seller-lessee from the sale of the assets that are leased back under a capital lease should be deferred and amortized over the lease term (or the economic life if either criteria (1) or (2) are satisfied) in proportion to the amortization of the leased assets.[26] For example, if Lessee, Inc. sells equipment having a book value of $580,000 and a fair value of $623,110 to Lessor, Inc. for $623,110 and leases the equipment back for $50,000 a year for 20 years, the profit of $43,110 should be amortized over the 20-year period at the same rate that the $623,110 is depreciated. Under an operating lease such profit or loss should be deferred and amortized in proportion to the rental payments over the period of time the assets are expected to be used by the lessee. If the leased asset is land only, the amortization shall be on a straight-line basis over the lease term.

The FASB requires, however, that when the fair value of the asset is **less** than the book value or carrying amount (undepreciated cost), a loss must be recognized immediately up to the amount of the difference between the book value and fair value. For example, if Lessee, Inc. sells equipment having a book value of $650,000 and a fair value of $623,110, the difference of $26,890 should be charged against current income.

Lessor   If the lease meets one of the criteria in Group I and both of the criteria in Group II (see page 969), the **purchaser-lessor** records the transaction as a purchase

---

[26]*Statement of Financial Accounting Standards No. 28,* "Accounting for Sales with Leasebacks" (Stamford, Conn.: FASB, 1979), however, requires the seller to recognize some profit or loss in certain limited circumstances.

and a direct financing lease. If the lease does not meet the criteria, the purchaser-lessor records the transaction as a purchase and an operating lease.

Sale-Leaseback Illustration

To illustrate the accounting treatment accorded a sale-leaseback transaction, assume that Lessee Corp. on January 1, 1981, sells aircraft having a carrying amount on its books of $75,500,000, to Lessor Corp. for $80,000,000, and immediately leases the aircraft back under the following conditions:

1. The term of the lease is 15 years, noncancelable, requiring equal rental payments of $10,487,443 at the beginning of each year.
2. The aircraft has a fair value of $80,000,000 on January 1, 1981, and an estimated economic life of 15 years.
3. Lessee Corp. has the option to renew the lease, one year at a time, at the same rental payments upon expiration of the original lease.
4. Lessee Corp. pays all executory costs.
5. Lessee Corp. depreciates similar aircraft that it owns on a straight-line basis over 15 years.
6. The annual payments assure the lessor a 12% return.
7. The incremental borrowing rate of Lessee Corp. is 12%.

This lease is a capital lease to Lessee Corp. because the lease term exceeds 75% of the estimated life of the aircraft and because the present value of the lease payments exceeds 90% of the fair value of the aircraft to the lessor. Assuming that collectibility of the lease payments is reasonably predictable, and that no important uncertainties exist in relation to unreimbursable costs yet to be incurred by the lessor, Lessor Corp. should classify this lease as a direct financing lease.

The typical journal entries to record the transactions relating to this lease for both Lessee Corp. and Lessor Corp. for the first year are presented below:

Lessee Corp.			**Lessor Corp.**		
Sale of Aircraft by Lessee to Lessor Corp., January 1, 1981					
Cash	80,000,000		Aircraft	80,000,000	
Aircraft		75,500,000	Cash		80,000,000
Unearned Profit on			Lease Payments		
Sale-Leaseback		4,500,000	Receivable	157,311,645	
Leased Aircraft Under			Aircraft		80,000,000
Capital Leases	80,000,000		Unearned Interest		
Obligations Under Capital			Income—Leases		77,311,645
Leases		80,000,000	($10,487,443 × 15 = $157,311,645)		
First Lease Payment, January 1, 1981					
Obligations Under			Cash	10,487,443	
Capital Leases	10,487,443		Lease Payments		
Cash		10,487,443	Receivable		10,487,443

Incurrence and Payment of Executory Costs by Lessee Corp. throughout 1981

		(No entry)
Insurance, Maintenance, Taxes, etc.	XXX	
Cash or Accounts Payable	XXX	

Depreciation Expense on the Aircraft, December 31, 1981

		(No entry)
Depreciation Expense	5,333,333	
Accumulated Depr.— Capital Leases ($80,000,000 ÷ 15)	5,333,333	

Amortization of Profit on Sale-Leaseback by Lessee Corp., December 31, 1981

		(No entry)
Unearned Profit on Sale-Leaseback	300,000	
Depreciation Expense ($4,500,000 ÷ 15)	300,000	

Note: A case might be made for crediting Revenue instead of Depreciation Expense.

Interest for 1981, December 31, 1981

Interest Expense— Capital Leases	8,341,507[a]	Unearned Interest Income	8,341,507	
Interest Payable	8,341,507	Interest Income—Leases		8,341,507[a]

[a]Partial Lease Amortization Schedule

Date	Annual Rental Payment	Interest 12%	Reduction of Balance	Balance
1/1/81				$80,000,000
1/1/81	$10,487,443	—	—	69,512,557
1/1/82	10,487,443	$8,341,507	$2,145,936	67,366,621

REPORTING LEASE DATA IN FINANCIAL STATEMENTS

Disclosures Required of the Lessee for Capitalized Leases

The FASB requires that the following information with respect to leases be disclosed in the lessee's financial statements or in the footnotes:

1. For **capital leases:**
   a. The gross amount of assets recorded under capital leases as of the date of each balance sheet presented, in the aggregate and by major classes according to nature or function. This information may be combined with comparable information for owned assets.
   b. Future minimum lease payments as of the date of the latest balance sheet presented, in the aggregate and for each of the five succeeding fiscal years, with separate deductions from the total for the amount representing executory costs including any profit thereon included in the minimum lease payments and for the amount of the imputed interest necessary to reduce the net minimum lease payments to present value.

c. The total of minimum sublease rentals to be received in the future under noncancelable subleases as of the date of the latest balance sheet presented.

d. Total contingent rentals (rentals on which the amounts are dependent on some factor other than the passage of time) actually incurred for each period for which an income statement is presented.

2. For **all leases,** a general description of the lessee's leasing arrangements including, but not limited to, the following:

a. The basis on which contingent rental payments are determined.

b. The existence and terms of renewal or purchase options and escalation clauses.

c. Restrictions imposed by lease agreements, such as those concerning dividends, additional debt, and further leasing.[27]

The following illustration of balance sheet and footnote disclosure by the lessee for all types of leases is adopted from Appendix D of **FASB Statement No. 13:**

Lessee Company
BALANCE SHEET

ASSETS			LIABILITIES		
	December 31,			December 31,	
	1981	1980		1981	1980
Leased property under capital leases, less accumulated amortization (Note 2)	XXX	XXX	Current: Obligations under capital leases (Note 2)	XXX	XXX
			Noncurrent: Obligations under capital leases (Note 2)	XXX	XXX

FOOTNOTES

Note 1—Description of Leasing Arrangements (omitted here)
Note 2—Capital Leases

The following is an analysis of the leased property under capital leases by major classes:

Classes of Property	Asset Balances at December 31,	
	1981	1980
Manufacturing plant	$XXX	$XXX
Store facilities	XXX	XXX
Other	XXX	XXX
	XXX	XXX
Less: Accumulated amortization	XXX	XXX
	$XXX	$XXX

[27]*Ibid.,* par. 15.

The following is a schedule by years of future minimum lease payments under capital leases, together with the present value of the net minimum lease payments as of December 31, 1981:

Year ending December 31:	
1982	$XXX
1983	XXX
1984	XXX
1985	XXX
1986	XXX
Later years	XXX
Total minimum lease payments	XXX
Less: Amount representing estimated executory costs (such as taxes, maintenance, and insurance) included in total minimum lease payments	XXX
Net minimum lease payments	XXX
Less: Amount representing interest	XXX
Present value of net minimum lease payments	$XXX

Note 3—Operating Leases

The following is a schedule by years of future minimum rental payments required under operating leases that have initial or remaining noncancelable lease terms in excess of one year as of December 31, 1981:

Year ending December 31:	
1982	$XXX
1983	XXX
1984	XXX
1985	XXX
1986	XXX
Later years	XXX
Total minimum payments required	$XXX

The following schedule shows the composition of total rental expense for all operating leases except those with terms of a month or less that were not renewed:

	Year ended December 31,	
	1981	1980
Minimun rentals	$ XXX	$ XXX
Contingent rentals	XXX	XXX
Less: Sublease rentals	(XXX)	(XXX)
	$ XXX	$ XXX

Disclosures Required by the Lessor

The FASB requires that lessors disclose in the financial statements or in the footnotes the following information when leasing "is a significant part of the lessor's business activities in terms of revenue, net income, or assets."[28]

1. For **operating leases**
   a. The cost and carrying amount, if different, of property on lease or held for leasing by major classes of property according to nature or function, and the amount of accumulated depreciation in total as of the date of the latest balance sheet presented.

[28]"Accounting for Leases," op. cit., par. 23.

    b. Minimum future rentals on noncancelable leases as of the date of the latest balance sheet presented, in the aggregate and for each of the five succeeding fiscal years.

    c. Total contingent rentals included in income for each period for which an income statement is presented.

2. For **sales-type and direct financing leases**

    a. The components of the net investment in sales-type and direct financing leases as of the date of each balance sheet presented:

        (1) Future minimum lease payments to be received, with separate deductions for (a) amounts representing executory costs included in the minimum lease payments and (b) the accumulated allowance for uncollectible minimum lease payments receivable.

        (2) The unguaranteed residual values accruing to the benefit of the lessor.

        (3) The unamortized balance of initial direct costs. (For direct financing leases only.)

        (4) Unearned income.

    b. Future minimum lease payments to be received for each of the five succeeding fiscal years as of the date of the latest balance sheet presented.

    c. The amount of unearned income included in income to offset initial direct costs charged against income for each period for which an income statement is presented. (For direct financing leases only.)

    d. Total contingent rentals included in income for each period for which an income statement is presented.

3. A general description of the lessor's leasing arrangements.

FASB Statement No. 13 contains the following illustrations of balance sheet and footnote disclosure by the lessor for operating, direct financing, and sales-type leases:

Lessor Company
BALANCE SHEET

ASSETS	December 31,	
	1981	1980
Current assets:		
Net investment in direct financing and sales-type leases (Note 2)	XXX	XXX
Noncurrent assets:		
Net investment in direct financing and sales-type leases (Note 2)	XXX	XXX
Property on operating leases and property held for leases (net of accumulated depreciation of $XXX and $XXX for 1981 and 1980, respectively) (Note 3)	XXX	XXX

FOOTNOTES

Note 1—Description of Leasing Arrangements

The company's leasing operations consist principally of the leasing of various types of heavy construction and mining equipment, data processing equipment, and transportation equipment. With the exception of the leases of transportation equipment, the bulk of the company's leases are classified as direct financing leases. The construction equipment and mining equipment leases expire over the next 10 years and the data processing equipment leases expire over the next 8 years. Transportation equipment (principally trucks) is leased under operating leases that expire during the next 3 years.

Note 2—Net Investment in Direct Financing and Sales-Type Leases

The following lists the components of the net investment in direct financing and sales-type leases as of December 31:

	1981	1980
Total minimum lease payments to be received*	$ XXX	$ XXX
Less: Amounts representing estimated executory costs (such as taxes, maintenance, and insurance) included in total minimum lease payments	(XXX)	(XXX)
Minimum lease payments receivable	XXX	XXX
Less: Allowance for uncollectibles	(XXX)	(XXX)
Net minimum lease payments receivable	XXX	XXX
Estimated residual values of leased property (unguaranteed)	XXX	XXX
Unearned income	(XXX)	(XXX)
Net investment in direct financing and sales-type leases	$ XXX	$ XXX

*Minimum lease payments do not include contingent rentals which may be received under certain leases of data processing equipment on the basis of hours of use in excess of stipulated minimums. Contingent rentals amounted to $XXX in 1981 and $XXX in 1980. At December 31, 1981, minimum lease payments for each of the five succeeding fiscal years are as follows: $XXX in 1982, $XXX in 1983, $XXX in 1984, $XXX in 1985, and $XXX in 1986.

Note 3—Property on Operating Leases and Property Held for Lease

The following schedule provides an analysis of the company's investment in property on operating leases and property held for lease by major classes and the status of the property as of December 31, 1981:

Investment by Major Classes of Property:	
Construction equipment	$ XXX
Mining equipment	XXX
Data processing equipment	XXX
Transportation equipment	XXX
Other	XXX
Investment	$ XXX
Status of Property:	
On operating leases	$ XXX
Held for lease	XXX
Investment	XXX
Accumulated depreciation	(XXX)
Net investment	$ XXX

Note 4—Rentals under Operating Leases

The following is a schedule by years of minimum future rentals on noncancelable operating leases as of December 31, 1981:

Year ending December 31:	
1982	$XXX
1983	XXX
1984	XXX
1985	XXX
1986	XXX
Later years	XXX
Total	$XXX

Lease Accounting—The Unsolved Problem

As indicated at the beginning of this chapter, lease accounting is currently a much abused area in which strenuous efforts are being made to circumvent **Statement No. 13.** In practice, the accounting rules for capitalizing leases have been rendered partially ineffective by the strong desire of lessees to resist capitalization. Leasing generally involves large dollar amounts which when capitalized materially increase reported liabilities and adversely affect the debt-to-equity ratio. Lease capitalization is also resisted because charges against income made in the early years of the lease term are higher under the capital lease method than under the operating method, frequently without tax benefit. As a consequence, "let's beat **Statement No. 13**" has become one of the most popular games in town.[29]

To avoid leased asset capitalization, lease agreements are designed, written, and interpreted so that none of the four capitalized lease criteria is satisfied from the lessee's viewpoint. Devising lease agreements in such a way has not been too difficult when the following specifications are met.

1. Make certain that the lease does not specify the transfer of title to the property to the lessee.
2. Do not write in a bargain purchase option.
3. Set the lease term at something less than 75% of the estimated economic life of the leased property.
4. Arrange for the present value of the minimum lease payments to be less than 90% of the fair value of the leased property.

But, the real challenge lies in disqualifying the lease as a capital lease to the lessee while having the same lease qualify as a capital (sales or financing) lease to the lessor. Unlike lessees, lessors try to avoid having lease arrangements classified as operating leases.

Avoiding the first three criteria is relatively simple, but it takes a little ingenuity to avoid the "90% recovery test" for the lessee while satisfying it for the lessor. Two of the factors involved in this effort are: (1) the use of the incremental borrowing rate by the lessee when it is higher than the implicit interest rate of the lessor, by making information about the implicit rate unavailable to the lessee; and (2) residual value guarantees. The residual value guarantee is probably the most popular device used by lessees and lessors. In fact, a whole new industry has emerged to circumvent symmetry between the lessee and the lessor in accounting for leases. The residual value guarantee has spawned numerous companies whose principal, or even sole, function is to guarantee the residual value of leased assets. These "third-party guarantors" (insurers), for a fee, assume the risk of deficiencies in leased asset residual value.[30]

---

[29]Richard Dieter, "Is Lessee Accounting Working." *The CPA Journal,* August 1979, p. 13–19. This article provides interesting examples of abuse of *Statement No. 13,* discusses the circumstances that led to the current situation, and proposes a solution for the confusion.

[30]As an aside, third party guarantors have experienced some difficulty lately. Lloyd's of London, for example, insured the fast growing U.S. computer-leasing industry in the amount of $2 billion against revenue losses and losses in residual value if leases were cancelled. Because of "overnight" technological improvements and the successive introductions of more efficient and less expensive computers by IBM, lessees in abundance cancelled their leases. As the market for second-hand computers becomes flooded and residual values plummet, third-party guarantor Lloyd's of London stands to lose millions. Much of the third party guarantee business was stimulated by the lessees' and lessors' desire to circumvent *FASB No. 13.*

Because the guaranteed residual value is included in the minimum lease payments for the lessor, the 90% recovery of fair market value test is satisfied and the lease is a nonoperating lease to the lessor. Because the residual value is guaranteed by a third party, the minimum lease payments of the lessee do not include the guarantee. Thus, by merely transferring some of the risk to a third party, lessees can alter substantially the accounting treatment by converting what would otherwise be capital leases to operating leases.

Much of this circumvention is encouraged by the nature of the criteria which stem from weaknesses in the basic objective of **Statement No. 13.** Accounting standard-setting bodies continue to have poor experience with arbitrary break points or other size and percentage criteria, i.e., rules like "90% of," "75% of," etc. Some accountants believe that a more workable solution would be to require capitalization of all leases that extend for some defined period (such as one year) on the basis that the lessee has acquired an asset (a property right) and a corresponding liability rather than on the basis that the lease transfers substantially all the risks and rewards of ownership.[31]

A change in the official view of the nature of leases may be forthcoming. At its March 6, 1979 meeting, a majority of the FASB expressed "the tentative view that, if **Statement 13** were to be reconsidered, they would support a property right approach in which all leases are included as 'rights to use property' and as 'lease obligations' in the lessee's balance sheet."[32] So we have come full circle, since that is the accounting view that was recommended by AICPA **Accounting Research Study No. 4** in 1962.

---

[31]"Is Lessee Accounting Working," *op. cit.,* p. 19.
[32]*Ibid.*

APPENDIX

Accounting for Leveraged
Leases

Leveraged leasing began in the late sixties and grew during the seventies. It has been estimated that more than $5 billion worth of capital equipment is financed annually through the use of leveraged leases, and there is every expectation that the use of this type of lease will continue to grow at a substantial rate.

The leverage lease is a complex financing arrangement that is entered into for various reasons. For example, in 1971 Anaconda Co. began building a plant in Kentucky, which management assumed would cost approximately $138 million and be fully owned by Anaconda Co.[1] As the company was arranging the financing, two events occurred which changed Anaconda's perspective on the situation. First, the government of Chile expropriated the company's copper mines, which led to a $356.3 million tax loss; second, Congress reinstated the investment credit. As a consequence, the depreciation, interest charges, and investment credit that would relate to ownership of the plant were only marginally beneficial to Anaconda Co. as a tax write-off because of the large tax losses already incurred. The company, therefore, decided to leverage lease the plant, because they could pass the tax benefits on to the lessor, and the lessor in turn could provide Anaconda Co. with a lower than normal rental payment.

Under a properly structured lease arrangement the lessor then has the tax benefits of the asset to use as a basis to shield taxable income. In addition, the lessor can concentrate the tax benefits by **leveraging** the lease. That is, the lessor of the property may finance a small percentage of the purchase price (with 100% ownership of the asset) and find debt participants who will finance the balance. The leveraged lease arrangement generally involves the following:

[1]Example taken from an article by Peter Vanderwicken, "The Powerful Logic of the Leasing Boom," *Fortune*, November 1973.

1. It meets the definition of a direct financing lease, except that the 90% of fair value criterion is not applicable.
2. Three participants in the lease arrangement—
   (a) An owner-lessor (equity participant).
   (b) A lessee (user of the asset).
   (c) A third-party long-term creditor (debt participant).
3. The owner-lessor provides a portion of the cost of the property to be leased, generally 20% to 40%.
4. Long-term creditors (generally financial institutions) provide the remaining portion (60 to 80%) of the cost of the equipment. The amount provided by these third-party creditors is generally called the **leveraged debt.** The leveraged debt is structured without recourse to the owner-lessor; it is secured by a pledge of lease payments or by a security interest in the property. For this reason, the interest rate obtained by the long-term creditors for the leveraged debt is based, in part, on the lessee's credit rating.
5. The asset is then purchased from the manufacturer or contractor by the lessor-owner and leased to the lessee. In return, the lessor-owner receives the rental payments, makes debt service payments (principal and interest) to the long-term creditors, and retains any difference. The residual value from the disposition of the asset at the end of the lease term is retained by the lessor. Generally, the lessor's net investment declines during the early years and rises during the later years of the lease. The lessor's return and early net cash inflow results from several sources: (1) lease rentals; (2) investment tax credit; and (3) income tax benefits such as depreciation (often accelerated) on the total cost of the property, interest expense on the debt, and possibly others.

The following diagram illustrates the relationship of the parties involved in a leveraged lease transaction.

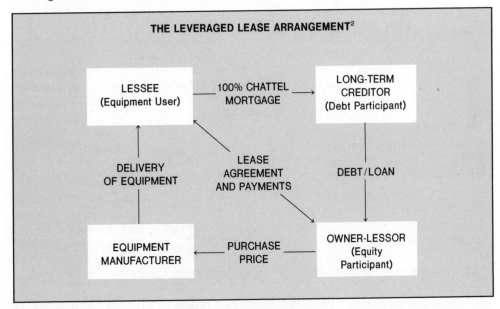

THE LEVERAGED LEASE ARRANGEMENT[2]

Typically, the lessor's investment (receivables, tax benefits, residual value, and unearned income) in a leveraged lease follows this pattern:

---

[2]Taken from "A Straightforward Approach to Leveraged Leasing," by Pierce R. Smith, *The Journal of Commercial Bank Lending* (July, 1973), pp. 40–47.

Early years—**positive,** based on initial investment in leased assets.

Middle years—**negative,** owing mainly to large income tax reductions due to investment credit, accelerated depreciation, and high interest payments.

Later years—**positive,** as investment credit has been used, accelerated depreciation reverses, and interest payments diminish.

Final year—**zero,** as residual value is realized upon sale of the asset.

To illustrate the mechanics of leveraged leases, assume that an individual in the 70% tax bracket purchases equipment at a cost of $1,000, financing 80% of the purchase price through long-term borrowing at an interest rate of 10%. The equipment is immediately leased for seven years at a yearly rental of $160, and $250 is received for the residual value of the equipment at the end of the lease. The investment credit is 10% on this property. The individual's **net investment,** after deducting the investment credit, is computed as follows:

Cost of equipment	$1,000
Less investment credit	100
	900
Amount borrowed	800
Net investment	$ 100

The following table displays the cash flows, ignoring the tax savings, that the lessor would receive on the net investment.

TABLE 1 DETERMINATION OF INTEREST AND PRINCIPAL REPAYMENT

Year	Lease Rentals and Residual Value	Payments to Creditor			Payment to (by) Lessor
		Interest	Principal	Total	
	(a)	(b)	(c)	(d)	(e)
Net investment					$(100)
1	$ 160	$ 80	$ 80	$ 160	-0-
2	160	72	88	160	-0-
3	160	65	95	160	-0-
4	160	58	102	160	-0-
5	160	53	107	160	-0-
6	160	47	113	160	-0-
7	160	43	117	160	-0-
End	250		98	98	152
	$1,370	$418	$800	$1,218	$ 52

As indicated in Table 1, the lessor receives a return of $152 for the initial $100 investment which computes out to a yield of 6.2%. If the tax savings related to the transaction are considered, however, the cash flows develop as shown on page 993.

Table 2 indicates that the lessor recovers the original investment in the second year and has the use of this money until Period 6. The yield then earned is 39% assuming reinvestment at that rate.

TABLE 2 DETERMINATION OF CUMULATIVE CASH FLOWS

Year	Lease Rentals	Interest	Expenses Depreciation	Total (b + c)	Tax Loss (Income) (d) − (a)	Tax Saving (Expense) (e) × 70%	Cumulative Cash Flow
	(a)	(b)	(c)	(d)	(e)	(f)	(g)
Net investment							$(100)
1	$ 160	$ 80	$188	$ 268	$108	$ 76	(24)
2	160	72	161	233	73	51	27
3	160	65	134	199	39	27	54
4	160	58	107	165	5	4	58
5	160	53	80	133	(27)	(19)	39
6	160	47	54	101	(59)	(41)	(2)
7	160	43	26	69	(91)	(64)	(66)
Residual value							152
	$1,120	$418	$750	$1,168	$ 48	$ 34	$ 86

The accounting problems associated with leveraged leasing are complex. The FASB requires recording income in leveraged leasing transactions by use of the **investment with separate phases method.** This approach states that the leveraged lease generates two distinct classes of earnings: primary earnings and earnings from reinvestment. In most leveraged leases, primary earnings are determined by (1) rental receipts net of operating and financial charges, (2) the investment tax credit, and (3) the residual value. Earnings from reinvestment arise from the fact that the large cash flows in the early years of the lease are shielded from payment of taxes because of deductions such as depreciation and, therefore, are available for reinvestment. The proposal is to allocate primary earnings to the years in which the investment is positive. During years in which the investment is negative, only the earnings on the reinvested funds are realized.

Lease income is therefore recognized at a level rate of return on the net investment (cost of asset less nonrecourse debt less investment credit) in those years in which the net investment at the beginning of the year is positive. When the net investment is negative, income is limited to earnings on the reinvested funds. As illustrated in Table 2 (Col. g), the lessor in most leveraged lease transactions quickly recovers the net investment, so that income on primary earnings will ordinarily be shown only in the earlier years of a leveraged lease contract. Earnings on reinvestment will be shown in the middle years, and then primary earnings will be shown in the later part of the lease when the investment is again positive.

In the income statement or the footnote, there should be separate presentation of:

1. Pretax income from the leveraged lease,
2. The tax effect of the pretax income in (1), and
3. The amount of the investment tax credit recognized as income.

In addition, disclosure should be made of all the components of the net investment reflected in the balance sheet.

Note: All **asterisked** questions, cases, exercises, or problems relate to material contained in the appendix to each chapter.

Questions

1. VanBuer Fertilizer, Inc. is expanding its operations and is in the process of selecting the method of financing this program. After some investigation, the company determines that it may (1) issue bonds and with the proceeds purchase the needed assets, or (2) lease the assets on a long-term basis.

   Without knowing the comparative costs involved, answer these questions:
   (a) What might be the advantages of leasing the assets instead of owning them?
   (b) What might be the disadvantages of leasing the assets instead of owning them?
   (c) In what way will the balance sheet be differently affected by leasing the assets as opposed to issuing bonds and purchasing the assets?

2. Gourmet Foods Corp. is considering leasing a significant amount of assets. The President, Peggy Graham, is attending an informal meeting in the afternoon with a potential lessor. Because her legal advisor cannot be reached, she has called on you, the controller, to brief her on the general provisions of lease agreements to which she should give consideration in such preliminary discussions with a possible lessor.

   Identify the general provisions of the lease agreement that the president should be told to include in her discussion with the potential lessor.

3. Identify the lease classifications for lessees and the criteria that must be met for each classification.

4. Identify the two recognized lease accounting methods for lessees and distinguish between them.

5. The Lawn Mower Company rents a warehouse on a month-to-month basis for the storage of its excess inventory. The company periodically must rent space whenever its production greatly exceeds actual sales. For several years the company officials have discussed building their own storage facility, but this enthusiasm wavers when sales increase sufficiently to absorb the excess inventory.

   What is the nature of this type of lease arrangement, and what accounting treatment should be accorded it?

6. What disclosures should be made by a lessee if the leased assets and the related obligation are not capitalized?

7. Differentiate between the "lessee's incremental borrowing rate" and the "lessor's implicit rate" in accounting for leases indicating when one or the other should be used.

8. Outline the accounting procedures involved in applying the operating method by a lessee.

9. Outline the accounting procedures involved in applying the capital lease method by a lessee.

10. Identify the lease classifications for lessors and the criteria that must be met for each classification.

11. Outline the accounting procedures involved in applying the operating method by a lessor.

12. Outline the accounting procedures involved in applying the direct financing method.

13. Microdot Company is a manufacturer and lessor of computer equipment. What should be the nature of its lease arrangements with lessees if the company wishes to account for its lease transactions as sales-type leases?

14. Vacuum Sweeper Corporation's lease arrangements qualify as sales-type leases at the time of entering into the transactions. How should the corporation recognize revenues and costs in these situations?

15. Why are present-value concepts appropriate and applicable in accounting for financing-type lease arrangements?

16. Jerry Moluf, M. D. (lessee) has a noncancelable 20-year lease with E. T. Elsner Realty, Inc., (lessor) for the use of a medical building. Taxes, insurance, and maintenance are paid by the lessee in addition to the fixed annual payments, of which the present value is equal to the fair market value of the leased property. At the end of the lease period, title becomes the lessee's at a nominal price.

    Considering the terms of the lease described above, comment on the nature of the lease transaction and the accounting treatment that should be accorded it by the lessee.

17. The residual value is the estimated fair value of the leased property at the end of the lease term.
    (a) Of what significance is (1) an unguaranteed and (2) a guaranteed residual value in the lessee's accounting for a capitalized lease transaction?
    (b) Of what significance is (1) an unguaranteed and (2) a guaranteed residual value in the lessor's accounting for a direct financing lease transaction?

18. How should changes in the estimated residual value be handled by the lessor?

19. Describe the effect of a "bargain purchase option" on accounting for a capital lease transaction by a lessee.

20. What are "initial direct costs" and how are they accounted for?

21. What is the nature of a "sale-leaseback" transaction?

*22. What distinguishes a leveraged lease from all other lease arrangements?

*23. What is the cash flow that the lessor realizes in a normal leveraged lease transaction?

Cases

C22-1 Milton Corporation entered into a lease arrangement with Foxy Leasing Corporation for a certain machine. Foxy's primary business is leasing and it is not a manufacturer or dealer. Milton will lease the machine for a period of three years which is 50% of the machine's economic life. Foxy will take possession of the machine at the end of the initial three-year lease and lease it to another smaller company that does not need the most current version of the machine. Milton does not guarantee any residual value for the machine and will not purchase the machine at the end of the lease term.

Milton's incremental borrowing rate is 10% and the implicit rate in the lease is 8½%. Milton has no way of knowing the implicit rate used by Foxy. Using either rate, the present value of the minimum lease payments is between 90% and 100% of the fair value of the machine at the date of the lease agreement.

Milton has agreed to pay all executory costs directly and no allowance for these costs is included in the lease payments.

Foxy is reasonably certain that Milton will pay all lease payments, and, because Milton has agreed to pay all executory costs, there are no important uncertainties regarding costs to be incurred by Foxy. Assume that no indirect costs are involved.

Instructions

(a) With respect to Milton (the lessee) answer the following:
    1. What type of lease has been entered into? Explain the reason for your answer.
    2. How should Milton compute the appropriate amount to be recorded for the lease or asset acquired?
    3. What accounts will be created or affected by this transaction and how will the lease or asset and other costs related to the transaction be matched with earnings?
    4. What disclosures must Milton make regarding this lease or asset?

(b) With respect to Foxy (the lessor) answer the following:
    1. What type of leasing arrangement has been entered into? Explain the reason for your answer.

2. How should this lease be recorded by Foxy and how are the appropriate amounts determined?

3. How should Foxy determine the appropriate amount of earnings to be recognized from each lease payment?

4. What disclosures must Foxy make regarding this lease?

(AICPA adapted)

Exercises

E22-1   Nancy Beasley Leasing Company leases a new machine that cost $36,000 to Patty Hart Corporation on a three-year noncancelable contract. Patty Hart Corporation agrees to assume all risks of normal ownership including such costs as insurance, taxes, and maintenance. The machine has a three-year useful life and no residual value. The lease was signed on January 1, 1981; Beasley Leasing Company expects to earn a 6% return on its investment. The annual rentals are payable on each December 31.

Instructions

(a) Discuss the nature of the lease arrangement and the accounting method each party to the lease should apply.

(b) Prepare an amortization schedule that would be suitable for both the lessor and the lessee and covers all the years involved.

E22-2   Stillwater Company enters into a lease agreement on July 1, 1980 for the purpose of leasing a machine to be used in its manufacturing operations. The following data pertain to this agreement:

1. The term of the noncancelable lease is 3 years, with no renewal option, and no residual value at the end of the lease term. Payments of $97,008.26 are due on June 30 of each year, beginning June 30, 1981.

2. The fair value of the machine on July 1, 1980 is $265,000. The machine has a remaining economic life of 5 years, with no salvage value. The machine reverts to the lessor upon the termination of the lease.

3. Stillwater Company elects to depreciate the machine on the straight-line method.

4. Stillwater Company's incremental borrowing rate is 8% per year. Stillwater does not have knowledge of the implicit rate computed by the lessor.

Instructions

Prepare the journal entries on the books of the lessee that relate to the lease agreement through June 30, 1983. The accounting period of Stillwater Company ends on December 31. (Assume that reversing entries are made.)

E22-3   On January 1, 1981, Judy Nolan Paper Co. signs a 10-year noncancelable lease agreement to lease a storage building from Temporary Storage Company. The following information pertains to this lease agreement:

1. The agreement requires equal rental payments of $120,000 at the end of each year.

2. The fair value of the building on January 1, 1981 is $753,855.

3. The building has an estimated economic life of 12 years, with an unguaranteed residual value of $10,000. Nolan Paper Co. depreciates similar buildings on the straight-line method.

4. The lease is nonrenewable. At the termination of the lease, the building reverts to the lessor.

5. Nolan Paper's incremental borrowing rate is 8% per year. The lessor's implicit rate is not known by Nolan Paper Co.

6. The yearly rental payment includes $8,227.86 of executory costs related to taxes on the property.

Instructions

Prepare the journal entries on the lessee's books to reflect the signing of the lease agreement and to record the payments and expenses related to this lease for the years 1981 and 1982.

E22-4 Lahey Housing Company leases an automobile with a fair value of $6,000 from Jerri Delaney Motors, Inc. on the following terms:

1. Noncancelable term of 50 months.
2. Rental of $140 per month (at end of each month; present value at 1% per month is $5,484).
3. Estimated residual value after 50 months is $850 (the present value at 1% per month is $516). Lahey Housing Company guarantees the residual value of $850.
4. Estimated economic life of the automobile is 60 months.
5. Lahey Housing Company's incremental borrowing rate is 12% a year (1% a month). Delaney's implicit rate is unknown.

Instructions

(a) What is the nature of this lease to Lahey Housing Company?
(b) What is the present value of the minimum lease payments?
(c) Record the lease on Lahey Housing Company's books at the date of inception.
(d) Record the first month's depreciation on Lahey Housing Company's books (assume straight-line).
(e) Record the first month's lease payment.

E22-5 Electric Car Company leases a car at fair value to a salesman on January 1, 1981. The term of the noncancelable lease is four years. The following information about the lease is provided:

1. Title to the car passes to the lessee upon the termination of the lease when residual value is estimated at $1,000.
2. The fair value of the car is $9,000. The cost of the car to Electric Car Company is $6,000. The car has an economic life of five years.
3. Electric Car Company desires a rate of return of 15% on its investment.
4. Collectibility of the lease payments is reasonably predictable. There are no important uncertainties surrounding the amount of costs yet to be incurred by the lessor.
5. Equal annual lease payments are due at the beginning of each lease year.

Instructions

(a) Prepare a lease amortization schedule for Electric Car Company for the four-year lease term.
(b) What type of lease is this? Discuss.
(c) Prepare the journal entries in 1981, 1982, and 1983 to record the lease agreement, the receipt of lease payments, and the recognition of income.

E22-6 Mavis Williams Leasing Company signs a lease agreement on January 1, 1981 to lease electronic equipment to Hamsmith Company at cost. The term of the noncancelable lease is two years and payments are required at the end of each year. The following information relates to this agreement:

1. Hamsmith Company has the option to purchase the equipment for $10,000 upon the termination of the lease.
2. The equipment has a cost of $60,000 to Mavis Williams Company; the useful economic life is two years, with a salvage value of $10,000.
3. Hamsmith Company is required to pay $5,000 each year to the lessor for executory costs.
4. Mavis Williams Company desires to earn a return of 8% on its investment.

5. Collectibility of the payments is reasonably predictable, and there are no important uncertainties surrounding the costs yet to be incurred by the lessor.

Instructions

    (a) Prepare the journal entries on the books of Mavis Williams Company to reflect the payments received under the lease, and to recognize income, for the years 1981 and 1982.

    (b) Assuming that Hamsmith Company exercises its option to purchase the equipment on December 31, 1982, prepare the journal entry to reflect the sale.

E22-7 On January 1, 1981, Rickshaw Corporation sells land to Ski-Daddle Corporation for $1,000,000, and immediately leases the land back. The relevant information is as follows:

1. The land was carried on Rickshaw's books at a value of $750,000.
2. The term of the noncancelable lease is 20 years; title will pass to Rickshaw.
3. The lease agreement requires equal rental payments of $101,852.18 at the end of each year.
4. The incremental borrowing rate of Rickshaw Corporation is 10%. Rickshaw is aware that Ski-Daddle Corporation set the annual rental to insure a rate of return of 8%.
5. The land has a fair value of $1,000,000 on January 1, 1981.
6. Rickshaw pays all executory costs. These costs consist of insurance and taxes amounting to $5,000 per year.

Instructions

Prepare the journal entries for both the lessee and the lessor for 1981 to reflect the sale and leaseback agreement.

Problems

P22-1 Lease-What-You-Like, Inc., agrees to rent Denise Rode Winery Corporation the equipment that it requires to expand its production capacity to meet customers' demands for its products. The lease agreement calls for five annual lease payments of $200,000 at the end of each year. On the date the capital lease begins, the lessee recognizes the existence of leased assets and the related lease obligation at the present value of the five annual payments discounted at a rate of 8%, $798,542. The lessee uses the effective-interest method of reducing lease obligations. The leased equipment has an estimated useful life of five years and no residual value; Rode Winery uses the sum-of-the-years'-digits method on similar equipment that it owns.

Instructions

    (a) What would be the total amount of the reduction in the lease obligation of the lessee during the first year? The second year?

    (b) Prepare the journal entry made by Rode Winery Corporation (lessee) on the date the lease begins.

    (c) Prepare the journal entries to record the lease payment and interest expense for the first year; the second year.

    (d) Prepare the journal entry at the end of the first full year to recognize depreciation of the leased equipment.

P22-2 Rob Isham Company leased a new crane to Hefty Products Company under a 5-year noncancelable contract starting January 1, 1981. Terms of the lease require payments of $10,000 each December 31. Isham will pay insurance, taxes, and maintenance charges on the crane, which has an estimated life of 12 years, a fair value of $80,000, and a cost to Isham Company of $80,000. The estimated fair value of the crane is expected to be $40,000 at the end of the lease term. No bargain purchase or renewal options are included in the contract. Both Isham and Hefty adjust and close books annually at December 31. Collectibility is reasonably certain and no uncertainties exist relative to unreimbursable lessor costs.

Instructions

(a) Identify the type of lease involved and give reasons for your classification. Discuss the accounting treatment that should be applied by both the lessee and the lessor.

operating
lease inc
lease expense

(b) Prepare all the entries related to the lease contract and leased asset for the year 1981 for the lessee and lessor, assuming:
1. Insurance $160.00
2. Taxes $80.00
3. Maintenance $490.00
4. Straight-line depreciation and salvage value of $2,000.

(c) Discuss what should be presented in the balance sheet and income statement and related footnotes of both the lessee and the lessor at December 31, 1981.

P22-3 Quincy & Northern Railroad and Electro-Motive Corporation enter into an agreement that requires Electro-Motive to build four diesel-electric engines to Quincy's specifications. Upon completion of the engines, Quincy has agreed to lease them for a period of 12 years and to assume all costs and risks of ownership. The lease is noncancelable, becomes effective on January 1, 1981, and requires annual rental payments each December 31 of $280,000.

Quincy's incremental borrowing rate is 13%, and the implicit interest rate used by Electro-Motive and known to Quincy is 12%. The total cost of building the four engines is $1,550,000. The economic life of the engines is estimated to be 12 years with residual value set at zero. The railroad depreciates similar equipment on a straight-line basis. At the end of the lease, the railroad assumes title to the engines. Collectibility is reasonably certain and no uncertainties exist relative to unreimbursable lessor costs.

Instructions

(Round all numbers to the nearest dollar.)

(a) Discuss the nature of this lease transaction from the viewpoints of both lessee and lessor.

(b) Prepare the journal entry or entries to record the transaction on January 1, 1981 on the books of the Quincy & Northern Railroad.

(c) Prepare the journal entry or entries to record the transaction on January 1, 1981 on the books of the Electro-Motive Corporation.

(d) Prepare the journal entries for both the lessee and lessor to record the first rental payment on December 31, 1981.

(e) Show the items and amounts that would be reported on the balance sheet (not footnotes) at December 31, 1981 for both the lessee and the lessor.

P22-4 On January 1, 1981, Rainbow Company contracts to lease equipment for five years, agreeing to make a payment of $70,000 (including the executory costs of $10,000) at the end of each year. The taxes, the insurance, and the maintenance, estimated at $10,000 a year, are the obligations of the lessee. The leased equipment is to be capitalized at $252,741. The asset is to be amortized on a straight-line basis while the obligation is to be reduced on an effective-interest basis. Rainbow Company's incremental borrowing rate is 8%, and the implicit rate in the lease is 6%, which is known by Rainbow. Title to the equipment transfers to Rainbow when the lease expires. The asset has an estimated useful life of five years and no residual value.

Instructions

(Round all numbers to the nearest dollar.)

(a) Explain the probable relationship of the $252,741 amount to the lease arrangement.

(b) Prepare the journal entry or entries that should be recorded on January 1, 1981 by Rainbow Company.

(c) Prepare the journal entry to record depreciation of the leased asset for the year 1981.

(d) Prepare the journal entry to record the lease payment of December 31, 1981.

(e) What amounts will appear on the lessee's December 31, 1981 balance sheet relative to the lease contract?

P22-5 Armaloy Company as lessee signed a lease agreement for equipment for 5 years, beginning December 31, 1980. Annual rental payments of $30,000 are to be made at the beginning of each lease year (December 31). The taxes, insurance, and the maintenance costs are the obligation of the lessee. The interest rate used by the lessor in setting the payment schedule is 8%; Armaloy's incremental borrowing rate is 10%. Armaloy is unaware of the rate being used by the lessor. At the end of the lease, Armaloy has the option to buy the equipment for $1, considerably below its then estimated fair value. The equipment has an estimated useful life of 8 years. Armaloy uses the straight-line method of depreciation on similar owned equipment.

Instructions

(Round all numbers to the nearest dollar.)

(a) Prepare the journal entry or entries, with explanations, that should be recorded on December 31, 1980 by Armaloy. (Assume no residual value.)

(b) Prepare the journal entry or entries, with explanations, that should be recorded on December 31, 1981 by Armaloy (prepare the lease amortization schedule for all five payments).

(c) Prepare the journal entry or entries, with explanations, that should be recorded on December 31, 1982 by Armaloy.

(d) What amounts would appear on the December 31, 1982 balance sheet of Armaloy relative to the lease arrangement?

P22-6 Cannon, Inc., was incorporated in 1979 to operate as a computer software service firm with an accounting fiscal year ending August 31. Cannon's primary product is a sophisticated on-line inventory-control system; its customers pay a fixed fee plus a usage charge for using the system.

Cannon has leased a large, BIG-I computer system from the manufacturer. The lease calls for a monthly rental of $30,000 for the 144 months (12 years) of the lease term. The estimated useful life of the computer is 15 years.

Each scheduled monthly rental payment includes $5,000 for full-service maintenance on the computer to be performed by the manufacturer. All rentals are payable on the first day of the month beginning with August 1, 1980, the date the computer was installed and the lease agreement was signed.

The lease is noncancelable for its 12-year term, and it is secured only by the manufacturer's chattel lien on the BIG-I system. On any anniversary date of the lease after August 1985, Cannon can purchase the BIG-I system from the manufacturer at 75% of the then current fair value of the computer.

This lease is to be accounted for as a capital lease by Cannon, and it will be depreciated by the straight-line method with no expected salvage value. Borrowed funds for this type of transaction would cost Cannon 12% per year (1% per month). Following is a schedule of the present value of $1 for selected periods discounted at 1% per period when payments are made at the beginning of each period.

Periods (months)	Present Value of $1 per Period Discounted at 1% per Period
1	1.000
2	1.990
3	2.970

143	76.658
144	76.899

Instructions

Prepare, in general journal form, all entries Cannon should have made in its accounting records during August 1980 relating to this lease. Give full explanations and show supporting computations for each entry. Remember, August 31, 1980, is the end of Cannon's fiscal accounting period and it will be preparing financial statements on that date. **Do not prepare closing entries.**

(AICPA adapted)

P22-7 Sammie Jones Dairy leases its milking equipment from Lois Fisk Finance Company under the following lease terms:

1. The lease term is five years, noncancelable, and requires equal rental payments of $46,474.17 due at the beginning of each year starting January 1, 1981.

2. The equipment has a fair value at the inception of the lease (January 1, 1981) of $201,023, an estimated economic life of five years, and a residual value (which is guaranteed by Jones Dairy) of $10,000.

3. The lease contains no renewable options and the equipment reverts to Fisk Finance Company upon termination of the lease.

4. Jones Dairy's incremental borrowing rate is 10% per year; the implicit rate of 9% is not known by Jones Dairy.

5. Jones Dairy depreciates similar equipment that it owns on a straight-line basis.

Instructions

(a) Describe the nature of the lease and in general discuss how Sammie Jones Dairy should account for the lease transaction.

(b) Prepare the journal entries at January 1, 1981.

(c) Prepare a lease amortization schedule covering the term of the lease.

(d) Prepare the journal entries at December 31, 1981 (Jones Dairy's year end).

(e) Prepare the journal entry at January 1, 1982.

(f) On December 31, 1985, the residual value of the equipment is $4,000. Jones Dairy returns to Fisk Finance the equipment and makes good on its residual value guarantee. Prepare the journal entry to record this final transaction of the lease.

P22-8 Panda Company manufactures a desk-type computer with an estimated economic life of 12 years and leases it to Cougar Company for a period of 10 years. The normal selling price of the equipment is $270,360, and its unguaranteed residual value at the end of the lease term is estimated to be $20,000. Cougar will pay annual payments of $40,000 at the beginning of each year and all maintenance, insurance, and taxes. Panda incurred costs of $200,000 in manufacturing the equipment and $6,000 in negotiating and closing the lease. Cougar has determined that the collectibility of the lease payments is reasonably predictable, that there will be no additional costs incurred, and that the implicit interest rate is 10%.

Instructions

(Round all numbers to the nearest dollar.)

(a) Discuss the nature of this lease in relation to the lessor and compute the amount of each of the following items:
   1. Gross investment.
   2. Unearned income.
   3. Sales price.
   4. Cost of sales.

(b) Prepare a 10-year lease amortization schedule.

(c) Prepare all of the lessor's journal entries for the first year.

P22-9   On February 1, 1978, Navajo Company buys land costing $300,000 and on that site has a larger shopping center constructed to its specifications at a cost of $2,700,000. The center is completed on December 27, 1980. On January 1, 1981, Navajo Company sells the shopping center property to Stargell Development Corporation for $3,000,000 cash and immediately signs an agreement to lease the entire property for 40 years, making annual payments of $306,778 on December 31. These payments are sufficient to repay the Stargell Development Corporation its cash outlay and to provide a 10% return on the investment. Title to the property will revert to Navajo Company at the termination of the lease. All maintenance and other services, and the cost of insurance, taxes, and utilities, are the responsibility of the lessee. The Navajo Company has decided to amortize the property on a straight-line basis.

Instructions

(Round all numbers to the nearest dollar.)

(a) From the information above, prepare for Navajo Company books journal entries (on an annual basis), with explanations, relative to the leased property for the year 1981.

(b) What accounts and amounts will appear in the December 31, 1981 financial statements of Navajo Company relative to the leased property?

(c) From the information above, prepare for Stargell Development Corporation books journal entries relative to the leased property for the year 1981.

P22-10   Cribkeep Company owns land having a cost basis of $55,000 on which it constructs a warehouse that is completed on January 1, 1981, at a cost of $404,799. On that date Cribkeep sells the warehouse and the land to Robert Morris Realty Inc. for $504,799 and simultaneously signs a lease under the following conditions:

1. Ten-years and noncancelable.
2. Fair values at 1/1/81—land $100,000; warehouse $404,799.
3. Estimated life of the warehouse is 20 years with no residual value.
4. Lease payments are $75,230 payable each December 31.
5. Cribkeep Company's incremental borrowing rate is 8%; the lessor uses it to compute the annual payments.
6. Lessee has the option to buy the warehouse for $1 at the end of the lease term.
7. Lessee depreciates similar assets using the straight-line method.
8. Lessee assumes responsibility for executory costs.
9. Collectibility of the payments is reasonably certain and no uncertainties exist relative to unreimbursable lessor costs.

Instructions

(Round all amounts to the nearest dollar.)

(a) Prepare a lease amortization schedule usable by both lessee and lessor through 1983 to record interest and reduction of principal.

(b) Prepare entries for the books of both the lessee and the lessor on January 1, 1981.

(c) Prepare entries for the books of both the lessee and the lessor for 1981 amortization and the first rental payment on December 31, 1981.

(d) Indicate the amounts and accounts that should appear on the December 31, 1981 balance sheet of both the lessee and the lessor.

(e) Prepare the footnotes that should accompany the December 31, 1981 financial statements of the lessee and the lessor.

P22-11   In 1978 the Intermountain Express Company negotiated and closed a long-term lease contract for newly constructed truck terminals and freight storage facilities. The buildings were erected to the company's specifications on land owned by the company. On January 1, 1979, Intermountain Express Company took possession of the leased properties. On January 1, 1979 and 1980, the company made cash payments of $1,200,000 that were recorded as rental expenses.

Although the terminals have a composite useful life of 40 years, the noncancelable lease runs for 20 years from January 1, 1979, with a bargain purchase option available upon expiration of the lease.

The 20-year lease is effective for the period January 1, 1979 through December 31, 1998. Advance rental payments of $1,000,000 are payable to the lessor on January 1 of each of the first 10 years of the lease term. Advance rental payments of $300,000 are due on January 1 for each of the last 10 years of the lease. The company has an option to purchase all of these leased facilities for $1 on December 31, 1998. It also must make annual payments to the lessor of $75,000 for property taxes and $125,000 for insurance. The lease was negotiated to assure the lessor a 6% rate of return.

Instructions

(Round all computations to the nearest dollar.)

(a) Prepare a schedule to compute for Intermountain Express Company the discounted present value of the terminal facilities and related obligation at January 1, 1979.

(b) Assuming that the discounted present value of terminal facilities and related obligation at January 1, 1979, was $10,000,000, prepare journal entries for Intermountain Express Company to record the:
1. Cash payment to the lessor on January 1, 1981.
2. Amortization of the cost of the leased properties for 1981 using the straight-line method and assuming a zero salvage value.
3. Accrual of interest expense at December 31, 1981.

Selected present value factors are as follows:

Periods	For an Ordinary Annuity of $1 at 6%	For $1 at 6%
1	.943396	.943396
2	1.833393	.889996
8	6.209794	.627412
9	6.801692	.591898
10	7.360087	.558395
19	11.158117	.330513
20	11.469921	.311805

(AICPA adapted)

P22-12   During 1981, Sharko Leasing Co. began leasing equipment to small manufacturers. Below is information regarding leasing arrangements.

1. Sharko Leasing Co. leases equipment with terms from 3 to 5 years depending upon the useful life of the equipment. At the expiration of the lease, the equipment will be sold to the lessee at 10% of the lessor's cost, the expected salvage value of the equipment.

2. The amount of the lessee's monthly payment is computed by multiplying the lessor's cost of the equipment by the payment factor applicable to the term of lease.

Term of lease	Payment factor
3 years	3.32%
4 years	2.63%
5 years	2.22%

3. The excess of the gross contract receivable for equipment rentals over the cost (reduced by the estimated salvage value at the termination of the lease) is recognized as revenue over the term of the lease under the sum-of-the-years'-digits method computed on a monthly basis.

4. The following leases were entered into during 1981:

Machine	Dates of Lease	Period of Lease	Machine Cost
Die	7/1/81–6/30/85	4 years	$45,000
Press	9/1/81–8/31/84	3 years	$30,000

Instructions

(a) Prepare a schedule of gross contracts receivable for equipment rentals at the dates of the lease for the die and press machines.

(b) Prepare a schedule of unearned lease income at December 31, 1981 for each machine lease.

(c) Prepare a schedule computing the present dollar value of lease payments receivable (gross investment) for equipment rentals at December 31, 1981. (The present dollar value of the "lease receivables for equipment rentals" is the outstanding amount of the gross lease receivables less the unearned lease income included therein.) Without prejudice to your solution to part (b), assume that the unearned lease income at December 31, 1981, was $14,500.

(AICPA adapted)

Accounting Changes and Error Analysis

ACCOUNTING CHANGES

Headlines such as the following often appear in the financial press:

"Pan American had April profit, tied to accounting move."
"Alexander & Baldwin to revise accounting, halt some operations."
"Aeronautical company revises estimates of service lives of Boeing 747s."
"Deficit would have been $20 million more if firm hadn't altered accounting."
"Change in reporting land sales of unit cited for 8.2 million deficit despite operating net."

Changes in accounting occur in practice because at the time financial statements are prepared, important future events or conditions may be in dispute or uncertain. Only several years later may it be possible to determine the adjustments needed to reflect the financial information properly. Accountants, in this situation, face the difficult problem of determining how changes in accounting can be reflected in the accounting records to facilitate analysis and understanding of financial statements. Trends shown in comparative financial statements and historical summaries are particularly affected by the manner in which changes in accounting are disclosed. This chapter discusses the different procedures used to account for (1) accounting changes and (2) error corrections.

The Different Types of Accounting Changes

Before the issuance of **APB Opinion No. 20,** "Accounting Changes" in 1971, companies had considerable flexibility in reporting changes affecting comparability in accounting reports. This flexibility was evidenced by alternative accounting treatments that were developed and used in essentially equivalent situations. For example, when the steel companies changed their methods of depreciating plant assets from accelerated depreciation to straight-line depreciation, the effect of the change was presented in different ways by different companies. The cumulative difference between the depreciation charges that had been recorded and what would have been recorded could have been reflected in the income statement of the period of the change. Similarly, the change could have been ignored, and the undepreciated asset balance simply depreciated on a straight-line basis in the future. Or, companies could simply have restated the prior periods on the basis that the straight-line approach had always been used. When such alternatives exist, comparability of the statements between periods and between companies is diminished and useful historical-trend data are obscured.

The APB's first step in this area was to establish categories for the different types of changes that occur in practice:[1]

A. **Types of Accounting Changes:**

  1. **Change in accounting principle.** A change from one generally accepted accounting principle to another generally accepted accounting principle: for example, a change in the method of depreciation from double-declining to straight-line depreciation of plant assets.

  2. **Change in accounting estimate.** A change that occurs as the result of new information or as additional experience is acquired. An example is a change in the estimate of the useful lives of depreciable assets.

  3. **Change in reporting entity.** A change from reporting as one type of entity to another type of entity: for example, changing specific subsidiaries comprising the group of companies for which consolidated financial statements are prepared.

B. **Correction of an Error in Previously Issued Financial Statements** (not an accounting change). Errors in financial statements that occur as a result of mathematical mistakes, mistakes in the application of accounting principles, or oversight or misuse of facts that existed at the time financial statements were prepared: for example, the incorrect application of the retail inventory method for determining the final inventory value.

Changes were classified into these categories because the individual characteristics of each category necessitate different methods of recognizing these changes in the financial statements. Each of these items is discussed separately to investigate its unusual characteristics and to determine how each item should be reflected in the accounts and how the information should be disclosed in comparative statements.

Changes in Accounting Principle

A change in accounting principle involves a change from one generally accepted accounting principle to another generally accepted accounting principle. The

---

[1]"Accounting Changes," *Opinions of the Accounting Principles Board No. 20* (New York: AICPA, 1971).

term "accounting principle" is defined to include changes in the method of application of an accounting principle. Below are examples of changes in accounting principles.

1. Changing the basis of inventory pricing from average cost to LIFO.
2. Changing the method of depreciation on plant assets from accelerated to straight-line or vice versa.
3. Changing the accounting for construction contracts from the completed contract to the percentage of completion.

A careful examination must be made in each circumstance to insure that a change in principle has occurred. **A change in accounting principle is not considered to result from the adoption of a new principle in recognition of events that have occurred for the first time or that were previously immaterial.** For example, adoption of a depreciation method for newly acquired plant assets different from the method or methods used for previously recorded assets of a similar class is not considered a change in accounting principle. Certain marketing expenditures that were previously immaterial and expensed in the period incurred may now be material and acceptably deferred and amortized without being considered a change in accounting principle. Finally, **if the accounting principle previously followed was not acceptable, or if the principle was applied incorrectly, a change to a generally accepted accounting principle is considered a correction of an error.** For example, a switch from the cash basis of accounting to the accrual basis is considered a correction of an error. If the company deducted salvage value when computing double-declining depreciation on plant assets and later recomputed depreciation without deduction of estimated salvage, a correction of an error occurs.

Three approaches have been suggested for reporting changes in accounting principles in the accounts:

Retroactively. The cumulative effect of the use of the new method on the financial statements at the beginning of the period is computed. A retroactive adjustment of the financial statements is then made, recasting the financial statements of prior years on a basis consistent with the newly adopted principle. Advocates of this position argue that only by restatement of prior periods can changes in accounting principles lead to comparable financial statements. If this approach is not used, the year previous to the change will be on the old method; the year of the change will reflect the entire cumulative adjustment in income; and the following year will present financial statements on the new basis without the cumulative effect of the change. The question is how can public confidence in financial statements be maintained when the periods are not on a comparable basis? Consistency is considered essential to providing meaningful earnings-trend data and other financial relationships necessary to evaluate the business.

Currently. The cumulative effect of the use of the new method on the financial statements at the beginning of the period is computed. This adjustment is then reported in the current year's income statement as a special item between the captions "extraordinary items" and "net income." Advocates of this position argue that restating financial statements for prior years results in a loss of confidence by investors in financial reports. How will a present or prospective investor react when told that the earnings computed five years ago are now entirely different? Restatement, if permitted, also might upset many contractual and other arrangements that were based on the old figures. For example, profit-sharing arrangements computed on the old basis might have to be recomputed and completely new distributions made, which might create numerous legal problems. Many practical difficulties also exist; the cost of restatement may be excessive, or restatement may be impossible on the basis of data available. Finally, some individuals argue that restatement permits possible manipulation of earnings, because changes having a favorable effect on income might be handled currently or in the future, but changes having an unfavorable effect might be handled retroactively.

Prospectively. No change is made in previously reported results. Opening balances are not adjusted, and no attempt is made to allocate charges or credits for prior events. Advocates of this position argue that once management presents to investors and to others financial statements based on acceptable accounting principles, they are final, because management cannot change prior periods by adopting a new principle. According to this line of reasoning, the cumulative adjustment in the current year is not appropriate, because this approach reflects in net income an amount that has little or no relationship to the current year's income or economic events.

Before the adoption of **APB Opinion No. 20,** all three of the approaches above were used. **APB Opinion No. 20,** however, settled this issue by establishing guidelines that are to be used, depending on the type of change in accounting principle involved. We have classified these changes in accounting principle into three categories:

1. Cumulative-Effect Type Accounting Change
2. Retroactive-Effect Type Accounting Change
3. Change to the LIFO Method of Inventory

Cumulative-Effect Type Accounting Change

The general requirement of **APB Opinion No. 20** was that the current or catch-up method should be used to account for changes in accounting principles. The basic requirements are as follows:

1. The current or catch-up approach should be employed. The cumulative effect of the adjustment should be reported in the income statement between the captions "extraordinary items" and "net income." The cumulative effect is not an extraordinary item but should be reported on a net-of-tax basis in a manner similar to that used for an extraordinary item.
2. Financial statements for prior periods included for comparative purposes should be presented as previously reported.
3. Income before extraordinary items and net income computed on a **pro forma (as if)** basis should be shown on the face of the income statement for all periods presented as if the newly adopted principle had been applied during all periods affected. Related earnings per share data should also be reported. The reader, then, has some understanding of how restated financial statements appear.[2] The pro forma amounts should include both (1) the direct effects of a change and (2) nondiscretionary adjustments in items based on income before taxes or net income (such as profit-sharing expense and certain royalties) that would have been recognized if the newly adopted principle had been followed in prior periods; related income tax effects should be recognized for both (1) and (2). If an income statement is presented for the current period only, the actual and pro forma amounts (including earnings per share) for the immediately preceding period should be disclosed.

To illustrate, assume that Hillstone, Inc. decided at the beginning of 1981 to change from the sum-of-the-years'-digits method of depreciation to the straight-line method for financial reporting on its plant assets. For tax purposes, the company has employed the sum-of-the-years'-digits method and will continue to do so.

[2]*Ibid.*, par. 21.

The assets originally cost $100,000 in 1979 and have an estimated useful life of four years. The data assumed for this illustration are:

Year	Sum-of-the-Years'-Digits Depreciation	Straight-Line Depreciation	Difference	Tax Effect 40%	Effect on Income (net of tax)
1979	$40,000	$25,000	$15,000	$6,000	$ 9,000
1980	$30,000	$25,000	5,000	2,000	3,000
			$20,000	$8,000	$12,000

The entry made to record this transaction in 1981 should be:

Accumulated Depreciation	20,000	
Deferred Income Taxes		8,000
Cumulative Effect of Change in Accounting Principle—Depreciation		12,000

The debit of $20,000 to Accumulated Depreciation is the excess of the sum-of-the-years'-digits depreciation over the straight-line depreciation. The Deferred Income Taxes of $8,000 are recorded to reflect interperiod tax allocation procedures. Prior to the change in accounting principle, sum-of-the-years'-digits was used for both tax and book purposes. However, if the straight-line method had been employed for book purposes in previous years, the excess of tax depreciation over book depreciation would have created credits to deferred income taxes totaling $8,000. The cumulative effect on income resulting from the difference between sum-of-the-years'-digits depreciation and straight-line depreciation is reduced by the tax on that difference.

The information is reported in comparative statements as follows:

Cumulative-Effect Type Accounting Change
Reporting the Change in Two-Year Comparative Statements

	1981	1980
Income before extraordinary item and cumulative effect of a change in accounting principles (assumed)	$120,000	$111,000
Extraordinary item (assumed)	(30,000)	10,000
Cumulative effect on prior years of retroactive application of new depreciation method (Note A)	12,000	
Net income	$102,000	$121,000
Per share amounts		
Earnings per share (100,000 shares)		
Income before extraordinary item and cumulative effect of a change in accounting principle	$1.20	$1.11
Extraordinary item	(0.30)	0.10
Cumulative effect on prior years of retroactive application of new depreciation method	0.12	
Net income	$1.02	$1.21

Pro forma (as if) *amounts*, assuming retroactive application
of new depreciation method:

	1981	1980
Income before extraordinary item	$120,000	$114,000[a]
Earnings per common share	$1.20	$1.14
Net income	$ 90,000	$124,000[b]
Earnings per common share	$0.90	$1.24

[a]The pro forma income before extraordinary item is computed as follows:

Income before extraordinary item (1980) not restated	$111,000
Excess of accelerated depreciation over straight-line depreciation (1980), net of tax	3,000
Pro forma income before extraordinary item (restated)	$114,000

[b]Net income is computed after adding or subtracting extraordinary items as follows:

	1981	1980
Income before extraordinary item	$120,000	$114,000
Extraordinary item	(30,000)	10,000
Net income	$ 90,000	$124,000

Note A. *Change in Depreciation Method for Plant Assets.* In 1981 depreciation of plant assets is computed by use of the straight-line method. In prior years, beginning in 1979, depreciation of plant equipment was computed by the sum-of-the-years'-digits. The new method of depreciation was adopted in recognition of . . . (state justification for the change of depreciation method) . . . and has been applied retroactively to equipment acquisitions of prior years. The effect of the change in 1981 was to decrease income before extraordinary item by approximately $3,000 (or three cents per share). The adjustment necessary for retroactive application of the new method, amounting to $12,000, is included in income of 1981. The pro forma amounts shown on the income statement have been adjusted for the effect of retroactive application on depreciation, and the pro forma effect for related income taxes.

It should be understood that the pro forma (as if) amounts are presented only as supplementary information. **Pro forma amounts permit financial statement users to determine the net income that would have been shown if the newly adopted principle had been in effect in the earlier periods.** This type of data provides useful information to an individual who is interested in assessing the trend in earnings over a period of time.

Retroactive-Effect Type Accounting Change

In special circumstances, a change in accounting principle may be handled retroactively. In such situations, the nature of and justification for the change and the effect on net income and related per-share amounts should be disclosed for each period presented. The five situations that require the restatement of all prior-period financial statements are:

1. A change from the LIFO inventory valuation method to another method.
2. A change in the method of accounting for long-term construction-type contracts.
3. A change to or from the "full-cost" method of accounting in the extractive industries.

4. Issuance of financial statements by a company for the first time to obtain additional equity capital, to effect a business combination, or to register securities. (This procedure may be used once and only once by closely held companies.)

5. A professional pronouncement recommends that a change in accounting principle be treated retroactively. For example, **FASB No. 11** requires that retroactive treatment be given for changes in "Accounting for Contingencies."[3]

Why did the APB provide for these exceptions? Although the reasons are varied, the major one is that reflecting the cumulative adjustment in the period of the change might have such a large effect on net income that the income figure would be misleading. A perfect illustration is the experience that Chrysler Corporation had when it changed its inventory accounting from LIFO to FIFO in 1970. If the change had been handled currently, Chrysler would have had to report a $53,500,000 adjustment to net income for 1970, which would have resulted in net income of $45,900,000 instead of a net loss of $7,600,000. Such situations lend support to restatement so that comparability is not seriously affected.

To illustrate, assume that Madsen Construction Co. has accounted for its income from long-term construction contracts using the completed-contract method. In 1981, the company changed to the percentage-of-completion method because the management believes that this approach provides a more appropriate measure of the income earned. For tax purposes (assume a 40% rate), the company has employed the completed-contract method and plans to continue using this method in the future.

The following information is available for analysis:

	Pre-tax Income from		Difference in Income		
Year	Percentage-of-Completion	Completed-Contract	Difference	Tax Effect 40%	Income Effect (net of tax)
Prior to 1980	$600,000	$400,000	$200,000	$80,000	$120,000
In 1980	180,000	160,000	20,000	8,000	12,000
Total at beginning of 1981	$780,000	$560,000	$220,000	$88,000	$132,000
In 1981	$200,000	$190,000	$ 10,000	$ 4,000	$ 6,000

The entry to record the change in 1981 would be:

Construction in Process	220,000	
Deferred Income Taxes		88,000
Retained Earnings		132,000

The Construction in Process account is increased by $220,000, representing the adjustment in prior years' income of $132,000 and the adjustment in prior years' tax expense of $88,000. The Deferred Income Taxes account is used to recognize interperiod tax allocation. If, in previous years, the percentage-of-completion method had been employed for accounting purposes while the completed-contract method was used for tax purposes, a difference of $220,000 between book income

---

[3]"Accounting for Contingencies—Transition Method," *Statement of the Financial Accounting Standards Board No. 11* (Stamford, Conn.: FASB, 1975).

and taxable income would have developed, on which $88,000 of tax would have been deferred.

The bottom portion of the income statement for Madsen Construction Co., giving effect to the retroactive change in accounting principle, would be as follows:

Retroactive-Effect Type Accounting Change Reporting the Change in Two-Year Comparative Statements		
Income Statement	1981	1980
Net income	$120,000[a]	$108,000[a]
Per Share Amounts		
Earnings per share (100,000 shares)	$1.20	$1.08

[a]The net income for the two periods is computed as follows:
1981 $200,000 − .40 ($200,000) = $120,000
1980 $180,000 − .40 ($180,000) = $108,000

The adjustment for the cumulative effect of the accounting change would be reported in the statement of retained earnings in comparative form as follows:

Statement of Retained Earnings	1981	1980
Balance at beginning of year, as previously reported	$1,696,000	$1,600,000
Add adjustment for the cumulative effect on prior years of applying retroactively the new method of accounting for long-term contracts (Note A)	132,000	120,000
Balance at beginning of year, as adjusted	1,828,000	1,720,000
Net income	120,000	108,000
	$1,948,000	$1,828,000

Note A. *Change in Method of Accounting for Long-Term Contracts.* The company has accounted for revenue and costs for long-term construction contracts by the percentage-of-completion method in 1981, whereas in all prior years revenue and costs were determined by the completed contract method. The new method of accounting for long-term contracts was adopted to recognize . . . (state justification for change in accounting principle) . . . and financial statements of prior years have been restated to apply the new method retroactively. For income tax purposes, the completed contract method has been continued. The effect of the accounting change on income of 1981 was an increase of $6,000 net of related taxes and on income of 1980 as previously reported was an increase of $12,000 net of related taxes. The balances of retained earnings for 1980 and 1981 have been adjusted for the effect of applying retroactively the new method of accounting.

Note that the foregoing two-year comparative statement has major differences from the earlier two-year comparative statement (pages 1009–1010). First, no pro forma information is necessary when changes in accounting principles are handled retroactively, because the income numbers for previous periods are restated. In other words, the pro forma method described in the previous section provides the same type of information as the retroactive method of this section. Second, a retained earnings statement was included in this two-year comparative statement to indicate the type of adjustment that is needed to restate the beginning balance of retained earnings. In 1980, the beginning balance was adjusted for the excess of the percentage-of-completion income over the completed-contract income prior to 1980 ($120,000). In 1981, the beginning balance was adjusted for the $120,000 plus the additional $12,000 for 1980.

No such adjustments are necessary when the current or catch-up method is employed, because the cumulative effect of the change on net income is reported in the income statement of the current year and no prior-period reports are restated. It is ordinarily appropriate to prepare a retained earnings statement when presenting comparative statements regardless of what type of accounting change is involved; an illustration was provided for the retroactive method only to explain the additional computations required.

Change to the LIFO Method of Inventory

APB Opinion No. 20 generally requires that the cumulative effect of any accounting change should be shown in the income statement between "extraordinary items" and "net income," except for the conditions mentioned in the preceding section. In addition, this rule does not apply when a company changes to the LIFO method of inventory valuation. In such a situation, the base-year inventory for all subsequent LIFO calculations is the opening inventory in the year the method is adopted. There is no restatement of prior years' income because it is just too impractical. A restatement to LIFO would be subject to assumptions as to the different years that the layers were established, and these assumptions would ordinarily result in the computation of a number of different earnings figures. The only adjustment necessary may be to restate the beginning inventory to a cost basis from a lower of cost or market approach. This type of adjustment was discussed in Appendix G of Chapter 9.

Disclosure then is limited to showing the effect of the change on the results of operations in the period of change. Also the reasons for omitting the computations of the cumulative effect and the pro forma amounts for prior years should be explained. Finally, the company should disclose the justification for the change to LIFO. A recent annual report of Ford Motor Company indicates the type of disclosure necessary.

Notes to Financial Statements

Note 1 (in part):

Inventory Valuation—inventories are stated at the lower of cost or market. In 1976, the Company changed its method of accounting from First-In, First-Out (FIFO) to Last-In, First-Out (LIFO) for most of its U.S. inventories. The cost of the remaining inventories is determined substantially on a FIFO basis. Under LIFO, the cost of goods sold is based on the most recent prices for raw material and other inventory items. The change reflects earnings more realistically by matching current costs with current revenues.

The change to LIFO reduced net income in 1976 by $81 million or $.86 a share. There is no effect on prior years' earnings resulting from the change to LIFO in 1976 and, accordingly, prior years' earnings have not been restated. If the FIFO method of inventory accounting had been used by the Company, inventories at December 31, 1976 would have been $166 million higher than reported.

In practice, many companies defer the formal adoption of LIFO until year end. Management thus has an opportunity to assess the impact that a change to LIFO will have on the financial statements and to evaluate the desirability of a change for tax purposes. As indicated in Chapter 8, many companies have changed to LIFO in recent years because of the advantages of this inventory valuation method in a period of inflation.

Change in Accounting Estimate

The preparation of financial statements requires estimating the effects of future conditions and events. Future conditions and events and their effects cannot be perceived with certainty; therefore, estimating requires the exercise of judgment. Accounting estimates will change as new events occur, as more experience is acquired, or as additional information is obtained. The following are examples of items that require estimates:

1. Uncollectible receivables.
2. Inventory obsolescence.
3. Useful lives and salvage values of assets.
4. Periods benefited by deferred costs.
5. Liabilities for warranty costs and income taxes.
6. Recoverable mineral reserves.

APB Opinion No. 20 requires that changes in estimates be handled prospectively; that is, no changes should be made in previously reported results. Opening balances are not adjusted, and no attempt is made to "catch-up" for prior periods. Financial statements of prior periods are not restated and pro forma amounts for prior periods are not reported. Instead, the effects of all changes in estimate are accounted for in (1) the period of change if the change affects that period only or (2) the period of change and future periods if the change affects both. This recommendation is consistent with **APB Opinions No. 9** and **No. 30,** and **FASB Statement No. 16,** which view changes in estimates as normal recurring corrections and adjustments, the natural result of the accounting process, and prohibits retroactive treatment.

The circumstances related to a change in estimate appear to be very different from those surrounding a change in accounting principle. If changes in estimates were handled on a retroactive basis, or catch-up basis, continual adjustments of prior years' income would occur. It seems proper to accept the view that because new conditions or circumstances exist, the revision fits the new situation and should be handled in the current and future periods.

To illustrate, machinery purchased for $20,000 was originally estimated to have a life of 10 years. Depreciation has been recorded for six years on a straight-line basis. On January 1, 1981, the estimate of the useful life of the asset is revised, so that the asset is considered to have a total life of 16 years. The accounts at the end of the sixth year are as follows:

Machinery	$20,000
Less: Accumulated Depreciation—Machinery	(12,000)
Book value of machinery	$ 8,000

The entry to record depreciation for the year 1981 is:

| Depreciation Expense | 800 | |
| Accumulated Depreciation—Machinery | | 800 |

The $800 depreciation charge is computed as follows:

$$\text{Depreciation charge} = \frac{\text{book value of asset}}{\text{remaining service life}} = \frac{\$20,000 - \$12,000}{16 \text{ years} - 6 \text{ years}}$$

Differentiating between a change in an estimate and a change in an accounting principle is sometimes difficult. When, for example, a company changes from deferring and amortizing certain marketing costs to recording them as an expense as incurred because future benefits of the cost have become doubtful, is it a change in principle or a change in estimate? In such a case, **whenever it is impossible to determine whether a change in principle or a change in estimate has occurred, the change should be considered a change in estimate.**

A similar problem occurs in differentiating between a change in estimate and a correction of an error, although the answer is more clear cut. How do we determine whether the information was overlooked in earlier periods (an error) or whether the information is now available for the first time (change in estimate)? Proper classification is important because corrections of errors have a different accounting treatment from that given changes in estimates. The general rule is that **careful estimates that later prove to be incorrect should be considered changes in estimate.** Only when the estimate was obviously computed incorrectly because of lack of expertise or in bad faith should the adjustment be considered an error. There is no clear demarcation line here and the accountant must use good judgment in light of all the circumstances.

Reporting a Change in Entity

An accounting change that results in financial statements that are actually the statements of a different entity should be reported by **restating** the financial statements of all prior periods presented to show the financial information for the new reporting entity for all periods.

Examples of a change in reporting entity are:

1. Presenting consolidated statements in place of statements of individual companies.
2. Changing specific subsidiaries comprising the group of companies for which consolidated financial statements are presented.
3. Changing the companies included in combined financial statements.
4. Accounting for a pooling of interests.

5. A change in the cost, equity, or consolidation method of accounting for subsidiaries and investments. A change in the reporting entity does not result from creation, cessation, purchase, or disposition of a subsidiary or other business unit.

The financial statements of the year in which the change in reporting entity is made should describe the nature of the change and the reason for it. The effect of the change on income before extraordinary items, net income, and earnings-per-share amounts should be disclosed for all periods presented. These disclosures need not be repeated in subsequent period financial statements. These situations are not illustrated in this textbook, but are presented in advanced accounting.

Reporting a Correction of an Error

APB Opinion No. 20 also discussed how a correction of an error should be handled in the financial statements, because no authoritative guidelines existed previously in this area. The conclusions of **APB Opinion No. 20** were reaffirmed in **FASB Statement No. 16,** issued in 1977.[4] No business, large or small, is immune from errors. The risk of material errors, however, may be reduced through the installation of good internal control and the application of sound accounting procedures.

The following are examples of accounting errors:

1. A change from an accounting principle that is **not** generally accepted to an accounting principle that is acceptable. The rationale adopted is that the prior periods were incorrectly presented because of the application of an improper accounting principle; for example, a change from the cash basis of accounting to the accrual basis.
2. Mathematical mistakes that result from adding, subtracting, and so on. An illustration is the totaling of the inventory count sheets incorrectly in computing the inventory value.
3. Changes in estimate that occur because the estimates are not prepared in good faith, for example, the adoption of a clearly unrealistic depreciation rate.
4. An oversight such as the failure to accrue or defer certain assets and liabilities at the end of the period.
5. A misuse of facts such as the failure to use salvage value in computing the depreciation base for the straight-line approach.
6. The incorrect classification of a cost as an expense instead of an asset and vice versa.

As soon as they are discovered, errors must be corrected by proper entries in the accounts and reflected in the financial statements. **FASB Statement No. 16 requires that corrections of errors be treated as prior-period adjustments,** be recorded in the year in which the error was discovered, and be reported in the financial statements as an adjustment to the beginning balance of retained earnings. If comparative statements are presented, the prior statements affected should be restated to correct for the error. The disclosures need not be repeated in the financial statements of subsequent periods.

To illustrate, in 1982 the bookkeeper for Sure Sale Company discovered that in 1981 the company failed to record in the accounts $20,000 of depreciation expense on a newly constructed building. The depreciation is correctly included in the tax return. Because of numerous timing differences, reported net income for 1981 was $150,000 and taxable income was $110,000. The following entry was made for income taxes (assume a 40% effective tax rate in 1981):

[4]"Prior Period Adjustments," *Statements of Financial Accounting Standards No. 16* (Stamford, Conn.: FASB, 1977), p. 5.

Income Tax Expense	60,000	
Income Tax Payable		44,000
Deferred Income Taxes		16,000

As a result of the $20,000 omission error in 1981:

Depreciation expense (1981) **was** understated	$20,000
Accumulated depreciation **is** understated	20,000
Income tax expense (1981) **was** overstated ($20,000 × 40%)	8,000
Net income (1981) **was** overstated	12,000
Deferred income taxes **is** overstated ($20,000 × 40%)	8,000

The entry made in 1982 to correct the omission of $20,000 of depreciation in 1981 would be:

<u>1982 Correcting Entry</u>

Retained Earnings	12,000	
Deferred Income Taxes	8,000	
Accumulated Depreciation—Buildings		20,000

The journal entry to record the correction of the error is the same whether single-period or comparative financial statements are prepared; however, presentation on the financial statements will differ. If single-period (noncomparative) statements are presented, the error should be reported as an adjustment to the opening balance of retained earnings of the period in which the error is discovered, as shown below:

Retained earnings, January 1, 1982:		
As previously reported		$350,000
Correction of an error (depreciation)	$20,000	
Less applicable income tax reduction	8,000	(12,000)
Adjusted balance of retained earnings, January 1, 1982		338,000
Add net income 1982		400,000
Retained earnings, December 31, 1982		$738,000

If comparative financial statements are prepared, adjustments should be made to correct the amounts for all affected accounts reported in the statements for all periods reported. The data for each year being presented should be restated to the correct basis, and any catch-up adjustment should be shown as a prior-period adjustment to retained earnings for the earliest period being reported. For example, in the case of Sure Sale Company, the error of omitting the depreciation of $20,000 in 1981, which was discovered in 1982, results in the restatement of the 1981 financial statements when presented in comparison with those of 1982. The following accounts in the 1981 financial statements (presented in comparison with those of 1982) would have been restated:

In the balance sheet:

Accumulated depreciation—buildings	$20,000 increase
Deferred income taxes	$8,000 decrease
Retained earnings, ending balance	$20,000 decrease

In the income statement:

Depreciation expense—buildings	$20,000 increase
Tax expense	$8,000 decrease
Net income	$12,000 decrease

In the statement of retained earnings:

Retained earnings, ending balance (due to lower net income for the period)	$12,000 decrease

The 1982 financial statements in comparative form with those of 1981 are prepared as if the error had not occurred. As a minimum, such comparative statements in 1982 would include a footnote calling attention to restatement of the 1981 statements and disclosing the effect of the correction on income before extraordinary items, net income, and the related per share amounts.

Summary of Accounting Changes and Corrections of Errors

The issuance of **APB Opinion No. 20** provided long-awaited guidelines for the orderly resolution of several significant and long-standing accounting problems. Yet, because of diversity in situations and characteristics of the items encountered in practice, the application of professional judgment is of paramount importance. In applying these guides, the primary objective is to serve the user of the financial statements; achieving such service requires accuracy, full disclosure,[5] and an absence of misleading inferences. The principal distinction and treatments presented in the earlier discussion are summarized below.

1. **Changes in accounting principle** (General Rule).
   Employ the current or catch-up approach by:
   a. Reporting current results on the new basis.
   b. Reporting the cumulative effect of the adjustment in the current income statement between the captions "extraordinary items" and "net income."
   c. Presenting prior-period financial statements as previously reported.
   d. Presenting pro forma data on income and earnings per share data for all prior periods presented.
2. **Changes in accounting principle** (Exceptions).
   Employ the retroactive approach by:
   a. Restating the financial statements of all prior periods presented.
   b. Disclosing in the year of the change the effect on net income and earnings per share for all prior periods presented.
   Employ the change to LIFO approach by:
   a. Not restating prior years' income.

---

[5]"Reporting on Consistency and Accounting Changes," *Statement on Auditing Procedure No. 53* discusses the various disclosure requirements related to changes in accounting. A change in accounting principle, a change in the reporting entity (special type of change in accounting principle), and a correction of an error involving a change in accounting principle require recognition in the auditor's report relative to consistency. A change in accounting estimate does not affect the auditor's opinion relative to consistency; however, if the estimate change has a material effect on the financial statements, disclosure may be required in a note to the financial statements. Error correction not involving a change in accounting principle does not require disclosure relative to consistency (New York: AICPA, 1972).

   b. Using opening inventory in the year the method is adopted as the base-year inventory for all subsquent LIFO computations.

   c. Disclosing the effect of the change on the current year, and the reasons for omitting the computation of the cumulative effect and pro forma amounts for prior years.

3. **Changes in estimate.**
   Employ the current and prospective approach by:
   a. Reporting current and future financial statements on the new basis.
   b. Presenting prior-period financial statements as previously reported.
   c. Making no adjustments to current period opening balances for purposes of catch-up, and making no pro forma presentations.

4. **Changes in entity.**
   Employ the retroactive approach by:
   a. Restating the financial statements of all prior periods presented.
   b. Disclosing in the year of change the effect on net income and earnings per share data for all prior periods presented.

5. **Changes due to error.**
   Employ the retroactive approach by:
   a. Correcting all prior-period statements presented.
   b. Restating the beginning balance of retained earnings for the first period presented when the error effects extend to a period prior to that one.

Changes in accounting principle are considered appropriate only when the enterprise demonstrates that the alternative generally accepted accounting principle that is adopted is *preferable* to the existing one. In applying **APB Opinion No. 20,** preferability among accounting principles should be determined on the basis of whether the new principle constitutes an improvement in financial reporting, not on the basis of the income tax effect alone. But it is not always easy to determine what is an improvement in financial reporting. **How does one measure preferability or improvement?** One enterprise might argue that a change in accounting principle from FIFO to LIFO inventory valuation better matches current costs and current revenues. Conversely, another enterprise might change from LIFO to FIFO because it wishes to report a more realistic balance sheet amount for inventory. How does an accountant determine which is the better of these two arguments? It appears that the auditor must have some "standard" or "objective" as a basis for determining the method that is preferable. Because the objectives of financial statements are still in the process of development, the problem of determining preferability continues to be a difficult one.

Initially the SEC took the position that the public accountant in the role of auditor should indicate whether a change in accounting principle was preferable. The SEC has modified this approach, noting that greater reliance may be placed on the management's judgment in assessing preferability. Even though the criterion of preferability is difficult to apply, the general guidelines established have acted as a deterrent to capricious changes in accounting principles. **If an FASB standard creates a new principle or expresses preference for or rejects a specific accounting principle, a change is considered clearly acceptable.** Similarly, other authoritative documents, such as AcSEC's statements of position and AICPA industry audit guides, are considered preferable accounting when a change in accounting principles is contemplated.[6]

---

[6]"Specialized Accounting and Reporting Principles and Practices in AICPA Statements of Position and Guides on Accounting and Auditing Matters," *Statement of Financial Accounting Standards No. 32* (Stamford, Conn.: FASB, 1979).

ERROR ANALYSIS

As indicated earlier, material errors are unusual in large corporations because internal control procedures coupled with the diligence of the accounting staff are ordinarily sufficient to find any major errors in the system. Smaller businesses may face a different problem. These enterprises may not be able to afford an internal audit staff, nor implement the necessary control procedures to insure that accounting data are always recorded accurately. The following discussion, therefore, applies primarily to smaller firms whose internal control systems are inappropriate or inefficient for processing the accounting data.

In practice, firms do not correct for errors discovered that do not have a significant effect on the presentation of the financial statements. For example, the failure to record accrued wages of $5,000 when the total payroll for the year is $1,750,000 and net income is $940,000 is not considered significant, and no correction is made. Obviously, defining materiality is difficult, and accountants must rely on their experience and judgment to determine whether adjustment is necessary for a given error. **All errors discussed in this section are assumed to be material and to require adjustment.**

The accountant must answer three questions in error analysis:

1. What type of error is involved?
2. What entries are needed to correct for the error?
3. How are financial statements to be restated once the error is discovered?

Type of Error Involved

As indicated earlier, **FASB Statement No. 16** requires that errors be treated as prior period adjustments and be reported in the current year as adjustments to the beginning balance of Retained Earnings. If comparative statements are presented, the prior statements affected should be restated to correct for the error.

Three types of errors can occur; because each error has its own peculiarities, differentiation among the types is important.

Balance Sheet Errors

These errors affect only the presentation of the real accounts, that is, the improper classification of an asset, liability, or stockholders' equity account. Examples are the classification of a short-term receivable as part of the investment section; the classification of a note payable as an account payable; and the classification of plant assets as inventory. Reclassification of the item to its proper position is needed when the error is discovered. If comparative statements that include the error year are prepared, the balance sheet for the error year is restated correctly.

Income Statement Errors

These errors affect only the presentation of the nominal accounts presented in the income statement. Errors involve the improper classification of revenues or expenses, such as recording interest revenue as part of sales; purchases as bad debt expense; and depreciation expense as interest expense. An income statement error has no effect on the balance sheet and no effect on net income; a reclassification entry is needed when the error is discovered, if it is discovered in the year it is made. If the error occurred in prior periods, no entry is needed at the date of discovery because the accounts for the current year are correctly stated. If comparative statements that include the error year are prepared, the income statement for the error year is restated correctly.

Balance Sheet and Income Statement Effect

The third type of error involves both the balance sheet and income statement. For example, assume that accrued wages payable were overlooked by the bookkeeper at the end of the accounting period. The effect of this error is to understate expenses, understate liabilities, and overstate net income for that period of time. This type of error affects both the balance sheet and the income statement and is classified in the following two ways—counterbalancing and noncounterbalancing.

Counterbalancing errors are errors that will be offset or corrected over two periods. In the previous illustration, the failure to record accrued wages is considered a counterbalancing error because over a two-year period the error will no longer be present. In other words the failure to record accrued wages in the previous period means: (1) net income for the first period is overstated; (2) accrued wages payable (a liability) is understated, and (3) wages expense is understated. In the next period, net income is understated; accrued wages payable (a liability) is correctly stated; and wages expense is overstated. For the **two years combined:** (1) net income is correct; (2) wages expense is correct; and (3) accrued wages payable at the end of the second year is correct. Most errors in accounting that affect both the balance sheet and income statement are counterbalancing errors.

Noncounterbalancing errors are errors that are not offset in the next accounting period; for example, the failure to capitalize equipment that has a useful life of five years. If we expense this asset immediately, expenses will be overstated in the first period but understated in the next four periods. At the end of the second period, the effect of the error is not fully offset. Net income is correct in the aggregate only at the end of five years, because the asset is fully depreciated at this point. Only in rare instances is an error never reversed; for example, when land is initially expensed. Because land is not depreciable, theoretically the error is never offset unless the land is sold.

Accountants define counterbalancing errors as errors that correct themselves over two periods, whereas noncounterbalancing errors are those that take longer than two periods to correct themselves. How these errors are handled in the accounting records is illustrated in the following sections.

Counterbalancing Errors

The usual types of counterbalancing errors are illustrated on the following pages. In studying these illustrations, a number of points should be remembered. First, determine whether or not the books have been closed for the period in which the error is found:

1. **The books have been closed.**
   a. If the error is already counterbalanced, no entry is necessary.
   b. If the error is not yet counterbalanced, an entry is necessary to adjust the present balance of retained earnings.
2. **The books have not been closed.**
   a. If the error is already counterbalanced and we are in the second year, an entry is necessary to correct the current period and to adjust the beginning balance of Retained Earnings.
   b. If the error is not yet counterbalanced, an entry is necessary to adjust the beginning balance of Retained Earnings.

Second, if comparative statements are presented, restatement of the amounts for comparative purposes is necessary. This situation occurs even if a correcting journal entry is not required. To illustrate, assume that Sanford's Cement Co. failed to accrue income in 1979 when earned, but recorded the income in 1980 when received. The error was discovered in 1982. No entry is necessary to correct for this error because the effects have been counterbalanced by the time the error is discovered in 1982. However, if comparative financial statements for 1979 through 1982 are presented, the accounts and related amounts for the years 1979 and 1980 should be restated correctly for financial reporting purposes.

Failure to Record Accrued Wages   On December 31, 1981, accrued wages in the amount of $1,500 were not recognized. The entry in 1982 to correct this error, assuming that the books have not been closed for 1982, is:

Retained Earnings	1,500	
Wages Expense		1,500

If the books have been closed for 1982, no entry is made because the error is counterbalanced.

Failure to Record Prepaid Expenses   In January, 1981, Hurley Enterprises purchased a two-year insurance policy costing $1,000; Insurance Expense was debited, and Cash was credited. No adjusting entries were made at the end of 1981.

The entry on December 31, 1982, to correct this error, assuming that the books have not been closed for 1982, is:

Insurance Expense	500	
Retained Earnings		500

If the books have been closed for 1982, no entry is made because the error is counterbalanced.

Overstatement of Prepaid Income   On December 31, 1981, Hurley Enterprises received $50,000 as a prepayment for renting certain office space for the following year. The entry made at the time of receipt of the rent payment was a debit to Cash and a credit to Rent Income. No adjusting entry was made as of December 31, 1981. The entry on December 31, 1982, to correct for this error, assuming that the books have not been closed for 1982, is:

| Retained Earnings | 50,000 | |
| Rent Income | | 50,000 |

If the books have been closed for 1982, no entry is made because the error is counterbalanced.

Overstatement of Accrued Income   On December 31, 1981, Hurley Enterprises accrued as interest income $8,000 that applied to 1982. The entry made on December 31, 1981, was to debit Accrued Interest Receivable and credit Interest Income. The entry on December 31, 1982, to correct for this error, assuming that the books have not been closed for 1982, is:

| Retained Earnings | 8,000 | |
| Interest Income | | 8,000 |

If the books have been closed for 1982, no entry is made because the error is counterbalanced.

Understatement of Ending Inventory   On December 31, 1981, the physical count of the inventory was understated by $25,000 because the inventory crew failed to count one warehouse of merchandise. The entry on December 31, 1982, to correct for this error, assuming that the books have not been closed for 1982, is:

| Inventory (beginning) | 25,000 | |
| Retained Earnings | | 25,000 |

If the books have been closed for 1982, no entry is made because the error is counterbalanced by the taking of the new inventory.

Overstatement of Purchases   Hurley Enterprise's accountant recorded a purchase of merchandise for $9,000 in 1981 that applied to 1982. The physical inventory for 1981 was correctly stated. The entry on December 31, 1982, to correct for this error, assuming that the books have not been closed for 1982, is:

| Purchases | 9,000 | |
| Retained Earnings | | 9,000 |

If the books have been closed for 1982, no entry is made because the error is counterbalanced.

Overstatement of Purchases and Inventories   Sometimes both the physical inventory and the purchases are incorrectly stated. Assume, as in the previous illustration, that purchases for 1981 are overstated by $9,000 and that inventory is overstated by the same amount. The entry on December 31, 1982, to correct for this error, assuming that the books have not been closed for 1982, is:

| Purchases | 9,000 | |
| Inventory | | 9,000[a] |

[a]The net income for 1981 is correctly computed because the overstatement of purchases was offset by the overstatement of ending inventory in the cost of goods sold computation.

If the books have been closed for 1982, no entry is made because the error is counterbalanced.

Noncounterbalancing Errors

Because such errors do not counterbalance over a two-year period, the entries are more complex and correcting entries are needed, even if the books have been closed.

Failure to Record Depreciation   Assume that Hurley Enterprises purchased a machine for $10,000 on January 1, 1981, that had an estimated useful life of five years. The accountant incorrectly expensed this machine in 1981. The error was discovered in 1982. If we assume that the company desires to use straight-line depreciation on this asset, the entry on December 31, 1982, to correct for this error, given that the books have not been closed, is:

Machinery	10,000	
Depreciation Expense	2,000	
Retained Earnings		8,000[a]
Accumulated Depreciation		4,000[a]

[a]Computations:

Retained Earnings

Overstatement of expense in 1981	$10,000
Proper depreciation for 1981 (20% × $10,000)	(2,000)
Retained earnings understated as of Dec. 31, 1981	$ 8,000

Accumulated Depreciation

Accumulated depreciation (20% × $10,000 × 2)	$ 4,000

If the books have been closed for 1982, the entry is:

Machinery	10,000	
Retained Earnings		6,000[a]
Accumulated Depreciation		4,000

[a]Computations:

Retained Earnings

Retained earnings understated as of Dec. 31, 1981	$ 8,000
Proper depreciation for 1982 (20% × $10,000)	(2,000)
Retained earnings understated as of Dec. 31, 1982	$ 6,000

Failure to Adjust for Bad Debts   Companies sometimes use a specific charge-off method in accounting for bad debt expense when a percentage of sales is more appropriate. Adjustments are often made to change from the specific write-off to some type of allowance method. Assume that Hurley Enterprises has recognized bad debt expense because the debts have actually become uncollectible as follows:

	1981	1982
From 1981 sales	$550	$690
From 1982 sales		700

Hurley estimates that an additional $1,400 will be charged off in 1983; $300 applicable to 1981 Sales and $1,100 to 1982 Sales. The entry on December 31, 1982, assuming that the books have not been closed for 1982, is:

Bad Debt Expense	410[a]	
Retained Earnings	990[a]	
Allowance for Doubtful Accounts		1,400

[a]Computations:

Allowance for doubtful accounts—additional $300 for 1981 sales and $1,100 for 1982 sales.
Bad debts and retained earnings balance:

	1981	1982
Bad debts charged for	$1,240	$ 700
Additional bad debts anticipated	300	1,100
Proper bad debt expense	1,540	1,800
Charges currently made to each period	(550)	(1,390)
Bad debt adjustment	$ 990	$ 410

If the books have been closed for 1982, the entry is:

Retained Earnings	1,400	
Allowance for Doubtful Accounts		1,400

Comprehensive Illustration: Numerous Errors

In some circumstances not one but a combination of errors occurs. A work sheet is therefore prepared to facilitate the analysis. To demonstrate the use of a work sheet, the following problem is presented for solution. The mechanics of the work sheet preparation should be obvious from the solution format.

The income statements of the Hudson Company for the years ended December 31, 1980, 1981, and 1982 indicate the following net incomes.

1980	$17,400
1981	20,200
1982	11,300

An examination of the accounting records of the Hudson Company for these years indicates that several errors were made in arriving at the net income amounts reported. The following errors were discovered:

a. Wages earned by workers but not paid at December 31 were consistently omitted from the records. The amounts omitted were

December 31, 1980	$1,000
December 31, 1981	1,400
December 31, 1982	1,600

These amounts were recorded as expenses when paid in the year following that in which they were earned.

b. The merchandise inventory on December 31, 1980, was overstated by $1,900 as the result of errors made in the footings and extensions on the inventory sheets.

c. Unexpired insurance of $1,200, applicable to 1982, was expensed on December 31, 1981.

d. Interest receivable in the amount of $240 was not recorded on December 31, 1981.

e. On January 2, 1981, a piece of equipment costing $3,900 was sold for $1,800. At the date of sale the equipment had accumulated depreciation pertaining to it of $2,400. The cash received was recorded as Miscellaneous Income in 1981. In addition, depreciation was recorded for this equipment in both 1981 and 1982 at the rate of 10% of cost.

Instructions Prepare a schedule showing the corrected net income amounts for the years ended December 31, 1980, 1981, and 1982. Each correction of the amount originally reported should be clearly labeled. In addition, indicate the balance sheet accounts affected as of December 31, 1982 (see page 1027).

Correcting entries **if the books have not been closed** on December 31, 1982 are:

Retained Earnings	1,400	
Wages Expense		1,400
(To correct improper charge to wages expense for 1982)		
Wages Expense	1,600	
Wages Payable		1,600
(To record proper wages expense for 1982)		
Insurance Expense	1,200	
Retained Earnings		1,200
(To record proper insurance expense for 1982)		
Interest Income	240	
Retained Earnings		240
(To correct improper credit to interest income in 1982)		
Retained Earnings	1,500	
Accumulated Depreciation	2,400	
Machinery		3,900
(To record write-off of machinery in 1981 and adjustment of retained earnings)		
Accumulated Depreciation	780	
Depreciation Expense		390
Retained Earnings		390
(To correct improper charge for depreciation expense in 1981 and 1982)		

If the books have been closed:

Retained Earnings	1,600	
Wages Payable		1,600
(To record proper wage expense for 1982)		
Retained Earnings	1,500	
Accumulated Depreciation	2,400	
Machinery		3,900
(To record write-off of machinery in 1981 and adjustment of retained earnings)		
Accumulated Depreciation	780	
Retained Earnings		780
(To correct improper charge for depreciation expense in 1981 and 1982)		

Preparation of Comparative Statements

Discussion of error analysis up to now has been concerned with the identification of the type of error involved and the accounting for its correction in the accounting records. The correction of the error should be presented on comparative financial statements. In addition, five- or ten-year summaries are given for the interested

Solution:	Worksheet Analysis of Changes in Net Income				Balance Sheet Correction at December 31, 1982		
	1980	1981	1982	Totals	Debit	Credit	Account
Net income as reported	17,400	20,200	11,300	48,900			
Wages unpaid, 12/31/80	(1,000)	1,000		-0-			
Wages unpaid, 12/31/81		(1,400)	1,400	-0-			
Wages unpaid, 12/31/82			(1,600)	(1,600)		1,600	Wages Payable
Inventory overstatement, 12/31/80	(1,900)	1,900		-0-			
Unexpired insurance, 12/31/81		1,200	(1,200)	-0-			
Interest receivable, 12/31/81		240	(240)	-0-			
Correction for entry made upon sale of equipment, 1/2/81[a]		(1,500)		(1,500)	2,400	3,900	Accumulated Depreciation Machinery
Overcharge of depreciation, 1981		390		390	390		Accumulated Depreciation
Overcharge of depreciation, 1982			390	390	390		Accumulated Depreciation
Corrected net income	14,500	22,030	10,050	46,580			

[a] Cost	$ 3,900
Accumulated depreciation	2,400
Book value	1,500
Proceeds from sale	1,800
Gain on sale	300
Income reported	(1,800)
Adjustment	$(1,500)

financial reader. The work sheet on page 1028 (Table 23–1) illustrates how a typical year's financial statements are restated given many different errors. The resulting balance sheet, income statement, and the correcting entries are not presented because they should be self-explanatory.

To illustrate, Reynolds and Sons operate a small retail outlet in the town of Prescott. Lacking expertise in accounting, they did not keep adequate records; as a result, many errors occurred in recording the accounting information. Presented on page 1028 is a work sheet that begins with the unadjusted trial balance of Reynolds and Sons; the correcting entries and their effect on the financial statements can be determined by examining the work sheet. Supplementary information, related to the correction of errors appears below and at the top of page 1029.

1. The bookkeeper inadvertently failed to record a cash receipt of $1,000 on the sale of merchandise in 1982.
2. Accrued wages expense at the end of 1981 was $2,500; at the end of 1982, $3,200. The company did not accrue for wages; all wages are charged to administrative expense.
3. The beginning inventory was understated by $5,400 because goods in transit at the end of last year were not counted. The proper purchase entry had been made.

TABLE 23-1 WORK SHEET ANALYSIS TO ADJUST FINANCIAL STATEMENTS FOR REYNOLDS AND SONS FOR THE YEAR 1982

	Trial Balance Unadjusted		Adjustments		Income Statement Adjusted		Balance Sheet Adjusted	
	Debit	Credit	Debit	Credit	Debit	Credit	Debit	Credit
Cash	3,100		(1) 1,000				4,100	
Accounts Receivable	17,600						17,600	
Notes Receivable	8,500						8,500	
Inventories, Jan. 1, 1982	34,000		(3) 5,400		39,400			
Property, Plant & Equip.	112,000			(7) 10,000ª			102,000	
Accumulated Depreciation		83,500	(7) 6,000ª (8) 2,000					75,500
Investments	24,300						24,300	
Accounts Payable		14,500	(6) 6,000					8,500
Notes Payable		10,000		(6) 6,000				16,000
Capital Stock		43,500						43,500
Retained Earnings		20,000	(4) 2,700ᵇ (7) 4,000ª (2) 2,500	(3) 5,400 (5) 600 (8) 800				17,600
Sales		94,000		(1) 1,000		95,000		
Purchases	21,000				21,000			
Selling Expenses	22,000			(4) 500ᵇ	21,500			
Administrative Expenses	23,000		(2) 700 (5) 600	(5) 400 (8) 1,200	22,700			
Totals	265,500	265,500						
Wages Payable				(2) 3,200				3,200
Allowance for Doubtful Accounts				(4) 2,200ᵇ				2,200
Unexpired Insurance			(5) 400				400	
Inventory, Dec. 31, 1982						40,000	40,000	
Net Income					30,400			30,400
Totals			31,300	31,300	135,000	135,000	196,900	196,900

Computations:

ªMachinery			ᵇBad Debts	1981	1982
Proceeds from sale	$7,000		Bad debts charged for	$2,400	$1,600
Book value of machinery	4,000		Additional bad debts anticipated	700	1,500
Gain on sale	3,000			3,100	3,100
Income credited	7,000		Charges currently made to each year	(400)	(3,600)
Retained earnings adjustment	$4,000		Bad debt adjustment	$2,700	$ (500)

4. No allowance had been set up for estimated uncollectible receivables. It is decided to set up such an allowance for the estimated probable losses as of December 31, 1982 for 1981 accounts of $700, and for 1982 accounts of $1,500. It is also decided to correct the charge against each year so that it shows the losses (actual and estimated) relating to that year's sales. Accounts have been written off to bad debt expense (selling expense) as follows:

	In 1981	In 1982
1982 Accounts		$1,600
1981 Accounts	$400	2,000

5. Unexpired insurance not recorded at the end of 1981, $600; at the end of 1982, $400. All insurance expense is charged to Administrative Expense.

6. An account payable of $6,000 should have been a note payable.

7. During 1981, an asset that cost $10,000 and had a book value of $4,000 was sold for $7,000. At the time of sale Cash was debited and Miscellaneous Income was credited for $7,000.

8. As a result of the last transaction, the company overstated depreciation expense (an administrative expense) in 1981 by $800 and in 1982 by $1,200.

9. In a physical count, the company determined the final inventory to be $40,000.

Questions

1. What are the advantages of employing the current or catch-up method for handling changes in accounting principle?

2. In recent years, **The Wall Street Journal** has indicated that many companies have changed their accounting principles. What are the major reasons why companies change accounting methods?

3. Define a change in estimate and provide an illustration. When is a change in accounting estimate effected by a change in accounting principle?

4. Discuss and illustrate how a correction of an error in previously issued financial statements should be handled.

5. Indicate how the following items are recorded in the accounting records in the current year.
   (a) Change from the cash basis to accrual basis of accounting.
   (b) Change from LIFO to FIFO method for inventory valuation purposes.
   (c) Change in the estimate of service lives for plant assets.
   (d) Large write-off of goodwill.
   (e) A change in depreciating plant assets from accelerated to the straight-line method.
   (f) Large write-off of inventories because of obsolescence.

6. State how each of the following items is reflected in the financial statements:
   (a) Charge for failure to record depreciation in a previous period.
   (b) Change from straight-line method of depreciation to sum-of-the-years'-digits.
   (c) Change from FIFO to LIFO method for inventory valuation purposes.
   (d) Litigation won in current year, related to prior period.
   (e) Change in the realizability of certain receivables.
   (f) Write-off of receivables.
   (g) Change from the percentage-of-completion to the completed-contract method for reporting net income.

7. Bold, Inc. has followed the practice of capitalizing certain marketing costs and amortizing these costs over their expected life. In the current year, the company determined that the future benefits from these costs were doubtful. Consequently, the company adopted the policy of expensing these costs as incurred. How should this accounting change be reported in the comparative financial statements?

8. The Madsen Construction Co. had followed the practice of expensing all materials assigned to a construction job without recognizing any salvage inventory. On December

31, 1981, it was determined that salvage inventory should be valued at $41,500. Of this amount, $20,000 arose during the current year. How should this change in accounting principle be reflected in the financial statements?

9. Bolman, Inc. wishes to change from the sum-of-the-years'-digits to the straight-line depreciation method for financial reporting purposes. The auditor indicates that a change would be permitted only if it is to a preferable method. What difficulties develop in assessing preferability?

10. Porter Enterprises controlled four domestic subsidiaries and one foreign subsidiary. Prior to the current year, Porter Enterprises had excluded the foreign subsidiary from consolidation. During the current year, the foreign subsidiary was included in the financial statements. How should this change in accounting principle be reflected in the financial statements?

11. Senn, Inc., a closely held corporation, is in the process of preparing financial statements to accompany an offering of its common stock. The company at this time has decided to switch from the accelerated depreciation to the straight-line method of depreciation to better present its financial operations. How should this change in accounting principle be reported in the financial statements?

12. Prior to 1981, Ivery, Inc. excluded manufacturing overhead costs from work in process and finished goods inventory. These costs have been expensed as incurred. In 1981, the company decided to change its accounting methods for manufacturing inventories to full costing by including these costs as product costs. Assuming that these costs are material, how should this change be reflected in the financial statements for 1980 and 1981?

13. Largo Company failed to record accrued salaries for 1978, $1,800; 1979, $2,100; and 1980, $4,200. What is the amount of the overstatement or understatement of Retained Earnings at December 31, 1981?

14. In January, 1980, installation costs of $7,000 on new machinery were charged to Repair Expense. Other costs of this machinery of $30,000 were correctly recorded and have been depreciated using the straight-line method with an estimated life of 10 years and no salvage value. At December 31, 1981, it is decided that the machinery has a useful life of 20 years, starting with January 1, 1981. What entry(ies) should be made in 1981 to correctly record transactions related to machinery, assuming the machinery has no salvage value? The books have not been closed for 1981.

15. An account payable of $9,000 for merchandise purchased on December 23, 1980 was recorded in January 1981. This merchandise was not included in inventory at December 31, 1980. What effect does this error have on reported net income for 1980? What entry should be made to correct for this error, assuming that the books are not closed for 1980?

16. On January 2, 1980, $100,000 of 10%, 20-year bonds were issued for $98,000. The $2,000 discount was charged to Interest Expense. The bookkeeper records interest only on the interest payment dates of January 1 and July 1. What is the effect on reported net income for 1980 of this error, assuming straight-line amortization of the discount? What entry is necessary to correct for this error, assuming that the books are not closed for 1980?

17. Equipment was purchased on January 2, 1980 for $14,000, but no portion of the cost has been charged to depreciation. The corporation wishes to use the straight-line method for these assets, which have been estimated to have a life of 10 years and no salvage value. What effect does this error have on net income in 1980? What entry is necessary to correct for this error, assuming that the books are not closed for 1980?

Cases

C23-1 Interlaken, Inc. has recently hired a new independent auditor who says she wants "to get everything straightened out." Consequently, she has proposed the following accounting changes in connection with the client's 1980 financial statements:

1. In the past, the client has spread preproduction costs in its furniture division over 5 years. Because its latest furniture is of the "fad" type, it appears that the largest volume of sales will occur during the first two years after introduction. Consequently, the client proposes to amortize preproduction costs on a per-unit basis, which will result in expensing most of such costs during the first 2 years after the furniture's introduction. If the new accounting method had been used prior to 1980, retained earnings at December 31, 1979, would have been $200,000 less.

2. For the nursery division the client proposes to switch from FIFO to LIFO inventories as it is believed that LIFO will provide a better matching of current costs with revenues. The effect of making this change on 1980 earnings will be an increase of $180,000. The client says that the effect of the change on December 31, 1979, retained earnings cannot be determined.

3. To achieve a better matching of revenues and expenses in its building construction division, the client proposes to switch from the completed-contract method of accounting to the percentage-of-completion method. Had the percentage-of-completion method been employed in all prior years, retained earnings at December 31, 1979, would have been $825,000 greater.

4. At December 31, 1979, the client had a receivable of $525,000 from Harris, Inc. on its balance sheet. Harris, Inc. has gone bankrupt, and no recovery is expected. The client proposes to write off the receivable as a prior period item.

5. The client proposes the following changes in depreciation policies:
   (a) For office furniture and fixtures it proposes to change from a 10-year useful life to an 8-year life. If this change had been made in prior years, retained earnings at December 31, 1979 would have been $100,000 less. The effect of the change on 1980 income alone is a reduction of $10,000.
   (b) For its manufacturing assets the client proposes to change from double-declining balance depreciation to straight line. If straight-line depreciation had been used for all prior periods, retained earnings would have been $190,000 greater at December 31, 1979. The effect of the change on 1980 income alone is a reduction of $12,000.
   (c) For its equipment in the leasing division the client proposes to adopt the sum-of-the-years'-digits depreciation method. The client had never used SYD before. The first year the client operated a leasing division was 1980. If straight-line depreciation were used, 1980 income would be $40,000 greater.

6. In preparing its 1979 statements, one of the client's bookkeepers overstated ending inventory by $115,000 because of a mathematical error. The client proposes to treat this item as a prior period adjustment.

Instructions

(a) For each of the changes described above decide whether:
   1. The change involves an accounting principle, accounting estimate, or correction of an error.
   2. Restatement of opening retained earnings is required.

(b) Do any of the changes require presentation of pro forma amounts?

(c) What would be the proper adjustment to the December 31, 1979, retained earnings? What would be the "cumulative effect" shown separately in the 1980 income statement?

C23-2 Listed below are three independent, **unrelated** sets of facts relating to accounting changes.

Situation I

A company determined that the depreciable lives of its fixed assets are too long at present to fairly match the cost of the fixed assets with the revenue produced. The company decided at the beginning of the current year to reduce the depreciable lives of all of its existing fixed assets by five years.

Situation II

Ronald Logan Company is in the process of having its first audit. The company's policy with regard to recognition of revenue is to use the installment method. However, *APB No. 10* states that the installment method of revenue recognition is not a generally accepted accounting principle except in certain circumstances, which are not present here. Mr. Logan, the president, is willing to change to an acceptable method.

Situation III

A company decides in January 1980 to adopt the straight-line method of depreciation for plant equipment. The straight-line method will be used for new acquisitions as well as for previously acquired plant equipment for which depreciation had been provided on an accelerated basis.

Instructions

For each of the situations described above, provide the information indicated below.

1. Type of accounting change.
2. Manner of reporting the change under current generally accepted accounting principles including a discussion, where applicable, of how amounts are computed.
3. Effect of the change on the balance sheet and income statement.

C23-3   Neil Jones, controller of Monte Corp., is aware that an opinion on accounting changes has been issued. After reading the opinion, he is confused and is not sure what action should be taken on the following items related to the Monte Corp. for the year 1980:

1. All equipment sold by Monte is subject to a three-year warranty. It has been estimated that the expense ultimately to be incurred on these machines is 1% of sales. In 1980, because of a production breakthrough, it is now estimated that ½ of 1% of sales is sufficient. In 1978 and 1979, warranty expense was computed as $20,000 and $25,000, respectively. The company now believes that these warranty costs should be reduced by 50%.

2. In 1980, the company decided to change its method of inventory pricing from average cost to the FIFO method. The effect of this change on prior years is to increase 1978 income by $30,000 and decrease 1979 income by $10,000.

3. In 1980, Monte decided to change its policy on accounting for certain marketing costs. Previously, the company had chosen to defer and amortize all marketing costs over at least five years because Monte believed that a return on these expenditures did not occur immediately. Recently, however, the time differential has considerably shortened, and Monte is now expensing the marketing costs as incurred.

4. In 1980, the company examined its entire policy relating to the depreciation of plant equipment. Plant equipment had normally been depreciated over a 15-year period, but recent experience has indicated that the company was incorrect in its estimates and that the assets should be depreciated over a 20-year period.

5. One division of Monte Corp., Wigwag, Inc., has consistently shown an increasing net income from period to period. On closer examination of their operating statement, it is noted that bad debt expense and inventory obsolescence charges are much lower than in other divisions. In discussing this with the controller of this division, it has been learned that the controller has increased his net income each period by knowingly making low estimates related to the write-off of receivables and inventory.

6. In 1980, the company purchased new machinery that should increase production dramatically. The company has decided to depreciate this machinery on an accelerated basis, even though other machinery is depreciated on a straight-line basis.

Instructions

Neil Jones has come to you, as his CPA, for advice about the situations above. Indicate the appropriate accounting treatment that should be given each of these situations.

C23-4 Various types of accounting changes can affect the financial statements of a business enterprise differently. Assume that the following list describes changes that have a material effect on the financial statements for the current year of your business enterprise.

1. Correction of a mathematical error in inventory pricing made in a prior period.
2. A change from prime costing to full absorption costing for inventory valuation.
3. A change from presentation of statements of individual companies to presentation of consolidated statements.
4. A change in the method of accounting for leases for tax purposes to conform with the financial accounting method. As a result, both deferred and current taxes payable changed substantially.
5. A change from the FIFO method of inventory pricing to the LIFO method of inventory pricing.
6. A change from the completed-contract method to the percentage-of-completion method of accounting for long-term construction-type contracts.
7. A change in the estimated useful life of previously recorded fixed assets based on newly acquired information.
8. A change from deferring and amortizing preproduction costs to recording such costs as an expense when incurred because future benefits of the costs have become doubtful. The new accounting method was adopted in recognition of the change in estimated future benefits.
9. A change from including the employer share of FICA taxes to including it with "Retirement benefits" on the income statement.

Instructions

Identify the type of change that is described in each item above and indicate whether the prior year's financial statements should be restated when presented in comparative form with the current year's statements. Ignore possible pro forma effects.

Exercises

E23-1 The Kelly Venture Co. purchased equipment on January 1, 1978 for $275,000. At that time it was estimated that the machine would have a 10-year life and no salvage value. On December 31, 1981, the firm's accountant found that the entry for depreciation expense had been omitted in 1979. In addition, management has informed the accountant that they plan to switch to straight-line depreciation, starting with the year 1981. At present, the company uses the sum-of-the-years'-digits method for depreciating equipment.

Instructions

Prepare the general journal entries the accountant should make at December 31, 1981.

E23-2 Maynard, Inc. purchased equipment for $120,000 which was estimated to have a useful life of eight years with a salvage value of $8,000 at the end of that time. Depreciation has been entered for five years on a straight-line basis. In 1981 it is determined that the total estimated life should be 12 years with a salvage value of $4,500 at the end of that time.

Instructions

(a) Prepare the entry (if any) to correct the prior years' depreciation.
(b) Prepare the entry to record depreciation for 1981.

E23-3 The Laughlin Corporation owns equipment that originally cost $240,000 and had an estimated useful life of 10 years. The equipment had no expected salvage value.

The two requirements below are independent and must be considered as entirely separate from each other.

Instructions

(a) After using the double-declining balance method for two years, the company decided to switch to the straight-line method of depreciation. Prepare the general journal entry(ies) necessary in the third year to properly account for (1) the change in accounting principle and (2) depreciation expense.

(b) After using the straight-line method for 2 years, the company determined that the useful life of the equipment is 12 years (two more than the original estimate). Prepare the general journal entry(ies) necessary to properly account for the depreciation expense in the third year.

E23-4 Cello Enterprises changed from the double-declining balance to the straight-line method in 1981 on all its plant assets. For tax purposes, the company has employed the double-declining balance method and it will continue to do so. The appropriate information related to this change is as follows:

Year	Double-declining Balance Depreciation	Straight-line Depreciation	Difference
1979	$300,000	$150,000	$150,000
1980	250,000	150,000	100,000
1981	200,000	150,000	50,000

Net income for 1980 was reported at $380,000; net income for 1981 was reported at $395,000, excluding any adjustment for the cumulative effect of a change in depreciation methods. The straight-line method of depreciation was employed in computing net income for 1981.

Instructions

(a) Assuming a tax rate of 45%, what is the amount of the cumulative effect adjustment in 1981?

(b) Prepare the journal entry(ies) to record the cumulative effect adjustment in the accounting records.

(c) Starting with income before cumulative effect of change in accounting principle, prepare the remaining portion of the income statement for 1980 and 1981. Indicate the pro forma net income that should be reported. Ignore per share computations and footnote disclosures.

E23-5 Wallace Company changed from the completed-contract to the percentage-of-completion method of accounting for long-term construction contracts during 1981. For tax purposes, the company employs the completed-contract method and will continue this approach in the future. The appropriate information related to this change is as follows:

Pretax income from:

	Percentage-of-completion	Completed-Contract	Difference
1980	$1,500,000	$1,300,000	$200,000
1981	1,400,000	1,100,000	300,000

Instructions

(a) Assuming that the tax rate is 40%, what is the amount of net income that would be reported in 1981?

(b) What entry(ies) are necessary to adjust the accounting records for the change in accounting principle?

E23-6 In 1981, the Braniff Corporation decided to change its method of inventory pricing from FIFO to average cost. The periodic inventory system is used, and the books have not been closed for 1981. Net income computed on a FIFO as compared to average cost basis for the four years involved is:

	FIFO	Average Cost
1978—	$12,000	$10,000
1979—	15,000	12,000
1980—	14,000	14,000
1981—	20,000	17,000

Instructions

(a) Indicate the journal entry necessary in 1981 to correct the records and show all appropriate information needed for reporting on a comparative basis.
(b) What journal entry (if any) is necessary in 1981 to correct the records and show all appropriate information needed for reporting on a comparative basis, assuming that the company changed to the LIFO method? Net income under the LIFO method would be: 1978, $8,000; 1979, $11,000; 1980, $13,000; 1981, $16,000.
(c) Assume that the company had used the LIFO method in previous years with the income as noted in (b) above, and that it decided to change to FIFO. Prepare the general journal entry necessary in 1981 to correct the records and show all appropriate information needed for reporting on a comparative basis.

E23-7 IC Industries utilizes periodic inventory procedures and on Dec. 31, 1981 decides to change from FIFO to LIFO. The following information is available in the company records:

			Units	Unit Cost
1980:	Beginning Inventory		3,000	$20
	Purchases:	#1	5,000	24
		#2	4,000	28
		#3	6,000	32
		#4	5,000	36
		#5	5,000	40
	Ending Inventory		6,000	
1981:	Beginning Inventory		6,000	
	Purchases:	#1	2,000	44
		#2	5,000	48
		#3	5,000	52
		#4	7,000	56
		#5	3,000	60
	Ending Inventory		11,000	

Instructions

(a) State the value at which IC Industries reports the ending inventory for 1981.
(b) Indicate what additional disclosures are necessary for this change (both within the body of the financial statements and in footnotes). Assume a 40% tax rate.

E23-8 The first audit of the books of Northeast Company was made for the year ended December 31, 1981. In examining the books, the auditor found that certain items had been overlooked or incorrectly handled in the last three years. These items are:

1. The Northeast Company purchased another company early in 1979 and recorded goodwill of $140,000. Northeast had not amortized goodwill since its value had not diminished.

2. In 1981, the company changed its basis of inventory pricing from FIFO to LIFO. The cumulative effect of this change was to decrease net income by $41,000. The company debited this cumulative effect to Retained Earnings. LIFO was used in computing income in 1981.

3. In 1981, the company wrote off $170,000 of inventory considered to be obsolete; this loss was charged directly to Retained Earnings.

4. At the beginning of 1979, the company purchased a machine for $72,000 (salvage value of $6,000) that had a useful life of six years. The bookkeeper used straight-line depreciation, but failed to deduct the salvage value in computing the depreciation base for the three years.

5. At the end of 1980, the company failed to accrue sales salaries of $75,000.

6. A tax lawsuit that involved the year 1979 was settled late in 1981. It was determined that the company owed an additional $75,000 in taxes related to 1979. The company did not record a liability in 1979 or 1980 because the possibility of loss was considered remote, and charged the $75,000 to a loss account in 1981.

Instructions

Prepare the journal entries necessary in 1981 to correct the books, assuming that the books have not been closed. The proper amortization period for goodwill is 40 years. Disregard effects of corrections on income tax.

E23-9   Seaver, Inc. acquired the following assets in January of 1978:

Equipment, estimated service life, 5 years; salvage value, $45,000	$270,000
Building, estimated service life, 30 years; no salvage value	$630,000

The equipment has been depreciated using the sum-of-the-years'-digits method for the first 3 years, both for financial reporting purposes and for income tax purposes. In 1981, the company decided to change the method of computing depreciation to the straight-line method for the equipment, but no change was made in the estimated service life or salvage value. It was also decided to change the total estimated service life of the building from 30 years to 39 years, with no change in the estimated salvage value. The building is depreciated on the straight-line method.

The company has 100,000 shares of capital stock outstanding. Results of operations for 1981 and 1980 are shown below:

	1981	1980
Income before cumulative effect of change in computing depreciation for 1981: depreciation for 1981 has been computed on the straight-line basis for both the equipment and building*	$406,000	$400,000
Income per share before cumulative effect of change in computing depreciation for 1981	$4.06	$4.00

*It should be noted that the computation for depreciation expense for 1981 and 1980 for the building was based on the original estimate of service life of 30 years.

Instructions

(a) Compute the cumulative effect of the change in accounting principle to be reported in the income statement for 1981, and prepare the journal entry to record the change. (Ignore tax effects.)

(b) Present comparative data for the years 1980 and 1981, starting with income before cumulative effect of accounting change. Prepare pro forma data. Do not prepare the footnote. (Ignore tax effects.)

E23-10 Presented below are the comparative statements for Erskine, Inc.

	1981	1980
Sales	$300,000	$250,000
Cost of sales	180,000	142,000
Gross profit	120,000	108,000
Expenses	77,000	68,000
Net income	$ 43,000	$ 40,000
Retained earnings (Jan. 1)	$150,000	$130,000
Net income	43,000	40,000
Dividends	(25,000)	(20,000)
Retained earnings (Dec. 31)	$168,000	$150,000

The following additional information is provided:

1. In 1981, Erskine decided to switch its depreciation method from sum-of-the-years'-digits to the straight-line method. The differences in the two depreciation methods for the assets involved are:

	1980	1981
Sum-of-the-years'-digits	$60,000	$50,000[a]
Straight-line	30,000	30,000

[a]The 1981 income statement contains depreciation expense of $50,000.

2. In 1981, the company discovered that the ending inventory for 1980 was overstated by $20,000; ending inventory for 1981 is correctly stated.

Instructions

(a) Prepare the revised income and retained earnings statement for 1980 and 1981, assuming comparative statements (ignore income tax effects). Do not prepare footnotes or pro forma amounts.

(b) Prepare the revised income and retained earnings statement for 1981, assuming a noncomparative presentation (ignore income tax effects). Do not prepare footnotes or pro forma amounts.

E23-11 Murdock Company's December 31 year-end financial statements contained the following errors:

	December 31, 1980	December 31, 1981
Ending inventory	$3,000 understated	$2,700 overstated
Depreciation expense	$ 600 understated	—

An insurance premium of $22,500 was prepaid in 1980 covering the years 1980, 1981, and 1982. The entire amount was charged to expense in 1980. In addition, on December 31, 1981, fully depreciated machinery was sold for $4,800 cash, but the entry was not recorded until 1982. There were no other errors during 1980 or 1981, and no corrections have been made for any of the errors. Ignore income tax considerations.

Instructions

(a) Compute the total effect of the errors on 1981 net income.

(b) Compute the total effect of the errors on the amount of Murdock's working capital at December 31, 1981.

(c) Compute the total effect of the errors on the balance of Murdock's retained earnings at December 31, 1981.

E23-12   The reported net incomes for the first two years of Tab Products, Inc. were as follows: 1980—$147,000; 1981—$185,000. Early in 1982, the following errors were discovered:

1. December 31, 1980 inventory was understated $40,000.
2. December 31, 1981 inventory was overstated $10,000.
3. Depreciation of equipment for 1980 was overstated $5,000.
4. Depreciation of equipment for 1981 was understated $19,000.

Instructions

Prepare the correcting entry necessary when these errors are discovered. Assume that the books are closed.

E23-13   When the records of the Brand Corporation were reviewed at the close of 1981, the errors listed below were discovered. For each item indicate by a check mark in the appropriate column whether the error resulted in an overstatement, an understatement, or had no effect on net income for the years 1980 and 1981.

	1980			1981		
Item	Over-statement	Under-statement	No Effect	Over-statement	Under-statement	No Effect
1) Failure to record amortization of patent in 1980.						
2) Failure to record accrued interest on notes payable in 1980; amount was recorded when paid in 1981.						
3) Failure to reflect supplies on hand on balance sheet at end of 1980.						
4) Failure to record the correct amount of ending 1980 inventory. The amount was overstated because of an error in calculation.						
5) Failure to record merchandise purchased in 1980. Merchandise was also omitted from ending inventory in 1980 but was not yet sold.						

E23-14   A partial trial balance of the Baldor Corporation is as follows on December 31, 1981:

	Dr.	Cr.
Supplies on hand	$ 2,000	
Accrued salaries and wages		$ 2,000
Accrued interest on investments	4,000	
Prepaid insurance	100,000	
Unearned rental income		-0-
Accrued interest payable		12,000

Additional adjusting data:

1. A physical count of supplies on hand on December 31, 1981 totaled $1,000.
2. Through oversight, the accrued salaries and wages account was not changed during 1981. Accrued salaries and wages on 12/31/81 amounted to $3,000.

3. The accrued interest on investments account was also left unchanged during 1981. Accrued interest on investments amounts to $3,800 on 12/31/81.

4. The unexpired portions of the insurance policies totaled $80,000 as of December 31, 1981.

5. $10,000 was received on January 1, 1981 for the rent of a building for both 1981 and 1982. The entire amount was credited to rental income.

6. Depreciation for the year was erroneously recorded as $2,000 rather than the correct figure of $20,000.

7. A further review of depreciation calculations of prior years revealed that depreciation of $6,000 was not recorded. It was decided that this oversight should be corrected by a prior period adjustment.

Instructions

(a) Assuming that the books have not been closed, what are the adjusting entries necessary at December 31, 1981?

(b) Assuming that the books have been closed, what are the adjusting entries necessary at December 31, 1981?

E23-15 The reported net income for Adler, Inc. for 1980 was $60,700 and $50,000 for 1981. However, the accountant noted that the following errors had been made:

1. Sales for 1980 included amounts of $20,000 which had been received in cash during 1980, but for which the related products were delivered in 1981. Title did not pass to the purchaser until 1981.

2. The inventory on December 31, 1980 was understated by $4,500.

3. The bookkeeper in recording interest expense for both 1980 and 1981 on bonds payable made the following entry on an annual basis:

Interest Expense	12,000	
Cash		12,000

The bonds have a face value of $200,000 and pay a stated interest rate of 6%. They were issued at a discount of $10,000 on January 1, 1980 to yield an effective interest rate of 7%. (Assume that the effective yield method should be used.)

4. Ordinary repairs to equipment had been erroneously charged to the Equipment account during 1980 and 1981. Repairs in the amount of $7,800 in 1980 and $7,200 in 1981 were so charged. The company applies a rate of 10% to the balance in the Equipment account at the end of the year in its determination of depreciation charges.

Instructions

Prepare a schedule showing the determination of corrected net income for 1980 and 1981.

E23-16 Presented below is the net income related to Hold, Inc.:

1981	1980	1979
$49,000	$39,000	$70,000

Assume that depreciation entries for 1981 have not been recorded. The following information is also available.

(a) Hold purchased a truck on January 1, 1978 for $10,000 with a $1,000 salvage value and a six-year life. The company debited an expense account and credited cash on the purchase date.

(b) During 1981, Hold changed from the straight-line method of depreciation for its building to the double-declining method. The following computations present depreciation on both bases:

	1981	1980	1979
Straight-line	$60,000	$60,000	$ 60,000
Double-declining	50,000	80,000	110,000

(c) Early in 1981, Hold determined that a piece of equipment purchased in January 1978 at a cost of $9,000 with an estimated life of five years and salvage of $1,500, is now estimated to continue in use until December 31, 1985 and will have a $750 salvage value. Hold, Inc. has been using straight-line depreciation.

(d) Hold won a court case in 1981 related to a patent infringement in 1978. Hold will collect its $8,000 settlement of the suit in 1982. The company had not recorded any entries related to this suit in previous periods.

(e) Hold, in reviewing its provision for uncollectibles during 1981, has determined that 1% of sales is the appropriate amount of bad debt expense to be charged to operations. The company had used ½ of 1% as its rate in 1980 and 1979 when the expense had been $4,500 and $3,000, respectively. The company would have recorded $6,000 of bad debt expense on December 31, 1981 under the old rate. An entry for bad debt expense in 1981 has not been recorded.

Instructions

For each of the foregoing accounting changes, errors, or prior period adjustments, present the journal entry(ies) Hold would have made to record them during 1981, assuming that the books have not been closed. If no entry is required, write "none."

Problems

P23-1 On December 31, 1981, before the books were closed, the management and accountants of Canon, Inc. made the following determinations about three depreciable assets:

1. Depreciable asset A was purchased January 2, 1978. It originally cost $82,500 and, for depreciation purposes, the straight-line method was originally chosen. The asset was originally expected to be useful for 10 years and have a zero salvage value. In 1981, the decision was made to change the depreciation method from straight-line to sum-of-the-years'-digits, and the estimates relating to useful life and salvage value remained unchanged.

2. Depreciable asset B was purchased January 3, 1977. It originally cost $45,000 and, for depreciation purposes, the straight-line method was chosen. The asset was originally expected to be useful for 10 years and have a zero salvage value. In 1981, the decision was made to shorten the total life of this asset to 8 years and to estimate the salvage value at $1,500.

3. Depreciable asset C was purchased January 5, 1976. The asset's original cost was $15,000, and this amount was entirely expensed in 1976. This particular asset has a 10-year useful life and no salvage value. The straight-line method was chosen for depreciation purposes.

Additional data:

1. Income in 1981 before depreciation expense amounted to $100,000.
2. Depreciation expense on assets other than A, B, and C totaled $20,000 in 1981.
3. Income in 1980 was reported at $200,000.
4. Ignore all income tax effects.
5. 100,000 shares of common stock were outstanding in 1980 and 1981.

Instructions

(a) Prepare all necessary entries in 1981 to record these determinations.

(b) Prepare comparative income statements for Canon, Inc. for 1980 and 1981, starting with income before the cumulative effects of any change in accounting principle.

(c) Prepare comparative retained earnings statements for Canon, Inc. for 1980 and 1981. The company had retained earnings of $100,000 at December 31, 1979.

P23-2 Noreen Co. decided in 1981 to change its method of depreciating plant assets to the straight-line method for book purposes. The previous method, the double-declining balance method, will be continued for tax purposes. The effect of the change on depreciation expense for each year since the company's inception is shown in Schedule I below.

In previous years the company recorded royalty income on the cash basis for both tax and book purposes. In 1981, at the auditor's insistence, the company decided to change its method and record this income when earned for book purposes. The effect of this change on royalty income for each year since the company's inception is shown in Schedule II on page 1042.

The average number of outstanding common shares (the only equity security) during 1980 and 1981 was 100,000.

Additional Information:

1. Assume a tax rate of 50% for all years.

2. Income for the year ended December 31, 1981, **before** depreciation expense, royalty income, and federal income tax was $126,000.

3. No dividends were paid or declared during 1981.

4. The statement of earnings and retained earnings for the year ended December 31, 1980, follows:

(Foregoing data omitted)	XXX
Net income	$200,000
Retained earnings, beginning of year	750,000
Retained earnings, end of year	$950,000

Schedule I

Depreciation Expense

Year Ended Dec. 31,	Double-Declining Balance	Straight-Line	Difference	Cumulative Difference
1974	$75,000	$37,500	$37,500	$ 37,500
1975	67,500	37,500	30,000	67,500
1976	60,500	37,500	23,000	90,500
1977	54,500	37,500	17,000	107,500
1978	74,000	50,000	24,000	131,500
1979	67,000	50,000	17,000	148,500
1980	60,000	50,000	10,000	158,500
1981	74,000	60,000	14,000	172,500

Schedule II

Royalty Income

Year Ended Dec. 31,	Cash Received	Income Earned	Difference	Cumulative Difference
1974	-0-	$ 30,000	$30,000	$ 30,000
1975	$ 45,000	60,000	15,000	45,000
1976	50,000	70,000	20,000	65,000
1977	75,000	50,000	(25,000)	40,000
1978	100,000	100,000	-0-	40,000
1979	100,000	150,000	50,000	90,000
1980	100,000	170,000	70,000	160,000
1981	200,000	250,000	50,000	210,000

Instructions

(a) Prepare a statement of income in comparative form for the year ended December 31, 1981. Footnotes are not required.

(b) Prepare a statement of retained earnings in comparative form for the year ended December 31, 1981. Footnotes are not required.

P23-3 Legg Enterprises was organized in late 1977 to manufacture and sell hosiery. At the end of its fourth year of operation, the company has been fairly successful, as indicated by the following reported net incomes.

1978	$150,000[a]
1979	195,000[b]
1980	230,000
1981	300,000

[a]Includes a $15,000 increase because of change in bad debt experience rate.

[b]Includes extraordinary gain of $30,000.

The company has decided to expand operations and has applied for a sizable bank loan. The bank officer has indicated that the records should be audited and presented in comparative statements to facilitate analysis by the bank. Legg, therefore, hired the auditing firm of Doublecheck Co. and has provided the following additional information.

1. In early 1979, Legg changed their estimate from 2 to 1% on the amount of bad debt expense to be charged to operations. Bad debt expense for 1978, if a 1% rate had been used, would have been $15,000. The company, therefore, restated its net income of 1978.

2. In 1981, the auditor discovered that the company had changed its method of inventory pricing from LIFO to FIFO. The effect on the income statements for the previous years is as follows:

	1978	1979	1980	1981
Net income unadjusted-LIFO basis	$150,000	$195,000	$230,000	$300,000
Net income unadjusted-FIFO basis	160,000	200,000	255,000	295,000
	$ 10,000	$ 5,000	$ 25,000	($ 5,000)

3. In 1979, the company changed its method of depreciation from the accelerated method to the straight-line approach. The company used the straight-line method in 1979. The effect on the income statement for the previous year is as follows:

	1978
Net income unadjusted (accelerated method)	$150,000
Net income unadjusted (straight-line method)	157,500
	$ 7,500

4. In 1981, the auditor discovered that:
   (a) The company incorrectly overstated the ending inventory by $24,000 in 1980.
   (b) A dispute developed in 1978 with the Internal Revenue Service over the deductibility of entertainment expenses. In 1978, the company was not permitted these deductions, but a tax settlement was reached in 1981 that allowed these expenses. As a result of the court's finding, tax expenses in 1981 were reduced by $7,500.

Instructions

(a) Indicate how each of these changes or corrections should be handled in the accounting records.

(b) Present comparative income statements for the years 1978 to 1981, starting with income before extraordinary items. Do not prepare pro forma amounts.

P23-4 The management of Grace Corporation has concluded, with the concurrence of its independent auditors, that results of operations would be more fairly presented if Grace changed its method of pricing inventory from last-in, first-out (LIFO) to average cost in 1980. Given below is the five-year summary of income and a schedule of what the inventories might have been if stated on the average cost method.

Grace Corporation
STATEMENT OF INCOME AND RETAINED EARNINGS
For the Years Ended May 31

	1976	1977	1978	1979	1980
Sales—net	$13,964	$15,506	$16,673	$18,221	$18,898
Cost of goods sold:					
Beginning inventory	1,000	1,100	1,000	1,115	1,237
Purchases	13,000	13,900	15,000	15,900	17,100
Ending inventory	(1,100)	(1,000)	(1,115)	(1,237)	(1,369)
Total	12,900	14,000	14,885	15,778	16,968
Gross profit	1,064	1,506	1,788	2,443	1,930
Administrative expenses	700	763	832	907	989
Income before taxes	364	743	956	1,536	941
Income taxes (50%)	182	372	478	768	471
Net income	182	371	478	768	470
Retained earnings—beginning	1,206	1,388	1,759	2,237	3,005
Retained earnings—ending	$ 1,388	$ 1,759	$ 2,237	$ 3,005	$ 3,475
Earnings per share	$ 1.82	$ 3.71	$ 4.78	$ 7.68	$ 4.70

Schedule of Inventory Balances Using Average Cost Method

Year ended May 31					
1975	1976	1977	1978	1979	1980
$900	$1,100	$1,060	$1,254	$1,452	$1,690

Instructions

Prepare comparative statements for the five years, assuming that Grace changed its method of inventory pricing to average cost. Indicate the effects on net income and earnings per share for the years involved. (All amounts except EPS are rounded down to the nearest dollar.)

P23-5 Davis Corporation has decided that in the preparation of its 1981 financial statements two changes will be made from the methods used in prior years:

1. *Depreciation.* Davis has always used the declining-balance method for tax and financial reporting purposes but has decided to change during 1981 to the straight-line method for financial reporting only. The effect of this change is as follows:

	Excess of Accelerated Depreciation Over Straight-line Depreciation
Prior to 1980	$1,300,000
1980	101,000
1981	99,000
	$1,500,000

Depreciation is charged to cost of sales and to selling, general, and administrative expenses on the basis of 75% and 25%, respectively.

2. *Bad debt expense.* In the past Davis has recognized bad debt expense equal to 1.5% of net sales. After careful review it has been decided that a rate of 2% is more appropriate for 1981. Bad debt expense is charged to selling, general, and administrative expenses.

The following information is taken from preliminary financial statements, prepared before giving effect to the two changes:

Davis Corporation
CONDENSED BALANCE SHEET
December 31, 1981
With Comparative Figures for 1980

	1981	1980
Assets		
Current assets	$43,561,000	$43,900,000
Plant assets, at cost	45,792,000	43,974,000
Less accumulated depreciation	23,761,000	22,946,000
	$65,592,000	$64,928,000
Liabilities and Stockholders' Equity		
Current liabilities	$21,124,000	$23,650,000
Long-term debt	15,154,000	14,097,000
Capital stock	11,620,000	11,620,000
Retained earnings	17,694,000	15,561,000
	$65,592,000	$64,928,000

Davis Corporation
INCOME STATEMENT
For the Year Ended December 31, 1981
With Comparative Figures for 1980

	1981	1980
Net sales	$80,520,000	$78,920,000
Cost of goods sold	54,847,000	53,074,000
	25,673,000	25,846,000
Selling, general, and administrative expenses	19,540,000	18,411,000
	6,133,000	7,435,000
Other income (expense), net	(1,198,000)	(1,079,000)
Income before income taxes	4,935,000	6,356,000
Income taxes	2,368,800	3,050,880
Net income	$ 2,566,200	$ 3,305,120

There have been no timing differences between any book and tax items prior to the changes above. The effective tax rate is 48%.

Instructions

Compute for the items listed below the amounts that would appear on the comparative (1981 and 1980) financial statements of Davis Corporation after adjustment for the two accounting changes. Show amounts for both 1981 and 1980 and prepare supporting schedules as necessary.

(a) Accumulated depreciation.

(b) Deferred income taxes (cumulative).

(c) Selling, general, and administrative expenses.

(d) Current portion of federal income tax expense.

(e) Deferred portion of federal income tax expense.

(f) Retained earnings.

(g) Pro forma net income.

(AICPA adapted)

P23-6 The Nimble Corporation has used the accrual basis of accounting for several years. A review of the records, however, indicates that some expenses and revenues have been handled on a cash basis because of errors made by an inexperienced bookkeeper. Income statements prepared by the bookkeeper reported $18,000 net income for 1980 and $20,000 net income for 1981. Further examination of the records reveals that the following items were handled improperly.

(a) Rent was received from a tenant in December 1980; the amount, $600, was recorded as income at that time even though the rental pertained to 1981.

(b) Wages payable on December 31 have been consistently omitted from the records of that date and have been entered as expenses when paid in the following year. The amounts of the accruals recorded in this manner were:

December 31, 1979	$ 720
December 31, 1980	1,020
December 31, 1981	650

(c) Invoices for office supplies purchased have been charged to expense accounts when received. Inventories of supplies on hand at the end of each year have been ignored, and no entry has been made for them.

December 31, 1979	$800
December 31, 1980	500
December 31, 1981	940

Instructions

Prepare a schedule that will show the corrected net income for the years 1980 and 1981. All items listed should be labeled clearly.

P23-7 The Noble Corporation is in the process of negotiating a loan for expansion purposes. The books and records have never been audited and the bank has requested that an audit be performed. Noble has prepared the following comparative financial statements for the years ended December 31, 1981, and 1980:

BALANCE SHEET

As of December 31, 1981 and 1980

	1981	1980
Assets		
Current assets		
Cash	$ 163,000	$ 82,000
Accounts receivable	392,000	296,000
Allowance for doubtful accounts	(37,000)	(18,000)
Marketable securities, at cost	78,000	78,000
Merchandise inventory	207,000	202,000
Total current assets	803,000	640,000
Plant assets		
Property, plant, and equipment	167,000	169,500
Accumulated depreciation	(121,600)	(106,400)
Total fixed assets	45,400	63,100
Total assets	$ 848,400	$703,100
Liabilities and Stockholders' Equity		
Liabilities		
Accounts payable	$ 121,400	$196,100
Stockholders' equity		
Common stock, par value $10, authorized 50,000 shares, issued and outstanding 20,000 shares	260,000	260,000
Retained earnings	467,000	247,000
Total stockholders' equity	727,000	507,000
Total liabilities and stockholders' equity	$ 848,400	$703,100

STATEMENT OF INCOME

For the Years Ended December 31, 1981 and 1980

	1981	1980
Sales	$1,000,000	$900,000
Cost of sales	430,000	395,000
Gross profit	570,000	505,000
Operating expenses	210,000	205,000
Administrative expenses	140,000	105,000
	350,000	310,000
Net income	$ 220,000	$195,000

During the course of the audit, the following additional facts were determined:

1. An analysis of collections and losses on accounts receivable during the past two years indicates a drop in anticipated losses due to bad debts. After consultation with management it was agreed that the loss experience rate on sales should be reduced from the recorded 2% to 1%, beginning with the year ended December 31, 1981.

2. An analysis of marketable securities revealed that this investment portfolio consisted entirely of short-term investments in marketable equity securities that were acquired in 1980. The total market valuation for these investments as of the end of each year was as follows:

December 31, 1980	$81,000
December 31, 1981	$62,000

3. The merchandise inventory at December 31, 1980, was overstated by $4,000 and the merchandise inventory at December 31, 1981, was overstated by $6,100.

4. On January 2, 1980, equipment costing $12,000 (estimated useful life of ten years and residual value of $1,000) was incorrectly charged to operating expenses. Noble records depreciation on the straight-line method. In 1981 fully depreciated equipment (with no residual value) that originally cost $17,500 was sold as scrap for $2,500. Noble credited the proceeds of $2,500 to property and equipment.

5. An analysis of 1980 operating expenses revealed that Noble charged to expense a three-year insurance premium of $2,700 on January 15, 1980.

Instructions

(a) Prepare the journal entries to correct the books at December 31, 1981. The books for 1981 have not been closed. Ignore income taxes.

(b) Prepare a schedule showing the computation of corrected net income for the years ended December 31, 1981 and 1980, assuming that any adjustments are to be reported on comparative statements for the two years. The first items on your schedule should be the net income for each year. Ignore income taxes. (Do not prepare financial statements.)

(AICPA adapted)

P23-8 You have been asked by a client to review the records of the Melba Company, a small manufacturer of precision tools and machines. Your client is interested in buying the business, and arrangements have been made for you to review the accounting records.

Your examination reveals the following:

1. The Melba Company commenced business on April 1, 1978, and has been reporting on a fiscal year ending March 31. The company has never been audited, but the annual statements prepared by the bookkeeper reflect the following income before closing and before deducting income taxes:

Year Ended March 31	Income Before Taxes
1979	$36,800
1980	57,200
1981	53,790

2. A relatively small number of machines have been shipped on consignment. These transactions have been recorded as ordinary sales and billed as such. On March 31 of each year, machines billed and in the hands of consignees amounted to:

1979	$ 6,110
1980	none
1981	5,343

Sales price was determined by adding 30% to cost. Assume that the consigned machines are sold the following year.

3. On March 30, 1980, two machines were shipped to a customer on a C.O.D. basis. The sale was not entered until April 5, 1980, when cash was received for $5,800. The machines were not included in the inventory at March 31, 1980. (Title passed on March 30, 1980.)

4. All machines are sold subject to a five-year warranty. It is estimated that the expense ultimately to be incurred in connection with the warranty will amount to ½ of 1% of sales. The company has charged an expense account for warranty costs incurred.

Sales per books and warranty costs were:

Year Ended March 31	Sales	Warranty Expense for Sales Made In			Total
		1979	1980	1981	
1979	$ 844,710	$680			$ 680
1980	905,000	320	$1,170		1,490
1981	1,604,110	290	1,450	$1,710	3,450

5. A review of the corporate minutes reveals the manager is entitled to a bonus of ½ of 1% of the income before deducting income taxes and the bonus. The bonuses have never been recorded or paid.

6. Bad debts have been recorded on a direct write-off basis. Experience of similar enterprises indicates that losses will approximate ¼ of 1% of sales. Bad debts written off were:

	Bad Debts Incurred on Sales Made In			
	1979	1980	1981	Total
1979	$670			$ 670
1980	720	$ 480		1,200
1981	200	1,700	$1,500	3,400

7. The bank deducts 6% on all contracts financed. Of this amount ½% is placed in a reserve to the credit of the Melba Company that is refunded to Melba as finance contracts are paid in full. The reserve established by the bank has not been reflected in the books of Melba. The excess of credits over debits (net increase) to the reserve account with Melba on the books of the bank for each fiscal year were as follows:

1979	$ 2,800
1980	3,750
1981	4,960
	$11,510

8. Commissions on sales have been entered when paid. Commissions payable on March 31 of each year were:

1979	$ 1,200
1980	700
1981	960

Instructions

(a) Present a schedule showing the revised income before income taxes for each of the years ended March 31, 1979, 1980, and 1981. Make computations to the nearest whole dollar.

(b) Prepare the journal entry or entries you would give the bookkeeper to correct the books. Assume the books have not yet been closed for the fiscal year ended March 31, 1981. Disregard correction of income taxes.

(AICPA adapted)

P23-9 You have been engaged to examine the financial statements of Zurich Corporation for the year ended December 31, 1981. In the course of your examination you have ascertained the following information:

1. A check for $1,500 representing the repayment of an employee advance was received on December 29, 1981, but was not recorded until January 2, 1982.

2. Zurich uses the allowance method of accounting for uncollectible trade accounts receivable. The allowance is based upon 3% of past due accounts (over 120 days) and 1% of current accounts as of the close of each month. Because of a changing economic climate, the amount of past due accounts has increased significantly, and management has decided to increase the percentage based on past due accounts to 5%. The following balances are available:

	As of November 30, 1981 Dr. (Cr.)	As of December 31, 1981 Dr. (Cr.)
Accounts receivable	$390,000	$430,000
Past due accounts (included in accounts receivable)	12,000	30,000
Allowance for uncollectible accounts	(28,000)	9,000

3. The merchandise inventory on December 31, 1980, did **not** include merchandise having a cost of $7,000 which was stored in a public warehouse. Merchandise having a cost of $3,000 was erroneously counted twice and included twice in the merchandise inventory on December 31, 1981. Zurich uses a periodic inventory system.

4. On January 2, 1981, Zurich had a new machine delivered and installed in its main factory. The cost of this machine was $97,000, and the machine is being depreciated on the straight-line method over an estimated useful life of 10 years. When the new machine was installed, Zurich paid for the following items which were not included in the cost of the machine, but were charged to repairs and maintenance:

Delivery expense	$ 2,500
Installation costs	8,000
Rearrangement of related equipment	4,000
	$14,500

5. On January 1, 1980, Zurich leased a building for 10 years at a monthly rental of $12,000. On that date, Zurich paid the landlord the following amounts:

Rent deposit	$ 6,000
First month's rent	12,000
Last month's rent	12,000
Installation of new walls and offices	80,000
	$110,000

The entire amount was charged to rent expense in 1980.

6. In January 1980, Zurich issued $200,000 of 8%, 10-year bonds at 97. The discount was charged to interest expense in 1980. Interest on the bonds is payable on December 31st of each year. Zurich has recorded interest expense of $22,000 for 1980 and $16,000 for 1981.

7. On May 3, 1981, Zurich exchanged 500 shares of treasury stock (its $50 par value common stock) for a parcel of land to be used as a site for a new factory. The treasury stock had cost $70 per share when it was acquired and on May 3, 1981, it had a fair

market value of $80 per share. Zurich received $2,000 when an existing building on the land was sold for scrap. The land was capitalized at $40,000, and Zurich recorded a gain of $5,000 on the sale of its treasury stock. Use the cost method. The sale of the building was credited to income.

8. The account "advertising and promotion expense" included an amount of $75,000 which represented the cost of printing sales catalogues for a special promotional campaign in January 1982.

9. Zurich adopted a pension plan on January 2, 1981, to be administered by a trustee. By use of actuarial computations, the annual normal pension cost was determined to be $70,000, and the present value of past service cost on that date was $900,000. The company has decided to use the maximum provision for pension expense and to fund past service cost. On December 31, 1981, Zurich remitted to the trustee $970,00 and charged this amount to the account "pension expense."

10. Zurich was named as a defendant in a lawsuit by a former customer. Zurich's counsel has advised management that Zurich has a good defense and that counsel does **not** anticipate that there will be any impairment of Zurich's assets or that any significant liabilities will be incurred as a result of this litigation. Management, however, wishes to be conservative and, therefore, has established a loss contingency of $100,000, reducing income.

Instructions

Prepare a schedule showing the effect of errors upon the financial statements for 1981. The items in the schedule should be presented in the same order as the facts are given with corresponding numbers 1 through 10. Use the following columnar headings for your schedule (the books have not been closed for 1981):

No.	Explanation	Income Statement Dr. (Cr.)	Balance Sheet December 31, 1981 Dr. (Cr.)	Account

(AICPA adapted)

Preparation and Analysis
of Financial Statements

Statement of Changes in Financial Position

How did Atlantic Richfield finance the large investment it made to drill for oil in the North Slope of Alaska? How will Boeing Aircraft finance the new B-757 and B-767 jet aircraft that it is building for the airline industry? How was Sears Industries Inc. able to purchase long-term assets recently in the same year that it sustained a net loss? How much of the proposed expansion by Marriott Hotels will be financed through the reinvestment of net income? These types of questions are often asked by investors, creditors, and internal management who are interested in the financial operations of a business enterprise. However, an examination of the balance sheet, income statement, and statement of retained earnings often fails to provide ready answers to questions of this type.

The balance sheet presents the status of the assets and equities as of a specific date; the income statement presents a summary of the nature and results of transactions affecting net income. The statement of retained earnings provides an analysis of changes in retained earnings. These statements present to a limited extent and in a fragmented manner information about the financial activities of an enterprise during the period. Comparative balance sheets help to show what new assets have been acquired or disposed of and what liabilities have been incurred or liquidated. The income statement provides information as to resources provided by operations. The statement of retained earnings provides information as to the resources used to pay dividends. None of these statements, however, presents a detailed summary of all the resources provided during the period and the uses to which they were put.

Evolution of a New Statement

A statement specifically designed to furnish this information is now issued by all major business enterprises as one of the primary financial statements. This statement, the **Statement of Changes in Financial Position,** is designed to present information on the financing and investing activities of a business enterprise. The evolution of this statement provides an interesting example of how the needs of financial statement users are met.

The statement originated in a simple analysis called the "Where-Got and Where-Gone Statement" that consisted of nothing more than a listing of the increases or decreases in the company's balance sheet items. After some years, the title of this statement was changed to "the funds statement." In 1961, the AICPA, recognizing the significance of this statement, sponsored research in this area that resulted in the publication of **Accounting Research Study No. 2,** entitled " 'Cash Flow' Analysis and the Funds Statements."[1] This study recommended that the funds statement be included in all annual reports to the stockholders and that it be covered by the auditor's opinion.

In 1963, **APB Opinion No. 3** was issued to provide some standards for the preparation and presentation of such statements. The Board recommended that the name be changed to "Statement of Source and Application of Funds" and said "that a statement of source and application of funds should be presented as supplementary information in financial reports. The inclusion of such information is not mandatory, and it is optional as to whether it should be covered in the report of the independent accountant."[2]

After the issuance of **APB Opinion No. 3,** support by the business community, the stock exchanges, and the SEC resulted in a substantial increase in the number of companies that presented statements of source and applications of funds.[3] The value of and demand for this type of information resulted in the issuance in 1971 of **APB Opinion No. 19,** which made it mandatory that a "statement of changes in financial position" be presented as an integral part of the financial statements and that it be covered by the auditor's opinion. The Board concluded

> ... that information concerning the financing and investing activities of a business enterprise and the changes in its financial position for a period is essential for financial statement users, particularly owners and creditors, in making economic decisions. When financial statements purporting to present both financial position (balance sheet) and results of operations (statement of income and retained earnings) are issued, a statement summarizing changes in financial position should also be presented as a basic financial statement for each period for which an income statement is presented. These conclusions apply to all profit-oriented business entities, whether or not the reporting entity normally classifies its assets and liabilities as current and noncurrent.[4]

[1]Perry Mason, "'Cash Flow' Analysis and the Funds Statement," *Accounting Research Study No. 2* (New York: AICPA, 1961).

[2]"The Statement of Source and Application of Funds," *Opinions of the Accounting Principles Board No. 3* (New York: AICPA, 1963), par. 8.

[3]*Accounting Trends and Techniques—1978,* for example, indicates that all 600 companies surveyed presented a statement of changes in financial position in 1977.

[4]"Reporting Changes in Financial Position," *Opinions of the Accounting Principles Board No. 19* (New York: AICPA, 1971), par. 7.

The Board recommended that the new title be "Statement of Changes in Financial Position," a title that has rapidly gained popularity.

What Is Meant by Changes in Financial Position?

The changes that occur in financial position from one period to another can be measured in several different ways. The more common approaches are discussed below.

Cash   Under this concept the changes in the cash balance that occur over a period of time are summarized. Any transaction that either increases or decreases cash is considered in preparing the final statement. For example, the purchase of land for cash is considered a change in financial position because it decreases cash. A transaction that has no effect on cash such as the purchase of land on credit is not reported. Using cash to measure changes in financial position has limitations, because many important transactions resulting in changes in financial position are of a noncash variety and are excluded from this statement. Concepts similar to cash such as (1) cash and temporary investments; (2) cash, temporary investments, and receivables (monetary assets); and (3) cash, temporary investments, and receivables minus current liabilities (net monetary assets), are sometimes suggested as means of measuring changes in financial position, but these concepts are not extensively employed in practice.[5]

Working Capital   Changes in financial position are most commonly measured in terms of working capital (current assets minus current liabilities). Any transaction that increases or decreases working capital is shown in the statement. For example, the purchase of land for cash or on short-term credit is reported in the changes statement because a change in working capital occurs. The use of working capital as the basis permits the exclusion of many routine transactions such as cash collections on accounts receivable and the purchase of inventory on credit. All of these transactions are summarized in the amount reported as "resources (working capital) provided by operations."

All Financial Resources   If working capital alone is used in measuring changes in financial position, some major financial transactions may be omitted. For example, issuing common stock for buildings or machinery has no effect on working capital, but it is a significant financial transaction that should be disclosed. For this reason the definition of changes in financial position was expanded to include **any change that significantly affects the financing and investing aspects of the enterprise.** This approach, called the **all financial resources concept,** expands the definition of resources beyond working capital to cover all significant financial occurrences. **APB Opinion No. 19** requires the use of the all financial resources concept, indicating that a company may explain its changes in resources using a concept such as cash, cash and temporary investments, or working capital, but that whatever con-

---

[5]*Accounting Trends and Techniques—1978* indicates that in 1977 only 43 out of 600 companies surveyed used cash and cash equivalent approaches in measuring changes in financial position while 557 of the companies surveyed analyzed the change in terms of working capital.

cept is followed, it must be adjusted to disclose significant financial transactions that would otherwise be omitted under this concept.

The statement of changes in financial position must be based upon the all financial resources concept; at the same time, most of these statements attempt to disclose the change in working capital. To accomplish these two objectives, the statement must identify and analyze two categories of items: (1) sources of working capital (inflows) and applications of working capital (outflows), and (2) sources and applications of resources that did not affect (flow through) working capital. Because the working capital concept, adjusted for other significant (nonworking capital) changes in resources, is used extensively in practice, it is employed as the basis for discussion in this chapter.

STATEMENT OF CHANGES IN FINANCIAL POSITION—WORKING CAPITAL APPROACH

Working Capital as a Fund

Working capital is the difference between current assets and current liabilities. As a fund, working capital is viewed as containing all current assets (increases in working capital) and all current liabilities (decreases in working capital). **Any transaction that results in a net increase in working capital is a "source" of working capital;** that is, it provides working capital. **Any transaction that results in a net decrease in working capital is a "use" of working capital;** that is, it applies working capital. Some transactions merely rearrange the internal content of working capital; that is, they neither increase nor decrease working capital. For example, the collection of cash from an account receivable, the payment of an account payable, and the purchase of inventory for cash or on short-term credit, are neither sources nor applications of working capital, because the net balance does not change. Thus, **in the analysis of working capital we must separate the transac-**

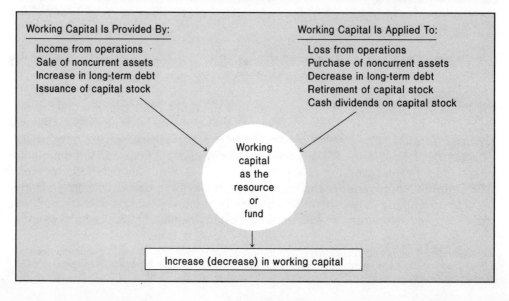

tions that cause changes in working capital from those that merely change the composition but not the total of working capital. It is the change in the working capital balance, along with other significant (nonworking capital) changes in resources, that the statement of changes in financial position reports.

The diagram on page 1056 illustrates the type of events and transactions that result in working capital being provided and applied.

First Illustration

To illustrate the preparation of a statement of changes in financial position, let us assume a very simple situation. The comparative account balances and the differences in account balances for Potter, Inc. are:

| | Potter, Inc. | | Differences | |
	Dec. 31, 1981	Dec. 31, 1980	Dr.	Cr.
Cash	$15,000	$10,000	$ 5,000	
Accounts receivable	65,000	80,000		$15,000
	$80,000	$90,000		
Accounts payable	$ 4,000	$20,000	16,000	
Common stock	50,000	50,000		
Retained earnings	26,000	20,000		6,000
	$80,000	$90,000	$21,000	$21,000

Assume that no dividends were declared or paid during the year and that the net income for the year was $6,000.

Presented on page 1058 is a statement of changes in financial position and a supporting schedule of working capital changes, prepared from the information presented above.

Net income from operations for the year was $6,000, and the additional resources provided by that source were applied to increase working capital by that same amount. As shown in the comparative balance sheets, however, the total assets decreased $10,000 during the year. The schedule of working capital changes indicates that the decrease in current assets of $10,000 was more than offset by a decrease in accounts payable of $16,000; thus, the net result is an increase in working capital of $6,000. **APB Opinion No. 19** requires that changes in the elements of working capital be analyzed in appropriate detail in a tabulation or schedule accompanying the statement or in the statement itself. This approach is mandatory because significant information often found in the schedule of working capital changes is not provided in the basic statement. To illustrate, assume that a company shifted its current assets from marketable securities into short-term receivables and that the assets involved were significant in relation to the total asset structure of the enterprise. This change in the composition of current assets should be described in the lower part of the statement of changes in financial position, or in supplemental information.

Potter, Inc.
STATEMENT OF CHANGES IN FINANCIAL POSITION
For the Year Ended December 31, 1981

Resources provided by
Operations $6,000

Resources applied to
Increase in working capital $6,000

SCHEDULE OF WORKING CAPITAL CHANGES

	Working Capital Change	
	Increase	Decrease
Current assets		
Cash	$ 5,000	
Accounts receivable		$15,000
Current liabilities		
Accounts payable	16,000	
Totals	21,000	15,000
Increase in working capital		6,000
	$21,000	$21,000

Second Illustration

Net income usually must be adjusted to arrive at resources provided by operations because certain expenses do not decrease working capital and some items of revenue and gain do not increase working capital. Depreciation expense, for example, does not cause a decrease in working capital during the current period. To direct attention to the effect of depreciation on the preparation of this statement, the information presented below has been condensed somewhat and the schedule of working capital changes has been omitted.

	Information Processing, Inc.			
	Dec. 31,	Dec. 31,	Differences	
Accounts	1981	1980	Dr.	Cr.
Current assets	$ 25,000	$ 20,000	$5,000	
Plant assets	80,000	80,000		
	$105,000	$100,000		
Accumulated depreciation	$ 11,000	$ 10,000		$1,000
Current liabilities	12,000	15,000	3,000	
Common stock	50,000	50,000		
Retained earnings	32,000	25,000		7,000
	$105,000	$100,000	$8,000	$8,000

Assume that no dividends were declared or paid during the year and that the net income for the year was $7,000. Examination of the columns for differences indicates that working capital increased $8,000 during the year as evidenced by an increase of $5,000 in current assets and a decrease of $3,000 in current liabilities. Where did this $8,000 increase in working capital come from? The other two items appearing in the differences columns above are $7,000 of net income for the year and a $1,000 increase in the accumulated depreciation; these two items total $8,000. The recording of depreciation, however, did not provide resources. A more accurate statement is that **the charge for depreciation expense that reduced net income did not require any current expenditure during the period.** Therefore, net income must be adjusted for such noncash or nonworking capital charges in order to disclose the total resources provided by operations. Total resources provided by operations is $8,000. The statement below reports this information.

Information Processing, Inc.
STATEMENT OF CHANGES IN FINANCIAL POSITION
For the Year Ended December 31, 1981

Resources provided by	
Operations:	
Net income for the year	$7,000
Add (or deduct) item not affecting working capital	
Depreciation on plant assets	1,000
	$8,000
Resources applied to	
Increase in working capital	$8,000

The statement should begin with net income or loss and add back or deduct items that did not use or provide working capital during the period. Items added or deducted in accordance with this procedure are not sources or uses of working capital, and the related caption should make that clear. An acceptable alternative that produces the same result is to start with total revenue that provided working capital and deduct operating costs and expenses that required the outlay of working capital during the period. In either case, the final amount should be appropriately described as resources provided from operations.

Other charges against income for the period that do not require the use of working capital may be treated in the same manner as depreciation. Bond discount amortized and amortization of patents or goodwill are examples of such charges that are illustrated later in this chapter.

Third Illustration

The preceding two illustrations were made very simple to illustrate specific points. A more comprehensive example follows:

| | Doral, Inc. | | | |
| | Dec. 31, | Dec. 31, | Differences | |
Accounts	1981	1980	Dr.	Cr.
Cash	$ 4,600	$ 3,000	$ 1,600	
Accounts receivable (net)	11,300	15,000		$ 3,700
Inventories	11,500	25,000		13,500
Prepaid expenses	1,200	1,000	200	
Land	34,000	40,000		6,000
Equipment	95,000	60,000	35,000	
	$157,600	$144,000		
Accumulated depreciation—equipment	$ 23,000	$ 20,000		$ 3,000
Accounts payable	4,000	10,000	6,000	
Dividends payable	5,500	5,000		500
Bonds payable (long-term)	13,500	6,000		7,500
Common stock	80,000	80,000		
Retained earnings	31,600	23,000		8,600
	$157,600	$144,000	$42,800	$42,800

Additional information concerning some of the differences:

1. Land carried at $6,000 was sold for $7,000 during the year; the gain of $1,000 was not considered an extraordinary item.
2. Equipment costing $40,000 was purchased during the year; equipment with a cost of $5,000 was sold at its book value of $1,500. Depreciation expense for the year was $6,500.
3. Bonds payable in the amount of $7,500 were issued for cash.
4. Net income for the year was $19,600; cash dividends of $11,000 were declared.

In preparing a statement of changes in financial position, a work sheet, described later, could be used, although it is possible to prepare the statement without using

Doral, Inc.		
SCHEDULE OF WORKING CAPITAL CHANGES		
For the Year Ended December 31, 1981		
	Working Capital Change	
Current Assets	Increase	Decrease
Increase in cash	$ 1,600	
Decrease in accounts receivable (net)		$ 3,700
Decrease in inventories		13,500
Increase in prepaid expenses	200	
Current Liabilities		
Decrease in accounts payable	6,000	
Increase in dividends payable		500
	7,800	17,700
Decrease in working capital	9,900	
	$17,700	$17,700

one. To prepare the statement without the use of a work sheet, it is necessary to analyze the differences that occur in the accounts from one period to the next.

The starting point in the development of the statement of changes in financial position is computation of the working capital change. The working capital change is computed as shown at the bottom of page 1060.

The schedule of working capital changes shown on page 1060 is somewhat different from the one used in the first illustration on page 1058. The repetition of the words "increase" or "decrease" in the left hand margin may be monotonous in this example, but it provides another example of how this schedule might be shown. This format should be used for problem material unless another approach is specifically requested.

After the decrease in working capital is computed, an analysis of the nonworking capital accounts is performed. An analysis of the retained earnings account is a good starting point because the net income is the first item reported on a statement of changes in financial position. Then the noncurrent assets, liabilities, and other stockholders' equity accounts should be analyzed.

Increase in Retained Earnings   Retained earnings increased $8,600 for Doral, Inc. as a result of net income of $19,600 less cash dividends of $11,000. The net income amount would be reported as follows:

Resources provided by	
Operations:	
Net income	$19,600

The cash dividends are reported as a use of resources as follows:

Resources applied to	
Cash dividends	$11,000

The appropriate time to indicate that resources are applied is at the time the cash dividend is declared. At the declaration date, the equity of the stockholders is decreased and a current obligation of the same amount is established. The subsequent payment of the dividend to the stockholders has no effect on working capital because the current liability and cash are reduced by the same amount.

Decrease in Land   The decrease in the balance of the land account from the beginning to the end of the year is $6,000. The resources provided by the sale of the land are $7,000; the gain of $1,000 is included in net income for the year. On the statement of changes in financial position, the following information is reported:

Resources provided by	
Sale of land	$7,000

The total proceeds from the sale of the land is reported as resources provided by sale of land. Note that the $1,000 gain on sale of the land is included in net income.

This gain of $1,000 must be deducted from net income when computing working capital provided by operations to avoid double counting.

Equipment and Related Depreciation Equipment costing $40,000 was purchased during the year; this purchase would be reported as follows:

Resources applied to	
Purchase of equipment	$40,000

In addition, equipment costing $5,000 was sold at its book value of $1,500. This transaction would be reported as follows:

Resources provided by	
Sale of equipment	$1,500

Depreciation expense for the year is $6,500 and would be reported as an item added back to net income to show working capital provided by operations. The difference of $3,000 in the Accumulated Depreciation—Equipment account is the net result of the increase of $6,500 from 1981 depreciation expense and the decrease of $3,500 from the sale of equipment.

Issuance of Bonds Payable Bonds in the amount of $7,500 were issued during the year. This transaction would be reported as follows:

Resources provided by	
Issuance of bonds payable	$7,500

Preparation of the Statement Combining the foregoing items that were illustrated separately, a complete statement of changes in financial position would be presented as shown on page 1063.

Source of Information for Statement

Below are important points to remember in the preparation of the statement of changes in financial position.

1. Comparative balance sheets provide the basic information from which the report is prepared. Additional information obtained from analyses of specific accounts is also included. All the information necessary to prepare a statement of changes in financial position is readily available and should not be difficult to assemble.

2. The increase or decrease in working capital (current assets less current liabilities) is shown in one amount in the statement. As this is sometimes the most significant item in the report, increases or decreases in the individual items comprising working capital are shown in a separate (supporting) schedule of changes in working capital, or included in the body of the statement, as illustrated later in this chapter.

3. Both increases and decreases of plant assets, investments, long-term debt, and contributed capital stock are shown in the statement. This requires supplementary information obtained by analysis of related accounts.

Doral, Inc.
STATEMENT OF CHANGES IN FINANCIAL POSITION
For the Year Ended December 31, 1981

Resources provided by		
Operations:		
Net income		$19,600
Add or (deduct) items not affecting working capital		
Gain on sale of land	$(1,000)	
Depreciation expense	6,500	5,500
Working capital provided by operations		25,100
Sale of land		7,000
Sale of equipment		1,500
Issuance of bonds payable		7,500
Total resources provided		41,100
Resources applied to		
Cash dividends	11,000	
Purchase of equipment	40,000	
Total resources applied		51,000
Decrease in working capital		$ 9,900

SCHEDULE OF WORKING CAPITAL CHANGES

| | Working Capital Change ||
	Increase	Decrease
Current Assets		
Increase in cash	$ 1,600	
Decrease in accounts receivable (net)		$ 3,700
Decrease in inventories		13,500
Increase in prepaid expenses	200	
Current Liabilities		
Decrease in accounts payable	6,000	
Increase in dividends payable		500
	7,800	17,700
Decrease in working capital	9,900	
	$17,700	$17,700

4. An analysis of the retained earnings account is necessary to derive data relative to resources provided and applied. The net increase or decrease in retained earnings without any explanation is a meaningless amount in the statement, for it might represent the effect of net income, dividends declared, appropriations of retained earnings, and "prior period" adjustments.

5. The statement includes all changes that have passed through working capital or have resulted in an increase or decrease in working capital and in addition, some significant financial transactions discussed later.

6. Writedowns, amortization charges, and similar "book" entries, such as depreciation of plant assets, are considered as neither sources nor applications of resources, because they have no effect on working capital. To the extent that they have entered into the determination of net income, however, they must be added back to or subtracted from net income to arrive at working capital provided by operations.

Special Problems in Statement Analysis

Some of the special problems related to preparing the statement of changes in financial position were discussed in connection with the preceding illustrations. Other problems that arise with some frequency in the preparation of this statement may be categorized as follows:

1. Adjustments similar to depreciation.
2. Nonworking capital (all financial resources) transactions.
3. Extraordinary items.
4. Net losses.
5. Reclassification of current and noncurrent items.

Adjustments Similar to Depreciation

Depreciation expense is the adjustment to net income that is made most commonly to arrive at working capital provided by operations. But there are numerous other expense or revenue items that do not affect working capital. Examples of expense items that must be added back to net income are the **amortization of intangible assets** such as goodwill and patents, and the **amortization of deferred charges** such as bond issue costs. These charges against income involve expenditures made in prior periods that are being amortized currently and reduce net income without affecting working capital in the current period. Also, **amortization of bond discount or premium** on long-term bonds payable affects the amount of interest expense, but neither affects working capital. As a result, amortization of these items should be added back to or subtracted from net income to arrive at working capital provided from operations.

In similar manner, **changes in deferred income taxes and deferred investment credit** accounts affect net income but have no effect on working capital. For example, Walt Disney Productions recently experienced an increase in its liability for deferred taxes of approximately $12,000,000. Tax expense was increased and net income was decreased by this amount, but the flow of working capital was not affected; therefore, $12,000,000 was added back to net income. Conversely, Grand Union Company recently had a decrease in its liability for deferred taxes of $814,000 and subtracted this amount from net income to arrive at working capital provided from operations.

A change related to an investment in common stock when the income or loss is accrued under the equity method is another common adjustment to net income. For example, Johns-Manville Corporation's equity in earnings of foreign subsidiaries recently increased by approximately 127 million dollars. Such an increase, however, is not represented by a working capital flow, so it was deducted from net income to arrive at working capital provided by operations. Similarly, Dictaphone Corporation's equity in the net losses of its foreign subsidiaries was $132,000, and this amount was added back to net income. If the company receives a dividend from its equity investee, resources provided from a cash dividend should be reported.

The following diagram illustrates the common types of adjustments that are made to net income to arrive at working capital provided by operations.

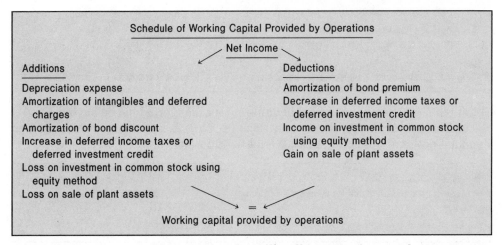

Schedule of Working Capital Provided by Operations

Net Income

Additions

Depreciation expense
Amortization of intangibles and deferred
  charges
Amortization of bond discount
Increase in deferred income taxes or
  deferred investment credit
Loss on investment in common stock using
  equity method
Loss on sale of plant assets

Deductions

Amortization of bond premium
Decrease in deferred income taxes or
  deferred investment credit
Income on investment in common stock
  using equity method
Gain on sale of plant assets

=

Working capital provided by operations

Some current asset adjustments such as the allocation of prepaid expenses are similar to depreciation in that they involve an allocation to expense during the current period but represent an expenditure made in a prior period. They are treated differently in the statement, however, because prepaid expenses are part of working capital, and the net increase or decrease in working capital is reported in the statement in one amount, whereas changes in long-term assets are shown separately.

The same holds true for any other charge or credit that might occur in the current asset or current liability section. For example, an increase in the allowance for doubtful accounts is a part of the computation of an increase or decrease in working capital without adjustment or special treatment. Similarly, a decrease in a current liability such as unearned revenue would be shown in the schedule of working capital changes but not as a separate adjustment to net income to arrive at working capital provided by operations.

Nonworking Capital Transactions

Up to now, we have concentrated on those items that flow through, or effect a change in, working capital. Under the all financial resources concept, the statement of changes in financial position must also include nonworking capital transactions that are considered significant financing and investing activities of an enterprise.

Nonworking Capital Transactions Reported The types of nonworking capital transactions that are commonly reported in the statement of changes in financial position are: (1) the issuance of long-term debt or equity securities to purchase noncurrent assets; (2) the conversion of long-term debt or preferred stock to common stock; (3) the acquisition of long-term assets through gift or donation or the forgiveness of a long-term obligation; and (4) the retirement of debt through a sinking fund classified as long-term. To illustrate, assume that Posture Furniture Company acquired a $200,000 warehouse in exchange for a long-term $200,000 mortgage note on the property. This transaction does not affect cash or working capital but it has a significant impact on resources and would be reported in the statement of changes in financial position as follows:

Resources provided by	
Issuance of mortgage note for building	$200,000
Resources applied to	
Purchase of building in exchange for long-term note	$200,000

For another illustration, assume that Houston, Inc. converted bonds having a par of $50,000 for 50,000 shares of common stock ($1 par). In a statement of changes in financial position, this information would be reported in the following manner:

Resources provided by	
Issuance of common stock for retirement of debt	$50,000
Resources applied to	
Retirement of debt through issuance of common stock	$50,000

This transaction resulted in the issuance of additional common stock and the retirement of long-term debt with no effect upon working capital or cash.

Nonworking Capital Transactions Not Reported Certain financial transactions that affect only nonworking capital accounts do not require reporting in the statement of changes in financial position because they do not provide or use resources. Examples of these types of transactions are **stock dividends, stock splits, and appropriations of retained earnings.** To illustrate, when a corporation declares a dividend distributable in *stock* instead of in *cash*, a transfer from Retained Earnings to Capital Stock and to Additional Paid-in Capital is usually made. **APB Opinion No. 19** recommends that this type of dividend not be disclosed in the statement of changes in financial position, because no change has occurred either in the amount or in the composition of stockholders' equity that has an effect on the resources of the enterprise.

Similarly, stock splits and appropriations of retained earnings do not represent either resources provided or resources applied; therefore, they should not be reported in a statement of changes in financial position.

Extraordinary Items

The statement of changes in financial position ordinarily begins with net income. Whenever extraordinary gains or losses are involved, the statement starts with income before extraordinary items. To this amount are added back or deducted items recognized in determining income or loss that did not use or provide working capital. These items should be subtotaled and appropriately labeled "working capital provided by operations for the year, exclusive of extraordinary item." This subtotal should be followed by the extraordinary item.

To illustrate, assume that Tandem Bike Company reported net income of $39,000, which included an extraordinary gain of $9,000 (net of $3,000 tax) resulting from the sale of their only investment in equity securities (book value $16,000). Depreciation expense was $4,000 for the period. In the statement of changes in financial position the following information would be reported:

Tandem Bike Company PARTIAL STATEMENT OF CHANGES IN FINANCIAL POSITION	
Resources provided by	
Operations:	
Income before extraordinary item	$30,000
Add (or deduct) items not affecting working capital	
Depreciation expense	4,000
Working capital provided by operations, exclusive of extraordinary item	34,000
Extraordinary item—gain on sale of investment (net of $3,000 tax)	9,000
	43,000
Book value of investment sold	16,000

Note that the extraordinary gain of $9,000 (net of $3,000 tax) is shown in a separate section as an extraordinary item. The book value of the investment ($16,000) is shown as an additional source to arrive at a total resources provided by sale of investment of $25,000.

Some accountants consider this type of presentation cumbersome. In practice the extraordinary gain and the proceeds of sale are often shown as one source item after "working capital provided by operations, exclusive of extraordinary item," as reported below:

Tandem Bike Company PARTIAL STATEMENT OF CHANGES IN FINANCIAL POSITION	
Resources provided by	
Operations:	
Income before extraordinary item	$30,000
Add (or deduct) items not affecting working capital	
Depreciation expense	4,000
Working capital provided by operations, exclusive of extraordinary item	34,000
Extraordinary item—sale of investment, including	
extraordinary gain of $9,000 (net of $3,000 tax)	25,000

In the latter illustration, the entire transaction is reported in one section of the statement. Because of its simplicity and ease of understanding, this format should be used for problem material unless another approach is requested. This format is also widely used in practice.

Net Losses

If an enterprise reports a net loss instead of a net income, the net loss must be adjusted for those items that do not result in a working capital inflow or outflow. The presentation in the statement of changes in financial position differs depending on whether the net loss after adjusting for the charges or credits not affecting working capital results in a negative or positive working capital from operations. For example, if the net loss was $50,000 and the total amount of charges to be added back was $60,000, then resources are provided by operations in the amount of $10,000, as shown in the computation on the next page.

Computation of Working Capital **Provided** by Operations		
Net loss		$(50,000)
Add (or deduct) items not affecting working capital		
Depreciation of plant assets	$55,000	
Amortization of patents	5,000	60,000
Working capital provided by operations		$ 10,000

A presentation similar to the above would appear in the resources **provided** section of the statement of changes in financial position. If the company experienced a net loss of $80,000 and the total amount of the charges to be added back is $25,000, the presentation would appear in the resources **applied** section as illustrated below:

Computation of Working Capital **Applied** to Operations	
Net loss	$(80,000)
Add (or deduct) items not affecting working capital	
Depreciation of plant assets	25,000
Working capital applied to operations	($55,000)

Reclassifications

A change that sometimes occurs in the long-term liability section is the reclassification of a part of the long-term debt obligation to the current liability section. In this situation, the transfer should be examined to determine its effect on working capital. Because a decrease in working capital occurs, working capital is considered to have been applied to retire long-term debt. For example, United Merchants and Manufacturers recently reported in their resources applied section approximately $10 million related to the reclassification of a long-term debt to a short-term obligation. In such cases, resources are considered applied to the retirement of long-term debt in the amount of $10 million. Similarly, if a long-term asset such as a sinking fund investment is transferred from long-term assets to short-term assets, working capital is considered to have been provided. The same principle would apply if marketable securities were reclassified from noncurrent to current assets. If a current asset such as a receivable is reclassified as long-term, resources are applied because working capital has decreased.

Comprehensive Illustration—Use of a Work Sheet

If numerous adjustments are necessary or if other complicating factors are present, many accountants prefer to use a work sheet to assemble and classify the data that will appear on the statement of changes in financial position. The work sheet is merely a device to aid in the preparation of the statement; its use is not required. The use of T-accounts or even the use of supplementary computations will often serve as suitable substitutes, and they may prove less time-consuming to anyone experienced in preparing such statements. The T-account approach is illustrated in the appendix to this chapter.

A work sheet for Hanes Corporation is presented on pages 1076 and 1077. **The important items to note as you study the illustration are:**

1. A working capital summary account is prepared to identify the working capital balance at both the beginning and the end of the year. A major purpose of the work sheet is to identify and organize the changes in working capital.

2. The other (nonworking capital) account balances listed on the work sheet are separated into those with debit balances and those with credit balances. The first column (far left) contains the beginning of the year balances and the last column (far right) contains the end of the year balances. The transactions that effected the changes in these accounts during the period are the reconciling items that appear between these two columns.

Hanes Corporation
COMPARATIVE BALANCE SHEET
December 31, 1981 and 1980

Assets	1981	1980	Difference Incr. or Decr.
Cash	$ 59,000	$ 66,000	7,000 Decr.
Accounts receivable (net)	104,000	51,000	53,000 Incr.
Inventories	493,000	341,000	152,000 Incr.
Prepaid expenses	16,500	17,000	500 Decr.
Investments in stock of Porter Co.			
(equity method)	18,500	15,000	3,500 Incr.
Land	131,500	82,000	49,500 Incr.
Equipment	187,000	142,000	45,000 Incr.
Accumulated depreciation—equipment	(29,000)	(31,000)	2,000 Decr.
Buildings	262,000	262,000	—
Accumulated depreciation—buildings	(74,100)	(71,000)	3,100 Incr.
Goodwill	7,600	10,000	2,400 Decr.
Total Assets	$1,176,000	$884,000	
Liabilities			
Accounts payable	$ 132,000	$131,000	1,000 Incr.
Accrued liabilities	40,500	38,000	2,500 Incr.
Dividends payable	2,500	1,000	1,500 Incr.
Income taxes payable	3,000	16,000	13,000 Decr.
Notes payable (long-term)	60,000	—	60,000 Incr.
Bonds payable	100,000	100,000	—
Premium on bonds payable	7,000	8,000	1,000 Decr.
Deferred income taxes (long-term)	9,000	6,000	3,000 Incr.
Total Liabilities	354,000	300,000	
Stockholders' Equity			
Common stock ($1.00 par)	60,000	50,000	10,000 Incr.
Additional paid-in capital	187,000	38,000	149,000 Incr.
Retained earnings	592,000	496,000	96,000 Incr.
Treasury stock	(17,000)	—	17,000 Incr.
Total stockholders' equity	822,000	584,000	
Total Liabilities and Stockholders' Equity	$1,176,000	$884,000	

3. The transactions for the current year are then examined to determine whether they affected resources provided or applied. After the transactions are analyzed and entered in the work sheet, all the differences between the beginning and ending balances should be reconciled.

4. The adjustments shown on the work sheet are not entered in any journal or posted to any account. They are not adjustments to correct accounts; they are merely adjustments for this work sheet to facilitate the preparation of a statement of changes in financial position. The totals of the reconciling transaction debit and credit columns should balance.

5. The bottom portion of the work sheet provides the information necessary to prepare the formal statement of changes in financial position (excluding the analysis of the changes in working capital).

To illustrate procedures for preparation of the work sheet, the financial statements and other data related to the Hanes Corporation are presented with the balance sheet on page 1069, the statement of income and retained earnings below and on page 1071, and the schedule of working capital changes on page 1071. Additional explanations related to preparation of the work sheet are provided throughout the discussion presented on pages 1072–1075.

Hanes Corporation COMBINED STATEMENT OF INCOME AND RETAINED EARNINGS For the Year Ended 1981	
Net sales	$524,500
Other income	3,500
Total revenues	528,000
Expense	
Cost of goods sold	310,000
Selling and administrative expense	47,000
Other expense and losses	12,000
Total expenses	369,000
Income before income tax and extraordinary item	159,000
Income Tax	
Current	47,000
Deferred	3,000
Income before extraordinary item	109,000
Gain on condemnation of land (net of tax)	8,000
Net income	117,000
Retained earnings, January 1	496,000
Less:	
Cash dividends	6,000
Stock dividend	15,000
Retained earnings, December 31	$592,000
Per Share:	
Income before extraordinary items	$1.98
Extraordinary item	.15
Net income	$2.13

Additional Information

(a) Other income of $3,500, represents Hanes Corporation's equity share in the net income of Porter Company, an equity investee. Hanes Corporation owns 22% of Porter Company.

(b) Land in the amount of $60,000 was purchased through the issuance of a long-term note; in addition, certain parcels of land were condemned, resulting in an $8,000 gain, net of $2,500 tax.

(c) An analysis of the equipment account and related accumulated depreciation indicates the following:

	Equipment Dr./(Cr.)	Accum. Dep. Dr./(Cr.)	Gain or Loss
Balance at end of 1980	$142,000	$(31,000)	
Purchases of equipment	53,000		
Sale of equipment	(8,000)	2,500	1,500L
Depreciation for the period		(11,500)	
Major repair charged to accumulated depreciation		11,000	
Balance at end of 1981	$187,000	$(29,000)	

(d) The change in the accumulated depreciation—building, goodwill, premium on bonds payable, and deferred income tax accounts resulted from depreciation and amortization entries.

(e) An analysis of the paid-in capital accounts in stockholders' equity discloses the following:

	Common Stock	Additional Paid-In Capital
Balance at end of 1980	$50,000	$ 38,000
Issuance of 2% stock dividend	1,000	14,000
Sale of stock for cash	9,000	135,000
Balance at end of 1981	$60,000	$187,000

Hanes Corporation
SCHEDULE OF WORKING CAPITAL CHANGES
For the Year Ended 1981

	Working Capital Change	
	Increase	Decrease
Current Assets		
Decrease in cash		$ 7,000
Increase in accounts receivable (net)	$ 53,000	
Increase in inventories	152,000	
Decrease in prepaid expenses		500
Current Liabilities		
Increase in accounts payable		1,000
Increase in accrued liabilities		2,500
Increase in dividends payable		1,500
Decrease in income taxes payable	13,000	
Totals	218,000	12,500
Increase in working capital		205,500
	$218,000	$218,000

Analysis of Working Capital Changes

As indicated earlier, the first step in the preparation of a statement of changes in financial position is to compute the increase or decrease in working capital for the year. The schedule of working capital changes for Hanes Corporation is presented at the bottom of page 1071. A major purpose of the statement of changes in financial position is to report the investing and financing activities that caused this increase in working capital of $205,500.

If a work sheet is employed, the beginning and ending balances of working capital are determined and entered on the work sheet. To illustrate, Hanes Corporation has $289,000 of working capital at the beginning of 1981 and $494,500 at the end of 1981 (as computed from the current items on the comparative balance sheet on page 1069). These two working capital amounts ($289,000 and $494,500) should be entered at the top of the work sheet as illustrated on page 1076.

Analysis of Work Sheet Transactions

The following discussion (from page 1072 through page 1075) provides an explanation of the individual adjustments that appear on the work sheet on pages 1076 and 1077.

Change in Retained Earnings   Net income for the period is comprised of "income before extraordinary item" and an "extraordinary gain." Income before the extraordinary item is $109,000 and the extraordinary gain is $8,000 (net of $2,500 tax) from condemnation of land that has a book value of $10,500. The entry on the work sheet for certain items affecting retained earnings would be as follows:

(1)

Resources Provided by Income before Extraordinary Item	109,000	
Resources Provided by Condemnation of Land (Gain)	8,000	
Retained Earnings		117,000

The resources provided by income before extraordinary item is reported at the bottom of the work sheet and is the starting point for preparation of the statement of changes in financial position. The resources provided by the condemnation of the land, gain of $8,000 (net of $2,500 tax), is entered separately at the bottom of the work sheet as a resource provided item. The book value ($10,500) part of this extraordinary item transaction is handled separately in preparing the work sheet.

Retained earnings was also affected by a stock dividend and a cash dividend. The retained earnings statement reports a stock dividend of $15,000. The work sheet entry for this transaction is as follows:

(2)

Retained Earnings	15,000	
Common Stock		1,000
Additional Paid-in Capital		14,000

The issuance of stock dividends is not considered to be either resources provided or resources applied; therefore, although this transaction is entered on the work sheet for reconciling purposes, it is not reported in the statement of changes.

The cash dividend of $6,000 requires the use of resources and is recorded in the work sheet by the following entry:

(3)

Retained Earnings	6,000	
Resources Applied to Cash Dividends		6,000

The beginning and ending balances of retained earnings are reconciled by the entry of the three items above.

Investment in Stock of Porter Co. The investment in the stock of Porter Co. increased $3,500, which reflects Hanes Corporation's share of the income earned by its equity investee during the current year. Although revenue, and therefore income per the income statement, was increased $3,500 by the accounting entry that recorded Hanes' share of Porter Co.'s net income, no working capital or resources were provided. The following work sheet entry is made:

(4)

Investment in Stock of Porter Co.	3,500	
Income before Extraordinary Item—		
Equity in Earnings of Porter Co.		3,500

Land Land in the amount of $60,000 was purchased through the issuance of a long-term note payable. Although this transaction did not affect working capital, it is considered a significant financial resource transaction that should be reported because both resources provided and resources applied are affected. Two entries are necessary to record this transaction on the work sheet.

(5)

Land	60,000	
Resources Applied to Purchase of Land—		
Issuance of Long-term Note		60,000
Resources Provided by Issuance of Long-term Note—		
Purchase of Land	60,000	
Note Payable		60,000

In addition to the all financial resources transactions involving the issuance of a note to purchase land, the land account was decreased by the condemnation proceedings. The work sheet entry to record the book value portion of this transaction is as follows:

(6)

Resources Provided by Condemnation of Land (Book Value)	10,500	
Land		10,500

The $10,500 of resources provided by condemnation plus the $8,000 gain recorded earlier constitute the total resources of $18,500 related to the condemnation. The land account balances are now reconciled.

Equipment and Accumulated Depreciation

An analysis of the equipment account and its related accumulated depreciation account shows that a number of financial transactions have affected these accounts. Equipment in the amount of $53,000 was purchased during the year. The entry to record this transaction on the work sheet is as follows:

(7)

Equipment	53,000	
Resources Applied to the Purchase of Equipment		53,000

In addition, equipment with a book value of $5,500 was sold at a loss of $1,500. The entry to record this transaction on the work sheet is as follows:

(8)

Resources Provided by Sale of Equipment	4,000	
Income before Extraordinary Item—Loss on Sale of Equipment	1,500	
Accumulated Depreciation—Equipment	2,500	
Equipment		8,000

The proceeds from the sale of the equipment provide working capital of $4,000. In addition, the loss on the sale of the equipment has reduced the income before extraordinary item, but has not affected working capital; therefore, it must be added back to income before extraordinary item to report accurately working capital provided by operations.

Depreciation on the equipment was reported at $11,500 and should be presented on the work sheet in the following manner:

(9)

Income before Extraordinary Item— Depreciation Expense	11,500	
Accumulated Depreciation—Equipment		11,500

The depreciation expense is added back to the income before extraordinary item because it reduced income but did not affect working capital.

Finally, a major repair to the equipment in the amount of $11,000 was charged to Accumulated Depreciation—Equipment. Because this expenditure required working capital, the following work sheet entry is made:

(10)

Accumulated Depreciation—Equipment	11,000	
Resources Applied to Major Repairs of Equipment		11,000

The balances in the equipment and related accumulated depreciation accounts are reconciled after adjustment for the foregoing items.

Other Nonworking Capital Charges or Credits   An analysis of the remaining accounts indicates that changes in the Accumulated Depreciation—Building, Goodwill, Premium on Bonds Payable, and Deferred Income Taxes balances resulted from charges or credits not affecting working capital. The following compound entry to the work sheet could be made for these nonworking capital, income-related items:

(11)

Income before Extraordinary Item—Depreciation Expense	3,100	
Income before Extraordinary Item—Amortization of Goodwill	2,400	
Income before Extraordinary Item—Deferred Income Taxes	3,000	
Premium on Bonds Payable	1,000	
Accumulated Depreciation—Buildings		3,100
Goodwill		2,400
Deferred Income Taxes		3,000
Income before Extraordinary Item—		
Bond Premium Amortization		1,000

Common Stock and Related Accounts   A comparison of the common stock balances and the additional paid-in capital balances shows that transactions during the year affected these accounts. First, a stock dividend of 2% was issued to stockholders. As indicated in the discussion of work sheet entry (2), no resources were provided or applied by the stock dividend transaction. In addition to the shares issued via the stock dividend, the Hanes Corporation sold shares of common stock at $16 per share. The work sheet entry to record this transaction is as follows:

(12)

Resources Provided by Sale of Common Stock	144,000	
Common Stock		9,000
Additional Paid-in Capital		135,000

Also, the company purchased shares of its common stock in the amount of $17,000. The work sheet entry to record this transaction is as follows:

(13)

Treasury Stock	17,000	
Resources Applied to Purchase of Treasury Stock		17,000

Final Summary Entry   The final entry to reconcile the change in working capital and to balance the work sheet is as follows:

(14)

Working Capital Summary	205,500	
Increase in Working Capital		205,500

The $205,500 amount is the difference between the beginning of the year and the end of the year working capital balance. That amount also appears on the schedule of working capital changes at the bottom of page 1071.

Once it has been determined that the differences between the beginning and ending balances per the work sheet columns have been accounted for, the reconciling transactions columns can be totaled, and they should balance. The statement of changes in financial position can be prepared entirely from the items and amounts that appear at the bottom of the work sheet in the form of "resources provided by" and "resources applied to." The difference between the resources provided and the resources applied should equal the change in working capital. This reconciliation provides evidence that the posting of the transactions during the period was performed accurately. However, the statement may still be incorrect if certain transactions were improperly analyzed.

Hanes Corporation
WORK SHEET FOR PREPARATION OF STATEMENT OF CHANGES IN FINANCIAL POSITION
For the Year Ended 1981

	Account Balance at End of 1980		Reconciling Transactions During 1981			Account Balance at End of 1981
			Debit		Credit	
Debits						
Working capital summary	$289,000	(14)	205,500			$494,500
Investments in stock of						
Porter Co. (equity method)	15,000	(4)	3,500			18,500
Land	82,000	(5)	60,000	(6)	10,500	131,500
Equipment	142,000	(7)	53,000	(8)	8,000	187,000
Buildings	262,000					262,000
Goodwill	10,000			(11)	2,400	7,600
Treasury stock	-0-	(13)	17,000			17,000
Total debits	$800,000					$1,118,100
Credits						
Accumulated depreciation—		(8)	2,500			
equipment	$ 31,000	(10)	11,000	(9)	11,500	29,000
Accumulated depreciation—						
buildings	71,000			(11)	3,100	74,100
Notes payable (long-term)	-0-			(5)	60,000	60,000
Bonds payable	100,000					100,000
Premium on bonds payable	8,000	(11)	1,000			7,000
Deferred income taxes	6,000			(11)	3,000	9,000
Common stock	50,000			(2)	1,000	
				(12)	9,000	60,000
Additional paid-in capital	38,000			(2)	14,000	
				(12)	135,000	187,000
Retained earnings	496,000	(2)	15,000			
		(3)	6,000	(1)	117,000	592,000
Total credits	$800,000		$374,500		$374,500	$1,118,100
Resources provided by Operations:						
Income before extraordinary item		(1)	109,000			
Equity in earnings of Porter Co.				(4)	3,500	
Loss on sale of equipment		(8)	1,500			Total
Depreciation expense—						resources
equipment		(9)	11,500			provided
Depreciation expense—						by
buildings		(11)	3,100			operations
Amortization of goodwill		(11)	2,400			$126,000
Deferred income taxes		(11)	3,000			
Amortization of bond premium				(11)	1,000	
Condemnation of land		(1)	8,000			
Condemnation of land		(6)	10,500			
Issuance of note payable to						
purchase land		(5)	60,000			
Sale of equipment		(8)	4,000			
Sale of common stock		(12)	144,000			

Resources applied to		
Payment of cash dividend	(3)	6,000
Purchase of land through issuance of note payable	(5)	60,000
Purchase of equipment	(7)	53,000
Major repairs of equipment	(10)	11,000
Purchase of treasury stock	(13)	17,000
Increase in working capital	(14)	205,500
$357,000		$357,000

Preparation of Statement   Presented below is a formal statement of changes in financial position. The schedule of working capital changes that appears on page 1071 may be incorporated into the statement by showing it at the bottom, or as a separate schedule accompanying the statement.

Hanes Corporation
STATEMENT OF CHANGES IN FINANCIAL POSITION
For the Year Ended December 31, 1981

Resources provided by		
Operations:		
Income before extraordinary item		$109,000
Add (or deduct) items not affecting working capital		
Equity in earnings of Porter Co.	$(3,500)	
Loss on sale of equipment	1,500	
Depreciation expense	14,600	
Amortization of goodwill	2,400	
Deferred income taxes	3,000	
Amortization of bond premium	(1,000)	17,000
Working capital provided by operations, exclusive of extraordinary item		126,000
Extraordinary item—Condemnation of land, including extraordinary gain of $8,000 (net of $2,500 tax)		18,500
Issuance of note payable to purchase land		60,000
Sale of equipment		4,000
Sale of common stock		144,000
Total resources provided		352,500
Resources applied to		
Cash dividends	6,000	
Purchase of land through issuance of note payable	60,000	
Purchase of equipment	53,000	
Major repairs of equipment	11,000	
Purchase of treasury stock	17,000	
Total resources applied		147,000
Increase in working capital		$205,500

The Tenneco Inc. financial statements on page 197 contain a comprehensive statement of changes in financial position prepared on a working capital basis. The example shown on page 1078 is taken from practice (Fairchild Camera and Instrument Corporation's 1978 Annual Report) and is almost identical in form and terminology to the illustrations in this chapter; study it carefully.

Fairchild Camera and Instrument Corporation and Subsidiaries

STATEMENT OF CHANGES IN FINANCIAL POSITION

	Year Ended	
	December 31, 1978	January 1, 1978
	(In thousands)	
Financial resources were provided by:		
Operations:		
Net income	**$24,764**	$11,162
Charges (credits) to income not affecting working capital:		
Depreciation and amortization	**22,708**	18,309
Deferred income taxes	**1,218**	2,111
Provision for employee benefits	**637**	1,645
Gain on disposition of fixed assets and security investments	**(2,308)**	(455)
Equity in undistributed earnings of joint venture	**—**	(592)
Financial resources provided by operations	**47,019**	32,180
Increase in common stock and additional paid-in capital	**591**	386
Proceeds from disposition of fixed assets and security investments	**6,697**	2,527
Increase in long-term debt:		
Financing of business acquisition	**3,689**	—
Capitalized lease obligations	**4,044**	792
Proceeds from long-term borrowings	**—**	7,071
Total financial resources provided	**62,040**	42,956
Financial resources were applied to:		
Expenditures for fixed assets, including capitalized leases	**29,472**	22,047
Cash dividends	**4,304**	4,292
Reduction of long-term debt	**10,092**	3,465
Long-term investments	**8,176**	5,842
Net noncurrent assets from business acquisitions	**7,586**	—
Other	**495**	(12)
Total financial resources applied	**60,125**	35,634
Increase in working capital	**$ 1,915**	$ 7,322
Changes in elements of working capital:		
Current assets—increase (decrease):		
Cash and temporary cash investments	**$16,207**	$16,143
Accounts and notes receivable	**22,847**	(9,560)
Inventories	**12,478**	(18,528)
Accumulated income tax prepayments	**1,071**	1,195
Prepaid expenses and other current assets	**(1,417)**	2,208
	51,186	(8,542)
Current liabilities—(increase) decrease:		
Notes payable to banks	**(10,685)**	4,806
Current installments of long-term debt	**(1,618)**	128
Accounts payable	**(8,368)**	1,888
Accruals—compensation, employee benefits and other	**(16,292)**	736
Estimated income taxes payable	**(12,308)**	8,306
	(49,271)	15,864
Increase in working capital	**$ 1,915**	$ 7,322

STATEMENT OF CHANGES IN FINANCIAL POSITION—CASH APPROACH

Although the working capital approach to preparing a statement of changes in financial position is most often employed for external reporting purposes, other approaches such as cash or cash and temporary investments are sometimes employed. For example, a statement of changes in financial position emphasizing a cash basis approach is useful to management and short-term creditors in assessing the enterprise's ability to meet cash operating needs. As Walter Wriston, chairman of the board of Citibank, recently noted, "Well, assets give you a warm feeling, but they don't generate cash. The first question I would ask any borrower these days is 'What is your breakeven cash flow?' That's the one thing we can't find out from your audit reports and it is the single most important question we ask."

Business managers and bankers are not the only parties interested in cash flow. **Investors and analysts are concerned that accrual accounting has become too far removed from the underlying cash flows of the enterprise.** They contend that accountants are using too many arbitrary allocation devices (deferred taxes, depreciation, amortization of intangibles, etc.) and are computing a net income figure that no longer provides an accurate assessment of the earning power of the enterprise. Because accounting statements take no cognizance of the inflation besetting the economy today, they look for a more concrete standard like cash flow to evaluate operating success or failure. And, in certain industries, such as real estate, the classification of assets into current and long-term has little meaning, so cash flow, not working capital, becomes the important resource to measure.

If the emphasis is on a statement of changes in financial position employing a cash basis approach, **changes in the elements of working capital (e.g., receivables, inventories, and payables) constitute sources and uses of cash and should be disclosed in appropriate detail in the body of the statement.**[6] This approach is different from the working capital approach, in which changes in working capital are reported separately in a tabulation accompanying the statement; the cash basis approach presents the cash provided by operations, not the working capital provided by operations.

Change from Accrual to Cash Basis

Adaptation to a cash basis approach from a working capital approach is relatively simple. Each working capital item is adjusted to show its effect on the income figure as if a cash basis instead of an accrual basis of income determination were employed. To illustrate, Hanes Corporation would make the conversion in the manner shown in the following schedule on page 1080.

---

[6]This statement, often called a cash flow statement, is sometimes prepared in the same manner as an income statement, indicating collections from customers minus related cash expenditures. This format is not illustrated because it is used infrequently in practice.

Hanes Corporation
SCHEDULE OF CHANGE FROM ACCRUAL TO CASH BASIS

Operations	Working Capital Provided	Cash Provided
Income before extraordinary item	$109,000	$109,000
Add items providing or not requiring working capital or cash		
Loss on sale of equipment	1,500	1,500
Depreciation expense	14,600	14,600
Amortization of goodwill	2,400	2,400
Deferred income taxes	3,000	3,000
Decrease in prepaid expenses		500
Increase in accounts payable		1,000
Increase in accrued liabilities		2,500
Deduct items requiring or not providing working capital or cash		
Equity in earnings of Porter Co.	(3,500)	(3,500)
Amortization of bond premium	(1,000)	(1,000)
Increase in accounts receivable (net)		(53,000)
Increase in inventories		(152,000)
Decrease in income taxes payable		(13,000)
Working capital and cash provided from operations, exclusive of extraordinary item	$126,000	$ (88,000)

Conversion to the cash basis of accounting requires that changes in each working capital item except cash be included along with nonworking capital items in the schedule.

Increase in Accounts Receivable (net)   When accounts receivable (net) increased during the current year, revenues on an accrual basis are higher than revenues on a cash basis, because goods sold on account are reported as revenues. To convert income on an accrual basis to income on a cash basis, the increase of $53,000 in accounts receivable must be deducted from income on an accrual basis.

Increase in Inventories   When inventory purchased exceeds inventory sold, cost of goods sold on an accrual basis is lower than cost of goods sold on a cash basis, because the cost of inventory on hand is deferred to the subsequent period. To convert income on an accrual basis to income on a cash basis, the increase of $152,000 in inventory must be deducted from income on an accrual basis.

Decrease in Prepaid Expenses   When prepaid expenses decrease during a period, expenses on an accrual basis income statement are higher than they are on a cash basis income statement, because prepaid expenses of a previous period have been amortized as a charge against current year's income. To convert income on an accrual basis to income on a cash basis, the decrease of $500 in prepaid expenses must be added to income on the accrual basis.

Increase in Accounts Payable and Accrued Liabilities   When accounts payable and accrued liabilities increase during a period, cost of goods sold and expenses on an accrual basis are higher than they are on a cash basis, because goods are purchased and expenses are incurred for which payment has not taken place. To convert income on an accrual basis to income on a cash basis, the increases of $1,000 in accounts payable and $2,500 in accrued liabilities must be added to income on the accrual basis.

Decrease in Income Taxes Payable   When income tax payable decreased during a period, expenses on an accrual basis are lower than expenses on a cash basis, because payment for income taxes exceeded the cost incurred for income taxes during the current period. To convert income on an accrual basis to income on a cash basis, the $13,000 decrease in income tax payable must be deducted from income on an accrual basis.

Hanes Corporation
STATEMENT OF CHANGES IN FINANCIAL POSITION (CASH BASIS)
For the Year Ended December 31, 1981

Resources provided by		
Operations:		
Income before extraordinary item		$109,000
Add (or deduct) items not affecting cash		
Equity in earnings of Porter Co.	$ (3,500)	
Loss on sale of equipment	1,500	
Depreciation expense	14,600	
Amortization of goodwill	2,400	
Deferred income taxes	3,000	
Amortization of bond premium	(1,000)	
Decrease in prepaid expenses	500	
Increase in accounts payable	1,000	
Increase in accrued liabilities	2,500	
Increase in accounts receivable (net)	(53,000)	
Increase in inventories	(152,000)	
Decrease in income taxes payable	(13,000)	(197,000)
Cash provided from operations, exclusive of extraordinary item		(88,000)
Extraordinary item—Condemnation of land, including extraordinary		
gain of $8,000 (net of $2,500 tax)		18,500
Issuance of note payable to purchase land		60,000
Sale of equipment		4,000
Sale of common stock		144,000
Total resources provided		138,500
Resources applied to		
Cash dividends	4,500	
Purchase of land through issuance of note payable	60,000	
Purchase of equipment	53,000	
Major repairs of equipment	11,000	
Purchase of treasury stock	17,000	
Total resources applied		145,500
Decrease in cash		$ 7,000

The increase in the dividends payable account is ignored in computing cash provided by operations. Because the dividend payable account increased $1,500, dividends must have been declared that have not been paid. As a result, only $4,500 (not $6,000) of dividends was paid and should be reported as a separate resource applied under the cash basis.

The statement of changes in financial position for Hanes Corporation emphasizing a cash basis approach is shown on page 1081.

A separate schedule of working capital changes is not needed when the cash concept is employed, because all the working capital changes are explained in the body of the statement. For illustration purposes, all working capital items, except for dividends payable, were assumed to affect operations. In certain situations, changes in working capital items might not affect operations. For example, changes in temporary investments and notes receivable and payable are items that may be presented in other parts of the statement.

Flexibility in Disclosure

The statement of changes in financial position has not been standardized in form and content to as great an extent as the balance sheet and income statement, except that certain major categories are normally included. The arrangement of items is usually kept flexible so that any significant changes that might develop in a particular year can be highlighted. Consequently many variations in content and form appear. Generally the statement is presented either in a balanced form (total sources equal applications) or in a form that highlights the change in working capital or cash.

APB Opinion No. 19 indicates that the statement may take the form that most usefully portrays the financing and investing aspects of the reporting entity. The opinion, however, specifies the following provisions:

1. A statement summarizing changes in financial position should be presented as a basic financial statement along with the balance sheet and statement of income.
2. The statement summarizing changes in financial position should be based on a broad concept embracing all changes in financial position (all financial resources).
3. The title to be used for summarizing changes in financial position is Statement of Changes in Financial Position.
4. The statement should prominently disclose working capital or cash provided from or used in operations for the period. Disclosure is considered most informative if the effect of extraordinary items is reported separately from the effects of ordinary items.
5. The statement should begin with income or loss before extraordinary items, if any, and add back (or deduct) items that did not use (or provide) working capital.
6. A schedule of changes in working capital should be in a tabulation accompanying the statement or in the statement itself.
7. Effects of financing and investing activities should be disclosed individually when material. For example, both outlays for acquisitions and proceeds from retirements of property should be reported; both long-term borrowings and repayments of long-term debt should be reported; and outlays for purchases of consolidated subsidiaries should be summarized by major assets obtained and obligations assumed.
8. Related items should be presented together where the result contributes to clarity. To illustrate, we might associate the retirement or sale of the old property with the purchase of new property. The proper approach is to deduct the proceeds from the sale of

the old property from the cost of the new. It is not considered proper to show the net amount, unless it is immaterial or unless it is part of a normal trade-in cycle to replace equipment.

Usefulness of Statement of Changes in Financial Position

Accountants have differing opinions about the best approach to follow in preparation of the statement of changes in financial position. Most favor the working capital approach that summarizes many of the transactions of the business into an increase or decrease in working capital. Others believe that a cash approach or some adaptation thereof is better because the users of financial statements are concerned with cash flows.[7] No matter which approach is adopted, it cannot be overemphasized that transactions such as the donation of land, bond conversions, and issuance of equity securities for property should still be disclosed to make the statement complete. Failure to disclose these transactions in the statement can mean that the statement does not adequately reflect the financing and investing activities of the enterprise.

Some of the many questions answered by a typical statement of changes in financial position are presented below:[8]

1. Where did the resources go?
2. Why were the dividends not larger?
3. How was it possible to distribute dividends in excess of current earnings or in the presence of a net loss for the period?
4. How did working capital increase even though there was a net loss for the period?
5. Why was money borrowed during the period?
6. How was the expansion in plant and equipment financed?
7. What happened to the proceeds from the sale of plant and equipment?
8. How was the retirement of debt accomplished?
9. What became of the assets derived from the increase in outstanding capital stock?
10. What became of the proceeds of the bond issue?
11. How was the increase in working capital financed?

These questions can be answered by a careful analysis of the statement of changes in financial position. Relationships that provide meaningful interpretations, such as the relation of resources generated internally to resources generated externally, can be developed. Related items, such as resources provided by operations to dividend distributions, can be analyzed.

---

[7]Recently the usefulness of the statement of changes in financial position has come under criticism. For example, one writer has recommended that the statement of changes in financial position as currently prepared should be discontinued and replaced with three required statements: a statement of cash receipts and payments, a statement of financing activities, and a statement of investing activities. See Lloyd C. Heath, *Accounting Research Monograph No. 3: Financial Reporting and the Evaluation of Solvency* (New York: AICPA, 1978). The FASB also has established a task force on fund flow analysis which suggests that new approaches to summarizing the investing and financing activities of an enterprise may be recommended. In addition, study groups are forming which are advocating a return to a more cash-oriented reporting system.

[8]Adapted from Perry Mason, "Cash Flow Analysis and the Funds Statement," *Accounting Research Study No. 2* (New York: AICPA, 1961).

Cash Flow From Operations

Opinion No. 19 also recommended that isolated statistics of cash flow and cash flow per share not be presented. The term *cash flow* is used by financial analysts to mean the total of the net income for the year plus or minus depreciation and other charges or credits to income not requiring current expenditures or cash receipts. In other words, it represents an amount that in the statement of changes in financial position is called "working capital provided by operations."

The so-called cash flow is usually calculated as follows:

Net income for the year	$30,000
Depreciation charged	8,000
Amortization of bond discount	3,000
"Cash flow"	$41,000

The amount of $41,000 is more accurately described as the working capital provided by operations and does not represent the net of cash received and disbursed, as the term "cash flow" seems to imply.

Most accountants generally agree that the term cash flow used in this manner is a misnomer: it is neither cash nor a flow. Preparation of the statement of changes in financial position emphasizing a cash approach requires making a great many adjustments, some of which are made in cash flow computations (e.g., depreciation), and some of which are not (e.g., increase or decrease in receivables and payables). Also, inflows and outflows such as those for debt expansion and debt repayment are ignored.

Often cash flow is divided by the number of shares outstanding to arrive at a cash flow per share or cash earnings per share, which is compared to earnings per share or to dividends per share. Some analysts believe that using cash flow per share instead of earnings per share helps to normalize the effect of the variances that occur because alternative accounting methods for capitalization and amortization of assets are used by different companies. The argument is that to obtain meaningful intercompany comparisons the factors that might be handled in alternative ways must be eliminated. To illustrate, assume that two firms in the same industry both earn revenue of $1,000, and incur labor and material costs of $600. Each firm has a delivery truck that costs $1,000 and has a useful life of 10 years. Firm A uses straight-line depreciation, and Firm B employs accelerated depreciation (double-declining method). Income statements for Firm A and Firm B for the first year the long-lived assets are used are presented at the top of page 1085.

For the year Firm A reports a net income of $150 and a cash flow of $250. Firm B reports a net income of $100 and a cash flow of $300. Some security analysts believe that the cash flow figure is a better measure for comparing the two firms for the period, because the cash flow offsets the variance in the depreciation charges that is allowed under generally accepted accounting principles. Firm A has the higher net income; Firm B has the higher cash flow. Analysts claim that a more rational investment decision can be made with this information than can be made if only the net income figure is presented.

Firm A			Firm B		
Revenue		$1,000	Revenue		$1,000
Costs			Costs		
Labor and material	600		Labor and material	600	
Depreciation	100	700	Depreciation	200	800
Income before taxes		300	Income before taxes		200
Income taxes 50%		150	Income taxes 50%		100
Net income		$ 150	Net income		$ 100
Cash flow		$ 250	Cash flow		$ 300

Cash flow data have certain limitations. First, **interindustry comparisons of cash flow data can be deceiving.** Cash flow comparisons do not measure the economic progress or efficiency of one firm in relation to another, because the enterprise that has the heaviest capital investment will normally have the highest cash flow. For example, cash flow cannot be used as a measure of comparability between a steel company and an electronics company.

Second, **interperiod comparisons of cash flow data also can be deceiving.** A firm is not necessarily in a better financial position in the current year than in the past year because its cash flow has increased.

The APB wisely recommended that isolated statistics of cash flow be avoided, particularly per share amounts. Cash flow is valid only in conjunction with the statement of changes in financial position to indicate the internal generation of resources; better terminology is "working capital provided by operations" or "resources provided by operations."

APPENDIX

The T-Account Approach to Preparation of the Statement of Changes in Financial Statements

Many accountants find the work sheet approach to preparing a statement of changes in financial position time-consuming and cumbersome. In some cases, the detail of a work sheet is not needed, and time does not permit for preparation of a work sheet. Therefore, the **T-account approach** for preparing a statement of changes in financial position has been devised. This procedure provides a quick and systematic method of accumulating the appropriate information to be presented in the formal statement of changes in financial position. The T-accounts used in this approach are not part of the general ledger or any other ledger; they are developed only for use in this process.

Illustration

To illustrate the T-account approach, we will use the information of the Hanes Corp. example presented on pages 1069–1075. When the T-account approach is employed, the net change in working capital for the period is computed by comparing the beginning and ending balances of the working capital accounts. After the net change is computed, a T-account for working capital is prepared and the net change in working capital is entered at the top of this account on the left if working capital increased, and on the right if it decreased (see illustration of T-account on page 1089). The T-account is then structured into four separate classifications: (1) Sources—Operations and (2) Sources—Other, both on the left; and (3) Applica-

ILLUSTRATION **1087**

tions—Operations and (4) Applications—Other, on the right. T-accounts are then set up for all nonworking capital items that have had activity during the period, with the net change entered at the top of each account. The objective of the T-account approach is to explain the net change in working capital through the various changes that have occurred in the nonworking capital accounts. The working capital T-account acts as a summarizing account. Most of the changes in the nonworking capital items are explained through the working capital account. Significant financial transactions that did not affect working capital are assumed to provide and apply working capital and are entered in this summary account to insure their inclusion in the final statement. To illustrate, a complete version of the T-account approach is presented on the following pages.

The following items caused the change in working capital (you should trace each entry to the accounts that are presented beginning on page 1089):

1. Net income for the period, comprised of income before extraordinary item of 109,000 and an extraordinary gain of $8,000 (net of tax), increased retained earnings $117,000. To avoid the detail of nonworking capital revenues and expenses, we employ a short-cut by starting with income before extraordinary item and then in subsequent entries adjust it to reflect resources provided by operations, exclusive of extraordinary item. In general journal form, the entry to report this increase and the extraordinary item would be:

Working Capital—Operations	109,000	
Working Capital—Other	8,000	
Retained Earnings		117,000

2. The retained earnings account also discloses stock dividends of $15,000. Because this transaction is not considered a significant investing or financing activity, the working capital account is not affected, and the following entry would be made:

Retained Earnings	15,000	
Common Stock		1,000
Additional Paid-in Capital		14,000

3. Further analysis of the retained earnings account indicates that a cash dividend of $6,000 was declared during the current period. The entry to record the transaction would be:

Retained Earnings	6,000	
Working Capital—Other		6,000

Note that the net change in the retained earnings balance of $96,000 is now reconciled. This reconciliation procedure is basic to the T-account approach because it insures that all appropriate transactions have been considered.

4. The equity in the earnings of Porter Co. must be subtracted from income before extraordinary item because this income item does not increase working capital. The journal entry to recognize this equity in the earnings of Porter Co. is as follows:

Investment in Stock of Porter Co.	3,500	
Working Capital—Operations		3,500

5. A note of $60,000 was issued to purchase land. Although this transaction did not affect working capital, it is a significant financial transaction that should be reported. The transaction is therefore assumed both to have increased working capital and to have decreased working capital in order to report this amount in the net working capital account. The following entry would be made:

Land	60,000	
Working Capital—Other		60,000
Working Capital—Other	60,000	
Note Payable		60,000

An alternative to this approach is simply to adjust the Land and Note Payable account, noting that in a formal preparation of a statement of changes in financial position, this transaction must be reported.

6. In addition, land with a book value of $10,500 was condemned. The entry to record this transaction is as follows:

Working Capital—Other	10,500	
Land		10,500

Note that adding the $10,500 book value of this condemnation to the $8,000 extraordinary gain net of $2,500 tax determined earlier provides total resources of $18,500 related to the condemnation.

7. Equipment and the related Accumulated Depreciation account indicate that a number of financial transactions affected these accounts. The first transaction is the purchase of equipment, which is recorded as follows:

Equipment	53,000	
Working Capital—Other		53,000

8. In addition, equipment with a book value of $5,500 was sold at a loss of $1,500. The entry to record this transaction is as follows:

Working Capital—Other	4,000	
Working Capital—Operations	1,500	
Accumulated Depreciation—Equipment	2,500	
Equipment		8,000

Note that the loss on the sale of the equipment has reduced the income before extraordinary item, but has not affected working capital. The loss must therefore be added back to income before extraordinary item to report accurately resources provided by operations.

9. Depreciation on the equipment of $11,500 must be recorded as follows:

Working Capital—Operations	11,500	
Accumulated Depreciation—Equipment		11,500

10. The major repair reduced working capital, so the necessary journal entry is as follows:

Accumulated Depreciation—Equipment	11,000	
Working Capital—Other		11,000

The equipment account and related accumulated depreciation account are now reconciled.

11. Analysis of the remaining accounts indicates changes in Accumulated Depreciation—Building, Premium on Bonds Payable, and Deferred Income Taxes that must be accounted for in determining the resources provided by operations, exclusive of extraordinary item. The entry to record these transactions is as follows:

ILLUSTRATION   **1089**

Working Capital—Operations	3,100	
Working Capital—Operations	2,400	
Working Capital—Operations	3,000	
Premium on Bonds Payable	1,000	
Accumulated Depreciation—Buildings		3,100
Goodwill		2,400
Deferred Income Taxes		3,000
Working Capital—Operations		1,000

12. Examination of the common stock account indicates that in addition to the stock dividend (transaction 2), common stock was issued at $16 per share. The entry to record this transaction is as follows:

Working Capital—Other	144,000	
Common Stock		9,000
Additional Paid-in Capital		135,000

13. The company also purchased treasury stock, which is recorded as follows:

Treasury Stock	17,000	
Working Capital—Other		17,000

After the entries above are posted to the appropriate accounts, the working capital account (shown below) is used as the basis for preparing the statement of changes in financial position. The debit side of the working capital account contains the resources provided and the credit side contains the resources applied. The difference between the two sides of the working capital account should reconcile to the increase or decrease in working capital. The completed statement of changes in financial position is presented on page 1077.

Working Capital

Increases		Decreases	
Net change	$205,500		
Sources—Operations:		Applications—Operations:	
1. Income before extraordinary item	109,000	4. Equity in earnings of Porter Co.	3,500
8. Loss on sale of equipment	1,500	11. Bond premium amortization	1,000
9. Depreciation expense	11,500		4,500
11. Depreciation expense	3,100		
11. Goodwill amortization	2,400		
11. Deferred income taxes	3,000		
	130,500		
Sources—Other:		Applications—Other:	
1. Condemnation of land	8,000	3. Cash dividends	6,000
2. Issuance of note	60,000	5. Purchase of land	60,000
6. Condemnation of land	10,500	7. Purchase of equipment	53,000
8. Sale of equipment	4,000	10. Major repair of equipment	11,000
12. Sale of common stock	144,000	13. Purchase of treasury stock	17,000
	226,500		147,000

Investment in Stock of Porter Co. (equity method)

Net change	$ 3,500		
4. Equity in earnings	3,500		

Land

Net change	$ 49,500		
5. Purchase of land	60,000	6. Condemnation	10,500

Equipment

Net change	$ 45,000		
7. Purchase	53,000	8. Sale of equipment	8,000

Accumulated Depreciation Equipment

Net change	$ 2,000		
8. Sale of equipment	2,500	9. Depreciation expense	11,500
10. Major repair	11,000		

Accumulated Depreciation—Buildings

		Net change	$ 3,100
		11. Depreciation expense	3,100

Goodwill

		Net change	$ 2,400
		11. Amortization of goodwill	2,400

Notes Payable

		Net change	$ 60,000
		5. Issuance of Note	60,000

Premium on Bonds Payable

Net change	$ 1,000		
11. Bond premium amortization	1,000		

Deferred Income Taxes

		Net change	$ 3,000
		11. Increase	3,000

Common Stock

		Net change	$ 10,000
		2. Stock dividend	1,000
		12. Sale of common stock	9,000

Additional Paid-In Capital

		Net change	$149,000
		2. Stock dividend	14,000
		12. Sale of common stock	135,000

Retained Earnings

		Net change	$ 96,000
2. Stock dividend	15,000	1. Net income	117,000
3. Cash dividend	6,000		

Treasury Stock

Net change	$ 17,000		
13. Purchase of treasury stock	17,000		

Summary of T-Account Approach

Short-cut approaches are often used with the T-account approach. For example, the journal entries may not be prepared because the transactions are obvious. Also, only the nonworking capital T-accounts that have a number of changes, such as Equipment, Accumulated Depreciation—Equipment, and Retained Earnings, need be presented in T-account form. Other more obvious changes in nonworking capital items can be simply determined by examining the comparative balance sheet and other related data. The T-account approach provides certain advantages over the work sheet method in that (1) a statement usually can be prepared much faster using the T-account method, and (2) the use of the T-account method helps in understanding the relationship between working capital and nonworking capital items. Conversely, the work sheet on highly complex problems provides a more orderly and systematic approach to preparing the statement of changes in financial position. In addition, in practice the work sheet is used extensively to insure that all items are properly accounted for.

The following steps are used in the T-account approach:

1. Determine the increase or decrease in working capital for the year.
2. Post the increase or decrease to the working capital T-account and establish four classifications within this account: Sources—Operations, Sources—Other, Applications—Operations, and Applications—Other.
3. Determine the increase or decrease in each nonworking capital account. Accounts that have no change can be ignored unless two transactions have occurred in the same account of the same amount, which is highly unlikely. A short-cut approach is to prepare T-accounts only for nonworking capital accounts that have a number of transactions. All other changes can be immediately posted to the working capital account after examining the additional information related to the changes in the balance sheet for a period.
4. Reconstruct entries in nonworking capital accounts and post them to the nonworking capital account affected and to the working capital T-account.
5. Using the postings from the working capital T-account, prepare the formal statement of changes in financial position.

One word of caution: the T-account approach will have to be modified if an all financial resources transaction occurs, such as the issuance of bonds to purchase a building. Although these transactions do not affect the working capital T-accounts directly, an assumption may be made that they affect working capital indirectly and can be reported in the working capital account as sources and uses. An alternative is simply to adjust the two accounts affected, remembering that these transactions must be reported on a formal statement of changes in financial position.

Questions

1. What is the purpose of the statement of changes in financial position? How does it differ from a balance sheet or income statement?
2. What are the common funds or approaches that are used as the basis in preparing a statement of changes in financial position? Which approach is recommended by **APB Opinion No. 19**? Why?
3. The following differences result from comparing the amounts in two successive balance sheets. Do the following items represent resources provided, resources applied, or neither?

	Differences		
	Debit	Credit	Explanation
(a) Long-term investment	$60,000		Bonds purchased
(b) Patents		$ 8,000	Amortization of patents
(c) Appropriation for plant expansion		30,000	Appropriation of retained earnings
(d) Common stock	15,000		Purchase of treasury stock
(e) Retained earnings	6,000		Net income of $10,000 and dividends of $16,000

4. The net income for the year for Saffian, Inc., is $150,000, but the statement of changes in financial position indicates that the resources provided by operations is $180,000. What might account for the difference?

5. Give three examples of financial transactions that would be omitted if a working capital concept not including all financial resources were used as the basis for preparing a statement of changes in financial position.

6. On a statement of changes in financial position, why is the amortization of prepaid expenses treated differently than the depreciation taken on a plant asset?

7. Give four examples of changes in the capital structure that do not appear on the statement of changes in financial position.

8. Give four examples of items added back to income before extraordinary items to arrive at working capital provided by operations.

9. Each of the following items must be considered in preparing a statement of changes in financial position for Rosenfield, Inc. for the year ended December 31, 1981. For each item state where it is to be shown in the statement, if at all.
   (a) Uncollectible accounts receivable in the amount of $6,000 were written off against the Allowance for Doubtful Accounts.
   (b) The company sustained a net loss for the year of $2,200. Depreciation amounted to $1,000 and patent amortization to $500.
   (c) Plant assets that had cost $10,000 six and a half years before and were being depreciated on a straight-line basis over 10 years with no estimated scrap value were sold for $3,000.
   (d) During the year 500 shares of common stock with a stated value of $30 a share were issued for $35 a share.

10. Farmer Enterprises has a net income for the year of $650,000. Included in this net income are: a gain on casualty (extraordinary item), net of tax of $60,000; depreciation expense of $130,000; and amortization of bond premium of $10,000. What amount should Farmer Enterprises report on its statement of changes in financial position for resources provided by operations, exclusive of extraordinary item?

11. Of what use is the statement of changes in financial position?

12. Mike Wallace, a student in intermediate accounting, decided that he would have no difficulty in preparing a statement of changes in financial position on the next exam if the problem were straightforward. He still, however, has difficulty understanding the following items. Explain how these items should be treated in a statement of changes in financial position.
   (a) Gain on the sale of marketable securities (current).
   (b) A common stock split.
   (c) The maturing portion of a long-term serial bond.
   (d) A long-term note given for the purchase of inventory.

13. Define the term "cash flow" from an accounting standpoint.

14. Discuss each of the following statements:
   (a) A large cash flow permits steady expansion and the regular payment of cash dividends.

(b) Cash flow provides a more significant indication of the results of a company's operations than does net income.

15. Why might a business concern use a statement of changes in financial position—cash approach? Does a separate schedule of working capital have to be included if a cash approach is adopted?

Cases

C24-1 Presented below is the financial statement related to the Holten Enterprises, Inc.:

Holten Enterprises, Inc.
STATEMENT SHOWING CAUSES
OF NET CHANGE IN WORKING CAPITAL

Funds were obtained from:		
Operations (net income transferred to retained earnings)		$180,001.73
Current assets used up in year's operations:		
Cash on hand and in banks	$34,427.12	
Postal stamps	20.00	34,447.12
Increase in common stock outstanding	10,000.00	
Increase in paid-in capital in excess of par	20,000.00	30,000.00
		$244,448.85
Funds were applied to:		
Payments of cash dividends		$ 35,442.00
Declaration of stock dividends (not yet issued)		27,400.00
Investment in additions to		
Accounts receivable—trade	$12,004.43	
Notes receivable—trade	2,500.00	
Inventories	101,442.21	
Marketable securities	10,440.00	
Cash surrender value of life insurance	1,141.25	
Fixed assets (net increase)	15,142.50	
Patents	20,000.00	
Prepaid expense	2,452.03	165,122.42
Payments of serial-bond maturities		10,000.00
Reduction in current liabilities		6,484.43
		$244,448.85

Instructions

You are to criticize the statement above, considering mainly its **function** and **content**. (There are differences of opinion concerning the general form of such a statement and the terminology used. You need not concern yourself with these matters in your criticism except where you believe them to be essential to the accomplishment of the statement's function.) Mention in your discussion specific items that the data supplied lead you to believe (1) may have been omitted incorrectly from the statement or (2) should have been excluded from the statement. For each item that you mention, give your reason for inclusion or deletion and state how you would treat the item. You need not prepare a revised statement.

C24-2 A. After considerable discussion and research in recent years concerning the reporting of changes in financial position (sources and applications of funds), **Accounting Principles Board Opinion No. 19** concluded:

. . . That the statement summarizing changes in financial position should be based on a broad concept embracing all changes in financial position and that the title of the statement should reflect this broad concept. The Board therefore recommends that the title be Statement of Changes in Financial Position.

Instructions

1. What are the two common meanings of "funds" as used when preparing the statement of changes in financial position? Explain.
2. What is meant by ". . . a broad concept embracing all changes in financial position . . ." as used by the Accounting Principles Board in its **Opinion No. 19**? Explain.

> B. Wilson Company is a young and growing producer of electronic measuring instruments and technical equipment. You have been retained by Wilson to advise it in the preparation of a statement of changes in financial position. For the fiscal year ended October 31, 1981, you have obtained the following information concerning certain events and transactions of Wilson.

1. A gain of $4,700 was realized on the sale of a machine; it originally cost $75,000, of which $25,000 was undepreciated on the date of sale.
2. On April 1, 1981, a freak flood caused an uninsured inventory loss of $93,000 ($180,000 loss, less reduction in income taxes of $87,000). This extraordinary loss was included in determining income as indicated in 6 below.
3. On July 3, 1981, building and land were purchased for $600,000; Wilson gave in payment $100,000 cash, $200,000 market value of its unissued common stock, and a $300,000 purchase-money mortgage.
4. On August 3, 1981, $800,000 face value of Wilson's 6% convertible debentures were converted into $140,000 par value of its common stock. The bonds were originally issued at face value.
5. The board of directors declared a $360,000 cash dividend on October 20, 1981, payable on November 18, 1981, to stockholders of record on November 5, 1981.
6. The amount of reported earnings for the fiscal year was $800,000, which included a deduction for an extraordinary loss of $93,000 (see item 2 above).
7. Depreciation expense of $300,000 was included in the earnings statement.
8. Uncollectible accounts receivable of $40,000 was written off against the allowance for doubtful accounts. Also, $43,000 of bad debts expense was included in determining income for the fiscal year, and the same amount was added to the allowance for doubtful accounts.

Instructions

Explain whether each of the 8 numbered items above is a source or use of working capital and explain how it should be disclosed in Wilson's statement of changes in financial position for the fiscal year ended October 31, 1981. If any item is neither a source nor a use of working capital, explain why it is **not** and indicate the disclosure, if any, that should be made of the item in Wilson's statement of changes in financial position for the fiscal year ended October 31, 1981.

C24-3 The following statement was prepared by the Notar Corporation's accountant:

The Notar Corporation
STATEMENT OF SOURCE AND APPLICATION OF FUNDS
For the Year Ended September 30, 1981

Source of funds	
Net income	$ 61,000
Depreciation and depletion	50,000
Increase in long-term debt	178,000
Common stock issued under employee option plans	5,000
Changes in current receivables and inventories, less current liabilities (excluding current maturities of long-term debt)	3,000
	$297,000

Application of funds	
Cash dividends	$ 33,000
Expenditures for property, plant, and equipment	202,000
Investments and other uses	9,000
Change in cash	53,000
	$297,000

The following additional information relating to the Notar Corporation is available for the year ended September 30, 1981:

1. The balance sheet of Notar Corporation distinguishes between current and noncurrent assets and liabilities.

2.
Depreciation expense	$ 48,000
Depletion expense	2,000
	$ 50,000

3.
Increase in long-term debt	$600,000
Retirement of debt	422,000
Net increase	$178,000

4. The corporation received $5,000 in cash from its employees on its employee stock option plans, and wage and salary expense attributable to the option plans was an additional $22,000.

5.
Expenditures for property, plant, and equipment	$212,000
Proceeds from retirements of property, plant, and equipment	10,000
Net expenditures	$202,000

6. A stock dividend of 10,000 shares of Notar Corporation common stock was distributed to common stockholders on April 1, 1981, when the per-share market price was $6 and par value was $1.

7. On July 1, 1981, when its market price was $5 per share, 16,000 shares of Notar Corporation common stock were issued in exchange for 4,000 shares of preferred stock.

Instructions

(a) In general, what are the objectives of a statement of the type shown above for the Notar Corporation? Explain.

(b) Identify the weaknesses in the form and format of the Notar Corporation's Statement of Changes in Financial Position without reference to the additional information.

(c) For each of the seven items of additional information for the Statement of Changes in Financial Position indicate the preferable treatment and explain why the suggested treatment is preferable.

(AICPA adapted)

Exercises

E24-1 Condensed financial data of the Casio Company for the years ended December 31, 1980 and December 31, 1981, are presented below:

Casio Company
COMPARATIVE POSITION STATEMENT DATA
as of December 31, 1980 and 1981

	1980	1981
Cash	$ 18,400	$124,800
Receivables, net	49,000	83,200
Inventories	61,900	92,500
Investments	100,000	90,000
Plant assets	220,000	240,000
	$449,300	$630,500
Accounts payable	$ 67,300	$100,000
Mortgage payable	73,500	50,000
Accumulated depreciation	50,000	30,000
Common stock	125,000	175,000
Retained earnings	133,500	275,500
	$449,300	$630,500

Casio Company
INCOME STATEMENT
For the Year Ended December 31, 1981

Sales	$320,000	
Interest and other revenue	20,000	$340,000
Less:		
Cost of goods sold	130,000	
Selling and administrative expenses	10,000	
Depreciation	22,000	
Income taxes	5,000	
Interest charges	3,000	
Loss on sale of plant assets	8,000	178,000
Net income		162,000
Dividends		20,000
Income retained in business		$142,000

Additional information:

New plant assets costing $80,000 were purchased during the year. Investments were sold at book value.

Instructions

From the foregoing information, prepare a statement of changes in financial position (working capital approach).

E24-2 Duke and Eden are equal partners in a service enterprise. Duke withdraws from the partnership at the end of 1981, terminating the partnership. Below you are given comparative financial data and other pertinent information.

	Dec. 31, 1980	Dec. 31, 1981	Increase or (Decrease)
Cash	$ 6,800	$ 7,400	$ 600
Receivables	7,800	10,300	2,500
Allowance for doubtful accounts	(900)	(1,000)	100
Marketable securities	5,000	5,000	—

Prepaid expenses	1,300	1,100	(200)
Land	10,000	10,000	—
Building and equipment	32,600	35,600	3,000
Accumulated depreciation	(3,800)	(5,300)	1,500
	$58,800	$63,100	
Accounts payable	$ 3,000	$ 2,600	(400)
Notes payable (short-term)	1,500	1,000	(500)
Accrued expenses	1,500	1,800	300
Mortgage payable	22,500	20,000	(2,500)
Duke, capital	19,200	22,500	3,300
Eden, capital	11,100	15,200	4,100
	$58,800	$63,100	

1. Equipment for $3,000 was purchased in 1981.
2. At the time of the termination, Duke makes withdrawals totaling $3,500; Eden has withdrawn $4,000.

Instructions

Prepare a statement of changes in financial position (working capital approach) for the year 1981.

E24-3 Comparative adjusted trial balances for Hershey, Inc., are presented below:

Hershey, Inc.
ADJUSTED TRIAL BALANCE

	Dec. 31, 1980		Dec. 31, 1981	
	Dr.	Cr.	Dr.	Cr.
Cash	$ 6,500		$ 8,200	
Marketable securities	20,000		22,000	
Receivables (net)	60,000		66,800	
Inventories	64,000		72,000	
Delivery equipment	30,000		33,500	
Accumulated depreciation—delivery equipment		$ 17,000		$ 21,000
Machinery	15,000		17,500	
Accumulated depreciation—machinery		8,500		10,500
Building	55,000		55,000	
Accumulated depreciation—buildings		7,000		15,000
Land	15,000		15,000	
Accounts payable		47,000		43,000
Accrued expenses		8,000		9,500
Long-term notes payable		10,000		5,000
Bonds payable		50,000		50,000
Common stock		65,000		65,000
Retained earnings		38,000		53,000
Sales		299,000		330,000
Cost of goods sold	220,000		245,000	
Operating expenses	48,000		51,000	
Income taxes	16,000		16,000	
	$549,500	$549,500	$602,000	$602,000

Instructions

Using the information above, prepare a statement of changes in financial position (working capital approach).

E24-4   Joe Kline, an ex-wrestler, now runs a gymnasium. The following information is presented to you for analysis.

Joe Kline, Inc.
CONDENSED COMPARATIVE BALANCE SHEET

	Dec. 31, 1980	Dec. 31, 1981
Net working capital	$10,300	$ 37,400
Athletic equipment	35,000	42,000
Accumulated depreciation—athletic equipment	(10,000)	(15,000)
Furniture	12,500	15,000
Accumulated depreciation—furniture	(4,000)	(7,000)
Building	27,000	57,000
Accumulated depreciation—building	(2,000)	(3,000)
Long-term investments (future building site)	29,200	34,200
	$98,000	$160,600
Long-term note payable	$ -0-	$ 1,200
Common stock ($10 par)	40,000	80,000
Premium on common stock	-0-	400
Retained earnings	58,000	79,000
	$98,000	$160,600

1. Athletic equipment that cost $14,000 and that has accumulated depreciation of $2,000, was sold for book value.
2. A piece of new athletic equipment that had a book value of $2,000 was discarded because of obsolescence.
3. No dividends were declared or paid.
4. An addition to the building was financed through the issuance of common stock at par $30,000.
5. All gains and losses resulting from transactions are found on the income statement.
6. Net income for 1981 was $21,000.

Instructions

Prepare a statement of changes in financial position (working capital approach) for 1981. A separate schedule of working capital changes is not required.

E24-5   Presented below are data taken from the records of the Healy Company.

	December 31, 1980	December 31, 1981
Current assets	$ 40,000	$ 80,000
Long-term investments	60,000	10,000
Plant assets	240,000	396,000
	$340,000	$486,000
Accumulated depreciation	$ 40,000	$ 30,000
Current liabilities	30,000	35,000
Bonds payable	-0-	100,000
Capital stock	250,000	250,000
Donated capital	-0-	36,000
Retained earnings	20,000	35,000
	$340,000	$486,000

1. Securities carried at a cost of $50,000 on December 31, 1980, were sold during 1981 for $40,000. The loss (not extraordinary) was incorrectly charged directly to Retained Earnings.
2. Plant assets which cost $50,000 and were 60% depreciated were sold during the year for $10,000. The loss (not extraordinary) was incorrectly charged directly to Retained Earnings.
3. Net income as reported on the income statement for the year was $50,000.
4. Dividends paid amounted to $15,000.
5. Depreciation charged for the year was $20,000.
6. Land was donated to Healy Company by the city. The land was worth $36,000. (Assume credit to Donated Capital is correct.)

Instructions

Prepare a statement of changes in financial position (working capital concept). No schedule of working capital changes is required.

E24-6 Comparative balance sheets at December 31, 1980 and 1981, for the Haas Company follow.

	1980	1981
Cash	$ 50,000	$ 54,000
Receivables	68,000	60,000
Inventory	112,000	110,000
Prepaid expenses	8,000	9,000
Plant assets	217,000	312,000
Accumulated depreciation	(63,000)	(86,000)
Patents	41,000	35,000
	$433,000	$494,000
Accounts payable	$ 83,000	$ 75,000
Taxes payable	65,000	70,000
Mortgage payable	100,000	—
Preferred stock	—	150,000
Additional paid-in capital—preferred	—	4,000
Common stock	150,000	150,000
Retained earnings	35,000	45,000
	$433,000	$494,000

1. The only entries in the Retained Earnings account are for dividends paid in the amount of $18,000 and for the net income for the year.
2. The income statement for 1981 is as follows:

Sales	$130,000
Cost of sales	94,000
Gross profit	36,000
Operating expenses	8,000
Net income	$ 28,000

3. The only entry in the Accumulated Depreciation account is the depreciation expense for the period.

Instructions

(a) From the information above, prepare a statement of changes in financial position (working capital approach).

(b) From the information above, prepare a statement of changes in financial position (cash approach).

E24-7   Neal, Inc., had the following condensed balance sheet at the end of operations for 1980.

Neal, Inc.
BALANCE SHEET
December 31, 1980

Current assets	$ 37,500	Current liabilities	$ 15,000
Investments	20,000	Long-term notes payable	25,500
Plant assets (net)	67,500	Bonds payable	25,000
Land	40,000	Capital stock	75,000
		Retained earnings	24,500
	$165,000		$165,000

During 1981 the following occurred:

1. A tract of land was purchased for $6,000.
2. Bonds payable in the amount of $5,000 were retired at par.
3. An additional $10,000 in capital stock was issued at par.
4. Dividends totaling $7,500 were paid to stockholders.
5. Net income for 1981 was $21,000 after allowing depreciation of $9,000.
6. Land was purchased through the issuance of $18,000 in bonds.
7. Neal, Inc., sold part of its investment portfolio for $10,300. This transaction resulted in a gain of $300 for the firm. The company often sells and buys securities of this nature.

Instructions

(a) Prepare a statement of changes in financial position for 1981. A supporting schedule of working capital changes need not be prepared.

(b) Prepare the condensed balance sheet for Neal, Inc., as it would appear at December 31, 1981. Assume that current liabilities remained at $15,000.

E24-8   The accounts below appear in the ledger of the Shank Company.

Machinery		Dr.	Cr.	Bal.
Jan. 1, 1981	Debit Balance			$100,000
Aug. 3	Purchases of Machinery	$30,000		130,000
Sept. 10	Cost of Machinery Constructed	20,000		150,000
Nov. 15	Machinery Sold		$40,000	110,000

Accumulated Depreciation—Machinery		Dr.	Cr.	Bal.
Jan. 1, 1981	Credit Balance			$ 60,000
Apr. 8	Extraordinary Repairs	$15,000		45,000
Nov. 15	Accum. Depreciation of Machinery Sold	18,000		27,000
Dec. 31	Depreciation for 1981		$ 8,000	35,000

Retained Earnings		Dr.	Cr.	Bal.
Jan. 1, 1981	Credit Balance			$ 30,000
Aug. 15	Dividends (cash)	$14,000		16,000
Dec. 31	Net Income for 1981		$ 9,000	25,000

Instructions

From the information given, prepare all adjustments that should be made on a work sheet for a statement of changes in financial position (working capital concept). The loss on sale of equipment (Nov. 15) was $9,000.

E24-9 Presented below is some information related to Hugh's International:

1. Some old office equipment was traded in on the purchase of some dissimilar office equipment and the following entry was made:

Office Equipment	2,500	
Accum. Depreciation—Office Equipment	1,500	
Office Equipment		2,000
Cash		1,700
Gain on Disposal of Plant Assets		300

The Gain on Disposal of Plant Assets was credited to current operations as ordinary income.

2. Dividends in the amount of $12,000, payable in cash, were declared near the end of the year, and an entry was made to record them. They are payable in January of next year.
3. The Appropriations for Bonded Indebtedness in the amount of $120,000 was returned to Retained Earnings during the year, because the bonds were retired during the year.
4. Convertible bonds payable of a par value of $200,000 were exchanged for unissued common stock of a par value of $200,000. The market price of both types of securities was par.
5. The net income for the year was $30,000.
6. Depreciation charged on the building was $8,000.
7. Organization costs in the amount of $5,000 was written off during the year as a charge to income.

Instructions

Show by journal entries the adjustments that would be made on a work sheet for a statement of changes in financial position.

E24-10 Below is the comparative balance sheet for the East Towne Corporation.

	Dec. 31, 1980	Dec. 31, 1981
Cash	$ 13,000	$ 15,500
Short-term investments	20,000	25,000
Accounts receivable	45,000	43,000
Allowance for doubtful accounts	(2,000)	(1,800)
Prepaid expenses	2,500	3,200
Inventories	65,000	73,000
Land	50,000	50,000
Buildings	75,000	100,000
Accumulated depreciation—buildings	(20,000)	(30,000)
Equipment	48,000	53,000
Accumulated depreciation—equipment	(16,000)	(19,000)
Delivery equipment	39,000	39,000
Accumulated depreciation—delivery equipment	(20,000)	(24,000)
Patents	-0-	10,000
	$299,500	$336,900

Accounts payable	$ 21,000	$ 26,000
Short-term notes payable	6,000	4,000
Accrued payables	5,000	3,000
Mortgage payable	50,000	65,000
Bonds payable	60,000	50,000
Capital stock	100,000	110,000
Additional paid-in capital	4,000	5,500
Retained earnings	53,500	73,400
	$299,500	$336,900

Dividends in the amount of $5,000 were declared and paid in 1981.

Instructions

From this information, prepare a work sheet for a statement of changes in financial position (working capital approach). Make reasonable assumptions as appropriate. Do not prepare a schedule of working capital changes.

E24-11   Presented below is information related to Winjum, Inc. for the years 1980 and 1981 to aid in preparing a statement of changes in financial position (cash concept).

Winjum, Inc.
BALANCE SHEETS

	December 31,	
Assets	1981	1980
Current assets:		
Cash	$ 150,000	$100,000
Marketable securities	40,000	
Accounts receivable—net	430,000	290,000
Merchandise inventory	330,000	210,000
Prepaid expenses	50,000	25,000
	1,000,000	625,000
Property, plant and equipment	565,000	300,000
Less accumulated depreciation	55,000	25,000
	510,000	275,000
	$1,510,000	$900,000
Equities		
Current liabilities:		
Accounts payable	$ 265,000	$220,000
Accrued expenses	70,000	65,000
Dividends payable	35,000	
	370,000	285,000
Note payable—due 1984	250,000	
Stockholders' equity:		
Common stock	600,000	450,000
Retained earnings	290,000	165,000
	890,000	615,000
	$1,510,000	$900,000

Winjum, Inc.
INCOME STATEMENTS

	Year Ended December 31,	
	1981	1980
Net sales—including service charges	$3,200,000	$2,000,000
Cost of goods sold	2,500,000	1,600,000
Gross profit	700,000	400,000
Expenses (including income taxes)	500,000	260,000
Net income	$ 200,000	$ 140,000

Additional information available included the following:

Although Winjum will report all changes in financial position, management has adopted a format emphasizing the flow of cash.

All accounts receivable and accounts payable relate to trade merchandise. Cash discounts are not allowed to customers but a service charge is added to an account for late payment. Accounts payable are recorded net and always are paid to take all of the discount allowed. The Allowance for Doubtful Accounts at the end of 1981 was the same as at the end of 1980; no receivables were charged against the Allowance during 1981.

The proceeds from the note payable were used to finance a new store building. Capital stock was sold to provide additional working capital.

Instructions

Compute the following for the year 1981:

(a) Cash collected from accounts receivable, assuming that all sales are on account.

(b) Cash payments made on accounts payable to suppliers, assuming that all purchases of inventory are on account.

(c) Cash dividend payment.

(d) Cash receipts which were not provided by operations.

(e) Cash payments for assets which were not reflected in operations.

E24-12 Delkamp, Inc., has recently decided to go public and has hired you as the independent CPA. One statement that the enterprise is anxious to have prepared is a statement of changes in financial position. Financial statements of Delkamp, Inc., for 1980 and 1981 are provided below.

COMPARATIVE BALANCE SHEETS

	12/31/80		12/31/81	
Cash		$ 16,000		$ 21,000
Accounts receivable		12,000		33,000
Merchandise inventory		34,000		22,000
Property, plant, and equipment	$80,000		$60,000	
Less accumulated depreciation	(26,000)	54,000	(22,000)	38,000
		$116,000		$114,000
Accounts payable		26,000		30,000
Federal income taxes payable		30,000		25,000
Bonds payable		30,000		35,000
Common stock		15,000		6,000
Retained earnings		15,000		18,000
		$116,000		$114,000

INCOME STATEMENT
For the Year Ended December 31, 1981

Sales		$220,000
Cost of sales		180,000
Gross profit		40,000
Selling expenses	$ 18,000	
Administrative expenses	6,000	24,000
Income from operations		16,000
Interest expense		5,000
Income before taxes		11,000
Income taxes		2,000
Net income		$ 9,000

The following additional data were provided:

1. Dividends for the year 1981 were $3,000.
2. During the year equipment was sold for $10,000. This equipment cost $20,000 originally and had a book value of $13,000 at the time of sale. The loss on sale was incorrectly charged to retained earnings.
3. All depreciation expense is in the selling expense category.

Instructions

(a) Prepare a statement of changes in financial position using a working capital approach.

(b) Prepare a statement of changes in financial position emphasizing a cash approach (often called the cash flow statement). All sales and purchases are on account.

E24-13 Covaleski Co. reported $180,000 of net income for 1981. The accountant, in preparing the statement of changes in financial position on a working capital basis, noted several items which might offset working capital provided by operations. These items are listed below:

1. Depreciation expense for 1981 is $20,000.
2. Covaleski Co. holds 40% of the Miller Company's common stock as a long-term investment. Miller Company reported $10,000 of net income for 1981.
3. Miller Company paid a total of $2,000 of cash dividends in 1981.
4. A comparison of Covaleski's December 31, 1980 and December 31, 1981 balance sheets indicates that the credit balance in Deferred Income Taxes (classified as a long-term liability) decreased $3,000.
5. During 1981, Covaleski declared a 10% stock dividend. One thousand shares of $10 par common stock were distributed. The market price at date of issuance was $20 per share.
6. During 1981, Covaleski purchased 100 shares of treasury stock at a cost of $20 per share. These shares were then resold at $25 per share.
7. During 1981, Covaleski sold 100 shares of IBM common at $250 per share. Acquisition cost of these shares was $150 per share. This investment was shown on Covaleski's December 31, 1980 balance sheet as a current asset.
8. During 1981, Covaleski changed from the straight-line method to the double-declining balance method of depreciation for its machinery. The debit to the Cumulative Effect account was for $16,000 net of tax.
9. During 1981, Covaleski revised its estimate for bad debts. Before 1981, Covaleski's bad debts expense was 1% of its net sales. In 1981, this percentage was increased to 1½%. Net sales for 1981 were $500,000.
10. During 1981, Covaleski issued 500 shares of its $10 par common stock for a patent. The market value of the shares on the date of the transaction was $23 per share.

Instructions

Prepare a schedule that shows working capital provided by operations.

E24-14 Each of the following items must be considered in preparing a statement of changes in financial position for Robin Shore Company for the year ended December 31, 1981.

1. An Appropriation for Contingencies in the amount of $30,000 was created by a charge against Retained Earnings.
2. Uncollectible accounts receivable in the amount of $2,000 were written off against the Allowance for Doubtful Accounts.
3. Investments that cost $12,000 when purchased four years earlier were sold for $10,500. The loss was considered ordinary.
4. Bonds payable with a par value of $24,000 on which there was unamortized bond premium of $1,800 were redeemed at 101. The gain was credited to income.
5. Fixed assets that had cost $10,000 six and one-half years before and were being depreciated on a 10-year basis with no estimated scrap value were sold for $3,000.
6. During the year, goodwill of $100,000 was completely written off against net income.
7. During the year, 500 shares of common capital stock with a stated value of $25 a share were issued for $30 a share.
8. The company sustained a net loss for the year of $1,800. Depreciation amounted to $900 and patent amortization was $400.

Instructions

For each item, state first where it is to be shown in the statement and then illustrate how you would present the necessary information, including the amount. Consider each item to be independent of the others. Assume that correct entries were made for all transactions as they took place.

E24-15 The president of a small factory has come to you for advice. The bookkeeper indicates that each year the business has been just about breaking even. In addition, the inventories, receivables, and payables have not varied much since the corporation was organized 10 years ago but that cash has been constantly increasing. The president thinks that the business has been making money and that there is an error. The president stated that there has been no sale of assets, refinancing of indebtedness, or change in corporate structure such as sale of stock.

Instructions

(a) Present briefly the **explanation** that you would give the president for the continued increase in cash.
(b) Give examples of transactions that illustrate your explanation.
(c) What financial statements would you prepare for the president?

Problems

P24-1 The following schedule showing **net** changes in balance-sheet accounts at December 31, 1981, compared to December 31, 1980, was prepared from the records of The Sodium Company. The statement of changes in financial position for the year ended December 31, 1981, has not yet been prepared.

Assets	Net Change Increase (Decrease)
Cash	$ 50,000
Accounts receivable, net	76,000
Inventories	37,000
Prepaid expenses	1,000
Property, plant and equipment, net	64,000
Total assets	$228,000

Liabilities

Accounts payable	$ (55,500)
Notes payable—current	(15,000)
Accrued expenses	33,000
Bonds payable	(28,000)
Less decrease in unamortized bond discount	1,200
Total liabilities	(64,300)

Stockholders' Equity

Common stock, $10 par value	500,000
Capital contributed in excess of par value	200,000
Retained earnings	(437,700)
Appropriation of retained earnings for possible future inventory price decline	30,000
Total stockholders' equity	292,300
Total liabilities and stockholders' equity	$228,000

Additional Information:

1. The net income for the year ended December 31, 1981, was $172,300. There were no extraordinary items.

2. During the year ended December 31, 1981, uncollectible accounts receivable of $26,400 were written off by a charge to allowance for doubtful accounts.

3. A comparison of property, plant and equipment as of the end of each year follows:

	December 31,		Net Increase (Decrease)
	1981	1980	
Property, plant and equipment	$570,500	$510,000	$60,500
Less: Accumulated depreciation	224,500	228,000	(3,500)
Property, plant and equipment, net	$346,000	$282,000	$64,000

During 1981, machinery was purchased at a cost of $45,000. In addition, machinery that was acquired in 1974 at a cost of $48,000 was sold for $3,600. At the date of sale, the machinery had an undepreciated cost of $4,200. The remaining increase in property, plant and equipment resulted from the acquisition of a tract of land for a new plant site.

4. The bonds payable mature at the rate of $28,000 every year.

5. In January 1981, the Company issued an additional 10,000 shares of its common stock at $14 per share upon the exercise of outstanding stock options held by key employees. In May 1981 (market price $14), the Company declared and issued a 5% stock dividend on its outstanding stock. During the year, a cash dividend was paid on the common stock. On December 31, 1981, there were 840,000 shares of common stock outstanding.

6. The appropriation of retained earnings for possible future inventory price decline was provided by a charge against retained earnings, in anticipation of an expected future drop in the market related to goods in inventory.

Instructions

(a) Prepare a statement of changes in financial position for the year ended December 31, 1981, based upon the information presented above. The statement should be prepared using a **working capital format.**

(b) Prepare a schedule of changes in working capital for the year 1981.

(AICPA adapted)

P24-2 The comparative balance sheets for Shapiro Corporation show the following information:

	December 31	
	1981	1980
Cash	$ 38,500	$ 4,000
Accounts receivable	12,000	9,000
Inventory	12,000	10,000
Investments	—	2,000
Building	—	25,000
Equipment	50,000	40,000
Patent	5,000	6,000
Totals	$117,500	$96,000
Allowance for doubtful accounts	$ 3,000	$ 4,000
Accumulated depreciation on equipment	2,000	5,000
Accumulated depreciation on building	—	10,000
Accounts payable	5,000	3,000
Dividends payable	—	7,000
Notes payable, short-term (nontrade)	3,000	4,000
Long-term notes payable	36,000	25,000
Common stock	38,000	34,000
Retained earnings	30,500	4,000
	$117,500	$96,000

Additional data related to 1981 are as follows:

1. Investments (long-term) were sold at $3,000 (net of tax) above their cost. The company has made similar sales and investments in the past.
2. Cash of $5,000 was paid for the acquisition of equipment.
3. A long-term note for $15,000 was issued for the acquisition of equipment.
4. Equipment which had cost $10,000 and was 50% depreciated at time of disposal was sold for $2,500 (net of tax).
5. $4,000 of the long-term note payable was paid by issuing common stock.
6. The only cash dividends paid were $7,000.
7. On January 1, 1981 the building was completely destroyed by a flood. Insurance proceeds on the building were $25,000 (net of tax).

Instructions

Prepare a statement of changes in financial position (working capital approach). No work sheet or schedule of working capital changes is required: Flood damage is unusual and infrequent in that part of the country.

P24-3 You have completed the field work in connection with your audit of the Nording Corporation for the year ended December 31, 1981. The following schedule shows the balance sheet accounts at the beginning and end of the year:

	Dec. 31, 1981	Dec. 31, 1980	Increase or (Decrease)
Cash	$ 282,400	$ 320,000	$ (37,600)
Accounts receivable	490,000	410,000	80,000
Inventory	695,000	660,000	35,000
Prepaid expenses	10,000	8,000	2,000
Investment in subsidiary	106,000	—	106,000
Cash surrender value of life insurance	2,100	1,800	300
Machinery	186,600	190,000	(3,400)

Buildings	566,500	507,500	59,000
Land	52,500	52,500	—
Patents	71,000	60,000	11,000
Goodwill	40,000	50,000	(10,000)
Bond discount and expense	4,680	—	4,680
	$2,506,780	$2,259,800	$ 246,980

	Dec. 31, 1981	Dec. 31, 1980	Increase or (Decrease)
Accrued taxes payable	$ 92,000	$ 80,000	$ 12,000
Accounts payable	301,280	280,000	21,280
Dividends payable	60,000	—	60,000
Bonds payable—8%	125,000	—	125,000
Bonds payable—12%	—	100,000	(100,000)
Allowance for doubtful accounts	45,300	40,000	5,300
Accumulated depreciation—building	407,000	400,000	7,000
Accumulated depreciation—machinery	141,000	130,000	11,000
Premium on bonds payable	—	1,600	(1,600)
Capital stock—no par	1,301,200	1,453,200	(152,000)
Additional paid-in capital	14,000	—	14,000
Appropriation for plant expansion	10,000	—	10,000
Retained earnings—unappropriated	10,000	(225,000)	235,000
	$2,506,780	$2,259,800	$ 246,980

STATEMENT OF RETAINED EARNINGS

January	1, 1981	Balance (deficit)	$(225,000)
March	31, 1981	Net income for first quarter of 1981	25,000
April	1, 1981	Transfer from paid-in capital	200,000
		Balance	0
December 31, 1981		Net income for last three quarters of 1981	80,000
		Dividend declared—payable January 20, 1982	(60,000)
		Appropriation for plant expansion	(10,000)
		Balance	$ 10,000

Your working papers contain the following information:

1. On April 1, 1981, the existing deficit was written off against capital stock created by reducing the stated value of the no-par stock.

2. On November 1, 1981, 8,000 shares of no-par stock were sold for $62,000. The board of directors voted to regard $6 per share as stated capital.

3. A patent was purchased for $16,000.

4. Machinery was purchased for $4,600 and installed in December, 1981. A check for this amount was sent to the vendor in January, 1982.

5. During the year, machinery that had a cost basis of $8,000 and on which there was accumulated depreciation of $5,000 was sold for $1,000. No other plant assets were sold during the year.

6. The 12%, 20-year bonds were dated and issued on January 2, 1969. Interest was payable on June 30 and December 31. They were sold originally at 104. These bonds were retired at 101 (net of tax) plus accrued interest on March 31, 1981.

7. The 8%, 40-year bonds were dated January 1, 1981, and were sold on March 31 at 97 plus accrued interest. Interest is payable semi-anually on June 30 and December 31. Expense of issuance was $1,020.

8. The Nording Corporation acquired 80% control in the Subsidiary Company on January 2, 1981, for $100,000. The income statement of the Subsidiary Company for 1981, shows a net income of $7,500.

9. Extraordinary repairs to buildings of $7,000 were charged to Accumulated Depreciation—Building.

Instructions

From the information above prepare a statement of changes in financial position (working capital approach). A work sheet is **not** necessary, but the principal computations should be supported by schedules or skeleton ledger accounts.

P24-4 The manager of Kapnick Manufacturing Company has reviewed the annual financial statements for the year 1981 and is unable to determine from a reading of the balance sheet the reasons for the changes in working capital during the year. You are presented the following balance sheets of Kapnick Manufacturing Company.

	12/31/81	12/31/80	Increase (Decrease)
Land	$ 140,000	$ 150,000	$ (10,000)
Machinery	330,000	200,000	130,000
Tools	40,000	70,000	(30,000)
Bond investment	18,000	15,000	3,000
Inventories	210,000	218,000	(8,000)
Goodwill	-0-	200,000	(200,000)
Buildings	810,000	560,000	250,000
Accounts receivable	180,000	92,000	88,000
Notes receivable—trade	21,000	27,000	(6,000)
Cash in bank	-0-	8,000	(8,000)
Cash on hand	2,000	1,000	1,000
Unexpired insurance—machinery	1,200	1,400	(200)
Unamortized bond discount	2,100	2,500	(400)
	$1,754,300	$1,544,900	$ 209,400
Capital stock ($100 par)	$ 700,000	$ 400,000	$ 300,000
Bonds payable	150,000	100,000	50,000
Accounts payable	58,000	52,000	6,000
Bank overdraft	4,000	-0-	4,000
Notes payable—trade	9,000	10,000	(1,000)
Bank loans—short term	5,500	6,800	(1,300)
Accrued interest	10,000	6,000	4,000
Accrued taxes	5,000	3,000	2,000
Allowance for doubtful accounts	4,500	2,300	2,200
Accumulated depreciation	271,200	181,000	90,200
Retained earnings	537,100	783,800	(246,700)
	$1,754,300	$1,544,900	$ 209,400

You are advised that the following transactions took place during the year:

1. The income statement for the year 1981 was:

Sales (net)		$1,250,000
Operating charges:		
Material and supplies	$250,000	
Direct labor	210,000	
Manufacturing overhead	181,500	
Depreciation	123,500	
Selling expenses	245,000	
General expenses	230,000	
Interest expense (net)	7,500	

Unusual items:

Write-off of goodwill	230,000	
Write-off of land	10,000	
Loss on machinery	1,200	1,488,700
Net loss		$ 238,700

2. A 2% cash dividend was declared and paid on the outstanding capital stock at 1/1/81.
3. There were no purchases or sales of tools. The cost of tools used is in depreciation.
4. Stock was sold during the year at $90; the discount was charged to Goodwill.
5. Old machinery that cost $4,500 was scrapped and written off the books. Accumulated depreciation on such equipment was $3,300.

Instructions

(a) Prepare a statement of changes in financial position using a working capital approach.
(b) Prepare a statement of changes in financial position using a cash basis approach. Assume that the bank loan—short term and bank overdraft were related to transactions involving the purchase of materials and supplies. All sales and purchases of inventory are made on account.

P24-5   The balance sheet of the Rose Company at December 31, 1980, is as follows:

Rose Company
BALANCE SHEET
December 31, 1980

Cash			$ 42,000
Receivables			108,000
Inventories			214,000
Prepaid expenses			28,000
Total current assets			392,000
Investments (long-term)			84,000
Land		$ 45,000	
Buildings	$570,000		
Less accum. depreciation	110,000	460,000	
Equipment	385,000		
Less accum. depreciation	180,000	205,000	710,000
Patents			122,000
			$1,308,000
Accounts payable			$ 85,000
Notes payable			120,000
Taxes payable			188,000
Total current liabilities			393,000
Bonds payable			500,000
Preferred stock		$200,000	
Common stock		200,000	
Retained earnings		15,000	415,000
			$1,308,000

The Rose Company's management predicts the following transactions for the coming year:

	4,300,000	
Sales (accrual basis)		$4,400,000
Payments for salaries, purchases, interest, taxes, etc. (cash basis)		(4,078,000)
Decrease in prepaid expenses		5,000
Increase in receivables		100,000
Increase in inventories		32,000
Depreciation:		
— Buildings		30,000
— Equipment		50,000
Patent amortization		10,000
Increase in accounts payable		20,000
Increase in taxes payable		90,000
Reduction in bonds payable		500,000
Sales of investments (all those held 12/31/80)		100,000
Issuance of common stock at par		200,000

Instructions

(a) Prepare a balance sheet as it will appear December 31, 1981, if all the anticipated transactions work out as expected.

(b) Prepare a statement of changes in financial position (working capital approach) for 1981, assuming that the expected 1981 transactions are all completed. Assume that the sale of investments is not an extraordinary item.

(c) Prepare a statement of changes in financial position (cash approach) for 1981, assuming that the expected 1981 transactions are all completed.

P24-6 The following financial data were furnished to you by the Everett Corporation:

1. A six-months note payable for $50,000 was issued toward the purchase of new equipment.
2. The long-term note payable requires the payment of $20,000 per year plus interest until paid.
3. Treasury stock was sold for $1,000 more than its cost.
4. All dividends were paid by cash.
5. All purchases and sales were on account.
6. The sinking fund will be used to retire the long-term bonds.
7. Equipment with an original cost of $15,000 was sold for $7,000.
8. Selling and General Expenses includes the following expenses:

Expired insurance	$ 2,000
Building depreciation	3,750
Equipment depreciation	19,250
Bad debts expense	4,000
Interest expense	18,000

Everett Corporation
COMPARATIVE TRIAL BALANCES
At Beginning and End of Fiscal Year Ended October 31, 1981

	October 31 1981	Increase	Decrease	November 1 1980
Cash	$ 226,000	$176,000		$ 50,000
Accounts receivable	148,000	48,000		100,000
Inventories	291,000		$ 9,000	300,000
Unexpired insurance	2,500	500		2,000
Long-term investments at cost	10,000		30,000	40,000
Sinking fund	90,000	10,000		80,000

Land and building	195,000			195,000
Equipment	215,000	125,000		90,000
Discount on bonds payable	8,500		500	9,000
Treasury stock at cost	5,000		5,000	10,000
Cost of goods sold	539,000			
Selling and general expenses	287,000			
Income tax	32,000			
Loss on sale of equipment	1,000			
Capital gains tax	3,000			
Total debits	$2,053,000			$876,000
Allowance for doubtful accounts	$ 8,000	$ 3,000		$ 5,000
Accumulated depreciation—building	26,250	3,750		22,500
Accumulated depreciation—equipment	39,750	12,250		27,500
Accounts payable	55,000		5,000	60,000
Notes payable—current	70,000	50,000		20,000
Accrued expenses payable	18,000	3,000		15,000
Taxes payable	35,000	25,000		10,000
Unearned revenue	1,000		8,000	9,000
Note payable—long-term	40,000		20,000	60,000
Bonds payable—long-term	250,000			250,000
Common stock	300,000	100,000		200,000
Appropriation for sinking fund	90,000	10,000		80,000
Unappropriated retained earnings	94,000		18,000	112,000
Paid-in capital in excess of par value	116,000	111,000		5,000
Sales	898,000			
Gain on sale of investments (ordinary)	12,000			
Total credits	$2,053,000			$876,000

Instructions

(a) Prepare schedules computing
   1. Collections of accounts receivable.
   2. Payments of accounts payable.

(b) Prepare a statement of changes in financial position—cash approach (sometimes called a cash flow statement) for Everett Corporation. Supporting computations should be in good form.

(AICPA adapted)

P24-7 Todd Company has prepared its financial statements for the year ended December 31, 1980, and for the three months ended March 31, 1981. You have been asked to prepare a statement of changes in financial position on a working capital basis for the three months ended March 31, 1981. The company's balance sheet data at December 31, 1980, and March 31, 1981, and its income statement data for the three months ended March 31, 1981, follow. You have previously satisfied yourself as to the correctness of the amounts presented.

Balance Sheet

	December 31, 1980	March 31, 1981
Cash	$ 25,300	$ 87,400
Marketable investments	16,500	7,300
Accounts receivable, net	24,320	49,320
Inventory	31,090	48,590
Total current assets	97,210	192,610
Land	40,000	18,700
Building	250,000	250,000
Equipment	—	81,500
Accumulated depreciation	(15,000)	(16,250)
Investment in 30%-owned company	61,220	67,100
Other assets	15,100	15,100
Total	$448,530	$608,760
Accounts payable	$ 21,220	$ 17,330
Dividend payable	—	8,000
Income taxes payable	—	34,616
Total current liabilities	21,220	59,946
Other liabilities	186,000	186,000
Bonds payable	50,000	115,000
Discount on bonds payable	(2,300)	(2,150)
Deferred income taxes	510	846
Preferred stock	30,000	—
Common stock	80,000	110,000
Dividends declared	—	(8,000)
Retained earnings	83,100	147,118
Total	$448,530	$608,760

	Income Statement Data for the Three Months Ended March 31, 1981
Sales	$242,807
Gain on sale of marketable investments	2,400
Equity in earnings of 30%-owned company	5,880
Gain on condemnation of land (extraordinary)	10,700
	$261,787
Cost of sales	$138,407
General and administrative expenses	22,010
Depreciation	1,250
Interest expense	1,150
Income taxes	34,952
	197,769
Net income	$ 64,018

Your discussion with the company's controller and a review of the financial records have revealed the following information:

1. On January 8, 1981, the company sold marketable securities for cash.

2. The company's preferred stock is convertible into common stock at a rate of one share of preferred for two shares of common. The preferred stock and common stock have par values of $2 and $1, respectively.

3. On January 17, 1981, three acres of land were condemned. An award of $32,000 in cash was received on March 22, 1981. Purchase of additional land as a replacement is not contemplated by the company. (Treated as a capital gain for tax purposes.)

4. On March 25, 1981, the company purchased equipment for cash.

5. On March 29, 1981, bonds payable were issued by the company at par for cash.

6. The company's tax rate is 40% for regular income and 20% for capital gains.

Instructions

Prepare in good form a statement of changes in financial position, including any supporting schedules needed, on a working capital basis for Todd Company for the three months ended March 31, 1981.

(AICPA adapted)

P24-8 This question concerns the various interrelationships among financial statements, accounts (or groups of accounts) among those statements, and accounts (or groups of accounts) within each statement. The following information is presented for Ross Company for the year ended December 31, 1981: (1) The Statement of Changes in Financial Position; (2) Selected information from the Income Statement; (3) Selected information regarding the January 1 and December 31 Balance Sheets; (4) Information regarding the correction of an error; (5) Partially completed Balance Sheets at January 1 (prior to restatement) and December 31. The omitted account and groups-of-account balances are numbered from (1) through (16) and can be calculated from the other information given.

STATEMENT OF CHANGES IN FINANCIAL POSITION

Working capital, January 1, 1981		$16,500
Add resources provided:		
Operations:		
Net loss for 1981	$(2,885)	
Adjustments not involving working capital:		
Bond premium amortization	(500)	
Deferred income taxes	(200)	
Depreciation expense	3,000	
Goodwill amortization for 1981	2,000	
Total from operations	1,415	
Portion of proceeds of equipment sold		
representing undepreciated cost	10,000	
Proceeds from reissue of treasury stock	11,400	
Par value of common stock issued to		
reacquire preferred stock	7,500	
Total resources provided	30,315	
Subtract resources applied:		
Purchase of land	14,715	
Current maturity of long-term bond debt	7,200	
Par value of preferred stock reacquired by		
issuing common stock	7,500	
Total resources applied	29,415	
Increase in working capital		900
Working capital, December 31, 1981		$17,400

Information from the Income Statement

Bad debt expense		$750
Bond interest expense (net of amortization of bond premium)		$ 3,500
Loss before tax adjustment		$(3,900)
Less:		
Income tax adjustment (refund due)	$815	
Deferred income taxes	200	1,015
Net loss after tax adjustment		$(2,885)

Information Regarding January 1 and December 31 Balance Sheets

The book value of the equipment sold was two-thirds of the cost of that equipment.

Selected Ratios

	January 1, 1981	December 31, 1981
	(prior to restatement)	
Current ratio	4 to 1 ?	3 to 1
Total stockholders' equity divided by total liabilities	4 to 3	?

Information Regarding the Correction of an Error

Ross Company had neglected to amortize $2,000 of goodwill in 1980. The correction of this material error has been appropriately made in 1981.

BALANCE SHEET

	January 1, 1981	December 31, 1981
	(prior to restatement)	
Current assets	$ 22,000	$ (5) 26,100 ✓ X
Building and equipment	92,000	(6) 77,000 ✓ ✓
Accumulated depreciation	(25,000)	(7) (23,000) ✓ X
Land	39,000 (1)	(8) 53,715 ✓ X
Goodwill	12,000	(9) 8000 ✓ X
Total assets	149,000 $ (?)	$ (?) 141,815 X
Current liabilities	5500 $ (2)	$ (10) 8,700 ✓ X
Bonds payable (8%)	50,000 (3)	(11) 42,800 ✓
Bond premium	2600 (?)	(12) 2800 ✓
Deferred income taxes	1900 (4)	1,700
Common stock	66,000	(13) 73,500 ✓
Paid-in capital	13,000	(14) 15,400 ✓
Preferred stock	16,000	(15) 8,500 ✓
Retained earnings (deficit)	(6,000)	(16) (0,885) ✓
Treasury stock (at cost)	(9,000)	0
Total liabilities and stockholders' equity	140,000 $ (?)	$ (?) 141,815

Instructions

Compute the correct balance for each balance sheet account or group of accounts that are shown as a question mark(?) Do not restate the January 1 balance sheet for the error.

Financial Reporting and
Changing Prices

It has often been said that only two things in life are certain—death and taxes. However, a third could probably now be added—inflation, that is, the value of every currency in the world steadily decreases. For example, during the decade of the 1970s, the compound annual inflation rate (the average) was 6.7% in the United States, 9% in France, 13.2% in Great Britain, 15% in Mexico, 28.3% in Brazil, 117.2% in Argentina, and 163.6% in Chile. Each of these increases in prices has been accompanied with a comparable decrease in the value of that country's currency.

In the United States prior to 1970 it was easy to ignore inflation's impact because the changes from year to year were considered insignificant. With the general price-level doubling between 1970 and 1980, this is no longer the case. In fact, as the diagram on page 1117 illustrates, we have been experiencing a significant decline in the purchasing power of the U.S. dollar over the period 1949–1978 when the rate of inflation is compounded. The effects of this phenomenon are substantial. Many companies are experiencing liquidity problems, even though they are reporting record net income figures, because they lack the necessary funds to replace their inventories and productive capacity. As one study recently noted, some companies (such as U.S. Steel and Jos. Schlitz Brewing) are paying out dividends in excess of net income after the income has been adjusted for price-level changes.[1]

As a consequence, the accounting and financial world is presented with challenges, decisions, and opportunities. Events and circumstances are causing accountants and others to be receptive to imaginative proposals for improvements in financial reporting. A difficult yet exciting and extensive experimental and educational process lies ahead. Before we have consensus on which changes to make and

[1]Mary Greenebaum, "How Securities Analysts are Adjusting to Inflation," *Fortune*, July 30, 1979, p. 112.

which new approaches to adopt, all of the parties concerned need to understand the alternatives and grasp what the new information is intended to portray. Such is the purpose of this chapter.

INFLATION IN THE UNITED STATES
(Based on Consumer Price Index)

Year	Consumer Price Index 1967 = 100[a]	Purchasing Power of Dollar 1979 = $1.00	Rate of Inflation[c]
945	53.9	$3.92	2.6%
946	58.5	3.61	8.6
947	66.9	3.16	14.2
948	72.1	2.93	7.8
949	71.4	2.96	(1.0)
950	72.1	2.93	1.0
951	77.8	2.72	7.9
952	79.5	2.66	2.2
953	80.1	2.64	.8
954	80.5	2.62	.5
955	80.2	2.63	(.3)
956	81.4	2.60	1.5
957	84.3	2.51	3.6
958	86.6	2.44	2.7
959	87.3	2.42	.8
960	88.7	2.38	1.6
961	89.6	2.36	1.0
962	90.6	2.33	1.1
963	91.7	2.30	1.2
964	92.9	2.27	1.3
965	94.5	2.24	1.7
966	97.2	2.17	2.9
967	100.0	2.11	2.9
968	104.2	2.03	4.2
969	109.8	1.92	5.4
970	116.3	1.82	5.9
971	121.3	1.74	3.7
972	125.3	1.69	3.3
973	133.1	1.59	6.2
974	147.4	1.43	10.7
975	161.2	1.31	9.4
976	170.5	1.24	5.7
977	181.5	1.16	6.4
978	195.4	1.08	7.7
979	211.2[b]	1.00 (Estimated)	8.1

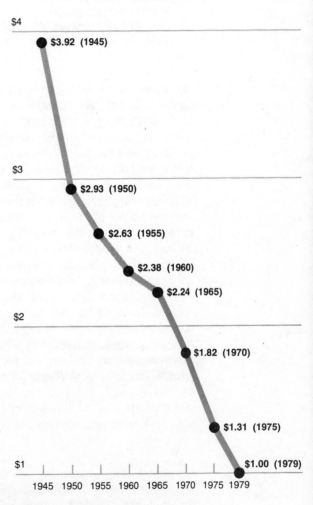

DECLINE IN THE PURCHASING POWER
OF THE DOLLAR
(Based on the Consumer Price Index)

$4 — $3.92 (1945)

$3 — $2.93 (1950) $2.63 (1955) $2.38 (1960) $2.24 (1965)

$2 — $1.82 (1970)

$1 — $1.31 (1975) $1.00 (1979)

1945 1950 1955 1960 1965 1970 1975 1979

Source: Handbook on Basic Economic Statistics, Bureau of Economic Statistics, Inc., Economic Statistics Bureau of ashington, D.C., April 1979, Vol. XXXIII, No. 4.
Estimated. Source: *Business Forecasts—1979,* Federal Reserve Bank of Richmond, p. 4.

$$\text{Rate of Inflation} = \frac{\text{Purch. Power of } \$_{t-1} - \text{Purch. Power of } \$_t}{\text{Purch. Power of } \$_t}$$

Alternative Financial Reporting Approaches

As indicated in Chapter 2, a long-standing principle of accounting holds that trans-actions should be recorded at historical cost. However, many accountants are unhappy with the present reporting model, noting that historical cost financial statements have severe limitations. Criticism is especially strong when one per-ceives the effects of double-digit inflation in the United States in 1974 and 1979. At such times cost is no longer adequate because the cost figures of a year ago are not comparable to current cost levels. To meet these criticisms, three different solu-tions have been offered.

1. **Constant dollar accounting**—Change the measuring unit but retain the historical cost reporting model.
2. **Current value accounting**—Retain the measuring unit but depart from the historical cost reporting model.
3. **Current value/constant dollar accounting**—Change the measuring unit and depart from the historical cost reporting model.

Constant Dollar Accounting (General Price-Level Model)   A dollar is valued in terms of its ability to purchase "a number of items in general," or more appropri-ately, its "purchasing power." If a dollar today cannot buy the same bundle of goods that a dollar bought a number of years ago, then inflation has occurred. This phenomenon has great relevance to accountants because we assume that our mea-suring unit (the dollar) is stable; unfortunately, the truth is that our measuring unit changes, and as it changes, distortions develop.

Those who advocate the adjustment of accounting data for changes in the pur-chasing power of the dollar, referred to as **constant dollar accounting** or **general price-level accounting,** ask the question: Is it possible to add 1960 dollars, 1972 dollars, and 1980 dollars and arrive at any meaningful sum because of the differ-ences in their purchasing power? Adding 20,000, 1960 dollars, with 30,000, 1972 dollars and 40,000, 1980 dollars may total 90,000 dollars, but the sum may have no more economic significance than the addition of 20,000 U.S. dollars to 30,000 French francs and 40,000 German marks for a total of 90,000 monetary units. The monetary units are just not equivalent.

Constant dollar accounting is historical cost data adjusted for changes in the unit of measurement. The advantages of this approach are that it is simple to compute, objective in nature, and easy to understand. If general price-level fluctuations are extreme enough to make cost data less useful than desired, financial statements adjusted for general price-level changes can be prepared from the historical cost data and used together with, or in place of, the cost-based statements.

Current Value Accounting   A second approach called current value accounting abandons historical cost as a basis for financial statements and shifts to some mea-sure of current value. Proponents of this approach argue that the problem is not with the unit of measure but rather with the historical cost model.

Their position is that users of financial statements are primarily interested in what the business is worth now, rather than what costs were incurred at some point in the past. Their argument is based on the notion of economic asset value, which conceptually is the present value of the future receipts from the particular asset in question.

Recognizing the practical problems of determining the present value of future cash flows, many contend that any objective approximation of economic value is more useful to financial statement readers than are historical cost figures. For many assets, current value figures are available on an objective basis, and it is argued that they are sufficiently close approximations to economic value to be useful. Investments in stocks and bonds quoted on a securities exchange, for example, provide current value information of obvious objectivity. Various staple commodities are also quoted on an open market price basis, and these prices could be used for valuing inventories. Some contend that there is a second-hand market for machinery and equipment sufficient to provide objective prices for many of these items. Where there are no quoted market prices, appraisals or specific index numbers may be used. Thus, for many assets an approximation of current value is available.

Current Value/Constant Dollar Accounting   A third group contends that both the unit of measurement and the historical cost model should be changed. As two writers noted in discussing constant dollar accounting: "We feel that the modification is a necessary one, but hope that the doctor, having cured the hangnail, does not fail to diagnose the pneumonia."[2] Advocates of this approach argue that the unit of measurement must be standardized (else we are using "a rubber ruler" in measuring dollars) and that after standardization some form of current value accounting should be employed. Only under this combined approach will the effects of real changes in enterprise wealth and earning power be determined.[3]

Professional Pronouncements

In 1963, the AICPA published **Accounting Research Study No. 6,** "Reporting the Financial Effects of Price-Level Changes," which recommended that constant dollar accounting information be reported on a supplemental basis.[4] Subsequently, the APB in 1969 noted that "general price-level adjusted financial statements present useful information that is not available from historical dollar statements" and therefore encouraged their use. However, the Board indicated that general price-level information was not required for fair presentation of financial position and results of operations.[5]

---

[2]Edgar O. Edwards and Philip W. Bell, *The Theory and Measurement of Business Income* (Berkeley: University of California Press, 1961), p. 16.

[3]For discussion that supports this approach, see Robert R. Sterling, "Relevant Financial Reporting in a Period of Changing Prices," *Journal of Accountancy*, February, 1975.

[4]Staff of the Accounting Research Division, "Reporting the Financial Effects of Price-Level Changes," *Accounting Research Study No. 6* (New York: AICPA, 1963).

[5]"Financial Statements Restated for General Price-Level Changes," *APB Statement No. 3* (New York: AICPA, 1969).

Owing to the relatively high rate of inflation experienced worldwide during the seventies and the expectation of continued significant inflation, several other countries have also undertaken studies to find better ways to report financial position, earning power, and cash flows. In May 1974 the Accounting Standards Steering Committee in the United Kingdom issued a proposal for constant dollar financial statements. It was followed in December 1974 by the Financial Accounting Standards Board in the United States and the Institute of Chartered Accountants in Australia, both of whom similarly proposed adoption of financial reporting in units of general purchasing power.[6] The Canadian Institute of Chartered Accountants issued a similar proposal in July 1975.

Just when it appeared that the business world was about to adopt constant dollar accounting, several fast-moving developments occurred. The Institute of Chartered Accountants in Australia in June 1975 took a different tack in a second proposal. It suggested a current-value approach to the valuation of assets in the balance sheet and a profit measurement based on matching revenue and expense, both expressed in current cost. Then in 1976, the Securities and Exchange Commission issued **ASR No. 190,** which required a modified form of current value accounting. Large publicly held companies were required to disclose the cost of replacing inventories and plant and equipment and to show what their cost of goods sold and depreciation expense would be if computed on a current replacement cost basis.[7]

Upon issuance of **ASR No. 190,** the FASB began to reevaluate its position concerning accounting for price-level changes. Many believed that it was important for the Board to take decisive action in this area, for otherwise the entire standard setting related to this issue would be developed by the SEC. In 1979 the FASB issued **Statement No. 33,** "Financial Reporting and Changing Prices," which requires certain large, publicly held enterprises to disclose supplementary information on both a constant dollar basis and a current cost basis.[8] In order to encourage experimentation in the development of techniques for accumulating, reporting, and analyzing data on the effects of price changes, the requirements of **Statement No. 33** are more flexible than is customary in Board statements.

CONSTANT DOLLAR ACCOUNTING

In addition to being a medium of exchange, the dollar has a "real" value that is determined by the amount of goods and services for which it can be exchanged. **This real value is commonly called purchasing power.** As the economy experiences periods of inflation (rising price levels) or deflation (declining price levels), the amount of goods and services for which a dollar can be exchanged changes; that is, the purchasing power of the dollar changes from one time period to the next.

For example, in 1969 ten gallons of regular gasoline cost $3.48. In 1979, ten gallons of regular gasoline cost approximately $9.68. Similarly, ten years ago the

---

[6]"Financial Reporting in Units of General Purchasing Power," *Exposure Draft* (Stamford, Conn.: FASB, 1974).

[7]"Disclosure of Certain Replacement Cost Data," *Accounting Series Release No. 190* (Washington: SEC, 1976). The requirement applies only to listed companies with inventories and gross plant aggregating more than $100 million and amounting to more than 10% of their total assets.

[8]"Financial Reporting and Changing Prices," *Statement of Financial Accounting Standards No. 33* (Stamford, Conn.: FASB, 1979).

median price of a new house was $25,000; today it is $64,000. Changes in the prices of gasoline and houses are examples of changes in the prices of specific items. The aggregation of specific prices at any particular time constitutes a **general price level.** A general price level change recognizes the change in the value of money in all its uses (often referred to as **general inflation**).

Fortunately, the need to measure purchasing power is neither new nor restricted to accounting. Various agencies of the United States government, like those of many foreign countries, publish indexes designed to measure changes in the general price level. When such indexes provide acceptable measures of general price-level changes, they can be used in accounting to adjust historical costs for changes in general purchasing power.

Measuring General Price-Level Changes

A price index is a weighted-average relation between money and a given set of goods and services. Constructing a price index that measures the change in purchasing power of the dollar is a complex problem; it involves the exercise of judgment in accumulating and appraising data.

It is fair to say, however, that the general indexes now available are reasonably useful to most persons and business managers as gauges of the change in the purchasing power of the dollar. The more widely used indexes of price change that are computed regularly by agencies of the U.S. government are:

1. The Gross National Product Implicit Price Deflator (GNP Deflator).
2. The Consumer Price Index for all Urban Consumers (CPI-U).
3. The Wholesale Price Index.
4. The Composite Construction Cost Index.
5. The 22 Commodity Spot Price Index.

The CPI-U reflects the average change in the retail prices of a fairly broad but select "basket" of consumer goods. It has been the most popular index because it is reported monthly (as opposed to the quarterly publication of the GNP Deflator) and it is not revised after its initial publication. As a result, **the FASB requires that the index used in constant dollar accounting be the CPI-U.**[9]

Restatement in Common Dollars

The procedure for restating the dollars of varying purchasing power reported in historical cost financial statements in dollars of current purchasing power is mathematically a simple, although sometimes time-consuming, process. The restatement (frequently called translation or conversion) is accomplished by multiplying the amount to be restated by a fraction, the numerator of which is the index for current prices and the denominator of which is the index for prices that prevailed at the date related to the amount being restated. For example, the cost of an asset acquired for $1,000 on June 30, 1970, is restated in terms of December 31, 1980, dollars as follows:

[9]*Ibid.*, par. 39.

$$\frac{1980 \text{ index}}{1970 \text{ index}} \times \$1000 = \text{cost of asset in terms of 1980 dollars}$$

Technically, the index at date of acquisition, June 30, 1970, should be used for the denominator. Because daily price-level indexes are not available, the average index for 1970 may be used. The average annual index may be used with satisfactory results in the absence of rampant inflation or deflation and, particularly, in the initial restatement when price-level adjustments are being made for the first time, a large number of amounts are to be adjusted, and the amounts to be restated are several years removed.

To further illustrate the method of restating historical dollars to current dollars, assume the following facts relative to acquired assets and the preparation of financial statements in 1980:

Year	Acquisition Cost	CPI-U Price Index
1959	$10,000	87
1967	$10,000	99
1974	$10,000	140
1980	$10,000	225 (Estimated)

To express all of these acquisition costs in terms of one year's prices, say 1980, the restatement process to restate all dollars to the dollar in existence in 1980 is:

1959	$10,000 × 225/87, or	$25,862
1967	10,000 × 225/99, or	22,727
1974	10,000 × 225/140, or	16,071
1980	10,000 × 225/225, or	10,000
	Total in terms of 1980 dollars	$74,660

Thus, the total acquisition cost of the assets, $40,000, is modified on a constant dollar basis to $74,660 in terms of year 1980 dollars.

Monetary and Nonmonetary Classifications

In preparing constant dollar financial statements, it is essential to distinguish between (1) the amounts that are by their nature already stated in current dollars and, therefore, require no restatement, and (2) the amounts that require restatement in order to be stated in terms of current dollars. The former are classified as **monetary items,** the latter as **nonmonetary items.**

Monetary assets include cash, contractual claims to a fixed amount of cash in the future, such as accounts and notes receivable, and investments that pay a fixed amount of interest or dividends and will be repaid at a fixed amount in the future (the date of repayment, however, need not be specified—as for an investment in preferred stock). **Monetary liabilities** include accounts and notes payable, accruals such as wages and interest payable, and long-term obligations payable in a fixed sum (including preferred stockholders' equity).

All assets and liabilities not classified as monetary items are classified as "nonmonetary" for constant dollar accounting purposes. **Nonmonetary assets** are the items whose prices in terms of the monetary unit may change over time: for example, inventories, investments in common stocks, property, plant and equipment, and deferred charges that represent costs expended in the past. **Nonmonetary liabilities** are obligations to provide given amounts of goods and services or an equivalent amount of purchasing power (even though the payment may be in the form of cash): for example, advances received on sales contracts, liabilities for rent collected in advance, and deferred credits that represent reductions of prior expense.

The importance of distinguishing between monetary and nonmonetary items in reporting the impact of changing price levels is demonstrated by Raymond J. Chambers:

> The importance of the distinction lies in the fact that monetary assets and nonmonetary assets are subject to quite different risks. Holdings of monetary assets are subject to the risk of changes in the purchasing power of money. If for whatever reasons, the general level of prices rises, the purchasing power of a unit of money tends to fall; a greater number of units is required to buy a given good. Clearly then, nonmonetary assets are subject to the same influences, but in the opposite direction. If the price level is expected to rise, it is clearly preferable to hold goods and to incur fixed obligations than it is to hold monetary assets.[10]

A list of the more common monetary and nonmonetary items is presented on page 1124. Note that inventories, property, plant, and equipment, and intangibles are nonmonetary in nature. Conversely, most liabilities are monetary because they involve a fixed claim to pay cash, except for liabilities that are liquidated through the exchange of goods or services. Stockholders' equity accounts such as common stock and additional paid-in capital are nonmonetary in nature. Retained earnings is computed separately each period by adding constant dollar net income less any dividends to the beginning balance of retained earnings.

Effects of Holding Monetary and Nonmonetary Items

Holders of money lose general purchasing power during inflation because a given amount of money buys progressively fewer goods and services. This same loss in purchasing power occurs when any "monetary" asset is held during a period of inflation. For instance, in the case of accounts or notes receivable, or any claim to a fixed amount of money, the amount of money expected to be received represents a diminishing amount of general purchasing power simply as a result of inflation. Similarly, accounts, notes, and bonds payable, or any fixed amount of money payable in the future becomes less burdensome during inflation because they are payable in dollars of reduced general purchasing power.

The resulting gains and losses have been variously described as "inflation gains or losses," "monetary gains or losses," "purchasing power gains and losses," and

[10]Raymond J. Chambers, *Accounting, Evaluation and Economic Behavior* (Englewood Cliffs, N.J.: Prentice-Hall, 1966), p. 196.

CLASSIFICATION OF MONETARY AND NON-MONETARY ITEMS*

MONETARY ITEMS:

Assets

Cash on hand and demand bank deposits
Time deposits
Preferred stock (nonconvertible and nonparticipating)
Bonds (other than convertible)
Accounts and notes receivable
Allowance for doubtful accounts
Loans to employees
Long-term receivables
Refundable deposits
Advances to unconsolidated subsidiaries
Cash surrender value of life insurance
Advances to suppliers (not on a fixed price contract)
Deferred income tax charges

Liabilities

Accounts and notes payable
Accrued expenses payable
Cash dividends payable
Advances from customers (not on a fixed price contract)
Accrued losses on firm purchase commitments
Refundable deposits
Bonds payable and long-term debt
Unamortized premium or discount on bonds or notes payable
Convertible bonds payable
Deferred income tax credits

NONMONETARY ITEMS:

Assets

Inventory (other than inventories used on contracts)
Investment in common stocks in most situations
Property, plant and equipment
Accumulated depreciation of property, plant and equipment
Purchase commitments (portion paid on fixed price contracts)
Patents, trademarks, licenses and formulas
Goodwill
Deferred property acquisition costs
Other intangible assets and deferred charges

Liabilities

Sales commitments (portion collected on fixed price contracts)
Obligations under warranties
Deferred investment tax credit

ITEMS REQUIRING INDIVIDUAL ANALYSIS:

Assets

Investment in preferred stock (convertible or participating) and convertible bonds
If the market values the security primarily as a bond, it is monetary; if it values the security primarily as a stock, it is nonmonetary.

Inventories
If the future cash receipts will not vary because of future changes in prices, they are monetary. Goods priced at market upon delivery are nonmonetary.

Prepaid insurance, advertising, rents and other prepayments
Claims to future services are nonmonetary. Prepayments that are deposits, advance payments or receivables are monetary because the prepayment does not obtain a given quantity of future services but rather is a fixed money offset.

Pension, sinking and other funds under enterprise control
The specific assets in the fund should be classified as monetary or nonmonetary.

Liabilities

Accrued vacation pay
If it is paid at the wage rates as of the vacation dates and if those rates may vary, it is nonmonetary. If they do not vary, then it is monetary.

Deferred revenue
Nonmonetary if an obligation to furnish goods or services is involved.

Accrued pension obligations
Fixed amounts payable to a fund are monetary; all other amounts are nonmonetary.

Special Items

Deferred income tax charges and credits
Deferred income tax charges and credits are considered monetary by the FASB. The position is inconsistent with *APB Opinion No. 11* which requires the deferred method instead of the liability approach. Because of practical difficulties of computing various layers at which deferred income taxes originated, the Board classified these items as monetary.

Preferred stock (stockholders' equity)
If, as is commonly the case, the preferred stockholders' equity is fixed in terms of the number of dollars to be paid in liquidation, then the aggregate par or stated value of the preferred stock may be treated (from the viewpoint of common stockholders' equity) as a monetary item.

*Adapted from "Financial Reporting and Changing Prices," *Statement of Financial Accounting Standards No. 33* (Stamford, Conn.: FASB, 1979).

"general price-level gains or losses." **The FASB in Statement No. 33 calls them "purchasing power gains or losses on net monetary items."**[11] Whatever their name, these explicit measurements of the gains and losses resulting from monetary assets and liabilities are the unique product of constant dollar adjustments of historical amounts.

To illustrate the effects of holding a monetary asset during a period of inflation, assume that you have the following balance sheet at the beginning of the period.

Balance Sheet (Beginning of Period)			
Cash	$100	Owners' equity	$100

If the general price level doubles during the year, and no transactions take place, then to be in the same economic position you should have the following balance sheet at the end of the year.

Balance Sheet (End of Period)			
Cash	$200	Owners' equity	$200

However, the fact is that you only have $100 and have experienced a purchasing power loss in holding monetary items in a period of inflation. Your balance sheet would be presented as follows on a constant dollar basis.

Balance Sheet (End of Period)			
Cash	$100	Owners' equity	$200
		Retained earnings	(100)
			$100

In summary, you have lost $100 in end-of-year dollars.

Nonmonetary items, on the other hand do not represent a fixed claim to receive or pay cash. If, for example, the price level doubles, and you hold inventory, the cost of the inventory should be adjusted because, like other nonmonetary items, it retains its purchasing power. To illustrate the effects of holding a nonmonetary asset during a period of inflation, assume that you have the following balance sheet at the beginning of the period.

Balance Sheet (Beginning of Period)			
Inventory	$100	Owners' equity	$100

---

[11]"Financial Reporting and Changing Prices," *op. cit.*

If the price level doubles and the inventory was purchased at the beginning of the period, then your balance sheet in constant dollars is as follows.

Balance Sheet (End of Period)			
Inventory	$200	Owners' equity	$200

In summary, monetary assets and liabilities are stated in dollars of current purchasing power in the historical dollar balance sheet; consequently, they will appear at the same amounts in current general price-level statements without being adjusted. The fact that the end of the current-year amounts are the same in historical dollars as in constant dollar statements does not obscure the fact, however, that purchasing power gains or losses result from holding them during a period of general price-level change. Conversely, nonmonetary items are reported at different amounts in the constant dollar statements than they are in the historical cost statements, assuming a change in the general price level.

Constant Dollar Accounting—Lia Corporation

When financial statements are being adjusted to constant dollars for the first time, it is necessary to analyze completely the amounts in each account to determine their year of origin. The initial adjustment process involves considerably more work than subsequent adjustments. When comparative financial statements are being adjusted, the previous period's amounts must be restated in terms of the price level at the latest statement date. If adjusted statements have been prepared for the previous year, the restatement of that year can be accomplished by multiplying each amount in the previous year's adjusted statements by the ratio of the current index to the index of the immediately preceding year.

To illustrate the procedures peculiar to constant dollar accounting, the accounts of Lia Corporation are presented on a historical cost basis in the form of abbreviated comparative balance sheets and an intervening income statement on page 1127 (Exhibit 1). Price-level changes are magnified to illustrate their effects. Only the first six items of additional information have relevance in computing a constant dollar set of financial statements. Assume that Lia Corporation started business on January 1, 1981.

Adjustment of Balance Sheet Items

Monetary Items   The amounts of the monetary items at the end of the year 12/31/81 do not need to be restated because they are reported in end-of-the-year dollars. The amounts at the beginning of the period, however, must be restated in order to express them in terms of purchasing power at the end of the year. These computations are shown on page 1128.

Exhibit 1
Lia Corporation
Comparative Balance Sheets
as of January 1, 1981 and December 31, 1981
(Historical Cost Basis)

	January 1, 1981	December 31, 1981
Cash, receivables, and other monetary assets	$ 200,000	$ 325,000
Inventories	250,000	300,000
Equipment (net)	150,000	140,000
Land	450,000	450,000
Total assets	$1,050,000	$1,215,000
Current liabilities (all monetary)	$ 100,000	$ 200,000
Long-term liabilities (all monetary)	650,000	650,000
Total liabilities	750,000	850,000
Common stock	300,000	300,000
Retained earnings	-0-	65,000
Total stockholders' equity	300,000	365,000
Total liabilities and stockholders' equity	$1,050,000	$1,215,000

Lia Corporation
Statement of Income and Retained Earnings
For the Year Ended December 31, 1981
(Historical Cost Basis)

Sales		$800,000
Cost of goods sold:		
Inventory, January 1, 1981	$250,000	
Purchases	520,000	
Goods available for sale	770,000	
Inventory, December 31, 1981	300,000	470,000
Gross profit		330,000
Selling and administrative expenses		170,000
Depreciation expense		10,000
Income before income taxes		150,000
Income taxes		75,000
Net income		75,000
Retained earnings, January 1, 1981		-0-
		75,000
Cash dividends		10,000
Retained earnings, December 31, 1981		$ 65,000

Additional related information: (Only the first six items have relevance in computing a constant dollar set of financial statements).

Constant Dollar Information

1. The following CPI-U index numbers are assumed for use in the illustration:

1/1/81	Opening of the business	100
1981	First-year average	160
12/31/81	Year-end	200

2. The inventory is priced on a first-in, first-out (FIFO) basis. The beginning inventory was purchased at the opening of the business. The ending inventory was acquired in November and December at a price level of 180.
3. Acquisition of the equipment and land took place at the opening of the business.
4. The equipment has a useful life of 15 years and is depreciated on a straight-line basis with no salvage value.
5. All revenue and expenses, except for that portion of the cost of goods sold represented by the beginning inventory are earned or incurred evenly throughout the year.
6. Dividends are declared and paid at the end of the year.

Current Cost Information

7. Cost of goods sold on a current cost basis at different dates during the year is $760,000 (assume incurred evenly). Current cost of the inventory at the end of 1981 is $500,000.
8. Current cost of the equipment at the end of 1981 excluding accumulated depreciation is $180,000. Net current cost is $168,000.
9. Current cost of the land at the end of 1981 is $900,000.
10. Historical cost and current cost are identical for the inventory, equipment, and land at the beginning of the year 1/1/81.
11. Selling and administrative expenses and income taxes are the same on both an historical and current cost basis.

Cash, receivables, and other monetary assets	
12/31/81 $325,000 × 200/200	$ 325,000
1/1/81 $200,000 × 200/100	$ 400,000
Current liabilities (all monetary)	
12/31/81 $200,000 × 200/200	$ 200,000
1/1/81 $100,000 × 200/100	$ 200,000
Long-term liabilities (all monetary)	
12/31/81 $650,000 × 200/200	$ 650,000
1/1/81 $650,000 × 200/100	$1,300,000

The balances of the monetary items at 12/31/81 are stated in terms of the price level on 12/31/81 and remain the same. The cash, receivables, and other monetary items had greater purchasing power on 1/1/81 than they now have on 12/31/81. Therefore, the 1/1/81 balances must be increased to 12/31/81 dollars to restate the beginning balances in end-of-year dollars. The current and long-term liabilities at 1/1/81 must also be converted to 12/31/81 dollars.

Inventories Inventories can present a special problem because restatement in terms of the current price level requires knowledge of the dates of acquisition and the historical cost. If the specific identification method is used, the identified number of historical dollars is multiplied by a fraction, the numerator of which is the current index and the denominator of which is the index for the date of acquisition. Typically, however, a FIFO, LIFO, or average-cost assumption is utilized. The price-level restatement should be consistent with that assumption. In this case it is assumed that the FIFO method is applied and that the year-end inventory consists of goods acquired during the last two months at an average index for those months:

12/31/81	Inventories—ending $300,000 × 200/180	$333,333
1/1/81	Inventories—beginning $250,000 × 200/100	$500,000

Equipment The equipment would be restated in end-of-year dollars as follows:

12/31/81	Equipment (net)—$140,000 × 200/100	$280,000
1/1/81	Equipment (net)—$150,000 × 200/100	$300,000

Land The restatement of the land in end-of-year dollars is the same on both balance sheets:

12/31/81	Land—$450,000 × 200/100	$900,000
1/1/81	Land—$450,000 × 200/100	$900,000

The computations above illustrate that while price-level restatements for equipment and land are straightforward, the initial restatement process can be tedious when a large number of items and acquisition dates are involved.

Common Stock and Retained Earnings The common stock account balances at 12/31/81 and at 1/1/81 are converted to end-of-year dollars as follows:

12/31/81	Common stock—$300,000 × 200/100	$600,000
1/1/81	Common stock—$300,000 × 200/100	$600,000

Retained earnings is computed as the amount needed to balance the balance sheet. The following balances are reported:

12/31/81	Retained earnings	$388,333
1/1/81	Retained earnings	-0-

Note that the amount of retained earnings at 12/31/81 should be reconcilable to the amount of restated income for the year 1981 taking into consideration dividends paid during the year (see Exhibit 2 page 1132).

In preparing constant dollar financial statements, common stock, additional paid-in capital, and retained earnings may all be viewed as stockholders' equity and treated as one residual, inseparable sum. Price-level adjusted common stockholders' equity may then be measured as the difference between (1) total **restated** assets and (2) total **restated** liabilities plus preferred stockholders' equity (if any):

12/31/81	Common stockholders' equity—$1,838,333 (assets) − $850,000 (liabilities) =	$988,333
1/1/81	Common stockholders' equity—$2,100,000 (assets) − $1,500,000 (liabilities) =	$600,000

The abbreviated comparative balance sheet of Lia Corporation prepared on a comprehensive constant dollar basis is presented on page 1132 (Exhibit 2).

Adjustment of Combined Income and Retained Earnings Statement Items

Sales Because sales were spread evenly over the year, the average index for 1981 may be used to restate sales to year-end dollars:

$$\$800,000 \times 200/160 = \$1,000,000$$

If sales (or other operating items) are seasonal or if the price-level changes are not reasonably constant during the year, quarterly sales (or other operating items) are restated using quarterly indexes.

Cost of Goods Sold The cost of goods sold can be restated in 12/31/81 dollars as follows:

Beginning inventory	$250,000 × 200/100 =	$	500,000
Purchases	520,000 × 200/160 =		650,000
Goods available for sale	770,000		1,150,000
Ending inventory	300,000 × 200/180 =		333,333
Cost of goods sold	$470,000		$ 816,667

Selling and Administrative Expenses Assuming that these expenses were incurred evenly throughout the period, they would be restated as follows:

$$\$170,000 × 200/160 = \$212,500$$

Depreciation Expense The equipment was purchased at the beginning of the year; depreciation expense should be restated to year-end dollars as follows:

$$\$10,000 × 200/100 = \$20,000$$

Income Taxes Assuming that these expenses were incurred evenly throughout the period, they would be restated as follows:

$$\$75,000 × 200/160 = \$93,750$$

Cash Dividends Cash dividends were paid to common stockholders at the end of the year when the index was 200. No adjustment is necessary, as the following computation illustrates:

$$\$10,000 × 200/200 = \$10,000$$

Purchasing Power Gain or Loss Analyzing the effects of price-level changes on monetary items reveals management's effectiveness in coping with such changes. The computation of the purchasing power gain or loss on net monetary items involves preparing a detailed statement of sources and uses of monetary items for the period under consideration, restated item by item. The method is shown on page 1131.

Lia Corporation
Computation of Purchasing Power Gain or Loss—1981
(End-of-Year-Dollars)

| | 1/1/81 | | | 12/31/81 |
	Historical	Index	Restated to 12/31/81 Dollars	Historical Stated in 12/31/81 Dollars
Net monetary items				
Cash, receivables, and other monetary assets	$ 200,000	× 200/100	$ 400,000	$ 325,000
Current liabilities (all monetary)	(100,000)	× 200/100	(200,000)	(200,000)
Long-term liabilities (all monetary)	(650,000)	× 200/100	(1,300,000)	(650,000)
Net monetary items	$(550,000)[a]		$(1,100,000)[b]	$ (525,000)[c]

	1981 Historical	Index		Restated to 12/31/81 Dollars
Net monetary items 1/1/81	$(550,000)[a]	× 200/100		$(1,100,000)[b]
Add (sources):				
Sales	800,000	× 200/160		1,000,000
	250,000			(100,000)
Deduct (uses):				
Purchases	520,000	× 200/160		650,000
Selling and administrative expenses	170,000	× 200/160		212,500
Income taxes	75,000	× 200/160		93,750
Cash dividends	10,000	× 200/200		10,000
Total uses	775,000			966,250
Net monetary items— historical—12/31/81	$(525,000)[c]			
Net monetary items— restated—12/31/81 (if there was no gain or loss)				(1,066,250)
Net monetary items— historical—12/31/81 (as above)				(525,000)[c]
Purchasing power gain on net monetary items				$ 541,250

In the computation above, those items that occurred continuously during the year (sales, purchases, selling and administrative expenses, and income taxes) are restated using the average index for the year; the isolated lump-sum use (payment of dividend) was restated using the index applicable to the date of occurrence.

The statement of income and retained earnings on a constant dollar basis is illustrated on page 1132 (Exhibit 2).

Exhibit 2
Lia Corporation
Comparative Balance Sheets
as of January 1, 1981 and December 31, 1981
(Constant Dollar Basis)

	January 1, 1981	December 31, 1981
Cash, receivables and other monetary assets	$ 400,000	$ 325,000
Inventories	500,000	333,333
Equipment (net)	300,000	280,000
Land	900,000	900,000
Total assets	$2,100,000	$1,838,333
Current liabilities (all monetary)	$ 200,000	$ 200,000
Long-term liabilities (all monetary)	1,300,000	650,000
Total liabilities	1,500,000	850,000
Common stock	600,000	600,000
Retained earnings	–0–	388,333
Total stockholders' equity	600,000	988,333
Total liabilities and stockholders' equity	$2,100,000	$1,838,333

Lia Corporation
Statement of Income and Retained Earnings
For the Year Ended December 31, 1981
(Constant Dollar Basis)

Sales		$1,000,000
Cost of goods sold		
Inventory, January 1, 1981	$ 500,000	
Purchases	650,000	
Goods available for sale	1,150,000	
Inventory, December 31, 1981	333,333	816,667
Gross profit		183,333
Selling and administrative expenses		212,500
Depreciation expense		20,000
Loss before income taxes		(49,167)
Income taxes		93,750
Loss before purchasing power gain on net		
monetary items		(142,917)
Purchasing power gain on net monetary items		541,250
Constant dollar net income		398,333
Retained earnings, January 1, 1981		–0–
Cash dividends		(10,000)
Retained earnings, December 31, 1981		$ 388,333

Advantages and Disadvantages of Constant Dollar Accounting

Constant dollar financial statements have been discussed widely within both the accounting profession and the business and financial community and lauded by many as the cure to reporting problems during periods of inflation or deflation. The following arguments have been submitted in support of preparing such statements:

1. Constant dollar accounting provides management with an **objectively** determined quantification of the impact of inflation on its business operations.
2. Constant dollar accounting eliminates the effects of inflation from financial information by requiring each enterprise to follow the same objective procedure and use the same price-level index, thereby **preserving comparability of financial statements between firms.**
3. Constant dollar accounting **enhances comparability between the financial statements of a single firm** by eliminating differences due to price-level changes and thereby improves trend analysis.
4. Constant dollar accounting eliminates the effects of price-level changes without having to develop a new structure of accounting; that is, it **preserves the historical cost-based accounting system** that is currently used and understood.
5. Constant dollar accounting **eliminates the necessity of and attraction to the "piecemeal" approaches** used in combating the effects of inflation of financial statements, namely, LIFO inventory costing and accelerated depreciation of property, plant, and equipment.

In spite of widespread publicity, discussion, and authoritative support both inside and outside the accounting profession, the preparation and public issuance of constant dollar financial statements up to this point has been negligible, probably because of the following disadvantages said to be associated with constant dollar financial statements.

1. The additional **cost** of preparing constant dollar statements is not offset by the benefit of receiving sufficient relevant information.
2. Constant dollar financial statements will cause **confusion** and be misunderstood by users.
3. Restating the "value" of nonmonetary items at historical cost adjusted for general price-level changes **is no more meaningful than historical cost alone,** that is, it suffers all the shortcomings of the historical cost method.
4. The reported purchasing power gain from monetary items is **misleading** because it does not necessarily represent successful management or provide funds for dividends, plant expansion, or other purposes.
5. Constant dollar accounting **assumes that the impact of inflation falls equally** on all businesses and on all classes of assets and costs, which is not true.

Probably the greatest deterrent to widespread and mandatory adoption of constant dollar accounting in the past is **what it is not;** constant dollar accounting is not present value, net realizable value, or current cost accounting, and therein lies much of the opposition to its use.

CURRENT VALUE ACCOUNTING

There is no single definition of value. **The value of anything is dependent upon answers to questions like: Value to whom? and Value for what purpose?** The determination of one value can at best be responsive to only one type of problem. Assets, defined as "things of value," cannot be represented by one number from which all types of economic decisions can be made. Value is what assets are worth to a particular person, for a particular purpose, at a particular point in time. Hence, the word is generally preceded by a descriptive adjective, such as, going-concern value, resale value, liquidation value, market value, present value, current value, fair value, book value, net realizable value, exit value, appraisal value, and others.

Value should not be confused with valuation, which in accounting is the assignment of dollar amounts to assets and liabilities. Value and valuation, however, are interrelated in that the accounting process of valuation results in the assignment of an amount that represents a value, generally either historical entry exchange value or historical exit exchange value, which in conventional accounting is cost and selling price, respectively. The point is, that the accounting process of valuation, because of its preoccupation with historical exchange prices, has contributed only a small portion of its information potential. Begging to be tapped at a time when inflation makes the existing historical basis of valuation obsolete are the other bases of valuation, namely, current value, replacement value, present value, reproduction value, net realizable value, appraisal value, etc. Determining which basis of valuation to adopt depends largely on the answers to the question: What is the objective of financial statements? Multiple answers may require multiple disclosures of values.

The Current Value Approach

The term **current value** has recently been adopted as the generic term representative of the process that reports an entity's resources and obligations on the basis of "present worth," using any of several means or techniques of evaluation. The three most commonly advocated **concepts of current value** are: (1) present value (discounted future cash flows), (2) net realizable value (current cash equivalents) and (3) current cost. The current value approach merely describes the objective that is accomplished through the application of selected techniques and methods to the individual items to be measured and reported. In similar manner the term "historical cost approach" merely represents the many concepts, methods, and techniques applied in preparing cost-based financial statements.

Present Value Present value (often referred to as **value in use**) relates to the future cash inflows and outflows that can be attributed to or related to the specific item or group of items being measured. As discussed in Chapter 6, present value is measured by discounting at an appropriate interest rate the future estimated net cash inflows, or cost savings, of the item being valued. Present value is frequently viewed as the ideal basis for current valuation of resources and obligations because it is most consistent with the user's objective of predicting future cash flows.[12] In most cases, however, except for monetary items, the direct measurement of present value is not feasible, owing perhaps to the lack of cash flow data or to complex interactions among several resources and obligations that invalidate cash flows as valuation tools for individual items.

Net Realizable Value A net realizable value model is based on the premise that **the value of the asset is the selling price of the asset in the market less cost of disposal,** instead of its purchase price or replacement cost.[13] Proponents of this

---

[12]See, for example, George J. Staubus, *A Theory of Accounting to Investors* (Berkeley: University of California Press, 1961), for an excellent exposition of this valuation system.

[13]See, for example, Chambers, *op. cit.*

approach believe that the market value or current cash equivalent is the best means available for measuring the value of enterprise assets and that changes in market value should be reported in net income immediately. The criticisms of this model are that some assets do not have a ready market price, that the computation of value is subjective, and that many assets are held for use, not sale, so that market value is not useful information. It should be noted that this approach generally assumes no forced or distress sale; "liquidation value" implies a forced or distressed sale value.

Current Cost   Current cost[14] is the cost of replacing the identical asset owned, that is, one of the same age and of the same operating capacity.[15] Current cost may be approximated in a variety of ways but often is computed by applying a **specific price index** to the historical cost or book value of assets. Specific price indexes are available for specific industries and for broad classifications of equipment and other plant assets. The application of specific price indexes to assets is computationally similar to the application of general price indexes. Because the current cost method is conceptually appealing, and because the FASB requires supplementary information on a current cost basis, our discussion of current cost procedures is extensive.

Current Cost—Simplified Illustration

To illustrate the current cost accounting model, assume that Andrea, Co. purchased inventory at the beginning of Period 1 for $100,000; the current cost of the inventory at the end of Period 1 is $125,000; at the end of Period 2 the current cost is $155,000; and the inventory is sold in Period 3 for $170,000 when the inventory has a current cost of $160,000. Net income under the current cost and historical cost models for the three periods would be reported as shown at the top of page 1136.

The total net income is the same over the three years using either the current cost or the historical cost approach. The current cost approach recognizes the income as the inventory increases in value, whereas the historical cost approach delays recognition until the inventory is sold. In this illustration, the term **holding gain is employed to measure the increase in current cost that arises from holding the inventory from period to period.**

---

[14]Although they are used interchangeably, a subtle but important distinction exists between current cost and replacement cost. Current cost is the current purchase price of an asset owned, whereas replacement cost is the current purchase price of assets which will replace existing assets. In many cases, such as inventories, current cost and replacement cost are the same, because replacement will be with similar assets. However, with long-term assets, significant differences can develop. For example, assume that a Boeing 727 aircraft is going to be replaced with a new Boeing 767. In computing the current cost of the Boeing 727, we would take the cost of the Boeing 767 and adjust that cost for the value of the differences in service potential due to differences in life, output capacity, and nature of service, including any operating cost savings associated with the new aircraft. However, under replacement cost only the difference in output capacity is considered and no allowances are made for differences in useful life or operating costs.

[15]For a complete discussion of current cost, see Lawrence Revsine, *Replacement Cost Accounting* (Englewood Cliffs, N.J.: Prentice-Hall, 1973); Edgar O. Edwards and Phillip W. Bell, *The Theory and Measurement of Business Income* (Berkeley: University of California Press, 1961); and James A. Largay, III, and John Leslie Livingstone, *Accounting for Changing Prices* (Santa Barbara, Wiley/Hamilton, 1976).

Andrea Co.
Comparison of Current Cost and Historical Cost

Current Cost Model

	Period 1	Period 2	Period 3
Revenues	$ -0-	$ -0-	$170,000
Cost of goods sold	-0-	-0-	160,000
Current cost income from continuing operations	-0-	-0-	10,000
Holding gain	25,000	30,000	5,000
Current cost net income	$25,000	$30,000	$ 15,000

Historical Cost Model

	Period 1	Period 2	Period 3
Revenue	$ -0-	$ -0-	$170,000
Cost of goods sold	-0-	-0-	100,000
Historical cost net income	$ -0-	$ -0-	$ 70,000

Current Cost—Complex Illustration

In a comprehensive current cost model, holding gains and losses are usually segregated between those that are realized and those that are unrealized. **Realized holding gains and losses** are the difference between the current cost and the historical cost of the asset sold or consumed during the period. **Unrealized holding gains and losses** relate to assets on hand at the end of the year. These gains and losses are the total increase in the current cost of the assets from the date they were acquired to the end of the current year. **The total holding gain recognized for any period will then be as follows:**

1. **the holding gains and losses realized during the year, and**
2. **the change in the unrealized holding gain or loss between the beginning and the end of the year.**

To illustrate, assume the same information as in the Andrea Co. in the preceding illustration. A current cost accounting system would report the following:

Andrea Co.
Comprehensive Approach

Current Cost Model

	Period 1	Period 2	Period 3
Revenues	$ -0-	$ -0-	$170,000
Cost of goods sold	-0-	-0-	160,000
Current cost income from continuing operations	-0-	-0-	10,000
Realized holding gain	-0-	-0-	60,000
Realized income	-0-	-0-	70,000
Unrealized holding gain (loss)	25,000	30,000	(55,000)
Current cost net income	$25,000	$30,000	$ 15,000

The realized holding gain in Period 3 is $60,000, the difference between the current cost of inventory ($160,000) and the historical cost of inventory ($100,000); it is reported when the asset is sold. The unrealized holding gain or loss reported in each period is the change in the total unrealized holding gain from one period to the next. For example in Period 2, the total unrealized holding gain at the beginning of the period is $25,000 and at the end of the period is $55,000. The unrealized holding gain reported in Period 2 is therefore $30,000 ($55,000 − $25,000). In Period 3 the total unrealized holding gain at the beginning of the period is $55,000 and at the end of the period is zero because the inventory is sold. As a result, an unrealized holding loss of $55,000 ($55,000 − $0) is reported in the third period.[16]

In the current cost model, three different income numbers are reported. **Current cost income from continuing operations** reflects current cost margins—sales revenues less the current cost of inputs. **Realized income** measures the total income realized during the year. Realized income and historical cost income are always the same. Classification within the income statement is different however because the current cost model subdivides historical cost income into two components— current cost income from continuing operations and realized holding gains. **Current cost net income** measures the total income of the enterprise for one period and takes into account both realized and unrealized holding gains. Many consider this income number to provide the most appropriate measure of whether an enterprise is successful from one period to the next.

Current Cost Accounting—Lia Corporation

To illustrate the current cost approach, assume the same historical information for Lia Corporation as that reported on page 1127 (Exhibit 1). The additional related information, **numbers 7–11,** is relevant for preparing current cost financial statements.

Adjustment of Balance Sheet Items

Preparation of the balance sheet on a current cost basis is relatively straightforward. The current cost of each item is reported without adjustment for any general price-level changes. The abbreviated comparative balance sheets for Lia Corporation would be presented as indicated on page 1140 (Exhibit 3).

All the monetary items are stated at face value. No adjustments to the beginning-of-the-year balances are necessary because they are not being reported on a constant dollar basis. The inventory, equipment, and land in both balance sheets are reported at their current cost. Common stock is not adjusted because the purchasing power of the dollar has not changed. The retained earnings is simply the difference between the assets and liabilities less the common stock. Retained earnings also can be computed by adding the beginning balance to the current cost net income less dividends for 1981. Dividends are not adjusted in a current cost system.

---

[16]This system is basically the approach adopted by Edwards and Bell (see footnote 15). Note that only the change in the unrealized holding gain is considered in computing current cost net income. If current cost net income included realized holding gains and total unrealized holding gains, you could be double counting because the realized holding gain would recognize unrealized holding gains of prior periods.

Adjustment of Income Statement Items

As indicated earlier the current cost income statement usually reports three types of income: current cost income (loss) from continuing operations, realized income (loss), and current cost net income (loss). If the data from the Lia Corporation are used, the following would be reported on the income statement.

Sales   Because revenues are stated at their current price when sold, their amount is the same in either an historical cost or a current cost system.

Sales	$800,000

Cost of Goods Sold   Current cost of goods sold as given in the additional information in Exhibit 1 is the result of adjusting the historical cost of goods sold to the current cost of these items at the date of sale.

Cost of goods sold	$760,000

Selling and Administrative Expenses   These expenses are reported at their current cost which in this case is the same as their historical cost.

Selling and administrative expenses	$170,000

Depreciation Expense   In a current cost accounting system, it is appropriate to assume that depreciation expense is incurred evenly through the year. As a result, average current cost balances should be used as the basis for computing depreciation.[17] In this case, depreciation expense on the equipment is computed and reported as follows:

$$\text{Average current cost balance} = \frac{\$150,000 + \$180,000}{2} = \$165,000$$

$$\text{Depreciation expense} = \$165,000 \div 15 = \$11,000$$

Income Taxes   These expenses are reported at their current cost, which is the same as their historical cost:

Income taxes	$75,000

Realized and Unrealized Holding Gains   To compute the realized and unrealized holding gain, the following information is pertinent:

---

[17]Note that some theorists would argue for depreciation expense to be reported on the basis of the ending balance. Our presentation is in accordance with *FASB Statement No. 33.*

Exhibit 3-A
Lia Corporation
Historical and Current Cost for Selected Items

	Historical Cost	Current Cost	Difference
Inventory 1/1/81	$250,000	$250,000	$ -0-
Inventory 12/31/81	300,000	500,000	200,000
Cost of goods sold	470,000	760,000	290,000
Purchases	520,000	520,000	-0-
Equipment (net), 1/1/81	150,000	150,000	-0-
Equipment (net), 12/31/81	140,000	168,000	28,000
Depreciation expense	10,000	11,000	1,000
Land 1/1/81	450,000	450,000	-0-
Land 12/31/81	450,000	900,000	450,000

Exhibit 3–B summarizes the computation of the unrealized and realized holding gains for Lia Corporation.

Exhibit 3-B
Lia Corporation
Summary of Unrealized and Realized Holding Gains

	Inventory	Equipment	Land	Total
Unrealized gains:				
at 12/31/81	$200,000	$28,000	$450,000	$678,000
at 1/1/81	-0-	-0-	-0-	-0-
Increase (decrease) in unrealized gains	200,000	28,000	450,000	678,000
Realized holding gains	290,000	1,000	-0-	291,000
Increase (decrease) in current cost of assets held during the year (total holding gains)	$490,000	$29,000	$450,000	$969,000

An explanation of the unrealized and realized holding gains follows:

Inventory, cost of goods sold, and purchases During the period, the company experienced an unrealized holding gain on its ending inventory of $200,000 ($500,000 − $300,000). In addition, a realized holding gain of $290,000 ($760,000 − $470,000) on the sale of products occurred. A holding gain on the purchases does not take place because at the date of purchase the historical cost and current cost are the same.

Equipment and depreciation expense The computation for the holding gains involving the equipment and related depreciation expense is complex. As indicated earlier, the current cost depreciation for the period is $11,000 computed on the average current cost balance for the year. The difference of $1,000 ($11,000 − $10,000) between the current cost depreciation and the historical cost depreciation is reported as a realized holding gain. A portion of the equipment which has appreciated in value is now consumed (depreciated), and a holding gain should be realized.

An additional complication, however, arises related to depreciation because the 12/31/81 balance sheet reports the equipment at a total current cost of $180,000, not $165,000 (average balance of current cost). In order to report the proper accumulated depreciation balance of $12,000 ($180,000 ÷ 15 years), a **catch-up depreciation charge** (often referred to as **backlog depreciation**) must be made. This catch-up depreciation charge is reported as a reduction of the unrealized holding gain on the equipment. The entry to record this catch-up depreciation is as follows:

Unrealized Holding Gain	1,000	
Accumulated Depreciation		1,000
($12,000 − $11,000)		

The problem of catch-up depreciation will arise whenever an average is used to compute depreciation and the year-end current cost is higher than the average.

In addition to the realized holding gain, an unrealized holding gain of $28,000, after deducting catch-up depreciation, must be recognized. This unrealized holding gain is the difference between the current cost of the equipment at the end of the year minus the current cost of the equipment at the beginning of the year adjusted for depreciation. No unrealized holding gains exist from previous periods.

Land   The current cost of the land has increased $450,000 ($900,000 − $450,000), and an unrealized holding gain in this amount should be recognized.

The current cost income statement for Lia Corporation is presented on page 1141, (Exhibit 3). The current cost loss from continuing operations and the realized holding gain when added together equal historical cost net income. An advantage of the current cost over the historical cost income statement is the segregation of income into these two components.

Exhibit 3
Lia Corporation
Comparative Balance Sheets
as of January 1 and December 31, 1981
(Current Cost Basis)

	January 1, 1981	December 31, 1981
Cash, receivables, and other monetary assets	$ 200,000	$ 325,000
Inventories	250,000	500,000
Equipment (net)	150,000	168,000
Land	450,000	900,000
Total assets	$1,050,000	$1,893,000
Current liabilities (all monetary)	100,000	200,000
Long-term liabilities (all monetary)	650,000	650,000
Total liabilities	750,000	850,000
Common stock	300,000	300,000
Retained earnings	-0-	743,000
Total stockholders' equity	300,000	1,043,000
Total liabilities and stockholders' equity	$1,050,000	$1,893,000

	(Exhibit 3)
Lia Corporation	
Statement of Income and Retained Earnings	
For the Year Ended December 31, 1981	
(Current Cost Basis)	
Sales	$ 800,000
Cost of goods sold	760,000
Gross profit	40,000
Selling and administrative expenses	170,000
Depreciation expense	11,000
Loss before income taxes	(141,000)
Income taxes	75,000
Current cost loss from continuing operations	(216,000)
Realized holding gain	291,000
Realized income	75,000
Unrealized holding gain	678,000
Current cost net income	753,000
Retained earnings, January 1, 1981	-0-
	753,000
Cash dividends	10,000
Retained earnings, December 31, 1981	$ 743,000

Comparison of Constant Dollar and Current Cost

The heading of this section was intentionally not worded "Constant Dollar **versus** Current Cost" because these two different bases of reporting financial information are not per se competing or conflicting methods. They are competing approaches only in the minds of their staunch proponents, who feel the adoption of one approach precludes the adoption of the other. This need not be so because constant dollar accounting and current cost accounting are complementary responses to different measurement problems.

Public confusion about the differences between and merits of these two approaches begins when accountants or other writers lump them together or discuss them on the implicit assumption that a choice has to be made between the two and that the real problem is deciding which to choose. A common misconception is that, because it is the less drastic departure from present historical cost accounting, constant dollar accounting is merely the first step toward current cost accounting. Conceptually, neither is an approximation of the other or a first step toward the other.

The basis of both constant dollar accounting and current cost accounting is the **theory of capital maintenance,** that is, that income is recognized only after capital is kept intact. Both recognize that when prices rise, the degree of capital maintenance may not be readily discernible unless some allowance is made for changes in prices. But the similarities cease at this point, because the two approaches view capital maintenance differently and, therefore, offer different treatments for the price change problem.[18]

[18]For a more complete discussion of the effect of price-level adjustments on capital maintenance, see Norman S. Featherson, "Inflation Accounting," *World,* Peat, Marwick, Mitchell & Co., Summer 1975.

The **objective of constant dollar accounting** is to maintain capital in terms of constant purchasing power as measured by a general index of the level of prices. This concept implies that the business must maintain at a constant level its ability to purchase a wide variety of goods and services throughout the economy. In the operation of a business, a certain amount of purchasing power is given up through the process of acquiring, producing, and selling goods over a period of time. The investors in and the managers of the business need to know whether the purchasing power sacrificed is being restored and maintained.

The **objective of current cost accounting** is to maintain capital in terms of operating capacity or the ability to provide goods and services at the same level at the end of a period as at the beginning. This approach assumes that all resources consumed or sold will be replaced with resources performing a similar function at the same or better level of production. This approach implies (1) the use of replacement or reproduction cost (using specific price-level indexes) for nonmonetary assets revalued at their specific current cost and (2) matching with revenues the sacrifice value of resources sold or consumed.

In summary, constant dollar accounting does not rest on the assumption that when a producer parts with a product, the assets and services consumed in producing it must be replaced in order to maintain the continuity of production. Instead, it relates the purchasing power of cash invested in assets to the purchasing power generated by those assets; it views replacement of the assets as new investment decisions that are not affected by decisions made in the past.[19]

Advantages and Disadvantages of Current Cost

A distinct advantage that current cost has over both historical cost and constant dollar accounting is that the specific changes (up and down) in individual items is considered. While the general level of prices may be increasing, specific items may be decreasing. Such items as calculators, tennis balls, watches, micro-wave ovens, and television sets, for example, have decreased in price, whereas the general level of prices has increased. Constant dollar accounting using a general price index does not make an allowance for these changes in prices as effectively as a current cost system does.

The major **arguments for** the use of a current cost approach are:

1. **Current cost provides a better measure of efficiency.** If, for example, depreciation is based on current costs, not historical costs, a better measure of operating efficiencies is obtained. For example, assume that you are a new manager in an operation that includes a number of assets purchased recently at current prices, and your performance is compared with that of someone in a similar job elsewhere who is using similar assets that were purchased five years ago when the price was substantially lower. You probably would contend that the five-year-old assets should be revalued because the other manager will show a lower depreciation charge and higher net income than you will.

2. **Current cost is an approximation of the service potential of the asset.** It is difficult if not impossible to determine the present discounted values of specific cash flows that will occur from the use of certain assets; but current cost frequently is a reasonable approximation of this value. As the current cost increases, the implication is that the enterprise has a holding gain (an increase from one period to another in the current

---

[19]*Ibid.*

cost of that item) because the aggregate value of the asset's service potential has increased.

3. **Current cost provides for the maintenance of physical capital.** Assume that an asset is purchased for one dollar, sold for two dollars, and replaced for two dollars. How much income should be reported and how much tax should be paid? Under traditional accounting procedures, one dollar of income would be earned (which is subject to tax and a claim for dividend distribution). If current cost is used, however, no income exists to be taxed and claims for dividend distributions would probably be fewer.

4. **Current cost provides an assessment of future cash flows.** Information on current cost margins may be useful for assessing future cash flows when the selling price of a product is closely related to its current cost. In addition, reporting holding gains (losses) may provide help in assessing future cash flows.

The major **arguments against** current cost adjustments are:

1. **The use of current cost is subjective because it is difficult to determine the exact current cost of all items at any point in time.** A good second-hand market for all types of assets does not exist. In most cases, the asset is not replaced with an identical asset; it is replaced with a better one, a faster one, an improved one, an altogether different one, or not replaced at all.

2. **The maintenance of physical capital is not the accountant's function.** It is generally conceded that it is management's function to ensure that capital is not impaired.

3. **Current cost is not always an approximation of the fair market value.** An asset's value is a function of the future cash flows generated by it. Current cost, however, does not necessarily measure an increase in the service potential of that asset.

CURRENT COST/CONSTANT DOLLAR

Some accountants contend that either a current cost system or a constant dollar system alone is not appropriate. Although current cost accounting measures changes in the current cost of assets held, it does nothing to reveal the extent to which the changes in the holding gains are real or fictitious if the purchasing power of the dollar is changing. To illustrate, assume that you purchased marketable securities for $100 and their current cost is $150. Under current cost accounting, an unrealized holding gain of $50 is recognized. But, suppose that the general price level increased 100% during the period of time you held the asset. Have you a gain? Actually the marketable securities should be restated to $200 ($100 × 200/100) and a holding loss of $50 should be recorded. Also, if only the current cost approach is used, the purchasing power gain or loss on net monetary items is omitted. As a result, many believe current cost should be combined with a constant dollar accounting system to properly reflect the effects of changing prices.

Current Cost/Constant Dollar Accounting—Lia Corporation

If current cost/constant dollar financial statements are prepared, all amounts in the financial statements must be stated at current cost in year-end dollars. The following illustration is based on Lia Corporation data on page 1127 (Exhibit 1) and all of the related additional information **(numbers 1–11).**

Adjustment of Balance Sheet Items

Because assets and liabilities are stated at current cost in year-end dollars on a current cost balance sheet, these items appear at the same amounts on a current cost/constant dollar balance sheet. The items that make up stockholders' equity will differ because under a current cost system common stock is not adjusted to end-of-the-year dollars, whereas under a current cost/constant dollar system, common stock is restated. In addition, retained earnings must be restated for current cost/constant dollar net income which includes a purchasing power gain or loss on net monetary items. The amounts reported on the comparative balance sheet on page 1147 (Exhibit 4) should be compared with the amounts on the balance sheets in Exhibits 2 and 3.

The 1/1/81 balance sheet is restated to end-of-the-year dollars. The balance sheet at 12/31/81 (Exhibit 4) is the same as the current cost balance sheet shown on page 1140 (Exhibit 3) with the exception of common stock and retained earnings. Common stock must be restated to 12/31/81 dollars and the retained earnings balance is determined by subtracting the liabilities and common stock balances from total assets. The retained earnings balance can also be determined by adding the current cost/constant dollar net income less dividends to beginning retained earnings.

Adjustment of Income Statement Items

To arrive at a current cost/constant dollar income statement, the current cost income statement must be adjusted to year-end dollars.

Sales and Related Expenses   Sales, cost of goods sold, selling and administrative expenses, depreciation expense and income taxes are adjusted to year-end dollars as follows:

Sales $800,000 × 200/160 =	$1,000,000
Cost of goods sold $760,000 × 200/160 =	$ 950,000
Selling and administrative expenses $170,000 × 200/160 =	$ 212,500
Depreciation expense $11,000 × 200/160 =	$ 13,750
Income taxes $75,000 × 200/160 =	$ 93,750
Note: All of the above items were stated in average dollars and must be adjusted to year-end dollars.	

Realized and Unrealized Holding Gains   To compute the realized and unrealized holding gain, net of inflation, the following information is pertinent:

Exhibit 4–A
Lia Corporation
Constant Dollar and Current Cost/Constant Dollar for Selected Items

	Constant Dollar*	Current Cost/ Constant Dollar**	Difference
Inventory 1/1/81	$500,000	$500,000	–0–
Inventory 12/31/81	333,333	500,000	$166,667
Cost of goods sold	816,667	950,000	133,333
Purchases	650,000	650,000	–0–
Equipment (net) 1/1/81	300,000	300,000	–0–
Equipment (net) 12/31/81	280,000	168,000	(112,000)
Depreciation expense	20,000	13,750	(6,250)
Land 1/1/81	900,000	900,000	–0–
Land 12/31/81	900,000	900,000	–0–

*All amounts taken from Exhibit 2.
**All amounts in this column are adjusted to year-end dollars.

Exhibit 4–B summarizes the computation of the unrealized and realized holding gains for Lia Corporation on a current cost/constant dollar basis:

Exhibit 4–B
Lia Corporation
Summary of Unrealized and Realized Holding Gains

	Inventory	Equipment	Land	Total
Unrealized gains, net of inflation				
at 12/31/81	$166,667	$(112,000)	$-0-	$ 54,667
at 1/1/81	–0–	–0–	–0–	–0–
Increase (decrease) in unrealized gains, net of inflation	166,667	(112,000)	–0–	54,667
Realized gains (losses), net of inflation	133,333	(6,250)	–0–	127,083
Increase (decrease) in current cost of assets held during the year, net of inflation (total holding gains, net of inflation)	$300,000	$(118,250)	$-0-	$181,750

An explanation of the unrealized and realized holding gains follows:

Inventory, cost of goods sold and purchases The beginning inventory is the same under both a constant dollar and current cost/constant dollar accounting system because the historical cost and current cost amounts were identical at the start of the business. An unrealized holding gain of $166,667 ($500,000 − $333,333) must be recognized on the ending inventory because the current cost/constant dollar basis exceeds the constant dollar basis. A realized holding gain of $133,333 must also be recognized for the difference between the current cost/constant dollar cost of goods sold $950,000 and the constant dollar cost of goods sold of $816,667. No holding gains result on the purchases because the historical cost and current cost amounts are identical.

Depreciation expense and equipment Depreciation expense on a constant dollar basis is $20,000, and on a current cost/constant dollar is $13,750 ($11,000 ×

200/160). A realized holding loss, net of inflation would therefore be recognized in the amount of $6,250 ($20,000 − $13,750). Because the current cost/constant dollar basis of the equipment at the end of the year is less than the constant dollar basis of the equipment at the end of the year by $112,000 ($280,000 − $168,000), an unrealized holding loss (net of inflation), of that amount must be recognized. No unrealized holding gain exists at the beginning of the year.

Land The current cost of the land has increased $450,000 to $900,000. The land restated on a constant dollar basis is also $900,000. As a result, no holding gain or loss is recognized.

Purchasing Power Gain or Loss The purchasing power gain on net monetary items of $541,250 as computed on page 1131 is already stated in year-end dollars and need not be adjusted. This purchasing power gain on net monetary items is added to current cost/constant dollar loss from continuing operations to arrive at the final net income on a current cost/constant dollar basis.

Advantages and Disadvantages of Current Cost/Constant Dollar Accounting

Many of the arguments indicated earlier for and against current cost and constant dollar accounting apply here. Some arguments that have particular relevance are presented below:

Arguments for Current Cost/Constant Dollar Accounting:

1. Current cost/constant dollar accounting both **stabilizes the measuring unit and provides current, comparable data.**
2. A current cost/constant dollar system provides **more information** than either system alone. Holding gains and losses adjusted for inflation and deflation are reported, as well as the purchasing power gain or loss on net monetary items.
3. Because it is not certain what is the most useful income figure, by providing these additional disclosures, users through **experimentation** will identify the most useful data.

Arguments against Current Cost/Constant Dollar Accounting:

1. The **cost** to prepare this information is significant and is perhaps not justified by the benefits received.
2. Very few people will understand the new data. Providing this additional information may be more harmful than helpful. More information is not always better information, because it **may confuse readers or lead to information overload.**
3. The conceptual superiority of the current cost/constant dollar accounting system is **untested and unproven.** For example, there is no body of literature that indicates that the information might lead to better predictions of cash flow.

FASB POSITION

FASB Statement No. 33

In late 1979, the long-awaited **FASB Statement No. 33** on "Financial Reporting and Changing Prices" was issued. The Board indicated that **no major changes should**

Exhibit 4
Lia Corporation
Comparative Balance Sheets
as of January 1 and December 31, 1981
(Current Cost/Constant Dollar Basis)

	January 1, 1981	December 31, 1981
Cash, receivables, and other monetary assets	$ 400,000	$ 325,000
Inventories	500,000	500,000
Equipment (net)	300,000	168,000
Land	900,000	900,000
Total assets	$2,100,000	$1,893,000
Current liabilities (all monetary)	$ 200,000	$ 200,000
Long-term liabilities (all monetary)	1,300,000	650,000
Total liabilities	1,500,000	850,000
Common stock	600,000	600,000
Retained earnings	-0-	443,000
Total stockholders' equity	600,000	1,043,000
Total liabilities and stockholders' equity	$2,100,000	$1,893,000

Lia Corporation
Statement of Income and Retained Earnings
For the Year Ended December 31, 1981
(Current Cost/Constant Dollar Basis)

Sales	$1,000,000
Cost of goods sold	950,000
Gross profit	50,000
Selling and administrative expenses	212,500
Depreciation expense	13,750
Loss before income taxes	(176,250)
Income taxes	93,750
Loss from continuing operations	(270,000)
Realized holding gain, net of inflation	127,083
Realized loss	(142,917)
Unrealized holding gain, net of inflation	54,667
	(88,250)
Purchasing power gain on net monetary items	541,250
Current cost/constant dollar net income	453,000
Retained earnings, January 1, 1981	-0-
	453,000
Cash dividends	10,000
Retained earnings, December 31, 1981	$ 443,000

be made to the primary financial statements at the present time but that something must be done to augment them with information about the effects of price changes. The statement requires two different types of disclosure—one on a constant dollar basis and the other on a current cost basis. Balance sheets and complete statements of income on either a current cost or a constant dollar basis are not required, although their presentation is encouraged. Certain enterprises are required to report the following:[20]

(a) Income from continuing operations on a constant dollar basis.
(b) The purchasing power gain or loss on net monetary items.

AND

(a) Income from continuing operations on a current cost basis.
(b) Current cost amounts of inventory and property, plant, and equipment at the end of the year.
(c) Increases or decreases in current cost amounts of inventory and property, plant, and equipment, net of inflation (same as total holding gain, net of inflation).

In addition, a five-year summary of selected financial data, including information on income, sales and other operating revenues, net assets, dividends per common share and market price per share must be reported. In the computation of net assets, only inventory and property, plant, and equipment need be adjusted for the effects of changing prices.

Because of the costs involved in preparing this information, only certain large public companies are required to present this information on a supplementary basis, although others are encouraged to do so.[21] Information related to changing prices is to be presented in supplementary statements, schedules, or supplementary notes in the financial reports along with the primary financial statements.

In summary, the Board is requiring companies to report both constant dollar and current cost information. What is proposed is a set of disclosures that fall short of requiring comprehensive financial statements of either of these approaches. Many will argue that the Board went too far; others will argue that the Board did not go far enough. Actually, the FASB had little choice. Some current cost disclosure was necessary to cause the SEC rescission of **ASR No. 190**.[22] In addition, given the continued high inflation rate, some form of constant dollar accounting has become imperative.

Partial Restatement Required

FASB Statement No. 33 does not require the preparation of comprehensive financial statements on a constant dollar or current cost basis. However, the Board encourages companies to experiment and to present financial statements on a comprehensive basis. If comprehensive financial statements are prepared, we believe that the financial statements presented earlier provide an appropriate basis for reporting this information. Little guidance is provided in **Statement No. 33** for companies that wish to present comprehensive financial statements, except that the minimum disclosures required for partial restatement must be present if comprehensive restatement occurs.

[20]"Financial Reporting and Changing Prices," *Statement of Financial Accounting Standards No. 33* (Stamford, Conn.: FASB, 1979).

[21]Large public companies are defined as enterprises having inventories and property, plant, and equipment (before deducting accumulated depreciation, depletion and amortization) amounting to more than 125 million or total assets amounting to more than $1 billion (after deducting accumulated depreciation).

[22]The SEC has voted to delete its replacement cost disclosure requirements when *FASB Statement No. 33* becomes effective.

Because accounting for changing prices is a complex issue, the Board simplifies the analysis in a number of ways. First, **restatement is necessary only for inventory, property, plant, and equipment, cost of goods sold, and depreciation and depletion expense;** sales and other revenues, and other expenses do not have to be adjusted. In addition, investments in subsidiaries, intangibles, and deferred charges and credits do not have to be restated. The Board takes this approach because the differences between historical cost and constant dollar or current cost amounts for inventories, property, plant and equipment are likely to be great.[23]

Second, the Board requires this limited information be reported in **average-for-the-year dollars** instead of year-end dollars. This approach has significant computational advantages in that revenues and expenses assumed to occur evenly throughout the year will be the same in historical as well as constant dollars. Current cost measures of cost of goods sold and depreciation expense also approximate measures in average-for-the-year dollars without further adjustment.[24] If comprehensive financial statements are prepared, they may be prepared in average-for-the-year dollars or end-of-the-year dollars. The problem with the use of average-for-the-year dollars when comprehensive financial statements are prepared is that the monetary items must be adjusted to average-for-the-year dollars and, therefore, will not be stated at the same amount as the historical cost balances.

Third, **no distinction is made between realized and unrealized holding gains and losses.** A total holding gain or loss, net of inflation referred to in the statement as the excess of the increase in specific prices over the increase in the general price-level, only need be presented.

FASB Position—Lia Corporation

To illustrate the constant dollar and current cost approach required by the FASB, assume the information for Lia Corporation on page 1127 (Exhibit 1). When a partial income statement is prepared in constant dollars, average-for-the-year dollars must be used. It should be emphasized that even if revenues and other expenses are not incurred evenly throughout the year, the FASB assumes an even incurrence to simplify the computations.

Adjustments to Income Statement Items

Sales Because sales are spread evenly through the year, they are incurred in average-for-the-year dollars. No adjustment is therefore necessary on a constant dollar basis or on a current cost basis. Sales are reported as follows:

Constant Dollar	$800,000
Current Cost	$800,000

Cost of Goods Sold The cost of goods sold can be restated in average-for-the-year dollars as follows:

---

[23]*Statement No. 33, op. cit.,* par. 202.
[24]*Ibid.,* par. 189.

Beginning inventory	$250,000 × 160/100 =	$400,000
Purchases	520,000 × 160/160 =	520,000
Goods available for sale	770,000	920,000
Ending inventory	300,000 × 160/180 =	266,667
Cost of goods sold	$470,000	$653,333

The current cost of goods sold is given as $760,000 and was incurred in average-for-the-year dollars. The following two amounts would be reported for cost of goods sold:

Constant Dollar	$653,333
Current Cost	$760,000

Selling and Administrative Expenses These expenses are incurred evenly throughout the year, and no adjustment is necessary on a constant dollar or current cost basis. These amounts are reported as follows:

Constant Dollar	$170,000
Current Cost	$170,000

Depreciation Expense The equipment was purchased at the beginning of the year and depreciation expense is restated to average-for-the-year dollars as follows:

$$\$10,000 \times 160/100 = \$16,000$$

As indicated earlier, the depreciation expense on a current cost basis was computed as follows:

$$\text{Average current cost balance} = \frac{\$150,000 + \$180,000}{2} = \$165,000$$

$$\text{Depreciation expense} = \$165,000 \div 15 = \$11,000$$

The following two amounts would then be reported as depreciation expense:

Constant Dollar	$16,000
Current Cost	$11,000

Income Taxes These expenses were incurred evenly throughout the year and are reported as follows:

Constant Dollar	$75,000
Current Cost	$75,000

In addition to income from continuing operations, a purchasing power gain or loss on net monetary items would have to be computed in reporting the constant dollar information. The method is shown below:

Lia Corporation
Computation of Purchasing Power Gain or Loss—1981
(Average-for-the-Year Dollars)

Net monetary items:	Historical	1/1/81 Index	Restated to average-for-the-year Dollars	12/31/81 Historical Stated in 12/31/81 Dollars
Cash, receivables, and other monetary assets	$ 200,000	× 160/100	320,000	325,000
Current liabilities (all monetary)	(100,000)	× 160/100	(160,000)	(200,000)
Long-term liabilities (all monetary)	(650,000)	× 160/100	(1,040,000)	(650,000)
Net monetary items	$(550,000)[a]		$ (880,000)[b]	$(525,000) [c]

	1981 Historical	Index	Restated to average-for-the-year Dollars
Net monetary items 1/1/81	$(550,000)[a]	× 160/100	(880,000) [b]
Add (sources):			
Sales	800,000	× 160/160	800,000
	250,000		(80,000)
Deduct (uses)			
Purchases	520,000	× 160/160	520,000
Selling and administrative expenses	170,000	× 160/160	170,000
Income taxes	75,000	× 160/160	75,000
Cash dividends	10,000	× 160/200	8,000
Total uses	775,000		773,000
Net monetary items— historical 12/31/81	$(525,000)[c]		
Net monetary items—restated			(853,000)
Net monetary items—historical adjusted to average-for-the-year dollars	$(525,000)	× 160/200	(420,000)
Purchasing power gain on net monetary items			$ 433,000

Note that use of the average-for-the-year dollar method simplifies the computation of the income from continuing operations and the purchasing power gain or loss on net monetary items because many items are not adjusted.

Adjustments of Balance Sheet Items

Although the FASB does not require a balance sheet, to compute the excess of the increase in specific prices over the increase in the general price level (total holding gain, net of inflation) a number of balance sheet items must be adjusted. Note that the FASB current cost approach states current cost in average-for-the-year dollars. The current cost of assets on hand at the end of the year must therefore be deflated to average-for-the-year dollars.

Inventory The inventory at the beginning of the year on an historical cost and current cost basis is the same. As a result, the beginning inventory is restated as follows:

Constant Dollar	$250,000 \times 160/100 = \$400,000$
Current Cost (FASB)	$250,000 \times 160/100 = \$400,000$

The ending inventory on an historical cost basis ($300,000) and on a current cost basis ($500,000) are not the same and are reported as follows:

Constant Dollar	$300,000 \times 160/180 = \$266,667$
Current Cost (FASB)	$500,000 \times 160/200 = \$400,000$

Equipment The equipment at the beginning of the year on an historical and current cost basis is identical. As a result, the beginning equipment is restated as follows:

Constant Dollar	$150,000 \times 160/100 = \$240,000$
Current Cost (FASB)	$150,000 \times 160/100 = \$240,000$

The equipment at the end of the year on an historical cost basis ($140,000) and on a current cost basis ($168,000) are different and are restated as follows:

Constant Dollar	$140,000 \times 160/100 = \$224,000$
Current Cost (FASB)	$168,000 \times 160/200 = \$134,400$

Land At the beginning of the year land on an historical cost basis and land on a current cost basis are identical. As a result, the land is restated as follows:

Constant Dollar	$450,000 \times 160/100 = \$720,000$
Current Cost (FASB)	$450,000 \times 160/100 = \$720,000$

At the end of the year land on an historical cost basis ($450,000) and land on a current cost basis ($900,000) are different. These items are restated as follows:

Constant Dollar	$450,000 × 160/100 = $720,000
Current Cost (FASB)	$900,000 × 160/200 = $720,000

Total Holding Gain   For computing the total holding gain (net of inflation) we now have the following data:

Exhibit 5–A
Lia Corporation
Constant Dollar and Current Cost for Selected Items

	Constant Dollar	Current Cost (FASB)	Difference
Inventory 1/1/81	$400,000	$400,000	-0-
Inventory 12/31/81	266,667	400,000	$133,333
Cost of goods sold	653,333	760,000	106,667
Purchases	520,000	520,000	-0-
Equipment 1/1/81	240,000	240,000	-0-
Equipment 12/31/81	224,000	134,400	(89,600)
Depreciation expense	16,000	11,000	(5,000)
Land 1/1/81	720,000	720,000	-0-
Land 12/31/81	720,000	720,000	-0-

Exhibit 5–B summarizes the computation of the total holding gain, net of inflation, using the FASB approach.

Exhibit 5–B
Lia Corporation
Summary of Unrealized and Realized Holding Gains

	Inventory	Equipment	Land	Total
Unrealized gains, net of inflation				
at 12/31/81	$133,333	$(89,600)	$-0-	$ 43,733
at 1/1/81	-0-	-0-	-0-	-0-
Increase (decrease) in unrealized gains, net of inflation	133,333	(89,600)	-0-	43,733
Realized gains (losses), net of inflation	106,667	(5,000)	-0-	101,667
Increase (decrease) in current cost of assets held during the year, net of inflation (total holding gain, net of inflation)	$240,000	$(94,600)	$-0-	$145,400

Another way to compute the $145,400 above is to restate the total holding gain (net of inflation) of $181,750 (Exhibit 4–B) to average-for-the-year dollars ($145,400 = $181,750 × 160/200). Note that if the total holding gain is $969,000 (Exhibit 3–B) and the total holding gain (net of inflation) is $145,400, the effect of inflation can then be measured as follows:

Increase in current cost (total holding gain)	$969,000
Increase in current cost (FASB)	145,400
Effect of inflation	$823,600

The partial income statement reporting constant dollar and current cost income from continuing operations is shown on page 1156 (Exhibit 5) with the information required in the five-year summary. Note that the purchasing power gain or loss on net monetary items as well as the excess of the specific increase in inventory, equipment, and land over the increase in the general price-level (total holding gain, net of inflation) are not added to income from continuing operations to arrive at total income. The reason is that some believe these items should be credited or debited directly to stockholders' equity. Others argue that these gains and losses should be reported as the last element in or immediately following net income. And still others argue that one of the two items should be income, but not the other. As a consequence, the Board decided that disclosure was the most important consideration and did not attempt to classify these items as either income or capital.

The FASB permits the information on changing prices to be presented in an income statement format or a **reconciliation format.** The reconciliation format is provided below and shows the adjustments to historical cost income from continuing operations to arrive at the inflation adjusted amounts. The computations are provided in the statement to indicate how the individual amounts are determined.

Lia Corporation
Statement of Income From Continuing Operations
Adjusted for Changing Prices
For the Year Ended December 31, 1981

Income from continuing operations, as reported in the income statement		$ 75,000
Adjustments to restate costs for the effect of general inflation		
Cost of goods sold ($653,333 − $470,000)	$183,333	
Depreciation expense ($16,000 − $10,000)	6,000	189,333
Loss from continuing operations adjusted for general inflation		114,333
Adjustments to reflect the difference between general inflation and changes in specific prices (current costs)		
Cost of goods sold ($760,000 − $653,333)	$106,667	
Depreciation expense ($11,000 − $16,000)	(5,000)	101,667
Loss from continuing operations adjusted for changes in specific prices		$216,000

(The remainder of the reconciliation would provide the same information as Exhibit 5 starting with purchasing power gain on net monetary items.)

Five Year Summary

In addition to reporting the constant dollar and current cost information for the current year, the FASB requires a five-year comparison of selected financial data adjusted for the effects of changing prices. The purpose of this summary is to provide the user of the financial statements with some idea of the trend in such items as earnings, dividends, and consumer prices. Using the Lia Corporation illustration, most of the information for this report has already been computed or is easily computed. The only additional computation that is necessary is the balance in net assets on a constant dollar and current cost basis. To determine the required amounts the difference between (a) constant dollar and historical cost and (b) current cost and historical cost for inventories, property, plant and equipment must be computed. These differences are added to net assets (stockholders' equity) and then converted to average-for-the-year dollars. This computation is shown below:

	Historical Cost Exhibit 1	Constant Dollar Exhibit 2	Current Cost Exhibit 3
	Lia Corporation Computation of Net Assets as of December 31, 1981		
Inventory	$300,000	$ 333,333	$ 500,000
Equipment (net)	140,000	280,000	168,000
Land	450,000	900,000	900,000
	$890,000	$1,513,333	$1,568,000
Net assets (stockholders' equity), 12/31/81, as stated in the financial statements (historial cost)		$365,000	$ 365,000
Inventory, equipment (net) and land			
Constant dollar amount		$1,513,333	
Historical cost amount		890,000	623,333
Current cost amount		$1,568,000	
Historical cost amount		890,000	678,000
Net assets 12/31/81—as stated in year-end dollars			
Constant dollar		$988,333	
Current cost			$1,043,000
Adjustment to average dollars			
Constant dollar $988,333 × 160/200		$790,666	
Current cost $1,043,000 × 160/200			$ 834,400

For purposes of the five-year summary it is assumed that 100,000 shares were outstanding for the year. This information is presented at the bottom of page 1156 (Exhibit 5).

Additional Highlights

Other matters of importance are as follows:

1. Use of recoverable amount.
2. Income taxes
3. Determination of current costs.

Exhibit 5
Lia Corporation
Statement of Income from Continuing Operations
Adjusted for Changing Prices
For the Year Ended December 31, 1981

	Historical Cost	Constant Dollar	Current Cost
Sales	$800,000	$ 800,000	$ 800,000
Cost of goods sold	470,000	653,333	760,000
Selling and administrative expense	170,000	170,000	170,000
Depreciation expense	10,000	16,000	11,000
Income taxes	75,000	75,000	75,000
	725,000	914,333	1,016,000
Income (loss) from continuing operations	$ 75,000	$(114,333)	$ (216,000)
Purchasing power gain on net monetary items		$ 433,000	$ 433,000
Increase in specific prices (current cost) of inventories, equipment and land held during the year*			$ 969,000
Effect of increase in general price-level**			$ 823,600
Excess of increase in specific price over increase in the general price-level			$ 145,400

*At December 31, 1981 current cost of the inventory was $500,000, equipment $168,000 and land $900,000.
**Presentation is not required by *FASB Statement No. 33.*

FIVE-YEAR COMPARISON OF SELECTED
SUPPLEMENTARY FINANCIAL DATA ADJUSTED FOR EFFECTS OF CHANGING PRICES

(In Average 1981 Dollars)

	Years Ended December 31,				
	1979	1978	1979	1980	1981
Net sales and other operating revenues	XX	XX	XX	XX	$ 800,000
Historical cost information adjusted for general inflation:					
Income (loss) from continuing operations					$(114,333)
Income (loss) from continuing operations per common share					$(1.14)
Net assets at year-end					$790,666
Current cost information:					
Income (loss) from continuing operations					$(216,000)
Income (loss) from continuing operations per common share					$(2.16)
Excess of increase in specific prices over increase in the general price level					$145,400
Net assets at year-end					$834,400
Purchasing power gain on net monetary items					$433,000
Cash dividends declared per common share					.10
Market price per common share at year-end					Not given
Average consumer price index					160

Recoverable Amount   The term recoverable amount means net realizable value or the present value (value in use) expected to be recoverable from the sale or use of the asset. The Board requires that when an asset or group of assets recoverable amount is **permanently lower** than historical cost in constant dollars or current cost, the recoverable amount should be used as the measure of the assets and of the expense associated with the use or sale of the assets for that measure of income. This concept is similar to that used for historical cost statements (lower of cost or market for inventories as an illustration). To state assets at a cost figure that is in excess of its recoverable amounts is inappropriate. A better approach is to recognize the loss immediately.

Income Taxes   The FASB requires that the total income tax be based on historical cost and be charged as an expense in arriving at income from continuing operations. The Board wishes to highlight the impact of the income taxes on overstated profits and thereby inform users of the excessive taxation that often occurs in a period of inflation. Others disagree with this approach and argue that a portion of the income taxes should be allocated to the realized holding gain. Still others contend that income taxes should be imputed on the unrealized holding gain as well. If the purpose is to disclose the economic change from one period to another, then many argue that the unrealized holding gain should have a tax effect associated with it.

The Board requires the reporting company to disclose that it made no adjustments to income tax expense for any timing differences that might arise as a result of restatement on a current cost basis. In addition, it must be disclosed that income tax expense has not been allocated between income from continuing operations and the increases or decreases in the current cost amounts of inventory and property, plant and equipment.

Determination of Current Costs   The FASB has identified the following bases for determining the current cost of inventories and property, plant, and equipment.

Direct pricing. Current invoice prices and vendors' and price lists or other quotations or estimates, are acceptable methods of valuing both inventories and property, plant and equipment.

Indexation. Either external or specific internal indexes might be used to value both inventories and property, plant, and equipment.

Standard costs. If these costs reflect current costs, they may be used to determine the current cost of inventories.

Keeping with the Board's attempt to simplify the computations, cost of goods sold measured on a LIFO basis is assumed to provide an acceptable approximation of cost of goods sold on a current cost basis if the effect of any decrease in inventory layers is excluded.

Comparative Analysis

Presented as Exhibit 6 (page 1159) is a comparative set of the financial statements prepared under the different valuation approaches illustrated in this chapter. First, note that the current cost and current cost/constant dollar **balance sheets** will be essentially the same except for differences in stockholders' equity. Second, the current year's monetary balances are unaffected, regardless of the valuation method employed if reported in year-end dollars. However, the nonmonetary items are adjusted, depending upon the method selected.

Examination of the **income statement** shows that Lia Corporation's profitability is the result of a purchasing power gain on net monetary items due principally to holding a large amount of debt during a period of price inflation. During a period of inflation, companies with large real estate holdings and large loans outstanding report higher income under constant dollar and current cost/constant dollar statements. Note also that Lia Corporation would report a loss from continuing operations on a constant dollar, current cost, current cost/constant dollar system, and the FASB approach but would still be paying income taxes. This presentation illustrates why many have contended that the historical cost income numbers are an illusion which vanish after phantom inventory profits are considered and depreciation expense is adjusted for the cost of replacing aging assets. The year 1974 provided a good illustration of this problem. As one article noted, "corporations were paying an effective tax rate of 63% on inflation adjusted profits, compared to what was thought to be only 41%. In addition, some companies increased dividends and ended up paying out 99% of their adjusted earnings." It was estimated that many manufacturing companies paid out more than 150% of their adjusted earnings.[25]

Finally, note that historical cost net income, $75,000, equals current cost realized income, $75,000, and that the constant dollar loss ($142,917) (purchasing gain or loss on net monetary items excluded), equals current cost/constant dollar realized loss, ($142,917). This occurrence in our illustration is not a coincidence; it demonstrates that the current cost approach segregates the historical cost income into two components—income (loss) from continuing operations and realized holding gain (loss).

Concluding Observations

Now that certain enterprises are required to report price-level information, the FASB will be able to determine whether some type of consensus will emerge in support of the appropriate method or methods of valuation. It is quite conceivable that some users will find all or some of the information provided by the FASB requirement helpful, whereas others will find little if any usefulness in these supplementary disclosures. The eventual resolution of this issue is dependent upon continued experimentation and analysis. This statement will have considerable impact upon the investment community.

Questions

1. What is constant dollar accounting? How does constant dollar accounting differ from current cost accounting?
2. Assume that the Consumer Price Index for Urban Consumers has increased to 130 from 100 three years ago. How many end of year dollars are needed today to purchase what $20,000 purchased three years ago?

[25]"The Profit Illusion," *Business Week*, March 19, 1979.

Exhibit 6
Lia Corporation
Comparative Analysis of Different Reporting Systems
December 31, 1981

Balance Sheet	Historical Cost (Exhibit 1)	Constant Dollar (Exhibit 2)	Current Cost (Exhibit 3)	Current Cost/ Constant Dollar (Exhibit 4)	FASB Approach (Exhibit 5) (Partial)
Cash, receivables and other monetary assets	$ 325,000	$ 325,000	$ 325,000	$ 325,000	NA
Inventories	300,000	333,333	500,000	500,000	500,000*
Equipment (net)	140,000	280,000	168,000	168,000	168,000
Land	450,000	900,000	900,000	900,000	900,000
Total assets	$1,215,000	$1,838,333	$1,893,000	$1,893,000	
Current liabilities (all monetary)	200,000	200,000	200,000	200,000	NA
Long-term liabilities (all monetary)	650,000	650,000	650,000	650,000	NA
Total liabilities	850,000	850,000	850,000	850,000	NA
Common stock	300,000	600,000	300,000	600,000	NA
Retained earnings	65,000	388,333	743,000	443,000	NA
Total stockholders' equity	365,000	988,333	1,043,000	1,043,000	NA
Total liabilities and stockholders' equity	$1,215,000	$1,838,333	$1,893,000	$1,893,000	

*The current cost of inventories and property, plant, and equipment must be disclosed.

Income Statement	Historical Cost (Exhibit 1)	Constant Dollar (Exhibit 2)	Current Cost (Exhibit 3)	Current Cost/ Constant Dollar (Exhibit 4)	FASB Approach (Exhibit 5) (Partial) Constant Dollar	FASB Approach (Exhibit 5) (Partial) Current Cost
Sales	$800,000	$1,000,000	$800,000	$1,000,000	$ 800,000	$ 800,000
Cost of goods sold	470,000	816,667	760,000	950,000	653,333	760,000
Gross profit	330,000	183,333	40,000	50,000	146,667	40,000
Selling and administrative expenses	170,000	212,500	170,000	212,500	170,000	170,000
Depreciation expense	10,000	20,000	11,000	13,750	16,000	11,000
Income taxes	75,000	93,750	75,000	93,750	75,000	75,000
Income (loss) from continuing operations	75,000	(142,917)	(216,000)	(270,000)	$(114,333)	$(216,000)
Realized holding gain (loss)	NA	NA	291,000	127,083		
Realized income (loss)	NA	NA	75,000	(142,917)		
Unrealized holding gain	NA	NA	678,000	54,667		
Specific increase (decrease) in inventories, equipment, land, net of inflation	NA	NA	NA	NA		$ 145,400
Purchasing power gain or (loss) on net monetary items	NA	541,250	NA	541,250	$ 433,000	$ 433,000
Net income	75,000	398,333	753,000	453,000		
Beginning retained earnings	-0-	-0-	-0-	-0-		
	75,000	398,333	753,000	453,000		
Cash dividends	10,000	10,000	10,000	10,000		
Ending retained earnings	$ 65,000	$ 388,333	$743,000	$ 443,000		

3. Distinguish between monetary and nonmonetary items. What is a purchasing power gain or loss on net monetary items?

4. What is a price index? How does a general price index differ from a specific price index?

5. If the general price-level is rising steadily, which of the following would be most realistically valued for balance sheet purposes: (a) inventories, (b) receivables, or (c) real estate?

6. Bill Wright purchased a 20-year, 10% bond at par for $1,000, collected interest annually during the life of the bond, and realized the principal amount of the bond at maturity. If the price level were twice as high at maturity date as it was at the date of purchase, how did Bill fare?

7. Sally Harris purchased a 20-year, 10% bond at par for $1,000, collected interest annually during the life of the bond, and realized the principal amount of the bond at maturity. If the price level were half as high at maturity date as it was at the date of purchase, how did Sally fare?

8. Classify each of the following as monetary or nonmonetary items:
    (a) Inventories
    (b) Discount on bonds payable
    (c) Accumulated depreciation—equipment
    (d) Accounts receivable
    (e) Deferred income taxes
    (f) Common stock
    (g) Bonds
    (h) Preferred stock (par value to be paid in liquidation)
    (i) Investment in common stock
    (j) Refundable deposits

9. Indicate whether a company gains or loses under each of the following conditions:
    (a) A company maintains equal amounts of monetary assets and monetary liabilities during a period of price-level increases.
    (b) A company maintains an excess of liabilities over monetary assets during a period of price-level increases.
    (c) A company maintains an excess of monetary assets over monetary liabilities during a period of price-level increases.
    (d) A company maintains an excess of monetary assets over monetary liabilities during a period of price-level decrease.

10. Assume a decade of rising prices. Would the following items give rise to (a) purchasing power gains, (b) purchasing power losses, or (c) neither purchasing power gains or losses?
    (a) Owning land during the period.
    (b) Holding a long-term note payable.
    (c) Holding cash in a pension fund.
    (d) Having preferred stock outstanding during the period.
    (e) Holding a note receivable.
    (f) Having patents during the period.
    (g) Having an investment in common stocks.

11. What are the major arguments in opposition to modifying financial statements for general price level changes?

12. Explain three commonly advocated concepts of current value.

13. Some theorists have argued that the present value of future discounted cash flows should be used as the basis for measuring assets and liabilities. What are the major disadvantages to this approach?

14. Many have noted that the major difference between constant dollar and current cost accounting is related to the view of capital maintenance. What is the theory of capital maintenance and how does the constant dollar approach differ from the current cost approach in this regard?

15. A comprehensive current cost model emphasizes three different income numbers. Explain the rationale for these three income numbers.

16. At the beginning of 1979, a company purchased inventory for $50,000. During the year, the company sold half this inventory for $50,000 at a time when the current cost of the inventory sold was $40,000. At the end of the year, the remaining inventory had a current cost of $55,000. Compute the current cost income from continuing operations, the realized holding gain, the unrealized holding gain and the current cost net income.

17. Hillery Enterprises has decided that it wishes to report current cost information related to its inventories. What approaches might be utilized to find the current cost for inventories?

18. Sample Industries purchased equipment at the beginning of the year for $70,000 that had an estimated life of ten years and no salvage value. The current cost of the equipment at the end of the year was $90,000. Assuming straight-line depreciation on a current cost basis, how much depreciation would be reported as a charge to current cost income from continuing operations? How much should be charged to the unrealized holding gain?

19. Many believe that if a partial or complete current cost income statement is prepared, income taxes should not be allocated to the realized or unrealized holding gain. Explain the rationale for this approach. Indicate the FASB position on this matter.

20. What are the major advantages of current cost accounting? Explain the difference between current cost accounting and replacement cost accounting.

21. Some argue that a current cost approach is not acceptable, unless the historical cost numbers are adjusted to a constant dollar basis. Explain the rationale for this approach.

22. On January 1, 1979, Info, Inc. had cash of $10,000 and inventories whose historical cost and current cost were $20,000. During the year, the general price level increased 15 percent on an even basis throughout the period and the current cost of the inventories at the end of the year was $30,000. Assuming that the company held these assets for the entire year, compute the unrealized holding gain if a current cost/constant dollar approach were employed and reported in (1) end-of-year dollars and (2) average-for-the-year dollars.

23. What are the major differences between the current cost/constant dollar approach and the current cost approach?

24. What are the major advantages of the current cost/constant dollar approach?

25. Recently, *FASB Statement No. 33* "Financial Reporting and Changing Prices" was issued. Indicate the major reporting requirements of this statement.

26. Why do you believe the FASB required a dual presentation (constant dollar and current cost) for reporting price-level effects?

Cases

C25-1 The general purchasing power of the dollar has declined considerably because of inflation in recent years. To account for this changing value of the dollar, many accountants suggest that financial statements should be adjusted for general price-level changes. Three independent, unrelated statements regarding general price-level adjusted financial statements follow. Each statement contains some fallacious reasoning.

Statement I

The accounting profession has not seriously considered price-level adjusted financial statements before because the rate of inflation usually has been so small from year-to-year that the adjustments would have been immaterial in amount. Price-level adjusted financial statements represent a departure from the historical-cost basis of accounting. Financial statements should be prepared on the basis of facts, not estimates.

Statement II

If financial statements were adjusted for general price-level changes, depreciation charges in the income statement would permit the recovery of dollars of current purchasing power and, thereby, equal the cost of new assets to replace the old ones. General price-level adjusted data would yield statement-of-financial-position amounts closely approximating current values. Furthermore, management can make better decisions if constant dollar financial statements are published.

Statement III

When adjusting financial data for general price-level changes, a distinction must be made between monetary and nonmonetary assets and liabilities, which, under the historical-cost basis of accounting, have been identified as "current" and "noncurrent." When using the historical-cost basis of accounting, no purchasing-power gain or loss is recognized in the accounting process, but when financial statements are adjusted for general price-level changes, a purchasing-power gain or loss will be recognized on monetary and nonmonetary items.

Instructions

Evaluate each of the independent statements and identify the areas of fallacious reasoning in each and explain why the reasoning is incorrect. Complete your discussion of each statement before proceeding to the next statement.

(AICPA adapted)

C25-2 Cola Corp., a manufacturer with large investments in plant and equipment, began operations in 1941. The company's history has been one of expansion in sales, production, and physical facilities. Recently, some concern has been expressed that the conventional financial statements do not provide sufficient information for decisions by investors. After consideration of proposals for various types of supplementary financial statements to be included in the 1980 annual report, management has decided to present a balance sheet as of December 31, 1980, and a statement of income and retained earnings for 1980, both restated for changes in the general price level.

Instructions

(a) On what basis can it be contended that Cola's conventional statements should be restated for changes in the general price level?

(b) Distinguish between financial statements restated for general price-level changes and current-value financial statements.

(c) Distinguish between monetary and nonmonetary assets and liabilities, as the terms are used in constant dollar accounting. Give examples of each.

(d) Outline the procedures Cola should follow in preparing the proposed supplementary statements. (Assume statements are computed in year end dollars.)

(e) Indicate the major similarities and differences between the proposed supplementary statements and the corresponding conventional statements.

(f) Assuming that in the future Cola will want to present comparative supplementary statements, can the 1980 supplementary statements be presented in 1981 without adjustment? Explain.

(AICPA adapted)

C25-3 The financial statements of a business entity could be prepared by using historical cost or current value as a basis. In addition, the basis could be stated in terms of unadjusted dollars or dollars restated for changes in purchasing power. The various permutations of these two separate and distinct areas are shown in the following matrix:

	Unadjusted Dollars	Dollars Restated for Changes in Purchasing Power
Historical cost	1	2
Current value	3	4

Block number 1 of the matrix represents the traditional method of accounting for transactions in accounting today, wherein the absolute (unadjusted) amount of dollars given up or received is recorded for the asset or liability obtained **(relationship between resources)**. Amounts recorded in the method described in block number 1 reflect the original cost of the asset or liability and do not give effect to any change in value of the unit of measure **(standard of comparison)**. This method assumes the validity of the accounting concepts of going concern and stable monetary unit. Any gain or loss (including holding and purchasing power gains or losses) resulting from the sale or satisfaction of amounts recorded under this method is deferred in its entirety until sale or satisfaction.

Instructions

For each of the remaining matrix blocks (2, 3 and 4) respond to the following questions. **Limit your discussion to nonmonetary assets only.**

(a) How will this method of recording assets affect the relationship between resources and the standard of comparison?

(b) What is the theoretical justification for using each method?

(c) How will each method of asset valuation affect the recognition of gain or loss during the life of the asset and ultimately from the sale or abandonment of the asset? Your response should include a discussion of the timing and magnitude of the gain or loss and conceptual reasons for any difference from the gain or loss computed using the traditional method.

(AICPA adapted)

C25-4   The controller for San-Tan, Inc. has recently hired you as assistant controller. Recognizing that you should be quite familiar with the recent pronouncement on accounting for changing prices, the controller shows you supplementary information that the auditors recommend be reported as supplementary data for the year. Part of the information is as follows:

San-Tan, Inc.
STATEMENT OF INCOME FROM CONTINUING
OPERATIONS ADJUSTED FOR CHANGING PRICES
For the Year Ended December 31, 1980

(In (000s) of Average 1980 Dollars)

Income from continuing operations, as reported in the income statement		$ 9,000
Adjustments to restate costs for the effect of general inflation		
Cost of goods sold	(7,384)	
Depreciation and amortization expense	(4,130)	(11,514)
Loss from continuing operations adjusted for general inflation		(2,514)
Adjustments to reflect the difference between general inflation and changes in specific prices (current costs)		
Cost of goods sold	(1,024)	
Depreciation and amortization expense	(5,370)	(6,394)
Loss from continuing operations adjusted for changes in specific prices		$ (8,908)
Purchasing power of net monetary items		$ 7,729

Increase in specific prices (current cost) of inventories and property, plant, and equipment held during the year[a]	$24,608
Effect of increase in general price level	18,959
Excess of increase in specific prices over increase in the general price level	$ 5,649

[a]At December 31, 1980 current cost of inventory was $65,700 and current cost of property, plant, and equipment, net of accumulated depreciation was $85,100.

Instructions

The controller is interested in the answer to the following questions:

(a) Why is the statement presented in average 1980 dollars?

(b) What is meant by general inflation?

(c) What is the difference in the two losses from continuing operations?

(d) Why are the other expenses such as officers salaries not reported on this statement?

(e) What is the purchasing power gain on net monetary items? (Explain.)

(f) Why are taxes not allocated to the increase in specific prices of inventories and property, plant and equipment?

(g) Must San-Tan, Inc. report this information in this manner, or are other alternatives available? (Assume that the company is required to present supplementary price-level data.)

Exercises

E25-1 You have been asked to prepare constant dollar financial statements for the Harris Company. At the end of the period for which statements are being prepared, the price index being used stands at 180. The index values prevailing when each item (amount) was first recorded on the books is shown below.

Item	Index	Item	Index
1. Accounts payable	160	5. Insurance expense	175
2. Equipment	135	6. Bonds payable (long-term)	140
3. Depreciation on equipment	—	7. Rent income	130 and 150
4. Land	180	8. Notes receivable (short-term)	178

Instructions

Indicate which of the items above would be raised, lowered, or remain unchanged on constant dollar statements as compared to the historical cost statements.

E25-2 Excerpts from the trial balance of Karin Haldeman Company as of December 31, 1981, when the price index was 125 include the following accounts.

Cash	$ 30,000
Notes receivable	50,000
Land	100,000
Building	400,000
Accounts payable	25,000
Bonds payable (due 1988)	200,000
Depreciation expense—building	10,000
Inventory (LIFO basis)	60,000
Sales (made evenly throughout the year)	400,000

During 1981, the average price index was 120. The land was purchased in 1973 when the price index was 90, and the building was constructed in 1977 when the index was 100. The bonds were issued November, 1976, when the index was 98. The LIFO inventory was built up during 1978 when the average index was 105.

Instructions

At what amounts would these accounts be presented in constant dollar financial statements in (1) end-of-year dollars and (2) average-for-the-year dollars?

E25-3 Presented below are selected price indices for specific dates or periods:

Dec. 31, 1953—100	June 30, 1980—201
Feb. 15, 1954—107	Dec. 31, 1980—213
Mar. 21, 1954—107	Average 1980—203
May 1, 1969—172	June 19, 1981—218
Sept. 23, 1973—187	Dec. 31, 1981—230
Dec. 31, 1976—195	Average 1981—220

1. Depreciation expense for 1981 (on equipment purchased March 21, 1954).
2. Sales made during 1981.
3. Investments in common stocks (purchased May 1, 1969).
4. Accounts payable (balance Dec. 31, 1981).
5. Bonds payable (issued Dec. 31, 1976, maturing Dec. 31, 1993).
6. Purchases made during 1981.
7. Interest expense (incurred evenly through 1981).
8. Allowance for doubtful accounts (balance Dec. 31, 1981).
9. Cash (on hand Dec. 31, 1981).
10. Equipment (purchased Mar. 21, 1954).
11. Common stock, $100 par, issued Dec. 31, 1953.
12. Land (acquired Feb. 15, 1954).
13. Preferred stock, 6% (issued Sept. 23, 1973).
14. Accounts receivable (balance Dec. 31, 1981).
15. Inventory (LIFO accumulated throughout 1980).

Instructions

Given the dates and respective price indices above, indicate what the numerator and the denominator would be to adjust the following items for price-level changes for presentation in a December 31, 1981, constant dollar balance sheet, in end-of-year dollars.

E25-4 Import Company purchased equipment for $60,000 on January 1, 1980, when the price index was 125. The equipment has an estimated life of 10 years with no scrap value. At December 31, 1980, the price index was 140 and at December 31, 1981, it was 150.

Instructions

(a) At what amounts is the equipment carried on constant dollar balance sheets at December 31, 1980, and December 31, 1981? (Assume amounts reported in end-of-year dollars.) Round answers to nearest dollar.

(b) What is the amount of depreciation expense (use the straight-line method) on the constant dollar income statements for the years ended December 31, 1980 and December 31, 1981? (Assume amounts reported in end-of-year dollars.)

(c) Assuming that the average price level in 1980 was 130 and in 1981 was 144, indicate the amount at which equipment and the related depreciation would be reported on the related financial statements for each of these years. (Assume average-for-the-year dollars is employed.)

E25-5 The Leland Company began operations on January 1, 1981. At that time merchandise was purchased for $40,000. Additional merchandise was purchased uniformly throughout the year for $210,000. The inventory at December 31, 1981 consists of goods purchased throughout December, at a cost of $29,000. Leland utilized a FIFO cost assumption. Assume the following price-level indices:

January 1, 1981	125
1981 Year Average	140
December, 1981, Average	145
December 31, 1981	150

Instructions

Compute the cost of goods sold as it would appear in a constant dollar income statement for 1981 in (1) end-of-year dollars and (2) average-for-the-year dollars.

E25-6 At the beginning of 1980, the Barrett Company had net monetary assets of $60,000. During the period, the following items increased or decreased this balance:

1. Sales of $200,000 were made evenly throughout the period.
2. Purchases of $150,000 were made evenly throughout the period.
3. Selling expenses (excluding depreciation) of $40,000 were incurred in the first quarter.
4. Equipment was purchased in the first quarter for $11,000 and dividends were paid on December 31 of $6,000.

   The Consumer Price Index for all Urban Consumers was as follows:

January 1, 1980	100
First quarter, 1980	110
Average 1980	120
December 31, 1980	140

Instructions

(a) Compute the purchasing power gain or loss on net monetary items for 1980 in end-of-year dollars.

(b) Compute the purchasing power gain or loss on net monetary items for 1980 in average-for-the-year dollars as required in *FASB Statement No. 33.*

E25-7 The books of Howard Company carried the following selected items on December 31.

	1981	1980
Net monetary items	$ 42,700	$ 30,500
Inventory (FIFO)	66,600	50,000
Plant and equipment	125,500	225,500
Accumulated depreciation—plant and equipment	30,000	85,000
Common stock, $10 par	100,000	100,000

Other relevant information:

1. Equipment costing $100,000 and having $60,000 of accumulated depreciation was sold on April 15, 1981 for its book value.
2. The company paid a $.10/share cash dividend on June 15, 1981 and December 15, 1981.
3. The following Consumer Price Indices for all Urban Consumers existed

December 31, 1980	110
April 15, 1981	105
June 15, 1981	110
December 15, 1981	125
December 31, 1981	125
Average for 1981	115

4. Assume that all other transactions that affect net monetary items such as sales occur evenly through 1981.

Instructions

(a) Compute the purchasing power gain or loss on net monetary items for 1981 in end-of-year dollars.

(b) Compute the purchasing power gain or loss on net monetary items for 1981 in average-for-the-year dollars as required by FASB Statement No. 33.

E25-8   Henshaw Manufacturing has equipment with the following costs and other information at the end of 1980:

	Cost	Acquisition Date	Acquisition Date Heavy Tools Price Index
Milling lathe	$50,000	January 10, 1977	100
Drill press	42,500	September 2, 1977	110
Finishing lathe	30,000	December 20, 1978	120
Sander	36,000	July 5, 1979	125

Each item has a useful life of 10 years and no salvage value. The company policy is to take straight-line depreciation on all equipment and to take one-half year's depreciation in the years of acquisition and disposal.

The current Heavy Tools Price Index is 140.

Instructions

Determine the net current cost of the equipment; that is, the gross cost less accumulated depreciation in end-of-year dollars. Do not compute depreciation expense.

E25-9   Salem Manufacturing Company owns a patent for a milling device. The device has a remaining life of four years. Salem estimates the future cash flows from the patent to be as follows:

Year	Cash Receipts Received at the End of Each Year	Cash Disbursements Made at the End of Each Year	Net Cash Inflows
1	$50,000	$20,000	$30,000
2	40,000	20,000	20,000
3	25,000	20,000	5,000
4	21,000	18,000	3,000

Instructions

(a) Assuming a 10% discount factor, determine the present value of the patent. (Round to nearest dollar.)

(b) Many contend that the present value of future cash flows is the proper method for valuation purposes. Speculate as to why this approach was not adopted in FASB Statement No. 33.

E25-10   Federal Systems, Inc. adopted a current cost system in its first year of operation. At the start of the first year, 1980, the company purchased $20,000 of inventory, and at the end of the year had an inventory of $12,000 on an historical cost basis and $19,000 on a current cost basis. At the time the inventory was sold, the current cost of the inventory was $11,000. Sales for the year were $15,000. Ignore all tax effects and assume that the Consumers Price Index for all Urban Consumers did not change over this period. Other expenses were $1,000 on both historical cost and current cost bases.

Instructions

(a) Prepare a current cost income statement.

(b) Prepare a current cost income statement in accordance with FASB Statement No. 33.

E25-11   Assume the same information as Exercise 25-10, and that the Consumer Price Index for all Urban Consumers was as follows:

Beginning of 1980	100
Average for 1980	120
End of 1980	150

Instructions

Compute the increase (decrease) in the current cost of inventory, less the effect of the increase in the general price-level. Assume that the current cost of goods sold was sold at the time when the general price-level was at the average for the year. The beginning inventory was acquired at the beginning price-level. The company is only presenting a partial income statement in accordance with *FASB Statement No. 33*.

E25-12   Presented below is the historical cost income statement of Williams, Inc.

Sales	$30,000
Cost of goods sold	12,000
Gross profit	18,000
Depreciation expense	2,000
Other expenses	6,000
Income before taxes	10,000
Income taxes (50%)	5,000
Net income	$ 5,000

Assume that the current cost of goods sold was $15,000 and that depreciation on a current cost basis was $5,000. Current cost and historical cost are the same on all other items. The general price level has not changed.

Instructions

(a) Prepare a current cost partial income statement per *FASB Statement No. 33*. Use the income statement format and assume that no unrealized holding gains exist.

(b) If a portion of the income tax were allocated to the realized holding gain, how would the income statement differ?

(c) What might be the rationale of the FASB for not allocating the income tax?

E25-13   Hoyt Enterprises is considering the adoption of a current cost system. Presented below is the enterprises' balance sheet at the end of the first year based on historical cost.

Hoyt Enterprises
BALANCE SHEET
as of December 31, 19xx

Cash	$25,000	Accounts Payable	$ 9,000
Inventory	42,000	Capital Stock	50,000
Land	16,000	Retained Earnings	24,000
	$83,000		$83,000

The following additional information is presented:

1. Cost of goods sold on an historical cost basis is $54,000; on a current cost basis $58,000.
2. No dividends were paid in the first year of operation.
3. Ending inventory on a current cost basis is $46,000; land on a current basis is $22,000 at the end of the year.
4. Operating expenses for the first year were $19,000.

Instructions

(a) Prepare an income statement for the current year on a (1) historical cost basis; (2) current cost basis. No unrealized holding gains exist at the beginning of the year.

(b) Prepare a balance sheet for the current year on a current cost basis.

E25-14

Fortune Corporation
INCOME STATEMENT
For the Year Ended December 31, 1981

		Historical
Sales		$ 950,000
Cost of goods sold:		
Inventory 1/1/81	$ 40,000	
Purchases	500,000	
	540,000	
Inventory 12/31/81	100,000	
Cost of goods sold		440,000
Gross profit		560,000
Depreciation	400,000	
Operating expenses	190,000	
Total expenses		590,000
Net loss		$ (80,000)

Additional information:

1. Revenues are earned and operating expenses are incurred evenly throughout the year.
2. Inventory was acquired during the last week of the year (FIFO basis).
3. Depreciable assets have a five-year life and were acquired as follows:

    January 1, 1978—$1,500,000
    January 1, 1980— 500,000

4. The Consumer Price Index for all Urban Consumers was as follows:

1/1/78	150
Average, 1978	140
1/1/80	125
Average, 1980	120
1/1/81	110
Average, 1981	100
12/31/81	80

5. The purchasing power loss on net monetary items was $19,000.

Instructions

(a) Using the data provided above, prepare a comprehensive constant dollar income statement in year-end dollars.

(b) What are the major differences between a comprehensive income statement on a constant dollar basis and a partial income statement on a constant dollar basis prepared in accordance with the provisions of *FASB Statement No. 33*?

E25-15 Presented below is information related to equipment purchased by Marshall Company.

Historical cost (acquired 7/1/80)	$10,000
Current cost 1/1/82 (gross)	12,000
Current cost 12/31/82 (25% increase in specific price index)	15,000
Accumulated depreciation 1/1/82:	
Historical cost	3,000
Current cost	3,600
Life of asset	5 years
Depreciation method	Straight-line

Instructions

(a) Compute the amount of depreciation expense that would be reported in arriving at income from continuing operations on a current cost basis per *FASB Statement No. 33*. (One-half year's depreciation was taken in the year of acquisition.)

(b) Compute the increase in current cost of equipment (holding gain) that will be reported per *FASB Statement No. 33*.

E25-16   Roller Enterprises purchased 100 bolts of cloth for $400 each on July 1, 1980. On December 15, 50 bolts were sold for $500 each, the current cost to replace the sold bolts was $450 each. On March 31, 1981, the remaining bolts were sold for $550 each; their current cost had risen to $510.

Instructions

Compute the current cost net income in 1980 and 1981. Indicate the realized and unrealized holding gains (losses) reported in each year. Ignore income taxes.

Problems

P25-1   The historical cost balance sheet for the Derek Holcomb Corporation is as follows:

Assets	12/31/79	12/31/80
Cash and accounts receivable	$ 80,000	$ 190,000
Inventory	500,000	520,000
Equipment	130,000	250,000
Accumulated depreciation—equipment	(11,500)	(30,500)
Building	800,000	800,000
Accumulated depreciation—building	(80,000)	(152,000)
	$1,418,500	$1,577,500

Liabilities and Owners' Equity		
Accounts payable	$ 40,000	$ 50,000
8% bonds payable	600,000	650,000
Preferred stock	100,000	100,000
Common stock	300,000	300,000
Retained earnings	378,500	477,500
	$1,418,500	$1,577,500

The following information is taken from the historical cost income statement:

Sales revenue	$1,000,000
Cost of goods sold	600,000
Selling and administrative expenses	29,000
Depreciation expense	91,000
Interest expense	64,000
Income taxes	16,000

The following additional information is provided:

1. Sales revenues and material purchases occurred uniformly throughout the year. The expenses, other than depreciation, were paid uniformly throughout the year.
2. The general price-level index at December 31, 1979 is 140; the average index for the year 1980 is 145; the index at December 31, 1980 is 150.
3. The inventories utilize a FIFO-cost assumption. The December 31, 1979 inventory consists of goods acquired during the last three months of the year; the average index during those three months was 135. The December 31, 1980 inventory consists of goods acquired during the last month of 1980; the average index for that month was 148.
4. The equipment account consists of the following:

Acquisition date	Amount	Index
6/ 5/78	$ 50,000	120
10/27/79	80,000	134
10/ 9/80	120,000	146
	$250,000	

Depreciation is calculated using the straight-line method, a useful life of 10 years, and no expected salvage value. Company policy is to take ½ year's depreciation in the year of acquisition or retirement.

5. The building was acquired in 1979, when the index was 130. The building has a 20-year life, with an estimated salvage value of $50,000. Depreciation is calculated using the double-declining balance method. Company policy with respect to buildings is to take a full year's depreciation in the year of acquisition.
6. Bonds with a face value of $600,000 were issued in 1962, when the company was organized. Bonds with a face value of $50,000 were issued in 1980, when the index was 143.
7. The preferred stock has a par value of $100, and a fixed liquidation value of $110.
8. The common stock was issued when the company was organized in 1962, when the index was 95.
9. Dividends of $101,000 were paid uniformly throughout the year.

Instructions

(a) Prepare a schedule computing the purchasing power gain or loss on net monetary items in end-of-year dollars.
(b) Prepare a constant dollar income statement in end-of-year dollars.
(c) Prepare a constant dollar balance sheet for 1980 in end-of-year dollars, and restate the 1979 balance sheet to the current end-of-year price level.
(d) Prepare a schedule computing the purchasing power gain or loss on net monetary items in average-for-the-year dollars as required by *FASB Statement No. 33*.

P25-2 Comparative balance sheets for the Hartwick Company on December 31, 1979, 1980, and 1981 are shown below:

	December 31,		
	1979	1980	1981
Cash	$ 20,000	$ 15,000	$ 30,000
Receivables	30,000	40,000	40,000
Merchandise	20,000	25,000	30,000
Plant (net)	65,000	65,000	64,750
Total	$135,000	$145,000	$164,750

Accounts Payable	$ 30,000	$ 30,000	$ 45,000
Capital Stock	80,000	80,000	80,000
Retained Earnings	25,000	35,000	39,750
Total	$135,000	$145,000	$164,750

Additional information is as follows:

1. The Consumers Price Index for all Urban Consumers for applicable years is

	Index Number
January 1, 1973	100
Last quarter, 1979	120
December 31, 1979	120
Average, 1980	130
Last quarter, 1980	140
December 31, 1980	150
Average, 1981	160
Last quarter, 1981	160
December 31, 1981	170

2. Sales were $200,000 in 1980 and $250,000 in 1981.
3. Purchases and sales were made regularly throughout the year.
4. Merchandise inventory was acquired in the last quarter of the year.
5. Plant assets were acquired for cash as follows:

January 1, 1973	$100,000
December 31, 1980	5,000
December 31, 1981	5,000
Total	$110,000

6. Depreciation is at the rate of 5% of cost each year, and no salvage value is assumed.
7. Cost of goods sold was $100,000 in 1980 and $125,000 in 1981.
8. Operating expenses were incurred throughout the year.
9. The company had paid no dividend since 1973.

Instructions

(a) Prepare income statements for 1980 and 1981 on an historical cost basis.
(b) Prepare income statements for 1980 and 1981 on a constant dollar basis. Both income statements should be stated in 12/31/81 dollars.

P25-3   RM and Associates is discussing the possibility of reporting its cost of goods sold and ending inventory on an historical cost, constant dollar, current cost, and current cost/constant dollar basis. Assume that you are given the following information with respect to RM and Associates.

	Historical Cost	Current Cost	Consumer Price Index for Urban Consumers
Beginning inventory	$ 40,000	$40,000	100
Purchases	160,000	*	120 (average)
Ending inventory	50,000	60,000	140

*Note: the current cost of goods sold is $180,000 (incurred evenly through the year).

Assume that the beginning and ending inventory were purchased when the general price-level indexes were 100 and 140 respectively. Purchases were made evenly throughout the year.

Instructions

    (a) Compute the cost of goods sold and ending inventory under an historical cost, constant dollar, current cost and current cost/constant dollar accounting system in year end dollars. (Hint: the conversion factor for 140/120 to be used is 1.167.)

    (b) At what amount would cost of goods sold and inventory be reported in accordance with *FASB Statement No. 33*, assuming that comprehensive financial statements are not prepared. (Hint: the conversion factor for 120/140 to be used is .857.)

    (c) Compute the increase in current cost of inventory, net of general inflation effects. Indicate the realized and unrealized holding gain, net of inflation. Compute in average-for-the-year dollars.

P25-4 Presented below is information related to the Frederick Company at the beginning of the year 1980:

Frederick Co.
BALANCE SHEET
as of January 1, 1980

Cash	$10,000	Common Stock	$30,000
Inventory	20,000	Retained Earnings	15,000
Land	15,000		
	$45,000		$45,000

Additional information related to transactions occurring in 1980.

Sales	$100,000
Purchases of inventory in 1980	60,000
Ending inventory, 12/31/80, historical cost	22,000
Ending inventory, 12/31/80, current cost	26,000
Cost of goods sold on current cost basis at different dates during the year (average current cost of goods sold the same)	65,000

Land's current cost increased to $19,000 during the year

Operating expenses on both an historical and current cost basis were $20,000.

All applicable transactions were on a cash basis and the company uses a perpetual system for recording inventories.

Current cost and historical cost are identical for the inventory and land at the beginning of the period.

Instructions

    (a) Prepare an income statement and balance sheet on an historical cost basis for 1980.

    (b) Prepare an income statement and balance sheet on a current cost basis for 1980.

    (c) Prepare the income statement information that is required to be presented under *FASB Statement No. 33* for current cost data in an income statement format for 1980. Assume no change in the Consumer Price Index for all Urban Consumers during the year.

    (d) Prepare the income statement information that is required to be presented under *FASB Statement No. 33* for current cost data for 1980 in a reconciliation format. Assume no change in the Consumer Price Index for all Urban Consumers during the year.

P25-5 Assume the same information as Problem 25-4 and that the following changes occurred in the Consumers Price Index for all Urban Consumers

Beginning of 1980	100
Average	130
End of 1980	180

Instructions

(a) Prepare an income statement and balance sheet on a constant dollar basis in end of year dollars. Assume that sales, purchases and operating expenses were incurred evenly throughout the year. Land and beginning inventory were acquired when the general price-level index was at 100. Ending inventory was comprised of goods purchased when the general price level was 130. (Hint: use the conversion factor of 1.3846 for the 180/130; do not use the fraction approach.) Round to nearest dollar.

(b) Assume the same information as (a), prepare an income statement and a balance sheet on a current cost/constant dollar basis in end of year dollars.

(c) Assume the same information as (a), prepare the partial income statement that is required to be presented under *FASB Statement No. 33* for constant dollar data in an (1) income statement format and (2) a reconciliation format. (Hint: use the conversion factor of .7222 for 130/180; do not use the fraction approach.)

(d) Assume the same information as (a), prepare the partial income statement that is required to be presented under *FASB Statement No. 33* for current cost data in an income statement format.

(e) Assume the same information as (a) and using the data in (c), prepare a partial income statement in a reconciliation format, starting with income from continuing operations as reported in the historical cost income statement.

P25-6   Presented below is information related to Hood, Inc.

1978   Purchased land for $40,000 cash on December 31.
Current cost at year end was $40,000.
1979   Held this land all year.
Current cost at year end was $52,000.
1980   October 31—sold this land for $68,000. Current cost of land at date of sale is $65,000.

General price-level index:

December 31, 1978	100
December 31, 1979	110
October 31, 1980	120

Instructions

(a) Determine the amount that the land would be stated on a balance sheet at December 31, 1978 and 1979 under the following assumptions (end-of-year dollars):
1. Constant dollar accounting
2. Current cost accounting
3. Current cost/constant dollar accounting

(b) Determine the following items (end-of-year dollars):
1. Constant dollar income for 1978, 1979, and 1980.
2. Unrealized holding gain (loss) on current cost basis for 1979.
3. Income from continuing operations on a current cost basis for 1980.
4. Realized holding gain (loss) on a current cost basis in 1980.
5. Realized holding gain (loss) on current cost/constant dollar basis for 1980.
6. Unrealized holding gain (loss) on current cost/constant dollar basis for 1980.

(c) Indicate the amount of income from continuing operations that would be reported under *FASB Statement No. 33* for 1978, 1979, and 1980. Assume that the general indexes presented above also reflect the average index for the year; that is 1978 average index equals 100; 1979 average index equals 110; 1980 average index equals 120.

P25-7 The Leggo Company started operations on January 1, 1980 with the following balance sheet:

Leggo Company
BALANCE SHEET
as of January 1, 1980

Cash	$10,000	Common stock	$40,000
Inventories	30,000	Paid-in capital	20,000
Equipment	20,000		
Total assets	$60,000		$60,000

Transaction data for 1980 were as follows:

Sales (cash)	$105,000
Purchases (cash)	60,000
Ending inventory, historical cost	45,000
Cash operating expenses (excludes depreciation)	20,000
Current cost of goods sold (incurred evenly through year)	55,000
Current cost of ending inventory at year end	50,000
Current cost of equipment at year end	
(five-year life—straight-line depreciation)	25,000
Income taxes (50% rate)	

Instructions

(a) Prepare a historical cost income statement and balance sheet for Leggo Company for 1980.

(b) Prepare a comprehensive current cost income statement and balance sheet for Leggo Company for 1980. Assume that the historical cost of the inventory and equipment is the same as its current cost at the beginning of 1980. Depreciation expense is computed on the average current cost asset balances. Charge catch-up depreciation to the unrealized holding gain. Operating expenses on an historical and current cost basis are the same.

P25-8 Assume the same data as Problem 25–7, and that the Consumer Price Index for all Urban Consumers is as follows:

Beginning of 1980	100
Average	120
End of 1980	150

Assume that all revenues, purchases, and expenses (excluding depreciation) and the ending inventory were incurred at the average price-level.

Instructions

(a) Prepare a constant dollar income statement and balance sheet for Leggo Company for 1980 in end-of-year dollars.

(b) Prepare a current cost/constant dollar income statement and balance sheet for Leggo Company for 1980 in end-of-year dollars.

(c) Prepare a constant dollar income statement and balance sheet for Leggo Company in average-for-the-year dollars.

(d) Prepare a current cost/constant dollar income statement and balance sheet for Leggo Company for 1980 in average-for-the-year dollars.

(e) Prepare a partial income statement in the reconciliation format as required by *FASB Statement No. 33.*

P25-9 Janet, Inc. is experimenting with the use of current cost in its accounting. At the beginning of 1980, the company purchased inventory that had a cost of $50,000, of which $30,000 was sold evenly during the year end at a sales price of $45,000. The general price level at the beginning of 1980 was 100 and at the end of the period was 150. The average price-level for the period was 120. It is estimated that the current cost of the inventory at the date of sale was $33,000 and the current cost of the ending inventory at December 31, 1980 is $22,000. Assume that the company has no other beginning inventory or purchases and uses a perpetual system. (Ignore income taxes.)

Instructions

(a) Prepare an income statement on an historical cost basis for the year 1980.

(b) Prepare an income statement on a constant dollar basis for the year 1980 in end-of-year dollars.

(c) Prepare a comprehensive income statement on a current cost basis for the year 1980.

(d) Prepare a comprehensive income statement on a current cost/constant dollar basis for the year 1980 in end-of-year dollars.

(e) Prepare, in an income statement format, income from continuing operations in accordance with *FASB Statement No. 33* and other related disclosures, where possible, for the year 1980.

(f) Prepare, in a reconciliation format, income from continuing operations in accordance with *FASB Statement No. 33* and other related disclosures, where possible, for the year 1980.

26

Basic Financial
Statement Analysis

The interpretation and evaluation of financial statement data require familiarity with the basic tools of financial statement analysis. Naturally, the type of financial analysis that takes place depends on the particular interest that the analyst (whether creditor, stockholder, potential investor, manager, government agency, or labor leader) has in the enterprise. For example, **short-term creditors,** such as banks, are primarily interested in the ability of the firm to pay its currently maturing obligations. The composition of the current assets and their relation to short-term liabilities are examined closely to evaluate the short-run solvency of the firm. **Bondholders,** on the other hand, look to more long-term indicators, such as the enterprise's capital structure, past and projected earnings, and changes in financial position. **Stockholders,** present or prospective, also are interested in many of the features considered by a long-term debtor. Their examination is focused on the earnings picture, because changes in it greatly affect the market price of their investment. Stockholders also are concerned with the financial position of the firm, because it affects indirectly the stability of the earnings.

The **management** of a company is of necessity concerned about the composition of its capital structure and about the changes and trends in earnings. This financial information has a direct influence on the type, amount, and cost of external financing that the company may obtain. In addition, the company finds financial information useful on a day-to-day operating basis in such areas as capital budgeting, breakeven analysis, variance analysis, gross margin analysis, and for internal control purposes.

The accountant's function is twofold: (1) to measure economic events and transactions and (2) to communicate economic information about them to interested parties. Thus far in this textbook we have discussed the measurement and reporting functions of accounting. But communication in accounting means more than just preparing the reports; accountants must also analyze and interpret financial statements.

Basic Measures of Financial Analysis

Various devices are used in the analysis of financial statement data to bring out the comparative and relative significance of the financial information presented. These devices include ratio analysis, comparative analysis, percentage analysis, and examination of related data. It is difficult to say that one device is more useful than another because every situation faced by the investment analyst is different, and the answers needed are often obtained only upon close examination of the interrelationships among all the data provided. Ratio analysis is the starting point in developing the information desired by the analyst.

Ratios can be classified as follows:

Liquidity Ratios. Measures of the short-run ability of the enterprise to pay its maturing obligations.

Activity Ratios. Measures of how effectively the enterprise is using the assets employed.

Profitability Ratios. Measures of the degree of success or failure of a given enterprise or division for a given period of time.

Coverage Ratios. Measures of the degree of protection for long-term creditors and investors.

Anetek Chemical Corporation
INCOME STATEMENT
For the Year Ended December 31
(000 Omitted)

	1981	1980
Sales and other revenue:		
Net sales	$1,600,000	$1,350,000
Interest income	25,000	20,000
Other income	50,000	30,000
Total revenue	1,675,000	1,400,000
Cost and other charges:		
Cost of goods sold	1,000,000	850,000
Depreciation and amortization	150,000	150,000
Selling and administrative expenses	225,000	150,000
Interest expense	50,000	25,000
Total	1,425,000	1,175,000
Income before taxes	250,000	225,000
Income taxes	100,000	75,000
Net income	$ 150,000	$ 150,000
Earnings per share[a]	$5.00	$4.50

[a]Additional information:
Number of shares outstanding in 1981 is thirty million shares.
Market price of Anetek's stock at end of 1981 is $60.
Cash dividend per share in 1981 is $2.25.
Correction of error in prior period $4.5 million.

The use of these ratios is illustrated through the following actual case example adopted from the annual report of a large chemical concern that we have disguised under the name of Anetek Chemical Corporation.

Anetek Chemical Corporation is a worldwide enterprise offering more than 1,400 products and services in the following major classifications: chemicals, plasters, pharmaceuticals, metals, agricultural chemicals, packaging, and industrial chemical cleaning. Anetek products are manufactured through the recovery and

Anetek Chemical
CONSOLIDATED BALANCE SHEET[a]
December 31
(000 omitted)

	1981	1980
Assets		
Current assets:		
Cash	$ 40,000	$ 25,000
Marketable securities (at cost)	100,000	75,000
Accounts receivable	350,000	300,000
Inventories (at lower of cost or market)	310,000	250,000
Total current assets	800,000	650,000
Investments (at cost)	300,000	325,000
Fixed assets:		
Property, plant and equipment (at cost)	2,000,000	1,900,000
Less—accumulated depreciation	(900,000)	(800,000)
	1,100,000	1,100,000
Goodwill	50,000	25,000
Total assets	$2,250,000	$2,100,000
Debt and Equity		
Current liabilities:		
Accounts payable	$ 125,000	$ 100,000
Notes payable	250,000	200,000
Accrued and other liabilities	200,000	150,000
Total current liabilities	575,000	450,000
Long-term debt:		
Bonds and notes payable	725,000	550,000
Total liabilities	1,300,000	1,000,000
Stockholders' equity:		
Common stock	150,000	150,000
Additional paid-in capital	550,000	650,000
Retained earnings	250,000	300,000
Total equity	950,000	1,100,000
Total debt and equity	$2,250,000	$2,100,000

[a]The footnotes and some detail that accompanied this statement are excluded for purposes of simplicity and brevity.

upgrading of chemicals found in underground brines, salt deposits, petroleum, and seawater. Production is accomplished through the intensive application of technology developed in large part by the company's own research organization. "Anetek" people number some 50,000 in 48 nations. The comparative financial statements of Anetek (pages 1178–1179) are the basis for all of the ratios. The ratios, like the financial statements, are computed with the last three digits (000) omitted.

Liquidity Ratios

The ability of a firm to meet its current debts is important in evaluating its financial position. For example, Anetek Chemical has current liabilities of $575,000. Can these current obligations be met when due? Certain basic ratios can be computed that provide some guides for determining the enterprise's short-term debt-paying ability.

1. Current Ratio   The current ratio is the ratio of total current assets to total current liabilities. Although the quotient is the dollars of current assets available to cover each dollar of current debt, it is most frequently expressed as a coverage of so many times. Sometimes it is called the working capital ratio, because working capital is the excess of current assets over current liabilities. The computation of the current ratio for Anetek is:

$$\text{Current Ratio} = \frac{\text{Current Assets}}{\text{Current Liabilities}} = \frac{\$800,000}{\$575,000} = 1.39 \text{ times}$$

$$\text{Industry Average}^1 = 2.30 \text{ times}$$

The current ratio of 1.39 to 1 compared with the industry average of 2.30 to 1 indicates that Anetek's safety factor to meet maturing short-term obligations is noticeably low. Does the relatively low current ratio indicate the existence of a liquidity problem? Or considering that the ratio is greater than 1 to 1, is the situation well in hand? The current ratio is only one measure of determining liquidity, and it does not answer all of the liquidity questions. How liquid are the receivables and inventory? What effect does the omission of the inventory have on the analysis of liquidity? To answer these and other questions, additional analysis of other related data is required.

2. Acid-Test Ratio   A satisfactory current ratio does not disclose the fact that a portion of the current assets may be tied up in slow-moving inventories. With inventories, especially raw material and work in process, there is a question of how long it will take to transform them into the finished product and what ultimately will be realized on the sale of the merchandise. Elimination of the inventories, along with any prepaid expenses, from the current assets might provide better information for the short-term creditor. Many analysts favor a "quick" or "acid-test"

---

[1]The industry average ratios are taken from Dun and Bradstreet, Inc., *Key Business Ratios in 25 Lines*, and Leo Troy's The *Almanac of Business and Industrial Financial Ratios*. The standard ratios provide some basis for comparison with other companies in the same industry.

ratio that relates total current liabilities to cash, marketable securities, and receivables. The acid-test ratio is computed for Anetek as follows:

$$\text{Acid-test Ratio} = \frac{\text{Cash} + \text{Marketable Securities} + \text{Net Receivables}}{\text{Current Liabilities}} = \frac{\$490,000}{\$575,000} = .85 \text{ times}$$

Industry Average = 1.20 times

The acid-test ratio for Anetek as compared with the industry average is low. This means that Anetek may have difficulty in meeting its short-term needs unless the firm is able to obtain additional current assets through conversion of some of its long-term assets, through additional financing, or through profitable operating results.

3. Defensive-Interval Ratio Neither the current ratio nor the acid-test ratio, however, gives a complete explanation of the current debt-paying ability of the company. The matching of current assets with current liabilities assumes that the current assets will be employed to pay off the current liabilities. Some investors argue that a better measure of liquidity is provided by the defensive-interval ratio. The defensive-interval ratio is computed by dividing defensive assets (cash, marketable securities, and net receivables) by projected daily expenditures from operations. This ratio measures the time span a firm can operate on present liquid assets without resorting to revenues from next year's income sources. Projected daily expenditures are computed by dividing cost of goods sold plus selling and administrative expenses and other ordinary cash expenses by 365 days.[2]

The defensive-interval measure for Anetek is:

$$\text{Defensive-Interval Measure} = \frac{\text{Defensive Assets}}{\text{Projected Daily Operational Expenditures (based on past expenditures) minus Noncash Charges}}$$

$$= \$490,000 \div \frac{\$1,525,000 - \$150,000}{365}$$

$$= 130 \text{ days}$$

Industry Average = 80 days

Whether this ratio provides a better measure of liquidity than the current ratio or acid-test ratio is difficult to evaluate, but it does provide another useful tool for analyzing the liquidity position of the enterprise.[3] This ratio establishes a safety factor or margin for the investor in determining the capability of the company to

---

[2]The only necessary adjustments to the total expense figure are deductions of any noncash charges such as depreciation and provisions for any known changes in planned operations from previous periods.

[3]For other approaches to measuring short-term liquidity, see Harold Bierman, "Measuring Financial Liquidity," *The Accounting Review* (October, 1960), pp. 628-632, where he argues for the ratio of net working capital to resources provided by operations; and James Walter, "Determination of Technical Solvency," *Journal of Business* (January, 1957), pp. 30-43, where he uses the ratio of resources provided by operations to current debt.

meet its basic operational costs.[4] It would appear that 130 days provides the company with a relatively high degree of protection, and tends to offset the weakness indicated by the low current and acid-test ratios.

Activity Ratios

Another way of evaluating liquidity is to determine how quickly certain assets can be turned into cash. How liquid, for example, are the receivables and inventory? In addition, this type of calculation provides information related to how efficiently the enterprise utilizes its assets. Activity ratios are computed for Anetek Chemical on the basis of receivables, inventories, and total assets.

4. Receivables Turnover   The receivables turnover ratio is computed by dividing net sales by average receivables outstanding during the year. Theoretically, the numerator should include only net credit sales. This information is frequently not available, however, and if the relative amounts of charge and cash sales remain fairly constant, the trend indicated by the ratio will still be valid. Unless seasonal factors are significant, average receivables outstanding can be computed from the beginning and ending balance of the trade receivables. Net receivables instead of gross receivables are used for the computation.

$$\text{Accounts Receivable Turnover} = \frac{\text{Net Sales}}{\text{Average Trade Receivables (net)}}$$

$$= \$1,600,000 \div \frac{\$350,000 + \$300,000}{2}$$

$$= 4.92 \text{ or every 74 days}$$

$$\text{Industry Average}[5] = 7.15 \text{ or every 51 days}$$

This information provides some indication of the quality of the receivables, and also an idea of how successful the firm is in collecting its outstanding receivables. The faster this turnover, the more credence the current ratio and acid-test ratio have in the financial analysis. If possible, an aging schedule should also be prepared to determine how long the receivables have been outstanding. It is possible that the receivables turnover is quite satisfactory, but this situation may have resulted because certain receivables have been collected quickly whereas others have been outstanding for a relatively long period. In Anetek's case, the receivables turnover appears low. The general rule used is that the time allowed for payment by the selling terms should not be exceeded by more than 10 or 15 days.

---

[4]See George H. Sorter and George Benston, "Appraising the Defensive Position of the Firm: The Interval Measure," *Accounting Review* (October, 1960), pp. 633–640; and Sidney Davidson, George H. Sorter, and Hemu Kalle, "Measuring the Defensive Position of a Firm," *Financial Analyst's Journal* (January-February, 1964), pp. 23–29.

[5]Often the receivables turnover is transformed to an average collection period. In this case, 4.92 is divided into 365 days to obtain 74 days. Several figures other than 365 could be used here; a most common alternative is 360 days. Because our industry average was based on 365, we used this figure in our computations.

5. Inventory Turnover   Inventory turnover is computed by dividing the average inventory into the cost of goods sold. The inventory turnover ratio for Anetek Chemical is:

$$\text{Inventory Turnover} = \frac{\text{Cost of Goods Sold}}{\text{Average Inventory}} = \frac{\$1,000,000}{\dfrac{\$310,000 + \$250,000}{2}}$$

$$= 3.57 \text{ times or every 102 days}$$

$$\text{Industry Average} = 4.62 \text{ or every 79 days}$$

The inventory turnover measures how quickly inventory is sold. Generally, the higher the inventory turnover, the better the enterprise is performing. It is possible, however, that the enterprise is incurring high "stockout costs" because not enough inventory is available. The ratio is useful because it provides a basis for determining whether obsolete inventory is present or pricing problems exist. In Anetek's case, the turnover ratio is lower than the industry average, indicating that some slow-moving inventory exists. Remember that this ratio is an average, which means that many goods may be turning over quite rapidly, whereas others may have failed to sell at all. In addition, it was assumed that an average of the beginning and ending inventory was representative of the average for the year. If this situation is not correct, additional computations must be made.

Because inventory is stated at cost, it must be divided into cost of sales (a cost figure) instead of into sales, which includes some margin of profit. Occasionally analysts use sales instead of cost of goods sold as a substitute, but this practice has no theoretical support unless inventories are valued at retail prices.

The method of inventory valuation can affect the computed turnover and the current ratio. The analyst should be aware of the different valuations that can be used in costing inventory (i.e., FIFO, LIFO, etc.) and the effect these different valuation procedures might have on the ratio.

6. Asset Turnover   The asset turnover ratio is determined by dividing average total assets into net sales for the period. The asset turnover for Anetek is:

$$\text{Asset Turnover} = \frac{\text{Net Sales}}{\text{Average Total Assets}} = \frac{\$1,600,000}{\dfrac{\$2,250,000 + \$2,100,000}{2}} = .74$$

$$\text{Industry Average} = .94$$

This ratio supposedly indicates how efficiently the company utilizes its assets. If the turnover ratio is high, the implication is that the company is using its assets effectively to generate sales. If the turnover ratio is low, the company either has to use its assets more efficiently or dispose of them. The problem with this turnover calculation is that it places a premium on using old assets because their book value is low. In addition, this ratio is affected by the depreciation method employed by the company. For example, a company that employs an accelerated method of depreciation will have a higher turnover than a company using straight-line, all other factors being equal. For these reasons, the ratio should not be the only one considered in evaluating the efficiency of the company in this area.

Profitability Ratios

Profitability ratios indicate how well the enterprise has operated during the year. These ratios answer such questions as: Was the net income adequate? What rate of return does it represent? What is the rate of net income by activities? What amount was paid in dividends? What amount was earned by different equity claimants? Generally, the ratios are either computed on the basis of sales or on an investment base such as total assets. Profitability is frequently used as the ultimate test of management effectiveness.

7. Profit Margin on Sales The profit margin on sales is computed by dividing net income by net sales for the period. Anetek's ratio is:

$$\text{Profit Margin on Sales} = \frac{\text{Net Income}}{\text{Net Sales}} = \frac{\$150,000}{\$1,600,000} = 9.4\%$$

$$\text{Industry Average} = 6\%$$

This ratio indicates that Anetek is achieving an above-average rate of profit on each sales dollar received. It provides some indication of the buffer available in case of higher costs or lower sales in the future. Employment of this ratio in conjunction with the asset turnover ratio offers an interplay that leads to a rate of return on total assets. This relationship is expressed as follows:

$$\text{Rate of Return on Assets} = \text{Profit Margin on Sales} \times \text{Asset Turnover}$$

$$\text{Rate of Return on Assets} = \frac{\text{Net Income}}{\text{Net Sales}} \times \frac{\text{Net Sales}}{\text{Average Total Assets}}$$

$$= \frac{\$150,000}{\$1,600,000} \times \frac{\$1,600,000}{\dfrac{\$2,250,000 + \$2,100,000}{2}}$$

$$= 6.9\%$$

The profit margin on sales does not answer the question of how profitable the enterprise was for a given time period. Only by determining how many times the assets turned over during a period of time is it possible to ascertain the amount of net income earned on the total assets.

Many enterprises have a small profit margin on sales and a high turnover (grocery and discount stores), whereas other enterprises have a relatively high profit margin but a low inventory turnover (jewelry and furniture stores).

One of the most interesting applications of this is called the du Pont system of financial control.[6] The basic components in the du Pont system are presented in the following diagram.

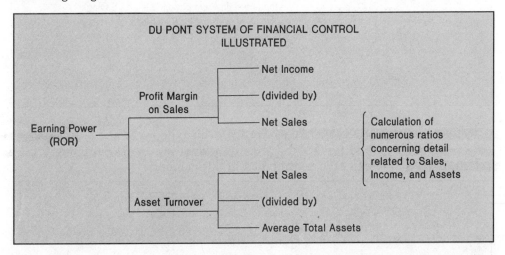

In this system, ratios can be defined in enough detail to give the analyst the information desired. The significant point is that all ratios can help explain the different effects leading to the rate of return on invested capital.

8. Rate of Return on Assets   As just indicated, this ratio is computed by using as a numerator net income and as a denominator average total assets. The ratio for Anetek is:

$$\text{Rate of Return on Assets} = \frac{\text{Net Income}}{\text{Average Total Assets}}$$

$$= \$150,000 \div \frac{\$2,250,000 + \$2,100,000}{2}$$

$$= 6.9\%$$

$$\text{Industry Average} = 5.6\%$$

Anetek's rate of return is slightly above the average of the industry and is a result of Anetek's relatively high profit margin.

Many contend that a better measure of the rate earned on the assets results from the use of net income before subtraction of the interest charge.[7] This ratio is computed by dividing net income before interest expense and dividends but after taxes by average total assets. Interest expense (net of tax effect), including discount amortization, is added back to income because the interest represents a cost of

[6]Descriptions of this system are available in T. C. Davis, *How the du Pont Organization Appraises Its Performance*, Financial Management Series, No. 94 (New York: American Management Association Treasurer's Dept., 1950); and C. A. Kline, Jr. and H. L. Hissler, "The du Pont Chart System for Appraising Operating Performance," *N.A.C.A. Bulletin* (August, 1953), pp. 1595–1619.

[7]For example, public utilities compute their rate of return on the basis of this approach.

securing additional assets and, therefore, should not be considered as a deduction in arriving at the amount of return on assets. The ratio for Anetek is:

$$\text{Rate of Return on Assets} = \frac{\text{Net Income} + \text{Interest Expense} - \text{Tax Savings}^8}{\text{Average Total Assets}}$$

$$= \frac{\$150,000 + \$50,000 - .40\,(\$50,000)}{\dfrac{\$2,250,000 + \$2,100,000}{2}}$$

$$= 8.3\%$$

9. Rate of Return on Common Stock Equity   This ratio is defined as net income after interest, taxes, and preferred dividends divided by average common stockholders' equity. Anetek's ratio is computed in this manner:

$$\text{Rate of Return on Common Stock Equity} = \frac{\text{Net Income minus Preferred Dividends}}{\text{Average Common Stockholders' Equity}}$$

$$= \$150,000 \div \frac{\$950,000 + \$1,100,000}{2}$$

$$= 14.6\%$$

$$\text{Industry Average} = 9.5\%$$

When the rate of return on total assets is lower than the rate of return on the common stockholders' investment, the enterprise is said to be trading on the equity at a gain. Trading on the equity increases the company's financial risk, but it enhances residual earnings whenever the rate of return on assets exceeds the cost of debt capital.

Whether the rate of return on total assets or the rate of return on common stock equity is a better measure of performance is difficult to evaluate. For example, when **Forbes** (a popular financial magazine) is asked to provide basic guidelines for profitability, it computes both ratios. The three companies listed below all rank fairly close in return on equity; however, they are not as close in rate of return on total assets.

COMPARISONS OF DIFFERENT TYPES PROFITABILITY INDEXES				
	5-Year Return on Common Equity		5-Year Return on Total Assets	
Company	Rank[a]	Percent	Rank	Percent
Avon Products	9	32.0	3	29.8
Northwest Industries	15	29.6	319	11.2
McDonald's	29	26.3	125	14.9
[a]Rank amongst 500 publicly owned U.S. companies.				

[8]The tax savings is computed by multiplying the interest expense by the effective tax rate. The effective tax rate is determined by dividing the provision for income taxes by income before taxes.

When these three companies are evaluated, Northwest Industries stands out as a company that is highly leveraged; that is, a great deal of debt is in its capital structure. Leveraging per se is not wrong, but in an economic downturn chances are that Northwest Industries would turn less profitable more quickly than the other two companies.

On the other hand, there are companies such as Maytag and Minnesota Mining and Manufacturing that have leveraged very little; can they be considered less profitable? For example, Maytag has a rate of return on assets of 27.4% (Rank 9) and rate of return on common equity of 27.5% (Rank 25). Is Maytag more or less profitable than Northwest Industries? It is a difficult question to evaluate and both ratios should be considered in the analysis.

Trading on the Equity   The expression "trading on the equity" describes the practice of using borrowed money at fixed interest rates or issuing preferred stock with constant dividend rates in hopes of obtaining a higher rate of return on the money used than the interest or preferred dividends paid. Because these issues must be given a prior claim on some or all of the corporate assets, the advantage to stockholders must come from borrowing at a lower rate of interest than the rate of return obtained by the corporation on the assets borrowed. If this can be done, the capital obtained from bondholders or preferred stockholders earns enough to pay the interest or preferred dividends, and to leave a margin for the common stockholders. When this condition exists, trading on the equity is profitable. A comparison of the rate of return on total assets with the rate paid to other than common stock claimants indicates the profitability of trading on the equity in any given case. To illustrate, Anetek's rate of return on total assets is 6.9%, whereas the rate of return on the stockholders' equity is 14.6%. Anetek traded on the equity at a gain. In essence, the liability claimants were paid a lower rate than 6.9%. Anetek is a very highly leveraged company which has achieved an excellent rate of return on common equity by using its debt effectively. A word of caution—trading on the equity is a two-way street: just as a company's gains can be magnified, so also can losses be magnified.

10. Earnings Per Share   The earnings per share figure is probably the ratio most used by investment analysts, yet it is one of the most deceptive. If no dilutive securities are present in the capital structure, then earnings per share is simply computed by dividing net income minus preferred dividends by the average number of shares of outstanding common stock. If, however, convertible securities, stock options, warrants, or other dilutive securities are included in the capital structure, (1) earnings per common and common equivalent shares and (2) fully diluted earnings per share figures may have to be used.[9] The computation for Anetek is:

$$\text{Earnings Per Share} = \frac{\text{Net Income Minus Preferred Dividends}}{\text{Weighted Shares Outstanding}} = \frac{\$150,000}{30,000} = \$5.00$$

[9]See Chapter 17 for a discussion of how dilutive securities should be handled to compute earnings per share.

Because no dilutive securities that are common stock equivalents or potentially dilutive securities are present in Anetek's capital structure, primary earnings per share and fully diluted earnings per share amounts need not be reported.

Certain dangers exist when the earnings per share ratio is computed. Often earnings per share can be increased simply by reducing the number of shares outstanding through the purchase of treasury stock. In addition, the earnings per share figure fails to recognize the probable increasing base of the stockholders' investment. That is, earnings per share, all other factors being equal, will probably increase year after year if the corporation reinvests earnings in the business because a larger earnings figure should be generated without a corresponding increase in the denominator, the number of shares outstanding. Because even the well-informed element of the public attaches such importance to earnings per share, caution must be exercised, and it should not be given more emphasis than it deserves. The common problem is that the per-share figure draws the investor's attention from the enterprise as a whole—which involves differing magnitudes of sales, costs, volumes, and invested capital—and concentrates too much attention on the single share of stock.

11. Price Earnings Ratio   The price earnings (P/E) ratio is an oft-quoted statistic used by analysts in discussing the investment possibility of a given enterprise. It is computed by dividing the market price of the stock by its earnings per share. For Anetek, the ratio is

$$\text{Price Earnings Ratio} = \frac{\text{Market Price of Stock}}{\text{Earnings Per Share}} = \frac{\$60}{\$5} = 12.0$$

The average price earnings ratio for all the stocks traded on the New York Stock Exchange in early 1979 was 8.6. A steady drop in a company's price earnings ratio indicates that investors are wary of the firm's growth potential. Some companies have high P/E multiples, while others have low multiples. For instance, Newmont Mining in 1979 enjoyed a P/E ratio of 27 while Bendix had a low P/E ratio of 6. The reason for this difference is linked to several factors: relative risk, stability of earnings, trends in earnings, and the market's perception of the growth potential of the stock. Analysts who believe a company will be able to generate future earnings at even higher levels than at present may value the stock higher than its present earnings may warrant and vice versa.

12. Payout Ratio   The payout ratio is the ratio of cash dividends to net income. If preferred stock is outstanding, this ratio is computed for common stockholders by dividing cash dividends paid to common stock by income available to common stockholders. Assuming that the cash dividends are $67,500, the payout ratio for Anetek is:

$$\text{Payout Ratio} = \frac{\text{Cash Dividends}}{\text{Net Income}} = \frac{\$67,500}{\$150,000} = 45\%$$

It is important to many investors that a fairly substantial payout ratio exist; however, speculators view appreciation in the value of the stock as more important. Generally, growth companies are characterized by low payout ratios because they reinvest most of their earnings. For example, Anetek has a rather high payout ratio when compared with Xerox, which normally pays out approximately 26% of earnings, but a relatively low payout ratio when compared with Standard Oil (Ohio), which normally pays out 80%.

Another closely related ratio that is often used is the dividend yield; it is simply the cash dividend per share divided by the market price of the stock. The cash dividend per share for Anetek is $2.25, so the dividend yield is 3.75% ($2.25/$60.00). This ratio affords investors some idea of the rate of return that will be received in the short run from their investment. In 1979, International Business Machines (IBM) stockholders experienced a modest yield of approximately 4.5%, while American Telephone and Telegraph (AT & T) stockholders experienced a yield of approximately 9.4%.

Coverage Ratios

The coverage ratios are computed to help in predicting the long-run solvency of the firm. These ratios are of interest primarily to bondholders who need some indication of the measure of protection available to them. In addition, they indicate part of the risk involved in investing in common stock because the more debt that is added to the capital structure, the more uncertain is the return on common stock.

13. Debt to Total Assets   This ratio provides the creditors with some idea of the corporation's ability to withstand losses without impairing the interests of creditors. The lower this ratio is, the more "buffer" there is available to creditors before the corporation becomes insolvent. From the creditor's point of view a low ratio of debt to total assets is desirable. The ratio for Anetek is:

$$\text{Debt to Total Assets} = \frac{\text{Debt}}{\text{Total Assets or Equities}} = \frac{\$1,300,000}{\$2,250,000} = 58\%$$

$$\text{Industry Average} = 38\%$$

There are other ways of expressing this ratio, such as the ratio of debt to stockholders' equity, the ratio of stockholders' equity to the sum of debt and stockholders' equity. Essentially, these ratios all provide the same answer to the question: How well protected are the creditors in the case of possible insolvency of the enterprise?[10] This ratio has a very definite effect on the company's ability to obtain additional financing. Anetek is highly leveraged; further growth through debt financing may not be possible.

14. Times Interest Earned   The times interest earned ratio is computed by dividing income before interest charges and taxes by the interest charge. This ratio stresses the importance of a company covering all interest charges. Note that the

---

[10]Additional protection, of course, is afforded through specified liens and collateral and through contractual restrictive covenants.

times interest earned ratio uses income before taxes because the ability to pay interest is not a function of the taxes to be paid. The ratio for Anetek is:

$$\text{Times Interest Earned} = \frac{\text{Income Before Taxes and Interest Charges}}{\text{Interest Charges}} = \frac{\$300,000}{\$50,000} = 6 \text{ times}$$

In this case Anetek's interest coverage is adequate.

If a company pays preferred dividends, the number of times the preferred dividends were earned is computed by dividing the net income for the year by the annual preferred dividend requirements.

15. Book Value Per Share   A much-used basis for evaluating the net worth and any changes in it from year to year is found in the book value or equity value per share of stock. Book value per share of stock is the amount each share would receive if the company were liquidated **on the basis of amounts reported on the balance sheet.** The figure loses much of its relevance if the valuations on the balance sheet do not approximate fair market value of the assets. It is computed by allocating the stockholders' equity items among the various classes of stock and then dividing the total so allocated to each class of stock by the number of shares outstanding.

The book value per common share for Anetek is:

$$\text{Book Value Per Share} = \frac{\text{Common Stockholders' Equity}}{\text{Outstanding Shares}} = \frac{\$950,000}{30,000} = \$31.67$$

Preferred stock is not a part of the capital structure of Anetek. When this type of security is present, an analysis of the covenants involving the preferred shares should be studied. If the preferred dividends are in arrears, and the preferred stock is participating, or if preferred stock has a redemption or liquidating value higher than its carrying amount, retained earnings must be allocated between the preferred and common stockholders.

To illustrate, assume that the following situation exists:

Stockholders' equity	Preferred	Common
Preferred stock, 5%	$300,000.00	
Common stock		$400,000.00
Excess of issue price over par of common stock		37,500.00
Retained earnings		162,582.00
Totals	$300,000.00	$600,082.00
Shares outstanding	3,000	4,000
Book value per share	$ 100.00	$ 150.02

In the computation above it is assumed that no preferred dividends are in arrears and that the preferred is not participating. Now assume that the same facts exist except that the 5% preferred is cumulative, participating up to 8%, and that dividends for three years before the current year are in arrears. The book value of each class of stock is then computed as follows, assuming that no action has yet been taken concerning dividends for the current year:

Stockholders' equity	Preferred	Common
Preferred stock[11], 5%	$300,000.00	
Common stock		$400,000.00
Excess of issue price over par of common stock		37,500.00
Retained earnings:		
Dividends in arrears (3 years at 5% a year)	45,000.00	
Current year dividends at 5%	15,000.00	20,000.00
Participating—additional 3%	9,000.00	12,000.00
Remainder to common		61,582.00
Totals	$369,000.00	$531,082.00
Shares outstanding	3,000	4,000
Book value per share	$ 123.00	$ 132.77

In connection with the book value computation, the analyst must know how to handle such items as the number of authorized and unissued shares, the number of treasury shares on hand, any commitments with respect to the issuance of unissued shares or the reissuance of treasury shares, and the relative rights and privileges of the various types of stock authorized. Although the book value per share figure is useful in some cases, in many instances it is not meaningful for decision-making purposes.

16. Cash Flow Per Share One of the most popular yet least understood ratios used today is cash flow per share. It is computed by dividing net income plus noncash charges (such as depreciation and amortization) by the number of shares of common stock outstanding. The cash flow per share for Anetek is:

$$\text{Cash Flow Per Share} = \frac{\text{Net Income} + \text{Noncash Adjustments}}{\text{Outstanding Shares}}$$

$$= \frac{\$150,000 + \$150,000}{30,000} = \$10.00$$

This amount represents neither the flow of cash through the enterprise nor the residual of the cash received minus the cash disbursed divided by the outstanding shares of stock. It is frequently used to determine approximately the amount of resources generated internally. For most purposes, however, "cash flow per share" is extremely misleading and too frequently used as a measure of "real" profitability. The profession "strongly recommends that isolated statistics of working capital or cash provided from operations, especially per share amounts, not be presented in annual reports to shareholders."[12]

---

[11]If the preferred stock has a liquidating preference as to assets, this is considered in determining book value. For example, if the preferred stockholder receives $360,000 at liquidation instead of $300,000, an additional $60,000 is allocated to the preferred.

[12]"Reporting Changes in Financial Position," *APB Opinion No. 19* (New York: AICPA, 1971), par. 15.

Comparative Analysis

In comparative analysis the same reports or data are presented for two or more different dates or periods so that like items may be compared. Ratio analysis provides only a single snapshot, the analysis being for one given point or period in time. In a comparative analysis, an investment analyst can concentrate on a given item and determine whether it appears to be growing or diminishing year by year and the proportion of such change to related items. Generally, companies present comparative financial statements.[13]

In addition, many companies include in their annual reports 5- or 10-year summaries of pertinent data that permit the reader to examine and analyze trends. **ARB No. 43** concluded that "the presentation of comparative financial statements in annual and other reports enhances the usefulness of such reports and brings out more clearly the nature and trends of current changes affecting the enterprise." An illustration of a 5-year condensed statement with additional supporting data as presented by Anetek Chemical Corporation is presented below.

Anetek Chemical Corporation
CONDENSED COMPARATIVE STATEMENTS
(000,000 omitted)

INCOME (000 omitted)	1981	1980	1979	1978	1977	10 Years Ago 1971	20 Years Ago 1961
Sales and other revenue:							
Net sales	$1,600.0	$1,350.0	$1,309.7	$1,176.2	$1,077.5	$636.2	$170.7
Other revenue	75.0	50.0	39.4	34.1	24.6	9.0	3.7
Total	1,675.0	1,400.0	1,349.1	1,210.3	1,102.1	645.2	174.4
Costs and other charges:							
Cost of sales	1,000.0	850.0	827.4	737.6	684.2	386.8	111.0
Depreciation and depletion	150.0	150.0	122.6	115.6	98.7	82.4	14.2
Selling and administrative expenses	225.0	150.0	144.2	133.7	126.7	66.7	10.7
Interest expense	50.0	25.0	28.5	20.7	9.4	8.9	1.8
Taxes on income	100.0	75.0	79.5	73.5	68.3	42.4	12.4
Total	1,525.0	1,250.0	1,202.2	1,081.1	987.3	587.2	150.1
Net income for the year	150.0	150.0	146.9	129.2	114.8	58.0	24.3
OTHER STATISTICS							
Earnings per share on common stock (in dollars)[a]	$ 5.00	$ 4.50	$ 4.09	$ 3.58	$ 3.11	$ 1.66	$ 1.06
Cash dividends per share paid to stockholders on common stock (in dollars)[a]	2.25	2.15	1.95	1.79	1.71	1.11	.25
Cash dividends declared on common stock	67.5	66.1	59.9	54.1	53.3	30.8	5.0
Stock dividend at approximate market value				46.8		27.3	
Taxes (major)	144.5	125.9	116.5	105.6	97.8	59.8	17.0
Wages paid	389.3	325.6	302.1	279.6	263.2	183.2	48.6
Cost of employee benefits	50.8	36.2	32.9	28.7	27.2	18.4	4.4
Number of employees at year end (thousands)	47.4	36.4	35.0	33.8	33.2	26.6	14.6
Additions to property	306.3	192.3	241.5	248.3	166.1	185.0	49.0

[a]Adjusted for stock splits and stock dividends.

[13]In 1978 all 600 companies surveyed in *Accounting Trends and Techniques* presented comparative 1976 amounts in their 1977 balance sheets and income statements.

Anetek Chemical Corporation
SUMMARY OF FINANCIAL RATIOS

Ratio	Formula for Computation	Computation
I. Liquidity		
1. Current ratio	$\dfrac{\text{Current assets}}{\text{Current liabilities}}$	$\dfrac{\$800,000}{\$575,000} = 1.39 \text{ times}$
2. Quick, or acid-test	$\dfrac{\text{Cash, marketable securities, and receivables}}{\text{Current liabilities}}$	$\dfrac{\$490,000}{\$575,000} = .85 \text{ times}$
3. Defensive-interval measure	$\dfrac{\text{Defensive assets}}{\text{Projected daily expenditures minus noncash expenditures}}$	$\dfrac{\$490,000}{\dfrac{\$1,525,000 - \$150,000}{365}} = 130 \text{ days}$
II. Activity		
4. Receivable turnover	$\dfrac{\text{Net sales}}{\text{Average trade receivables (net)}}$	$\dfrac{\$1,600,000}{\dfrac{\$350,000 + \$300,000}{2}} = 4.92 \text{ times, every } 74 \text{ days}$
5. Inventory turnover	$\dfrac{\text{Cost of goods sold}}{\text{Average inventory}}$	$\dfrac{\$1,000,000}{\dfrac{\$310,000 + \$250,000}{2}} = 3.57 \text{ times, every } 102 \text{ days}$
6. Asset turnover	$\dfrac{\text{Net sales}}{\text{Average total assets}}$	$\dfrac{\$1,600,000}{\dfrac{\$2,250,000 + \$2,100,000}{2}} = .74 \text{ times}$
III. Profitability		
7. Profit margin on sales	$\dfrac{\text{Net income}}{\text{Net sales}}$	$\dfrac{\$150,000}{\$1,600,000} = 9.4\%$
8. Rate of return on assets	$\dfrac{\text{Net income}}{\text{Average total assets}}$	$\dfrac{\$150,000}{\dfrac{\$2,250,000 + \$2,100,000}{2}} = 6.9\%$
9. Rate of return on common stock equity	$\dfrac{\text{Net income minus preferred dividends}}{\text{Average common stockholders' equity}}$	$\dfrac{\$150,000}{\dfrac{\$950,000 + \$1,100,000}{2}} = 14.6\%$
10. Earnings per share	$\dfrac{\text{Net income}}{\text{Weighted shares outstanding}}$	$\dfrac{\$150,000}{30,000} = \$5.00$
11. Price earnings ratio	$\dfrac{\text{Market price of stock}}{\text{Earnings per share}}$	$\dfrac{\$60}{\$5} = 12 \text{ times}$
12. Payout ratio	$\dfrac{\text{Cash dividends}}{\text{Net income}}$	$\dfrac{\$67,500}{\$150,000} = 45\%$
IV. Coverage		
13. Debt to total assets	$\dfrac{\text{Debt}}{\text{Total assets or equities}}$	$\dfrac{\$1,300,000}{\$2,250,000} = 58\%$
14. Times interest earned	$\dfrac{\text{Income before interest charges and taxes}}{\text{Interest charges}}$	$\dfrac{\$300,000}{\$50,000} = 6 \text{ times}$
15. Book value per share	$\dfrac{\text{Common stockholders' equity}}{\text{Outstanding shares}}$	$\dfrac{\$950,000}{30,000} = \$31.67$
16. Cash flow per share	$\dfrac{\text{Income plus noncash adjustments}}{\text{Outstanding shares}}$	$\dfrac{\$150,000 + \$150,000}{30,000} = \$10.00$

Percentage Analysis

Analysts also use percentage analysis to help them evaluate an enterprise. Percentage analysis consists of reducing a series of related amounts to a series of percentages of a given base. All items in an income statement are frequently expressed as a percentage of sales or sometimes as a percentage of cost of goods sold; a balance sheet may be analyzed on the basis of total assets. This analysis facilitates comparison and is helpful in evaluating the relative size of items or the relative change in items. To illustrate, here is a comparative analysis of the expense section of Anetek for the last two years.

	Anetek Chemical			
	1981	1980	Difference	% Change Inc. (dec.)
Cost of sales	$1,000.0	$850.0	$150.0	17.6
Depreciation and depletion	150.0	150.0	0	0
Selling and administrative expenses	225.0	150.0	75.0	50.0
Interest expense	50.0	25.0	25.0	100.0
Taxes	100.0	75.0	25.0	33.3

This approach, normally called a **horizontal analysis,** indicates the proportionate change over a period of time. It is especially useful in evaluating a trend situation, because absolute changes are often deceiving.

Another approach, called **vertical analysis,** is the expression of each item on a financial statement in a given period to a base figure. For example, Anetek Chemical's income statement using this approach appears below.

Anetek Chemical INCOME STATEMENT (000,000 omitted)		
	Amount	Percentage of Total Revenue
Net sales	$1,600.0	96%
Other revenue	75.0	4
Total revenue	1,675.0	100
Less		
Cost of goods sold	1,000.0	60
Depreciation and depletion	150.0	9
Selling and administrative expenses	225.0	13
Interest expense	50.0	3
Income tax	100.0	6
Total expenses	1,525.0	91
Net income	$ 150.0	9

A variation in vertical analysis, referred to as **common-size analysis,** is the presentation of percentages without the dollar amounts given.

Limitations of Ratio Analysis

Because a ratio can be computed precisely, it is easy to attach a high degree of reliability or significance to it. Financial analysis involves many alternative approaches though, and ratio analysis is only one of several means of gaining an understanding about a business enterprise from the financial data. Different and supplementary approaches such as careful investigation of footnotes, examination of the company's accounting policies, analysis of product-line breakdowns, and inspection of interim data are discussed in the next chapter.

The reader of financial statements must understand the basic limitations associated with ratio analysis when evaluating an enterprise. As analytical tools, ratios are attractive because they are simple and convenient. Frequently decisions are based on only these simple computations involving relationships between financial data. The ratios are only as good as the data upon which they are based.

The analyst must recognize that traditional financial statements are not adjusted for price-level changes. Depending on the type and age of the assets involved, inflation or deflation can greatly affect financial data.

In addition, cost-based financial statements do not reveal unrealized gains and losses on different asset balances. This shortcoming is especially true in regard to investments in other companies or in natural resources that are carried at cost. Upon sale of such investments or resources, a large gain or loss may be realized. For example, Superior Oil Company at one time owned 1.4% of Texaco, Inc., which it carried at the cost of approximately 64 million dollars, although the fair market value of the investment was almost twice that figure or approximately $118 million. Such significant information is often overlooked in the enthusiasm for computing precise ratios.

Also, investors must remember that where estimated items (such as depreciation and amortization) are significant, income ratios lose some of their credibility. Income recognized before the termination of the life of the business is an approximation. In analyzing the income statement, the user should be cognizant of the uncertainty surrounding the computation of net income. "The physicist has long since conceded that the location of an electron is best expressed by a probability curve. Surely an abstraction like earnings per share is even more subject to the rules of probability and risk."[14]

Probably the greatest criticism of ratio analysis is the difficult problem of achieving comparability among firms in a given industry. Achieving comparability among firms that apply different accounting procedures is difficult and requires that the analyst (1) identify basic differences existing in their accounting and (2) adjust the balances to achieve comparability.

Basic differences in accounting usually involve one of the following areas:

1. Inventory valuation (FIFO, LIFO, Average Cost).
2. Depreciation methods, particularly the use of straight-line versus accelerated depreciation.
3. Capitalization versus expense of certain costs, particularly costs involved in developing natural resources.
4. Pooling versus purchase in accounting for business combinations.

[14]Richard E. Cheney, "How Dependable Is the Bottom Line?" *The Financial Executive* (January, 1971), p. 12.

5. Capitalization of leases versus noncapitalization.
6. Investments in common stock carried at cost, equity, and sometimes market.
7. Differing treatments of pension costs.
8. Questionable practices of defining discontinued operations and extraordinary items.

The use of these different alternatives can make quite a significant difference in the ratios computed. For example, in the brewing industry, Anheuser-Busch recently noted that if it had used average cost for inventory valuation instead of LIFO, inventories would have increased approximately $33,000,000; such an increase would have a substantive impact on the current ratio. Several studies have already been made analyzing the impact of different accounting methods on financial statement analysis. The differences in income that can develop are staggering in some cases, depending on the company's accounting policies.[15] The average investor may find it difficult to grasp all these differences, but investors must be aware of the potential pitfalls if they are to be able to make the proper adjustments.

Recent Studies Related to Ratio Analysis

One of the more interesting approaches to ratio analysis has been the recent introduction of prediction models to determine whether a company is headed for bankruptcy or increased profitability. Several studies have been partially successful in using a combination of ratios to predict a possible bankruptcy situation whereas attempts to determine profitability have met with dismal failure.

One major study has forecast failure up to two years prior to the occurrence of bankruptcy with prediction accuracy diminishing as the time differential increases.[16] In this study, five variables were selected as a basis for prediction: working capital to total assets, retained earnings to total assets, market value of equity to book value of total debt, earnings before taxes and interest to total assets, and sales to total assets. Some of these ratios have been discussed in this chapter; others are computed without great difficulty.

A similar study also found ratios quite useful in predicting bankruptcy.[17] The ratio of cash flow to total debt was considered the best ratio predictor. The study showed how financial ratios can be used to predict failure five years prior to failure. In a later study, using the same data, it was concluded that nonliquid measures such as net income ratios were much better predictors than liquid ratios such as the current ratio or acid-test ratio.

Such studies indicate the potential that ratio analysis holds. Although this type of analysis has many limitations, the merits of ratio analysis as a method for analyzing a business situation should be recognized.

---

[15]Examples of such descriptive studies are: Curtis L. Norton and Ralph E. Smith, "A Comparison of General Price Level and Historical Cost Financial Statements in the Prediction of Bankruptcy, *The Accounting Review* (January, 1979), pp. 72–87. Robert Alan Cerf, "Price Level Changes and Financial Ratios," *Journal of Business* (July, 1957), pp. 180–192, and Thomas A. Nelson, "Capitalizing Leases—The Effect on Financial Ratios," *Journal of Accountancy* (July, 1963), pp. 49–58.

[16]Edward Altman, "Financial Ratios, Discriminant Analysis and the Prediction of Corporate Bankruptcy," *Journal of Finance* (September, 1968), pp. 589–590.

[17]William H. Beaver, "Financial Ratios as Predictors of Failure," Empirical Research in Accounting, Selected Studies, 1966, *Journal of Accounting Research*, pp. 71–127; and William H. Beaver, "Alternative Accounting Measures as Predictors of Failures," *The Accounting Review* (January, 1968), pp. 113–122. See also E. B. Deakin, "Discriminate Analysis of Predictors of Business Failure," *Journal of Accounting Research* (Spring, 1972), pp. 167–179.

APPENDIX

Fundamental Analysis versus Capital Market Analysis

The approach presented in this chapter assumes that a present or potential stockholder analyzes financial information to determine whether a common stock is under- or overvalued. This approach, often referred to as **fundamental analysis,** attempts to find the **intrinsic value** of the security, which is defined as "that value which is justified by the facts, e.g., assets, earnings, dividends, definite prospects including the factor of management."[1] An investor who, therefore, finds a common stock that has an intrinsic value higher than the current market price will buy or continue to hold this security. Conversely, if the intrinsic value of the common stock is lower than the current market price, the investor will sell or not purchase the stock. The assumption of fundamental analysis is that by careful investigation, under- and overvalued common stocks may be detected and appropriate investment decisions made.

To illustrate, Del Monte Corporation's stock recently dropped from $29 to $23 per share—this drop was attributed to the fact that its most recent earnings had dropped from $2.16 to $1.65. However, certain analysts concluded after careful investigation that Del Monte's income would have increased 48 cents instead of declining 51 cents if not for some nonrecurring charges that had little to do with the operations of the business. Apparently many other investors arrived at the same conclusion because the stock price increased 87% to $44 a share a short time later. This example demonstrates that many believe that fundamental analysis is the most useful technique in analyzing financial statements.

[1]Benjamin Graham, David L. Dodd, and Sidney Cottle, *Security Analysis: Principles and Techniques,* 4th ed. (New York: McGraw-Hill Book Co., 1962), p. 28.

Proponents of **capital market analysis** believe that the current market price of the common stock at any given point in time reflects all available public information and, therefore, analysis of financial statements will not enable an investor to find an under- or overvalued security. The implication of this approach is that attempts to "beat the market" through fundamental analysis are fruitless because the market is efficient with respect to incorporating publicly available information into the common stock price. It should be emphasized that capital market analysis states only that the current price reflects publicly available information such as that found in financial statements; if you happen to have inside information, you may be able to use it advantageously.

What then does an investor do who believes that the capital market is efficient with respect to publicly available information? To answer this question, we have to recognize that **an investor in common stock is interested in determining the return that would be received and the risk level that would be assumed if the common stock were purchased.** The return on each share of common stock is measured by the change in the market price plus the dividend payment received; the risk level is computed by assessing the probability of achieving a desired return. It follows that the higher the return, the greater the risk and vice versa. A rational investor will attempt to achieve the highest return possible, given the risk level assumed.

In fundamental analysis, it is extremely difficult to determine the risk level that an investor is assuming. Although an analysis of the financial condition of the business enterprise provides indications as to the possible variability in the returns from the common stock, no theory of risk measurement has been well formulated. This is not the case in capital market analysis. A capital market advocate notes that the risk (variability) associated with the return on a common stock is comprised of two components, a **systematic risk** and an **unsystematic risk.** The systematic risk, often referred to as **beta,** measures the average change in a common stock's return for each change in the return on the market as a whole. For example, if a common stock has a beta of one, a 10 percent increase in the market would mean that a 10 percent increase in the return on that common stock should be expected. Conversely, if a common stock has a beta of a negative one, the return on the security moves directly opposite to changes in the overall market. The nonsystematic risk, however, cannot be correlated with any factor and is considered random. By acquiring a portfolio of stocks, the investor can avoid this unsystematic risk entirely because over a number of stocks this risk component cancels and is eliminated from consideration.

The implication of capital market analysis is that an investor should be concerned with the acquisition of a portfolio of common stocks and not with the purchase of an individual security. Purchase of a number of stocks provides two important advantages. First, the investor can eliminate the unsystematic risk because this component cancels out for a number of stocks. Second, the investor can determine the risk level desired and hopefully can attain this level. If an investor prefers less risk, the investor should establish a portfolio of common stocks with a low beta; if a higher return is desired, a higher beta portfolio should be selected.

To illustrate the difference between fundamental analysis and capital market analysis, assume that you are interested in purchasing some shares of General Motors stock. Adherents of fundamental analysis would suggest that you analyze the financial statements of General Motors to determine its intrinsic value or what you think "the stock is worth." Comparison of the present price to its intrinsic value will then provide the answer as to whether this stock should be purchased. Proponents of capital market analysis, however, would argue that you should determine the beta of General Motors stock and how this beta interacts with the other stocks held in your portfolio. If the purchase of General Motors stock increases the beta in your portfolio, and if you desire this additional risk, then the appropriate investment decision is evident.

It should be emphasized that capital market analysis is highly controversial in the investment community. Only after continual experimentation will the financial community be able to determine its conceptual validity.

Questions

1. A close friend of yours, who is an English major and who has not had any college courses or any experience in business, is receiving the financial statements from companies in which he has minor investments (acquired for him by his now deceased father). He asks you what general prerequisites and understanding are necessary to interpret and to evaluate the financial statement data that he is receiving. What would you tell him?

2. "The significance of financial statement data is not in the amount alone." Discuss the meaning of this statement.

3. Distinguish between ratio analysis and percentage analysis relative to the interpretation of financial statements. What is the value of these two types of analysis?

4. The controller of a Fortune 500 chemical company has requested you to include in your report certain balance sheet and income statement ratios so that comparisons may be made. Indicate the types or categories of ratios that might be provided and explain their significance.

5. Of what significance is the current ratio? If this ratio is too low, what may it signify? Can this ratio be too high? Explain.

6. How does the acid-test ratio differ from the current ratio? How are they similar? Of what benefit is the defensive interval ratio?

7. In calculating inventory turnover, why is cost of goods sold used as the numerator? As the inventory turnover increases, what increasing risk does the business assume?

8. Answer each of the questions in the following unrelated situations:
   (a) The current ratio of a company is 4:1 and its acid-test ratio is 1:1. If the inventories and prepaid items amount to $450,000, what is the amount of current liabilities?
   (b) A company had an average inventory last year of $185,000 and its inventory turnover was 4.2. If sales volume and unit cost remain the same this year as last and inventory turnover is 7.0 this year, what will average inventory have to be during the current year?
   (c) A company has current assets of $80,000 (of which $30,000 is inventory and prepaid items) and current liabilities of $20,000. What is the current ratio? What is the acid-test ratio? If the company borrows $10,000 cash from a bank on a 120-day loan, what will its current ratio be? What will the acid-test ratio be?
   (d) A company has current assets of $500,000 and current liabilities of $240,000. The board of directors declares a cash dividend of $60,000. What is the current ratio after the declaration, but before payment? What is the current ratio after the payment of the dividend?

9. What is the relationship of the asset turnover ratio to the rate of return on assets?

10. What primary factors should the board of directors consider in selecting a method of financing plant expansion?

11. One member of the board of directors suggests that the corporation maximize trading on equity, that is, using stockholders' equity as a basis for borrowing additional funds at a lower rate of interest than the expected earnings from the use of the borrowed funds.
    (a) Explain how a change in income tax rates affects trading on equity.
    (b) Explain how trading on equity affects earnings per share of common stock.
    (c) Under what circumstances should a corporation seek to trade on equity to a substantial degree?

12. Explain the meaning of the following terms:
    (a) Payout ratio.
    (b) Earnings per share.
    (c) Dividend yield.
    (d) Price-earnings ratio.

13. What is meant by book value? Of what significance is preferred stock in the computation of book value?

14. Of what importance are the following ratios in financial analysis?
    (a) Stockholders' equity to total assets or equity.
    (b) Debt to total assets or equities.
    (c) Times interest earned.
    (d) Ratio of plant assets to long-term liabilities.

15. Discuss the inherent limitations of single-year statements for purposes of analysis and interpretation. Include in your discussion the extent to which these limitations are overcome by the use of comparative statements.

16. Comparative balance sheets and comparative income statements that show a firm's financial history for each of the last 10 years may be misleading. Discuss the factors or conditions that might contribute to misinterpretations. Include a discussion of the additional information and supplementary data that might be included in or provided with the statements to prevent misinterpretations.

17. Explain the meaning of the following terms: (a) common-size analysis, (b) vertical analysis, (c) horizontal analysis, (d) percentage analysis.

18. What are the limitations for ratio analysis?

19. A student who just completed his first finance course commented, "We didn't use ratio analysis; our instructor indicated that ratio analysis was no longer fashionable." Discuss.

20. Some believe that the stock market is efficient with respect to incorporating publicly available information into the stock price. What implication does this statement have for financial statement analysis?

Cases

C26-1 As the CPA for Schaefer Retailers, you have been requested to develop some key ratios from the comparative financial statements. This information is to be used to convince creditors that Schaefer Retailers is solvent and to support the use of going-concern valuation procedures in the financial statements.

The data requested and the computations developed from the financial statements follow:

	1981	1980
Current ratio	2.5 times	2 times
Acid-test ratio	.7 times	1.2 times
Property, plant, and equipment to stockholders' equity	2.6 times	2.3 times
Sales to stockholders' equity	2.5 times	2.8 times
Net income	Up 30%	Down 10%
Earnings per share	$3.12	$2.40
Book value per share	Up 5%	Up 8%

Instructions

(a) Schaefer Retailers asks you to prepare a list of brief comments stating how each of these items supports the solvency and going-concern potential of the business. The company wishes to use these comments to support its presentation of data to its creditors. You are to prepare the comments as requested, giving the implications and the limitations of each item separately, and then the collective inference that may be drawn from them about Schaefer's solvency and going-concern potential.

(b) Having done as the client requested in part (a), prepare a brief listing of additional ratio-analysis-type data for this client which you think its creditors are going to ask for to supplement the data provided in part (a). Explain why you think the additional data will be helpful to these creditors in evaluating the client's solvency.

(c) What warnings should you offer these creditors about the limitations of ratio analysis for the purposes stated here?

C26-2 Tyson Foods, Inc. went public three years ago. The board of directors will be meeting shortly after the end of the year to decide on a dividend policy. In the past, growth has been financed primarily through the retention of earnings. A stock or a cash dividend has never been declared. Presented below is a brief financial summary of Tyson Foods, Inc. operations.

| | ($000 omitted) | | | | |
	1981	1980	1979	1978	1977
Sales	$10,000	$8,000	$7,000	$3,000	$2,000
Net income	$ 1,500	$ 800	$ 400	$ 500	$ 100
Average total assets	$11,000	$9,500	$5,500	$2,100	$1,500
Current assets	$ 4,000	$3,000	$1,500	$ 600	$ 500
Working capital	$ 1,800	$1,600	$ 600	$ 250	$ 200
Common shares:					
Number of shares outstanding (000)	1,000	1,000	1,000	10	10
Average market price	$9	$6	$4	—	—

Instructions

(a) Suggest factors to be considered by the board of directors in establishing a dividend policy.

(b) Compute the rate of return on assets, profit margin on sales, earnings per share, and price-earnings ratio for each of the five years for Tyson Foods, Inc.

(c) Comment on the appropriateness of declaring a cash dividend at this time, using the ratios computed in part (b) as a major factor in your analysis.

C26-3 The transactions listed below relate to Seller, Inc. You are to assume that on the date on which each of the transactions occurred the corporation's accounts showed only common stock ($100 par) outstanding, a current ratio of 2½:1 and a substantial net income for the year to date (before giving effect to the transaction concerned). On that date the book value per share of stock was $146.48.

Each numbered transaction is to be considered completely independent of the others, and its related answer should be based on the effect(s) of that transaction alone. Assume that all numbered transactions occurred during 1981 and that the amount involved in each case is sufficiently material to distort reported net income if improperly included in the determination of net income. Assume further that each transaction was recorded in accordance with generally accepted accounting principles and, where applicable, in conformity with the all-inclusive concept of the income statement.

For each of the numbered transactions you are to decide whether it:

(a) Increased the corporation's 1981 net income.

(b) Decreased the corporation's 1981 net income.

(c) Increased the corporation's total retained earnings directly (i.e., not via net income).

(d) Decreased the corporation's total retained earnings directly.

(e) Increased the corporation's current ratio.

(f) Decreased the corporation's current ratio.

(g) Increased each stockholder's proportionate share of total owner's equity.

(h) Decreased each stockholder's proportionate share of total owner's equity.

(i) Increased each stockholder's equity per share of stock (book value).

(j) Decreased each stockholder's equity per share of stock (book value).

(k) Had none of the foregoing effects.

Instructions

List the numbers 1 through 10. Select as many letters as you deem appropriate to reflect the effect(s) of each transaction as of the date of the transaction by printing beside the transaction number the letter(s) that identifies that transaction's effect(s).

Transactions

1. The corporation paid a cash dividend which had been recorded in the accounts at time of declaration.

2. Litigation involving Seller, Inc., as defendant was settled in the corporation's favor, with the plaintiff paying all court costs and legal fees. The corporation had appropriated retained earnings in 1975 as a special contingency appropriation for this court action, and the board directs abolition of the appropriation.

3. The corporation received a check for the proceeds of an insurance policy from the company with which it is insured against theft of trucks. No entries concerning the theft had been made previously, and the proceeds reduce but do not cover completely the loss.

4. Treasury stock, which had been repurchased at and carried at $102 per share, was issued as a stock dividend. In connection with this distribution, the board of directors of Seller, Inc. had authorized a transfer from retained earnings to permanent capital of an amount equal to the aggregate market value ($104 per share) of the shares issued. No entries relating to this dividend had been made previously.

5. In January the board directed the write-off of certain patent rights that had suddenly and unexpectedly become worthless.

6. The corporation wrote off all of the unamortized discount and issue expense applicable to bonds that it refinanced in 1981.

7. Treasury stock originally repurchased and carried at $101 per share was sold for cash at $103.50 per share.

8. The corporation sold at a profit land and a building that had been idle for some time. Under the terms of the sale, the corporation received a portion of the sales price in cash immediately, the balance maturing at six-month intervals.

9. The board of directors authorized the write-up of certain fixed assets to values established in a competent appraisal.

10. The corporation called in all its outstanding shares of stock and exchanged them for new shares on a 2-for-1 basis, reducing the par value at the same time to $50 per share.

(AICPA adapted)

C26-4 The Finance Committee of the Stout Corporation was established to appraise and screen departmental requests for plant expansions and improvements at a time when these requests totaled $10 million. The committee then sought your professional advice and help in establishing the minimum performance standards that it should demand of these projects in the way of anticipated rates of return before interest and taxes.

The Stout Corporation is a closely held family corporation in which the stockholders exert an active and unified influence on the management. At this date, the company has no long-term debt and has 1,000,000 shares of common capital stock outstanding which were sold at $20 per share. It is currently earning $5 million (Income before interest and taxes) per year. The applicable tax rate is 50%.

If the projects under consideration are approved, management is confident that the $10 million of required funds can be obtained either:

1. **By Borrowing:** via the medium of an issue of $10 million, 10%, 20-year bonds.
2. **By Equity Financing:** via the medium of an issue of 500,000 shares of common stock to the general public. It is expected and anticipated that the ownership of these 500,000 shares will be widely dispersed and scattered.

The company has been earning 12½% return after taxes. The management and the dominant stockholders consider this rate of earnings to be a fair price-earnings ratio (8 times earnings) as long as the company remains free of long-term debt. A lowering of the price-earnings ratio to six and two-thirds times earnings constitutes an adequate adjustment to compensate for the risk of carrying $10 million of long-term debt. They believe that this reflects, and is consistent with, current market appraisals.

Instructions

(a) Prepare columnar schedules comparing minimum returns, considering interest, taxes, and earnings ratio, which should be produced by each alternative to maintain the present capitalized value per share (of $20).

(b) What minimum rate of return on new investment is necessary for each alternative to maintain the present capitalized value per share (of $20)?

(AICPA adapted)

C26-5   The owners of R. L. Jefferson Company, a closely held corporation, have offered to sell their 100% interest in the company's common stock at an amount equal to the book value of the common stock. They will retain their interest in the company's preferred stock.

The president of the Heilmut Corporation, your client, would like to combine the operations of the R. L. Jefferson Company with the Metal Products Division, and she is seriously considering having Heilmut Corporation buy the common stock of the R. L. Jefferson Company. She questions the use of "book value" as a basis for the sale, however, and has come to you for advice.

Instructions

Draft a report to your client. Your report should cover the following points:

(a) Define book value. Explain its significance in establishing a value for a business that is expected to continue in operation indefinitely.

(b) Describe the procedure for computing book values of ownership equities.

(c) Why should your client consider the R. L. Jefferson Company's accounting policies and methods in his evaluation of the company's reported book value? List the areas of accounting policy and method relevant to this evaluation.

(d) What factors, other than book value, should your client recognize in determining a basis for the sale?

(AICPA adapted)

*C26-6   Two students are discussing the merits of ratio analysis as a basis for financial analysis. In discussing the valuation of common stock, one student notes that many securities sell too high in normal markets. These stocks, often referred to as "blue chip" stocks—the prosperous leaders of the industry—have a popularity that is not supported by their assets and earnings. It seems that certain companies and certain industries attract a bullishness that overvalues the stock. Through fundamental analysis, therefore, we can determine whether this stock is overvalued in relation to its intrinsic value.

The second student argues that this type of analysis is no longer used in the investment community for evaluating common stocks. The student notes that a new theory of investment selection based on capital market analysis is now used extensively. Unfortunately, the student cannot explain this concept except to indicate that it has something to do with "beta" and a "portfolio of stocks."

Instructions

(a) Define the term "intrinsic value" and explain why an investment analyst would be interested in finding this value.

(b) Explain the term "beta" and its importance to the theory of capital market analysis.

(c) Why is a portfolio of stocks necessary in the capital market analysis approach to selection of common stocks?

Exercises

E26-1 The Morgan Company has been operating for several years, and on December 31, 1981, presented the following balance sheet:

Morgan Company
BALANCE SHEET
December 31, 1981

Cash	$ 20,000	Accounts payable	$ 70,000
Receivables	60,000	Mortgage payable	100,000
Inventories	60,000	Common stock ($1.00 par)	120,000
Plant assets (net)	180,000	Retained earnings	30,000
	$320,000		$320,000

The net income for 1981 was $20,000. Projected **annual** operational expenditures (based on past data) exclusive of depreciation are $45,000. Assume that total assets are the same in 1980 and 1981.

Instructions

Compute each of the following ratios. For each of the five indicate the manner in which it is computed and its significance as a tool in the analysis of the financial soundness of the company.

1. Current ratio.
2. Acid-test ratio.
3. Defensive interval measure.
4. Debt to total assets.
5. Rate of return on assets.

E26-2 Presented below is information related to Hunt Corporation:

Hunt Corporation
BALANCE SHEET
December 31, 1981

Cash		$ 40,000	Notes payable (short-term)	$ 50,000
Receivables	$100,000		Accounts payable	26,000
less allowance	10,000	90,000	Accrued liabilities	5,000
Inventories		130,000	Capital stock (par $5) 50,000	250,000
Prepaid insurance		3,000	Retained earnings	112,000
Land		20,000		
Equipment (net)		160,000		
		$443,000		$443,000

STATEMENT OF INCOME
Year Ended December 31, 1981

Sales		$1,000,000
Cost of Sales		
Inventory, Jan. 1, 1981	$100,000	
Purchases	790,000	
Cost of goods available for sale	890,000	
Inventory, Dec. 31, 1981	130,000	
Cost of goods sold		760,000
Gross Profit on Sales		240,000
Operating Expenses		170,000
Net Income		$ 70,000

Instructions

(a) Compute the following ratios or relationships of the Hunt Corporation. Assume that the ending account balances are representative unless the information provided indicates differently.   *CA/CL*
1. Current ratio.   *CGS / average inventory*
2. Inventory turnover.
3. Receivables turnover.   *net sales / avg trade receivables*
4. Earnings per share.   *net inc / net sales*
5. Profit margin on sales.   *NI - pref div / avg cs equity*
6. Rate of return on common stock equity on December 31, 1981.

(b) Indicate for each of the following transactions whether the transaction would improve, weaken, or have no effect on the current ratio of the Hunt Corporation at December 31, 1981.
1. Write-off an uncollectible account receivable, $2,000.
2. Purchase additional capital stock for cash.
3. Pay $20,000 on notes payable (short-term)
4. Collect $20,000 on accounts receivable.
5. Buy equipment on account.
6. Give an existing creditor a short-term note in settlement of account.

E26-3   Financial information for the Blakely Company is presented below.

	12/31/81	12/31/80
Assets		
Cash	$ 140,000	$ 122,000
Receivables (net)	240,000	198,000
Inventories	1,200,000	1,000,000
Short-term investments	200,000	400,000
Prepaid items	60,000	80,000
Land	300,000	300,000
Building and equipment (net)	2,000,000	1,820,000
	$4,140,000	$3,920,000
Equities		
Accounts payable	$ 500,000	$ 420,000
Notes payable	200,000	200,000
Accrued liabilities	100,000	100,000
Bonds payable due 1986	800,000	800,000
Common stock	2,000,000	2,000,000
Retained earnings	540,000	400,000
	$4,140,000	$3,920,000

Blakely Company
COMPARATIVE INCOME STATEMENT
Years Ended December 31, 1981 and 1980

	1981	1980
Sales	$4,000,000	$3,600,000
Cost of goods sold	3,300,000	2,970,000
Gross profit	700,000	630,000
Operating expenses	480,000	400,000
Net income	$ 220,000	$ 230,000

Instructions

From these data compute as many ratios presented in the chapter as possible. Assume that the ending account balances for 1980 are representative unless the information provided indicates differently. The beginning inventory for 1980 was $800,000.

E26-4 Shown below is the equity section of the balance sheet for Senn Company and Carter Company. Each has assets totaling $4,000,000.

Senn Co.		Carter Co.	
Current liabilities	$ 300,000	Current liabilities	$ 500,000
Long-term debt, 5%	1,500,000	Common stock ($20 par)	2,800,000
Common stock ($20 par)	1,600,000	Retained earnings	700,000
Retained earnings	600,000		
	$4,000,000		$4,000,000

For the last two years each company has earned the same income before interest and taxes.

	Senn Co.	Carter Co.
Income before interest and taxes	$432,000	$432,000
Interest expense	84,000	12,000
	348,000	420,000
Income taxes (40%)	139,200	168,000
Net income	$208,800	$252,000

Instructions

(a) Which company is more profitable in terms of return on total assets?
(b) Which company is more profitable in terms of return on stockholders' equity?
(c) Which company has the greater net income per share of stock? Why?
(d) From the point of view of income, is it advantageous to the stockholders of the Senn Co. to have the long-term debt outstanding? Why?

E26-5 The controller of Columbus Merchandise Company finds that, although the company continues to earn about the same net income year after year, the rate of return on stockholders' equity is decreasing. Most of the profits are permitted to remain in the business so that total assets are increasing year by year, but there is very little increase in net income. As the recently hired chief accountant, you are requested to assist the controller in locating the difficulty and to suggest remedial measures.

Among the matters of interest that you find is the following:

	Inventory Dec. 31	Cost of Goods Sold
1978	$257,000	$2,850,000
1979	292,000	2,650,000
1980	365,000	2,800,000
1981	407,000	2,980,000

Instructions

(a) What conclusions can be reached on the basis of this information only?

(b) What further investigation does it suggest? State exactly how you would proceed.

(c) If your conclusions are confirmed in the additional investigation, what recommendations would you make concerning remedial measures?

E26-6   Presented below is information related to Hardy, Inc.

Operating income	$ 240,000
Bond interest expense	90,000
	150,000
Income taxes	78,000
Net income	$ 72,000
Bonds payable	$1,500,000
Common stock	525,000
Appropriation for contingencies	75,000
Retained earnings, unappropriated	300,000

Instructions

Is Hardy, Inc. trading on the equity successfully? Explain.

E26-7   L. N. Roland Company's condensed financial statements provide the following information:

Balance Sheet

	Dec. 31, 1981	Dec. 31, 1980
Cash	$ 40,000	$ 60,000
Accounts receivable (net)	100,000	80,000
Marketable securities (short-term)	80,000	40,000
Inventories	440,000	360,000
Prepaid expenses	3,000	7,000
Total current assets	$ 663,000	$ 547,000
Property, plant, and equipment (net)	637,000	653,000
Total assets	$1,300,000	$1,200,000
Current liabilities	200,000	160,000
Bonds payable	400,000	400,000
Common stockholders' equity	700,000	640,000
Total liabilities and stockholders' equity	$1,300,000	$1,200,000

Income Statement
For the Year Ended 1981

Sales	$1,000,000
Cost of goods sold	(700,000)
Gross profit	300,000
Selling and administrative expense	(106,000)
Interest expense	
(including $1,500 amortization of bond discount)	(24,000)
Net income	$ 170,000

Instructions

(a) Determine the following:
1. Current ratio at December 31, 1981.
2. Acid-test ratio at December 31, 1981.
3. Accounts receivable turnover for 1981.
4. Inventory turnover for 1981.
5. Rate of return on assets for 1981.
6. Rate of return on common stock equity for 1981.

(b) Prepare a brief evaluation of the financial condition of the L. N. Roland Company and of the adequacy of its profits.

E26-8 As loan analyst for the Shorewood National Bank, you have been presented the following information:

Assets

	Potter Co.	Feller Co.
Cash	$ 85,000	$ 250,000
Receivables	137,000	212,000
Inventories	450,000	460,000
Total current assets	672,000	922,000
Other assets	485,000	627,000
Total assets	$1,157,000	$1,549,000

Liabilities and Capital

	Potter Co.	Feller Co.
Current liabilities	$ 250,000	$ 320,000
Long-term liabilities	400,000	500,000
Capital stock and retained earnings	507,000	729,000
Total liabilities and capital	$1,157,000	$1,549,000
Annual sales	$1,000,000	$1,500,000
Rate of gross profit on sales	30%	40%

Each of these companies has requested a loan of $50,000 for six months with no collateral offered. Inasmuch as your bank has reached its quota for loans of this type, only one of these requests is to be granted.

Instructions

Which of the two companies, as judged by the information given above, would you recommend as the better risk and why? Assume that the ending account balances are representative of the entire year.

E26-9 Thorpe Company is a wholesale distributor of professional equipment and supplies. The company's sales have averaged about $900,000 annually for the three-year period 1978–1980. The firm's total assets at the end of 1980 amounted to $850,000.

The president of Thorpe Company has asked the controller to prepare a report that summarizes the financial aspects of the company's operations for the past three years. This report will be presented to the Board of Directors at their next meeting.

In addition to comparative financial statements, the controller has decided to present a number of relevant financial ratios which can assist in the identification and interpretation of trends. At the request of the controller, the accounting staff has calculated the following ratios for the three-year period 1978–1980:

	1978	1979	1980
Current ratio	2.00	2.13	2.18
Acid-test (quick) ratio	1.20	1.10	0.97
Accounts receivable turnover	9.72	8.57	7.13
Inventory turnover	5.25	4.80	3.80
Percent of total debt to total assets	44	41	38
Percent of long-term debt to total assets	25	22	19
Sales to fixed assets (fixed asset turnover)	1.75	1.88	1.99
Sales as a percent of 1978 sales	1.00	1.03	1.06
Gross margin percentage	40.0	38.6	38.5
Net income to sales	7.8%	7.8%	8.0%
Return on total assets	8.5%	8.6%	8.7%
Return on stockholders' equity	15.1%	14.6%	14.1%

In the preparation of his report, the controller has decided first to examine the financial ratios independently of any other data to determine if the ratios themselves reveal any significant trends over the three-year period.

Instructions

(a) The current ratio is increasing while the acid-test (quick) ratio is decreasing. Using the ratios provided, identify and explain the contributing factor(s) for this apparently divergent trend.

(b) In terms of the ratios provided, what conclusion(s) can be drawn regarding the company's use of financial leverage during the 1978–1980 period?

(c) Using the ratios provided, what conclusion(s) can be drawn regarding the company's net investment in plant and equipment?

(CMA adapted)

E26-10   Ringlund, Inc. began operations in January 1979 and reported the following results for each of its three years of operations:

1979	$160,000 net loss
1980	$ 20,000 net loss
1981	$600,000 net income

At December 31, 1981, the Ringlund, Inc. capital accounts were as follows:

6% cumulative preferred stock, par value $100; authorized, issued, and outstanding 10,000 shares	$1,000,000
Common stock, par value $1.00; authorized 1,000,000 shares; issued and outstanding 500,000 shares	$ 500,000

Ringlund, Inc. has never paid a cash or stock dividend. There has been no change in the capital accounts since Ringlund began operations. The appropriate state law permits dividends only from retained earnings.

Instructions

(a) Compute the book value of the common stock and preferred stock at December 31, 1981.

(b) Compute the book value of the common stock and preferred stock at December 31, 1981, assuming that the preferred stock has a liquidating value of $105 per share.

E26-11   Presented below is information related to the Tuna Company for 1981:

Sales	$600,000
Net income	60,000
Average total assets	260,000
Average stockholders' equity	100,000
Market price of stock at year-end	$60 per share
Cash dividend per share	$2.00
Earnings per share	$3.00

Instructions

(a) Compute the following ratios for 1981:
   1. Profit margin on sales.
   2. Rate of return on stockholders' equity.
   3. Rate of return on total assets.
   4. Dividend yield.
   5. Price-earnings ratio.
(b) Compute the following for 1982, assuming that all other factors remain constant:
   1. Total sales if the profit margin on sales is 13%.
   2. Average total assets if the asset turnover is three times.
   3. Net income if the earnings per share is $3.50.
   4. Rate of return on stockholders' equity, assuming that stockholders' equity increases 10 percent.
   5. Asset turnover, assuming that average total assets increase $40,000.

Problems

P26-1   Presented below are comparative balance sheets for the Edmonds Company.

Edmonds Company
COMPARATIVE BALANCE SHEET
December 31, 1981 and 1980

	December 31	
Assets	1981	1980
Cash	$ 100,000	$ 230,000
Accounts receivable (net)	220,000	190,000
Investments	200,000	150,000
Inventories	860,000	900,000
Prepaid expense	30,000	20,000
Fixed assets	2,400,000	2,000,000
Accumulated depreciation	(810,000)	(700,000)
	$3,000,000	$2,790,000
Liabilities and Stockholders' Equity		
Accounts payable	$ 40,000	$ 30,000
Accrued expenses	150,000	170,000
Bonds payable	400,000	200,000
Capital stock	2,000,000	2,000,000
Retained earnings	410,000	390,000
	$3,000,000	$2,790,000

Instructions

(a) Prepare a comparative balance sheet of the Edmonds Company showing the percent each item is of the total.

(b) Prepare a comparative balance sheet of the Edmonds Company showing the dollar change and the percent change for each item.

(c) Of what value is the additional information provided in part (a)?

(d) Of what value is the additional information provided in part (b)?

P26-2   The Alvarez Corporation has been operating successfully for a number of years. The balance sheet of the company as of December 31 is presented here.

The Alvarez Corporation
BALANCE SHEET
December 31, 1981

Assets			Equities		
Current assets			Current liabilities		
Cash		$ 50,000	Notes payable		$ 80,000
Accounts receivable (net)		140,000	Accounts payable		77,000
Notes receivable		80,000	Taxes payable		61,000
Inventories		270,000	Total current liabilities		218,000
Prepaid items		20,000			
Total current assets		560,000	Long-term bank loan, due in		
Fixed assets			1984, 9% interest		140,000
Land	$ 30,000		Stockholders' equity		
Building (net)	165,000		Common stock		
Equipment (net)	330,000		($10 par)	$350,000	
Total fixed assets		525,000	Retained		
		$1,085,000	earnings	377,000	727,000
					$1,085,000

This balance sheet indicates that the bulk of the company's growth has been financed by the common stockholders, because more than $377,000 of past net income of the company has been retained and is now invested in various operating assets. For the last three years the company has earned an average net income of $110,000 after interest ($15,000) and taxes ($61,000).

The board of directors has been considering an expansion of operations. Estimations indicate that the company can double its volume of operations with an additional investment of about $750,000. Of this amount $500,000 would be used to add to the present building, to purchase new equipment, and to reorganize certain operations. The remaining amount would be needed for working capital—inventories and higher receivables. Competitive conditions are such that the added volume can probably be sold at the existing prices and that income before taxes and interest will total $360,000. The tax rate of about 40% on income after interest will continue.

Three alternative plans for financing the expansion are under consideration:

1. Sell enough additional stock to raise $750,000. For this purpose it is estimated the stock would sell at $30 per share.

2. Sell 20-year bonds at 10% interest, totaling $590,000. In addition, sell 10,000 shares of additional stock at a price of $30 per share. Use part of the proceeds to pay off the present long-term bank loan.

3. Sell 20-year bonds at 10% interest, totaling $700,000. Use part of the proceeds to pay off present long-term bank loans. The remaining funds are to be provided by short-term creditors. The cost of these funds (in interest and discounts not taken) is estimated at $20,000 a year.

Assume that the financing alternative selected will take place immediately.

Instructions

(a) Compute the current ratio under each plan and compare it with the present current ratio.

(b) Compute earnings per share under each plan and compare with the present earnings per share.

(c) Compute the rate of return on common stock equity under each plan and compare with the present return.

(d) Compute the ratio of debt to total equity under each plan and compare it with the present ratio.

P26-3 The stockholders' equity in the Beach Manufacturing, Inc. is as follows:

Preferred stock—6% cumulative, nonparticipating, $100 par value			
Authorized 10,000 shares; issued 5,000 shares	$500,000		
Less 500 shares in treasury	50,000		
Outstanding, 4,500 shares	450,000		
Common stock, $1.00 par value			
Authorized 1,000,000 shares; issued 900,000 shares	900,000		
Capital in excess of par	115,000	$1,465,000	
Capital arising from the acquisition of preferred stock below par value		4,000	
Retained earnings			
Appropriation for contingencies	46,000		
Appropriation for sinking fund	280,000		
Appropriation for possible inventory decline	75,000		
Unrestricted	414,000	815,000	$2,284,000

Instructions

Compute the book value per share of the common and preferred stock under each of the following conditions:

(a) As stated above, assume that there are no preferred stock dividends in arrears.

(b) Assume the same situation as stated above except that preferred stock dividends are $66,000 in arrears including the current year.

(c) Assume the same situation as in (a) except that the preferred stock is fully participating, based on the ratio of the total par value of the respective stocks outstanding.

(d) Assume the same situation as in (a) except that, instead of retained earnings, the company has a deficit of $130,000.

P26-4 Erdman Corporation's management is concerned over the corporation's current financial position and return on investment. They request your assistance in analyzing their financial statements, and furnish the following statements:

Erdman Corporation
STATEMENT OF WORKING CAPITAL DEFICIT
December 31, 1981

Current liabilities		$224,500
Less current assets:		
Cash	$ 5,973	
Accounts receivable (net)	80,100	
Inventory	113,125	199,198
Working capital deficit		$ 25,302

Erdman Corporation
INCOME STATEMENT
For the Year Ended December 31, 1981

Sales (90,500 units)	$760,200
Cost of goods sold	452,500
Gross profit	307,700
Selling and administrative expenses, including $22,980 depreciation	155,660
Income before income taxes	152,040
Income taxes	74,000
Net income	$ 78,040

Additional information:

Assets other than current assets consist of land, building, and equipment with a book value of $352,950 on December 31, 1981. Assume that ending account balances are representative of amounts existing throughout the year.

Instructions

Assuming that Erdman Corporation operates 300 days per year, compute the following (use 300 days in all computations):

1. Accounts receivable turnover.
2. Inventory turnover.
3. Number of days' operations (working capital provided by operations) to cover the working capital deficit.
4. Return on total assets as a product of asset turnover and the profit margin on sales (profit margin ratio).

P26-5 The Data Terminal Company is planning to invest $10,000,000 in an expansion program which is expected to increase income before interest and taxes by $2,500,000. The company currently is earning $5 per share on 1,000,000 shares of common stock outstanding. The capital structure prior to the investment is:

Debt	$10,000,000
Equity	30,000,000
	$40,000,000

The expansion can be financed by sale of 200,000 shares at $50 net each, or by issuing long-term debt at a 6% interest cost. The firm's recent income statement was as follows:

Sales	$101,000,000
Variable cost	$ 60,000,000
Fixed cost	30,500,000
	$ 90,500,000
Income before interest and taxes	$ 10,500,000
Interest	500,000
Income before income taxes	$ 10,000,000
Income taxes (50%)	5,000,000
Net income	$ 5,000,000

Instructions

(a) Assuming that the firm maintains its current income and achieves the anticipated income from the expansion, what will be the earnings per share (1) if the expansion is financed by debt? (2) if the expansion is financed by equity?

(b) At what level of income before interest and taxes will the earnings per share under either alternative be the same amount?

(c) The choice of financing alternatives influences the earnings per share. The choice might also influence the earnings multiple used by the "market." Discuss the factors inherent in choice between the debt and equity alternatives that might influence the earnings multiple. Be sure to indicate the direction in which these factors might influence the earnings multiple.

(CMA adapted)

P26-6 The Morris Company is listed on the New York Stock Exchange. The market value of its common stock was quoted at $10 per share at December 31, 1981, and 1980. Morris's balance sheet at December 31, 1981, and 1980, and statement of income and retained earnings for the years then ended are presented below:

Morris Company
BALANCE SHEET

	December 31,	
	1981	1980
Assets		
Current assets:		
Cash	$ 3,500,000	$ 3,600,000
Marketable securities, at cost which approximates market	13,000,000	11,000,000
Accounts receivable, net of allowance for doubtful accounts	105,000,000	95,000,000
Inventories, lower of cost or market	126,000,000	154,000,000
Prepaid expenses	2,500,000	2,400,000
Total current assets	250,000,000	266,000,000
Property, plant, and equipment, net of accumulated depreciation	311,000,000	308,000,000
Investments, at equity	2,000,000	3,000,000
Long-term receivables	14,000,000	16,000,000
Goodwill and patents, net of accumulated amortization	6,000,000	6,500,000
Other assets	7,000,000	8,500,000
Total assets	$590,000,000	$608,000,000
Liabilities and Stockholders' Equity		
Current liabilities:		
Notes payable	$ 5,000,000	$ 15,000,000
Accounts payable	38,000,000	48,000,000
Accrued expenses	24,500,000	27,000,000
Income taxes payable	1,000,000	1,000,000
Payments due within one year on long-term debt	6,500,000	7,000,000
Total current liabilities	75,000,000	98,000,000
Long-term debt	169,000,000	180,000,000
Deferred income taxes	74,000,000	67,000,000
Other liabilities	9,000,000	8,000,000

Stockholders' equity:

Common stock, par value $1.00 per share; authorized 20,000,000 shares; issued and outstanding 10,000,000 shares	10,000,000	10,000,000
5% cumulative preferred stock, par value $100.00 per share; $100.00 liquidating value; authorized 50,000 shares; issued and outstanding 40,000 shares	4,000,000	4,000,000
Additional paid-in capital	107,000,000	107,000,000
Retained earnings	142,000,000	134,000,000
Total stockholders' equity	263,000,000	255,000,000
Total liabilities and stockholders' equity	$590,000,000	$608,000,000

Morris Company
STATEMENT OF INCOME AND RETAINED EARNINGS

	Year ended December 31,	
	1981	1980
Net sales	$600,000,000	$500,000,000
Costs and expenses:		
Cost of goods sold	490,000,000	400,000,000
Selling, general, and administrative expenses	66,000,000	60,000,000
Other, net	7,000,000	6,000,000
Total costs and expenses	563,000,000	466,000,000
Income before income taxes	37,000,000	34,000,000
Income taxes	16,800,000	15,800,000
Net income	20,200,000	18,200,000
Retained earnings at beginning of period	134,000,000	126,000,000
Dividends on common stock	12,000,000	10,000,000
Dividends on preferred stock	200,000	200,000
Retained earnings at end of period	$142,000,000	$134,000,000

Instructions

On the basis of the information above, compute the following for 1981 only:

(a) Current (working capital) ratio.

(b) Quick (acid-test) ratio.

(c) Number of days' sales in average receivables, assuming a business year consisting of 300 days and all sales on account.

(d) Inventory turnover.

(e) Book value per share of common stock, assuming that there is no dividend arrearage on the preferred stock.

(f) Earnings per share on common stock.

(g) Price-earnings ratio on common stock.

(h) Dividend-payout ratio on common stock.

45- 55

P26-7 Near the close of your audit, the treasurer of Clausing Corporation, your client, informs you that the company is planning to acquire the Nelson Corporation and requests that you prepare certain financial statistics for 1981 and 1980 from the following statements of Nelson Corporation.

Nelson Corporation
BALANCE SHEET
December 31, 1981 and 1980

Assets	1981	1980
Current assets		
Cash	$ 1,610,000	$ 1,387,000
Marketable securities, at cost (market value $550,000)	510,000	
Accounts receivable, less allowance for doubtful accts.:		
1981, $125,000; 1980, $110,000	4,075,000	3,669,000
Inventories, at lower of cost or market	7,250,000	7,050,000
Prepaid expenses	125,000	218,000
Total current assets	13,570,000	12,324,000
Plant and equipment, at cost		
Land and buildings	13,500,000	13,500,000
Machinery and equipment	9,250,000	8,520,000
Total plant and equipment	22,750,000	22,020,000
Less accumulated depreciation	13,470,000	12,549,000
Total plant and equipment—net	9,280,000	9,471,000
Long-term receivables	250,000	250,000
Other assets	25,000	75,000
Total assets	$23,125,000	$22,120,000

Liabilities and Stockholders' Equity

	1981	1980
Current liabilities		
Accounts payable	$ 2,950,000	$ 3,426,000
Accrued expenses	1,575,000	1,644,000
Federal taxes payable	875,000	750,000
Current maturities on long-term debt	500,000	500,000
Total current liabilities	5,900,000	6,320,000
Other liabilities		
5% sinking-fund debentures, due January 1, 1992		
($500,000 redeemable annually)	5,000,000	5,500,000
Deferred taxes on income, related to depreciation	350,000	210,000
Total other liabilities	5,350,000	5,710,000
Capital stock		
Preferred stock, $1.00 cumulative, $20 par, preference on		
liquidation $100 per share (authorized: 100,000 shares;		
issued and outstanding: 50,000 shares)	1,000,000	1,000,000
Common stock, $1.00 par (authorized: 900,000 shares;		
issued and outstanding; 1981, 550,000 shares;		
1980, 500,000 shares)	550,000	500,000
Capital in excess of par value of common stock	3,075,000	625,000
Retained earnings	7,250,000	7,965,000
Total stockholders' equity	11,875,000	10,090,000
Total liabilities and stockholders' equity	$23,125,000	$22,120,000

Nelson Corporation
STATEMENT OF INCOME AND RETAINED EARNINGS
For the Years Ended December 31, 1981 and 1980

	1981	1980
Revenues		
Net sales	$48,400,000	$41,700,000
Royalties	70,000	25,000
Interest	30,000	
Total	48,500,000	41,725,000
Costs and expenses		
Cost of goods sold	31,460,000	29,190,000
Selling, general and administrative	12,090,000	8,785,000
Interest on 5% sinking-fund debentures	275,000	300,000
Income taxes	2,315,000	1,695,000
Total	46,140,000	39,970,000
Net income	2,360,000	1,755,000
Retained earnings, beginning of year	7,965,000	6,760,000
Total	10,325,000	8,515,000
Dividends paid		
Preferred stock, $1.00 per share in cash	50,000	50,000
Common stock:		
Cash—$1.00 per share	525,000	500,000
Stock—(10%)—50,000 shares at market value		
of $50 per share	2,500,000	
Total	3,075,000	550,000
Retained earnings, end of year	$ 7,250,000	$ 7,965,000

Additional information:

1. The inventory at January 1, 1980, was $6,850,000.

2. The market prices of the common stock at December 31, 1981 and 1980 were $73.50 and $47.75, respectively.

3. The cash dividends for both preferred and common stock were declared and paid in June and December of each year. The stock dividend on common stock was declared and distributed in August, 1981.

4. Plant and equipment sales and retirements during 1981 and 1980 were $375,000 and $425,000, respectively. The related depreciation allowances were $215,000 in 1981 and $335,000 in 1980. At December 31, 1979, the plant and equipment asset balance was $21,470,000, and the related depreciation allowances were $11,650,000.

Instructions

Prepare a schedule computing the following selected statistics for 1981 and 1980. The current equivalent number of shares outstanding as of the respective year-end dates should be utilized in computing per-share statistics. (The current equivalent shares means the number of shares outstanding in the prior period adjusted retroactively for the stock dividend.)

At December 31:

1. Current ratio.
2. Acid-test (quick) ratio.
3. Book value per common share.

Year ended December 31:

1. Gross margin rate.

2. Inventory turnover rate.
3. Times interest earned (before taxes).
4. Earnings per common share.
5. Common stock price-earnings ratio (end of year value).
6. Gross capital expenditures.

(AICPA adapted)

60-85

P26-8 Keene Corporation has in recent years maintained the following relationships among the data on its financial statements:

1.	Gross profit rate on net sales	40%
2.	Net profit margin on net sales	10%
3.	Rate of selling expenses to net sales	20%
4.	Accounts receivable turnover	8 per year
5.	Inventory turnover	6 per year
6.	Acid-test ratio	2 to 1
7.	Current ratio	3 to 1
8.	Quick asset composition: 8% cash, 32% marketable securities, 60% accounts receivable	
9.	Asset turnover	2 per year
10.	Ratio of total assets to intangible assets	20 to 1
11.	Ratio of accumulated depreciation to cost of fixed assets	1 to 3
12.	Ratio of accounts receivable to accounts payable	1.5 to 1
13.	Ratio of working capital to stockholders' equity	1 to 1.6
14.	Ratio of total debt to stockholders' equity	1 to 2

The corporation had a net income of $120,000 for 1981 which resulted in earnings of $5.20 per share of common stock. Additional information includes the following:

1. Capital stock authorized, issued (all in 1973), and outstanding:
   Common, $10 per share par value, issued at 10% premium
   Preferred, 6% nonparticipating, $100 per share par value, issued at a 10% premium
2. Market value per share of common at December 31, 1981: $78
3. Preferred dividends paid in 1981: $3,000
4. Times interest earned in 1981: 33
5. The amounts of the following were the same at December 31, 1981, as at January 1, 1981: inventory, accounts receivable, 5% bonds payable—due 1983, and total stockholders' equity
6. All purchases and sales were "on account."

Instructions

(a) Prepare in good form the condensed (1) balance sheet and (2) income statement for the year ending December 31, 1981, presenting the amounts you would expect to appear on Keene's financial statements (ignoring income taxes). Major captions appearing on Keene's balance sheet are: Current Assets, Property, plant, and equipment, Intangible Assets, Current Liabilities, Long-term Liabilities, and Stockholders' Equity. In addition to the accounts divulged in the problem, you should include accounts for Prepaid Expenses, Accrued Expenses, and Administrative Expenses.

(b) Compute the following for 1981 (show your computations):
   1. Rate of return on common stockholders' equity.
   2. Price-earnings ratio for common stock.
   3. Dividends paid per share of common stock.
   4. Dividends paid per share of preferred stock.
   5. Dividend yield on common stock.

(AICPA adapted)

Full Disclosure in Financial Reporting

Accountants have long recognized that attempting to present all essential information about an enterprise in a balance sheet, income statement, and statement of changes in financial position is an extremely difficult if not impossible task. As indicated in Chapter 2, the profession has adopted a **full disclosure principle** that generally calls for reporting in financial statements any financial facts significant enough to influence the judgment of an informed reader. But such a principle can be difficult to put into operation. In some situations the benefits of disclosure may be apparent but the costs uncertain, while in other instances the costs may be certain but the benefits of disclosure not so apparent.

The costs of disclosure cannot be dismissed. For example, *The Wall Street Journal* indicated that if governmental reporting rules in segmented reporting were adopted, a company like Fruehauf would have to increase its accounting staff 50%, from 300 to 450 individuals. Many accountants and managers believe that the present reporting requirements are so substantial that users have a difficult time absorbing the information; they charge the profession with engaging in **information overload.** Conversely, others contend that even more information is needed to assess an enterprise's financial position and earnings potential.

The complexity of this situation is highlighted by such recent financial disasters as Penn Central, W. T. Grant, or Franklin National Bank. Was the information presented about these companies not comprehensible? Was it buried? Was it too technical? Or was it simply not there? No easy answers are forthcoming. One problem is that the profession is still in the process of developing the guidelines that tell whether a given transaction should be disclosed and what format this disclosure should take. Different users want different information, and it becomes exceedingly difficult to develop disclosure policies that meet their varied objectives.[1]

A substantial increase in disclosure requirements has occurred recently. The SEC has issued more **Accounting Series Releases** in the last seven years than in its previous history. And, as illustrated throughout this textbook, the FASB has issued many standards that have substantial disclosure provisions. The reasons for this increase in disclosure requirements are varied; some of them are listed below.

Complexity of the Business Environment The difficulty of distilling economic events into summarized reports has been magnified by the increasing complexity of business operations in such areas as leasing, business combinations, pensions, financing arrangements, revenue recognition, and deferred taxes. As a result, **footnotes** are used extensively to explain these transactions and their future effects.

Necessity for Timely Information Today, more than ever before, information that is current and predictive is being demanded. For example, more complete **interim data** are required. And published financial forecasts, long avoided and even feared by some accountants, are recommended by the SEC.

Accounting as a Control and Monitoring Device The government has recently sought more information and public disclosure of such phenomena as **management compensation, environmental pollution, related party transactions, errors and irregularities,** and **illegal activities.** A "post-Watergate" concern is expressed in many of these newer disclosure requirements, and, accountants and auditors have been selected as the agents to assist in controlling and monitoring these concerns. A trend toward **differential disclosure** also is occurring. For example, the SEC requires that certain substantive information be reported to it that is not found in annual reports to stockholders. And the FASB, recognizing that certain disclosure requirements are costly and unnecessary for certain companies, has eliminated reporting requirements for nonpublic enterprises in such areas as earnings per share and segmented reporting.

The purpose of this chapter is to acquaint you with (1) the general types of disclosure currently required, (2) some recent trends in financial reporting, and (3) the breadth of responsibility that has been placed on the accounting profession.

Read the Footnotes!

Footnotes are an integral part of the financial statements of a business enterprise, but they are often overlooked because they are highly technical and often appear in small print. Footnotes are the accountant's means of more fully disclosing data relevant to the interpretation of the statements. Information pertinent to specific financial statement items can be explained in qualitative terms, and supplementary data of a quantitative nature can be provided to expand the information in the financial statements. Restrictions imposed by financial arrangements or basic contractual agreements also can be explained in footnotes. It is generally conceded

[1]See, for example, Stephen Buzby, "The Nature of Adequate Disclosure," *The Journal of Accountancy* (April, 1974) for an interesting discussion of issues related to disclosure.

that, although footnotes may be technical and difficult to understand, they provide meaningful information for the user of the financial statements.

Footnotes can generally be classified in the following way.

Disclosure of Accounting Methods Used   Often footnotes answer such questions as: What method of depreciation is used on plant assets? What valuation method is employed on inventories? What amortization policy is followed in regard to intangible assets? How is the investment credit handled for plant assets? And, how are marketing costs handled for financial reporting purposes?

Refer to Appendix E following Chapter 5 for an illustration of footnote disclosure of accounting methods and other footnotes accompanying the audited financial statements of Tenneco Inc.

Some of the footnotes for Anetek Chemical Corporation are used for illustration purposes. Following the quoted footnote is an analysis of the information provided by the footnote.

> *Principles of Consolidation*—The financial statements include all significant subsidiaries on a full consolidation basis. During 1981, several minor acquisitions were consummated. One acquisition was accounted for as a pooling of interests; the others were accounted for as purchases. The effect of these acquisitions on the results of operations was not material.

Analysis. This footnote discloses that the company acquired several other businesses during the year. Because the acquisitions are acknowledged not to be material, it is not important that the differing effects of the "purchase" and "pooling of interests" method be understood. When the mergers or acquisitions during the period are material, the difference between "purchase" accounting and "pooling of interests" accounting could have significant effects on the balance sheet and income statement. The general subject of accounting for combinations is covered in advanced accounting. From this footnote the reader can determine that a part of the company's growth is attributable to external growth through business combinations as opposed to internal growth.

> *Goodwill*—The excess of the cost of investments in consolidated subsidiaries over their net assets at dates of acquisition is carried as goodwill. All goodwill is amortized over a five-year period on a straight-line basis.

Analysis. Anetek is apparently taking a fairly conservative policy regarding amortization of goodwill. Comparison of this amortization policy with that of other chemical companies might provide some interesting insights into the accounting philosophy and policies employed by Anetek. Is the income of a company that amortizes goodwill over a 40-year period comparable with the income of a company that amortizes goodwill over a 5-year period?

Disclosure of Gain or Loss Contingencies   In some cases, enterprises have either gain or loss contingencies that are not disclosed in the body of the financial statements. As indicated in earlier chapters, these contingencies may take a variety of forms such as pending lawsuits, either favorable or unfavorable, a contingent liability on an accommodation endorsement, and possible renegotiation refunds on government contracts. A footnote from Anetek's balance sheet is presented below:

> *Loss Contingencies*—In February 1978, when the United States Resources Commission reported finding mercury residues in fish, Anetek Chemical launched a "crash" program to make sure of emission control related to mercury emission. Several damage suits related to mercury have been lodged against Anetek. Anetek Chemical feels they are not legally liable and, therefore, are contesting these suits.
>
> Other suits have been started against the company and certain subsidiaries because of alleged product damage and other claims. All suits are being contested and the amount of uninsured liability thereunder, if any, is considered to be immaterial.

Analysis. The nature of various suits in relation to ecological matters is explained to the investor. The opinion of the company regarding possible damages is also considered. In addition, other litigative matters at this time do not seem to be material and do not have a substantially adverse effect on Anetek's financial posi-

Long-Term Debt & Available Credit Facilities (a) **Details of long-term debt**	(000 omitted) December 31 1981	1980
Promissory notes		
4.5%, final maturity 1998	$ 50,000	$ 85,000
5.0%, final maturity 1999	45,000	150,000
Debentures		
4.35%, final maturity 1996	50,000	60,000
6.70%, final maturity 2006	100,000	100,000
7.75%, final maturity 2007	100,000	100,000
8.875%, final maturity 2008	100,000	
8.90%, final maturity 2008	100,000	
Debentures, subordinate convertible, 3% due 1990		
(1981—22,184 common shares reserved)	5,000	5,000
Notes payable under revolving credit agreements		
Due 1984 (total available facility $225,000,000)	50,000	50,000
Due 1986 (total available facility $110,000,000)	50,000	50,000
Other (various rates and maturities):		
Foreign currency loans	50,000	35,000
Dollar loans	25,000	15,000
Total	$725,000	$650,000

The promissory notes and debentures are payable generally in annual installments beginning at various dates.

Agreements relating to the issuance of the 8.875% and 8.90% debentures provide for delivery of $8,000,000 and $18,000,000 principal amounts, respectively, subsequent to December 31, 1981. The debentures are recorded as debt when proceeds are received.

Installments (stated in millions) due on long-term debt in the five years after 1981 are: 1982, $62.0; 1983, $31.6; 1984, $46.2; 1985, $39.5; 1986, $83.6.

(b) **Available credit facilities at year end:**

In addition to the revolving credit agreements referenced above, the company had a 1.0 billion Deutsche mark agreement with a group of major German banks exercisable through 1986. Of the German credit facility, 30.0 million Deutsche marks were in use at December 31, 1981.

tion. The investor should read this section carefully, reading even between the lines, to measure the potential impact of contingencies.

Examination of Credit Claims An investor normally finds it extremely useful to determine the nature and cost of creditorship claims. The liability section in the balance sheet can provide the major types of liabilities outstanding only in the aggregate. Footnote schedules regarding such obligations provide additional information about how the company is financing its operations, the costs that will have to be borne in future periods, and the timing of future cash outflows as shown on page 1222.

   Analysis. The footnote discloses the composition and details of the outstanding long-term debt. For example, the company has promissory notes, debentures, convertible debentures, and other notes payable, ranging in cost from 3% to approximately 9%. In addition, the amount of debt to be retired in installments is disclosed. The interest rates represent a fixed annual cost. The maturity dates indicate when large cash outlays will have to be made or refinancing will have to take place.

Claims of Equity Holders Many companies present in the body of the balance sheet the number of shares authorized, issued, and outstanding and the par value for each type of equity security. Such data may also be presented in a footnote. Beyond that, the most common type of equity footnote disclosure relates to contracts and senior securities outstanding that might affect the various claims of the residual equity holders: for example, the existence of outstanding stock options, outstanding convertible debt and convertible preferred stock. In addition, it is necessary to disclose to equity claimants certain types of restrictions currently in force. Generally, these types of restrictions involve the amount of earnings available for dividend distribution.

Stockholders' Equity

At December 31, 1981 authorized capital stock consisted of 100,000,000 common shares and 25,000,000 preferred shares of $5 par and $1.00 par per share, respectively.

The changes in the number and amount of issued shares of common stock during 1981 were:

	Shares	Amount
Issued January 1	29,812,750	$157,152,870
Sold to employees	166,583	832,915
Awarded as restricted stock	18,705	93,525
Conversion of debentures	1,962	9,810
Issued December 31	30,000,000	$158,089,120

At December 31, 1981, there were 30,000,000 shares of common stock outstanding. None of the preferred shares have been issued.

In May 1981, the company made an offering of common stock to its employees at $57.75 a share, payable generally through payroll deductions. At December 31, 1981, there were unfilled subscriptions for 151,541 shares which may be cancelled at the option of the employee. Partial payments on these subscriptions aggregating $4,814,000 are included in current liabilities.

The stockholders authorized in 1980 an Award Plan providing for the granting, during the ensuing 10-year period, of 350,000 shares of Restricted or Deferred Stock, or a combination thereof, to selected employees in lieu of cash for services. During 1981, 18,705 shares of Restricted Stock were issued and 745 shares of Deferred Stock were awarded. At December 31, 1981, there were 312,635 shares available for grant. The Plan also extended to May 1987 the previous authority for granting dividend units.

The stockholders previously authorized plans for granting options to purchase common stock at the fair market value at the date of grant to officers and key employees. The options must be exercised within five years from the date of issuance. Changes during 1981 in the number of shares under option were:

	1981 Option Plan	1981 Incentive Plan	Dividend Units*
Options:			
Outstanding January 1	300,247	82,350	61,420
Granted	30,000		
Expired or terminated	1,500	15,600	
Outstanding December 31	328,747	66,750	61,420
Not optional			
December 31	71,253		188,580
Price range on			
Outstanding options	$61.44 to	$60.00 to	
at December 31	87.99	76.25	

*A dividend unit is the right to receive for a specified period cash payments equivalent in value to cash dividends paid during such period on one share of common stock.

In computing earnings per share, no adjustment was made for common shares issuable under stock purchase and option plans or upon conversion of 3% debentures because there would be no material dilutive effect.

Analysis. This footnote provides information about (1) the capital changes during the year and (2) the compensation plans related to employees, officers, and key executives. This footnote indicates the magnitude of the changes that occurred in the equity section during the year and also the potential changes that may develop from existing contractual arrangements. For example, the number of shares outstanding during the year changed very little, even though some shares were sold to employees and some conversion of debentures occurred. In addition, at present the dilutive effect of existing contractual arrangements outstanding in the form of convertible debenture bonds and stock options is not material (less than 3%).

Executory Commitments An enterprise often becomes involved in several executory contracts. When two parties commit themselves to some undertaking on the basis of a signed contract but neither party has yet performed, the contract is executory. Examples in accounting are pension agreements, lease arrangements, and purchase commitments. Most companies do not recognize these items in the accounts, although many accountants believe that these items should be recorded, notwithstanding the difficult valuation problems. Everyone agrees that some type of disclosure is necessary because these commitments will affect the cash flow of the enterprise in the future. An example of Anetek's commitments is as follows:

Retirement Plans and Other Commitments—The company and certain subsidiaries have plans to provide retirement benefits for eligible employees. The company's plan was amended effective January 1, 1981 to extend coverage to substantially all full-time employees and to provide additional benefits. The cost of the plan was $14,398,000 in 1981 and $13,634,000 in 1980. The company's policy is to accrue and fund pension cost as computed by its actuary. Pension fund assets exceed the actuarially computed value of vested benefits.

The total cost of pension plans for all companies in the consolidated group in 1981 and 1980 was $17,177,000 and $14,987,000 respectively.

At December 31, 1980, the company and its subsidiaries were lessees under various lease agreements. While the majority of these leases will expire during the next eight years, it is expected that they will be renewed or replaced by leases on other properties and facilities. The rental payments (stated in millions) due in cash five years after 1981 are: 1982, $36.3; 1983, $31.9; 1984, $30.5; 1985, $28.1; 1986, $25.9.

Analysis. Examination indicates that the company is computing pension expense on an actuarial basis instead of on a pay-as-you-go basis. In addition, the fact that pension assets exceed the computed value of vested benefits suggests that pension obligations are not a problem at this point.

The company also discloses in this footnote that certain fixed assets have been leased and sets out the payment amounts and due dates over the next five years. This information is valuable to a credit grantor, because a lease is similar to a liability in that the future payments on a lease represent future obligations.

Disclosure of Accounting Policies

Recently, much discussion has occurred relating to the publication in annual reports to stockholders of a statement that identifies the accounting policies that have a significant impact on reported profitability and financial condition. Accounting policies of a given entity are the specific accounting principles and methods currently employed and considered most appropriate in the circumstances to present fairly the financial statements of the enterprise. Current practice, therefore, **requires a description of accounting treatments** in a separate statement of accounting policies for such items as basis of consolidation, depreciation methods, inventory valuation techniques, amortization of intangibles, and handling of investment credits.

The following table shows the nature of information frequently disclosed in summaries of accounting policies and the number of survey companies (out of 600) disclosing such information.

Disclosure of Accounting Policies[2]

	No. of Companies
Consolidation basis	584
Depreciation methods	581
Inventory pricing	557
Interperiod tax allocation	546
Property	504
Employee benefits	360
Amortization of intangibles	320
Earnings per share calculation	295
Translation of foreign currency	238

The illustration on page 1228 is taken from the 1978 annual report of Northwest Industries, Inc. (Also see Tenneco, Inc.'s summary of accounting policies on pages 198–199.)

The APB in **Opinion No. 22,** "Disclosure of Accounting Policies," concluded that information about the accounting policies adopted and followed by a reporting entity is essential for financial statement users in making economic decisions. It

	CONSOLIDATED INCOME STATEMENT AND RESULTING EARNINGS PER SHARE BASED ON TWO DIFFERENT BUT ACCEPTED SETS OF ACCOUNTING TECHNIQUES	
Item	Method A (Conservative)	Method B (Liberal)
Net sales	$240,809,200	$243,924,600
Cost of goods sold	201,287,300	199,248,200
Gross profit	39,521,900	44,676,400
Other operating income		1,191,000
	39,521,900	45,867,400
Selling, general, and administrative expenses	24,210,700	26,468,300
	15,311,200	19,399,100
Other income (expenses)		
Interest expense	(1,810,900)	(1,873,400)
Net income—subsidiaries	538,000	
Amortization of goodwill	(180,000)	(10,000)
Miscellaneous	(259,000)	(229,200)
	(1,711,900)	(2,112,600)
Income before income taxes	13,599,300	17,286,500
State income taxes	638,000	812,900
Federal income taxes—deferred		348,900
Federal income taxes—current	5,238,000	6,440,000
Charges equivalent to tax reductions from:		
Investment tax credits	775,000	
Tax loss carryovers	990,000	297,000
	7,641,000	7,898,800
Net income	$ 5,958,300	$ 9,387,700
Earnings per share	$1.99	$3.14

[2]*Accounting Trends and Techniques—1978* (New York: AICPA, 1978), p. 45.

DIFFERING ACCOUNTING TECHNIQUES

Inventories

A uses last-in, first-out;
B uses first-in, first-out.
    Difference—$1,196,500

Goodwill from Acquisition

A amortizes over 10 years;
B amortizes over 40 years.
    Difference—$170,000

Taxes on Subsidiary Profits

A makes provision as
    income earned;
B makes no provision until
    dividends received.
    Difference—$43,000

Depreciation

A uses sum-of-the-years'-
    digits;
B uses straight-line.
    Difference—$253,100

Acquisition Depreciation

A uses "larger" base in
    purchase;
B uses "smaller" base
    pooling of interests.
    Difference—$63,800

Investment Tax Credits

A amortizes over useful lives
    of equipment;
B credits against current
    taxes.
    Difference—$656,000

Marketing Expenses

A charges as incurred;
B amortizes over 3 years.
    Difference—$191,500

Acquisition Loss Carryovers

B applies against federal
    income taxes to extent
    of pooling of interest.
    Difference—$693,000

Unfunded Pension Costs

A amortizes over 18 years;
B does not amortize.
    Difference—$50,500

Acquisition

A treats as purchase;
B treats as pooling of
    interest.
    Difference (see
    related items)

Retirement Allowances

A accrues and expenses prior
    to retirement;
B does not accrue
    expense until
    allowance paid.
    Difference—$120,000

Total Difference: $3,429,400

recommended that when financial statements are issued, a statement identifying the accounting policies adopted and followed by the reporting entity should also be presented as an integral part of the financial statements. The APB believed that the disclosure should be given in a separate Summary of Significant Accounting Policies preceding the notes to the financial statements or as the initial note.

The benefit of this recommendation to the investor is obvious. Reporting the accounting policies of all companies gives the investor some basis for determining whether a particular company is following the same accounting policies as other companies, whether conservative or liberal accounting policies are adopted, and whether these policies are consistently applied from year to year. The illustration presented above shows the differences in net income that can occur in accounting for one set of transactions given variations in accounting principles.[3] This example provides evidence that an analyst can be seriously misled if variations are ignored in the accounting principles employed by one business enterprise from another.

[3]"What are Earnings? The Growing Credibility Gap," *Forbes* (May 15, 1967), pp. 28–29.

Northwest Industries, Inc. and Subsidiaries
SUMMARY OF SIGNIFICANT ACCOUNTING POLICIES

Principles of Consolidation The consolidated financial statements include the accounts of the company and all of its subsidiaries.

Coca-Cola Bottling Company of Los Angeles has been included in the consolidated financial statements from November 1, 1977, the effective date of acquisition. If 1977 consolidated results had included Coca-Cola of Los Angeles on a full year basis, estimated pro forma results would have been as follows (in thousands of dollars except earnings per share): net sales $2,089,200; operating earnings, $296,900; net earnings, $132,800; and earnings per share, $4.31.

Inventories Approximately 64% of total inventories at December 31, 1978, and 68% of inventories at December 31, 1977, are stated at the lower of cost (first-in, first-out or average) or market. Market represents current replacement cost by purchase or reproduction, or net realizable value. The remaining inventories are stated on the last-in, first-out (Lifo) cost method. The Lifo cost was lower than the replacement cost of these inventories by approximately $96,800,000 at December 31, 1978, and $79,900,000 at December 31, 1977. Inventory costs include material, labor and factory overhead.

Property, Plant and Equipment Property, plant and equipment is stated at cost. Depreciation is based on the straight-line method over the estimated useful lives of depreciable assets. Cost and accumulated depreciation for property retired or disposed of are removed from the accounts. Gain or loss on disposal is credited or charged to earnings. Property, plant and equipment secured by financing leases are capitalized.

Intangible Assets In compliance with current generally accepted accounting principles, approximately $234,000,000 of the original cost in excess of book value of companies acquired is being amortized over 40 years on the straight-line method. Accumulated amortization amounted to $13,600,000 and $7,700,000 at December 31, 1978 and 1977, respectively. However, in the opinion of management, no diminution in value has occurred. Patents and trademarks are being amortized over their remaining lives on the straight-line method.

Earnings Per Share Earnings per share is determined by dividing earnings available to common shares by average common shares. Earnings available to common shares consists of net earnings, plus interest on subordinated debentures of $200,000 and $300,000 in 1978 and 1977, respectively, used in connection with assumed warrant exercises, less dividends on noncovertible preferred stock of $3,800,000 in 1978. Average common shares consist of common shares outstanding and common shares that would result if all dilutive options and warrants were assumed to be exercised and all convertible preferred shares were assumed to be converted. Cash proceeds from the assumed exercises of options were assumed to be used to acquire common stock for the treasury at the higher of year-end or average market price in each of the years, and the warrants were assumed to be exercised using 7.5% subordinated debentures.

All share and per share information in this report reflects a two-for-one common stock split that became effective June 29, 1978.

Income Taxes The effective income tax rate for 1978 was 44% and for 1977 was 45%. The items causing the variances from the statutory federal income tax rate of 48% were:

	1978	1977
Investment tax credit (flow through method)	4.7%	3.6%
Foreign earnings and taxes	0.6	0.8
State income taxes net of federal tax benefit	(1.7)	(1.6)
Amortization of excess cost	(1.0)	(0.5)
Minority expense	(0.2)	(0.3)
Other—net	1.6	1.0
Total	4.0%	3.0%

Deferred income taxes are provided for all significant items which are reported for tax purposes in different periods than in the statement of earnings. The effects of such items are as follows (in thousands of dollars):

	1978	1977
Depreciation and amortization expense	$13,300	$13,400
Deferred income items	1,500	3,400
Other—net	(1,200)	500
Total deferred income taxes	$13,600	$17,300

Pension Plans The company and its subsidiaries have numerous pension plans, which cover substantially all employees. Annual pension expense charged against operations approximated $18,200,000 and $15,500,000 in 1978 and 1977, respectively, which included amortization of prior service cost over various periods of not more than 40 years. All plans, except two, fund accrued pension costs. The unfunded prior service cost based on the most recent actuarial reviews amounted to approximately $93,000,000, of which $18,500,000 has been accrued. The vested portion of the prior service cost exceeded the pension funds and balance sheet accruals by approximately $28,000,000.

Disclosure of Special Transactions or Events

Related party transactions, errors and irregularities, and illegal acts pose especially sensitive and difficult problems for the accountant. The accountant/auditor who has responsibility for reporting on these types of transactions has to be extremely careful that the rights of the reporting company and the needs of users of the financial statements are properly balanced.

Related party transactions arise when a business enterprise engages in transactions in which one of the transacting parties has the ability to influence significantly the policies of the other, or in which a nontransacting party has the ability to influence the policies of the two transacting parties.[4]

Transactions such as borrowing or lending monies at abnormally low or high interest rates, real estate sales at amounts that differ significantly from appraisal value, exchanges of nonmonetary assets, and transactions involving enterprises that have no economic substance suggest that related parties may be involved. The accountant is expected to report the economic substance rather than the legal form of these transactions and to make adequate disclosures. Because it is often difficult to separate the economic substance from the legal form, disclosure is used extensively in this area. Companies involved in related party transactions usually **disclose the nature of the relationship and the nature and amount of the transaction.** Amounts due from or to related parties, as well as the terms of settlement, are also commonly disclosed.

Examples of the disclosure of related party transactions are shown below:

Winnebago Industries, Inc.

NOTES TO CONSOLIDATED FINANCIAL STATEMENTS
Note 8: Related Party Transactions—On May 13, 1976, the Company purchased a jet aircraft from an officer of the Company for $900,000. Three independent appraisals of the current value of the aircraft were utilized in determining the purchase price.

Chart House Inc.

Note 7: Related Party Transactions—The Company provides computer services to the First National Bank of Lafayette, of which William E. Trotter, II, Chairman of the Board, and Braxton I. Moody, III, Vice Chairman of the Board and Chief Executive Officer, are substantial shareholders. During 1978 and 1977, respectively, the Company received $301,000 and $319,000 for computer services rendered to the First National Bank of Lafayette.

The Company has various leases for office space with an entity owned by Messrs. Moody and Trotter for terms of up to 5 years (renewable through 1995) requiring rental payments of approximately $222,000 per year.

---

[4]"Related Party Transactions," *Statement on Auditing Standards No. 6* (New York: AICPA, 1975).

Cannon Mills Company

NOTES TO FINANCIAL STATEMENTS

Note 2: Related Party Transactions—The Company, in the normal course of business, sells cotton and certain manufactured products and provides administrative and selling services to companies in which it holds minority investments and purchases from certain of them cotton, yarn, and manufacturing services. Such sales and purchases are consummated at competitive prices and for fiscal 1977 amounted to $23,600,000 and $120,800,000, respectively, and for fiscal 1976 amounted to $19,700,000 and $97,100,000, respectively.

Loans, principally in connection with these activities, are made among the companies for short durations with interest charged at the rate of 6% per annum. The loans receivable from these related companies at December 29, 1977 and December 30, 1976 totalled $1,000,166 and $200,834, respectively, and are included in accounts receivable. The loans payable to the related companies at December 30, 1976 totalled $400,000 and are included in accounts payable.

Errors are defined as unintentional mistakes, whereas **irregularities** are intentional distortions of financial statements.[5] As indicated in earlier sections of this textbook, when errors are discovered, the financial statements should be corrected. The same treatment should be given irregularities. The discovery of irregularities, however, gives rise to a whole different set of suspicions, procedures, and responsibilities on the part of the accountant/auditor.

Illegal acts encompass such items as illegal political contributions, bribes, kickbacks, and other violations of laws and regulations.[6] In these situations, the accountant/auditor must evaluate the adequacy of disclosure in the financial statements. For example, if revenue is derived from an illegal act that is considered material in relation to the financial statements, this information should be disclosed. Passage of the Foreign Corrupt Practices Act of 1977 has had a significant impact upon the accounting profession, and its implications are not yet completely clear.

Many companies are involved in related party transactions; errors and irregularities, and illegal acts, however, are the exception rather than the rule. Disclosure plays a very important role in these areas because the transaction or event is more qualitative than quantitative and involves more subjective than objective evaluation. The users of the financial statements, however, must be provided with some indication of the existence and nature of these transactions where material. These items are generally revealed through disclosures, modifications in the auditor's report, or in reports of changes in auditors. See Tenneco's "Questionable Payments" footnote on page 205 for a disclosure of two charges of illegal acts.

Disclosure of Social Responsibility

The social responsibility of business has received a great deal of public attention in recent years. The public and local, state, and federal governments have urged that businesses make a more adequate response to current issues of social concern than they have in the past. For example, the SEC has already required listed corporations to file a report if pollution expenditures have a material effect on earnings.

---

[5]"The Independent Auditor's Responsibility for the Detection of Errors and Irregularities," *Codification of Statements on Auditing Standards* (New York: AICPA, 1979), pp. 117–124.

[6]"Illegal Acts of Clients," *Statement on Auditing Standards No. 17* (New York: AICPA, 1977).

Some investment funds, such as Dreyfus Third Century Fund, have been incorporated to invest only in "socially responsible" companies. The Council on Economic Priorities has been established as an independent research organization to inquire into the social activities of private enterprises. The United Church of Christ uses various criteria for determining the social consciousness of a corporation before investing church funds.

The information related to social expenditures as presented in current financial reports is haphazard. Expenditures for the following types of items are generally considered "social awareness expenditures":

> Assistance to educational institutions
> Grants to hospitals, health and other community related activities
> Aid to minority groups or enterprises
> Contributions to charitable foundations
> Aid to unemployed and related programs
> Assistance in urban development

The following diagram illustrates the extent of disclosure for the Fortune 500 companies:[7]

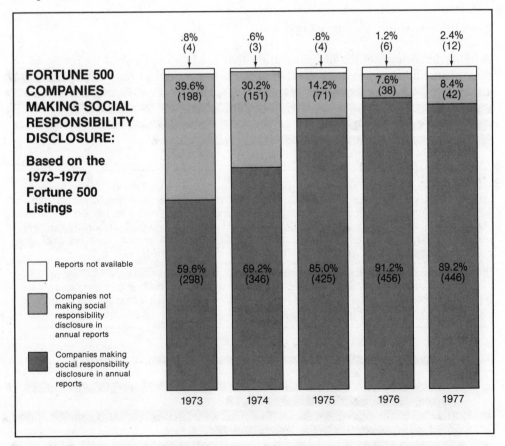

FORTUNE 500 COMPANIES MAKING SOCIAL RESPONSIBILITY DISCLOSURE:

Based on the 1973–1977 Fortune 500 Listings

	1973	1974	1975	1976	1977
Reports not available	.8% (4)	.6% (3)	.8% (4)	1.2% (6)	2.4% (12)
Companies not making social responsibility disclosure in annual reports	39.6% (198)	30.2% (151)	14.2% (71)	7.6% (38)	8.4% (42)
Companies making social responsibility disclosure in annual reports	59.6% (298)	69.2% (346)	85.0% (425)	91.2% (456)	89.2% (446)

[7]Ernst and Ernst, *Social Responsibility Disclosure—1978 Survey*, page 3.

Recently the SEC concluded that the following types of environmental information should be disclosed in filings with their agency.

1. The material effects that compliance with federal, state, and local environmental protection laws may have upon capital expenditures, earnings, and competitive position.
2. Litigation commenced or known to be contemplated against registrants by a government authority pursuant to federal, state, and local environmental regulatory provisions.
3. All other environmental information of which the average, prudent investor ought reasonably to be informed.

As yet, no standards or requirements have been proposed for the measurement and reporting of the social responsibilities assumed by individual enterprises by the FASB. To some investors, it is a matter of importance whether a company is adopting affirmative policies with regard to environmental matters or is simply doing the minimum to assure legal compliance.

Examination of the Auditor's Report

Another important source of information that is often overlooked by investors in their examination of the financial statements is the auditor's report. An **auditor** is a professional who conducts an independent examination of the accounting data presented by the business enterprise. If the auditor is satisfied that the financial statements represent the financial position and results of operations, an **opinion** is expressed on audited statements in the following manner:

> We have examined the consolidated balance sheet of Anetek Chemical Corporation and its subsidiary companies as of December 31, 1981 and the related consolidated statements of income, stockholders' equity, and changes in financial position for the year then ended. Our examination was made in accordance with generally accepted auditing standards, and accordingly included such tests of the accounting records and such other auditing procedures as we considered necessary in the circumstances.
>
> In our opinion, such financial statements present fairly the financial position of the companies at December 31, 1981 and the results of their operations and the changes in financial position for the year then ended, in conformity with generally accepted accounting principles applied on a basis consistent with that of the preceding year.

In preparing this report, the auditor follows these reporting standards:

1. The report shall state whether the financial statements are presented in accordance with generally accepted accounting principles.
2. The report shall state whether such principles have been consistently observed in the current period in relation to the preceding period.
3. Informative disclosures in the financial statements are to be regarded as reasonably adequate unless otherwise stated in the report.

4. The report shall contain either an expression of opinion regarding the financial statements taken as a whole or an assertion to the effect that an opinion cannot be expressed. When an overall opinion cannot be expressed, the reasons therefore should be stated. In all cases where an auditor's name is associated with financial statements, the report should contain a clear-cut indication of the character of the auditor's examination, if any, and the degree of responsibility being taken.

In short, these standards require that an auditor state in the opinion that generally accepted accounting principles have been followed and that they have been applied on a basis consistent with that of the preceding year. In most cases, the auditor issues a standard **unqualified** or **"clean"** opinion; that is, the auditor believes that the financial statements do present fairly the financial statements on a basis consistent with that used in the preceding year. There are situations in which the auditor, however, is required to (1) express a **qualified** opinion, (2) express an **adverse** opinion, or (3) **disclaim** an opinion.

A qualified opinion contains an exception to the standard opinion; ordinarily the exception is not of sufficient magnitude to invalidate the statements as a whole; if it were, an adverse opinion would be rendered. The usual circumstances in which the auditor may deviate form the standard unqualified short-form report on financial statements are as follows:

1. The scope of the examination is limited or affected by conditions or restrictions.
2. The statements do not fairly present financial position or results of operations because of:
    (a) Lack of conformity with generally accepted accounting principles and standards.
    (b) Inadequate disclosure.
3. Accounting principles and standards are not consistently applied.
4. Unusual uncertainties exist concerning future developments, the effects of which cannot be reasonably estimated or otherwise resolved satisfactorily.

If the auditor is confronted with one of the situations noted above, the opinion must be qualified. A qualification is one of two types, a "subject to" or an "except for." A **subject to** qualification is used when the qualification results from an uncertainty that would materially affect the financial statements, such as serious deficiencies in working capital, litigation in which the company is a defendant, and threatened expropriation. An **except for** qualification is used in all other cases mentioned above.

An adverse opinion is required in any report in which the exceptions to fair presentation are so material that in the independent auditor's judgment a qualified opinion is not justified. In such a case, the financial statements taken as a whole are not presented in accordance with generally accepted accounting principles. Adverse opinions are rare, because most enterprises change their accounting to conform with the auditor's desires. A disclaimer of an opinion is normally issued for one of two reasons: (1) the auditor has gathered so little information on the financial statements that no opinion can be expressed, or (2) the auditor concludes on the basis of the evaluation that the ability of the company to continue on a going-concern basis is highly questionable because of financing or operating problems.

The qualified (subject to) opinion shown at the top of page 1234 was issued because of "costs and expenses related to factors not presently determinable."

Board of Directors and Stockholders
Scovill Manufacturing Company

We have examined the consolidated balance sheet of Scovill Manufacturing Company and consolidated subsidiaries as of December 25, 1977 and December 26, 1976, and the related consolidated statements of earnings, stockholders' equity and changes in financial position for the fiscal years then ended. Our examinations were made in accordance with generally accepted auditing standards and, accordingly, included such tests of the accounting records and such other auditing procedures as we considered necessary in the circumstances.

As described in Note B, the Company made provision in 1975 for loss on disposition of its Metals and General Products division. While it is management's opinion, with which we concur, that the balance of the provision at December 25, 1977 is more than adequate to cover all future costs and expenses which may arise as a result of the disposition, the ultimate amount of such costs and expenses is dependent on factors which are not presently determinable.

In our opinion, subject to the effect on the financial statements of determining the ultimate amount of costs and expenses referred to in the preceding paragraph, the financial statements referred to above present fairly the consolidated financial position of Scovill Manufacturing Company and consolidated subsidiaries at December 25, 1977 and December 26, 1976, and the consolidated results of their operations and changes in financial position for the fiscal years then ended, in conformity with generally accepted accounting principles applied on a consistent basis.—*Report of Independent Auditors.*

Another illustration of how a close reading of the auditor's report can warn the investor of possible disaster in the future is an annual report of Lockheed Aircraft that stated:

In our opinion, subject to the realization of the work-in-process inventories and accounts receivable described in Note 2, the statements mentioned above present fairly, ... except for the change in accounting for administrative and general expenses and independent research and development costs described in Note 1.

The change in accounting in Note 1 increased earnings by $22 million out of a total of $44 million reported as net income for the year. Note 2 had to do with the costs associated within the C-5 aircraft. Essentially, the question revolved around the ultimate realizability of receivables and inventory related to construction of this aircraft. If Lockheed could not collect on these claims, the company would be in financial difficulty running into hundreds of millions of dollars.

The auditor's report stated in part:

As discussed in Notes 2 and 3, the company is faced with contingencies of extraordinary magnitudes arising from disputes with, and claims against, the U.S. Government as well as uncertainty as to its commercial TriStar program. These items are material to both the financial position and the results of the operations of the company, and their resolution may significantly affect its future. In our opinion, subject to the effect of the matters referred to in the preceding paragraph....

Our point should be clear: the sophisticated analyst should examine closely the auditor's report in conjunction with the examination of the other financial data. Although the information usually can be found in other parts of the financial statements, the auditor's report can be a convenient and useful source of highly pertinent information.

Management's Responsibilities for Financial Statements

The public accounting profession has attempted for many years to educate the public to the fact that a company's management has the primary responsibility for the preparation, integrity, and objectivity of the company's financial statements. Only in the last couple of years have management letters acknowledging such responsibility appeared in annual reports to stockholders. Presented below is the management letter that served as a prelude to the 1978 financial statements of General Motors Corporation.

**GENERAL MOTORS CORPORATION
AND CONSOLIDATED SUBSIDIARIES**

CONSOLIDATED FINANCIAL STATEMENTS

Responsibilities for Financial Statements

The following financial statements of General Motors Corporation and Consolidated Subsidiaries were prepared by the management which is responsible for their integrity and objectivity. The statements have been prepared in conformity with generally accepted accounting principles and, as such, include amounts based on judgments of management.

Management is further responsible for maintaining a system of internal controls, including internal accounting controls, that contains organizational arrangements that provide an appropriate division of responsibility and is designed to assure that the books and records reflect the transactions of the companies and that its established policies and procedures are carefully followed. The system is constantly reviewed for its effectiveness and is augmented by written policies and guidelines, a strong program of internal audit, and the careful selection and training of qualified personnel.

Deloitte Haskins & Sells, independent certified public accountants, are engaged to examine the financial statements of General Motors Corporation and its subsidiaries and issue reports thereon. Their examination is conducted in accordance with generally accepted auditing standards and includes a review of internal controls and a test of transactions. The Accountants' Report appears on page 27.

The Board of Directors, through the Audit Committee of the Board, is responsible for assuring that management fulfills its responsibilities in the preparation of the financial statements and for engaging the independent public accountants with whom the Committee reviews the scope of the audits and the accounting principles to be applied in financial reporting. The Audit Committee meets regularly (separately and jointly) with the independent public accountants, representatives of management, and the internal auditors to review the activities of each and to ensure that each is properly discharging its responsibilities. To ensure complete independence, Deloitte Haskins & Sells have full and free access to meet with the Audit Committee, without management representatives present, to discuss the results of their examination and their opinions on the adequacy of internal controls and the quality of financial reporting.

[signature]

Chairman

[signature]

Chief Financial Officer

Reporting for Diversified (Conglomerate) Companies

In the last two decades business enterprises have evidenced an increasing tendency to diversify their operations. As a result, investors and investment analysts have sought more information concerning the details behind conglomerate financial statements. Particularly, they are requesting revenue and income information on the **individual** segments that comprise the **total** business income figure. In addition, some attention has also been given to the segmentation of the balance sheet and statement of changes in financial position for the various divisions or subsidiaries comprising the consolidated group.

An illustration of segmentation is presented in the following example of an office equipment and auto parts company.

Office Equipment and Auto Parts Company INCOME STATEMENT DATA (in millions)			
	Consolidated	Office Equipment	Auto Parts
Net sales	$78.8	$18.0	$60.8
Manufacturing costs:			
Inventories, beginning	12.3	4.0	8.3
Materials and services	38.9	10.8	28.1
Wages	12.9	3.8	9.1
Inventories, ending	(13.3)	(3.9)	(9.4)
	50.8	14.7	36.1
Selling and administrative expense	12.1	1.6	10.5
Total operating expenses	62.9	16.3	46.6
Operating income	15.9	1.7	14.2
Income taxes	(9.3)	(1.0)	(8.3)
Net income	$ 6.6	$ .7	$ 5.9

If only the consolidated figures are available to the analyst, much information regarding the composition of these figures is hidden in aggregated figures. There is no way to tell from the consolidated data the extent to which the differing product lines **contribute to the company's profitability, risk, and growth potential.**[8] For example, in the illustration above, if the office equipment segment is deemed a risky venture, the segmentation provides useful information for purposes of making an informed investment decision.

Companies have been somewhat hesitant to disclose segmented data for the reasons listed below.

1. Without a thorough knowledge of the business and an understanding of such important factors as the competitive environment and capital investment requirements, the investor may find the segment information meaningless or even draw improper conclusions about the reported earnings of the segments.

2. Additional disclosure may harm reporting firms because it may be helpful to competitors, labor unions, suppliers, and certain government regulatory agencies.

[8]One writer has shown that data provided on a segmental basis allows an analyst to predict future total sales and earnings better than data presented on a nonsegmental basis. See D. W. Collins, "Predicting Earnings with Sub-Entity Data: Some Further Evidence," *Journal of Accounting Research* (Spring, 1976).

3. Additional disclosure may discourage management from taking intelligent business risks because segments reporting losses or unsatisfactory earnings may cause stockholder dissatisfaction with management.

4. The wide variation among firms in the choice of segments, cost allocation, and other accounting problems limits the usefulness of segment information.

5. The investor is investing in the company as a whole and not in the particular segments, and it should not matter how any single segment is performing if the overall performance is satisfactory.

6. Certain technical problems, such as classification of segments and allocation of segment revenues and cost (especially "common costs"), are formidable.

On the other hand, the advocates of segmented disclosures offer these reasons:

1. Segment information is needed by the investor to make an intelligent investment decision regarding a diversified company.
   (a) Sales and earnings of individual segments are needed to forecast consolidated profits because of the differences between segments in growth rate, risk, and profitability.
   (b) Segment reports disclose the nature of a company's businesses and the relative size of the components as an aid in evaluating the company's investment worth.

2. The absence of segmented reporting by a diversified company may put its unsegmented, single product-line competitors at a competitive disadvantage because the conglomerate may obscure information that its competitors must disclose.

Since the issuance of **FASB Statement No. 14** in 1976, however, enterprises that issue a complete set of financial statements have been required to disclose as part of those statements certain information relating to: the enterprise's operations in different industries, its foreign operations, its export sales, and its major customers.[9] The basic requirements of the statement are as follows:

1. Information required to be reported is to be prepared on the same accounting basis and by the same accounting principles used in the enterprise's consolidated financial statements.

2. A number of methods might be used to identify industry segments such as the Standard Industrial Classification manual, currently existing profit centers, or relating common risk factors to products or product groups. The Board concluded that none of these methods by itself is suitable and that management should exercise its judgment in determining industry segments. Industry segments should be determined on a worldwide basis where practicable.

3. Each industry segment that is significant to the enterprise as a whole must report certain information. It is significant if it satisfies **one or more** of the following tests in each period for which financial statements are presented:

---

[9]"Financial Reporting for Segments of a Business Enterprise," *Statement of Financial Accounting Standards No. 14* (Stamford, Conn.: FASB, 1976), par. 3. A number of pronouncements have been issued since 1976 that modify certain disclosure requirements. "Financial Reporting for Segments of a Business Enterprise—Interim Financial Statements," *Statement of Financial Accounting Standards No. 18* (Stamford, Conn.: FASB, 1977) indicates that segment information need not be presented in interim reports. "Suspension of the Reporting of Earnings per Share and Segment Information by Nonpublic Enterprises," *Statement of Financial Accounting Standards No. 21* (Stamford, Conn.: FASB, 1978) states that a nonpublic company is not required to disclose segmental data. "Reporting Segment Information in Financial Statements that are Presented in Another Enterprise's Financial Report," *Statement of Financial Accounting Standards No. 24* (Stamford, Conn.: FASB, 1978) eliminates the requirement for the disclosure of segmental data in the separate financial statements of a parent company or affiliate that also presents consolidated or combined financial statements. "Disclosure of Information About Major Customers," *Statement of Financial Accounting Standards No. 30* (Stamford, Conn.: FASB, 1979) requires that the amount of sales to an individual domestic government or foreign government be disclosed when those revenues are 10 percent or more of the enterprise's revenues.

(a) Its revenues are 10% or more of the combined revenues of all industry segments.

(b) Its operating profit or loss is 10% or more of the **greater,** in absolute amount, of either:

    (i) the combined operating profit of all industry segments that did not incur a loss; or

    (ii) the combined operating loss of all industry segments that did incur a loss; or

(c) Its identifiable assets are 10% or more of the combined identifiable assets of all industry segments.

4. The statement requires that the following information be presented for each reportable segment and in the aggregate for the remaining industry segments:

Revenues—Sales to unaffiliated customers and to other industry segments are to be separately disclosed. The basis of accounting for intersegment sales or transfers must be described and consistently applied.

Profitability—Operating profit or loss must be disclosed for each reportable segment. To the extent that an unusual amount of income or expense or an unusual or infrequently occurring item **(APB Opinion No. 30)** are included in the industry segment profitability, the nature and amount shall be explained. Disclosure of changes in accounting principles **(APB Opinion No. 20)** should be explained and attributed to the reportable segment.

Identifiable Assets—Identifiable assets of an industry segment must be disclosed for each reportable segment. Disclosure of additional information on certain assets may be desirable for some reportable segments.

Such information may be included within the body of the financial statements, in the notes to the financial statements, or in a separate schedule included as an integral part of the financial statements. At a minimum, revenues and operating profit or loss must be reconciled to corresponding amounts in the consolidated statement of operations and identifiable assets reconciled to consolidated total assets.

The trend is toward greater segmented financial disclosure when an enterprise consists of two or more segments in distinctly different lines of business or otherwise clearly subject to different trends and risks. Certain accounting problems do exist, however, which still have not been resolved completely.

Definition of a Segment   The first major problem in accounting for a diversified enterprise is to define the reporting basis. For example, **should the company provide information on a legal-entity basis, a geographical basis, an organizational-units basis, type-of-customer basis, or an industry-grouping basis?** Each of these approaches has certain benefits, yet all of them have disadvantages as well.

For example, setting the divisions up on the basis of legal entities has the advantage of providing a fairly clean and defined set of entities. Often these entities are set up merely to hold properties, meet certain governmental regulations, or provide tax shelters, however. In these situations, the corporation operates the businesses on a much different basis and uses the legal entities only for questions of form rather than substance.

A second possible alternative is in terms of geographical distribution. This approach has some validity, particularly in comparing national and international business but, in general, it appears that more appropriate bases might be selected. A very similar approach is by type of customer, normally government versus nongovernment. Again, such information is valuable in certain circumstances, but its application appears to be relatively restricted to a small number of companies.

A general view that seems to prevail among accountants is that the enterprise should be free to select the breakdown that best represents the underlying activities of the business. An organizational unit approach probably reflects this point of view, because enterprises normally devise some way of relating responsibilities to various segments of the business. The problem with using this procedure is that the organizational unit is continually changing as operations are expanded or contracted. A problem of comparability between periods can develop.

In addition to the problem of determining the basis for identifying the segments, there is the question of what percentage to use. As indicated earlier, a 10% factor is applied to one of the following items: revenue, income or loss, or identifiable assets. But these criteria are still subject to interpretation. For example, Weyerhaeuser Co. indicates that except for certain real estate ventures, everything else relates to paper production, so no additional disclosure is necessary. Other timber companies have broken down their segments into such categories as pulp and paper, packaging products, and wood products and have provided operating data. In general, however, the disclosure requirements associated with **FASB Statement No. 14** appear quite reasonable and the flexibility afforded management seems desirable. Management is in the best position to judge which is the most meaningful breakdown of its divisional data, and with experimentation useful information should be forthcoming.

Allocation of Common Costs One of the critical problems in providing segmented income statements for conglomerate companies is the allocation of common costs. Common costs are those incurred for the benefit of more than one segment and whose interrelated nature prevents a completely objective division of costs among segments. For example, the president's salary is very difficult to allocate to various segments. The significance of common costs is indicated by a Financial Executive Research Foundation survey that shows that the average ratio of common costs to net sales is greater than that of net income to net sales.

Many different bases for allocation have been suggested, such as sales, gross profit, assets employed, investment, and marginal income. The choice of basis is difficult because it can materially influence the relative profitability of the segments.

The use of a **defined profit** concept has been suggested. Defined profit is the excess of segment revenues over directly chargeable segment expense. Common costs in this framework are charged against total company defined profits but not against any individual segments. This approach is not used at present and it is unlikely that this concept will be implemented because no final earnings figures ever occur for separate divisions.

Transfer Pricing Problems Transfer pricing is the practice of charging a price for goods "sold" between divisions or subsidiaries of a company, commonly called intracompany transfers. A transfer price system is used for several reasons, but the primary objective is to measure the performance and profitability of a given segment of the business in relation to other segments. In addition, a pricing system is needed to insure control over the flow of goods through the enterprise.

Transfer pricing is not a problem of the same magnitude as common costs, but it still is very significant in many business enterprises. At present, different ap-

DRESSER INDUSTRIES (DRESSER)

The financial information by industry segment for the year ended October 31, 1978 is summarized as follows (in millions):

INDUSTRY SEGMENTS

	Petroleum Operations	Energy Processing & Conversion	Refractories & Minerals Operations	Construction & Mining Equipment	Industrial Specialty Products	Adjustments & Eliminations	Consolidated
Sales and service revenues to unaffiliated customers	$883.7	$704.9	$340.1	$561.8	$563.5	$ —	$3,054.0
Intersegment sales and service revenues	2.4	4.3	4.1	5.0	8.9	(24.7)	—
Total sales and service revenues	$886.1	$709.2	$344.2	$566.8	$572.4	$(24.7)	$3,054.0
Operating profit	$146.7	$144.6	$ 40.9	$ 56.7	$ 57.3	$ (.5)	$ 445.7
Equity in net income of unconsolidated subsidiaries and affiliates							2.7
General corporate expenses							(49.0)
Interest expense, net							(20.7)
Earnings before taxes							$ 378.7
Identifiable assets	$593.6	$276.1	$221.8	$456.6	$313.3	$(12.8)	$1,848.6
Equity investments							48.0
Corporate assets							458.7
Total assets							$2,355.3
Capital expenditures	$ 54.5	$ 12.4	$ 26.0	$ 12.1	$ 13.5		$ 118.5
Corporate capital expenditures							4.3
Total capital expenditures							$ 122.8
Depreciation, depletion and amortization	$ 35.3	$ 10.6	$ 15.1	$ 21.5	$ 13.3		$ 95.8
Corporate depreciation, depletion and amortization							4.7
Total depreciation, depletion and amortization							$ 100.5

proaches to transfer pricing are used. Some firms transfer the goods at market prices; others use cost plus a fixed fee; and some use variable cost. In some situations, the company lets the division bargain for the price of the item in question.

In evaluating a specific division, we must consider the transfer pricing problem. If, for example, Division A sells certain goods to Division B using a market price instead of cost, the operating results of both divisions are affected. Transfer pricing in many situations does not occur on an arm's-length basis and, therefore, the final results of a given division must be suspect. In practice, there are at present no defined guides in regard to a company's disclosure of its method of transfer pricing for external reporting purposes.

Illustrations of Segmented Reporting Although many problems exist with segmented reporting, the information provided by revenue and profit breakdowns is considered useful by most investors. Sample schedules (above) taken from Dresser Industries' corporate report show the different product-line breakdowns disclosed.

The financial information by geographic area for the year ended October 31, 1978 is summarized as follows (in millions):

GEOGRAPHIC AREA

	United States	Canada	Latin America	Europe	Mid East Far East & Africa	Adjustments & Eliminations	Consolidated
Sales and service revenues to unaffiliated customers	$2,345.0	$131.1	$111.1	$280.7	$186.1	$ —	$3,054.0
Intergeographic area sales and service revenues	92.7	20.1	10.7	35.2	7.0	(165.7)	—
Total sales and service revenues	$2,437.7	$151.2	$121.8	$315.9	$193.1	$(165.7)	$3,054.0
Operating profit	$ 346.8	$ 8.7	$ 17.5	$ 48.4	$ 24.4	$ (.1)	$ 445.7
Equity in net income of unconsolidated subsidiaries and affiliates							2.7
General corporate expenses							(49.0)
Interest expense, net							(20.7)
Earnings before taxes							$ 378.7
Identifiable assets	$1,419.5	$108.1	$ 66.7	$226.6	$119.9	$ (92.2)	$1,848.6
Equity investments							48.0
Corporate assets							458.7
Total assets							$2,355.3

United States export sales by geographic area are as follows (in millions):

Canada	$ 47.8
Latin America	95.6
Europe	42.4
Mid East, Far East and Africa	188.3
Total	$374.1

Reporting on Forecasts

In recent years, the investing public's demand for more and better information has focused on disclosure of corporate expectations for the future through publication of earnings forecasts. Financial forecasts have therefore become the subject of intensive discussion with journalists, corporate executives, the SEC, financial analysts, accountants, and others making their views known. Predictably, there are strong arguments on either side. Listed below are some of the arguments.

Arguments for requiring published forecasts:

1. Investment decisions are based on future expectations; therefore, information about the future facilitates better decisions.
2. Forecasts are already circulated informally, but are uncontrolled, frequently misleading, and not available equally to all investors. This confused situation should be brought under control.
3. Circumstances now change so rapidly that historical information is no longer adequate for prediction.

Arguments against requiring published forecasts:

1. No one can foretell the future. Therefore forecasts, while conveying an impression of precision about the future, will inevitably be wrong.
2. Organizations will strive only to meet their published forecasts, not to produce results that are in the stockholders' best interest.
3. When forecasts are not proved to be accurate, there will be recriminations and probably legal actions.
4. Disclosure of forecasts will be detrimental to organizations, because it will fully inform not only investors, but also competitors (foreign and domestic).[10]

In 1978, the SEC indicated that companies are **permitted** (not required) to include profit projections in reports filed with that agency.[11] The SEC guidelines indicate that

1. Management has the option to provide good-faith projections, provided it has some reasonable basis for the projection. Disclosure of the assumptions used to prepare the forecast would be helpful. The most probable amount or the most reasonable range for the items projected should be used.
2. Projections should include at least these financial items: revenues, net income, and earnings per share, although disclosure is not limited to these items. Management should select the period over which the items should be projected. It is recommended that management indicate whether updates will be furnished.
3. Outside reviews of the projections may be included. If a review is included, the qualifications of the reviewer, extent of the review and relationship between the reviewer and the company should be described.

To encourage management to disclose this type of information, the SEC has issued a "safe harbor" rule. The safe harbor rule provides protection to an enterprise that presents an erroneous projection as long as the projections were prepared on a reasonable basis and were disclosed in good faith.[12]

Experience in Great Britain   Great Britain has permitted financial forecasts for years, and the results have been fairly successful. Some significant differences exist between the English and the American business and legal environment,[13] but probably none that could not be overcome if influential interests in this country cooperated to produce an atmosphere conducive to quality forecasting. A typical British forecast adapted from a construction company's report to support a public offering of stock is as follows:

[10]Joseph P. Cummings, *Financial Forecasts and the Certified Public Accountant* (New York: Peat, Marwick, Mitchell & Co., Nov. 30, 1972).

[11]"Guides for Disclosure of Projections of Future Economic Performance," *Release No. 5992* (Washington: SEC, Nov. 7, 1978).

[12]"Safe-Harbor Rule for Projections," *Release No. 5993* (Washington: SEC, 1979).

[13]The British system, for example, does not permit litigation on forecasted information, and the solicitor (lawyer) is not permitted to work on a contingent fee basis. See "A Case for Forecasting—The British Have Tried It and Find That It Works," *World* (New York: Peat, Marwick, Mitchell & Co., Autumn 1978), pp. 10–13.

> Profits have grown substantially over the past 10 years and directors are confident of being able to continue this expansion. . . . While the rate of expansion will be dependent on the level of economic activity in Ireland and in England, the group is well structured to avail itself of opportunities as they arise, particularly in the field of property development, which is expected to play an increasingly important role in the group's future expansion.
>
> Profits before taxation for the half year ended 30th June 1977 was 402,000 pounds. On the basis of trading experiences since that date and the present level of sales and completions, the directors expect that in the absence of unforeseen circumstances, the group's profits before taxation for the year to 31st December 1977 will be not less than 960,000 pounds. . . .
>
> No dividends will be paid in respect of the year December 31, 1977. In a full financial year, on the basis of above forecasts (not including full year profits) it would be the intention of the board, assuming current rates of tax, to recommend dividends totaling 40% (of after-tax profits), of which 15% payable would be as an interest dividend in November 1978 and 25% in final dividend in June 1979.

A general narrative-type forecast issued by a U.S. corporation appeared as follows:

> On the basis of promotions planned by the company for the second half of fiscal 1976, net earnings for that period are expected to be approximately the same as those for the first half of fiscal 1976, with net earnings for the third quarter expected to make the predominant contribution to net earnings for the second half of fiscal 1976.

Questions of Liability   What happens if a company does not meet its forecasts? Are the company and the auditor going to be sued? If a company, for example, projects an earnings increase of 15% and achieves only 5%, should the stockholder be permitted to have some judicial recourse against the company? One court case involving Monsanto Chemical Corporation has provided some guidelines. In this case, Monsanto predicted that sales would increase 8 to 9% and that earnings would rise 4 to 5%. In the last part of the year, the demand for Monsanto's products dropped as a result of a business turndown and, therefore, the company's earnings declined instead of increasing. The company was sued because the projected earnings figure was erroneous, but the judge dismissed the suit because the forecasts were the best estimates of qualified people whose intents were honest.

As indicated earlier, the SEC's "safe harbor" rules are intended to protect enterprises that provide good-faith projections. However, much concern exists as to how the SEC and the courts will interpret such terms as "good faith" and "reasonable assumptions" when erroneous projections mislead users of this information.

Many Unresolved Problems   In addition to the question of liability, several other issues must be resolved before earnings projections should be made mandatory. The role and responsibility of the CPA as an attestor of forecasts must be determined. Should forecasts consist of general expectations or detailed disclosures? Should a single value ($1.50) or a range of values ($1.50 $\pm$ $.20) be presented? What should be the length of the period to be forecasted?

Because forecasts are needed and desired, they will, in fact, be supplied.[14] The unregulated supply of forecasts in the past has been unsatisfactory. Formal standards for preparation, review, and dissemination of forecasts are needed to resolve the above-noted questions and to rectify the unsatisfactory condition existing at present.

Financial forecasts provide such highly relevant investment information that the demand for them will not subside. Although there are some disadvantages to requiring forecasts, they are outweighed by the advantages. We believe that the publication of forecasts is a natural and inevitable extension of corporate disclosure.

Interim Reports

One further source of information for the investor is interim reports, which are reports that cover periods of less than one year. At one time, interim reports were referred to as the forgotten reports; such is no longer the case. The stock exchanges, the SEC, and the accounting profession have taken an active role in developing guidelines for the presentation of interim information. The SEC mandates that certain companies file a Form 10Q, which requires a company to disclose quarterly data similar to that disclosed in the annual report. It also requires those companies to disclose selected quarterly information in notes to the annual financial statements.[15] A recent annual report of General Motors illustrates the disclosure of selected quarterly data:

Selected Quarterly Data—General Motors Corporation							
	1978 Quarters				1977 Quarters		
	1st	2nd	3rd	4th	1st	2nd	3rd	4th
Dollars in Millions								
Net sales	$14,867.2	$17,026.1	$13,583.3	$17,744.5	$13,552.9	$14,880.6	$11,426.8	$15,101.0
Net income	869.6	1,106.3	527.9	1,004.2	903.4	1,096.6	402.0	935.5
Per Share Amounts								
Earned	3.03	3.86	1.84	3.51	3.14	3.82	1.40	3.26
Dividends	1.00	1.50	1.00	2.50	0.85	1.85	0.85	3.25
Stock Price Range*								
High	62.50	66.88	66.50	65.50	78.50	71.00	70.75	70.88
Low	57.13	59.25	58.00	53.75	66.38	65.88	64.75	61.13

*The principal market is the New York Stock Exchange and prices are based on the Composite Tape.

Also, the APB issued **Opinion No. 28,** which attempted to narrow the reporting alternatives related to interim reports.[16] Finally, the FASB is currently in the process of formulating improved interim reporting standards.

---

[14]It might be noted that AcSEC has issued a statement of position on financial forecasts, providing guidance to those who choose to issue information related to the future. "Presentation and Disclosure of Financial Forecasts," *AcSEC Statement of Position 75-4* (New York: AICPA, 1975). The AICPA's Management Advisory Services Division has also issued a statement dealing with guidelines for systems to prepare financial forecasts: "Guidelines for Systems for the Preparation of Financial Forecasts," *Management Advisory Services Executive Committee, Guideline Series No. 3* (New York: AICPA, 1975).

[15]"Disclosure of Interim Results for Registrants," *ASR No. 177* (Washington: SEC, 1975).

[16]"Interim Financial Reporting," *Opinions of the Accounting Principles Board No. 28* (New York: AICPA, 1973).

Because of the short-term nature of these reports, however, there is considerable controversy as to the general approach that should be employed. One group **(discrete view)** believes that each interim period should be treated as a separate accounting period; deferrals and accruals would therefore follow the principles employed for annual reports. Accounting transactions should be reported as they occur, and expense recognition should not change with the period of time covered. Conversely, another group **(integral view)** believes that the interim report is an integral part of the annual report and that deferrals and accruals should take into consideration what will happen for the entire year. In this approach, estimated expenses are assigned to parts of a year on the basis of sales volume or some other activity base. At present, many companies follow the discrete approach for certain types of expenses and the integral approach for others because the standards currently employed in practice are vague and lead to differing interpretations.

Interim Reporting Requirements

APB Opinion No. 28 indicates that the same acounting principles used for annual reports should be employed for interim reports. Revenues should be recognized in interim periods on the same basis as they are for annual periods. For example, if the installment sales method is used as the basis for recognizing income on an annual basis, then the installment basis should also be applied to interim reports as well. Also, cost directly associated with revenues (product costs), such as materials, labor and related fringe benefits, and manufacturing overhead should be treated in the same manner for interim reports as for annual reports.

Companies generally should use the same inventory pricing methods (FIFO, LIFO, etc.) for interim reports that they use for annual reports. However, the following exceptions are appropriate at interim reporting periods:

1. Companies may use the gross profit method for interim inventory pricing, but disclosure of the method and adjustments to reconcile with annual inventory are necessary.
2. When LIFO inventories are liquidated at an interim date and expected to be replaced by year-end, cost of goods sold should include the expected cost of replacing the liquidated LIFO base and not give effect to the interim liquidation.
3. Inventory market declines should not be deferred beyond the interim period unless they are temporary and no loss is expected for the fiscal year.
4. Planned variances under a standard cost system which are expected to be absorbed by year-end ordinarily should be deferred.

Costs and expenses other than product costs, often referred to as *period costs,* are often charged to the interim period as incurred, but may be allocated among interim periods on the basis of an estimate of time expired, benefit received, or activity associated with the periods. Considerable latitude is exercised in accounting for these costs in interim periods, and many believe more definitive guidelines are needed.

Regarding disclosure, the following interim data should be reported as a minimum:

1. Sales or gross revenues, provision for income taxes, extraordinary items, cumulative effect of a change in accounting principles or practices, and net income.
2. Primary and fully diluted earnings per share where appropriate.

3. Seasonal revenue, cost, or expenses.
4. Significant changes in estimates or provisions for income taxes.
5. Disposal of a segment of a business and extraordinary, unusual, or infrequently occurring items.
6. Contingent items.
7. Changes in accounting principles or estimates.
8. Significant changes in financial position.

The Board also encourages but does not require companies to publish a balance sheet and a statement of changes in financial position. When this information is not presented, significant changes in such items as liquid assets, net working capital, long-term liabilities, and stockholders' equity should be disclosed. To illustrate the type of summarized disclosure presented, the interim report for Mark Controls Corporation for the first quarter of 1979 is presented on page 1247.

Unique Problems of Interim Reporting

In **APB Opinion No. 28,** the Board indicated that it favored the integral approach. However, within this broad guideline, a number of unique reporting problems develop related to the following items.

Advertising and Similar Costs　The general guidelines are that costs such as advertising should be deferred in an interim period if the benefits extend beyond that period; otherwise they should be expensed as incurred. But such a determination is difficult, and even if they are deferred, how should they be allocated between quarters? Because of the vague guidelines in this area, accounting for advertising varies widely. Some companies in the food industry, such as Nabisco and Pillsbury, charge advertising costs as a percentage of sales and adjust to actual at year-end, whereas General Foods and Kellogg's expense these costs as incurred.

The same type of problem relates to such items as social security taxes, research and development costs, and major repairs. For example, should the company expense social security costs (payroll taxes) on the highly paid personnel early in the year or allocate and spread them to subsequent quarters? Should a major repair that occurs later in the year be anticipated and allocated proportionately to earlier periods?

Expenses Subject to Year-end Adjustment　Allowance for bad debts, executive bonuses, pension costs, and inventory shrinkage are often not known with a great deal of certainty until year-end. **These costs should be estimated and allocated in the best possible way to interim periods.** It should be emphasized that companies use a variety of allocation techniques to accomplish this objective.

Income Taxes　Not every dollar of corporate taxable income is assessed at the same tax rate. For example, in 1979 the following corporate tax rate structure was applicable:

Taxable Income	Tax Rate
$0　　—$25,000	17%
$25,000—$50,000	20%
$50,000—$75,000	30%
$75,000—$100,000	40%
Over　　$100,000	46%

MARK CONTROLS CORPORATION

**Report to the
Stockholders for
The Three Months
Ended March 31, 1979**

	Three Months Ended March 31,	
	1979	**1978**
SUMMARY INCOME STATEMENT		
Net Sales	$ 53,251,000	$ 49,435,000
Costs, Expenses and Other Income, Net	52,239,000	47,505,000
Income Before Income Taxes	$ 1,012,000	$ 1,930,000
Income Taxes	400,000	900,000
Net Income	$ 612,000	$ 1,030,000
Net Income per Common Share (1)	$ .11	$ .27
SUMMARY BALANCE SHEET	**March 31,**	**December 31,**
ASSETS	**1979**	**1978**
Current Assets:		
Cash	$ 758,000	$ 4,393,000
Accounts Receivable, Net	46,279,000	42,943,000
Income Tax Refund Receivable	1,750,000	1,750,000
Inventories	47,353,000	43,957,000
Other	1,917,000	2,168,000
Total Current Assets	$ 98,057,000	$ 95,211,000
Investment in Affiliate	1,300,000	1,219,000
Property, Plant and Equipment, Net	36,356,000	36,172,000
	$135,713,000	$132,602,000
LIABILITIES AND STOCKHOLDERS' EQUITY		
Current Liabilities:		
Notes Payable	$ 2,387,000	$ —
Current Maturities of Long-Term Debt	1,280,000	1,280,000
Accounts Payable and Accrued Expenses	28,376,000	32,018,000
Accrued Income Taxes	3,586,000	3,378,000
Billings on Uncompleted Contracts in Excess		
of Related Costs	4,693,000	4,693,000
Total Current Liabilities	$ 40,322,000	$ 41,369,000
Long-Term Debt	37,772,000	34,303,000
Deferred Income Taxes and Other Liabilities	4,074,000	3,565,000
Deferred Gain	914,000	948,000
Stockholders' Equity	52,631,000	52,417,000
	$135,713,000	$132,602,000

(1) Primary net income per common share was computed by dividing net income, less preferred dividend requirements of $322,000, by the weighted average number of common shares outstanding and common equivalent shares. Shares issuable under the Company's stock option plan are classified as common equivalent shares. Shares used in the computation were 2,622,526 in 1979 and 2,631,833 in 1978. No dilution results from the assumed conversion of the Series A Convertible Preferred Stock.

(2) The above summary financial statements should be read in conjunction with the Company's 1978 Annual Report for a description of accounting policies and various other financial matters discussed in the notes to the 1978 financial statements.

The above figures are unaudited.

This progressive aspect of business income taxes poses a problem in preparing **interim financial statements.** Should the income to date be annualized and the proportionate income tax accrued for the period to date? Or should the first amount of income earned be taxed at the lower rate of tax applicable to such income? Prior to 1974, companies generally followed the marginal principle and accrued the tax applicable to each additional dollar of income. The marginal principle was especially applied to businesses having a seasonal or uneven income pattern on the justification that the interim accrual of tax is based on the actual results to date. In 1973, however, the APB in **Opinion No. 28** on "Interim Financial Reporting" recommended that "at the end of each interim period the company should make its best estimate of the effective tax rate expected to be applicable for the full fiscal year. The rate so determined should be used in providing for income taxes on a current year-to-date basis."[17]

Because businesses did not similarly apply this general guideline in accounting for similar situations, the FASB issued **Interpretation No. 18** in 1977. This interpretation requires that the **estimated annual effective tax rate** be applied to the year-to-date "ordinary" income at the end of each interim period to compute the year-to-date tax. Further, the **interim period tax** related to "ordinary" income shall be the difference between the amount so computed and the amounts reported for previous interim periods of the fiscal period.[18]

Extraordinary Items   Extraordinary items consist of unusual and nonrecurring material gains and losses. In the past, they were handled in interim reports in one of three ways: (1) absorbed entirely in the quarter in which they occurred; (2) pro rated over the four quarters; or (3) disclosed only by footnote. **The required approach is to charge or credit the loss or gain in the quarter that it occurs instead of attempting some arbitrary multiple-period allocation.** This approach is consistent with the way in which extraordinary items are currently handled on an annual basis; no attempt is made to prorate the extraordinary items over several years. Some accountants favor the omission of extraordinary items from the quarterly net income because they believe that inclusion of extraordinary items that may be large in proportion to interim results naturally distorts the predictive value of interim reports. Many accountants, however, consider this approach inappropriate because it deviates from the actual situation.

Changes in Accounting   What happens if a company decides to change an accounting principle in the third quarter of a fiscal year? Should the cumulative effect adjustment be charged or credited to that quarter? Presentation of a cumulative effect in the third quarter may be misleading because of the inherent subjectivity associated with the first two quarters' reported income. In addition, a ques-

---

[17]"Interim Financial Reporting," *Opinions of the Accounting Principles Board No. 28* (New York: AICPA, 1973), par. 19. The estimated annual effective tax rate should reflect anticipated investment tax credits, foreign tax rates, percentage depletion, capital gains rates, and other available tax planning alternatives.

[18]"Accounting for Income Taxes in Interim Periods," *FASB Interpretation No. 18* (Stamford, Conn.: FASB, March 1977), par. 9. "Ordinary" income (or loss) refers to "income (or loss) from continuing operations before income taxes (or benefits)" excluding extraordinary items, discontinued operations, and cumulative effects of changes in accounting principles.

tion arises as to whether such a change might not be used to manipulate a given quarter's income. As a result, **FASB Statement No. 3** was issued indicating that **if a cumulative effect change occurs in other than the first quarter, no cumulative effect should be recognized in those quarters.**[19] **Rather, the cumulative effect at the beginning of the year should be computed and the first quarter restated.** Subsequent quarters would not report a cumulative effect adjustment.

Earnings Per Share   Interim reporting of earnings per share has all the problems inherent in computing and presenting annual earnings per share, and then some. If shares are issued in the third period, EPS for the first two periods will not be indicative of year-end EPS. If an extraordinary item is present in one period and new equity shares are sold in another period, the EPS figure for the extraordinary item will change for the year. On an annual basis only one EPS figure is associated with an extraordinary item and that figure does not change; the interim figure is subject to change. **For purposes of computing earnings per share and making the disclosure determinations required by APB Opinion No. 28, each interim period should stand alone, that is, all applicable tests should be made for that single period.**

Seasonality   Seasonality occurs when sales are compressed into one short period of the year while certain costs are fairly evenly spread throughout the year. For example, the natural gas industry has its heavy sales in the winter months, as contrasted with the beverage industry, which has its heavy sales in the summer months.

The problem of seasonality is related to the matching concept in accounting. Expenses should be matched against the revenues they create. In a seasonal business, wide fluctuations in profits occur because off-season sales do not absorb the company's fixed costs (e.g., manufacturing, selling, and administrative costs that tend to remain fairly constant regardless of sales or production).

To illustrate why seasonality is a problem, assume the following information:

Selling price per unit	$1
Annual sales for the period	
(projected and actual)	
100,000 units @ $1.00	$100,000
Manufacturing costs:	
Variable	10¢ per unit
Fixed	20¢ per unit or $20,000 for the year
Nonmanufacturing costs:	
Variable	10¢ per unit
Fixed	30¢ per unit or $30,000 for the year

Sales for four quarters and the year (projected and actual) were:

---

[19]"Reporting Accounting Changes in Interim Financial Statements," *Statement of the Financial Accounting Standards Board No. 3* (Stamford, Conn.: FASB, 1974). This standard also provides guidance related to a LIFO change and accounting changes made in the fourth quarter of a fiscal year where interim data are not presented.

		Percent of Sales
1st Quarter	$ 20,000	20
2nd Quarter	5,000	5
3rd Quarter	10,000	10
4th Quarter	65,000	65
Total for the Year	$100,000	100%

Under the present accounting framework, the income statements for the quarters might be as presented as follows:

	1st Qtr	2nd Qtr	3rd Qtr	4th Qtr	Year
Sales	$20,000	$ 5,000	$10,000	$65,000	$100,000
Manufacturing costs					
Variable	(2,000)	(500)	(1,000)	(6,500)	(10,000)
Fixed[a]	(4,000)	(1,000)	(2,000)	(13,000)	(20,000)
	14,000	3,500	7,000	45,500	70,000
Nonmanufacturing costs					
Variable	(2,000)	(500)	(1,000)	(6,500)	(10,000)
Fixed[b]	(7,500)	(7,500)	(7,500)	(7,500)	(30,000)
Net income	$ 4,500	($ 4,500)	($ 1,500)	$31,500	$ 30,000

[a]The fixed manufacturing costs are inventoried, so that equal amounts of fixed costs do not appear during each quarter.
[b]The fixed nonmanufacturing costs are not inventoried so that equal amounts of fixed costs appear during each quarter.

An investor who uses the first quarter's results can be misled. If the first quarter's earnings are $4,500, should this figure be multiplied by four to predict annual earnings of $18,000? Or, as the analysis suggests, inasmuch as $20,000 in sales is 20% of the predicted sales for the year, net income for the year should be $22,500 ($4,500 × 5). Either figure is obviously wrong, and after the second quarter's results occur, the investor may become even more confused.

The problem with the conventional approach is that the fixed nonmanufacturing costs are not charged in proportion to sales. Some enterprises have adopted a way of avoiding this problem by making all fixed nonmanufacturing costs follow the sales pattern, as shown below:

	1st Qtr	2nd Qtr	3rd Qtr	4th Qtr	Year
Sales	$20,000	$ 5,000	$10,000	$65,000	$100,000
Manufacturing costs					
Variable	(2,000)	(500)	(1,000)	(6,500)	(10,000)
Fixed	(4,000)	(1,000)	(2,000)	(13,000)	(20,000)
	14,000	3,500	7,000	45,500	70,000
Nonmanufacturing costs					
Variable	(2,000)	(500)	(1,000)	(6,500)	(10,000)
Fixed	(6,000)	(1,500)	(3,000)	(19,500)	(30,000)
Net income	$ 6,000	$ 1,500	$ 3,000	$19,500	$ 30,000

This approach solves some of the problems of interim reporting; sales in the first quarter are 20% of total sales for the year, and net income in the first quarter is 20% of total income. In this case, as in the previous example, the investor cannot reply on multiplying any given quarter by four, but can use comparative data or rely on some estimate of sales in relation to income for a given period.

The greater the degree of seasonality experienced by a company, the greater the possibility for distortion. Because no definitive guidelines are available for handling such items as the fixed nonmanufacturing costs, variability in income can be substantial. To alleviate this problem, the profession recommends that companies subject to material seasonal variations disclose the seasonal nature of their business and consider supplementing their interim reports with information for 12-month periods ended at the interim date for the current and preceding years.

The two illustrations above highlight the difference between the **discrete** and **integral** viewpoint. The fixed nonmanufacturing expenses would be expensed as incurred under the discrete viewpoint, but under the integral method they would be charged to income on the basis of some measure of activity.

Continuing Controversy   The profession has developed some standards for interim reporting. But much still has to be done. The FASB is currently studying the issue, and recommendations should soon be forthcoming. As yet, it is unclear whether the discrete, integral, or some combination of these two methods will be proposed.

Discussion also persists concerning the independent auditor's involvement in interim reports. Many auditors are reluctant to express an opinion on interim financial information, arguing that the data are too tentative and subjective. Conversely, an increasing number of individuals advocate some type of examination of interim reports. A compromise may be a limited review of interim reports that provides some assurance that an examination has been conducted by an outside party and that the published information appears to be in accord with generally accepted accounting principles.[20]

Criteria for Making Accounting and Reporting Choices

Throughout this textbook and especially in this chapter we have stressed the need to make judicial choices between alternative accounting concepts, methods, and means of disclosures. You probably are surprised and even discouraged at the large number of choices among acceptable alternatives that accountants are required to make. As "a help to those who have to choose from among such alternatives," the FASB has issued "Qualitative Characteristics: Criteria for Selecting and Evaluating Financial Accounting and Reporting Policies."[21] This recent pronouncement is an addition to its series on "concept statements." The qualitative criteria

---

[20]For example, the AICPA has been involved in developing guidelines for the review of interim reports. "Limited Review of Interim Financial Statements," *Statement on Auditing Standards No. 24* (New York: AICPA, 1979) sets standards for the review of interim reports.

[21]"Qualitative Characteristics: Criteria for Selecting and Evaluating Financial Accounting and Reporting Policies," Exposure draft of *Proposed Statement of Financial Accounting Concepts* (Stamford, Conn.: FASB, August 9, 1979).

offered by the FASB for selecting and evaluating financial accounting and reporting policies and methods are: decision usefulness, relevance, reliability, timeliness, understandability, neutrality, verifiability, representational faithfulness, comparability, completeness, consistency, and materiality.

The FASBs concepts statements on objectives of financial reporting, elements of financial statements (in proposal stage), and qualitative criteria for selecting financial accounting policies, are somewhat reminiscent of other false starts at developing a theoretical framework for accounting practice. Nevertheless, the profession must continue its vigilance to develop a sound foundation upon which accounting standards and practice can be built. As Aristotle said: "The correct beginning is more than half the whole."

Questions

1. Some financial writers have described the 1970s as the age of disclosure. What is the full disclosure principle in accounting? Why has disclosure increased substantially in the last ten years?

2. What are the major advantages of footnotes? What type of items are usually reported in footnotes?

3. A recent annual report of a major steel company states: "Income tax expense includes provision for deferred income taxes of 8.8 million in 1979 and 13.1 million in 1978. Tax expense was reduced by a flow-through of the allowable investment credit of 7.3 million in 1979 and 3.1 million in 1978." What does this footnote mean?

4. The auditor for Seattle, Inc. is debating whether the major categories of property, plant, and equipment and related accumulated depreciation should be reported in a footnote or in the summary of significant accounting policies. What would be your recommendation? Why?

5. What type of disclosure or accounting do you believe is necessary for the following items:
   (a) The client reports an extraordinary item (net of tax) correctly on the income statement. No other mention is made of this item in the annual report.
   (b) The client expects to recover a substantial amount in connection with a pending refund claim for a prior year's taxes. Although the claim is being contested, counsel for the company has confirmed the client's expectation of recovery expectation.
   (c) Because of a general increase in the number of labor disputes and strikes, both within and outside the industry, there is an increased likelihood that the client will suffer a costly strike in the near future.

6. Arendt Co. is liable for a 7% mortgage payable of $24,600, secured by land and buildings, which is payable in semiannual installments (including principal and interest) of $4,500. Indicate the balance sheet presentation of long-term debt, current maturities, and indicate in general terms the necessary disclosure.

7. The SEC requires a reconciliation beween the effective tax rate and the federal government's statutory rate. Of what benefit is such a disclosure requirement?

8. At the beginning of 1981, Sloan Enterprises entered into an eight-year nonrenewable lease agreement. Provisions in the lease require the client to make substantial reconditioning and restoration expenditures at the end of the lease. What type of disclosure do you believe is necessary for this type of situation?

9. A recent annual report of Dane Industries states: "The company and its subsidiaries have long-term leases expiring on various dates after December 31, 1981. Amounts

payble under such commitments, without reduction for related rental income, are expected to average approximately $5,711,000 annually for the next three years. Related rental income from certain subleases to others is estimated to average $3,094,000 annually for the next three years." What information is provided by this footnote?

10. An annual report of Ford Motor Corporation states: "Net income a share is computed based upon the average number of shares of capital stock of all classes outstanding. Additional shares of common stock may be issued or delivered in the future on conversion of outstanding convertible debentures, exercise of outstanding employee stock options, and for payment of defined supplemental compensation. Had such additional shares been outstanding, net income a share would have been reduced by 10¢ in the current year and 3¢ in the previous year.

"As a result of capital stock transactions by the company during the current year, (primarily the purchase of Class A Stock from Ford Foundation), net income a share was increased by 6¢." What information is provided by this footnote?

11. The following information was described in a footnote of Tobin Packing Co. "During August 1977 Halco Products Corporation purchased 311,003 shares of the Company's common stock which constitutes approximately 35% of the stock outstanding. Halco has since obtained representation on the Board of Directors.

"An affiliate of Halco Products Corporation acts as a food broker for the Company in the greater New York City marketing area. The commissions for such services after August 1977 amounted to approximately $20,000." Why is this information disclosed?

12. What approaches might be employed to disclose "social awareness" expenditures?

13. What is the difference between a CPA's unqualified opinion or "clean" opinion and a qualified one?

14. When does a CPA render a "subject to" qualified opinion? When does a CPA render an adverse opinion?

15. What are diversified companies? What accounting problems are related to diversified companies?

16. The controller for Conglomerate, Inc. recently commented: "If I have to disclose our segments individually, the only people who will gain are our competitors and the only people that will lose are our present stockholders." Evaluate this comment.

17. Explain the following terms:
    (a) Industry segment.
    (b) Common cost.
    (c) Identifiable assets.
    (d) Defined profit.

18. One student of Intermediate Accounting was heard to remark after a class discussion on diversified reporting: "All this is very confusing to me. First we are told that there is merit in presenting the consolidated results and now we are told that it is better to show segmental results. I wish they would make up their minds." Evaluate this comment.

19. A financial writer noted recently: "There are substantial arguments for including earnings projections in annual reports and the like. The most compelling is that it would give anyone interested something now available to only a relatively select few—like large shareholders, creditors and attentive bartenders." Identify some arguments against providing earnings projections.

20. What are interim reports? Why are balance sheets often not provided with interim data?

21. What are the accounting problems related to the presentation of interim data?

22. Aprilnair, Inc., a closely held corporation, has decided to go public. The controller, Mark Miller, is concerned with presenting interim data when a LIFO inventory valuation is used. What problems are encountered with LIFO inventories when quarterly data are presented?

23. What approaches have been suggested to overcome the seasonal problem related to interim reporting?

24. "The financial statements of a company are management's, not the accountant's." Discuss the implications of this statement.

Cases

C27-1 LOC Container Corporation is in the process of preparing its annual financial statements for the fiscal year ended April 30, 1980. Because all of LOC Container's shares are traded intrastate, the company does not have to file any reports with the Securities and Exchange Commission. The company manufactures plastic, glass, and paper containers for sale to food and drink manufacturers and distributors.

LOC Container Corporation maintains separate control accounts for its raw materials, work-in-process, and finished goods inventories for each of the three types of containers. The inventories are valued at the lower of cost or market.

The company's property, plant, and equipment are classified in the following major categories: land, office buildings, furniture and fixtures, manufacturing facilities, manufacturing equipment, leasehold improvements. All fixed assets are carried at cost. The depreciation methods employed depend upon the type of asset (its classification) and when it was acquired.

LOC Container Corporation plans to present the inventory and fixed asset amounts in its April 30, 1980, balance sheet as shown below.

Inventories	$1,659,609
Property, plant, and equipment (net of depreciation)	$3,578,475

Instructions

What information regarding Inventories and Property, plant, and equipment must be disclosed by LOC Container Corporation in the audited financial statements issued to stockholders, either in the body or the notes, for the 1979–1980 fiscal year?

(CMA adapted)

C27-2 Presented below are three independent situations.

Situation I

A company offers a one-year warranty for the product that it manufactures. A history of warranty claims has been compiled and the probable amount of claims related to sales for a given period can be determined.

Situation II

Subsequent to the date of a set of financial statements, but prior to the issuance of the financial statements, a company enters into a contract that will probably result in a significant loss to the company. The amount of the loss can be reasonably estimated.

Situation III

A company has adopted a policy of recording self-insurance for any possible losses resulting from injury to others by the company's vehicles. The premium for an insurance policy for the same risk from an independent insurance company would have an annual cost of $2,000. During the period covered by the financial statements, there were no accidents involving the company's vehicles that resulted in injury to others.

Instructions

Discuss the accrual or type of disclosure necessary (if any) and the reason(s) why such disclosure is appropriate for each of the three independent sets of facts above.

(AICPA adapted)

C27-3 You are completing an examination of the financial statements of the Lenox Manufacturing Corporation for the year ended February 28, 1981. Lenox's financial statements have not been examined previously. The controller of Lenox has given you the following draft of proposed footnotes to the financial statements:

The Lenox Manufacturing Corporation
NOTES TO FINANCIAL STATEMENTS
Year Ended February 28, 1981

Note 1. With the approval of the Commissioner of Internal Revenue, the company changed its method of accounting for inventories from the first-in first-out method to the last-in first-out method on March 1, 1980. In the opinion of the company the effects of this change on the pricing of inventories and cost of goods manufactured were not material in the current year but are expected to be material in future years.

Note 2. The investment property was recorded at cost until December, 1980, when it was written up to its appraisal value. The company plans to sell the property in 1981, and an independent real estate agent in the area has indicated that the appraisal price can be realized. Pending completion of the sale the amount of the expected gain on the sale has been recorded in an unearned income account.

Note 3. The stock dividend described in our May 24, 1980, letter to stockholders has been recorded as a 105 for 100 stock split-up. Accordingly, there were no changes in the stockholders' equity account balances from this transaction.

Note 4. For many years the company has maintained a pension plan for certain of its employees. Prior to the current year, pension expense was recognized as payments were made to retired employees. There was no change in the plan in the current year, but on the recommendation of its auditor, the company provided $64,000, based on an actuarial estimate, for pensions to be paid in the future to current employees.

Instructions

For each of the notes above discuss the note's adequacy and needed revisions, if any, of the financial statements or the note.

C27-4   Atlantic, Inc. produces electronic components for sale to manufacturers of radios, television sets, and phonographic systems. In connection with her examination of Atlantic's financial statements for the year ended December 31, 1981, Sue Davis, CPA, completed field work two weeks ago. Ms. Davis now is evaluating the significance of the following items prior to preparing her auditor's report. Except as noted, none of these items have been disclosed in the financial statements or footnotes.

Item 1

Recently Atlantic interrupted its policy of paying cash dividends quarterly to its stockholders. Dividends were paid regularly through 1980, discontinued for all of 1981 to finance equipment for the company's new plant, and resumed in the first quarter of 1982. In the annual report dividend policy is to be discussed in the president's letter to stockholders.

Item 2

A 10-year loan agreement, which the company entered into three years ago, provides that dividend payments may not exceed net income earned after taxes subsequent to the date of the agreement. The balance of retained earnings at the date of the loan agreement was $298,000. From that date through December 31, 1981, net income after taxes has totaled $360,000 and cash dividends have totaled $130,000. On the basis of these data the staff auditor assigned to this review concluded that there was no retained earnings restriction at December 31, 1981.

Item 3

The company's new manufacturing plant building, which cost $600,000 and has an estimated life of 25 years, is leased from the Sixth National Bank at an annual rental of $100,000. The company is obligated to pay property taxes, insurance, and maintenance. At the conclusion of its 10-year noncancellable lease, the company has the option of purchasing the property for $1.00. In Atlantic's income statement the rental payment is reported on a separate line.

Item 4

A major electronics firm has introduced a line of products that will compete directly with Atlantic's primary line, now being produced in the specially designed new plant. Because of manufacturing innovations, the competitor's line will be of comparable quality but priced 50% below Atlantic's line. The competitor announced its new line during the week following completion of field work. Ms. Davis read the announcement in the newspaper and discussed the situation by telephone with Atlantic executives. Atlantic will meet the lower prices that are high enough to cover variable manufacturing and selling expenses but will permit recovery of only a portion of fixed costs.

Instructions

For each of the items above discuss any additional disclosures in the financial statements and footnotes that the auditor should recommend to her client. (The cumulative effect of the four items should not be considered.)

C27-5 You have completed your audit of FMC Corporation and its consolidated subsidiaries for the year ended December 31, 1981, and were satisfied with the results of your examination. You have examined the financial statements of FMC Corporation for the past three years. The corporation is now preparing its annual report to stockholders. The report will include the consolidated financial statements of FMC Corporation and its subsidiaries and your short-form auditor's report. During your audit the following matters came to your attention:

1. The Internal Revenue Service is currently examining the corporation's 1978 federal income tax return and is questioning the amount of a deduction claimed by the corporation's domestic subsidiary for a loss sustained in 1978. The examination is still in process, and any additional tax liability is indeterminable at this time. The corporation's tax counsel believes that there will be no substantial additional tax liability.

2. A vice-president who is also a stockholder resigned on December 31, 1981, after an argument with the president. The vice-president is soliciting proxies from stockholders and expects to obtain sufficient proxies to gain control of the board of directors so that a new president will be appointed. The president plans to have a footnote prepared that would include information of the pending proxy fight, management's accomplishments over the years, and an appeal by management for the support of stockholders.

3. In 1981 the corporation changed its method of accounting for the investment credit. An investment credit of $121,000 deferred in prior years was credited to income and the full 1981 investment credit of $50,000 was recorded as a reduction of income tax expense. As a result, net income after taxes for 1981 was increased by $45,000. You approved of this change as an acceptable alternative accounting treatment.

Instructions

(a) Prepare the footnotes, if any, that you would suggest for the items listed above.

(b) State your reasons for not making disclosure by footnote for each of the listed items for which you did not prepare a footnote.

(AICPA adapted)

C27-6 In a recent annual report of Republic Steel, the following was reported:

"In the Cleveland District, a major improvement in air emission control was made possible by the completion of the first phase of construction of a giant suppressed combustion pollution control system for the basic oxygen furnaces.

"The system, believed to be the first of its type ever installed on an existing steelmaking complex, replaces a bank of electrostatic precipitators which will be used to control other emissions that occur in the steelmaking process. The total system is expected to become fully operational this spring."

Instructions

(a) Do you believe that Republic should disclose information of this nature?

(b) How might an enterprise measure its socially responsible activities?

C27-7 The excerpt below is taken from a letter to the editor in **Barron's**.

Businessman's Fantasy
To the Editor:

I have this fantasy about corporate social responsibility. David Loehwing's coverage of the Berkeley seminar on the same subject published in your November 27 issue prompts me to share it with your readers. It goes like this.

The company president is reporting this sad litany to the Board of Directors: "One of the major products of our manufacturing division has been recalled and the loss will nick earnings per share by 50 cents. There is also a good chance that a class action suit by Nader's group will attempt to obtain substantial damages for those who have been injured by the product.

"Our Smoke Rise plant was shut down by the State environmental health agency due to inadequate emission controls. This will increase the already excessive delay in shipments of another important product to wholesalers. There will also be substantial costs of retooling another plant to handle interim manufacture until pollution control equipment can be installed at Smoke Rise.

"The 75-mile relocation of the company's headquarters to its new site (within five minutes of the president's country home) has been completed. It will be necessary, however, to replace 25% of the work force, mostly lower salaried and minority employes, who have refused to move due to lack of housing under $50,000 as well as the de facto pattern of racial discrimination in the area.

"I think all of you have seen the newspaper story reporting on our firm's sub rosa $20,000 contribution to a television campaign designed to defeat the State environmental initiative. This scurrilous disclosure caused about 12,000 of our retail customers to return their credit cards. I'm sorry to report that sales of our retail division dropped $100,105 in the month following this incident.

"The company recruiter recently visited 10 graduate schools of business on a swing around the country. Five candidates scheduled interviews; two showed up but neither indicated interest in working for a company that had no objective but to maximize profits.

"Three members of the Creek Indian Nation hijacked our corporate airplane but agreed to fly it back from their reservation on condition that the company scrap a new TV advertising campaign built around a seedy character called "Indian Joe." Ad agency billings for creative and production expenses of $250,000 have been incurred and will have to be written off if we want the plane returned.

"These temporary and totally unanticipated difficulties will cut our earnings about 75% in the third quarter. The future, however, has never been brighter for your company," the president concluded.

The Board takes this cheerful news and then elects the president to the position of chairman emeritus of the honorary executive committee of the Board of Directors. The company press release indicates that his only responsibility in this "new and challenging post" is to handle company contributions to charitable organizations.

Barron's reports that his successor is a "hard-nosed" type and predicts that things will get fixed pronto and many executive heads will roll. At his first Board meeting, the new C.E.O. announces two dramatic steps to begin the turnaround.

"The formula for determining the amount of company contributions will be cut from .8% to .1% of pretax corporate profits.

"Our next move will be to run an institutional campaign in print media including Army Times, Rotarian, Saint Anthony Messenger, Daughters of America Magazine, Readers Digest, American Rifleman, Country Club Golfer, Boy's Life and Yachting. The theme of the new campaign will be PROFITS, NOT PEOPLE and the goal is to reestablish broad public confidence in the corporation. The agency has retained Milton Friedman on a consulting basis to provide creative ideas for the campaign," the new president announces.

The Board members settle confidently and comfortably into their arm chairs—it's clear that they have found exactly the right man they need for the work at hand.... FRANK KOCH
Public Affairs Director
Syntex Corp.
Palo Alto, Calif.
* * *

Instructions

(a) What points is Mr. Koch making?

(b) How should a company inform the public of its "social awareness" expenditures?

C27-8 Harness Corporation acquired a large tract of land in a small town approximately 10 miles from Capital City. The company executed a firm contract on November 15, 1980, for the construction of a one-mile race track, together with related facilities. The track and facilities were completed December 15, 1981. On December 31, 1981, a 12% installment note of $100,000 was issued along with other consideration in settlement of the construction contract. Installments of $50,000 fall due on December 31 of each of the next two years. The company planned to pay the notes from cash received from operations and from sale of additional capital stock.

The company adopted the double-declining balance method of computing depreciation. No depreciation was taken in 1981 because all racing equipment was received in December after the completion of the track and facilities.

The land on which the racing circuit was constructed was acquired at various dates for a total of $43,000, and its approximate market value on December 31, 1981, is $60,000.

Through the sale of tickets to spectators, parking fees, concession income, and income from betting, the company officials anticipated that approximately $175,000 is taken in during the typical year's racing season. Cash expenses for a racing season were estimated at $123,000.

You have made an examination of the financial condition of Harness Corporation as of December 31, 1981. The balance sheet as of that date and statement of operations follow.

Harness Corporation
BALANCE SHEET
December 31, 1981

Assets

Cash		$ 14,500
Accounts receivable		1,000
Prepaid expenses		7,500
Property (at cost)		
Land	$ 43,000	
Grading and track improvements	68,200	
Grandstand	100,000	
Buildings	60,000	
Racing equipment	40,000	311,200
Organization costs		300
Total assets		$334,500

Liabilities and Stockholders' Equity

Accounts payable	$ 22,000
Installment note payable—12%	100,000
Stockholders' equity	
Capital stock, par value $1.00 per share,	
authorized 200,000, issued and outstanding 47,800 shares	47,800
Capital in excess of par, representing amounts paid	
in over par value of capital stock	174,700
Retained earnings (deficit)	(10,000)
Total liabilities and stockholders' equity	$334,500

Harness Corporation
STATEMENT OF INCOME
For the Period from Inception, December 1, 1978
to December 31, 1981

Income	
Profit on sales of land	$ 5,000
Other	100
	5,100
General and administrative expenses	15,100
Net loss for the period	$10,000

On January 15, 1982, legislation that declared betting to be illegal was enacted by the state legislature and was signed by the governor. A discussion with management on January 17 about the effect of the legislation revealed that it is now estimated that revenue will be reduced to approximately $48,000 and cash expenses will be reduced to one-third the original estimate.

Instructions

(Disregard federal income tax implications.)

(a) Prepare the explanatory notes to accompany the balance sheet.

(b) What opinion do you believe the auditor should render? Discuss.

(AICPA adapted)

C27-9   Carllock Corporation, a publicly traded company, is preparing the interim financial data which it will issue to its stockholders and the Securities and Exchange Commission (SEC) at the end of the first quarter of the 1980–1981 fiscal year. Carllock's financial accounting department has compiled the following summarized revenue and expense data for the first quarter of the year:

Sales	$10,000,000
Cost of goods sold	6,000,000
Variable selling expenses	300,000
Fixed selling expenses	500,000

Included in the fixed selling expenses was the single lump-sum payment of $400,000 for television advertisements for the entire year.

Instructions

(a) Carllock Corporation must issue its quarterly financial statements in accordance with generally accepted accounting principles regarding interim financial reporting.
  1. Explain whether Carllock should report its operating results for the quarter as if the quarter were a separate reporting period in and of itself or if the quarter were an integral part of the annual reporting period.
  2. State how the sales, cost of goods sold, and fixed selling expenses would be reflected in Carllock Corporation's quarterly report prepared for the first quarter of the 1980–1981 fiscal year. Briefly justify your presentation.

(b) What financial information, as a minimum, must Carllock Corporation disclose to its stockholders in its quarterly reports?

(CMA adapted)

Monday   30-35

C27-10 The following statement is an excerpt from Paragraphs 9 and 10 of **Accounting Principles Board (APB) Opinion No. 28**, "Interim Financial Reporting":

Interim financial information is essential to provide investors and others with timely information as to the progress of the enterprise. The usefulness of such information rests on the relationship that it has to the annual results of operations. Accordingly, the Board has concluded that each interim period should be viewed primarily as an integral part of an annual period.

In general, the results for each interim period should be based on the accounting principles and practices used by a enterprise in the preparation of its latest annual financial statements unless a change in an accounting practice or policy has been adopted in the current year. The Board has concluded, however, that certain accounting principles and practices followed for annual reporting purposes may require modification at interim reporting dates so that the reported results for the interim period may better relate to the results of operations for the annual period.

Instructions

Listed below are six (6) independent cases on how accounting facts might be reported on an individual company's interim financial reports. For each of these cases, state whether the method proposed to be used for interim reporting would be acceptable under generally accepted accounting principals applicable to interim financial data. Support each answer with a brief explanation.

1. Hanover Company was reasonably certain they would have an employee strike in the third quarter. As a result, they shipped heavily during the second quarter but plan to defer the recognition of the sales in excess of the normal sales volume. The deferred sales will be recognized as sales in the third quarter when the strike is in progress. Hanover Company management thinks this is more nearly representative of normal second- and third-quarter operations.

2. Aruba Company takes a physical inventory at year-end for annual financial statement purposes. Inventory and cost of sales reported in the interim quarterly statements are based on estimated gross profit rates, because a physical inventory would result in a cessation of operations. Aruba Company does have reliable perpetual inventory records.

3. Bayes Company is planning to report one-fourth of its pension expense each quarter.

4. Rapid Company wrote inventory down to reflect lower of cost or market in the first quarter of 1980. At year-end the market exceeds the original acquisition cost of this inventory. Consequently, management plans to write the inventory back up to its original cost as a year-end adjustment.

5. Peabody Company realized a large gain on the sale of investments at the beginning of the second quarter. The company wants to report one-third of the gain in each of the remaining quarters.

6. Lance Company has estimated its annual audit fee. They plan to prorate this expense equally over all four quarters.

40

(CMA adapted)

C27-11 The Dines Manufacturing Company, a California corporation listed on the Pacific Coast Stock Exchange, budgeted activities for 1981 as follows:

	Amount	Units
Net sales	$6,000,000	1,000,000
Cost of goods sold	3,600,000	1,000,000
Gross margin	$2,400,000	
Selling, general, and administrative expenses	1,400,000	
Operating income	$1,000,000	
Nonoperating revenues and expenses	–0–	
Income before income taxes	$1,000,000	
Estimated income taxes (current and deferred)	550,000	
Net income	$ 450,000	
Earnings per share of common stock	$4.50	

Dines has operated profitably for many years and has experienced a seasonal pattern of sales volume and production similar to the following ones forecasted for 1981. Sales volume is expected to follow a quarterly pattern of 10%, 20%, 35%, 35%, respectively, because of the seasonality of the industry. Also, owing to production and storage capacity limitations, it is expected that production will follow a pattern of 20%, 25%, 30%, 25%, per quarter, respectively.

At the conclusion of the first quarter of 1981, the controller of Dines has prepared and issued the following interim report for public release:

	Amount	Units
Net sales	$ 600,000	100,000
Cost of goods sold	360,000	100,000
Gross margin	$ 240,000	
Selling, general, and administrative expenses	275,000	
Operating loss	$ (35,000)	
Loss from warehouse fire	(175,000)	
Loss before income taxes	$(210,000)	
Estimated income taxes	–0–	
Net loss	$(210,000)	
Loss per share of common stock	$(2.10)	

The following additional information is available for the first quarter just completed, but was not included in the public information released:

1. The company uses a standard cost system in which standards are set at currently attainable levels on an annual basis. At the end of the first quarter there was underapplied fixed factory overhead (volume variance) of $50,000 that was treated as an asset at the end of the quarter. Production during the quarter was 200,000 units, of which 100,000 were sold.

2. The selling, general, and administrative expenses were budgeted on a basis of $900,000 fixed expenses for the year plus $0.50 variable expenses per unit of sales.

3. Assume that the warehouse fire loss met the conditions of an extraordinary loss. The warehouse had an undepreciated cost of $320,000; $145,000 was recovered from insurance on the warehouse. No other gains or losses are anticipated this year from similar events or transactions, and Dines had no similar losses in preceding years; thus, the full loss will be deductible as an ordinary loss for income tax purposes.

4. The effective income tax rate, for federal and state taxes combined, is expected to average 55% of earnings before income taxes during 1981. There are no permanent differences between pretax accounting earnings and taxable income.

5. Earnings per share were computed on the basis of 100,000 shares of capital stock outstanding. Dines has only one class of stock issued, no long-term debt outstanding, and no stock option plan.

Instructions

(a) Without reference to the specific situation described above, what are the standards of disclosure for interim financial data (published interim financial reports) for publicly traded companies? Explain.

(b) Identify the weaknesses in form and content of Dines' interim report without reference to the additional information.

(c) For each of the five items of additional information, indicate the preferable treatment for each item for interim reporting purposes and explain why that treatment is preferable.

(AICPA adapted)

C27-12 Recently, the following article appeared in the *Wall Street Journal:*

WASHINGTON—The Securities and Exchange Commission staff issued guidelines for companies grappling with the problem of dividing up their business into industry segments for their annual reports.

An industry segment is defined by the Financial Accounting Standards Board as a part of an enterprise engaged in providing a product or service or a group of related products or services primarily to unaffiliated customers for a profit.

Although conceding that the process is a "subjective task" that "to a considerable extent, depends on the judgment of management," the SEC staff said companies should consider the nature of the products, the nature of their production and their markets and marketing methods to determine whether products and services should be grouped together or in separate industry segments.

Instructions

(a) What does financial reporting for segments of a business enterprise involve?

(b) Identify the reasons for requiring financial data to be reported by segments.

(c) Identify the possible disadvantages of requiring financial data to be reported by segments.

(d) Identify the accounting difficulties inherent in segment reporting.

C27-13 The most recently published statement of consolidated income of Schiff Industries, Inc., appears below:

Charles Mann, a representative of a firm of security analysts, visited the central headquarters of Schiff Industries for the purpose of obtaining more information about the company's operations.

In the annual report Schiff's president stated that Schiff was engaged in the pharmaceutical, food-processing, toy-manufacturing, and metal-working industries. Mr. Mann complained that the published income statement was of limited utility in his analysis of the firm's operations. He said that Schiff should have disclosed separately the profit earned in each of its component industries. Further, he maintained that several items appearing on the statement of consolidated retained earnings should have been included on the income statement; a gain of $633,400 on the sale of the furniture division in early March of the current year and an assesment for additional income taxes of $164,900 resulting from an examination of the returns covering the years ended March 31, 1977 and 1978 (normally recurring).

Schiff Industries, Inc.
STATEMENT OF CONSOLIDATED INCOME
For the Year Ended March 31, 1980

Net sales	$38,041,200
Other revenue	407,400
Total revenue	38,448,600
Cost of products sold	27,173,300
Selling and administrative expenses	8,687,500
Interest expense	296,900
Total cost and expenses	36,157,700
Income before income taxes	2,290,900
Income taxes	1,005,200
Net income	$ 1,285,700

Instructions

(a) Explain what is meant by a "conglomerate" company.

(b) 1. Discuss the accounting problems involved in measuring net profit by industry segments within a company.

   2. With reference to Schiff Industries' statement of consolidated income, identify the specific items where difficulty might be encountered in measuring profit by each of its industry segments, and explain the nature of the difficulty.

(c) 1. What criteria should be applied in determining whether a gain or loss should be excluded from the determination of net income?

   2. What criteria should be applied in determining whether a gain or loss that is properly includable in the determination of net income should be included in the results of ordinary operations or shown separately as an extraordinary item after all other items of revenue and expense?

   3. How should the gain on the sale of the furniture division and the assessment of additional taxes each be presented in Schiff's financial statements?

(AICPA adapted)

 C27-14 A recent article in *Barron's* noted:

Okay. Last fall, someone with a long memory and an even longer arm reached into that bureau drawer and came out with a moldy cheese sandwich and the equally moldy notion of corporate forecasts. We tried to find out what happened to the cheese sandwich—but, rats!, even recourse to the Freedom of Information Act didn't help. However, the forecast proposal was dusted off, polished up and found quite serviceable. The SEC, indeed, lost no time in running it up the old flagpole—but no one was very eager to salute. Even after some of the more objectionable features—compulsory corrections and detailed explanations of why the estimates went awry—were peeled off the original proposal.

Seemingly, despite the Commission's smiles and sweet talk, those craven corporations were still afraid that an honest mistake would lead down the primrose path to consent decrees and class action suits. To lay to rest such qualms, the Commission last week approved a "Safe Harbor" rule that, providing the forecasts were made on a reasonable basis and in good faith, protected corporations from litigation should the projections prove wide of the mark (as only about 99% are apt to do).

Instructions

(a) What are the arguments for preparing profit forecasts?

(b) What is the purpose of the "safe harbor" rule?

(c) Why are corporations concerned about presenting profit forecasts?

Index